D1390359

THEORY OF STRATEGIC MANAGEMENT

with Cases

GARETH R. JONES
Texas A&M University

CHARLES W. L. HILL
University of Washington

THEORY OF STRATEGIC MANAGEMENT

with Cases

10th edition

Australia · Brazil · Japan · Korea · Mexico · Singapore · Spain · United Kingdom · United States

**Theory of Strategic Management with Cases,
Tenth International Edition**
Gareth R. Jones and Charles W. L. Hill

Vice President of Editorial, Business:
Jack W. Calhoun

Publisher: Erin Joyner

Sr. Acquisitions Editor: Michele Rhoades

Editorial Assistant: Tammy Grega

Developmental Editor: Suzanna Bainbridge

Marketing Manager: Jonathan Monahan

Marketing Coordinator: Julia Tucker

Marketing Communications Manager:
Jim Overly

Content Project Manager: Jana Lewis

Assoc. Media Editor: Rob Ellington

Manufacturing Planner: Ron Montmongery

Production Service: S4 Carlisle Publishing
Services

Copyeditor: Kelly Lydick

Sr. Art Director: Tippy McIntosh

Cover Designer: Patti Hudepohl

Internal Designer: Beckmeyer Design, Inc.

Cover Photo Credits:

　b/w image: JoLin/iStockphoto

　color image: Shutterstock Images/
Patrick Poendl

© 2013, 2010 South-Western, Cengage Learning

ALL RIGHTS RESERVED. No part of this work covered by the copyright
herein may be reproduced, transmitted, stored or used in any form or by
any means graphic, electronic, or mechanical, including but not limited to
photocopying, recording, scanning, digitizing, taping, Web distribution,
information networks, or information storage and retrieval systems,
except as permitted under Section 107 or 108 of the 1976 United States
Copyright Act, or applicable copyright law of another jurisdiction, without
the prior written permission of the publisher.

For permission to use material from this text or product,
submit all requests online at **www.cengage.com/permissions**
Further permissions questions can be emailed to
permissionrequest@cengage.com

Exam *View*® is a registered trademark of eInstruction Corp. Windows is
a registered trademark of the Microsoft Corporation used herein under
license. Macintosh and Power Macintosh are registered trademarks of
Apple Computer, Inc. used herein under license.
© 2008 Cengage Learning. All Rights Reserved.

Library of Congress Control Number: 2012931470

International Edition:
ISBN-13: 978-1-133-58465-0
ISBN-10: 1-133-58465-9

Cengage Learning International Offices

Asia
www.cengageasia.com
tel: (65) 6410 1200

Australia/New Zealand
www.cengage.com.au
tel: (61) 3 9685 4111

Brazil
www.cengage.com.br
tel: (55) 11 3665 9900

India
www.cengage.co.in
tel: (91) 11 4364 1111

Latin America
www.cengage.com.mx
tel: (52) 55 1500 6000

UK/Europe/Middle East/Africa
www.cengage.co.uk
tel: (44) 0 1264 332 424

**Represented in Canada by
Nelson Education, Ltd.**
tel: (416) 752 9100/(800) 668 0671
www.nelson.com

Cengage Learning is a leading provider of customized learning solutions
with office locations around the globe, including Singapore, the United
Kingdom, Australia, Mexico, Brazil, and Japan. Locate your local office at:
www.cengage.com/global

For product information: **www.cengage.com/international**
Visit your local office: **www.cengage.com/global**
Visit our corporate website: **www.cengage.com**

Printed in Canada
1 2 3 4 5 6 7 18 17 16 15 14 13 12

Brief Contents

1

2

3

4

5

Contents

③

Chapter 13   Implementing Strategy in Companies that Compete Across Industries and Countries   461

PART FIVE   CASES IN STRATEGIC MANAGEMENT

5

Cases

Preface

In the tenth edition of our book, *Theory of Strategic Management with Cases*, we continue with our mission to provide students the most current and up-to-date account of the changes taking place in the world of business strategy and management. The fast-changing domestic and global environment continues to pressure organizations and their managers to find new and improved ways to respond in order to maintain and increase their performance. In revising our book, we continue to strive to make our text relevant and interesting to students. It encourages students to make the effort necessary to assimilate the text material because they find it useful and relevant. We continue to mirror the changes taking place in strategic management practices by incorporating recent important developments into our text and by providing vivid, current examples of the way managers of well-known companies—large and small—have responded to the dramatic changes in the competitive environment that have been taking place since the turn of the century.

Since the Ninth Edition was published, this book has strengthened its position as a market leader in the Strategic Management market. This tells us that we continue to meet the expectations of existing users and attract many new users to our book. It is clear that most strategy instructors share with us a concern for our currency in the text and its examples to ensure that cutting-edge issues and new developments in strategic management are continually addressed.

Just as in the last edition, our objective in writing the Tenth Edition has been to maintain all that was good about prior editions. As we move steadily into the second decade of the 21st Century, we continue to refine our approach by expanding our discussion of established strategic management issues and adding new material as management trends develop to present a more complete, clear, and current account of strategic management. We believe that the result is a book that is more closely aligned with the needs of today's professors and students and with the realities of competition in the global environment.

Comprehensive and Up-to-Date Coverage

We have updated many of the features throughout the chapters, including all new Opening Cases, Running Cases, and a Focus on Dell feature. In this edition, we have made no changes to the number or sequencing of our chapters. However, we have made many significant changes inside each chapter to refine and update our presentation of strategic management. Continuing real-world changes in strategic management practices such as the increased use of cost reduction strategies like global outsourcing, ethical issues, and lean production, and a continued emphasis on business model as the driver of differentiation and competitive advantage have lead to many changes in our approach.

Throughout the revision process, we have been careful to preserve the *balanced and integrated* nature of our account of strategic management. As we have continued to add new material, we have also shortened or deleted coverage of out-of-date or less important models and concepts to help students identify and focus on the core concepts and issues in the field. We have also paid close attention to retaining the book's readability.

Finally, it is important to emphasize that we have overhauled the case selection. The cases are all either new to this edition, or revised and updated versions of cases that appeared in prior editions. As always, we have used a tight screen to filter out irrelevant cases, and we believe that the selection we offer is the best on the market. We would like to extend our gratitude to the case authors who have contributed to this edition: Isaac Cohen (*San Jose State University*), Alan N. Hoffman (*Bentley College*), Frank Shipper (*Salisbury University*), Anne Lawrence (*San Jose State University*), Vivek Gupta (*Indian School of Business*), and Debapratim Purkayastha (*Indian School of Business*).

Practicing Strategic Management: An Interactive Approach

We have received a lot of positive feedback about the usefulness of the end-of-chapter exercises and assignments in the Practicing Strategic Management section of our book. They offer a wide range of hands-on and digital learning experiences for students. Following the Chapter Summary and Discussion Questions, each chapter contains the following exercises and assignments:

- **Ethical Dilemma**. This feature has been developed to highlight the importance of ethical decision making in today's business environment. With today's current examples of questionable decision making (as seen in companies like Countrywide Financial during the 2007-2009 global financial crisis), we hope to equip students with the tools they need to be strong ethical leaders.

- **Small Group Exercise**. This short (20-minute) experiential exercise asks students to divide into groups and discuss a scenario concerning some aspect of strategic management. For example, the scenario in Chapter 11 asks students to identify the stakeholders of their educational institution and evaluate how stakeholders' claims are being and should be met.

- The **Strategy Sign-On** section is new to this edition and presents an opportunity for students to explore the latest data through digital research activities.
  - First, the Article File requires students to search business articles to identify a company that is facing a particular strategic management problem. For instance, students are asked to locate and research a company pursuing a low-cost or a differentiation strategy, and to describe this company's strategy, its advantages and disadvantages, and the core competencies required to pursue it. Students' presentations of their findings lead to lively class discussions.
  - Then, the **Strategic Management Project: Developing Your Portfolio** asks students to choose a company to study through the duration of the semester. At the end of every chapter, students analyze the company using the series of questions provided at the end of every chapter. For example, students might select Ford Motor Co. and, using the series of chapter questions, collect information on Ford's top managers, mission, ethical position, domestic and

global strategy and structure, and so on. Students write a case study of their company and present it to the class at the end of the semester. In the past, we also had students present one or more of the cases in the book early in the semester, but now in our classes, we treat the students' own projects as the major class assignment and their case presentations as the climax of the semester's learning experience.

- **Closing Case Study.** A short closing case provides an opportunity for a short class discussion of a chapter-related theme.

In creating these exercises, it is not our intention to suggest that they should *all* be used for *every* chapter. For example, over a semester, an instructor might combine a group of Strategic Management Projects with five to six Article File assignments while incorporating eight to ten Small Group Exercises in class.

We have found that our interactive approach to teaching strategic management appeals to students. It also greatly improves the quality of their learning experience. Our approach is more fully discussed in the *Instructor's Resource Manual*.

Strategic Management Cases

The twenty-two cases that we have selected for this edition will appeal, we are certain, to students and professors alike, both because these cases are intrinsically interesting and because of the number of strategic management issues they illuminate. The organizations discussed in the cases range from large, well-known companies, for which students can do research to update the information, to small, entrepreneurial business that illustrate the uncertainty and challenge of the strategic management process. In addition, the selections include many international cases, and most of the other cases contain some element of global strategy. Refer to the Contents for a complete listing of the cases with brief descriptions.

To help students learn how to effectively analyze and write a case study, we continue to include a special section on this subject. It has a checklist and an explanation of areas to consider, suggested research tools, and tips on financial analysis.

We feel that our entire selection of cases is unrivaled in breadth and depth, and we are grateful to the other case authors who have contributed to this edition.

Teaching and Learning Aids

Taken together, the teaching and learning features of *Theory of Strategic Management with Cases* provide a package that is unsurpassed in its coverage and that supports the integrated approach that we have taken throughout the book.

For the Instructor

- **The Instructor's Resource Manual: Theory.** For each chapter, we provide a clearly focused synopsis, a list of teaching objectives, a comprehensive lecture outline, teaching notes for the *Ethical Dilemma* feature, suggested answers to discussion questions, and comments on the end-of-chapter activities. Each Opening Case,

Strategy in Action boxed feature, and Closing Case has a synopsis and a corresponding teaching note to help guide class discussion.

- **Case Teaching Notes** include a complete list of case discussion questions as well as a comprehensive teaching note for each case, which gives a complete analysis of case issues.

- **ExamView Test Bank** offers a set of comprehensive true/false, multiple-choice, and essay questions for each chapter in the book. The mix of questions has been adjusted to provide fewer fact-based of simple memorization items and to provide more items that rely on synthesis or application. Also, more items now reflect real or hypothetical situations in organizations. Every question is keyed to the Learning Objectives outlined in the text and includes an answer and text page reference.

- **DVD program** highlights a collection of 13 new BBC videos. These new videos are short, compelling, and timely illustrations of today's management world. Topics include Brazil's growing global economy, the aftermath of BP's oil spill, Zappos.com, the Southwest merger with AirTrans, and more. Available on the DVD and Instructor Web site. Detailed case write-ups including questions and suggested answers appear in the Instructor's Resource Manual. Assignable and auto-gradable exercises accompany these videos in CengageNow.

- **CourseMate, text companion website.** This dynamic interactive learning tool includes student and instructor resources. For instructors, you can download electronic versions of the instructor supplements from the password-protected section of the site, including the Instructor's Resource Manual, Test Bank, PowerPoint® presentations, and Case Notes. To access companion resources, please visit www.cengagebrain.com. On the CengageBrain.com homepage, use the search box at the top of the page to search for the ISBN of your title (from the back cover of your book). This will take you to the product page where free companion resources can be found.

- **CengageNow.** This robust online course management system gives you more control in less time and delivers better student outcomes—NOW. CengageNow™ includes teaching and learning resources organized around lecturing, creating assignments, casework, quizzing, and gradework to track student progress and performance. Multiple types of quizzes, including video quizzes that cover the videos found in the accompanying DVD, are assignable and gradable. We also include assignable and gradable Business & Company Resource Center (BCRC) quizzes that direct students to Gale articles to find expansive, current event coverage for companies featured in the Opening and Closing Cases in the text. Flexible assignments, automatic grading, and a gradebook option provide more control while saving you valuable time. A Personalized Study diagnostic tool empowers students to master concepts, prepare for exams, and become more involved in class.

- **The Business & Company Resource Center (BCRC.)** Put a complete business library at your students' fingertips! This premier online business research tool allows you and your students to search thousands of periodicals, journals, references, financial data, industry reports, and more. This powerful research tool saves time for students—whether they are preparing for a presentation or writing a reaction paper. You can use the BCRC to quickly and easily assign readings or research projects. Visit http://www.cengage.com/bcrc to learn more about this indispensable tool. For this text in particular, BCRC will be especially useful in further researching the featured companies.

- **Global Economic Watch.** The current global economic crisis leaves more and more questions unanswered every day and presents "one of the most teachable moments of the century." South-Western delivers the solution. The Global Economic Crisis Resource Center is an online one-stop shopping location that provides educators with current news, journal articles, videos, podcasts, PowerPoint slides, test questions, and much more.

For the Student

- **CourseMate, text companion website** includes chapter summaries, learning objectives, web quizzes, glossary, and flashcards.

- **CengageNow** includes learning resources organized around lecturing, creating assignments, casework, quizzing, and gradework to track student progress and performance. Multiple types of quizzes, including video quizzes that cover the videos found in the accompanying DVD, are assignable and gradable. We also include assignable and gradable Business & Company Resource Center (BCRC) quizzes that direct students to Gale articles to find expansive, current event coverage for companies featured in the Opening and Closing Cases in the text. Flexible assignments, automatic grading, and a gradebook option provide more control while saving you valuable time. A Personalized Study diagnostic tool empowers students to master concepts, prepare for exams, and become more involved in class.

- **The Business & Company Resource Center (BCRC.)** A complete business library at your fingertips! This premier online business research tool allows you to search thousands of periodicals, journals, references, financial data, industry reports, and more. This powerful research tool saves time—whether preparing for a presentation or writing a reaction paper. You can use the BCRC to quickly and easily research projects. Visit http://www.cengage.com/bcrc to learn more about this indispensable tool. For this text in particular, BCRC will be especially useful in further researching the featured companies.

Acknowledgements

This book is the product of far more than two authors. We are grateful to our Acquisitions Editor, Michele Rhoades; our developmental editor, Suzanna Bainbridge; our content project manager, Jana Lewis; and our Marketing Manager, Jon Monahan, for their help in developing and promoting the book and for providing us with timely feedback and information from professors and reviewers, which allowed us to shape the book to meet the needs of its intended market. We are also grateful to the case authors for allowing us to use their materials. We also want to thank the departments of management at the University of Washington and Texas A&M University for providing the setting and atmosphere in which the book could be written, and the students of these universities who react to and provide input for many of our ideas. In addition, the following reviewers of this and earlier editions gave us valuable suggestions for improving the manuscript from its original version to its current form:

Andac Arikan, *Florida Atlantic University*

Ken Armstrong, *Anderson University*

Richard Babcock, *University of San Francisco*

Kunal Banerji, *West Virginia University*

Kevin Banning, *Auburn University- Montgomery*

Glenn Bassett, *University of Bridgeport*

Thomas H. Berliner, *The University of Texas at Dallas*

Bonnie Bollinger, *Ivy Technical Community College*

Richard G. Brandenburg, *University of Vermont*

Steven Braund, *University of Hull*

Philip Bromiley, *University of Minnesota*

Geoffrey Brooks, *Western Oregon State College*

Jill Brown, *Lehigh University*

Amanda Budde, *University of Hawaii*

Lowell Busenitz, *University of Houston*

Sam Cappel, *Southeastern Louisiana University*

Charles J. Capps III, *Sam Houston State University*

Don Caruth, *Texas A&M Commerce*

Gene R. Conaster, *Golden State University*

Steven W. Congden, *University of Hartford*

Catherine M. Daily, *Ohio State University*

Robert DeFillippi, *Suffolk University Sawyer School of Management*

Helen Deresky, *SUNY—Plattsburgh*

Fred J. Dorn, *University of Mississippi*

Gerald E. Evans, *The University of Montana*

John Fahy, *Trinity College, Dublin*

Patricia Feltes, *Southwest Missouri State University*

Bruce Fern, *New York University*

Mark Fiegener, *Oregon State University*

Chuck Foley, *Columbus State Community College*

Isaac Fox, *Washington State University*

Craig Galbraith, *University of North Carolina at Wilmington*

Scott R. Gallagher, *Rutgers University*

Eliezer Geisler, *Northeastern Illinois University*

Gretchen Gemeinhardt, *University of Houston*

Lynn Godkin, *Lamar University*

Sanjay Goel, *University of Minnesota—Duluth*

Robert L. Goldberg, *Northeastern University*

James Grinnell, *Merrimack College*

Russ Hagberg, *Northern Illinois University*

Allen Harmon, *University of Minnesota—Duluth*

Ramon Henson, *Rutgers University*

David Hoopes, *California State University—Dominguez Hills*

Todd Hostager, *University of Wisconsin—Eau Claire*

David Hover, *San Jose State University*

Graham L. Hubbard, *University of Minnesota*

Tammy G. Hunt, *University of North Carolina at Wilmington*

James Gaius Ibe, *Morris College*

W. Grahm Irwin, *Miami University*

Homer Johnson, *Loyola University—Chicago*

Jonathan L. Johnson, *University of Arkansas Walton College of Business Administration*

Marios Katsioloudes, *St. Joseph's University*

Robert Keating, *University of North Carolina at Wilmington*

Geoffrey King, *California State University—Fullerton*

Rico Lam, *University of Oregon*

Robert J. Litschert, *Virginia Polytechnic Institute and State University*

Franz T. Lohrke, *Louisiana State University*

Paul Mallette, *Colorado State University*

Daniel Marrone, *SUNY Farmingdale*

Lance A. Masters, *California State University—San Bernardino*

Robert N. McGrath, *Embry-Riddle Aeronautical University*

Charles Mercer, *Drury College*

Van Miller, *University of Dayton*

Tom Morris, *University of San Diego*

Joanna Mulholland, *West Chester University of Pennsylvania*

James Muraski, *Marquette University*

John Nebeck, *Viterbo University*

Jeryl L. Nelson, *Wayne State College*

Louise Nemanich, *Arizona State University*

Francine Newth, *Providence College*

Don Okhomina, *Fayetteville State University*

Phaedon P. Papadopoulos, *Houston Baptist University*

John Pappalardo, *Keen State College*

Paul R. Reed, *Sam Houston State University*

Rhonda K. Reger, *Arizona State University*

Malika Richards, *Indiana University*

Simon Rodan, *San Jose State*

Stuart Rosenberg, *Dowling College*

Douglas Ross, *Towson University*

Ronald Sanchez, *University of Illinois*

Joseph A. Schenk, *University of Dayton*

Brian Shaffer, *University of Kentucky*

Leonard Sholtis, *Eastern Michigan University*

Pradip K. Shukla, *Chapman University*

Mel Sillmon, *University of Michigan—Dearborn*

Dennis L. Smart, *University of Nebraska at Omaha*

Barbara Spencer, *Clemson University*

Lawrence Steenberg, *University of Evansville*

Kim A. Stewart, *University of Denver*

Ted Takamura, *Warner Pacific College*

Scott Taylor, *Florida Metropolitan University*

Thuhang Tran, *Middle Tennessee University*

Bobby Vaught, *Southwest Missouri State*

Robert F. Vichas, *Florida Atlantic University*

John Vitton, *University of North Dakota*

Edward Ward, *St. Cloud State University*

Kenneth Wendeln, *Indiana University*

Daniel L. White, *Drexel University*
Edgar L. Williams, Jr., *Norfolk State University*
Jun Zhao, *Governors State University*

Gareth R. Jones
Charles W. L. Hill

Dedication

For Nicholas and Julia and Morgan and Nia

– Gareth R. Jones

To my children, Elizabeth, Charlotte, and Michelle

– Charles W. L. Hill

THEORY OF STRATEGIC MANAGEMENT

with Cases

10th edition

1

Strategic Leadership: Managing the Strategy-Making Process for Competitive Advantage

Dell Inc.

Dell Inc., the personal computer company started by Michael Dell in his University of Texas dorm room, was one of the great success stories of the 1990s and early 2000s. Between the mid-1990s and 2007, Dell's average return on invested capital (ROIC) was a staggering 48.3%, far more than the profitability of competing producers of personal computers (see Figure 1.1a). Clearly, for much of this period Dell had a sustained competitive advantage over its rivals. However, beginning in 2007, Dell's profitability declined, while several of its competitors, including Apple and Hewlett-Packard, improved their performance. Even more striking, from 2005 onwards, Dell's earnings per share have not grown, while those of Hewlett-Packard showed steady growth, and Apple's soared (see Figure 1.1b). From where did Dell's competitive advantage come? Why did it start to erode after the mid-2000s? What actions must Dell need to take to arrest the decline in its performance?

Dell's competitive advantage was based on a business model of selling directly to customers. By cutting out wholesalers and retailers, Dell gained the profit these wholesalers and retailers would have otherwise received. Dell gave part of these profits back to customers in the form of lower prices, which increased sales volumes and market share gains, and boosted profit growth. Moreover, Dell's sophisticated Website allowed customers to mix-and-match product

LEARNING OBJECTIVES
After reading this chapter you should be able to:
- Explain what is meant by "competitive advantage"
- Discuss the strategic role of managers at different levels within an organization
- Identify the primary steps in a strategic planning process
- Discuss the common pitfalls of planning, and how those pitfalls can be avoided
- Outline the cognitive biases that might lead to poor strategic decisions, and explain how these biases can be overcome
- Discuss the role strategic leaders play in the strategy-making process

Figure 1.1a Profitability of U.S. Computer Companies 2001–2010

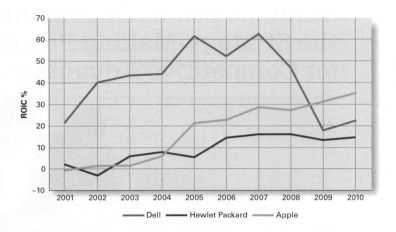

Figure 1.1b Earnings Per Share Growth of U.S. Computer Companies 2001–2010

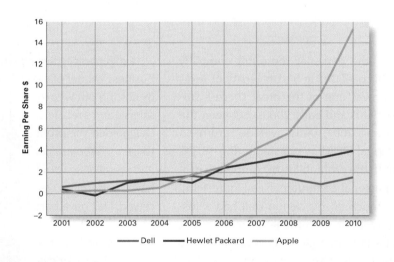

features such as microprocessors, memory capacity, monitors, internal hard drives, DVD drives, and keyboard and mouse formats, in order for customers to personalize their own computer system. The ability to customize orders provided Dell with repeat customers.

Another reason for Dell's competitive advantage was the way it managed its supply chain to minimize the costs of holding inventory. Dell uses the Internet to feed real-time information about order flow to its suppliers, who then have up-to-the-minute information about demand trends for the components they produce, and volume expectations for the upcoming 4–12 weeks. Dell's suppliers use this information to adjust their production schedules, manufacturing just enough components for Dell's needs, and shipping them via the most appropriate transportation mode to ensure that the parts arrive just in time for production. Dell succeeded in decreasing inventory to the lowest level in the industry. In 2006, it was turning its inventory over every 5 days, compared to an average of 41 days at key competitor Hewlett-Packard. High industry turnover can be a major source of competitive advantage in the computer industry, where component costs account for 75% of revenues and typically fall by 1% per week due to rapid obsolescence.

Why, then, did Dell's competitive advantage erode in the later half of the 2000s? There are several reasons. First, a large portion of Dell's sales came from business customers. During the 2008–2009 recession, demand from businesses slumped. Second, Hewlett-Packard gained share in the business market by selling not only personal computers, but a "bundle" that included a combination of PCs, servers, printers, storage devices, network equipment, and consulting services that helped businesses install, manage, and service this equipment. In other words, Hewlett-Packard repositioned itself as a provider of information technology hardware *and* consulting services. Dell lacked the assets to respond to this strategy. Third, to grow its consumer business, Dell needed to sell through retail channels such as Walmart and Best Buy, where profit margins were much lower (some consumers like to purchase online, many still do not). Finally, Apple gained share from Dell in the consumer market by differentiating its products through design and ease of use. Apple created the impression that products from rivals such as Dell were cheap commodity boxes that lacked styling and elegance.

Dell has responded to these challenges by attempting to expand its offerings in order to compete more effectively with companies such as Hewlett-Packard. It has purchased several companies, including a maker of storage devices, and Perot Systems, an information technology consulting company. But is this enough? Dell was once the industry leader, but is now playing catch up. Its competitive advantage has eroded and the company is struggling to find the right strategy to regain this advantage.[1]

Jason Cox/Alamy

Overview

Why do some companies succeed while others fail? Why did Dell do so well during the 1990s and the first half of the 2000s? How did Apple return from near obsolence in the late 1990s and become the dominant technology company of today? Why has Walmart been able to persistently outperform its well-managed rivals? In the airline industry, how has Southwest Airlines managed to keep increasing its revenues and profits through both good times and bad, while rivals such as United Airlines have had to seek bankruptcy protection? What explains the persistent growth and profitability of Nucor Steel, now the largest steel maker in America, during a period when many of its once larger rivals disappeared into bankruptcy?

In this book, we argue that the strategies that a company's managers pursue have a major impact on its performance relative to its competitors. A **strategy** is a set of related actions that managers take to increase their company's performance. For most, if not all, companies, achieving superior performance relative to rivals is the ultimate challenge. If a company's strategies result in superior performance, it is said to have a competitive advantage. Dell's strategies produced superior performance from the mid-1990s until the mid-2000s; as a result, Dell enjoyed competitive advantage over its rivals. How did Dell achieve this competitive advantage? As explained in the Opening Case, it was due to the successful pursuit of varying strategies implemented by Dell's managers. These strategies enabled the company to lower its cost structure, charge low prices, gain market share, and become more profitable than its rivals. Dell lost its competitive advantage in the later half of the 2000s, and is now pursuing strategies to attempt to regain that advantage. We will return to the example of Dell several times throughout this book in a Running Case that examines various aspects of Dell's strategy and performance.

This book identifies and describes the strategies that managers can pursue to achieve superior performance and provide their company with a competitive advantage. One of its central aims is to give you a thorough understanding of the analytical techniques and skills necessary to identify and implement strategies successfully. The first step toward achieving this objective is to describe in more detail what superior performance and competitive advantage mean and to explain the pivotal role that managers play in leading the strategy-making process.

Strategic leadership is about how to most effectively manage a company's strategy-making process to create competitive advantage. The strategy-making process is the process by which managers select and then implement a set of strategies that aim to achieve a competitive advantage. **Strategy formulation** is the task of selecting strategies, whereas **strategy implementation** is the task of putting strategies into action, which includes designing, delivering, and supporting products; improving the efficiency and effectiveness of operations; and designing a company's organization structure, control systems, and culture.

By the end of this chapter, you will understand how strategic leaders can manage the strategy-making process by formulating and implementing strategies that enable a company to achieve a competitive advantage and superior performance. Moreover, you will learn how the strategy-making process can go wrong, and what managers can do to make this process more effective.

Strategic Leadership, Competitive Advantage, and Superior Performance

Strategic leadership is concerned with managing the strategy-making process to increase the performance of a company, thereby increasing the value of the enterprise to its owners, its shareholders. As shown in Figure 1.2, to increase shareholder value, managers must pursue strategies that increase the profitability of the company and ensure that profits grow (for more details, see the Appendix to this chapter). To do this, a company must be able to outperform its rivals; it must have a competitive advantage.

Strategy

A set of related actions that managers take to increase their company's performance.

Strategic leadership

Creating competitive advantage through effective management of the strategy-making process.

Strategy formulation

Selecting strategies based on analysis of an organization's external and internal environment.

Strategy implementation

Putting strategies into action.

Figure 1.2 Determinants of Shareholder Value

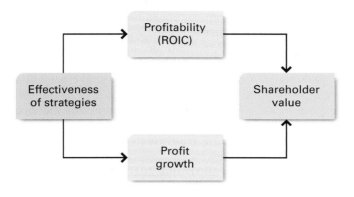

Superior Performance

Maximizing shareholder value is the ultimate goal of profit-making companies, for two reasons. First, shareholders provide a company with the risk capital that enables managers to buy the resources needed to produce and sell goods and services. **Risk capital** is capital that cannot be recovered if a company fails and goes bankrupt. In the case of Dell, for example, shareholders provided the company with capital to build its assembly plants, invest in information systems, and build its order-taking and customer support system. Had Dell failed, its shareholders would have lost their money; their shares would have been worthless. Thus, shareholders will not provide risk capital unless they believe that managers are committed to pursuing strategies that provide a good return on their capital investment. Second, shareholders are the legal owners of a corporation, and their shares, therefore, represent a claim on the profits generated by a company. Thus, managers have an obligation to invest those profits in ways that maximize shareholder value. Of course, as explained later in this book, managers must behave in a legal, ethical, and socially responsible manner while working to maximize shareholder value.

By **shareholder value**, we mean the returns that shareholders earn from purchasing shares in a company. These returns come from two sources: (a) capital appreciation in the value of a company's shares and (b) dividend payments.

For example, between January 2 and December 31, 2010, the value of one share in Verizon Communications increased from $30.97 to $35.78, which represents a capital appreciation of $4.81. In addition, Verizon paid out a dividend of $1.93 per share during 2010. Thus, if an investor had bought one share of Verizon on January 2 and held on to it for the entire year, the return would have been $6.74 ($4.81 + $1.93), an impressive 21.8% return on her investment. One reason Verizon's shareholders did so well during 2010 was that investors came to believe that managers were pursuing strategies that would both increase the long-term profitability of the company and significantly grow its profits in the future.

Risk capital

Equity capital for which there is no guarantee that stockholders will ever recoup their investment or ear a decent return.

Shareholder value

Returns that shareholders earn from purchasing shares in a company.

One way of measuring the **profitability** of a company is by the return that it makes on the capital invested in the enterprise.[2] The return on invested capital (ROIC) that a company earns is defined as its net profit over the capital invested in the firm (profit/capital invested). By net profit, we mean net income after tax. By capital, we mean the sum of money invested in the company: that is, stockholders' equity plus debt owed to creditors. So defined, profitability is the result of how efficiently and effectively managers use the capital at their disposal to produce goods and services that satisfy customer needs. A company that uses its capital efficiently and effectively makes a positive return on invested capital.

The **profit growth** of a company can be measured by the increase in net profit over time. A company can grow its profits if it sells products in markets that are growing rapidly, gains market share from rivals, increases the amount it sells to existing customers, expands overseas, or diversifies profitably into new lines of business. For example, between 2001 and 2010, Apple increased its net profit from $25 million to $14.02 billion. It was able to do this because the company (a) expanded its product offering to include the iPod, iPhone, and iPad; (b) successfully differentiated its products based on design, ease of use, and brand; and (c) as a result, took market share from rivals such as Dell. Due to the increase in net profit, Apple's earnings per share increased from $0.04 to $15.15, making each share more valuable, and leading, in turn, to appreciation in the value of Apple's shares.

Together, profitability and profit growth are the principal drivers of shareholder value (see the Appendix to this chapter for details). To both boost profitability and grow profits over time, managers must formulate and implement strategies that give their company a competitive advantage over rivals.

Managers face a key challenge: to simultaneously generate high profitability and increase the profits of the company. Companies that have high profitability but profits that are not growing, will not be as highly valued by shareholders as a company that has both high profitability and rapid profit growth (see the Appendix for details). This was the situation that Dell faced in the later part of the 2000s. As a result, its shares lost significant value between 2007 and 2010. At the beginning of 2007, Dell's shares were trading at approximately $27. By the end of 2010, they were trading at about $14. Although the company was still profitable, Dell's shares had lost almost half of their value because it was not growing its profits over time (see the Opening Case for details). At the same time, managers need to be aware that if they grow profits but profitability declines, that too will not be as highly valued by shareholders. What shareholders want to see, and what managers must try to deliver through strategic leadership, is *profitable growth*: that is, high profitability and sustainable profit growth. This is not easy, but some of the most successful enterprises of our era have achieved it—companies such as Apple, Google and Walmart.

Competitive Advantage and a Company's Business Model

Managers do not make strategic decisions in a competitive vacuum. Their company is competing against other companies for customers. Competition is a rough-and-tumble process in which only the most efficient and effective companies win out. It is a race without end. To maximize shareholder value, managers must formulate and implement strategies that enable their company to outperform rivals—that give it a competitive advantage. A company is said to have a **competitive advantage** over its

---

Profitability

The return a company makes on the capital invested in the enterprise.

Profit growth

The increase in net profit over time.

Competitive advantage

The achieved advantage over rivals when a company's profitability is greater than the average profitability of firms in its industry.

rivals when its profitability is greater than the average profitability and profit growth of other companies competing for the same set of customers. The higher its profitability relative to rivals, the greater its competitive advantage will be. A company has a **sustained competitive advantage** when its strategies enable it to maintain above-average profitability for a number of years. As discussed in the Opening Case, Dell had a significant and sustained competitive advantage over rivals between 1995 and 2005, but after 2005, that advantage began to erode.

If a company has a sustained competitive advantage, it is likely to gain market share from its rivals and thus grow its profits more rapidly than those of rivals. In turn, competitive advantage will also lead to higher profit growth than that shown by rivals.

The key to understanding competitive advantage is appreciating how the different strategies managers pursue over time can create activities that fit together to make a company unique or different from its rivals and able to consistently outperform them. A **business model** is managers' conception of how the set of strategies their company pursues should work together as a congruent whole, enabling the company to gain a competitive advantage and achieve superior profitability and profit growth. In essence, a business model is a kind of mental model, or gestalt, of how the various strategies and capital investments a company makes should fit together to generate above-average profitability and profit growth. A business model encompasses the totality of how a company will:

- Select its customers.
- Define and differentiate its product offerings.
- Create value for its customers.
- Acquire and keep customers.
- Produce goods or services.
- Lower costs.
- Deliver goods and services to the market.
- Organize activities within the company.
- Configure its resources.
- Achieve and sustain a high level of profitability.
- Grow the business over time.

The business model at Dell during its height, for example, was based on the idea that costs could be lowered by selling directly to customers, and avoiding using a distribution channel (see the Opening Case). The cost savings attained as a result of this model was then passed on to consumers in the form of lower prices, which enabled Dell to gain market share from rivals. For the best part of a decade, this business model proved superior to the established business model in the industry—selling computers through retailers.

Industry Differences in Performance

It is important to recognize that in addition to its business model and associated strategies, a company's performance is also determined by the characteristics of the industry in which it competes. Different industries are characterized by different competitive conditions. In some industries, demand is growing rapidly, and in others it is contracting. Some industries might be beset by excess capacity and persistent price wars, others by strong demand and rising prices. In some, technological change

Sustained competitive advantage

A company's strategies enable it to maintain above-average profitability for a number of years.

Business model

The conception of how strategies should work together as a whole to enable the company to achieve competitive advantage.

might be revolutionizing competition; others may be characterized by stable technology. In some industries, high profitability among incumbent companies might induce new companies to enter the industry, and these new entrants might subsequently depress prices and profits in the industry. In other industries, new entry might be difficult, and periods of high profitability might persist for a considerable time. Thus, the different competitive conditions prevailing in different industries may lead to differences in profitability and profit growth. For example, average profitability might be higher in some industries and lower in other industries because competitive conditions vary from industry to industry.

Figure 1.3 shows the average profitability, measured by ROIC, among companies in several different industries between 2002 and 2010. The pharmaceutical industry had a favorable competitive environment: demand for drugs was high and competition was generally not based on price. Just the opposite was the case in the air transport industry, which was extremely price competitive. Exactly how industries differ is discussed in detail in Chapter 2. For now, it is important to remember that the profitability and profit growth of a company are determined by two main factors: its relative success in its industry and the overall performance of its industry relative to other industries.[3]

Performance in Nonprofit Enterprises

A final point concerns the concept of superior performance in the nonprofit sector. By definition, nonprofit enterprises such as government agencies, universities, and charities are not in "business" to make profits. Nevertheless, they are expected to

Figure 1.3   Return on Invested Capital in Selected Industries, 2002–2010

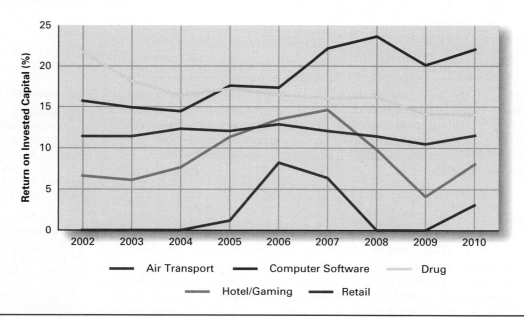

Source: Value Line Investment Survey.

use their resources efficiently and operate effectively, and their managers set goals to measure their performance. The performance goal for a business school might be to get its programs ranked among the best in the nation. The performance goal for a charity might be to prevent childhood illnesses in poor countries. The performance goal for a government agency might be to improve its services while not exceeding its budget. The managers of nonprofits need to map out strategies to attain these goals. They also need to understand that nonprofits compete with each other for scarce resources, just as businesses do. For example, charities compete for scarce donations, and their managers must plan and develop strategies that lead to high performance and demonstrate a track record of meeting performance goals. A successful strategy gives potential donors a compelling message about why they should contribute additional donations. Thus, planning and thinking strategically are as important for managers in the nonprofit sector as they are for managers in profit-seeking firms.

Strategic Managers

Managers are the linchpin in the strategy-making process. It is individual managers who must take responsibility for formulating strategies to attain a competitive advantage and for putting those strategies into effect. They must lead the strategy-making process. The strategies that made Dell so successful were not chosen by some abstract entity known as "the company"; they were chosen by the company's founder, Michael Dell, and the managers he hired. Dell's success was largely based on how well the company's managers performed their strategic roles. In this section, we look at the strategic roles of different managers. Later in the chapter, we discuss strategic leadership, which is how managers can effectively lead the strategy-making process.

In most companies, there are two primary types of managers: **general managers**, who bear responsibility for the overall performance of the company or for one of its major self-contained subunits or divisions, and **functional managers**, who are responsible for supervising a particular function, that is, a task, activity, or operation, such as accounting, marketing, research and development (R&D), information technology, or logistics.

A company is a collection of functions or departments that work together to bring a particular good or service to the market. If a company provides several different kinds of goods or services, it often duplicates these functions and creates a series of self-contained divisions (each of which contains its own set of functions) to manage each different good or service. The general managers of these divisions then become responsible for their particular product line. The overriding concern of general managers is the success of the whole company or division under their direction; they are responsible for deciding how to create a competitive advantage and achieve high profitability with the resources and capital they have at their disposal. Figure 1.4 shows the organization of a **multidivisional company**, that is, a company that competes in several different businesses and has created a separate self-contained division to manage each. As you can see, there are three main levels of management: corporate, business, and functional. General managers are found at the first two of these levels, but their strategic roles differ depending on their sphere of responsibility.

General managers

Managers who bear responsibility for the overall performance of the company or for one of its major self-contained subunits or divisions.

Functional managers

Managers responsible for supervising a particular function, that is, a task, activity, or operation, such as accounting, marketing, research and development (R&D), information technology, or logistics.

Multidivisional company

A company that competes in several different businesses and has created a separate self-contained division to manage each.

Figure 1.4 Levels of Strategic Management

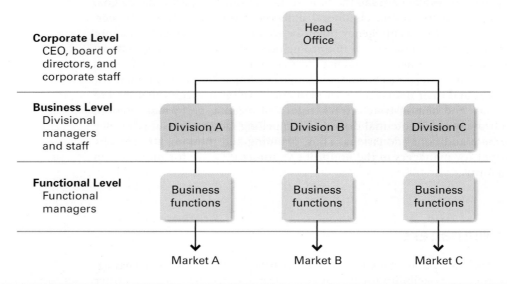

© Cengage Learning 2013

Corporate-Level Managers

The corporate level of management consists of the chief executive officer (CEO), other senior executives, and corporate staff. These individuals occupy the apex of decision making within the organization. The CEO is the principal general manager. In consultation with other senior executives, the role of corporate-level managers is to oversee the development of strategies for the whole organization. This role includes defining the goals of the organization, determining what businesses it should be in, allocating resources among the different businesses, formulating and implementing strategies that span individual businesses, and providing leadership for the entire organization.

Consider General Electric (GE) as an example. GE is active in a wide range of businesses, including lighting equipment, major appliances, motor and transportation equipment, turbine generators, construction and engineering services, industrial electronics, medical systems, aerospace, aircraft engines, and financial services. The main strategic responsibilities of its CEO, Jeffrey Immelt, are setting overall strategic goals, allocating resources among the different business areas, deciding whether the firm should divest itself of any of its businesses, and determining whether it should acquire any new ones. In other words, it is up to Immelt to develop strategies that span individual businesses; his concern is with building and managing the corporate portfolio of businesses to maximize corporate profitability.

It is the CEO's specific responsibility (in this example, Immelt) to develop strategies for competing in the individual business areas, such as financial services. The development of such strategies is the responsibility of the general managers in these different businesses, or business-level managers. However, it is Immelt's responsibility to probe the strategic thinking of business-level managers to make sure that they are pursuing robust business models and strategies that will contribute toward the maximization of GE's long-run profitability, to coach and motivate those managers, to reward them for attaining or exceeding goals, and to hold them accountable for poor performance.

Corporate-level managers also provide a link between the people who oversee the strategic development of a firm and those who own it (the shareholders). Corporate-level managers, and particularly the CEO, can be viewed as the agents of shareholders.[4] It is their responsibility to ensure that the corporate and business strategies that the company pursues are consistent with maximizing profitability and profit growth. If they are not, then the CEO is likely to be called to account by the shareholders.

Business-Level Managers

A **business unit** is a self-contained division (with its own functions—e.g., finance, purchasing, production, and marketing departments) that provides a product or service for a particular market. The principal general manager at the business level, or the business-level manager, is the head of the division. The strategic role of these managers is to translate the general statements of direction and intent that come from the corporate level into concrete strategies for individual businesses. Whereas corporate-level general managers are concerned with strategies that span individual businesses, business-level general managers are concerned with strategies that are specific to a particular business. At GE, a major corporate goal is to be first or second in every business in which the corporation competes. Then, the general managers in each division work out for their business the details of a business model that is consistent with this objective.

Functional-Level Managers

Functional-level managers are responsible for the specific business functions or operations (human resources, purchasing, product development, customer service, etc.) that constitute a company or one of its divisions. Thus, a functional manager's sphere of responsibility is generally confined to one organizational activity, whereas general managers oversee the operation of an entire company or division. Although they are not responsible for the overall performance of the organization, functional managers nevertheless have a major strategic role: to develop functional strategies in their area that help fulfill the strategic objectives set by business- and corporate-level general managers.

In GE's aerospace business, for instance, manufacturing managers are responsible for developing manufacturing strategies consistent with corporate objectives. More-over, functional managers provide most of the information that makes it possible for business- and corporate-level general managers to formulate realistic and attainable strategies. Indeed, because they are closer to the customer than is the typical general manager, functional managers themselves may generate important ideas that subsequently become major strategies for the company. Thus, it is important for general managers to listen closely to the ideas of their functional managers. An equally great responsibility for managers at the operational level is strategy implementation: the execution of corporate- and business-level plans.

The Strategy-Making Process

We can now turn our attention to the process by which managers formulate and implement strategies. Many writers have emphasized that strategy is the outcome of a formal planning process and that top management plays the most important role

Business unit

A self-contained division that provides a product or service for a particular market.

in this process.[5] Although this view has some basis in reality, it is not the whole story. As we shall see later in the chapter, valuable strategies often emerge from deep within the organization without prior planning. Nevertheless, a consideration of formal, rational planning is a useful starting point for our journey into the world of strategy. Accordingly, we consider what might be described as a typical formal strategic planning model for making strategy.

A Model of the Strategic Planning Process

The formal strategic planning process has five main steps:

1. Select the corporate mission and major corporate goals.
2. Analyze the organization's external competitive environment to identify opportunities and threats.
3. Analyze the organization's internal operating environment to identify the organization's strengths and weaknesses.
4. Select strategies that build on the organization's strengths and correct its weaknesses in order to take advantage of external opportunities and counter external threats. These strategies should be consistent with the mission and major goals of the organization. They should be congruent and constitute a viable business model.
5. Implement the strategies.

The task of analyzing the organization's external and internal environments and then selecting appropriate strategies constitutes strategy formulation. In contrast, as noted earlier, strategy implementation involves putting the strategies (or plan) into action. This includes taking actions consistent with the selected strategies of the company at the corporate, business, and functional levels; allocating roles and responsibilities among managers (typically through the design of organization structure); allocating resources (including capital and money); setting short-term objectives; and designing the organization's control and reward systems. These steps are illustrated in Figure 1.5 (which can also be viewed as a plan for the rest of this book).

Each step in Figure 1.5 constitutes a sequential step in the strategic planning process. At step 1, each round, or cycle, of the planning process begins with a statement of the corporate mission and major corporate goals. The existing business model of the company shapes this statement. The mission statement, then, is followed by the foundation of strategic thinking: external analysis, internal analysis, and strategic choice. The strategy-making process ends with the design of the organizational structure and the culture and control systems necessary to implement the organization's chosen strategy. This chapter discusses how to select a corporate mission and choose major goals. Other parts of strategic planning are reserved for later chapters, as indicated in Figure 1.5.

Some organizations go through a new cycle of the strategic planning process every year. This does not necessarily mean that managers choose a new strategy each year. In many instances, the result is simply to modify and reaffirm a strategy and structure already in place. The strategic plans generated by the planning process generally project over a period of 1–5 years, and the planis updated, or rolled forward, every year. In most organizations, the results of the annual strategic planning process are used as input into the budgetary process for the coming year so that strategic planning is used to shape resource allocation within the organization.

Figure 1.5 Main Components of the Strategic Planning Process

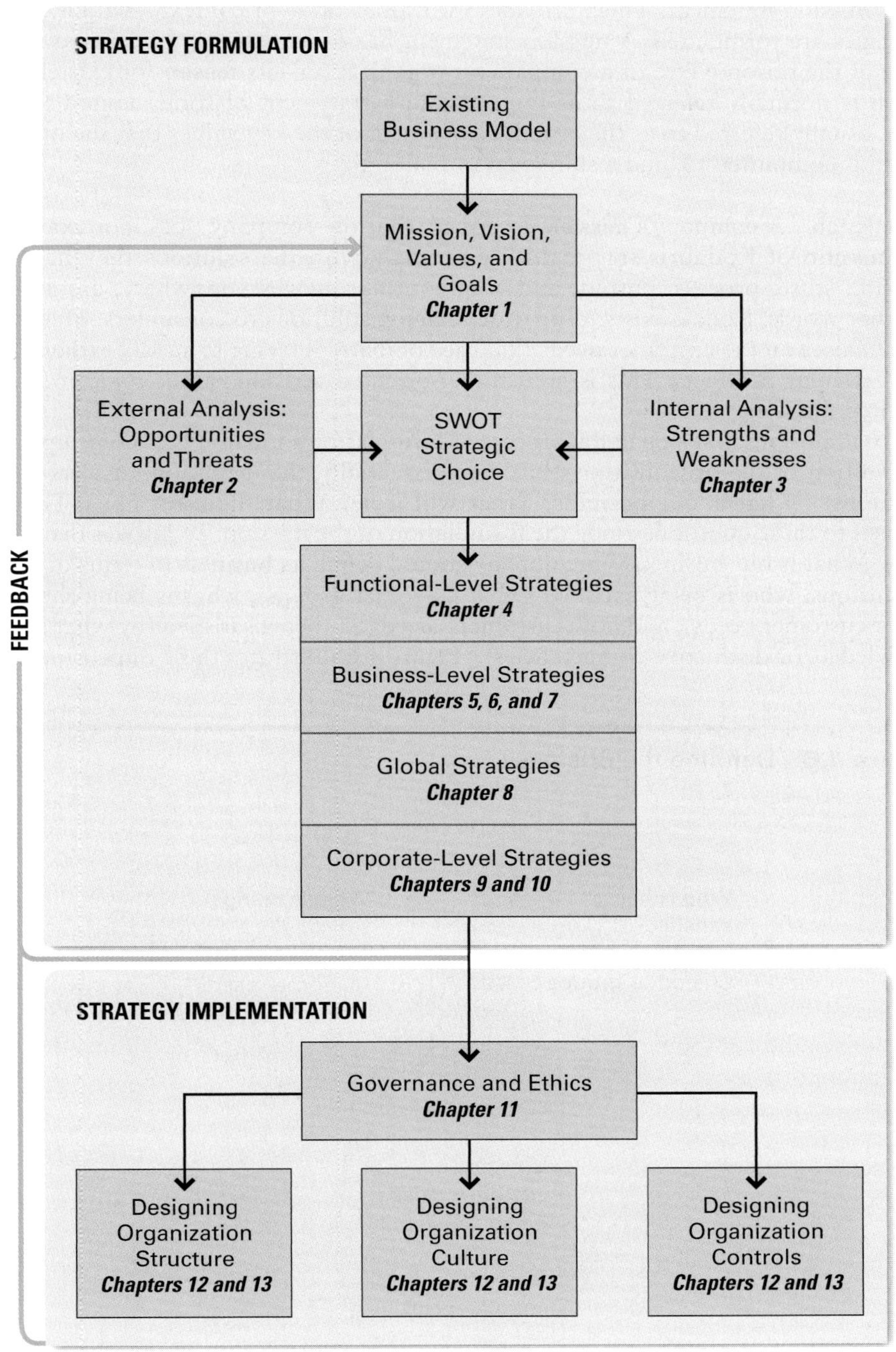

© Cengage Learning 2013

Mission Statement

The first component of the strategic management process is crafting the organization's mission statement, which provides the framework—or context—within which strategies are formulated. A mission statement has four main components: a statement of the raison d'être of a company or organization—its reason for existence—which is normally referred to as the mission; a statement of some desired future state, usually referred to as the vision; a statement of the key values that the organization is committed to; and a statement of major goals.

The Mission   A company's **mission** describes what the company does. For example, the mission of Kodak is to provide "customers with the solutions they need to capture, store, process, output, and communicate images—anywhere, anytime."[6] In other words, Kodak exists to provide imaging solutions to consumers. This mission focuses on the customer needs that the company is trying to satisfy rather than on particular products. This is a customer-oriented mission rather than product-oriented mission.

An important first step in the process of formulating a mission is to come up with a definition of the organization's business. Essentially, the definition answers these questions: "What is our business? What will it be? What should it be?"[7] The responses to these questions guide the formulation of the mission. To answer the question, "What is our business?" a company should define its business in terms of three dimensions: who is being satisfied (what customer groups), what is being satisfied (what customer needs), and how customers' needs are being satisfied (by what skills, knowledge, or distinctive competencies).[8] Figure 1.6 illustrates these dimensions.

> **Mission**
> The purpose of the company, or a statement of what the company strives to do.

Figure 1.6   Defining the Business

This approach stresses the need for a *customer-oriented* rather than a *product-oriented* business definition. A product-oriented business definition focuses on the characteristics of the products sold and the markets served, not on which kinds of customer needs the products are satisfying. Such an approach obscures the company's true mission because a product is only the physical manifestation of applying a particular skill to satisfy a particular need for a particular customer group. In practice, that need may be served in many different ways, and a broad customer-oriented business definition that identifies these ways can safeguard companies from being caught unaware by major shifts in demand.

By helping anticipate demand shifts, a customer-oriented mission statement can also assist companies in capitalizing on changes in their environment. It can help answer the question, "What will our business be?" Kodak's mission statement—to provide "customers with the solutions they need to capture, store, process, output, and communicate images"—is a customer-oriented statement that focuses on customer needs rather than a particular product (or solution) for satisfying those needs, such as chemical film processing. For this reason, from the early-1990s onward the mission statement has driven Kodak's choice to invest in digital imaging technologies, which replaced much of its traditional business based on chemical film processing.

The need to take a customer-oriented view of a company's business has often been ignored. Business history is peppered with the ghosts of once-great corporations that did not define their business, or defined it incorrectly, so that ultimately they declined. In the 1950s and 1960s, many office equipment companies, such as Smith Corona and Underwood, defined their businesses as being the production of typewriters. This product-oriented definition ignored the fact that they were really in the business of satisfying customers' information-processing needs. Unfortunately for those companies, when a new form of technology appeared that better served customer needs for information processing (computers), demand for typewriters plummeted. The last great typewriter company, Smith Corona, went bankrupt in 1996, a victim of the success of computer-based word-processing technology.

In contrast, IBM correctly foresaw what its business would be. In the 1950s, IBM was a leader in the manufacture of typewriters and mechanical tabulating equipment using punch-card technology. However, unlike many of its competitors, IBM defined its business as providing a means for *information processing and storage*, rather thanonly supplying mechanical tabulating equipment and typewriters.[9] Given this definition, the company's subsequent moves into computers, software systems, office systems, and printers seem logical.

Vision The **vision** of a company defines a desired future state; it articulates, often in bold terms, what the company would like to achieve. Nokia, the world's largest manufacturer of mobile (wireless) phones, has been operating with a very simple but powerful vision for some time: "If it can go mobile, it will!" This vision implied that not only would voice telephony go mobile, but also a host of other services based on data, such as imaging and Internet browsing. This vision led Nokia to become a leader in developing mobile handsets that not only can be used for voice communication but that also take pictures, browse the Internet, play games, and manipulate personal and corporate information.

Values The **values** of a company state how managers and employees should conduct themselves, how they should do business, and what kind of organization they should build to help a company achieve its mission. Insofar as they help drive and shape

---

Vision

The articulation of a company's desired achievements or future state.

Values

A statement of how employees should conduct themselves and their business to help achieve the company mission.

behavior within a company, values are commonly seen as the bedrock of a company's organizational culture: the set of values, norms, and standards that control how employees work to achieve an organization's mission and goals. An organization's culture is commonly seen as an important source of its competitive advantage.[10] (We discuss the issue of organization culture in depth in Chapter 12.) For example, Nucor Steel is one of the most productive and profitable steel firms in the world. Its competitive advantage is based, in part, on the extremely high productivity of its work force, which the company maintains is a direct result of its cultural values, which in turn determine how it treats its employees. These values are as follows:

- "Management is obligated to manage Nucor in such a way that employees will have the opportunity to earn according to their productivity."
- "Employees should be able to feel confident that if they do their jobs properly, they will have a job tomorrow."
- "Employees have the right to be treated fairly and must believe that they will be."
- "Employees must have an avenue of appeal when they believe they are being treated unfairly."[11]

At Nucor, values emphasizing pay-for-performance, job security, and fair treatment for employees help to create an atmosphere within the company that leads to high employee productivity. In turn, this has helped to give Nucor one of the lowest cost structures in its industry, and helps to explain the company's profitability in a very price-competitive business.

In one study of organizational values, researchers identified a set of values associated with high-performing organizations that help companies achieve superior financial performance through their impact on employee behavior.[12] These values included respect for the interests of key organizational stakeholders: individuals or groups that have an interest, claim, or stake in the company, in what it does, and in how well it performs.[13] They include stockholders, bondholders, employees, customers, the communities in which the company does business, and the general public. The study found that deep respect for the interests of customers, employees, suppliers, and shareholders was associated with high performance. The study also noted that the encouragement of leadership and entrepreneurial behavior by mid- and lower-level managers and a willingness to support change efforts within the organization contributed to high performance. Companies that emphasize such values consistently throughout their organization include Hewlett-Packard, Walmart, and PepsiCo. The same study identified the values of poorly performing companies— values that, as might be expected, are not articulated in company mission statements: (1) arrogance, particularly to ideas from outside the company; (2) a lack of respect for key stakeholders; and (3) a history of resisting change efforts and "punishing" mid- and lower-level managers who showed "too much leadership." General Motors was held up as an example of one such organization. According to the research, a mid- or lower-level manager who showed too much leadership and initiative there was not promoted!

Major Goals

Having stated the mission, vision, and key values, strategic managers can take the next step in the formulation of a mission statement: establishing major goals. A goal is a precise and measurable desired future state that a company attempts to realize.

In this context, the purpose of goals is to specify with precision what must be done if the company is to attain its mission or vision.

Well-constructed goals have four main characteristics[14]:

- They are precise and measurable. Measurable goals give managers a yardstick or standard against which they can judge their performance.
- They address crucial issues. To maintain focus, managers should select a limited number of major goals to assess the performance of the company. The goals that are selected should be crucial or important ones.
- They are challenging but realistic. They give all employees an incentive to look for ways of improving the operations of an organization. If a goal is unrealistic in the challenges it poses, employees may give up; a goal that is too easy may fail to motivate managers and other employees.[15]
- They specify a time period in which the goals should be achieved, when that is appropriate. Time constraints tell employees that success requires a goal to be attained by a given date, not after that date. Deadlines can inject a sense of urgency into goal attainment and act as a motivator. However, not all goals require time constraints.

Well-constructed goals also provide a means by which the performance of managers can be evaluated.

As noted earlier, although most companies operate with a variety of goals, the primary goal of most corporations is to maximize shareholder returns, and doing this requires both high profitability and sustained profit growth. Thus, most companies operate with goals for profitability and profit growth. However, it is important that top managers do not make the mistake of overemphasizing current profitability to the detriment of long-term profitability and profit growth.[16] The overzealous pursuit of current profitability to maximize short-term ROIC can encourage such misguided managerial actions as cutting expenditures judged to be nonessential in the short run—for instance, expenditures for research and development, marketing, and new capital investments. Although cutting current expenditure increases current profitability, the resulting underinvestment, lack of innovation, and diminished marketing can jeopardize long-run profitability and profit growth.

To guard against short-run decision-making, managers need to ensure that they adopt goals whose attainment will increase the long-run performance and competitiveness of their enterprise. Long-term goals are related to such issues as product development, customer satisfaction, and efficiency, and they emphasize specific objectives or targets concerning such details as employee and capital productivity, product quality, innovation, customer satisfaction, and customer service.

External Analysis

The second component of the strategic management process is an analysis of the organization's external operating environment. The essential purpose of the external analysis is to identify strategic opportunities and threats within the organization's operating environment that will affect how it pursues its mission. Strategy in Action 1.1 describes how an analysis of opportunities and threats in the external environment led to a strategic shift at Time Inc.

Three interrelated environments should be examined when undertaking an external analysis: the industry environment in which the company operates, the country or national environment, and the wider socioeconomic or macroenvironment.

STRATEGY IN ACTION

1.1

Strategic Analysis at Time Inc.

Time Inc., the magazine publishing division of media conglomerate Time Warner, has a venerable history. Its magazine titles include *Time*, *Fortune*, *Sports Illustrated*, and *People*, all long-time leaders in their respective categories. By the mid-2000s, however, Time Inc. recognized that it needed to change its strategy. By 2005, circulation at *Time* had decreased by 12%; *Fortune*, by 10%; and *Sports Illustrated*, by 17%.

An external analysis revealed what was happening. The readership of Time's magazines was aging. Increasingly, younger readers were getting what they wanted from the Web. This was both a *threat* for Time Inc., since its Web offerings were not strong, and an *opportunity*, because with the right offerings, Time Inc. could capture this audience. Time also realized that advertising dollars were migrating rapidly to the Web, and if the company was going to maintain its share, its Web offerings had to be every bit as good as its print offerings.

An internal analysis revealed why, despite multiple attempts, Time had failed to capitalize on the opportunities offered by the emergence of the Web. Although Time had tremendous *strengths*, including powerful brands and strong reporting, development of its Web offerings had been hindered by a serious *weakness*—an editorial culture that regarded Web publishing as a backwater. At *People*, for example, the online operation use to be "like a distant moon" according to managing editor Martha Nelson. Managers at Time Inc. had also been worried that Web offerings would cannibalize print offerings and help to accelerate the decline in the circulation of magazines, with dire financial consequences for the company. As a result of this culture, efforts to move publications onto the Web were underfunded or were stymied entirely by a lack of management attention and commitment.

It was Martha Nelson at *People* who, in 2003, showed the way forward for the company. Her *strategy* for overcoming the *weakness* at Time Inc., and better exploiting

opportunities on the Web, started with merging the print and online newsrooms at *People*, removing the distinction between them. Then, she relaunched the magazine's online site, made major editorial commitments to Web publishing, stated that original content should appear on the Web, and emphasized the importance of driving traffic to the site and earning advertising revenues. Over the next 2 years, page views at People.com increased fivefold.

Ann Moore, the CEO at Time Inc., formalized this strategy in 2005, mandating that all print offerings should follow the lead of People.com, integrating print and online newsrooms and investing significantly more resources in Web publishing. To drive this home, Time hired several well-known bloggers to write for its online publications. The goal of Moore's strategy was to neutralize the cultural *weakness* that had hindered online efforts in the past at Time Inc., and to redirect resources to Web publishing.

In 2006, Time made another strategic move designed to exploit the opportunities associated with the Web when it started a partnership with the 24-hour news channel, CNN, putting all of its financial magazines onto a site that is jointly owned, CNNMoney.com. The site, which offers free access to *Fortune*, *Money*, and *Business 2.0*, quickly took the third spot in online financial Websites behind Yahoo! finance and MSN. This was followed with a redesigned Website for *Sports Illustrated* that has rolled out video downloads for iPods and mobile phones.

To drive home the shift to Web-centric publishing, in 2007 Time announced another change in strategy—it would sell off 18 magazine titles that, while good performers, did not appear to have much traction on the Web. Ann Moore stated that going forward Time would be focusing its energy, resources, and investments on the company's largest and most profitable brands: brands that have demonstrated an ability to draw large audiences in digital form.

Source: A. Van Duyn, "Time Inc. Revamp to Include Sale of 18 Titles," *Financial Times*, September 13, 2006, p. 24; M. Karnitsching, "Time Inc. Makes New Bid to be Big Web Player," *Wall Street Journal,* March 29, 2006, p. B1; M. Flamm, "Time Tries the Web Again," *Crain's New York Business,* January 16, 2006, p. 3.

Analyzing the industry environment requires an assessment of the competitive structure of the company's industry, including the competitive position of the company and its major rivals. It also requires analysis of the nature, stage, dynamics, and history of the industry. Because many markets are now global markets, analyzing the industry environment also means assessing the impact of globalization on competition within an industry. Such an analysis may reveal that a company should move some production facilities to another nation, that it should aggressively expand in emerging markets such as China, or that it should beware of new competition from emerging nations. Analyzing the macroenvironment consists of examining macroeconomic, social, government, legal, international, and technological factors that may affect the company and its industry. We look at external analysis in Chapter 2.

Internal Analysis

Internal analysis, the third component of the strategic planning process, focuses on reviewing the resources, capabilities, and competencies of a company. The goal is to identify the strengths and weaknesses of the company. For example, as described in Strategy in Action 1.1, an internal analysis at Time Inc. revealed that while the company had strong well-known brands such as *Fortune*, *Money*, *Sports Illustrated*, and *People* (a strength), and strong reporting capabilities (another strength), it suffered from a lack of editorial commitment to online publishing (a weakness). We consider internal analysis in Chapter 3.

SWOT Analysis and the Business Model

The next component of strategic thinking requires the generation of a series of strategic alternatives, or choices of future strategies to pursue, given the company's internal strengths and weaknesses and its external opportunities and threats. The comparison of strengths, weaknesses, opportunities, and threats is normally referred to as a **SWOT analysis**.[17] The central purpose is to identify the strategies to exploit external opportunities, counter threats, build on and protect company strengths, and eradicate weaknesses.

At Time Inc., managers saw the move of readership to the Web as both an *opportunity* that they must exploit and a *threat* to Time's established print magazines. Managers recognized that Time's well-known brands and strong reporting capabilities were *strengths* that would serve it well online, but that an editorial culture that marginalized online publishing was a *weakness* that had to be fixed. The *strategies* that managers at Time Inc. came up with included merging the print and online newsrooms to remove distinctions between them; investing significant financial resources in online sites; and entering into a partnership with CNN, which already had a strong online presence.

More generally, the goal of a SWOT analysis is to create, affirm, or fine-tune a company-specific business model that will best align, fit, or match a company's resources and capabilities to the demands of the environment in which it operates. Managers compare and contrast the various alternative possible strategies against each other and then identify the set of strategies that will create and sustain a competitive advantage. These strategies can be divided into four main categories:

- *Functional-level strategies*, directed at improving the effectiveness of operations within a company, such as manufacturing, marketing, materials management, product development, and customer service. We review functional-level strategies in Chapter 4.
- *Business-level strategies*, which encompasses the business's overall competitive theme, the way it positions itself in the marketplace to gain a competitive advantage, and the different positioning strategies that can be used in different

SWOT analysis

The comparison of strengths, weaknesses, opportunities, and threats.

industry settings—for example, cost leadership, differentiation, focusing on a particular niche or segment of the industry, or some combination of these. We review business-level strategies in Chapters 5, 6, and 7.

- *Global strategies*, which addresses how to expand operations outside the home country to grow and prosper in a world where competitive advantage is determined at a global level. We review global strategies in Chapter 8.
- *Corporate-level strategies*, which answer the primary questions: What business or businesses should we be in to maximize the long-run profitability and profit growth of the organization, and how should we enter and increase our presence in these businesses to gain a competitive advantage? We review corporate-level strategies in Chapters 9 and 10.

The strategies identified through a SWOT analysis should be congruent with each other. Thus, functional-level strategies should be consistent with, or support, the company's business-level strategy and global strategy. Moreover, as we explain later in this book, corporate-level strategies should support business-level strategies. When combined, the various strategies pursued by a company should constitute a complete, viable business model. In essence, a SWOT analysis is a methodology for choosing between competing business models, and for fine-tuning the business model that managers choose. For example, when Microsoft entered the videogame market with its Xbox offering, it had to settle on the best business model for competing in this market. Microsoft used a SWOT type of analysis to compare alternatives and settled on a "razor and razor blades" business model in which the Xbox console is priced below cost to build sales (the "razor"), while profits are made from royalties on the sale of games for the Xbox (the "blades").

Strategy Implementation

Once managers have chosen a set of congruent strategies to achieve a competitive advantage and increase performance, managers must put those strategies into action: strategy has to be implemented. Strategy implementation involves taking actions at the functional, business, and corporate levels to execute a strategic plan. Implementation can include, for example, putting quality improvement programs into place, changing the way a product is designed, positioning the product differently in the marketplace, segmenting the marketing and offering different versions of the product to different consumer groups, implementing price increases or decreases, expanding through mergers and acquisitions, or downsizing the company by closing down or selling off parts of the company. These and other topics are discussed in detail in Chapters 4 through 10.

Strategy implementation also entails designing the best organization structure and the best culture and control systems to put a chosen strategy into action. In addition, senior managers need to put a governance system in place to make sure that all within the organization act in a manner that is not only consistent with maximizing profitability and profit growth, but also legal and ethical. In this book, we look at the topic of governance and ethics in Chapter 11; we discuss the organization structure, culture, and controls required to implement business-level strategies in Chapter 12; and discuss the structure, culture, and controls required to implement corporate-level strategies in Chapter 13.

The Feedback Loop

The feedback loop in Figure 1.5 indicates that strategic planning is ongoing: it never ends. Once a strategy has been implemented, its execution must be monitored to determine the extent to which strategic goals and objectives are actually being achieved, and to what degree competitive advantage is being created and sustained. This information and knowledge is returned to the corporate level through feedback loops, and becomes the input for the next round of strategy formulation and implementation. Top managers can then decide whether to reaffirm the existing business model and the existing strategies and goals, or suggest changes for the future. For example, if a strategic goal proves too optimistic, the next time, a more conservative goal is set. Or, feedback may reveal that the business model is not working, so managers may seek ways to change it. In essence, this is what happened at Time Inc. (see Strategy in Action 1.1).

Strategy as an Emergent Process

The planning model suggests that a company's strategies are the result of a plan, that the strategic planning process is rational and highly structured, and that top management orchestrates the process. Several scholars have criticized the formal planning model for three main reasons: the unpredictability of the real world, the role that lower-level managers can play in the strategic management process, and the fact that many successful strategies are often the result of serendipity, not rational strategizing. These scholars have advocated an alternative view of strategy making.[18]

Strategy Making in an Unpredictable World

Critics of formal planning systems argue that we live in a world in which uncertainty, complexity, and ambiguity dominate, and in which small chance events can have a large and unpredictable impact on outcomes.[19] In such circumstances, they claim, even the most carefully thought-out strategic plans are prone to being rendered useless by rapid and unforeseen change. In an unpredictable world, being able to respond quickly to changing circumstances, and to alter the strategies of the organization accordingly, is paramount. The dramatic rise of Google, for example, with its business model-based revenues earned from advertising links associated with search results (the so-called pay-per-click business model), disrupted the business models of companies that made money from online advertising. Nobody could foresee this development or plan for it, but companies had to respond to it, and rapidly. Companies with a strong online advertising presence, including Yahoo.com and Microsoft's MSN network, rapidly changed their strategies to adapt to the threat Google posed. Specifically, both companies developed their own search engines and copied Google's pay-per-click business model. According to critics of formal systems, such a flexible approach to strategy-making is not possible within the framework of a traditional strategic planning process, with its implicit assumption that an organization's strategies only need to be reviewed during the annual strategic planning exercise.

Autonomous Action: Strategy Making by Lower-Level Managers

Another criticism leveled at the rational planning model of strategy is that too much importance is attached to the role of top management, particularly the CEO.[20] An alternative view is that individual managers deep within an organization can—and often do—exert a profound influence over the strategic direction of the firm.[21] Writing with Robert Burgelman of Stanford University, Andy Grove, the former CEO of Intel, noted that many important strategic decisions at Intel were initiated not by top managers but by the autonomous action of lower-level managers deep within Intel who, on their own initiative, formulated new strategies and worked to persuade top-level managers to alter the strategic priorities of the firm.[22] These strategic decisions included the decision to exit an important market (the DRAM memory chip market) and to develop a certain class of microprocessors (RISC-based microprocessors) in direct contrast to the stated strategy of Intel's top managers. Another example of autonomous action, this one at Starbucks, is given in Strategy in Action 1.2.

Autonomous action may be particularly important in helping established companies deal with the uncertainty created by the arrival of a radical new technology that changes the dominant paradigm in an industry.[23] Top managers usually rise to preeminence by successfully executing the established strategy of the firm. Therefore, they may have an emotional commitment to the status quo and are often unable to see things from a different perspective. In this sense, they can be a conservative force that promotes inertia. Lower-level managers, however, are less likely to have the same commitment to the status quo and have more to gain from promoting new technologies and strategies. They may be the first ones to recognize new strategic opportunities and lobby for strategic change. As described in Strategy in Action 1.3, this seems to have been the case at discount stockbroker, Charles Schwab, which had to adjust to the arrival of the Web in the 1990s.

STRATEGY IN ACTION

Starbucks' Music Business

Anyone who has walked into a Starbucks cannot help but notice that, in addition to various coffee beverages and food, the company also sells music CDs. Most Starbucks stores now have racks displaying about 20 CDs. The interesting thing about Starbucks' entry into music retailing is that it was not the result of a formal planning process. The company's journey into music retailing started in the late 1980s when Tim Jones, then the manager of a Starbucks in Seattle's University Village, started to bring his own tapes of music compilations into the store to play. Soon Jones was getting requests for copies from customers. Jones told this to Starbucks' CEO, Howard Schultz, and suggested that Starbucks start to sell its own music. At first, Schultz was skeptical but after repeated lobbying efforts by Jones, he eventually took up the suggestion. Today, Starbucks not only sells CDs, it also provides music downloading at its "Hear Music" Starbucks stores, outlets where customers can listen to music from Starbucks' 200,000-song online music library while sipping their coffee and burning their own CDs.

Source: S. Gray and E. Smith. "Coffee and Music Create a Potent Mix at Starbucks," *Wall Street Journal*, July 19, 2005, p. A1.

STRATEGY IN ACTION

A Strategic Shift at Charles Schwab

In the mid-1990s, Charles Schwab was the most successful discount stockbroker in the world. Over 20 years, it had gained share from full-service brokers like Merrill Lynch by offering deep discounts on the commissions charged for stock trades. Although Schwab had a nationwide network of branches, most customers executed their trades through a telephone system called TeleBroker. Others used online proprietary software, Street Smart, which had to be purchased from Schwab. It was a business model that worked well—then along came E*Trade.

Bill Porter, a physicist and inventor, started the discount brokerage firm E*Trade in 1994 to take advantage of the opportunity created by the rapid emergence of the World Wide Web. E*Trade launched the first dedicated Website for online trading: E*Trade had no branches, no brokers, and no telephone system for taking orders, and thus it had a very low-cost structure. Customers traded stocks over the company's Website. Due to its low-cost structure, E*Trade was able to announce a flat $14.95 commission on stock trades, a figure significantly below Schwab's average commission, which at the time was $65. It was clear from the outset that E*Trade and other online brokers, such as Ameritrade, who soon followed, offered a direct threat to Schwab. Not only were their cost structures and commission rates considerably lower than Schwab's, but the ease, speed, and flexibility of trading stocks over the Web suddenly made Schwab's Street Smart trading software seem limited and its telephone system antiquated.

Deep within Schwab, William Pearson, a young software specialist who had worked on the development of Street Smart, immediately saw the transformational power of the Web. Pearson believed that Schwab needed to develop its own Web-based software, and quickly. Try as he might, though, Pearson could not get the attention of his supervisor. He tried a number of other executives but found little support. Eventually he approached Anne Hennegar, a former Schwab manager who now worked as a consultant to the company. Hennegar suggested that Pearson meet with Tom Seip, an executive vice president at Schwab who was known for his ability to think outside the box. Hennegar approached Seip on Pearson's behalf, and Seip responded positively, asking her to set up a meeting. Hennegar and Pearson arrived expecting to meet only Seip, but to their surprise, in walked Charles Schwab, his chief operating officer, David Pottruck, and the vice presidents in charge of strategic planning and electronic brokerage.

As the group watched Pearson's demo, which detailed how a Web-based system would look and work, they became increasingly excited. It was clear to those in the room that a Web-based system using real-time information, personalization, customization, and interactivity all advanced Schwab's commitment to empowering customers. By the end of the meeting, Pearson had received a green light to start work on the project. A year later, Schwab launched its own Web-based offering, eSchwab, which enabled Schwab clients to execute stock trades for a low flat-rate commission. eSchwab went on to become the core of the company's offering, enabling it to stave off competition from deep discount brokers like E*Trade.

Source: John Kador, *Charles Schwab: How One Company Beat Wall Street and Reinvented the Brokerage Industry*, (John Wiley & Sons: New York, 2002); Erick Schonfeld, "Schwab Puts It All Online," *Fortune* December 7, 1998, pp. 94–99.

Serendipity and Strategy

Business history is replete with examples of accidental events that help to push companies in new and profitable directions. What these examples suggest is that many successful strategies are not the result of well-thought-out plans, but of serendipity—stumbling across good things unexpectedly. One such example occurred at 3M during the 1960s. At that time, 3M was producing fluorocarbons for sale as coolant liquid in air conditioning equipment. One day, a researcher working with fluorocarbons in a 3M lab spilled some of the liquid on her shoes. Later that day when she spilled coffee over her shoes, she watched with interest as the coffee formed into little beads of liquid and then ran off her shoes without leaving a stain. Reflecting on this phenomenon, she realized that a fluorocarbon-based liquid might turn out to be useful for protecting fabrics from liquid stains, and so the idea for Scotchgard was born. Subsequently, Scotchgard became one of 3M's most profitable products, and took the company into the fabric protection business, an area within which it had never planned to participate.[24]

Serendipitous discoveries and events can open all sorts of profitable avenues for a company. But some companies have missed profitable opportunities because serendipitous discoveries or events were inconsistent with their prior (planned) conception of what their strategy should be. In one of the classic examples of such myopia, a century ago, the telegraph company Western Union turned down an opportunity to purchase the rights to an invention made by Alexander Graham Bell. The invention was the telephone, a technology that subsequently made the telegraph obsolete.

Intended and Emergent Strategies

Henry Mintzberg's model of strategy development provides a more encompassing view of what strategy actually is. According to this model, illustrated in Figure 1.7, a company's realized strategy is the product of whatever planned strategies are actually put into action (the company's deliberate strategies) and of any unplanned, or emergent, strategies. In Mintzberg's view, many planned strategies are not implemented because of unpredicted changes in the environment (they are unrealized). Emergent strategies are the unplanned responses to unforeseen circumstances. They arise from autonomous action by individual managers deep within the organization, from serendipitous discoveries or events, or from an unplanned strategic shift by top-level managers in response to changed circumstances. They are not the product of formal top-down planning mechanisms.

Figure 1.7 Emergent and Deliberate Strategies

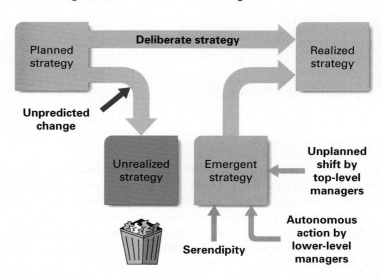

Source: Adapted from H. Mintzberg and A. McGugh, *Administrative Science Quarterly*, Vol. 30. No 2, June 1985.

Mintzberg maintains that emergent strategies are often successful and may be more appropriate than intended strategies. In the classic description of this process, Richard Pascale described how this was the case for the entry of Honda Motor Co. into the U.S. motorcycle market.[25] When a number of Honda executives arrived in Los Angeles from Japan in 1959 to establish a U.S. operation, their original aim (intended strategy) was to focus on selling 250-cc and 350-cc machines to confirmed motorcycle enthusiasts rather than 50-cc Honda Cubs, which were a big hit in Japan. Their instinct told them that the Honda 50s were not suitable for the U.S. market, where everything was bigger and more luxurious than in Japan.

However, sales of the 250-cc and 350-cc bikes were sluggish, and the bikes themselves were plagued by mechanical failure. It looked as if Honda's strategy was going to fail. At the same time, the Japanese executives who were using the Honda 50s to run errands around Los Angeles were attracting a lot of attention. One day, they got a call from a Sears, Roebuck and Co. buyer who wanted to sell the 50-cc bikes to a broad market of Americans who were not necessarily motorcycle enthusiasts. The Honda executives were hesitant to sell the small bikes for fear of alienating serious bikers, who might then associate Honda with "wimpy" machines. In the end, however, they were pushed into doing so by the failure of the 250-cc and 350-cc models.

Honda had stumbled onto a previously untouched market segment that would prove huge: the average American who had never owned a motorbike. Honda had also found an untried channel of distribution: general retailers rather than specialty motorbike stores. By 1964, nearly one out of every two motorcycles sold in the United States was a Honda.

The conventional explanation for Honda's success is that the company redefined the U.S. motorcycle industry with a brilliantly conceived intended strategy. The fact was that Honda's intended strategy was a near-disaster. The strategy that emerged did so not through planning but through unplanned action in response to unforeseen circumstances. Nevertheless, credit should be given to the Japanese management for recognizing the strength of the emergent strategy and for pursuing it with vigor.

The critical point demonstrated by the Honda example is that successful strategies can often emerge within an organization without prior planning, and in response to unforeseen circumstances. As Mintzberg has noted, strategies can take root wherever people have the capacity to learn and the resources to support that capacity.

In practice, the strategies of most organizations are likely a combination of the intended and the emergent. The message for management is that it needs to recognize the process of emergence and to intervene when appropriate, relinquishing bad emergent strategies and nurturing potentially good ones.[26] To make such decisions, managers must be able to judge the worth of emergent strategies. They must be able to think strategically. Although emergent strategies arise from within the organization without prior planning—that is, without completing the steps illustrated in Figure 1.5 in a sequential fashion—top management must still evaluate emergent strategies. Such evaluation involves comparing each emergent strategy with the organization's goals, external environmental opportunities and threats, and internal strengths and weaknesses. The objective is to assess whether the emergent strategy fits the company's needs and capabilities. In addition, Mintzberg stresses that an organization's capability to produce emergent strategies is a function of the kind of corporate culture that the organization's structure and control systems foster. In other words, the different components of the strategic management process are just as important from the perspective of emergent strategies as they are from the perspective of intended strategies.

Strategic Planning in Practice

Despite criticisms, research suggests that formal planning systems do help managers make better strategic decisions. A study that analyzed the results of 26 previously published studies came to the conclusion that, on average, strategic planning has a positive impact on company performance.[27] Another study of strategic planning in 656 firms found that formal planning methodologies and emergent strategies both form part of a good strategy formulation process, particularly in an unstable environment.[28] For strategic planning to work, it is important that top-level managers plan not only within the context of the current competitive environment but also within the context of the future competitive environment. To try to forecast what that future will look like, managers can use scenario-planning techniques to project different possible futures. They can also involve operating managers in the planning process and seek to shape the future competitive environment by emphasizing strategic intent.

Scenario Planning

One reason that strategic planning may fail over longer time periods is that strategic managers, in their initial enthusiasm for planning techniques, may forget that the future is entirely unpredictable. Even the best-laid plans can fall apart if unforeseen contingencies occur, and that happens all the time. The recognition that uncertainty makes it difficult to forecast the future accurately led planners at Royal Dutch Shell to pioneer the scenario approach to planning.[29] **Scenario planning** involves formulating plans that are based upon "what-if" scenarios about the future. In the typical scenario-planning exercise, some scenarios are optimistic and some are pessimistic. Teams of managers are asked to develop specific strategies to cope with each scenario. A set of indicators is chosen as signposts to track trends and identify the probability that any particular scenario is coming to pass. The idea is to allow managers to understand the dynamic and complex nature of their environment, to think through problems in a strategic fashion, and to generate a range of strategic options that might be pursued under different circumstances.[30] The scenario approach to planning has spread rapidly among large companies. One survey found that over 50% of the *Fortune* 500 companies use some form of scenario-planning methods.[31]

The oil company Royal Dutch Shell has, perhaps, done more than most to pioneer the concept of scenario planning, and its experience demonstrates the power of the approach.[32] Shell has been using scenario planning since the 1980s. Today, it uses two primary scenarios to anticipate future demand for oil and refine its strategic planning. . The first scenario, called "Dynamics as Usual," sees a gradual shift from carbon fuels (such as oil) to natural gas, and eventually, to renewable energy. The second scenario, "The Spirit of the Coming Age," looks at the possibility that a technological revolution will lead to a rapid shift to new energy sources.[33] Shell is making investments that will ensure profitability for the company, regardless of which scenario comes to pass, and it is carefully tracking technological and market trends for signs of which scenario is becoming more likely over time.

The great virtue of the scenario approach to planning is that it can push managers to think outside the box, to anticipate what they might need to do in different situations. It can remind managers that the world is complex and unpredictable, and to place a premium on flexibility, rather than on inflexible plans based on assumptions about the future (which may or may not be correct). As a result of scenario planning, organizations might pursue one dominant strategy related to the scenario

Scenario planning

Formulating plans that are based upon "what-if" scenarios about the future.

that is judged to be most likely, but they make some investments that will pay off if other scenarios come to the fore (see Figure 1.8). Thus, the current strategy of Shell is based on the assumption that the world will only gradually shift way from carbon-based fuels (its "Dynamics as Usual" scenario), but the company is also hedging its bets by investing in new energy technologies and mapping out a strategy to pursue should the second scenario come to pass.

Decentralized Planning

A mistake that some companies have made in constructing their strategic planning process has been to treat planning exclusively as a top management responsibility. This ivory tower approach can result in strategic plans formulated in a vacuum by top managers who have little understanding or appreciation of current operating realities. Consequently, top managers may formulate strategies that do more harm than good. For example, when demographic data indicated that houses and families were shrinking, planners at GE's appliance group concluded that smaller appliances were the wave of the future. Because they had little contact with home-builders and retailers, they did not realize that kitchens and bathrooms were the two rooms that were not shrinking. Nor did they appreciate that families with couples who both worked wanted big refrigerators to cut down on trips to the supermarket. GE ended up wasting a lot of time designing small appliances with limited demand.

The ivory tower concept of planning can also lead to tensions between corporate-, business-, and functional-level managers. The experience of GE's appliance group is again illuminating. Many of the corporate managers in the planning group were recruited from consulting firms or top-flight business schools. Many of the functional managers took this pattern of recruitment to mean that corporate managers did not believe they were smart enough to think through strategic problems for themselves. They felt shut out of the decision-making process, which they believed

Figure 1.8 Scenario Planning

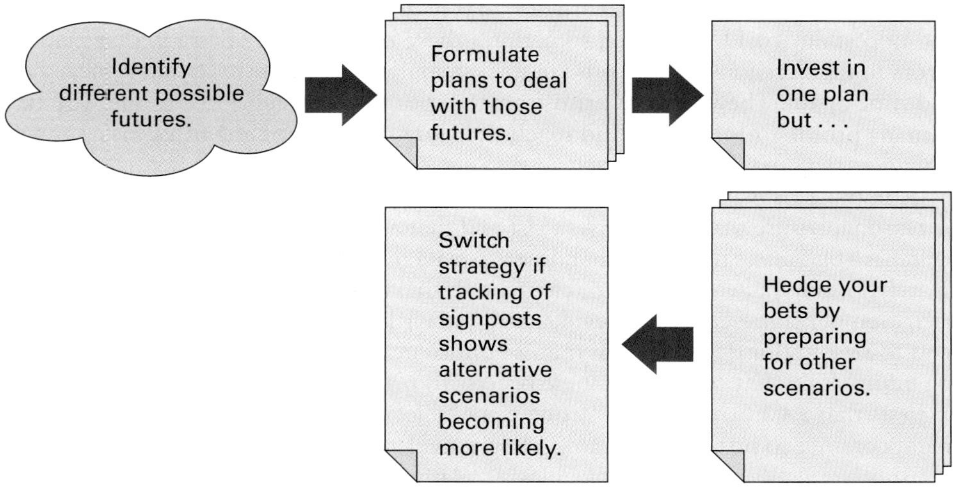

to be unfairly constituted. Out of this perceived lack of procedural justice grew an us-vs.-them mindset that quickly escalated into hostility. As a result, even when the planners were correct, operating managers would not listen to them. For example, the planners correctly recognized the importance of the globalization of the appliance market and the emerging Japanese threat. However, operating managers, who then saw Sears, Roebuck and Co. as the competition, paid them little heed. Finally, ivory tower planning ignores the important strategic role of autonomous action by lower-level managers and by serendipity.

Correcting the ivory tower approach to planning requires recognizing that successful strategic planning encompasses managers at all levels of the corporation. Much of the best planning can and should be done by business and functional managers who are closest to the facts; in other words, planning should be decentralized. Corporate-level planners should take on roles as facilitators who help business and functional managers do the planning by setting the broad strategic goals of the organization and providing the resources required to identify the strategies that might be required to attain those goals.

Strategic Decision Making

Even the best-designed strategic planning systems will fail to produce the desired results if managers do not effectively use the information at their disposal. Consequently, it is important that strategic managers learn to make better use of the information they have, and understand why they sometimes make poor decisions. One important way in which managers can make better use of their knowledge and information is to understand how common cognitive biases can result in poor decision-making.[34]

Cognitive Biases and Strategic Decision Making

Cognitive biases

Systematic errors in human decision making that arise from the way people process information.

Prior hypothesis bias

A cognitive bias that occurs when decision makers who have strong prior beliefs tend to make decisions on the basis of these beliefs, even when presented with evidence that their beliefs are wrong.

Escalating commitment

A cognitive bias that occurs when decision makers, having already committed significant resources to a project, commit even more resources after receiving feedback that the project is failing.

The rationality of decision-making is bound by one's cognitive capabilities.[35] Humans are not supercomputers, and it is difficult for us to absorb and process large amounts of information effectively. As a result, when we make decisions, we tend to fall back on certain rules of thumb, or heuristics, that help us to make sense out of a complex and uncertain world. However, sometimes these rules lead to severe and systematic errors in the decision-making process.[36] Systematic errors are those that appear time and time again. They seem to arise from a series of **cognitive biases** in the way that humans process information and reach decisions. Because of cognitive biases, many managers may make poor strategic decisions.

A number of biases have been verified repeatedly in laboratory settings, so we can be reasonably sure that these biases exist and that all people prone to them.[37] The **prior hypothesis bias** refers to the fact that decision makers who have strong prior beliefs about the relationship between two variables tend to make decisions on the basis of these beliefs, even when presented with evidence that their beliefs are incorrect. Moreover, they tend to seek and use information that is consistent with their prior beliefs while ignoring information that contradicts these beliefs. To place this bias in a strategic context, it suggests that a CEO, who has a strong prior belief that a certain strategy makes sense, might continue to pursue that strategy despite evidence that it is inappropriate or failing.

Another well-known cognitive bias, **escalating commitment**, occurs when decision makers, having already committed significant resources to a project, commit even more resources even if they receive feedback that the project is failing.[38] This may be an irrational response; a more logical response would be to abandon the project and move on (i.e., to cut your losses and exit), rather than escalate commitment. Feelings of personal responsibility for a project seemingly induce decision makers to stick with a project despite evidence that it is failing.

A third bias, **reasoning by analogy**, involves the use of simple analogies to make sense out of complex problems. The problem with this heuristic is that the analogy may not be valid. A fourth bias, **representativeness**, is rooted in the tendency to generalize from a small sample or even a single vivid anecdote. This bias violates the statistical law of large numbers, which says that it is inappropriate to generalize from a small sample, let alone from a single case. In many respects, the dot-com boom of the late 1990s was based on reasoning by analogy and representativeness. Prospective entrepreneurs saw some of the early dot-com companies such as Amazon and Yahoo! achieve rapid success, at least judged by some metrics. Reasoning by analogy from a very small sample, they assumed that any dot-com could achieve similar success. Many investors reached similar conclusions. The result was a massive wave of start-ups that jumped into the Internet space in an attempt to capitalize on the perceived opportunities. That the vast majority of these companies subsequently went bankrupt, proving that the analogy was wrong and that the success of the small sample of early entrants was no guarantee that all dot-coms would succeed.

A fifth cognitive bias is referred to as **the illusion of control**, or the tendency to overestimate one's ability to control events. General or top managers seem to be particularly prone to this bias: having risen to the top of an organization, they tend to be overconfident about their ability to succeed. According to Richard Roll, such overconfidence leads to what he has termed the hubris hypothesis of takeovers.[39] Roll argues that top managers are typically overconfident about their ability to create value by acquiring another company. Hence, they end up making poor acquisition decisions, often paying far too much for the companies they acquire. Subsequently, servicing the debt taken on to finance such an acquisition makes it all but impossible to make money from the acquisition.

The **availability error** is yet another common bias. The availability error arises from our predisposition to estimate the probability of an outcome based on how easy the outcome is to imagine. For example, more people seem to fear a plane crash than a car accident, and yet statistically one is far more likely to be killed in a car on the way to the airport than in a plane crash. People overweigh the probability of a plane crash because the outcome is easier to imagine, and because plane crashes are more vivid events than car crashes, which affect only small numbers of people at one time. As a result of the availability error, managers might allocate resources to a project with an outcome that is easier to imagine, than to one that might have the highest return.

Techniques for Improving Decision Making

The existence of cognitive biases raises a question: how can critical information affect the decision-making mechanism so that a company's strategic decisions are realistic and based on thorough evaluation. Two techniques known to enhance strategic thinking and counteract cognitive biases are devil's advocacy and dialectic inquiry.[40]

Devil's advocacy requires the generation of a plan, and a critical analysis of that plan. One member of the decision-making group acts as the devil's advocate, emphasizing all the reasons that might make the proposal unacceptable. In this way, decision makers can become aware of the possible perils of recommended courses of action.

Reasoning by analogy

Use of simple analogies to make sense out of complex problems.

Representativeness

A bias rooted in the tendency to generalize from a small sample or even a single vivid anecdote.

Illusion of control

A cognitive bias rooted in the tendency to overestimate one's ability to control events.

Availability error

A bias that arises from our predisposition to estimate the probability of an outcome based on how easy the outcome is to imagine.

Devil's advocacy

A technique in which one member of a decision-making team identifies all the considerations that might make a proposal unacceptable.

Dialectic inquiry is more complex because it requires the generation of a plan (a thesis) and a counter-plan (an antithesis) that reflect plausible but conflicting courses of action.[41] Strategic managers listen to a debate between advocates of the plan and counter-plan and then decide which plan will lead to higher performance. The purpose of the debate is to reveal the problems with definitions, recommended courses of action, and assumptions of both plans. As a result of this exercise, strategic managers are able to form a new and more encompassing conceptualization of the problem, which then becomes the final plan (a synthesis). Dialectic inquiry can promote strategic thinking.

Another technique for countering cognitive biases is the outside view, which has been championed by Nobel Prize winner Daniel Kahneman and his associates.[42] The **outside view** requires planners to identify a reference class of analogous past strategic initiatives, determine whether those initiatives succeeded or failed, and evaluate the project at hand against those prior initiatives. According to Kahneman, this technique is particularly useful for countering biases such as the illusion of control (hubris), reasoning by analogy, and representativeness. For example, when considering a potential acquisition, planners should look at the track record of acquisitions made by other enterprises (the reference class), determine if they succeeded or failed, and objectively evaluate the potential acquisition against that reference class. Kahneman argues that such a reality check against a large sample of prior events tends to constrain the inherent optimism of planners and produce more realistic assessments and plans.

Strategic Leadership

One of the key strategic roles of both general and functional managers is to use all their knowledge, energy, and enthusiasm to provide strategic leadership for their subordinates and develop a high-performing organization. Several authors have identified a few key characteristics of good strategic leaders that do lead to high performance: (1) vision, eloquence, and consistency; (2) articulation of a business model; (3) commitment; (4) being well informed; (5) willingness to delegate and empower; (6) astute use of power; and (7) emotional intelligence.[43]

Vision, Eloquence, and Consistency

One of the key tasks of leadership is to give an organization a sense of direction. Strong leaders seem to have a clear and compelling vision of where the organization should go, are eloquent enough to communicate this vision to others within the organization in terms that energize people, and consistently articulate their vision until it becomes part of the organization's culture.[44]

In the political arena, John F. Kennedy, Winston Churchill, Martin Luther King, Jr., and Margaret Thatcher have all been regarded as examples of visionary leaders. Think of the impact of Kennedy's sentence, "Ask not what your country can do for you, ask what you can do for your country," of King's "I have a dream" speech, and of Churchill's "we will never surrender." Kennedy and Thatcher were able to use their political office to push for governmental actions that were consistent with their vision. Churchill's speech galvanized a nation to defend itself against an aggressor, and King was able to pressure the government from outside to make changes within society.

Examples of strong business leaders include Microsoft's Bill Gates; Jack Welch, the former CEO of General Electric; and Sam Walton, Walmart's founder. For years,

Dialectic inquiry

The generation of a plan (a thesis) and a counter-plan (an antithesis) that reflect plausible but conflicting courses of action.

Outside view

Identification of past successful or failed strategic initiatives to determine whether those initiatives will work for project at hand.

Bill Gates' vision of a world in which there would be a Windows-based personal computer on every desk was a driving force at Microsoft. More recently, that vision has evolved into one of a world in which Windows-based software can be found on any computing device, from PCs and servers to videogame consoles (Xbox), cell phones, and hand-held computers. At GE, Jack Welch was responsible for articulating the simple but powerful vision that GE should be first or second in every business in which it competed, or it should exit from that business. Similarly, it was Walmart founder Sam Walton who established and articulated the vision that has been central to Walmart's success: passing on cost savings from suppliers and operating efficiencies to customers in the form of everyday low prices.

Articulation of the Business Model

Another key characteristic of good strategic leaders is their ability to identify and articulate the business model the company will use to attain its vision. A business model is managers' conception of how the various strategies that the company pursues fit together into a congruent whole. At Dell, for example, it was Michael Dell who identified and articulated the basic business model of the company: the direct sales business model. The various strategies that Dell has pursued over the years have refined this basic model, creating one that is very robust in terms of its efficiency and effectiveness. Although individual strategies can take root in many different places in an organization, and although their identification is not the exclusive preserve of top management, only strategic leaders have the perspective required to make sure that the various strategies fit together into a congruent whole and form a valid and compelling business model. If strategic leaders lack a clear conception of the company's business model (or what it should be), it is likely that the strategies the firm pursues will not fit together, and the result will be lack of focus and poor performance.

Commitment

Strong leaders demonstrate their commitment to their vision and business model by actions and words, and they often lead by example. Consider Nucor's former CEO, Ken Iverson. Nucor is a very efficient steel maker with perhaps the lowest cost structure in the steel industry. It has achieved 30 years of profitable performance in an industry where most other companies have lost money due to a relentless focus on cost minimization. In his tenure as CEO, Iverson set the example: he answered his own phone, employed only one secretary, drove an old car, flew coach class, and was proud of the fact that his base salary was the lowest of the Fortune 500 CEOs (Iverson made most of his money from performance-based pay bonuses). This commitment was a powerful signal to employees that Iverson was serious about doing everything possible to minimize costs. It earned him the respect of Nucor employees and made them more willing to work hard. Although Iverson has retired, his legacy lives on in the cost-conscious organization culture that has been built at Nucor, and like all other great leaders, his impact will last beyond his tenure.

Being Well Informed

Effective strategic leaders develop a network of formal and informal sources who keep them well informed about what is going on within their company. At Starbucks, for example, the first thing that former CEO Jim Donald did every morning was call

5–10 stores, talk to the managers and other employees there, and get a sense for how their stores were performing. Donald also stopped at a local Starbucks every morning on the way to work to buy his morning coffee. This has allowed him to get to know individual employees there very well. Donald found these informal contacts to be a very useful source of information about how the company was performing.[45]

Similarly, Herb Kelleher, the founder of Southwest Airlines, was able to gauge the health of his company by dropping in unannounced on aircraft maintenance facilities and helping workers perform their tasks. Herb Kelleher would also often help airline attendants on Southwest flights, distributing refreshments and talking to customers. One frequent flyer on Southwest Airlines reported sitting next to Kelleher three times in 10 years. Each time, Kelleher asked him (and others sitting nearby) how Southwest Airlines was doing in a number of areas, in order to spot trends and inconsistencies.[46]

Using informal and unconventional ways to gather information is wise because formal channels can be captured by special interests within the organization or by gatekeepers—managers who may misrepresent the true state of affairs to the leader. People like Donald and Kelleher who constantly interact with employees at all levels are better able to build informal information networks than leaders who closet themselves and never interact with lower-level employees.

Willingness to Delegate and Empower

High-performance leaders are skilled at delegation. They recognize that unless they learn how to delegate effectively, they can quickly become overloaded with responsibilities. They also recognize that empowering subordinates to make decisions is a good motivational tool and often results in decisions being made by those who must implement them. At the same time, astute leaders recognize that they need to maintain control over certain key decisions. Thus, although they will delegate many important decisions to lower-level employees, they will not delegate those that they judge to be of critical importance to the future success of the organization, such as articulating the company's vision and business model.

The Astute Use of Power

In a now classic article on leadership, Edward Wrapp noted that effective leaders tend to be very astute in their use of power.[47] He argued that strategic leaders must often play the power game with skill and attempt to build consensus for their ideas rather than use their authority to force ideas through; they must act as members of a coalition or its democratic leaders rather than as dictators. Jeffery Pfeffer has articulated a similar vision of the politically astute manager who gets things done in organizations through the intelligent use of power.[48] In Pfeffer's view, power comes from control over resources that are important to the organization: budgets, capital, positions, information, and knowledge. Politically astute managers use these resources to acquire another critical resource: critically placed allies who can help them attain their strategic objectives. Pfeffer stresses that one does not need to be a CEO to assemble power in an organization. Sometimes junior functional managers can build a surprisingly effective power base and use it to influence organizational outcomes.

Emotional Intelligence

Emotional intelligence is a term that Daniel Goleman coined to describe a bundle of psychological attributes that many strong and effective leaders exhibit:[49]

- Self-awareness—the ability to understand one's own moods, emotions, and drives, as well as their effect on others.
- Self-regulation—the ability to control or redirect disruptive impulses or moods, that is, to think before acting.
- Motivation—a passion for work that goes beyond money or status and a propensity to pursue goals with energy and persistence.
- Empathy—the ability to understand the feelings and viewpoints of subordinates and to take those into account when making decisions.
- Social skills—friendliness with a purpose.

According to Goleman, leaders who possess these attributes—who exhibit a high degree of emotional intelligence—tend to be more effective than those who lack these attributes. Their self-awareness and self-regulation help to elicit the trust and confidence of subordinates. In Goleman's view, people respect leaders who, because they are self-aware, recognize their own limitations and, because they are self-regulating, consider decisions carefully. Goleman also argues that self-aware and self-regulating individuals tend to be more self-confident and therefore better able to cope with ambiguity and are more open to change. A strong motivation exhibited in a passion for work can also be infectious, helping to persuade others to join together in pursuit of a common goal or organizational mission. Finally, strong empathy and social skills can help leaders earn the loyalty of subordinates. Empathetic and socially adept individuals tend to be skilled at remedying disputes between managers, better able to find common ground and purpose among diverse constituencies, and better able to move people in a desired direction compared to leaders who lack these skills. In short, Goleman argues that the psychological makeup of a leader matters.

Ethical Dilemma

You are the general manager of a home mortgage-lending business within a large diversified financial services firm. In the firm's mission statement, there is a value that emphasizes the importance of acting with integrity at all time. When you asked the CEO what this means, she told you that you should "do the right thing, and not try to do all things right." This same CEO has also set your challenging profitability and growth goals for the coming year. The CEO has told you that the goals are "non-negotiable." If you satisfy those goals, you will earn a large bonus and may get promoted. If you fail to meet the goals, it may negatively affect your career at the company. You know, however, that satisfying the goals will require you to lower lending standards, and it is possible that your unit will lend money to some people whose ability to meet their mortgage payments is questionable. If people do default on their loans, however, your company will be able to seize their homes, and resell them, which mitigates the risk.

What should you do?

Summary of Chapter

1. A strategy is a set of related actions that managers take to increase their company's performance goals.
2. The major goal of companies is to maximize the returns that shareholders receive from holding shares in the company. To maximize shareholder value, managers must pursue strategies that result in high and sustained profitability and also in profit growth.
3. The profitability of a company can be measured by the return that it makes on the capital invested in the enterprise. The profit growth of a company can be measured by the growth in earnings per share. Profitability and profit growth are determined by the strategies managers adopt.
4. A company has a competitive advantage over its rivals when it is more profitable than the average for all firms in its industry. It has a sustained competitive advantage when it is able to maintain above-average profitability over a number of years. In general, a company with a competitive advantage will grow its profits more rapidly than its rivals.
5. General managers are responsible for the overall performance of the organization, or for one of its major self-contained divisions. Their overriding strategic concern is for the health of the total organization under their direction.
6. Functional managers are responsible for a particular business function or operation. Although they lack general management responsibilities, they play a very important strategic role.
7. Formal strategic planning models stress that an organization's strategy is the outcome of a rational planning process.

8. The major components of the strategic management process are: defining the mission, vision, and major goals of the organization; analyzing the external and internal environments of the organization; choosing a business model and strategies that align an organization's strengths and weaknesses with external environmental opportunities and threats; and adopting organizational structures and control systems to implement the organization's chosen strategies.
9. Strategy can emerge from deep within an organization in the absence of formal plans as lower-level managers respond to unpredicted situations.
10. Strategic planning often fails because executives do not plan for uncertainty and because ivory tower planners lose touch with operating realities.
11. In spite of systematic planning, companies may adopt poor strategies if cognitive biases are allowed to intrude into their decision-making processes.
12. Devil's advocacy, dialectic inquiry, and the outside view are techniques for enhancing the effectiveness of strategic decision-making.
13. Good leaders of the strategy-making process have a number of key attributes: vision, eloquence, and consistency; ability to craft a business model; commitment; being well informed; a willingness to delegate and empower; political astuteness; and emotional intelligence.

Discussion Questions

1. Discuss the accuracy of the following statement: Formal strategic planning systems are irrelevant for firms competing in high-technology industries where the pace of change is so rapid that plans are routinely made obsolete by unforeseen events.
2. What are the strengths of formal strategic planning? What are its weaknesses?
3. To what extent do you think that cognitive biases may have contributed to the global financial crisis that gripped financial markets in 2008–2009? Explain your answer.
4. Pick the current or a past president of the United States and evaluate his performance against the leadership characteristics discussed in the text. On the basis of this comparison, do you think that the president was/is a good strategic leader? Why or why not?
5. What do you think are the sources of sustained superior profitability?
6. What do we mean by strategy? How is a business model different from a strategy?

Practicing Strategic Management

Small-Group Exercises

Small-Group Exercise Designing a Planning System

Break up into groups of 3–5 each and discuss the following scenario. Appoint one group member as a spokesperson who will communicate the group's findings to the class when called on to do so by the instructor.

You are a group of senior managers working for a fast-growing computer software company. Your product allows users to play interactive role-playing games over the Internet. In the past 3 years, your company has gone from being a start-up enterprise with 10 employees and no revenues to a company with 250 employees and revenues of $60 million. It has been growing so rapidly that you have not had time to create a strategic plan, but now your board of directors is telling you that they want to see a plan, and they want the plan to drive decision-making and resource allocation at the company. They want you to design a planning process that will have the following attributes:

1. It will be democratic, involving as many key employees as possible in the process.
2. It will help to build a sense of shared vision within the company about how to continue to grow rapidly.
3. It will lead to the generation of 3–5 key strategies for the company.
4. It will drive the formulation of detailed action plans, and these plans will be subsequently linked to the company's annual operating budget.

Design a planning process to present to your board of directors. Think carefully about who should be included in this process. Be sure to outline the strengths and weaknesses of the approach you choose, and be prepared to justify why your approach might be superior to alternative approaches.

Strategy Sign-On

Article File 1

At the end of every chapter in this book is an article file task. The task requires you to search newspapers or magazines in the library for an example of a real company that satisfies the task question or issue.

Your first article file task is to find an example of a company that has recently changed its strategy. Identify whether this change was the outcome of a formal planning process or whether it was an emergent response to unforeseen events occurring in the company's environment.

Strategic Management Project: Developing Your Portfolio 1

To give you practical insight into the strategic management process, we provide a series of strategic modules; one is at the end of every chapter in this book. Each module asks you to collect and analyze information relating to the material discussed in that chapter. By completing these strategic modules, you will gain a clearer idea of the overall strategic management process.

The first step in this project is to pick a company to study. We recommend that you focus on the same company throughout the book. Remember also that we will be asking you for information about the corporate and international strategy of your company as well as its structure. We strongly recommend that you pick a company for which such information is likely to be available.

There are two approaches that can be used to select a company to study, and your instructor will tell you which one to follow. The first approach is to pick a well-known company that has a lot of information written about it. For example, large publicly held companies such as IBM, Microsoft, and Southwest Airlines are routinely covered in the business and financial press. By going to the library at your university, you should be able to track down a great deal of information on such companies. Many libraries now have comprehensive Web-based electronic data search facilities such as ABI/Inform, the Wall Street Journal Index, the F&S Index, and the LexisNexis databases. These enable you to identify any article that has been written in the business press on the company of your choice within the past few years. A number of non-electronic data sources are also available and useful. For example, F&S Predicasts publishes an annual list of articles relating to major companies that appeared in the national and international business press. S&P Industry Surveys is also a great source for basic industry data, and Value Line Ratings and Reports contain good summaries of a firm's financial position and future prospects. Collect full financial information on the company that you pick. This information can be accessed from Web-based electronic databases such as the EDGAR database, which archives all forms that publicly quoted companies have to file with the Securities and Exchange Commission (SEC); for example, 10-K filings can be accessed from the SEC's EDGAR database. Most SEC forms for public companies can now be accessed from Internet-based financial sites, such as Yahoo!'s finance site (www.finance.yahoo.com/).

A second approach is to choose a smaller company in your city or town to study. Although small companies are not routinely covered in the national business press, they may be covered in the local press. More important, this approach can work well if the management of the company will agree to talk to you at length about the strategy and structure of the company. If you happen to know somebody in such a company or if you have worked there at some point, this approach can be very worthwhile. However, we do not recommend this approach unless you can get a substantial amount of guaranteed access to the company of your choice. If in doubt, ask your instructor before making a decision. The primary goal is to make sure that you have access to enough interesting information to complete a detailed and comprehensive analysis.

Your assignment for Module 1 is to choose a company to study and to obtain enough information about it to carry out the following instructions and answer the questions:

1. Give a short account of the history of the company, and trace the evolution of its strategy. Try to determine whether the strategic evolution of your company is the product of intended strategies, emergent strategies, or some combination of the two.
2. Identify the mission and major goals of the company.
3. Do a preliminary analysis of the internal strengths and weaknesses of the company and the opportunities and threats that it faces in its environment. On the basis of this analysis, identify the strategies that you think the company should pursue. (You will need to perform a much more detailed analysis later in the book.)
4. Who is the CEO of the company? Evaluate the CEO's leadership capabilities.

CLOSING CASE

Planning for Rise of Cloud Computing at Microsoft

Microsoft is one of the world's largest and most successful computer software enterprises. It's strength is based upon two businesses: Windows, the operating system which resides upon more than 90% of the world's personal computers; and Office, the most widely used suite of office productivity software in the world. These two monopolies generate much of the $22 billion in free cash flow that Microsoft generated in 2010, and are the major reason for the company's stellar 2010 return on invested capital of 38.57%. Both monopolies are also under threat from the rise of a new computing paradigm know as "cloud computing."

For the last 20 years, individuals and enterprises have stored their data and run their applications on their own computer hardware. Individuals have stored data and installed applications onto their own machines. Enterprises have stored data and installed applications onto their own networks of servers and clients. The vast majority of clients (desktops and laptops) have run Windows. A large proportion of servers have also used the Windows server operating system by Microsoft.

However, with the rise of high bandwidth (very fast) Internet connections, it is becoming increasingly attractive to store data and run applications remotely "*in the cloud*" on server farms that are owned by other enterprises. The largest owners of server farms today are Amazon, Google, and Microsoft. Server farms are vast collections of

thousands of computer servers. Each server farm can cost $500 million to construct. Data can be stored and applications "hosted" on server farms. Individuals and enterprises can access these server farms to run their applications from anyplace, anytime, so long as they have an Internet connection. The applications no longer need to reside on their own machines. In fact, all that is needed to run applications is a Web browser. In other words, you may no longer need Windows on your machine to run applications that are "hosted" on a server farm. The Windows monopoly is therefore under threat. In the future, an individual using a laptop that is running a non-Windows operating system, such as Apple's OS X, Google's Android, or Linux, could conceivably run applications hosted on server farms through their Web browser.

There are compelling economic reasons why enterprises might want to move their applications to the cloud. First, they no longer need to purchase their own servers and maintain them, which reduces information technology hardware costs. Second, they no longer need to pay for applications upfront; instead they can adopt a pay-as-you-go approach, in the same way that you pay for electricity from a utility company. This is very attractive, since there is good evidence that corporations overspend on applications, purchasing excess software that is rarely used. Third, server farms can balance workloads very efficiently, spreading out application runtime from numerous customers, thereby optimizing capacity utilization (in contrast, most enterprises must have enough servers for peak load periods, meaning that most of the time they have excess capacity). This means that server farms can run applications at lower costs, and some of those cost savings can be passed onto customers in the form of lower prices.

Microsoft first recognized the potential importance of cloud computing in 2006–2007. At that time, the business was tiny. However, through its environmental scanning, Microsoft quickly realized that over time, the economics of cloud computing would become increasingly attractive. The company's strategic managers also understood the negative implications for their Windows business. The introduction of Google apps in 2008 underlined this. Google apps is a collection of Office-like software, including Word Processing, spreadsheets, and presentation software, that is hosted on Google's server farms, and that enterprises and individuals can access and run through a Web browser. You don't need Windows to run Google apps, and moreover, Google apps represent a direct threat to Microsoft's lucrative Office business.

Microsoft saw the rise of cloud computing as both a threat to their existing business, and an opportunity to grow a new business. The company decided that it had little choice but to aggressively invest in cloud computing. Moreover, the company realized that it had several strengths that it could draw upon in order to build a cloud computing business. It already had built server farms to run its search, X-Box live, and Hotmail businesses, so it knew how to do that. Many enterprises that used Microsoft applications would likely want to continue using them on the cloud, which gave the company an inherent advantage. The company had a significant cash horde that could be used to finance investments in cloud computing, and, had a wealth of software talent that could be used to write applications for cloud computing.

Beginning in 2008, Microsoft charted out a strategy for cloud computing. First, the company made heavy investments in large-scale server farms. Second, the company developed a new operating system to run applications on the cloud. Know as "Azure," this operating system is specifically designed to distribute workloads across large numbers of servers in order to optimize capacity utilization. Third, the company started to rewrite many of its own applications to run in Azure and moved them to the cloud. For example, enterprises can now sign up for Office Live, which is a cloud based version of Office that is run through a Web browser and hosted on Microsoft server farms. Fourth, the company embraced a change in its business model. The traditional business model for most Microsoft applications has required enterprises to pay an annual licensing fee for the number of copies of an application that they install on machines. The new business model is a pay-as-you-go structure for applications like Office Live that are hosted on Microsoft's server farms.

Fifth, Microsoft realized that one of the impediments that corporations face when moving their own customized applications to the cloud is the cost of rewriting the applications to run on a cloud based operating system, such as Azure. To manage this, the company invested in the development of "tools" that would help programmers complete the transition in a cost efficient manner. Finally, Microsoft understood that for security reasons, some enterprises had to maintain control over data on de dicated servers (e.g., regulations require banks to do this). In such cases, Microsoft decided to offer its enterprise customers a "private cloud," which is a collection of servers packed into a container, running Azure, and hosting applications that are dedicated to just that enterprise. Private clouds enable enterprises to gain many of the economic advantages of cloud computing, without moving all data and applications to a "public cloud."

By 2011, the cloud was starting to gain attention. Although it only represented about 5% of the $1.5 trillion in global information technology spending in 2010, numerous companies were starting to announce their investment in cloud services. In the first quarter of 2011 alone, IBM, Hewlett-Packard, and Dell Inc. all announced their intentions to increase their investments in cloud computing infrastructure and applications. This is an emerging market that is posed for rapid growth in the years ahead. Microsoft hopes that through proactive strategic planning, it has positioned the company to do well in this new environment.[50]

Case Discussion Questions

1. If Microsoft does not build a cloud computing business, what might happen to the company over the next decade? Why did the company decide that it had little choice but to invest in cloud computing?

2. The case talks about Microsoft's strengths, which might help it to build a cloud computing business. It does not talk about weaknesses. Can you think of any weaknesses that the company might have?

3. How does the business model for cloud computing differ from the traditional business model used by companies such as Microsoft? What are the implications of this new business model for Microsoft's future financial performance?

4. To develop its cloud computing business, Microsoft implemented a self-contained unit within its organization dedicated to that task. Why do you think that it did this?

5. Cloud computing is still in its infancy. If business history teaches us anything, it is that events often do not turn out the way that planners thought they would. Given this, might it have been better for Microsoft do adopt a "wait and see" attitude? What would have been the benefits of delaying investments? What would have been the costs?

APPENDIX TO CHAPTER: ENTERPRISE VALUATION, ROIC, AND GROWTH

The ultimate goal of strategy is to maximize the value of a company to its shareholders (subject to the important constraints that this is done in a legal, ethical, and socially responsible manner). The two main drivers of enterprise valuation are return on invested capital (ROIC) and the growth rate of profits, g.[51]

ROIC is defined as net operating profits less adjusted taxes (NOPLAT) over the invested capital of the enterprise (IC), where IC is the sum of the company's equity and debt (the method for calculating adjusted taxes need not concern us here). That is:

$$ROIC = NOPLAT/IC$$

where:

NOPLAT = revenues − cost of goods sold
− operating expenses − depreciation
charges − adjusted taxes
IC = value of shareholders' equity + value of debt

The growth rate of profits, g, can be defined as the percentage increase in net operating profits (NOPLAT) over a given time period. More precisely:

$$g = [(NOPLAT_{t+1} - NOPLAT_t)/NOPLAT_t] \times 100$$

Note that if NOPLAT is increasing over time, earnings per share will also increase so long as (a) the number of shares stays constant, or (b) the number of shares outstanding increases more slowly than NOPLAT.

The valuation of a company can be calculated using discounted cash flow analysis and applying it to future expected free cash flows (free cash flow in a period is defined as NOPLAT—net investments). It can be shown that the valuation of a company so calculated is related to the company's weighted average cost of capital (WACC), which is the cost of the equity and debt that the firm uses to finance its business, and the company's ROIC. Specifically:

- If ROIC > WACC, the company is earning more than its cost of capital and it is creating value.
- If ROIC = WACC, the company is earning its cost of capital and its valuation will be stable.
- If ROIC < WACC, the company is earning less than its cost of capital and it is therefore destroying value.

A company that earns more than its cost of capital is even more valuable if it can grow its NOPLAT over time. Conversely, a firm that is not earning its cost of capital destroys value if it grows its NOPLAT. This critical relationship between ROIC, g, and value is shown in Table A1.

In Table A1, the figures in the cells of the matrix represent the discounted present values of future free cash flows for a company that has a starting NOPLAT of $100, invested capital of $1,000, a cost of capital of 10%, and a 25-year time horizon after which ROIC = cost of capital. Table A1ROIC, Growth and Valuation

NOPLAT Growth g	ROIC 7.5%	ROIC 10.0%	ROIC 12.5%	ROIC 15.0%	ROIC 20
3%	887	1000	1058	1113	1170
6%	708	1000	1117	1295	1442
9%	410	1000	1354	1591	1886

The important points revealed by this exercise are as follows:

1. A company with an already high ROIC can create more value by increasing its profit growth rate rather than pushing for an even higher ROIC. Thus, a company with an ROIC of 15% and a 3% growth rate can create more value by increasing its profit growth rate from 3% to 9% than it can by increasing ROIC to 20%.
2. A company with a low ROIC destroys value if it grows. Thus, if ROIC = 7.5%, a 9% growth

rate for 25 years will produce less value than a 3% growth rate. This is because unprofitable growth requires capital investments, the cost of which cannot be covered. Unprofitable growth destroys value.

3. The best of both worlds is high ROIC and high growth.

Very few companies are able to maintain an ROIC > WACC and grow NOPLAT over time, but there are some notable examples, including Dell, Microsoft, and Walmart. Because these companies have generally been able to fund their capital investment needs from internally generated cash flows, they have not had to issue more shares to raise capital. Thus, growth in NOPLAT has translated directly into higher earnings per share for these companies, making their shares more attractive to investors and leading to substantial share-price appreciation. By successfully pursuing strategies that result in a high ROIC and growing NOPLAT, these firms have maximized shareholder value.

Notes

[1]Source: S. Scherreik, "How Efficient is that Company," *Business Week*, December 23, 2003, pp. 94–95; Dell Computer Corporation 10K, March 2006; A. Serwer, "Dell's Midlife Crisis," *Fortune*, November 28, 2005, pp. 147–151; L. Lee, "Dell: Facing up to Past Mistakes," *Business Week*, June 19, 2006, p. 35; K. Allison, "Can Dell Succeed in Getting its Mojo Back?" *Financial Times*, June 29, 2006, p. 19; David Kirkpatrick, "Dell in the Penalty Box," *Fortune*, September 18, 2006, pp. 70–74; "Rebooting Their Systems," *The Economist*, March 12, 2011, pp. 73–74; R. Karlgaard, "Michael Reinvents Dell," *Forbes*, May 9, 2011, p. 32.

[2]There are several different ratios for measuring profitability, such as return on invested capital, return on assets, and return on equity. Although these different measures are highly correlated with each other, finance theorists argue that the return on invested capital is the most accurate measure of profitability. See Tom Copeland, Tim Koller, and Jack Murrin, *Valuation: Measuring and Managing the Value of Companies* (New York: Wiley, 1996).

[3]Trying to estimate the relative importance of industry effects and firm strategy on firm profitability has been one of the most important areas of research in the strategy literature during the past decade. See Y. E. Spanos and S. Lioukas, "An Examination of the Causal Logic of Rent Generation," *Strategic Management* 22 (10) (October 2001): 907–934; and R. P. Rumelt, "How Much Does Industry Matter?" *Strategic Management* 12 (1991): 167–185. See also A. J. Mauri and M. P. Michaels, "Firm and Industry Effects Within Strategic Management: An Empirical Examination," *Strategic Management* 19 (1998): 211–219.

[4]This view is known as "agency theory." See M. C. Jensen and W. H. Meckling, "Theory of the Firm: Managerial Behavior, Agency Costs and Ownership Structure," *Journal of Financial Economics* 3 (1976): 305–360; and E. F. Fama, "Agency Problems and the Theory of the Firm," *Journal of Political Economy* 88 (1980): 375–390.

[5]K. R. Andrews, *The Concept of Corporate Strategy* (Homewood, IL: Dow Jones Irwin, 1971); H. I. Ansoff, *Corporate Strategy* (New York: McGraw-Hill, 1965); C. W. Hofer and D. Schendel, *Strategy Formulation: Analytical Concepts* (St. Paul, MN: West, 1978). See also P. J. Brews and M. R. Hunt, "Learning to Plan and Planning to Learn," *Strategic Management* 20 (1999): 889–913; and R. W. Grant, "Planning in a Turbulent Environment," *Strategic Management* 24 (2003): 491–517.

[6]www.kodak.com/US/en/corp/careers/why/valuesmission.jhtml.

[7]These three questions were first proposed by P. F. Drucker, *Management—Tasks, Responsibilities, Practices* (New York: Harper & Row, 1974), pp. 74–94.

[8]Derek F. Abell, *Defining the Business: The Starting Point of Strategic Planning* (Englewood Cliffs, NJ: Prentice-Hall, 1980).

[9]P. A. Kidwell and P. E. Ceruzzi, *Landmarks in Digital Computing* (Washington, DC: Smithsonian Institute, 1994).

[10]J. C. Collins and J. I. Porras, "Building Your Company's Vision," *Harvard Business Review* (September–October 1996): 65–77.

[11]www.nucor.com/.

[12]See J. P. Kotter and J. L. Heskett, *Corporate Culture and Performance* (New York: Free Press, 1992). For similar work, see Collins and Porras, "Building Your Company's Vision."

[13]E. Freeman, *Strategic Management: A Stakeholder Approach* (Boston: Pitman Press, 1984).

[14]M. D. Richards, *Setting Strategic Goals and Objectives* (St. Paul, MN: West, 1986).

[15]E. A. Locke, G. P. Latham, and M. Erez, "The Determinants of Goal Commitment," *Academy of Management Review* 13 (1988): 23–39.

[16]R. E. Hoskisson, M. A. Hitt, and C. W. L. Hill, "Managerial Incentives and Investment in R&D in Large Multiproduct Firms," *Organization Science* 3 (1993): 325–341.

[17]Andrews, *Concept of Corporate Strategy;* Ansoff, *Corporate Strategy;* Hofer and Schendel, *Strategy Formulation.*

[18]For details, see R. A. Burgelman, "Intraorganizational Ecology of Strategy Making and Organizational Adaptation: Theory and Field Research," *Organization Science* 2 (1991): 239–262; H. Mintzberg, "Patterns in Strategy Formulation," *Management Science* 24 (1978): 934–948; S. L. Hart, "An Integrative Framework for Strategy Making Processes," *Academy of Management Review* 17 (1992): 327–351; G. Hamel, "Strategy as Revolution," *Harvard Business Review* 74 (July–August 1996): 69–83; and R. W. Grant, "Planning in a Turbulent Environment," *Strategic Management Journal* 24 (2003): 491–517. See also G. Gavetti, D. Levinthal, and J. W. Rivkin, "Strategy Making in Novel and Complex Worlds: The Power of Analogy," *Strategic Management Journal,* 26 (2005): 691–712.

[19]This is the premise of those who advocate that complexity and chaos theory should be applied to strategic management. See S. Brown and K. M. Eisenhardt, "The Art of Continuous Change: Linking Complexity Theory and Time Based Evolution in Relentlessly Shifting Organizations," *Administrative Science Quarterly* 29 (1997): 1–34; and R. Stacey and D. Parker, *Chaos, Management and Economics* (London: Institute for Economic Affairs, 1994). See also H. Courtney, J. Kirkland, and P. Viguerie, "Strategy Under Uncertainty," *Harvard Business Review* 75 (November–December 1997): 66–79.

[20]Hart, "Integrative Framework"; Hamel, "Strategy as Revolution."

[21]See Burgelman, "Intraorganizational Ecology," and Mintzberg, "Patterns in Strategy Formulation."

[22]R. A. Burgelman and A. S. Grove, "Strategic Dissonance," *California Management Review* (Winter 1996): 8–28.

[23]C. W. L. Hill and F. T. Rothaermel, "The Performance of Incumbent Firms in the Face of Radical Technological Innovation," *Academy of Management Review* 28 (2003): 257–274.

[24]This story was related to the author by George Rathmann, who at one time was head of 3M's research activities.

[25]Richard T. Pascale, "Perspectives on Strategy: The Real Story Behind Honda's Success," *California Management Review* 26 (1984): 47–72.

[26]This viewpoint is strongly emphasized by Burgelman and Grove, "Strategic Dissonance."

[27]C. C. Miller and L. B. Cardinal, "Strategic Planning and Firm Performance: A Synthesis of More Than Two Decades of Research," *Academy of Management Journal* 37 (1994): 1649–1665. Also see P. R. Rogers, A. Miller, and W. Q. Judge, "Using Information Processing Theory to Understand Planning/Performance Relationships in the Context of Strategy," *Strategic Management* 20 (1999): 567–577.

[28]P. J. Brews and M. R. Hunt, "Learning to Plan and Planning to Learn," *Strategic Management Journal* 20 (1999): 889–913.

[29]P. Cornelius, A. Van de Putte, and M. Romani, "Three Decades of Scenario Planning at Shell," *California Management Review*, 48 (2005): 92–110.

[30]H. Courtney, J. Kirkland, and P. Viguerie, "Strategy Under Uncertainty," *Harvard Business Review* 75 (November–December 1997): 66–79.

[31]P. J. H. Schoemaker, "Multiple Scenario Development: Its Conceptual and Behavioral Foundation," *Strategic Management Journal* 14 (1993): 193–213.

[32]P. Schoemaker, P. J. H. van der Heijden, and A. J. M. Cornelius, "Integrating Scenarios into Strategic Planning at Royal Dutch Shell," *Planning Review* 20(3) (1992): 41–47; I. Wylie, "There is no alternative to…" *Fast Company*, July 2002, pp. 106–111.

[33]"The Next Big Surprise: Scenario Planning," *The Economist* (October 13, 2001), p. 71.

[34]See C. R. Schwenk, "Cognitive Simplification Processes in Strategic Decision Making," *Strategic Management* 5 (1984): 111–128; and K. M. Eisenhardt and M. Zbaracki, "Strategic Decision Making," *Strategic Management* 13 (Special Issue, 1992): 17–37.

[35]H. Simon, *Administrative Behavior* (New York: McGraw-Hill, 1957).

[36]The original statement of this phenomenon was made by A. Tversky and D. Kahneman, "Judgment Under Uncertainty: Heuristics and Biases," *Science* 185 (1974): 1124–1131. See also D. Lovallo and D. Kahneman, "Delusions of Success: How Optimism Undermines Executives' Decisions," *Harvard Business Review* 81 (July 2003): 56–67; and J. S. Hammond, R. L. Keeny, and H. Raiffa, "The Hidden Traps in Decision Making," *Harvard Business Review* 76 (September–October 1998): 25–34.

[37]Schwenk, "Cognitive Simplification Processes," pp. 111–128.

[38]B. M. Staw, "The Escalation of Commitment to a Course of Action," *Academy of Management Review* 6 (1981): 577–587.

[39]R. Roll, "The Hubris Hypotheses of Corporate Takeovers," *Journal of Business* 59 (1986): 197–216.

[40]See R. O. Mason, "A Dialectic Approach to Strategic Planning," *Management Science* 13 (1969): 403–414; R. A. Cosier and J. C. Aplin, "A Critical View of Dialectic Inquiry in Strategic Planning," *Strategic Management* 1 (1980): 343–356; and I. I. Mintroff and R. O. Mason, "Structuring III—Structured Policy Issues: Further Explorations in a Methodology for Messy Problems," *Strategic Management* 1 (1980): 331–342.

⁴¹Mason, "A Dialectic Approach," pp. 403–414.

⁴²Lovallo and Kahneman, "Delusions of Success."

⁴³For a summary of research on strategic leadership, see D. C. Hambrick, "Putting Top Managers Back into the Picture," *Strategic Management* 10 (Special Issue, 1989): 5–15. See also D. Goldman, "What Makes a Leader?" *Harvard Business Review* (November–December 1998): 92–105; H. Mintzberg, "Covert Leadership," *Harvard Business Review* (November–December 1998): 140–148; and R. S. Tedlow, "What Titans Can Teach Us," *Harvard Business Review* (December 2001): 70–79.

⁴⁴N. M. Tichy and D. O. Ulrich, "The Leadership Challenge: A Call for the Transformational Leader," *Sloan Management Review* (Fall 1984): 59–68; F. Westley and H. Mintzberg, "Visionary Leadership and Strategic Management," *Strategic Management* 10 (Special Issue, 1989): 17–32.

⁴⁵Comments were made by Jim Donald at a presentation to University of Washington MBA students.

⁴⁶B. McConnell and J. Huba. *Creating Customer Evangelists* (Chicago: Dearborn Trade Publishing, 2003).

⁴⁷E. Wrapp, "Good Managers Don't Make Policy Decisions," *Harvard Business Review* (September–October 1967): 91–99.

⁴⁸J. Pfeffer, *Managing with Power* (Boston: Harvard Business School Press, 1992). H2: Emotional Intelligence

⁴⁹D. Goleman, "What Makes a Leader?" *Harvard Business Review* (November–December 1998): 92–105.

⁵⁰Sources: (1) Field interviews. (2) A. Vance, "The Cloud: Battle of the Tech Titans," *Bloomberg Business Week*, March 3, 2011. (3) R. Harms and M. Yamartino, "The Economics of the Cloud," *Microsoft White Paper*, November 2010.

⁵¹Sources: C. Y. Baldwin, *Fundamental Enterprise Valuation: Return on Invested Capital*, Harvard Business School Note 9-801-125, July 3, 2004; T. Copeland et al., *Valuation: Measuring and Managing the Value of Companies* (New York: Wiley, 2000).

2

External Analysis: The Identification of Opportunities and Threats

erel photography/istockphoto.com

The United States Airline Industry

The U.S. airline industry has long struggled to make a profit. In the 1990s, investor Warren Buffet famously quipped that the airline industry would have been more fortunate if the Wright Brothers had crashed at Kitty Hawk. Buffet's point was that the airline industry had cumulatively lost more money than it had made—it has always been an economically deleterious proposition. Buffet once made the mistake of investing in the industry when he took a stake in USAir. A few years later, he was forced to write off 75% of the value of that investment. He told his shareholders that if he ever invested in another airline, they should shoot him.

The 2000s have not been kinder to the industry. The airline industry lost $35 billion between 2001 and 2006. It managed to earn meager profits in 2006 and 2007, but lost $24 billion in 2008 as oil and jet fuel prices surged throughout the year. In 2009, the industry lost $4.7 billion as a sharp drop in business travelers—a consequence of the deep recession that followed the global financial crisis—more than offset the beneficial effects of falling oil prices. In 2010, however, the industry returned to profitability, making a slim $3.7 billion in net profit on revenues of $114 billion.

Why has the industry been so unprofitable? Analysts point to a number of factors. Over the years larger carriers such as United, Delta, American, Continental, and USAir have been hurt by low cost budget carriers entering the industry, including Southwest Airlines, Jet Blue, AirTran Airways, and Virgin America. These new entrants have used nonunion labor, often fly just one type of aircraft (which reduces maintenance costs), have focused on the most lucrative routes, typically fly point-to-point (unlike the incumbents who have historically routed passengers through hubs), and compete by offering very low fares. New entrants have helped to create a situation of excess capacity in the industry, and taken share from the incumbent airlines, whose cost structure was often much higher (primarily due to higher labor costs).

The incumbents have had little choice but to respond to fare cuts, and the result has been a protracted industry price war. To complicate matters, the rise of Internet travel sites such as Expedia, Travelocity, and Orbitz has made it much easier for consumers to comparison shop, and has helped to keep fares low.

Beginning in 2001, higher oil prices have complicated matters. Fuel costs accounted for 25% of total revenues in 2009 (labor costs accounted for 26%; together they are the two biggest variable expense items). From 1985 to 2001, oil prices traded in a range between $15 and $25 a barrel. Then, prices began to rise due to strong demand from developing nations including China and India, hitting a high of $147 a barrel in mid-2008. The price for jet fuel, which stood at $0.57 a gallon in December 2001, hit a high of $3.70 a gallon in July 2008, plunging the industry deep into the red. Although oil prices and fuel prices subsequently fell, they remain far above historic levels. For 2010, jet fuel averaged $2.22 a gallon.

Many airlines went bankrupt in the 2000s, including Delta, Northwest, United, and US Airways. The larger airlines continued to fly, however, as they reorganized under chapter 11 bankruptcy laws, and excess capacity persisted in the industry. These companies thereafter came out of bankruptcy protection with lower labor costs, but generating revenue still remained challenging for them.

The late 2000s have been characterized by a wave of mergers in the industry. In 2008, Delta and Northwest merged. In 2010, United and Continental merged, and Southwest Airlines announced plans to acquire AirTran. The driving forces behind these mergers include the desire to reduce excess capacity and lower costs by eliminating duplication. To the extent that they are successful, they could lead to a more stable pricing environment in the industry, and higher profit rates. That, however, remains to be seen.[1]

Overview

Strategy formulation begins with an analysis of the forces that shape competition within the industry in which a company is based. The goal is to understand the opportunities and threats confronting the firm, and to use this understanding to identify strategies that will enable the company to outperform its rivals. **Opportunities** arise when a company can take advantage of conditions in its environment to formulate and implement strategies that enable it to become more profitable. For example, as discussed in the Opening Case, the *opportunity* to merge with other carriers has represented a strategic opportunity for established airlines in the U.S. airline

Opportunities

Elements and conditions in a company's environment that allow it to formulate and implement strategies that enable it to become more profitable.

industry. **Threats** arise when conditions in the external environment endanger the integrity and profitability of the company's business. Rising prices for oil, and hence jet fuel, is a major threat to the profitability of carriers in the U.S. airline industry (see the Opening Case).

This chapter begins with an analysis of the industry environment. First, it examines concepts and tools for analyzing the competitive structure of an industry and identifying industry opportunities and threats. Second, it analyzes the competitive implications that arise when groups of companies within an industry pursue similar or different kinds of competitive strategies. Third, it explores the way an industry evolves over time, and the changes present in competitive conditions. Fourth, it looks at the way in which forces in the macroenvironment affect industry structure and influence opportunities and threats. By the end of the chapter, you will understand that a company must either fit its strategy to the external environment in which it operates, or be able to reshape the environment to its advantage through its chosen strategy in order to succeed.

Defining an Industry

An industry can be defined as a group of companies offering products or services that are close substitutes for each other—that is, products or services that satisfy the same basic customer needs. A company's closest competitors—its rivals—are those that serve the same basic customer needs. For example, carbonated drinks, fruit punches, and bottled water can be viewed as close substitutes for each other because they serve the same basic customer needs for refreshing, cold, nonalcoholic beverages. Thus, we can talk about the soft drink industry, whose major players are Coca-Cola, PepsiCo, and Cadbury Schweppes. Similarly, desktop computers and notebook computers satisfy the same basic need that customers have for computer hardware on which to run personal productivity software, browse the Internet, send e-mail, play games, and store, display, or manipulate digital images. Thus, we can talk about the personal computer industry, whose major players are Dell, Hewlett-Packard, Lenovo (the Chinese company which purchased IBM's personal computer business), and Apple.

External analysis begins by identifying the industry within which a company competes. To do this, managers must start by looking at the basic customer needs their company is serving—that is, they must take a customer-oriented view of their business rather than a product-oriented view (see Chapter 1). An industry is the supply side of a market, and companies within the industry are the suppliers. Customers are the demand side of a market, and are the buyers of the industry's products. The basic customer needs that are served by a market define an industry's boundary. It is very important for managers to realize this, for if they define industry boundaries incorrectly, they may be caught flat-footed by the rise of competitors that serve the same basic customer needs but with different product offerings. For example, Coca-Cola long saw itself as part of the soda industry—meaning carbonated soft drinks—whereas it actually was part of the soft drink industry, which includes noncarbonated soft drinks. In the mid-1990s, the rise of customer demand for bottled water and fruit drinks began to cut into the demand for sodas, which caught Coca-Cola by surprise. Coca-Cola moved quickly to respond to these threats, introducing its own brand of water, Dasani, and acquiring orange juice maker Minute Maid. By defining its industry boundaries too narrowly, Coke almost missed the rapid rise of noncarbonated soft drinks within the soft drinks market.

Threats

Elements in the external environment that could endanger the integrity and profitability of the company's business.

Industry and Sector

An important distinction should be made between an industry and a sector. A sector is a group of closely related industries. For example, as illustrated in Figure 2.1, the computer sector comprises several related industries: the computer component industries (e.g., the disk drive industry, the semiconductor industry, and the modem industry), the computer hardware industries (e.g., the personal computer industry, the hand-held computer industry, which includes smart phones such as the Apple iPhone and slates such as Apple's iPad, and the mainframe computer industry), and the computer software industry. Industries within a sector may be involved with one another in many different ways. Companies in the computer component industries are the suppliers of firms in the computer hardware industries. Companies in the computer software industry provide important complements to computer hardware: the software programs that customers purchase to run on their hardware. Companies in the personal, hand-held, and mainframe industries indirectly compete with each other because all provide products that are, to one degree or another, substitutes for each other.

Industry and Market Segments

It is also important to recognize the difference between an industry and the market segments within that industry. Market segments are distinct groups of customers within a market that can be differentiated from each other on the basis of their individual attributes and specific demands. In the beer industry, for example, there are three primary segments: consumers who drink long-established mass-market brands (e.g., Budweiser); weight conscious consumers who drink less-filling low-calorie mass-market brands (e.g., Coors Light); and consumers who prefer premium-priced

Figure 2.1 The Computer Sector: Industries and Segments

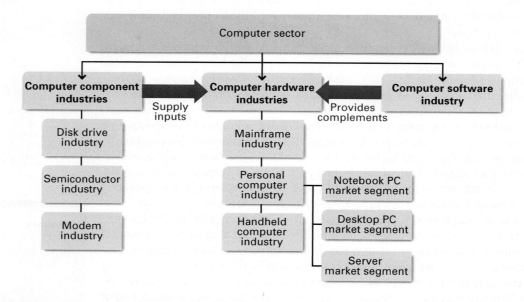

"craft beer" offered by micro-breweries and many importers. Similarly, in the personal computer industry, there are different market segments in which customers desire desktop machines, lightweight portable machines, or servers that sit at the center of a network of personal computers (see Figure 2.1). Personal computer makers recognize the existence of these different segments by producing a range of product offerings that appeal to customers in the different segments. Customers in all of these market segments, however, share a common need for devices on which to run personal software applications.

Changing Industry Boundaries

Industry boundaries may change over time as customer needs evolve, or as emerging new technologies enable companies in unrelated industries to satisfy established customer needs in new ways. We have noted that during the 1990s, as consumers of soft drinks began to develop a taste for bottled water and noncarbonated fruit-based drinks, Coca-Cola found itself in direct competition with the manufacturers of bottled water and fruit-based soft drinks: all were in the same industry.

For an example of how technological change can alter industry boundaries, consider the convergence that is currently taking place between the computer and telecommunications industries. Historically, the telecommunications equipment industry has been considered an entity distinct from the computer hardware industry. However, as telecommunications equipment has moved from analog technology to digital technology, this equipment increasingly resembles computers. The result is that the boundaries between these different industries are now blurring. A digital wireless smart phone such as Apple's iPhone, for example, is nothing more than a small handheld computer with a wireless connection and telephone capabilities. Thus, Samsung and Motorola, which manufacture wireless phones, are now finding themselves competing directly with traditional computer companies such as Apple and Microsoft.

Industry competitive analysis begins by focusing upon the overall industry in which a firm competes before market segments or sector-level issues are considered. Tools that managers can use to perform industry analysis are discussed in the following sections: *competitive forces model, strategic group analysis*, and *industry life-cycle analysis*.

Competitive Forces Model

Once the boundaries of an industry have been identified, managers face the task of analyzing competitive forces within the industry environment in order to identify opportunities and threats. Michael E. Porter's well-known framework, known as "The Five Forces Model," has helped managers with this analysis.[2] An extension of his model, shown in Figure 2.2, focuses on *six* forces that shape competition within an industry: (1) the risk of entry by potential competitors, (2) the intensity of rivalry among established companies within an industry, (3) the bargaining power of buyers, (4) the bargaining power of suppliers, (5) the closeness of substitutes to an industry's products and (6) the power of complement providers (Porter did not recognize this sixth force).

When developing his model, Porter argued that as the forces grow stronger, they limit the ability of established companies to raise prices and earn greater profits. Within Porter's framework, a strong competitive force can be regarded as

Figure 2.2 Competitive Forces

Source: Adapted from "How Competitive Forces Shape Strategy," by Michael E. Porter, Harvard Business Review, March/April 1979.

a threat because it depresses profits. A weak competitive force can be viewed as an opportunity because it allows a company to earn greater profits. The strength of the forces may change overtime as industry conditions change. Managers face the task of recognizing how changes in the forces give rise to new opportunities and threats, and formulating appropriate strategic responses. In addition, it is possible for a company, through its choice of strategy, to alter the strength of one or more of the forces to its advantage. This is discussed in the following chapters.

Risk of Entry by Potential Competitors

Potential competitors are companies that are not currently competing in an industry, but have the capability to do so if they choose. For example, cable television companies have recently emerged as potential competitors to traditional phone companies. New digital technologies have allowed cable companies to offer telephone service over the same cables that transmit television shows.

Established companies already operating in an industry often attempt to discourage potential competitors from entering the industry because as more companies enter, it becomes more difficult for established companies to protect their share of the market and generate profits. A high risk of entry by potential competitors represents a threat to the profitability of established companies. For most of the last two decades, the risk of potential entry into the U.S. airline industry has been high; entrants have included Jet Blue in 2000, and Virgin America in 2007. These entrants have helped to drive down prices and profits in the industry (see the Opening case). If the risk of new entry is low, established companies can take advantage of this opportunity, raise prices, and earn greater returns.

The risk of entry by potential competitors is a function of the height of barriers to entry, that is, factors that make it costly for companies to enter an industry. The greater the costs potential competitors must bear to enter an industry, the greater the barriers to entry, and the weaker this competitive force. High entry barriers may keep potential competitors out of an industry even when industry profits are high. Important barriers to entry include: economies of scale, brand loyalty, absolute cost advantages, customer switching costs, and government regulation.[3] An important strategy is building barriers to entry (in the case of incumbent firms) or finding ways to circumvent those barriers (in the case of new entrants). We shall discuss this topic in more detail in subsequent chapters.

Ed Brown/Alamy

For most of the last two decades, the risk of potential entry into the U.S. airline industry has been high; entrants have included Jet Blue in 2000, and Virgin America in 2007. These entrants have helped to drive down prices and profits in the industry (see the Opening case).

Economies of Scale   Economies of scale arise when unit costs fall as a firm expands its output. Sources of scale economies include: (1) cost reductions gained through mass-producing a standardized output; (2) discounts on bulk purchases of raw material inputs and component parts; (3) the advantages gained by spreading fixed production costs over a large production volume; and (4) the cost savings associated with distributing marketing and advertising costs over a large volume of output. If the cost advantages from economies of scale are significant, a new company that enters the industry and produces on a small scale suffers a significant cost disadvantage relative to established companies. If the new company decides to enter on a large scale in an attempt to obtain these economies of scale, it must raise the capital required to build large-scale production facilities and bear the high risks associated with such an investment. In addition, an increased supply of products will depress prices and result in vigorous retaliation by established companies, which constitutes a further risk of large-scale entry. For these reasons, the threat of entry is reduced when established companies have economies of scale.

Brand Loyalty   Brand loyalty exists when consumers have a preference for the products of established companies. A company can create brand loyalty by continuously advertising its brand-name products and company name, patent protection of its products, product innovation achieved through company research and development programs, an emphasis on high quality products, and exceptional after-sales service. Significant brand loyalty makes it difficult for new entrants to take market share away from established companies. Thus, it reduces the threat of entry by potential competitors; they may see the task of breaking down well-established customer preferences as too costly. In the mass-market segments of the beer industry, for example, the brand loyalty enjoyed by Anheuser Busch (Budweiser), Molson Coors (Coors), and SBA-Miller (Miller) is such that new entry into these segments of the industry is very difficult. Hence, most new entrants have focused on the premium segment of the industry, where established brands have less of a hold. (For an example of how a

Economies of scale

Reductions in unit costs attributed to a larger output.

Brand loyalty

Preference of consumers for the products of established companies.

company circumvented brand-based barriers to entry in the market for carbonated soft drinks, see Strategy in Action 2.1.)

Absolute Cost Advantages   Sometimes established companies have an **absolute cost advantage** relative to potential entrants, meaning that entrants cannot expect to match the established companies' lower cost structure. Absolute cost advantages arise from three main sources: (1) superior production operations and processes due to accumulated experience, patents, or trade secrets; (2) control of particular inputs required for production, such as labor, materials, equipment, or management skills, that are limited in their supply; and (3) access to cheaper funds because existing companies represent lower risks than new entrants. If established companies have an absolute cost advantage, the threat of entry as a competitive force is weaker.

Customer Switching Costs   **Switching costs** arise when a customer invests time, energy, and money switching from the products offered by one established company to the products offered by a new entrant. When switching costs are high, customers can be locked in to the product offerings of established companies, even if new entrants offer better products.[4] A familiar example of switching costs concerns the costs associated with switching from one computer operating system to another. If a person currently uses Microsoft's Windows operating system and has a library of related software applications (e.g., word-processing software, spreadsheet, games) and document files, it is expensive for that person to switch to another computer operating system. To effect the change, this person would need to purchase a new set of software applications and convert all existing document files to the new system's format. Faced with such an expense of money and time, most people are unwilling to make the switch unless the competing operating system offers a substantial leap forward in performance. Thus, the higher the switching costs, the higher the barrier to entry for a company attempting to promote a new computer operating system.

Government Regulations   Historically, government regulation has constituted a major entry barrier into many industries. For example, until the mid-1990s, U.S. government regulation prohibited providers of long-distance telephone service from competing for local telephone service and vice versa. Other potential providers of telephone service, including cable television service companies such as Time Warner and Comcast (which could have used their cables to carry telephone traffic as well as TV signals), were prohibited from entering the market altogether. These regulatory barriers to entry significantly reduced the level of competition in both the local and long-distance telephone markets, enabling telephone companies to earn higher profits than they might have otherwise. All this changed in 1996 when the government significantly deregulated the industry. In the months that followed this repeal of policy, local, long-distance, and cable TV companies all announced their intention to enter each other's markets, and a host of new players entered the market. The Five Forces Model predicts that falling entry barriers due to government deregulation will result in significant new entry, an increase in the intensity of industry competition, and lower industry profit rates, and that is what occurred here.

In summary, if established companies have built brand loyalty for their products, have an absolute cost advantage over potential competitors, have significant scale economies, are the beneficiaries of high switching costs, or enjoy regulatory protection, the risk of entry by potential competitors is greatly diminished; it is a weak competitive force. Consequently, established companies can charge higher prices, and industry

Absolute cost advantage

A cost advantage that is enjoyed by incumbents in an industry and that new entrants cannot expect to match.

Switching costs

Costs that consumers must bear to switch from the products offered by one established company to the products offered by a new entrant.

2.1 STRATEGY IN ACTION

Circumventing Entry Barriers into the Soft Drink Industry

Two companies have long dominated the soft drink industry: Coca-Cola and PepsiCo. By spending large sums of money on advertising and promotion, these two giants have created significant brand loyalty and made it very difficult for new competitors to enter the industry and take market share away. When new competitors try to enter, both companies have responded by cutting prices, forcing the new entrant to curtail expansion plans.

However, in the early 1990s, the Cott Corporation, then a small Canadian bottling company, worked out a strategy for entering the soft drink market. Cott's strategy was deceptively simple. The company initially focused on the cola segment of the soft drink market. Cott entered a deal with Royal Crown Cola for exclusive global rights to its cola concentrate. RC Cola was a small player in the U.S. cola market. Its products were recognized as high-quality, but RC Cola had never been able to effectively challenge Coke or Pepsi. Next, Cott entered an agreement with a Canadian grocery retailer, Loblaw, to provide the retailer with its own private-label brand of cola. The Loblaw private-label brand, known as "President's Choice," was priced low, became very successful, and took shares from both Coke and Pepsi.

Emboldened by this success, Cott decided to try and convince other retailers to carry private-label cola. To retailers, the value proposition was simple because, unlike its major rivals, Cott spent almost nothing on advertising and promotion. This constituted a major source of cost savings, which Cott passed on to retailers in the form of lower prices.

Retailers found that they could significantly undercut the price of Coke and Pepsi colas and still make better profit-margins on private-label brands than on branded colas.

Despite this compelling value proposition, few retailers were willing to sell private-label colas for fear of alienating Coca-Cola and Pepsi, whose products were a major draw for grocery store traffic. Cott's breakthrough came in the 1990s when it signed a deal with Walmart to supply the retailing giant with a private-label cola called "Sam's Choice" (named after Walmart founder Sam Walton). Walmart proved to be the perfect distribution channel for Cott. The retailer was just beginning to appear in the grocery business, and consumers went to Walmart—not to buy branded merchandise—but to get low prices. As Walmart's grocery business grew, so did Cott's sales. Cott soon added other flavors to its offering, such as lemon lime soda, which would compete with 7-Up and Sprite. Moreover, by the late 1990s, other U.S. grocers pressured by Walmart had also started to introduce private-label sodas, and often turned to Cott to supply their needs.

By 2010, Cott had become a $1.8 billion company. Cott captured over 6% of the U.S. soda market up from almost nothing a decade earlier, and held onto a 15% share of sodas in grocery stores, its core channel. The underachievers in this process have been Coca-Cola and PepsiCo, who are now facing the steady erosion of their brand loyalty and market share as consumers increasingly came to recognize the high quality and low price of private-label sodas.

Source: A. Kaplan, *"Cott Corporation,"* Beverage World, June 15, 2004, p. 32; J. Popp, *"2004 Soft Drink Report,"* Beverage Industry, March 2004, pp. 13–18L; Sparks, *"From Coca-Colinization to Copy Catting: The Cott Corporation and Retailers Brand Soft Drinks in the UK and US,"* Agribusiness, March 1997, pp. 153–127 Vol 13, Issue 2; E. Cherney, *"After Flat Sales, Cott Challenges Pepsi, Coca-Cola,"* Wall Street Journal, January 8, 2003, pp. B1, B8; Anonymous, "Cott Corporation: Company Profile," *Just Drinks*, August 2006, pp. 19–22.

profits are, therefore, higher. Evidence from academic research suggests that the height of barriers to entry is one of the most important determinants of profit rates within an industry.[5] Clearly, it is in the interest of established companies to pursue strategies consistent with raising entry barriers to secure these profits. Additionally, potential new entrants must find strategies that allow them to circumvent barriers to entry.

Rivalry Among Established Companies

The second of Porter's Five Forces is the intensity of rivalry among established companies within an industry. Rivalry refers to the competitive struggle between companies within an industry in order to gain market share from each other. The competitive struggle can be fought using price, product design, advertising and promotional spending, direct-selling efforts, and after-sales service and support. Intense rivalry implies lower prices or more spending on non–price-competitive strategies, or both. Because intense rivalry lowers prices and raises costs, it squeezes profits out of an industry. Thus, intense rivalry among established companies constitutes a strong threat to profitability. Alternatively, if rivalry is less intense, companies may have the opportunity to raise prices or reduce spending on non–price-competitive strategies, leading to a higher level of industry profits. The intensity of rivalry among established companies within an industry is largely a function of four factors: (1) industry competitive structure, (2) demand conditions, (3) cost conditions, and (4) the height of exit barriers in the industry.

Industry Competitive Structure The competitive structure of an industry refers to the number and size distribution of companies in it, something that strategic managers determine at the beginning of an industry analysis. Industry structures vary, and different structures have different implications for the intensity of rivalry. A fragmented industry consists of a large number of small or medium-sized companies, none of which is in a position to determine industry price. A consolidated industry is dominated by a small number of large companies (an oligopoly) or, in extreme cases, by just one company (a monopoly), and companies often are in a position to determine industry prices. Examples of fragmented industries are agriculture, dry cleaning, health clubs, real estate brokerage, and sun tanning parlors. Consolidated industries include the aerospace, soft drink, automobile, pharmaceutical, stockbrokerage, and beer industries. In the beer industry, for example, the top three firms account for 80% of industry sales.

Low-entry barriers and commodity-type products that are difficult to differentiate characterize many fragmented industries. This combination tends to result in boom-and-bust cycles as industry profits rapidly rise and fall. Low-entry barriers imply that new entrants will flood the market, hoping to profit from the boom that occurs when demand is strong and profits are high. The explosive number of video stores, health clubs, and sun-tanning parlors that arrived on the market during the 1980s and 1990s exemplifies this situation.

Often the flood of new entrants into a booming, fragmented industry creates excess capacity, and companies start to cut prices in order to use their spare capacity. The difficulty companies face when trying to differentiate their products from those of competitors can exacerbate this tendency. The result is a price war, which depresses industry profits, forces some companies out of business, and deters potential new entrants. For example, after a decade of expansion and booming profits, many health clubs are now finding that they have to offer large discounts in order to maintain their memberships. In general, the more commodity-like an industry's product, the more vicious the price war will be. The bust part of this cycle continues until overall industry capacity is brought into line with demand (through bankruptcies), at which point prices may stabilize again.

A fragmented industry structure, then, constitutes a threat rather than an opportunity. Most booms are relatively short-lived because the ease of new entry leads to excess capacity which often results in price wars and bankruptcies. Because it is often difficult to differentiate products in these industries, trying to minimize costs is the best strategy for a company so it will be profitable in a boom, and survive any subsequent bust. Alternatively, companies might try to adopt strategies that change the underlying structure of fragmented industries and lead to a consolidated industry structure in which the level of industry profitability is increased. (Exactly how companies can do this is something we shall consider in later chapters.)

In consolidated industries, companies are interdependent because one company's competitive actions (changes in price, quality, etc.) directly affect the market share of its rivals, and thus their profitability. When one company makes a move, this generally "forces" a response from its rivals, and the consequence of such competitive interdependence can be a dangerous competitive spiral. Rivalry increases as companies attempt to undercut each other's prices, or offer customers more value in their products, pushing industry profits down in the process. The fare wars that have periodically created havoc in the airline industry provide a good illustration of this process (see the Opening case).

Companies in consolidated industries sometimes seek to reduce this threat by following the prices set by the dominant company in the industry.[6] However, companies must be careful, for explicit face-to-face price-fixing agreements are illegal. (Tacit, indirect agreements, arrived at without direct or intentional communication, are legal.) Instead, companies set prices by watching, interpreting, anticipating, and responding to one another's strategies. However, tacit price-leadership agreements often break down under adverse economic conditions, as has occurred in the breakfast cereal industry, profiled in Strategy in Action 2.2.

Industry Demand   The level of industry demand is the second determinant of the intensity of rivalry among established companies (competitive structure being the first). Growing demand from new customers or additional purchases by existing customers tend to moderate competition by providing greater scope for companies to compete for customers. Growing demand tends to reduce rivalry because all companies can sell more without taking market share away from other companies. High industry profits are often the result. Conversely, declining demand results in increased rivalry as companies fight to maintain market share and revenues (as in the breakfast cereal industry example). Demand declines when customers exit the marketplace, or when each customer purchases less. When this is the case, a company can only grow by taking market share away from other companies. Thus, declining demand constitutes a major threat, for it increases the extent of rivalry between established companies.

Cost Conditions   The cost structure of firms in an industry is a third determinant of rivalry. In industries where fixed costs are high, profitability tends to be highly leveraged to sales volume, and the desire to grow volume can spark intense rivalry. Fixed costs are the costs that must be paid before the firm makes a single sale. For example, before they can offer service, cable TV companies must lay cable in the ground; the cost of doing so is a fixed cost. Similarly, to offer express courier service, a company such as FedEx must first invest in planes, package-sorting facilities, and delivery trucks—all fixed costs that require significant capital investments. In industries where the fixed costs of production are high, firms cannot cover their fixed costs and will not be profitable if sales volume is low. Thus they have an incentive to cut their prices and/or increase promotional spending to drive up sales volume in order to cover fixed costs. In situations where demand is not growing fast enough and too many companies are simultaneously engaged in the same actions (cutting prices and/ or raising promotional spending in an attempt to cover fixed costs), the result can be intense rivalry and lower profits. Research suggests that the weakest firms in an industry often initiate such actions, precisely because they are struggling to cover their fixed costs.[7]

STRATEGY IN ACTION

Price Wars in the Breakfast Cereal Industry

For decades, the breakfast cereal industry was one of the most profitable in the United States. The industry has a consolidated structure dominated by Kellogg's, General Mills, and Kraft Foods with its Post brand. Strong brand loyalty, coupled with control over the allocation of supermarket shelf space, helped to limit the potential for new entry. Meanwhile, steady demand growth of about 3% per annum kept industry revenues expanding. Kellogg's, which accounted for over 40% of the market share, acted as the price leader in the industry. Every year Kellogg's increased cereal prices, its rivals followed, and industry profits remained high.

This favorable industry structure began to change in the 1990s when growth in demand slowed—and then stagnated—as a latte and bagel or muffin replaced cereal as the American morning fare. Then, the rise of powerful discounters such as Walmart, (which entered the grocery industry in 1994) began to aggressively promote their own cereal brands, and priced their products significantly below the brand-name cereals. As the decade progressed, other grocery chains such as Kroger's started to follow suit, and brand loyalty in the industry began to decline as customers realized that a $2.50 bag of wheat flakes from Walmart tasted about the same as a $3.50 box of Cornflakes from Kellogg's. As sales of cheaper store-brand cereals began to take off, supermarkets, no longer as dependent on brand names to bring traffic into their stores, began to demand lower prices from the branded cereal manufacturers.

For several years, manufacturers of brand-name cereals tried to hold out against these adverse trends, but in the mid-1990s, the dam broke. In 1996, Kraft (then owned by Philip Morris) aggressively cut prices by 20% for its Post brand in an attempt to gain market share. Kellogg's soon followed with a 19% price cut on two-thirds of its brands, and General Mills quickly did the same. The decades of tacit price collusion were officially over. If breakfast cereal companies were hoping that price cuts would stimulate demand, they were wrong. Instead, demand remained flat while revenues and margins followed price decreases, and operating margins at Kellogg's dropped from 18% in 1995 to 10.2% in 1996, a trend also experienced by the other brand-name cereal manufacturers.

By 2000, conditions had only worsened. Private-label sales continued to make inroads, gaining over 10% of the market. Moreover, sales of breakfast cereals started to contract at 1% per annum. To cap it off, an aggressive General Mills continued to launch expensive price-and-promotion campaigns in an attempt to take share away from the market leader. Kellogg's saw its market share slip to just over 30% in 2001, behind the 31% now held by General Mills. For the first time since 1906, Kellogg's no longer led the market. Moreover, profits at all three major producers remained weak in the face of continued price discounting.

In mid-2001, General Mills finally blinked and raised prices a modest 2% in response to its own rising costs. Competitors followed, signaling—perhaps—that after a decade of costly price warfare, pricing discipline might once more emerge in the industry. Both Kellogg's and General Mills tried to move further away from price competition by focusing on brand extensions, such as Special K containing berries and new varieties of Cheerios. Efforts with Special K helped Kellogg's recapture market leadership from General Mills, and, more importantly, the renewed emphasis on non-price competition halted years of damaging price warfare.

However, after a decade of relative peace, price wars broke out in 2010 once more in this industry. The trigger, yet again, appears to have been falling demand for breakfast cereals due to the consumption of substitutes, such as a quick trip to the local coffee shop. In the third quarter of 2010, prices fell by 3.6%, and unit volumes by 3.4%, leading to falling profit rates at Kellogg's. Both General Mills and Kellogg's announced plans to introduce new products in 2011 in an attempt to boost demand and raise prices.

Sources: G. Morgenson, "Denial in Battle Creek," *Forbes,* October 7, 1996, p. 44; J. Muller, "Thinking out of the Cereal Box," *Business Week,* January 15, 2001, p. 54; A. Merrill, "General Mills Increases Prices," *Star Tribune,* June 5, 2001, p. 1D; S. Reyes, "Big G, Kellogg's Attempt to Berry Each Other," *Brandweek,* October 7, 2002, p. 8; M. Andrejczak, "Kellogg's Profit Hurt by Cereal Price War," *Market Watch,* November 2, 2010.

Exit Barriers   Exit barriers are economic, strategic, and emotional factors that prevent companies from leaving an industry.[8] If exit barriers are high, companies become locked into an unprofitable industry where overall demand is static or declining. The result is often excess productive capacity, leading to even more intense rivalry and price competition as companies cut prices attempting to obtain the customer orders needed to use their idle capacity and cover their fixed costs.[9] Common exit barriers include the following:

- Investments in assets such as specific machines, equipment, or operating facilities that are of little or no value in alternative uses, or cannot be later sold. If the company wishes to leave the industry, it must write off the book value of these assets.
- High fixed costs of exit, such as severance pay, health benefits, or pensions that must be paid to workers who are being made redundant when a company ceases to operate.
- Emotional attachments to an industry, such as when a company's owners or employees are unwilling to exit from an industry for sentimental reasons or because of pride.
- Economic dependence on the industry because a company relies on a single industry for its entire revenue and all profits.
- The need to maintain an expensive collection of assets at or above a minimum level in order to participate effectively in the industry.
- Bankruptcy regulations, particularly in the United States, where Chapter 11 bankruptcy provisions allow insolvent enterprises to continue operating and to reorganize under this protection. These regulations can keep unprofitable assets in the industry, result in persistent excess capacity, and lengthen the time required to bring industry supply in line with demand. (This occurred in the U.S. airline industry, see the Opening Case).

As an example of exit barriers and effects in practice, consider the express mail and parcel delivery industry. Key players in this industry, such as FedEx and UPS, rely entirely upon the delivery business for their revenues and profits. They must be able to guarantee their customers that they will deliver packages to all major localities in the United States, and much of their investment is specific to this purpose. To meet this guarantee, they need a nationwide network of air routes and ground routes, an asset that is required in order to participate in the industry. If excess capacity develops in this industry, as it does from time to time, FedEx cannot incrementally reduce or minimize its excess capacity by deciding not to fly to and deliver packages in Miami, for example, because that portion of its network is underused. If it did, it would no longer be able to guarantee to its customers that packages could be delivered to all major locations in the United States, and its customers would switch to another carrier. Thus, the need to maintain a nationwide network is an exit barrier that can result in persistent excess capacity in the air express industry during periods of weak demand. Finally, both UPS and FedEx managers and employees are emotionally tied to this industry because they both were first movers, in the ground and air segments of the industry, respectively, and because their employees are also major owners of their companies' stock and they are dependent financially on the fortunes of the delivery business.

The Bargaining Power of Buyers

The third of Porter's Five Forces is the bargaining power of buyers. An industry's buyers may be the individual customers who consume its products (end-users) or the companies that distribute an industry's products to end-users, such as retailers and wholesalers. For example, while soap powder made by Procter & Gamble and Unilever is consumed by end-users, the principal buyers of soap powder are supermarket chains and discount stores, which resell the product to end-users. The bargaining power of buyers refers to the ability of buyers to bargain down prices charged by companies in the industry, or to raise the costs of companies in the industry by demanding better product quality and service. By lowering prices and raising costs, powerful buyers can squeeze profits out of an industry. Powerful buyers, therefore, should be viewed as a threat. Alternatively, when buyers are in a weak bargaining position, companies in an industry can raise prices and perhaps reduce their costs by lowering product quality and service, thus increasing the level of industry profits. Buyers are most powerful in the following circumstances:

- When the industry that is supplying a particular product or service is composed of many small companies and the buyers are large and few in number. These circumstances allow the buyers to dominate supplying companies.
- When the buyers purchase in large quantities. In such circumstances, buyers can use their purchasing power as leverage to bargain for price reductions.
- When the supply industry depends upon buyers for a large percentage of its total orders.
- When switching costs are low so that buyers can pit the supplying companies against each other to force down prices.
- When it is economically feasible for buyers to purchase an input from several companies at once so that buyers can pit one company in the industry against another.
- When buyers can threaten to enter the industry and independently produce the product thus supplying their own needs, also a tactic for forcing down industry prices.

The automobile component supply industry, whose buyers are large manufacturers such as GM, Ford, and Toyota, is a good example of an industry in which buyers have strong bargaining power, and thus a strong competitive threat. Why? The suppliers of auto components are numerous and typically smaller in scale; their buyers, the auto manufacturers, are large in size and few in number. Additionally, to keep component prices down, both Ford and GM have used the threat of manufacturing a component themselves rather than buying it from auto component suppliers. The automakers use their powerful position to pit suppliers against one another, forcing down the prices for component parts and demanding better quality. If a component supplier objects, the automaker can use the threat of switching to another supplier as a bargaining tool.

Another issue is that the relative power of buyers and suppliers tends to change in response to changing industry conditions. For example, changes now taking place in the pharmaceutical and health care industries are allowing major buyers of pharmaceuticals (hospitals and health maintenance organizations) to gain power over the suppliers of pharmaceuticals and demand lower prices.

The Bargaining Power of Suppliers

The fourth of Porter's five competitive forces is the bargaining power of suppliers—the organizations that provide inputs into the industry, such as materials, services, and labor (which may be individuals, organizations such as labor unions, or companies that supply contract labor). The bargaining power of suppliers refers to the ability of suppliers to raise input prices, or to raise the costs of the industry in other ways—for example, by providing poor-quality inputs or poor service.

Powerful suppliers squeeze profits out of an industry by raising the costs of companies in the industry. Thus, powerful suppliers are a threat. Conversely, if suppliers are weak, companies in the industry have the opportunity to force down input prices and demand higher-quality inputs (such as more productive labor). As with buyers, the ability of suppliers to make demands on a company depends on their power relative to that of the company. Suppliers are most powerful in these situations:

- The product that suppliers sell has few substitutes and is vital to the companies in an industry.
- The profitability of suppliers is not significantly affected by the purchases of companies in a particular industry, in other words, when the industry is not an important customer to the suppliers.
- Companies in an industry would experience significant switching costs if they moved to the product of a different supplier because a particular supplier's products are unique or different. In such cases, the company depends upon a particular supplier and cannot pit suppliers against each other to reduce prices.
- Suppliers can threaten to enter their customers' industry and use their inputs to produce products that would compete directly with those of companies already in the industry.
- Companies in the industry cannot threaten to enter their suppliers' industry and make their own inputs as a tactic for lowering the price of inputs.

An example of an industry in which companies are dependent upon a powerful supplier is the personal computer industry. Personal computer firms are heavily dependent on Intel, the world's largest supplier of microprocessors for PCs. Intel's microprocessor chips are the industry standard for personal computers. Intel's competitors, such as Advanced Micro Devices (AMD), must develop and supply chips that are compatible with Intel's standard. Although AMD has developed competing chips, Intel still supplies approximately 85% of the chips used in PCs primarily because only Intel has the manufacturing capacity required to serve a large share of the market. It is beyond the financial resources of Intel's competitors, such as AMD, to match the scale and efficiency of Intel's manufacturing systems. This means that while PC manufacturers can purchase some microprocessors from Intel's rivals, most notably AMD, they still must turn to Intel for the bulk of their supply. Because Intel is in a powerful bargaining position, it can charge higher prices for its microprocessors than if its competitors were stronger and more numerous (i.e., if the microprocessor industry were fragmented).

Substitute Products

The final force in Porter's model is the threat of substitute products: the products of different businesses or industries that can satisfy similar customer needs. For example, companies in the coffee industry compete indirectly with those in the tea and soft drink industries because all three serve customer needs for nonalcoholic drinks. The existence of close substitutes is a strong competitive threat because this limits the price that companies in one industry can charge for their product, which also limits industry profitability. If the price of coffee rises too much relative to that of tea or soft drinks, coffee drinkers may switch to those substitutes.

If an industry's products have few close substitutes (making substitutes a weak competitive force) then companies in the industry have the opportunity to raise prices and earn additional profits. Thus, there is no close substitute for microprocessors, which gives companies like Intel and AMD the ability to charge higher prices than if there were substitutes for microprocessors.

A Sixth Force: Complementors

Andrew Grove, the former CEO of Intel, has argued that Porter's Five Forces Model ignores a sixth force: the power, vigor, and competence of complementors.[10] Complementors are companies that sell products that add value to (complement) the products of companies in an industry because, when used together, the use of the combined products better satisfies customer demands. For example, the complementors to the personal computer industry are the companies that make software applications to run on the computers. The greater the supply of high-quality software applications running on these machines, the greater the value of personal computers to customers, the greater the demand for PCs, and the greater the profitability of the personal computer industry.

Grove's argument has a strong foundation in economic theory, which has long argued that both substitutes and complements influence demand in an industry.[11] Moreover, recent research has emphasized the importance of complementary products in determining demand and profitability in many high-technology industries, such as the computer industry in which Grove made his mark.[12] When complements are an important determinant of demand for an industry's products, industry profits critically depend upon an adequate supply of complementary products. When the number of complementors is increasing and producing attractive complementary products, demand increases and profits in the industry can broaden opportunities for creating value. Conversely, if complementors are weak, and are not producing attractive complementary products, they can become a threat, slowing industry growth and limiting profitability.

Summary

The systematic analysis of forces in the industry environment using the Porter framework is a powerful tool that helps managers to think strategically. It is important to recognize that one competitive force often affects others, and all forces need to be considered when performing industry analysis. Industry analysis inevitably leads managers to think systematically about strategic choices. How will these choices be affected by the forces of industry competition? How will these choices affect the five forces and change conditions in the industry? For an example of industry analysis using Competitive Forces model framework see the Focus on Dell feature.

Strategic Groups Within Industries

Companies in an industry often differ significantly from one another with regard to the way they strategically position their products in the market. Factors such as the distribution channels they use, the market segments they serve, the quality of their products, technological leadership, customer service, pricing policy, advertising policy, and promotions affect product position. As a result of these differences, within most industries, it is possible to observe groups of companies

FOCUS ON D∅LL

Dell Inc. and the Personal Computer Industry

The global personal computer industry is very competitive. At the end of 2010, Hewlett-Packard was market leader with a global share of 19.4% followed by Dell Inc. with 12%, Acer with 11.5%, Lenovo with 9.5% and Toshiba with 5.8%. Apple had 4.5% of the market, although in the U.S. its share was closer to 9%, (and among U.S. consumers, Apple's market share is around 25%). A long tail of small companies accounts for the remainder of the market, and some focus on local markets and make unbranded "white box" computers.

The long tail of small companies reflects relatively low barriers to entry. The open architecture of the personal computer means that key components—such as an Intel compatible microprocessor, a Windows operating system, memory chips, a hard drive, and other similar hardware—can be purchased easily on the open market. Assembly is easy, requiring very little capital equipment or technical skills, and economies of scale in production are not particularly significant. Although small entrants lack the brand name recognition of the market share leaders, they survive in the industry by pricing their machines a few hundred dollars below market leaders and capturing the demand of price sensitive consumers. This puts constant pressure on brand name companies and the prices they can charge.

Moreover, most buyers view the product offerings of different branded companies as very close substitutes for each other, so competition between them often defaults to price. Consequently, the average selling price of a PC has fallen from around $1,700 in 1999 to under $750 in 2010, and projections are that it may continue to fall, fueled in part by aggressive competition between Dell and Hewlett Packard.

The constant downward pressure on prices makes it hard for personal computer companies to bring in big gross margins, and results in lower profitability (with the exception of Apple, which has successfully differentiated its offering).

The downward pressure on prices has been exacerbated by slowing demand growth in many developed nations, including the world's largest market, the United States, where the market is now mature and demand is limited to replacement demand plus expansion in the overall population. There is also a pronounced cyclical aspect to demand from businesses. Demand growth was just 4% in 2009, for example, due to a global recession, but it jumped to 14% in 2010 as the economy recovered.

Personal computer companies have long had to deal with two very powerful suppliers—Microsoft, which supplies the industry standard operating system, Windows, and Intel, the supplier of the industry standard microprocessor. Microsoft and Intel have been able to charge relatively high prices for their products, which has raised input costs for personal computer manufacturers, and reduced their profitability.

A new substitute has also appeared—slate format computers led by Apple's iPad. Due to the booming popularity of the iPad, analysts predict that demand for laptops will slow in the years ahead and both consumers and businesses will increasingly use slates like the iPad to satisfy their mobile computing needs.

In sum, the personal computer industry is an intensely competitive one. The combination of low-entry barriers, intense rivalry among established companies, slowing demand growth, buyers who are indifferent between the offerings of various companies (and often look at price before anything else), powerful suppliers who have raised the prices for key inputs, and new substitutes, all make it difficult for established companies to earn a decent profits. Against this background, the performance of Dell over the last decade has generally been very strong, illustrating exactly how strong the company's business model and competitive advantage has historically been.

Source: T.W. Smith, *Standard & Poor's Industry Surveys, Computers: Hardware,* April 21, 2011. M. Dickerson, "Plain PCs sitting pretty," *Los Angeles Times,* December 11, 2005, page C1. *IDC Press Release,* "Long Term PC Outlook Improves," September 14, 2006.

in which each company follows a business model that is similar to that pursued by other companies in the group, but different from the business model followed by companies in other groups. These different groups of companies are known as strategic groups.[13]

Normally, the basic differences between the business models that companies in different strategic groups use can be captured by a relatively small number of strategic factors. For example, in the pharmaceutical industry, two primary strategic groups stand out (see Figure 2.3).[14] One group, which includes such companies as Merck, Eli Lilly, and Pfizer, is characterized by a business model based on heavy R&D spending, and a focus on developing new, proprietary, blockbuster drugs. The companies in this proprietary strategic group are pursuing a high-risk, high-return strategy because basic drug research is difficult and expensive. Bringing a new drug to market can cost up to $800 million in R&D money and a decade of research and clinical trials. The risks are high because the failure rate in new drug development is very high: only 1 out of every 5 drugs entering clinical trials is eventually approved by the U.S. Food and Drug Administration. However, this strategy has potential for a high-return because a single successful drug can be patented, giving the innovator a monopoly on the production and sale of the drug for the life of the patent (patents are issued for 20 years). This allows proprietary companies to charge a high price for the patented drug, earning them millions, if not billions, of dollars over the lifetime of the patent.

The second strategic group might be characterized as the generic drug strategic group. This group of companies, which includes Forest Labs, Mylan Labs, and Watson Pharmaceuticals, focuses on the manufacture of generic drugs: low-cost copies of drugs that were developed by companies in the proprietary group, which now have expired patents. Low R&D spending, production efficiency, and an emphasis on low prices characterize the business models of companies in this strategic group. They are pursuing a low-risk, low-return strategy. It is low risk because these companies are not investing millions of dollars in R&D, and low return because they cannot charge high prices for their products.

Figure 2.3 Strategic Groups in the Pharmaceutical Industry

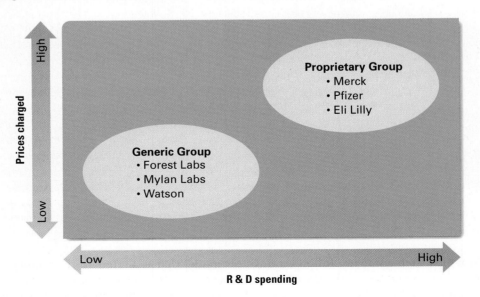

Implications of Strategic Groups

The concept of strategic groups has a number of implications for the identification of opportunities and threats within an industry. First, because all companies in a strategic group are pursuing a similar business model, customers tend to view the products of such enterprises as direct substitutes for each other. Thus, a company's closest competitors are those in its strategic group, not those in other strategic groups in the industry. The most immediate threat to a company's profitability comes from rivals within its own strategic group. For example, in the retail industry, there is a group of companies that might be characterized as discounters. Included in this group are Walmart, Kmart, Target, and Fred Meyer. These companies compete vigorously with each other, rather than with other retailers in different groups, such as Nordstrom or The Gap. Kmart, for example, was driven into bankruptcy in the early 2000s, not because Nordstrom or The Gap took its business, but because Walmart and Target gained share in the discounting group by virtue of their superior strategic execution of the discounting business model.

A second competitive implication is that different strategic groups can have different relationships to each of the competitive forces; thus, each strategic group may face a different set of opportunities and threats. Each of the following can be a relatively strong or weak competitive force depending on the competitive positioning approach adopted by each strategic group in the industry: the risk of new entry by potential competitors; the degree of rivalry among companies within a group; the bargaining power of buyers; the bargaining power of suppliers; and the competitive force of substitute and complementary products. For example, in the pharmaceutical industry, companies in the proprietary group historically have been in a very powerful position in relation to buyers because their products are patented and there are no substitutes. Also, rivalry based on price competition within this group has been low because competition in the industry depends upon which company is first to patent a new drug ("patent races"), not around drug prices. Thus, companies in this group have been able to charge high prices and earn high profits. In contrast, companies in the generic group have been in a much weaker position because many companies are able to produce different versions of the same generic drug after patents expire. Thus, in this strategic group, products are close substitutes, rivalry has been high, and price competition has led to lower profits than the companies in the proprietary group.

The Role of Mobility Barriers

It follows from these two issues that some strategic groups are more desirable than others because competitive forces open up greater opportunities and present fewer threats for those groups. Managers, after analyzing their industry, might identify a strategic group where competitive forces are weaker and higher profits can be made. Sensing an opportunity, they might contemplate changing their business model and move to compete in that strategic group. However, taking advantage of this opportunity may be difficult because of mobility barriers between strategic groups.

Mobility barriers are within-industry factors that inhibit the movement of companies between strategic groups. They include the barriers to entry into a group and the barriers to exit from a company's existing group. For example, Forest Labs would encounter mobility barriers if it attempted to enter the proprietary group in the pharmaceutical industry because it lacks R&D skills, and building these skills would be an expensive proposition. Over time, companies in different groups develop different cost structures, skills and competencies that allow them different pricing options and choices. A company contemplating entry into another strategic group must evaluate whether it has the ability to imitate, and outperform, its potential competitors in that strategic group. Managers must determine if it is cost-effective to overcome mobility barriers before deciding whether the move is worthwhile.

In summary, an important task of industry analysis is to determine the sources of the similarities and differences among companies in an industry, and to understand the nature of competition in an industry. This analysis often reveals new opportunities to compete in an industry by developing new products to better meet the needs of customers. It can also reveal emerging threats that can be effectively countered by changing competitive strategy. This issue is taken up in Chapters 5, 6, and 7, which examine crafting competitive strategy in different kinds of markets to build a competitive advantage over rivals and best satisfy customer needs.

Industry Life-Cycle Analysis

Changes that take place in an industry over time are an important determinant of the strength of the competitive forces in the industry (and of the nature of opportunities and threats). The similarities and differences between companies in an industry often become more pronounced over time, and its strategic group structure frequently changes. The strength and nature of each of the competitive forces also change as an industry evolves, particularly the two forces of risk of entry by potential competitors and rivalry among existing firms.[15]

A useful tool for analyzing the effects that industry evolution has on competitive forces is the industry life-cycle model. This model identifies five sequential stages in the evolution of an industry that lead to five distinct kinds of industry environment: embryonic, growth, shakeout, mature, and decline (see Figure 2.4). The task managers face is to anticipate how the strength of competitive forces will change as the industry environment evolves, and to formulate strategies that take advantage of opportunities as they arise and that counter emerging threats.

Embryonic Industries

An embryonic industry refers to an industry just beginning to develop (e.g., personal computers and biotechnology in the 1970s, wireless communications in the 1980s, Internet retailing in the early 1990s, and nanotechnology today). Growth at this stage is slow because of factors such as buyers' unfamiliarity with the industry's product, high prices due to the inability of companies to reap any significant scale economies, and poorly developed distribution channels. Barriers to entry tend to be based on access to key technological know-how rather than cost economies or brand loyalty. If the core know-how required to compete in the industry is complex and difficult to grasp, barriers to entry can be quite high, and established companies will be protected from potential competitors. Rivalry in embryonic industries is based not so much on price as on educating customers, opening up distribution channels, and perfecting the design of the product. Such rivalry can be intense, and the company that is the first to solve design problems often has the opportunity to develop a significant market position. An embryonic industry may also be the creation of one company's innovative efforts, as happened with microprocessors (Intel), vacuum

Figure 2.4 Stages in the Industry Life-Cycle

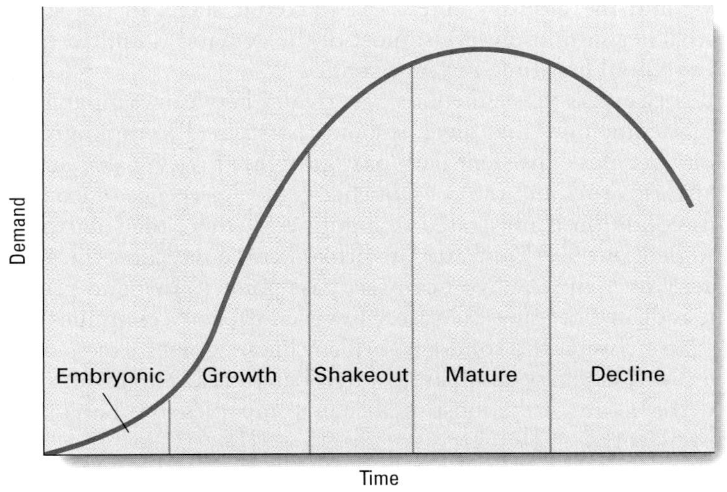

© Cengage Learning 2013

cleaners (Hoover), photocopiers (Xerox), small package express delivery (FedEx) and Internet search engines (Google). In such circumstances, the developing company has a major opportunity to capitalize on the lack of rivalry and build a strong hold on the market.

Growth Industries

Once demand for the industry's product begins to increase, the industry develops the characteristics of a growth industry. In a growth industry, first-time demand is expanding rapidly as many new customers enter the market. Typically, an industry grows when customers become familiar with the product, prices fall because experience and scale economies have been attained, and distribution channels develop. The U.S. wireless telephone industry remained in the growth stage for most of the 1990s. In 1990, there were only 5 million cellular subscribers in the nation. By 2010, this figure had increased to about 306 million.

Normally, the importance of control over technological knowledge as a barrier to entry has diminished by the time an industry enters its growth stage. Because few companies have yet to achieve significant scale economies or built brand loyalty, other entry barriers tend to be relatively low as well, particularly early in the growth stage. Thus, the threat from potential competitors is typically highest at this point. Paradoxically, however, high growth usually means that new entrants can be absorbed into an industry without a marked increase in the intensity of rivalry. Thus, rivalry tends to be relatively low. Rapid growth in demand enables companies to expand their revenues and profits without taking market share away from competitors. A strategically aware company takes advantage of the relatively benign environment of the growth stage to prepare itself for the intense competition of the coming industry shakeout.

Industry Shakeout

Explosive growth cannot be maintained indefinitely. Sooner or later, the rate of growth slows, and the industry enters the shakeout stage. In the shakeout stage, demand approaches saturation levels: most of the demand is limited to replacement because few potential first-time buyers remain.

As an industry enters the shakeout stage, rivalry between companies becomes intense. Typically, companies that have become accustomed to rapid growth continue to add capacity at rates consistent with past growth. However, demand is no longer growing at historic rates, and the consequence is the emergence of excess productive capacity. This condition is illustrated in Figure 2.5, where the solid curve indicates the growth in demand over time and the broken curve indicates the growth in productive capacity over time. As you can see, past point t_1, demand growth becomes slower as the industry becomes mature. However, capacity continues to grow until time t_2. The gap between the solid and broken lines signifies excess capacity. In an attempt to use this capacity, companies often cut prices. The result can be a price war, which drives many of the most inefficient companies into bankruptcy: enough to deter any new entry.

Mature Industries

The shakeout stage ends when the industry enters its mature stage: the market is totally saturated, demand is limited to replacement demand, and growth is low or zero. The growth that remains comes from population expansion, bringing new customers into the market or increasing replacement demand.

As an industry enters maturity, barriers to entry increase, and the threat of entry from potential competitors decreases. As growth slows during the shakeout, companies can no longer maintain historic growth rates merely by holding on to their market share. Competition for market share develops, driving down prices and often

Figure 2.5   Growth in Demand and Capacity

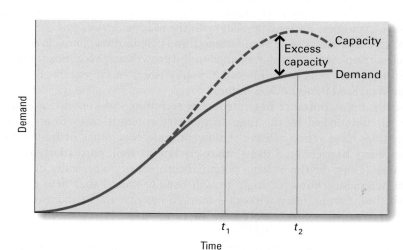

producing a price war, as has happened in the airline and personal computer industries. To survive the shakeout, companies begin to focus on minimizing costs and building brand loyalty. The airlines, for example, tried to cut operating costs by hiring nonunion labor, and build brand loyalty by introducing frequent-flyer programs. Personal computer companies have sought to build brand loyalty by providing excellent after-sales service and working to lower their cost structures. By the time an industry matures, the surviving companies are those that have brand loyalty and efficient low-cost operations. Because both these factors constitute a significant barrier to entry, the threat of entry by potential competitors is often greatly diminished. High entry barriers in mature industries can give companies the opportunity to increase prices and profits—although this does not always occur.

As a result of the shakeout, most industries in the maturity stage have consolidated and become oligopolies. Examples include the beer industry, breakfast cereal industry, and pharmaceutical industry. In mature industries, companies tend to recognize their interdependence and try to avoid price wars. Stable demand gives them the opportunity to enter into price-leadership agreements. The net effect is to reduce the threat of intense rivalry among established companies, thereby allowing greater profitability. Nevertheless, the stability of a mature industry is always threatened by further price wars. A general slump in economic activity can depress industry demand. As companies fight to maintain their revenues in the face of declining demand, price-leadership agreements break down, rivalry increases, and prices and profits fall. The periodic price wars that occur in the airline industry, for example, appear to follow this pattern.

Declining Industries

Eventually, most industries enter a stage of decline: growth becomes negative for a variety of reasons, including technological substitution (e.g., air travel instead of rail travel), social changes (greater health consciousness impacting tobacco sales), demographics (the declining birthrate damaging the market for baby and child products), and international competition (low-cost foreign competition helped pushed the U.S. Steel industry into decline). Within a declining industry, the degree of rivalry among established companies usually increases. Depending on the speed of the decline and the height of exit barriers, competitive pressures can become as fierce as in the shakeout stage.[16] The largest problem in a declining industry is that falling demand leads to the emergence of excess capacity. In trying to use this capacity, companies begin to cut prices, thus sparking a price war. The U.S. Steel industry experienced these problems during the 1980s and 1990s because steel companies tried to use their excess capacity despite falling demand. The same problem occurred in the airline industry in the 1990–1992 period, in 2001–2005, and again in 2008–2009 as companies cut prices to ensure that they would not be flying with half-empty planes (i.e., they would not be operating with substantial excess capacity—see the Opening Case). Exit barriers play a part in adjusting excess capacity. The greater the exit barriers, the harder it is for companies to reduce capacity, and the greater the threat of severe price competition.

Summary

In summary, a third task of industry analysis is to identify the opportunities and threats that are characteristic of different kinds of industry environments in order to develop an effective business model and competitive strategy. Managers have to tailor their strategies to changing industry conditions. They must also learn to recognize the crucial points in an industry's development, so they can forecast when the shakeout stage of an industry might begin, or when an industry might be moving into decline. This is also true at the level of strategic groups, for new embryonic groups may emerge because of shifts in customer needs and tastes, or because some groups may grow rapidly due to changes in technology, while others will decline as their customers defect.

Limitations of Models for Industry Analysis

The competitive forces, strategic groups, and life-cycle models provide useful ways of thinking about and analyzing the nature of competition within an industry to identify opportunities and threats. However, each has its limitations, and managers must be aware of their shortcomings.

Life-Cycle Issues

It is important to remember that the industry life-cycle model is a generalization. In practice, industry life-cycles do not always follow the pattern illustrated in Figure 2.4. In some cases, growth is so rapid that the embryonic stage is skipped altogether. In others, industries fail to get past the embryonic stage. Industry growth can be revitalized after long periods of decline through innovation or social change. For example, the health boom brought the bicycle industry back to life after a long period of decline.

The time span of these stages can also vary significantly from industry to industry. Some industries can stay in maturity almost indefinitely if their products become basic necessities of life, as is the case for the car industry. Other industries skip the mature stage and go straight into decline, as in the case of the vacuum tube industry. Transistors replaced vacuum tubes as a major component in electronic products despite that the vacuum tube industry was still in its growth stage. Still other industries may go through several shakeouts before they enter full maturity, as appears to currently be happening in the telecommunications industry.

Innovation and Change

Over any reasonable length of time, in many industries competition can be viewed as a process driven by innovation.[17] Innovation is frequently the major factor in industry evolution and causes a company's movement through the industry life-cycle. Innovation is attractive because companies that pioneer new products, processes, or strategies can often earn enormous profits. Consider the explosive growth of Toys"R"Us, Dell, and Walmart. In a variety of different ways, all of these companies were innovators. Toys"R"Us pioneered a new way of selling toys (through large discount warehouse-type stores), Dell pioneered an entirely new way of selling personal computers (directly via telephone and then the Web), and Walmart pioneered the low-price discount superstore concept.

Successful innovation can transform the nature of industry competition. In recent decades, one frequent consequence of innovation has been to lower the fixed costs of production, thereby reducing barriers to entry and allowing new, and smaller, enterprises to compete with large established organizations. For example, two decades ago, large integrated steel companies such as U.S. Steel, LTV, and Bethlehem Steel dominated the steel industry. The industry was a typical oligopoly, dominated by a small number of large producers, in which tacit price collusion was practiced. Then along came a series of efficient mini-mill producers such as Nucor and Chaparral Steel, which used a new technology: electric arc furnaces. Over the past 20 years, they have revolutionized the structure of the industry. What was once a consolidated industry is now much more fragmented and price competitive. U.S. Steel now has only a 12% market share, down from 55% in the mid-1960s. In contrast, the mini-mills as a group now hold over 40% of the market, up from 5% 20 years ago.[18] Thus, the mini-mill innovation has reshaped the nature of competition in the steel industry.[19] A competitive forces model applied to the industry in 1970 would look very different from a competitive forces model applied in 2010.

Michael Porter talks of innovations as "unfreezing" and "reshaping" industry structure. He argues that after a period of turbulence triggered by innovation, the structure of an industry once more settles down into a fairly stable pattern, and the five forces and strategic group concepts can once more be applied.[20] This view of the evolution of industry structure is often referred to as "punctuated equilibrium."[21] The punctuated equilibrium view holds that long periods of equilibrium (refreezing), when an industry's structure is stable, are punctuated by periods of rapid change (unfreezing) when industry structure is revolutionized by innovation.

Figure 2.6 shows what punctuated equilibrium might look like for one key dimension of industry structure: competitive structure. From time t_0 to t_1, the competitive structure of the industry is a stable oligopoly, and few companies share the market. At time t_1, a major new innovation is pioneered either by an existing company or a new entrant. The result is a period of turbulence between t_1 and t_2. Afterward, the

Figure 2.6   Punctuated Equilibrium and Competitive Structure

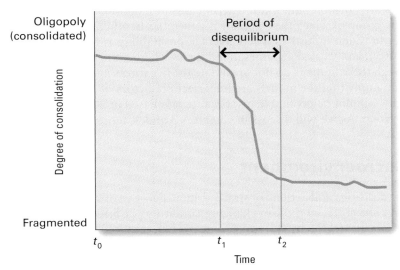

industry settles into a new state of equilibrium, but now the competitive structure is far more fragmented. Note that the opposite could have happened: the industry could have become more consolidated, although this seems to be less common. In general, innovations seem to lower barriers to entry, allow more companies into the industry, and as a result lead to fragmentation rather than consolidation.

During a period of rapid change when industry structure is being revolutionized by innovation, value typically migrates to business models based on new positioning strategies.[22] In the stockbrokerage industry, value migrated from the full-service broker model to the online trading model. In the steel industry, the introduction of electric arc technology led to a migration of value away from large, integrated enterprises and toward small mini-mills. In the book-selling industry, value has migrated first away from small boutique "bricks-and-mortar" booksellers toward large bookstore chains like Barnes & Noble, and more recently towards online bookstores such as amazon.com. Because the competitive forces and strategic group models are static, they cannot adequately capture what occurs during periods of rapid change in the industry environment when value is migrating.

Company Differences

Another criticism of industry models is that they overemphasize the importance of industry structure as a determinant of company performance, and underemphasize the importance of variations or differences among companies within an industry or a strategic group.[23] As we discuss in the next chapter, there can be enormous variance in the profit rates of individual companies within an industry. Research by Richard Rumelt and his associates, for example, suggests that industry structure explains only about 10% of the variance in profit rates across companies.[24] This implies that individual company differences explain much of the remainder. Other studies have estimated the explained variance at about 20%, which is still not a large figure.[25] Similarly, a growing number of studies have found only weak evidence linking strategic group membership and company profit rates, despite that the strategic group model predicts a strong link.[26] Collectively, these studies suggest that a company's individual resources and capabilities are far more important determinants of its profitability than the industry or strategic group of which the company is a member. In other words, there are strong companies in tough industries where average profitability is low (e.g., Nucor in the steel industry), and weak companies in industries where average profitability is high.

Although these findings do not invalidate the five forces and strategic group models, they do imply that the models are imperfect predictors of enterprise profitability. A company will not be profitable just because it is based in an attractive industry or strategic group. As we will discuss in Chapters 3 and 4, more is required.

The Macroenvironment

Just as the decisions and actions of strategic managers can often change an industry's competitive structure, so too can changing conditions or forces in the wider macroenvironment, that is, the broader economic, global, technological, demographic, social, and political context in which companies and industries are embedded (see Figure 2.7). Changes in the forces within the macroenvironment can have a direct impact on any or all of the forces in Competitive Forces model, thereby altering the relative strength of these forces as well as the attractiveness of an industry.

Figure 2.7 The Role of the Macroenvironment

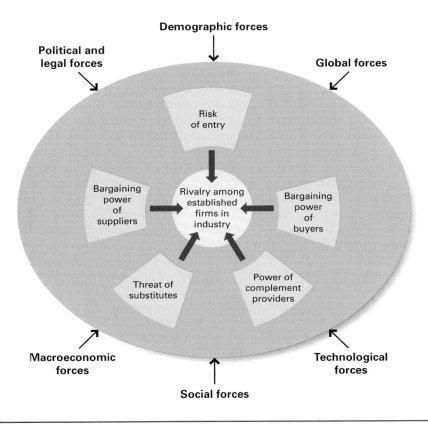

Macroeconomic Forces

Macroeconomic forces affect the general health and well-being of a nation or the regional economy of an organization, which in turn affect companies' and industries' ability to earn an adequate rate of return. The four most important macroeconomic forces are the growth rate of the economy, interest rates, currency exchange rates, and inflation (or deflation) rates. Economic growth, because it leads to an expansion in customer expenditures, tends to ease competitive pressures within an industry. This gives companies the opportunity to expand their operations and earn higher profits. Because economic decline (a recession) leads to a reduction in customer expenditures, it increases competitive pressures. Economic decline frequently causes price wars in mature industries.

Interest rates can determine the demand for a company's products. Interest rates are important whenever customers routinely borrow money to finance their purchase of these products. The most obvious example is the housing market, where mortgage rates directly affect demand. Interest rates also have an impact on the sale of autos, appliances, and capital equipment, to give just a few examples. For companies in such industries, rising interest rates are a threat, and falling rates an opportunity. Interest rates are also important as they influence a company's cost of capital, and therefore its ability to raise funds and invest in new assets. The lower that interest rates are, the lower the cost of capital for companies, and the more investment there can be.

Currency exchange rates define the comparative value of different national currencies. Movement in currency exchange rates has a direct impact on the competitiveness of a company's products in the global marketplace. For example, when the value of the dollar is low compared to the value of other currencies, products made in the United States are relatively inexpensive and products made overseas are relatively expensive. A low or declining dollar reduces the threat from foreign competitors while creating opportunities for increased sales overseas. The fall in the value of the dollar against several major currencies during 2004–2008 helped to make the United States steel industry more competitive.

Price inflation can destabilize the economy, producing slower economic growth, higher interest rates, and volatile currency movements. If inflation continues to increase, investment planning will become hazardous. The key characteristic of inflation is that it makes the future less predictable. In an inflationary environment, it may be impossible to predict with any accuracy the real value of returns that can be earned from a project 5 years later. Such uncertainty makes companies less willing to invest, which in turn depresses economic activity and ultimately pushes the economy into a recession. Thus, high inflation is a threat to companies.

Price deflation also has a destabilizing effect on economic activity. If prices fall, the real price of fixed payments goes up. This is damaging for companies and individuals with a high level of debt who must make regular fixed payments on that debt. In a deflationary environment, the increase in the real value of debt consumes more household and corporate cash flows, leaving less for other purchases and depressing the overall level of economic activity. Although significant deflation has not been seen since the 1930s, in the 1990s it started to take hold in Japan and in 2008–2009 there were concerns that it might remerge in the United States as the country plunged into a deep recession.

Global Forces

Over the last half-century there have been enormous changes in the world's economic system. We review these changes in some detail in Chapter 8 when we discuss global strategy. For now, the important points to note are that barriers to international trade and investment have tumbled, and more and more countries have enjoyed sustained economic growth. Economic growth in places like Brazil, China, and India has created large new markets for companies' goods and services and is giving companies an opportunity to grow their profits faster by entering these nations. Falling barriers to international trade and investment have made it much easier to enter foreign nations. For example, 20 years ago, it was almost impossible for a Western company to set up operations in China. Today, Western and Japanese companies are investing around $100 billion a year in China. By the same token, however, falling barriers to international trade and investment have made it easier for foreign enterprises to enter the domestic markets of many companies (by lowering barriers to entry), thereby increasing the intensity of competition and lowering profitability. Because of these changes, many formerly isolated domestic markets have now become part of a much larger, more competitive global marketplace, creating a myriad threats and opportunities for companies.

Technological Forces

Over the last few decades the pace of technological change has accelerated.[27] This has unleashed a process that has been called a "perennial gale of creative destruction."[28] Technological change can make established products obsolete overnight and simultaneously create a host of new product possibilities. Thus, technological change is both creative and destructive—both an opportunity and a threat.

Most importantly, impacts of technological change can impact the height of barriers to entry and therefore radically reshape industry structure. For example, the Internet lowered barriers to entry into the news industry. Providers of financial news must now compete for advertising dollars and customer attention with new Internet-based media organizations that developed during the 1990s and 2000s, such as TheStreet.com, The Motley Fool, Yahoo!'s financial section, and most recently, Google news. Advertisers now have more choices due to the resulting increase in rivalry, enabling them to bargain down the prices that they must pay to media companies.

Demographic Forces

Demographic forces are outcomes of changes in the characteristics of a population, such as age, gender, ethnic origin, race, sexual orientation, and social class. Like the other forces in the general environment, demographic forces present managers with opportunities and threats and can have major implications for organizations. Changes in the age distribution of a population are an example of a demographic force that affects managers and organizations. Currently, most industrialized nations are experiencing the aging of their populations as a consequence of falling birth and death rates and the aging of the baby-boom generation. As the population ages, opportunities for organizations that cater to older people are increasing; the home health care and recreation industries, for example, are seeing an upswing in demand for their services. As the baby-boom generation from the late-1950s to the early-1960s has aged, it has created a host of opportunities and threats. During the 1980s, many baby boomers were getting married and creating an upsurge in demand for the customer appliances normally purchased by couples marrying for the first time. Companies such as Whirlpool Corporation and GE capitalized on the resulting upsurge in demand for washing machines, dishwashers, dryers, and the like. In the 1990s, many of these same baby boomers were beginning to save for retirement, creating an inflow of money into mutual funds, and creating a boom in the mutual fund industry. In the next 20 years, many of these same baby boomers will retire, creating a boom in retirement communities.

Social Forces

Social forces refer to the way in which changing social mores and values affect an industry. Like the other macroenvironmental forces discussed here, social change creates opportunities and threats. One of the major social movements of recent decades has been the trend toward greater health consciousness. Its impact has been immense, and companies that recognized the opportunities early have often reaped significant gains. Philip Morris, for example, capitalized on the growing health consciousness trend when it acquired Miller Brewing Company, and then redefined competition in the beer industry with its introduction of low-calorie beer (Miller Lite).

Similarly, PepsiCo was able to gain market share from its rival, Coca-Cola, by being the first to introduce diet colas and fruit-based soft drinks. At the same time, the health trend has created a threat for many industries. The tobacco industry, for example, is in decline as a direct result of greater customer awareness of the health implications of smoking.

Political and Legal Forces

Political and legal forces are outcomes of changes in laws and regulations, and significantly affect managers and companies. Political processes shape a society's laws, which constrain the operations of organizations and managers and thus create both opportunities and threats.[29] For example, throughout much of the industrialized world, there has been a strong trend toward deregulation of industries previously controlled by the state, and privatization of organizations once owned by the state. In the United States, deregulation of the airline industry in 1979 allowed 29 new airline companies to enter the industry between 1979 and 1993. The increase in passenger-carrying capacity after deregulation led to excess capacity on many routes, intense competition, and fare wars. To respond to this more competitive task environment, airlines needed to look for ways to reduce operating costs. The development of hub-and-spoke systems, the rise of nonunion airlines, and the introduction of no-frills discount service are all responses to increased competition in the airlines' task environment. Despite these innovations, the airline industry still experiences intense fare wars, which have lowered profits and caused numerous airline company bankruptcies (see Opening Case). The global telecommunications service industry is now experiencing the same kind of turmoil following the deregulation of that industry in the United States and elsewhere.

Ethical Dilemma

You are a strategic analyst at a successful hotel enterprise that has been generating substantial excess cash flow. Your CEO instructed you to analyze the competitive structure of closely related industries to find one that the company could enter, using its cash reserve to build up a sustainable position. Your analysis, using the competitive forces model, suggests that the highest profit opportunities are to be found in the gambling industry. You realize that it might be possible to add casinos to several of your existing hotels, lowering entry costs into this industry. However, you personally have strong moral objections to gambling.

Should your own personal beliefs influence your recommendations to the CEO?

Summary of Chapter

1. An industry can be defined as a group of companies offering products or services that are close substitutes for each other. Close substitutes are products or services that satisfy the same basic customer needs.

2. The main technique used to analyze competition in the industry environment is the Five Forces Model. When considering this model, some argue for a sixth competitive force of some significance. That sixth forth helps determine the Competitive Forces model. The five forces are: (1) the risk of new entry by potential competitors, (2) the extent of rivalry among established firms, (3) the bargaining power of buyers, (4) the bargaining power of suppliers, (5) the threat of substitute products. The stronger each force is, the more competitive the industry and the lower the rate of return that can be earned, and (6) the power of complement providers.

3. The risk of entry by potential competitors is a function of the height of barriers to entry. The higher the barriers to entry are, the lower is the risk of entry and the greater are the profits that can be earned in the industry.

4. The extent of rivalry among established companies is a function of an industry's competitive structure, demand conditions, cost conditions, and barriers to exit. Strong demand conditions moderate the competition among established companies and create opportunities for expansion. When demand is weak, intensive competition can develop, particularly in consolidated industries with high exit barriers.

5. Buyers are most powerful when a company depends on them for business, but they are not dependent on the company. In such circumstances, buyers are a threat.

6. Suppliers are most powerful when a company depends on them for business, but they are not dependent on the company. In such circumstances, suppliers are a threat.

7. Substitute products are the products of companies serving customer needs similar to the needs served by the industry being analyzed. When substitute products are very similar to one another, companies can charge a lower price without losing customers to the substitutes.

8. The power, vigor, and competence of complementors can be a significant competitive force. Powerful and vigorous complementors may have a strong positive impact on demand in an industry.

9. Most industries are composed of strategic groups: groups of companies pursuing the same or a similar strategy. Companies in different strategic groups pursue different strategies.

10. The members of a company's strategic group constitute its immediate competitors. Because different strategic groups are characterized by different opportunities and threats, a company may improve its performance by switching strategic groups. The feasibility of doing so is a function of the height of mobility barriers.

11. Industries go through a well-defined life cycle: from an embryonic stage, through growth, shakeout, and maturity, and eventually decline. Each stage has different implications for the competitive structure of the industry, and each gives rise to its own set of opportunities and threats.

12. The competitive forces (adapted from the Five Forces model), strategic group, and industry life-cycles models all have limitations. The competitive forces and strategic group models present a static picture of competition that deemphasizes the role of innovation. Yet innovation can revolutionize industry structure and completely change the strength of different competitive forces. The competitive forces and strategic group models have been criticized for deemphasizing the importance of individual company differences. A company will not be profitable just because it is part of an attractive industry or strategic group; much more is required. The industry life-cycle model is a generalization that is not always followed, particularly when innovations revolutionize an industry.

13. The macroenvironment affects the intensity of rivalry within an industry. Included in the macroenvironment are the macroeconomic environment, the global environment, the technological environment, the demographic and social environment, and the political and legal environment.

Discussion Questions

1. Identify a growth industry, a mature industry, and a declining industry. For each industry, identify the following: (1) the number and size distribution of companies, (2) the nature of barriers to entry, (3) the height of barriers to entry, and (4) the extent of product differentiation. What do these factors tell you about the nature of competition in each industry? What are the implications for the company in terms of opportunities and threats?

2. Under what environmental conditions are price wars most likely to occur in an industry? What are the implications of price wars for a company? How should a company try to deal with the threat of a price war?

3. Assess the impact of macroenvironmental factors on the likely level of enrollment at your university over the next decade. What are the implications of these factors for the job security and salary level of your professors?

4. Discuss the Competitive Forces model (Figure 2.2) with reference to what you know about the U.S. beer industry (see the Opening case). What does the model tell you about the level of competition in this industry?

Practicing Strategic Management

Small-Group Exercises

Small-Group Exercise: Competing with Microsoft

Break into groups of 3–5 people, and discuss the following scenario. Appoint one group member as a spokesperson who will communicate your findings to the class.

You are a group of managers and software engineers at a small start-up. You have developed a revolutionary new operating system for personal computers that offers distinct advantages over Microsoft's Windows operating system: it takes up less memory space on the hard drive of a personal computer; it takes full advantage of the power of the personal computer's microprocessor, and in theory can run software applications much faster than Windows; it is much easier to install and use than Windows; and it responds to voice instructions with an accuracy of 99.9%, in addition to input from a keyboard or mouse. The operating system is the only product offering that your company has produced.

Complete the following exercises:

1. Analyze the competitive structure of the market for personal computer operating systems. On the basis of this analysis, identify what factors might inhibit adoption of your operating system by customers.

2. Can you think of a strategy that your company might pursue, either alone or in conjunction with other enterprises, in order to "beat Microsoft"? What will it take to execute that strategy successfully?

Strategy Sign-On

Article File 2

Find an example of an industry that has become more competitive in recent years. Identify the reasons for the increase in competitive pressure.

Strategic Management Project: Developing Your Portfolio 2 This module requires you to analyze the industry environment in which your company is based using the information you have already gathered:

1. Apply the Five Forces Model to the industry in which your company is based. What does this model tell you about the nature of competition in the industry?
2. Are any changes taking place in the macroenvironment that might have an impact, positive or negative, on the industry in which your company is based? If so, what are these changes, and how might they affect the industry?
3. Identify any strategic groups that might exist in the industry. How does the intensity of competition differ across these strategic groups?
4. How dynamic is the industry in which your company is based? Is there any evidence that innovation is reshaping competition or has done so in the recent past?
5. In what stage of its life cycle is the industry in which your company is based? What are the implications of this for the intensity of competition now? In the future?
6. Is your company part of an industry that is becoming more global? If so, what are the implications of this change for competitive intensity?
7. Analyze the impact of national context as it pertains to the industry in which your company is based. Does national context help or hinder your company in achieving a competitive advantage in the global marketplace?

CLOSING CASE

The United States Steel Industry

For decades, the United States steel industry was in deep economic malaise. The problems of the industry were numerous. Beginning in the 1970s, falling trade barriers allowed cost-efficient foreign producers to sell steel in the United States, and they were taking market share away from once dominant integrated steel makers, such as U.S. Steel, Bethlehem Steel, and Wheeling-Pittsburg.

To make matters worse for incumbents, there was also new domestic competition in the form of mini-mills. Mini-mills were small steel makers who used electric arc furnaces to smelt and produce scrap steel , often at a significantly lower cost than

large established companies. Because they did not use iron ore, mini-mills did not need to invest in blast furnaces to smelt iron ore (blast furnaces are very capital intensive). The average mini-mill was approximately one tenth of the size of a large integrated mill, used nonunion labor, and was typically located in rural communities where labor costs were relatively low. Scrap steel was in plentiful supply and priced low. Initially, most mini-mills produced low-grade construction steel, although they have moved into higher-grade steel in recent years.

If the expansion in supply from foreign companies and mini-mills wasn't enough, demand for steel was also contracting as customers switched to substitutes, including aluminum, plastics, and composites. The combination of growing supply and shrinking demand resulted in excess capacity. Indeed, at one time, as much as 45 % of the steel-making capacity in the United States was excess to requirements. As steel makers struggled with excess capacity, they slashed their prices to try and capture more demand and cover their fixed costs, only to be matched by rivals. The result was intense price competition and low profits. In addition, customers, for whom steel was mostly a commodity type input, could easily switch demand from company to company, and they used this leverage to further bargain down prices. To make matters worse, established steel makers were typically unionized, and a combination of high wage rates and inflexible work rules raised labor costs, making it even more difficult to make a profit in this brutally competitive industry. Strong unions, together with the costs of closing a plant, were also an impediment to reducing excess capacity in the industry.

The steel industry rarely made money. Many of the old integrated steel making companies ultimately went bankrupt, including Bethlehem Steel and Wheeling-Pittsburg. Then, in the early 2000s, things started to change. There was a surge in demand for steel from the rapidly developing economies of China, India, Russia, and Brazil. By 2004, China alone was consuming almost one third of all steel produced worldwide, and demand there was growing by more than 20% per year. Moreover, two decades of bankruptcies and consolidation had finally removed much of the excess capacity from the industry, not just in the United States, but also worldwide. In the United States, the producers that survived the decades of restructuring were efficient enterprises with productive workforces and new technology. Now finally competitive, for the first time, steel producers were able to hold their own against foreign imports. A decline in the value of the U.S. dollar after 2001 helped make steel imports relatively more expensive, and helped to create demand for steel exports *from* the United States.

As a result of this changed competitive environment, prices and profits surged. Hot rolled steel plate, for example, was priced at $260 per ton in June of 2003. By June of 2008, it had increased to $1225 per ton! In 2003, U.S. Steel, the country's largest steel producer, lost $406 million. In 2008 it made $2 billion in net profit. Nucor Steel, long regarded as the most efficient steel maker in the country, saw its profits increase from $63 million to $1.8 billion over the same period.

However, in late 2008 and 2009 demand for steel slumped again as a deep recession gripped the United States and many other nations following the global financial crisis. U.S. Steel makers cut their production from 108 million tons in 2007 to just 65.5 million tons in 2009. In 2009, the industry lost money. Even Nucor, long considered the most efficient steel maker in the United States, recorded a $293 million loss, while U.S. Steel lost $1.9 billion. The following year brought a recovery, however, with production rebounding 44% on the back of stronger demand trends. This enabled many steel makers to cover their fixed costs and start to make money again. Nucor, for example, made $134 million in 2009.

Sources: S. James, "Lofty Steel Prices Could Keep Climbing," *Herald Tribune*, May 19, 2008; *The Economist*, "A Changed Game," July 15, 2006, pp. 61–62; M. Gene, "U.S. Steel is on a Roll," *Business Week*, June 30, 2008, p. 20; L.J. Larkin, *Standard & Poors Industry Survey, Metals: Industrial*, February 17, 2011.

Case Discussion Questions

1. Using the information contained in the case, conduct a five-forces analysis of the U.S. Steel industry. What conclusion can you draw from this?
2. Do you think there are any strategic groups in the U.S. Steel industry? What might they be? How might the nature of competition vary from group to group?
3. Demand for steel is very cyclical. Why do you think this is the case? What might steel makers do to better cope with the cyclical nature of demand?
4. Given the nature of competition in the U.S. steel industry, what must a steel maker focus on in order to be profitable?

Notes

[1] J. Corridore, *Standard & Poors Industry Surveys: Airlines*, December 30, 2010. B. Kowitt, "High Anxiety," *Fortune*, April 27, 2009, p.14. "Shredding Money," *The Economist*, September 20, 2008.

[2] M. E. Porter, *Competitive Strategy* (New York: Free Press, 1980).

[3] J. E. Bain, *Barriers to New Competition* (Cambridge, MA: Harvard University Press, 1956). For a review of the modern literature on barriers to entry, see R. J. Gilbert, "Mobility Barriers and the Value of Incumbency," in R. Schmalensee and R. D. Willig (eds.), *Handbook of Industrial Organization*, vol. 1 (Amsterdam: North-Holland, 1989). See also R. P. McAfee, H. M. Mialon, and M. A. Williams, "What Is a Barrier to Entry?" *American Economic Review* 94 (May 2004): 461–468.

[4] A detailed discussion of switching costs and lock in can be found in C. Shapiro and H. R. Varian, *Information Rules: A Strategic Guide to the Network Economy* (Boston: Harvard Business School Press, 1999).

[5] Most of this information on barriers to entry can be found in the industrial organization economics literature. See especially the following works: Bain, *Barriers to New Competition*; M. Mann, "Seller Concentration, Barriers to Entry and Rates of Return in 30 Industries," *Review of Economics and Statistics* 48 (1966): 296–307; W. S. Comanor and T. A. Wilson, "Advertising, Market Structure and Performance," *Review of Economics and Statistics* 49 (1967): 423–440; Gilbert, "Mobility Barriers"; and K. Cool, L.-H. Roller, and B. Leleux, "The Relative Impact of Actual and Potential Rivalry on Firm Profitability in the Pharmaceutical Industry," *Strategic Management Journal* 20 (1999): 1–14.

[6] For a discussion of tacit agreements, see T. C. Schelling, *The Strategy of Conflict* (Cambridge, MA: Harvard University Press, 1960).

[7] M. Busse, "Firm Financial Condition and Airline Price Wars," *Rand Journal of Economics* 33 (2002): 298–318.

[8] For a review, see F. Karakaya, "Market Exit and Barriers to Exit: Theory and Practice," *Psychology and Marketing* 17 (2000): 651–668.

[9] P. Ghemawat, *Commitment: The Dynamics of Strategy* (Boston: Harvard Business School Press, 1991).

[10] A. S. Grove, *Only the Paranoid Survive* (New York: Doubleday, 1996).

[11] In standard microeconomic theory, the concept used for assessing the strength of substitutes and complements is the cross elasticity of demand.

[12] For details and further references, see Charles W. L. Hill, "Establishing a Standard: Competitive Strategy and Technology Standards in Winner Take All Industries," *Academy of Management Executive* 11 (1997): 7–25; and Shapiro and Varian, *Information Rules*.

[13] The development of strategic group theory has been a strong theme in the strategy literature. Important contributions include the following: R. E. Caves and Michael E. Porter, "From Entry Barriers to Mobility Barriers," *Quarterly Journal of Economics* (May 1977): 241–262; K. R. Harrigan, "An Application of Clustering for Strategic Group Analysis," *Strategic Management Journal* 6 (1985): 55–73; K. J. Hatten and D. E. Schendel, "Heterogeneity Within an Industry: Firm Conduct in the U.S. Brewing Industry, 1952–71," *Journal of Industrial Economics* 26 (1977): 97–113; Michael E. Porter, "The Structure Within Industries and Companies' Performance," *Review of Economics and Statistics* 61 (1979): 214–227. See also K. Cool and D. Schendel, "Performance Differences Among Strategic Group Members," *Strategic Management Journal* 9 (1988): 207–233; A. Nair and S. Kotha, "Does Group Membership Matter? Evidence from the Japanese Steel Industry," *Strategic Management Journal* 20 (2001): 221–235; and G. McNamara, D. L. Deephouse, and R. A. Luce, "Competitive Positioning Within and Across a Strategic Group Structure," *Strategic Management Journal* 24 (2003): 161–180.

[14] For details on the strategic group structure in the pharmaceutical industry, see K. Cool and I. Dierickx, "Rivalry, Strategic Groups, and Firm Profitability," *Strategic Management Journal* 14 (1993): 47–59.

[15] Charles W. Hofer argued that life-cycle considerations may be the most important contingency when formulating business strategy. See Hofer, "Towards a Contingency Theory of Business Strategy," *Academy of Management Journal* 18 (1975): 784–810. There is empirical evidence to support this view. See C. R. Anderson and C. P. Zeithaml, "Stages of the Product Life Cycle, Business Strategy, and Business Performance," *Academy of Management Journal* 27 (1984): 5–24; and D. C. Hambrick and D. Lei, "Towards an Empirical Prioritization of Contingency Variables for Business Strategy," *Academy of Management Journal* 28 (1985): 763–788. See also G. Miles, C. C. Snow, and M. P. Sharfman, "Industry Variety and Performance," *Strategic Management Journal* 14 (1993): 163–177; G. K. Deans, F. Kroeger, and S. Zeisel, "The Consolidation Curve," *Harvard Business Review* (December 2002): 2–3. Vol 80.

[16] The characteristics of declining industries have been summarized by K. R. Harrigan, "Strategy Formulation in Declining Industries," *Academy of Management Review* 5 (1980): 599–604. See also J. Anand and H. Singh, "Asset Redeployment, Acquisitions and Corporate Strategy in Declining Industries," *Strategic Management Journal* 18 (1997): 99–118.

[17] This perspective is associated with the Austrian school of economics, which goes back to Schumpeter. For a summary of this school and its implications for strategy, see R. Jacobson, "The Austrian School of Strategy," *Academy of Management Review* 17 (1992): 782–807; and C. W. L. Hill and D. Deeds, "The Importance of Industry Structure for the Determination of Industry Profitability: A Neo-Austrian Approach," *Journal of Management Studies* 33 (1996): 429–451.

[18] "A Tricky Business," *Economist,* June 30, 2001, pp. 55–56.

[19] D. F. Barnett and R. W. Crandall, *Up from the Ashes* (Washington, D.C.: Brookings Institution, 1986).

[20] M. E. Porter, *The Competitive Advantage of Nations* (New York: Free Press, 1990).

[21] The term *punctuated equilibrium* is borrowed from evolutionary biology. For a detailed explanation of the concept, see M. L. Tushman, W. H. Newman, and E. Romanelli, "Convergence and Upheaval: Managing the Unsteady Pace of Organizational Evolution," *California Management Review* 29:1 (1985): 29–44; C. J. G. Gersick, "Revolutionary Change Theories: A Multilevel

Exploration of the Punctuated Equilibrium Paradigm," *Academy of Management Review* 16 (1991): 10–36; and R. Adner and D. A. Levinthal, "The Emergence of Emerging Technologies," *California Management Review* 45 (Fall 2002): 50–65.

[22]A. J. Slywotzky, *Value Migration: How to Think Several Moves Ahead of the Competition* (Boston: Harvard Business School Press, 1996).

[23]Hill and Deeds, "Importance of Industry Structure."

[24]R. P. Rumelt, "How Much Does Industry Matter?" *Strategic Management Journal* 12 (1991): 167–185. See also A. J. Mauri and M. P. Michaels, "Firm and Industry Effects Within Strategic Management: An Empirical Examination," *Strategic Management Journal* 19 (1998): 211–219.

[25]See R. Schmalensee, "Inter-Industry Studies of Structure and Performance," in Schmalensee and Willig (eds.), *Handbook of Industrial Organization.* Similar results were found by A. N. McGahan and M. E. Porter, "How Much Does Industry Matter, Really?" *Strategic Management Journal* 18 (1997): 15–30.

[26]For example, see K. Cool and D. Schendel, "Strategic Group Formation and Performance: The Case of the U.S. Pharmaceutical Industry, 1932–1992," *Management Science* (September 1987): 1102–1124.

[27]See M. Gort and J. Klepper, "Time Paths in the Diffusion of Product Innovations," *Economic Journal* (September 1982): 630–653. Looking at the history of 46 products, Gort and Klepper found that the length of time before other companies entered the markets created by a few inventive companies declined from an average of 14.4 years for products introduced before 1930 to 4.9 years for those introduced after 1949.

[28]The phrase was originally coined by J. Schumpeter, *Capitalism, Socialism and Democracy* (London: Macmillan, 1950), p. 68.

[29]For a detailed discussion of the importance of the structure of law as a factor explaining economic change and growth, see D. C. North, *Institutions, Institutional Change, and Economic Performance* (Cambridge: Cambridge University Press, 1990).

3 Internal Analysis: Distinctive Competencies, Competitive Advantage, and Profitability

erel photography/istockphoto.com

Rebuilding Competitive Advantage at Starbucks—Howard Schultz's Second Act

The growth of Starbucks is the stuff of business legend. In the 1980s, when the company had only a handful of stores, the company's director of marketing, Howard Schultz, returned from a trip to Italy enchanted with the Italian coffeehouse experience. Schultz, who later purchased the company and became CEO, persuaded the owners to experiment with the coffeehouse format, and the Starbucks experience was born. The strategy was to sell the company's own premium roasted coffee and freshly brewed espresso-style coffee beverages, along with a variety of pastries, coffee accessories, and other products, in a tastefully designed coffeehouse setting. The idea was to transform the act of buying and drinking coffee into a social experience. The stores were to be "third places," where people could meet and talk, or relax and read. The company focused on providing superior customer service. Reasoning that motivated

employees provide the best customer service, Starbucks' executives devoted much attention to employee hiring and training programs, and progressive compensation policies that gave full-time and part-time employees stock option grants and medical benefits.

This formula was the bedrock of Starbucks' competitive advantage. Starbucks went from obscurity to one of the best-known brands in the United States within a decade. Between

LEARNING OBJECTIVES
After reading this chapter you should be able to:
- Discuss the source of competitive advantage
- Identify and explore the role of efficiency, quality, innovation, and customer responsiveness in building and maintaining a competitive advantage
- Explain the concept of the value chain
- Understand the link between competitive advantage and profitability
- Explain what impacts the durability of a company's competitive advantage

1995 and 2005, Starbucks added U.S. stores at an annual rate of 27%, reaching almost 12,000 total locations. It also expanded aggressively internationally. Schultz himself stepped down from the CEO role in 2000, although he remained chairman.

By 2008, however, the company was hitting serious headwinds. Competitors from small boutique coffeehouses to chains like Tully's and Peet's Coffee, and even McDonald's, were beginning to erode Starbucks' competitive advantage. Although the company was still adding stores at a break neck pace, same store sales started to fall. Profitability, measured by return on invested capital (ROIC), slumped from around 21% to just 8.6% in 2008. The stock price tumbled.

At this point, Howard Schultz fired the CEO, and again reclaimed the position. His strategy was to return Starbucks to its roots. He wanted the company to reemphasize the creation of value through great customer experience, and he wanted the company to do that as efficiently as possible. He first closed all Starbucks' stores for a day, and retrained baristas in the art of making coffee. A number of other changes followed. The company redesigned many of its stores to give them a contemporary feel. It stopped selling breakfast sandwiches because Schultz thought that the smell detracted from the premium coffeehouse experience. Instead of grinding enough coffee for an entire day, he told employees to grind more coffee each time a new pot was brewed to create the aroma of freshly brewed coffee. He gave store managers more freedom to decide specific things, such as the type of artwork that would be displayed in the stores. Starbucks also dramatically expanded its fair trade policy, purchasing its coffee beans from growers who adhered to environmentally friendly policies, and it promoted this to customers.

To reduce costs, Schultz announced the closure of 600 underperforming U.S. stores. Starbucks used the threat of possible closure to renegotiate many store leases at lower rates. It cut back on the number of suppliers of pastries and negotiated volume discounts. A lean thinking team was created and it was tasked with the job of improving employee productivity; baristas needed to become more efficient. The team found that by making simple changes, such as placing commonly ordered syrup flavors closer to where drinks are made, they could shave several seconds off the time it took to make a drink, and give employees more time to interact with customers. Faster customer service meant higher customer satisfaction.

The results have been impressive. What was once nearly dismissed as a stale brand, has been reinvigorated. Starbucks' revenues are growing again, and their profitability has increased, with ROIC reaching an impressive 24.19% in 2010.[1]

Overview

hy, within a particular industry or market, do some companies outperform others? What is the basis of their (sustained) competitive advantage? The Opening Case provides some clues. Starbucks' innovative adoption of the Italian coffeehouse format provided an original competitive advantage. Starbucks had created something radically new in the United States: a third place social experience based around the consumption of coffee. This *innovation* was reinforced by an

emphasis on *customer responsiveness*, particularly with regard to the *quality* of the entire experience. By 2008, however, the company was losing its competitive advantage. Howard Schultz, the original creator of Starbucks' strategy, returned to the company as CEO. Under his leadership, Starbucks took actions to rebuild its brand, to improve the quality of the Starbucks experience for customers, and to do both as *efficiently* as possible. As you will see in this chapter, efficiency, customer responsiveness, quality, and innovation are the building blocks of competitive advantage.

This chapter focuses on internal analysis, which is concerned with identifying the strengths and weaknesses of the company. Internal analysis, coupled with an analysis of the company's external environment, gives managers the information they need to choose the business model and strategies that will enable their company to attain a sustained competitive advantage. Internal analysis is a 3-step process. First, managers must understand the process by which companies create value for customers and profit for the company. Managers must also understand the role of resources, capabilities, and distinctive competencies in this process. Second, they need to understand the importance of superior efficiency, innovation, quality, and customer responsiveness when creating value and generating high profitability. Third, they must be able to analyze the sources of their company's competitive advantage to identify what drives the profitability of their enterprise, and where opportunities for improvement might lie. In other words, they must be able to identify how the strengths of the enterprise boost its profitability and how any weaknesses lead to lower profitability.

Three more critical issues in internal analysis are addressed in this chapter. First: What factors influence the durability of competitive advantage? Second: Why do successful companies sometimes lose their competitive advantage? Third: How can companies avoid competitive failure and sustain their competitive advantage over time?

After reading this chapter, you will understand the nature of competitive advantage and why managers need to perform internal analysis (just as they must conduct industry analysis), to achieve superior performance and profitability.

The Roots of Competitive Advantage

A company has a *competitive advantage* over its rivals when its profitability is greater than the average profitability of all companies in its industry. It has a *sustained competitive advantage* when it is able to maintain above-average profitability over a number of years (as Walmart has done in the retail industry and Starbucks has done in the restaurant industry). The primary objective of strategy is to achieve a sustained competitive advantage, which in turn will result in superior profitability and profit growth. What are the sources of competitive advantage, and what is the link between strategy, competitive advantage, and profitability?

Distinctive Competencies

Competitive advantage is based upon distinctive competencies. **Distinctive competencies** are firm-specific strengths that allow a company to differentiate its products from those offered by rivals, and/or achieve substantially lower costs than its rivals. Starbucks, for example, has a distinctive competence in managing coffee shops, which creates value for customers, leads to higher employee productivity and lower costs (see the Opening case). Similarly, it can be argued that Toyota, which historically has been the stand out performer in the automobile industry, has distinctive competencies in the development and operation of manufacturing processes (although the company has struggled somewhat since 2008). Toyota has pioneered an entire range of manufacturing techniques, such as just-in-time inventory systems, self-managing teams, and reduced setup times for complex equipment. These competencies, collectively known as the "Toyota lean production system," helped the company attain superior efficiency and product quality as the basis of its competitive advantage in the global automobile industry.[2] Distinctive competencies arise from two complementary sources: resources and capabilities.[3]

Resources **Resources** refer to the assets of a company. A company's resources can be divided into two types: tangible and intangible resources. **Tangible resources** are physical entities, such as land, buildings, manufacturing plants, equipment, inventory, and money. **Intangible resources** are nonphysical entities that are created by managers and other employees, such as brand names, the reputation of the company, the knowledge that employees have gained through experience, and the intellectual property of the company, including patents, copyrights, and trademarks.

Resources are particularly *valuable* when they enable a company to create strong demand for its products, and/or to lower its costs. Toyota's valuable *tangible resources* include the equipment associated with its lean production system, much of which has been engineered specifically by Toyota for exclusive use in its factories. These valuable tangible resources allow Toyota to lower its costs, relative to competitors. Similarly, Microsoft has a number of valuable *intangible resources*, including its brand name and the software code that comprises its Windows operating system. These valuable resources allow Microsoft to sell more of its products, relative to competitors.

Valuable resources are more likely to lead to a sustainable competitive advantage if they are *rare*, in the sense that competitors do not possess them, and difficult for rivals to imitate; that is, if there are *barriers to imitation* (we will discuss the source of barriers to imitation in more detail later in this chapter). For example, the software code underlying Windows is *rare* because only Microsoft has full access to it. The code is also difficult to imitate. A rival cannot simply copy the software code underlying Windows and sell a repackaged version of Windows because the code is protected by copyright law, and reproducing it is illegal.

Capabilities **Capabilities** refer to a company's resource coordinating skills and productive use. These skills reside in an organization's rules, routines, and procedures, that is, the style or manner through which it makes decisions and manages its internal processes to achieve organizational objectives.[4] More generally, a company's capabilities are the product of its organizational structure, processes, control systems and hiring systems. They specify how and where decisions are made within a company, the kind of behaviors the company rewards, and the company's cultural norms and values. (We will discuss how organizational structure and control systems help a company obtain capabilities in Chapters 12 and 13.) Capabilities are intangible. They reside not in individuals, but in the way individuals interact, cooperate, and make decisions within the context of an organization.[5]

Distinctive competencies

Firm-specific strengths that allow a company to differentiate its products and/or achieve substantially lower costs to achieve a competitive advantage.

Resources

Assets of a company.

Tangible resources

Physical entities, such as land, buildings, equipment, inventory, and money.

Intangible resources

Nonphysical entities such as brand names, company reputation, experiential knowledge and intellectual property, including patents, copyrights, and trademarks.

Capabilities

A company's skills at coordinating its resources and putting them to productive use.

Like resources, capabilities are particularly valuable if they enable a company to create strong demand for its products, and/or to lower its costs. The competitive advantage of Southwest Airlines is based largely upon its capability to select, motivate and manage its workforce in such a way that leads to high employee productivity and lower costs (see Opening case). As with resources, valuable capabilities are also more likely to lead to a sustainable competitive advantage if they are both *rare* and protected from copying by *barriers to imitation*.

Resources, Capabilities and Competencies   The distinction between resources and capabilities is critical to understanding what generates a distinctive competency. A company may have firm-specific and valuable resources, but unless it also has the capability to use those resources effectively, it may not be able to create a distinctive competency. Additionally, it is important to recognize that a company may not need firm-specific and valuable resources to establish a distinctive competency so long as it has capabilities that no other competitor possesses. For example, the steel mini-mill operator Nucor is widely acknowledged to be the most cost-efficient steel maker in the United States. Its distinctive competency in low-cost steel making does not come from any firm-specific and valuable resources. Nucor has the same resources (plant, equipment, skilled employees, know-how) as many other mini-mill operators. What distinguishes Nucor is its unique capability to manage its resources in a highly productive way. Specifically, Nucor's structure, control systems, and culture promote efficiency at all levels within the company.

In sum, for a company to possess a distinctive competency, it must—at a minimum—have either (1) a firm-specific and valuable resource, and the capabilities (skills) necessary to take advantage of that resource, or (2) a firm-specific capability to manage resources (as exemplified by Nucor). A company's distinctive competency is strongest when it possesses both firm-specific and valuable resources and firm-specific capabilities to manage those resources.

The Role Of Strategy   Figure 3.1 illustrates the relationship of a company's strategies, distinctive competencies, and competitive advantage. Distinctive competencies shape the strategies that the company pursues, which lead to competitive advantage

Figure 3.1   Strategy, Resources, Capabilities, and Competencies

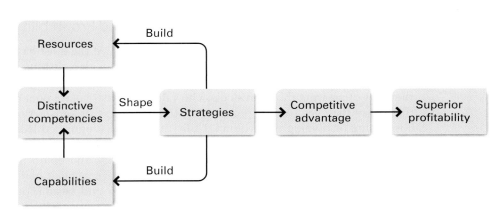

and superior profitability. However, it is also very important to realize that the strategies a company adopts can build new resources and capabilities or strengthen the existing resources and capabilities of the company, thereby enhancing the distinctive competencies of the enterprise. Thus, the relationship between distinctive competencies and strategies is not a linear one; rather, it is a reciprocal one in which distinctive competencies shape strategies, and strategies help to build and create distinctive competencies.[6]

The history of The Walt Disney Company illustrates the way this process works. In the early 1980s, Disney suffered a string of poor financial years that culminated in a 1984 management shakeup when Michael Eisner was appointed CEO. Four years later, Disney's sales had increased from $1.66 billion to $3.75 billion, its net profits from $98 million to $570 million, and its stock market valuation from $1.8 billion to $10.3 billion. What brought about this transformation was the company's deliberate attempt to use its resources and capabilities more aggressively: Disney's enormous film library, its brand name, and its filmmaking skills, particularly in animation. Under Eisner, many old Disney classics were re-released, first in movie theaters and then on video, earning the company millions in the process. Then Eisner reintroduced the product that had originally made Disney famous: the full-length animated feature. Putting together its brand name and in-house animation capabilities, Disney produced a stream of major box office hits, including *The Little Mermaid, Beauty and the Beast, Aladdin, Pocahontas,* and *The Lion King.* Disney also started a cable television channel, the Disney Channel, to use this library and capitalize on the company's brand name. In other words, Disney's existing resources and capabilities shaped its strategies.

Through his choice of strategies, Eisner also developed new competencies in different parts of the business. In the filmmaking arm of Disney, for example, Eisner created a new low-cost film division under the Touchstone label, and the company had a string of low-budget box office hits. It entered into a long-term agreement with the computer animation company Pixar to develop a competency in computer-generated animated films. This strategic collaboration produced several hits, including *Toy Story* and *Monsters, Inc.* (in 2004 Disney acquired Pixar). In sum, Disney's transformation was based not only on strategies that took advantage of the company's existing resources and capabilities, but also on strategies that built new resources and capabilities, such as those that underlie the company's competency in computer-generated animated films.

Competitive Advantage, Value Creation, and Profitability

Competitive advantage leads to superior profitability. At the most basic level, a company's profitability depends on three factors: (1) the value customers place on the company's products, (2) the price that a company charges for its products, and (3) the costs of creating those products. The value customers place on a product reflects the *utility* they get from a product, or, the happiness or satisfaction gained from consuming or owning the product. Utility must be distinguished from price. Utility is something that customers receive from a product. It is a function of the attributes of the product, such as its performance, design, quality, and point-of-sale and after-sale service. For example, most customers would place a much higher utility value on a top-end Lexus car from Toyota than on a low-end basic economy car from Kia (they would value it more), precisely because they perceive Lexus to have better performance and superior design, quality, and service. A company that strengthens the utility (or value) of its products in the eyes of customers has more pricing options: it can raise prices to reflect that utility (value) or hold prices lower to induce more customers to purchase its products, thereby expanding unit sales volume.

Regardless of the pricing option a company may choose, that price is typically less than the utility value placed upon the good or service by the customer. This is because the customer captures some of that utility in the form of what economists call a *consumer surplus*.[7] The customer is able to do this because the company is competing with other companies for the customer's business, therefore, the company must charge a lower price than it could were it a monopoly supplier. Moreover, it is normally impossible to segment the market to such a degree that the company can charge each customer a price that reflects that individual's unique assessment of the utility of a product—what economists refer to as a customer's reservation price. For these reasons, the point-of-sale price tends to be less than the utility value placed on the product by many customers. Nevertheless, remember the basic principle here: the more utility that consumers get from a company's products or services, the more pricing options it has.

These concepts are illustrated in Figure 3.2: U is the *average* utility value per unit of a product to a customer, P is the average price per unit that the company decides to charge for that product, and C is the average unit cost of producing that product (including actual production costs and the cost of capital investments in production systems). The company's average profit per unit is equal to $P–C$, and the consumer surplus is equal to $U–P$. In other words, $U–P$ is a measure of the value the consumer captures, and $P–C$ is a measure of the value the company captures. The company makes a profit so long as P is more than C, and its profitability will be greater the lower C is relative to P. Bear in mind that the difference between U and i is in part determined by the intensity of competitive pressure in the marketplace; the lower the competitive pressure's intensity, the higher the price that can be charged relative to U, but the difference between U and P is also determined by the company's pricing choice.[8] As we shall see, a company may choose to keep prices low relative to volume because lower prices enable the company to sell more products, attain scale economies, and boost its profit margin by lowering C relative to P.

Figure 3.2 Value Creation per Unit

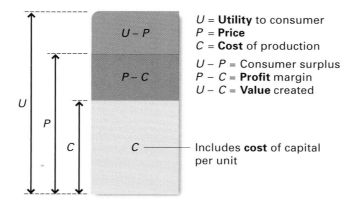

© Cengage Learning 2013

Also, note that the value created by a company is measured by the difference between the utility a consumer gets from the product (U) and the costs of production (C), that is, U–C. A company creates value by converting factors of production that cost C into a product from which customers receive a utility of U. A company can create more value for its customers by lowering C or making the product more attractive through superior design, performance, quality, service, etc. When customers assign a greater utility to the product (U increases), they are willing to pay a higher price (P increases). This discussion suggests that a company has a competitive advantage and high profitability when it creates more value for its customers than rivals.[9]

The company's pricing options are captured in Figure 3.3. Suppose a company's current pricing option is the one pictured in the middle column of Figure 3.3. Imagine that the company decides to pursue strategies to increase the utility of its product offering from U to U^* in order to boost its profitability. Increasing utility initially raises production costs because the company must spend money in order to increase product performance, quality, service, and other factors. Now there are two different pricing options that the company can pursue. Option 1 is to raise prices to reflect the higher utility: the company raises prices more than its costs increase, and profit per unit (P–C) increases. Option 2 involves a very different set of choices: the company lowers prices in order to expand unit volume. Generally, customers recognize that they are getting a great bargain because price is now much lower than utility (the consumer surplus has increased), so they rush out to buy more (demand has increased). As unit volume expands due to increased demand, the company is able to realize scale economies and reduce its average unit costs. Although creating the extra utility initially costs more and prices are lowered, profit margins widen because the average per-unit cost of production falls as volume increases and scale economies are attained.

Figure 3.3 Value Creation and Pricing Options

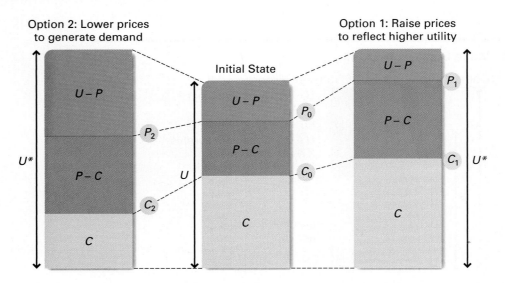

Managers must understand the dynamic relationships among utility, pricing, demand, and costs in order to make decisions that will maximize competitive advantage and profitability. Option 2 in Figure 3.3, for example, may not be a viable strategy if demand did not increase rapidly with lower prices, or if few economies of scale will result by increasing volume. Managers must understand how value creation and pricing decisions affect demand, as well as how unit costs change with increases in volume. In other words, they must have a good grasp of the demand for the company's product and its cost structure at different levels of output if they are to make decisions that maximize profitability.

Consider the automobile industry. According to a 2008 study by Oliver Wyman, Toyota made $922 in profit on every vehicle it manufactured in North America in 2007. General Motors, in contrast, lost $729 on every vehicle it made.[10] What accounts for the difference? First, Toyota had the best reputation for quality in the industry. According to annual surveys issued by J.D. Power, Toyota consistently topped the list in terms of quality, while GM cars were—at best—in the middle of the pack. Higher quality equaled a higher utility and now allows Toyota to charge 5% to 10% higher prices than General Motors for equivalent cars. Second, Toyota had a lower cost per vehicle than General Motors, in part because of its superior labor productivity. For example, in Toyota's North American plants, it took an average of 30.37 employee hours to build one car, compared to 32.29 at GM plants in North America. The 1.94 hour productivity advantage meant lower total labor costs for Toyota and, hence, a lower overall cost structure. Therefore, as summarized in Figure 3.4, Toyota's advantage over GM came from greater utility (U), which allowed the company to charge a higher price (P) for its cars, and from a lower cost structure (C), which taken together implies greater profitability per vehicle ($P - C$).

Toyota's pricing decisions are guided by its managers' understanding of the relationships between utility, prices, demand, and costs. Given its ability to build more utility into its products, Toyota could have charged even higher prices than illustrated in Figure 3.4, but that might have led to lower sales volume, fewer scale economies, higher unit costs, and lower profit margins. Toyota's managers sought to find the pricing option that enabled the company to maximize its profits given their assessment of demand for its products and its cost function. Thus, to create superior

---

Figure 3.4 Comparing Toyota and General Motors

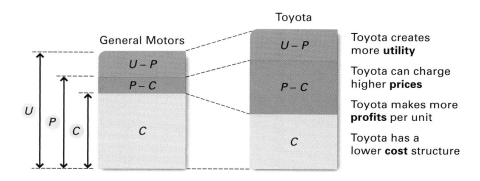

value, a company does not need to tout the lowest cost structure in an industry, nor create the product with the highest utility in the eyes of customers. All that is necessary is that the gap between perceived utility (U) and costs of production (C) is greater than the gap attained by competitors.

Note that Toyota has differentiated itself from General Motors by its superior quality, which allows it to charge higher prices, and its superior productivity translates into a lower cost structure. Thus, its competitive advantage over General Motors is the result of strategies that have led to distinctive competencies, resulting in greater differentiation and a lower cost structure.

Indeed, at the heart of any company's business model is the combination of congruent strategies aimed at creating distinctive competencies that (1) differentiate its products in some way so that its consumers derive more utility from them, which gives the company more pricing options, and (2) result in a lower cost structure, which also gives it a broader range of pricing choices.[11] Achieving superior profitability and a sustained competitive advantage requires the right choices regarding utility through differentiation and pricing (given the demand conditions in the company's market), and the company's cost structure at different levels of output. This issue is addressed in detail in the following chapters.

The Value Chain

Value chain

The idea that a company is a chain of activities that transforms inputs into outputs that customers value.

All of the functions of a company—such as production, marketing, product development, service, information systems, materials management, and human resources—have a role in lowering the cost structure and increasing the perceived utility (value) of products through differentiation. As the first step in examining this concept, consider the value chain, which is illustrated in Figure 3.5.[12] The term **value chain** refers to the idea that a company is a chain of activities that transforms inputs into outputs that customers value. The transformation process involves both primary activities and support activities that add value to the product.

Figure 3.5 The Value Chain

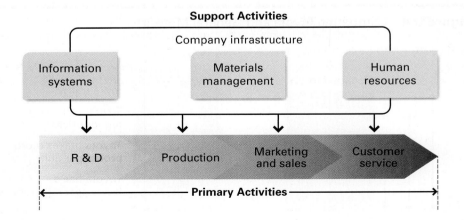

Primary Activities

Primary activities include the design, creation, and delivery of the product, the product's marketing, and its support and after-sales service. In the value chain illustrated in Figure 3.5, the primary activities are broken down into four functions: research and development, production, marketing and sales, and customer service.

Research and Development　　Research and development (R&D) refers to the design of products and production processes. Although we think of R&D as being associated with the design of physical products and production processes in manufacturing enterprises, many service companies also undertake R&D. For example, banks compete with each other by developing new financial products and new ways of delivering those products to customers. Online banking and smart debit-cards are two examples of the fruits of new-product development in the banking industry. Earlier examples of innovation in the banking industry included ATM machines, credit cards, and debit cards.

By creating superior product design, R&D can increase the functionality of products, making them more attractive to customers, and thereby adding value. Alternatively, the work of R&D may result in more efficient production processes, thereby lowering production costs. Either way, the R&D function can help to lower costs or raise the utility of a product and permit a company to charge higher prices. At Intel, for example, R&D creates value by developing ever more powerful microprocessors and helping to pioneer ever more efficient manufacturing processes (in conjunction with equipment suppliers).

It is important to emphasize that R&D is not just about enhancing the features and functions of a product, it is also about the elegance of a product's design, which can create an impression of superior value in the minds of consumers. For example, part of Apple's success with the iPod has been based upon the elegance and appeal of the iPod design, which has turned a piece of electronic equipment into a fashion accessory. For another example of how design elegance can create value, see Strategy in Action 3.1, which discusses value creation at the fashion house Burberry.

Production　　Production refers to the creation process of a good or service. For physical products, this generally means manufacturing. For services such as banking or retail operations, "production" typically takes place while the service is delivered to the customer, as when a bank makes a loan to a customer. By performing its activities efficiently, the production function of a company helps to lower its cost structure. For example, the efficient production operations of Honda and Toyota help those automobile companies achieve higher profitability relative to competitors such as General Motors. The production function can also perform its activities in a way that is consistent with high product quality, which leads to differentiation (and higher value) and lower costs.

Marketing and Sales　　There are several ways in which the marketing and sales functions of a company can help to create value. Through brand positioning and advertising, the marketing function can increase the value that customers perceive to be contained in a company's product (and thus the utility they attribute to the product). Insofar as these help to create a favorable impression of the company's product in the minds of customers, they increase utility. For example, the French company Perrier persuaded U.S. customers that slightly carbonated bottled water was worth $1.50 per bottle rather than a price closer to the $0.50 that it cost to collect, bottle,

Primary activities

Activities related to the design, creation, and delivery of the product, its marketing, and its support and after-sales service.

and distribute the water. Perrier's marketing function increased the perception of utility that customers ascribed to the product. Similarly, by helping to re-brand the company and its product offering, the marketing department at Burberry helped to create value (see Strategy in Action 3.1). Marketing and sales can also create value by discovering customer needs and communicating them back to the R&D function of the company, which can then design products that better match those needs.

Customer Service   The role of the service function of an enterprise is to provide after-sales service and support. This function can create superior utility by solving customer problems and supporting customers after they have purchased the product. For example, Caterpillar, the U.S.-based manufacturer of heavy earthmoving equipment, can ship spare parts to any location in the world within 24 h, thereby minimizing the amount of downtime its customers have to face if their Caterpillar equipment malfunctions. This is an extremely valuable support capability in an industry where downtime is very expensive. The extent of customer support has helped to increase the utility that customers associate with Caterpillar products, and therefore, the price that Caterpillar can charge for its products.

STRATEGY IN ACTION

Value Creation at Burberry

When Rose Marie Bravo, the highly regarded President of Saks Fifth Avenue, announced in 1997 that she was leaving to become CEO of ailing British fashion house Burberry, people thought she was crazy. Burberry, best known as a designer of raincoats with their trademark tartan linings, had been described as an outdated, stuffy business with a fashion cachet of almost zero. When Bravo stepped down in 2006, she was heralded in Britain and the United States as one of the world's best managers. In her tenure at Burberry, she had engineered a remarkable turnaround, leading a transformation of Burberry into what one commentator called an "achingly hip" high end fashion brand whose famous tartan bedecks everything from raincoats to bikinis, and handbags to luggage in a riot of color from pink to blue to purple. In less than a decade, Burberry had become one of the most valuable luxury fashion brands in the world.

When asked how she achieved the transformation, Bravo explains that there was hidden value in the brand, which was unleashed by constant creativity and innovation. Bravo hired world class designers to redesign Burberry's tired fashion line and bought in Christopher Bailey, one of the very best, to lead the design team. The marketing department worked closely with advertisers to develop hip ads that would appeal to a younger well-healed audience. The ads featured supermodel Kate Moss promoting the line, and Burberry hired a top fashion photographer to shoot Moss in Burberry. Burberry exercised tight control over distribution, pulling its products from stores whose image was not consistent with the Burberry brand, and expanding its own chain of Burberry stores.

Bravo also noted that "creativity doesn't just come from designers . . . ideas can come from the sales floor, the marketing department, even from accountants, believe it or not. People at whatever level they are working have a point of view and have something to say that is worth listening to." Bravo emphasized the importance of teamwork. "One of the things I think people overlook is the quality of the team. It isn't one person, and it isn't two people. It is a whole group of people—a team that works cohesively toward a goal—that makes something happen or not." She notes that her job is to build the team and then motivate the team, "keeping them on track, making sure that they are following the vision".

Source: Quotes from S. Beatty. "Bass Talk: Plotting Plaid's Future," *Wall Street Journal,* September 9, 2004, page B1. Also see C.M. Moore and G. Birtwistle, "The Burberry Business Model," *International Journal of Retail and Distribution Management,* 32, 2004, pp. 412–422; M. Dickson, "Bravo's legacy in transforming Burberry," *Financial Times,* October 6, 2005, p. 22.

Support Activities

The **support activities** of the value chain provide inputs that allow the primary activities to take place. These activities are broken down into four functions: materials management (or logistics), human resources, information systems, and company infrastructure (see Figure 3.5).

Materials Management (Logistics)   The materials-management (or logistics) function controls the transmission of physical materials through the value chain, from procurement through production and into distribution. The efficiency with which this is carried out can significantly lower cost, thereby creating more profit. Dell Inc. has a very efficient materials-management process. By tightly controlling the flow of component parts from its suppliers to its assembly plants, and into the hands of consumers, Dell has dramatically reduced its inventory holding costs. Lower inventories equate to lower costs, and hence greater profitability. Another company that has benefited from very efficient materials management, the Spanish fashion company Zara, is discussed in Strategy in Action 3.2.

Human Resources   There are a number of ways in which the human resource function can help an enterprise to create more value. This function ensures that the company has the right combination of skilled people to perform its value creation activities effectively. It is also the job of the human resource function to ensure that people are adequately trained, motivated, and compensated to perform their value creation tasks. If the human resources are functioning well, employee productivity rises (which lowers costs) and customer service improves (which raises utility), thereby enabling the company to create more value.

Information Systems   Information systems are, primarily, the electronic systems for managing inventory, tracking sales, pricing products, selling products, dealing with customer service inquiries, and so on. Information systems, when coupled with the communications features of the Internet, are holding out the promise of being able to improve the efficiency and effectiveness with which a company manages its other value creation activities. Again, Dell uses Web-based information systems to efficiently manage its global logistics network and increase inventory turnover. World-class information systems are also an aspect of Zara's competitive advantage (see Strategy in Action 3.2).

Company Infrastructure   Company infrastructure is the companywide context within which all the other value creation activities take place: the organizational structure, control systems, and company culture. Because top management can exert considerable influence upon shaping these aspects of a company, top management should also be viewed as part of the infrastructure of a company. Indeed, through strong leadership, top management can shape the infrastructure of a company and, through that, the performance of all other value creation activities that take place within it. A good example of this process is given in Strategy in Action 3.1, which looks at how Rose Marie Bravo helped to engineer a turnaround at Burberry.

The Building Blocks of Competitive Advantage

Four factors help a company to build and sustain competitive advantage—superior efficiency, quality, innovation, and customer responsiveness. Each of these factors is the product of a company's distinctive competencies. Indeed, in a very real sense they are

> **Support activities**
> Activities of the value chain that provide inputs that allow the primary activities to take place.

STRATEGY IN ACTION

Competitive Advantage at Zara

The fashion retailer Zara is one of Spain's fastest growing and most successful companies with sales of some $10 billion, and a network of 2,800 stores in 64 countries. Zara's competitive advantage centers around one thing—speed. While it takes most fashion houses 6–9 months to go from design to having merchandise delivered to a store, Zara can complete the entire process in just 5 weeks. This rapid response time enables Zara to quickly respond to changing fashions.

Zara achieves this by breaking many of the rules of operation in the fashion business. While most fashion houses outsource production, Zara has its own factories and keeps approximately half of its production in-house. Zara also has its own designers and own stores. Its designers are in constant contact with the stores, to track what is selling on a real time basis through information systems, and talk to store managers once a week to get their subjective impressions of what is "hot." This information supplements data gathered from other sources, such as fashion shows.

Drawing on this information, Zara's designers create approximately 40,000 new designs a year from which 10,000 are selected for production. Zara then purchases basic textiles from global suppliers, but performs capital-intensive production activities in its own factories. These factories use computer-controlled machinery to cut

pieces for garments. Zara does not produce in large volumes to attain economies of scale—instead it produces in small lots. Labor-intensive activities, such as sewing, are performed by sub-contractors located close to Zara's factories. Zara makes a practice of retaining more production capacity than necessary, so that if a new fashion trend emerges, it can quickly respond by designing garments and ramping up production.

Once a garment has been made, it is delivered to one of Zara's own warehouses, and then shipped to its own stores once a week. Zara deliberately under-produces products, supplying small batches of products in hot demand before quickly shifting to the next fashion trend. Often its merchandise sells out quickly. The empty shelves in Zara stores create a scarcity value—which helps to generate demand. Customers quickly snap up products they like because they know these styles may soon be out of stock, and never produced again.

As a result of this strategy, which is supported by competencies in design, information systems, and logistics management, Zara carries fewer inventories than competitors (Zara's inventory equals about 10% of sales, compared to 15% at rival stores like The Gap and Benetton). This means fewer price reductions to move products that haven't sold, and higher profit margins.

Source: Staff Reporter, "Shining Examples," *The Economist: A Survey of Logistics,* June 17, 2006, pp. 4–6; K. Capell et al, "Fashion Conquistador," *Business Week,* September 4, 2006, pp. 38–39; K. Ferdows et al, "Rapid Fire Fulfillment," *Harvard Business Review,* 82 (November 2004) pp. 101–107.

"generic" distinctive competencies. These generic competencies allow a company to (1) differentiate its product offering, and hence offer more utility to its customers, and (2) lower its cost structure (see Figure 3.6). These factors can be considered generic distinctive competencies because any company, regardless of its industry or the products or services it produces, can pursue these competencies. Although each one is discussed sequentially below, all are highly interrelated, and the important ways these competencies affect each other should be noted. For example, superior quality can lead to superior efficiency, and innovation can enhance efficiency, quality, and responsiveness to customers.

Efficiency

In one sense, a business is simply a device for transforming inputs into outputs. Inputs are basic factors of production such as labor, land, capital, management, and technological know-how. Outputs are the goods and services that the business produces. The simplest measure of efficiency is the quantity of inputs that it takes to produce a given output, that is, efficiency = outputs/inputs. The more efficient a company is, the fewer inputs required to produce a particular output.

Figure 3.6 Building Blocks of Competitive Advantage

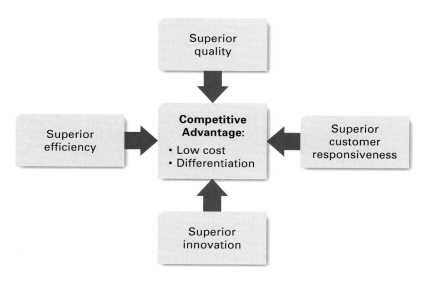

The most common measure of efficiency for many companies is employee efficiency. **Employee productivity** refers to the output produced per employee. For example, if it takes General Motors 30 h of employee time to assemble a car, and it takes Ford 25 h, we can say that Ford has higher employee productivity than GM, and is more efficient. As long as other factors are equal, such as wage rates, we can assume from this information that Ford will have a lower cost structure than GM. Thus, employee productivity helps a company attain a competitive advantage through a lower cost structure.

Quality as Excellence and Reliability

A product can be thought of as a bundle of attributes.[13] The attributes of many physical products include their form, features, performance, durability, reliability, style, and design.[14] A product is said to have *superior quality* when customers perceive that its attributes provide them with higher utility than the attributes of products sold by rivals. For example, a Rolex watch has attributes—such as design, styling, performance, and reliability—that customers perceive as being superior to the same attributes in many other watches. Thus, we can refer to a Rolex as a high-quality product: Rolex has differentiated its watches by these attributes.

When customers evaluate the quality of a product, they commonly measure it against two kinds of attributes: those related to *quality as excellence* and those related to *quality as reliability*. From a quality-as-excellence perspective, the important attributes are things such as a product's design and styling, its aesthetic appeal, its features and functions, the level of service associated with the delivery of the product, and so on. For example, customers can purchase a pair of imitation leather boots for $20 from Walmart, or they can buy a handmade pair of butter-soft leather boots from Nordstrom for $500. The boots from Nordstrom will have far superior

Employee productivity
The output produced per employee.

styling, feel more comfortable, and look much better than those from Walmart. The utility consumers will get from the Nordstrom boots will in all probability be much greater than the utility derived from the Walmart boots, but of course, they will have to pay far more for them. That is the point: when excellence is built into a product offering, consumers must pay more to own or consume it.

With regard to quality as reliability, a product can be said to be reliable when it consistently performs the function it was designed for, performs it well, and rarely, if ever, breaks down. As with excellence, reliability increases the utility a consumer gets from a product, and thus the price the company can charge for that product. Toyota's cars, for example, have the highest reliability ratings in the automobile industry, and therefore consumers are prepared to pay more for them than for cars that are very similar in other attributes. As we shall see, increasing product reliability has been the central goal of an influential management philosophy that came out of Japan in the 1980s and is commonly referred to as **total quality management**.

The position of a product against two dimensions, reliability and other attributes, can be plotted on a figure similar to Figure 3.7. For example, a Lexus has attributes—such as design, styling, performance, and safety features—that customers perceive as demonstrating excellence in quality and that are viewed as being superior to most other cars. Lexus is also a very reliable car. Thus, Lexus has a very high overall quality, which means that the car offers consumers significant utility—and that gives Toyota the option of charging a premium price for the Lexus. Toyota also produces another very reliable vehicle, the Toyota Corolla, but this model is aimed at less wealthy customers and lacks many of the superior attributes of the Lexus. Although the Corolla is also a high-quality car with regard to its reliability, it is not as high quality as a Lexus with regard to its overall excellency. At the other end of the spectrum, we can find poor-quality products that have both low reliability and

Total quality management

Increasing product reliability so that it consistently performs as it was designed to and rarely breaks down.

Figure 3.7 A Quality Map for Automobiles

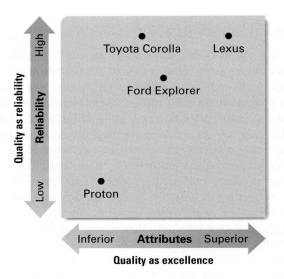

inferior attributes, such as poor design, performance, and styling. An example is the Proton, which is built by the Malaysian car firm of the same name. The design of the car is over a decade old and has a dismal reputation for styling and safety. Moreover, Proton's reliability record is one of the worst of any car, according J.D. Power.[15]

The concept of quality applies whether we are talking about Toyota automobiles, clothes designed and sold by the Gap, the customer service department of Citibank, or the ability of airlines to arrive on time. Quality is just as relevant to services as it is to goods.[16] The impact of high product quality on competitive advantage is two-fold.[17] First, providing high-quality products increases the utility those products provide to customers, which gives the company the option of charging a higher price for the products. In the automobile industry, for example, Toyota can charge a higher price for its cars because of the higher quality of its products.

Second, greater efficiency and lower unit costs associated with reliable products of high quality impact competitive advantage. When products are reliable, less employee time is wasted making defective products, or providing substandard services, and less time has to be spent fixing mistakes—which means higher employee productivity and lower unit costs. Thus, high product quality not only enables a company to differentiate its product from that of rivals, but, if the product is reliable, it also lowers costs.

The importance of reliability in building competitive advantage has increased dramatically over the past decade. The emphasis many companies place on reliability is so crucial to achieving high product reliability, that it can no longer be viewed as just one way of gaining a competitive advantage. In many industries, it has become an absolute imperative for a company's survival.

Innovation

Innovation refers to the act of creating new products or processes. There are two main types of innovation: product innovation and process innovation. **Product innovation** is the development of products that are new to the world or have superior attributes to existing products. Examples are Intel's invention of the microprocessor in the early 1970s, Cisco's development of the router for routing data over the Internet in the mid-1980s, and Apple's development of the iPod, iPhone, and iPad in the 2000s. **Process innovation** is the development of a new process for producing products and delivering them to customers. Examples include Toyota, which developed a range of new techniques collectively known as the "Toyota lean production system" for making automobiles: just-in-time inventory systems, self-managing teams, and reduced setup times for complex equipment.

Product innovation creates value by creating new products, or enhanced versions of existing products, that customers perceive as having more utility, thus increasing the company's pricing options. Process innovation often allows a company to create more value by lowering production costs. Toyota's lean production system, for example, helped to boost employee productivity, thus giving Toyota a cost-based competitive advantage.[18] Similarly, Staples' dramatically lowered the cost of selling office supplies by applying the supermarket business model to retail office supplies. Staples passed on some of this cost saving to customers in the form of lower prices, which enabled the company to increase its market share rapidly.

In the long run, innovation of products and processes is perhaps the most important building block of competitive advantage.[19] Competition can be viewed as a process driven by innovations. Although not all innovations succeed, those that do can be a major source of competitive advantage because, by definition, they give

Product innovation

Development of products that are new to the world or have superior attributes to existing products.

Process innovation

Development of a new process for producing products and delivering them to customers.

a company something unique—something its competitors lack (at least until they imitate the innovation). Uniqueness can allow a company to differentiate itself from its rivals and charge a premium price for its product, or, in the case of many process innovations, reduce its unit costs far below those of competitors.

Customer Responsiveness

To achieve superior responsiveness to customers, a company must be able to do a better job than competitors of identifying and satisfying its customers' needs. Customers will then attribute more utility to its products, creating a differentiation based on competitive advantage. Improving the quality of a company's product offering is consistent with achieving responsiveness, as is developing new products with features that existing products lack. In other words, achieving superior quality and innovation is integral to achieving superior responsiveness to customers.

Another factor that stands out in any discussion of responsiveness to customers is the need to customize goods and services to the unique demands of individual customers or customer groups. For example, the proliferation of soft drinks and beers can be viewed partly as a response to this trend. Automobile companies have become more adept at customizing cars to the demands of individual customers. For instance, following the lead of Toyota, the Saturn division of General Motors builds cars to order for individual customers, letting them choose from a wide range of colors and options.

An aspect of responsiveness to customers that has drawn increasing attention is **customer response time:** the time that it takes for a good to be delivered or a service to be performed.[20] For a manufacturer of machinery, response time is the time it takes to fill customer orders. For a bank, it is the time it takes to process a loan, or that a customer must stand in line to wait for a free teller. For a supermarket, it is the time that customers must stand in checkout lines. For a fashion retailer, it is the time required to take a new product from design inception to placement in a retail store (see Strategy in Action 3.2 for a discussion of how the Spanish fashion retailer Zara minimizes this). Customer survey after customer survey has shown slow response time to be a major source of customer dissatisfaction.[21]

Other sources of enhanced responsiveness to customers are superior design, superior service, and superior after-sales service and support. All of these factors enhance responsiveness to customers and allow a company to differentiate itself from its less responsive competitors. In turn, differentiation enables a company to build brand loyalty and charge a premium price for its products. Consider how much more people are prepared to pay for next-day delivery of Express Mail, compared to delivery in 3–4 days. In 2011, a 2-page letter sent by overnight Express Mail within the United States cost about $10, compared to $0.44 for regular mail. Thus, the price premium for express delivery (reduced response time) was $9.56, or a premium of 2,272% over the regular price.

Business Models, The Value Chain, and Generic Distinctive Competencies

Customer response time

Time that it takes for a good to be delivered or a service to be performed.

As noted in Chapter 1, a business model is a managers' conception, or gestalt, of how the various strategies that a firm pursues fit together into a congruent whole, enabling the firm to achieve a competitive advantage. More precisely, a business model represents the way in which managers configure the value chain of the firm through strategy, as well as the investments they make to support that configuration, so that they can build the distinctive competencies necessary to attain the efficiency, quality, innovation, and customer responsiveness required to support the firm's low-cost or differentiated position, thereby achieving a competitive advantage and generating superior profitability (see Figure 3.8).

For example, the primary strategic goal of Walmart is to be the lowest-cost operator offering a wide display of general merchandise in the retail industry. Walmart's business model involves offering general merchandise in a self-service supermarket type of setting. Walmart's strategies flesh out this business model and help the company to attain its strategic goal. For example, to reduce costs, Walmart limits investments in the fittings and fixtures of its stores. One of the keys to generating sales and lowering costs in this setting is rapid inventory turnover, which is achieved through strategic investments in logistics and information systems. Walmart makes major investments in process innovation to improve the effectiveness of its information and logistics systems, which enables the company to respond to customer demands for low-priced goods, and to do so in a very efficient manner.

Walmart's business model is very different from retailers such as Nordstrom. Nordstrom's business model is to offer high quality, and high-priced apparel, in a full-service and sophisticated setting. This implies differences in the way the value chain is configured. Nordstrom devotes far more attention to in-store customer service than Walmart does, which implies significant investments in its salespeople. Moreover, Nordstrom invests far more in the furnishings and fittings for its stores, compared to Walmart, whose stores have a basic warehouse feel to them. Nordstrom recaptures the costs of this investment by charging higher prices for higher-quality

Figure 3.8   Competitive Advantage and the Value Creation Cycle

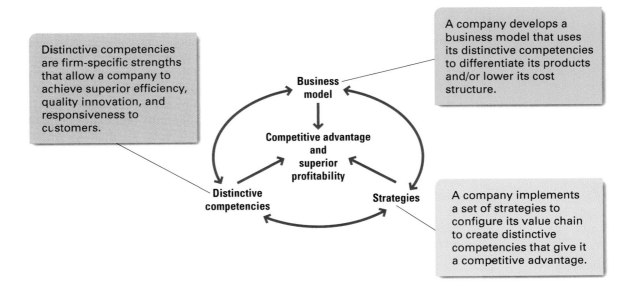

merchandise. Although Walmart and Nordstrom both sell apparel (Walmart is in fact the biggest seller of apparel in the United States), their business models imply very different positions in the marketplace, and very different configurations of value chain activities and investments.

Analyzing Competitive Advantage and Profitability

If a company's managers are to perform a good internal analysis, they must be able to analyze the financial performance of their company, identifying how its strategies contribute (or not) to profitability. To identify strengths and weaknesses effectively, they must be able to compare, or benchmark, the performance of their company against competitors, as well as against the historic performance of the company itself. This will help them determine whether they are more or less profitable than competitors and whether the performance of the company has been improving or deteriorating through time; whether their company strategies are maximizing the value being created; whether their cost structure is out of alignment compared to competitors; and whether they are using the resources of the company to the greatest effect.

As we noted in Chapter 1, the key measure of a company's financial performance is its profitability, which captures the return that a company is generating on its investments. Although several different measures of profitability exist, such as return on assets and return on equity, many authorities on the measurement of profitability argue that ROIC is the best measure because "it focuses on the true operating performance of the company."[22] (However, return on assets is very similar in formulation to return on invested capital.)

ROIC is defined as net profit over invested capital, or ROIC = net profit/invested capital. Net profit is calculated by subtracting the total costs of operating the company away from its total revenues (total revenues total costs). *Net profit* is what is left over after the government takes its share in taxes. *Invested capital* is the amount that is invested in the operations of a company: property, plant, equipment, inventories, and other assets. Invested capital comes from two main sources: interest-bearing debt and shareholders' equity. Interest-bearing debt is money the company borrows from banks and those who purchase its bonds. Shareholders' equity is the money raised from selling shares to the public, plus earnings that the company has retained in prior years (and which are available to fund current investments). ROIC measures the effectiveness with which a company is using the capital funds that it has available for investment. As such, it is recognized to be an excellent measure of the value a company is creating.[23]

A company's ROIC can be algebraically divided into two major components: return on sales and capital turnover.[24] Specifically:

$$\text{ROIC} = \text{net profits/invested capital}$$
$$= \text{net profits/revenues} \times \text{revenues/ invested capital}$$

where net profits/revenues is the return on sales, and revenues/invested capital is capital turnover. Return on sales measures how effectively the company converts revenues into profits. Capital turnover measures how effectively the company employs its invested capital to generate revenues. These two ratios can be further divided into some basic accounting ratios, as shown in Figure 3.9 (these ratios are defined in Table 3.1).[25]

Figure 3.9 says that a company's managers can increase ROIC by pursuing strategies that increase the company's return on sales. To increase the company's return

Figure 3.9 Drivers of Profitability (ROIC)

© Cengage Learning 2013

Table 3.1 Definitions of Basic Accounting Terms

Term	Definition	Source
Cost of Goods Sold (COGS)	Total costs of producing products.	Income statement
Sales, General, and Administrative Expenses (SG&A)	Costs associated with selling products and administering the company.	Income statement
R&D Expenses (R&D)	Research and development expenditure.	Income statement
Working Capital	The amount of money the company has to "work" with in the short term: Current assets—current liabilities	Balance sheet
Property, Plant, and Equipment (PPE)	The value of investments in the property, plant, and equipment that the company uses to manufacture and sell its products. Also known as *fixed capital*.	Balance sheet
Return on Sales (ROS)	Net profit expressed as a percentage of sales. Measures how effectively the company converts revenues into profits.	Ratio
Capital Turnover	Revenues divided by invested capital. Measures how effectively the company uses its capital to generate revenues.	Ratio
Return on Invested Capital (ROIC)	Net Profit divided by invested capital.	Ratio
Net Profit	Total revenues minus total costs before tax.	Income statement
Invested Capital	Interest bearing debt plus shareholders equity.	Balance sheet

© Cengage Learning 2013

on sales, they can pursue strategies that reduce the cost of goods sold (COGS) for a given level of sales revenues (COGS/sales); reduce the level of spending on sales force, marketing, general, and administrative expenses (SG&A) for a given level of sales revenues (SG&A/sales); and reduce R&D spending for a given level of sales revenues (R&D/sales). Alternatively, they can increase return on sales by pursuing strategies that increase sales revenues more than they increase the costs of the business, as measured by COGS, SG&A, and R&D expenses. That is, they can increase the return on sales by pursuing strategies that lower costs or increase value through differentiation, and thus allow the company to increase its prices more than its costs.

Figure 3.9 also tells us that a company's managers can boost the profitability of their company by obtaining greater sales revenues from their invested capital, thereby increasing capital turnover. They do this by pursuing strategies that reduce the amount of working capital, such as the amount of capital invested in inventories, needed to generate a given level of sales (working capital/sales) and then pursuing strategies that reduce the amount of fixed capital that they have to invest in plant, property, and equipment (PPE) to generate a given level of sales (PPE/sales). That is, they pursue strategies that reduce the amount of capital that they need to generate every dollar of sales, and therefore, their cost of capital. Recall that cost of capital is part of the cost structure of a company (see Figure 3.2), so strategies designed to increase capital turnover also lower the cost structure.

To see how these basic drivers of profitability help us to understand what is going on in a company and to identify its strengths and weaknesses, let us compare the financial performance of Dell against one of its most effective competitors, Apple. This is done in the next *Focus on Dell* feature.

The Durability of Competitive Advantage

The next question we must address is how long a competitive advantage will last once it has been created. In other words: What is the durability of competitive advantage given that other companies are also seeking to develop distinctive competencies that will give them a competitive advantage? The answer depends on three factors: barriers to imitation, the capability of competitors, and the general dynamism of the industry environment.

Barriers to Imitation

A company with a competitive advantage will earn higher-than-average profits. These profits send a signal to rivals that the company has valuable, distinctive competencies allowing it to create superior value. Naturally, its competitors will try to identify and imitate that competency, and insofar as they are successful, ultimately their increased success may whittle away the company's superior profits.[26]

How quickly rivals will imitate a company's distinctive competencies is an important issue, because the speed of imitation has a bearing on the durability of a company's competitive advantage. Other factors being equal, the more rapidly competitors imitate a company's distinctive competencies, the less durable its competitive advantage will be, and the more important it is that the company endeavor to improve its competencies to stay one step ahead of imitators. It is important to stress at the outset that a competitor can imitate almost any distinctive competency. The critical issue is time: the longer it takes competitors to imitate a distinctive competency,

FOCUS ON D∢LL

③

COMPARING DELL INC. AND APPLE

Dell and Apple are very close in size. In 2010, Dell generated $61 billion in sales, and Apple $65 billion. For the 2010 financial year, Dell earned a ROIC of 20.41%, while Apple earned 29.32%. Although Dell has improved its performance since 2008, and its ROIC is respectable, it remains less profitable than Apple. The difference between the profitability of these two enterprises can be understood in terms of the impact of their strategies on the various ratios identified in Figure 3.9. The differences are summarized in Figure 3.10.

First, note that Dell's return on sales (ROS) is much lower than Apple's. This is because Dell's COGS as a percentage of sales are much higher than Apple's (81.47% against 60.6%). Dell, in other words, does not (or cannot) put a big markup

on the goods that it sells. Dell is perceived as producing commodity-like products. Apple has successfully created a strong brand. Apple's products are perceived as delivering high value to consumers. Consequently, Apple has a much larger markup over COGS, which reflects its successful differentiation strategy.

Second, Apple spends about 2.5 times as much as a percentage of sales on R&D as Dell (Apple spends 2.73% of its sales revenue on R&D, Dell spends 1.07%). Dell's low R&D to sales ratio reflects the fact that it is producing commodity-like PC boxes. It is not trying to differentiate itself through product design. Apple is differentiating by product design, hence Apple's greater R&D spending.

Figure 3.10 Comparing Dell Inc. and Apple

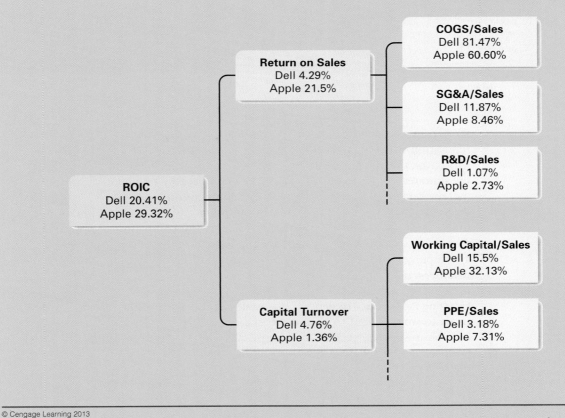

(continued)

FOCUS ON D&LL (*continued*)

Dell excels, however, in its efficient use of capital. Dell generates $4.76 for every $1 of capital invested in the business, against $1.36 for Apple. Dell's working capital to sales ratio is also much lower than Apple's. Dell, in other words, has less capital tied up in inventory than Apple. This reflects Dell's build to order strategy. Dell does not need to fill a retail channel with inventory. Moreover, it takes order information received over its Website, and through telephone sales, and transmits that instantaneously to suppliers located throughout the world, who then adjust their own production schedules accordingly. Dell coordinates the entire process so that parts arrive at Dell's assembly plants just when they are required and not before. They are quickly assembled at the plants, and the complete products are shipped out the door in a few days. As a result, Dell turns over its inventory much more rapidly than Apple does. Put another way, Apple has a large amount of capital tied up in parts inventory waiting to be assembled into computers, and in finished inventory that is in distribution, or sitting in retail channels. Dell does not.

Dell's working capital requirements are reduced even further because many of its customers pay by credit card.

The cards are charged when a machine leaves Dell's factory, which is long before Dell must pay its suppliers, enabling Dell to use this money to finance its day-to-day operations.

On the other hand, we should not forget that Apple is a vertically integrated enterprise, which sells a portion of its products through its own Apple stores. Since Apple has capital tied up in the inventory on display in its stores, we would expect its working capital ratio to be higher. In addition, since Apple owns retail stores, it is expected to have a higher PPE/sales ratio. In other words, Apple's choice of strategy has made it less efficient than Dell with regard to capital productivity, but more than makes up for this by the high margins that it can place on the goods it sells due to its successful differentiation strategy.

It is also worth noting that at the end of 2010, Apple had $27 billion in cash and short-term investments on its balance sheet, whereas Dell had $14.4 billion. If Apple had decided to give some of that cash back to shareholders in 2011 in the form of stock buybacks or dividend payouts, its capital turnover ratio would have been much better, and its ROIC higher still. Presumably, Apple has strategic reasons for hording cash on its balance sheet.

Source: Calculated by the author from 2010 company 10K statements.

the greater the opportunity the company has to build a strong market position and reputation with customers—which are then more difficult for competitors to attack. Moreover, the longer it takes to achieve an imitation, the greater the opportunity for the imitated company to improve on its competency or build other competencies, thereby remaining one step ahead of the competition.

Barriers to imitation are a primary determinant of the speed of imitation. Barriers to imitation are factors that make it difficult for a competitor to copy a company's distinctive competencies; the greater the barriers to imitation, the more sustainable a company's competitive advantage.[30] Barriers to imitation differ depending on whether a competitor is trying to imitate resources or capabilities.

Imitating Resources   In general, the easiest distinctive competencies for prospective rivals to imitate tend to be those based on possession of firm-specific and valuable tangible resources, such as buildings, manufacturing plants, and equipment. Such resources are visible to competitors and can often be purchased on the open market. For example, if a company's competitive advantage is based on sole possession of efficient-scale manufacturing facilities, competitors may move fairly quickly to establish similar facilities. Although Ford gained a competitive advantage over General Motors in the 1920s by first adopting assembly line manufacturing technology to produce automobiles, General Motors quickly imitated that innovation, competing away Ford's distinctive competency in the process. A similar process is occurring

> **Barriers to imitation**
>
> Factors that make it difficult for a competitor to copy a company's distinctive competencies.

in the auto industry now, as companies try to imitate Toyota's famous production system. However, Toyota has slowed down the rate of imitation by not allowing competitors access to its latest equipment.

Intangible resources can be more difficult to imitate. This is particularly true of brand names, which are important because they symbolize a company's reputation. In the heavy earthmoving equipment industry, for example, the Caterpillar brand name is synonymous with high quality and superior after-sales service and support. Similarly, the St. Michael's brand name used by Marks & Spencer, Britain's largest clothing retailer, symbolizes high-quality but reasonably priced clothing. Customers often display a preference for the products of such companies because the brand name is an important guarantee of high quality. Although competitors might like to imitate well-established brand names, the law prohibits them from doing so.

Marketing and technological know-how are also important intangible resources and can be relatively easy to imitate. The movement of skilled marketing personnel between companies may facilitate the general dissemination of marketing know-how. For example, in the 1970s, Ford was acknowledged as the best marketer among the big three U.S. auto companies. In 1979, it lost a lot of its marketing know-how to Chrysler when its most successful marketer, Lee Iacocca, joined Chrysler and subsequently hired many of Ford's top marketing people to work with him at Chrysler. More generally, successful marketing strategies are relatively easy to imitate because they are so visible to competitors. Thus, Coca-Cola quickly imitated PepsiCo's Diet Pepsi brand with the introduction of its own brand, Diet Coke.

With regard to technological know-how, the patent system in theory should make technological know-how relatively immune to imitation. Patents give the inventor of a new product a 20-year exclusive production agreement. However, this is not always the case. In electrical and computer engineering, for example, it is often possible to invent and circumnavigate the patent process: that is, produce a product that is functionally equivalent but does not rely on the patented technology. One study found that 60% of patented innovations were successfully invented around in 4 years.[28] This suggests that, in general, distinctive competencies based on technological know-how can be relatively short-lived.

Imitating Capabilities Imitating a company's capabilities tends to be more difficult than imitating its tangible and intangible resources, chiefly because capabilities are based on the way in which decisions are made and processes managed deep within a company. It is hard for outsiders to discern them.

The invisible nature of capabilities would not be enough to halt imitation; competitors could still gain insights into how a company operates by hiring people away from that company. However, a company's capabilities rarely reside in a single individual. Rather, they are the product of how numerous individuals interact within a unique organizational setting.[29] It is possible that no one individual within a company may be familiar with the totality of a company's internal operating routines and procedures. In such cases, hiring people away from a successful company in order to imitate its key capabilities may not be helpful.

Capability of Competitors

According to work by Pankaj Ghemawat, a major determinant of the capability of competitors to rapidly imitate a company's competitive advantage is the nature of the competitors' prior strategic commitments.[30] By strategic commitment, Ghemawat means a company's commitment to a particular way of doing business—that is, to developing a particular set of resources and capabilities. Ghemawat states that once a company has made a strategic commitment, it will have difficulty responding to new competition if doing so requires a break with this commitment. Therefore, when competitors have long-established commitments to a particular way of doing business, they may be slow to imitate an innovating company's competitive advantage. Its competitive advantage will be relatively durable as a result.

The U.S. automobile industry again offers an example. From 1945 to 1975, General Motors, Ford, and Chrysler, dominated this stable oligopoly, and all three companies directed their operations to the production of large cars, which American customers demanded at the time. When the market shifted from large cars to small, fuel-efficient vehicles during the late 1970s, U.S. companies lacked the resources and capabilities required to produce these cars. Their prior commitments had built the wrong kind of skills for this new environment. As a result, foreign producers, particularly the Japanese, stepped into the market breach by providing compact, fuel-efficient, high-quality low-cost cars. U.S. auto manufacturers failed to react quickly to the distinctive competency of Japanese auto companies, gaving them time to build a strong market position and brand loyalty, which subsequently proved difficult to attack.

Another determinant of the ability of competitors to respond to a company's competitive advantage is the absorptive capacity of competitors.[31] **Absorptive capacity** refers to the ability of an enterprise to identify, value, assimilate, and use new knowledge. For example, in the 1960s, 1970s, and 1980s Toyota developed a competitive advantage based on its innovation of lean production systems. Competitors such as General Motors were slow to imitate this innovation, primarily because they lacked the necessary absorptive capacity. General Motors was such a bureaucratic and inward-looking organization that it was very difficult for the company to identify, value, assimilate, and use the knowledge underscoring lean production systems. Long after General Motors had identified and understood the importance of lean production systems, it was still struggling to assimilate and use that new knowledge. Put differently, internal forces of inertia can make it difficult for established competitors to respond to rivals whose competitive advantage is based on new products or internal processes—that is, on innovation.

Together, factors such as existing strategic commitments and low absorptive capacity limit the ability of established competitors to imitate the competitive advantage of a rival, particularly when that competitive advantage is based on innovative products or processes. This is why value often migrates away from established competitors and toward new enterprises that are operating with new business models when innovations reshape the rules of industry competition.

Industry Dynamism

A dynamic industry environment is one that changes rapidly. We examined the factors that determine the dynamism and intensity of competition in an industry in Chapter 2 when we discussed the external environment. The most dynamic industries tend to be those with a very high rate of product innovation—for instance, the customer electronics industry and the personal computer industry. In dynamic industries, the rapid rate of innovation means that product life-cycles are shortening and that competitive advantage can be fleeting. A company that has a competitive advantage today may find its market position outflanked tomorrow by a rival's innovation.

Absorptive capacity
The ability of an enterprise to identify, value, assimilate, and use new knowledge.

In the personal computer industry, the rapid increase in computing power during the past two decades has contributed to a high degree of innovation and a turbulent environment. Reflecting the persistence of computer innovation, Apple had an industrywide competitive advantage due to its innovation in the late 1970s and early 1980s. In 1981, IBM seized the advantage by introducing its first personal computer. By the mid-1980s, IBM had lost its competitive advantage to high-power "clone" manufacturers, such as Compaq, that had beaten IBM in the race to introduce a computer based on Intel's 386 chip. In the 1990s, Compaq subsequently lost its competitive advantage to Dell, which pioneered new low-cost ways of delivering computers to customers using the Internet as a direct selling device. In recent years, Apple has again seized the initiative with its innovative product designs and successful differentiation strategy.

Summary

The durability of a company's competitive advantage depends upon the height of barriers to imitation, the capability of competitors to imitate its innovation, and the general level of dynamism in the industry environment. When barriers to imitation are low, capable competitors abound, and innovations are rapidly being developed within a dynamic environment, then competitive advantage is likely to be transitory. But even within such industries, companies can build a more enduring competitive advantage—if they are able to make investments that build barriers to imitation.

Avoiding Failure and Sustaining Competitive Advantage

How can a company avoid failure and escape the traps that have snared so many once successful companies? How can managers build a sustainable competitive advantage? Much of the remainder of this book addresses these questions. Here, we outline a number of key points that set the scene for the coming discussion.

Why Companies Fail

When a company loses its competitive advantage, its profitability falls. The company does not necessarily fail; it may just have average or below-average profitability and can remain in this mode for a considerable time, although its resource and capital base is shrinking. Failure implies something more drastic. A failing company is one whose profitability is substantially lower than the average profitability of its competitors; it has lost the ability to attract and generate resources and its profit margins and invested capital are rapidly shrinking.

Why does a company lose its competitive advantage and fail? This question is particularly pertinent because some of the most successful companies of the last half-century have seen their competitive position deteriorate at one time or another. IBM, General Motors, American Express, Digital Equipment, and Sears, (among many others) which all were astute examples of managerial excellence, have gone through periods of poor financial performance, during which any competitive advantage was distinctly lacking. We explore three related reasons for failure: inertia, prior strategic commitments, and the Icarus paradox.

Inertia   The inertia argument states that companies find it difficult to change their strategies and structures in order to adapt to changing competitive conditions.[32] IBM is a classic example of this problem. For 30 years, it was viewed as the world's most successful computer company. Then, in only a few years, its success turned into a disaster: it lost $5 billion in 1992, and laid off more than 100,000 employees. The underlying cause of IBM's troubles was a dramatic decline in the cost of computing power as a result of innovations in microprocessors. With the advent of powerful low-cost microprocessors, the locus of the computer market shifted from mainframes to small, low-priced personal computers, leaving IBM's huge mainframe operations with a diminished market. Although IBM had a significant presence in the personal computer market, it had failed to shift the focus of its efforts away from mainframes and toward personal computers. This failure meant deep trouble for one of the most successful companies of the twentieth century. (IBM has now executed a very successful turnaround repositioning itself as a provider of information technology infrastructure and solutions.)

It appears that one reason companies find it so difficult to adapt to new environmental conditions is the role of capabilities in causing inertia. Organizational capabilities—the way a company makes decisions and manages its processes—can be a source of competitive advantage, but they are often difficult to change. IBM always emphasized close coordination among operating units and favored decision-making processes that stressed consensus among interdependent operating units as a prerequisite for decisions to go forward.[33] This capability was a source of advantage for IBM during the 1970s, when coordination among its worldwide operating units was necessary to develop, manufacture, and sell complex mainframes. But the slow-moving bureaucracy that it had spawned was a source of failure in the 1990s, when organizations needed to readily adapt to rapid environmental change.

Capabilities are difficult to change because distribution of power and influence is embedded within the established decision-making and management processes of an organization. Those who play key roles in a decision-making process clearly have more power. It follows that changing the established capabilities of an organization means changing its existing distribution of power and influence. Most often, those whose power and influence would diminish resist such change; proposals for change trigger turf battles. Power struggles and the hierarchical resistance associated with trying to alter the way in which an organization makes decisions and manages its process—that is, trying to change its capabilities—bring on inertia. This is not to say that companies cannot change. However, those who feel threatened by change often resist it; change in most cases is induced by a crisis. By then, the company may already be failing, as exemplified by IBM.

Prior Strategic Commitments   A company's prior strategic commitments not only limit its ability to imitate rivals but may also cause competitive disadvantage.[34] IBM, for instance, had major investments in the mainframe computer business, so when the market shifted, it was stuck with significant resources specialized to that particular business: its manufacturing facilities largely produced mainframes, its research organization was similarly specialized, as was its sales force. Because these resources were not well suited to the newly emerging personal computer business, IBM's difficulties in the early 1990s were in a sense inevitable. Its prior strategic commitments locked it into a business that was shrinking. Shedding these resources inevitably caused hardship for all organization stakeholders.

The Icarus Paradox   Danny Miller has postulated that the roots of competitive failure can be found in what he termed "The Icarus Paradox."[35] Icarus is a figure in Greek mythology who used a pair of wings, made for him by his father, to escape from an island where he was being held prisoner. He flew so well that he climbed higher and higher, ever closer to the sun, until the heat of the sun melted the wax that held his wings together, and he plunged to his death in the Aegean Sea. The paradox is that his greatest asset, his ability to fly, caused his demise. Miller argues that the same paradox applies to many once successful companies. According to Miller, many companies become so dazzled by their early success that they believe more of the same type of effort is the way to future success. As a result, they can become so specialized and myopic that they lose sight of market realities and the fundamental requirements for achieving a competitive advantage. Sooner or later, this leads to failure. For example, Miller argues that Texas Instruments and Digital Equipment Corporation (DEC), achieved early success through engineering excellence. But thereafter, they became so obsessed with engineering details that they lost sight of market realities. (The story of DEC's demise is summarized in Strategy in Action 3.3.)

STRATEGY IN ACTION

The Road To Ruin at DEC

Digital Equipment Corporation (DEC) was one of the premier computer companies of the 1970s and 1980s. DEC's original success was founded on the minicomputer, a cheaper, more flexible version of its mainframe cousins that Ken Olson and his brilliant team of engineers invented in the 1960s. They then improved on their original minicomputers until they could not be beat for quality and reliability. In the 1970s, their VAX series of minicomputers was widely regarded as the most reliable series of computers ever produced, and DEC was rewarded by high profit rates and rapid growth. By 1990, it was number 27 on the Fortune 500 list of the largest corporations in America.

Buoyed by its success, DEC turned into an engineering monoculture: its engineers became idols; its marketing and accounting staff, however, were barely tolerated. Component specs and design standards were all that senior managers understood. Technological fine-tuning became such an obsession that the customer's needs for smaller, more economical, user-friendly computers were ignored. DEC's personal computers, for example, bombed because they were out of touch with the needs of customers. The company failed to respond to the threat to its core market, presented by the rise of computer workstations and client-server architecture. Ken Olson was known for dismissing such new products. He once said, "We always say that customers are right, but they are not always right." Perhaps. But DEC, blinded by its early success, failed to remain responsive to its customers and to changing market conditions. In another famous statement, when asked about personal computers in the early 1980s, Olson said: "I can see of no reason why anybody would ever want a computer on their desk."

By the early 1990s, DEC was in deep trouble. Olson was forced out in July 1992, and the company lost billions of dollars between 1992 and 1995. It returned to profitability in 1996, primarily because its turnaround strategy, aimed at reorienting the company to serve the areas that Olson had dismissed, was a success. In 1998, Compaq purchased DEC (which Hewlett-Packard later purchased) and DEC disappeared from the business landscape as an independent entity.

Sources: D. Miller, *The Icarus Paradox* (New York: HarperBusiness, 1990); P. D. Llosa, "We Must Know What We Are Doing," *Fortune,* November 14, 1994, p. 68.

Steps to Avoid Failure

Given that so many pitfalls await companies, the question arises as to how strategic managers can use internal analysis to find and escape them. We now look at several tactics that managers can use.

Focus on the Building Blocks of Competitive Advantage   Maintaining a competitive advantage requires a company to continue focusing on all four generic building blocks of competitive advantage—efficiency, quality, innovation, and responsiveness to customers—and to develop distinctive competencies that contribute to superior performance in these areas. Miller's Icarus paradox promotes the message that many successful companies become unbalanced in their pursuit of distinctive competencies. DEC, for example, focused on engineering quality at the expense of almost everything else, including, most importantly, responsiveness to customers. Other companies fail to focus on any distinctive competency at all.

Institute Continuous Improvement and Learning   Change is constant and inevitable. Today's source of competitive advantage may soon be rapidly imitated by capable competitors or made obsolete by the innovations of a rival. In a dynamic, fast-paced environment, the only way that a company can maintain a competitive advantage over time is to continually improve its efficiency, quality, innovation, and responsiveness to customers. The way to do this is to recognize the importance of learning within the organization.[36] The most successful companies are not those that stand still, resting on their laurels. Companies that are always seeking ways to improve their operations and constantly upgrade the value of their distinctive competencies or create new competencies are the most successful. General Electric and Toyota, for example, have reputations as learning organizations; they are continually analyzing the processes that underlie their efficiency, quality, innovation, and responsiveness to customers. Learning from prior mistakes and seeking out ways to improve processes over time is the primary objective. This approach has enabled Toyota, for instance, to continually upgrade its employee productivity and product quality, and stay ahead of imitators.

Track Best Industrial Practice and Use Benchmarking   Identifying and adopting best industrial practice is one of the best ways to develop distinctive competencies that contribute to superior efficiency, quality, innovation, and responsiveness to customers. Only in this way will a company be capable of building and maintaining the resources and capabilities that underpin excellence in efficiency, quality, innovation, and responsiveness to customers. (We discuss what constitutes best industrial practice in some depth in Chapter 4.) It requires tracking the practice of other companies, and perhaps the best way to do so is through benchmarking: measuring the company against the products, practices, and services of some of its most efficient global competitors.

Overcome Inertia   Overcoming the internal forces that are a barrier to change within an organization is one of the key requirements for maintaining a competitive advantage. Identifying barriers to change is an important first step. Once barriers are identified, implementing change to overcome these barriers requires good leadership, the judicious use of power, and appropriate subsequent changes in organizational structure and control systems.

The Role of Luck   A number of scholars have argued that luck plays a critical role in determining competitive success and failure.[37] In its most extreme version, the luck argument devalues the importance of strategy altogether. Instead, it states that in the face of uncertainty, some companies just happen to choose the correct strategy.

Although luck may be the reason for a company's success in particular cases, it is an unconvincing explanation for the persistent success of a company. Recall our argument that the generic building blocks of competitive advantage are superior efficiency, quality, innovation, and responsiveness to customers. In addition, keep in mind that competition is a process in which companies are continually trying to outdo each other in their ability to achieve high efficiency, superior quality, outstanding innovation, and rapid responsiveness to customers. It is possible to imagine a company getting lucky and coming into possession of resources that allow it to achieve excellence within one or more of these dimensions. It is difficult, however, to imagine how sustained excellence within any of these four dimensions could be produced by anything other than conscious effort—that is, by strategy. Luck may indeed play a role in success, and managers must always exploit a lucky break. However, to argue that success is entirely a matter of luck is to strain credibility. As the prominent banker of the early 20th century, J. P. Morgan, once said, "The harder I work, the luckier I seem to get." Managers who strive to formulate and implement strategies that lead to a competitive advantage are more likely to be lucky.

Ethical Dilemma

unionization at your company (the workforce is not unionized). Although she acknowledges that this approach does lead to high employee turnover, she argues that the jobs are low skilled, and that it is easy to replace someone who leaves.

Your friend manages a retailer that has a history of superior profitability. She believes that one of the principle sources of competitive advantage for her enterprises are low labor costs. The low labor costs are due to her hiring of minimum wage workers, the decision not to give them any benefits (such as health benefits), and her consistent opposition to

Is your friend's approach to doing business ethical? Are their ways of achieving low labor costs that do not rely upon the hiring of minimum wage workers? Would you council your friend to use an alternative approach?

Summary of Chapter

1. Distinctive competencies are the firm-specific strengths of a company. Valuable distinctive competencies enable a company to earn a profit rate that is above the industry average.
2. The distinctive competencies of an organization arise from its resources (its financial, physical, human, technological, and organizational assets) and capabilities (its skills at coordinating resources and putting them to productive use).
3. In order to achieve a competitive advantage, a company needs to pursue strategies that build on its existing resources and capabilities and formulate strategies that build additional resources and capabilities (develop new competencies).
4. The source of a competitive advantage is superior value creation.
5. To create superior value (utility) a company must lower its costs or differentiate its product so that it creates more value and can charge a higher price, or do both simultaneously.
6. Managers must understand how value creation and pricing decisions affect demand and how costs change with increases in volume. They must have a good grasp of the demand conditions in the company's market, and the cost structure of the company at different levels of output if they are to make decisions that maximize the profitability of their enterprise.
7. The four building blocks of competitive advantage are efficiency, quality, innovation, and responsiveness to customers. These are generic distinctive competencies. Superior efficiency enables a company to lower its costs; superior quality allows it to charge a higher price and lower its costs; and superior customer service lets it charge a higher price. Superior innovation can lead to higher prices, particularly in the case of product innovations, or lower unit costs, and in the case of process innovations.
8. If a company's managers are to perform a good internal analysis, they need to be able to analyze the financial performance of their company, identifying how the strategies of the company relate to its profitability, as measured by the return on invested capital.
9. The durability of a company's competitive advantage depends on the height of barriers to imitation, the capability of competitors, and environmental dynamism.
10. Failing companies typically earn low or negative profits. Three factors seem to contribute to failure: organizational inertia in the face of environmental change, the nature of a company's prior strategic commitments, and the Icarus paradox.
11. Avoiding failure requires a constant focus on the basic building blocks of competitive advantage: continuous improvement, identification and adoption of best industrial practice, and victory over inertia.

Discussion Questions

1. Which is more important in explaining the success and failure of companies: strategizing or luck?
2. It is possible for a company to be the lowest-cost producer in its industry and simultaneously have an output that is the most valued by customers. Discuss this statement.
3. Why is it important to understand the drivers of profitability, as measured by the return on invested capital?
4. When is a company's competitive advantage most likely to endure over time?
5. What are the primary implications of the material discussed in this chapter for strategy formulation?

Practicing Strategic Management

Small-Group Exercises

Small-Group Exercise: Analyzing Competitive Advantage

Break up into groups of 3–5 people. Drawing on the concepts introduced in this chapter, analyze the competitive position of your business school in the market for business education. Then answer the following questions:

1. Does your business school have a competitive advantage?
2. If so, upon what is this advantage based, and is this advantage sustainable?
3. If your school does not have a competitive advantage in the market for business education, identify the inhibiting factors that are holding it back.
4. How might the Internet change the way in which business education is delivered?
5. Does the Internet pose a threat to the competitive position of your school in the market for business education, or is it an opportunity for your school to enhance its competitive position?

Strategy Sign-On

Article File 3

Find a company that has sustained its competitive advantage for more than 10 years. Identify the source or sources of this competitive advantage, and explain why it has lasted so long.

Strategic Management Project: Developing Your Portfolio 3 This module deals with the competitive position of your company. With the information you have available, perform the tasks and answer the questions listed:

1. Identify whether your company has a competitive advantage or disadvantage in its primary industry. (Its primary industry is the one in which it has the most sales.)
2. Evaluate your company against the four generic building blocks of competitive advantage: efficiency, quality, innovation, and responsiveness to customers. How does this exercise help you understand the performance of your company relative to its competitors?
3. What are the distinctive competencies of your company?
4. What roles have prior strategies played in shaping the distinctive competencies of your company? What has been the role of luck?
5. Do the strategies your company is currently pursuing build on its distinctive competencies? Are they an attempt to build new competencies?
6. What are the barriers to imitating the distinctive competencies of your company?
7. Is there any evidence that your company finds it difficult to adapt to changing industry conditions? If so, why do you think this is the case?

CLOSING CASE
Regaining McDonald's Competitive Advantage

McDonald's is an extraordinarily successful enterprise. It began in 1955, when the legendary Ray Kroc decided to franchise the McDonald brothers' fast food concept. Since its inception, McDonald's has grown into the largest restaurant chain in the world with almost 32,000 stores in 120 countries.

For decades, McDonald's experience in success was grounded in a simple formula: give consumers value for money, good quick service, and consistent quality in a clean environment, and they will return time and time again. To deliver value for money and consistent quality, it standardized the process of order taking, making food, and providing service. Standardized processes raised the productivity of employees while ensuring that customers had the same experience in all branches of the restaurant. McDonald's also developed close ties with wholesalers and food producers, managing its supply chain to reduce costs. As it became larger, its buying power enabled McDonald's to realize economies of scale in purchasing, and to pass on cost savings to customers in the form of low-priced meals, which drove forward demand. There was also the ubiquity of McDonald's; their restaurants could be found everywhere. This accessibility, coupled with the consistent experience and low prices, drove brand loyalty.

The formula worked well until the late-1990s and early-2000s. By then, McDonald's was under attack for contributing to obesity. Its low-priced high-fat foods were dangerous claimed critics. The company's image was tarnished by the best selling book, "Fast Food Nation," and thereafter by the documentary, "Super Size Me" which featured a journalist who rapidly gained weight by only eating at McDonald's "super size" meals for a month. By 2002, sales were stagnating and profits were falling. It seemed that McDonald's had lost its edge.

What followed was a classic corporate makeover that has enabled the company to regain its competitive advantage. First, there was a change in top-level management. Then there was a shift of emphasis. McDonald's scrapped its super-size menu and added healthier options, such as salads and apple slices. Executives mined data to discover what people were eating, and they found that people were eating more chicken and less beef. Based on this data, McDonald's decided to emphasize chicken, and added grilled chicken sandwiches, wraps with chicken, Southern style chicken sandwiches, and most recently, chicken for breakfast to their menu. To be clear, the company still sells an awful lot of low cost "dollar meals" consisting of cheeseburgers and fries. During the recessionary environment of 2008–2009, sales of dollar-menus surged. However, chicken sales doubled at McDonald's between 2002 and 2008 and the company now buys more chicken than beef. The company also decided to use only white chicken meat, ending customer's speculation about the "mystery meat" found in chicken McNuggets.

The company also shifted its emphasis on beverages. For decades, drinks were an afterthought at McDonald's, but executives couldn't help but note the raid growth of Starbucks. So in 2006, McDonald's decided to offer better coffee, including lattes. McDonald's improved the quality of its coffee by purchasing high-quality beans, using better equipment, and filtering its water. The company did not lose sight of the need to keep costs low and service quick, however, and continues to add coffee making machines that produce lattes and cappuccinos in 45 s, at the push of a button. Starbucks it is not, but for many people, a latte from the McDonald's drive through window is comparable. Today, the latte machines have been installed in almost half of the stores in the United States.

Additionally, a change in the restaurant's design has given it a face lift. Sleek new buildings with trendy furnishings and lights, wide screen TVs, and Wi-Fi connections are replacing the aging design, which is incrementally being phased out. The idea is to raise the perception of quality, and thereby capture more customers.

So far, the changes appear to be working. Both sales and profits have been growing at a healthy rate, despite a difficult economic environment. In 2010, net profits were $4.9 billion, up from $1.7 billion in 2002, while revenues expanded from $15.4 billion to $24 billion. Profitability has also improved, with McDonald's return on invested capital increasing from 9.4% in 2002 to 18%–19% in 2008–2010.[38]

Case Discussion Questions

1. How important are efficiency, quality, customer responsiveness, and innovation to McDonald's competitive position?
2. Does McDonald's have any distinctive competencies? If so, how do they impact the business?
3. Is McDonald's pursuing a low cost strategy, or a differentiation strategy?
4. Why did McDonald's start to lose its competitive advantage in the 2000s? What did it do to halt the erosion in its competitive position? What does this teach you about the sustainability of competitive advantage?

Notes

[1] J. Jargon, "Latest Starbucks Buzzword: Lean Japanese Techniques," *Wall Street Journal*, August 4, 2009, p. A1; J. Adamy, "Starbucks Moves to Cut Costs, Retain Customers," *Wall Street Journal*, December 5, 2008, p. B3; "Coffee Wars," *The Economist*, December 1, 2008, pp. 57–59; R. Lowenstein, "What Latte Lost its Luster," *Wall Street Journal*, March 29, 2011, p. A17.

[2] M. Cusumano, *The Japanese Automobile Industry* (Cambridge, MA: Harvard University Press, 1989); S. Spear and H. K. Bowen, "Decoding the DNA of the Toyota Production System," *Harvard Business Review* (September–October 1999): 96–108.

[3] The material in this section relies on the resource-based view of the company. For summaries of this perspective, see J. B. Barney, "Company Resources and Sustained Competitive Advantage," *Journal of Management* 17 (1991): 99–120; J. T. Mahoney and J. R. Pandian, "The Resource-Based View Within the Conversation of Strategic Management," *Strategic Management Journal* 13 (1992): 63–380; R. Amit and P. J. H. Schoemaker, "Strategic Assets and Organizational Rent," *Strategic Management Journal* 14 (1993): 33–46; M. A. Peteraf, "The Cornerstones of Competitive Advantage: A Resource-Based View," *Strategic Management Journal* 14 (1993): 179–191; B. Wernerfelt, "A Resource Based View of the Company," *Strategic Management Journal* 15 (1994): 171–180; and K. M. Eisenhardt and J. A. Martin, "Dynamic Capabilities: What Are They?" *Strategic Management Journal* 21 (2000): 1105–1121.

[4] J. B. Barney, "Company Resources and Sustained Competitive Advantage", *Journal of Management*, 1991, 17, pp 99–120.

[5] For a discussion of organizational capabilities, see R. R. Nelson and S. Winter, *An Evolutionary Theory of Economic Change* (Cambridge, MA: Belknap Press, 1982).

[6] W. Chan Kim and R. Mauborgne, "Value Innovation: The Strategic Logic of High Growth," *Harvard Business Review* (January–February 1997): 102–115.

[7] The concept of consumer surplus is an important one in economics. For a more detailed exposition, see D. Besanko, D. Dranove, and M. Shanley, *Economics of Strategy* (New York: Wiley, 1996).

[8] However, $P = U$ only in the special case when the company has a perfect monopoly and it can charge each customer a unique price that reflects the utility of the product to that customer (i.e., where perfect price discrimination is possible). More generally, except in the limiting case of perfect price discrimination, even a monopolist will see most customers capture some of the utility of a product in the form of a consumer surplus.

[9] This point is central to the work of Michael Porter. See M. E. Porter, *Competitive Advantage* (New York: Free Press, 1985). See also P. Ghemawat, *Commitment: The Dynamic of Strategy* (New York: Free Press, 1991), chap. 4.

[10] Oliver Wyman, The Harbor Report, 2008. http://www.oliverwyman.com/ow/automotive.htm

[11] Porter, *Competitive Advantage*.

[12] Ibid.

[13] This approach goes back to the pioneering work by K. Lancaster: *Consumer Demand, a New Approach* (New York: 1971).

[14] D. Garvin, "Competing on the Eight Dimensions of Quality," *Harvard Business Review* (November–December 1987): 101–119; P. Kotler, *Marketing Management* (Millennium ed.) (Upper Saddle River, NJ: Prentice-Hall, 2000).

[15] "Proton Bomb," *Economist*, May 8, 2004, p. 77.

[16] C. K. Prahalad and M. S. Krishnan, "The New Meaning of Quality in the Information Age," *Harvard Business Review* (September–October 1999): 109–118.

[17] See D. Garvin, "What Does Product Quality Really Mean," *Sloan Management Review* 26 (Fall 1984): 25–44; P. B. Crosby, *Quality Is Free* (New York: Mentor, 1980); A. Gabor, *The Man Who Discovered Quality* (New York: Times Books, 1990).

[18] M. Cusumano, *The Japanese Automobile Industry* (Cambridge, MA: Harvard University Press, 1989); S. Spear and H. K. Bowen, "Decoding the DNA of the Toyota Production System," *Harvard Business Review* (September–October 1999): 96–108.

[19] Kim and Mauborgne, "Value Innovation."

[20] G. Stalk and T. M. Hout, *Competing Against Time* (New York: Free Press, 1990).

[21] Ibid.

[22]Tom Copeland, Tim Koller, and Jack Murrin, *Valuation: Measuring and Managing the Value of Companies* (New York: Wiley, 1996). See also S. F. Jablonsky and N. P. Barsky, *The Manager's Guide to Financial Statement Analysis* (New York: Wiley, 2001).

[23]Copeland, Koller, and Murrin, *Valuation.*

[24]This is done as follows. Signifying net profit by π, invested capital by K, and revenues by R, then ROIC $= \pi/K$. If we multiply through by revenues, R, this becomes $R \times (\pi/K) = (\pi \times R)/(K \times R)$, which can be rearranged as $\pi/R \times R/K$. π/R is the return on sales and R/K capital turnover.

[25]Note that Figure 3.9 is a simplification and ignores some other important items that enter the calculation, such as depreciation/sales (a determinant of ROS) and other assets/sales (a determinant of capital turnover).

[26]This is the nature of the competitive process. For more detail, see C. W. L. Hill and D. Deeds, "The Importance of Industry Structure for the Determination of Company Profitability: A Neo-Austrian Perspective," *Journal of Management Studies,* 33 (1996): 429–451.

[27]As with resources and capabilities, so the concept of barriers to imitation is also grounded in the resource-based view of the company. For details, see R. Reed and R. J. DeFillippi, "Causal Ambiguity, Barriers to Imitation, and Sustainable Competitive Advantage," *Academy of Management Review* 15 (1990): 88–102.

[28]E. Mansfield, "How Economists See R&D," *Harvard Business Review* (November–December 1981): 98–106.

[29]S. L. Berman, J. Down, and C. W. L. Hill, "Tacit Knowledge as a Source of Competitive Advantage in the National Basketball Association," *Academy of Management Journal* (2002): 13–33.

[33]P. Ghemawat, *Commitment: The Dynamic of Strategy* (New York: Free Press, 1991).

[31]W. M. Cohen and D. A. Levinthal, "Absorptive Capacity: A New Perspective on Learning and Innovation," *Administrative Science Quarterly* 35 (1990): 128–152.

[32]M. T. Hannah and J. Freeman, "Structural Inertia and Organizational Change," *American Sociological Review* 49 (1984): 149–164.

[33]See "IBM Corporation," Harvard Business School Case #180–034.

[34]Ghemawat, *Commitment.*

[35]D. Miller, *The Icarus Paradox* (New York: HarperBusiness, 1990).

[36]P. M. Senge, *The Fifth Discipline: The Art and Practice of the Learning Organization* (New York: Doubleday, 1990).

[37]The classic statement of this position was made by A. A. Alchain, "Uncertainty, Evolution, and Economic Theory," *Journal of Political Economy* 84 (1950): 488–500.

[38]A. Martin, "McDonald's, the Happiest Meal is Hot Profits," *New York Times,* January 11, 2009; M. Vella, "A New Look for McDonald's," *Business Week Online,* December 4, 2008; M. Warner, "Salads or No, Cheap Burgers Revive McDonald's," *New York Times,* April 19, 2006.

4 Building Competitive Advantage Through Functional-Level Strategy

erei.photography/istockphoto.com

Lean Production at Virginia Mason

In the early-2000s, Seattle's Virginia Mason Hospital was not performing as well as it should have been. Financial returns were low, patient satisfaction was subpar; too many errors were occurring during patient treatment, and staff moral was suffering. Gary Kaplan, the CEO, was wondering what to do about this when he experienced a chance encounter with Ian Black, the director of lean thinking at Boeing. Black told Kaplan that Boeing had been implementing aspects of Toyota's famous lean production system in its aircraft assembly operations, and Boeing was seeing positive results. Kaplan soon became convinced that the same system that had helped Toyota build more reliable cars at a lower cost could also be applied to health care to improve patient outcomes at a lower cost.

In 2002, Kaplan and a team of executives began annual trips to Japan to study the Toyota production system. They learned that "lean" meant doing without things that were not needed; it meant removing unnecessary steps in a process so that tasks were performed more

efficiently. It meant eliminating waste and elements that didn't add value. Toyota's system applied to health care meant improving patient outcomes through more rapid treatment, and eliminating errors in the treatment process.

Kaplan and his team returned from Japan believing in the value of lean production. They quickly set about applying what they had learned to Virginia Mason. Teams were created to look at individual processes in what Virginia Mason called "rapid process improvement workshops." The teams, which included doctors as well as other employees, were freed from their normal duties for 5 days. They learned the methods of lean production, analyzed systems and processes, tested proposed changes, and were empowered to implement the chosen change the following week.

The gains appeared quickly, reflecting the fact that there was a lot of inefficiency in the hospital. One of the first changes involved the delay between a doctor's referral to a specialist and the patient's first consultation with that specialist. By examining the process, it was found that secretaries, whose job it was to arrange these referrals, were not needed. Instead, the doctor would send a text message to the consultant the instant he decided that a specialist was required. The specialist then needed to respond within 10 minutes, even if only to confirm the receipt of the message. Delays in referral-to-treatment time dropped by 68% as a consequence of this simple change, which improved patient satisfaction.

On another occasion, a team in the radiation oncology department mapped out the activities that the department performed when processing a patient, eliminating time wasted during employee performance. By removing unnecessary work-flow activities, patient time spent in the department fell from 45 minutes to just 15 minutes. A similar exercise at Virginia Mason's back clinic cut treatment time from an average of 66 days to just 12.

By 2010, Virginia Mason was claiming that lean production had transformed the hospital into a more efficient, customer responsive organization, where medical errors during treatment had been significantly reduced. Among other gains, lean processes reduced annual inventory costs by more than $1 million, reduced the time it took to report lab tests to a patient by more than 85%, freed up the equivalent of 77 full-time employee positions through more efficient processes, and reduced staff walking distance by 60 miles a day, giving both doctors and nurses more time to spend with patients. These, and many other similar changes lowered costs, increased the organization's customer responsiveness, improved patient outcomes, and increased the financial performance of the hospital.[1]

Overview

In this chapter, we take a close look at **functional-level strategies:** those aimed at improving the effectiveness of a company's operations and its ability to attain superior efficiency, quality, innovation, and customer responsiveness.

It is important to keep in mind the relationships between functional strategies, distinctive competencies, differentiation, low cost, value creation, and profitability (see Figure 4.1). Distinctive competencies shape the functional-level strategies that a company can pursue. Managers, through their choices related to functional-level strategies, can build resources and capabilities that enhance a company's distinctive competencies. Also, note that a company's ability to attain superior efficiency, quality, innovation, and customer responsiveness will determine if its product offering is differentiated from that of rivals, and if it has a low-cost structure. Recall that companies that increase the utility consumers get from their

Functional-level strategies

Strategy aimed at improving the effectiveness of a company's operations and its ability to attain superior efficiency, quality, innovation, and customer responsiveness.

Figure 4.1 The Roots of Competitive Advantage

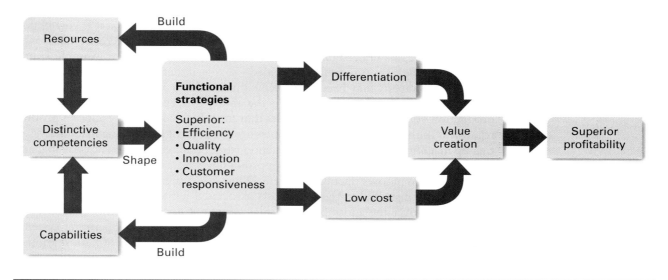

products through differentiation, while simultaneously lowering their cost structure, create more value than their rivals—and this leads to a competitive advantage, superior profitability, and profit growth.

The Opening Case illustrates some of these relationships. By adopting lean production techniques, employees at Virginia Mason Hospital in Seattle increased productivity, reduced medical errors (which increased reliability), and improved patient satisfaction through faster treatment. The resulting gains in efficiency enabled Virginia Mason to reduce its costs, while improved reliability and superior customer responsiveness enabled the hospital to differentiate itself from other hospitals in the region. This meant higher patient volumes and better financial performance.

Much of this chapter is devoted to looking at the basic strategies that can be adopted at the functional level to improve competitive position, as the Virginia Mason example illustrates. By the end of this chapter, you will understand how functional-level strategies can be used to build a sustainable competitive advantage.

Achieving Superior Efficiency

A company is a device for transforming inputs (labor, land, capital, management, and technological know-how) into outputs (the goods and services produced). The simplest measure of efficiency is the quantity of inputs that it takes to produce a given output; that is, efficiency = outputs/inputs. The more efficient a company, the fewer the inputs required to produce a given output, and therefore, the lower its cost structure. Put another way, an efficient company has higher productivity, and therefore lower costs, than its rivals. Here we review the steps that companies can take at the functional level to increase their efficiency and thereby lower cost structure.

Efficiency and Economies of Scale

Economies of scale, as we learned in Chapter 2, are unit cost reductions associated with a large scale of output. You will recall from the last chapter that it is very important for managers to understand how the cost structure of their enterprise varies with output because this understanding should help to drive strategy. For example, if unit costs fall significantly as output is expanded—that is, if there are significant economies of scale—a company may benefit by keeping prices down and increasing volume.

One source of economies of scale is the ability to spread fixed costs over a large production volume. **Fixed costs** are costs that must be incurred to produce a product regardless of the level of output; examples are the costs of purchasing machinery, setting up machinery for individual production runs, building facilities, advertising, and R&D. For example, Microsoft spent approximately $5 billion to develop the latest version of its Windows operating system, Windows 7. It can realize substantial scale economies by distributing the fixed costs associated with developing the new operating system over the enormous unit sales volume it expects for this system (95% of the world's 250 million personal computers use a Microsoft operating system). These scale economies are significant because of the trivial incremental (or marginal) cost of producing additional copies of Windows 7: once the master copy has been produced, additional DVD's containing the operating system can be produced for a few cents. The key to Microsoft's efficiency and profitability (and that of other companies with high fixed costs and trivial incremental or marginal costs) is to increase sales rapidly enough that fixed costs can be spread out over a large unit volume and substantial scale economies can be realized.

Another source of scale economies is the ability of companies producing in large volumes to achieve a greater division of labor and specialization. Specialization is said to have a favorable impact on productivity, primarily because it enables employees to become very skilled at performing a particular task. The classic example of such economies is Ford's Model T car. The Model T Ford was introduced in 1923, and was the world's first mass-produced car. Until 1923, Ford had made cars using an expensive hand-built craft production method. Introducing mass-production techniques allowed the company to achieve greater division of labor (it split assembly into small, repeatable tasks) and specialization, which boosted employee productivity. Ford was also able to distribute the fixed costs of developing a car and setting up production machinery over a large volume of output. As a result of these economies, the cost of manufacturing a car at Ford fell from $3,000 to less than $900 (in 1958 dollars).

These examples illustrate that economies of scale can boost profitability, as measured by return on invested capital (ROIC), in a number of ways. Economies of scale exist in production, sales and marketing, and R&D, and the overall effect of realizing scale economies is to reduce spending as a percentage of revenues on cost of goods sold (COGS), sales, general, and administrative expenses (SG&A), and R&D expenses, thereby boosting return on sales and, by extension, ROIC (see Figure 3.9). In addition, by making more intensive use of existing capacity, a company can increase the amount of sales generated from its property, plant, and equipment (PPE), thereby reducing the amount of capital it needs to generate a dollar of sales, and increasing its capital turnover and its ROIC.

The concept of scale economies is illustrated in Figure 4.2, which illustrates that as a company increases its output, unit costs decrease. This process comes to an end at an output of Q1, where all scale economies are exhausted. Indeed, at outputs of

Fixed costs

Costs that must be incurred to produce a product regardless of the level of output.

Figure 4.2 Economies and Diseconomies of Scale

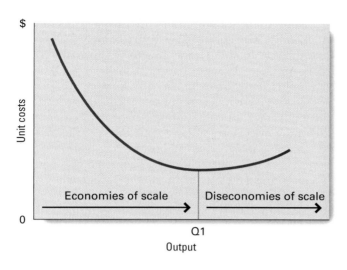

greater than Q1, the company may encounter **diseconomies of scale**, which are the unit cost increases associated with a large scale of output. Diseconomies of scale occur primarily because of increased bureaucracy associated with large-scale enterprises and the managerial inefficiencies that can result.[2] Larger enterprises have a tendency to develop extensive managerial hierarchies in which dysfunctional political behavior is commonplace. Information about operating matters can accidentally and deliberately be distorted by the number of managerial layers through which the information must travel to reach top decision makers. The result is poor decision-making. Therefore, past a specific point—such as Q1 in Figure 4.2—inefficiencies result from such developments, and outweigh any additional gains from economies of scale. As output expands unit costs begin to rise.

Managers must know the extent of economies of scale, and where diseconomies of scale begin to occur. At Nucor Steel, for example, the realization that diseconomies of scale exist has led to the company's decision to build plants that only employ 300 individuals or less. The belief is that it is more efficient to build 2 plants, each employing 300 people, than one plant employing 600 people. Although the larger plant may theoretically make it possible to reap greater scale economies, Nucor's management believes that larger plants would suffer from the diseconomies of scale associated with larger organizational units.

Efficiency and Learning Effects

Learning effects are cost savings that come from learning by doing. Labor, for example, learns by repetition how to best carry out a task. Therefore, labor productivity increases over time, and unit costs decrease as individuals learn the most efficient way to perform a particular task. Equally important, management in new manufacturing facilities typically learns over time how best to run the new operation. Hence, production costs decline because of increasing labor productivity and management

Diseconomies of scale

Unit cost increases associated with a large scale of output.

Learning effects

Cost savings that come from learning by doing.

efficiency. Japanese companies such as Toyota are noted for making learning a central part of their operating philosophy.

Learning effects tend to be more significant when a technologically complex task is repeated because there is more to learn. Thus, learning effects will be more significant in an assembly process that has 1,000 complex steps than in a process with 100 simple steps. Although learning effects are normally associated with the manufacturing process, there is every reason to believe that they are just as important in service industries. For example, one famous study of learning in the health care industry discovered that more experienced medical providers posted significantly lower mortality rates for a number of common surgical procedures, suggesting that learning effects are at work in surgery.[3] The authors of this study used the evidence to argue in favor of establishing regional referral centers for the provision of highly specialized medical care. These centers would perform many specific surgical procedures (such as heart surgery), replacing local facilities with lower volumes and presumably higher mortality rates. Another recent study found strong evidence of learning effects in a financial institution. This study looked at a newly established document-processing unit with 100 staff members and found that, over time, documents were processed much more rapidly as the staff learned the process. Overall, the study concluded that unit costs decreased every time the cumulative number of documents processed doubled.[4] Strategy in Action 4.1 looks at the determinants of differences in learning effects across a sample of hospitals performing cardiac surgery.

In terms of the unit cost curve of a company, economies of scale imply a movement along the curve (say, from A to B in Figure 4.3). The realization of learning effects implies a downward shift of the entire curve (B to C in Figure 4.3) as both labor and management become more efficient over time at performing their tasks at every level of output. In accounting terms, learning effects in a production setting will reduce the cost of goods sold as a percentage of revenues, enabling the company to earn a higher return on sales, and return on invested capital.

Figure 4.3 The Impact of Learning and Scale Economies on Unit Costs

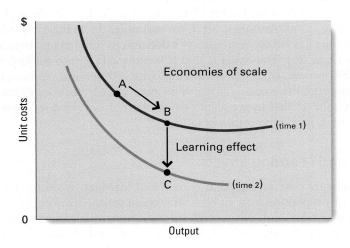

STRATEGY IN ACTION

4.1

Learning Effects in Cardiac Surgery

A study carried out by researchers at the Harvard Business School tried to estimate the importance of learning effects in the case of a specific new technology for minimally invasive heart surgery that was approved by the Federal regulators in 1996. The researchers looked at 16 hospitals and obtained data on the operations for 660 patients. They examined how the time required to undertake the procedure varied with cumulative experience. Across the 16 hospitals, they found that average time decreased from 280 minutes for the first procedure with the new technology, to 220 minutes once a hospital had performed 50 procedures (note that not all of the hospitals performed 50 procedures, and the estimates represent an extrapolation based on the data).

Next, the study observed differences across hospitals; here they found evidence of very large differences in learning effects. One hospital, in particular, stood out. This hospital, which they called "Hospital M," reduced its net procedure time from 500 minutes on case 1 to 132 minutes by case 50. Hospital M's 88 minutes procedure time advantage over the average hospital at case 50 meant a cost savings of approximately $2,250 per case, which allowed surgeons at the hospital to complete one more revenue generating procedure per day.

The researchers tried to find out why Hospital M was so superior. They noted that all hospitals had similar state-of-the-art operating rooms, all used the same set of FDA approved devices, all adopting surgeons completed the same training courses, and all surgeons came from highly respected training hospitals. Follow up interviews, however, suggested that Hospital M differed in how it implemented the new procedure. The adopting surgeon handpicked the team that would perform the surgery. It had significant prior experience working together which was a key criterion for team members, and the team trained together to perform the new surgery. Before undertaking a single procedure, the entire team met with the operating room nurses and anesthesiologists to discuss the procedure. In addition, the adopting surgeon mandated that the surgical team and surgical procedure was stable in the early cases. The initial team completed 15 procedures before any new members were added or substituted, and completed 20 cases before the procedures were modified. The adopting surgeon also insisted that the team meet prior to each of the first 10 cases, and after the first 20 cases to debrief.

The picture that emerges is one of a core team that was selected and managed to maximize the gains from learning. Unlike other hospitals where team members and procedures were less consistent, and where there was not the same attention to briefing, debriefing and learning, surgeons at Hospital M learned much faster, and ultimately achieved higher productivity than their peers in other institutions. Clearly, differences in the implementation of the new procedure were very significant.

Source: G.P. Pisano, R.M.J. Bohmer, A.C. Edmondson, "Organizational Differences in Rates of Learning: Evidence from the Adoption of Minimally Invasive Cardiac Surgery," *Management Science*, 47 (2001): 752–768.

No matter how complex the task is, however, learning effects typically die out after a limited period of time. Indeed, it has been suggested that they are very important only during the start-up period of a new process, and cease after 2 or 3 years.[5] When changes occur to a company's production system—as a result of merger or the use of new information technology, for example—the learning process must begin again.

Efficiency and the Experience Curve

The **experience curve** refers to the systematic lowering of the cost structure, and consequent unit cost reductions, that have been observed to occur over the life of a product.[6] According to the experience-curve concept, per-unit manufacturing costs for a product typically decline by some characteristic amount each time accumulated output of the product is doubled (accumulated output is the total output of a product since its introduction). This relationship was first observed in the aircraft industry,

> **Experience curve**
>
> The systematic lowering of the cost structure, and consequent unit cost reductions, that have been observed to occur over the life of a product.

where it was found that each time the accumulated output of airframes doubled, unit costs declined to 80% of their previous level.[7] As such, the fourth airframe typically cost only 80% of the second airframe to produce, the eighth airframe only 80% of the fourth, the sixteenth only 80% of the eighth, and so on. The outcome of this process is a relationship between unit manufacturing costs and accumulated output similar to the illustration in Figure 4.4. Economies of scale and learning effects underlie the experience-curve phenomenon. Put simply, as a company increases the accumulated volume of its output over time, it is able to realize both economies of scale (as volume increases) and learning effects. Consequently, unit costs and cost structure fall with increases in accumulated output.

The strategic significance of the experience curve is clear: increasing a company's product volume and market share will lower its cost structure relative to its rivals. In Figure 4.4, company B has a cost advantage over company A because of its lower cost structure, and because it is farther down the experience curve. The concept is very important in industries that mass-produce a standardized output, for example, the manufacture of semiconductor chips. A company that wishes to become more efficient and lower its cost structure must try to move down the experience curve as quickly as possible. This means constructing efficient scale manufacturing facilities (even before it has generated demand for the product), and aggressively pursuing cost reductions from learning effects. It might also need to adopt an aggressive marketing strategy, cutting prices drastically, and stressing heavy sales promotions and extensive advertising in order to build up demand and accumulated volume as quickly as possible. The need to be aware of the relationship of demand, price options, and costs noted in Chapter 3 is clear.

A company is likely to have a significant cost advantage over its competitors because of its superior efficiency once it is down the experience curve. For example, it has been argued that Intel uses such tactics to ride down the experience curve and gain a competitive advantage over its rivals in the market for microprocessors.[8]

Figure 4.4 The Experience Curve

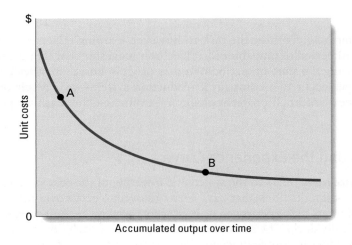

However, there are three reasons why managers should not become complacent about efficiency-based cost advantages derived from experience effects. First, because neither learning effects nor economies of scale are sustained forever, the experience curve is likely to bottom out at some point; it must do so by definition. When this occurs, further unit cost reductions from learning effects and economies of scale will be difficult to attain. Over time, other companies can lower their cost structures and match the cost leader. Once this happens, a number of low-cost companies can have cost parity with each other. In such circumstances, a sustainable competitive advantage must rely on strategic factors other than the minimization of production costs by using existing technologies—factors such as better responsiveness to customers, product quality, or innovation.

Second, as noted in Chapter 2, changes that are always taking place in the external environment disrupt a company's business model, so cost advantages gained from experience effects can be made obsolete by the development of new technologies. The price of television picture tubes followed the experience-curve pattern from the introduction of television in the late 1940s until 1963. The average unit price dropped from $34 to $8 (in 1958 dollars) in that time. However, the advent of color TV interrupted the experience curve. To make picture tubes for color TVs, a new manufacturing technology was required, and the price of color TV tubes shot up to $51 by 1966. Then, the experience curve reappeared as it did earlier. The price dropped to $48 in 1968, $37 in 1970, and $36 in 1972.[9] In short, technological change can alter the rules of the game, requiring that former low-cost companies take steps to reestablish their competitive edge.

Third, producing a high volume of output does not necessarily give a company a lower cost structure. Different technologies have different cost structures. For example, the steel industry has two alternative manufacturing technologies: an integrated technology, which relies on the basic oxygen furnace, and mini-mill technology, which depends on the electric arc furnace. Whereas the basic oxygen furnace requires high volumes of production to attain maximum efficiency, mini-mills are cost efficient at relative low volumes. Even when both technologies are producing at the most efficient output levels, steel companies with basic oxygen furnaces do not have a cost advantage over mini-mills. Consequently, the pursuit of experience economies by an integrated company using basic oxygen technology may not bring the kind of cost advantages that a naive reading of the experience-curve phenomenon might lead the company to expect. There have been significant periods of time when integrated companies have not been able to get enough orders to run at optimum capacity. As a consequence, their production costs have been considerably higher than those of mini-mills.[10] In many industries, new flexible manufacturing technologies hold out the promise of allowing small manufacturers to produce at unit costs comparable to those of large assembly-line operations.

Efficiency, Flexible Production Systems, and Mass Customization

Central to the concept of economies of scale is the idea that a lower cost structure, through the mass production of a standardized output, is the best way to achieve high efficiency. The tradeoff implicit in this idea is between unit costs and product variety. Producing greater product variety from a factory implies shorter production runs, which implies an inability to realize economies of scale and higher costs. That is, a wide product variety makes it difficult for a company to increase its production efficiency and thus reduce its unit costs. According to this logic, the way to increase efficiency and achieve a lower cost structure is to limit product variety and produce a standardized product in large volumes (see Figure 4.5a).

This view of production efficiency has been challenged by the rise of flexible production technologies. The term **flexible production technology**—or lean production, as it is sometimes called—covers a range of technologies designed to reduce setup times for complex equipment, increase the use of individual machines through better scheduling, and improve quality control at all stages of the manufacturing process.[11] Flexible production technologies allow the company to produce a wider variety of end products at a unit cost that at one time could be achieved only through the mass production of a standardized output (see Figure 4.5b). Research suggests that the adoption of flexible production technologies may increase efficiency and lower unit costs relative to what can be achieved by the mass production of a standardized output, while at the same time enabling the company to customize its product offering to a much greater extent than was once thought possible. The term **mass customization** has been coined to describe the company's ability to use flexible manufacturing technology to reconcile two goals that were once thought to be incompatible: low cost, and differentiation through product customization.[12] For an extended example of the benefits of mass customization, see Strategy in Action 4.2, which looks at mass customization at Lands' End.

Flexible machine cells are a common flexible production technology. A flexible machine cell is a grouping of various types of machinery, a common materials handler, and a centralized cell controller (a computer). Each cell normally contains 4–6 machines capable of performing a variety of operations, but is dedicated to producing a family of parts or products. The settings on the machines are computer controlled, which allows each cell to quickly alternate between the production of different parts and products.

Flexible production technology (or, lean production)

A range of technologies designed to reduce setup times for complex equipment, increase the use of individual machines through better scheduling, and improve quality control at all stages of the manufacturing process.

Mass customization

The use of flexible manufacturing technology to reconcile two goals that were once thought to be incompatible: low cost, and differentiation through product customization.

Figure 4.5 Tradeoff Between Costs and Product Variety

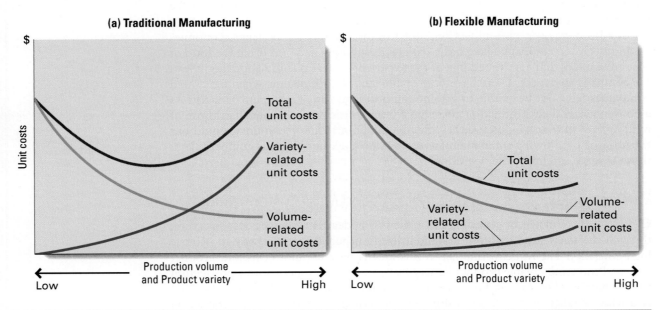

STRATEGY IN ACTION

Mass Customization at Lands' End

Years ago, almost all clothing was made to individual order by a tailor (a job shop production method). Then, in the 20th century, techniques for mass production, mass marketing, and mass selling were becoming commonplace. Production in the industry shifted toward larger volume and less variety based on standardized sizes. The benefits of production cost reductions were enormous, but the customer did not always win. Lower prices were offset against the difficulty of finding clothes that fit as well as those that were tailored. People come in a bewildering variety of shapes and sizes, but normally when they go into a store to purchase a shirt, they get to pick between just four sizes; small, medium, large, and extra large! It is estimated the current sizing categories in clothing fit only about one third of the population. All others wear clothes that fit less than ideally.

The mass production system has drawbacks for apparel manufacturers and retailers as well. Year after year, apparel firms find themselves saddled with billions of dollars in excess inventory that is either thrown away or put on fire sale, because retailers had too many items of the wrong size and color. To try and solve this problem, Lands' End has been experimenting with mass customization techniques.

To purchase customized clothes from Lands' End, the customer provides information on the Lands' End Website by answering a series of 15 questions (for pants) or 25 questions (for shirts) denoting everything from waist to inseam. The process takes about 20 minutes the first time, but once the data is saved by Lands' End, it can be quickly accessed for repeat purchases. This data is then analyzed by an algorithm that pinpoints a customer's physical dimensions. The results of this analysis are input into a huge database of typical sizes to create a unique, customized pattern. The analysis is done automatically by a computer, which then transmits the order to one of five contract manufacturing plants in the United States and elsewhere. There, the clothing order is cuts and sewn, and the finished garment is shipped directly to the customer.

Today customization is available for most categories of Lands' End clothing. Approximately 40% of the company's online shoppers choose a customized garment over the standard-sized equivalent when given the choice. Although prices for customized clothes are at least $20 higher and they take approximately 3–4 weeks to arrive, customized clothing reportedly accounts for a rapidly growing percentage of Lands' End's $500 million online business. Lands' End states that its profit margins are roughly the same for customized clothes as regular clothes, but the reductions in inventories that come from matching demand to supply account for additional cost savings. Moreover, customers who choose made-to-order clothing appear to be more loyal; reordering rates are 34% higher than for buyers of standard sized clothing.

Source: J. Schlosser, "Cashing in on the New World of Me," *Fortune*, December 13, 2004, pp. 244–249; V. S. Borland, "Global Technology in the Twenty First Century," *Textile World*, January 2003, pp. 42–56; www.landsend.com.

Improved capacity utilization and reductions in work-in-progress (that is, stockpiles of partly finished products) and waste are major efficiency benefits of flexible machine cells. Improved capacity utilization arises from the reduction in setup times and from the computer-controlled coordination of production flow between machines, which eliminates bottlenecks. The tight coordination between machines also reduces work-in-progress. Reductions in waste are due to the ability of computer-controlled machinery to identify ways to transform inputs into outputs while producing a minimum of unusable waste material. Freestanding machines might be in use 50% of the time; the same machines when grouped into a cell can be used more than 80% of the time and produce the same end product with half the waste, thereby increasing efficiency and resulting in lower costs.

The effects of installing flexible production technology on a company's cost structure can be dramatic. Ford Motor Company is currently introducing flexible production technologies into its automotive plants around the world. These new technologies should allow Ford to produce multiple models from the same line and to switch production from one model to another much more quickly than in the past. In total, Ford took $2 billion out of its cost structure between 2006 and 2010 through flexible manufacturing, and is striving to take out more.[13]

More generally, in terms of the profitability framework developed in Chapter 3, flexible production technology should boost profitability (measured by ROIC) by reducing the cost of goods sold as a percentage of revenues, reducing the working capital needed to finance work-in-progress (because there is less of it), and reducing the amount of capital that needs to be invested in property, manufacturing plants, and equipment to generate a dollar of sales (because less space is needed to store inventory).

Marketing and Efficiency

The marketing strategy that a company adopts can have a major impact on efficiency and cost structure. **Marketing strategy** refers to the position that a company takes with regard to pricing, promotion, advertising, product design, and distribution. Some of the steps leading to greater efficiency are fairly obvious. For example, moving down the experience curve to achieve a lower cost structure can be facilitated by aggressive pricing, promotions, and advertising—all of which are the task of the marketing function. Other aspects of marketing strategy have a less obvious—but no less important impact—on efficiency. One important aspect is the relationship of customer defection rates, cost structure and unit costs.[14]

Customer defection rates (or "churn rates") are the percentage of a company's customers who defect every year to competitors. Defection rates are determined by customer loyalty, which in turn is a function of the ability of a company to satisfy its customers. Because acquiring a new customer entails one-time fixed costs for advertising, promotions, and related tasks, there is a direct relationship between defection rates and costs. The longer a company retains a customer, the greater the volume of customer-generated unit sales that can be set against these fixed costs, and the lower the average unit cost of each sale. Thus, lowering customer defection rates allows a company to achieve a lower cost structure.

One consequence of the defection-cost relationship depicted is illustrated in Figure 4.6. Because of the relatively high fixed costs of acquiring new customers, serving customers who stay with the company only for a short time before switching to competitors often leads to a loss on the investment made to acquire those customers. The longer a customer stays with the company, the more the fixed costs of acquiring that customer can be distributed over repeat purchases, boosting the profit per customer. Thus, there is a positive relationship between the length of time that a customer stays with a company and profit per customer. If a company can reduce customer defection rates, it can make a much better return on its investment in acquiring customers, and thereby boost its profitability. In terms of the profitability framework developed in Chapter 3, reduced customer defection rates mean that the company can spend less on sales, general, and administrative expenses to generate a dollar of sales revenue, which increases both return on sales and return on invested capital.

For an example, consider the credit card business.[15] Most credit card companies spend an average of $50 per customer for recruitment and new account set up. These costs are derived from the advertising required to attract new customers, the credit checks required for each customer, and the mechanics of setting up an account and issuing a card. These one-time fixed costs can be recouped only if a customer stays with the company for at least 2 years. Moreover, when customers stay a second year,

Marketing strategy

The position that a company takes with regard to pricing, promotion, advertising, product design, and distribution.

Customer defection rates (or churn rates)

Percentage of a company's customers who defect every year to competitors.

Figure 4.6 The Relationship between Customer Loyalty and Profit per Customer

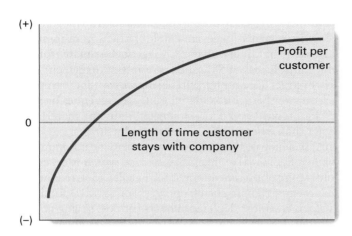

they tend to increase their use of the credit card, which raises the volume of revenues generated by each customer over time. As a result, although the credit card business loses $50 per customer in year 1, it makes a profit of $44 in year 3 and $55 in year 6.

Another economic benefit of long-time customer loyalty is the free advertising that customers provide for a company. Loyal customers can dramatically increase the volume of business through referrals. A striking example is Britain's largest retailer, the clothing and food company Marks & Spencer, whose success is built on a well-earned reputation for providing its customers with high-quality goods at reasonable prices. The company has generated such customer loyalty that it does not need to advertise in Britain, a major source of cost saving.

The key message, then, is that reducing customer defection rates and building customer loyalty can be major sources of a lower cost structure. One study has estimated that a 5 % reduction in customer defection rates leads to the following increases in profits per customer over average customer life: 75% in the credit card business, 50% in the insurance brokerage industry, 45% in the industrial laundry business, and 35% in the computer software industry.[16]

A central component of developing a strategy to reduce defection rates is to identify customers who have defected, find out why they defected, and act on that information so that other customers do not defect for similar reasons in the future. To take these measures, the marketing function must have information systems capable of tracking customer defections.

Materials Management, Just-In-Time, and Efficiency

The contribution of materials management (logistics) to boosting the efficiency of a company can be just as dramatic as the contribution of production and marketing. Materials management encompasses the activities necessary to get inputs and components to a production facility (including the costs of purchasing inputs), through the production process, and out through a distribution system to the end-user.[17] Because there are so many sources of cost in this process, the potential for reducing costs through more efficient materials-management strategies is enormous. For a typical manufacturing company, materials and transportation costs account for 50% to 70% of its revenues, so even a small reduction in these costs can have a substantial impact on profitability. According to one estimate, for a company with revenues of $1 million, a ROIC of 5%, and materials-management costs that amount to 50% of sales revenues (including purchasing costs), increasing total profits by $15,000 would require either a 30% increase in sales revenues or a 3% reduction in materials costs.[18] In a typical competitive market, reducing materials costs by 3% is usually much easier than increasing sales revenues by 30%.

Improving the efficiency of the materials-management function typically requires the adoption of a **just-in-time** (JIT) inventory system, which is designed to economize on inventory holding costs by scheduling components to arrive at a manufacturing plant just in time to enter the production process, or to have goods arrive at a retail store only when stock is almost depleted. The major cost saving comes from increasing inventory turnover, which reduces inventory holding costs, such as warehousing and storage costs, and the company's need for working capital. For example, through efficient logistics, Walmart can replenish the stock in its stores at least twice a week; many stores receive daily deliveries if they are needed. The typical competitor replenishes its stock every 2 weeks, so it must carry a much higher inventory and requires more working capital per dollar of sales. Compared to its competitors, Walmart can maintain the same service levels with a lower investment in inventory, a major source of its lower cost structure. Thus, faster inventory turnover has helped Walmart achieve an efficiency-based competitive advantage in the retailing industry.[19]

More generally, in terms of the profitability model developed in Chapter 3, JIT inventory systems reduce the need for working capital (since there is less inventory to finance) and the need for fixed capital to finance storage space (since there is less to store), which reduces capital needs, increases capital turnover, and, by extension, boosts the return on invested capital.

The drawback of JIT systems is that they leave a company without a buffer stock of inventory. Although buffer stocks are expensive to store, they can help a company prepare for shortages on inputs brought about by disruption among suppliers (for instance, a labor dispute at a key supplier), and can help a company respond quickly to increases in demand. However, there are ways around these limitations. For example, to reduce the risks linked to dependence on just one supplier for an important input, a company might decide to source inputs from multiple suppliers.

Recently, the efficient management of materials and inventory has been recast in terms of **supply-chain management**: the task of managing the flow of inputs and components from suppliers into the company's production processes to minimize inventory holding and maximize inventory turnover. Dell, whose goal is to streamline its supply chain to such an extent that it "replaces inventory with information," is exemplary in terms of supply-chain management.

R&D Strategy and Efficiency

The role of superior research and development (R&D) in helping a company achieve a greater efficiency and a lower cost structure is twofold. First, the R&D function can boost efficiency by designing products that are easy to manufacture. By cutting down

Just-in-time

System of economizing on inventory holding costs by scheduling components to arrive just in time to enter the production process or as stock is depleted.

Supply-chain management

The task of managing the flow of inputs and components from suppliers into the company's production processes to minimize inventory holding and maximize inventory turnover.

on the number of parts that make up a product, R&D can dramatically decrease the required assembly time, which results in higher employee productivity, lower costs, and higher profitability. For example, after Texas Instruments redesigned an infrared sighting mechanism that it supplies to the Pentagon, it found that it had reduced the number of parts from 47 to 12, the number of assembly steps from 56 to 13, the time spent fabricating metal from 757 minutes per unit to 219 minutes per unit, and unit assembly time from 129 minutes to 20 minutes. The result was a substantial decline in production costs. Design for manufacturing requires close coordination between the production and R&D functions of the company. Cross-functional teams that contain production and R&D personnel who work jointly can best achieve this.

Pioneering process innovations is the second way in which the R&D function can help a company achieve a lower cost structure. A process innovation is a new, unique way that production processes can operate to improve their efficiency. Process innovations have often been a major source of competitive advantage. Toyota's competitive advantage is based partly on the company's invention of new flexible manufacturing processes that dramatically reduce setup times. This process innovation enabled Toyota to obtain efficiency gains associated with flexible manufacturing systems years ahead of its competitors.

Human Resource Strategy and Efficiency

Employee productivity is one of the key determinants of an enterprise's efficiency, cost structure, and profitability.[20] Productive manufacturing employees can lower the cost of goods sold as a percentage of revenues, a productive sales force can increase sales revenues for a given level of expenses, and productive employees in the company's R&D function can boost the percentage of revenues generated from new products for a given level of R&D expenses. Thus, productive employees lower the costs of generating revenues, increase the return on sales, and, by extension, boost the company's return on invested capital. The challenge for a company's human resource function is to devise ways to increase employee productivity. Among its choices are: using certain hiring strategies; training employees; organizing the work force into self-managing teams; and linking pay to performance.

Hiring Strategy   Many companies that are well known for their productive employees devote considerable attention to hiring. Southwest Airlines hires people who have a positive attitude and who work well in teams because it believes that people who have a positive attitude will work hard and interact well with customers, therefore helping to create customer loyalty. Nucor hires people who are self-reliant and goal-oriented, because its employees, who work in self-managing teams, require these skills to perform well. As these examples suggest, it is important to be sure that the hiring strategy of the company is consistent with its own internal organization, culture, and strategic priorities. The people a company hires should have attributes that match the strategic objectives of the company.

Employee Training   Employees are a major input into the production process. Those who are highly skilled can perform tasks faster and more accurately, and are more likely to learn the complex tasks associated with many modern production methods than individuals with lesser skills. Training upgrades employee skill levels, bringing the company productivity-related efficiency gains from learning and experimentation.[21]

Self-Managing Teams   The use of **self-managing teams**, whose members coordinate their own activities and make their own hiring, training, work, and reward decisions, has been spreading rapidly. The typical team comprises 5–15 employees who produce an entire product or undertake an entire task. Team members learn all team tasks and rotate from job to job. Because a more flexible work force is one result, team members can fill in for absent coworkers and take over managerial duties such as scheduling work and vacation, ordering materials, and hiring new members. The greater responsibility thrust on team members and the empowerment it implies are seen as motivators. (Empowerment is the process of giving lower-level employees decision-making power.) People often respond well to being given greater autonomy and responsibility. Performance bonuses linked to team production and quality targets work as an additional motivator.

The effect of introducing self-managing teams is reportedly an increase in productivity of 30% or more and a substantial increase in product quality. Further cost savings arise from eliminating supervisors and creating a flatter organizational hierarchy, which also lowers the cost structure of the company. In manufacturing companies, perhaps the most potent way to lower the cost structure is to combine self-managing teams with flexible manufacturing cells. For example, after the introduction of flexible manufacturing technology and work practices based on self-managing teams, a General Electric plant in Salisbury, North Carolina, increased productivity by 250% compared with GE plants that produced the same products 4 years earlier.[22]

Still, teams are no panacea; in manufacturing companies, self-managing teams may fail to live up to their potential unless they are integrated with flexible manufacturing technology. Also, teams place a lot of management responsibilities upon team members, and helping team members to cope with these responsibilities often requires substantial training—a fact that many companies often forget in their rush to drive down costs. Haste can result in teams don't work out as well as planned.[23]

Pay For Performance   It is hardly surprising that linking pay to performance can help increase employee productivity, but the issue is not quite so simple as just introducing incentive pay systems. It is also important to define what kind of job performance is to be rewarded and how. Some of the most efficient companies in the world, mindful that cooperation among employees is necessary to realize productivity gains, link pay to group or team (rather than individual) performance. Nucor Steel divides its work force into teams of about 30, with bonus pay, which can amount to 30% of base pay, linked to the ability of the team to meet productivity and quality goals. This link creates a strong incentive for individuals to cooperate with each other in pursuit of team goals; that is, it facilitates teamwork.

Information Systems and Efficiency

With the rapid spread of computer use, the explosive growth of the Internet and corporate intranets (internal corporate computer networks based on Internet standards), and the spread of high-bandwidth fiber optics and digital wireless technology, the information systems function is moving to center stage in the quest for operating efficiencies and a lower cost structure.[24] The impact of information systems on productivity is wide ranging and potentially affects all other activities of a company. For example, Cisco Systems has been able to realize significant cost savings by moving its ordering and customer service functions online. The company has just 300 service agents handling all of its customer accounts, compared to the 900 it would need if sales

Self-managing teams

Teams where members coordinate their own activities and make their own hiring, training, work, and reward decisions.

were not handled online. The difference represents an annual saving of $20 million a year. Moreover, without automated customer service functions, Cisco calculates that it would need at least 1,000 additional service engineers, which would cost around $75 million.[25] Dell Inc. also makes extensive use of the Internet to lower its cost structure, and to differentiate itself from rivals (see the *Focus on Dell* in this chapter).

Like Cisco and Dell, many companies are using Web-based information systems to reduce the costs of coordination between the company and its customers and the company and its suppliers. By using Web-based programs to automate customer and supplier interactions, they can substantially reduce the number of people required to manage these interfaces, thereby reducing costs. This trend extends beyond high-tech

FOCUS ON DELL ④

Dell's Utilization of the Internet

Dell Inc. is famous for being the first company to implement online selling in the PC industry. Launched in June 1994, by 2010 more than 85% of Dell's computers were sold online. According to Michael Dell: "as I saw it, the Internet offered a logical extension of the direct (selling) model, creating even stronger relationships with our customers. The Internet would augment conventional telephone, fax, and face-to-face encounters, and give our customers the information they wanted faster, cheaper, and more efficiently." Dell's Website allows consumers to customize their orders to a degree that would have been unfathomable in the pre-Web era. Customers can mix-and-match product features such as microprocessors, memory, monitors, internal hard drives, CD and DVD drives, keyboard and mouse formats, and more, in order to purchase the system that best suits their individual requirements. By allowing customers to configure their order, Dell increases its customer responsiveness, thereby differentiating itself from rivals. Dell has also moved much of its customer service functions to the Web, reducing the need for telephone calls to customer service representatives, and saving costs in the process. Each week, some 200,000 people access Dell's trouble shooting tips online. Each of these visits to Dell's Website saves the company a potential $15, which is the average cost of a technical support call. If just 10% of these online visitors were to call Dell by telephone instead, it would cost the company $15.6 million per year.

Dell also uses the Internet to manage its supply chain, feeding real time information about order flow to its suppliers. Dell's suppliers use this information to better schedule their own production on a real time basis, providing components to Dell on a just-in-time basis, thereby taking inventory out of the system and reducing Dell's need for working capital and space to store the inventory. Dell's ultimate goal is to drive all inventories out of the supply chain apart from that in transit between suppliers and Dell, effectively replacing inventory with information. By doing so, Dell can drive significant costs out of its system.

Internet based customer ordering and procurement systems have also allowed the company to synchronize demand and supply to an extent that few other companies can. For example, if Dell sees that it is running out of a particular component, say 17 inch monitors from Panasonic, it can manipulate demand by offering a 19 inch model at a lower price until Panasonic delivers more 17 inch monitors. By taking steps to fine tune the balance between demand and supply, Dell can meet customers' expectations and maintain its differential advantage. Moreover, balancing supply and demand allows the company to minimize excess and obsolete inventory. Dell writes off between 0.05% and 0.1% of total materials costs in excess or obsolete inventory. It's competitors write off between 2% and 3%, which gives Dell a significant cost advantage.

Source: B.Gates. *Business @ the Speed of Thought.* (New York: Warner Books, 1999. Anonymous, "Enter the Eco-system: From Supply Chain to Network." *The Economist,* November 11, 2000; Anonymous, "Dell's Direct Initiative." *Country Monitor,* June 7, 2000, p. 5; Michael Dell. *Direct from Dell: Strategies that Revolutionized an Industry.* (New York: Harper Business, 1999); Staff reporter, "Survey: Shining Examples," *The Economist,* June 17, 2006, pp. 4–5.

companies. Banks and financial service companies are finding that they can substantially reduce costs by moving customer accounts and support functions online. Such a move reduces the need for customer service representatives, bank tellers, stockbrokers, insurance agents, and others. For example, it costs an average of about $1.07 to execute a transaction at a bank, such as shifting money from one account to another; executing the same transaction over the Internet costs $0.01.[26]

Similarly, the theory behind Internet-based retailers such as amazon.com, is that replacing physical stores and their supporting personnel with an online virtual store and automated ordering and checkout processes, allows a company to take significant costs out of the retailing system. Cost savings can also be realized by using Web-based information systems to automate many internal company activities, from managing expense reimbursements to benefits planning and hiring processes, thereby reducing the need for internal support personnel.

Infrastructure and Efficiency

A company's infrastructure—that is, its structure, culture, style of strategic leadership, and control system—determines the context within which all other value creation activities take place. It follows that improving infrastructure can help a company increase efficiency and lower its cost structure. Above all, an appropriate infrastructure can help foster a companywide commitment to efficiency, and promote cooperation among different functions in pursuit of efficiency goals. These issues are addressed at length in later chapters.

For now, it is important to note that strategic leadership is especially important in building a companywide commitment to efficiency. The leadership task is to articulate a vision that recognizes the need for all functions of a company to focus on improving efficiency. It is not enough to improve the efficiency of production, or of marketing, or of R&D in a piecemeal fashion. Achieving superior efficiency requires a companywide commitment to this goal that must be articulated by general and functional managers. A further leadership task is to facilitate the cross-functional cooperation needed to achieve superior efficiency. For example, designing products that are easy to manufacture requires that production and R&D personnel communicate; integrating JIT systems with production scheduling requires close communication between materials management and production; and designing self-managing teams to perform production tasks requires close cooperation between human resources and production.

Summary

Table 4.1 summarizes the primary roles that various functions must take to achieve superior efficiency. Keep in mind that achieving superior efficiency is not something that can be tackled on a function-by-function basis. It requires an organization-wide commitment and an ability to ensure close cooperation among functions. Top management, by exercising leadership and influencing the infrastructure, plays a significant role in this process.

Achieving Superior Quality

In Chapter 3, we noted that quality can be thought of in terms of two dimensions: *quality as reliability* and *quality as excellence*. High-quality products are reliable, do well the job for which they were designed, and are perceived by consumers to

Table 4.1 Primary Roles of Value Creation Functions in Achieving Superior Efficiency

Value Creation Function	Primary Roles
Infrastructure (leadership)	1. Provide company-wide commitment to efficiency
	2. Facilitate cooperation among functions
Production	1. Where appropriate, pursue economies of scale and learning economics
	2. Implement flexible manufacturing systems
Marketing	1. Where appropriate, adopt aggressive marketing to ride down the experience curve
	2. Limit customer defection rates by building brand loyalty
Materials management	1. Implement JIT systems
	2. Implement supply-chain coordination
R&D	1. Design products for ease of manufacture
	2. Seek process innovations
Information systems	1. Use information systems to automate processes
	2. Use information systems to reduce costs of coordination
Human resources	1. Institute training programs to build skills
	2. Implement self-managing teams
	3. Implement pay for performance

© Cengage Learning 2013

have superior attributes. We also noted that superior quality provides a company with two advantages. First, a strong reputation for quality allows a company to differentiate its products from those offered by rivals, thereby creating more utility in the eyes of customers, and giving the company the option of charging a premium price for its products. Second, eliminating defects or errors from the production process reduces waste, increases efficiency, lowers the cost structure of the company, and increases its profitability. For example, reducing the number of defects in a company's manufacturing process will lower the cost of goods sold as a percentage of revenues, thereby raising the company's return on sales and return on invested capital. In this section, we look in more depth at what managers can do to enhance the reliability and other attributes of the company's product offering.

Attaining Superior Reliability

The principal tool that most managers now use to increase the reliability of their product offering is the Six Sigma quality improvement methodology. The Six Sigma methodology is a direct descendant of the total quality management (TQM) philosophy that was widely adopted, first by Japanese companies and then by American companies, during the 1980s and early 1990s.[27] The TQM concept was developed by a number of American management consultants, including W. Edwards Deming, Joseph Juran, and A. V. Feigenbaum.[28]

Originally, these consultants won few converts in the United States. However, managers in Japan embraced their ideas enthusiastically, and even named their premier annual prize for manufacturing excellence after Deming. The philosophy underlying TQM, as articulated by Deming, is based on the following five-step chain reaction:

1. Improved quality means that costs decrease because of less rework, fewer mistakes, fewer delays, and better use of time and materials.
2. As a result, productivity improves.
3. Better quality leads to higher market share and allows the company to raise prices.
4. Higher prices increase the company's profitability and allow it to stay in business.
5. Thus, the company creates more jobs.[29]

Deming identified a number of steps that should be part of any quality-improvement program: A company should have a clear plan to specify its goal and how it is going to get there.

1. Management should embrace the philosophy that mistakes, defects, and poor-quality materials are not acceptable and should be eliminated.
2. Quality of supervision should be improved by allowing more time for supervisors to work with employees, and giving employees appropriate skills for the job.
3. Management should create an environment in which employees will not fear reporting problems or recommending improvements.
4. Work standards should not only be defined as numbers or quotas, but should also include some notion of quality to promote the production of defect-free output.
5. Management is responsible for training employees in new skills to keep pace with changes in the workplace.
6. Achieving better quality requires the commitment of everyone in the company.

Western businesses were blind to the importance of the TQM concept until Japan rose to the top rank of economic powers in the 1980s. Since that time, quality improvement programs have spread rapidly throughout Western industry. Strategy in Action 4.3 describes one of the most successful implementations of a quality improvement process, General Electric's Six Sigma program.

Despite such instances of spectacular success, quality improvement practices are not universally accepted. A study by the American Quality Foundation found that only 20% of U.S. companies regularly review the consequences of quality performance, compared with 70% of Japanese companies.[30] Another study, this one by Arthur D. Little, found that only 36% of 500 American companies using TQM, believed that TQM was increasing their competitiveness.[31] A primary reason for this, according to the study, was that many companies had not fully understood or embraced the TQM concept. They were looking for a quick fix, whereas implementing a quality improvement program requires a long-term commitment.

STRATEGY IN ACTION

General Electric's Six Sigma Quality Improvement Process

Six Sigma, a quality and efficiency program adopted by several major corporations, including Motorola, General Electric, and AlliedSignal, aims to reduce defects, boost productivity, eliminate waste, and cut costs throughout a company. "Sigma" comes from the Greek letter that statisticians use to represent a standard deviation from a mean: the higher the number of sigmas, the smaller the number of errors. At Six Sigma, a production process would be 99.99956% accurate, creating just 3.4 defects per million units. Although it is almost impossible for a company to achieve such perfection, several companies strive toward that goal.

General Electric is perhaps the most well-known adopter of the Six Sigma program. Under the direction of long-serving CEO Jack Welch, GE spent nearly $1 billion to convert all of its divisions to the Six Sigma method.

One of the first products designed using Six Sigma processes was a $1.25 million diagnostic computer tomography (CT) scanner, the LightSpeed VCT, which produces rapid three-dimensional imagines of the human body. The new scanner captures multiple images simultaneously, requiring only 20 seconds to do full-body scans that once took 3 minutes—important because patients must remain perfectly still during the scan. GE spent $50 million to run 250 separate Six Sigma analyses designed to improve the reliability and lower the manufacturing cost of the new scanner. Its efforts were rewarded when LightSpeed VCT's first customers soon noticed that it ran without downtime between patients—a testament to the reliability of the machine.

Achieving that reliability took immense work. GE's engineers deconstructed the scanner into its basic components and tried to improve the reliability of each component through a detailed step-by-step analysis. For example, the most important part of CT scanners is the vacuum tubes that focus x-ray waves. The tubes that GE used in previous scanners, which cost $60,000 each, suffered from low reliability. Hospitals and clinics wanted the tubes to operate for 12 hours a day for at least 6 months, but typically they lasted only half that long. Moreover, GE was scrapping some $20 million in tubes each year because they failed preshipping performance tests, and a disturbing number of faulty tubes were slipping past inspection, only to be determined as dysfunctional upon arrival.

To try to solve the reliability problem, the Six Sigma team took the tubes apart. They knew that one problem was a petroleum-based oil used in the tubes to prevent short circuits by isolating the anode (which has a positive charge) from the negatively charged cathode. The oil often deteriorated after a few months, leading to short circuits, but the team did not know why. By using statistical "what-if" scenarios on all parts of the tube, the researchers learned that the lead-based paint on the inside of the tube was contaminating the oil. Acting on this information, the team developed a paint that would preserve the tube and protect the oil.

By pursuing this and other improvements, the Six Sigma team was able to extend the average life of a vacuum tube in the CT scanner from 3 months to over 1 year. Although the improvements increased the cost of the tube from $60,000 to $85,000, the increased cost was outweighed by the reduction in replacement costs, making it an attractive proposition for customers.

DOUG KANTER/AFP/Getty Images

Sources: C. H. Deutsch, "Six-Sigma Enlightenment," *New York Times,* December 7, 1998, p. 1; J. J. Barshay, "The Six-Sigma Story," *Star Tribune,* June 14, 1999, p. 1; D. D. Bak, "Rethinking Industrial Drives," *Electrical/Electronics Technology,* November 30, 1998, p. 58.

Table 4.2   Roles Played by Different Functions in Implementing Reliability Improvement Methodologies

Infrastructure (leadership)	1. Provide leadership and commitment to quality
	2. Find ways to measure quality
	3. Set goals and create incentives
	4. Solicit input from employees
	5. Encourage cooperation among functions
Production	1. Shorten production runs
	2. Trace defects back to the source
Marketing	1. Focus on the customer
	2. Provide customers' feedback on quality
Materials management	1. Rationalize suppliers
	2. Help suppliers implement quality-improvement methodologies
	3. Trace defects back to suppliers
R&D	1. Design products that are easy to manufacture
Information systems	1. Use information systems to monitor defect rates
Human resources	1. Institute quality-improvement training programs
	2. Identify and train "black belts"
	3. Organize employees into quality teams

© Cengage Learning 2013

Implementing Reliability Improvement Methodologies

Among companies that have successfully adopted quality improvement methodologies, certain imperatives stand out. These are discussed below in the order in which they are usually tackled in companies implementing quality improvement programs. What needs to be stressed first, however, is that improvement in product reliability is a cross-functional process. Its implementation requires close cooperation among all functions in the pursuit of the common goal of improving quality; it is a process that works across functions. The roles played by the different functions in implementing reliability improvement methodologies are summarized in Table 4.2.

First, it is important that senior managers agree to a quality improvement program and communicate its importance to the organization. Second, if a quality improvement program is to be successful, individuals must be identified to lead the program. Under the Six Sigma methodology, exceptional employees are identified and put through a "black belt" training course on the Six Sigma methodology. The black belts are taken out of their normal job roles, and assigned to work solely on Six Sigma projects for the next 2 years. In effect, the black belts become internal consultants *and* project leaders. Because they are dedicated to Six Sigma programs, the black belts are not distracted from the task at hand by day-to-day operating responsibilities. To make a black belt assignment attractive, many companies now endorse the program as an advancement in a career path. Successful black belts might not return to their prior job after 2 years, but could instead be promoted and given more responsibility.

Third, quality improvement methodologies preach the need to identify defects that arise from processes, trace them to their source, find out what caused the defects, and make corrections so that they do not recur. Production and materials management are primarily responsible for this task. To uncover defects, quality improvement methodologies rely upon the use of statistical procedures to pinpoint variations in the quality of goods or services. Once variations have been identified, they must be traced to their respective sources and eliminated.

One technique that helps greatly in tracing defects to the source is reducing lot sizes for manufactured products. With short production runs, defects show up immediately. Consequently, they can quickly be sourced, and the problem can be addressed. Reducing lot sizes also means that when defective products are produced, there will not be a large number produced, thus decreasing waste. Flexible manufacturing techniques can be used to reduce lot sizes without raising costs. JIT inventory systems also play a part. Under a JIT system, defective parts enter the manufacturing process immediately; they are not warehoused for several months before use. Hence, defective inputs can be quickly spotted. The problem can then be traced to the supply source and corrected before more defective parts are produced. Under a more traditional system, the practice of warehousing parts for months before they are used may mean that suppliers produce large numbers of defects before entering the production process.

Fourth, another key to any quality improvement program is to create a metric that can be used to measure quality. In manufacturing companies, quality can be measured by criteria such as defects per million parts. In service companies, suitable metrics can be devised with a little creativity. For example, one of the metrics Florida Power & Light uses to measure quality is meter-reading errors per month.

Fifth, once a metric has been devised, the next step is to set a challenging quality goal and create incentives for reaching it. Under Six Sigma programs, the goal is 3.4 defects per million units. One way of creating incentives to attain such a goal is to link rewards, such as bonus pay and promotional opportunities, to the goal.

Sixth, shop floor employees can be a major source of ideas for improving product quality, so these employees must participate and must be incorporated into a quality improvement program.

Seventh, a major source of poor-quality finished goods is poor-quality component parts. To decrease product defects, a company must work with its suppliers to improve the quality of the parts they supply.

Eighth, the more assembly steps a product requires, the more opportunities there are for mistakes. Thus, designing products with fewer parts is often a major component of any quality improvement program.

Finally, implementing quality improvement methodologies requires organization-wide commitment and substantial cooperation among functions. R&D must cooperate with production to design products that are easy to manufacture; marketing must cooperate with production and R&D so that customer problems identified by marketing can be acted on; and human resource management must cooperate with all the other functions of the company in order to devise suitable quality-training programs.

Improving Quality as Excellence

As we stated in Chapter 3, a product is comprised of different attributes, and reliability is just one attribute, albeit an important one. Products can also be *differentiated* by attributes that collectively define product excellence. These attributes include the form, features, performance, durability, and styling of a product. In addition, a company can create quality as excellence by emphasizing attributes of the service associated with the product, such as ordering ease, prompt delivery, easy installation, the availability of customer training and consulting, and maintenance services. Dell Inc., for example, differentiates itself on ease of ordering (via the Web), prompt delivery, easy installation, and the ready availability of customer support and maintenance services. Differentiation can also be based on the attributes of the people in the company with whom customers interact when making a product purchase, such as their competence, courtesy, credibility, responsiveness, and communication. Singapore Airlines, for example, enjoys an excellent reputation for quality service, largely because passengers perceive their flight attendants as competent, courteous, and responsive to their needs. Thus, we can talk about the product attributes, service attributes, and personnel attributes associated with a company's product offering (see Table 4.3).

For a product to be regarded as high in the excellence dimension, a company's product offering must be seen as superior to that of rivals. Achieving a perception of high quality on any of these attributes requires specific actions by managers. First, it is important for managers to collect marketing intelligence indicating which of these attributes are most important to customers. For example, consumers of personal computers may place a low weight on durability because they expect their PC to be made obsolete by technological advances within 3 years, but they may place a high weight on features and performance. Similarly, ease of ordering and timely delivery may be very important attributes for customers of online booksellers (as they indeed are for customers of amazon.com), whereas customer training and consulting may be very important attributes for customers who purchase complex business-to-business software to manage their relationships with suppliers.

Second, once the company has identified the attributes that are important to customers, it needs to design its products (and the associated services) in such a way that those attributes are embodied in the product. It also needs to make sure that personnel in the company are appropriately trained so that the correct attributes are emphasized during design creation. This requires close coordination between marketing and product development (the topic of the next section) and the involvement of the human resource management function in employee selection and training.

Table 4.3 Attributes Associated with a Product Offering

Product Attributes	Service Attributes	Associated Personnel Attributes
Form	Ordering ease	Competence
Features	Delivery	Courtesy
Performance	Installation	Credibility
Durability	Customer training	Reliability
Reliability	Customer consulting	Responsiveness
Style	Maintenance and repair	Communication

© Cengage Learning 2013

Third, the company must decide which of the significant attributes to promote and how best to position them in the minds of consumers, that is, how to tailor the marketing message so that it creates a consistent image in the minds of customers.[32] At this point, it is important to recognize that although a product might be differentiated on the basis of six attributes, covering all of those attributes in the company's communication messages may lead to an unfocused message. Many marketing experts advocate promoting only one or two central attributes to customers. For example, Volvo consistently emphasizes the safety and durability of its vehicles in all marketing messages, creating the perception in the minds of consumers (backed by product design) that Volvo cars are safe and durable. Volvo cars are also very reliable and have high performance, but the company does not emphasize these attributes in its marketing messages. In contrast, Porsche emphasizes performance and styling in all of its marketing messages; thus, a Porsche is positioned differently in the minds of consumers than Volvo. Both are regarded as high-quality products because both have superior attributes, but the attributes that each of the two companies have chosen to emphasize are very different; they are differentiated from the average car in different ways.

Finally, it must be recognized that competition is not stationary, but instead continually produces improvement in product attributes, and often the development of new-product attributes. This is obvious in fast-moving high-tech industries where product features that were considered leading edge just a few years ago are now obsolete—but the same process is also at work in more stable industries. For example, the rapid diffusion of microwave ovens during the 1980s required food companies to build new attributes into their frozen food products: they had to maintain their texture and consistency while being cooked in the microwave; a product could not be considered high quality unless it could do that. This speaks to the importance of having a strong R&D function in the company that can work with marketing and manufacturing to continually upgrade the quality of the attributes that are designed into the company's product offerings. Exactly how to achieve this is covered in the next section.

Achieving Superior Innovation

In many ways, innovation is the most important source of competitive advantage. This is because innovation can result in new products that better satisfy customer needs, can improve the quality (attributes) of existing products, or can reduce the costs of making products that customers want. The ability to develop innovative new products or processes gives a company a major competitive advantage that allows it to: (1) *differentiate* its products and charge a premium price; and/or (2) *lower its cost structure* below that of its rivals. Competitors, however, attempt to imitate successful innovations and often succeed. Therefore, maintaining a competitive advantage requires a continuing commitment to innovation.

Successful new product launches are major drivers of superior profitability. Robert Cooper reviewed more than 200 new product introductions and found that of those classified as successes, some 50% achieve a return on investment in excess of 33%, half have a payback period of 2 years or less, and half achieve a market share in excess of 35%.[33] Many companies have established a track record for successful innovation. Among them Sony, whose successes include the Walkman, the Compact Disc, and the PlayStation; Nokia, which has been a leader in the development of wireless phones; Pfizer, a drug company that during the 1990s and early 2000s produced 8 new blockbuster drugs; 3M, which has applied its core competency in tapes and adhesives to developing a wide range of new products; Intel, which has consistently managed to lead in the development of innovative new microprocessors to run personal computers; and Cisco Systems, whose innovations helped to pave the way for the rapid growth of the Internet.

The High Failure Rate of Innovation

Although promoting innovation can be a source of competitive advantage, the failure rate of innovative new products is high. Research evidence suggests that only 10%–20% of major R&D projects give rise to commercial products.[34] Well-publicized product failures include Apple's Newton, a personal digital assistant; Sony's Betamax format in the video player and recorder market; and Sega's Dream-cast videogame console. While many reasons have been advanced to explain why so many new products fail to generate an economic return, five explanations for failure repeatedly appear.[35]

First, many new products fail because the demand for innovations is inherently uncertain. It is impossible to know prior to market introduction whether the new product has tapped an unmet customer need, and if there sufficient market demand to justify manufacturing the product. While good market research can reduce the uncertainty about likely future demand for a new technology, that uncertainty cannot be fully eradicated; a certain failure rate is to be expected.

Second, new products often fail because the technology is poorly commercialized. This occurs when there is definite customer demand for a new product, but the product is not well-adapted to customer needs because of factors such as poor design and poor quality. For instance, the failure of Apple to establish a market for the Newton, a hand-held personal digital system that the company introduced in the 1990s, can be traced to poor commercialization of a potentially attractive technology. Apple predicted a $1 billion market for the Newton, but sales failed to materialize when it became clear that the Newton's handwriting software, an attribute that Apple chose to emphasize in its marketing promotions, could not adequately recognize messages written on the Newton's message pad.

Third, new products may fail because of poor positioning strategy. **Positioning strategy** is the specific set of options a company adopts for a product based upon four main dimensions of marketing: price, distribution, promotion and advertising, and product features. Apart from poor product quality, another reason for the failure of the Apple Newton was poor positioning strategy. The Newton was introduced at such a high initial price (close to $1,000) that, even if the technology had been adequately commercialized, there likely would have been few buyers.

Fourth, many new product introductions fail because companies often make the mistake of marketing a technology for which there is not enough demand. A company can become blinded by the wizardry of a new technology and fail to determine whether there is customer demand for the product.

Finally, companies fail when products are slowly marketed. The more time that elapses between initial development and final marketing—the slower "cycle time"—the more likely it is that a competitor will beat the company to market, and gain a first-mover advantage.[36] In the car industry, General Motors has suffered from being a slow innovator. Its typical product development cycle has been about 5 years, compared with 2–3 years at Honda, Toyota, and Mazda, and 3–4 years at Ford. Because GM cars are based on 5-year-old technology and design concepts, they are already out of date when they reach the market.

Positioning strategy

The specific set of options a company adopts for a product based upon four main dimensions of marketing: price, distribution, promotion and advertising, and product features.

Reducing Innovation Failures

One of the most important things that managers can do to reduce the high failure rate associated with innovation is to make sure that there is tight integration between R&D, production and marketing.[37] Tight cross-functional integration can help a company ensure that

1. Product development projects are driven by customer needs.
2. New products are designed for ease of manufacture.
3. Development costs are reduced.
4. The time it takes to develop a product and bring it to market is minimized.
5. Close integration between R&D and marketing is achieved to ensure that product development projects are driven by the needs of customers.

A company's customers can be a primary source of new product ideas. The identification of customer needs, and particularly unmet needs, can set the context within which successful product innovation takes place. As the point of contact with customers, the marketing function can provide valuable information. Moreover, integrating R&D and marketing is crucial if a new product is to be properly commercialized—otherwise, a company runs the risk of developing products for which there is little or no demand.

Integration between R&D and production can help a company to ensure that products are designed with manufacturing requirements in mind. Design for manufacturing lowers manufacturing costs and leaves less room for mistakes; thus it can lower costs and increase product quality. Integrating R&D and production can help lower development costs and speed products to market. If a new product is not designed with manufacturing capabilities in mind, it may prove too difficult to build with existing manufacturing technology. In that case, the product will need to be redesigned, and both overall development costs and time to market may increase significantly. Making design changes during product planning can increase overall development costs by 50% and add 25% to the time it takes to bring the product to market.[38]

One of the best ways to achieve cross-functional integration is to establish cross-functional product development teams composed of representatives from R&D, marketing, and production. The objective of a team should be to oversee a product development project from initial concept development to market introduction. A number of attributes appear to be important in order for a product development team to function effectively and meet all its development milestones.[39]

First, a heavyweight project manager—one who has high status within the organization and the power and authority required to secure the financial and human resources that the team needs to succeed—should lead the team and be dedicated primarily, if not entirely, to the project. The leader should believe in the project (a champion) and be skilled at integrating the perspectives of different functions and helping personnel from different functions work together for a common goal. The leader should also be able to act as an advocate of the team to senior management.

Second, the team should be composed of at least one member from each key function or position. Individual team members should have a number of attributes, including an ability to contribute functional expertise, high standing within their function, a willingness to share responsibility for team results, and an ability to put functional advocacy aside. It is generally preferable if core team members are 100% dedicated to the project for its duration. This ensures that their focus is upon the project, not upon their ongoing individual work.

Third, the team members should be physically co-located to create a sense of camaraderie and facilitate communication. Fourth, the team should have a clear plan and clear goals, particularly with regard to critical development milestones and development budgets. The team should have incentives to attain those goals; for example, pay bonuses when major development milestones are attained. Fifth, each team needs to develop its own processes for communication, as well as conflict resolution. For example, one product development team at Quantum Corporation, a California-based manufacturer of disk drives for personal computers, mandated that all major decisions would be made and conflicts resolved during meetings that were held every Monday afternoon. This simple rule helped the team to meet its development goals.[40]

Finally, there is sufficient evidence that developing competencies in innovation requires managers to proactively learn from their experience with product development, and to incorporate the lessons from past successes and failures into future new product development processes.[41] This is easier said than done. To learn, managers need to undertake an objective assessment process after a product development project has been completed, identifying key success factors and the root causes of failures, and allocating resources toward repairing failures. Leaders also must admit their own failures if they are to encourage other team members to responsibly identify what they did wrong. Strategy in Action 4.4 looks at how Corning learned from a prior mistake to develop a potentially promising new product.

The primary role that the various functions play in achieving superior innovation is summarized in Table 4.4. The table makes two matters clear. First, top management must bear primary responsibility for overseeing the entire development process.

Table 4.4   Functional Roles for Achieving Superior Innovation

Value Creation Function	Primary Roles
Infrastructure (leadership)	1. Manage overall project (i.e., manage the development function)
	2. Facilitate cross-functional cooperation
Production	1. Cooperate with R&D on designing products that are easy to manufacture
	2. Work with R&D to develop process innovations
Marketing	1. Provide market information to R&D
	2. Work with R&D to develop new products
Materials management	No primary responsibility
R&D	1. Develop new products and processes
	2. Cooperate with other functions, particularly marketing and manufacturing, in the development process
Information systems	1. Use information systems to coordinate cross-functional and cross-company product development work
Human resources	1. Hire talented scientists and engineers

STRATEGY IN ACTION

Corning—Learning From Innovation Failures

In 1998, Corning, then the world's largest supplier of fiber-optic cable, decided to diversify and develop and manufacture of DNA microarrays (DNA chips). DNA chips are used to analyze the function of genes, and are an important research tool in pharmaceutical drug development processes. Corning tried to develop a DNA chip that could print all 28,000 human genes onto a set of slides. By 2000, Corning had invested over $100 million in the project and its first chips were on the market, but the project was a failure and in 2001 it was pulled.

What went wrong? Corning was late to market—a critical mistake. Affymetrix, which had been in the businesses since the early 1990s, dominated the market. By 2000, Affymetrix's DNA chips were the dominant design—researchers were familiar with them, they performed well, and few people were willing to switch to chips from unproven competitors. Corning was late because it adhered to its long established innovation processes, which were not entirely appropriate in the biological sciences. In particular, Corning's own in-house experts in the physical sciences insisted on sticking to rigorous quality standards that customers and life scientists felt where higher than necessary. These quality standards proved to be very difficult to achieve, and as a result, the product launch was delayed, giving Affymetrix time to consolidate its hold on the market. Additionally, Corning failed to allow potential customers to review prototypes of its chips, and consequently, it missed incorporating some crucial features that customers wanted.

After reviewing this failure, Corning decided that in the future, it needed to bring customers into the development process earlier. The company also needed to hire additional outside experts if it planned to diversify into an area where it lacked competencies—and to allow those experts extensive input in the development process.

The project was not a total failure, however, for through it Corning discovered a vibrant and growing market—the market for drug discovery. By combining what it had learned about drug discovery with another failed business, photonics, which manipulates data using light waves, Corning created a new product called "Epic." Epic is a revolutionary technology for drug testing that uses light waves instead of fluorescent dyes (the standard industry practice). Epic promises to accelerate the process of testing potential drugs and saving pharmaceutical companies valuable R&D money. Unlike its DNA microarray project, Corning had 18 pharmaceutical companies test Epic before development was finalized. Corning used this feedback to refine Epic. The company believes that ultimately Epic could generate $500 million annually.

Source: V. Govindarajan and C. Trimble, "How Forgetting Leads to Innovation," *Chief Executive*, March 2006, pp. 46–50. J. McGregor, "How Failure Breads Success," *Business Week*, July 10, 2006, pp. 42–52.

This entails both managing the development process and facilitating cooperation among the functions. Second, the effectiveness of R&D in developing new products and processes depends upon its ability to cooperate with marketing and production.

Achieving Superior Responsiveness To Customers

To achieve superior responsiveness to customers, a company must give customers what they want, when they want it, and at a price they are willing to pay—so long as the company's long-term profitability is not compromised in the process. Customer responsiveness is an important differentiating attribute that can help to build brand loyalty. Strong product differentiation and brand loyalty give a company more pricing options; it can charge a premium price for its products, or keep prices low to sell more goods and services to customers. Whether prices are at a premium or kept low, the company that is the most responsive to its customers' needs will have the competitive advantage.

Achieving superior responsiveness to customers means giving customers value for money, and steps taken to improve the efficiency of a company's production process and the quality of its products should be consistent with this aim. In addition, giving customers what they want may require the development of new products with new features. In other words, achieving superior efficiency, quality, and innovation are all part of achieving superior responsiveness to customers. There are two other prerequisites for attaining this goal. First, a company must develop a competency in listening to its customers, focusing on its customers, and in investigating and identifying their needs. Second, it must constantly seek better ways to satisfy those needs.

Focusing on the Customer

A company cannot be responsive to its customers' needs unless it knows what those needs are. Thus, the first step to building superior responsiveness to customers is to motivate the entire company to focus on the customer. The means to this end are: demonstrating leadership, shaping employee attitudes, and using mechanisms for making sure that the needs of the customer are known within the company.

Demonstrating Leadership   Customer focus must begin at the top of the organization. A commitment to superior responsiveness to customers brings attitudinal changes throughout a company that can only be built through strong leadership. A mission statement that puts customers first is one way to send a clear message to employees about the desired focus. Another avenue is top management's own actions. For example, Tom Monaghan, the founder of Domino's Pizza, stays close to the customer by eating Domino's pizza regularly, visiting as many stores as possible every week, running some deliveries himself, and insisting that other top managers do the same.[42]

Shaping Employee Attitudes   Leadership alone is not enough to attain a superior customer focus. All employees must see the customer as the focus of their activity, and be trained to focus on the customer—whether their function is marketing, manufacturing, R&D, or accounting. The objective should be to make employees think of themselves as customers—to put themselves in customers' shoes. From that perspective, employees become better able to identify ways to improve the quality of a customer's experience with the company.

To reinforce this mindset, incentive systems within the company should reward employees for satisfying customers. For example, senior managers at the Four Seasons hotel chain, who pride themselves on customer focus, like to tell the story of Roy Dyment, a doorman in Toronto who neglected to load a departing guest's briefcase into his taxi. The doorman called the guest, a lawyer, in Washington, D.C., and found that he desperately needed the briefcase for a morning meeting. Dyment hopped on a plane to Washington and returned it—without first securing approval from his boss. Far from punishing Dyment for making a mistake and for not checking with management before going to Washington, the Four Seasons responded by naming Dyment Employee of the Year.[43] This action sent a powerful message to Four Seasons employees, stressing the importance of satisfying customer needs.

Knowing Customer Needs   "Know thy customer" is one of the keys to achieving superior responsiveness to customers. Knowing the customer not only requires that employees think like customers themselves; it also demands that they listen to what customers have to say and, This involves bringing in customers' opinions by soliciting feedback from customers on the company's goods and services, and by building information systems that communicate the feedback to the relevant people.

For an example, consider direct-selling clothing retailer Lands' End. Through its catalog, the Internet, and customer service telephone operators, Lands' End actively solicits comments from its customers about the quality of its clothing and the kind of merchandise they want it to supply. Indeed, it was customers' insistence that initially prompted the company to move into the clothing segment. Lands' End formerly supplied equipment for sailboats through mail-order catalogs. However, it received so many requests from customers to include outdoor clothing in its offering that it responded by expanding the catalog to fill this need. Soon clothing became its main business, and Lands' End ceased selling the sailboat equipment. Today, the company continues to pay close attention to customer requests. Every month, a computer printout of customer requests and comments is reported to managers. This feedback helps the company to fine-tune the merchandise it sells; new lines of merchandise are frequently introduced in response to customer requests.[44]

Satisfying Customer Needs

Once customer focus is an integral part of the company, the next requirement is to satisfy the customer needs that have been identified. As already noted, efficiency, quality, and innovation are crucial competencies that help a company satisfy customer needs. Beyond that, companies can provide a higher level of satisfaction if they differentiate their products by (1) customizing them, where possible, to the requirements of individual customers, and (2) reducing the time it takes to respond to or satisfy customer needs.

Customization   Customization means varying the features of a good or service to tailor it to the unique needs or tastes of groups of customers, or—in the extreme case—individual customers. Although extensive customization can raise costs, the development of flexible manufacturing technologies has made it possible to customize products to a much greater extent than was feasible 10–15 years ago, without experiencing a prohibitive rise in cost structure (particularly when flexible manufacturing technologies are linked with Web-based information systems). For example, online retailers such as amazon.com have used Web-based technologies to develop a homepage customized for each individual user. When a customer accesses amazon.com, he or she is offered a list of recommended books and music to purchase based on an analysis of prior buying history—a powerful competency that gives amazon.com a competitive advantage.

The trend toward customization has fragmented many markets, particularly customer markets, into ever-smaller niches. An example of this fragmentation occurred in Japan in the early 1980s when Honda dominated the motorcycle market there. Second-place Yamaha had decided to surpass Honda's lead. It announced the opening of a new factory that, when operating at full capacity, would make Yamaha the world's largest manufacturer of motorcycles. Honda responded by proliferating its product line, and increasing its rate of new-product introduction. At the start of what became known as the "motorcycle wars," Honda had 60 motorcycles in its product line. Over the next 18 months thereafter, it rapidly increased its range to 113 models, customizing them to ever-smaller niches. Honda was able to accomplish this without bearing a prohibitive cost penalty due to its competency in flexible manufacturing. The flood of Honda's customized models pushed Yamaha out of much of the market, effectively stalling its bid to overtake Honda.[45]

Response Time   Supplying customers with what they want, when they want it requires speed of response to customer demands. To gain a competitive advantage, a company must often respond to customer demands very quickly, whether the transaction is a furniture manufacturer's delivery of a product once it has been ordered, a bank's processing of a loan application, an automobile manufacturer's delivery of a spare part for a car that broke down, or the wait in a supermarket checkout line. We live in a fast-paced society, where time is a valuable commodity. Companies that can satisfy customer demands for rapid response build brand loyalty, differentiate their products, and can charge higher prices for products.

Increased speed often lets a company choose a premium pricing option, as the mail delivery industry illustrates. The air express niche of the mail delivery industry is based on the notion that customers are often willing to pay substantially more for overnight Express Mail than for regular mail. Another example of the value of rapid response is Caterpillar, the manufacturer of heavy earthmoving equipment, which can deliver a spare part to any location in the world within 24 hours. Downtime for heavy construction equipment is very costly, so Caterpillar's ability to respond quickly in the event of equipment malfunction is of prime importance to its customers. As a result, many customers have remained loyal to Caterpillar despite the aggressive low-price competition from Komatsu of Japan.

In general, reducing response time requires: (1) a marketing function that can quickly communicate customer requests to production; (2) production and materials-management functions that can quickly adjust production schedules in response to unanticipated customer demands; and (3) information systems that can help production and marketing in this process.

Table 4.5 summarizes the steps different functions must take if a company is to achieve superior responsiveness to customers. Although marketing plays a critical role in helping a company attain this goal (primarily because it represents the point of contact with the customer) Table 4.5 shows that the other functions also have major roles. Achieving superior responsiveness to customers requires top management to lead in building a customer orientation within the company.

Table 4.5 Primary Roles of Different Functions in Achieving Superior Responsiveness to Customers

Value Creation Function	Primary Roles
Infrastructure (leadership)	• Through leadership by example, build a company-wide commitment to responsiveness to customers
Production	• Achieve customization through implementation of flexible manufacturing • Achieve rapid response through flexible manufacturing
Marketing	• Know the customer • Communicate customer feedback to appropriate functions
Materials management	• Develop logistics systems capable of responding quickly to unanticipated customer demands (JIT)
R&D	• Bring customers into the product development process
Information systems	• Use Web-based information systems to increase responsiveness to customers
Human resources	• Develop training programs that get employees to think like customers themselves

Ethical Dilemma

given that the organization also works its people very hard?

Is it ethical for Walmart to pay its employees minimum wage and to oppose unionization,

Are Walmart's employment and compensation practices for lower-level employees ethical?

Summary of Chapter

1. A company can increase efficiency through a number of steps: exploiting economies of scale and learning effects; adopting flexible manufacturing technologies; reducing customer defection rates; implementing just-in-time systems; getting the R&D function to design products that are easy to manufacture; upgrading the skills of employees through training; introducing self-managing teams; linking pay to performance; building a companywide commitment to efficiency through strong leadership; and designing structures that facilitate cooperation among different functions in pursuit of efficiency goals.

2. Superior quality can help a company lower its costs, differentiate its product, and charge a premium price.

3. Achieving superior quality demands an organization-wide commitment to quality, and a clear focus on the customer. It also requires metrics to measure quality goals and incentives that emphasize quality, input from employees regarding ways in which quality can be improved, a methodology for tracing defects to their source and correcting the problems that produce them, a rationalization of the company's supply base, cooperation with the suppliers that remain to implement total quality management programs, products that are designed for ease of manufacturing, and substantial cooperation among functions.

4. The failure rate of new-product introductions is high because of factors such as: uncertainty, poor commercialization, poor positioning strategy, slow cycle time, and technological myopia.

5. To achieve superior innovation, a company must build skills in basic and applied research; design good processes for managing development projects; and achieve close integration between the different functions of the company, primarily through the adoption of cross-functional product development teams and partly parallel development processes.

6. To achieve superior responsiveness to customers often requires that the company achieve superior efficiency, quality, and innovation.

7. To achieve superior responsiveness to customers, a company must give customers what they want, when they want it. It must ensure a strong customer focus, which can be attained by: emphasizing customer focus through leadership; training employees to think like customers; bringing customers into the company through superior market research; customizing products to the unique needs of individual customers or customer groups; and responding quickly to customer demands.

Discussion Questions

1. From what perspective might innovation be called "the single most important building block" of competitive advantage?

2. Over time, will the adoption of Six Sigma quality improvement processes give a company a competitive advantage, or will it be required only to achieve parity with competitors?

3. How are the four generic building blocks of competitive advantage related to each other?

4. What role can top management play in helping a company achieve superior efficiency, quality, innovation, and responsiveness to customers?

Practicing Strategic Management

 **Small-Group Exercises**

Small-Group Exercise: Identifying Excellence

Break up into groups of 3–5 people, and appoint one group member as a spokesperson who will communicate your findings to the class.

You are the management team of a start-up company that will produce hard drives for the personal computer industry. You will sell your product to manufacturers of personal computers (original equipment manufacturers). The disk drive market is characterized by rapid technological change, product life-cycles of only 6–9 months, intense price competition, high fixed costs for manufacturing equipment, and substantial manufacturing economies of scale. Your customers, the original equipment manufacturers, issue very demanding technological specifications that your product must comply with. They also pressure you to deliver your product on time so that it fits in within their company's product introduction schedule.

1. In this industry, what functional competencies are the most important for you to build?
2. How will you design your internal processes to ensure that those competencies are built within the company?

 Strategy Sign-On

Article File 4

Choose a company that is widely regarded as excellent. Identify the source of its excellence, and relate it to the material discussed in this chapter. Pay particular attention to the role played by the various functions in building excellence.

Strategic Management Project: Developing Your Portfolio 4

This module deals with the ability of your company to achieve superior efficiency, quality, innovation, and responsiveness to customers. With the information you have at your disposal, answer the questions and perform the tasks listed:

1. Is your company pursuing any of the efficiency-enhancing practices discussed in this chapter?
2. Is your company pursuing any of the quality-enhancing practices discussed in this chapter?
3. Is your company pursuing any of the practices designed to enhance innovation discussed in this chapter?
4. Is your company pursuing any of the practices designed to increase responsiveness to customers discussed in this chapter?
5. Evaluate the competitive position of your company with regard to your answers to questions 1–4. Explain what, if anything, the company must do to improve its competitive position.

CLOSING CASE

Productivity Improvement at United Technologies Corporation

In 2007, George David, the long-time CEO of United Technologies Corporation (UTC), retired. He could look back upon a very impressive 15 years at the helm of a company, during which time revenues tripled while net profits went up tenfold. Today, UTC is a $60 billion per annum diversified manufacturing enterprise whose businesses include jet-engine maker Pratt & Whitney, air-conditioning business Carrier, and Otis Elevators.

A major source of the profit surge over the last 15 years has been productivity improvements.

At the heart of these improvements is a program known as Achieve Competitive Excellence (ACE). This program was the result of collaboration between George David and a Japanese quality consultant, Yuzuru Ito, who at one time was a quality expert at Matsushita, the Japanese consumer electronics giant. David recruited Ito in order to figure out why Otis' elevators performed so poorly compared to those from rival Mitsubishi. Otis products required a building owner to call a mechanic an average of 40 times per year, while Mitsubishi's elevators required service only 0.5 times a year. What Ito uncovered was a range of problems including poor design, poor manufacturing practices, and a lack of quality control inside Otis' factories. Ito explained to David how poor quality damaged employee productivity, because time was wasted building defective products. Poor quality also hurt demand because customers were less likely to buy products from a company with a poor reputation for quality.

The solution to these problems at Otis included: designing elevators so that they were easier to manufacture, which led to fewer errors in the assembly process; reconfiguring the manufacturing process; and empowering factory-floor employees to identify and fix quality problems. For example, by changing the placement of elevator parts, and allowing assembly line workers to access them more easily, Otis took $300 off the cost of each elevator, which led to worldwide annual savings of $27 million. In addition, the production processes was streamlined, requiring fewer steps, less reaching and movement for workers, and easier access to parts—all of which boosted productivity.

ACE evolved out of the experience at Otis and was subsequently rolled out company wide. The main thrust of ACE is built around the belief that every person should be involved with continuous improvement, from top executives to the most junior workers. ACE "pilots" are production-line workers who learn a quality improvement process in just days, and then are empowered to implement and lead their work groups through that process. They learn to pinpoint potential problems, ranging from fundamental design flaws in a product, such as misplaced bolts, to a co-worker's fatigue from staying up with a newborn all night.

As the program was implemented across the company, the results were impressive. At Carrier, the number of employees decreased by 10%, the square footage assigned to manufacturing was reduced by 50%, and, despite these decreases, production increased by 70%. At Pratt & Whitney, dramatic improvements in the quality of jet engines were registered. The average time between part-failure in a jet engine went from 2,500 hours to 170,000 hours—a huge improvement resulting from better design and manufacturing processes. Customers noticed these quality improvements, and increased their purchases of United Technologies Corporation products, driving forward revenues and profits.[46]

Case Discussion Questions

1. How did poor quality at United Technologies' Otis unit damage the company's financial performance and competitive position?
2. Why do you think quality was so poor at Otis?
3. What did UTC learn by repairing the quality problems at Otis? How did it leverage this learning to improve the performance of the entire corporation?
4. What general principles about competitive advantage and strategy can be drawn from this case?

Notes

[1]C. Black, "To Build a Better Hospital, Virginia Mason Takes Lessons from Toyota Plants," *Seattle PI*, March 14, 2008; P. Neurath, "Toyota Gives Virginia Mason Docs a Lesson in Lean," *Puget Sound Business Journal*, September 14, 2003; K. Boyer and R. Verma, *Operations and Supply Chain Management for the 21st Century*, Cengage, 2009.

[2]G. J. Miller, *Managerial Dilemmas: The Political Economy of Hierarchy* (Cambridge: Cambridge University Press, 1992).

[3]H. Luft, J. Bunker, and A. Enthoven, "Should Operations Be Regionalized?" *New England Journal of Medicine* 301 (1979): 1364–1369.

[4]S. Chambers and R. Johnston, "Experience Curves in Services," *International Journal of Operations and Production Management* 20 (2000): 842–860.

[5]G. Hall and S. Howell, "The Experience Curve from an Economist's Perspective," *Strategic Management Journal* 6 (1985): 197–212; M. Lieberman, "The Learning Curve and Pricing in the Chemical Processing Industries," *RAND Journal of Economics* 15 (1984): 213–228; R. A. Thornton and P. Thompson, "Learning from Experience and Learning from Others," *American Economic Review* 91 (2001): 1350–1369.

[6]Boston Consulting Group, *Perspectives on Experience* (Boston: Boston Consulting Group, 1972); Hall and Howell, "The Experience Curve," pp. 197–212; W. B. Hirschmann, "Profit from the Learning Curve," *Harvard Business Review* (January–February 1964): 125–139.

[7]A. A. Alchian, "Reliability of Progress Curves in Airframe Production," *Econometrica* 31 (1963): 679–693.

[8]M. Borrus, L. A. Tyson, and J. Zysman, "Creating Advantage: How Government Policies Create Trade in the Semi-Conductor Industry," in P. R. Krugman (ed.), *Strategic Trade Policy and the New International Economics* (Cambridge, MA: MIT Press, 1986); S. Ghoshal and C. A. Bartlett, "Matsushita Electrical Industrial (MEI) in 1987," Harvard Business School Case #388–144 (1988).

[9]W. Abernathy and K. Wayne, "Limits of the Learning Curve," *Harvard Business Review* 52 (September–October 1974): pp. 59–69.

[10]D. F. Barnett and R. W. Crandall, *Up from the Ashes: The Rise of the Steel Minimill in the United States* (Washington, DC: Brookings Institution, 1986).

[11]See P. Nemetz and L. Fry, "Flexible Manufacturing Organizations: Implications for Strategy Formulation," *Academy of Management Review* 13 (1988): 627–638; N. Greenwood, *Implementing Flexible Manufacturing Systems* (New York: Halstead Press, 1986); J. P. Womack, D. T. Jones, and D. Roos, *The Machine That Changed the World* (New York: Rawson Associates, 1990); and R. Parthasarthy and S. P. Seith, "The Impact of Flexible Au-

tomation on Business Strategy and Organizational Structure," *Academy of Management Review* 17 (1992): 86–111.

[12]B. J. Pine, *Mass Customization: The New Frontier in Business Competition* (Boston: Harvard Business School Press, 1993); S. Kotha, "Mass Customization: Implementing the Emerging Paradigm for Competitive Advantage," *Strategic Management Journal* 16 (1995): 21–42; J. H. Gilmore and B. J. Pine II, "The Four Faces of Mass Customization," *Harvard Business Review* (January–February 1997): 91–101.

[13]P. Waurzyniak, "Ford's Flexible Push," *Manufacturing Engineering*, September 2003, pp. 47–50.

[14]F. F. Reichheld and W. E. Sasser, "Zero Defections: Quality Comes to Service," *Harvard Business Review* (September–October 1990): 105–111.

[15]The example comes from ibid.

[16]Ibid.

[17]R. Narasimhan and J. R. Carter, "Organization, Communication and Coordination of International Sourcing," *International Marketing Review* 7 (1990): 6–20.

[18]H. F. Busch, "Integrated Materials Management," *IJDP & MM* 18 (1990): 28–39.

[19]G. Stalk and T. M. Hout, *Competing Against Time* (New York: Free Press, 1990).

[20]See Peter Bamberger and Ilan Meshoulam, *Human Resource Strategy: Formulation, Implementation, and Impact* (Thousand Oaks, CA: Sage, 2000); P. M. Wright and S. Snell, "Towards a Unifying Framework for Exploring Fit and Flexibility in Human Resource Management," *Academy of Management Review* 23 (October 1998): 756–772.

[21]A. Sorge and M. Warner, "Manpower Training, Manufacturing Organization, and Work Place Relations in Great Britain and West Germany," *British Journal of Industrial Relations* 18 (1980): 318–333; R. Jaikumar, "Postindustrial Manufacturing," *Harvard Business Review* (November–December 1986): 72–83.

[22]J. Hoerr, "The Payoff from Teamwork," *Business Week*, July 10, 1989, pp. 56–62.

[23]"The Trouble with Teams," *Economist*, January 14, 1995, p. 61.

[24]T. C. Powell and A. Dent-Micallef, "Information Technology as Competitive Advantage: The Role of Human, Business, and Technology Resource," *Strategic Management Journal* 18 (1997): 375–405; B. Gates, *Business @ the Speed of Thought* (New York: Warner Books, 1999).

[25]"Cisco@speed," *Economist*, June 26, 1999, p. 12; S. Tully, "How Cisco Mastered the Net," *Fortune*, August 17, 1997, pp. 207–210; C. Kano, "The Real King of the Internet," *Fortune*, September 7, 1998, pp. 82–93.

[26]Gates, *Business @ the Speed of Thought.*

[27]See the articles published in the special issue of the *Academy of Management Review on Total Quality Management* 19:3 (1994); The following article provides a good overview of many of the issues involved from an academic perspective: J. W. Dean and D. E. Bowen, "Management Theory and Total Quality," *Academy of Management Review* 19 (1994): 392–418; See also T. C. Powell, "Total Quality Management as Competitive Advantage," *Strategic Management Journal* 16 (1995): 15–37.

[28]For general background information, see "How to Build Quality," *Economist,* September 23, 1989, pp. 91–92; A. Gabor, *The Man Who Discovered Quality* (New York: Penguin, 1990); and P. B. Crosby, *Quality Is Free* (New York: Mentor, 1980).

[29]W. E. Deming, "Improvement of Quality and Productivity Through Action by Management," *National Productivity Review* 1 (Winter 1981–1982): 12–22.

[30]J. Bowles, "Is American Management Really Committed to Quality?" *Management Review* (April 1992): 42–46.

[31]O. Port and G. Smith, "Quality," *Business Week*, November 30, 1992, pp. 66–75; See also "The Straining of Quality," *Economist,* January 14, 1995, pp. 55–56.

[32]A. Ries and J. Trout, *Positioning: The Battle for Your Mind* (New York: Warner Books, 1982).

[33]R. G. Cooper, *Product Leadership* (Reading, MA: Perseus Books, 1999).

[34]See: R.G. Cooper, *Product Leadership*. (Reading, MA: Perseus Books, 1999); A. L. Page, PDMA's New product development practices survey: Performance and best practices. PDMA 15th Annual International Conference, Boston, MA, October 16, 1991; E. Mansfield, "How Economists See R&D," *Harvard Business Review* (November–December 1981): 98–106.

[35]S. L. Brown and K. M. Eisenhardt, "Product Development: Past Research, Present Findings, and Future Directions," *Academy of Management Review* 20 (1995): 343–378; M. B. Lieberman and D. B. Montgomery, "First Mover Advantages," *Strategic Management Journal* 9 (Special Issue, Summer 1988): 41–58; D. J. Teece, "Profiting from Technological Innovation: Implications for Integration, Collaboration, Licensing and Public Policy," *Research Policy* 15 (1987): 285–305; G. J. Tellis and P. N. Golder, "First to Market, First to Fail?" *Sloan Management Review* (Winter 1996): 65–75; G.A. Stevens, J. Burley, "Piloting the Rocket of Radical Innovation," *Research Technology Management*, 46 (2003): 16–26.

[36]G. Stalk and T. M. Hout, *Competing Against Time* (New York: Free Press, 1990).

[37]K. B. Clark and S. C. Wheelwright, *Managing New Product and Process Development* (New York: Free Press, 1993); M. A. Schilling and C. W. L. Hill, "Managing the New Product Development Process," *Academy of Management Executive* 12:3 (August 1998): 67–81.

[38]O. Port, "Moving Past the Assembly Line," *Business Week,* (Special Issue, Reinventing America, 1992): 177–180.

[39]K. B. Clark and T. Fujimoto, "The Power of Product Integrity," *Harvard Business Review* (November–December 1990): 107–118; Clark and Wheelwright, *Managing New Product and Process Development;* Brown and Eisenhardt, "Product Development"; Stalk and Hout, *Competing Against Time.*

[40]C. Christensen, "Quantum Corporation—Business and Product Teams," Harvard Business School Case, #9–692–023.

[41]H. Petroski, *Success Through Failure: The Paradox of Design* (Princeton, NJ: Princeton University Press, 2006); See also A.C. Edmondson, "Learning From Mistakes is Easier Said Than Done," *Journal of Applied Behavioral Science*, 40 (2004) pp. 66–91.

[42]S. Caminiti, "A Mail Order Romance: Lands' End Courts Unseen Customers," *Fortune,* March 13, 1989, pp. 43–44.

[43]Sellers, "Getting Customers to Love You."

[44]Caminiti, "A Mail Order Romance," pp. 43–44.

[45]Stalk and Hout, *Competing Against Time.*

[46]D. Brady, "The Unsung CEO," *Business Week,* October 25, 2004, pp. 74–84; E. Cevallos, "Productivity and Leadership Insights from George David" *Ezine Articles,* August 25, 2007; G. G. Marcial, "United Technologies: Going UP?" *Business Week*, November 21, 2005, pp. 156.

5 Building Competitive Advantage Through Business-Level Strategy

Zynga Finds a New Strategy to Compete in Online Social Gaming

Zynga Inc., based in San Francisco, is the most popular maker of online social games—a rapidly growing and highly competitive segment of the game software and content industry. Every month, 1 out of 10 users of the Web play one or more of Zynga's 55 games, which include *FarmVille, CityVille, Zynga poker,* and *Mafia Wars.* About 4/5 of the U.S. population, approximately 250 million people, plays its games each month.

In 2011, Zynga released its newest online game, *Empires & Allies,* which expanded the company's repertoire, moving it into a new gaming arena—"action and strategy" games, which have been dominated by leading game developer, Electronic Arts (EA), (whose blockbuster games include *Crysis 2, Star Wars: The Old Republic, The Sims,* and *Portal 2).* Microsoft, Nintendo, and Sony are also major developers of action games that can be played on their proprietary gaming consoles—the Xbox, Wii, and PlayStation, respectively. Today, many of the

games these companies develop can also be purchased and played on desktop PCs, laptops, and mobile computing devices such as smartphones and tablets.

LEARNING OBJECTIVES
After reading this chapter, you should be able to:
- Explain why a company must define its business, and how managers do this through choices about which customer groups, customer needs, and distinctive competencies to pursue
- Define competitive positioning and explain the tradeoffs between differentiation, cost, and pricing options
- Identify the choices managers make to pursue a business model based on a combination of the primary generic business-level strategies: cost leadership, differentiation, and focus
- Explain why each business model allows a company to outperform its rivals, reach the value-creation frontier, and obtain above average profitability
- Discuss why some companies can successfully make the competitive positioning decisions that allow them to sustain their competitive advantage over time while others cannot

Leading game developers like EA and Sony utilize a business model that innovates block-buster games, which will sell millions of copies at a price of $50–$75 each game, generating billions of dollars in revenues and profits. Each game is produced by a team of hundreds of developers, who may work for 2 years (or more) to create a new game before it is finally released for sale. The popularity of the games the team creates determines the success of established game developers; as such, they are pursuing a differen-tiation strategy based on creating a unique prod-uct that can be sold at a premium price.

How did Zynga manage to enter and successfully compete in the highly competitive social gaming industry against giants such as EA and Nintendo? Its principal founder, Mark Pincus, armed with only $29 million in venture capital, decided to pursue a focused differen-tiation strategy to develop games using an approach that was unique within the software gaming industry. Pincus' approach was to start small, and hire 20 or more game developers to work interactively in teams of 10–15 members to continuously create, develop, and then perfect new games such as *FarmVille*. As each new game was launched, and revenue from online users started to roll in, Pincus could recruit new teams of game developers. By 2011, Zynga employed over 1,200 game developers and designers, and promoted a relaxed, university campus-like en-vironment in which employees could even bring their dogs to work if they chose.

Mark Skaggs, Zynga's Senior Vice President of product design, describes the company's strategy toward game making as "fast, light, and right."[1] Zynga's games take only a few weeks or months to design because the company's de-veloping teams work in self-managed groups that, today, may have up to 30 members. The ongoing developmental work of each team member (and the changes that are made to games) is immediately obvious to other team members. All team members are connected through interactive real-time software that allows evaluation of game changes, and how those changes will affect the entire game. Team members can continuously approve, dis-approve, or find alternative ways to improve a game's functionality and objectives. Devel-opers can also add new features to a game to captivate Zynga's hundreds of millions of online users when the game is released—the key to its differentiated appeal.

Another aspect of strategy that works well for Zynga is its competency to continuously cus-tomize every game it develops to better appeal to the likes and dislikes of its users—even *after* the game has been released online! Unlike other leading game-makers who cannot change their games after they have been released, much of Zynga's game development takes place *after* a game is released. Zynga's designers work around-the-clock to enhance content, correct errors, test new features, and constantly modify a new game based upon real-time feedback de-tailing how game players are "interacting" with the game. This feedback allows developers to discover what users enjoy the most, and modify games accordingly.

One of Zynga's unique competences is its ability to track the performance of each feature and design element of a game through "A/B test-ing." Zynga creates two different groups of on-line players—"A" and "B"—to test the games that are being developed. The responses of players in groups A and B to a game that has been modified or improved with new features are monitored. By tallying how many players click on the new feature, Zynga can collect data about whether players like the game, and what they want in a game. Its developers can then continuously change the dynamics of the game, according to this data, and make the game more satisfy-ing to users. The result is that Zynga's online games increasingly improve over time; they become more appealing to users as a result. As Greg Black, *Empires & Allies'* lead game designer says, "We can mine our users and see in real-time what they like to do."[2] So, for example, while the first thousands of *Empires & Allies* players were learning how to play the game and conquer the virtual rivals on their computer screens, the game's developers were watching their efforts and using the players' real-time experiences to continually craft and improve the way the game is played, making it more exciting.

This amazing interactive approach to online game development is quite different to the approach of the industry leaders—who have been losing market share as a result and so is the way it monetizes or obtains revenues from its unique business model. In Zynga's business model, all its online games are provided free of charge to hundreds of millions of online users—but to use each game's advanced or unique features, users must pay a fee, or agree to participate in one or more online marketing exercises. The popularity of online social games is based on the number of daily active users, which in Zynga's case is 50–60 million a day (it has an audience of 240 million players on Facebook alone). So, if

only 2%–5% of Zynga's players spend money on the extra game features that can be purchased cheaply—often for nickels or dimes—Zynga's 50 million users a day are generating revenues over $900 million per year. The more games that Zynga encourages users to play, the more money it earns! When the company announced a public offering of its shares in June 2011, analysts estimated the company could be worth as much as $20 billion. In December 2011 the company raised $1 billion that valued the whole company at over $10 billion. Thus, Zynga's focused differentiation strategy has made it one of the leaders in the gaming industry. It is most accurate to describe Zynga as a *differentiator*.

David Paul Morris/Bloomberg via Getty Image

Overview

As the Opening Case suggests, the companies that dominate an industry can never take a leading position for granted. A new competitor can emerge with an innovative or superior business-level strategy that can change the industry's competition. By 2011, online social gaming industry leaders such as EA, Sony, and Nintendo were experiencing major problems due to the increased use of mobile computing devices. Smartphones and laptops—now being used for gaming purposes—were negatively affecting the leading gaming companies, which were losing their competitive advantage. This chapter examines how a company selects, pursues, and maintains a business model that will allow it to compete effectively in an industry and increase its profitability over time. A successful business model results from business-level strategies that create a competitive advantage over rivals, and achieve superior performance in an industry.

In Chapter 2, we examined how the competitive forces at work inside an industry affect its profitability. As industry forces change, they change the profitability of an industry and, thus, the profitability of any particular business model. Industry analysis is vital in formulating a successful business model because it determines: (1) how existing companies will decide to change their business-level strategies to improve the performance of their business model over time; (2) whether established companies outside an industry may decide to create a business model to enter it; and (3) whether entrepreneurs can devise a business model that will allow them to compete successfully against existing companies in an industry.

In Chapter 3, we examined how competitive advantage depends upon a business model that allows a company to achieve superior efficiency, quality, innovation, and customer responsiveness—the building blocks of competitive advantage. In Chapter 4, we discussed how every function of a company must develop the distinctive competencies that allow it to implement a business model that will lead to superior performance and competitive advantage in an industry.

In this chapter, we examine the competitive decisions involved in creating a business model that will attract and retain customers and continue to do so over time, so that a company enjoys increasing profitability. To create a successful business model, strategic managers must (1) formulate business-level strategies that will allow a company to attract customers and lead them away from other companies in the industry (its competitors), and (2) implement the business-level strategies, which involves the use of functional-level strategies to increase responsiveness to customers, efficiency, innovation, and quality. As the Opening Case suggests, Zynga used the opportunities offered by real-time interactive social gaming to create new, innovative game experiences, and become more responsive to its customers—game users. It has increased its competitive advantage and profitability as a result.

By the end of this chapter, you will be able to distinguish between the different types of principal generic business models and business-level strategies that a company uses to obtain a competitive advantage over its rivals. You will also understand why, and under what circumstances, strategic leaders of companies like Zynga, Sony, Apple, IBM, and Ford change their company's strategies over time to pursue different business models and try to increase their competitive advantage over industry rivals.

Competitive Positioning and The Business Model

To create a successful business model, managers must choose a set of business-level strategies that work together to give a company a competitive advantage over its rivals; that is, they must optimize competitive positioning. As we noted in Chapter 1, to craft a successful business model, a company must first define its business, which entails decisions about: (1) customer needs, or what is to be satisfied; (2) customer groups, or who is to be satisfied; and (3) distinctive competencies, or how customer needs are to be satisfied.[3] The decisions managers make regarding these three elements determine which set of strategies will be formulated and implemented to put a company's business model into action and create value for customers. Consequently, we need to examine the principal choices facing managers as they make these three decisions.

Formulating the Business Model: Customer Needs and Product Differentiation

Customer needs are desires, wants, or cravings that can be satisfied by means of the attributes or characteristics of a product (a good or service). For example, a person's craving for something sweet can be satisfied by a box of Godiva chocolates, a carton of Ben & Jerry's ice cream, a Snickers bar, or a spoonful of sugar. Two factors determine which product a customer chooses to satisfy these needs: (1) the way a product is differentiated from other products of its type so that it is appealing and (2) the price of the product. All companies must differentiate their products to attract customers. Some companies, however, decide to offer customers low-priced products and do not engage in much product differentiation. Companies that seek to create something *unique* about their product differentiate their products to a much greater degree than others so that they satisfy customers' needs in ways other products cannot.

Product differentiation is the process of designing products to satisfy customers' needs. A company obtains a competitive advantage when it creates, makes, and sells a product that better satisfies customer needs than its rivals. Then the four building blocks of competitive advantage come into play; a company's decision to pursue one or more of these building blocks will determine its approach to product differentiation. If managers devise strategies to differentiate a product by innovation, excellent quality, or responsiveness to customers, they are choosing a business model based on offering customers *differentiated products*. Conversely, if managers base their business model on finding ways to increase efficiency and reliability to reduce costs, they are choosing a business model based on offering customers *low-priced products*.

Creating unique or distinctive products can be achieved in a myriad of ways, which explains why there are usually many different companies competing within one industry. Distinctiveness obtained from the physical characteristics of a product commonly results from pursuing innovation or quality, such as when a company focuses on developing state-of-the-art car safety systems, or on engineering a sports utility vehicle (SUV) to give it sports car-like handling—something Porsche and BMW strive to achieve. Similarly, companies might attempt to design cars with features such as butter-soft, hand-sewn leather interiors, fine wood fittings, and sleek, exciting body-styling to appeal to customers' psychological needs, such as a personal need for prestige and status, or to declare a particular "lifestyle," something for which Mercedes-Benz and Lexus strive.[4]

Differentiation has another important aspect. Companies that invest their resources to create something distinct or different about their products can often charge a higher or *premium* price for their product. For example, superb design or technical sophistication allows companies to charge more for their products because customers are willing to pay these higher prices. Porsche and Mercedes-Benz buyers pay a high premium price to enjoy their sophisticated vehicles, as do customers of Godiva chocolates, which retail for about $26 a pound—much more than, say, a box of Whitman's candies or a Hershey's chocolate bar.

Consider the high-price segment of the car market, in which customers are willing to pay more than $35,000 to satisfy their needs for a "personal luxury vehicle." In this segment, Cadillac, Mercedes-Benz, Infiniti, BMW, Jaguar, Lexus, Lincoln, Audi, Volvo, Acura, and others are engaged in a continuing battle to design the "perfect" luxury vehicle—the one that best meets the needs of those who want such a

Product differentiation

The process of designing products to satisfy customers' needs.

vehicle. Over time, the companies that attract the most luxury car buyers—because they have designed the cars that possess the innovative features, or excellent quality and reliability these customers desire the most—are the companies that achieve a sustained competitive advantage over rivals. For example, some customers value a sporty ride and performance handling; Mercedes-Benz and BMW, because of cutting-edge technical design, can offer this driving experience better than other carmakers. Toyota's Lexus division is well known for the smoothness and quietness of its cars, and their exceptional reliability. Lexus cars consistently outrank all other cars in published reliability rankings, and this excellence appeals to a large group of customers who appreciate these qualities. Infinity's reputation for sportiness and reliability has increased steadily in the 2010s, as has its market share, and both Bentley and Rolls-Royce, which produce prestige cars, can sell all they can make. Other luxury carmakers have not fared so well. Cadillac, Lincoln, Audi, Acura, Saab, and Volvo have found it more difficult to differentiate their cars, which sometimes compare unfavorably to their rivals in terms of ride, comfort, safety, or reliability. Although these less successful companies still sell many cars, customers often find their needs better satisfied by the attributes and qualities of their rivals' cars. It is the latter that can sustain their competitive advantage over time. Luxury carmakers, however, must still be concerned with efficiency because price affects a buying decision, even for highly differentiated products. Luxury carmakers compete to offer customers the car with the ride, performance, and features that provide them with the most value (best satisfies their needs) given the price of the car. Thus, Lexus cars are always several thousand dollars less than comparable cars, and Toyota can price these cars lower because of its low cost structure. For example, the Lexus LS460 at about $70,000 costs at least $20,000 less than a similarly equipped BMW 7 Series or a Mercedes S Class, its closest rivals. Most customers are discriminating and align price with differentiation, even in the luxury segment of the car market, therefore BMW and Mercedes must offer customers something that justifies their vehicles' higher prices.

At every price range in the car market—under $15,000, from $15,000–$25,000, from $25,000–$35,000, and the luxury segment above $35,000—many models of cars compete to attract customers. For each price range, a carmaker must decide how to best differentiate a particular car model to suit the needs of customers within that price range. Typically, the more differentiated a product, the more it will cost to design and produce, and so, differentiation leads to a higher cost structure. Therefore, if a carmaker is to stay within the $15,000–$25,000 price range and simultaneously design and produce a differentiated car with a competitive advantage that allows it to outperform its rivals in the same price range, its managers must make difficult choices. They must forecast what features customers will value most; for example, they may decide to forego sporty styling in order to increase safety features so that the car will not cost too much to produce; this allows the company to make a profit *and* sell the car for less than $25,000.

In sum, when devising a business model, strategic managers are always constrained by the need to differentiate their products against the need to keep their cost structure under control in order to offer a product at a competitive price—a price that gives customers as much or more value than the products of its rivals. Companies that have built a competitive advantage through innovation, quality, and reliability can differentiate their products more successfully than their rivals. In turn, because customers perceive there is more value in a company's products, the company can charge a premium price, as Cadillac and Lincoln used to be able to do.

Formulating the Business Model: Customer Groups and Market Segmentation

The second important choice involved in formulating a successful business model is to decide which kind of product(s) to offer to which customer group(s). Customer groups are the sets of people who share a similar need for a particular product. Because a particular product usually satisfies several different kinds of desires and needs, many different customer groups typically coexist in a market. In the car market, for example, some customers need basic transportation, some desire top-of-the-line luxury, and others want the thrill of driving a sports car; these are three of the customer groups in the car market.

In the athletic shoe market, the two primary customer groups are those who use the shoes for sporting purposes and those who like to wear the shoes because they are casual and comfortable. Within each customer group, there are often subgroups comprised of people who have a more focused, specific need for a product. Within the group of people who buy athletic shoes for sporting purposes, for example, are subgroups of people who buy shoes suited to a specific kind of activity, such as running, aerobics, walking, and soccer (see Figure 5.1).

A company searching for a successful business model must classify customers according to the similarities or differences in their needs in order to decide what kinds of products to develop for different kinds of customers. The marketing function performs research to discover a group of customers' primary need for a product, how they will use it, and their income or buying power (to determine the balance between differentiation and price). Other important attributes of a group are then identified to more narrowly target the customers' specific needs. Once a group of customers who share a similar or specific need for a product has

Figure 5.1 Identifying Customer Groups and Market Segments

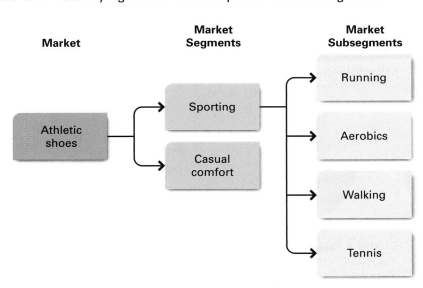

been identified, this group is treated as a market segment. Companies then decide whether to make and sell a product designed to satisfy the specific needs of a particular customer segment.

Three Approaches to Market Segmentation   **Market segmentation** is the way a company decides to classify its customers, based on important differences in their needs or preferences, to gain a competitive advantage.[5] First, the company must segment the market according to how much customers are able and willing to pay for a particular product, such as the different price ranges for cars mentioned earlier. Once price has been considered, customers can be segmented according to the specific needs that are being satisfied by a particular product, such as the economy, luxury, or speed of cars mentioned in the earlier example.

In crafting a business model, managers must think strategically about which segments they are going to compete within, and how they will differentiate their products for each segment. In other words, once market segments have been identified, a company must decide how *responsive it should be to the needs of customers in the different segments* to obtain a competitive advantage. This decision determines a particular company's product range. There are three primary approaches toward market segmentation in devising a business model (see Figure 5.2):

> **Market segmentation**
>
> The way a company decides to group customers based on important differences in their needs to gain a competitive advantage.

1. First, a company might choose *not* to recognize that different market segments exist and make a product targeted at the average or typical customer. In this case, customer responsiveness is at a *minimum*, and competitive advantage is achieved through low price, not differentiation.
2. Second, a company can choose to recognize the differences between customer groups and create a product targeted toward most (or all) of the different market segments. In this case, customer responsiveness is *high* and products are being *customized* to meet the specific needs of customers in each group. Competitive advantage is obtained through differentiation, not low price.
3. Third, a company might choose to target only *1 or 2 market segments* and devote its resources to developing products for customers in these segments. In

Figure 5.2 Three Approaches to Market Segmentation

No Market Segmentation
A product is targeted at the "average customer."

High Market Segmentation
A different product is offered to each market segment.

Focused Market Segmentation
A product is offered to one or a few market segments.

this case, a company may be highly responsive to the needs of customers in only these segments, or it may offer a bare-bones product to undercut companies who do focus on differentiation and charge lower prices. Competitive advantage may be obtained through a focus on low price *or* differentiation.

Because a company's cost structure and operating costs increase when it makes a different product for each market segment—rather than just one product for the entire market—why would a company devise a business model based on serving customers in multiple market segments? The answer is that although operating costs increase, the decision to produce a range of products closely aligned with customers' needs in different market segments attracts additional customers (because responsiveness to customers increases), and, therefore, sales revenues and profits increase. A car company that offers a wide range of cars customized to the needs of customers in different market segments increases the total number of cars it can sell. As long as a company's revenues increase faster than its operating costs while its product range expands, profitability increases.

This does *not* mean that all companies should decide to produce a wide range of products aimed at each market segment. Profitability increases to the degree that there are significant differences in customer needs for a product in a particular market or industry. In some industries, such as cars, customer needs differ widely. There are considerable differences in buyers' primary needs for a car: income levels, lifestyles, ages, etc. For this reason, major global carmakers broaden their product range and make vehicles to serve most market segments because this increases profitability. A company that produces only a single model, compared with a company that produces 25 models, may therefore find itself at a serious competitive disadvantage.

On the other hand, in some markets, customers have similar needs for a product, and so the relative price of competing products drives their buying choices. In this situation, a company that strives to gain a competitive advantage by using its resources to make and sell a single product as inexpensively as possible might be the most profitable. The average customer buys the product because it's "OK" and good "value for the money." This is the business model followed by companies that specialize in making low-cost products, such as BIC, which makes low-cost razors and ballpoint pens, and Arm & Hammer, which makes baking soda. Most people use these products in the same way. This is also the business model followed by companies like Walmart, whose goal is to purchase products from suppliers as cheaply as possible, and then sell the products to customers at the lowest possible prices. BIC and Walmart do not segment the market; they decide to serve the needs of customers who want to buy products as inexpensively as possible. Walmart promises everyday low prices and price rollbacks; BIC promises the lowest-priced razor blades that acceptably work.

The third approach to market segmentation is to target a product at only 1 or 2 market segments. To pursue this approach, a company must develop something very special or distinctive about its product to attract a large share of customers in those particular market segments. In the car market, for example, Rolls-Royce and Porsche target their products at specific market segments. Porsche, for example, targets its well-known sports cars at buyers in the high-priced sports car segment. In a similar way, specialty retailers compete for customers in a particular market segment, such as the segment composed of affluent people who can afford to buy expensive handmade clothing, or people who enjoy wearing "trendy" shoes or jeans. A retailer might also specialize in a particular style of clothing, such as western wear, beachwear, or accessories. In many markets, these are enormous opportunities for small companies to specialize in satisfying the needs of a specific market segment. Often, these companies can better satisfy their customers' needs because they understand how customer needs change over time.

Market segmentation is an evolving, ongoing process that presents considerable opportunities for strategic managers to improve their company's business model. For example, in the car industry, savvy strategists often identify a "new" customer group whose specific needs have not been met; these customers have had to "satisfice" and buy a model that does not exactly meet their needs, but is a reasonable compromise. A car company can decide to treat this group as a new market segment and create a product designed to meet their specific needs, and, if it makes the right choice, it has a blockbuster product. This strategy resulted in the creation of new vehicles such as the minivan; the SUV; crossover vehicles like the Honda Pilot, Toyota Scion, or Dodge Journey; and hybrid vehicles such as the Toyota Prius and Honda Insight. In the case of SUVs, many car buyers were looking for a more rugged, powerful vehicle capable of carrying many passengers or towing heavy loads. Buyers like the comfort of a car, but also the qualities of a pickup truck. Carmakers created the SUV market segment by creating a new vehicle that would meet both these needs. If managers are mistaken, however, and design a product for a market segment that is much smaller than they expected, the opposite can occur. After oil prices soared, U.S. carmakers ceased production of many gas-guzzling vehicles such as the luxury Lincoln truck and Excursion SUV, and cut production of other models after customer demand collapsed; even Toyota had to suspend production of its Tundra pickup.

Implementing the Business Model: Building Distinctive Competencies

To develop a successful business model, strategic managers must devise a set of strategies that determine (1) how to differentiate and price their product, and (2) how much to segment a market and how wide a range of products to develop. Whether these strategies will result in a profitable business model depends upon a strategic manager's ability to implement the business model, that is, to choose strategies that will create products that provide customers with the most value, while keeping the cost structure viable (because of the need to be price competitive).

In practice, this involves deciding how to invest a company's capital to build and shape distinctive competencies, resulting in a competitive advantage based on superior efficiency, quality, innovation, and/or responsiveness to customers. Hence, implementing a company's business model sets into motion *the specific set of functional-level strategies needed to create a successful differentiation and low-cost business strategy.* We discussed how functional strategies might build competitive advantage in Chapter 4. The better the fit between a company's business strategy and its functional-level strategies, the more value and profit can create, as the example of Krispy Kreme Doughnuts profiled in Strategy in Action 5.1 suggests.

Competitive Positioning and Business-Level Strategy

Figure 5.3 presents a way of thinking about the competitive positioning decisions that strategic managers make when creating a successful business model.[6] The decision to differentiate a product increases its perceived value to customers, and market demand for the product then increases. Differentiation is expensive, however;

STRATEGY IN ACTION

Krispy Kreme Doughnuts Are Hot Again

Founded in 1937 in Newington, Connecticut, Krispy Kreme is a leading specialty retailer of premium quality yeast-raised doughnuts. Krispy Kreme's doughnuts have a broad customer following, and command a premium price because of their unique taste and quality. The way this company has developed competences to increase its operating efficiency and responsiveness to customers is instructive. Krispy Kreme calls its store production operations "doughnut theater" because all stores are designed so that customers can see and smell the doughnuts while they are being made by impressive company-built doughnut-making machines.

What are elements of its production competency? The story begins with the 70-year-old company's secret doughnut recipe that it keeps locked in a vault. None of its franchisees know the recipe for making its dough, and Krispy Kreme sells the ready-made dough and other ingredients to its individual stores. The machines used to make the doughnuts are company designed and produced, so no doughnut maker can imitate its unique cooking methods, and thus create a similar competing product. The doughnut-making machines are designed

to produce a wide variety of different kinds of doughnuts in small quantities, and each store makes and sells between 4,000 and 10,000 dozen doughnuts per day.

Krispy Kreme constantly refines its production system to improve the efficiency of its small-batch operations. For example, it redesigned its doughnut machine to include a high-tech extruder that uses air pressure to force the doughnut dough into rows of rings or shells. Employees formerly had to adjust air pressure manually as the dough load lightened; now this is all done automatically. A redesigned doughnut "icer" dips finished pastries into a puddle of chocolate frosting; employees had to dunk the doughnuts two at a time—by hand—before the machine was invented. Although these innovations may seem minute, across almost 600 stores worldwide that make billions of doughnuts, the seemingly small changes total significant gains in productivity—and more satisfied customers. Clearly, Krispy Kreme has developed a niche in the fast food industry, commanding a premium price for its superior products; it is pursuing a focused strategy (as discussed later) which resulted in a soaring stock price in 2011.

Figure 5.3 Competitive Positioning at the Business Level

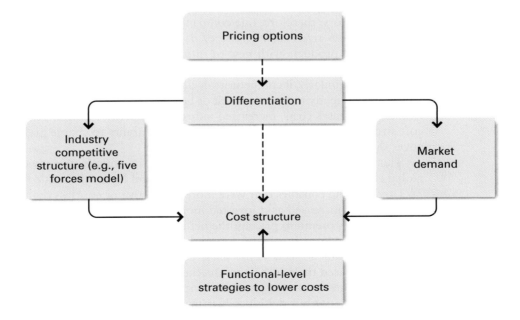

including strategies to improve product quality, support a higher level of service, or increase innovation increase operating costs. Therefore, the decision to increase product differentiation also increases a company's cost structure and results in a higher unit cost. (In some cases, if increased demand for the product allows a company to manufacture large volumes of the product and achieve economies of scale, these economies can offset some of these extra costs; this effect is indicated by the dashed line in Figure 5.3.)

To maximize profitability, managers must choose a premium pricing option that compensates for the extra costs of product differentiation, but which is not so high that it inhibits the increase in expected demand (to prevent customers from deciding that the extra differentiation is not worth the higher price). Once again, to increase profitability, managers must search for additional ways to reduce the cost structure, but not harm the differentiated appeal of its products. There are many specific functional strategies a company can adopt to achieve this. For example, Nordstrom, the luxury department store retailer, differentiates itself in the retail clothing industry by providing a high-quality shopping experience with elegant store operations and a high level of customer service—all of which raise Nordstrom's cost structure. However, Nordstrom can still lower its cost structure by, for example, managing its inventories efficiently and increasing inventory turnover. Also, Nordstrom's employees are highly responsive to customers, which results in higher demand and more customers, which means that sales per square foot increase. This revenue enables the company to make more efficient use of its facilities and salespeople, which leads to scale economies and lower costs. Thus, no matter at what level of differentiation a company chooses to pursue in its business model, the company must always recognize how its cost structure will vary as a result of its differentiation choice, and additional specific strategies it adopts to lower its cost structure. In other words, *differentiation and cost structure decisions affect one another.*

A last main issue shown in Figure 5.3 concerns the impact of the industry's competitive structure on a company's differentiation, cost structure, and pricing choices. Recall that strategies are developed in an industry environment full of watchful and agile competitors; therefore, one company's choice of competitive positioning is always made *with reference to those of its competitors.* If, for example, competitors begin to offer products with new or improved features, a company may be forced to increase its level of differentiation to remain competitive, even if this reduces its profitability. Similarly, if competitors decide to develop products for new market segments, the company must follow suit or become uncompetitive. Thus, because differentiation increases costs, increasing industry competition can increase a company's cost structure. When that happens, a company's ability to charge premium prices to cover these high costs may fall.

This is what happened to Sony when it lost its competitive advantage as other global electronics companies, such as Samsung and Nintendo, made flat screen LCD TVs and gaming consoles that were more innovative or cost less than Sony's. Sony's cost structure increased as it invested more resources to compete, but it was unable to maintain its premium pricing; the net result was that it became unprofitable. Of course, Sony's competitors experienced the opposite situation because although their innovative products, such as 3D flatscreen TVs, smartphones, and the Wii gaming console, increased their cost structure, the technological lead they obtained allowed them to charge customers premium prices, which has made these companies the most profitable within these product markets. This is why competitive advantage can change so quickly in an industry, and why it is vital to make the right product positioning choices. In sum, maximizing the profitability of a company's business model is about making the right choices with regard to value creation through differentiation, cost structure, and pricing, given the level of customer demand for its particular product and overall competitive conditions in the industry.

Competitive Positioning: Generic Business-Level Strategies

As we previously discussed, a successful business model is the result of how a company formulates and implements a set of strategies to achieve appropriate differentiation, cost, and pricing options. Although no diagram could encompass all the complexities involved in business-level strategy decisions, Figure 5.4 represents a way to bring together the three factors involved when developing a successful business model. In the figure, the vertical and horizontal axes represent the decisions of strategic managers to position a company's products with respect to the tradeoff between differentiating products (higher costs/higher prices), and achieving the lowest cost structure or cost leadership (lower costs/lower prices). The curve connecting these axes represents the value creation frontier, that is, the maximum amount of value that the products of different companies within an industry can

Figure 5.4 Competitive Positioning and the Value Creation Frontier

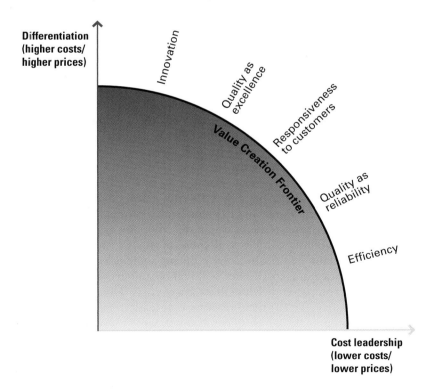

provide to customers at any one time using the different business models. Companies on the value creation frontier are those that have built and maintained the most successful business models in a particular industry over time—they have a competitive advantage and above average profitability.

As Figure 5.4 illustrates, the value creation frontier is reached by pursuing one or more of the four building blocks of competitive advantage (quality has been split into its two components), which are listed from top to bottom according to how much they can contribute to the creation of a differentiation or cost-leadership advantage. Innovation, a costly process that results in unique products, is nearest the differentiation axis, followed by quality as excellence, customer responsiveness, and quality as reliability; efficiency, with its focus on lowering the cost structure, is closest to the cost-leadership axis.

To reach the value creation frontier and achieve above-average profitability, a company must formulate and implement a business model based on one, or a combination of, three generic business-level strategies: cost leadership, differentiation, and focused. A **generic business-level strategy** gives a company a specific form of competitive position and advantage in relation to its rivals, which results in above-average profitability.[7] *Generic* means that all companies can potentially pursue these strategies regardless of whether they are manufacturing, service, or nonprofit enterprises; they are also generic because they can be pursued across different kinds of industries.[8]

Cost Leadership

A company pursuing a **cost-leadership** business model chooses strategies that do everything possible to lower its cost structure so that the company can make and sell goods or services at a lower cost than its competitors. These strategies include functional strategies designed to improve its operating performance, and competitive strategies intended to influence industry competition in its favor. Using the cost-leadership model, a company will seek to achieve a competitive advantage and above-average profitability by developing a model that positions it on the value creation frontier as close as possible to the lower costs/lower prices axis.

Two advantages accrue to a company pursuing cost leadership. First, because the company has lower costs, it will be more profitable than its closest competitors—the companies that compete for the same set of customers and charge similarly low prices for their products. Second, the cost leader gains a competitive advantage because it is able to charge a *lower price* than its competitors due to lower cost structure. Offering customers the same kind of value from a product at a lower price than another attracts many more customers; even if the company has chosen a lower price option, the increased volume of sales will cause profits to surge. If the company's competitors try to reclaim lost business by reducing their prices, and all companies start to compete on price, the cost leader will still be able to withstand competition better than the other companies because of its lower costs. The cost leader is likely to win any competitive struggle. For these reasons, cost leaders are likely to earn above-average profits. A company becomes a cost leader when its strategic managers make the competitive positioning decisions discussed next.

Competitive Positioning Decisions The cost leader chooses a low-to-moderate level of product differentiation relative to its competitors. Differentiation is expensive; the more a company spends resources to make its products distinctive, the more its

Generic business-level strategy

A strategy that gives a company a specific form of competitive position and advantage vis-à-vis its rivals that results in above-average profitability.

Cost-leadership

A business model that pursues strategies that work to lower its cost structure so it can make and sell products at a lower cost than its competitors.

costs rise.[9] The cost leader aims for a "sufficient" level of differentiation obtainable at low cost.[10] Walmart, for example, does not spend hundreds of millions of dollars on store design to create an attractive shopping experience like chains such as Macy's, Dillard's, or Nordstrom's. As Walmart explains in its mission statement: "We think of ourselves as buyers for our customers, and we apply our considerable strengths to get the best value for you." Such value is not obtained by building lavish stores.[11] Cost leaders often wait until customers want a feature or service before providing it. For example, a cost leader like Vizio or Phillips is never the first to offer state-of-the-art picture or sound quality; LCD TV capabilities are only increased when it is obvious that customers demand the upgrade—or when competitors begin to offer the feature first.

The cost leader also ignores the many different market segments in an industry. It positions its products to appeal to the "average" customer, while avoiding the high costs of developing and selling a wide range of products tailored to the needs of different market segments. When targeting the average customer, companies aim to provide the smallest number of products that will attract the largest number of customers—something at the heart of Dell's approach to building its PCs, or Walmart's approach to stocking its stores. Although customers may not get exactly the products they want, they are attracted primarily by the cost leader's lower prices.

To implement cost leadership, the overriding goal of the cost leader must be to choose strategies to increase its efficiency and lower its cost structure compared with its rivals. The development of distinctive competencies in manufacturing, materials management, and IT is central to achieving this goal. For example, manufacturing companies that pursue a cost-leadership strategy focus on doing everything they can to continually ride or move down the experience curve to continuously lower cost structure. Achieving a cost-leadership position requires a company to develop skills in flexible manufacturing, adopt efficient materials-management techniques, and do all it can to increase inventory turnover and reduce the cost of goods sold. (Table 4.1 outlined the ways in which a company's functions can be used to increase efficiency.)

Consequently, the primary goal is to reduce the operating costs of the manufacturing and materials-management functions, and to allow the other functions to shape their distinctive competencies and help achieve this. The sales function, for example, may focus on capturing large, stable sets of customer orders so that manufacturing can make longer production runs and obtain economies of scale that reduce costs. Similarly, Dell provides its online PC customers with a limited set of options to choose from, so that it can provide customized PCs at a low cost.

By contrast, companies supplying services, such as retail stores like Walmart, must develop distinctive competencies in the specific functions that contribute most to their cost structure. For Walmart, this is the cost of purchasing products, so the logistics or materials-management function becomes most important for reducing product costs. Walmart continually takes advantage of advances in IT to lower the costs associated with transferring products from manufacturers to customers, just as Dell, the cost leader in the PC industry, uses the Internet to lower the cost of selling its computers. Choosing an organizational structure and culture to implement this strategy in the most cost efficient way is another major source of cost savings in pursuing cost leadership. Thus, a low-cost strategy implies minimizing the number of managers in the hierarchy and the rigorous use of budgets to control production and selling costs.

Competitive Advantages and Disadvantages   Porter's Five Forces Model, discussed in Chapter 2, explains why companies that employ each of the business models successfully reach the value creation frontier shown in Figure 5.4 and achieve a competitive advantage and above-average profitability. Recall that the five forces are: threats from competitors, powerful suppliers, powerful buyers, substitute products, and new entrants. The cost leader has an advantage over industry competitors because it has a lower cost structure. Its lower costs also mean that it will be less affected than its competitors by increases in the price of inputs if there are powerful suppliers, and less affected by the lower prices it can charge if powerful buyers exist. Moreover, because cost leadership usually requires a large market share, the cost leader purchases in relatively large quantities, increasing its bargaining power over suppliers, just as Walmart does. If substitute products arrive on the market, the cost leader can reduce its price to compete with the substitute products and retain its market share. Finally, the leader's cost advantage constitutes a barrier to entry because other companies are unable to enter the industry and match the leader's low costs or prices. The cost leader is, therefore, in a relatively safe position as long as it can maintain its low-cost advantage.

The principal dangers of the cost-leadership approach arise when competitors are able to develop new strategies that lower their cost structure and beat the cost leader at its own game. For instance, if technological change makes experience-curve economies obsolete, new companies may apply lower-cost technologies that give them a cost advantage. The steel mini-mills discussed in Chapter 4 pursued this strategy to obtain a competitive advantage. Competitors may also obtain a cost advantage from labor-cost savings. Global competitors located in countries overseas often have very low labor costs; wage costs in the United States are roughly 600% more than they are in Malaysia, China, or Mexico. Most United States companies now assemble their products abroad as part of their low-cost strategy; many are forced to outsource simply to compete and stay in business.

Competitors' ability to easily imitate the cost leader's methods is another threat to the cost-leadership strategy. For example, companies in China routinely disassemble the electronic products of Japanese companies, such as Sony and Panasonic, to see how they are designed and assembled. Then, using inexpensive Chinese-made components and domestic labor, they manufacture clones of these products and flood the U.S. market with lower-priced items, including flatscreen TVs, laptops, and mobile phones.

Finally, a danger arises if a strategic manager's single-minded desire to reduce costs (in order to remain the cost leader) results in decisions that might lower costs, but also drastically reduces demand for its products because customers either do not like the new products, or experience poor customer service. In 2011, for example, Research In Motion's new BlackBerry smartphones and tablet computers were not well-received by its loyal users, and as sales fell, stock value also plunged.

Focused Cost Leadership

focused cost leadership

A business model based on using cost leadership to compete for customers by offering low-priced products to only one, or a few, market segments.

A cost leader is not always a large, national company that targets the average customer. Sometimes a company can pursue a **focused cost leadership** business model based on combining the cost leadership and focused business-level strategies to compete for customers in just one, or a few, market segments. Focused cost leaders concentrate on a narrow market segment, which may be defined geographically, by type of customer, or by segment of the product line.[12] In Figure 5.5, focused cost

Figure 5.5 Generic Business Models and the Value Creation Frontier

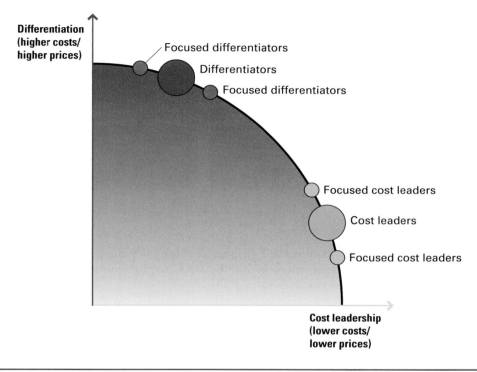

leaders are shown as the smaller circles next to the cost leader's circle. For example, because a geographic niche can be defined by region or even by locality, a cement-making company, a carpet-cleaning business, or a pizza chain could pursue a cost-leadership strategy in one or more cities in a region. Figure 5.6 compares a focused cost-leadership business model with a pure cost-leadership model.

If a company uses a focused cost-leadership approach, it competes against the cost leader in the market segments where it can operate at no cost disadvantage. For example, in local lumber, cement, bookkeeping, or pizza delivery markets, the focuser may have lower materials or transportation costs than the national cost leader. The focuser may also have a cost advantage because it is producing complex or custom-built products that do not lend themselves easily to economies of scale in production, and, therefore, offer few cost-saving possibilities. The focused cost leader concentrates on small-volume custom products, for which it has a cost advantage, and leaves the large-volume standardized market to the national cost leader—for example, low-priced Mexican food specials versus Big Macs.

Because it has no cost disadvantage in its market segments, a focused cost leader also operates on the value creation frontier, and therefore earns above-average profits. Such a company has great opportunity to enlarge its market segment and compete against companies pursuing cost-leadership or differentiated strategies. Ryanair, for example, was the first focused low-cost airline in Europe, and began by offering low-priced flights only between Dublin and London. Because no other airline company was a cost leader in the European market, Ryanair was able to rapidly expand

Figure 5.6 Why Focus Strategies are Different

	Offers products to only one group of customers	Offers products to many kinds of customers
Offers low-priced products to customers	Focused cost-leadership strategy	Cost-leadership strategy
Offers unique or distinctive products to customers	Focused differentiation strategy	Differentiation strategy

© Cengage Learning 2013

its operations, and in 2011, it is the European cost leader. Similarly, Southwest Airlines began as a focused cost leader within the Texas market, but today is a leading U.S. airline company, as we discuss later in this chapter.

Because a focused company makes and sells only a relatively small quantity of a product, its cost structure will often be higher than that of the cost leader. In some industries, such as automotive, this can make it very difficult—or impossible—to compete with the cost leader. Sometimes, however, targeting a new market segment, or implementing a business model in a superior way—such as adopting a more advanced technology—focused companies can become a threat to large cost leaders. For example, flexible manufacturing systems have opened up many new opportunities for focused companies because small production runs become possible at a lower cost. The steel mini-mills discussed in Chapter 4 provide another appropriate example of how a focused company, in this case Nucor, specializes in one market can grow so efficiently that it becomes *the* cost leader. Similarly, the growth of the Internet has opened up many new opportunities for focused companies to develop business models based on positioning as the cost leader compared to bricks-and-mortar companies. The success of Amazon.com shows how a company can effectively craft and implement a business model to become the cost leader. First Global Xpress, discussed in Strategy in Action 5.2, is an interesting example of how a company can create a business model to become the focused cost leader in an industry.

Implications and Conclusions To pursue cost leadership, strategic managers need to devote enormous efforts toward incorporating all the latest information, materials management, and manufacturing technology into their operations, in order to find new ways to reduce costs. Often, as discussed in Chapter 4, using new technology will also increase product quality and responsiveness to customers. A low-cost approach requires ongoing strategic thinking to ensure the business model is aligned with changing environmental opportunities and threats.

Strategic managers in companies throughout their industry observe the cost leader, and will move quickly to imitate its innovations; they also want to reduce their company's costs. Today, a differentiator cannot allow a cost leader to gain too great a cost advantage; the leader might then be able to use its high profits to invest

STRATEGY IN ACTION

First Global Xpress Delivers Packages Faster, Cheaper, and Greener

First Global Xpress (FGX) is a small, $10 million global package shipping company. FGX claims it can ship packages from the 12 largest U.S. cities on the East Coast anywhere around the globe 24 hours faster and more reliably (its package loss rate is 1% compared to the industry average, over 8%) than large competitors such as FedEx and UPS. Also, FGX claims it can ship its customers' packages at a 20% lower cost than its large rivals, and ship them in a "greener way" because it uses less fuel oil, noting 30% savings in CO_2 emissions. How has FGX become so efficient?

First, large shipping companies like FedEx and DHL rely on a "hub-and-spoke" package distribution system; no matter where a package is collected, and no matter its destination, it must pass through a central hub first. At the central hub, packages from all over the United States are sorted for shipment to their final destination. This means that a customer's shipment, for example, from New York to London, must take two different flights—one flight to arrive at a hub, in this case Memphis, Tennessee, and another flight to arrive at its final destination, England. FGX does not own any aircraft; it has been rapidly forming alliances with over 100 different global airlines that can ship

its customers' packages directly from city to city—from New York to London, for example—which saves time and money. Commercial airlines do charge a fee for this service, but when demand for global air travel is declining and fuel costs are rising, forming an alliance with FGX is profitable for these airline companies. As a result, airlines such as United Continental Airlines, Virgin Atlantic, and Airfrance are willing to work closely with FGX to ensure that packages are shipped directly and reliably to their destination cities. Because FGX partners with airlines that use direct flights, FGX can also claim that it is providing services "in a more socially responsible, greener way."

FGX hopes to quickly grow and offer its shipping services from U.S. cities such as Chicago, Houston, and Los Angeles in the future. Its CEO, Justin Brown, claims: "Over the next 5 years FGX plans to keep growing, replicating its model for clients worldwide. Every day, FGX offers you the chance to save money, cut time off of your deliveries, and reduce your carbon footprint—all through the simple solution of shipping direct." Keeping its value chain operations lean and efficient so that it can continue to pursue its low-cost strategy is the challenge facing FGX managers.

Sources: www.fgx.com; Company Overview, 2011.

more in product differentiation and beat the differentiator at its own competitive game. Toyota and Honda, for example, both began as focused cost leaders, manufacturing reliable low-priced vehicles. Cars sold well at both companies, and they each then reinvested profits to design and manufacture new car models that increasingly became differentiated in features and quality. Today, Toyota and Honda, with cars in every market segment, pursue a differentiation strategy, although Toyota still has the lowest cost structure of any carmaker worldwide.

A cost leader must also imitate the strategic moves of its differentiated competitors, and increase the quality and features of its products when they do, to prosper in the long run. Low-priced products, such as Timex watches and BIC razors, cannot be too inferior to the more expensive Seiko watches or Gillette razors if the lower costs/ lower prices model is to succeed. Companies in an industry observe the strategies (and changes to those strategies) that their rivals are pursuing. So, for example, if Seiko or Swatch introduce a new type of LCD watch dial, or Gillette begins to make a 3- or 4-bladed razor, managers at Timex and BIC will respond within months by incorporating these innovations in their low-priced products, if required. This type of situation is also very common in the high-priced women's fashion industry. When famous designers, such as Gucci and Dior, have unveiled their spring and fall collections, their designs are copied and the plans are transmitted to factories in Malaysia. There, workers are ready to manufacture low-priced imitations that will reach low-price clothing retail stores around the world within months.

Differentiation

A company pursuing a **differentiation** business model pursues business-level strategies that allow it to create a unique product—one that customers perceive as different or distinct in some important way. A differentiator (i.e., a differentiated company) gains a competitive advantage because it has the ability to satisfy customers' needs in a way that its competitors cannot, which, in turn, allows it to charge a premium price for its product. The ability to increase revenues by charging premium prices (rather than by reducing costs, as the cost leader does) allows the differentiator to reach the value frontier, outperform its competitors, and achieve superior profitability, as shown in Figure 5.5. Customers pay a premium price when they believe the product's differentiated qualities are worth the extra money; differentiated products, therefore, are priced as high as customers are willing to pay.

Mercedes-Benz cars are more expensive than the cars of its closest rivals because customers believe they offer more features and confer more status on their owners. Similarly, a BMW is not much more expensive to produce than a Honda, but BMW's higher price is determined by customers who want its distinctive sporty ride and the prestige of owning a BMW. (In fact, in Japan, BMW prices its entry cars quite modestly to attract young, well-heeled Japanese customers from Honda.) Similarly, Rolex watches do not cost much to produce—their design has not changed very much over the years—and their gold content represents only a small fraction of their price. Customers, however, purchase a Rolex because of the distinct qualities they perceive it has: beautiful design, and the ability to hold its value, as well as to confer status upon its wearer.

Competitive Positioning Decisions   A differentiator invests its resources to gain a competitive advantage from superior innovation, excellent quality, and responsiveness to customer needs—the three principal routes to high product differentiation. For example, Procter & Gamble claims that its product quality is high, and that Ivory soap is 99.44% pure. Toyota stresses reliability and the best repair record of any carmaker. IBM promotes the quality service its well-trained sales force provides. Innovation is commonly the source of differentiation for technologically complex products, and many people pay a premium price for new and innovative products, such as a state-of-the-art gaming PC or console, or car.

When differentiation is based on responsiveness to customers, a company offers comprehensive after-sales service and product repair. This is an especially important consideration for complex products such as cars and domestic appliances, which are likely to break down periodically. Dell, Whirlpool, and BMW, for example, all excel in responsiveness to customers. In service organizations, quality-of-service attributes are also very important. Neiman Marcus, Nordstrom, and FedEx can charge premium prices because they offer an exceptionally high level of service. Firms of lawyers, accountants, and consultants stress the service aspects of their operations to clients: their knowledge, professionalism, and reputation.

Finally, a product's appeal to customers' psychological desires is a source of differentiation. The appeal can be prestige or status, as it is with Rolls-Royce cars and Rolex watches; safety of home and family, as with Aetna or Prudential Insurance; or providing a superior shopping experience, as with Target and Macy's. Differentiation can also be tailored to age groups and socioeconomic groups; differentiation can be based on an endless list of demographics.

Differentiation

A business model that pursues business-level strategies that allow it to create a unique product, one that customers perceive as different or distinct in some important way.

A company pursuing a business model based on differentiation pursues strategies to differentiate itself along as many competitive dimensions as possible. The less a company resembles its rivals, the more the company is protected from competition, and the wider is its market appeal. Thus, BMWs offer more than prestige; they also offer technological sophistication, luxury, reliability, and good (although very expensive) repair service. These varied dimensions of differentiation all help to increase sales.

Generally, a differentiator chooses to divide its market into many segments and offer different products in each segment, such as the way that Apple and Toyota do. For example, Apple has several versions of its iPods and laptops at different price points to attract the largest number of customers possible. Strategic managers recognize how much revenues can be increased when each of a company's products, targeted at different market segments, can attract more customers. A differentiator, however, only targets the market segments in which customers are willing to pay a premium price. Apple, for example, produces many laptop models, but it targets only the niches from mid-priced to high-priced; its lowest-priced model is still a few hundred dollars above that of its low-cost competitors such as Acer or Dell.

Finally, in choosing how to implement its business model, a differentiated company concentrates on developing distinctive competencies in the functions that provide the source of its competitive advantage. Differentiation on the basis of innovation and technological competency depends on the R&D function, as discussed in Chapter 4. Efforts to improve service to customers depend upon the quality of the sales and the customer service function.

Pursuing a business model based on differentiation is expensive, so a differentiator has a cost structure that is higher than a cost leader's. Building new competencies in the functions necessary to sustain a company's differentiated appeal does not mean neglecting the cost structure, however. Even differentiators benchmark how cost leaders operate to find ways to imitate their cost-saving innovations while preserving their products' differentiated appeal. A differentiator must control its cost structure to ensure that product prices do not exceed the price customers are willing to pay for them—something that Sony has failed to do. Also, superior profitability is a function of a company's cost structure, so it is important to keep costs under control, but not to reduce costs so much that a company loses the source of its differentiated appeal.[13] The owners of the famous Savoy Hotel in London, England, faced this problem. The Savoy's reputation has always been based upon the incredibly high level of service it offers its customers. Three hotel employees serve the needs of each guest, and in every room, a guest can summon a waiter, maid, or valet by pressing a button at bedside. The cost of offering this level of service is so exorbitant, that the hotel makes less than 1% net profit every year, despite the fact that each room costs at least $500 a night![14] Its owners attempt to find ways to reduce costs and increase profits, but if the number of hotel staff (the main source of the Savoy's high costs), is reduced, the hotel's main source of differentiated appeal will be destroyed.

Competitive Advantages and Disadvantages Porter's Five Forces Model explains the reason why the differentiation business model also allows a company to obtain a competitive advantage and reach the value creation frontier. Differentiation protects a company from competitors when customers develop brand loyalty for its products—the valuable asset that allows the company to charge a premium price. Because the differentiated company's strategy is directed toward the premium price it can charge (rather than toward costs), powerful suppliers become less of a problem, especially as differentiators can often pass along price increases to loyal customers. Thus, a differentiator can tolerate moderate increases in input prices better than the cost leader can. Differentiators are unlikely to experience problems with powerful buyers because they offer a distinctive product that commands brand loyalty—and only they can supply that product. Differentiation and brand loyalty also create a barrier to entry for other companies seeking to enter the industry. A new company must find a way to make its product distinctive enough to be able to compete, which involves an expensive investment in building some type of distinctive competence. Finally, substitute products are only a threat if a competitor can develop a product that satisfies a customer need similar to the need met by the differentiator's product, causing customers to switch to the new product. This can happen; wired phone companies have suffered as mobile phone companies offer an attractive wireless product. In addition, lower-cost alternative ways of making phone calls through PCs and the Internet have increasingly become popular.

The major problems with a differentiation strategy are related to how well strategic managers can maintain a product's perceived difference or distinctness to customers and still maintain premium pricing. In the 2000s, it was easier than ever for agile competitors to imitate and copy successful differentiators. This has happened across many industries, such as retailing, computers, cars, home electronics, telecommunications, and pharmaceuticals. Patents and first-mover advantages (the advantages of being the first company to market a product or service) last only so long, and as the overall quality of competing products increases, brand loyalty and prices decline. The way in which Apple continues to grow its differentiation advantage in the mobile computing and entertainment industry is profiled in Strategy in Action 5.3.

Implications and Conclusions   A business model based on differentiation requires a company to make strategic choices that reinforce one another, and together increase the value of a good or service in the eyes of customers. When a product has distinctness, differentiators can charge a premium price. The disadvantages of pursuing differentiation are the ease with which competitors can imitate a differentiator's product, and the difficulty of maintaining a premium price. When differentiation stems from the design or physical features of the product, differentiators are at great risk because imitation is easy; over time, products such as LCD TVs and smartphones become commodity-like products, and customers become increasingly price sensitive. However, when differentiation stems from functional-level strategies that lead to superior service or reliability, or from any intangible source, such as FedEx's guarantee or the prestige of a Rolex, a company is much more secure within the marketplace. It is difficult to imitate intangible products, and a differentiator can often reap the benefits of premium prices for an indefinite period of time. Nevertheless, all differentiators must be aware of imitators, and be careful not to charge a premium price that is higher than customers are willing to pay.

Focused differentiation

A business model based on using differentiation to focus on competing customers by making unique to customized products for only one, or a few, market segments.

Focused Differentiation

A company that pursues a business model based on **focused differentiation** chooses to combine the differentiation and focused, generic business-level strategies, to specialize in making distinctive products for 1 or 2 market segments. All the means of differentiation that are open to the differentiator are also available to the focused differentiator. The focused company will develop a business model that allows it to successfully position itself to compete with the differentiator in just one, or a few,

STRATEGY IN ACTION

Apple's Growing Differentiation Advantage

Steve Jobs, Apple's longtime CEO, has always been obsessed with developing state-of-the-art products that are powerful, elegant, and easy to use. In the early 1990s, Jobs was forced out of Apple because its directors believed he lacked the desire and skills necessary to develop and manufacture low-cost, inexpensive PCs, and, therefore, challenge Michael Dell's cost leadership strategy.

After leaving Apple, Jobs used his wealth to begin new ventures such as NeXT, a company that would develop the most powerful PCs in the world; and Pixar, a computer animation company that became a huge success after making blockbuster movies such as *Toy Story* and *Finding Nemo*. At NeXT and Pixar, Jobs perceived his main role to be managing the future product development strategies of both these companies, to create a stream of innovative products.

Meanwhile, Apple was struggling to compete against Dell's low-cost PCs, its performance was plummeting, and its future looked doubtful. Apple's directors, realizing that Jobs' commitment to differentiation was now its only chance of survival, asked Jobs to resume as CEO at Apple. In 1996, Jobs agreed—providing Apple would purchase NeXT for $400 million, and use its powerful operating system and software as the basis of a new line of innovative Apple Mac PCs.

Upon becoming CEO in 1997, Jobs' first step was to create a clear vision and set of goals to energize Apple employees to develop state-of-the art, stylish PCs and related digital equipment. Jobs shifted Apple's strategy to focused differentiation—it would now only compete in the super-premium PC market niche. He created a team structure that allowed programmers and engineers to pool their skills and develop new PCs, using the NeXT technology. A wide range of futuristic, PC-related products, including laptops and printers, quickly followed Apple's sleek new line of iMac PCs , and Apple's sales began to rapidly increase.

Jobs investigated new opportunities using the R&D and engineering competencies of its employees to develop new kinds of differentiated products. Pixar had exposed Jobs to the potential of digital entertainment products, and he realized that digital MP3 music players would be a perfect extension to Apple's product line. These players made Apple's PCs more valuable; they were now machines that could run programs, and serve as a device upon which users could store their huge music libraries. In 2003, Apple introduced its iPod music player, and

at the same time, it announced its own new online music store called "iTunes," from which people could download songs for $0.99 each. The iPod was a spectacular success, and over the years, Jobs has kept his designers continuously focused on developing new generations of the iPod. Apple's differentiation advantage increased as its new models became more compact, more powerful, and more versatile than previous models. By 2006, Apple had gained control of 70% of the digital music player market and 80% of the online music download business—and its stock price soared to a new record level.

The next milestone in Jobs' attempt to build Apple's differentiation advantage came in 2007, when he announced Apple had used its competencies to develop a revolutionary new smartphone, the "iPhone," to directly compete with Nokia and BlackBerry smartphones. Once again, Apple's engineering teams not only developed the new phone's hardware and software, but also built an online iPhone applications platform where users could download iPhone applications and make their phones more useful, such as to engage in social networking. By 2011, over 2 million iPhone applications had been developed, and iPhone users had downloaded over 3 billion applications. Apple is now the smartphone market leader. Once again, Jobs was careful to defend Apple's differentiation advantage by continuously improving the iPhone, for example, new models came out once or twice a year.

Then in 2010, Jobs orchestrated another coup when he announced that Apple would introduce a new advanced tablet computer, the "iPad," which he claimed would revolutionize the way users interacted with the WWW, e-mail, photos, and videos, and which would also have a wireless reading application to compete directly against Amazon.com's successful Kindle wireless reader. After the iPad was released customers swarmed to buy it, and following his differentiation strategy, when the iPad2 was launched in 2011, every other electronics company was rushing to develop their own competing version.

By 2011, Apple's stock had soared to over $400 per share as its product teams continuously unveiled new and improved versions of its iMac, iPod, iPhone, and iPad. In October 2011 the company's stock became the most valuable in the world as a result of Job's successful differentiation strategy—of course how long this will last depends on its ability to sustain its competitive advantage.

segments. For example, Porsche, a focused differentiator, competes against Toyota and BMW, but only in the sports car and luxury SUV segments of the car market.

For the focused differentiator, selecting a market segment means deciding to focus on one type of customer, such as serving only the very rich, the very young, or the very adventurous; or to focus on only one kind of product in a particular market, such as organic or vegetarian foods, very fast cars, luxury designer clothes, or exclusive sunglasses. Focused differentiators reach the value frontier when they have developed a distinctive product that better meets the needs of customers in a particular segment than the differentiator (Figure 5.5). A competitive advantage may result, for example, because a focused differentiator possesses better knowledge (than the differentiator) about the needs of a small customer set (such as sports car buyers), or superior expertise in a particular field (such as corporate law, management consulting, or Website management for retail customers or restaurants). Similarly, a focused differentiator might develop superior skills in responsiveness to customers because of its ability to serve the particular needs of regional or industry customers in ways that would be very expensive for a national differentiator. Finally, concentration on a narrow range of products sometimes allows a focuser to develop innovations more quickly than a large differentiator.

The focuser does not attempt to serve all market segments, because that would bring the company into direct competition with the differentiator. Instead, it concentrates on building market share in one, or a few, market segments; if it is successful, it may begin to serve additional market segments, and incrementally decrease the differentiator's competitive advantage. However, if it is too successful at what it does, or if it does try to compete with the differentiator, it may encounter difficulties because the differentiator has the resources to imitate the focused company's business model. For example, when Ben & Jerry's innovated luxury ice cream, their huge success led other companies like Häagen-Dazs and Godiva to reveal competing products. A good example of the way competition is changing, even among focused differentiators that make a similar luxury product, is the designer clothing company profiled in Strategy in Action 5.4.

In sum, a focused differentiator can protect its competitive advantage in a market segment to the extent that it can provide a good or service that its rivals cannot, for example, by being close to its customers and responding to their changing needs. However, a focused company cannot easily move to another market segment; if its market segment disappears because of technological change or changes in customers' tastes, a major danger is presented. For example, fewer people today want a DVD player—even if the player is a state-of-the-art model—because newer digital technologies, such as those that can download movies directly from the Internet using set-top boxes, are available. Similarly, corner diners have almost become archaic because they are unable to compete with the low prices and speed of service at fast-food chains like McDonald's, or the upscale atmosphere of Starbucks.

The Dynamics of Competitive Positioning

Companies that successfully pursue one of the business models discussed earlier in this chapter are able to outperform their rivals, and reach the value creation frontier. They have developed the business-level strategies that result in competitive advantage and above-average profitability, and are the most successful and well-known companies in their industry. Although some companies are able to develop the business

STRATEGY IN ACTION

Zara Uses IT to Change the World of Fashion

Well-known fashion houses like Chanel, Dior, Gucci, and Armani charge thousands of dollars for the fashionable suits and dresses that they introduce twice yearly, in the fall and spring. Because only the very wealthy can afford such differentiated and expensive clothing, to expand demand for its products, most luxury designers produce less expensive lines of clothing and accessories that are sold in upscale fashion retailers such as Neiman Marcus, Nordstrom, and Saks Fifth Avenue. In the 2000s, however, these luxury designers (which all pursue focused differentiation), were under increasing pressure from small, agile fashion designers, such as England's Jaeger and Laura Ashley, and Spain's Zara, that have developed capabilities in using IT that allow them to pursue a focused differentiation strategy but at a much lower cost than the luxury fashion houses. This has allowed them to circumvent barriers to entry into the high fashion segment and develop well-received brand names that still command a premium price.

Zara, in particular, has achieved significant success. Zara's sales have soared because it created innovative information and materials management systems to keep its cost structure low, while reducing time to market.

The result is that Zara can produce fashionable clothes at lower prices, and sell them quickly by making them available in its own chain of clothing stores. Major fashion houses, like Dior and Gucci, can take 6 or more months to design their collections, and 3–6 more months before their moderately priced lines become available in upscale retailers. Zara's designers closely watch the trends in the high-fashion industry, and the kinds of innovations that the major houses are introducing. Then, using sophisticated IT that links Zara's designers to its suppliers and clothing manufacturers abroad, the company can create a new collection in only 5 weeks, and these clothes can then be made in 1 week and delivered to stores soon thereafter. This short time to market makes Zara very flexible, and allows it to compete effectively in the rapidly changing fashion market, where customer tastes quickly evolve.

Because of the quick manufacturing-to-sales cycle and just-in-time fashion, Zara has been able to offer its collections at comparatively low prices and still make profits that are the envy of the fashion clothing industry. In 2011, its global stores were still rapidly increasing in number, and its profits and stock price rising accordingly.

Source: C. Vitzthum, "Just-in-Time-Fashion," *Wall Street Journal*, May 18, 2001, p. B1, B4; www.zara.com, 2002–2011.

---

model and the strategies that allow them to reach the value creation frontier, many other companies cannot, and so achieve only average or below-average profitability. For example, the most successful companies in the retail industry, such as Neiman Marcus, Target, and Walmart, have reached the value frontier; but their competitors, Saks, JCPenney, and Sears/Kmart have not.

Additionally, few companies are able to continuously outperform their rivals and remain on the value frontier over time. For example, high-performing companies such as Sony and Dell that were on the frontier a few years ago have lost their competitive advantage to rivals such as Samsung, Apple, and HP. Companies, such as Honda, Walmart, and Apple, that have maintained their position on the frontier are rare. Why is it so hard for companies to sustain their competitive advantage over time and remain on the frontier?

To understand why some companies perform better than others, and why the performance of one company can increase or decrease over time, it is necessary to understand the dynamics involved in successfully positioning a company's business model so that it can compete in an industry. In this section, we first explore another business model that helps explain why some companies are able to sustain and increase their competitive advantage over time. Second, we examine how the business model a company pursues places it in a strategic group composed of other companies that compete in a similar way, and how the model has a major affect on a company's profitability over time. Finally, we examine some competitive dynamics that explain why companies encounter major problems that can affect their success.

Competitive Positioning for Superior Performance: Broad Differentiation

Companies that pursue cost leadership pursue a different business model and different strategies than companies that choose differentiation, yet each business model is a path to superior performance and profitability. As we emphasize throughout this chapter, regardless of the business model a company pursues, it must control its cost structure if it is to maintain and increase its profitability; at the same time, it also must find ways to differentiate its product in some way to attract customers. This is particularly important in today's marketplace because intense global competition from companies abroad, and rapid technological changes that allow competitors to develop strategies provide companies with some type of superior differentiation or cost advantage. In this dynamic situation, a company that can *combine* the strategies necessary to successfully pursue both cost leadership *and* differentiation will develop the most competitive and profitable business model in its industry.

Today, the most successful companies in an industry are often the companies that have developed strategies for achievement; these companies are the most profitable because they can offer customers quality products at reasonable prices, that is, they offer customers a superior "value proposition" compared to their rivals.

Broad differentiators—occupy the middle segment of the value-creation frontier, that is, companies that have developed business-level strategies to better differentiate their products and lower their cost structures *simultaneously*. Broad differentiators operate on the value frontier because they have chosen a level of differentiation that gives them a competitive advantage in the market segments they have targeted, and they have achieved this *in a way that has allowed them to lower their cost structure over time* (see Figure 5.7). Thus, although they may have higher costs than cost leaders, and offer a less differentiated product than differentiators, they have found a competitive position that offers their customers more value than industry rivals. Broad differentiators continually use their distinctive competencies to increase their product range, and they search for new market segments to enter to increase their market share and profits. At the same time, they work continuously to find ways to lower their cost structure and increase their profitability. For example, companies such as Apple, Amazon.com, and eBay have used the Internet as a way to become broad differentiators. These companies have been rapidly expanding the range of products they offer customers, and taking advantage of their highly efficient information and/or materials-management systems to decrease costs compared to bricks-and-mortar retailers.

Importantly, broad differentiators that have developed the business-level strategies that enable them to reach this highly profitable position become an increasing threat to both differentiators and cost leaders over time. These companies make differentiated products so that they can charge higher prices than the cost leader, but they can also charge lower (but still premium) prices than differentiators because their cost structures are lower. The result is that many customers perceive the value of the products offered by the broad differentiator as worth the higher price compared with the cost leader. At the same time, customers who are reluctant to pay the

Broad differentiators

Companies that have developed business-level strategies to better differentiate their products and lower their cost structures simultaneously to offer customers the most value.

Figure 5.7 The Broad Differentiation Business Model

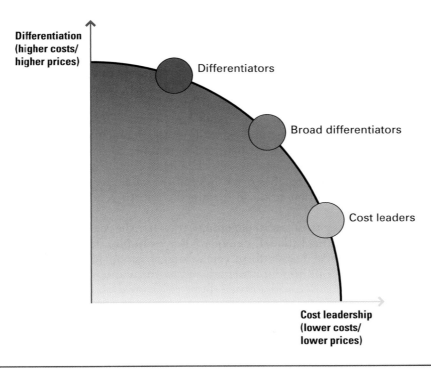

© Cengage Learning 2013

high premium prices of a differentiator's products decide that the lower price of the broad differentiator's product more than makes up for the loss of the "extra" differentiated features of the luxury premium-priced products. In other words, customers choose LCD TVs from Samsung (a broad differentiator) over Vizio (a cost leader) or Sony (a differentiator); or a bottle of Pantene shampoo from Procter & Gamble (a broad differentiator) over a bottle from Estée Lauder (a differentiator) or Walmart (a cost leader).

As a result, if strategic managers have the skills to pursue this business model successfully, broad differentiators steadily increase their market share and profitability over time. This provides them with more capital to reinvest in their business to continually improve their business model. For example, their growing profits allow broad differentiators to invest in new technology that both increases their differentiation advantage and lowers their cost structure, which weakens the competitive position of their rivals. As they build their competitive advantage and become able to offer customers a better value proposition, they push the value creation frontier to the right and knock their competitors off the frontier, so they become less profitable.

Competitive Positioning and Strategic Groups

New developments such as: (1) technological innovations that permit increased product differentiation; (2) the identification of new customer groups and market segments; and (3) the discovery of superior ways to lower cost structure, continually change the competitive forces at work in an industry. In such a dynamic situation, the competitive position of companies can rapidly change. Higher performing companies are able to gain if they can position themselves competitively to pursue broad differentiation. Poorer performing companies often do not realize how fast their competitive position is deteriorating because of their rivals' strategies, and sometimes discover it is too late to rebuild their business models. Strategic group analysis, which we discussed in Chapter 2, is a tool that managers can use to better understand the dynamics of competitive positioning, in order to change their business models and maintain above-average profitability.

A company's business model determines how it will compete for customers in one or more market segments, and typically several companies compete for the same group of customers. This means that, over time, companies competing for the same customer group become rivals locked in a competitive struggle. The goal is to be the company that reaches or pushes out the value frontier by pursuing the business-level strategies that result in sustained competitive advantage and above average profitability.

Within most industries, **strategic groups**, that is, the set of companies that pursue a similar business model, emerge.[15] For example, those companies that compete to be the cost leader form one strategic group in an industry, those that seek some form of differentiation advantage form another group, and those companies that have developed a broad differentiation strategy form yet another. Companies pursuing focused differentiation or focused cost leadership also form strategic groups.

The concept of strategic groups has several implications for competitive positioning. First, strategic managers must map their competitors according to their choice of specific business model, for example, cost leadership and focused cost leadership. The managers must identify the differences among the specific set of strategies each company uses to pursue the same business model to explain their differences in profitability. How has one company better identified which particular customer needs to satisfy or customer groups to serve? How has the company worked to develop a particular distinctive competence? Strategic managers can then use the knowledge gleaned from questions such as these to better position their business model and become closer to customers, differentiate themselves from their competitors, or learn how to reduce costs. Careful strategic-group analysis allows managers to uncover the most important ways to compete for customers in one or more market segments, and this analysis also helps to reveal what strategies are needed in the future to maintain a competitive advantage.

Second, once a company has mapped its rivals, it can better understand how changes taking place in the industry are affecting its competitive advantage from a differentiation and cost-structure perspective. The company can also identify opportunities and threats. Often a company's nearest rivals are the competitors in its strategic group that are pursuing a similar business model. Customers tend to view the products of such companies as direct substitutes for one another. Thus, a major threat to a company's profitability can arise from within its own strategic group when its rivals find ways to improve product differentiation and get closer to customers, or lower their cost structure. This is why companies today benchmark their closest competitors on major performance dimensions to determine if they are falling behind in some important aspect. For example, UPS and FedEx are constantly examining one another's performance.

Strategic groups

The set of companies that pursue a similar business model and compete for the same group of customers.

In sum, strategic-group analysis involves identifying and charting the business models and business-level strategies that industry rivals are pursuing. Managers can then determine which strategies are successful or unsuccessful, and why a particular business model is or is not working. Importantly, managers can also analyze how the relative competitive position of industry rivals (both those pursuing the same business model and those pursuing different business models), is changing over time. This knowledge allows managers to either fine-tune or radically alter their business models and strategies to improve their competitive position and reach or remain on the value frontier.

Failures in Competitive Positioning

Successful competitive positioning requires that a company achieve a fit between its strategies and its business model. Thus, a cost leader cannot strive for high-level market segmentation and provide a wide range of products as a differentiator does, because this strategy would increase its cost structure too much, causing the company to lose its low-cost advantage. Similarly, a differentiator with a competency in innovation that tries to reduce its R&D costs, or a differentiator with a competency in after-sales service that seeks to economize on its sales force to lower costs, is placing the company in a risky position by using the wrong strategies to implement its business model.

To pursue a successful business model, managers must be careful to ensure that the set of business-level strategies they have formulated and implemented are working in harmony to support each other, and do not result in conflicts that ruin the competitive position a company is aiming for through its choice of business model. Many companies, through neglect, ignorance, or error—perhaps because of the Icarus paradox discussed in Chapter 3—do not work to continuously improve their business model, do not perform strategic-group analysis, and often fail to identify and respond to changing opportunities and threats in the industry environment. As a result, a company's business model begins to fail because its business-level strategies do not work together, and its profitability starts to decline. This happened to Sony when competitors such as Samsung, Apple, and Panasonic began to use outsourcing to lower their cost structures in order to offer customers lower priced products. By pursuing its differentiation strategy, Sony spent billions to develop innovative products that when introduced, had already been surpassed by those of Apple or Samsung. Sony lost its competitive position, its performance rapidly declined, and it became unprofitable. If a company cannot recover quickly, it may be taken over by its competitors or go bankrupt—in 2011, many analysts were forecasting that both Nokia and Research In Motion might soon experience a similar outcome.

These companies lost their position on the value frontier, either because they have lost the source of their competitive advantage, or because their rivals have found ways to push out the value creation frontier and leave them behind. Sometimes these companies initially pursued a successful cost-leadership or differentiation business model, but then gradually began to pursue business-level strategies that worked against them. Unfortunately, it seems that most companies lose control of their business models over time, often because they become large, complex companies that are difficult to manage, or because the environment is changing faster than they can change their business model. Adjusting product and market strategies to

FOCUS ON D∅LL

How Dell is Changing its Business-level Strategies to Create Value for Customers

In 2005, Dell had a market value of over $100 billion, more than HP and Apple combined; but by 2011, its value had dropped to $30 billion, while Apple's was $300 billion, and HP's was $75 billion![16] Why? Dell's value chain management practices failed in the 2000s primarily because it lost its focus on the customer, and its managers could not innovate the kinds of PCs and mobile computing devices that customers desired. Dell became the leading global PC manufacturer because its mastery in both materials management and supply chain management allowed it to obtain computer components, assemble them into final products, and sell them to customers far more efficiently than its competitors. At its peak, for example, Dell had a 20% cost advantage over HP and Apple because it assembled its computers at low-cost locations around the globe. It also instructed its suppliers to station parts warehouses next to its factories to take advantage of "just-in-time" inventory systems, which lowered its production costs.

Dell was able to achieve this enormous efficiency advantage only by sacrificing its ability to customize its PCs to customers' needs—that is, to be flexible in meeting their needs. Just as Henry Ford told customers they could have any Model T car color they wanted "as long as it is black," Dell's computers were uniformly a color such as beige or black because standardization is an important way for costs to remain low. At the same time, standardization increases quality and reliability because workers become experts at assembling a product when they continuously perform the same work tasks, such as assembling the same set of PC components into the final product. Customers were happy to purchase Dell's products because they were much less expensive than those of its rivals; recall from Chapter 1 that Dell also pioneered direct phone sales to sell its computers at rock-bottom prices.

Dell's problems steadily increased in the 2000s because its rival companies learned how to manage their own supply chains, and outsourced PC manufacturing to reduce costs. Unlike Dell, HP and Apple have always made innovation an important component of their value chain management strategies. These companies have consistently spent billions of dollars to innovate new and improved components and products. Although innovation put HP and Apple at a cost disadvantage in the past (because R&D increases total costs), today their competence allows them to satisfy customer needs for more stylish, powerful, versatile PCs and portable digital devices. This has given HP and Apple a competitive

advantage over Dell—hence the dramatic change in the values of these companies during the 2000s.

Michael Dell returned as CEO in 2007, when he realized that his company was quickly losing its competitive advantage because Apple and HP could manage their values chains while being more responsive to customers by offering them innovative, customized products that better satisfied their needs. To help him revive the company, Dell hired a new team of value chain management experts from companies such as IBM, GE, and Motorola. In particular, he hired Ronald Garriques, the former head of Motorola's mobile devices division, who had led the successful launch of the Razr cell phone, to lead Dell's consumer division. Michael Dell realized that participating in the new world of mobile digital computing would be key to Dell's future success; he asked Garriques to develop innovative new lines of desktop, laptop, and mobile digital devices that could successfully compete against those of Apple and HP.

Garriques immediately ended projects he felt would not result in the flexible computing solutions customers wanted, and he formed new teams of engineers, instructing them to design a new generation of innovative computing products. He also began to manage Dell's value chain in order to focus on meeting customer needs, and he demanded that engineers design products that could be increasingly customized. At the same time, Dell could not lose its focus on efficiency; Garriques also changed how it managed its supply chain. By 2011, Dell had closed down all its global and U.S. factories, and had outsourced production to Asian companies. Garriques also decided Dell had to find new ways to distribute its products and it began to sell its PCs to retailers such as Walmart to reach more customers and compete with HP. HP found retail to be a highly profitable distribution strategy despite that it meant lower profit margins.

Dell has since introduced new lines of desktops and laptops, and a tablet computer to compete with Apple. However, in 2011, although its sales and profits had improved, the company still did not meet analysts' projected estimates.[17] Some analysts worried that Dell lacked strong value-chain skills in R&D and marketing to compete with Apple and HP; others believed its low-cost rivals like Acer and Lenovo would be able to offer customers the lowest prices in the future. Whether Dell and his top management team can find ways to develop new competencies in value chain management to regain its competitive advantage and once again become the leading global PC maker remains a question.

suit changing industry conditions may not be enough. This is why it is so important that managers *think strategically*. The way in which Dell became stuck in the middle as it lost its position on the value creation frontier, and how it is trying to recover its competitive advantage is discussed in *Focus on Dell*.

There are many factors that can cause a focused company to make competitive positioning errors. Although some focused companies may spectacularly succeed for a time, a focuser may make a major error if, in its rush to implement its business model, it over expands and loses control of its business model. Differentiators can also fail in the market and end up stuck in the middle if focused competitors attack their markets with more valuable or low-cost products that blunt their competitive edge. This happened to Sony when companies like Apple and Samsung introduced products that better met customer needs. No company is safe in the jungle of competition, and each must constantly be on the lookout to take advantage of new opportunities as they arise.

In sum, strategic managers must employ the tools discussed in this book to continually monitor how well the business-level strategies they use to implement their company's business model are working. There is no more important task than ensuring that their company is optimally positioned against its rivals to compete for customers. And, as we have discussed, the constant changes occurring in the external environment, as well as the actions of competitors who work to develop superior business-level strategies, make competitive positioning a complex, demanding task that requires the highest degree of strategic thinking. That is why companies pay tens of millions of dollars a year to CEOs and other top managers who have demonstrated their ability to create and sustain successful business models.

Ethical Dilemma

left while others have banded together, threatening to leave if their demands aren't met. Consequently, you stand to lose your competitive advantage.

You are a top manager of a small company that has pioneered the development of software that allows Web users to interface online in real time. A major rival recognized the value of your product and offered to buy your company at a price you think is inadequate. When you refused to sell your company, the rival began recruiting your top software engineers to obtain their specialized knowledge. One engineer

Is it ethical for you to apply for a court order preventing engineers from leaving to join your competitor? Is it ethical for your competitor to recruit your employees to obtain their knowledge? Given your answers to these questions, should you allow the differentiator to purchase your company and take over your market niche?

Summary of Chapter

1. To create a successful business model, managers must choose business-level strategies that give the company a competitive advantage over its rivals; that is, they must optimize competitive positioning. They must first decide on: (a) customer needs, or what is to be satisfied; (b) customer groups, or who is to be satisfied; and (c) distinctive competencies, or how customer needs are to be satisfied. These decisions determine which strategies managers formulate and implement to put a company's business model into action.

2. Customer needs are desires, wants, or cravings that can be satisfied through the attributes or characteristics of a product. Customers choose a product based on (a) the way a product is differentiated from other products of its type, and (b) the price of the product. Product differentiation is the process of designing products to satisfy customers' needs in ways that competing products cannot. Companies that create something distinct or different can often charge a higher, or premium, price for their products.

3. If managers devise strategies to differentiate a product by innovation, excellent quality, or responsiveness to customers, they are choosing a business model based on offering customers differentiated products. If managers base their business model on finding ways to reduce costs, they are choosing a business model based on offering customers low-priced products.

4. The second main strategy in formulating a successful business model is to decide what kind of product(s) to offer to which customer group(s). Market segmentation is the way a company decides to group customers, based on important differences in their needs or preferences, to gain a competitive advantage.

5. There are three main approaches toward market segmentation. First, a company might choose to ignore differences and make a product targeted at the average (or typical) customer. Second, a company can choose to recognize the differences between customer groups and make a product targeted toward most or all of the different market segments. Third, a company might choose to target only 1 or 2 market segments.

6. To develop a successful business model, strategic managers must devise a set of strategies that determine (a) how to differentiate and price their product and (b) how much to segment a market and how wide a range of products to develop. Whether these strategies will result in a profitable business model will depend upon a strategic manager's ability to provide customers with the most value while keeping the cost structure viable.

7. The value creation frontier represents the maximum amount of value that the products of different companies inside an industry can give customers at any one time by using different business models. Companies on the value frontier are those that have the most successful business models in a particular industry.

8. The value creation frontier can be reached by choosing among four *generic competitive strategies*: cost leadership, focused cost leadership, differentiation, and focused differentiation.

9. A cost-leadership business model is based upon lowering the company's cost structure so it can make and sell goods or services at a lower cost than its rivals. A cost leader is often a large, national company that targets the average customer. Focused cost leadership means developing the correct strategies to serve just 1 or 2 market segments.

10. A differentiation business model is based on creating a product that customers perceive as different or distinct in some important way. Focused differentiation is providing a differentiated product for just 1 or 2 market segments.

11. The middle of the value creation frontier is occupied by broad differentiators, which have pursued their differentiation strategy in a way that has also allowed them to lower their cost structure over time.

12. Strategic-group analysis helps companies in an industry better understand the dynamics of competitive positioning. In strategic-group analysis, managers identify and chart the business models and business-level strategies their industry rivals are pursuing. Then they can determine which strategies are successful or unsuccessful, and why a certain business model is or is not working. In

turn, this allows managers to either fine-tune or radically alter their business models and strategies to improve their competitive position.

13. Many companies, through neglect, ignorance, or error, do not work to continually improve their business model, do not perform strategic-group analysis, and often fail to identify and respond to changing opportunities and threats. As a result, their business-level strategies do not cohesively work together, their business model begins to fail, and profitability starts to decline. No task is more important than ensuring that one's company is optimally positioned against its rivals to compete for customers.

Discussion Questions

1. What are some of the reasons companies lose control over their business models, and thus their competitive advantage, over time?

2. Why is strategic-group analysis important for superior competitive positioning?

3. What strategies does a company need to develop to become a broad differentiator? In what ways does this provide the company with a competitive advantage over cost leaders? Over differentiators?

4. How do changes in the environment affect the success of a company's business model?

5. What is the value creation frontier? How does each of the four generic business models allow a company to reach this frontier?

6. How can companies pursuing cost leadership and differentiation lose their place on the value frontier? In what ways can companies regain their competitive advantage?

7. Why does each generic business model require a different set of business-level strategies? Give examples of pairs of companies in: (a) the computer industry; (b) the electronics industry; and (c) the fast-food industry that pursue different types of business models.

Practicing Strategic Management

Small-Group Exercises

Experiential Exercise: Finding a Strategy for a Restaurant

Break up into groups of 3–5 people and discuss the following scenario. You are a group of partners contemplating opening a new restaurant in your city. You are trying to decide how to position your restaurant to give it the best competitive advantage.

1. Create a strategic-group map of the restaurants in your city by analyzing their generic business models and strategies. What are the similarities or differences between these groups?

2. Identify which restaurants you think are the most profitable. Discuss why.

3. On the basis of this analysis, decide what kind of restaurant you want to open, and why.

Strategy Sign-On

Article File 5

Find an example (or several examples) of a company pursuing one of the generic business models. What set of business-level strategies does the company use to formulate and implement its business model? How successful has the company been?

Strategic Management Project: Developing Your Portfolio 5

This part of the project focuses on the nature of your company's business model and business-level strategies. If your company operates in more than one business, concentrate on either its core, or most central or most important, businesses. Using all the information you have collected on your company so far, answer the following questions:

1. How differentiated are the products or services of your company? What is the basis of their differentiated appeal?
2. What is your company's strategy toward market segmentation? If it segments its market, on what basis does it do so?
3. What distinctive competencies does your company have? (Use the information on functional-level strategy in the previous chapter to answer this question.) Is efficiency, quality, innovation, responsiveness to customers, or a combination of these factors, the main driving force in your company?
4. What generic business model is your company pursuing? How has it formulated and implemented a set of business-level strategies to pursue this business model?
5. What are the advantages and disadvantages associated with your company's choice of business model and strategies?
6. Is your company a member of a strategic group in an industry? If so, which one?
7. How could you improve your company's business model and strategies to strengthen its competitive advantage?

CLOSING CASE

Southwest Airlines Forges Ahead

The importance of continuously improving efficiency is very clear in the airline industry. During the recent financial crisis, most major airlines were reporting billions of dollars in losses as a result of rising fuel prices, but one airline, Southwest Airlines, was only reporting lower profits. In fact, Southwest has long been the most profitable U.S. airline, despite that its fares have been 25% or more *below* those of its rivals. The major reason for its high performance is its never-ending quest to increase operating efficiency.[18]

Since its inception, Southwest Airlines focused on developing an operating structure that lowers the cost of inputs and the cost of converting inputs into outputs, which are on-time flights that satisfy customers. How does it do this? First, Southwest carefully selects its human resource inputs; only 3% of those who are interviewed each year are hired. Its existing employees do all the hiring—to make certain the potential new employee fits into Southwest's culture, and is a team player with a great attitude. This is a vital strategy because employees are expected to have a positive, helping attitude toward passengers and to other fellow employees. To increase efficiency, all of Southwest's employees are expected to work as a team to prepare everything necessary to speed the departure of its planes. Efficiency in the airline industry is measured by the time each plane spends in the air, not the time stationed at the gate, and Southwest can land an aircraft and have it back in the air in 30 to 45 minutes—a much shorter time than its rivals. Southwest needs fewer employees than other airlines to efficiently run its fleet of planes, which means major cost savings.

It also uses other inputs efficiently; for example, it only flies one kind of plane, the Boeing 737, which means that far less pilot training is required, and maintenance costs are reduced. Southwest planes mainly fly into low-cost lower-trafficked airports instead of highly congested city airports where landing charges are typically much higher, and plane turnaround is much slower. It also operates what is called a "hub-and-spoke" network, meaning its planes typically touch down at least once before they reach the final destination, allowing planes to more easily fill with passengers, and make better use of resources. Finally,

Southwest has never offered passengers meals or other free perks, a policy that all airlines have now copied to reduce costs as fuel prices soar. Although the company has experimented with assigned seating, boarding is on a first-come, first-served basis, which additionally simplifies its procedures.

Southwest works to streamline and simplify all of its operating procedures in order to improve efficiency. Coordination between its employees, however, is the only thing that makes it possible for its lean and simplified procedures to work. And as we discussed earlier, coordination is not enough for operating structures to efficiently work; employees must also be motivated to work hard and cooperate. Southwest has, since it first began operating, motivated employees by offering a generous profit-sharing plan which includes stock in the company—a measure of how well the company cohesively performs. Today employees own over 20% of Southwest's stock, and this is a clear indicator that its continuous concern to design an operating structure that improves efficiency has paid off. In 2011, Southwest purchased JetBlue, its closest low-cost competitor, to expand its national route structure, and both these airlines are consistently rated as the highest in customer satisfaction.[19]

Case Discussion Questions

1. Why has Southwest's business model and strategies changed over time?
2. In what ways is Southwest trying to improve its competitive advantage in 2011?

Notes

[1] www.zynga.com, 2011.

[2] Ibid.

[3] D. F. Abell, *Defining the Business: The Starting Point of Strategic Planning* (Englewood Cliffs, NJ: Prentice-Hall, 1980), 169.

[4] R. Kotler, *Marketing Management*, 5th ed. (Englewood Cliffs, NJ: Prentice-Hall, 1984); M. R. Darby and E. Karni, "Free Competition and the Optimal Amount of Fraud," *Journal of Law and Economics* 16 (1973): 67–86.

[5] Abell, *Defining the Business*, 8.

[6] Some of the theoretical underpinnings for this approach can be found in G. R. Jones and J. Butler, "Costs, Revenues, and Business Level Strategy," *Academy of Management Review* 13 (1988): 202–213; and C. W. L. Hill, "Differentiation versus Low Cost or Differentiation and Low Cost: A Contingency Framework," *Academy of Management Review* 13 (1988): 401–412.

[7] Many authors have discussed cost leadership and differentiation as basic competitive approaches—for example, F. Scherer, *Industrial Market Structure and Economic Performance*, 10th ed. (Boston: Houghton Mifflin, 2000). The basic cost-leadership/

differentiation dimension has received substantial empirical support; see, for example, D. C. Hambrick, "High Profit Strategies in Mature Capital Goods Industries: A Contingency Approach," *Academy of Management Journal* 26 (1983): 687–707.

[8]C. Campbell-Hunt, "What Have We Learned about Generic Competitive Strategy: A Meta-Analysis," *Strategic Management Journal* 21 (2000): 127–154.

[9]M. E. Porter, *Competitive Advantage: Creating and Sustaining Superior Performance* (New York: Free Press, 1985), 37.

[10]Ibid., 13–14.

[11]www.walmart.com, 2011.

[12]M. E. Porter, *Competitive Strategy: Techniques for Analyzing Industries and Competitors* (New York: Free Press, 1980), 46.

[13]W. K. Hall, "Survival Strategies in a Hostile Environment," *Harvard Business Review* 58 (1980): 75–85; Hambrick, "High Profit Strategies," 687–707.

[14]J. Guyon, "Can the Savoy Cut Costs and Be the Savoy?" *Wall Street Journal*, October 25, 1994, B1; www.savoy.com, 2011.

[15]The development of strategic-group theory has been a strong theme in the strategy literature. Important contributions include R. E. Caves and M. E. Porter, "From Entry Barriers to Mobility Barriers," *Quarterly Journal of Economics* (May 1977): 241–262; K. R. Harrigan, "An Application of Clustering for Strategic Group Analysis," *Strategic Management Journal* 6 (1985): 55–73; K. J. Hatten and D. E. Schendel, "Heterogeneity Within an Industry: Company Conduct in the U.S. Brewing Industry, 1952–1971," *Journal of Industrial Economics* 26(1982): 97–113; and M. E. Porter, "The Structure within Industries and Companies Performance," *Review of Economics and Statistics* 61 (1979): 214–227.

[16]www.google.com/finance, 2011.

[17]www.dell.com, 2011.

[18]www.southwest.com, 2011.

[19]www.consumerreports.com, May 2011.

6 Business-Level Strategy and the Industry Environment

erel.photography/istockphoto.com

Groupon's Strategy to Become the Leader in the Online Coupon Industry

In 2010, Google offered to buy Groupon, the online "daily deal" coupon startup company for $6 billion—an astonishingly high offer many analysts said—but Groupon rejected Google's offer, leaving analysts surprised. Why? Groupon's founders decided that they could make much more money from their new company if they could develop strategies to allow the company to stay ahead of potential competitors (such as Google), and establish it as the dominant company in this segment of the online advertising market. Facebook had refused early takeover offers from companies such as Microsoft and Google, and Facebook's initial public offering was expected to exceed $120 billion! If Facebook could do this, so could Groupon.

Groupon was originally a website called "The Point" founded by Andrew Mason in 2007, which was designed to allow a sufficient number of people to connect online and participate as members in a joint endeavor. When enough people joined, a "tipping point" was reached that allowed them to act as a *group*, and to take advantages of opportunities that could not be obtained by any single person acting alone. As Mason stated in a letter to prospective investors in 2011: "I started The Point to empower the little guy and solve the world's unsolvable problems."[1] A big idea. It quickly became clear to Mason that Internet users really liked the opportunity to act together and get great deals on location-specific

LEARNING OBJECTIVES

After reading this chapter, you should be able to:

- Explain why strategic managers need to align their business models with the conditions that exist in different kinds of industry environments
- Identify the strategies managers can develop to increase profitability in fragmented industries
- Discuss the special problems that exist in embryonic and growth industries and how companies can develop successful business models to effectively compete
- Understand competitive dynamics in mature industries and discuss the strategies managers can develop to increase profitability even when competition is intense
- Outline the different strategies that companies in declining industries can use to support their business models and profitability

goods and services; online coupons that changed day-by-day brought people together.

Mason transformed The Point into "Groupon," and quickly began hiring software engineers and salespeople who shared his vision: people acting together to increase their buying power. As Mason wrote: ". . . as an antidote to a common ailment for U.S. city-dwellers there's so much cool stuff to do, but the choice can be overwhelming. With so many options, sometimes the easiest thing is to go to a familiar restaurant, or just stay at home and watch a movie. As a result, we miss out on trying all the cool things our cities have to offer."[2] In 2009, Groupon's online coupon service was launched in major cities around the United States, and the strategy was focused upon providing one specific coupon that offered big discounts on a particular good or service each day, in a specific geographic location. Groupon's strategy was now based on leveraging its member's collective buying power to obtain great deals from companies that online customers found hard to resist. Its strategy was clear—it needed to expand its user base. To do this, Groupon had to attract companies that were anxious to captivate new customers by offering good deals and samples of their goods and services, such as restaurants or recreational experiences. To increase Groupon's user base and encourage users to buy its coupons it had to offer them protection; so Groupon promises that if users feel disappointed they can call it to obtain a refund. Groupon's website states that nothing is more important than treating customers well; the companies offering coupons know they must also work to attract and keep Groupon users—their customers.

Groupon's revenues increased 15 times between 2009 and 2011 as its user base grew to 50 million spearheaded by Mason's vision and business-level strategy. While global sales were nonexistent in March 2010 they were 53% of Groupon's revenues by March 2011, just 1 year

later. Its explosive growth led Google to realize the potential of Groupon to leverage its own competences in Internet advertising in new ways, and build its online advertising market share.

However, when Groupon refused Google's offer it took on a major risk: it is pursuing a focused differentiation strategy based on becoming the leader in online coupon sales. If it succeeds, it will become a major online differentiator worth tens of billions of dollars. However, the risk for Groupon is what barriers to entry exist to stop any other leading Internet differentiator—such as Google, Amazon.com, or Facebook (which has over 750,000 million active users)—from imitating Groupon's approach to offering online coupons and stealing its customers?

Groupon cannot patent its online coupon idea, so how is this embryonic company going to attract and retain the growing number of Web users who are attracted to the online coupon market, which is the only way it can

epa european pressphoto agency b.v./Alamy

increase its market share and become the established leader? Mason's strategy has included soliciting tens of millions of dollars from private investors, pursuing an initial stock offering, and then using the money to launch an aggressive global expansion plan to stay ahead of competitors. Being the "first mover" in a new market is a major strategic advantage; so pouring money into sales and marketing and software development to improve its online storefront and allow Groupon to remain the global leader is worth it. Amazon.com and eBay, for example, grew in this same way—they spent billions to become the online retail portals of choice, and now reap the benefits of their innovative strategies.

In 2011, however, Groupon faced the prospect of cutthroat competition from Internet giants. For example, Google announced the launch of an online coupon service that will offer discounts from restaurants and other merchants if enough people agree to buy the coupons. This service, called "Google Offers" is similar to the daily deals offered by Groupon. Google has been testing its new online coupon service in Portland, Oregon, and will rapidly expand to large cities such as New York and San Francisco in the near future. Google also unveiled a new mobile payment service that allows users to pay for products directly through their smartphones. Similarly, LivingSocial.com, funded by Amazon.com, is rushing into this market as are other new Internet startups!

Only time will tell if Groupon can maintain its leadership over this niche of the online advertising market or whether competitors will crush it. Will Groupon's refusal to take Google's $6 billion buyout offer in 2010 seem like a gigantic mistake?

Overview

As competition in the growing online coupon industry suggests, new startups can often find a market niche to enter, and then compete with leading industry companies who then face new problems in order to maintain their dominant positions over time. Even if strategic managers do create a successful business model and become the leading differentiator like Google, or become the cost leader like Walmart, managers still face another challenge: the need to continuously develop and improve their business-level strategies to sustain their competitive advantage. As the industry environment changes over the industry life cycle, the kinds of opportunities and threats that face a company change; its business model and strategies must adapt to meet the changing industry environment.

This chapter first examines how companies in fragmented industries can develop new kinds of business-level strategies to strengthen their business models. It then considers the challenges of developing and sustaining a competitive advantage in embryonic, growth, mature, and declining industries. By the end of this chapter, you will understand how forces in the changing industry environment require managers to pursue new kinds of strategies to strengthen their company's business model, and keep it at the value creation frontier where the most profit is earned.

Strategies in Fragmented Industries

A **fragmented industry** is one composed of a large number of small- and medium-sized companies, for example, the dry cleaning, restaurant, health club, and legal services industries. There are several reasons that an industry may consist of many small companies rather than a few large ones.[3]

First, low barriers to entry characterize fragmented industries because these industries lack economies of scale. Many homebuyers, for example, prefer dealing with local real estate agents, whom they perceive as having better local knowledge than national chains. Second, in some industries, there may even be diseconomies of scale. In the restaurant business, for example, customers often prefer the unique food and style of a popular local restaurant, rather than the standardized offerings of some national chain. Third, low-entry barriers that permit new companies to constantly enter also keep an industry fragmented. The restaurant industry exemplifies this situation. The costs of opening a restaurant are moderate, and can be shouldered by a single entrepreneur. High transportation costs, too, can keep an industry fragmented, and local or regional production may be the only efficient way to satisfy customers' needs—as in the dirt, cement, brick, or custom glass industries. Finally, an industry may be fragmented because customer needs are so specialized that only a small amount of a product is required, hence, there is no scope for a large mass-production operation to satisfy the market. Custom-made jewelry or catering is an example of this.

If these conditions exist in many fragmented industries, the focus business model will be the most profitable to pursue. Companies may specialize by customer group, customer need, or geographic region so that many small specialty companies operate in local or regional markets. All kinds of specialized or custom-made products—furniture, clothing, hats, boots, houses, etc.—fall into this category, as do all small service operations that cater to personalized customer needs, such as laundries, restaurants, health clubs, and furniture rental stores.

However, strategic managers are eager to gain the cost advantages of pursuing cost leadership, or the sales revenue-enhancing advantages, of differentiation by circumventing the competitive conditions that have allowed focus companies to dominate an industry. Essentially, companies search for the business model and strategies that will allow them to *consolidate* a fragmented industry to obtain the above average profitability possible in a consolidated industry. These companies include large retailers, such as Walmart and Target, and fast-food chains such as McDonald's and Subway; repair shops such as Midas, Inc.; and lawyers, consultants, and tax preparers.

To grow, consolidate their industries, and become industry leaders, these companies have developed strategies—such as chaining, franchising, horizontal merger, and using the Internet and IT—to realize the advantages of a cost-leadership or differentiation business model. By pursuing these business models many focus companies lost their competitive advantage and have disappeared (Figure 6.1).

Chaining

Companies such as Walmart and Midas pursue a **chaining** strategy to obtain the advantages of cost leadership. They establish networks of linked merchandising outlets that are interconnected by IT and function as one large company. The enormous buying power that these companies possess through the chain of nationwide stores

---

Fragmented industry

An industry composed of a large number of small- and medium-sized companies.

Chaining

A strategy designed to obtain the advantages of cost leadership by establishing a network of linked merchandising outlets interconnected by IT that functions as one large company.

Figure 6.1 Strategies for Consolidating a Fragmented Industry

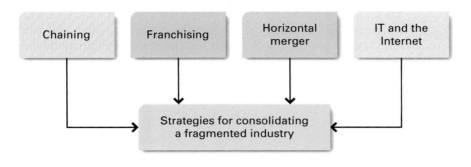

© Cengage Learning 2013

allows them to negotiate large price reductions with suppliers and promote their competitive advantage. They can overcome the barrier of high transportation costs by establishing regional distribution centers that can economize on inventory costs and maximize responsiveness to the needs of regional stores and customers. They also realize economies of scale by sharing managerial skills across the chain, and they can use nationwide, rather than local, advertising.

Thus, by chaining, companies achieve the cost and differentiation advantages enjoyed by industry leaders; they, in fact, often become the new industry leaders. For example, the chaining strategy has been used in a wide range of retail industries, Staples and Office Depot use this strategy in office supplies; Best Buy in electronics retailing; Home Depot in building supplies; among others. In each industry, the companies that use chaining to pursue a business model based on cost leadership or differentiation changed its competitive structure to their advantage—consolidating the industry and weakening the six forces of competition in the process.

Franchising

Like chaining, franchising is a business-level strategy that allows companies, particularly service companies such as McDonald's or Century 21 Real Estate, to enjoy the competitive advantages that result from cost leadership or differentiation. In **franchising**, the franchisor (parent company) grants to its franchisees the right to use the parent's name, reputation, and business model in a particular location or area in return for a sizable franchise fee and often a percentage of the profits.[4]

Because franchisees essentially own their businesses, they are strongly motivated to make the company-wide business model work effectively, and ensure that quality and standards are consistently high so that customers' needs are always satisfied—which is one particular advantage of this strategy. Such motivation is particularly critical for a differentiator that must continually work to maintain its unique or distinctive appeal. In addition, franchising lessens the financial burden of swift expansion, which permits rapid growth of the company. Finally, a nationwide franchised company can reap the advantages of large-scale advertising, as well as economies in purchasing, management, and distribution, as McDonald's does very efficiently in pursuing its cost-leadership model.

Franchising

A strategy in which the franchisor grants to its franchisees the right to use the franchisor's name, reputation, and business model in return for a franchise fee and often a percentage of the profits.

Horizontal Merger

Companies such as Anheuser-Busch (now part of European giant In Bev), Macy's, and Kroger chose a strategy of *horizontal merger* to consolidate their respective industries. For example, Macy's arranged the merger of regional store chains to become one of the largest U.S. clothing companies. By pursuing horizontal merger, companies are able to obtain economies of scale and secure a national market for their product. As a result, they are able to pursue a cost-leadership or a differentiation business model (although Macy's has been struggling to pursue its differentiation model effectively). The many important strategic implications of horizontal merger are discussed in detail in Chapter 9.

Using Information Technology and the Internet

The development of new IT often gives a company the opportunity to develop new business strategies to consolidate a fragmented industry. Amazon.com and eBay, for example, use the Internet and associated e-commerce strategies, making it possible to pursue a cost-leadership model and so increasingly consolidate the fragmented auction and bookselling industries. Before eBay, the auction business was extremely fragmented; local auctions in cities were the principal way in which people could dispose of their antiques and collectibles. By harnessing the Internet, eBay can now assure sellers that they are getting increased visibility for their collectibles, and are more likely to receive higher prices for the items they sell. Similarly, Amazon.com's success in the book market has accelerated the consolidation of the retail book industry; thousands of small bookstores closed because they could not compete by price or selection and by 2011 even a major bookseller such as Border's was forced into bankruptcy.

The challenge in a fragmented industry is to figure out and implement the best set of strategies to overcome a fragmented market to achieve the competitive advantages associated with pursuing one of the different business models. It is difficult to identify any major service activities—from consulting and accounting firms to businesses satisfying the smallest customer need, such as beauty parlors and car repair shops—that have not been consolidated by companies seeking a more profitable business model.

Strategies in Embryonic and Growth Industries

As Chapter 2 discusses, an embryonic industry is one that is just beginning to develop, and a growth industry is one in which first-time demand is rapidly expanding as many new customers enter the market. In choosing the strategies needed to pursue a business model, embryonic and growth industries pose special challenges because new groups of customers with different kinds of needs emerge. Strategic managers must be aware of the way competitive forces in embryonic and growth industries change over time because managers frequently need to build and develop new kinds of competencies, refine their business models, in order to effectively compete in the future.

Most embryonic industries emerge when a technological innovation creates a new product opportunity. For example, after 1875 continuing innovations in the internal combustion engine led to the development of ever more efficient "moving vehicles" and the rise of new industries manufacturing products such as motorcars, motorbuses, and motorbikes. In 1975, the PC industry was born after Intel developed new microprocessor (CPU) technology that allowed companies to build the world's first PCs; this spawned the growth of the PC software industry that took off after Microsoft developed an operating system for IBM.[5] Customer demand for the products of an embryonic industry is initially limited for a variety of reasons. Reasons for slow growth in market demand include: (1) the limited performance and poor quality of the first products; (2) customer unfamiliarity with what the new product can do for them; (3) poorly developed distribution channels to get the product to customers; (4) a lack of complementary products to increase the value of the product for customers; and (5) high production costs because of small volumes of production. Strategic managers who understand how markets develop are in a much better position to pursue a business model and strategies that will lead to a sustained competitive advantage.

Customer demand for the first cars, for example, was limited by their poor performance (they were no faster than a horse, far noisier, and frequently broke down), a lack of important complementary products (such as a network of paved roads and gas stations), and high production costs that made these cars an expensive luxury. Similarly, demand for the first PCs was limited because buyers had to know how to program computers to use them; there were no software programs to purchase that could run on the original PCs. Because of such problems, early demand for the products of embryonic industries come from a small set of technologically savvy customers willing and able to tolerate, and even enjoy, imperfections in their new purchase. Computer geeks who derive great joy out of tinkering with their (still) imperfect PCs and try to find ways to make their PCs work better are the customers that buy next-generation PCs—laptops, smartphones, or even "ultrabooks"—as they become available.

An industry moves from the embryonic stage to the growth stage when a mass market (one in which large numbers of customers enter the market) starts to develop for its product. Mass markets start to develop when three things happen: (1) ongoing technological progress makes a product easier to use, and increases its value for the average customer; (2) complementary products are developed that also increase its value; and (3) companies in the industry work to find ways to reduce the costs of making the new products so they can lower their prices and stimulate high demand.[6] For example, the mass market for cars emerged and the demand for cars surged when: (1) technological progress increased the performance of cars; (2) a network of paved roads and gas stations was established; and (3) Henry Ford began to mass produce cars, something that dramatically reduced production costs, which allowed him to reduce car prices. Similarly, the mass market for PCs emerged when technological advances made the computers easier to use, a supply of complementary software (such as spreadsheets and word processing programs) was developed, and companies in the industry (such as Dell) began to use mass production to build PCs at a low cost.

The Changing Nature of Market Demand

Strategic managers who understand how the demand for a product is affected by the changing needs of customers can focus on developing new strategies that will protect and strengthen their business models, such as building competencies to lower manufacturing costs or speed product development. In most product markets, the changing needs of customers lead to the S-shaped growth curve in Figure 6.2, which illustrates how different groups of customers with different needs enter the market over time. The curve is S-shaped because as the stage of market development moves from embryonic to mature, customer demand first accelerates then decelerates as the market approaches the saturation point—where most customers have already purchased the product. This curve has major implications for a company's differentiation, cost, and pricing competitive positioning decisions.

The first group of customers to enter the market is referred to as *innovators*. Innovators are "technocrats," people who are delighted to be the first to purchase and experiment with a product based on a new technology—even if it is imperfect and expensive. Frequently, innovators have technical talents and interests and that makes them want to "own" and develop the technology because it is so new. In the PC market, the first customers were software engineers and computer hobbyists who wanted to write computer code at home.[7]

Early adopters are the second group of customers to enter the market; they understand that the technology may have important future applications and are willing to experiment with it to see if they can pioneer new uses for the technology. Early adopters are often people who envision how the technology may be used in the future, and they try to be the first to profit from its use. Jeff Bezos, the founder of Amazon.com, was an early adopter of Internet technology. In 1994, before anyone else, he saw that the Internet could be used in innovative ways to sell books.

Both innovators and early adopters enter the market while the industry is in its embryonic stage. The next group of customers, the *early majority*, forms the leading wave or edge of the mass market, and their entry into the market signifies the beginning of the growth stage. Customers in the early majority are practical, understanding the new technology. They weigh the benefits of adopting its new products against their costs, and wait to enter the market until they are confident they will benefit. When the early majority decide to enter the market, a large number of new buyers may be expected. This is what happened in the PC market after IBM's introduction

Figure 6.2   Market Development and Customer Groups

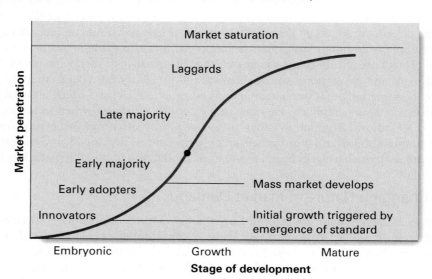

of the PC in 1981. For the early majority, IBM's entry into the market signaled that the benefits of adopting the new PC technology would be worth the cost to purchase and time spent to learn how to use a PC. The growth of the PC market was further strengthened by the development of applications that added value to the PC, such as new spreadsheet and word processing programs. These applications transformed the PC from a hobbyist's toy into a business productivity tool.

When the mass market reaches a critical mass, with about 30% of the potential market penetrated, the next group of customers enters the market. This group is characterized as the *late majority*, the customers who purchase a new technology or product only when it is obvious the technology has great utility and is here to stay. A typical late majority customer group is the "older" set of customers, familiar with their own technology such as the wired telephone, but unfamiliar with the advantages of the new technology (e-mail and so on) that began to enter the PC market in the mid-1990s. However, observing other people who were buying PCs to send e-mail and browse the Web, helped this older demographic group overcome their hesitancy to purchase PCs. By 2002, approximately 65% of U.S. homes had at least one PC, suggesting that the market was approaching saturation. The entry of the late majority signals the end of the growth stage.

Laggards, the last group of customers to enter the market, are people who are inherently conservative and unappreciative of the uses of new technology—such as online stock trading or playing CityVille. Laggards frequently refuse to adopt new products even when the benefits are obvious, or unless they are forced to do so by circumstances—for example, due to work-related reasons. People who use typewriters rather than computers to write letters and books or insist on using fountain pens rather than "micro" ballpoints would be considered laggards—except for people who use differentiated, luxury products such as Montblanc pens or Rolex watches.

In Figure 6.3, the bell-shaped curve represents the total market, and the divisions in the curve show the average percentage of buyers who fall into each of these customer

Figure 6.3 Market Share of Different Customer Segments

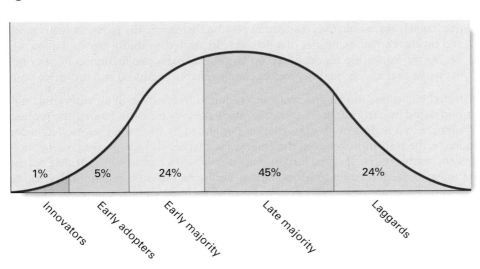

groups. Note that early adopters are a very small percentage of the market; hence, the figure illustrates a vital competitive dynamic—the highest market demand and industry profits arise when the early and late majority groups enter the market. Additionally, research has found that although early pioneering companies succeed in attracting innovators and early adopters, many of these companies often *fail* to attract a significant share of early and late majority customers, and ultimately go out of business.

Strategic Implications: Crossing the Chasm

Why are pioneering companies often unable to create a business model that allows them to be successful over time and remain as market leaders? *Innovators and early adopters have very different customer needs from the early majority*. In an influential book, Geoffrey Moore argues that because of the differences in customer needs between these groups, the business-level strategies required for companies to succeed in the emerging mass market are quite different from those required to succeed in the embryonic market.[8] Pioneering companies that do not change the strategies they use to pursue their business model will therefore lose their competitive advantage to those companies that implement new strategies to remain on the value creation frontier. New strategies are often required to strengthen a company's business model as a market develops over time for the following reasons:

- Innovators and early adopters are technologically sophisticated customers willing to tolerate the limitations of the product; the early majority, however, value ease of use and reliability. Companies competing in an embryonic market typically pay more attention to increasing the performance of a product than to its ease of use and reliability. Those competing in a mass market need to make sure that the product is reliable and easy to use. Thus, the product development strategies required for success are different as a market develops over time.
- Innovators and early adopters are typically reached through specialized distribution channels, and products are often sold by word of mouth. Reaching the early majority requires mass-market distribution channels and mass media advertising campaigns that require a different set of marketing and sales strategies.
- Because innovators and the early majority are relatively few in number and are not particularly price sensitive, companies serving them typically pursue a focus model and produce small quantities of a product. To serve the rapidly growing mass market, a cost-leadership model based on large-scale mass production may be critical to ensure that a high-quality product can be reliably produced at a low price point.

In sum, the business model and strategies required to compete in an embryonic market populated by early adopters and innovators are very different from those required to compete in a high-growth mass market populated by the early majority. As a consequence, the transition between the embryonic market and the mass market is not a smooth, seamless one. Rather, it represents a *competitive chasm* or gulf that companies must cross. According to Moore, many companies do not or cannot develop the right business model; they fall into the chasm and go out of business. Thus, although embryonic markets are typically populated by a large number of small companies, once the mass market begins to develop, the number of companies sharply decreases.[9]

Figure 6.4, which compares the strategies of AOL Time Warner and Prodigy Communications, illustrates Moore's thesis by showing that a chasm exists between innovators and the early majority, that is, between the embryonic market and the rapidly growing mass market. Note also that other chasms exist between other sets

Figure 6.4 The Chasm: AOL and Prodigy

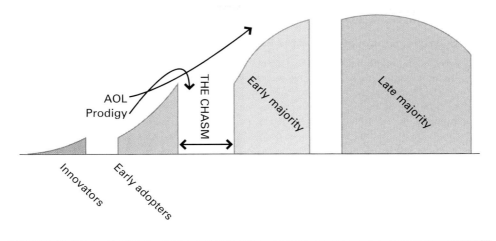

of customers; these also represent important changes in customer demand that require changes in business-level strategy (e.g., a different approach to market segmentation). To successfully cross a chasm, Moore implied a company must continually work to develop the right strategies and build new competencies to create a business model that will allow it to cross the chasm, succeed, and prosper. Strategy in Action 6.1 describes how one company, AOL, successfully built a business model to cross a chasm, and how another company, Prodigy, failed.

The implication is clear: to cross this chasm successfully, managers must correctly identify the customer needs of the first wave of early majority users—the leading edge of the mass market. Then they must alter their business models by developing new strategies to redesign products and create distribution channels and marketing campaigns to satisfy the needs of the early majority. They must have a suitable product available at a reasonable price to sell to the early majority when they begin to enter the market in large numbers. At the same time, the industry pioneers must abandon their outdated, focused business model that was solely directed at the needs of innovators and early adopters. Focusing on the outdated model will lead managers to ignore the needs of the early majority—and the need to develop the strategies necessary to pursue a differentiation or cost-leadership business model in order to remain a dominant industry competitor.

Strategic Implications of Market Growth Rates

Strategic managers must understand a final important issue in embryonic and growth industries: different markets develop at different rates. The speed at which a market develops can be measured by its growth rate, that is, the rate at which customers in that market purchase the industry's product. A number of factors explain the variation in market growth rates for different products, and thus the speed with which a particular industry develops. It is important for strategic managers to understand the source of these differences; their choice of business model and strategies can accelerate or retard the rate at which a particular market grows.[10] In other words, business-level strategy is a major determinant of industry profitability.

STRATEGY IN ACTION

AOL, Prodigy, and the Chasm between Innovators and the Early Majority

Before America Online (AOL) became a household name, Prodigy Communications was a market leader. When its online network was launched in 1990, Prodigy's business model was differentiation, and its goal was to build the largest proprietary online shopping network. It quickly attracted 500,000 users. Competition was low at this time; the largest competitor, CompuServe, was conservatively managed, and it pursued a focused business model based on servicing the needs of technical and financial users. There was one smaller competitor, AOL, but as one Prodigy executive commented, "It was just a little thing off to the side." Ten years later, that "little thing" had become the largest online service in the world—with 33 million members—and Prodigy had been forced to exit the online business altogether.

Why did Prodigy fail? The company appeared to be focusing on the mass market; its target customers were not computer-oriented early adopters but typical middle-class Americans. And its business model to sell products online seemed correct; surely this ultimately had to become a major Internet application. The problem was that Prodigy's managers did not choose the right set of strategies to formulate its business model and attract the early majority; they did not understand the full range of needs customers were trying to satisfy by using the Internet.

One of the surprise early drivers of customer demand for online services, and a major factor in creating the mass market, was e-mail. To attract the early majority, AOL's strategy was to offer its members unlimited e-mail storage, but Prodigy charged its members a fee for sending more than 30 e-mails per month—a big difference in business strategy. Chat rooms were another important online service application that customers were increasingly embracing. AOL saw chat rooms as an important feature to satisfy customer needs; its strategy was to quickly develop the software that soon made chat rooms one of its most popular services. Prodigy's attorneys, however, feared it might be held legally liable for comments made in chat rooms, or events that arose from chat exchanges between users. They discouraged Prodigy from offering this service. This censorship, lack of chat rooms, and charges for e-mail rankled its members, and they began to switch to AOL.

By 1996, the battle was effectively over: AOL was growing by leaps and bounds, and Prodigy was losing customers at a rapid pace because it had not developed the right set of strategies to pursue a differentiation business model that allowed it to remain on the value frontier. AOL, correctly sensed the way customer needs were changing, provided a differentiated product that met those needs, crossed the chasm with ease.

Source: www.aol.com (2011); Kara Swisher, *aol.com* (New York: Random House, 1998).

The first factor that accelerates customer demand is a new product's *relative advantage*, that is, the degree to which a new product is perceived as better at satisfying customer needs than the product it supersedes. For example, the early growth in demand for cell phones was partly driven by their economic benefits. Studies showed that because business customers could always be reached by cell phone, they made better use of their time—for example, by not showing up at a meeting that had been cancelled at the last minute—and saved 2 hours per week in time that would otherwise have been wasted. For busy executives, the early adopters, the productivity benefits of owning a cell phone outweighed the costs. Cellphones also rapidly diffused for social reasons, in particular, because they conferred glamour or prestige upon their users (something that also drives demand for the most advanced kinds of smartphones and tablet computers today).

Another factor driving growth in demand is *compatibility*, the degree to which a new product is perceived as being consistent with the current needs or existing values of potential adopters. Demand for cellphones grew rapidly because their operation was compatible with the prior experience of potential adopters who used traditional landline phones. *Complexity*, the degree to which a new product is perceived as difficult to understand and use, is a third factor. Early PCs with their clunky operating system interfaces were complex to use, and therefore slow to be adopted. The first cellphones were simple to use and were quickly adopted. A fourth factor is *trialability*, the degree to which potential customers can experiment with a new product during a hands-on trial basis. Many people first used cellphones when borrowing them from colleagues to make calls and positive experiences helped accelerate growth rates. In contrast, early PCs were more difficult to experiment with because they were rare and expensive and because some training was needed in how to use them. These complications led to slower growth rates for PCs. A final factor is *observability*, the degree to which the results of using and enjoying a new product can be seen and appreciated by other people. Originally, the Palm Pilot, then the BlackBerry, and now the iPhone and Galaxy rapidly diffused because it became obvious how their users could put them to so many different uses—and today the development of so many new apps is driving their rapid adoption by all groups of users.

Thus, strategic managers must be sure to devise strategies that help to educate customers about the value of their products if they are to grow their company's market share over time.

When a market is rapidly growing, and the popularity of a new product increases or spreads in a way that is analogous to a *viral model of infection*, a related strategic issue arises. Lead adopters (the first customers who buy a product) in a market become "infected" or enthused with the product, as exemplified by BlackBerry or iPhone users. Subsequently, lead adopters infect other people by telling others about the advantages of products. After observing the benefits of the product, these people also adopt and use the product. Companies promoting new products can take advantage of viral diffusion by identifying and aggressively courting opinion leaders in a particular market—the customers whose views command respect. For example, when the manufacturers of new high-tech medical equipment, such as MRI scanners, start to sell a new product, they try to get well-known doctors at major research and teaching hospitals to use the product first. Companies may give these opinion leaders (the doctors) free machines for their research purposes, and work closely with the doctors to further develop the technology. Once these opinion leaders commit to the product and give it their stamp of approval, other doctors at additional hospitals often follow.

In sum, understanding competitive dynamics in embryonic and growth industries is an important strategic issue. The ways in which different kinds of customer groups emerge and the ways in which customer needs change are important determinants of the strategies that need to be pursued to make a business model successful over time. Similarly, understanding the factors that affect a market's growth rate allows managers to tailor their business model to a changing industry environment. (More about competition in high-tech industries is discussed in the next chapter.)

Navigating Through the Life Cycle to Maturity

Another crucial business decision that strategic managers face at each stage of the industry life cycle is which investment strategy to pursue. An investment strategy determines the amount and type of resources and capital—human, functional, and financial—that must be spent to configure a company's value chain so that it can successfully pursue a business model over time.[11] When deciding on an investment strategy, managers must evaluate the potential return (on invested capital) from investing in a particular business model against the cost. In this way, they can determine whether pursuing a certain business model is likely to be profitable, and how the profitability of a particular business model will change as competition within the industry changes.

Two factors are crucial in choosing an investment strategy: (1) the competitive advantage a company's business model gives it in an industry relative to its competitors; and (2) the stage of the industry's life cycle in which the company is competing.[12] In determining the strength of a company's relative competitive position, market share and distinctive competencies become important. A large market share signals greater potential returns from future investment because it suggests a company has brand loyalty and is in a strong position to grow its profits in the future. Similarly, the more difficult it is to imitate a company's distinctive competencies, such as those in R&D or manufacturing and marketing, the more sustainable is the competitive advantage supplied by its business model—and the greater the likelihood that investment in it will lead to higher profitability. These two attributes also reinforce one another; for example, a large market share may help a company create and develop distinctive competencies that strengthen its business model over time because high demand allows it to ride or move down the experience curve and lower its cost structure. Also, a large market share may create a large cash flow that allows a company to invest more to develop competencies in R&D or elsewhere. In general, companies with the largest market share and the strongest distinctive competencies are in the best position to build and sustain their competitive advantage. Companies with small market shares and little ability to develop distinctive competencies are in a much weaker competitive position.[15]

Because different kinds of opportunities and threats are found in each life-cycle stage, the stage of the industry life cycle also influences a company's choice of how much to invest in its business model. Each stage, therefore, has different implications for the investment of resources needed to obtain a competitive advantage. Competition is strongest in the shakeout stage of the life cycle and least important in the embryonic stage, for example. The *risks* associated with pursuing a certain business model change over time. The difference in risk explains why the potential returns from investing in a particular business model depend on the life-cycle stage.

Embryonic Strategies

In the embryonic stage, all companies, weak and strong, emphasize the development of a distinctive competency to build a successful business model. During this stage, investment needs are great because a company has to establish a competitive advantage. Many fledgling companies in the industry are seeking resources to develop a distinctive competency. Thus, the appropriate business-level investment strategy is a **share-building strategy**. The aim is to build market share by developing a stable and distinct competitive advantage to attract customers who have no knowledge of the company's products.

Companies require large amounts of capital to develop R&D or sales and service competencies. They cannot generate much of this capital internally. Thus, a company's success depends on its ability to demonstrate a distinctive competency to attract outside investors, or venture capitalists. If a company gains the resources to develop a distinctive competency, it will be in a relatively stronger competitive position. If it fails, its only option may be to exit the industry. In fact, companies in weak competitive positions at all stages in the life cycle may choose to exit the industry to cut their losses.

Share-building strategy

A strategy that aims to build market share by developing a competitive advantage to attract customers by providing them with knowledge of the company's products.

Growth Strategies

At the growth stage, the task facing a company is to strengthen its business model to provide the competitive foundation it needs to survive the coming shakeout. Thus, the appropriate investment strategy is the **growth strategy**. The goal is to maintain its relative competitive position in a rapidly expanding market and, if possible, to increase it—in other words, to grow with the expanding market. However, other companies are entering the market and catching up with the industry's innovators. As a result, the companies that first enter the market with a particular kind of product often require successive waves of capital infusion to maintain the momentum generated by their success in the embryonic stage. For example, differentiators need to engage in extensive R&D to maintain their technological lead, and cost leaders need to invest in state-of-the-art machinery and computers to obtain new experience-curve economies. All this investment to strengthen their business model is very expensive. And, as we discussed previously, many companies fail to recognize the changing needs of customers in the market and invest their capital in ways that do not lead to the distinctive competencies required for long-term success.

The growth stage is also the time when companies attempt to secure their grip over customers in existing market segments, and simultaneously enter new segments to increase their market share. Increasing the level of market segmentation to become a broad differentiator is expensive as well. A company has to invest resources to develop a new sales and marketing competency, for example. Consequently, at the growth stage, companies must make investment decisions about the relative advantages of differentiation, cost-leadership, or focus business models given their financial needs and relative competitive position. If one or a few companies have emerged as the clear cost leaders, for example, other companies might realize that it is futile to compete head-to-head with these companies and instead decide to pursue a growth strategy using a differentiation or focus approach and invest resources in developing other competencies. As a result, strategic groups start to develop in an industry as each company seeks the best way to invest its scarce resources to maximize its competitive advantage.

Companies must spend a lot of money just to keep up with growth in the market, and finding additional resources to develop new competencies is a difficult task for strategic managers. Consequently, companies in a weak competitive position at this stage engage in a **market concentration** strategy to find a viable competitive position. They seek to specialize in some way and adopt a focus business model to reduce their investment needs. If these companies are very weak, they may also choose to exit the industry and sell out to a stronger competitor.

Shakeout Strategies

By the shakeout stage, customer demand is increasing, and competition by price or product characteristics becomes intense. Companies in strong competitive positions need resources to invest in a **share-increasing strategy** to attract customers from weak companies exiting the market. In other words, companies attempt to maintain and increase market share despite fierce competition. The way companies invest their resources depends on their business model.

For cost leaders, because of the price wars that can occur, investment in cost control is crucial if they are to survive the shakeout stage; cost leaders must do all they can to reduce their cost structure. Differentiators in a strong competitive position

Growth strategy

A strategy designed to allow a company to maintain its relative competitive position in a rapidly expanding market and, if possible, to increase it.

Market concentration

When a company specializes in some way and adopts a focus business model to reduce investment needs and searches for a viable and sustainable competitive position.

Share-increasing Strategy

When a company focuses its resources to invest in product development and marketing to become a dominant industry competitor.

choose to forge ahead and increase their market share by investing in marketing, and they are likely to develop a sophisticated after-sales service network. Differentiators in a weak position reduce their investment burden by withdrawing to a focused model, the market concentration strategy, to specialize in serving the needs of customers in a particular market segment. A market concentration strategy indicates that a company is trying to turn around its business to survive long term.

Weak companies exiting the industry engage in a harvest strategy. A company using a **harvest strategy** must limit or decrease its investment in a business and extract or "milk" its investment as much as it can. For example, a company reduces to a minimum the assets it employs in the business and forgoes investment to reduce its cost structure.[13] Then the company "harvests" all the sales revenues it can profitably obtain before it liquidates its assets and exits the industry. Companies that have lost their cost-leadership position to more efficient companies are more likely to pursue a harvest strategy because a smaller market share means higher costs and they are unable to move to a focus strategy. Differentiators, in contrast, have a competitive advantage in this stage if they can move to a focus model.

Maturity Strategies

By the maturity stage, companies want to reap the rewards of their previous investments in developing the business models that have made them dominant industry competitors. Until now, profits have been reinvested in the business, and dividends have been small. Investors in leading companies have obtained their rewards through the appreciation of the value of their stock, because the company has reinvested most of its capital to maintain and increase market share. As market growth slows in the maturity stage, a company's investment strategy depends on the level of competition in the industry and the source of the company's competitive advantage.

In industries in which competition is high because of technological change or low barriers to entry, companies need to defend their competitive position. Strategic managers need to continue to heavily invest in building the company's business model to maintain its competitive advantage. Both cost leaders and differentiators adopt a **hold-and-maintain strategy** to defend their business models and ward off threats from focused companies that might be attempting to grow and compete with the industry leaders. They expend resources to develop their distinctive competency to remain the market leaders. For example, differentiated companies may invest in improved after-sales service, and low-cost companies may invest in the latest production technologies.

It is at this point that many companies realize the benefits that can be obtained by investing resources to become broad differentiators and protect themselves from aggressive competitors (both at home and abroad) that are watching for any opportunity or perceived weakness to take the lead in the industry. Differentiators enter new market segments to increase their market share; they also take advantage of their growing profits to develop flexible manufacturing systems to reduce their production costs. Cost leaders also begin to enter more market segments and increase product differentiation to expand their market share. For example, Gallo moved from the bulk wine segment and began marketing premium wines and wine coolers to take advantage of its low production costs. Soon Gallo's new premium brands, such as Falling Leaf chardonnay, became best-selling wines in the United States. With time, the competitive positions of the leading differentiators and cost leaders lose their distinctiveness, and the pattern of industry competition changes yet again, as we discuss in the next section.

Harvest strategy

When a company reduces to a minimum the assets it employs in a business to reduce its cost structure and extract or "milk" maximum profits from its investment.

Hold-and-maintain strategy

When a company expends resources to develop its distinctive competency to remain the market leader and ward off threats from other companies that are attempting to usurp its leading position.

Strategy in Mature Industries

As a result of fierce competition in the shakeout stage, an industry becomes consolidated; hence, a mature industry is commonly dominated by a small number of large companies. Although they may also contain many medium-sized companies and a host of small, specialized companies, the large companies determine the nature of competition in the industry because they can influence the six competitive forces. Indeed, these large companies hold their leading positions because they have developed the most successful business models and strategies in an industry.

By the end of the shakeout stage, companies have learned how important it is to analyze each other's business model and strategies. They also know that if they change their strategies, their actions are likely to stimulate a competitive response from industry rivals. For example, a differentiator that starts to lower its prices because it has adopted a more cost-efficient technology not only threatens other differentiators, but may also threaten cost leaders that see their competitive advantage being eroded. Hence, by the mature stage of the life cycle, companies have learned the meaning of competitive independence.

As a result, in mature industries, business-level strategy revolves around understanding how established companies *collectively* attempt to reduce the strength of industry competition in order to preserve both company and industry profitability. Interdependent companies can help protect their competitive advantage and profitability by adopting strategies and tactics, first, to deter entry into an industry, and second, to reduce the level of rivalry within an industry.

Strategies to Deter Entry: Product Proliferation, Price Cutting, and Maintaining Excess Capacity

Companies can use three main methods to deter entry by potential rivals and hence maintain and increase industry profitability: product proliferation, price cutting, and maintaining excess capacity (see Figure 6.5). Of course, *potential entrants* will try to circumvent such entry-deterring strategies by incumbent companies. Competition is rarely a one-way street.

Figure 6.5　Strategies for Deterring Entry of Rivals

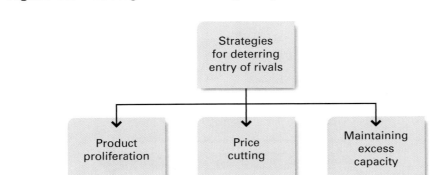

Product Proliferation   As we noted earlier, in the maturity stage, most companies move to increase their market share by producing a wide range of products targeted at different market segments. Sometimes, however, to reduce the threat of entry, existing companies ensure that they are offering a product targeted at every segment in the market. This creates a barrier to entry because potential competitors find it hard to break into an industry and establish a "beachhead" when there is no obvious group of customers whose needs are not being met by existing companies.[14] This strategy of "filling the niches," or catering to the needs of customers in all market segments to deter entry, is known as **product proliferation**.

Because large U.S. carmakers were so slow to fill the small-car niches (they did *not* pursue a product proliferation strategy), they were vulnerable to the entry of the Japanese into these market segments in the 1980s. Ford and GM had no excuse for this situation, for in their European operations, they had a long history of small-car manufacturing. Managers should have seen the opening and filled it 10 years earlier, but the (mistaken) view was that "small cars mean small profits." Better small profits than no profits! In the soap and detergent industry, on the other hand, competition is based on the production of new kinds of soaps and detergents to satisfy customer's desires or create new desires. Thus, the number of soaps and detergents, and especially the way they are packaged (powder, liquid, or tablets), proliferates, making it very difficult for prospective entrants to attack a new market segment. Figure 6.6 indicates how product proliferation can deter entry. It depicts product space in the restaurant industry along two dimensions: atmosphere, which ranges from fast food to candlelight dining, and food quality, which ranges from average to gourmet. The circles represent product spaces filled by restaurants located along the

Product proliferation

The strategy of "filling the niches," or catering to the needs of customers in all market segments to deter entry by competitors.

Figure 6.6   Product Proliferation in the Restaurant Industry

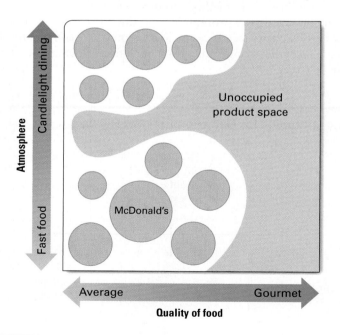

two dimensions. Accordingly, McDonald's is situated in the average quality/fast food area. A gap in the product space provides a potential entrant or an existing rival an opportunity to enter the market and make inroads. The shaded unoccupied product space represents areas where new restaurants could enter the market. When all the product spaces are filled, this barrier to entry makes it much more difficult for a new company to gain a foothold in the market and differentiate itself. This barrier can develop in any market, not just with food chains. Even an industry leader like Google can make a major mistake in not filling the niches—or recognizing the threat a new niche poses quickly enough—as Strategy in Action 6.2 describes.

STRATEGY IN ACTION

Google is Threatened by the Online Social Networking Niche

Google's rapid growth rate necessitated the hiring of more than 80,000 employees in the last 3 years; by 2011 it employed over 136,000 people and had more than doubled in size. Google's growth resulted from its entry into an increasing number of different niches in the Internet software industry as industry competition became increasingly fierce; new entry was increasing fast in online advertising, online search and web-browsing, mobile computing, and smartphones.

After Larry Page, one of Google's founders, took over Eric Schmidt's position as CEO in 2011, Schmidt admitted that his biggest mistake as CEO was that he had not recognized the major challenge posed by new online social networking sites such as Twitter and, in particular, Facebook, whose user base had grown from 40 million users in 2007 to 750 million by 2011. Google's search technology cannot search within Facebook's pages, so while Facebook was able to create a huge library of specific details about the interests of its members to sell to online advertisers, Google was unable to tap into this goldmine. Why is this so important? Because targeted online advertising is the key to earning higher sales revenues, and by 2011, Facebook's own targeted advertising program to its 700 million users was earning billions of dollars. It seemed that Facebook's rapid growth into online advertising would choke off Google's attempts to remain the leader so they would become fierce competitors in the online advertising market—hence Google's desire to buy Groupon (see Opening Case).

In early 2011 the issue facing Larry Page and his top management team was to rapidly develop new strategies to advance Google's competence in social networking—it had to find ways to integrate the strategies of all its different software product groups to promote its competence in social networking. Page created a new top management committee—all of Google's product group's team leaders are now required to meet once a week with Page to further integration and keep the company on track to succeed in social networking.

Page's task is not easy: each of Google's different software product groups are led by strong, charismatic leaders who aggressively pursue their own strategic agendas, and the primary problem is getting these managers to work together. For example, Google's Android smartphone department had to find ways to cooperate with the Chrome web-browser department to further social networking and the search department had to find ways to coordinate with the advertising department to find ways to target customers at the city level. Page made clear that he viewed this challenge as vital and he linked a substantial part of each managers' and employees' annual bonus and stock options (often worth millions of dollars) to how well the company's online social networking strategies succeeded in the future.

In the summer of 2011 Google opened its new Google+ social networking service to selected users, and after ironing out the initial software problems by September 2011 every Web user could open their own Google+ account. The new service received positive reviews and grew in popularity—so much so that Facebook was forced to expand its offerings and find new ways to compete against Google+. The race is on to see which company will dominate in this highly important advertising market in the 2010s.

Sources: www.google.com, 2011; www.facebook.com, 2011.

Price Cutting   In some situations, pricing strategies can be used to deter other companies' entry, thus protecting the profit margins of companies already in an industry. One entry-deterring strategy is to cut prices every time a new company enters the industry or, even better, cut prices every time a potential entrant is *contemplating* entry, and then raise prices once the new or potential entrant has withdrawn. The goal is to send a signal to potential entrants that new entry will be met with price cuts. If incumbent companies in an industry consistently pursue such a strategy, potential entrants will learn that their entry will instigate a price war, the threat of new entry will be reduced, average prices will remain higher, and industry profitability will increase. However, a price-cutting strategy will not deter an entrant that plans to adopt a new technology that will give it a cost advantage over established companies, or an entrant that has pioneered a new business model that its managers expect will also give it a competitive advantage. In fact, many of the most successful entrants into mature industries are companies that have done this. For example, the Japanese car companies were able to enter the United States market because they had pioneered new lean manufacturing technologies that provided a cost and quality advantage over established U.S. car companies.

A second price-cutting strategy involves initially charging a high price for a product and seizing short-term profits, but then aggressively cutting prices to build market share *and* simultaneously deter potential entrants.[15] The incumbent companies thus signal to potential entrants that if they enter the industry, the incumbents will use their competitive advantage to drive prices down to a level at which new companies will be unable to cover their costs. This pricing strategy also allows a company to move down the experience curve and obtain substantial economies of scale. Because costs fall with prices, profit margins can still be maintained. However, this strategy is unlikely to deter a strong potential competitor—an established company that is trying to find profitable investment opportunities in other industries. It is difficult, for example, to imagine 3M as afraid to enter an industry because companies threaten to drive down prices. A company such as 3M has the resources to withstand short-term losses to achieve long-term success. Hence, when faced with such a scenario, it may be in the interests of incumbent companies to gracefully accept new entry; gradually giving up market share to the new entrants to prevent price wars from developing, and thus maintaining good profits.

Maintaining Excess Capacity   A third competitive technique that allows companies to deter entry involves maintaining excess capacity, that is, maintaining the physical capability to produce more product than customers currently demand. Existing industry companies may deliberately develop some limited amount of excess capacity to warn potential entrants that if they enter the industry, existing firms can retaliate by increasing output and forcing prices down until entry would become unprofitable. However, the threat to increase output must be *credible*; that is, companies in an industry must quickly and collectively be able to increase production levels if entry appears likely.

Strategies to Manage Rivalry

Beyond seeking to deter entry, companies also wish to develop strategies to manage their competitive interdependence and decrease price rivalry. Unrestricted competition over prices reduces both company and industry profitability. Several strategies are available to companies to manage industry rivalry. The most important are: price signaling, price leadership, nonprice competition, and capacity control (Figure 6.7).

Figure 6.7 Strategies for Managing Industry Rivalry

Price Signaling   A company's ability to choose the price option that leads to superior performance is a function of several factors, including the strength of demand for a product and the intensity of competition between rivals. Price signaling is a first method by which companies attempt to control rivalry among competitors to allow the *industry* to choose the most favorable pricing option.[16] **Price signaling** is the process by which companies increase or decrease product prices to convey their intentions to other companies and influence the way other companies price their products.[17] Companies use price signaling to improve industry profitability.

Companies may use price signaling to announce that they will vigorously respond to hostile competitive moves that threaten them. For example, they may signal that if one company starts to aggressively cut prices, they will respond in kind. A *tit-for-tat strategy* is a well-known price signaling maneuver in which a company does exactly what its rivals do: if its rivals cut prices, the company follows; if its rivals raise prices, the company follows. By consistently pursuing this strategy over time, a company sends a clear signal to its rivals that it will mirror any pricing moves they make; sooner or later, rivals will learn that the company will always pursue a tit-for-tat strategy. Because rivals know that the company will match any price reductions and cutting prices will only reduce profits, price cutting becomes less common in the industry. Moreover, a tit-for-tat strategy also signals to rivals that price increases will be imitated, growing the probability that rivals will initiate price increases to raise profits. Thus, a tit-for-tat strategy can be a useful way of shaping pricing behavior in an industry.[18]

The airline industry is a good example of the power of price signaling when prices typically rise and fall depending upon the current state of customer demand. If one carrier signals the intention to lower prices, a price war frequently ensues as other carriers copy one another's signals. If one carrier feels demand is strong, it tests the waters by signaling an intention to increase prices, and price signaling becomes a strategy to obtain uniform price increases. Nonrefundable tickets or charges for a second bag, another strategy adopted to allow airlines to charge higher prices, also originated as a market signal by one company that was quickly copied by all other companies in the industry (it is estimated that extra bag charges have so far allowed airlines to raise over $1 billion in revenues). Carriers have recognized that they can

Price signaling

The process by which companies increase or decrease product prices to convey their intentions to other companies and influence the price of an industry's products.

stabilize their revenues and earn interest on customers' money if they collectively act to force customers to assume the risk of buying airline tickets in advance. In essence, price signaling allows companies to give one another information that enables them to understand each other's competitive product or market strategy and make coordinated, price-competitive moves.

Price Leadership   When one company assumes the responsibility for setting the pricing option that maximizes industry profitability, they assume the position as price leader—a second tactic used to reduce price rivalry between companies in a mature industry.[19] Formal price leadership, or when companies jointly set prices, is illegal under antitrust laws, therefore, the process of **price leadership** is often very subtle. In the car industry, for example, prices are set by imitation. The price set by the weakest company—that is, the company with the highest cost structure—is often used as the basis for competitors' pricing. Thus, in the past, U.S. carmakers set their prices and Japanese carmakers then set their prices in response to the U.S. prices. The Japanese are happy to do this because they have lower costs than U.S. carmakers, and still make higher profits without having to compete on price. Pricing is determined by market segment. The prices of different auto models in a particular range indicate the customer segments that the companies are targeting, and the price range the companies believe the market segment can tolerate. Each manufacturer prices a model in the segment with reference to the prices charged by its competitors, not by reference to competitors' costs. Price leadership also allows differentiators to charge a premium price.

Although price leadership can stabilize industry relationships by preventing head-to-head competition and raising the level of profitability within an industry, it has its dangers. It helps companies with high cost structures, allowing them to survive without needing to implement strategies to become more productive and efficient. In the long term, such behavior makes them vulnerable to new entrants that have lower costs because they have developed new low-cost production techniques. This is what happened in the U.S. car industry. After decades of tacit price fixing, and GM as the price leader, U.S. carmakers were subjected to growing low-cost overseas competition that was threatening their survival. In 2009, the U.S. government decided to bail out Chrysler and GM by loaning them billions of dollars after the financial crisis, while forcing them to enter, and then emerge from, bankruptcy. This dramatically lowered the cost structures of these companies, and has made them more competitive today (as well as Ford that obtained similar benefits while managing to avoid bankruptcy). In 2011, all these U.S. carmakers reported increased sales and profits.

Nonprice Competition   A third very important aspect of product and market strategy in mature industries is the use of **nonprice competition** to manage rivalry within an industry. The use of strategies to try to prevent costly price cutting and price wars does not preclude competition by product differentiation. In many industries, product-differentiation strategies are the principal tools companies use to deter potential entrants and manage rivalry within their industry.

Product differentiation allows industry rivals to compete for market share by offering products with different or superior features, such as smaller, more powerful, or more sophisticated computer chips, as AMD, Intel, and NVIDIA compete to offer, or by applying different marketing techniques as Procter & Gamble, Colgate, and Unilever do. In Figure 6.8, product and market segment dimensions are used to identify four nonprice competitive strategies based on product differentiation: market

Price leadership

When one company assumes the responsibility for determining the pricing strategy that maximizes industry profitability.

Nonprice competition

The use of product differentiation strategies to deter potential entrants and manage rivalry within an industry.

Figure 6.8 Four Nonprice Competitive Strategies

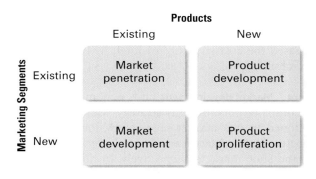

---

penetration, product development, market development, and product proliferation. (Note that this model applies to new market segments, *not* new markets.)[20]

Market Penetration   When a company concentrates on expanding market share in its existing product markets, it is engaging in a strategy of **market penetration**.[21] Market penetration involves heavy advertising to promote and build product differentiation. For example, Intel has actively pursued penetration with its aggressive marketing campaign of "Intel Inside." In a mature industry, advertising aims to influence customers' brand choice and create a brand-name reputation for the company and its products. In this way, a company can increase its market share by attracting its rival's customers. Because brand-name products often command premium prices, building market share in this situation is very profitable.

In some mature industries—for example, soap and detergent, disposable diapers, and brewing—a market-penetration strategy becomes a long-term strategy.[22] In these industries, all companies engage in intensive advertising and battle for market share. Each company fears that if it does not advertise, it will lose market share to rivals who do. Consequently, in the soap and detergent industry, Procter & Gamble spends more than 20% of sales revenues on advertising, with the aim of maintaining, and perhaps building, market share. These huge advertising outlays constitute a barrier to entry for prospective competitors.

Product Development   **Product development** is the creation of new or improved products to replace existing ones.[23] The wet-shaving industry depends on product replacement to create successive waves of customer demand, which then create new sources of revenue for companies in the industry. Gillette, for example, periodically unveils a new and improved razor, such as its vibrating razor (that competes with Schick's 4-bladed razor), to try to boost its market share. Similarly, in the car industry, each major car company replaces its models every 3–5 years to encourage customers to trade in old models and purchase new ones.

Product development is crucial for maintaining product differentiation and building market share. For instance, the laundry detergent Tide has gone through more than 50 changes in formulation during the past 40 years to improve its performance. The product is always advertised as Tide, but it is a different product each year.

Market penetration

When a company concentrates on expanding market share to strengthen its position in its existing product markets.

Product development

The creation of new or improved products to replace existing products.

Refining and improving products is a crucial strategy companies use to fine-tune and improve their business models in a mature industry, but this kind of competition can be as vicious as a price war because it is very expensive and can dramatically increase a company's cost structure. This happened in the chip industry where intense competition to make the fastest or most powerful chip and become the market leader has dramatically increased the cost structure of Intel, AMD, and NVIDIA and sharply reduced their profitability.

Market Development   **Market development** finds new market segments for a company's products. A company pursuing this strategy wants to capitalize on the brand name it has developed in one market segment by locating new market segments in which to compete—just as Mattel and Nike do by entering many different segments of the toy and shoe markets, respectively. In this way, companies can leverage the product differentiation advantages of their brand name. The Japanese auto manufacturers provide an interesting example of the use of market development. When each manufacturer entered the market, they offered a car model aimed at the economy segment of the auto market, such as the Toyota Corolla and the Honda Accord. Then, these companies upgraded each model over time; now each company is directed at a more expensive market segment. The Honda Accord is a leading contender in the mid-sized car segment, and the Toyota Corolla fills the small-car segment. By redefining their product offerings, Japanese manufacturers have profitably developed their market segments and successfully attacked their United States rivals, wresting market share from these companies. Although the Japanese used to compete primarily as cost leaders, market development has allowed them to become differentiators as well. In fact, as we noted in the previous chapter, Toyota has used market development to become a broad differentiator. Figure 6.9 illustrates how, over time, Toyota has used market development to create a vehicle for almost every segment of the car market, something discussed in Strategy in Action 6.3.[24]

Market development

When a company searches for new market segments for a company's existing products to increase sales.

Figure 6.9 Toyota's Product Lineup

Price	Utility Vehicles (SUVs)	Passenger/ Sports Sedans	Passenger Vans	Personal Luxury Vehicles	Sporty Cars	Pickup Trucks
$11–$20K	Scion xB	Camry, Matrix, Corolla, Prism, Scion xA			Celica GT	Tacoma
$21–$30K	RAV4- 4Runner, Highlander	Venza, Avalon	Sienna	Avalon	MR2, Spyder	Tundra
$31–$45K	Sequoia, RX330	GS 300, IS 300		ES 330	Camry, Solara	Tundra Double Cab
$46–$75K	Land Cruiser GX, LX	GS 430		LS 430	SC 430	

STRATEGY IN ACTION

Toyota Uses Market Development to Become the Global Leader

The car industry has always been one of the most competitive in the world because of the huge revenues and profits that are at stake. Given the difficult economic conditions in the late-2000s, it is hardly surprising that rivalry has increased as global carmakers struggle to develop new car models that better satisfy the needs of particular groups of buyers. One company at the competitive forefront is Toyota.

Toyota produced its first car 40 years ago, the ugly, boxy vehicle that was, however, it was cheap. As the quality of its car became apparent, sales increased. Toyota, which was then a focused cost leader, reinvested its profits into improving the styling of its vehicles, and into efforts to continually reduce production costs. Over time, Toyota has taken advantage of its low cost structure to make an ever-increasing range of reasonably priced vehicles tailored to different segments of the car market. The company's ability to begin with the initial design stage, and move to the production stage in 2–3 years allowed it to make new models available faster than its competitors, and capitalize on the development of new market segments.

Toyota has been a leader in positioning its entire range of vehicles to take advantage of new, emerging market segments. In the SUV segment, for example, its first offering was the expensive Toyota Land Cruiser, even then priced at over $35,000. Realizing the need for SUVs in lower price ranges, it next introduced the 4Runner, priced at $20,000 and designed for the average SUV customer; the RAV4, a small SUV in the low $20,000 range, followed; then came the Sequoia, a bigger, more powerful version of the 4Runner in the upper $20,000 range. Finally, taking the technology from its Lexus division, it introduced the luxury Highlander SUV in the low $30,000 range. Today it offers 6 SUV models, each offering a particular combination of price, size, performance, styling, and luxury to appeal to a particular customer group within the SUV segment of the car market. In a similar way, Toyota positions its sedans to appeal to the needs of different sets of customers. For example, the Camry is targeted at the middle of the market to customers who can afford to pay about $25,000 and want a balance of luxury, performance, safety, and reliability.

Toyota's broad differentiation business model is geared toward making a range of vehicles that optimizes the amount of value it can create for different groups of customers. At the same time, the number of models it makes is constrained by the need to keep costs under strict control so it can make car-pricing options that will generate maximum revenues and profits. Because competition in each car market segment is now intense, all global carmakers need to balance the advantages of showcasing more cars to attract customers against the increasing costs that result when the number of different car models they make expands to suit the needs of different customers.

Product Proliferation **Product proliferation** can be used to manage rivalry within an industry and also to deter entry. The strategy of product proliferation generally means that large companies in an industry all have a product in each market segment (or niche) and compete head-to-head for customers. If a new niche develops, such as SUVs, designer sunglasses, or shoe-selling websites, the leader gets a first-mover advantage—but soon thereafter, all the other companies catch up. Once again, competition is stabilized, and rivalry within the industry is reduced. Product proliferation thus allows the development of stable industry competition based on product differentiation, not price—that is, nonprice competition based on the development of new products. The competitive battle is over a product's perceived uniqueness, quality, features, and performance, not over its price.

The way in which Nike has used these nonprice competitive strategies to strengthen its differentiation business model is highly instructive. Bill Bowerman, a former University of Oregon track coach, and Phil Knight, an entrepreneur in search of a profitable business opportunity founded Nike, now headquartered in Beaverton, Oregon. Bowerman's dream was to create a new type of sneaker tread that would

> **Product proliferation**
>
> When a company develops many different products for different market segments to manage rivalry and deter entry into the industry.

enhance a runner's traction and speed, and after studying the waffle iron in his home, he came up with the idea for Nike's "waffle tread." Bowerman and Knight made this shoe, and began by selling it out of car trunks at track meets. Nike has since grown into a company that sells almost 45% of the shoes sold in the global $50 billion athletic footwear and apparel industries each year and made more than $2 billion in profit in 2011.

Nike's amazing success came from its business model, which was always based on differentiation; its strategy was to innovate state-of-the-art athletic shoes and then to publicize the qualities of its shoes through dramatic "guerrilla" marketing. Nike's marketing is designed to persuade customers that its shoes are not only superior, but also a high-fashion statement and a necessary part of a lifestyle based on sporting or athletic interests. Nike's strategy to emphasize the uniqueness of its product obviously paid off as its market share soared. However, the company received a shock in 1998, when its sales suddenly began to fall; it was becoming more and more difficult to design new shoes that its existing customers perceived to be significantly better and worth their premium price—in other words, its strategy of market penetration and product development was no longer paying off. Phil Knight recruited a team of talented top managers from leading consumer products companies to help him change Nike's business model in some fundamental ways.

In the past, Nike shunned sports like golf, soccer, rollerblading, and so on, and focused most of its efforts on making shoes for the track and basketball market segments. However, when its sales started to fall, it realized that using marketing to increase sales in a particular market segment (market penetration) could only grow sales and profits so much. Nike decided to take its existing design and marketing competencies and began to craft new lines of shoes for new market segments. In other words, it began to pursue market development and product proliferation as well as the other nonprice strategies. For example, it revamped its aerobics shoes, launched a line of soccer shoes, and perfected the company's design over time; by the mid-2000s, it took over as the market leader from its archrival Adidas. Nike's strategies significantly strengthened its differentiation business model, which is why its market share and profitability have continued to increase, and also why they are the envy of competitors.

Capacity Control Although nonprice competition helps mature industries avoid the cutthroat price cutting that reduces company and industry levels of profitability, price competition does periodically occur when excess capacity exists in an industry. Excess capacity arises when companies collectively produce too much output; to dispose of it, they cut prices. When one company cuts prices, other companies quickly do the same because they fear that the price cutter will be able to sell its entire inventory, while they will be left with unwanted goods. The result is a developing price war.

Excess capacity may be caused by a shortfall in demand, as when a recession lowers the demand for cars and causes car companies to give customers price incentives to purchase new cars. In this situation, companies can do nothing but wait for better times. By and large, however, excess capacity results from companies within an industry simultaneously responding to favorable conditions; they all invest in new plants to be able to take advantage of the predicted upsurge in demand. Paradoxically, each individual company's effort to outperform the others means that, collectively, companies create industry overcapacity, which hurts all companies.

Although demand is rising, the consequence of each company's decision to increase capacity is a surge in industry capacity, which drives down prices. To prevent the accumulation of costly excess capacity, companies must devise strategies that let them control—or at least benefit from—capacity expansion programs. Before we examine these strategies, however, we need to consider in greater detail the factors that cause excess capacity.[25]

Factors Causing Excess Capacity   The problem of excess capacity often derives from technological developments. Sometimes new low-cost technology can create an issue because all companies invest in it simultaneously to prevent being left behind. Excess capacity occurs because the new technology can produce more than the old. In addition, new technology is often introduced in large increments, which generates overcapacity. For instance, an airline that needs more seats on a route must add another plane, thereby adding hundreds of seats even if only 50 are needed. To take another example, a new chemical process may efficiently operate at the rate of only 1,000 gallons per day, whereas the previous process was efficient at 500 gallons per day. If all companies within an industry change technologies, industry capacity may double, and enormous problems can potentially result.

Overcapacity may also be caused by competitive factors within an industry. Entry into an industry is one such a factor. The recent economic recession caused global overcapacity and the price of steel plunged; with global recovery the price has increased. Sometimes the age of a company's physical assets is the source of the problem. For example, in the hotel industry, given the rapidity with which the quality of hotel room furnishings decline, customers are always attracted to new hotels. When new hotel chains are built alongside the old chains, excess capacity can result. Often, companies are simply making simultaneous competitive moves based on industry trends—but these moves lead to head-to-head competition. Most fast-food chains, for instance, establish new outlets whenever demographic data shows population increases. However, companies seem to forget that all other chains use the same data—they are not anticipating their rivals' actions. Thus, a certain locality that has few fast-food outlets may suddenly have several new outlets being built at the same time. Whether all the outlets can survive depends upon the growth rate of customer demand, but most often the least popular outlets close down.

Choosing a Capacity-Control Strategy   Given the various ways in which capacity can expand, companies clearly need to find some means of controlling it. If companies are always plagued by price cutting and price wars, they will be unable to recoup the investments in their generic strategies. Low profitability within an industry caused by overcapacity forces not only the weakest companies but also sometimes the major players to exit the industry. In general, companies have two strategic choices: (1) each company individually must try to preempt its rivals and seize the initiative, or (2) the companies must collectively find indirect means of coordinating with each other so that they are all aware of the mutual effects of their actions.

To *preempt* rivals, a company must forecast a large increase in demand in the product market and then move rapidly to establish large-scale operations that will be able to satisfy the predicted demand. By achieving a first-mover advantage, the company may deter other firms from entering the market because the preemptor will usually be able to move down the experience curve, reduce its costs, and, therefore, its prices as well—and threaten a price war if necessary.

This strategy, however, is extremely risky, for it involves investing resources before the extent and profitability of the future market are clear. Groupon, profiled in the opening case, is doing this. A preemptive strategy is also risky if it does not deter competitors, and they decide to enter the market—another major threat facing Groupon. If competitors can develop a stronger generic strategy, or have more resources, such as Google or Microsoft, they can make the preemptor suffer. Thus, for the strategy to succeed, the preemptor must generally be a credible company with enough resources to withstand a possible advertising/price war.

To *coordinate* with rivals as a capacity-control strategy, caution must be exercised because collusion on the timing of new investments is illegal under antitrust law. However, tacit coordination is practiced in many industries as companies attempt to understand and forecast one another's competitive moves. Generally, companies use market signaling to secure coordination. They make announcements about their future investment decisions in trade journals and newspapers. In addition, they share information about their production levels and their forecasts of demand within an industry to bring supply and demand into equilibrium. Thus, a coordination strategy reduces the risks associated with investment in the industry. This is very common in the chemical refining and oil businesses, where new capacity investments frequently cost hundreds of millions of dollars.

Strategies in Declining Industries

Sooner or later, many industries enter into a decline stage, in which the size of the total market begins to shrink. Examples are the railroad industry, the tobacco industry, and the steel industry. Industries start declining for a number of reasons, including technological change, social trends, and demographic shifts. The railroad and steel industries began to decline when technological changes brought viable substitutes for their products. The advent of the internal combustion engine drove the railroad industry into decline, and the steel industry fell into decline with the rise of plastics and composite materials. As for the tobacco industry, changing social attitudes toward smoking, which come from growing concerns about the health effects of smoking, have caused the decline.

The Severity of Decline

When the size of the total market is shrinking, competition tends to intensify in a declining industry, and profit rates tend to fall. The intensity of competition in a declining industry depends on four critical factors, which are indicated in Figure 6.10. First, the intensity of competition is greater in industries in which decline is rapid, opposed to industries such as tobacco, in which decline is slow and gradual.

Second, the intensity of competition is greater in declining industries in which exit barriers are high. Recall from Chapter 2 that high exit barriers keep companies locked into an industry, even when demand is falling. The result is the emergence of excess productive capacity and, hence, an increased probability of fierce price competition.

Third, and related to the previous point, the intensity of competition is greater in declining industries in which fixed costs are high (as in the steel industry). The reason is that the need to cover fixed costs, such as the costs of maintaining productive

Figure 6.10   Factors that Determine the Intensity of Competition in Declining Industries

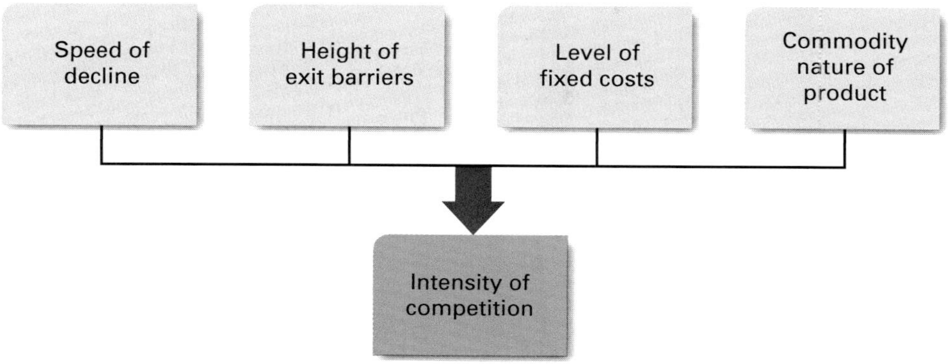

© Cengage Learning 2013

capacity, can make companies try to use any excess capacity they have by slashing prices, which can trigger a price war.

Finally, the intensity of competition is greater in declining industries in which the product is perceived as a commodity (as it is in the steel industry) in contrast to industries in which differentiation gives rise to significant brand loyalty, as was true (until very recently) of the declining tobacco industry.

Not all segments of an industry typically decline at the same rate. In some segments, demand may remain reasonably strong despite decline elsewhere. The steel industry illustrates this situation. Although bulk steel products, such as sheet steel, have suffered a general decline, demand has actually risen for specialty steels, such as those used in high-speed machine tools. Vacuum tubes provide another example. Although demand for the tubes collapsed when transistors replaced them as a key component in many electronics products, vacuum tubes still had some limited applications in radar equipment for years afterward. Consequently, demand in this vacuum tube segment remained strong despite the general decline in the demand for vacuum tubes. The point, then, is that there may be pockets of demand in an industry in which demand is declining more slowly than in the industry as a whole—or where demand is not declining at all. Price competition may be far less intense among the companies serving pockets of demand than within the industry as a whole.

Choosing a Strategy

There are four main strategies that companies can adopt to deal with decline: (1) a **leadership strategy**, by which a company seeks to become the dominant player in a declining industry; (2) a **niche strategy**, which focuses on pockets of demand that are declining more slowly than the industry as a whole; (3) a **harvest strategy**, which optimizes cash flow; and (4) a **divestment strategy**, by which a company sells the business to others. Figure 6.11 provides a simple framework for guiding strategic choice. Note that the intensity of competition in the declining industry is measured on the vertical axis, and a company's strengths relative to remaining pockets of demand are measured on the horizontal axis.

Leadership strategy

When a company develops strategies to become the dominant player in a declining industry.

Niche strategy

When a company focuses on pockets of demand that are declining more slowly than the industry as a whole to maintain profitability.

Harvest strategy

When a company reduces investment in its business in order to optimize current cash flow.

Divestment strategy

When a company decides to exit an industry by selling off its business assets to another company.

Figure 6.11   Strategy Selection in a Declining Industry

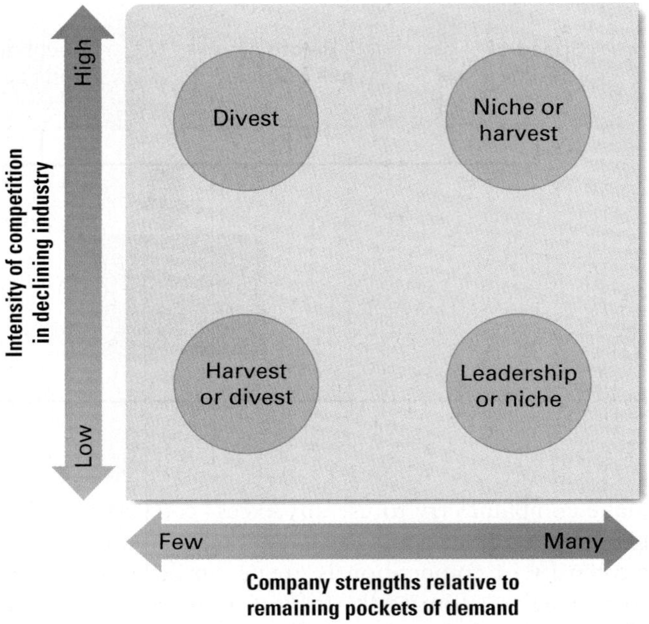

© Cengage Learning 2013

Leadership Strategy   A leadership strategy aims at growing in a declining industry by picking up the market share of companies that are leaving the industry. A leadership strategy makes most sense when (1) the company has distinctive strengths that allow it to capture market share in a declining industry and (2) the speed of decline and the intensity of competition in the declining industry are moderate. Philip Morris has pursued this strategy in the tobacco industry. Through aggressive marketing, Philip Morris has increased its market share in a declining industry and earned enormous profits in the process.

The tactical steps companies might use to achieve a leadership position include using aggressive pricing and marketing to build market share, acquiring established competitors to consolidate the industry, and raising the stakes for other competitors, for example, by making new investments in productive capacity. Competitive tactics such as these, signal to other competitors that the company is willing and able to stay and compete in the declining industry. These signals may persuade other companies to exit the industry, which would further enhance the competitive position of the industry leader. Strategy in Action 6.4 offers an example of a company, Richardson Electronics, one of the last companies in the vacuum tube business, which has prospered by taking a leadership position in a declining industry.

Niche Strategy   A niche strategy focuses on pockets of demand in the industry in which demand is stable, or declining less rapidly than the industry as a whole. This strategy makes sense when the company has some unique strengths relative to those niches in which demand remains relatively strong. As an example, consider Naval,

STRATEGY IN ACTION

How to Make Money in the Vacuum Tube Business

At its peak in the early-1950s, the vacuum tube business was a major industry in which companies such as Westinghouse, GE, RCA, and Western Electric had a large stake. Then the transistor was invented, making most vacuum tubes obsolete, and one by one, all the large companies manufacturing vacuum tubes exited the industry. One company, however, Richardson Electronics, not only stayed in the business, but also demonstrated that high returns are possible in a declining industry. Richardson bought the remains of a dozen companies in the United States and Europe as those companies exited the vacuum tube industry, despite that it was, primarily, a distribution company with some manufacturing capabilities. Today, Richardson has a warehouse that stocks more than 10,000 different types of vacuum tubes. The company is the world's only supplier of many of these tubes, which explains why its gross profit margin is approximately 35% to 40%.

Richardson remains in business—and prospers—because vacuum tubes are vital parts of some older electronic equipment that would be costly to replace with solid-state equipment. In addition, vacuum tubes still outperform semiconductors in some limited applications, including radar and welding machines. The U.S. government, GE, and GM are big customers of Richardson.

Speed is the essence of Richardson's business. The company's Illinois warehouse offers overnight delivery to at least 40,000 customers, and it processes 650 orders a day at an average price of $550. Customers such as GM do not really care whether a vacuum tube costs $250 or $350; what they care about is the $40,000 to $50,000 downtime loss that they face when a key piece of welding equipment is not working. By quickly responding to the demands of customers, and because they are the only major supplier of many types of vacuum tubes, Richardson has placed itself in a position that many companies in growing industries would envy: a monopoly position. However, a new company, Westrex Corporation, was formed to take advantage of the growing popularity of vacuum tubes in high-end stereo systems, and today it is directly competing with Richardson in some market segments. Clearly, good profits can be made even in a declining industry.

Sources: P. Haynes, "Western Electric Redux," *Forbes,* January 26, 1998, 46–47; www.westrexcorp.com, 2011; www.ge.com, 2011.

a company that manufactures whaling harpoons (and small guns to fire them) and makes adequate profits. This might be considered rather odd because the world community has outlawed whaling. However, Naval survived the terminal decline of the harpoon industry by focusing on the one group of people who are still allowed to hunt whales, although only in very limited numbers: North American Inuits. Inuits are permitted to hunt bowhead whales, provided that they do so only for food and not for commercial purposes. Naval is the sole supplier of small harpoon whaling guns to Inuit communities, and its monopoly position allows the company to earn a healthy return in this small market.

Harvest Strategy   As we noted earlier, a harvest strategy is the best choice when a company wishes to exit a declining industry and optimize cash flow in the process. This strategy makes the most sense when the company foresees a steep decline and intense future competition, or when it lacks strengths relative to remaining pockets of demand in the industry. A harvest strategy requires the company to halt all new investments in capital equipment, advertising, R&D, etc. The inevitable result is that the company will lose market share, but because it is no longer investing in the business, initially its positive cash flow will increase. Essentially, the company is accepting cash flow in exchange for market share. Ultimately, cash flow will start to decline, and when that occurs, it makes sense for the company to liquidate the business. Although this strategy can be very appealing in theory, it can be somewhat difficult to put into practice. Employee morale in a business that is declining may suffer. Furthermore, if customers realize what the company is doing, they may rapidly defect. Then, market share may decline much faster than the company expects.

Divestment Strategy   A divestment strategy rests on the idea that a company can recover most of its investment in an underperforming business by selling it early, before the industry has entered into a steep decline. This strategy is appropriate when the company has few strengths relative to whatever pockets of demand are likely to remain in the industry and when the competition in the declining industry is likely to be intense. The best option may be to sell to a company that is pursuing a leadership strategy in the industry. The drawback of the divestment strategy is that its success depends upon the ability of the company to spot industry decline before it becomes detrimental, and to sell while the company's assets are still valued by others.

Ethical Dilemma

the cost of ingredients, which will reduce product quality; another is to reduce the content of the products while maintaining the size of the packaging; a third is to slightly change an existing product and then offer it as a "new" premium brand that can be sold at a higher price.

A team of marketing managers for a major differentiated consumer products company has been instructed by top managers to develop new strategies to increase the profitability of the company's products. One idea is to lower

Do you think it is ethical to pursue these strategies and present them to management? In what ways could these strategies backfire and cause the company harm?

Summary of Chapter

1. In fragmented industries composed of a large number of small- and medium-sized companies, the principal forms of competitive strategy are using the Internet, chaining, franchising, and horizontal merger.

2. In embryonic and growth industries, strategy is partly determined by market demand. Innovators and early adopters have different needs than the early and the late majority, and a company must

have the right strategies in place to cross the chasms and survive. Similarly, managers must understand the factors that affect a market's growth rate so that they can tailor their business model to a changing industry environment.

3. Companies need to navigate the difficult road from growth to maturity by choosing an investment strategy that supports their business models. In choosing this strategy, managers must

consider the company's competitive position in the industry and the stage of the industry's life cycle. Some main types of investment strategy are share building, growth, market concentration, share increasing, harvest, and hold-and-maintain.

4. Mature industries are composed of a few large companies whose actions are so highly interdependent that the success of one company's strategy depends upon the responses of its rivals.

5. The principal strategies used by companies in mature industries to deter entry are product proliferation, price cutting, and maintaining excess capacity.

6. The principal strategies used by companies in mature industries to manage rivalry are price signaling, price leadership, nonprice competition, and capacity control.

7. In declining industries, in which market demand has leveled off or is decreasing, companies must tailor their price and nonprice strategies to the new competitive environment. Companies also need to manage industry capacity to prevent the emergence of capacity expansion problems.

8. There are four main strategies a company can pursue when demand is falling: leadership, niche, harvest, and divestment. The strategic choice is determined by the severity of industry decline and the company's strengths relative to the remaining pockets of demand.

Discussion Questions

1. Discuss how companies can use: (a) product differentiation, and (b) capacity control to manage rivalry and increase an industry's profitability.

2. What kinds of strategies might: (a) a small pizza place operating in a crowded college market, and (b) a detergent manufacturer seeking to unveil new products in an established market use to strengthen their business models?

3. Why are industries fragmented? What are the primary ways in which companies can turn a fragmented industry into a consolidated industry?

4. What are the key problems in maintaining a competitive advantage in embryonic and growth industry environments? What are the dangers associated with being the leader in an industry?

5. What investment strategies should be made by: (a) differentiators in a strong competitive position, and (b) differentiators in a weak competitive position, while managing a company's growth through the life cycle?

Practicing Strategic Management

 Small-Group Exercises

How to Keep the Salsa Hot

Break into groups of 3–5 people and discuss the following scenario. Appoint one group member as a spokesperson who will communicate your findings to the class. You are the managers of a company that has pioneered a new kind of salsa for chicken that has taken the market by storm. The salsa's differentiated appeal has been based on a unique combination of spices and packaging that has allowed you to charge a premium price. Over the past 3 years, your company's salsa has achieved a national reputation, and now major food companies such as Kraft and Nabisco, seeing the potential of this market segment, are beginning to introduce new salsas of their own, imitating your product.

1. Describe your business model and the strategies you are pursuing.
2. Describe the industry's environment in which you are competing.
3. What kinds of competitive strategies could you adopt to strengthen your business model in this kind of environment?

Strategy Sign-On

Article File 6

Choose a company (or group of companies) in a particular industry environment and explain how it has adopted a competitive strategy to protect or enhance its business-level strategy.

Strategic Management Project: Developing Your Portfolio 6

This part of the project considers how conditions in the industry environment affect the success of your company's business model and strategies. With the information you have available, perform the tasks and answer the questions listed:

1. In what kind of industry environment (e.g., embryonic, mature, etc.) does your company operate? Use the information from Strategic Management Project: Module 2 to answer this question.
2. Discuss how your company has attempted to develop strategies to protect and strengthen its business model. For example, if your company is operating in an embryonic industry, how has it attempted to increase its competitive advantage over time? If it operates in a mature industry, discuss how it has tried to manage industry competition.
3. What new strategies would you advise your company to pursue to increase its competitive advantage? For example, how should your company attempt to differentiate its products in the future, or lower its cost structure?
4. On the basis of this analysis, do you think your company will be able to maintain its competitive advantage in the future? Why or why not?

CLOSING CASE

From Holiday Inns to the InterContinental Hotels Group

The history of the Holiday Inn motel chain is one of the great success stories in United States business. Its founder, Kemmons Wilson, while vacationing in the early-1950s, found the motels he stayed in to be small, expensive, and of unpredictable quality. This discovery, along with an unprecedented amount of highway travel due to the new, integrated interstate highway program, triggered a realization: there was an unmet customer need—a gap in the market for quality accommodations.[26] Holiday Inn was founded to meet that need. From the beginning, Holiday Inn set the standard for offering motel features such as air-conditioning and icemakers while keeping room rates reasonable. These amenities enhanced the motels' popularity, and motel franchising, which was Wilson's own invention, made rapid expansion possible. By 1960, Holiday Inn hotels could be found in virtually every major city and on every major highway. Before the 1960s ended, more than 1,000 were in full operation, and occupancy rates averaged 80%. The concept of mass accommodation had arrived.

Holiday Inn offered a service that appealed to the average traveler, who wanted a standardized product (a room) at an average price—the middle of the hotel room market. But by the 1970s, travelers were beginning to make different demands on hotels and motels. Some wanted luxury and were willing to pay higher prices for better accommodations and service. Others sought low prices and accepted rock-bottom quality and service in exchange for luxury. As the market fragmented into different groups of customers with different needs, Holiday Inn continued to offer an undifferentiated, average-cost, average-quality product.

Although Holiday Inn missed the change in the market and failed to respond appropriately to it, the competition did not. Companies such as Hyatt siphoned off the top end of the market, where quality and service sold rooms. Chains such as Motel 6 and Days Inn captured the basic-quality, low-price end of the market. Many specialty chains that appealed to business travelers, families, or self-caterers (people who wanted to cook in their hotel rooms) were in between. Holiday Inn's position was attacked from all directions. As occupancy rates drastically dropped and competition increased, profitability declined.

Wounded but not dead, Holiday Inn began a "counterattack." The original chain was upgraded to suit quality-oriented travelers. Then, to meet the needs of different types of travelers, Holiday Inn created new hotel and motel chains: the luxury Crowne Plaza; Hampton Inn serving the low-priced end of the market; and the all-suite Embassy Suites. Thus, Holiday Inn attempted to meet the demands of the many niches, or segments, of the hotel market that have emerged as customers' needs have changed over time. These moves were successful in the early-1990s, and Holiday Inn has since grown to become one of the largest suppliers of hotel rooms in the industry. However, by the late-1990s, falling revenues made it clear that with intense competition from other chains such as Marriott, Holiday Inn was once again losing its differentiated appeal.[27]

In the fast-changing hotel and lodging market, positioning each hotel brand or chain to maximize customer demand is a continuing endeavor. In 2000, the pressure on all hotel chains to adapt to the challenges of global competition and to become globally differentiated brands led to the purchase of Holiday Inn, and its incorporation into the InterContinental Hotels Group chain. Today, more than 3,200 hotels around the globe, flying the flags of Holiday Inn, Holiday Inn Express, Crowne Plaza, Candlewood Suites, Staybridge Suites, and luxury InterContinental Hotels and Resorts are positioning to offer the services, amenities, and lodging experiences that will cater to every travel occasion and guest need.[28] In the 2010s, the company is continuing its massive modernization campaign in the United States to evolve the existing full-service Holiday Inns to their next inception. InterContinental Hotels plans to make available a hotel room to meet the need of every segment of the lodging market anywhere in the world.

Case Discussion Questions

1. Why did Holiday Inn's business model and strategies change over time?
2. How has competition changed the strategies behind the InterContinental Hotels Group's business model over time?

3. In what ways is it using nonprice strategies to improve its competitive advantage?

Notes

[1] www.groupon.com, 2011.

[2] Ibid.

[3] M. E. Porter, *Competitive Strategy: Techniques for Analyzing Industries and Competitors* (New York: Free Press, 1980), pp. 191–200.

[4] S. A. Shane, "Hybrid Organizational Arrangements and Their Implications for Firm Growth and Survival: A Study of New Franchisors," *Academy of Management Journal* 1 (1996): 216–234.

[5] Microsoft is often accused of not being an innovator, but the fact is that Gates and Allen wrote the first commercial software program for the first commercially available personal computer. Microsoft was the first mover in their industry. See P. Freiberger and M. Swaine, *Fire in the Valley* (New York: McGraw-Hill, 2000).

[6] J. M. Utterback, *Mastering the Dynamics of Innovation* (Boston: Harvard Business School Press, 1994).

[7] See Freiberger and Swaine, *Fire in the Valley*.

[8] G. A. Moore, *Crossing the Chasm* (New York: HarperCollins, 1991).

[9] Utterback, *Mastering the Dynamics of Innovation*.

[10] E. Rogers, *Diffusion of Innovations* (New York: Free Press, 1995).

[11] C. W. Hofer and D. Schendel, *Strategy Formulation: Analytical Concepts* (St. Paul, MN: West, 1978).

[12] Ibid.

[13] Ibid.

[14] J. Brander and J. Eaton, "Product Line Rivalry," *American Economic Review* 74 (1985): 323–334.

[15] Ibid.

[16] Porter, *Competitive Strategy*, 76–86.

[17] O. Heil and T. S. Robertson, "Towards a Theory of Competitive Market Signaling: A Research Agenda," *Strategic Management Journal* 12 (1991): 403–418.

[18] R. Axelrod, *The Evolution of Cooperation* (New York: Basic Books, 1984).

[19] F. Scherer, *Industrial Market Structure and Economic Performance*, 10th ed. (Boston: Houghton Mifflin, 2000), chap. 8.

[20] The model differs from Ansoff's model for this reason.

[21] H. I. Ansoff, *Corporate Strategy* (London: Penguin Books, 1984), pp. 97–100.

[22] R. D. Buzzell, B. T. Gale, and R. G. M. Sultan, "Market Share: A Key to Profitability," *Harvard Business Review* (January–February 1975): 97–103; R. Jacobson and D. A. Aaker, "Is Market Share All That It's Cracked Up to Be?" *Journal of Marketing* 49 (1985): 11–22.

[23] Ansoff, *Corporate Strategy*, 98–99.

[24] Figure copyright © Gareth R. Jones, 2011.

[25] The next section draws heavily on Marvin B. Lieberman, "Strategies for Capacity Expansion," *Sloan Management Review* 8 (1987): 19–27; Porter, *Competitive Strategy*, 324–338.

[26] "The Holiday Inns Trip; A Breeze for Decades, Bumpy Ride in the 1980s," *Wall Street Journal*, February 11, 1987, 1; U.S. Bureau of Labor Statistics, U.S. Industrial Output (Washington, DC: U.S. Government Printing Office, 1986).

[27] M. Gleason and A. Salomon, "Fallon's Challenge: Make Holiday Inn More 'In,'" *Advertising Age*, September 2, 1996, 14; J. Miller, "Amenities Range from Snacks to Technology," *Hotel and Motel Management*, July 3, 1996, 38–40.

[28] www.ichotelsgroup.com, 2011.

7

Strategy and Technology

erel photography/istockphoto.com

The Rise of Cloud Computing

There is a paradigm shift beginning in the world of computing. Over the next decade, increasing numbers of businesses will stop purchasing their own computer servers and mainframes, and instead move their applications and data to "the cloud." The cloud is a metaphor for large data centers or "server farms"—collections of hundreds of thousands of co-located and interlinked computer servers. Corporations will be able to "host" their data and applications on cloud computing providers' servers. To run an application hosted on the cloud, all a person will need is a computing device with a Web browser and an Internet connection.

There are significant cost advantages associated with shifting data and applications to the cloud. Business will no longer need to invest in information technology hardware that rapidly becomes obsolete. Cloud providers will instead be responsible for maintenance costs of servers and hardware. Moreover, businesses will no longer need to purchase many software applications. Instead, businesses will utilize a pay-as-you-go pricing model for any applications that they use, which also holds out the promise of

reducing costs. (Some studies have concluded that 70% of software purchased by corporations is either underutilized, or, not used at all.) The Brookings Institute estimates that companies could reduce their information technology costs by as much as 50% by moving to the cloud.

Early adopters of cloud computing services have included Inter-Continental Hotel Group (IHG), which has 650,000 rooms in 4,400 hotels around the world. Rather than upgrade its own information technology hardware, IHG has decided to move its central reservation system onto server farms owned by Amazon.com, the online retail store that is also emerging as an early leader in the cloud computing market.

LEARNING OBJECTIVES
After reading this chapter you should be able to:
- Understand the tendency toward standardization in many high-technology markets
- Describe the strategies that firms can use to establish their technology as the standard in a market
- Explain the cost structure of many high-technology firms, and articulate the strategic implications of this structure
- Explain the nature of technological paradigm shifts and their implications for enterprise strategy

Similarly, Netflix has decided to utilize Amazon's cloud services for distributing its movies digitally, rather than investing in its own server farms. Another early user of cloud services is Starbucks, which has moved its entire corporate e-mail system off its servers and onto Microsoft's cloud computing system.

Amazon and Microsoft are two of the early leaders in the embryonic cloud computing market. The other significant player is Google. All three companies had to build large server farms to run parts of their own businesses (online retail in the case of Amazon, and Web searching capabilities in the case of Google and Microsoft). When these corporations soon realized that they could rent out capacity on these server farms to other businesses, the concept of cloud computing was born. Other companies that have announced their intentions to enter the cloud computing market as providers of hosting services include IBM and Hewlett-Packard.

Right now the cloud is small—estimates suggest that it accounts for just 5% of the $1.5 trillion in corporate information technology spending in 2010. But many analysts believe that this share will grow very rapidly. Amazon, with an estimated $750 million in revenue from cloud services, is currently the leading company. Both Microsoft and Google, recognizing how crucial the cloud will become, are investing heavily in this technology.

Microsoft has developed an operating system, known as Windows Azure, which is designed to run software applications very efficiently on server farms, allocating workloads and balancing capacity across hundreds of thousands of servers. Microsoft is rewriting many of its own applications, such as Office and SQL server, to run on Azure. The belief is that this will help the company retain existing clients as they transition their data and applications from their own servers onto the cloud. Microsoft has also developed tools to help clients write their own custom applications for the cloud; they have recognized that the shift to the cloud threatens its existing Windows monopoly, and that its best strategy is to try and become the dominant company on the cloud.

Microsoft's rivals are not idly standing by. Google, for example, has developed a cloud-based operating system, Google App Engine, which will allow clients to efficiently run their custom software applications on the cloud. Amazon, too, has its own cloud-based operating system, known as "EC2." Other companies, including IBM and VM Ware, are developing similar software. Software applications that are written for one cloud based system operating system will not run on another cloud operating system without a complete rewrite—meaning that there will be significant switching costs involved in moving an application from one cloud provider to another. This strongly suggests that we are witnessing the beginnings of a format war in cloud computing, much like the format war during the early-1990s between Microsoft, IBM, and Apple to dominate the desktop computer—a war that Microsoft won with its Windows Operating System. If business history is any guild, at most only 2–3 formats will survive, with most other formats falling by the wayside.[1]

Overview

The paradigm shift that is beginning to occur in the computer industry with the development of cloud computing, and the beginnings of a format war between Microsoft, Google, Amazon, IBM, VM Ware, and others, to develop the dominant cloud operating system, is typical of the nature of competition in high-technology industries (see the Opening Case). In this chapter, we will take a close look at the nature of competition and strategy in high-technology industries. Technology refers to the body of scientific knowledge used in the production of goods or services. High-technology (high-tech) industries are those in which the underlying scientific knowledge that companies in the industry use is rapidly advancing, and by implication, so are the attributes of the products and services that result from its application. The computer industry is often thought of as the quintessential example of a high-technology industry. Other industries often considered high-tech are: telecommunications, where new technologies based on wireless and the Internet have proliferated in recent years; consumer electronics, where the digital technology underlying products from high definition DVD players to videogame terminals and digital cameras is advancing rapidly; pharmaceuticals, where new technologies based on cell biology, recombinant DNA, and genomics are revolutionizing the process of drug discovery; power generation, where new technologies based on fuel cells and cogeneration may change the economics of the industry; and aerospace, where the combination of new composite materials, electronics, and more efficient jet engines are giving birth to a new era of super-efficient commercial jet aircraft such as Boeing's 787.

This chapter focuses on high-technology industries for a number of reasons. First, technology is accounting for an ever-larger share of economic activity. Estimates suggest that 12%–15% of total economic activity in the United States is accounted for by information technology industries.[2] This figure actually underestimates the true impact of technology on the economy, because it ignores the other high-technology areas we just mentioned. Moreover, as technology advances, many low-technology industries are becoming more high-tech. For example, the development of biotechnology and genetic engineering transformed the production of seed corn, long considered a low-technology business, into a high-technology business. Retailing was once considered a low technology business, but the shift to online retailing, led by companies like Amazon.com, has changed this. In addition, high-technology products are making their way into a wide range of businesses; today most automobiles contain more computing power than the multimillion-dollar mainframe computers used in the Apollo space program, and the competitive advantage of physical stores, such as Walmart, is based on their use of information technology. The circle of high-technology industries is both large and expanding, and technology is revolutionizing aspects of the product or production system even in industries not typically considered high-tech.

Although high-tech industries may produce very different products, when developing a business model and strategies that will lead to a competitive advantage and superior profitability and profit growth, they often face a similar situation. For example, "winner-take-all" format wars are common in many high-technology industries, such as the consumer electronics and computer industries (see the Opening Case for an example of an emerging format war). This chapter examines the competitive features found in many high-tech industries and the kinds of strategies that companies must adopt to build business models that will allow them to achieve superior profitability and profit growth.

By the time you have completed this chapter, you will have an understanding of the nature of competition in high-tech industries, and the strategies that companies can pursue to succeed in those industries.

Technical Standards and Format Wars

Especially in high-tech industries, ownership of **technical standards**—a set of technical specifications that producers adhere to when making the product, or a component of it—can be an important source of competitive advantage.[3] Indeed, in many cases the source of product differentiation is based on the technical standard. Often, only one standard will dominate a market, so many battles in high-tech industries involve companies that are competing to set the standard. For example, Microsoft Windows is the dominant operating system for personal computers, residing on over 90% of the world's PCs.

Battles to set and control technical standards in a market are referred to as **format wars**—essentially, battles to control the source of differentiation, and thus the value that such differentiation can create for the customer. Because differentiated products often command premium prices and are often expensive to develop, the competitive stakes are enormous. The profitability and survival of a company may depend on the outcome of the battle. For example, the outcome of the battle now being waged over the establishment and ownership of the operating system for cloud computing will help determine which companies will be leaders in that marketplace (see the Opening Case).

Examples of Standards

A familiar example of a standard is the layout of a computer keyboard. No matter what keyboard you purchase, the letters are all arranged in the same pattern.[4] The reason is quite obvious. Imagine if each computer maker changed the ways the keys were laid out—if some started with QWERTY on the top row of letters (which is indeed the format used and is known as the QWERTY format), some with YUHGFD, and some with ACFRDS. If you learned to type on one layout, it would be irritating and time-consuming to have to relearn on a YUHGFD layout. The standard format (QWERTY) it makes it easy for people to move from computer to computer because the input medium, the keyboard, is set in a standard way.

Another example of a technical standard can be seen in the dimensions of containers used to ship goods on trucks, railcars, and ships: all have the same basic dimensions—the same height, length, and width—and all make use of the same locking mechanisms to hold them onto a surface or to bolt against each other. Having a standard ensures that containers can easily be moved from one mode of transportation to another—from trucks, to railcars, to ships, and back to railcars. If containers lacked standard dimensions and locking mechanisms, it would suddenly become much more difficult to ship containers around the world. Shippers would need to make sure that they had the right kind of container to go on the ships and trucks and railcars scheduled to carry a particular container around the world—a very complicated process.

Technical standards

A set of technical specifications that producers adhere to when making the product, or a component of it.

Format wars

Battles to control the source of differentiation, and thus the value that such differentiation can create for the customer.

Consider, finally, the personal computer. Most share a common set of features: an Intel or Intel-compatible microprocessor, random access memory (RAM), a Microsoft operating system, an internal hard drive, a DVD drive, a keyboard, a monitor, a mouse, a modem, and so on. We call this set of features the dominant design for personal computers (a **dominant design** refers to a common set of features or design characteristics). Embedded in this design are several technical standards (see Figure 7.1). For example, there is the Wintel technical standard based on an Intel microprocessor and a Microsoft operating system. Microsoft and Intel "own" that standard, which is central to the personal computer. Developers of software applications, component parts, and peripherals such as printers adhere to this standard when developing their own products because this guarantees that their products will work well with a personal computer based on the Wintel standard. Another technical standard for connecting peripherals to the PC is the Universal Serial Bus (or USB), established by an industry standards-setting board. No one owns it; the standard is in the public domain. A third technical standard is for communication between a PC and the Internet via a modem. Known as TCP/IP, this standard was also set by an industry association and is in the public domain. Thus, as with many other products, the PC is actually based on several technical standards. It is also important to note that when a company owns a standard, as Microsoft and Intel do with the Wintel standard, it may be a source of competitive advantage and high profitability.

Benefits of Standards

Standards emerge because there are economic benefits associated with them. First, a technical standard helps to guarantee compatibility between products and their complements. For example, containers are used with railcars, trucks, and ships, and

Dominant design

Common set of features or design characteristics.

Figure 7.1 Technical Standards for Personal Computers

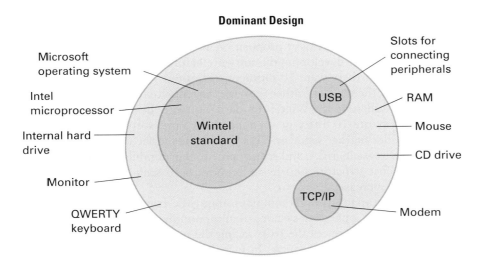

PCs are used with software applications. Compatibility has the tangible economic benefit of reducing the costs associated with making sure that products work well with each other.

Second, having a standard can help to reduce confusion in the minds of consumers. A few years ago, several consumer electronics companies were vying with each other to produce and market the first generation of DVD players, and they were championing different variants of the basic DVD technology—different standards—that were incompatible with each other; a DVD disk designed to run on a DVD player made by Toshiba would not run on a player made by Sony, and vice versa. The companies feared that selling these incompatible versions of the same technology would produce confusion in the minds of consumers, who would not know which version to purchase and might decide to wait and see which technology would dominate the marketplace. With lack of demand, the technology might fail to gain traction in the marketplace and would not be successful. To avoid this possibility, the developers of DVD equipment established a standard-setting body for the industry, the DVD Forum, which established a common technical standard for DVD players and disks that all companies adhered to. The result was that when DVDs were introduced, there was a common standard and no confusion in consumers' minds. This helped to boost demand for DVD players, making this one of the fastest-selling technologies of the late-1990s and early-2000s.

Third, the emergence of a standard can help to reduce production costs. Once a standard emerges, products that are based on the standard design can be mass-produced, enabling the manufacturers to realize substantial economies of scale while lowering their cost structures. The fact that there is a central standard for PCs (the Wintel standard) means that the component parts for a PC can be mass-produced. A manufacturer of internal hard drives, for example, can mass-produce drives for Wintel PCs, and so can realize substantial scale economies. If there were several competing and incompatible standards, each of which required a unique type of hard drive, production runs for hard drives would be shorter, unit costs would be higher, and the cost of PCs would increase.

Fourth, the emergence of standards can help to reduce the risks associated with supplying complementary products, and thus increase the supply for those complements. Consider the risks associated with writing software applications to run on personal computers. This is a risky proposition, requiring the investment of considerable sums of money for developing the software before a single unit is sold. Imagine what would occur if there were 10 different operating systems in use for PCs, each with only 10% of the market, rather than the current situation, where over 90% of the world's PCs adhere to the Wintel standard. Software developers would be faced with the need to write 10 different versions of the same software application, each for a much smaller market segment. This would change the economics of software development, increase its risks, and reduce potential profitability. Moreover, because of their higher cost structure and fewer economies of scale, the price of software programs would increase.

Thus, although many people complain about the consequences of Microsoft's near monopoly of PC operating systems, that monopoly does have at least one good effect: it substantially reduces the risks facing the makers of complementary products and the costs of those products. In fact, standards lead to both low-cost and differentiation advantages for individual companies and can help raise the level of industry profitability.

Establishment of Standards

Standards emerge in an industry in three primary ways. First, when the benefits of establishing a standard are recognized, companies in an industry might lobby the government to mandate an industry standard. In the United States, for example, the Federal Communications Commission (FCC), after detailed discussions with broadcasters and consumer electronics companies, has mandated a single technical standard for digital television broadcasts (DTV) and required broadcasters to have capabilities in place for broadcasting digital signals based on this standard by 2006. The FCC took this step because it believed that without government action to set the standard, the DTV rollout would be very slow. With a standard set by the government, consumer electronics companies can have greater confidence that a market will emerge, and this should encourage them to develop DTV products.

Second, technical standards are often set by cooperation among businesses, without government help, and often through the medium of an industry association such as the DVD Forum. Companies cooperate in this way when they decide that competition to create a standard might be harmful because of the uncertainty that it would create in the minds of consumers.

When the government or an industry association sets standards , these standards fall into the **public domain**, meaning that any company can freely incorporate the knowledge and technology upon which the standard is based into its products. For example, no one owns the QWERTY format, and therefore no one company can profit from it directly. Similarly, the language that underlies the presentation of text and graphics on the Web, hypertext markup language (HTML), is in the public domain; it is free for all to use. The same is true for TCP/IP, the communications standard used for transmitting data on the Internet.

Often, however, the industry standard is selected competitively by the purchasing patterns of customers in the marketplace—that is, by market demand. In this case, the strategy and business model a company has developed for promoting its technological standard are of critical importance because ownership of an industry standard that is protected from imitation by patents and copyrights is a valuable asset—a source of sustained competitive advantage and superior profitability. Microsoft and Intel, for example, both owe their competitive advantage to their ownership of a specific technological standard or format. **Format wars** occur when two or more companies compete against each other to get their designs adopted as the industry standard. Format wars are common in high-tech industries where standards are important. The Wintel standard became the dominant standard for PCs only after Microsoft and Intel won format wars against Apple's proprietary system, and later against IBM's OS/2 operating system. The Opening Case describes how a number of firms are engaged in a format war in the cloud computing business. There is also a format war ongoing today between in the smartphone business as Apple, Google, Research in Motion, and Microsoft all battle to get their respective operating systems and phones adopted as the industry standard.

Network Effects, Positive Feedback, and Lockout

There has been a growing realization that when standards are set by competition between companies promoting different formats, network effects are a primary determinant of how standards are established.[5] **Network effects** arise in industries where the size of the "network" of complementary products is a primary determinant of

Public domain

Government- or association-set standards of knowledge or technology that any company can freely incorporate into its product.

Network effects

The network of complementary products as a primary determinant of the demand for an industry's product.

demand for an industry's product. For example, the demand for automobiles early in the 20th century was an increasing function of the network of paved roads and gas stations. Similarly, the demand for telephones is an increasing function of the multitude of other numbers that can be called with that phone; that is, of the size of the telephone network (the telephone network is the complementary product). When the first telephone service was introduced in New York City, only 100 numbers could be called. The network was very small because of the limited number of wires and telephone switches, which made the telephone a relatively useless piece of equipment. But, as an increasing number of people got telephones, and as the network of wires and switches expanded, the telephone connection gained value. This led to an upsurge in demand for telephone lines, which further increased the value of owning a telephone, setting up a positive feedback loop.

To understand why network effects are important in the establishment of standards, consider the classic example of a format war: the battle between Sony and Matsushita to establish their respective technologies for videocassette recorders (VCRs) as the standard in the marketplace. Sony was first to market with its Betamax technology, followed by Matsushita with its VHS technology. Both companies sold VCR recorder-players, and movie studios issued films prerecorded on VCR tapes for rental to consumers. Initially, all tapes were issued in Betamax format to play on Sony's machine. Sony did not license its Betamax technology, preferring to make all of the player-recorders itself. When Matsushita entered the market, it realized that to make its VHS format players valuable to consumers, it would need to encourage movie studios to issue movies for rental on VHS tapes. The only way to do that, Matsushita's managers reasoned, was to increase the installed base of VHS players as rapidly as possible. They believed that the greater the installed base of VHS players, the greater the incentive for movie studios to issue films on VHS format tapes for rental. As more prerecorded VHS tapes were made available for rental, the VHS player became more valuable to consumers, and therefore, the demand for VHS players increased (see Figure 7.2). Matsushita wanted to exploit a positive feedback loop.

Figure 7.2 Positive Feedback in the Market for VCRs

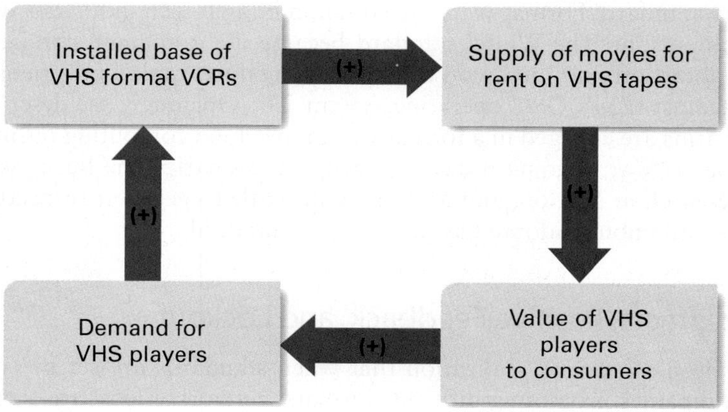

To do this, Matsushita chose a licensing strategy under which any consumer electronics company was allowed to manufacture VHS format players under license. This strategy worked. A large number of companies signed on to manufacture VHS players, and soon far more VHS players were available for purchase in stores than Betamax players. As sales of VHS players started to grow, movie studios issued more films for rental in VHS format, and this stoked demand. Before long, it was clear to anyone who entered a video rental store that there were more VHS tapes available for rent, and fewer Betamax tapes available. This served to reinforce the positive feedback loop, and ultimately Sony's Betamax technology was shut out of the market. The pivotal difference between the two companies was strategy: Matsushita chose a licensing strategy, and Sony did not. As a result, Matsushita's VHS technology became the de facto standard for VCRs, while Sony's Betamax technology was locked out.

The general principle that emerges from this example is that when two or more companies are competing with each other to get technology adopted as a standard in an industry, and when network effects and positive feedback loops are important, *the company that wins the format war will be the one whose strategy best exploits positive feedback loops*. This is a very important strategic principle in many high-technology industries, particularly computer hardware, software, telecommunications, and consumer electronics. Microsoft is where it is today because it exploited a positive feedback loop. Dolby presents us with another example of a company that exploited a positive feedback loop (see Strategy in Action 7.1).

As the market settles on a standard, an important implication of the positive feedback process occurs: companies promoting alternative standards can become locked out of the market when consumers are unwilling to bear the switching costs required to abandon the established standard and adopt the new standard. In this context, switching costs are the costs that consumers must bear to switch from a product based on one technological standard to a product based on another technological standard.

For illustration, imagine that a company developed an operating system for personal computers that was both faster and more stable than the current standard in the marketplace, Microsoft Windows. Would this company be able to gain significant market share from Microsoft? Only with great difficulty. Consumers choose personal computers not for their operating system, but for the applications that run on the operating system. A new operating system would initially have a very small installed base, so few developers would be willing to take the risks in writing word processing programs, spreadsheets, games, and other applications for that operating system. Because there would be very few applications available, consumers who did make the switch would have to bear the switching costs associated with giving up some of their applications—something that they might be unwilling to do. Moreover, even if applications were available for the new operating system, consumers would have to bear the costs of purchasing those applications, another source of switching costs. In addition, they would have to bear the costs associated with learning to use the new operating system, yet another source of switching costs. Thus, many consumers would be unwilling to switch even if the new operating system performed better than Windows, and the company promoting the new operating system would be locked out of the market.

However, consumers will bear switching costs if the benefits of adopting the new technology outweigh the costs of switching. For example, in the late-1980s and

7.1 STRATEGY IN ACTION

How Dolby Became the Standard in Sound Technology

Inventor Ray Dolby's name has become synonymous with superior sound in home theater systems, movie theaters, and recording studios. The technology produced by his company, Dolby Laboratories, is part of nearly every music cassette and cassette recorder, prerecorded videotape, and, most recently, DVD movie disk and player. Since 1976, close to 1.5 billion audio products that use Dolby's technology have been sold worldwide. More than 44,000 movie theaters now show films in Dolby Digital Surround Sound, and nearly 50 million Dolby Digital home theater receivers have been sold since 1999. Dolby technology has become the irrefutable industry standard for high-quality sound in the music and film industry. How did Dolby build this technology?

In 1965, Ray Dolby founded Dolby Laboratories in London (the company's headquarters moved to San Francisco in 1976). Dolby, who had a PhD in physics from Cambridge University (England), had invented a technology for reducing the background hiss in professional tape recording without compromising the quality of the material being recorded. Dolby reached an agreement to license his noise-reduction technology to KLH, a highly regarded American producer of audio equipment (record players and tape decks), for the consumer market in 1968. Soon thereafter, other manufacturers of consumer equipment started to approach Dolby requesting to license the technology. Dolby briefly considered manufacturing record players and tape decks for the consumer market, but as he later commented: "I knew that if we entered that market and tried to make something like a cassette deck, we would be in competition with any licensee that we took on . . . So we had to stay out of manufacturing in that area in order to license in that area."

Dolby adopted a licensing business model, and then had to determine how much to charge as a licensing fee. He knew his technology was valuable, but he also understood that charging a high fee would encourage manufacturers to invest in developing their own noise-reduction technology rather than license. He decided to charge a modest fee to reduce the incentive that manufacturers would have to develop their own technology. Then Dolby needed to decide to which companies the technology would be licensed. Dolby wanted the Dolby name associated with superior sound, so he needed to make sure that licensees adhered to his quality standards. To ensure these standards would be met, the company set up a formal quality control program for its licensees' products. Licensees must agree to have their products tested by Dolby, and the licensing agreement states that companies cannot sell products that do not pass Dolby's quality tests. By preventing products with substandard performance from reaching the market, Dolby can maintain the quality image of products featuring Dolby technology and trademarks. Today, Dolby Laboratories tests hundreds of samples of licensed products every year under this program. By ensuring that the Dolby name is associated with superior sound quality, Dolby's strategy has increased the power of the Dolby brand, making it very valuable to license.

Another key aspect of Dolby's strategy was developed in 1970, when Dolby began to promote the idea of releasing prerecorded cassettes encoded with Dolby noise-reduction technology. These cassettes had very low levels of noise when played on players equipped with Dolby noise-reduction technology. Dolby decided to license the technology on prerecorded tapes for free, instead collecting licensing fees just from the sales of tape players that used Dolby technology. This strategy was hugely successful and set up a positive feedback loop that helped to make Dolby technology ubiquitous. Growing sales of prerecorded tapes encoded with Dolby technology created a demand for tape players that contained Dolby technology, and as the installed base of tape players with Dolby technology grew, the proportion of prerecorded tapes that were encoded with Dolby technology surged—further boosting demand for players incorporating Dolby technology. By the mid-1970s, virtually all prerecorded tapes were encoded with Dolby noise-reduction technology. This strategy remains in effect today for all media recorded with Dolby technology, and encompasses not only videocassettes but also videogames and DVD releases encoded with Dolby Surround or Dolby Digital.

Andrew Harrer/Bloomberg via Getty Image

STRATEGY IN ACTION (*continued*)

As a result of its licensing and quality assurance strategies, Dolby has become the standard for high-quality sound in the consumer electronics and film industries. It continues to push the boundaries of sound-reduction technology (it has been a leader in digital sound since the mid-1980s) and has successfully extended its noise-reduction franchise, first into films, then into DVD and videogame technology, and finally onto the Web, where it has licensed its digital technology to a wide range of media companies for digital music delivery and digital audio players, such as those built into personal computers and hand-held music players. Dolby has also licensed its technology for use in Sony's Blu-ray High Definition DVDs, and the company estimates that as of 2010, its sound technology was embedded in nearly 60% of global TV shipments.

Sources: M. Snider, "Ray Dolby, Audio Inventor," *USA Today,* December 28, 2000, p. D3; D. Dritas, "Dealerscope Hall of Fame: Ray Dolby," *Dealerscope* (January 2002): 74–76; J. Pinkerton, "At Dolby Laboratories: A Clean Audio Pipe," *Dealerscope* (December 2000): 33–34; Company history archived at www.dolby.com; L. Himelstein, "Dolby Gets Ready to Make a Big Noise," *Business Week,* February 9, 2004, p. 78. D. Pomerantz, "Seeing in Dolby," *Forbes,* January 30, 2006, p. 56; M. Holt, "New Generation of Technology Creates Opportunity and Risks for Dolby's Dominant Position," *Morning Star Stock Report,* May 9, 2011.

early-1990s, millions of people switched from analog record players to digital CD players despite that switching costs were significant: consumers had to purchase the new player technology, and many people purchased duplicate copies of their favorite musical recordings. Nevertheless, people made the switch because for many, the perceived benefit—the incredibly better sound quality associated with CDs—outweighed the costs of switching.

As this switching process continued, a positive feedback loop started to develop, and the installed base of CD players grew, leading to an increase in the number of musical recordings issued on CDs, as opposed to, or, in addition to vinyl records. The installed base of CD players got so big that mainstream music companies began to issue recordings only in CD format. Once this occurred, even those who did not want to switch to the new technology were required to if they wished to purchase new music recordings. The music industry standard had shifted: new technology had locked in as the standard, and the old technology was locked out.

Extrapolating from this example, it can be argued that despite its dominance, the Wintel standard for personal computers could one day be superseded if a competitor finds a way of providing sufficient benefits that enough consumers are willing to bear the switching costs associated with moving to a new operating system. Indeed, there are signs that Apple is starting to chip away at the dominance of the Wintel standard, primarily by using elegant design and ease of use as tools to get people to bear the costs of switching from Wintel computers to Apple machines.

Strategies for Winning a Format War

From the perspective of a company pioneering a new technological standard in a marketplace where network effects and positive feedback loops operate, the key question becomes: "What strategy should we pursue to establish our format as the dominant one?"

The various strategies that companies should adopt in order to win format wars are centered upon *finding ways to make network effects work in their favor and against their competitors.* Winning a format war requires a company to build the installed base for its standard as rapidly as possible, thereby leveraging the positive feedback loop, inducing consumers to bear switching costs, and ultimately locking the market into its technology. It requires the company to jump-start and then accelerate demand for its technological standard or format such that it becomes established as quickly as possible as the industry standard, thereby locking out competing formats. There are a number of key strategies and tactics that can be adopted to try to achieve this.[6]

Ensure a Supply of Complements

It is important for the company to make sure that, in addition to the product itself, there is an adequate supply of complements. For example, no one will purchase the Sony PlayStation 3 unless there is an adequate supply of games to run on that machine. Companies typically take two steps to ensure an adequate supply of complements.

First, they may diversify into the production of complements and seed the market with sufficient supply to help jump-start demand for their format. Before Sony produced the original PlayStation in the early-1990s, for example, it established its own in-house unit to produce videogames for the PlayStation. When it launched the PlayStation, Sony also simultaneously issued 16 games to run on the machine, giving consumers a reason to purchase the format. Second, companies may create incentives or make it easy for independent companies to produce complements. Sony also licensed the right to produce games to a number of independent game developers, charged the developers a lower royalty rate than they had to pay to competitors (such as Nintendo and Sega), and provided them with software tools that made it easier for them to develop the games (note that Apple is now doing the same thing with its smartphones—see the Opening Case). Thus, the launch of the Sony PlayStation was accompanied by the simultaneous launch of approximately 30 games, which quickly helped to stimulate demand for the machine.

Leverage Killer Applications

Killer applications are applications or uses of a new technology or product that are so compelling that they persuade customers to adopt the new format or technology in droves, thereby "killing" demand for competing formats. Killer applications often help to jump-start demand for the new standard. For example, the killer applications that induced consumers to sign up to online services such as AOL in the 1990s were e-mail, chat rooms, and the ability to browse the Web.

Ideally, the company promoting a technological standard will also want to develop their own killer applications—that is, develop the appropriate complementary products. However, it may also be able to leverage the applications that others develop. For example, the early sales of the IBM PC following its 1981 introduction were primarily driven by IBM's decision to license two important software programs for the PC: VisiCalc (a spreadsheet program) and EasyWriter (a word processing program), both developed by independent companies. IBM saw that they were driving rapid adoption of rival personal computers, such as the Apple II, so it quickly licensed software, produced versions that would run on the IBM PC, and sold these programs as complements to the IBM PC, a strategy that was very successful.

Killer applications

Applications or uses of a new technology or product that are so compelling that customers adopt them in droves, killing the competing formats.

Aggressive Pricing and Marketing

A common tactic to jump-start demand is to adopt a **razor and blade strategy:** pricing the product (razor) low in order to stimulate demand and increase the installed base, and then trying to make high profits on the sale of complements (razor blades), which are priced relatively high. This strategy owes its name to Gillette, the company that pioneered this strategy to sell its razors and razor blades. Many other companies have followed this strategy—for example, Hewlett-Packard typically sells its printers at cost but makes significant profits on the subsequent sales of its replacement cartridges. In this case, the printer is the "razor," and it is priced low to stimulate demand and induce consumers to switch from their existing printer, while the cartridges are the "blades," which are priced high to make profits. The inkjet printer represents a proprietary technological format because only HP cartridges can be used with HP printers; cartridges designed for competing inkjet printers, such as those sold by Canon, will not work in HP printers. A similar strategy is used in the videogame industry: manufacturers price videogame consoles at cost to induce consumers to adopt their technology, while they make profits on the royalties received from the sales of games that run on the game system.

Aggressive marketing is also a key factor in jump-starting demand to get an early lead in an installed base. Substantial upfront marketing and point-of-sales promotion techniques are often used to try to attract potential early adopters who will bear the switching costs associated with adopting the format. If these efforts are successful, they can be the start of a positive feedback loop. Again, the Sony PlayStation provides a good example. Sony co-linked the introduction of the PlayStation with nationwide television advertising aimed at its primary demographic (18- to 34-year-olds) and in-store displays that allowed potential buyers to play games on the machine before making a purchase.

Cooperate with Competitors

Companies have been close to simultaneously introducing competing and incompatible technological standards a number of times. A good example is the compact disk. Initially four companies—Sony, Philips, JVC, and Telefunken—were developing CD players using different variations of the underlying laser technology. If this situation had persisted, they might have introduced incompatible technologies into the marketplace; a CD made for a Philips CD player would not play on a Sony CD player. Understanding that the nearly simultaneous introduction of such incompatible technologies can create significant confusion among consumers, and often lead them to delay their purchases, Sony and Philips decided to join forces and cooperate on developing the technology. Sony contributed its error correction technology, and Philips contributed its laser technology. The result of this cooperation was that momentum among other players in the industry shifted toward the Sony–Philips alliances; JVC and Telefunken were left with little support. Most important, recording labels announced that they would support the Sony–Philips format but not the Telefunken or JVC format. Telefunken and JVC subsequently decided to abandon their efforts to develop CD technology. The cooperation between Sony and Philips was important because it reduced confusion in the industry and allowed a single format to rise to the fore, which accelerated adoption of the technology. The cooperation was a win-win situation for both Philips and Sony, which eliminated the competitors and were able to share in the success of the format.

Razor and blade strategy

Pricing the product low in order to stimulate demand and pricing complements high.

License the Format

Licensing the format to other enterprises so that those others can produce products based on the format is another strategy often adopted. The company that pioneered the format gains from the licensing fees that return to it, as well as from the enlarged supply of the product, which can stimulate demand and help accelerate market adoption. This was the strategy that Matsushita adopted with its VHS format for the VCR. In addition to producing VCRs at its own factory in Osaka, Matsushita let a number of other companies produce VHS format players under license, and so VHS players were more widely available. (Sony decided not to license its competing Betamax format and produced all Betamax format players itself.) More people purchased VHS players, which created an incentive for film companies to issue more films in VHS format (rather than Betamax format), which further increased demand for VHS players—and hence helped Matsushita to lock in VHS as the dominant format in the marketplace. Sony, ironically the first to market, saw its position marginalized by the reduced supply of the critical complement—prerecorded films—and ultimately withdrew Betamax players from the consumer marketplace.

Dolby, as we saw in Strategy in Action 7.1, adopted a similar licensing strategy to get its noise-reduction technology adopted as the technological standard in the music and film industries. By charging a modest licensing fee for use of the technology in recording equipment and forgoing licensing fees on media recorded using Dolby technology, Dolby deliberately sought to reduce the financial incentive that potential competitors might have to develop their own, possibly superior, technology. Dolby calculated that adopting a licensing strategy to limit the incentive of competitors to enter the market would maximize its long-term profitability.

The correct strategy to pursue in a particular scenario requires that the company consider all of these different strategies and tactics and pursue those that seem most appropriate given the competitive circumstances prevailing in the industry and the likely strategy of rivals. Although there is no single best combination of strategies and tactics, the company must keep the goal of rapidly increasing the installed base of products based on its standard at the front of its mind. By helping to jump-start demand for its format, a company can induce consumers to bear the switching costs associated with adopting its technology and leverage any positive feedback process that might exist. It is also important not to pursue strategies that have the opposite effect. For example, pricing high to capture profits from early adopters, who tend not to be as price sensitive as later adopters, can have the unfortunate effect of slowing demand growth and allowing a more aggressive competitor pick up share and establish its format as the industry standard.

Costs in High-Technology Industries

In many high-tech industries, the fixed costs of developing the product are very high, but the costs of producing one extra unit of the product are very low. This is most obvious in the case of software. For example, it reportedly cost Microsoft $5 billion to develop Windows Vista, the latest version of its Windows operating system, but the cost of producing one more copy of Windows Vista is virtually zero. Once the Windows Vista program was complete, Microsoft duplicated its master disks and sent the copies to PC manufacturers, such as Dell Computer, which then installed a copy of Windows Vista onto every PC sold. Microsoft's cost was, effectively, zero, and yet the company receives a significant licensing fee for each copy of Windows Vista installed on a PC.[7] For Microsoft, the marginal cost of making one more copy of Windows 7 is close to zero, although the fixed costs of developing the product were around $5 billion.

Many other high-technology products have similar cost economics: very high fixed costs and very low marginal costs. Most software products share these features, although if the software is sold through stores, the costs of packaging and distribution will raise the marginal costs, and if it is sold by a sales force direct to end-users, this too will raise the marginal costs. Many consumer electronics products have the same basic economics. The fixed costs of developing a DVD player or a video-game console can be very expensive, but the costs of producing an incremental unit are very low. Similarly, the fixed costs of developing a new drug can run to over $800 million, but the marginal cost of producing each additional pill is at most a few cents.

Comparative Cost Economics

To grasp why this cost structure is strategically important, a company must understand that, in many industries, marginal costs rise as a company tries to expand output (economists call this the *law of diminishing returns*). To produce more of a good, a company must hire more labor and invest in more plant and machinery. At the margin, the additional resources used are not as productive, so this leads to increasing marginal costs. However, the law of diminishing returns often does not apply in many high-tech settings, such as the production of software, or sending bits of data through a digital telecommunications network.

Consider two companies, α and β (see Figure 7.3). Company α is a conventional producer and faces diminishing returns, so as it tries to expand output, its

Figure 7.3   Cost Structures in High-Technology Industries

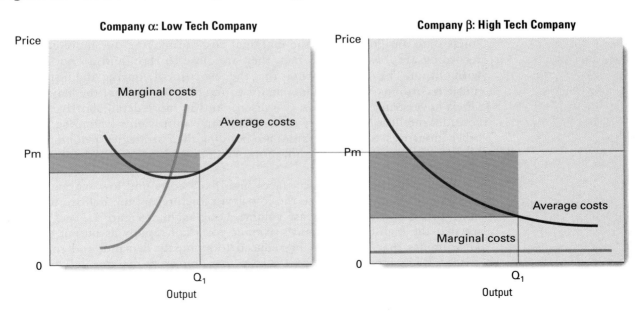

marginal costs rise. Company β is a high-tech producer, and its marginal costs do not rise at all as output is increased. Note that in Figure 7.3, company β's marginal cost curve is drawn as a straight line near to the horizontal axis, implying that marginal costs are close to zero and do not vary with output, whereas company α's marginal costs rise as output is expanded, illustrating diminishing returns. Company β's flat and low marginal cost curve means that its average cost curve will continuously fall over all ranges of output as it spreads its fixed costs out over greater volume. In contrast, the rising marginal costs encountered by company α mean that its average cost curve is the U-shaped curve familiar from basic economics texts. For simplicity, assume that both companies sell their product at the same price, Pm, and both sell exactly the same quantity of output, 0 – Q1. You will see from Figure 7.3 that at an output of Q1, company β has much lower average costs than company α and as a consequence is making far more profit (profit is the shaded area in Figure 7.3).

Strategic Significance

If a company can shift from a cost structure where it encounters increasing marginal costs to one where fixed costs may be high but marginal costs are much lower, its profitability may increase. In the consumer electronics industry, such a shift has been playing out for two decades. Musical recordings were once based on analog technology where marginal costs rose as output expanded due to diminishing returns (as in the case of company α in Figure 7.3). Since the 1980s, digital systems such as CD players have replaced analog systems. Digital systems are software based, and this implies much lower marginal costs of producing one more copy of a recording. As a result, music companies have been able to lower prices, expand demand, and see their profitability increase (their production system has more in common with company β in Figure 7.3).

This process is still unfolding. The latest technology for copying musical recordings is based on distribution over the Internet (e.g., by downloading songs onto an iPod). Here, the marginal costs of making one more copy of a recording are lower still. In fact, they are close to zero, and do not increase with output. The only problem is that the low costs of copying and distributing music recordings have created a major copyright problem that the major music labels have struggled to solve (we discuss this in more detail shortly when we consider intellectual property rights). The same shift is now beginning to affect other industries. Some companies are building their strategies around trying to exploit and profit from this shift. For an example, Strategy in Action 7.2 looks at SonoSite.

When a high-tech company faces high fixed costs and low marginal costs, its strategy should emphasize the low-cost structure option: deliberately drive down prices in order to increase volume. Look again at Figure 7.3 and you will see that the high-tech company's average costs fall rapidly as output expands. This implies that prices can be reduced to stimulate demand, and so long as prices fall less rapidly than average costs, per unit profit margins will expand as prices fall. This is a consequence of the firm's low marginal costs that do not rise with output. This strategy of pricing low to drive volume and reap wider profit margins is central to the business model of some very successful high-technology companies, including Microsoft.

STRATEGY IN ACTION

Lowering the Cost of Ultrasound Equipment Through Digitalization

The ultrasound unit has been an important piece of diagnostic equipment in hospitals for some time. Ultrasound units use the physics of sound to produce images of soft tissues in the human body. Ultrasounds can produce detailed three-dimensional color images of organs and, by using contrast agents, track the flow of fluids through an organ. A cardiologist, for example, can use an ultrasound in combination with contrast agents injected into the bloodstream to track the flow of blood through a beating heart. In addition to the visual diagnosis, ultrasound also produces an array of quantitative diagnostic information of great value to physicians.

Modern ultrasound units are sophisticated instruments that cost about $250,000–$300,000 each for a top-line model. They are fairly bulky instruments, weighing approximately 300 pounds, and are wheeled around hospitals on carts.

A few years ago, a group of researchers at ATL, one of the leading ultrasound companies, proposed an idea for reducing the size and cost of a basic machine. They theorized that it might be possible to replace up to 80% of the solid circuits in an ultrasound unit with software, and in the process significantly shrink the size and reduce the weight of machines, thereby producing portable ultrasound units. Moreover, by digitalizing much of the ultrasound (replacing hardware with software), they could considerably decrease the marginal costs of making additional units, and would thus be able to make a better profit at much lower price points.

The researchers reasoned that a portable and inexpensive ultrasound unit would find market opportunities in totally new niches. For example, a small, inexpensive ultrasound unit could be placed in an ambulance or carried into battle by an army medic, or purchased by family physicians for use in their offices. Although they realized that it would be some time, perhaps decades, before such small, inexpensive machines could attain the image quality and diagnostic sophistication of top-of-the-line machines, they saw the opportunity in terms of creating market niches that previously could not be served by ultrasound companies because of the high costs and bulk of the product.

The researchers later became part of a project team within ATL, and thereafter became an entirely new company, SonoSite. In late-1999, SonoSite introduced their first portable product, which weighed just 6 pounds and cost about $25,000. SonoSite targeted niches that full-sized ultrasound products could not reach: ambulatory care and foreign markets that could not afford the more expensive equipment. In 2010, the company sold over $275 million of product. In the future, SonoSite plans to include additional features and greater image quality in the small hand-held machines, primarily by improving the software. This could allow these machines to penetrate U.S. hospital markets currently purchasing the established technology, much as client–server systems based on PC technology replaced mainframes for some functions in business corporations.

Source: Interviews by Charles W. L. Hill.

Capturing First-Mover Advantages

In high-technology industries, companies often compete by striving to be the first to develop revolutionary new products, that is, to be a **first mover**. By definition, the first mover that creates a revolutionary product is in a monopoly position. If the new product satisfies unmet consumer needs and demand is high, the first mover can capture significant revenues and profits. Such revenues and profits signal to potential rivals that imitating the first mover makes money. Figure 7.4 implies that in the absence of strong barriers to imitation, imitators will rush into the market created by the first mover, competing away the first mover's monopoly profits and leaving all participants in the market with a much lower level of returns.

Despite imitation, some first movers have the ability to capitalize on and reap substantial first-mover advantages—the advantages of pioneering new technologies and products that lead to an enduring competitive advantage. Intel introduced the world's

Figure 7.4 The Impact of Imitation on Profits of a First Mover

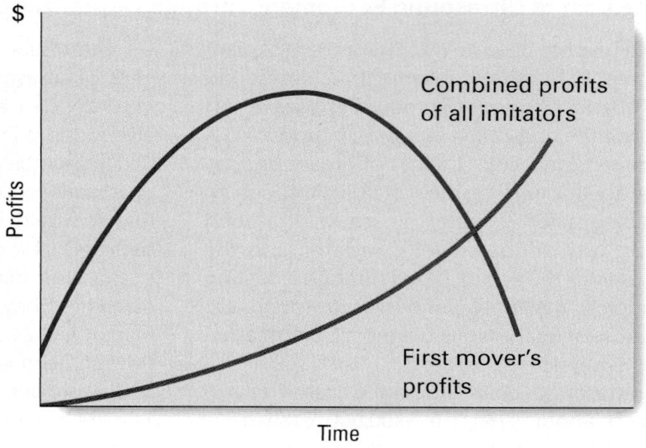

first microprocessor in 1971, and today, still dominates the microprocessor segment of the semiconductor industry. Xerox introduced the world's first photocopier and for a long time enjoyed a leading position in the industry. Cisco introduced the first Internet protocol network router in 1986, and still leads the market for that equipment today. Microsoft introduced the world's first software application for a personal computer in 1979, Microsoft BASIC, and it remains a dominant force in PC software.

Some first movers can reap substantial advantages from their pioneering activities that lead to an enduring competitive advantage. They can, in other words, limit or slow the rate of imitation.

But there are plenty of counterexamples suggesting that first-mover advantages might not be easy to capture and, in fact, that there might be **first-mover disadvantages**—the competitive disadvantages associated with being first. For example, Apple was the first company to introduce a hand-held computer, the Apple Newton, but the product failed; a second mover, Palm, succeeded where Apple had failed (although Apple has recently had major success as a first mover with the first true tablet computer, the iPad). In the market for commercial jet aircraft, DeHavilland was first to market with the Comet, but it was the second mover, Boeing, with its 707 jetliner, that went on to dominate the market.

Clearly, being a first mover does not by itself guarantee success. As we shall see, the difference between innovating companies that capture first-mover advantages and those that fall victim to first-mover disadvantages in part incites the strategy that the first mover pursues. Before considering the strategy issue, however, we need to take a closer look at the nature of first-mover advantages and disadvantages.[8]

First-Mover Advantages

There are five primary sources of first-mover advantages.[9] First, the first mover has an opportunity to exploit network effects and positive feedback loops, locking consumers into its technology. In the VCR industry, Sony could have exploited network

First-mover disadvantages

Competitive disadvantages associated with being first.

effects by licensing its technology, but instead the company ceded its first-mover advantage to the second mover, Matsushita.

Second, the first mover may be able to establish significant brand loyalty, which is expensive for later entrants to break down. Indeed, if the company is successful in this endeavor, its name may become closely associated with the entire class of products, including those produced by rivals. People still talk of "Xeroxing" when they will make a photocopy, or "FedExing" when they will be sending a package by overnight mail, and when we want to search for something on the Web, we "Google" it.

Third, the first mover may be able to increase sales volume ahead of rivals and thus reap cost advantages associated with the realization of scale economies and learning effects (see Chapter 4). Once the first mover has these cost advantages, it can respond to new entrants by cutting prices in order to retain its market share and still earn significant profits.

Fourth, the first mover may be able to create switching costs for its customers that subsequently make it difficult for rivals to enter the market and take customers away from the first mover. Wireless service providers, for example, will give new customers a "free" wireless phone, but customers must sign a contract agreeing to pay for the phone if they terminate the service contract within a specified time period, such as 1 or 2 years. Because the real cost of a wireless phone may run from $100 to $200, this represents a significant switching cost that later entrants must overcome.

Finally, the first mover may be able to accumulate valuable knowledge related to customer needs, distribution channels, product technology, process technology, and so on. Knowledge so accumulated can it an advantage that later entrants might find difficult or expensive to match. Sharp, for example, was the first mover in the commercial manufacture of active matrix liquid crystal displays used in laptop computers. The process for manufacturing these displays is very difficult, with a high rejection rate for flawed displays. Sharp has accumulated such an advantage with regard to production processes that it has been very difficult for later entrants to match it on product quality, and therefore, on costs.

First-Mover Disadvantages

Balanced against these first-mover advantages are a number of disadvantages.[10] First, the first mover has to bear significant pioneering costs that later entrants do not. The first mover must pioneer the technology, develop distribution channels, and educate customers about the nature of the product. All of this can be expensive and time-consuming. Later entrants, by way of contrast, might be able to free-ride on the first mover's investments in pioneering the market and customer education. That is, they do not have to bear the pioneering costs of the first mover.

Related to this, first movers are more prone to make mistakes because there are so many uncertainties in a new market. Later entrants may learn from the mistakes made by first movers, improve on the product or the way in which it is sold, and come to market with a superior offering that captures significant market share from the first mover. For example, one of the reasons that the Apple Newton failed was that the handwriting software in the hand-held computer failed to recognize human handwriting. The second mover in this market, Palm, learned from Apple's error. When it introduced the PalmPilot, it used software that recognized letters written in a particular way, Graffiti, and then persuaded customers to learn this method of inputting data into the hand-held computer.

Third, first movers run the risk of building the wrong resources and capabilities because they are focusing on a customer set that is not going to be characteristic of the mass market. This is the crossing the chasm problem that we discussed in the previous chapter. You will recall that the customers in the early market—those we categorized as innovators and early adopters—have different characteristics from the first wave of the mass market, the early majority. The first mover runs the risk of directing its resources and capabilities to the needs of innovators and early adopters, and not being able to switch when the early majority enters the market. As a result, first movers run a greater risk of plunging into the chasm that separates the early market from the mass market.

Finally, the first mover may invest in inferior or obsolete technology. This can happen when its product innovation is based on underlying technology that is rapidly advancing. By basing its product on an early version of the technology, it may become locked into something that rapidly becomes obsolete. In contrast, later entrants may be able to leapfrog the first mover and introduce products that are based on later versions of the underlying technology. This happened in France during the 1980s when, at the urging of the government, France Telecom introduced the world's first consumer online service, Minitel. France Telecom distributed crude terminals to consumers for free, which connected to the phone line and could be used to browse phone directories. Other simple services were soon added, and before long the French could shop, bank, make travel arrangements, and check weather and news "online"—years before the Web was invented. The problem was that by the standards of the Web, Minitel was very crude and inflexible, and France Telecom, as the first mover, suffered. The French were very slow to adopt personal computers and the Internet primarily because Minitel had such a presence. As late as 1998, only 1/5 of French households had a computer, compared with 2/5 in the United States, and only 2% of households were connected to the Internet, compared to over 30% in the United States. As the result of a government decision, France Telecom, and the entire nation of France, was slow to adopt a revolutionary new online medium—the Web—because they were the first to invest in a more primitive version of the technology.[11]

Strategies for Exploiting First-Mover Advantages

First movers must strategize and determine how to exploit its lead and capitalize on first-mover advantages to build a sustainable long-term competitive advantage while simultaneously reducing the risks associated with first-mover disadvantages. There are three basic strategies available: (1) develop and market the innovation; (2) develop and market the innovation jointly with other companies through a strategic alliance or joint venture; and (3) license the innovation to others and allow them develop the market.

The optimal choice of strategy depends on the answers to three questions:

1. Does the innovating company have the complementary assets to exploit its innovation and capture first-mover advantages?
2. How difficult is it for imitators to copy the company's innovation? In other words, what is the height of barriers to imitation?
3. Are there capable competitors that could rapidly imitate the innovation?

Complementary Assets Complementary assets are the assets required to exploit a new innovation and gain a competitive advantage.[12] Among the most important complementary assets are competitive manufacturing facilities capable of handling rapid growth in customer demand while maintaining high product quality. State-of-the-art manufacturing facilities enable the first mover to quickly move down the experience curve without encountering production bottlenecks or problems with the quality of the product. The inability to satisfy demand because of these problems, however, creates the opportunity for imitators to enter the marketplace. For example, in 1998, Immunex was the first company to introduce a revolutionary new biological treatment for rheumatoid arthritis. Sales for this product, Enbrel, very rapidly increased, reaching $750 million in 2001. However, Immunex had not invested in sufficient manufacturing capacity. In mid-2000, it announced that it lacked the capacity to satisfy demand and that bringing additional capacity on line would take at least 2 years. This manufacturing bottleneck gave the second mover in the market, Johnson & Johnson, the opportunity to rapidly expand demand for its product, which by early-2002, was outselling Enbrel. Immunex's first-mover advantage had been partly eroded because it lacked an important complementary asset, the manufacturing capability required to satisfy demand.

Complementary assets also include marketing know-how, an adequate sales force, access to distribution systems, and an after-sales service and support network. All of these assets can help an innovator build brand loyalty and more rapidly achieve market penetration.[13] In turn, the resulting increases in volume facilitate more rapid movement down the experience curve and the attainment of a sustainable cost-based advantage due to scale economies and learning effects. EMI, the first mover in the market for CT scanners, ultimately lost out to established medical equipment companies, such as GE Medical Systems, because it lacked the marketing know-how, sales force, and distribution systems required to effectively compete in the world's largest market for medical equipment, the United States.

Developing complementary assets can be very expensive, and companies often need large infusions of capital for this purpose. That is why first movers often lose out to late movers that are large, successful companies in other industries with the resources to quickly develop a presence in the new industry. Microsoft and 3M exemplify companies that have moved quickly to capitalize on the opportunities when other companies open up new product markets, such as compact disks or floppy disks. For example, although Netscape pioneered the market for Internet browsers with the Netscape Navigator, Microsoft's Internet Explorer ultimately dominated that market.

Height of Barriers to Imitation   Recall from Chapter 3 that barriers to imitation are factors that prevent rivals from imitating a company's distinctive competencies and innovations. Although any innovation can be copied, the higher the barriers are, the longer it takes for rivals to imitate the innovation, and the more time the first mover has to build an enduring competitive advantage.

Barriers to imitation give an innovator time to establish a competitive advantage and build more enduring barriers to entry in the newly created market. Patents, for example, are among the most widely used barriers to imitation. By protecting its photocopier technology with a thicket of patents, Xerox was able to delay any significant imitation of its product for 17 years. However, patents are often easy to "invent around." For example, one study found that this happened to 60% of patented innovations within 4 years.[14] If patent protection is weak, a company might try to slow imitation by developing new products and processes in secret. The most famous example of this approach is Coca-Cola, which has kept the formula for Coke a secret for generations. But Coca-Cola's success in this regard is an exception. A study of 100 companies has estimated that rivals learn about a company's decision to develop a major new product or process and its related proprietary information within about 12–18 months of the original development decision.[15]

Capable Competitors   Capable competitors are companies that can move quickly to imitate the pioneering company. Competitors' capability to imitate a pioneer's innovation depends primarily on two factors: (1) R&D skills; and (2) access to complementary assets. In general, the greater the number of capable competitors with access to the R&D skills and complementary assets needed to imitate an innovation, the more rapid imitation is likely to be.

In this context, R&D skills refer to the ability of rivals to reverse-engineer an innovation in order to find out how it works and quickly develop a comparable product. As an example, consider the CT scanner. GE bought one of the first CT scanners produced by EMI, and its technical experts reverse-engineered the machine. Despite the product's technological complexity, GE developed its own version, which allowed it to quickly imitate EMI and replace EMI as the major supplier of CT scanners.

Complementary assets, or the access that rivals have to marketing, sales know-how, and manufacturing capabilities is one of the key determinants of the rate of imitation. If would-be imitators lack critical complementary assets, not only will they have to imitate the innovation, but they may also need to imitate the innovator's complementary assets. This is expensive, as AT&T discovered when it tried to enter the personal computer business in 1984. AT&T lacked the marketing assets (sales force and distribution systems) necessary to support personal computer products. The lack of these assets and the time it takes to build the assets partly explains why: 4 years after it entered the market, AT&T had lost $2.5 billion and still had not emerged as a viable contender. It subsequently exited this business.

Three Innovation Strategies   The way in which these three factors—complementary assets, height of barriers to imitation, and the capability of competitors—influence the choice of innovation strategy is summarized in Table 7.1. The competitive strategy of developing and marketing the innovation alone makes most sense when: (1) the innovator has the complementary assets necessary to develop the innovation; (2) the barriers to imitating a new innovation are high; and (3) the number of capable competitors is limited. Complementary assets allow rapid development and promotion of the innovation. High barriers to imitation give the innovator time to establish a competitive advantage and build enduring barriers to entry through

Table 7.1   Strategies for Profiting from Innovation

Strategy	Does the Innovator Have the Required Complementary Assets?	Likely Height of Barriers to Imitation	Number of Capable Competitors
Going it alone	Yes	High	Very few
Entering into an alliance	No	High	Moderate number
Licensing the innovation	No	Low	Many

brand loyalty or experience-based cost advantages. The fewer the capable competitors there are, the less likely it is that any one of them will succeed in circumventing barriers to imitation and quickly imitating the innovation.

The competitive strategy of developing and marketing the innovation jointly with other companies through a strategic alliance or joint venture makes most sense when: (1) the innovator lacks complementary assets; (2) barriers to imitation are high; and (3) there are several capable competitors. In such circumstances, it makes sense to enter into an alliance with a company that already has the complementary assets—in other words, with a capable competitor. Theoretically, such an alliance should prove to be mutually beneficial, and each partner can share in high profits that neither could earn on its own. Moreover, such a strategy has the benefit of co-opting a potential rival. For example, had EMI teamed with a capable competitor to develop the market for CT scanners, such as GE Medical Systems, instead of going it alone, the company might have been able to build a more enduring competitive advantage, and also have co-opted a potentially powerful rival into its camp.

The third strategy, licensing, makes most sense when: (1) the innovating company lacks the complementary assets; (2) barriers to imitation are low; and (3) there are many capable competitors. The combination of low barriers to imitation and many capable competitors makes rapid imitation almost certain. The innovator's lack of complementary assets further suggests that an imitator will soon capture the innovator's competitive advantage. Given these factors, because rapid diffusion of the innovator's technology through imitation is inevitable, the innovator can at least share in some of the benefits of this diffusion by licensing out its technology.[16] Moreover, by setting a relatively modest licensing fee, the innovator may be able to reduce the incentive that potential rivals have to develop their own competing, and possibly superior, technology. This seems to have been the strategy Dolby adopted to get its technology established as the standard for noise reduction in the music and film businesses (see Strategy in Action 7.1).

Technological Paradigm Shifts

Technological paradigm shifts occur when new technologies that revolutionize the structure of the industry, dramatically alter the nature of competition, and require companies to adopt new strategies in order to survive. A good example of a paradigm shift is the evolution of photography from chemical to digital printing processes. For over half a century, the large incumbent enterprises in the photographic industry such as Kodak and Fujifilm have generated most of their revenues from selling and processing film using traditional silver halide technology. The rise of digital photography has been a huge disruptive threat to their business models. Digital cameras do not use film, the mainstay of Kodak's and Fuji's business. In addition, these cameras are more like specialized computers than conventional cameras, and are therefore based on scientific knowledge in which Kodak and Fuji have little expertise. Although both Kodak and Fuji have heavily invested in the development of digital cameras, they are facing intense competition from companies such as Sony, Canon, and Hewlett-Packard, which have developed their own digital cameras; from software developers such as Adobe and Microsoft, which make software for manipulating digital images; and from printer companies such as Hewlett-Packard and Canon, which are making the printers that consumers can use to print high-quality pictures from home. As digital substitution gathers speed in the photography

Technological paradigm

Shifts in new technologies that revolutionize the structure of the industry, dramatically alter the nature of competition, and require companies to adopt new strategies in order to survive.

industry, it is not clear that the traditional incumbents will be able to survive this shift; the new competitors might rise to dominance in the new market.

Kodak and Fuji are hardly the first large incumbents to be felled by a technological paradigm shift in their industry. In the early-1980s, the computer industry was revolutionized by the arrival of personal computer technology, which gave rise to client–server networks that replaced traditional mainframe and minicomputers for many business uses. Many incumbent companies in the mainframe era, such as Wang, Control Data, and DEC, ultimately did not survive, and even IBM went through a decade of wrenching changes and large losses before it reinvented itself as a provider of e-business solutions. Instead, new entrants such as Microsoft, Intel, Dell, and Compaq rose to dominate this new computer industry.

Today, many believe that the advent of cloud computing is ushering in a paradigm shift in the computer industry (see the Opening Case). Microsoft, the dominant incumbent in the PC software business, is very vulnerable to this shift. If the center of computing does move to the cloud, with most date and applications stored there, and if all one needs to access data and run applications is a Web browser, then the value of a PC operating system such as Windows is significantly reduced. Microsoft understands this as well as anyone, which is why the company is pushing aggressively into the cloud computing market with Windows Azure.

Examples such as these raise four questions:

1. When do paradigm shifts occur, and how do they unfold?
2. Why do so many incumbents go into decline following a paradigm shift?
3. What strategies can incumbents adopt to increase the probability that they will survive a paradigm shift and emerge on the other side of the market abyss created by the arrival of new technology as a profitable enterprise?
4. What strategies can new entrants into a market adopt to profit from a paradigm shift?

We shall answer each of these questions in the remainder of this chapter.

Paradigm Shifts and the Decline of Established Companies

Paradigm shifts appear to be more likely to occur in an industry when one, or both, of the following conditions are in place.[17] First, the established technology in the industry is mature and approaching or at its "natural limit," and second, a new "disruptive technology" has entered the marketplace and is taking root in niches that are poorly served by incumbent companies using the established technology.

The Natural Limits to Technology   Richard Foster has formalized the relationship between the performance of a technology and time in terms of what he calls the technology S-curve (see Figure 7.5).[18] This curve shows the relationship over time of cumulative investments in R&D and the performance (or functionality) of a given technology. Early in its evolution, R&D investments in a new technology tend to yield rapid improvements in performance as basic engineering problems are solved. After a time, diminishing returns to cumulative R&D begin to set in, the rate of improvement in performance slows, and the technology starts to approach its natural limit, where further advances are not possible. For example, one can argue that there was more improvement in the first 50 years of the commercial aerospace business following the pioneering flight by the Wright Brothers than there has been in the second 50 years. Indeed, the venerable Boeing 747 is based on a 1960s design. In

Figure 7.5 The Technology S-Curve

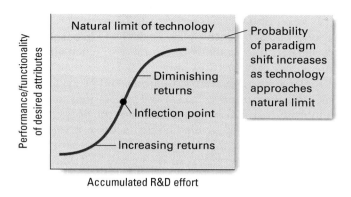

Natural limit of technology

Probability of paradigm shift increases as technology approaches natural limit

Performance/functionality of desired attributes

Diminishing returns

Inflection point

Increasing returns

Accumulated R&D effort

© Cengage Learning 2013

commercial aerospace, therefore, we are now in the region of diminishing returns and may be approaching the natural limit to improvements in the technology of commercial aerospace.

Similarly, it can be argued that we are approaching the natural limit to technology in the performance of silicon-based semiconductor chips. Over the past two decades, the performance of semiconductor chips has been increased dramatically; companies can now manufacture a larger amount of transistors in one single, small silicon chip. This process has helped to increase the power of computers, lower their cost, and shrink their size. But we are starting to approach limits to the ability to shrink the width of lines on a chip and therefore pack ever more transistors onto a single chip. The limit is imposed by the natural laws of physics. Light waves are used to help etch lines onto a chip, and one cannot etch a line that is smaller than the wavelength of light being used. Semiconductor companies are already using light beams with very small wavelengths, such as extreme ultraviolet, to etch lines onto a chip, but there are limits to how far this technology can be pushed, and many believe that we will reach those limits within the decade. Does this mean that our ability to make smaller, faster, cheaper computers is coming to an end? Probably not. It is more likely that we will find another technology to replace silicon-based computing and enable us to continue building smaller, faster, cheaper computers. In fact, several exotic competing technologies are already being developed that may replace silicon-based computing. These include self-organizing molecular computers, three-dimensional microprocessor technology, quantum computing technology, and using DNA to perform computations.[19]

What does all of this have to do with paradigm shifts? According to Foster, when a technology approaches its natural limit, research attention turns to possible alternative technologies, and sooner or later one of those alternatives might be commercialized and replace the established technology. That is, the probability that a paradigm shift will occur increases. Thus, sometime in the next decade or two, another paradigm shift might shake up the foundations of the computer industry as exotic computing technology replaces silicon-based computing. If history is any guide, if and when this happens, many of the incumbents in today's computer industry will go into decline, and new enterprises will rise to dominance.

Foster pushes this point a little further, noting that, initially, the contenders for the replacement technology are not as effective as the established technology in producing the attributes and features that consumers demand in a product. For example, in the early years of the 20th century, automobiles were just beginning to be produced. They were valued for their ability to move people from place to place, but so was the horse and cart (the established technology). When automobiles originally appeared, the horse and cart was still quite a bit better than the automobile (see Figure 7.6). After all, the first cars were slow, noisy, and prone to breakdown. Moreover, they needed a network of paved roads and gas stations to be really useful, and that network didn't yet exist. For most applications, the horse and cart was still the preferred mode of transportation—including the fact that it was cheaper.

However, this comparison ignored the fact that in the early 20th century, automobile technology was at the very start of its S-curve and was about to experience dramatic improvements in performance as major engineering problems were solved (and those paved roads and gas stations were built). In contrast, after 3,000 years of continuous improvement and refinement, the horse and cart was almost definitely at the end of its technological S-curve. The result was that the rapidly improving automobile soon replaced the horse and cart as the preferred mode of transportation. At time T_1 in Figure 7.6, the horse and cart was still superior to the automobile. By time T_2, the automobile had surpassed the horse and cart.

Foster notes that because the successor technology is initially less efficient than the established technology, established companies and their customers often make the mistake of dismissing it, only to be surprised by its rapid performance improvement. A final point here is that often there is not one potential successor technology but a swarm of potential successor technologies, only one of which might ultimately rise to the fore (see Figure 7.7). When this is the case, established companies are put at a disadvantage. Even if they recognize that a paradigm shift is imminent, companies may not have the resources to invest in all the potential replacement

Figure 7.6 Established and Successor Technologies

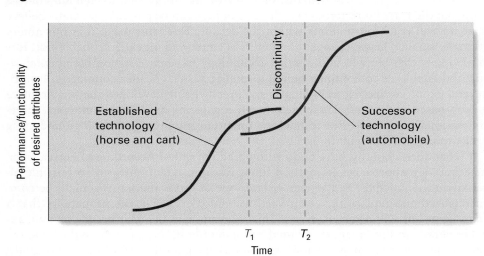

Figure 7.7   Swarm of Successor Technologies

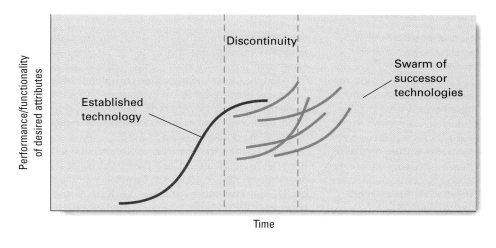

technologies. If they invest in the wrong one, something that is easy to do given the uncertainty that surrounds the entire process, they may be locked out of subsequent development.

Disruptive Technology   Clayton Christensen has built on Foster's insights and his own research to develop a theory of disruptive technology that has become very influential in high-technology circles.[20] Christensen uses the term disruptive technology to refer to a new technology that gets its start away from the mainstream of a market and then, as its functionality improves over time, invades the main market. Such technologies are disruptive because they revolutionize industry structure and competition, often causing the decline of established companies. They cause a technological paradigm shift.

Christensen's greatest insight is that established companies are often aware of the new technology but do not invest in it because they listen to their customers, and their customers do not want it. Of course, this arises because the new technology is early in its development, and only at the beginning of the S-curve for that technology. Once the performance of the new technology improves, customers will want it, but by this time it is new entrants (as opposed to established companies), that have accumulated the required knowledge to bring the new technology into the mass market. Christensen supports his view by several detailed historical case studies, one of which is summarized in Strategy in Action 7.3.

In addition to listening too closely to their customers, Christensen also identifies a number of other factors that make it very difficult for established companies to adopt a new disruptive technology. He notes that many established companies decline to invest in new disruptive technologies because initially they serve such small market niches that it seems unlikely there would be an impact on the company's revenues and profits. As the new technology starts to improve in functionality and invade the main market, their investment can often be hindered by the difficult implementation of a new business model required to exploit the new technology.

STRATEGY IN ACTION

Disruptive Technology in Mechanical Excavators

Excavators are used to dig out foundations for large buildings, trenches to lay large pipes for sewers and related components, and foundations and trenches for residential construction and farm work. Prior to the 1940s, the dominant technology used to manipulate the bucket on a mechanical excavator was based on a system of cables and pulleys. Although these mechanical systems could lift large buckets of earth, the excavators themselves were quite large, cumbersome, and expensive. Thus, they were rarely used to dig small trenches for house foundations, irrigation ditches for farmers, and projects of similar scale. In most cases, these small trenches were dug by hand.

In the 1940s, a new technology made its appearance: hydraulics. In theory, hydraulic systems had certain advantages over the established cable and pulley systems. Most important, their energy efficiency was higher: for a given bucket size, a smaller engine would be required using a hydraulic system. However, the initial hydraulic systems also had drawbacks. The seals on hydraulic cylinders were prone to leak under high pressure, effectively limiting the size of bucket that could be lifted. Notwithstanding this drawback, when hydraulics first appeared, many of the incumbent firms in the mechanical excavation industry took the technology seriously enough to ask their primary customers whether they would be interested in hydraulic products. Since the primary customers of incumbents needed excavators with large buckets to dig out the foundations for buildings and large trenches, their reply was negative. For this customer set, the hydraulic systems of the 1940s were neither reliable nor powerful enough. Consequently, after consulting with their customers, these established companies in the industry made the strategic decision not to invest in hydraulics. Instead, they continued to produce excavation equipment based on the dominant cable and pulley technology.

A number of new entrants, which included J. I. Case, John Deere, J. C. Bamford, and Caterpillar, pioneered hydraulic excavation equipment. Because of the limits on bucket size imposed by the seal problem, these companies initially focused on a poorly served niche in the market that could make use of small buckets: residential contractors and farmers. Over time, these new entrants were able to solve the engineering problems associated with weak hydraulic seals, and as they did this, they manufactured excavators with larger buckets. Ultimately, they invaded the market niches served by the old-line companies: general contractors that dug the foundations for large buildings, sewers, and large-scale projects. At this point, Case, Deere, Caterpillar, and similar companies rose to dominance in the industry, while the majority of established companies from the prior era lost share. Of the 30 or so manufacturers of cable-actuated equipment in the United States in the late-1930s, only four survived to the 1950s.

Source: Adapted from Christensen, *The Innovator's Dilemma*

Both of these points can be illustrated by reference to one more example: the rise of online discount stockbrokers during the 1990s, such as Ameritrade and E*TRADE, which made use of a new technology—the Internet—to allow individual investors to trade stocks for a very low commission fee, whereas full-service stockbrokers, such as Merrill Lynch, which required that orders be placed through a stockbroker who earned a commission for performing the transaction, did not.

Christensen also notes that a new network of suppliers and distributors typically grow alongside the new entrants. Not only do established companies initially ignore disruptive technology, so do their suppliers and distributors. This creates an opportunity for new suppliers and distributors to enter the market to serve the new entrants. As the new entrants grow, so does the associated network. Ultimately, Christensen suggests, the new entrants and their network may replace not only established enterprises, but also the entire network of suppliers and distributors associated with established companies. Taken to its logical extreme, this view suggests that disruptive technologies may result in the demise of the entire network of enterprises associated with established companies in an industry.

The established companies in an industry that is being rocked by a technological paradigm shift often must cope with internal inertia forces that limit their ability to adapt, but the new entrants do not, and thereby have an advantage. New entrants do not have to deal with an established, conservative customer set, and an obsolete business model. Instead, they can focus on optimizing the new technology, improving its performance, and riding the wave of disruptive technology into new market segments until they invade the main market and challenge the established companies. By then, they may be well equipped to surpass the established companies.

Strategic Implications for Established Companies

Although Christensen has uncovered an important tendency, it is by no means written in stone that all established companies are doomed to fail when faced with disruptive technologies, as we have seen with IBM and Merrill Lynch. Established companies must meet the challenges created by the emergence of disruptive technologies.[21]

First, having access to the knowledge about how disruptive technologies can revolutionize markets is a valuable strategic asset. Many of the established companies that Christensen examined failed because they took a myopic view of the new technology and asked their customers the wrong question. Instead of asking: "Are you interested in this new technology?" they should have recognized that the new technology was likely to improve rapidly over time and instead have asked: "Would you be interested in this new technology if it improves its functionality over time?" If established enterprises had done this, they may have made very different strategic decisions.

Second, it is clearly important for established enterprises to invest in newly emerging technologies that may ultimately become disruptive technologies. Companies have to hedge their bets about new technology. As we have noted, at any time, there may be a swarm of emerging technologies, any one of which might ultimately become a disruptive technology. Large, established companies that are generating significant cash flows can, and often should, establish and fund central R&D operations to invest in and develop such technologies. In addition, they may wish to acquire newly emerging companies that are pioneering potentially disruptive technologies, or enter into alliances with others to jointly develop the technology. The strategy of acquiring companies that are developing potentially disruptive technology is one that Cisco Systems, a dominant provider of Internet network equipment, is famous for pursuing. At the heart of this strategy must be a recognition on behalf of the incumbent enterprise that it is better for the company to develop disruptive technology and then cannibalize its established sales base than to have the sales base taken away by new entrants.

However, Christensen makes a very important point: even when established companies undertake R&D investments in potentially disruptive technologies, they often fail to commercialize those technologies because of internal forces that suppress change. For example, managers that are currently generating the most cash in one part of the business may claim that they need the greatest R&D investment to maintain their market position, and may lobby top management to delay investment in a new technology. This can be a powerful argument when, early in the S-curve, the long-term prospects of a new technology are very unclear. The consequence, however, may be that the company fails to build a competence in the new technology, and will suffer accordingly.

In addition, Christensen argues that the commercialization of new disruptive technology often requires a radically different value chain with a completely different cost structure—a new business model. For example, it may require a different manufacturing system, a different distribution system, and different pricing options, and may involve very different gross margins and operating margins. Christensen argues that it is almost impossible for two distinct business models to coexist within the same organization. When companies try to implement both models, the already established model will almost inevitably suffocate the model associated with the disruptive technology.

The solution to this problem is to separate out the disruptive technology and create an autonomous operating division solely for this new technology. For example, during the early-1980s, HP built a very successful laser jet printer business. Then ink jet technology was invented. Some employees at HP believed that ink jet printers would cannibalize sales of laser jet printers, and consequently argued that HP should not produce ink jet printers. Fortunately for HP, senior management saw ink jet technology for what it was: a potential disruptive technology. Instead of choosing not to invest in ink jet technology, they allocated significant R&D funds toward its commercialization. Furthermore, when the technology was ready for market introduction, they established an autonomous ink jet division at a different geographical location, including manufacturing, marketing, and distribution departments. HP senior managers accepted that the ink jet division might take sales away from the laser jet division and decided that it was better for an HP division to cannibalize the sales of another HP division, than allow those sales to be cannibalized by another company. Happily for HP, ink jets cannibalize sales of laser jets only on the margin, and both laser jet and ink jet printers have profitable market niches. This felicitous outcome, however, does not detract from the message of this example: if a company is developing a potentially disruptive technology, the chances for success will be enhanced if it is placed in a stand-alone product division and given its own mandate.

Strategic Implications for New Entrants

Christensen's work also holds implications for new entrants. The new entrants, or attackers, have several advantages over established enterprises. Pressures to continue the existing out-of-date business model do not hamstring new entrants, which do not need to worry about product cannibalization issues. They do not need to worry about their established customer base, or about relationships with established suppliers and distributors. Instead, they can focus all their energies on the opportunities offered by the new disruptive technology, move along the S-curve of technology improvement, and rapidly grow with the market for that technology. This does not mean that the new entrants do not have problems to solve. They may be constrained by a lack of capital or must manage the organizational problems associated with rapid growth; most important, they may need to find a way to take their technology from a small out-of-the-way niche into the mass market.

Perhaps one of the most important issues facing new entrants is choosing whether to partner with an established company, or go it alone in an attempt to develop and profit from a new disruptive technology. Although a new entrant may enjoy all of the advantages of the attacker, it may lack the resources required to fully exploit them. In such a case, the company might want to consider forming a strategic alliance with a larger, established company to gain access to those resources. The main issues here are the same as those discussed earlier when examining the three strategies that companies can pursue to capture first-mover advantages: go it alone, enter into a strategic alliance, or license its technology.

Ethical Dilemma

Your company is in a race with two other enterprises to develop a new technological standard for streaming high-definition video over the Internet. The three technologies are incompatible with each other, and switching costs are presumed to be high. You know that your technology is significantly inferior to the technology being developed by your rivals, but you strongly suspect that you will be the first to the market. Moreover, you know that by bundling your product with one that your company already sells (which is very popular among computer users) you should be able to ensure wide early adoption. You have even considered initially pricing the product at zero in order to ensure rapid take up, thereby shutting out the superior technology that your rivals are developing. You are able to do this because you make so much money from your other products. Once the market has locked into your offering, the strategy will be to raise the price on your technology.

One of your colleagues has suggested that it is not ethical for your company to use its financial muscle and bundling strategies to lock out a superior technology in this manner. Why do you think he makes this argument?

Do you agree with him? Why?

Can you think of a real-world situation that is similar to this case?

Summary of Chapter

1. Technical standards are important in many high-tech industries: they guarantee compatibility, reduce confusion in the minds of customers, allow for mass production and lower costs, and reduce the risks associated with supplying complementary products.

2. Network effects and positive feedback loops often determine which standard will dominate a market.

3. Owning a standard can be a source of sustained competitive advantage.

4. Establishing a proprietary standard as the industry standard may require the company to win a format war against a competing and incompatible standard. Strategies for doing this include producing complementary products, leveraging killer applications, using aggressive pricing and marketing, licensing the technology, and cooperating with competitors.

5. Many high-tech products are characterized by high fixed costs of development but very low or zero marginal costs of producing one extra unit of output. These cost economics create a presumption in favor of strategies that emphasize aggressive pricing to increase volume and drive down average total costs.

6. It is very important for a first mover to develop a strategy to capitalize on first-mover advantages. A company can choose from three strategies: develop and market the technology itself, do so jointly with another company, or license the technology to existing companies. The choice depends

on the complementary assets required to capture a first-mover advantage, the height of barriers to imitation, and the capability of competitors.

7. Technological paradigm shifts occur when new technologies come along that revolutionize the structure of the industry, dramatically alter the nature of competition, and require companies to adopt new strategies in order to succeed.

8. Technological paradigm shifts are more likely to occur when progress in improving the established technology is slowing because of diminishing returns and when a new disruptive technology is taking root in a market niche.

9. Established companies can deal with paradigm shifts by investing in technology or setting up a stand-alone division to exploit the technology.

Discussion Questions

1. Reread the opening case on the emerging format war for high definition DVD players. On the basis of the information contained in this case, which company do you think will most likely win this format war: Sony or Toshiba? Why?

2. What is different about high-tech industries? Were all industries once high tech?

3. You are a manager for a major music record label. Last year, music sales declined by 10%, primarily because of very high piracy rates for CDs. Your boss has asked you to develop a strategy for reducing piracy rates. What would you suggest that the company do?

4. You work for a small company that has the leading position in an embryonic market. Your boss believes that the company's future is ensured because it has a 60% share of the market, the lowest cost structure in the industry, and the most reliable and highest-valued product. Write a memo to your boss outlining why the assumptions posed might be incorrect.

5. You are working for a small company that has developed an operating system for PCs that is faster and more stable than Microsoft's Windows operating system. What strategies might the company pursue to unseat Windows and establish its own operating system as the dominant technical standard in the industry?

6. Why are standards so important in high-tech industries? What are the competitive implications of this?

Practicing Strategic Management

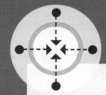

Small-Group Exercises

Small-Group Exercise: Digital Books

Break up into groups of 3–5 people, and discuss the following scenario. Appoint one group member as a spokesperson who will communicate your findings to the class.

You are a group of managers and software engineers at a small start-up that has developed software that enables customers to easily download and view digital books on a variety of digital devices, including PCs, iPods, and e-book readers. The same software also allows customers to share digital books using peer-to-peer technology (the same technology that allows people to share music files on the Web), and to "burn" digital books onto DVDs.

1. How do you think the market for this software is likely to develop? What factors might inhibit adoption of this software?

2. Can you think of a strategy that your company might pursue in combination with book publishers that will enable your company to increase revenues and the film companies to reduce piracy rates?

Strategy Sign-On

Article File 7

Find an example of an industry that has undergone a technological paradigm shift in recent years. What happened to the established companies as that paradigm shift unfolded?

Strategic Management Project: Developing Your Portfolio 7

This module requires you to analyze the industry environment in which your company is based and determine if it is vulnerable to a technological paradigm shift. With the information you have at your disposal, answer the following questions:

1. What is the dominant product technology used in the industry in which your company is based?
2. Are technical standards important in your industry? If so, what are they?
3. What are the attributes of the majority of customers purchasing the product of your company (e.g., early adopters, early majority, late majority)? What does this tell you about the strategic issues that the company is likely to face in the future?
4. Did the dominant technology in your industry diffuse rapidly or slowly? What drove the speed of diffusion?
5. Where is the dominant technology in your industry on its S-curve? Are alternative competing technologies being developed that might give rise to a paradigm shift in your industry?
6. Are intellectual property rights important to your company? If so, what strategies is it adopting to protect those rights? Is it doing enough?

CLOSING CASE

The Format War in Smartphone Operating Systems

There is a format war underway in the smartphone business as a number of companies battle for dominance in what is fast evolving into the next large high-technology market. Smartphones are wireless handsets with extended data capabilities, allowing users to browse the Internet, send e-mails, and run a growing number of applications, including spreadsheets, restaurant locators, and games and music players. The development of smartphones is rapidly transforming wireless handsets into powerful general purpose computing devices that can perform many of the functions we typically associate with desktop and laptop computers. Operating systems that reside on the devices and run all of the onboard functions and applications are a key feature of smartphones.

The main competitors in this market include: Research In Motion (RIM), with its BlackBerry phones; Apple, with the iPhone; Microsoft with its Windows phones; and Google with the Android phone. In 2010, over 300 million smartphones were sold worldwide, which represents an increase of 74% over 2009. While Research In Motion and Apple make both the phone and the operating system (OS), and sell the integrated bundle to end users, Microsoft and Google only make the operating system, and partner with various hardware manufacturers to sell phones to end users. All companies sell their phones in conjunction with wireless service providers.

Apple and RIM are both in business to make money from the sale of their devices. Google and Microsoft see the smartphone business as a crucial complement to their search businesses. As more people adopt smartphones, an increasing number of search queries will be made from smartphones. Both Google and Microsoft want their OS to run on as many phones as possible so that their respective particular search offerings are the default choice on a given smartphone. In other words, Microsoft and Google both see diffusion of the smartphone OS as a way of increasing revenues from the fast growing mobile search business.

The introduction of Apple's iPhone was one of the key developments in this market. This revolutionary device, with its elegant touch screen interface, Apple OS, and multimedia capabilities, helped to redefine the smartphone business, and rapidly started to create a mass market for these devices. Prior to the iPhone, most adopters had been business users. Now, increasingly, they are consumers.

By early-2011, phones using Google's Android operating system had a 38% share of the U.S. market, Apple's had a 26.6% share, RIM had a 24.7% share, and Microsoft had a 5.8% share. Google's Android OS has been rapidly gaining share. Apple, too, has positive market momentum. Conversely, RIM and Microsoft are losing share. The irony of this is that RIM and Microsoft both had smartphone offerings before Apple and Google, but their phones primarily targeted business users.

Many observers believe that the same trends toward the standardization of operating systems seen in the PC industry will now occur in the smartphone business, with the market eventually settling on 2–3 dominant systems. Apple's strategy with its iPhone is consistent with the attainment of such a goal. Apple was the first to realize that the available applications add significant value to a smartphone. To further this strategy, it provided tools to software developers to help them create applications for the iPhone, and developed a unique way of distributing those applications: Apple's online App store.

Apple is not having it all its own way, however. Other companies are pursuing a similar strategy. Google, RIM, and Microsoft have all copied Apple's strategy for application development and distribution, providing tools and opening their own app stores.

Interestingly, the world's largest wireless handset manufacturer, Nokia, has performed poorly in this space. Nokia does sell smartphones that use its Symbian operating system. However, these phones lack the features and functions of other smartphones, and many people do not consider the Nokia models to be true smartphones. Recognizing its inability to compete effectively with Apple and Google in particular, Nokia has now entered into an alliance with Microsoft, and is currently developing a line of smartphones that will use Microsoft's OS.[22]

Case Discussion Questions

1. Microsoft and RIM were selling smartphones several years before Apple and Google entered the market. Why then do you think Apple and Google's Android phones are now starting to dominate the market?

2. Why did Apple place such emphasis on the applications that run on the iPhone? What is it trying to achieve by heavily promoting applications? Why did other companies rush to copy Apple's strategies?

3. Apple and Google are pursuing different strategies—Apple sells the device and the OS as a bundle (the iPhone), whereas Google does not make devices and licenses its Android OS phones to other device makers. Both companies are gaining share. What does this teach about the right strategy for prevailing in a format war?

4. Microsoft and Nokia have both been losing share in the smartphone business. They have now decided to enter into an alliance. How are they hoping to reshape competition in the smartphone business? Do you think they will succeed?

5. Google licenses its Android OS to phone manufacturers for free. Why would it do this?

6. What do you think the structure of the smartphone market will look like a decade from now?

Notes

[1]R. Harms and M. Yamartino, "The Economics of the Cloud," *Microsoft White Paper*, November 2011. A. Vance, "The Cloud: Battle of the Tech Titans," *Bloomberg Business Week*, March 3, 2011. K. D. Schwartz, "Cloud Computing Can Generate Massive Savings for Agencies," *Federal Computer Week*, January 2011.

[2]Data from Bureau of Economic Analysis, *Survey of United States Current Business*, 2006. Available online at http://www.bea.gov/

[3]J. M. Utterback, *Mastering the Dynamics of Innovation* (Boston: Harvard Business School Press, 1994). C. Shapiro and H. R. Varian, *Information Rules: A Strategic Guide to the Network Economy* (Boston: Harvard Business School Press, 1999).

[4]The layout is not universal, although it is widespread. The French, for example, use a different layout.

[5]For details, see Charles W. L. Hill, "Establishing a Standard: Competitive Strategy and Technology Standards in Winner Take All Industries," *Academy of Management Executive* 11 (1997): 7–25; Shapiro and Varian, *Information Rules*; B. Arthur, "Increasing Returns and the New World of Business," *Harvard Business Review* (July–August 1996): 100–109; G. Gowrisankaran and J. Stavins, "Network Externalities and Technology Adoption: Lessons from Electronic Payments," *Rand Journal of Economics* 35 (2004): 260–277; and V. Shankar and B. L. Bayus, "Network Effects and Competition: An Empirical Analysis of the Home Video Game Industry," *Strategic Management Journal* 24 (2003): 375–394. R. Casadesus-Masanell and P. Ghemawat, "Dynamic Mixed Duopoly: A Model Motivated by Linux vs Windows," *Management Science*, 52 (2006): 1072–1085.

[6]See Shapiro and Varian, *Information Rules*; Hill, "Establishing a Standard"; and M. A. Shilling, "Technological Lockout: An Integrative Model of the Economic and Strategic Factors Driving Technology Success and Failure," *Academy of Management Review* 23(2) (1998): 267–285.

[7]Microsoft does not disclose the per unit licensing fee that it receives from original equipment manufacturers, although media reports speculate it is around $50 a copy.

[8]Much of this section is based on Charles W. L. Hill, Michael Heeley, and Jane Sakson, "Strategies for Profiting from Innovation," in *Advances in Global High Technology Management* 3 (Greenwich, CT: JAI Press, 1993), pp. 79–95.

[9]M. Lieberman and D. Montgomery, "First Mover Advantages," *Strategic Management Journal* 9 (Special Issue, Summer 1988): 41–58.

[10]W. Boulding and M. Christen, "Sustainable Pioneering Advantage? Profit Implications of Market Entry Order?" *Marketing Science* 22 (2003): 371–386; C. Markides and P. Geroski, "Teaching Elephants to Dance and Other Silly Ideas," *Business Strategy Review* 13 (2003): 49–61.

[11]J. Borzo, "Aging Gracefully," *Wall Street Journal*, October 15, 2001, p. R22.

[12]The importance of complementary assets was first noted by D. J. Teece. See D. J. Teece, "Profiting from Technological Innovation," in D. J. Teece (ed.), *The Competitive Challenge* (New York: Harper & Row, 1986), pp. 26–54.

[13]M. J. Chen and D. C. Hambrick, "Speed, Stealth, and Selective Attack: How Small Firms Differ from Large Firms in Competitive Behavior," *Academy of Management Journal* 38 (1995): 453–482.

[14]E. Mansfield, M. Schwartz, and S. Wagner, "Imitation Costs and Patents: An Empirical Study," *Economic Journal* 91 (1981): 907–918.

[15]E. Mansfield, "How Rapidly Does New Industrial Technology Leak Out?" *Journal of Industrial Economics* 34 (1985): 217–223.

[16]This argument has been made in the game theory literature. See R. Caves, H. Cookell, and P. J. Killing, "The Imperfect Market for Technology Licenses," *Oxford Bulletin of Economics and Statistics* 45 (1983): 249–267; N. T. Gallini, "Deterrence by Market Sharing: A Strategic Incentive for Licensing," *American Economic Review* 74 (1984): 931–941; C. Shapiro, "Patent Licensing and R&D Rivalry," *American Economic Review* 75 (1985): 25–30.

[17]M. Christensen, *The Innovator's Dilemma* (Boston: Harvard Business School Press, 1997); R. N. Foster, *Innovation: The Attacker's Advantage* (New York: Summit Books, 1986).

[18]Foster, *Innovation*.

[19]Ray Kurzweil, *The Age of the Spiritual Machines* (New York: Penguin Books, 1999).

[20]See Christensen, *The Innovator's Dilemma*; C. M. Christensen and M. Overdorf, "Meeting the Challenge of Disruptive Change," *Harvard Business Review* (March–April 2000): 66–77.

[21] Charles W. L. Hill and Frank T. Rothaermel, "The Performance of Incumbent Firms in the Face of Radical Technological Innovation," *Academy of Management Review* 28 (2003): 257–274;

F. T. Rothaermel and Charles W. L. Hill, "Technological Discontinuities and Complementary Assets: A Longitudinal Study of Industry and Firm Performance," *Organization Science* 16(1): 52–70.

[22] *The Economist*, "Battle for the Smart phone's Soul," November 22, 2008, pp. 76–77; Canalys, "Global smartphone shipments Rise 28 %," Press Release, November 6, 2008, www.canalys.com/pr/2008/r2008112.htm; N. Wingfield, "iPhone Software Sales Take Off," *Wall Street Journal*, August 11, 2008, p. B1; comScore press release, "comScore reports May 2011 U.S. Mobile Subscriber Market Share," July 5, 2011.

Strategy in the Global Environment

erel photography/istockphoto.com

Avon Products

In 1999, Andrea Jung became CEO of Avon Products, the beauty products company famous for its direct sales model, and for 6 years after her appointment, Avon's revenues grew in excess of 10% per annum. Profits tripled, making Jung a Wall Street favorite. Then, in 2005, the success story started to become ugly. Avon, which derives as much as 70% of its revenues from international markets, mostly in developing nations, suddenly began losing sales across the globe. A ban on direct sales had hurt its business in China (the Chinese government had accused companies that used a direct sales model of engaging in pyramid schemes and of creating "cults"). To compound matters, economic weakness in Eastern Europe, Russia, and Mexico, all drivers of Avon's success, stalled growth in those areas. The dramatic turn of events took investors by surprise. In May 2005, Jung had told investors that Avon would exceed Wall Street's targets for the year. By September, she was rapidly backpedaling and Avon stock fell 45%.

With her position in jeopardy, Jung began to reevaluate Avon's global strategy. Up until this point, the company had expanded primarily by replicating its U.S. strategy and organization in other countries. When it entered a nation, it gave country managers considerable autonomy. All used the Avon brand and adopted the direct sales model that has been the company's hallmark. The result was an army of 5 million Avon representatives around the world, all independent contractors, who sold the company's skin care and makeup products. However, many country managers also set up their own local manufacturing operations and supply chains, were responsible for local marketing, and developed their own new products. In Jung's words, "they were the king or queen of every decision." The result was a lack of consistency in marketing strategy from nation to nation, extensive duplication of manufacturing operations and supply chains, and a profusion of new products—many of which were not profitable. In Mexico, for example, the roster of products for sale had ballooned to 13,000. Moreover, the company had 15 layers of management, making accountability and communication of employees problematic. There was also a distinct lack of data-driven analysis of new product opportunities, with country managers often making decisions based on their intuition or gut feeling.

Jung's turnaround strategy involved several elements. To help transform Avon, she hired seasoned managers from well-known global consumer products companies such as Procter & Gamble and Unilever. She restructured the organization to improve employee communication, performance visibility, and accountability, reducing the number of management layers to just 8, and laying off 30% of managers in the process. Manufacturing was consolidated in a number of regional centers and supply chains were rationalized, eliminating duplication and reducing costs by over $1 billion per annum. Rigorous return on investment criteria was introduced to evaluate product profitability. As a consequence, 25% of Avon's products were discontinued, and new product decisions were centralized at Avon's headquarters. Jung also invested in centralized product development to introduce new blockbuster products that could be positioned as global brands. And, Jung pushed the company to emphasize its value proposition in every national market, which could be characterized as high quality at low prices.

By 2007, this strategy was beginning to yield dividends. The company's performance improved and growth resumed. It didn't hurt that Jung, a Chinese-American who speaks Mandarin, was instrumental in persuading Chinese authorities, to rescind its ban on direct sales, allowing Avon to recruit 400,000 new representatives in China. Then, in 2008 and 2009,

the global financial crisis hit, however, Jung's reaction was positive. She viewed the crisis as an opportunity for Avon to expand its business. In 2009, Avon ran ads around the world aimed at recruiting sales representatives. In the ads, female sales representatives talked about working for Avon. "I can't get laid off, I can't get fired," is what one said. Phones started to incessantly ring, and Avon was able to quickly expand its global sales force. Jung also instituted an aggressive pricing strategy, while packaging was redesigned for a more elegant look at no additional cost. The idea was to emphasize the "value for money" that the Avon products represented. Well-known celebrities were used in ads to help market the company's products, and Avon pushed it representatives to use online social networking sites as a medium for representatives to market themselves. The result was in the difficult years of 2008–2010 during which Avon gained global market share and it financial performance improved.

Overview

This chapter begins with a discussion of ongoing changes in the global competitive environment and discusses models managers can use for analyzing competition in different national markets. Next, the chapter discusses the various ways in which international expansion can increase a company's profitability and profit growth. It also looks at the advantages and disadvantages of different strategies companies can pursue to gain a competitive advantage in the global marketplace. This is followed by a discussion of two related strategic issues: (1) how managers decide which foreign markets to enter, when to enter them, and on what scale; and (2) what kind of vehicle or method a company should use to expand globally and enter a foreign country. Once a company has entered a foreign market, it becomes a **multinational company**, that is, a company that does business in two or more national markets. The vehicles that companies can employ to enter foreign markets and become multinationals include exporting, licensing, setting up a joint venture with a foreign company, and setting up a wholly owned subsidiary. The chapter closes with a discussion of the benefits and costs of entering into strategic alliances with other global companies.

Avon Products, profiled in the opening case, gives us a preview of some issues that we will explore in this chapter. Like many other companies, Avon moved into other countries because it recognized opportunities for huge growth in other locations. The company thought it could create value by transferring Avon's brand, products, and direct sales model to other countries and by giving country managers considerable autonomy to develop local markets abroad. This worked for decades, but by 2005 the company was running into significant headwinds. Avon's costs were too high, a result of extensive manufacturing duplication across national markets. It had too many products, many of which were not profitable, and there was a lack of consistency in marketing messages and branding across nations. In response, CEO Andrea Jung changed the strategy of the company. The autonomy of local country managers was reduced, and she consolidated manufacturing and reduced the product line by 25%, while emphasizing global brands and a global marketing strategy. This change in strategy helped Avon to remove over $1 billion from its cost structure while fueling an expansion in sales.

As we shall see later in this chapter, many other companies have made a similar shift in the last two decades, moving from what can be characterized as a *localization strategy*, where local country managers have considerable autonomy over manufacturing and marketing, to a *global strategy*, where the corporate center exercises more control over manufacturing, marketing, and product development decisions. The tendency to make such a shift in many international businesses is a response to the globalization of markets. We shall discuss this process later in the chapter.

By the time you have completed this chapter, you will have a good understanding of the various strategic issues that companies face when they decide to expand their operations abroad to achieve competitive advantage and superior profitability.

The Global and National Environments

Fifty years ago, most national markets were isolated from one another by significant barriers to international trade and investment. In those days, managers could focus on analyzing only those national markets in which their company competed. They

> **Multinational company**
>
> A company that does business in two or more national markets.

did not need to pay much attention to entry by global competitors, for there were few and entry was difficult. Nor did they need to pay much attention to entering foreign markets, since that was often prohibitively expensive. All of this has now changed. Barriers to international trade and investment have tumbled, huge global markets for goods and services have been created, and companies from different nations are entering each other's home markets on an unprecedented scale, increasing the intensity of competition. Rivalry can no longer be understood merely in terms of what happens within the boundaries of a nation; managers now need to consider how globalization is impacting the environment in which their company competes and what strategies their company should adopt to exploit the unfolding opportunities and counter competitive threats. In this section, we look at the changes ushered in by falling barriers to international trade and investment, and we discuss a model for analyzing the competitive situation in different nations.

The Globalization of Production and Markets

The past half-century has seen a dramatic lowering of barriers to international trade and investment. For example, the average tariff rate on manufactured goods traded between advanced nations has fallen from around 40% to under 4%. Similarly, in nation after nation, regulations prohibiting foreign companies from entering domestic markets and establishing production facilities, or acquiring domestic companies, have been removed. As a result of these two developments, there has been a surge in both the volume of international trade and the value of foreign direct investment. The volume of world merchandise trade has grown faster than the world economy since 1950.[1] From 1970 to 2010, the volume of world merchandise trade expanded 28-fold, outstripping the expansion of world production, which grew about 8 times in real terms. Moreover, between 1992 and 2010, the total flow of foreign direct investment from all countries increased over 500% while world trade by value grew by some 145% and world output by around 40%.[2] These trends have led to the globalization of production and the globalization of markets.[3]

The globalization of production has been increasing as companies take advantage of lower barriers to international trade and investment to disperse important parts of their production processes around the globe. Doing so enables them to take advantage of national differences in the cost and quality of factors of production such as labor, energy, land, and capital, which allows companies to lower their cost structures and boost profits. For example, foreign companies build nearly 30% of the Boeing Company's commercial jet aircraft, the 777. For its next jet airliner model, the 787, Boeing is pushing this trend even further, with nearly 65% of the total value of the aircraft scheduled to be outsourced to foreign companies, 35% of which will go to 3 major Japanese companies, and another 20% going to companies located in Italy, Singapore, and the United Kingdom.[4] Part of Boeing's rationale for outsourcing so much production to foreign suppliers is that these suppliers are the best in the world at performing their particular activity. Therefore, the result of having foreign suppliers build specific parts is a better final product and higher profitability for Boeing.

As for the globalization of markets, it has been argued that the world's economic system is moving from one in which national markets are distinct entities, isolated from each other by trade barriers and barriers of distance, time, and culture, toward a system in which national markets are merging into one huge global marketplace. Increasingly, customers around the world demand and use the same basic product offerings. Consequently, in many industries, it is no longer meaningful to talk about the German market, the U.S. market, or the Chinese market; there is only the global market. The global acceptance of Coca-Cola, Citigroup credit cards, blue jeans, Starbucks, McDonald's hamburgers, the Nokia wireless phone, and Microsoft's Windows operating system are examples of this trend.[5]

The trend toward the globalization of production and markets has several important implications for competition within an industry. First, industry boundaries do not stop at national borders. Because many industries are becoming global in scope, competitors and potential future competitors exist not only in a company's home market, but also in other national markets. Managers who analyze only their home market can be caught unprepared by the entry of efficient foreign competitors. The globalization of markets and production implies that companies around the globe are finding their home markets under attack from foreign competitors. For example, in Japan, American financial institutions such as J.P. Morgan have been making inroads against Japanese financial service institutions. In the United States, Finland's Nokia has taken market share from Motorola in the market for wireless phone handsets (see Strategy in Action 8.1). In the European Union, the once dominant Dutch company Philips has seen its market share in the customer electronics industry taken by Japan's JVC, Matsushita, and Sony.

Second, the shift from national to global markets has intensified competitive rivalry in many industries. National markets that once were consolidated oligopolies, dominated by 3 or 4 companies and subjected to relatively little foreign competition, have been transformed into segments of fragmented global industries in which a large number of companies battle each other for market share in many countries. This rivalry has threatened to drive down profitability and has made it more critical for companies to maximize their efficiency, quality, customer responsiveness, and innovative ability. The painful restructuring and downsizing that has been occurring at companies such as Kodak is as much a response to the increased intensity of global competition as it is to anything else. However, not all global industries are fragmented. Many remain consolidated oligopolies, except that now they are consolidated global (rather than national) oligopolies. In the videogame industry, for example, 3 companies are battling for global dominance, Microsoft from the United States and Nintendo and Sony from Japan. In the market for wireless handsets, Nokia of Finland does global battle against Motorola of the United States, Samsung and LG from South Korea, HTC from China, and more recently, Apple with its iPhone, Research In Motion of Canada with their BlackBerry and other phones using Google's Android operating system.

Finally, although globalization has increased both the threat of entry and the intensity of rivalry within many formerly protected national markets, it has also created enormous opportunities for companies based in those markets. The steady decline in barriers to cross-border trade and investment has opened up many once protected national markets to companies based outside these nations. Thus, for example, in recent years, western European, Japanese, and U.S. companies have accelerated their investments in the nations of Eastern Europe, Latin America, and Southeast Asia as they try to take advantage of growth opportunities in those areas.

National Competitive Advantage

Despite the globalization of production and markets, many of the most successful companies in certain industries are still clustered in a small number of countries. For example, many of the world's most successful biotechnology and computer

STRATEGY IN ACTION

Finland's Nokia

The wireless phone market is one of the great growth stories of the last 20 years. Starting from a low base in 1990, annual global sales of wireless phones surged to reach around 1.3 billion units in 2010. By the end of that year, the number of wireless subscriber accounts worldwide was around 4.5 billion, up from less than 10 million in 1990. Nokia is one of the dominant players in the world market for mobile phones with approximately 37% of the market share in 2010.

Nokia's roots are in Finland, not typically a country that comes to mind when one talks about leading-edge technology companies. In the 1980s, Nokia was a rambling Finnish conglomerate with activities that embraced tire manufacturing, paper production, consumer electronics, and telecommunications equipment. By the 2000s, Nokia had transformed into a focused telecommunications equipment manufacturer with a global reach and a 1/3 share of the global market for wireless phones. How has this former conglomerate emerged to take a global leadership position in wireless telecommunications equipment? Much of the answer is in the history, geography, and political economy of Finland and its Nordic neighbors.

In 1981, the Nordic nations cooperated to create the world's first international wireless telephone network. They had good reason to become pioneers: it cost far too much to install a traditional wire line telephone service in those sparsely populated and inhospitably cold countries. The same features made telecommunications all the more valuable: owners of remote northern houses and people driving through the Arctic winter needed a telephone to summon help if emergency services were necessary. As a result, Sweden, Norway, and Finland became the first nations in the world to take wireless telecommunications seriously. They found, for example, that although it cost up to $800 per subscriber to bring a traditional wire line service to remote locations, the same locations could be linked by wireless cellular for only $500 per person. As a consequence, 12% of people in Scandinavia owned cellular phones by 1994, compared with less than 6% in the United States, the world's second most developed market. This lead continued over the next decade. By the end of 2005, 90%

of the population in Finland owned a wireless phone, compared with 70% in the United States.

Nokia, a long-time telecommunications equipment supplier, was well positioned to take advantage of this development from the start, but there were also other forces at work that helped Nokia develop its competitive edge. Unlike almost every other developed nation, Finland has never had a national telephone monopoly. Instead, the country's telephone services have long been provided by about 50 autonomous local telephone companies, whose elected boards set prices by referendum (which naturally means low prices). This army of independent and cost-conscious telephone service providers prevented Nokia from taking anything for granted in its home country. With typical Finnish pragmatism, its customers were willing to buy from the lowest-cost supplier, whether that was Nokia, Ericsson, Motorola, or some other company. This situation contrasted sharply with what prevailed in most developed nations until the late-1980s and early-1990s; domestic telephone monopolies typically purchased equipment from a dominant local supplier, or made the equipment themselves. Nokia responded to this competitive pressure by doing everything possible to drive down its manufacturing costs while remaining at the leading edge of wireless technology.

However, there are now problems on the horizon for Nokia. In the last few years it has lost leadership in the lucrative market for smartphones to companies such as Apple and BlackBerry. While Nokia's market share is still strong, its margins are being compressed. For too long the company adhered to the idea that handsets were mainly for calling people, and failed to notice that Web-based applications were driving demand for products like the iPhone. Why did the one time technology leader make this mistake? According to some critics, Nokia was too isolated from Web-based companies, and other consumer electronics enterprises, whereas Apple, based in Silicon Valley, was surrounded by them. This meant that unlike Apple (and Google, whose Android operating system powers many smartphones), Nokia wasn't exposed to the mix of innovative ideas swirling around Silicon Valley. Location, initially a Nokia advantage, had now become a disadvantage.

Source: Lessons from the "Frozen North," *Economist*, October 8, 1994, pp. 76–77; "A Finnish Fable," *Economist*, October 14, 2000; D. O'Shea and K. Fitchard, "The First 3 billion is Always the Hardest," *Wireless Review* 22 (September 2005), pp. 25–31; P. Taylor, "Big Names Dominate in Mobile Phones," *Financial Times*, September 29, 2006, p. 26; and Nokia Website at www.nokia.com; M. Lynn, "The Fallen King of Finland," *Bloomberg Business Week*, September 20, 2010.

companies are based in the United States, and many of the most successful customer electronics companies are based in Japan, Taiwan, and South Korea. Germany is the base for many successful chemical and engineering companies. These facts suggest that the nation-state within which a company is based may have an important bearing on the competitive position of that company in the global marketplace.

In a study of national competitive advantage, Michael Porter identified four attributes of a national or country-specific environment that have an important impact on the global competitiveness of companies located within that nation:[6]

- *Factor endowments*: A nation's position in factors of production such as skilled labor or the infrastructure necessary to compete in a given industry
- *Local demand conditions*: The nature of home demand for the industry's product or service
- *Related and supporting industries*: The presence or absence in a nation of supplier industries and related industries that are internationally competitive
- *Firm strategy, structure, and rivalry*: The conditions in the nation governing how companies are created, organized, and managed, and the nature of domestic rivalry

Porter speaks of these four attributes as constituting the "diamond," arguing that companies from a given nation are most likely to succeed in industries or strategic groups in which the four attributes are favorable (see Figure 8.1). He also argues that the diamond's attributes form a mutually reinforcing system in which the effect of one attribute is dependent on the state of others.

Figure 8.1 National Competitive Advantage

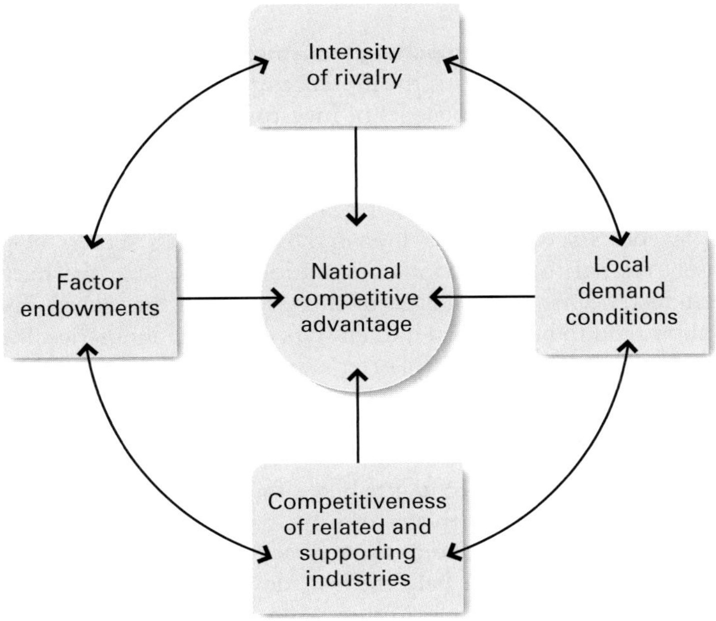

Source: Adapted from M. E. Porter, "The Competitive Advantage of Nations," *Harvard Business Review,* March–April 1990, 77.

Factor Endowments   Factor endowments—the cost and quality of factors of production—are a prime determinant of the competitive advantage that certain countries might have in certain industries. Factors of production include basic factors, such as land, labor, capital, and raw materials, and advanced factors, such as technological know-how, managerial sophistication, and physical infrastructure (roads, railways, and ports). The competitive advantage that the United States enjoys in biotechnology might be explained by the presence of certain advanced factors of production—for example, technological know-how—in combination with some basic factors, which might be a pool of relatively low-cost venture capital that can be used to fund risky start-ups in industries such as biotechnology.

Local Demand Conditions   Home demand plays an important role in providing the impetus for "upgrading" competitive advantage. Companies are typically most sensitive to the needs of their closest customers. Thus, the characteristics of home demand are particularly important in shaping the attributes of domestically made products and creating pressures for innovation and quality. A nation's companies gain competitive advantage if their domestic customers are sophisticated and demanding and pressure local companies to meet high standards of product quality and produce innovative products. Japan's sophisticated and knowledgeable buyers of cameras helped stimulate the Japanese camera industry to improve product quality and introduce innovative models. A similar example can be found in the cellular phone equipment industry, where sophisticated and demanding local customers in Scandinavia helped push Nokia of Finland and Ericsson of Sweden to invest in cellular phone technology long before demand for cellular phones increased in other developed nations. As a result, Nokia and Ericsson, together with Motorola, became significant players in the global cellular telephone equipment industry. The case of Nokia is reviewed in more depth in Strategy in Action 8.1.

Competitiveness of Related and Supporting Industries   The third broad attribute of national advantage in an industry is the presence of internationally competitive suppliers or related industries. The benefits of investments in advanced factors of production by related and supporting industries can spill over into an industry, thereby helping it achieve a strong competitive position internationally. Swedish strength in fabricated steel products (such as ball bearings and cutting tools) has drawn on strengths in Sweden's specialty steel industry. Switzerland's success in pharmaceuticals is closely related to its previous international success in the technologically related dye industry. One consequence of this process is that successful industries within a country tend to be grouped into clusters of related industries. Indeed, this is one of the most pervasive findings of Porter's study. One such cluster is the German textile and apparel sector, which includes high-quality cotton, wool, synthetic fibers, sewing machine needles, and a wide range of textile machinery.

Intensity of Rivalry   The fourth broad attribute of national competitive advantage in Porter's model is the intensity of rivalry of firms within a nation. Porter makes two important points here. First, different nations are characterized by different management ideologies, which either help them or do not help them to build national competitive advantage. For example, Porter noted the predominance of engineers in top management at German and Japanese firms. He attributed this to these firms' emphasis on improving manufacturing processes and product design. In contrast, Porter noted a predominance of people with finance backgrounds leading many U.S.

firms. He linked this to U.S. firms' lack of attention to improving manufacturing processes and product design. He argued that the dominance of finance led to an overemphasis on maximizing short-term financial returns. According to Porter, one consequence of these different management ideologies was a relative loss of U.S. competitiveness in those engineering-based industries where manufacturing processes and product design issues are all-important (such as the automobile industry).

Porter's second point is that there is a strong association between vigorous domestic rivalry and the creation and persistence of competitive advantage in an industry. Rivalry compels companies to look for ways to improve efficiency, which makes them better international competitors. Domestic rivalry creates pressures to innovate, improve quality, reduce costs, and invest in upgrading advanced factors. All this helps to create world-class competitors. The stimulating effects of strong domestic competition are clear in the story of the rise of Nokia of Finland in the market for wireless handsets and telephone equipment (see Strategy in Action 8.1).

Using the Framework The framework just described can help managers to identify from where their most significant global competitors are likely to originate. For example, there is an emerging cluster of computer service and software companies in Bangalore, India, that includes two of the fastest-growing information technology companies in the world, Infosys and Wipro. These companies are emerging as aggressive competitors in the global market. Indeed, there are signs that this is now happening; both companies have recently opened up offices in the European Union and United States so they can better compete against IBM and EDS (Electronic Data Systems), and both are gaining share in the global market place.

The framework can also be used to help managers decide where they might want to locate certain productive activities. Seeking to take advantage of U.S. expertise in biotechnology, many foreign companies have set up research facilities in San Diego, Boston, and Seattle, where U.S. biotechnology companies tend to be clustered. Similarly, in an attempt to take advantage of Japanese success in customer electronics, many U.S. electronics companies have set up research and production facilities in Japan, often in conjunction with Japanese partners.

Finally, the framework can help a company assess how tough it might be to enter certain national markets. If a nation has a competitive advantage in certain industries, it might be challenging for foreigners to enter those industries. For example, the highly competitive retailing industry in the United States has proved to be a very difficult industry for foreign companies to enter. Successful foreign retailers such as Britain's Marks & Spencer and Sweden's IKEA have found it tough going into the United States because the U.S. retailing industry is the most competitive in the world.

Increasing Profitability and Profit Growth Through Global Expansion

Here we look at a number of ways in which global expansion can enable companies to increase and rapidly grow profitability. At the most basic level, global expansion increases the size of the market in which a company is competing, thereby boosting profit growth. Moreover, as we shall see, global expansion offers opportunities for reducing the cost structure of the enterprise or adding value through differentiation, thereby potentially boosting profitability.

Expanding the Market: Leveraging Products

A company can increase its growth rate by taking goods or services developed at home and selling them internationally; almost all multinationals started out doing this. Procter & Gamble, for example, developed most of its best-selling products at home and then sold them around the world. Similarly, from its earliest days, Microsoft has always focused on selling its software around the world. Automobile companies like Ford, Volkswagen, and Toyota also grew by developing products at home and then selling them in international markets. The returns from such a strategy are likely to be greater if indigenous competitors in the nations a company enters lack comparable products. Thus, Toyota has grown its profits by entering the large automobile markets of North America and Europe and by offering products that are differentiated from those offered by local rivals (Ford and GM) by their superior quality and reliability.

It is important to note that the success of many multinational companies is based not just on the goods or services that they sell in foreign nations, but also upon the distinctive competencies (unique skills) that underlie the production and marketing of those goods or services. Thus, Toyota's success is based on its distinctive competency in manufacturing automobiles, and international expansion can be seen as a way of generating greater returns from this competency. Similarly, Procter & Gamble's global success was based on more than its portfolio of consumer products; it was also based on the company's skills in mass-marketing consumer goods. P&G grew rapidly in international markets between 1950 and 1990 because it was one of the most skilled mass-marketing enterprises in the world and could "outmarket" indigenous competitors in the nations it entered. Global expansion was, therefore, a way of generating higher returns from its competency in marketing.

Furthermore, one could say that because distinctive competencies are the most valuable aspects of a company's business model, the successful global expansion of manufacturing companies like Toyota and P&G was based on the ability to transfer aspects of the business model and apply it to foreign markets.

The same can be said of companies engaged in the service sectors of an economy, such as financial institutions, retailers, restaurant chains, and hotels. Expanding the market for their services often means replicating their business model in foreign nations (albeit with some changes to account for local differences, which we will discuss in more detail shortly). Starbucks, for example, is rapidly expanding outside of the United States by taking the basic business model it developed at home and using that as a blueprint for establishing international operations.

Realizing Cost Economies from Global Volume

In addition to growing profits more rapidly, a company can realize cost savings from economies of scale, thereby boosting profitability, by expanding its sales volume through international expansion. Such scale economies come from several sources. First, by spreading the fixed costs associated with developing a product and setting up production facilities over its global sales volume, a company can lower its average unit cost. Thus, Microsoft can garner significant scale economies by spreading the $5 billion it cost to develop Windows Vista over global demand.

Second, by serving a global market, a company can potentially utilize its production facilities more intensively, which leads to higher productivity, lower costs, and greater profitability. For example, if Intel sold microprocessors only in the United

States, it might only be able to keep its factories open for 1 shift, 5 days a week. But by serving a global market from the same factories, it might be able to utilize those assets for 2 shifts, 7 days a week. In other words, the capital invested in those factories is used more intensively if Intel sells to a global—as opposed to a national—market, which translates into higher capital productivity and a higher return on invested capital.

Third, as global sales increase the size of the enterprise, its bargaining power with suppliers increases, which may allow it to bargain down the cost of key inputs and boost profitability that way. For example, Walmart has been able to use its enormous sales volume as a lever to bargain down the price it pays to suppliers for merchandise sold through its stores.

In addition to the cost savings that come from economies of scale, companies that sell to a global rather than a local marketplace may be able to realize further cost savings from learning effects. We first discussed learning effects in Chapter 4, where we noted that employee productivity increases with cumulative increases in output over time. (e.g., it costs considerably less to build the 100th aircraft from a Boeing assembly line than the 10th because employees learn how to perform their tasks more efficiently over time). By selling to a global market, a company may be able to increase its sales volume more rapidly, and thus the cumulative output from its plants, which in turn should result in accelerated learning, higher employee productivity, and a cost advantage over competitors that are growing more slowly because they lack international markets.

Realizing Location Economies

Earlier in this chapter we discussed how countries differ from each other along a number of dimensions, including differences in the cost and quality of factors of production. These differences imply that some locations are more suited than others for producing certain goods and services.[7] **Location economies** are the economic benefits that arise from performing a value creation activity in the optimal location for that activity, wherever in the world that might be (transportation costs and trade barriers permitting). Locating a value creation activity in the optimal location for that activity can have one of two effects: (1) it can lower the costs of value creation, helping the company achieve a low-cost position; or (2) it can enable a company to differentiate its product offering, which gives it the option of charging a premium price or keeping prices low and using differentiation as a means of increasing sales volume. Thus, efforts to realize location economies are consistent with the business-level strategies of low cost and differentiation. In theory, a company that realizes location economies by dispersing each of its value creation activities to the optimal location for that activity should have a competitive advantage over a company that bases all of its value creation activities at a single location. It should be able to better differentiate its product offering and lower its cost structure more than its single-location competitor. In a world where competitive pressures are increasing, such a strategy may well become an imperative for survival.

For an example of how this works in an international business, consider Clear-Vision, a manufacturer and distributor of eyewear. Started in the 1970s by David Glassman, the firm now generates annual gross revenues of more than $100 million. Not exactly small, but no corporate giant either, ClearVision is a multinational firm with production facilities on three continents and customers around the world. ClearVision began its move toward becoming a multinational company in the 1980s. At that time, the U.S. dollar was strong, making U.S.-based manufacturing very

Location economies

The economic benefits that arise from performing a value creation activity in an optimal location.

expensive. Low-priced imports were taking an ever-larger share of the U.S. eyewear market, and ClearVision realized it could not survive unless it also began to import. Initially, the firm bought eye glasses from independent overseas manufacturers, primarily in Hong Kong. However, it became dissatisfied with these suppliers' product quality and delivery. As ClearVision's volume of imports increased, Glassman decided that the best way to guarantee quality and delivery was to set up Clear-Vision's own manufacturing operation overseas. Accordingly, ClearVision found a Chinese partner, and together they opened a manufacturing facility in Hong Kong, with ClearVision as the majority shareholder.

The choice of the Hong Kong location was influenced by its combination of low labor costs, a skilled work force, and tax breaks from the Hong Kong government. The firm's objective at this point was to lower production costs by locating value-creation activities at an appropriate location. After a few years, however, increasing industrialization and a growing labor shortage had pushed up wage rates so high that it was no longer a low-cost location. In response, Glassman and his Chinese partner moved part of their manufacturing to a plant in mainland China to take advantage of the lower wage rates there. Again, the goal was to lower production costs. The parts for eyewear frames manufactured at this plant are shipped to the Hong Kong factory for final assembly and then distributed to markets in North and South America. The Hong Kong factory now employs 80 people and the China plant between 300 and 400 people.

At the same time, ClearVision was looking for opportunities to invest in foreign eyewear firms with reputations for fashionable design and high quality. Its objective was not to reduce production costs but to launch a line of high-quality, differentiated, "designer" eyewear. ClearVision did not have the design capability in-house to support such a line, but Glassman knew that certain foreign manufacturers did. As a result, ClearVision invested in factories in Japan, France, and Italy, holding a minority shareholding in each case. These factories now supply eyewear for ClearVision's Status Eye division, which markets high-priced designer eyewear.[8]

Some Caveats   Introducing transportation costs and trade barriers complicates this process somewhat. New Zealand might have a comparative advantage for low-cost car assembly operations, but high transportation costs make it an uneconomical location from which to serve global markets. Factoring transportation costs and trade barriers into the cost equation helps explain why many U.S. companies have been shifting their production from Asia to Mexico. Mexico has three distinct advantages over many Asian countries as a location for value creation activities: low labor costs; Mexico's proximity to the large U.S. market, which reduces transportation costs; and the North American Free Trade Agreement (NAFTA), which has removed many trade barriers between Mexico, the United States, and Canada, increasing Mexico's attractiveness as a production site for the North American market. Thus, although the relative costs of value creation are important, transportation costs and trade barriers also must be considered in location decisions.

Another caveat concerns the importance of assessing political and economic risks when making location decisions. Even if a country looks very attractive as a production location when measured against cost or differentiation criteria, if its government is unstable or totalitarian, companies are usually well advised not to base production there. Similarly, if a particular national government appears to be pursuing inappropriate social or economic policies, this might be another reason for not basing production in that location, even if other factors look favorable.

Leveraging the Skills of Global Subsidiaries

Initially, many multinational companies develop the valuable competencies and skills that underpin their business model in their home nation and then expand internationally, primarily by selling products and services based on those competencies. However, for more mature multinational enterprises that have already established a network of subsidiary operations in foreign markets, the development of valuable skills can just as well occur in foreign subsidiaries.[9] Skills can be created anywhere within a multinational's global network of operations, wherever people have the opportunity and incentive to try new ways of doing things. The creation of skills that help to lower the costs of production, or to enhance perceived value and support higher product pricing, is not the monopoly of the corporate center.

Leveraging the skills created within subsidiaries and applying them to other operations within the firm's global network may create value. For example, McDonald's is increasingly finding that its foreign franchisees are a source of valuable new ideas. Faced with slow growth in France, its local franchisees have begun to experiment with the menu, layout, and theme of restaurants. Gone are the ubiquitous Golden Arches; gone too are many of the utilitarian chairs and tables and other plastic features of the fast-food giant. Many McDonald's restaurants in France now have hardwood floors, exposed brick walls, and even armchairs. Half of the 930 or so outlets in France have been upgraded to a level that would make them unrecognizable to an American. The menu, too, has been changed to include premier sandwiches, such as chicken on focaccia bread, priced some 30% higher than the average hamburger. In France, this strategy seems to be working. Following these changes, increases in same-store sales rose from 1% annually to 3.4%. Impressed with the impact, McDonald's executives are now considering adopting similar changes at other McDonald's restaurants in markets where same-store sales growth is sluggish, including the United States.[10]

For the managers of a multinational enterprise, this phenomenon creates important new challenges. First, managers must have the humility to recognize that valuable skills can arise anywhere within the firm's global network, not just at the corporate center. Second, they must establish an incentive system that encourages local employees to acquire new competencies. This is not as easy as it sounds. Creating new competencies involves a degree of risk. Not all new skills add value. For every valuable idea created by a McDonald's subsidiary in a foreign country, there may be several failures. The management of the multinational must install incentives that encourage employees to take necessary risks, and the company must reward people for successes and not sanction them unnecessarily for taking risks that did not pan out. Third, managers must have a process for identifying when valuable new skills have been created in a subsidiary, and finally, they need to act as facilitators, helping to transfer valuable skills within the firm.

Cost Pressures and Pressures for Local Responsiveness

Companies that compete in the global marketplace typically face two types of competitive pressures: *pressures for cost reductions and pressures to be locally responsive* (see Figure 8.2).[11] These competitive pressures place conflicting demands on a company. Responding to pressures for cost reductions requires that a company attempt to minimize its unit costs. To attain this goal, it may have to base its productive

Figure 8.2   Pressures for Cost Reductions and Local Responsiveness

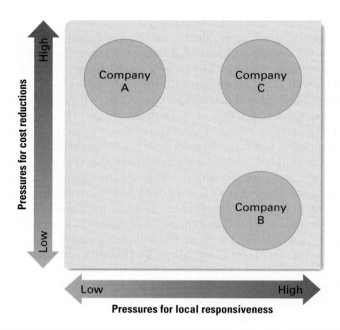

© Cengage Learning 2013

activities at the most favorable low-cost location, wherever in the world that might be. It may also need to offer a standardized product to the global marketplace in order to realize the cost savings that come from economies of scale and learning effects. On the other hand, responding to pressures to be locally responsive requires that a company differentiate its product offering and marketing strategy from country to country in an effort to accommodate the diverse demands arising from national differences in consumer tastes and preferences, business practices, distribution channels, competitive conditions, and government policies. Because differentiation across countries can involve significant duplication and a lack of product standardization, it may raise costs.

While some companies, such as Company A in Figure 8.2, face high pressures for cost reductions and low pressures for local responsiveness, and others, such as Company B, face low pressures for cost reductions and high pressures for local responsiveness, many companies are in the position of Company C. They face high pressures for both cost reductions and local responsiveness. Dealing with these conflicting and contradictory pressures is a difficult strategic challenge, primarily because local responsiveness tends to raise costs.

Pressures for Cost Reductions

In competitive global markets, international businesses often face pressures for cost reductions. To respond to these pressures, a firm must try to lower the costs of value creation. A manufacturer, for example, might mass-produce a standardized product at an optimal location in the world to realize economies of scale and location economies. Alternatively, it might outsource certain functions to low-cost foreign suppliers in an attempt to reduce costs. Thus, many computer companies have outsourced their telephone-based customer service functions to India, where qualified technicians who speak English can be hired for a lower wage rate than in the United States. In the same vein, a retailer like Walmart might push its suppliers (who are manufacturers) to also lower their prices. (In fact, the pressure that Walmart has placed on its suppliers to reduce prices has been cited as a major cause of the trend among North American manufacturers to shift production to China.)[12] A service business, such as a bank, might move some back-office functions, such as information processing, to developing nations where wage rates are lower.

Cost reduction pressures can be particularly intense in industries producing commodity-type products where meaningful differentiation on nonprice factors is difficult and price is the main competitive weapon. This tends to be the case for products that serve universal needs. Universal needs exist when the tastes and preferences of consumers in different nations are similar if not identical, such as for bulk chemicals, petroleum, steel, sugar, and similar products. Pressures for cost reductions also exist for many industrial and consumer products: for example, hand-held calculators, semiconductor chips, personal computers, and liquid crystal display screens. Pressures for cost reductions are also intense in industries where major competitors are based in low-cost locations, where there is persistent excess capacity, and where consumers are powerful and face low switching costs. Many commentators have argued that the liberalization of the world trade and investment environment in recent decades, by facilitating greater international competition, has generally increased cost pressures.[13]

Pressures for Local Responsiveness

Pressures for local responsiveness arise from differences in consumer tastes and preferences, infrastructure and traditional practices, distribution channels, and host government demands. Responding to pressures to be locally responsive requires that a company differentiate its products and marketing strategy from country to country to accommodate these factors, all of which tend to raise a company's cost structure.

Differences in Customer Tastes and Preferences Strong pressures for local responsiveness emerge when customer tastes and preferences differ significantly between countries, as they may for historic or cultural reasons. In such cases, a multinational company's products and marketing message must be customized to appeal to the tastes and preferences of local customers. The company is then typically pressured to delegate production and marketing responsibilities and functions to a company's overseas subsidiaries.

For example, the automobile industry in the 1980s and early-1990s moved toward the creation of "world cars." The idea was that global companies such as General Motors, Ford, and Toyota would be able to sell the same basic vehicle globally, sourcing it from centralized production locations. If successful, the strategy would have enabled automobile companies to reap significant gains from global scale economies. However, this strategy frequently ran aground upon the hard rocks of consumer reality. Consumers in different automobile markets have different tastes and preferences, and these require different types of vehicles. North American consumers show a strong demand for pickup trucks. This is particularly true in the South and West where many families have a pickup truck as a second or third car. But in

European countries, pickup trucks are seen purely as utility vehicles and are purchased primarily by firms rather than by individuals. As a consequence, the product mix and marketing message need to be tailored to take into account the different nature of demand in North America and Europe.

Some commentators have argued that customer demands for local customization are on the decline worldwide.[14] According to this argument, modern communications and transport technologies have created the conditions for a convergence of the tastes and preferences of customers from different nations. The result is the emergence of enormous global markets for standardized consumer products. The worldwide acceptance of McDonald's hamburgers, Coca-Cola, GAP clothes, Nokia cell phones, and Sony television sets, all of which are sold globally as standardized products, are often cited as evidence of the increasing homogeneity of the global marketplace.

Others, however, consider this argument to be extreme. For example, Christopher Bartlett and Sumantra Ghoshal have observed that in the consumer electronics industry, buyers reacted to an overdose of standardized global products by showing a renewed preference for products that are differentiated to local conditions.[15]

Differences in Infrastructure and Traditional Practices   Pressures for local responsiveness also arise from differences in infrastructure or traditional practices among countries, creating a need to customize products accordingly. To meet this need, companies may have to delegate manufacturing and production functions to foreign subsidiaries. For example, in North America, consumer electrical systems are based on 110 volts, whereas in some European countries 240-volt systems are standard. Thus, domestic electrical appliances must be customized to take this difference in infrastructure into account. Traditional social practices also often vary across nations. For example, in Britain, people drive on the left-hand side of the road, creating a demand for right-hand-drive cars, whereas in France and the rest of Europe, people drive on the right-hand side of the road (and therefore want left-hand-drive cars). Obviously, automobiles must be customized to take this difference in traditional practices into account.

Although many of the country differences in infrastructure are rooted in history, some are quite recent. For example, in the wireless telecommunications industry, different technical standards are found in different parts of the world. A technical standard known as GSM is common in Europe, and an alternative standard, CDMA, is more common in the United States and parts of Asia. The significance of these different standards is that equipment designed for GSM will not work on a CDMA network, and vice versa. Thus, companies such as Nokia, Motorola, and Ericsson, which manufacture wireless handsets and infrastructure such as switches, need to customize their product offering according to the technical standard prevailing in a given country.

Differences in Distribution Channels   A company's marketing strategies may have to be responsive to differences in distribution channels among countries, which may necessitate delegating marketing functions to national subsidiaries. In the pharmaceutical industry, for example, the British and Japanese distribution system is radically different from the U.S. system. British and Japanese doctors will not accept or respond favorably to a U.S.-style high-pressure sales force. Thus, pharmaceutical companies must adopt different marketing practices in Britain and Japan compared with the United States—soft sell versus hard sell.

Similarly, Poland, Brazil, and Russia all have similar per capita income on a purchasing power parity basis, but there are big differences in distribution systems across the three countries. In Brazil, supermarkets account for 36% of food retailing, in Poland for 18%, and in Russia for less than 1%.[16] These differences in channels require that companies adapt their own distribution and sales strategy.

Host Government Demands   Finally, economic and political demands imposed by host country governments may require local responsiveness. For example, pharmaceutical companies are subject to local clinical testing, registration procedures, and pricing restrictions, all of which make it necessary that the manufacturing and marketing of a drug should meet local requirements. Moreover, because governments and government agencies control a significant portion of the health care budget in most countries, they are in a powerful position to demand a high level of local responsiveness.

More generally, threats of protectionism, economic nationalism, and local content rules (which require that a certain percentage of a product should be manufactured locally) dictate that international businesses manufacture locally. As an example, consider Bombardier, the Canadian-based manufacturer of railcars, aircraft, jet boats, and snowmobiles. Bombardier has 12 railcar factories across Europe. Critics of the company argue that the resulting duplication of manufacturing facilities leads to high costs and helps explain why Bombardier makes lower profit margins on its railcar operations than on its other business lines. In reply, managers at Bombardier argue that in Europe, informal rules with regard to local content favor people who use local workers. To sell railcars in Germany, they claim, you must manufacture in Germany. The same goes for Belgium, Austria, and France. To try to address its cost structure in Europe, Bombardier has centralized its engineering and purchasing functions, but it has no plans to centralize manufacturing.[17]

Choosing a Global Strategy

Pressures for local responsiveness imply that it may not be possible for a firm to realize the full benefits from economies of scale and location economies. It may not be possible to serve the global marketplace from a single low-cost location, producing a globally standardized product and marketing it worldwide to achieve economies of scale. In practice, the need to customize the product offering to local conditions may work against the implementation of such a strategy. For example, automobile firms have found that Japanese, American, and European consumers demand different kinds of cars, and this necessitates producing products that are customized for local markets. In response, firms like Honda, Ford, and Toyota are pursuing a strategy of establishing top-to-bottom design and production facilities in each of these regions so that they can better serve local demands. Although such customization brings benefits, it also limits the ability of a firm to realize significant scale economies and location economies.

In addition, pressures for local responsiveness imply that it may not be possible to leverage skills and products associated with a firm's distinctive competencies wholesale from one nation to another. Concessions often have to be made to local conditions. Despite being depicted as "poster child" for the proliferation of standardized global products, even McDonald's has found that it has to customize its product offerings (its menu) in order to account for national differences in tastes and preferences.

Given the need to balance the cost and differentiation (value) sides of a company's business model, how do differences in the strength of pressures for cost reductions versus those for local responsiveness affect the choice of a company's strategy? Companies typically choose among four main strategic postures when competing internationally: a global standardization strategy, a localization strategy, a transnational strategy, and an international strategy.[18] The appropriateness of each strategy varies with the extent of pressures for cost reductions and local responsiveness. Figure 8.3 illustrates the conditions under which each of these strategies is most appropriate.

Global Standardization Strategy

Companies that pursue a **global standardization strategy** focus on increasing profitability by reaping the cost reductions that come from economies of scale and location economies; that is, their business model is based on pursuing a low-cost strategy on a global scale. The production, marketing, and R&D activities of companies pursuing a global strategy are concentrated in a few favorable locations. These companies try not to customize their product offering and marketing strategy to local conditions because customization, which involves shorter production runs and the duplication of functions, can raise costs. Instead, they prefer to market a standardized product worldwide so that they can reap the maximum benefits from economies of scale. They also tend to use their cost advantage to support aggressive pricing in world markets. Dell is a good example of a company that pursues such a strategy (see the Focus on Dell).

> **Global standardization strategy**
>
> A business model based on pursuing a low-cost strategy on a global scale.

Figure 8.3 Four Basic Strategies

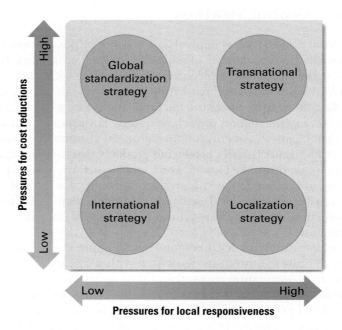

© Cengage Learning 2013

FOCUS ON DELL

8

Dell's Global Business Strategy

Dell has been expanding its presence outside of the United States since the early-1990s. In fiscal 2010, over 40% of Dell's $52 billion in revenue was generated outside of the United States. Dell's strategic goal is to be the low cost player in the global industry. It does not alter its business model from country to country—but instead uses the same direct selling and supply chain model that worked so well in the United States. Dell is thus pursuing a global standardization strategy.

Dell's basic approach to overseas expansion has been to serve foreign markets from a handful of regional manufacturing facilities, each established as a wholly owned subsidiary. To support its global business, it operates 3 final assembly facilities in the United States, 1 in Brazil (serving South America), Poland (serving Europe), Malaysia (serving SE Asia), China (serving China), and India. Each of these plants is large enough to attain significant economies of scale. When demand in a region gets large enough, Dell considers opening a second plant—thus it has 3 plants in the United States to serve North America and 3 in Asia.

Each plant uses exactly the same supply chain management processes that have made Dell famously efficient. Taking advantage of its supply chain management software, Dell schedules production of every line in every factory around the world every 2 hours. Every factory is run with no more than a few hours of inventory on hand, including work in progress. To serve Dell's global factories, many of Dell's largest suppliers have also located their facilities close to Dell's manufacturing plants so that they can better meet the company's demands for just-in-time inventory.

Dell has set up customer service centers in each region to handle phone and online orders and to provide technical assistance. In general, each center serves an entire region, which Dell has found to be more efficient than locating a customer service center in each country where the company does business. Beginning in 2001, Dell started to experiment with outsourcing some of its customer service functions for English language customers to call centers in India. Although the move helped the company to lower costs, it also led to dissatisfaction from customers, particularly in the United States, who could not always follow the directions given over the phone from someone with a thick regional accent. Subsequently, Dell moved its call centers for English language businesses back to the United States and the United Kingdom Dell continues to invest in Indian call centers for its retail customers, however, and in 2006, announced that it was opening a fourth Indian call center.

Sources: Dell Corporation 2010 10K. Staff Reporter, "Dell Inc: Call Center in India to Expand to 2,500 Workers from 800," *Wall Street Journal* (2006), p. A6.

This strategy makes most sense when there are strong pressures for cost reductions and demand for local responsiveness is minimal. Increasingly, these conditions prevail in many industrial goods industries, whose products often serve universal needs. In the semiconductor industry, for example, global standards have emerged, creating enormous demands for standardized global products. Accordingly, companies such as Intel, Texas Instruments, and Motorola all pursue a global strategy.

These conditions are not always found in many consumer goods markets, where demands for local responsiveness remain high. However, even some consumer goods companies are moving toward a global standardization strategy in an attempt to drive down their costs. Procter & Gamble, which is featured in the next Strategy in Action feature, is one example of such a company.

Localization Strategy

A **localization strategy** focuses on increasing profitability by customizing the company's goods or services so that the goods provide a favorable match to tastes and preferences in different national markets. Localization is most appropriate when

Localization strategy

Strategy focused on increasing profitability by customizing the company's goods or services so that the goods provide a favorable match to tastes and preferences in different national markets.

there are substantial differences across nations with regard to consumer tastes and preferences, and where cost pressures are not too intense. By customizing the product offering to local demands, the company increases the value of that product in the local market. On the downside, because it involves some duplication of functions and smaller production runs, customization limits the ability of the company to capture the cost reductions associated with mass-producing a standardized product for global consumption. The strategy may make sense, however, if the added value associated with local customization supports higher pricing, which would enable the company to recoup its higher costs, or if it leads to substantially greater local demand, enabling the company to reduce costs through the attainment of scale economies in the local market.

MTV is a good example of a company that has had to pursue a localization strategy. If MTV localized its programming to match the demands of viewers in different nations, it would have lost market share to local competitors, its advertising revenues would have fallen, and its profitability would have declined. Thus, even though it raised costs, localization became a strategic imperative at MTV.

At the same time, it is important to realize that companies like MTV still have to closely monitor costs. Companies pursuing a localization strategy still need to be efficient and, whenever possible, capture some scale economies from their global reach. As noted earlier, many automobile companies have found that they have to customize some of their product offerings to local market demands—for example, by producing large pickup trucks for U.S. consumers and small fuel-efficient cars for Europeans and Japanese. At the same time, these companies try to get some scale economies from their global volume by using common vehicle platforms and components across many different models and by manufacturing those platforms and components at efficiently scaled factories that are optimally located. By designing their products in this way, these companies have been able to localize their product offering, yet simultaneously capture some scale economies.

Transnational Strategy

We have argued that a global standardization strategy makes most sense when cost pressures are intense and demands for local responsiveness limited. Conversely, a localization strategy makes most sense when demands for local responsiveness are high but cost pressures are moderate or low. What happens, however, when the company simultaneously faces both strong cost pressures and strong pressures for local responsiveness? How can managers balance out such competing and inconsistent demands? According to some researchers, pursuing what has been called a transnational strategy is the answer.

Two of these researchers, Christopher Bartlett and Sumantra Ghoshal, argue that in today's global environment, competitive conditions are so intense that, to survive, companies must do all they can to respond to pressures for both cost reductions and local responsiveness. They must try to realize location economies and economies of scale from global volume, transfer distinctive competencies and skills within the company, and simultaneously pay attention to pressures for local responsiveness.[19]

Moreover, Bartlett and Ghoshal note that, in the modern multinational enterprise, distinctive competencies and skills do not reside just in the home country but can develop in any of the company's worldwide operations. Thus, they maintain that the flow of skills and product offerings should not be all one way, from home company to foreign subsidiary. Rather, the flow should also be from foreign subsidiary to home country and from foreign subsidiary to foreign subsidiary. Transnational companies, in other words, must also focus on leveraging subsidiary skills.

In essence, companies that pursue a **transnational strategy** are trying to develop a business model that simultaneously achieves low costs, differentiates the product offering across geographic markets, and fosters a flow of skills between different subsidiaries in the company's global network of operations. As attractive as this may sound, the strategy is not an easy one to pursue because it places conflicting demands on the company. Differentiating the product to respond to local demands in different geographic markets raises costs, which runs counter to the goal of reducing costs. Companies like Ford and ABB (one of the world's largest engineering conglomerates) have tried to embrace a transnational strategy and have found it difficult to implement in practice.

Indeed, how best to implement a transnational strategy is one of the most complex questions that large global companies are grappling with today. It may be that few if any companies have perfected this strategic posture. But some clues to the right approach can be derived from a number of companies. Consider, for example, the case of Caterpillar. The need to compete with low-cost competitors such as Komatsu of Japan forced Caterpillar to look for greater cost economies. However, variations in construction practices and government regulations across countries meant that Caterpillar also had to be responsive to local demands. Therefore, Caterpillar confronted significant pressures for cost reductions and for local responsiveness.

To deal with cost pressures, Caterpillar redesigned its products to use many identical components and invested in a few large-scale component-manufacturing facilities, sited at favorable locations, to fill global demand and realize scale economies. At the same time, the company augments the centralized manufacturing of components with assembly plants in each of its major global markets. At these plants, Caterpillar adds local product features, tailoring the finished product to local needs. Thus, Caterpillar is able to realize many of the benefits of global manufacturing while reacting to pressures for local responsiveness by differentiating its product among national markets.[20] Caterpillar started to pursue this strategy in 1979, and over the next 20 years, it succeeded in doubling output per employee, significantly reducing its overall cost structure in the process. Meanwhile, Komatsu and Hitachi, which are still wedded to a Japan-centric global strategy, have seen their cost advantages evaporate and have been steadily losing market share to Caterpillar.

However, building an organization capable of supporting a transnational strategy is a complex and challenging task. Indeed, some would say it is too complex because the strategy implementation problems of creating a viable organizational structure and set of control systems to manage this strategy are immense. We shall return to this issue in Chapter 13.

International Strategy

Sometimes it is possible to identify multinational companies that find themselves in the fortunate position of being confronted with low cost pressures and low pressures for local responsiveness. Typically, these enterprises are selling a product that serves universal needs, but because they do not face significant competitors, they are not confronted with pressures to reduce their cost structure. Xerox found itself in this position in the 1960s after its invention and commercialization of the photocopier. Strong patents protected the technology comprising the photocopier, so for several years Xerox did not face competitors—it had a monopoly. Because the product was

Transnational strategy

A business model that simultaneously achieves low costs, differentiates the product offering across geographic markets, and fosters a flow of skills between different subsidiaries in the company's global network of operations.

highly valued in most developed nations, Xerox was able to sell the same basic product all over the world and charge a relatively high price for it. At the same time, because it did not face direct competitors, the company did not have to deal with strong pressures to minimize its costs.

Historically, companies like Xerox have followed a similar developmental pattern as they build their international operations. They tend to centralize product development functions such as R&D at home. However, companies also tend to establish manufacturing and marketing functions in each major country or geographic region in which they do business. Although they may undertake some local customization of product offering and marketing strategy, this tends to be rather limited in scope. Ultimately, in most international companies, the head office retains tight control over marketing and product strategy.

Other companies that have pursued this strategy include Procter & Gamble, which had historically always developed innovative new products in Cincinnati and thereafter transferred them wholesale to local markets. Microsoft is another company that has followed a similar strategy. The bulk of Microsoft's product development work takes place in Redmond, Washington, where the company is headquartered. Although some localization work is undertaken elsewhere, this is limited to producing foreign-language versions of popular Microsoft programs such as Office.

Changes in Strategy over Time

The Achilles heal of the international strategy is that, over time, competitors inevitably emerge, and if managers do not take proactive steps to reduce their cost structure, their company may be rapidly outflanked by efficient global competitors. This is exactly what happened to Xerox. Japanese companies such as Canon ultimately invented their way around Xerox's patents, produced their own photocopying equipment in very efficient manufacturing plants, priced the machines below Xerox's products, and rapidly took global market share from Xerox. Xerox's demise was not due to the emergence of competitors, for ultimately that was bound to occur, but rather to its failure to proactively reduce its cost structure in advance of the emergence of efficient global competitors. The message in this story is that an international strategy may not be viable in the long term, and to survive, companies that are able to pursue it need to shift toward a global standardization strategy, or perhaps a transnational strategy, ahead of competitors (see Figure 8.4).

The same can be said about a localization strategy. Localization may give a company a competitive edge, but if it is simultaneously facing aggressive competitors, the company will also need to reduce its cost structure—and the only way to do that may be to adopt a transnational strategy. Thus, as competition intensifies, international and localization strategies tend to become less viable, and managers need to orient their companies toward either a global standardization strategy or a transnational strategy. The next Strategy in Action feature describes how this process occurred at Coca-Cola.

The Choice of Entry Mode

Any firm contemplating entering a different national market must determine the best mode or vehicle for such entry. There are five primary choices of entry mode: exporting, licensing, franchising, entering into a joint venture with a host country company,

Figure 8.4 Changes over Time

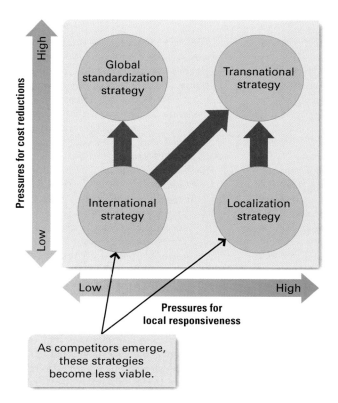

and setting up a wholly owned subsidiary in the host country. Each mode has its advantages and disadvantages, and managers must weigh these carefully when deciding which mode to use.[21]

Exporting

Most manufacturing companies begin their global expansion as exporters and only later switch to one of the other modes for serving a foreign market. Exporting has two distinct advantages: it avoids the costs of establishing manufacturing operations in the host country, which are often substantial, and it may be consistent with scale economies and location economies. By manufacturing the product in a centralized location and then exporting it to other national markets, the company may be able to realize substantial scale economies from its global sales volume. That is how Sony came to dominate the global television market, how many Japanese auto companies originally made inroads into the U.S. auto market, and how Samsung gained share in the market for computer memory chips.

There are also a number of drawbacks to exporting. First, exporting from the company's home base may not be appropriate if there are lower-cost locations for manufacturing the product abroad (i.e., if the company can achieve location

STRATEGY IN ACTION

The Evolving Strategy of Coca-Cola

Coca-Cola, the iconic American soda maker, has long been among the most international of enterprises. The company made its first move outside the United States in 1902, when it entered Cuba. By 1929, Coke was marketed in 76 countries. In World War II, Coke struck a deal to supply the U.S. military with Coca-Cola, wherever soldiers might be stationed. During this era, the company built 63 bottling plants around the world. Its global push continued after the war, fueled in part by the belief that the U.S. market would eventually reach maturity and by the perception that huge growth opportunities were overseas. By 2008, more than 59,000 of the company's 71,000 employees were located in 200 countries outside of the United States, and 73% of Coke's case volume was in international markets.

Through until the early-1980s, Coke's strategy could best be characterized as one of considerable localization. Local operations were granted a high degree of independence to oversee operations as managers saw fit. This changed in the 1980s and 1990s under the leadership of Roberto Goizueta, a talented Cuba immigrant who became the CEO of Coke in 1981. Goizueta placed renewed emphasis on Coke's flagship brands, which were extended with the introduction of Diet Coke, Cherry Coke, and similar flavors. His prime belief was that the main difference between the United States and international markets was the lower level of penetration in the latter, where consumption per capita of colas was only 10–15% of the U.S. figure. Goizueta pushed Coke to become a global company, centralizing a great deal of management and marketing activities at the corporate headquarters in Atlanta, focusing on core brands, and taking equity stakes in foreign bottlers so that the company could exert more strategic control over them. This one-size-fits-all strategy was built around standardization and the realization of economies of scale by, for example, using the same advertising message worldwide.

Goizueta's global strategy was adopted by his successor, Douglas Ivester, but by the late-1990s, the drive toward a one-size-fits-all strategy was running out of steam, as smaller, more nimble local competitors that were marketing local beverages began to halt the Coke growth engine. When Coke began failing to hit its financial targets for the first time in a generation, Ivester resigned in 2000 and was replaced by Douglas Daft. Daft instituted a 180 degree shift in strategy. Daft's belief was that Coke needed to put more power back in the hands of local country managers. He thought that strategy, product development, and marketing should be tailored to local needs. He laid off 6,000 employees, many of them in Atlanta, and granted country managers much greater autonomy. Moreover, in a striking move for a marketing company, he announced that the company would stop using global advertisements, and he placed advertising budgets and control over creative content back in the hands of country managers.

Ivester's move was, in part, influenced by the experience of Coke in Japan, the company's second most profitable market, where the best selling Coca-Cola product is not a carbonated beverage, but a canned cold coffee drink, Georgia Coffee, that is sold in vending machines. The Japanese experience seemed to signal that products should be customized to local tastes and preferences and that Coke would do well to decentralize more decision-making authority to local managers.

However, the shift toward localization didn't produce the growth that had been expected, and by 2002, the trend was moving back toward more central coordination, with Atlanta exercising *oversight* over marketing and product development in different nations outside the United States But this time, it was not the one-size-fits-all ethos of the Goizueta era. Under the leadership of Neville Isdell, who became CEO in March 2004, senior managers at the head office now review and help to guide local marketing and product development. However, Isdell has also adopted the belief that strategy (including pricing, product offerings, and marketing message) should be varied from market to market to match local conditions. Isdell's position, in other words, represents a midpoint between the strategy of Goizueta and of Daft. Moreover, Isdell has stressed the importance of leveraging good ideas across nations, for example, such as Georgia Coffee. Having seen the success of this beverage in Japan, in October 2007, Coke entered into a strategic alliance with Illycaffè, one of Italy's premier coffee makers, to build a global franchise for canned or bottled cold coffee beverages. Similarly, in 2003, the Coke subsidiary in China developed a low cost noncarbonated orange-based drink that has rapidly become one of the best selling drinks in that nation. Seeing the potential of the drink, Coke is now rolling it out in other Asian countries. It has been a huge hit in Thailand, where it was launched in 2005, and seems to be gaining traction in India, where it was launched in 2007.

Source: "Orange Gold," *The Economist*, March 3, 2007, p. 68. P. Bettis, "Coke Aims to Give Pepsi a Routing in Cold Coffee War," *Financial Times*, October 17, 2007, p. 16; P. Ghemawat, *Redefining Global Strategy* (Boston: Harvard Business School Press, 2007); D. Foust, "Queen of Pop," *Business Week*, August 7, 2006, pp. 44–47.

economies by moving production elsewhere). Thus, particularly in the case of a company pursuing a global standardization or transnational strategy, it may pay to manufacture in a location where conditions are most favorable from a value creation perspective and then export from that location to the rest of the globe. This is not so much an argument against exporting, as an argument against exporting from the company's home country. For example, many U.S. electronics companies have moved some of their manufacturing to Asia because low-cost but highly skilled labor is available there. They export from Asia to the rest of the globe, including the United States.

Another drawback is that high transport costs can make exporting uneconomical, particularly in the case of bulk products. One way of alleviating this problem is to manufacture bulk products on a regional basis, thereby realizing some economies from large-scale production while limiting transport costs. Many multinational chemical companies manufacture their products on a regional basis, serving several countries in a region from one facility.

Tariff barriers, too, can make exporting uneconomical, and a government's threat to impose tariff barriers can make the strategy very risky. Indeed, the implicit threat from the U.S. Congress to impose tariffs on Japanese cars imported into the United States led directly to the decision by many Japanese auto companies to set up manufacturing plants in the United States.

Finally, a common practice among companies that are just beginning to export also poses risks. A company may delegate marketing activities in each country in which it does business to a local agent, but there is no guarantee that the agent will act in the company's best interest. Often, foreign agents also carry the products of competing companies and thus have divided loyalties. Consequently, agents may not perform as well as the company would if it managed marketing itself. One way to solve this problem is to set up a wholly owned subsidiary in the host country to handle local marketing. In this way, the company can reap the cost advantages that arise from manufacturing the product in a single location and exercise tight control over marketing strategy in the host country.

Licensing

International licensing is an arrangement whereby a foreign licensee purchases the rights to produce a company's product in the licensee's country for a negotiated fee (normally, royalty payments on the number of units sold). The licensee then provides most of the capital necessary to open the overseas operation.[22] The advantage of licensing is that the company does not have to bear the development costs and risks associated with opening up a foreign market. Licensing therefore can be a very attractive option for companies that lack the capital to develop operations overseas. It can also be an attractive option for companies that are unwilling to commit substantial financial resources to an unfamiliar or politically volatile foreign market where political risks are particularly high.

Licensing has three serious drawbacks, however. First, it does not give a company the tight control over manufacturing, marketing, and strategic functions in foreign countries that it needs to have in order to realize scale economies and location economies—as companies pursuing both global standardization and transnational strategies try to do. Typically, each licensee sets up its manufacturing operations. Hence, the company stands little chance of realizing scale economies and location economies by manufacturing its product in a centralized location. When these economies are likely to be important, licensing may not be the best way of expanding overseas.

Second, competing in a global marketplace may make it necessary for a company to coordinate strategic moves across countries so that the profits earned in one country can be used to support competitive attacks in another. Licensing, by its very nature, severely limits a company's ability to coordinate strategy in this way. A licensee is unlikely to let a multinational company take its profits (beyond those due in the form of royalty payments) and use them to support an entirely different licensee operating in another country.

Third, there is risk associated with licensing technological know-how to foreign companies. For many multinational companies, technological know-how forms the basis of their competitive advantage, and they would want to maintain control over how this competitive advantage is put to use. By licensing its technology, a company can quickly lose control over it. RCA, for instance, once licensed its color television technology to a number of Japanese companies. The Japanese companies quickly assimilated RCA's technology and then used it to enter the U.S. market. Now the Japanese have a bigger share of the U.S. market than the RCA brand does.

There are ways of reducing this risk. One way is by entering into a cross-licensing agreement with a foreign firm. Under a cross-licensing agreement, a firm might license some valuable intangible property to a foreign partner and, in addition to a royalty payment, also request that the foreign partner license some of its valuable know-how to the firm. Such agreements are reckoned to reduce the risks associated with licensing technological know-how, since the licensee realizes that if it violates the spirit of a licensing contract (by using the knowledge obtained to compete directly with the licensor), the licensor can do the same to it. Put differently, cross-licensing agreements enable firms to hold each other hostage, thereby reducing the probability that they will behave opportunistically toward each other.[23] Such cross-licensing agreements are increasingly common in high-technology industries. For example, the U.S. biotechnology firm Amgen has licensed one of its key drugs, Neupogen, to Kirin, the Japanese pharmaceutical company. The license gives Kirin the right to sell Neupogen in Japan. In return, Amgen receives a royalty payment, and through a licensing agreement, it gains the right to sell certain Kirin products in the United States.

Franchising

In many respects, franchising is similar to licensing, although franchising tends to involve longer term commitments than licensing. Franchising is basically a specialized form of licensing in which the franchiser not only sells intangible property to the franchisee (normally a trademark) but also insists that the franchisee agree to abide by strict rules governing how it does business. The franchiser will often assist the franchisee to run the business on an ongoing basis. As with licensing, the franchiser typically receives a royalty payment, which amounts to a percentage of the franchisee revenues.

Whereas licensing is a strategy pursued primarily by manufacturing companies, franchising, which resembles it in some respects, is a strategy employed chiefly by service companies. McDonald's provides a good example of a firm that has grown by using a franchising strategy. McDonald's has set down strict rules as to how franchisees should operate a restaurant. These rules extend to control the menu, cooking methods, staffing policies, and restaurant design and location. McDonald's also organizes the supply chain for its franchisees and provides management training and financial assistance.[24]

The advantages of franchising are similar to those of licensing. Specifically, the franchiser does not need to bear the development costs and risks associated with opening up a foreign market on its own, for the franchisee typically assumes those costs and risks. Thus, using a franchising strategy, a service company can build up a global presence quickly and at a low cost.

The disadvantages of franchising are less pronounced than in licensing. Because service companies often use franchising, there is no reason to consider the need for coordination of manufacturing to achieve experience curve and location economies. But franchising may inhibit the firm's ability to take profits out of one country to support competitive attacks in another. A more significant disadvantage of franchising is quality control. The foundation of franchising arrangements is that the firm's brand name conveys a message to consumers about the quality of the firm's product. Thus, a business traveler checking in at a Four Seasons hotel in Hong Kong can reasonably expect the same quality of room, food, and service that would be received in New York, or Hawaii, or Ontario, Canada. The Four Seasons name is supposed to guarantee consistent product quality. This presents a problem in that foreign franchisees may not be as concerned about quality as they are supposed to be, and the result of poor quality can extend beyond lost sales in a particular foreign market to a decline in the firm's worldwide reputation. For example, if the business traveler has a bad experience at the Four Seasons in Hong Kong, the traveler may never go to another Four Seasons hotel and may urge colleagues to do likewise. The geographical distance of the firm from its foreign franchisees can make poor quality difficult to detect. In addition, the numbers of franchisees—in the case of McDonald's, tens of thousands—can make quality control difficult. Due to these factors, quality problems may persist.

To reduce this problem, a company can set up a subsidiary in each country or region in which it is expanding. The subsidiary, which might be wholly owned by the company, or a joint venture with a foreign company, then assumes the rights and obligations to establish franchisees throughout that particular country or region. The combination of proximity and the limited number of independent franchisees that need to be monitored reduces the quality control problem. Besides, because the subsidiary is at least partly owned by the company, the company can place its own managers in the subsidiary to ensure the kind of quality monitoring it wants. This organizational arrangement has proved very popular in practice; it has been used by McDonald's, KFC, and Hilton Worldwide to expand international operations, to name just three examples.

Joint Ventures

Establishing a joint venture with a foreign company has long been a favored mode for entering a new market. One of the most famous long-term joint ventures is the Fuji–Xerox joint venture to produce photocopiers for the Japanese market. The most typical form of joint venture is a 50/50 joint venture, in which each party takes a 50% ownership stake, and a team of managers from both parent companies shares operating control. Some companies have sought joint ventures in which they have a majority shareholding (e.g., a 51% to 49% ownership split), which permits tighter control by the dominant partner.[25]

Joint ventures have a number of advantages. First, a company may feel that it can benefit from a local partner's knowledge of a host country's competitive conditions, culture, language, political systems, and business systems. Second, when the development costs and risks of opening up a foreign market are high, a company might gain by sharing these costs and risks with a local partner. Third, in some countries, political considerations make joint ventures the only feasible entry mode. Historically, for example, many U.S. companies found it much easier to obtain permission to set up operations in Japan if they joined with a Japanese partner than if they tried to enter on their own. This is why Xerox originally teamed up with Fuji to sell photocopiers in Japan.

Despite these advantages, there are major disadvantages with joint ventures. First, as with licensing, a firm that enters into a joint venture risks giving control of its technology to its partner. Thus, a proposed joint venture in 2002 between Boeing and Mitsubishi Heavy Industries to build a new wide-body jet raised fears that Boeing might unwittingly give away its commercial airline technology to the Japanese. However, joint-venture agreements can be constructed to minimize this risk. One option is to hold majority ownership in the venture. This allows the dominant partner to exercise greater control over its technology—but it can be difficult to find a foreign partner who is willing to settle for minority ownership. Another option is to "wall off" from a partner technology that is central to the core competence of the firm, while sharing other technology.

A second disadvantage is that a joint venture does not give a firm the tight control over subsidiaries that it might need to realize experience curve or location economies. Nor does it give a firm the tight control over a foreign subsidiary that it might need for engaging in coordinated global attacks against its rivals. Consider the entry of Texas Instruments (TI) into the Japanese semiconductor market. When TI established semiconductor facilities in Japan, it did so for the dual purpose of checking Japanese manufacturers' market share and limiting the cash they had available for invading TI's global market. In other words, TI was engaging in global strategic coordination. To implement this strategy, TI's subsidiary in Japan had to be prepared to take instructions from corporate headquarters regarding competitive strategy. The strategy also required the Japanese subsidiary to run at a loss if necessary. Few if any potential joint-venture partners would have been willing to accept such conditions, since it would have necessitated a willingness to accept a negative return on investment. Indeed, many joint ventures establish a degree of autonomy that would make such direct control over strategic decisions all but impossible to establish.[26] Thus, to implement this strategy, TI set up a wholly owned subsidiary in Japan.

Wholly Owned Subsidiaries

A wholly owned subsidiary is one in which the parent company owns 100% of the subsidiary's stock. To establish a wholly owned subsidiary in a foreign market, a company can either set up a completely new operation in that country or acquire an established host country company and use it to promote its products in the host market.

Setting up a wholly owned subsidiary offers three advantages. First, when a company's competitive advantage is based on its control of a technological competency, a wholly owned subsidiary will normally be the preferred entry mode, since it reduces the company's risk of losing this control. Consequently, many high-tech companies prefer wholly owned subsidiaries to joint ventures or licensing arrangements. Wholly owned subsidiaries tend to be the favored entry mode in the semiconductor, computer, electronics, and pharmaceutical industries. Second, a wholly owned subsidiary gives a company the kind of tight control over operations in different countries that it needs if it is going to engage in global strategic coordination—taking profits from one country to support competitive attacks in another.

Third, a wholly owned subsidiary may be the best choice if a company wants to realize location economies and the scale economies that flow from producing a standardized output from a single or limited number of manufacturing plants. When pressures on costs are intense, it may pay a company to configure its value chain in such a way that value added at each stage is maximized. Thus, a national subsidiary may specialize in manufacturing only part of the product line or certain components of the end product, exchanging parts and products with other subsidiaries in the company's global system. Establishing such a global production system requires a high degree of control over the operations of national affiliates. Different national operations must be prepared to accept centrally determined decisions as to how they should produce, how much they should produce, and how their output should be priced for transfer between operations. A wholly owned subsidiary would have to comply with these mandates, whereas licensees or joint venture partners would most likely shun such a subservient role.

On the other hand, establishing a wholly owned subsidiary is generally the most costly method of serving a foreign market. The parent company must bear all the costs and risks of setting up overseas operations—in contrast to joint ventures, where the costs and risks are shared, or licensing, where the licensee bears most of the costs and risks. But the risks of learning to do business in a new culture diminish if the company acquires an established host country enterprise. Acquisitions, however, raise a whole set of additional problems, such as trying to marry divergent corporate cultures, and these problems may more than offset the benefits. (The problems associated with acquisitions are discussed in Chapter 10.)

Choosing an Entry Strategy

The advantages and disadvantages of the various entry modes are summarized in Table 8.1. Inevitably, there are trade-offs in choosing one entry mode over another. For example, when considering entry into an unfamiliar country with a track record of nationalizing foreign-owned enterprises, a company might favor a joint venture with a local enterprise. Its rationale might be that the local partner will help it establish operations in an unfamiliar environment and speak out against nationalization should the possibility arise. But if the company's distinctive competency is based on proprietary technology, entering into a joint venture might mean risking loss of control over that technology to the joint venture partner, which would make this strategy unattractive. Despite such hazards, some generalizations can be offered about the optimal choice of entry mode.

Distinctive Competencies and Entry Mode When companies expand internationally to earn greater returns from their differentiated product offerings, entering markets where indigenous competitors lack comparable products, the companies are pursuing an international strategy. The optimal entry mode for such companies depends to some degree upon the nature of their distinctive competency. In particular, we need to distinguish between companies with a distinctive competency in technological know-how and those with a distinctive competency in management know-how.

If a company's competitive advantage—its distinctive competency—derives from its control of proprietary technological know-how, licensing and joint venture arrangements should be avoided if possible to minimize the risk of losing control of

Table 8.1 The Advantages and Disadvantages of Different Entry Modes

Entry Mode	Advantages	Disadvantages
Exporting	• Ability to realize location- and scale-based economies	• High transport costs • Trade barriers • Problems with local marketing agents
Licensing	• Low development costs and risks	• Inability to realize location- and scale-based economies • Inability to engage in global strategic coordination • Lack of control over technology
Franchising	• Low development costs and risks	• Inability to engage in global strategic coordination • Lack of control over quality
Joint Ventures	• Access to local partner's knowledge • Shared development costs and risks • Political dependency	• Inability to engage in global strategic coordination • Inability to realize location- and scale-based economies • Lack of control over technology
Wholly Owned Subsidiaries	• Protection of technology • Ability to engage in global strategic coordination • Ability to realize location- and scale-based economies	• High costs and risks

© Cengage Learning 2013

that technology. Thus, if a high-tech company is considering setting up operations in a foreign country in order to profit from a distinctive competency in technological know-how, it should probably do so through a wholly owned subsidiary.

However, this should not be viewed as a hard and fast rule. For instance, a licensing or joint venture arrangement might be structured in such a way as to reduce the risks that a company's technological know-how will be expropriated by licensees or joint venture partners. (We consider this kind of arrangement in more detail later in the chapter when we discuss the issue of structuring strategic alliances.) To take another exception to the rule, a company may perceive its technological advantage as only transitory and expect rapid imitation of its core technology by competitors. In this situation, the company might want to license its technology as quickly as possible to foreign companies in order to gain global acceptance of its technology before imitation occurs.[27] Such a strategy has some advantages. By licensing its technology to competitors, the company may deter them from developing their own, possibly superior, technology. It also may be able to establish its technology as the dominant design in the industry (as Matsushita did with its VHS format for VCRs), ensuring a steady stream of royalty payments. Such situations aside, however, the attractions of licensing are probably outweighed by the risks of losing control of technology, and therefore, licensing should be avoided.

The competitive advantage of many service companies, such as McDonald's or Hilton Worldwide, is based on management know-how. For such companies, the risk of losing control of their management skills to franchisees or joint venture partners is not that great. The reason is that the valuable asset of such companies is their brand name, and brand names are generally well protected by international laws pertaining to trademarks. Given this fact, many of the issues that arise in the case of technological know-how do not arise in the case of management know-how. As a result, many service companies favor a combination of franchising and subsidiaries to control franchisees within a particular country or region. The subsidiary may be wholly owned or a joint venture. In most cases, however, service companies have found that entering into a joint venture with a local partner in order to set up a controlling subsidiary in a country or region works best because a joint venture is often politically more acceptable and brings a degree of local knowledge to the subsidiary.

Pressures for Cost Reduction and Entry Mode   The greater the pressures for cost reductions, the more likely that a company will want to pursue some combination of exporting and wholly owned subsidiaries. By manufacturing in the locations where factor conditions are optimal and then exporting to the rest of the world, a company may be able to realize substantial location economies and substantial scale economies. The company might then want to export the finished product to marketing subsidiaries based in various countries. Typically, these subsidiaries would be wholly owned and have the responsibility for overseeing distribution in a particular country. Setting up wholly owned marketing subsidiaries is preferable to a joint venture arrangement or using a foreign marketing agent because it gives the company the tight control over marketing that might be required to coordinate a globally dispersed value chain. In addition, tight control over a local operation enables the company to use the profits generated in one market to improve its competitive position in another market. Hence companies pursuing global or transnational strategies prefer to establish wholly owned subsidiaries.

Global Strategic Alliances

Global strategic alliances are cooperative agreements between companies from different countries that are actual or potential competitors. Strategic alliances range from formal joint ventures, in which two or more companies have an equity stake, to short-term contractual agreements, in which two companies may agree to cooperate on a particular problem (such as developing a new product).

Advantages of Strategic Alliances

Companies enter into strategic alliances with competitors to achieve a number of strategic objectives.[28] First, strategic alliances may facilitate entry into a foreign market. For example, many firms feel that if they are to successfully enter the Chinese market, they need a local partner who understands business conditions, and who has good connections. Thus, in 2004, Warner Brothers entered into a joint venture

Global strategic alliances

Cooperative agreements between companies from different countries that are actual or potential competitors.

with two Chinese partners to produce and distribute films in China. As a foreign film company, Warner found that if it wanted to produce films on its own for the Chinese market it had to go through a complex approval process for every film. It also had to farm out distribution to a local company, which made doing business in China very difficult. Due to the participation of Chinese firms, however, the joint-venture films will require a streamlined approval process, and the venture will be able to distribute any films it produces. Moreover, the joint venture will be able to produce films for Chinese TV, something that foreign firms are not allowed to do.[29]

Second, strategic alliances allow firms to share the fixed costs (and associated risks) of developing new products or processes. An alliance between Boeing and a number of Japanese companies to build Boeing's latest commercial jetliner, the 787, was motivated by Boeing's desire to share the estimated $8 billion investment required to develop the aircraft. (For another example of cost sharing, see Strategy in Action 8.3 which discusses the strategic alliances between Cisco and Fujitsu.)

Third, an alliance is a way to bring together complementary skills and assets that neither company could easily develop on its own.[30] In 2003, for example, Microsoft and Toshiba established an alliance aimed at developing embedded microprocessors (essentially tiny computers) that can perform a variety of entertainment functions in an automobile (e.g., run a back-seat DVD player or a wireless Internet connection). The processors will run a version of Microsoft's Windows CE operating system. Microsoft brings its software engineering skills to the alliance and Toshiba its skills in developing microprocessors.[31] The alliance between Cisco and Fujitsu was also formed to share know-how (see Strategy in Action 8.3).

Fourth, it can make sense to form an alliance that will help firms establish technological standards for the industry that will benefit the firm. For example, in 1999, Palm Inc., the leading maker of personal digital assistants (PDAs), entered into an alliance with Sony under which Sony agreed to license and use Palm's operating system in Sony PDAs. The motivation for the alliance was in part to help establish Palm's operating system as the industry standard for PDAs, rather than a rival Windows-based operating system from Microsoft.[32]

Disadvantages of Strategic Alliances

The advantages we have discussed can be very significant. Despite this, some commentators have criticized strategic alliances on the grounds that they give competitors a low-cost route to new technology and markets.[33] For example, a few years ago some commentators argued that many strategic alliances between U.S. and Japanese firms were part of an implicit Japanese strategy to keep high-paying, high-value-added jobs in Japan while gaining the project engineering and production process skills that underlie the competitive success of many U.S. companies.[34] They argued that Japanese success in the machine tool and semiconductor industries was built on U.S. technology acquired through strategic alliances. And they argued that U.S. managers were aiding the Japanese by entering alliances that channel new inventions to Japan and provide a U.S. sales and distribution network for the resulting products. Although such deals may generate short-term profits, so the argument goes, in the long term, the result is to "hollow out" U.S. firms, leaving them with no competitive advantage in the global marketplace.

These critics have a point; alliances have risks. Unless a firm is careful, it can give away more than it receives. But there are so many examples of apparently successful alliances between firms—including alliances between U.S. and Japanese firms—that

STRATEGY IN ACTION

Cisco and Fujitsu

In late 2004, Cisco Systems, the world's largest manufacturer of Internet routers entered into an alliance with the Japanese computer, electronics and telecommunications equipment firm, Fujitsu. The stated purpose of the alliance was to jointly develop next generation high-end routers for sales in Japan. Routers are the digital switches that sit at the heart of the Internet and direct traffic—they are in effect, the traffic cops of the Internet. Although Cisco has long held the leading share in the market for routers—it pioneered the original router technology—it faces increasing competition from other firms such as Juniper Networks and China's fast growing Huawei Technologies. At the same time, demand in the market is shifting as an increasing number of telecommunications companies adopt Internet-based telecommunications services. While Cisco has long had a strong global presence, the company's management also felt that it needed to have a better presence in Japan, which is shifting rapidly to second generation high-speed internet-based telecommunications networks.

By entering into an alliance with Fujitsu, Cisco feels it can achieve a number of goals. First, both firms can pool their R&D efforts, which will enable them to share complementary technology and develop products more rapidly, thereby gaining an advantage over competitors. Second, by combining Cisco's proprietary leading edge router technology with Fujitsu's production expertise, the companies believe that they can produce products that are more reliable than those currently offered. Third, Fujitsu will give Cisco a stronger sales presence in Japan. Fujitsu has good relationships with Japan's telecommunications companies and a well-earned reputation for reliability. It will leverage these assets to sell the routers produced by the alliance, which will be co-branded as Fujitsu–Cisco products. Fourth, sales may be further enhanced by bundling the co-branded routers together with other telecommunications equipment that Fujitsu sells, and marketing an entire solution to customers. Fujitsu sells many telecommunications products, but lacks a strong presence in routers. Cisco is strong in routers, but lacks strong offerings elsewhere. This combination of the two company's products will enable Fujitsu to offer Japan's telecommunications companies "end-to-end" communications solutions. Because many companies prefer to purchase their equipment from a single provider, this strategy should increase sales.

The alliance introduced its first products in May 2006. If it is successful, both firms should benefit. Development costs will be lower than if they did not cooperate. Cisco will grow its sales in Japan, and Fujitsu can use the co-branded routers to fill out its product line and sell more bundles of products to Japan's telecommunications companies.

Source: "Fujitsu, Cisco Systems to Develop High-end Routers for Web Traffic," *Knight Ridder Tribune Business News,* December 6, 2004, p. 1. "Fujitsu and Cisco Introduce New High Performance Routers for IP Next Generation Networks," *JCN Newswire,* May 25, 2006.

this position appears extreme. It is difficult to see how the Microsoft–Toshiba alliance, the Boeing–Mitsubishi alliance for the 787, or the Fuji–Xerox alliance fit the critics' thesis. In these cases, both partners seem to have gained from the alliance. Why do some alliances benefit both firms while others benefit one firm and hurt the other? The next section provides an answer to this question.

Making Strategic Alliances Work

The failure rate for international strategic alliances is quite high. For example, one study of 49 international strategic alliances found that 2/3 run into serious managerial and financial troubles within 2 years of their formation, and that although many of these problems are ultimately solved, 33% are rated as failures by the parties involved.[35] The success of an alliance seems to be a function of three main factors: partner selection, alliance structure, and the manner in which the alliance is managed.

Partner Selection One of the keys to making a strategic alliance work is to select the right kind of partner. A good partner has three principal characteristics. First, a good partner helps the company achieve strategic goals such as achieving market access, sharing the costs and risks of new-product development, or gaining access to critical core competencies. In other words, the partner must have capabilities that the company lacks and that it values. Second, a good partner shares the firm's vision for the purpose of the alliance. If two companies approach an alliance with radically different agendas, the chances are great that the relationship will not be harmonious and the partnership will end.

Third, a good partner is unlikely to try to exploit the alliance opportunistically for its own ends—that is, to expropriate the company's technological know-how while giving away little in return. In this respect, firms with reputations for fair play to maintain probably make the best partners. For example, IBM is involved in so many strategic alliances that it would not pay the company to trample over individual alliance partners (in the mid-2000s IBM reportedly had more than 150 major strategic alliances).[36] This would tarnish IBM's reputation of being a good ally and would make it more difficult for IBM to attract alliance partners. Because IBM attaches great importance to its alliances, it is unlikely to engage in the kind of opportunistic behavior that critics highlight. Similarly, their reputations make it less likely (but by no means impossible) that such Japanese firms as Sony, Toshiba, and Fuji, which have histories of alliances with non-Japanese firms, would opportunistically exploit an alliance partner.

To select a partner with these three characteristics, a company needs to conduct some comprehensive research on potential alliance candidates. To increase the probability of selecting a good partner, the company should collect as much pertinent, publicly available information about potential allies as possible; collect data from informed third parties, including companies that have had alliances with the potential partners, investment bankers who have had dealings with them, and some of their former employees; and get to know potential partners as well as possible before committing to an alliance. This last step should include face-to-face meetings between senior managers (and perhaps middle-level managers) to ensure that the chemistry is right.

Alliance Structure Having selected a partner, the alliance should be structured so that the company's risk of giving too much away to the partner is reduced to an acceptable level. Figure 8.5 depicts the four safeguards against opportunism by alliance partners that we discuss here. (**Opportunism**, which is often defined as self-interest seeking with guile, includes the "expropriation" of technology or markets.) First, alliances can be designed to make it difficult (if not impossible) to transfer technology not meant to be transferred. Specifically, the design, development, manufacture, and service of a product manufactured by an alliance can be structured to "wall off" sensitive technologies to prevent their leakage to the other participant. In the alliance between General Electric and Snecma to build commercial aircraft engines, for example, GE reduced the risk of "excess transfer" by walling off certain steps of the production process. The modularization effectively cut off the transfer of what GE regarded as key competitive technology while permitting Snecma access to final assembly. Similarly, in the alliance between Boeing and the Japanese to build the 767, Boeing walled off research, design, and marketing functions considered central to its competitive position, while allowing the Japanese

Opportunism

Seeking one's own self-interest often through the use of guile.

Figure 8.5 Structuring Alliances to Reduce Opportunism

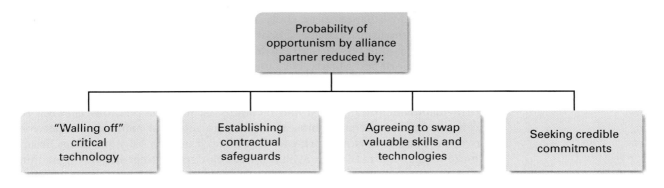

© Cengage Learning 2013

to share in production technology. Boeing also walled off new technologies not required for 767 production.[37]

Second, contractual safeguards can be written into an alliance agreement to guard against the risk of opportunism by a partner. For example, TRW has three strategic alliances with large Japanese auto component suppliers to produce seat belts, engine valves, and steering gears for sale to Japanese-owned auto assembly plants in the United States. TRW has clauses in each of its alliance contracts that bar the Japanese firms from competing with TRW to supply U.S.-owned auto companies with component parts. By doing this, TRW protects itself against the possibility that the Japanese companies are entering into the alliances merely as a means of gaining access to the North American market to compete with TRW in its home market.

Third, both parties in an alliance can agree in advance to exchange skills and technologies that the other covets, thereby ensuring a chance for equitable gain. Cross-licensing agreements are one way to achieve this goal.

Fourth, the risk of opportunism by an alliance partner can be reduced if the firm extracts a significant credible commitment from its partner in advance. The long-term alliance between Xerox and Fuji to build photocopiers for the Asian market perhaps best illustrates this. Rather than enter into an informal agreement or a licensing arrangement (which Fujifilm initially wanted), Xerox insisted that Fuji invest in a 50/50 joint venture to serve Japan and East Asia. This venture constituted such a significant investment in people, equipment, and facilities that Fujifilm was committed from the outset to making the alliance work in order to earn a return on its investment. By agreeing to the joint venture, Fuji essentially made a credible commitment to the alliance. Given this, Xerox felt secure in transferring its photocopier technology to Fuji.

Managing the Alliance Once a partner has been selected and an appropriate alliance structure agreed on, the task facing the company is to maximize the benefits from the alliance. One important ingredient of success appears to be sensitivity to cultural differences. Many differences in management style are attributable to cultural differences, and managers need to make allowances for these when dealing with their partner. Beyond this, maximizing the benefits from an alliance seems to involve building trust between partners and learning from partners.[38]

Managing an alliance successfully requires building interpersonal relationships between the firms' managers, or what is sometimes referred to as relational capital.[39] This is one lesson that can be drawn from a successful strategic alliance between Ford and Mazda. Ford and Mazda set up a framework of meetings within which their managers not only discuss matters pertaining to the alliance, but also have time to get to know one another better. The belief is that the resulting friendships help build trust and facilitate harmonious relations between the two firms. Personal relationships also foster an informal management network between the firms. This network can then be used to help solve problems arising in more formal contexts (such as in joint committee meetings between personnel from the two firms).

Academics have argued that a major determinant of how much acquiring knowledge a company gains from an alliance is its ability to learn from its alliance partner.[40] For example, in a study of 15 strategic alliances between major multinationals, Gary Hamel, Yves Doz, and C. K. Prahalad focused on a number of alliances between Japanese companies and Western (European or American) partners.[41] In every case in which a Japanese company emerged from an alliance stronger than its Western partner, the Japanese company had made a greater effort to learn. Few Western companies studied seemed to want to learn from their Japanese partners. They tended to regard the alliance purely as a cost-sharing or risk-sharing device, rather than as an opportunity to learn how a potential competitor does business.

For an example of an alliance in which there was a clear learning asymmetry, consider the agreement between General Motors and Toyota Motor Corp. to build the Chevrolet Nova. This alliance was structured as a formal joint venture, New United Motor Manufacturing, in which both parties had a 50% equity stake. The venture owned an auto plant in Fremont, California. According to one of the Japanese managers, Toyota achieved most of its objectives from the alliance: "We learned about U.S. supply and transportation. And we got the confidence to manage U.S. workers." All that knowledge was then quickly transferred to Georgetown, Kentucky, where Toyota opened a plant of its own in 1988. By contrast, although General Motors got a new product, the Chevrolet Nova, some GM managers complained that their new knowledge was never put to good use inside GM. They say that they should have been kept together as a team to educate GM's engineers and workers about the Japanese system. Instead, they were dispersed to different GM subsidiaries.[42]

When entering an alliance, a company must take some measures to ensure that it learns from its alliance partner and then puts that knowledge to good use within its own organization. One suggested approach is to educate all operating employees about the partner's strengths and weaknesses and make clear to them how acquiring particular skills will bolster their company's competitive position. For such learning to be of value, the knowledge acquired from an alliance must be diffused throughout the organization—which did not happen at GM. To spread this knowledge, the managers involved in an alliance should be used as a resource in familiarizing others within the company about the skills of an alliance partner.

Ethical Dilemma

Your company has established a manufacturing subsidiary in Southern China. Labor costs at this factory are much lower than in your home market. Employees also work 10 hours a day, 6 days a week, with mandatory overtime often pushing that to 12 hours a day. They are paid the local minimum wage. The factory also does not adhere to the same standards for environmental protection and employee safety as those mandated in your home nation. On a visit to the factory, you notice these things and ask the expatriate manager who heads up the operation if he should be doing some thing to improve working conditions and environmental protection. He replies that his view is that "when in Rome, do as the Romans do." He argues that the situation at the factory is normal for China, and he is complying at with all local regulations and laws. Moreover, he notes that the company established this subsidiary to have a low cost manufacturing base. Improving working conditions and environmental standards beyond those mandated by local laws would not be consistent with this goal.

Is the position taken by the expatriate manager the correct one? Is it ethical? What are the potential negative consequences, if any, of continuing to operate in this manner? What benefits might there be to the company of taking steps to raise working conditions and environmental protection beyond those mandated by local regulations?

Summary of Chapter

1. For some companies, international expansion represents a way of earning greater returns by transferring the skills and product offerings derived from their distinctive competencies to markets where indigenous competitors lack those skills. As barriers to international trade have fallen, industries have expanded beyond national boundaries and industry competition and opportunities have increased.

2. Because of national differences, it pays a company to base each value creation activity it performs at the location where factor conditions are most conducive to the performance of that activity. This strategy is known as focusing on the attainment of location economies.

3. By building sales volume more rapidly, international expansion can help a company gain a cost advantage through the realization of scale economies and learning effects.

4. The best strategy for a company to pursue may depend on the kind of pressures it must cope with: pressures for cost reductions or for local responsiveness. Pressures for cost reductions are greatest in industries producing commodity-type products,

where price is the main competitive weapon. Pressures for local responsiveness arise from differences in consumer tastes and preferences, as well as from national infrastructure and traditional practices, distribution channels, and host government demands.

5. Companies pursuing an international strategy transfer the skills and products derived from distinctive competencies to foreign markets, while undertaking some limited local customization.

6. Companies pursuing a localization strategy customize their product offering, marketing strategy, and business strategy to national conditions.

7. Companies pursuing a global standardization strategy focus on reaping the cost reductions that come from scale economies and location economies.

8. Many industries are now so competitive that companies must adopt a transnational strategy. This involves a simultaneous focus upon reducing costs, transferring skills and products, and being locally responsive. Implementing such a strategy may not be easy.

9. There are five different ways of entering a foreign market: exporting, licensing, franchising, entering into a joint venture, and setting up a wholly owned subsidiary. The optimal choice among entry modes depends on the company's strategy.

10. Strategic alliances are cooperative agreements between actual or potential competitors. The advantages of alliances are that they facilitate entry into foreign markets, enable partners to share the fixed costs and risks associated with new products and processes, facilitate the transfer of complementary skills between companies, and help companies establish technical standards.

11. The drawbacks of a strategic alliance are that the company risks giving away technological know-how and market access to its alliance partner while getting very little in return.

12. The disadvantages associated with alliances can be reduced if the company selects partners carefully, paying close attention to reputation, and structures the alliance in order to avoid unintended transfers of know-how.

Discussion Questions

1. Are the following global standardization industries, or industries where localization is more important: bulk chemicals, pharmaceuticals, branded food products, moviemaking, television manufacture, personal computers, airline travel, and fashion retailing?

2. What kind of companies stand to gain the most from entering into strategic alliances with potential competitors? Why?

3. Plot the position of the following companies on Figure 8.3: Microsoft, Google, Coca-Cola, Dow Chemicals, Pfizer, and McDonald's. In each case, justify your answer.

4. Discuss how the need for control over foreign operations varies with the strategy and distinctive competencies of a company. What are the implications of this relationship for the choice of entry mode?

5. Licensing proprietary technology to foreign competitors is the best way to give up a company's competitive advantage. Discuss.

Practicing Strategic Management

Small Group Exercises

Small-Group Exercise: Developing a Global Strategy

Break into groups of 3–5 people, and discuss the following scenario. Appoint one group member as a spokesperson who will communicate your findings to the class. You work for a company in the soft drink industry that has developed a line of carbonated fruit-based drinks. You have already established a significant presence in your home market, and now you are planning the global strategy development of the company in the soft drink industry. You need to decide the following:

1. What overall strategy to pursue: a global standardization strategy, a localization strategy, an international strategy, or a transnational strategy
2. Which markets to enter first
3. What entry strategy to pursue (e.g., franchising, joint venture, wholly owned subsidiary)
4. What information do you need to make this kind of decision? Considering what you do know, what strategy would you recommend?

Strategy Sign-On

Article File 8

Find an example of a multinational company that in recent years has switched its strategy from a localization, international, or global standardization strategy to a transnational strategy. Identify why the company made the switch and any problems that the company may be encountering while it tries to change its strategic orientation.

Strategic Management Project: Developing Your Portfolio 8

This module requires you to identify how your company might profit from global expansion, the strategy that your company should pursue globally, and the entry mode that it might favor. With the information you have at your disposal, answer the questions regarding the following two situations:

Your company is already doing business in other countries.

1. Is your company creating value or lowering the costs of value creation by realizing location economies, transferring distinctive competencies abroad, or realizing cost economies from the economies of scale? If not, does it have the potential to do so?
2. How responsive is your company to differences among nations? Does it vary its product and marketing message from country to country? Should it?
3. What are the cost pressures and pressures for local responsiveness in the industry in which your company is based?
4. What strategy is your company pursuing to compete globally? In your opinion, is this the correct strategy, given cost pressures and pressures for local responsiveness?
5. What major foreign market does your company serve, and what mode has it used to enter this market? Why is your company active in these markets and not others? What are the advantages and disadvantages of using this mode? Might another mode be preferable?

Your company is not yet doing business in other countries.

1. What potential does your company have to add value to its products or lower the costs of value creation by expanding internationally?

2. On the international level, what are the cost pressures and pressures for local responsiveness in the industry in which your company is based? What implications do these pressures have for the strategy that your company might pursue if it chose to expand globally?
3. What foreign market might your company enter, and what entry mode should it use to enter this market? Justify your answer.

CLOSING CASE

THE EVOLVING STRATEGY IBM

IBM's CEO, Sam Palmisano, likes to talk about the evolution of global strategy at one of the world's largest computer enterprises. According to Palmisano, when IBM first started to expand internationally, it did so in the classic "international" pattern of many enterprises, undertaking most of its activities at home, and selling its products internationally through overseas sales offices. By the time Palmisano joined IBM in 1972, however, it had already moved away from this model, and was by then a classic "multinational" enterprise, with small branches in major national markets around the world. This structure made sense for IBM in the 1970s, given that many markets were still segmented from each other by high barriers to cross border trade, and given that national differences in business practices often required considerable localization.

In recent decades, however, IBM has been moving away from this model and toward one that Palmisano characterizes as a "globally integrated enterprise." In his words: "We are locating work and operations anywhere in the world based on economics, expertise, and the right business environment. We are integrating those operations horizontally and globally. We use to have separate supply chains in different markets. Now we have one supply chain, a global one. Our R&D has been global for many years, with research and software development carried out in labs around the world. But in our professional services businesses, where we use to think about our human capital—our people—in terms of countries, and regions, and business units, we now manage and deploy them as one global asset."

Thus today's IBM locates its semiconductor R&D and manufacturing operations in upstate New York and Vermont, and its global procurement center is in China. Global services delivery is in India, while many of the services that support IBM's external and internal Websites are in places like Ireland and Brazil. The people at each of these centers are not focused on their national markets; they are leading integrated global operations.

This strategic shift was a response to three things; the globalization of the world economy, the global nature of many of IBM's customers, who were shifting towards a global integration strategy, and the emergence of fierce competition from enterprises in emerging markets such as China and India. India is a good example; in the 1990s a trio of Indian outsourcing firms, Tata Consulting Services, Infosys, and Wipro started to take share away from IBM in its core information technology services business. The Indians enjoyed an advantage based on a large supply of highly educated, but relative inexpensive, engineering, and managerial talent. IBM felt that to compete, it needed to adopt the low cost model being pioneered in India. In the mid-2000s, it bought Daksh, an Indian firm that was a smaller version of India's big three information technology services firms. IBM has invested heavily in its Indian unit, building it into a large global business with leading market share that now effectively competes on cost and quality against its Indian rivals. While Palmisano notes that the original motivation for expanding in India was to gain access to low cost labor, he argues that the skill base in India is just as important now—if not more so. IBM can find a large supply of highly skilled people in India who can staff its global services operations, and move seamlessly around the world. It doesn't hurt that most Indians have a good command of the English language, which has become the de facto language of business in much of the world.

Looking forward, Palmisano stresses that IBM is still fairly early in its journey to become a fully integrated global enterprise. The big thrust going forward will be on developing the human capital of the enterprise—helping to produce managers and engineers who see themselves as global professionals and global citizens, who are able to move effortlessly around the world, and do business effectively in a wide range of national contexts.[43]

Case Discussion Questions

1. In the 1970s and 1980s Palmisano states that IBM was organized as a classic multinational enterprise. What does this mean? Why do you think IBM was organized that way? What were the advantages of this kind of strategic orientation?
2. By the 1990s, the classic multinational strategic orientation was no longer working well for IBM. Why not?
3. What are the strategic advantages of IBM's globally integrated enterprise strategy? What kind of organizational changes do you think had to be made at IBM to make this strategy a reality?
4. According to the strategic choice framework introduced in this chapter, what strategy do you think IBM is pursuing today?

Notes

[1] World Trade Organization, *International Trade Trends and Statistics, 2005* (Geneva: WTO, 2006), and WTO press release, "World Trade for 2005: Prospects for 2006," April 11, 2006, available at www.wto.org.

[2] World Trade Organization, *International Trade Statistics, 2010* (Geneva: WTO, 2010), and United Nations, *World Investment Report, 2010*.

[3] P. Dicken, *Global Shift* (New York: Guilford Press, 1992).

[4] D. Pritchard, "Are Federal Tax Laws and State Subsidies for Boeing 7E7 Selling America Short?" *Aviation Week*, April 12, 2004, pp. 74–75.

[5] T. Levitt, "The Globalization of Markets," *Harvard Business Review*, May–June 1983, pp. 92–102.

[6] M. E. Porter, *The Competitive Advantage of Nations* (New York: Free Press, 1990). See also R. Grant, "Porter's Competitive Advantage of Nations: An Assessment," *Strategic Management Journal* 7 (1991), pp. 535–548.

[7] Porter, *Competitive Advantage of Nations*.

[8] Example is disguised. Comes from interviews by Charles Hill.

[9] See J. Birkinshaw and N. Hood, "Multinational Subsidiary Evolution: Capability and Charter Change in Foreign Owned Subsidiary Companies," *Academy of Management Review* 23 (October 1998), pp. 773–795; A. K. Gupta and V. J. Govindarajan, "Knowledge Flows Within Multinational Corporations," *Strategic Management Journal* 21 (2000), pp. 473–496; V. J. Govindarajan and A. K. Gupta, *The Quest for Global Dominance* (San Francisco: Jossey-Bass, 2001); T. S. Frost, J. M. Birkinshaw, and P. C. Ensign, "Centers of Excellence in Multinational Corporations," *Strategic Management Journal* 23 (2002), pp. 997–1018; and U. Andersson, M. Forsgren, and U. Holm, "The Strategic Impact of External Networks," *Strategic Management Journal* 23 (2002), pp. 979–996.

[10] S. Leung, "Armchairs, TVs and Espresso: Is It McDonald's?" *Wall Street Journal* (2002), pp. A1, A6.

[11] C. K. Prahalad and Yves L. Doz, *The Multinational Mission: Balancing Local Demands and Global Vision* (New York: Free Press, 1987). See also J. Birkinshaw, A. Morrison, and J. Hulland, "Structural and Competitive Determinants of a Global Integration Strategy," *Strategic Management Journal* 16 (1995), 637–655.

[12] J. E. Garten, "Walmart Gives Globalization a Bad Name," *Business Week*, March 8, 2004, p. 24.

[13] Prahalad and Doz, *Multinational Mission*. Prahalad and Doz actually talk about local responsiveness rather than local customization.

[14] Levitt, "Globalization of Markets."

[15] C. A. Bartlett and S. Ghoshal, *Managing Across Borders* (Boston: Harvard Business School Press, 1989).

[16] W. W. Lewis. *The Power of Productivity* (Chicago: University of Chicago Press, 2004).

[17] C. J. Chipello, "Local Presence Is Key to European Deals," *Wall Street Journal* (1998) p. A15.

[18] Bartlett and Ghoshal, *Managing Across Borders*.

[19] Ibid.

[20] T. Hout, M. E. Porter, and E. Rudden, "How Global Companies Win Out," *Harvard Business Review,* September–October 1982, pp. 98–108.

[21] This section draws on numerous studies, including: C. W. L. Hill, P. Hwang, and W. C. Kim, "An Eclectic Theory of the Choice of International Entry Mode," *Strategic Management Journal* 11 (1990), pp. 117–28; C. W. L. Hill and W. C. Kim, "Searching for a Dynamic Theory of the Multinational Enterprise: A Transaction Cost Model," *Strategic Management Journal* 9 (Special Issue on Strategy Content, 1988), pp. 93–104; E. Anderson and H. Gatignon, "Modes of Foreign Entry: A Transaction Cost Analysis and Propositions," *Journal of International Business Studies* 17 (1986), pp. 1–26; F. R. Root, *Entry Strategies for International Markets* (Lexington: D. C. Heath, 1980); A. Madhok, "Cost, Value and Foreign Market Entry: The Transaction and the Firm," *Strategic Management Journal* 18 (1997), pp. 39–61; K. D. Brouthers and L. B. Brouthers, "Acquisition or Greenfield Start-Up?" *Strategic Management Journal* 21, no. 1 (2000), pp. 89–97; X. Martin and R. Salmon, "Knowledge Transfer Capacity and Its Implications for the Theory of the Multinational Enterprise," *Journal of International Business Studies* (2003), p. 356; and A. Verbeke, "The Evolutionary View of the MNE and the Future of Internalization Theory," *Journal of International Business Studies* (2003), pp. 498–515.

[22] F. J. Contractor, "The Role of Licensing in International Strategy," *Columbia Journal of World Business* (Winter 1982): pp. 73–83.

[23] O. E. Williamson, *The Economic Institutions of Capitalism* (New York: Free Press, 1985).

[24] Andrew E. Serwer, "McDonald's Conquers the World," *Fortune* 1994, pp. 103–116.

[25] For an excellent review of the basic theoretical literature of joint ventures, see B. Kogut, "Joint Ventures: Theoretical and Empirical Perspectives," *Strategic Management Journal* 9 (1988), pp. 319–32. More recent studies include T. Chi, "Option to Acquire or Divest a Joint Venture," *Strategic Management Journal* 21, no. 6 (2000), pp. 665–88; H. Merchant and D. Schendel, "How Do International Joint Ventures Create Shareholder Value?" *Strategic Management Journal* 21, no. 7 (2000), pp. 723–37; H. K. Steensma and M. A. Lyles, "Explaining IJV Survival in a Transitional Economy though Social Exchange and Knowledge Based Perspectives," *Strategic Management Journal* 21, no. 8 (2000), pp. 831–51; and J. F. Hennart and M. Zeng, "Cross Cultural Differences and Joint Venture Longevity," *Journal of International Business Studies* 2002, pp. 699–717.

[26] J. A. Robins, S. Tallman, and K. Fladmoe-Lindquist, "Autonomy and Dependence of International Cooperative Ventures," *Strategic Management Journal* 2002, pp. 881–902.

[27] C. W. L. Hill, "Strategies for Exploiting Technological Innovations," *Organization Science* 3 (1992): 428–441.

[28] See K. Ohmae, "The Global Logic of Strategic Alliances," *Harvard Business Review,* March–April 1989, pp. 143–154; G. Hamel, Y. L. Doz, and C. K. Prahalad, "Collaborate with Your Competitors and Win!" *Harvard Business Review,* January–February 1989, 133–139; W. Burgers, C. W. L. Hill, and W. C. Kim, "Alliances in the Global Auto Industry," *Strategic Management Journal* 14 (1993): 419–432; and P. Kale, H. Singh, and H. Perlmutter, "Learning and Protection of Proprietary Assets in Strategic Alliances: Building Relational Capital," *Strategic Management Journal* 21 (2000), pp. 217–237.

[29] L. T. Chang, "China Eases Foreign Film Rules," *The Wall Street Journal* (2004), p. B2.

[30] B. L. Simonin, "Transfer of Marketing Knowhow in International Strategic Alliances," *Journal of International Business Studies* (1999), pp. 463–91, and J. W. Spencer, "Firms' Knowledge Sharing Strategies in the Global Innovation System," *Strategic Management Journal* 24 (2003), pp. 217–33.

[31] C. Souza, "Microsoft Teams with MIPS, Toshiba," *EBN* 2003, p. 4.

[32] M. Frankel, "Now Sony Is Giving Palm a Hand," *Business Week*, November 29, 2000, p. 50.

[33] Kale, Singh, and Perlmutter, "Learning and Protection of Proprietary Assets."

[34] R. B. Reich and E. D. Mankin, "Joint Ventures with Japan Give Away Our Future," *Harvard Business Review*, March–April 1986, pp. 78–90.

[35] J. Bleeke and D. Ernst, "The Way to Win in Cross-Border Alliances," *Harvard Business Review,* November–December 1991, 127–135.

[36] E. Booker and C. Krol, "IBM Finds Strength in Alliances," *B to B* (2003), pp. 3, 27.

[37] W. Roehl and J. F. Truitt, "Stormy Open Marriages Are Better," *Columbia Journal of World Business* (Summer 1987), 87–95.

[38] See T. Khanna, R. Gulati, and N. Nohria, "The Dynamics of Learning Alliances: Competition, Cooperation, and Relative Scope," *Strategic Management Journal* 19 (1998), pp. 193–210, and P. Kale, H. Singh, H. Perlmutter, "Learning and Protection of Proprietary Assets in Strategic Alliances: Building Relational Capital," *Strategic Management Journal* 21 (2000), pp. 217–37.

[39] Kale, Singh, and Perlmutter, "Learning and Protection of Proprietary Assets."

[40]Hamel, Doz, and Prahalad, "Collaborate with Competitors"; Khanna, Gulati, and Nohria, "The Dynamics of Learning Alliances: Competition, Cooperation, and Relative Scope"; and E. W. K. Tang, "Acquiring Knowledge by Foreign Partners from International Joint Ventures in a Transition Economy: Learning by Doing and Learning Myopia," *Strategic Management Journal* 23 (2002), pp. 835–54.

[41]Hamel, Doz, and Prahalad, "Collaborate with Competitors."

[42] B. Wysocki, "Cross Border Alliances Become Favorite Way to Crack New Markets," *Wall Street Journal* (1990), p. A1.

[43] "The Empire Fights Back," *The Economist* (2008), pp. 12–16; S. Palmisano, "The Globally Integrated Enterprise" *Vital Speeches of the Day* (2007), pp. 449–453; S. Hamm, "IBM vs Tata: Which is More American?" *Business Week* (2008), p. 28.

9

Corporate-Level Strategy: Horizontal Integration, Vertical Integration, and Strategic Outsourcing

erel.photography/istockphoto.com

The Rapid Consolidation of the U.S. Airline Industry

In July, 2008, American Airlines (AA) was the largest air carrier in the world, and it competed against five other established U.S. airlines as well as newer airlines such as Southwest and JetBlue. Then, oil prices, which are approximately 35% of an airline's total operating costs, were rising, and the recent financial recession occurred that led to a significant decrease in the number of business travelers (who are the most lucrative source of revenue for an airline). These circumstances led to billions of dollars in losses for most major U.S. airlines, including American and JetBlue. Southwest, however, was the exception because it has always pursued a cost-leadership strategy and so been able to withstand falling ticket prices and rising costs better than the older, more established airlines.

With many major airlines facing bankruptcy, the Justice Department began to look more favorably upon requests by airlines to merge their operations, expand their route structures, and

reduce their cost structures. The downside for passengers of merger and horizontal integration, of course, is that if there are fewer airlines, the remaining carriers are able to reduce the number of flights they offer and

LEARNING OBJECTIVES

After reading this chapter, you should be able to:

- Discuss how corporate-level strategy can be used to strengthen a company's business model and business-level strategies
- Define horizontal integration and discuss the primary advantages and disadvantages associated with this corporate-level strategy
- Explain the difference between a company's internal value chain and the industry value chain
- Define horizontal integration and describe the primary advantages and disadvantages associated with this corporate-level strategy
- Describe why, and under what conditions, cooperative relationships such as strategic alliances and outsourcing may become a substitute for vertical integration

services they provide—and the result is that ticket prices increase. For example, industry consolidation makes it easier for carriers to announce changes such as charging for a second checked bag or the right to be seated first all of which provide airlines with additional sources of revenue.

Nevertheless, by 2009 the Justice Department, which had allowed the proposed merger between Delta and Northwest Airlines to proceed, resulted in the new Delta becoming the largest U.S. airline. Then in 2010, the merger between United and Continental Airlines was also approved, and by 2011, the newly merged United-Continental Airlines was competing with Delta to become the largest U.S. carrier. American Airlines, by that time, was now number three after its proposal to merge with British Airways (and become the largest global airline) was not approved for antitrust reasons—despite that the global airline industry was also rapidly consolidating.

By 2011, the largest U.S. airlines had achieved their goal of reducing costs and increasing their profits; they had slashed the number of flights they offered, mothballed hundreds of older planes, laid off thousands of employees, and instituted new surcharges for fuel, baggage, and even for carrying pets onboard.

However, not only the oldest and largest U.S. airlines had participated in the movement to horizontally integrate the U.S. airline industry but also long-time cost leader and the most profitable of U.S. airlines, Southwest Airlines, had been rapidly expanding its route structure during the 2000s. For example, while its rivals lost billions, Southwest made a $439 million profit in 2010, which continued its string of unbroken consecutive annual profits—a huge increase over its 2009 profit of $99 million.

Southwest now served most major U.S. cities, and its managers also saw an opportunity to expand market share and simultaneously keep its cost structure low by acquiring its biggest low-cost rival, JetBlue. JetBlue's major presence on the east coast was a market in which Southwest was still a minor player. When Southwest's takeover of JetBlue was approved in 2011, it also became one of the largest U.S. carriers. What was Southwest's new strategy in the now rapidly consolidating industry?

Many analysts, watching Southwest's ever changing online fares, noted that it, too, was raising fares in response to the moves of other airlines. Although it had not instituted charges for second checked bags yet, analysts wondered if it would simply use its low-cost structure to outperform its high-cost rivals, and only reduce prices when falling demand warranted the reduction. In an interview in 2011, Herb Kelleher, Southwest's founder, commented on the consolidation of the industry, but he also noted that because of rising fuel prices, airlines could do little but find new ways to increase revenues or reduce costs in order for the industry as a whole to regain its profitability. Perhaps in response to the new way analysts were looking at Southwest's pricing practices in June 2011, the company announced large, across-the-board airfare sales to celebrate its 40th year in business. If Southwest's success continues and fuel prices continue to rise, it will be interesting to see where this carrier ranks among the largest U.S. airlines in the years ahead—and how many airlines will still be operating.

Overview

The overriding goal of managers is to maximize the value of a company for its shareholders. The way in which companies in the airline industry developed strategies to acquire and merge with other airlines is an example of the way corporate-level strategy can be employed to increase both company and industry profitability; Southwest is a master at this game.

In general, corporate-level strategy involves choices strategic managers must make: (1) deciding in which businesses and industries a company should compete; (2) which value creation activities it should perform in those businesses; and (3) how it should enter, consolidate, or exit businesses or industries to maximize long-term profitability. When formulating corporate-level strategy, managers must adopt a long-term perspective and consider how changes taking place in an industry and in its products, technology, customers, and competitors will affect their company's current business model and its future strategies. They then decide how to implement specific corporate-level strategies that redefine their company's business model to allow it to increase its competitive advantage in a changing industry environment by taking advantage of opportunities and countering threats. Thus, the principal goal of corporate-level strategy is to enable a company to sustain or promote its competitive advantage and profitability in its present business—*and in any new businesses or industries that it chooses to enter*.

This chapter is the first of two that describes the role of corporate-level strategy in repositioning and redefining a company's business model. We discuss three corporate-level strategies—horizontal integration, vertical integration, and strategic outsourcing—that are primarily directed toward improving a company's competitive advantage and profitability in its current business or industry. Diversification, which entails entry into new kinds of businesses or industries, is examined in the next chapter, along with guidelines for choosing the most profitable way to enter new businesses or industries, or to exit others. By the end of this chapter and the next, you will understand how the different levels of strategy contribute to the creation of a successful and profitable business or multibusiness model. You will also be able to distinguish between the types of corporate strategies managers use to maximize long-term company profitability.

Corporate-Level Strategy and the Multibusiness Model

The choice of corporate-level strategies is the final part of the strategy formulation process. Corporate-level strategies drive a company's business model over time and determine which types of business- and functional-level strategies managers will choose to maximize long-term profitability. The relationship between business-level strategy and functional-level strategy was discussed in Chapter 5. Strategic managers develop a business model and strategies that use their company's distinctive competencies to strive for a cost-leadership position and/or to differentiate its products. Chapter 8 described how global strategy is also an extension of these basic principles.

In this chapter and the next, we repeatedly emphasize that to increase profitability, a corporate-level strategy should enable a company or one or more of its business divisions or units *to perform value-chain functional activities (1) at a lower cost and/or (2) in a way that results in increased differentiation.* Only when it selects the appropriate corporate-level strategies can a company choose the pricing option (lowest, average, or premium price) that will allow it to maximize profitability. In addition, corporate-level strategy will increase profitability if it helps a company reduce industry rivalry by reducing the threat of damaging price competition. In sum, a company's corporate-level strategies should be chosen to promote the success of its business-level strategies, which allows it to achieve a sustainable competitive advantage, leading to higher profitability.

Many companies choose to expand their business activities beyond one market or industry and enter others. When a company decides to expand into new industries, it must construct its business model at two levels. First, it must develop a business model and strategies for each business unit or division in every industry in which it competes. Second, it must also develop a higher-level *multibusiness model* that justifies its entry into different businesses and industries. This multibusiness model should explain how and why entering a new industry will allow the company to use its existing functional competencies and business strategies to increase its overall profitability. This model should also explain any other ways in which a company's involvement in more than one business or industry can increase its profitability. IBM, for example, might argue that its entry into online computer consulting, data storage, and cloud computing enables it to offer its customers a lineup of computer services, which allows it to better compete with HP, Oracle, or Amazon. com. Apple might argue its entry into digital music and entertainment has given it a commanding lead over rivals such as Sony or Microsoft (which ended sales of its Zune music player in October 2011).

This chapter first focuses on the advantages of staying inside one industry by pursuing horizontal integration. It then looks at why companies use vertical integration and expand into new industries. In the next chapter, we examine two principal corporate strategies companies use to enter new industries to increase their profitability, related and unrelated diversification, and several other strategies companies may use to enter and compete in new industries.

Horizontal Integration: Single-Industry Corporate Strategy

Managers use corporate-level strategy to identify which industries their company should compete in to maximize its long-term profitability. For many companies, profitable growth and expansion often entail finding ways to successfully compete within a single market or industry over time. In other words, a company confines its value-creation activities to just one business or industry. Examples of such single-business companies include McDonald's, with its focus on the global fast-food business, and Walmart, with its focus on global discount retailing.

Staying within one industry allows a company to focus all of its managerial, financial, technological, and functional resources and capabilities on competing successfully in one area. This is important in fast-growing and changing industries in which demands on a company's resources and capabilities are likely to be substantial, but where the long-term profits from establishing a competitive advantage are also likely to be substantial.

A second advantage of staying within a single industry is that a company "sticks to the knitting," meaning that it stays focused on what it knows and does best. A company does not make the mistake of entering new industries in which its existing resources and capabilities create little value and/or where a whole new set of competitive industry forces—new competitors, suppliers, and customers—present unanticipated threats. Coca-Cola, like many other companies, has committed this strategic error in the past. Coca-Cola once decided to expand into the movie business and acquired Columbia Pictures; it also acquired a large California winemaker. It soon found it lacked the competencies to successfully compete in these new industries and had not foreseen the strong competitive forces that existed in these industries from movie companies such as Paramount and winemakers such as Gallo. Coca-Cola concluded that entry into these new industries had reduced rather than created value and lowered its profitability; it divested or sold off these new businesses at a significant loss.

Even when a company stays in one industry, sustaining a successful business model over time can be difficult because of changing conditions in the environment, such as advances in technology that allow new competitors into the market, or because of changing customer needs. A decade ago, the strategic issue facing telecommunications providers was how to shape their landline phone services to best meet customer needs in local and long-distance telephone service. When a new kind of product—wireless telephone service—emerged and quickly gained in popularity, landline providers like Verizon and AT&T had to quickly change their business models, lower the price of landline service, merge with wireless companies, and offer broadband services to ensure their survival.

Even within one industry, it is very easy for strategic managers to fail to see the "forest" (changing nature of the industry that results in new product/market opportunities) for the "trees" (focusing only on how to position current products). A focus on corporate-level strategy can help managers anticipate future trends and then change their business models to position their companies to compete successfully in a changing environment. Strategic managers must not become so committed to improving their company's *existing* product lines that they fail to recognize *new* product opportunities and threats. Apple has been so successful because it did recognize the increasing number of product opportunities offered by digital entertainment. The task for corporate-level managers is to analyze how new emerging technologies will impact their business models, how and why these technologies might change customer needs and customer groups in the future, and what kinds of new distinctive competencies will be needed to respond to these changes.

One corporate-level strategy that has been widely used to help managers strengthen their company's business model is horizontal integration, the strategy discussed in the opening case on the airline industry. **Horizontal integration** is the process of acquiring or merging with industry competitors to achieve the competitive advantages that arise from a large size and scope of operations. An **acquisition** occurs when one company uses its capital resources, such as stock, debt, or cash, to purchase another company, and a **merger** is an agreement between equals to pool their operations and create a new entity.

Mergers and acquisitions are common in most industries. In the aerospace industry, Boeing merged with McDonnell Douglas to create the world's largest aerospace company; in the pharmaceutical industry, Pfizer acquired Warner-Lambert to become the largest pharmaceutical firm; and global airlines are increasingly merging their operations as the opening case suggests. The pace of mergers and acquisitions

Horizontal integration

The process of acquiring or merging with industry competitors to achieve the competitive advantages that arise from a large size and scope of operations.

Acquisition

When a company uses its capital resources to purchase another company.

Merger

An agreement between two companies to pool their resources and operations and join together to better compete in a business or industry.

has been rising as companies try to gain a competitive advantage over their rivals. The reason for this is that horizontal integration often significantly improves the competitive advantage and profitability of companies whose managers choose to stay within one industry and focus on managing its competitive position to keep the company at the value-creation frontier.

Benefits of Horizontal Integration

In pursuing horizontal integration, managers decide to invest their company's capital resources to purchase the assets of industry competitors to increase the profitability of its single-business model. Profitability increases when horizontal integration (1) lowers the cost structure, (2) increases product differentiation, (3) replicates the business model, (4) reduces rivalry within the industry, and (5) increases bargaining power over suppliers and buyers.

Lower Cost Structure   Horizontal integration can lower a company's cost structure because it creates increasing *economies of scale*. Suppose five major competitors exist, each of which operates a manufacturing plant in some region of the United States, but none of the plants operate at full capacity. If one competitor buys another and closes that plant, it can operate its own plant at full capacity and reduce its manufacturing costs. Achieving economies of scale is very important in industries that have a high fixed-cost structure. In such industries, large-scale production allows companies to spread their fixed costs over a large volume, and in this way drive down average unit costs. In the telecommunications industry, for example, the fixed costs of building advanced 4G and LTE broadband networks that offer tremendous increases in speed are enormous, and to make such an investment profitable, a large volume of customers is required. Thus, companies such as AT&T and Verizon purchased other telecommunications companies to acquire their customers, increase their customer base, increase utilization rates, and reduce the cost of servicing each customer. In 2011, AT&T was attempting to acquire T-Mobile, but the outcome was uncertain because of anti-trust concerns. Similar considerations were involved in the hundreds of acquisitions that have taken place in the pharmaceutical industry in the last decade because of the need to realize scale economies in R&D and sales and marketing. The fixed costs of building a nationwide pharmaceutical sales force are enormous and pharmaceutical companies such as Pfizer and Merck must possess a wide portfolio of drugs to sell to effectively make use of their sales forces.

A company can also lower its cost structure when horizontal integration allows it to *reduce the duplication of resources* between two companies, such as by eliminating the need for two sets of corporate head offices, two separate sales teams, etc. Lowering costs was one reason why U.S. airlines have been engaging in horizontal integration as discussed in the opening case; it is also a major reason that justified HP's acquisition of Compaq as discussed in the following Focus on Dell.

Increased Product Differentiation   Horizontal integration may also increase profitability when it increases product differentiation, for example, by increasing the flow of innovative new products that a company's sales force can sell to customers at premium prices. Desperate for new drugs to fill its pipeline, for example, Eli Lilly paid $6.5 billion to ImClone Systems to acquire its new cancer preventing drugs in order to outbid rival Bristol-Myers Squibb. Google, anxious to provide its users with

FOCUS ON D⊄LL ⑨

Beating Dell: Why HP Acquired Compaq

HP (formerly Hewlett-Packard) shocked the business world when it announced that it was going to acquire rival PC maker Compaq. To justify the acquisition, HP claimed that it would yield a number of benefits. First, there would be significant cost savings of $2.5 billion per year by eliminating redundant administrative functions and laying off 15,000 employees. In addition, combining the PC businesses of HP and Compaq would enable HP to capture significant scale economies and compete more efficiently with Dell—the market leader in the early-2000s. The same would be true in the computer server and storage businesses, areas in which Dell was gaining share. Critics, however, were quick to point out that Dell's competitive advantage was based on its cost-leadership business model, which resulted from the efficient management of its supply chain—an area in which both HP and Compaq lagged behind Dell. Although achieving economies of scale is desirable, would the merger allow HP to reduce its cost structure and increase its supply-chain efficiency? If HP could not improve its PC business model to match Dell's low costs, the merger would not provide any real benefit.

By the mid-2000s, HP announced that it had achieved its cost savings target and that it was continuing to find ways to reduce the duplication of resources in the merged company, however, the profit margins on the sale of its PCs were still below those obtained by Dell. By 2007, however, HP astonished analysts when it announced much higher profit margins on its PC sales and higher profits across the company. Why? HP was now outsourcing more PC production to specialist companies in Taiwan and China and differentiating its PCs so they were much more attractive than Dell's "black box" desktop and laptop design . The result was that competitive advantage in the PC industry was moving away from Dell and toward HP.

Dell was now forced to find ways to differentiate its PCs and defend its position against HP—and increasingly, Apple had become the leader in offering state-of-the-art computers. Dell purchased upscale PC maker Alienware, and it also began to open Dell PC stores—an imitation of Apple's strategy—which proved to be a disaster. To find more cost savings, Dell also began to use AMD's cheaper processing chips and broke its long-term exclusive tie to Intel.

None of these strategies worked; Dell continued to lose market share to HP whose stock price rose to record highs. Then, HP came under attack after Apple, in its continuous quest to innovate desktops and laptops, began to gain market share from HP. At the same time, both Dell and HP have come under attack from low-cost PC makers Acer and Lenovo. The battle in the PC industry has become fierce, and in 2011, both Dell and HP were under attack as they worked to find new ways to lower costs and differentiate their products to compete effectively against rivals such as Oracle, Apple, and IBM.

online coupons, offered to pay $6 billion for Groupon to fill this niche in its online advertising business in order to increase its differentiation advantage—and reduce industry rivalry.

Horizontal integration may also increase differentiation when it allows a company to combine the product lines of merged companies so that it can offer customers a wider range of products that can be bundled together. **Product bundling** involves offering customers the opportunity to purchase a range of products at a single combined price. This increases the value of a company's product line because customers often obtain a price discount when purchasing a set of products at one time, and customers become used to dealing with only one company and its representatives. A company may obtain a competitive advantage from increased product differentiation.

Another way to increase product differentiation is through **cross-selling**, which is when a company takes advantage of or "leverages" its established relationship with customers by way of acquiring additional product lines or categories that it can sell to customers. In this way, a company increases differentiation because it can provide a "total solution" and satisfy all of a customer's specific needs. Cross-selling and becoming a total solution provider is an important rationale for horizontal integration in the computer sector, where IT companies attempt to increase the value of their offerings by satisfying all of the hardware and service needs of corporate customers. Providing a total solution saves customers time and money because they do not have to work with several suppliers, and a single sales team can ensure that all the components of a customer's IT seamlessly work together. When horizontal integration increases the differentiated appeal and value of the company's products, the total solution provider gains market share. This was the business model Oracle pursued when it acquired many IT software companies as discussed in Strategy in Action 9.1.

Replicating the Business Model   Given the many ways in which horizontal integration can be used to increase product differentiation and lower cost structure, a company that can replicate its successful business model in new *market segments* within its industry can also increase its profitability. In the retail industry, for example, Walmart opened its chain of Sam's Clubs using its low-cost/low-price discount retail business model to enter into the even-lower-priced warehouse segment. It also expanded the range of products it offers customers when it entered the supermarket business and

STRATEGY IN ACTION

Larry Ellison Wants Oracle to Become the Biggest and the Best

Oracle Corporation, based in Redwood Shores, California, is the world's largest maker of database software and the third-largest global software company after Microsoft and IBM. This commanding position is not enough for Oracle, however, which has set its sights on becoming the global leader in the corporate applications software market. In this market, Germany's SAP, with 45% of the market, is the acknowledged leader, and Oracle, with 25%, is a distant second. Corporate applications are a fast growing and highly profitable market, however, and Oracle has been snapping up leading companies in this segment. Its goal is to quickly build the distinctive competencies it needs to expand the range of products that it can offer to its existing customers and attract new customers to compete with SAP.

Beginning in the mid-2000s Oracle's CEO Larry Ellison has spent over $29 billion to acquire more than 20 leading suppliers of corporate software and hardware, including 2 of the top 5 companies: PeopleSoft, a leading human resource management (HRM) software supplier it bought for $10 billion, and Siebel Systems, a leader in customer relationship management (CRM) software, that it purchased for $5.8 billion.

Oracle expects several competitive advantages to result from its use of acquisitions to pursue the corporate strategy of horizontal integration. First, it is now able to bundle the best software applications of these acquired companies—with Oracle's own first-class set of corporate and database software programs—to create a new integrated software suite that will allow companies to manage all their functional activities, such as accounting, marketing, sales, HRM, CRM, and supply-chain management. Second, through these acquisitions, Oracle obtained access to thousands of new customers—especially the medium and small companies that use the software of the companies it acquired. All of these companies have become potential customers for Oracle's other database and corporate software offerings, and, therefore, its market share has steadily increased during the 2010s. Third, Oracle's acquisitions have consolidated the corporate software industry. By taking over some of its largest rivals, Oracle has become the second-largest supplier of corporate software and is better positioned to compete with leader SAP. As a result, its stock price has soared in the 2010s—at a much faster rate than archrival SAP.

Sources: www.oracle.com, 2011; www.sap.com, 2011.

established a nationwide chain of Walmart supercenters that sell groceries as well as all the clothing, toys, and electronics sold in regular Walmart stores. It has also replicated its business model globally by acquiring supermarket chains in several countries, such as Mexico, the United Kingdom, and Japan, where it used its efficient global materials-management practices to pursue its cost-leadership strategy. In the United States, Walmart has also been experimenting with new kinds of small-size supermarkets to expand its presence in the supermarket industry segment; these smaller stores compete with the growing popularity of "dollar stores" that have been taking its customers.[1]

Reduced Industry Rivalry   Horizontal integration can help to reduce industry rivalry in two ways. First, acquiring or merging with a competitor helps to *eliminate excess capacity* in an industry, which, as we discuss in Chapter 6, often triggers price wars. By taking excess capacity out of an industry, horizontal integration creates a more benign environment in which prices might stabilize—or even increase.

Second, by reducing the number of competitors in an industry, horizontal integration often makes it easier to implement *tacit price coordination* between rivals, that is, coordination reached without communication. (Explicit communication to fix prices is illegal.) In general, the larger the number of competitors in an industry, the more difficult it is to establish informal pricing agreements—such as price leadership by the dominant company—which reduces the possibility that a price war will erupt. By increasing industry concentration and creating an oligopoly, horizontal integration can make it easier to establish tacit coordination among rivals.

Both of these motives also seem to have been behind Oracle's many software acquisitions. There was significant excess capacity in the corporate software industry, and major competitors were offering customers discounted prices that had led to a price war and falling profit margins. Oracle hoped to be able to eliminate excess industry that would reduce price competition. By 2009, it was clear that the major corporate software competitors were focusing on finding ways to better differentiate their product suites to prevent a price war and continuing to make major acquisitions to help the company build competitive advantage.

Increased Bargaining Power   Finally, some companies use horizontal integration because it allows them to obtain bargaining power over suppliers or buyers and increase their profitability at the expense of suppliers or buyers. By consolidating the industry through horizontal integration, a company becomes a much larger buyer of suppliers' products and uses this as leverage to bargain down the price it pays for its inputs, thereby lowering its cost structure. Walmart, for example, is well known for pursuing this strategy. Similarly, by acquiring its competitors, a company gains control over a greater percentage of an industry's product or output. Other things being equal, the company then has more power to raise prices and profits because customers have less choice of suppliers and are more dependent on the company for their products—something both Oracle and SAP are striving for to protect their customer base. When a company has greater ability to raise prices to buyers or bargain down the price paid for inputs, it has obtained increased market power.

Problems with Horizontal Integration

Although horizontal integration can strengthen a company's business model in several ways, there are problems, limitations, and dangers associated with pursuing this corporate-level strategy. *Implementing* a horizontal integration strategy is not an easy task for managers. As we discuss in Chapter 10, there are several reasons why mergers and acquisitions may fail to result in higher profitability: problems associated with merging very different company cultures, high management turnover in the acquired company when the acquisition is a hostile one, and a tendency of managers to overestimate the potential benefits from a merger or acquisition and underestimate the problems involved in merging their operations.

When a company uses horizontal integration to become a dominant industry competitor, in an attempt to keep using the strategy to continue to grow business, the company comes into conflict with the Federal Trade Commission (FTC), the government agency responsible for enforcing antitrust laws. Antitrust authorities are concerned about the potential for abuse of market power; more competition is generally better for consumers than less competition. The FTC is concerned when a few companies within one industry try to make acquisitions that will allow them to raise consumer prices above the level that would exist in a more competitive situation, and thus abuse their market power. The FTC also wishes to prevent dominant companies from using their market power to crush potential competitors, for example, by cutting prices when a new competitor enters the industry and forcing the competitor out of business, then raising prices after the threatening company has been eliminated.

Because of these concerns, any merger or acquisition the FTC perceives as creating too much consolidation, and the *potential* for future abuse of market power, may, for antitrust reasons, be blocked. The proposed merger between the two dominant satellite radio companies Sirius and XM was blocked for months until it became clear that customers had many other ways to obtain high-quality radio programming, for example, through their computers and cell phones, so substantial competition would still exist in the industry. In 2011, AT&T's attempt to acquire T-Mobile was facing similar hurdles, although as the opening case discussed, airlines have been permitted to merge in order to reduce their cost structures.

Vertical Integration: Entering New Industries to Strengthen the "Core" Business Model

Many companies that use horizontal integration to strengthen their business model and improve their competitive position also use the corporate-level strategy of vertical integration for the same purpose. When pursuing vertical integration, however, a company is entering new industries to support the business model of its "core" industry, that is, the industry which is the primary source of its competitive advantage and profitability. At this point, therefore, a company must formulate a multibusiness model that explains how entry into a new industry using vertical integration will enhance its long-term profitability. The model that justifies the pursuit of vertical integration is based on a company entering industries that *add value* to its core products because this increases product differentiation and/or lowers its cost structure, thus increasing its profitability.

A company pursuing a strategy of **vertical integration** expands its operations either backward into an industry that produces inputs for the company's products (*backward vertical integration*) or forward into an industry that uses, distributes, or sells the company's products (*forward vertical integration*). To enter an industry, it may establish its own operations and build the value chain needed to compete

Vertical integration

When a company expands its operations either backward into an industry that produces inputs for the company's products (*backward vertical integration*) or forward into an industry that uses, distributes, or sells the company's products.

effectively in that industry, or it may acquire a company that is already in the industry. A steel company that supplies its iron ore needs from company-owned iron ore mines illustrates backward integration. A PC maker that sells its laptops through company-owned retail outlets illustrates forward integration. For example, Apple entered the retail industry in 2001 when it decided to establish a chain of Apple stores to sell its PCs and iPods. IBM is a highly vertically integrated company; it integrated backward into the chip and memory disk industry to produce the components that work inside its mainframes and servers, and integrated forward into the computer software and consulting services industries.

Figure 9.1 illustrates four *main* stages in a typical raw materials-to-customer value-added chain. For a company based in the final assembly stage, backward integration means moving into component parts manufacturing and raw materials production. Forward integration means moving into distribution and sales (retail). At each stage in the chain, *value is added* to the product, meaning that a company at one stage takes the product produced in the previous stage and transforms it in some way so that it is worth more to a company at the next stage in the chain and, ultimately, to the customer. It is important to note that each stage of the value-added chain is a separate industry or industries in which many different companies are competing. Moreover, within each industry, every company has a value chain composed of the value-creation activities we discussed in Chapter 3: R&D, production, marketing, customer service, and so on. In other words, we can think of a value chain that runs *across* industries, and embedded within that are the value chains of companies *within* each industry.

As an example of the value-added concept, consider how companies in each industry involved in the production of a PC contribute to the final product (Figure 9.2). The first stage in the chain includes raw materials companies that make specialty ceramics, chemicals, and metal, such as Kyocera of Japan, which manufactures the ceramic substrate for semiconductors. Companies at the first stage in the chain sell their products to the makers of PC component products, such as Intel and AMD, who transform the ceramics, chemicals, and metals they purchase into PC components such as microprocessors, disk drives, and memory chips. In the process, companies *add value* to the raw materials they purchase. At the third stage, the manufactured components are then sold to PC makers such as Apple, Dell, and HP, and these companies decide which of the components to purchase and assemble to *add value* to the final PCs (that they make or outsource to a contract manufacturer).

Figure 9.1 Stages in the Raw-Materials-to-Customer Value-Added Chain

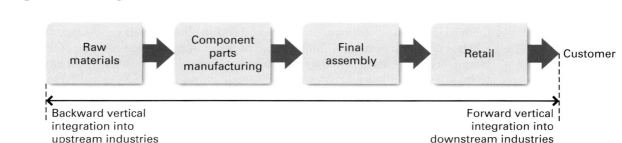

Figure 9.2 The Raw-Materials-to-Customer Value-Added Chain in the PC Industry

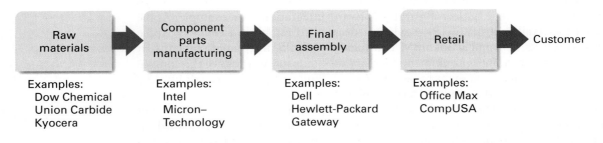

Examples:
Dow Chemical
Union Carbide
Kyocera

Examples:
Intel
Micron–
Technology

Examples:
Dell
Hewlett-Packard
Gateway

Examples:
Office Max
CompUSA

© Cengage Learning 2013

At stage four, the finished PCs are then either sold directly to the final customer over the Internet, or sold to retailers such as Best Buy and Staples, which distribute and sell them to the final customer. Companies that distribute and sell PCs also *add value* to the product because they make the product accessible to customers and provide customer service and support.

Thus, companies in different industries add value at each stage in the raw-materials-to-customer chain. Viewed in this way, vertical integration presents companies with a choice about (and within) which industries in the raw-materials-to-customer chain to operate and compete. This choice is determined by how much establishing operations at a stage in the value chain will increase product differentiation or lower costs—and therefore increase profitability—as we discuss in the following.

Increasing Profitability through Vertical Integration

As noted earlier, a company pursues vertical integration to strengthen the business model of its original or core business and to improve its competitive position.[2] Vertical integration increases product differentiation, lowers costs, or reduces industry competition when it (1) facilitates investments in efficiency-enhancing specialized assets, (2) protects product quality, and (3) results in improved scheduling.

Facilitating Investments in Specialized Assets A specialized asset is one that is designed to perform a specific task and whose value is significantly reduced in its next-best use.[3] The asset may be a piece of equipment that has a firm-specific use or the know-how or skills that a company or employees have acquired through training and experience. Companies invest in specialized assets because these assets allow them to lower their cost structure or to better differentiate their products, which facilitates premium pricing. A company might invest in specialized equipment to lower manufacturing costs, as Toyota does, for example, or it might invest in an advanced technology that allows it to develop better-quality products than its rivals, as Apple does. Thus, specialized assets can help a company achieve a competitive advantage at the business level.

Just as a company invests in specialized assets in its own industry to build competitive advantage, it is often necessary that suppliers invest in specialized assets to produce the inputs that a specific company needs. By investing in these assets, a supplier can make higher-quality inputs that provide its customers with a differentiation advantage, or inputs at a lower cost so it can charge its customers a lower price to keep their business. However, it is often difficult to persuade companies in adjacent stages of the raw materials-to-customer value-added chain to make investments in specialized assets. Often, to realize the benefits associated with such investments, a company must vertically integrate and enter into adjacent industries and invest its own resources. Why does this happen?

Imagine that Ford has developed a unique energy-saving electrical engine system that will dramatically increase fuel efficiency and differentiate Ford's cars from those of its rivals, giving it a major competitive advantage. Ford must decide whether to make the system in-house (vertical integration) or contract with a supplier such as a specialist outsourcing manufacturer to make the new engine system. Manufacturing these new systems requires a substantial investment in specialized equipment that can be used only for this purpose. In other words, because of its unique design, the equipment cannot be used to manufacture any other type of electrical engine for Ford or any other carmaker. Thus this is an investment in specialized assets.

Consider this situation from the perspective of the outside supplier deciding whether or not to make this investment. The supplier might reason that once it has made the investment, it will become dependent on Ford for business because *Ford is the only possible customer for the electrical engine made by this specialized equipment.* The supplier realizes that this puts Ford in a strong bargaining position and that Ford might use its buying power to demand lower prices for the engines. Given the risks involved, the supplier declines to make the investment in specialized equipment.

Now consider Ford's position. Ford might reason that if it outsources production of these systems to an outside supplier, it might become too dependent on that supplier for a vital input. Because specialized equipment is required to produce the engine systems, Ford cannot switch its order to other suppliers. Ford realizes that this increases the bargaining power of the supplier, which might use its bargaining power to demand higher prices.

The situation of *mutual dependence* that would be created by the investment in specialized assets makes Ford hesitant to allow outside suppliers to make the product and makes suppliers hesitant to undertake such a risky investment. The problem is a lack of trust—neither Ford nor the supplier can trust the other to operate fairly in this situation. The lack of trust arises from the risk of **holdup**; that is, being taken advantage of by a trading partner *after* the investment in specialized assets has been made.[4] Because of this risk, Ford reasons that the only cost-effective way to get the new engine systems is for it to make the investment in specialized assets and manufacture the engine in-house.

To generalize from this example, if achieving a competitive advantage requires one company to make investments in specialized assets so it can trade with another, *the risk of holdup* may serve as a deterrent, and the investment may not take place. Consequently, the potential for higher profitability from specialization will be lost. To prevent such loss, companies vertically integrate into adjacent stages in the value chain. Historically, the problems surrounding specific assets have driven automobile companies to vertically integrate backward into the production of component parts, steel companies to vertically integrate backward into the production of iron, computer companies to vertically integrate backward into chip production, and aluminum companies to vertically integrate backward into bauxite mining. The way specific asset issues have led to vertical integration in the global aluminum industry is discussed in Strategy in Action 9.2.

Holdup

When a company is taken advantage of by another company it does business with after it has made an investment in expensive specialized assets to better meet the needs of the other company.

STRATEGY IN ACTION

Specialized Assets and Vertical Integration in the Aluminum Industry

The metal content and chemical composition of bauxite ore, used to produce aluminum, vary from deposit to deposit, so each type of ore requires a specialized refinery—that is, the refinery must be designed for a particular type of ore. Running one type of bauxite through a refinery designed for another type reportedly increases production costs from 20% to 100%. Thus, the value of an investment in a specialized aluminum refinery and the cost of the output produced by that refinery depend on receiving the right kind of bauxite ore.

Imagine that an aluminum company must decide whether to invest in an aluminum refinery designed to refine a certain type of ore. Also assume that the ore is extracted by a company that owns a single bauxite mine. Using a different type of ore would raise production costs by 50%. Therefore, the value of the aluminum company's investment is dependent on the price it must pay the bauxite company for this material. Recognizing this, once the aluminum company has made the investment in a new refinery, what is to stop the bauxite company from raising prices? Nothing. Once it has made the

investment, the aluminum company is locked into its relationship with its bauxite supplier. The bauxite supplier can increase prices because it knows that as long as the increase in the total production costs of the aluminum company is less than 50%, the aluminum company will continue to buy its ore. Thus, once the aluminum company has made the investment, the bauxite supplier can *hold up* the aluminum company.

How can the aluminum company reduce the risk of holdup? The answer is by purchasing the bauxite supplier. If the aluminum company can purchase the bauxite supplier's mine, it no longer needs to fear that bauxite prices will be increased after the investment in an aluminum refinery has been made. In other words, vertical integration eliminates the risk of holdup, making the specialized investment worthwhile. In practice, it has been argued that these kinds of considerations have driven aluminum companies to pursue vertical integration to such a degree that, according to one study, more than 90% of the total volume of bauxite is transferred within vertically integrated aluminum companies.

Source: J.F. Hennart, "Upstream Vertical Integration in the Aluminum and Tin Industries," *Journal of Economic Behavior and Organization* 9 (1988): 281–299; www.alcoa.com, 2011.

Enhancing Product Quality By entering industries at other stages of the value-added chain, a company can often enhance the quality of the products in its core business and strengthen its differentiation advantage. For example, the ability to control the reliability and performance of complex components such as engine and transmission systems may increase a company's competitive advantage in the luxury sedan market and enable it to charge a premium price. Conditions in the banana industry also illustrate the importance of vertical integration in maintaining product quality. Historically, a problem facing food companies that import bananas has been the variable quality of delivered bananas, which often arrive on the shelves of U.S. supermarkets too ripe or not ripe enough. To correct this problem, major U.S. food companies such as Del Monte have integrated backward and now own banana plantations, putting them in control over the banana supply. As a result, they can distribute and sell bananas of a standard quality at the optimal time to better satisfy customers. Knowing they can rely on the quality of these brands, customers are also willing to pay more for them. Thus, by vertically integrating backward into plantation ownership, banana companies have built customer confidence, which has, in turn, enabled them to charge a premium price for their product.

The same considerations can promote forward vertical integration. Ownership of retail outlets may be necessary if the required standards of after-sales service for complex products are to be maintained. For example, in the 1920s, Kodak owned the retail outlets that distributed its photographic equipment because the company felt that few existing retail outlets had the skills necessary to sell and service its complex equipment. By the 1930s, new retailers had emerged that could provide satisfactory distribution and service for Kodak products, so it left the retail industry.

McDonald's has also used vertical integration to protect product quality and increase efficiency. By the 1990s, McDonald's faced a problem: after decades of rapid growth, the fast food market was beginning to show signs of market saturation. McDonald's responded to the slowdown by rapidly expanding abroad. In 1980, 28% of the chain's new restaurant openings were abroad; in 1990 it was 60%, and by 2000, 70%. In 2011, more than 12,000 restaurants in 110 countries exist outside the United States.[5] Replication of its value-creation skills was the key to successful global expansion and spurred the growth of McDonald's in the countries and world regions in which it operates. McDonald's U.S. success was built on a formula of close relations with suppliers, nationwide marketing might, and tight control over store-level operating procedures.

The biggest global problem McDonald's has faced is replicating its U.S. supply chain in other countries; its domestic suppliers are fiercely loyal to the company because their fortunes are closely linked to its success. McDonald's maintains very rigorous specifications for all the raw ingredients it uses—the key to its consistency and quality control. Outside of the United States, however, McDonald's has found suppliers far less willing to make the investments required to meet its specifications. In Great Britain, for example, McDonald's had problems getting local bakeries to produce the hamburger bun. After experiencing quality problems with two local bakeries, McDonald's had to vertically integrate backward and build its own bakeries to supply its British stores. When McDonald's decided to operate in Russia, it found that local suppliers lacked the capability to produce ingredients of the quality it demanded. It was then forced to vertically integrate through the local food industry on a heroic scale, importing potato seeds and bull semen and indirectly managing dairy farms, cattle ranches, and vegetable plots. It also needed to construct the world's largest food-processing plant at a huge cost. In South America, McDonald's also purchased huge ranches in Argentina, upon which it could raise its own cattle. In short, vertical integration has allowed McDonald's to protect product quality and reduce its global cost structure.[6]

Improved Scheduling Sometimes important strategic advantages can be obtained when vertical integration makes it quicker, easier, and more cost-effective to plan, coordinate, and schedule the transfer of a product, such as raw materials or component parts, between adjacent stages of the value-added chain.[7] Such advantages can be crucial when a company wants to realize the benefits of JIT inventory systems. For example, in the 1920s, Ford profited from the tight coordination and scheduling that backward vertical integration made possible. Ford integrated backward into steel foundries, iron ore shipping, and iron ore production—it owned mines in Upper Michigan! Deliveries at Ford were coordinated to such an extent that iron ore unloaded at Ford's steel foundries on the Great Lakes was turned into engine blocks within 24 hours, which lowered Ford's cost structure.

Very often, the improved scheduling that vertical integration makes possible also enables a company to respond better to sudden changes in the supply or demand for a particular product. For example, if demand drops, a company can quickly cut production of components; when demand increases, a company can quickly increase production capacity to more rapidly release its products into the marketplace.[8]

Problems with Vertical Integration

Vertical integration can often be used to strengthen a company's business model and increase profitability. However, the opposite can occur when vertical integration results in (1) an increasing cost structure, (2) disadvantages that arise when technology is changing fast, and (3) disadvantages that arise when demand is unpredictable. Sometimes these disadvantages are so great that vertical integration, rather than increasing profitability, may actually reduce it—in which case a company engages in **vertical disintegration** and exits industries adjacent to its core industry in the industry value chain. For example, Ford, which was highly vertically integrated, sold all its companies involved in mining iron ore and making steel when more efficient and specialized steel producers emerged that were able to supply lower-priced steel.

Increasing Cost Structure   Although vertical integration is often undertaken to lower a company's cost structure, it can raise costs if, over time, a company makes mistakes, such as continuing to purchase inputs from company-owned suppliers when low-cost independent suppliers that can supply the same inputs exist. For decades, for example, GM's company-owned suppliers made more than 60% of the component parts for its vehicles; this figure was far higher than any other major carmaker, which is why GM became such a high-cost carmaker. In the 2000s, it vertically disintegrated by selling off many of its largest component operations, such as Delhi, its electrical components supplier. Thus, vertical integration can be a major disadvantage when company-owned suppliers develop a higher cost structure than those of independent suppliers. Why would a company-owned supplier develop such a high cost structure?

Company-owned or "in-house" suppliers know that they can always sell their components to the car-making divisions of their company—they have a "captive customer." Because company-owned suppliers do not have to compete with independent, outside suppliers for orders, they have much less *incentive* to look for new ways to reduce operating costs or increase component quality. Indeed, in-house suppliers simply pass on cost increases to the car-making divisions in the form of higher **transfer prices**, the prices one division of a company charges other divisions for its products. Unlike independent suppliers, which constantly need to increase their efficiency to protect their competitive advantage, in-house suppliers face no such competition, and the resulting rising cost structure reduces a company's profitability.

The term *bureaucratic costs* refers to the costs of solving the transaction difficulties that arise from managerial inefficiencies and the need to manage the handoffs or exchanges between business units to promote increased differentiation, or to lower a company's cost structure. Bureaucratic costs become a significant component of a company's cost structure because considerable managerial time and effort must be spent to reduce or eliminate managerial inefficiencies, such as those that result when company-owned suppliers lose their incentive to increase efficiency or innovation.

Technological Change   When technology is changing fast, vertical integration may lock a company into an old, inefficient technology and prevent it from changing to a new one that would strengthen its business model.[9] Consider Sony, which had integrated backward to become the leading manufacturer of the now outdated cathode ray tubes (CRT) used in TVs and computer monitors. Because Sony was locked into the outdated CRT technology, it was slow to recognize that the future was flatscreen LCD screens and did not exit the CRT business. Sony's resistance to change in technology forced it to enter into a strategic alliance with Samsung to

---

Vertical disintegration

When a company decides to exit industries either forward or backward in the industry value chain to its core industry to increase profitability.

Transfer pricing

The price that one division of a company charges another division for its products, which are the inputs the other division requires to manufacture its own products.

supply the LCD screens that are used in its BRAVIA TVs. As a result, Sony lost its competitive advantage and has experienced a major loss in TV market share. Thus, vertical integration can pose a serious disadvantage when it prevents a company from adopting new technology, or changing its suppliers or distribution systems to match the requirements of changing technology.

Demand Unpredictability Suppose the demand for a company's core product, such as cars or washing machines, is predictable, and a company knows how many units it needs to make each month or year. Under these conditions, vertical integration allows a company to schedule and coordinate efficiently the flow of products along the industry value-added chain and may result in major cost savings. However, suppose the demand for cars or washing machines wildly fluctuates and is unpredictable. If demand for cars suddenly plummets, the carmaker may find itself burdened with warehouses full of component parts it no longer needs, which is a major drain on profitability—something that has hurt major carmakers during the recent recession. Thus, vertical integration can be risky when demand is unpredictable because it is hard to manage the volume or flow of products along the value-added chain.

For example, a PC maker might vertically integrate backward to acquire a supplier of memory chips so that it can make exactly the number of chips it needs each month. However, if demand for PCs falls because of the popularity of mobile computing devices, the PC maker finds itself locked into a business that is now inefficient because it is not producing at full capacity, and therefore, its cost structure starts to rise.

The Limits of Vertical Integration

Although there are many ways that vertical integration can strengthen a company's business model, it may weaken when (1) bureaucratic costs increase because company-owned suppliers lack the incentive to reduce operating costs and (2) changing technology or uncertain demand reduces a company's ability to change its business model to protect its competitive advantage. It is clear that strategic managers must carefully assess the advantages and disadvantages of expanding the boundaries of their company by entering adjacent industries, either backward (upstream) or forward (downstream), in the industry value-added chain. Moreover, although the decision to enter a new industry to make crucial component parts may have been profitable in the past, it may make no economic sense today because so many low-cost global component parts suppliers exist that compete for the company's business. The risks and returns on investing in vertical integration must be continually evaluated, and companies should be as willing to vertically disintegrate, as vertically integrate, to strengthen their core business model.

Alternatives to Vertical Integration: Cooperative Relationships

Is it possible to obtain the differentiation and cost-savings advantages associated with vertical integration without having to bear the problems and costs associated with this strategy? In other words, is there another corporate-level strategy that managers can use to obtain the advantages of vertical integration while allowing other companies to perform upstream and downstream activities? Today, companies have found that they can realize many of the benefits associated with vertical integration by entering into *long-term cooperative relationships* with companies in industries along the value-added chain. **Strategic alliances** are long-term agreements between two or more companies to jointly develop new products or processes that benefit all companies concerned. The advantages and disadvantages of strategic alliances are discussed in Chapter 8, in which we contrast the benefits of using strategic alliances against those obtained if a company decides to enter only into short-term contracts with other companies.

Short-Term Contracts and Competitive Bidding

Many companies use short-term contracts that last for a year or less to establish the price and conditions under which they will purchase raw materials or components from suppliers or sell their final products to distributors or retailers. A classic example is the carmaker that uses a *competitive bidding strategy,* in which independent component suppliers compete to be chosen to supply a particular component, such as brakes, made to agreed-upon specifications, at the lowest price. For example, GM typically solicits bids from global suppliers to produce a particular component and awards a 1-year contract to the supplier that submits the lowest bid. At the end of the year, the contract is once again put out for competitive bid, and once again the lowest cost supplier is most likely to win the bid.

The advantage of this strategy for GM is that suppliers are forced to compete over price, which drives down the cost of its car components. However, GM has no long-term commitment to outside suppliers—and it drives a hard bargain. For this reason, suppliers are unwilling to make the expensive long-term investment in specialized assets that are required to produce higher-quality or better-designed component parts over time. In addition, suppliers will be reluctant to agree upon the tight scheduling that makes it possible to use a JIT inventory system because this may help GM lower its costs but will increase a supplier's costs and reduce its profitability.

As a result, short-term contracting does not result in the specialized investments that are required to realize differentiation and cost advantages *because it signals a company's lack of long-term commitment to its suppliers.* Of course, this is not a problem when there is minimal need for cooperation, and specialized assets are not required to improve scheduling, product quality, or reduce costs. In this case, competitive bidding may be optimal. However, when there is a need for cooperation, something that is becoming increasingly significant today, the use of short-term contracts and competitive bidding can be a serious drawback.

Strategic Alliances and Long-Term Contracting

Strategic alliances

Long-term agreements between two or more companies to jointly develop new products or processes that benefit all companies which are a part of the agreement.

Unlike short-term contracts, strategic alliances between buyers and suppliers are long-term, cooperative relationships; both companies agree to make specialized investments and work jointly to find ways to lower costs or increase product quality so that they both gain from their relationship. A strategic alliance becomes a *substitute* for vertical integration because it creates a relatively stable long-term partnership that allows both companies to obtain the same kinds of benefits that result from vertical integration. However, it also avoids the problems (bureaucratic costs) that arise from managerial inefficiencies that result when a company owns its own suppliers, such as those that arise because of a lack of incentives, or when a company becomes locked into an old technology even when technology is rapidly changing.

Consider the cooperative relationships that often were established decades ago, which many Japanese carmakers have with their component suppliers (the *keiretsu* system), which exemplifies the benefits of successful long-term contracting. Japanese carmakers and suppliers cooperate to find ways to maximize the "value added" they can obtain from being a part of adjacent stages of the value chain. For example, they do this by jointly implementing JIT inventory systems, or sharing future component-parts designs to improve quality and lower assembly costs. As part of this process, suppliers make substantial investments in specialized assets to better serve the needs of a particular carmaker, and the cost savings that result are shared. Thus, Japanese carmakers have been able to capture many of the benefits of vertical integration without having to enter the component industry.

Similarly, component suppliers also benefit because their business and profitability grow as the companies they supply grow, and they can invest their profits in investing in ever more specialized assets.[10] An interesting example of this is the computer chip outsourcing giant Taiwan Semiconductor Manufacturing Company (TSMC) that makes the chips for many companies, such as NVIDIA, Acer, and AMD. In 2009, the cost of investing in the machinery necessary to build a state-of-the-art chip factory can exceed $10 billion. TSMC is able to make this huge (risky) investment because it has developed cooperative long-term relationships with its computer chip partners. All parties recognize that they will benefit from this outsourcing arrangement, which does not preclude some hard bargaining between TSMC and the chip companies, because all parties want to maximize their profits and reduce their risks. An interesting example of how strategic alliances can go wrong and lead to major problems occurred in 2011, as discussed in Strategy in Action 9.3.

Building Long-Term Cooperative Relationships

How does a company create a long-term strategic alliance with another company when the fear of holdup exists, and the possibility of being cheated arises if one company makes a specialized investment with another company? How do companies such as GM or Nissan manage to develop such profitable, enduring relationships with their suppliers?

There are several strategies companies can adopt to promote the success of a long-term cooperative relationship and lessen the chance that one company will renege on its agreement and cheat the other. One strategy is for the company that makes the specialized investment to demand a *hostage* from its partner. Another is to establish a *credible commitment* from both companies that will result in a trusting, long-term relationship.[11]

Hostage Taking   **Hostage taking** is essentially a means of guaranteeing that each partner will keep its side of the bargain. The cooperative relationship between Boeing and Northrop Grumman illustrates this type of situation. Northrop is a major subcontractor for Boeing's commercial airline division, providing many components for its aircraft. To serve Boeing's special needs, Northrop has had to make substantial investments in specialized assets, and, in theory, because of this investment, Northrop has become dependent on Boeing—which can threaten to change orders to other suppliers as a way of driving down Northrop's prices. In practice, Boeing is highly unlikely to make a change of suppliers because it is, in turn, a major supplier to Northrop's defense division and provides many parts for its Stealth aircraft; it also has made major investments in specialized assets to serve Northrop's needs. Thus, the companies

Hostage taking

A means of exchanging valuable resources to guarantee that each partner to an agreement will keep its side of the bargain.

STRATEGY IN ACTION

Apple, Samsung, and Nokia Battle in the Smartphone Market

For several years, Apple had formed a strategic alliance with Samsung to make the proprietary chips it uses in its iPhones and iPads, which are based on the designs of British chip company ARM Holdings, the company that dominates the smartphone chip industry. Samsung used its low-cost skills in chip-making to make Apple's new chips—despite that Samsung was one of Apple's competitors since it also makes its own smartphones. In 2010, Samsung introduced its new generation of Galaxy smartphones and tablet computers that do not use the same chip as Apple's, but perform similar functions, look similar to Apple's products, and have proven to be very popular with customers globally.

In 2011, Apple decided that its alliance with Samsung had allowed that company to imitate the designs of its smartphones and tablet computers and it sued Samsung, arguing that it had infringing on the patents and specialized knowledge that protected them. The alliance between the two companies quickly dissolved as Samsung countersued Apple, arguing that Apple had infringed upon Samsung's own patented designs, and analysts expect Apple to turn to another company to make its chips in the future. At the same time, Nokia, which has spent $60 billion on R&D to develop new smartphone technology in the last decade, was suing Apple! Nokia claimed that Apple had violated its patents and this had allowed it to innovate the iPhone so quickly. Apple countersued Nokia, arguing that Nokia had violated its patents, in particular the touch-screen technology for which it is now so well known. In June 2011, however, Apple agreed to settle with Nokia and to pay Nokia billions of dollars for the right to license its patents and use its technology. Then, also in June 2011, Apple was awarded a patent that protected its touch-screen technology and it looked like a new round of lawsuits would begin between these smartphone companies to dominate this highly profitable and growing market.

Sources: www.samsung.com, 2011; www.nokia.com, 2011; www.apple.com, 2011.

---

are *mutually dependent*; each company holds a hostage—the specialized investment the other has made. Thus, Boeing is unlikely to renege on any pricing agreements with Northrop because it knows that Northrop would respond the same way.

Credible Commitments   A **credible commitment** is a believable promise or pledge to support the development of a long-term relationship between companies. Consider the way GE and IBM developed such a commitment. GE is one of the major suppliers of advanced semiconductor chips to IBM, and many of the chips are customized to IBM's requirements. To meet IBM's specific needs, GE has had to make substantial investments in specialized assets that have little other value. As a consequence, GE is dependent on IBM and faces a risk that IBM will take advantage of this dependence to demand lower prices. In theory, IBM could back up its demand by threatening to switch its business to another supplier. However, GE reduced this risk by having IBM enter into a contractual agreement that committed IBM to purchase chips from GE for a 10-year period. In addition, IBM agreed to share the costs of the specialized assets needed to develop the customized chips, thereby reducing the risks associated with GE's investment. Thus, by publicly committing itself to a long-term contract and putting some money into the chip development process, IBM made a *credible commitment* that it would continue to purchase chips from GE. When a company violates a credible commitment with its partners, the results can be dramatic, as discussed in Strategy in Action 9.4.

Credible commitment

A believable promise or pledge to support the development of a long-term relationship between companies.

Maintaining Market Discipline   Just as a company pursuing vertical integration faces the problem that its company-owned suppliers might become inefficient, a company that forms a strategic alliance with an independent component supplier runs the

STRATEGY IN ACTION

Ebay's Changing Commitment to Its Sellers

Since its founding in 1995, eBay has always cultivated good relationships with the millions of sellers that advertise their goods for sale on its Website. Over time, however, to increase its revenues and profits, eBay has steadily increased the fees it charges sellers to list their products on its sites, to insert photographs, to use its PayPal online payment service, and for other additional services. Although this has caused some grumbling among sellers because it reduced their profit margins, eBay increasingly engages in extensive advertising to attract millions more buyers to its Website, so sellers can receive better prices and also increase their total profits. As a result, they remained largely satisfied with eBay's fee structure.

These policies changed when a new CEO, John Donohue, took the place of eBay's long-time CEO, Meg Whitman, who had built the company into a dot.com giant. By 2008, eBay's profits had not increased rapidly enough to keep its investors happy, and its stock price plunged. To increase performance, one of Donohue's first moves was to announce a major overhaul of eBay's fee structure and feedback policy. The new fee structure would reduce upfront seller listing costs, but increase back-end commissions on completed sales and payments. For smaller sellers that already had thin profit margins, these fee hikes were painful. In addition, in the future, eBay announced it would block sellers from leaving negative feedback about buyers—feedback such as buyers didn't pay for the goods they purchased, or buyers took too long to pay for goods. The feedback system that eBay had originally developed had been a major source of its success; it allowed buyers to be certain they were dealing with reputable sellers—and vice versa. All sellers and buyers have feedback scores that provide them with a reputation as good—or bad—individuals to do business with, and these scores helped reduce the risks involved in online transactions. Donohue claimed this change was implemented in order to improve the buyer's experience because many buyers had complained that if

they left negative feedback for a seller, the seller would then leave negative feedback for the buyer!

Together, however, throughout 2009, these changes resulted in conflict between eBay and its millions of sellers, who perceived they were being harmed by these changes. Their bad feelings resulted in a revolt. Blogs and forums all over the Internet were filled with messages claiming that eBay had abandoned its smaller sellers, and was pushing them out of business in favor of high-volume "powersellers" who contributed more to eBay's profits. Donohue and eBay received millions of hostile e-mails, and sellers threatened they would do business elsewhere, such as on Amazon.com and Yahoo!, two companies that were both trying to break into eBay's market. Sellers also organized a 1-week boycott of eBay during which they would list no items with the company to express their dismay and hostility! Many sellers did shut down their eBay online storefronts and moved to Amazon.com, which claimed in 2011 that its network of sites had overtaken eBay in monthly unique viewers or "hits" for the first time. The bottom line was that the level of commitment between eBay and its sellers had fallen dramatically; the bitter feelings produced by the changes eBay had made were likely to result in increasing problems that would hurt its future performance.

Realizing that his changes had backfired, Donohue reversed course and eliminated several of eBay's fee increases and revamped its feedback system; sellers and buyers can now respond to one another's comments in a fairer way. These changes did improve hostility and smooth over the bad feelings between sellers and eBay, but the old "community relationship" it had enjoyed with sellers in its early years largely disappeared. As this example suggests, finding ways to maintain cooperative relationships—such as by testing the waters in advance and asking sellers for their reactions to fee and feedback changes—could have avoided many of the problems that arose.

Sources: www.eBay.com, 2011.

risk that its alliance partner might become inefficient over time, resulting in higher component costs or lower quality. This also happens because the outside supplier knows it does not need to compete with other suppliers for the company's business. Consequently, a company seeking to form a mutually beneficial, long-term strategic alliance needs to possess some kind of power that it can use to discipline its partner—should the need arise.

A company holds two strong cards over its supplier partner. First, all contracts, including long-term contracts, are periodically renegotiated, usually every 3–5 years, so the supplier knows that if it fails to live up to its commitments, its partner may refuse to renew the contract. Second, many companies that form long-term relationships with suppliers use **parallel sourcing policies**—that is, they enter into long-term contracts with at least *two* suppliers for the *same* component (this is Toyota's policy, for example).[12] This arrangement protects a company against a supplier that adopts an uncooperative attitude because the supplier knows that if it fails to comply with the agreement, the company can switch *all* its business to its other supplier partner. When both the company and its suppliers recognize that the parallel sourcing policy allows a supplier to be replaced at short notice, most suppliers behave because the policy brings market discipline into their relationship.

The growing importance of JIT inventory systems as a way to reduce costs and enhance quality and differentiation is increasing the pressure on companies to form strategic alliances in a wide range of industries. The number of strategic alliances formed each year, especially global strategic alliances, is increasing, and the popularity of vertical integration is falling because so many low-cost global suppliers exist in countries like Malaysia, Korea, and China.

Strategic Outsourcing

Vertical integration and strategic alliances are alternative ways of managing the value chain *across industries* to strengthen a company's core business model. However, just as low-cost suppliers of component parts exist, so today many *specialized companies* exist that can perform one of a company's *own value-chain activities* in a way that contributes to a company's differentiation advantage or that lowers its cost structure. For example, one specialist chip outsourcer, Taiwanese giant TSMC was discussed earlier; two other huge global contract manufacturers are Flextronics and Jabil Circuit.

Strategic outsourcing is the decision to allow one or more of a company's value-chain activities or functions to be performed by independent specialist companies that focus all their skills and knowledge on just one kind of activity. The activity to be outsourced may encompass an entire function, such as the manufacturing function, or it may be just one kind of activity that a function performs. For example, many companies outsource the management of their pension systems while keeping other HRM activities within the company. When a company chooses to outsource a value-chain activity, it is choosing to focus on a *fewer* number of value-creation activities to strengthen its business model.

There has been a clear move among many companies to outsource activities that managers regard as being "noncore" or "nonstrategic," meaning they are not a source of a company's distinctive competencies and competitive advantage.[13] The vast majority of companies outsource manufacturing or some other value-chain activity to domestic or overseas companies today; some estimates are that over 60% of all global product manufacturing is outsourced to manufacturing specialists because of pressures to reduce costs. Some well-known companies that outsource include Nike, which does not make its athletic shoes; Gap Inc., which does not make its jeans and clothing; and Apple, which assembles none of its own products. These products are made under contract at low-cost, global locations by contract manufacturers that specialize in low-cost assembly—and many problems can arise as a result, as Strategy in Action 9.5 discusses.

Parallel sourcing policy

A policy in which a company enters into long-term contracts with at least two suppliers for the same component to prevent any problems of opportunism.

Strategic outsourcing

The decision to allow one or more of a company's value-chain activities to be performed by independent, specialist companies that focus all their skills and knowledge on just one kind of activity to increase performance.

STRATEGY IN ACTION

Apple Tries to Protect its New Products and the Workers Who Make Them

Apple's PCs and mobile computing devices are assembled by huge specialist outsourcing companies abroad, especially Foxconn, a subsidiary of Taiwan's giant outsourcer, Hon Hai Precision Industry controlled by its secretive multibillionaire CEO, Terry Gou. Foxconn operates several huge factories in mainland China that each employ hundreds of thousands of workers.

Apple has long been known for its concern for secrecy; it strives to keep the details of its new or improved products, such as its updated iPhone4S launched in October 2011, hidden while under development. Steve Job's, who also passed away in October 2011, was always concerned to protect Apple's secrets. His concern for security led Apple to sue a college student who published a Website that had obtained details of its future products; it has also brought legal action against many bloggers who reveal details about its new products. Even in its own U.S. product engineering units Apple has strict rules that prevent engineers from discussing the project they are working on with engineers from other units to prevent information flowing between engineering units and so protect product secrecy.

Apple has also developed uncompromising rules that govern how its outsourcers should protect product secrecy. To keep its business, outsourcers like Foxconn go to extreme lengths to follow Apple's rules and follow stringent security guidelines in their manufacturing plants to keep the details of Apple's new products secret. For example, Apple dictates that the final product should not be assembled until as late as possible to meet its launch date; so while workers learn how to assemble components, they have no idea what collection of components will go into the final product. Also, Foxconn strictly controls its factories to make it easier to enforce such rules. For example, Foxconn's massive plant in Longhua, China employs over 350,000 workers who are discouraged from leaving the factory; it offers them a full array of low-cost services such as canteens, dormitories, and recreational facilities. If employees leave the plant they are searched and metal detectors are used to ensure they do not take components with them, and they are also scanned when they return. Truck drivers who deliver components to the factory are also scanned, as well as anyone else who enters the factory. Apple's contracts include a confidentiality clause with stiff penalties in the event of a security breach, and

Apple's inspectors perform surprise factory visits to ensure outsourcers follow its rules.

While Apple insists its outsourcers create elaborate "secrecy" walls around their assembly plants, these same walls make it much more difficult to enforce the extensive and well-publicized rules Apple has developed regarding the fair and equitable treatment of employees who work in these gigantic "sweatshops." For example, in 2006, after reports claimed Foxconn was not following Apple's rules regarding employee treatment, Apple audited its factories and found many violations that were never publicly disclosed. Apple has been criticized for allowing its products to be made at plants with poor employment practices—despite the fact that it claims to enforce many rules governing how employees should be treated. In 2010, Apple announced that new audits had revealed that child labor had been used in Foxconn's and other Chinese factories that made its iPods and other electronic devices: "In each of the three facilities, we required a review of all employment records for the year as well as a complete analysis of the hiring process to clarify how under-age people had been able to gain employment." Also, Apple admitted that sweatshop-like conditions existed inside these factories and at least 55 of the 102 factories had ignored rules that employees should work no more than 60 hours per week. Apple said another of its outsourcers had repeatedly falsified its records to conceal child labor practices and long employee hours; it terminated all contracts with that company: "When we investigated, we uncovered records and conducted worker interviews that revealed excessive working hours and 7 days of continuous work."

Apple's ethical position came under increased scrutiny in 2010 when it was widely publicized that at Foxconn's biggest factory in Shenzhen, which assembles Apple's iPhone, 11 workers had committed suicide by jumping off buildings within a period of 12 months. Once again Apple sent inspectors, including its COO, to investigate and within months Foxconn's Terry Gou announced that it would almost double workers' wages and improve working conditions to improve employee morale. These circumstances beg the questions: Which rules does Apple spend the most time and effort to develop and enforce? Which rules does it regard as being most important—the rules that protect the secrecy of its products, or the rules that protect the rights of the workers who make those products?

Source: www.apple.com, 2011.

Although manufacturing is the most common form of strategic outsourcing, as we noted earlier, many other kinds of noncore activities are also outsourced. Microsoft has long outsourced its entire customer technical support operation to an independent company, as does Dell. Both companies have extensive customer support operations in India staffed by skilled operatives who are paid a fraction of what their U.S. counterparts earn. BP outsourced almost all of its human resource function to Exult, a San Antonio company, in a 5-year deal worth $600 million; a few years later Exult won a 10-year, $1.1 billion contract to handle HRM activities for all Bank of America's 150,000 employees. Similarly, American Express outsourced its entire IT function to IBM in a 7-year deal worth $4 billion, and the IT outsourcing market in North America was worth more than $250 billion by 2009.[14] In 2006, IBM announced it was outsourcing its purchasing function to an Indian company to save $2 billion a year, and it has steadily increased its use of outsourcing ever since. For example, in 2009, IBM announced it would lay off 5,000 IT employees in the United States and move their jobs to India.[15]

Companies engage in strategic outsourcing to strengthen their business models and increase their profitability. The process of strategic outsourcing typically begins with strategic managers identifying the value-chain activities that form the basis of a company's competitive advantage; these are obviously kept within the company to protect them from competitors. Managers then systematically review the noncore functions to assess whether independent companies that specialize in those activities can perform them more effectively and efficiently. Because these companies specialize in particular activities, they can perform them in ways that lower costs or improve differentiation. If managers decide there are differentiation or cost advantages, these activities are outsourced to those specialists.

This is illustrated in Figure 9.3, which shows the primary value-chain activities and boundaries of a company before and after it has pursued strategic outsourcing. In this example, the company decided to outsource its production and customer service

Figure 9.3   Strategic Outsourcing of Primary Value Creation Functions

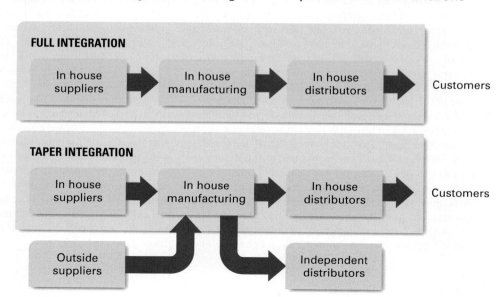

functions to specialist companies, leaving only R&D and marketing and sales within the company. Once outsourcing has been executed, the relationships between the company and its specialists are then often structured as long-term contractual relationships, with rich information sharing between the company and the specialist organization to which it has contracted the activity. The term **virtual corporation** has been coined to describe companies that have pursued extensive strategic outsourcing.[16]

Benefits of Outsourcing

Strategic outsourcing has several advantages. It can help a company to (1) lower its cost structure, (2) increase product differentiation,[17] and (3) focus on the distinctive competencies that are vital to its long-term competitive advantage and profitability.

Lower Cost Structure Outsourcing will reduce costs when the price that must be paid to a specialist company to perform a particular value-chain activity is less than what it would cost the company to internally perform that activity in-house. Specialists are often able to perform an activity at a lower cost than the company, because they are able to realize scale economies or other efficiencies not available to the company. For example, performing HRM activities, such as managing benefit and pay systems, requires a significant investment in sophisticated HRM IT; purchasing these IT systems represents a considerable fixed cost for one company. But, by aggregating the HRM IT needs of many individual companies, companies that specializes in HRM, such as Exult and Paychex, can obtain huge economies of scale in IT that any single company could not hope to achieve. Some of these cost savings are then passed to the client companies in the form of lower prices, which reduces their cost structure. A similar dynamic is at work in the contract manufacturing business. Once again, manufacturing specialists like Foxconn, Flextronics, and Jabil Circuit make large capital investments to build efficient-scale manufacturing facilities, but then are able to spread those capital costs over a huge volume of output, and drive down unit costs so that they can make a specific product—an Apple iPod or Motorola XOOM, for example—at a lower cost than the company.

Specialists are also likely to obtain the cost savings associated with learning effects much more rapidly than a company that performs an activity just for itself (see Chapter 4 for a review of learning effects). For example, because a company like Flextronics is manufacturing similar products for several different companies, it is able to build up *cumulative* volume more rapidly, and it learns how to manage and operate the manufacturing process more efficiently than any of its clients could. This drives down the specialists' cost structure and also allows them to charge client companies a lower price for a product than if they made that product in-house.

Specialists are also often able to perform activities at lower costs than a specific company because many are based in low-cost global locations. Nike, for example, outsources the manufacture of its running shoes to companies based in China because of much lower wage rates—although wages have doubled in China since 2010. Still, a Chinese-based specialist can assemble shoes, a very labor-intensive activity, at a much lower cost than could be done in the U S. Although Nike could establish its own operations in China to manufacture running shoes, it would require a major capital investment and limit its ability to switch production to an even lower-cost location later, for example, Vietnam. And many companies are moving to Vietnam because wage rates are lower there. So, for Nike and most other consumer goods companies, outsourcing manufacturing activity to lower costs and give the company the flexibility to switch to a more favorable location if labor costs change is the most efficient way to handle production.

Virtual corporation

When companies pursued extensive strategic outsourcing to the extent that they only perform the central value-creation functions that lead to competitive advantage.

Enhanced Differentiation　A company may also be able to differentiate its final products better by outsourcing certain noncore activities to specialists. For this to occur, the *quality* of the activity performed by specialists must be greater than if that same activity was performed by the company. On the reliability dimension of quality, for example, a specialist may be able to achieve a lower error rate in performing an activity, precisely because it focuses solely on that activity and has developed a strong distinctive competency in it. Again, this is one advantage claimed for contract manufacturers. Companies like Flextronics have adopted Six Sigma methodologies (see Chapter 4) and driven down the defect rate associated with manufacturing a product. This means they can provide more reliable products to their clients, which can now differentiate their products on the basis of their superior quality.

A company can also improve product differentiation by outsourcing to specialists when they stand out on the excellence dimension of quality. For example, the excellence of Dell's U.S. customer service is a differentiating factor, and Dell outsources its PC repair and maintenance function to specialist companies. A customer who has a problem with a product purchased from Dell can get excellent help over the phone, and if there is a defective part in the computer, a maintenance person will be dispatched to replace the part within a few days. The excellence of this service differentiates Dell and helps to guarantee repeat purchases, which is why HP has worked hard to match Dell's level of service quality. In a similar way, carmakers often outsource specific kinds of vehicle component design activities, such as microchips or headlights, to specialists that have earned a reputation for design excellence in this particular activity.

Focus on the Core Business　A final advantage of strategic outsourcing is that it allows managers to focus their energies and their company's resources on performing those core activities that have the most potential to create value and competitive advantage. In other words, companies can enhance their core competencies and are able to push out the value frontier and create more value for their customers. For example, Cisco Systems remains the dominant competitor in the Internet router industry because it has focused on building its competencies in product design, marketing and sales, and supply-chain management. Companies that focus on the core activities essential for competitive advantage in their industry are better able to drive down the costs of performing those activities, and better differentiate their final products.

Risks of Outsourcing

Although outsourcing noncore activities has many benefits, there are also risks associated with it, risks such as holdup and the possible loss of important information when an activity is outsourced. Managers must assess these risks before they decide to outsource a particular activity, although, as we discuss the following, these risks can be reduced when the appropriate steps are taken.

Holdup　In the context of outsourcing, holdup refers to the risk that a company will become too dependent upon the specialist provider of an outsourced activity and that the specialist will use this fact to raise prices beyond some previously agreed-upon rate. As with strategic alliances, the risk of holdup can be reduced by outsourcing to several suppliers and pursuing a parallel sourcing policy, as Toyota and Cisco do. Moreover, when an activity can be performed well by any one of several different providers, the threat that a contract will not be renewed in the future is normally sufficient to keep the chosen provider from exercising bargaining power over the company. For example, although IBM enters into long-term contracts to provide IT services to a wide range of companies, it would be unadvisable to attempt to raise prices after the contract has been signed because it knows full well that such an action would reduce its chance of getting the contract renewed in the future. Moreover, because IBM has many strong competitors in the IT services business, such as Accenture, Capgemini, and HP, it has a very strong incentive to deliver significant value to its clients.

МАКДОНАЛДС

Sign/Alamy

Loss of Information A company that is not careful can lose important competitive information when it outsources an activity. For example, many computer hardware and software companies have outsourced their customer technical support function to specialists. Although this makes good sense from a cost and differentiation perspective, it may also mean that a critical point of contact with the customer, and a source of important feedback, is lost. Customer complaints can be useful pieces of information and valuable inputs into future product design, but if those complaints are not clearly communicated to the company by the specialists performing the technical support activity, the company can lose the information. Again, this is not an argument against outsourcing. Rather, it is an argument for ensuring that there is appropriate communication between the outsourcing specialist and the company. At Dell, for example, a great deal of attention is paid to making sure that the specialist responsible for providing technical support and onsite maintenance collects and communicates all relevant data regarding product failures and other problems to Dell, so that Dell can design better products.

Ethical Dilemma

Google pursued a strategy of horizontal integration and has bought hundreds of small software companies to become the dominant online advertising company and a major software provider for PCs and mobile computing devices. Google has been accused of using its monopoly power to overcome or undermine its rivals, such as Yahoo! and perhaps Groupon, and in 2011, it was under investigation from the FTC. Google's managers have responded that online advertising costs have actually fallen because its search engine technology allows it to better target customers; it has given many products away for free such as its Chrome Web browser and Android software, and dramatically improved other online offerings.

If you were on a committee charged with deciding whether Google has behaved in an unethical manner, what kind of criteria would you use to determine the outcome?

Summary of Chapter

1. A corporate strategy should enable a company, or one or more of its business units, to perform one or more of the value creation functions at a lower cost or in a way that allows for differentiation and a premium price.

2. The corporate-level strategy of horizontal integration is pursued to increase the profitability of a company's business model by (a) reducing costs, (b) increasing the value of the company's products through differentiation, (c) replicating the business model, (d) managing rivalry within the industry to reduce the risk of price warfare, and (e) increasing bargaining power over suppliers and buyers.

3. There are two drawbacks associated with horizontal integration: (a) the numerous pitfalls associated with making mergers and acquisitions and (b) the fact that the strategy can bring a company into direct conflict with antitrust authorities.

4. The corporate-level strategy of vertical integration is pursued to increase the profitability of a company's "core" business model in its original industry. Vertical integration can enable a company to achieve a competitive advantage by helping build barriers to entry, facilitating investments in specialized assets, protecting product quality, and helping to improve scheduling between adjacent stages in the value chain.

5. The disadvantages of vertical integration include increasing bureaucratic costs if a company-owned or in-house supplier becomes lazy or inefficient, and it reduces flexibility when technology is changing fast or demand is uncertain.

6. Entering into a long-term contract can enable a company to realize many of the benefits associated with vertical integration without having to bear the same level of bureaucratic costs. However, to avoid the risks associated with becoming too dependent upon its partner, it needs to seek a credible commitment from its partner or establish a mutual hostage-taking situation.

7. The strategic outsourcing of noncore value creation activities may allow a company to lower its costs, better differentiate its products, and make better use of scarce resources, while also enabling it to respond rapidly to changing market conditions. However, strategic outsourcing may have a detrimental effect if the company outsources important value creation activities or becomes too dependent upon the key suppliers of those activities.

Discussion Questions

1. What value-creation activities should a company outsource to independent suppliers? What are the risks involved in outsourcing these activities?

2. Why was it profitable for GM and Ford to integrate backward into component-parts manufacturing in the past, and why are both companies now buying more of their parts from outside suppliers?

3. What steps would you recommend that a company take to build mutually beneficial long-term cooperative relationships with its suppliers?

4. What is the difference between a company's internal value chain and the industry value chain? What is the relationship between vertical integration and the industry value chain?

5. Under what conditions might horizontal integration be inconsistent with the goal of maximizing profitability?

Practicing Strategic Management

Small Group Exercises

Small-Group Exercise: Comparing Vertical Integration Strategies

Break up into small groups of 3–5 people, and discuss the following scenario. Appoint one group member as a spokesperson who will communicate your findings to the class. Read the following description of the activities of Seagate Technologies and Quantum Corporation, both of which manufacture computer disk drives. On the basis of this description, outline the pros and cons of a vertical integration strategy. Which strategy do you think makes most sense in the context of the computer disk drive industry?

Quantum Corporation and Seagate Technologies are major producers of disk drives for PCs and workstations. The disk drive industry is characterized by sharp fluctuations in the level of demand, intense price competition, rapid technological change, and product life cycles of only 12–18 months. Quantum and Seagate have pursued very different vertical integration strategies to meet this challenge.

Seagate is a vertically integrated manufacturer of disk drives, both designing and manufacturing the bulk of its own disk drives. On the other hand, Quantum specializes in design; it outsources most of its manufacturing to a number of independent suppliers, including, most importantly, Matsushita Kotobuki Electronics (MKE) of Japan. Quantum makes only its newest and most expensive products in-house. Once a new drive is perfected and ready for large-scale manufacturing, Quantum turns over manufacturing to MKE. MKE and Quantum have cemented their partnership over 8 years. At each stage in designing a new product, Quantum's engineers send the newest drawings to a production team at MKE. MKE examines the drawings and proposes changes that make new disk drives easier to manufacture. When the product is ready for manufacture, 8–10 Quantum engineers travel to MKE's plant in Japan for at least 1 month to work on production ramp-up.

Strategy Sign-On

Article File 9

Find an example of a company whose horizontal or vertical integration strategy appears to have dissipated rather than created value. Identify why this has been the case and what the company should do to rectify the situation.

Strategic Management Project: Module 9

This module requires you to assess the horizontal and vertical integration strategy being pursued by your company. With the information you have at your disposal, answer the questions and perform the tasks listed:

1. Has your company ever pursued a horizontal integration strategy? What was the strategic reason for pursuing this strategy?
2. How vertically integrated is your company? In what stages of the industry value-chain does it operate?
3. Assess the potential for your company to increase profitability through vertical integration. In reaching your assessment, also consider the bureaucratic costs of managing vertical integration.
4. On the basis of your assessment in question 3, do you think your company should (a) outsource some operations that are currently performed in-house or (b) bring some operations in-house that are currently outsourced? Justify your recommendations.
5. Is your company involved in any long-term cooperative relationships with suppliers or buyers? If so, how are these relationships structured? Do you think that these relationships add value to the company? Why?
6. Is there any potential for your company to enter into (additional) long-term cooperative relationships with suppliers or buyers? If so, how might these relationships be structured?

CLOSING CASE
News Corp Forges Ahead

News Corp CEO Rupert Murdoch engineered acquisition or divestiture decisions for more than 50 years. Murdoch has created 1 of the 4 largest and most powerful entertainment media companies in the world. What strategies did Murdoch use to create his media empire?[18] Murdoch was born into a newspaper family; his father owned and ran the *Adelaide News,* an Australian regional newspaper, and when his father died in 1952, Murdoch took control. He quickly enlarged the customer base by acquiring more Australian newspapers. One of these had connections to a major British "pulp" newspaper, and Murdoch used a sensational, *National Enquirer*-like, business model to establish his new newspaper, *The Sun,* as a leading British tabloid.

Murdoch's reputation as an entrepreneur grew because he showed that he could create a much higher return (ROIC) on the media assets he controlled than his competitors. This enabled him to borrow increasing amounts of money, which he used to purchase well-known newspapers such as the *British Sunday Telegraph,* and then his first U.S. newspaper, the *San Antonio Express.* Pursuing his sensational business model further, he launched the *National Star.* His growing profits and reputation allowed him to continue to borrow money, and in 1977, he bought the *New York Post.* Four years later, in 1981, he engineered a new coup when he bought *The Times* and *Sunday Times,* Britain's leading conservative publications—a far cry from *The Sun* tabloid.

Murdoch's strategy of horizontal integration through mergers allowed him to create one of the world's biggest newspaper empires. He realized, however, that industries in the entertainment and media sector can be divided into those that provide media content or "software" (newspapers, movies, and television programs) and those that provide the media channels or "hardware" necessary to bring software to customers (movie theaters, TV channels, TV cable, and satellite broadcasting).

Murdoch decided that he could create the most profit by becoming involved in both the media software *and* hardware industries, that is, the entire value chain of the entertainment and media sector. This strategy of vertical integration gave him control over all the different industries, joining together like links in a chain that converted inputs—such as stories—into finished products like newspapers, books, TV shows, and movies.

In the 1980s, Murdoch began purchasing global media companies in both the software and hardware stages of the entertainment sector. He also launched new ventures of his own. For example, sensing the potential of satellite broadcasting, in 1983 he launched Sky, the first satellite TV channel in the United Kingdom. He also began a new strategy of horizontal integration by purchasing companies that owned television stations; for Metromedia, which owned seven stations that reached more than 20% of U.S. households, he paid $1.5 billion. He scored another major coup in 1985 when he bought Twentieth Century Fox Studios, a premium movie content provider. As a result, he had Fox's huge film library and its creative talents to make new films and TV programming.

In 1986, Murdoch decided to create the FOX Broadcasting Company and buy or create his own U.S. network of FOX affiliates that would show programming developed by his own FOX movie studios. After a slow start, the FOX network gained popularity with sensational shows like *The Simpsons*, which was FOX's first blockbuster program. Then, in 1994, FOX purchased the sole rights to broadcast all NFL games for more than $1 billion, thereby shutting out NBC. FOX became the "fourth network," which has forged and, with Murdoch's sensational business model, was one of the first to create the "reality" programming that has been popular in the 2000s.

By 2005, Murdoch's business model, based on strategies of horizontal and vertical integration, had created a global media empire. The company's profitability has ebbed and flowed because of the massive debt needed to fund Murdoch's acquisitions, debt that has frequently brought his company near to financial ruin. However, in 2009, his company is still a market leader because he engineered so many new Internet acquisitions, such as MySpace, Rotten Tomatoes, and other popular Websites that he has used to create even more value from his media assets.[19]

Case Discussion Questions

1. What kind of corporate-level strategies did News Corp pursue to build its multibusiness model?

2. What are the advantages and disadvantages associated with these strategies?

Notes

[1] www.walmart.com, 2011.

[2] This is the essence of Chandler's argument. See A. D. Chandler, *Strategy and Structure* (Cambridge: MIT Press, 1962). The same argument is also made by J. Pfeffer and G. R. Salancik, *The External Control of Organizations* (New York: Harper & Row, 1978). See also K. R. Harrigan, *Strategic Flexibility* (Lexington: Lexington Books, 1985); K. R. Harrigan, "Vertical Integration and Corporate Strategy," *Academy of Management Journal* 28 (1985): 397–425; and F. M. Scherer, *Industrial Market Structure and Economic Performance* (Chicago: Rand McNally, 1981).

[3] O. E. Williamson, *The Economic Institutions of Capitalism*. For recent empirical work that uses this framework, see L. Poppo and T. Zenger, "Testing Alternative Theories of the Firm: Transaction Cost, Knowledge Based, and Measurement Explanations for Make or Buy Decisions in Information Services," *Strategic Management Journal* 19 (1998): 853–878.

[4] Williamson, *Economic Institutions of Capitalism*.

[5] www.mcdonalds.com, 2011.

[6] Ibid.

[7] A. D. Chandler, *The Visible Hand* (Cambridge: Harvard University Press, 1977).

[8] J. Pitta, "Score One for Vertical Integration," *Forbes*, January 18, 1993, 88–89.

[9] Harrigan, *Strategic Flexibility*, 67–87. See also A. Afuah, "Dynamic Boundaries of the Firm: Are Firms Better Off Being

Vertically Integrated in the Face of a Technological Change?" *Academy of Management Journal* 44 (2001): 1121–1228.

[10]X. Martin, W. Mitchell, and A. Swaminathan, "Recreating and Extending Japanese Automobile Buyer-Supplier Links in North America," *Strategic Management Journal* 16 (1995): 589–619; C. W. L. Hill, "National Institutional Structures, Transaction Cost Economizing, and Competitive Advantage," *Organization Science* 6 (1995): 119–131.

[11]Williamson, *Economic Institutions of Capitalism*. See also J. H. Dyer, "Effective Inter-Firm Collaboration: How Firms Minimize Transaction Costs and Maximize Transaction Value," *Strategic Management Journal* 18 (1997): 535–556.

[12]Richardson, "Parallel Sourcing."

[13]W. H. Davidow and M. S. Malone, *The Virtual Corporation* (New York: Harper & Row, 1992).

[14]J. Krane, "American Express Hires IBM for $4 Billion," *Columbian*, February 26, 2002, E2; www.ibm.com, 2011.

[15]www.ibm.com, 2011.

[16]Davidow and Malone, *The Virtual Corporation*.

[17]Ibid; H. W. Chesbrough and D. J. Teece, "When Is Virtual Virtuous? Organizing for Innovation," *Harvard Business Review*, January–February 1996, 65–74; J. B. Quinn, "Strategic Outsourcing: Leveraging Knowledge Capabilities," *Sloan Management Review* (Summer 1999): 9–21.

[18]www.newscorp.com, 2011.

[19]Ibid.

10

Corporate-Level Strategy: Related and Unrelated Diversification

VF Corp. Acquires Timberland to Realize the Benefits from Related Diversification

In June 2011, U.S.-based VF Corp., the global apparel and clothing maker, announced that it would acquire Timberland, the U.S.-based global footwear maker, for $2 billion, which was a 40% premium on Timberland's stock price.[1] VF is the maker of such established clothing brands as Lee and Wrangler Jeans, Nautica, lucy activewear, Kipling, and outdoor apparel makers such as The North Face, JanSport, and Eagle Creek. Timberland is well known for its tough waterproof leather footwear, such as its best-selling hiking boots and its classic boat shoes; it also licenses the right to make clothing and accessories under its brand name. Obviously, Timberland's stockholders were thrilled that they had made a 40% profit overnight on their investment; but why would a clothing maker purchase a footwear company that primarily competes in a different industry?

The reason, according to VF's CEO Eric Wiseman, is that the Timberland deal would be a "transformative" acquisition that would add footwear to VF's fastest-growing division, the outdoor and action sports business, which had achieved a 14% gain in revenues in 2010 and contributed $3.2 billion of VF's total revenues of $7.7 billion.[2] By combining the products of the clothing and footwear division, Wiseman claimed that VF could almost double Timberland's profitability by increasing its global sales by at least 15%. At the same time, the addition of the Timberland brand would increase the sales of VF's outdoor brands such as The North Face by 10%. The result would be a major increase in VF's revenues and profitability—an argument its investors agreed with because while the stock price of a company that acquires another company normally declines after the announcement, VF's stock price soared by 10%!

Why would this merger of two very different companies result in so much more value being created? The first reason is that it would allow the company to offer an extended range of outdoor products—clothing, shoes, backpacks, and accessories—which could all be packaged together, distributed to retailers, and marketed and sold to customers. The result would be substantial cost savings because purchasing, distribution, and marketing costs would now be shared between the different brands or product lines in VF's expanded portfolio. In addition, VF would be able to increasingly differentiate its outdoor products by, for example, linking its brand The North Face with the Timberland brand, so customers purchasing outdoor clothing would be more likely to purchase Timberland hiking boots and related accessories such as backpacks offered by VF's other outdoor brands.

In addition, although Timberland is a well-known popular brand in the United States, it generates more than 50% of its revenues from global sales (especially in high growth markets like China), and it has a niche presence in many countries such as the United Kingdom and Japan.[3] VF only generates 30% of its revenues from global sales; by taking advantage of the commonalities between its outdoor brands, VF argued that purchasing Timberland would increase its sales in overseas markets and also increase the brand recognition and sales of its other primary brands such as Wrangler Jeans and Nautica. For example, hikers could wear VF's Wrangler or Lee Jeans, as well as The North Face clothing, at the same time they put on their Timberland hiking boots. In short, Timberland's global brand cachet and the synergies between the two companies' outdoor lifestyle products would result in major new value creation. Thus, the acquisition would allow VF to increase the global differentiated appeal of all its brands, resulting in lower costs. VF would be able to negotiate better deals with specialist outsourcing companies abroad, and economies of scale would result from reduced global shipping and distribution costs.[4]

CEO Wiseman expects that the addition of Timberland to VF's outdoor and action sports business, which includes brands such as Vans, JanSport, and Eastpak that already make up 50% of the company's total revenues, will grow to more than 65% by 2015, adding $1 billion to its revenues. Given that global sales comprise only 30% of VF's sales, but 50% of Timberland's, the combined company will immediately obtain 35% of its revenue from international markets and allow VF to "build the premier portfolio of outdoor brands." Outdoor clothing, such as fleece vests and hiking pants, was VF's fastest growing segment in 2010 with sales up 16%. In a conference call to analysts Wiseman said that:

"Timberland has been our Number 1 acquisition priority. It knits together two powerful companies into a new global player in the outdoor and action sports space."

Before the Timberland acquisition, VF was highly diversified across brands, product categories, and channels of distribution—another reason analysts expect the combined company to create more value. Timberland owns more than 800 branded stores, for example, especially in outlet malls, and it has a well-established online storefront. The Timberland acquisition will increase the range of products VF can distribute and sell through its many distribution channels, so that many synergies and cost savings will result. In addition, VF allows the managers of each of its brands or divisions to pursue the business-level strategies that will increase their product's differentiated appeal. Because managers of the Timberland brand will be given similar freedom, many new innovative products may be introduced and sold. Finally, although each of its brands or product divisions is given autonomy, Wiseman insists that VF's organizational structure leverages the advantage of centralized purchasing, distribution, and IT to reduce costs across the organization.

Thus, the many advantages of VF's diversification into the shoe business explain why the stock price of both companies shot up after the announcement of the acquisition. Will these value-creation avenues be achieved? Only time will tell as VF's strategic managers attempt to actualize the claimed synergies that will result from the acquisition.

Overview

The Opening Case discusses how VF Corp. acquired Timberland to pursue the corporate-level strategy of related diversification to increase its ability to create value and profitability. VF Corp.'s new *multibusiness model* is based upon giving the managers of each of the company's individual product brands or divisions, such as The North Face, the opportunity to pursue the business model that leads to differentiation and a competitive advantage in the markets in which they operate. At the same time, VF Corp. intends to use the competencies of its central corporate purchasing, distribution, and IT functions to reduce costs and increase global sales.

In this chapter, we continue to discuss how companies can strengthen their business models by pursuing the corporate-level strategies of related and unrelated diversification. A diversification strategy is based upon a company's decision to enter one or more new industries to take advantage of its existing distinctive competencies and business model. We examine the different kinds of multibusiness models upon which related and unrelated diversification are based. Then, we discuss three different ways companies can implement a diversification strategy: internal new ventures, acquisitions, and joint ventures. By the end of this chapter, you will understand the advantages and disadvantages associated with strategic managers' decisions to diversify and enter new markets and industries.

Increasing Profitability through Diversification

Diversification is the process of entering new industries, distinct from a company's core or original industry, to make new kinds of products that can be sold profitably to customers in these new industries. A multibusiness model based on diversification aims to find ways to use a company's existing strategies and distinctive competencies to make products that are highly valued by customers in the new industries it enters. A **diversified company** is one that makes and sells products in two or more different or distinct industries (industries *not* in adjacent stages of an industry value chain as in vertical integration). In each industry a company enters, it establishes an operating division or business unit, which is essentially a self-contained company that makes and sells products to customers in one of more industry market segments. On the other hand, when a company like VF acquires another organization like Timberland, it is buying a company that already has well-established business units or divisions, in this case in the footwear industry. As in the case of the corporate strategies discussed in Chapter 9, a diversification strategy should enable a company or its individual business units to perform one or more of the value-chain functions: (1) at a lower cost, (2) in a way that allows for differentiation and gives the company pricing options, or (3) in a way that helps the company to manage industry rivalry better–*in order to increase profitability*.

The managers of most companies often consider diversification when they are generating *free cash flow*, that is, cash in excess of that required to fund new investments in the company's current business and meet existing debt commitments.[5] In other words, free cash flow is cash beyond that needed to make profitable new investments in its existing business. When a company's successful business model is generating so much free cash flow and profits managers must decide whether to return that cash to shareholders in the form of higher dividend payouts–or to invest it in diversification. That is, to find new industries to enter where they can use their company's capital to create even more free cash flow or profit in the future. In theory, any free cash flow belongs to the company's owners—its shareholders. So, for diversification to be profitable a company's return on investing free cash flow to pursue diversification opportunities, that is, its future ROIC, *must* exceed the return that stockholders could obtain by investing that capital in a diversified portfolio of stocks and bonds. If its future ROIC would not exceed the return from a diversified portfolio it would be in the best interests of shareholders for the company to return excess cash to them through higher dividends, rather than for managers to pursue a diversification strategy. Thus, a diversification strategy is *not* consistent with maximizing returns to shareholders unless the multibusiness model that managers use to justify entry into a new industry (such as VF's strategy discussed in the opening case) will significantly increase the value a company can create so that its stock price will rise in the future.

There are five primary ways in which pursuing a multibusiness model based on diversification can increase company profitability. Diversification can increase profitability when strategic managers (1) transfer competencies between business units in different industries, (2) leverage competencies to create business units in new industries, (3) share resources between business units to realize synergies or economies of scope, (4) use product bundling, and (5) utilize *general* organizational competencies that increase the performance of *all* a company's business units.

Diversification

The process of entering new industries, distinct from a company's core or original industry, to make new kinds of products for customers in new markets.

Diversified company

A company that makes and sells products in two or more different or distinct industries.

Transferring Competencies

Transferring competencies involves taking a distinctive competency developed by a business unit in one industry and implanting it in a business unit operating in another industry. The second business unit is often one a company has acquired. Companies that base their diversification strategy on transferring competencies aim to use one or more of their existing distinctive competencies in a value-chain activity—for example, in manufacturing, marketing, materials management, or R&D—to significantly strengthen the business model of the acquired business unit or company. For example, over time, Philip Morris developed distinctive competencies in product development, consumer marketing, and brand positioning that had made it a leader in the tobacco industry. Sensing a profitable opportunity, it acquired Miller Brewing, which at the time was a relatively small player in the brewing industry. Then, to create valuable new products in the brewing industry, Philip Morris transferred some of its best marketing experts to Miller, where they applied the skills acquired at Philip Morris to turn around Miller's lackluster brewing business (see Figure 10.1). The result was the creation of Miller Light, the first "light" beer, and a marketing campaign that helped to push Miller from number 6 to number 2 in market share in the brewing industry.

Companies that base their diversification strategy on transferring competencies tend to acquire new businesses *related* to their existing business activities because of commonalities between one or more of their value-chain functions. A **commonality** is some kind of skill or attribute, which, when it is shared or used by two or more business units, allows both businesses to operate more effectively and efficiently and create more value for customers.

For example, Miller Brewing was related to Philip Morris's tobacco business because it was possible to create important marketing commonalities; both beer and tobacco are mass market consumer goods in which brand positioning, advertising,

Transferring competencies

The process of taking a distinctive competency developed by a business unit in one industry and implanting it in a business unit operating in another industry.

Commonality

Some kind of skill or competency that when shared by two or more business units allows them to operate more effectively and create more value for customers.

Figure 10.1 Transfer of Competencies at Philip Morris

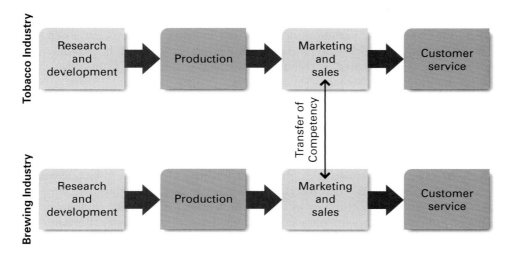

and product development skills are crucial to create successful new products. In general, such competency transfers increase profitability when they either (1) lower the cost structure of one or more of a diversified company's business units or (2) enable one or more of its business units to better differentiate their products, both of which give business unit pricing options to lower a product's price to increase market share or to charge a premium price.

For competency transfers to increase profitability, the competencies transferred must involve value-chain activities that become an important source of a specific business unit's competitive advantage in the future. In other words, the distinctive competency being transferred must have real strategic value. However, all too often companies assume that *any* commonality between their value chains is sufficient for creating value. When they attempt to transfer competencies, they find the anticipated benefits are not forthcoming because the different business units did not share some important attribute in common. For example, Coca-Cola acquired Minute Maid, the fruit juice maker, to take advantage of commonalities in global distribution and marketing, and this acquisition has proved to be highly successful. On the other hand, Coca-Cola once acquired the movie studio, Columbia Pictures, because it believed it could use its marketing prowess to produce blockbuster movies. This acquisition was a disaster, cost Coca-Cola billions in losses, and Columbia was eventually sold to Sony, which was then able to base many of its successful PlayStation games on the hit movies the studio produced.

Leveraging Competencies

Leveraging competencies involves taking a distinctive competency developed by a business unit in one industry and using it to create a *new* business unit or division in a different industry. For example, Apple leveraged its competencies in PC hardware and software to enter the smartphone industry. Once again, the multibusiness model is based on the premise that the set of distinctive competencies that are the source of a company's competitive advantage in one industry might be applied to create a differentiation or cost-based competitive advantage for a new business unit or division in a different industry. For example, Canon used its distinctive competencies in precision mechanics, fine optics, and electronic imaging to produce laser jet printers, which, for Canon, was a new business in a new industry. Its competencies enabled it to produce high-quality (differentiated) laser printers that could be manufactured at a low cost, which created its competitive advantage, and made Canon a leader in the printer industry.

The difference between leveraging competencies and transferring competencies is that leveraging competencies, means an entirely *new* business unit is being created, whereas transferring competencies involves the sharing of competencies between two *existing* businesses. This difference is important because each strategy is based on a different multibusiness model. Companies such as 3M, Apple, and Canon, which leverage competencies to establish new business units, tend to be *technology-based* companies that use their R&D competencies to create new business units and take advantage of opportunities in diverse industries. In contrast, companies that transfer competencies are often the leading companies in one industry that enter new industries by acquiring established companies—such as VF Corp. These companies then transfer their strong set of competencies, for example, in global distribution or marketing, to the acquired companies to increase their competitive advantage and profitability, as Philip Morris did with Miller Brewing.

Leveraging competencies

The process of taking a distinctive competency developed by a business unit in one industry and using it to create a new business unit in a different industry.

Many companies have based their diversification strategy on leveraging their competencies to create new business units in different industries. Microsoft leveraged its skills in software development and marketing to create two business units in new industries, its online network MSN, and Xbox video game units. Microsoft's managers believed this diversification strategy was in the best interests of shareholders because the company's competencies would enable it to attain a competitive advantage in the online and video game industries. The results of this strategy have been mixed; in 2003 when Microsoft first broke its profits down by business unit, it turned out that the software business was generating almost all its profits, and most other business units were losing money! Its competitive situation has improved somewhat since, and its Xbox 360 has captured market share from Sony, although the popularity of the Wii and the emergence of Apple as a dominant competitor has hurt Microsoft. In its online business, the increasing popularity of Google's search engine made Microsoft's Websites far less popular, although it has been fighting back with its Bing search engine. Then, in 2011 it announced that it would acquire Skype, the VOIP phone and video service provider; apparently Skype will differentiate its platform from Google's.

Sharing Resources and Capabilities

A third way in which two or more business units that operate in different industries can increase a diversified company's profitability is when the shared resources and capabilities results in economies of scope, or synergies.[6] **Economies of scope** arise when one or more of a diversified company's business units are able to realize cost-saving or differentiation synergies because they can more effectively pool, share, and utilize expensive resources or capabilities, such as skilled people, equipment, manufacturing facilities, distribution channels, advertising campaigns, and R&D laboratories. If business units in different industries can share a common resource or function, they can collectively lower their cost structure; the idea behind synergies is that $2+2=5$ not 4 in terms of value created.[7] For example, the costs of GE's consumer products advertising, sales, and service activities, reduces costs *across* product lines because they are spread over a wide range of products such as light bulbs, appliances, air conditioning, furnaces. There are two major sources of these cost reductions.

First, when companies can share resources or capabilities across business units, as VF intends to do, it lowers their cost structure compared to a company that operates in only one industry and bears the full costs of developing resources and capabilities. For example, P&G makes disposable diapers, toilet paper, and paper towels, which are all paper-based products that customers value for their ability to absorb fluids without disintegrating. Because these products need the same attribute—absorbency—P&G can share the R&D costs associated with developing and making even more advanced absorbent paper-based products across the three distinct businesses (only two are shown in Figure 10.2). Similarly, because all these products are sold to retailers, P&G can use the same sales force to sell all their products (see Figure 10.2). In contrast, P&G competitors that make only one or two of these products cannot share these costs across industries, so their cost structure is higher. As a result, P&G has lower costs; it can use its marketing function to better differentiate its products, and it achieves a higher ROIC than companies that operate only in one or a few industries—which are unable to obtain economies of scope from the ability to share resources and obtain synergies across business units.

Economies of scope

The synergies that arise when one or more of a diversified company's business units are able to lower costs or increase differentiation because they can more effectively pool, share, and utilize expensive resources or capabilities.

Figure 10.2   Sharing Resources at Proctor & Gamble

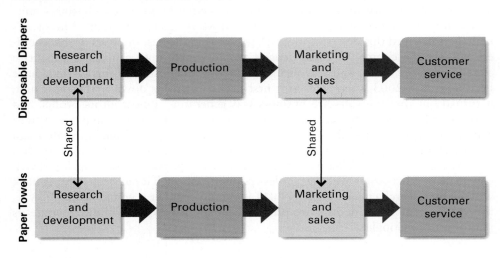

© Cengage Learning 2013

Once again, diversification to obtain economies of scope is possible only when there are *significant* commonalities between one or more of the value-chain functions in a company's different business units or divisions that result in synergies that increase profitability. In addition, managers must be aware that the costs of coordination necessary to achieve synergies or economies of scope within a company may sometimes be *higher* than the value that can be created by such a strategy.[8] Consequently, diversification based on obtaining economies of scope should be pursued only when the sharing of competencies will result in *significant* synergies that will achieve a competitive advantage for one or more of a company's new or existing business units.

Using Product Bundling

In the search for new ways to differentiate products, more and more companies are entering into industries that provide customers with new products that are connected or related to their existing products. This allows a company to expand the range of products it produces in order to be able to satisfy customers' needs for a complete package of related products. This is currently happening in telecommunications in which customers are increasingly seeking package prices for wired phone service, wireless phone service, high-speed access to the Internet, VOIP phone service, television programming, online gaming, video-on-demand, or any combination of these services. To meet this need, large phone companies such as AT&T and Verizon have been acquiring other companies that provide one or more of these services, while cable companies such as Comcast have acquired, or formed strategic alliances, with companies that can offer their customers a package of these services. In 2010, for example, Comcast acquired GE's NBC division to gain control of its library of content programming. The goal, once again, is to bundle products to offer customers lower prices and/or a superior set of services.

Just as manufacturing companies strive to reduce the number of their component suppliers to reduce costs and increase quality, as VF plans to do with Timberland, so the final customer wants to obtain the convenience and reduced price of a bundle of related products—such as from Google or Microsoft's cloud-based commercial, business-oriented online applications. Another example of product bundling comes from the medical equipment industry in which companies that, in the past, made one kind of product, such as operating theater equipment, ultrasound devices, magnetic imaging or X-ray equipment, and have now merged or been acquired to allow a larger diversified company to provide hospitals with a complete range of medical equipment. This industry consolidation has also been driven by hospitals and HMOs that wish to obtain the convenience and lower prices that often follow from forming a long-term contract with a single supplier.

Utilizing General Organizational Competencies

General organizational competencies transcend individual functions or business units and are found at the top or corporate level of a multibusiness company. Typically, **general organizational competencies** are the result of the skills of a company's top managers and functional experts. When these general competencies are present—and many times they are not—they help each business unit within a company perform at a higher level than it could if it operated as a separate or independent company—this increases the profitability of the *entire* corporation, something that VF hopes to achieve as discussed in the opening case.[9] Three kinds of general organizational competencies help a company increase its performance and profitability: (1) entrepreneurial capabilities, (2) organizational design capabilities, and (3) strategic capabilities.

Entrepreneurial Capabilities   A company that generates significant excess cash flow can take advantage of it only if its managers are able to identify new opportunities and act on them to create a stream of new and improved products, in its current industry and in new industries. Some companies seem to have a greater capability to stimulate their managers to act in entrepreneurial ways than others, for example, Apple, 3M, Google, and Samsung.[10]

These companies are able to promote entrepreneurship because they have an organizational culture that stimulates managers to act entrepreneurially. As a result, these companies are able to create profitable new business units more quickly than other companies; this allows them to take advantage of profitable opportunities for diversification. We discuss one of the strategies required to generate profitable new businesses later in this chapter: internal new venturing. For now, it is important to note that to promote entrepreneurship, a company must (1) encourage managers to take risks, (2) give them the time and resources to pursue novel ideas, (3) not punish managers when a new idea fails, and (4) make sure that its free cash flow is not wasted in pursuing too many risky new ventures that have a low probability of generating a profitable return on investment. Strategic managers face a significant challenge in achieving all four of these objectives. On the one hand, a company must encourage risk taking, and on the other hand, it must limit the number of risky ventures in which it engages.

Companies that possess strong entrepreneurial capabilities achieve this balancing act. For example, 3M's goal of generating 40% of its revenues from products introduced within the past 4 years focuses managers' attention on the need to develop new products and enter new businesses. 3M's long-standing commitment to help its

General organizational competencies

Competencies that result from the skills of a company's top managers that help every business unit within a company perform at a higher level than it could if it operated as a separate or independent company.

customers solve problems also ensures that ideas for new businesses are customer focused. The company's celebration of employees who have created successful new businesses helps to reinforce the norm of entrepreneurship and risk taking. Similarly, there is a norm that failure should not be punished but viewed as a learning experience.

Capabilities in Organizational Design   **Organizational design skills** are a result of manager's ability to create a structure, culture, and control systems that motivate and coordinate employees to perform at a high level. Organizational design is a major factor that influences a company's entrepreneurial capabilities; it is also an important determinant of a company's ability to create the functional competencies that give it a competitive advantage. The way strategic managers make organizational design decisions such as how much autonomy to give to managers lower in the hierarchy, what kinds of norms and values should be developed to create an entrepreneurial culture, and even how to design its headquarters buildings to encourage the free flow of ideas, are important determinant of a diversified company's ability to profit from its multibusiness model. Effective organizational structure and controls create incentives that encourage business unit (divisional) managers to maximize the efficiency and effectiveness of their units. Moreover, good organizational design helps prevent strategic managers from missing out on profitable new opportunities, as happens when employees become so concerned to protect their company's competitive position in *existing* industries that they lose sight of new or improved ways to do business and gain profitable opportunities to enter new industries.

The last two chapters of this book look at organizational design in depth. To profit from pursuing the corporate-level strategy of diversification, a company must be able to continuously manage and change its structure and culture to motivate and coordinate its employees to work at a high level and develop the resources and capabilities upon which its competitive advantage depends. The ever-present need to align a company's structure with its strategy is a complex, never-ending task, and only top managers with superior organizational design skills can do it.

Superior Strategic Management Capabilities   For diversification to increase profitability, a company's top managers must have superior capabilities in strategic management. They must possess the intangible, hard-to-define governance skills that are required to manage different business units in a way that enables these units to perform better than they would if they were independent companies.[11] These governance skills are a rare and valuable capability. However, certain CEOs and top managers seem to have them; they have developed the aptitude of managing multiple businesses simultaneously and encouraging the top managers of those business units to devise strategies and achieve superior performance. Examples of CEOs who possess superior strategic management capabilities include Jeffrey Immelt at GE, Steve Jobs at Apple, and Larry Ellison at Oracle.

An especially important governance skill in a diversified company is the ability to diagnose the underlying source of the problems of a poorly performing business unit, and then to understand how to proceed to solve those problems. This might involve recommending new strategies to the existing top managers of the unit or knowing when to replace them with a new management team that is better able to fix the problems. Top managers who have such governance skills tend to be very good at probing business unit managers for information and helping them to think through strategic problems, as the example of United Technologies Corporation (UTC) discussed in Strategy in Action 10.1 suggests.

Organizational design skills

The ability of the managers of a company to create a structure, culture, and control systems that motivate and coordinate employees to perform at a high level.

10.1 STRATEGY IN ACTION

United Technologies Has an "ACE" in Its Pocket

United Technologies Corporation (UTC), based in Hartford, Connecticut, is a *conglomerate*, a company that owns a wide variety of other companies that operate separately in many different businesses and industries. Some of the companies in UTC's portfolio are better known than UTC itself, such as Sikorsky Aircraft Corporation; Pratt & Whitney, the aircraft engine and component maker; Otis Elevator Company; Carrier Air Conditioning; and Chubb, the security and lock maker that UTC acquired in 2003. Today, investors frown upon companies like UTC that own and operate companies in widely different industries. There is a growing perception that managers can better manage a company's business model when the company operates as an independent or stand-alone entity. How can UTC justify holding all these companies together in a conglomerate? Why would this lead to a greater increase in total profitability than if they operated as independent companies? In the last decade, the boards of directors and CEOs of many conglomerates, such as Tyco and Textron, have realized that by holding diverse companies together they were reducing, not increasing, the profitability of their companies. As a result, many conglomerates have been broken up and their individual companies spun off to allow them to operate as separate, independent entities.

UTC's CEO George David claims that he has created a unique and sophisticated multibusiness model that adds value across UTC's diverse businesses. David joined Otis Elevator as an assistant to its CEO in 1975, but within 1 year, UTC acquired Otis.[12] The 1970s was a decade when a "bigger is better" mindset ruled corporate America, and mergers and acquisitions of all kinds were seen as the best way to grow profits. UTC sent David to manage its South American operations and later gave him responsibility for its Japanese operations. Otis had formed an alliance with Matsushita to develop an elevator for the Japanese market, and the resulting "Elevonic 401," after being installed widely in Japanese buildings, proved to be a disaster. It broke down much more often than elevators made by other Japanese companies, and customers were concerned about the reliability and safety of this model.

Matsushita was extremely embarrassed about the elevator's failure and assigned one of its leading total quality management (TQM) experts, Yuzuru Ito, to head a team of Otis engineers to find out why it performed so poorly. Under Ito's direction, all the employees—managers, designers, and production workers—who had produced the elevator analyzed why the elevators were malfunctioning. This intensive study led to a total redesign of the elevator, and when their new and improved elevator was launched worldwide, it met with great success. Otis's share of the global elevator market dramatically increased, and David was named president of UTC in 1992. He was given the responsibility to cut costs across the entire corporation, including its important Pratt & Whitney division, and his success in reducing UTC's cost structure and increasing its ROIC led to his appointment as CEO in 1994.

Now responsible for all of UTC's diverse companies, David decided that the best way to increase UTC's profitability, which had been declining, was to find ways to improve efficiency and quality in *all* its constituent companies. He convinced Ito to move to Hartford and take responsibility for championing the kinds of improvements that had by now transformed the Otis division. Ito began to develop UTC's TQM system, also known as "Achieving Competitive Excellence," or ACE.

ACE is a set of tasks and procedures that are used by employees from the shop floor to top managers to analyze all aspects of the way a product is made. The goal is to find ways to improve *quality and reliability*, to *lower the costs* of making a product and, especially, to find ways to make the next generation of a particular product perform better—in other words, to encourage *technological innovation*. David makes every employee in every function and at every level personally responsible for achieving the incremental, step-by-step gains that result in state-of-the-art innovative and efficient products that allow a company to dominate its industry.

David calls these techniques "process disciplines," and he has used them to increase the performance of all UTC companies. Through these techniques, he has created the extra value for UTC that justifies it owning and operating such a diverse set of businesses. David's success can be seen in the performance that his company has achieved in the decade since he took control: he has quadrupled UTC's earnings per share, and its sales and profits have soared. UTC has been in the top three performers of the companies that make up the Dow Jones industrial average for most of the 2000s, and the company has consistently outperformed GE, another huge conglomerate, in its return to investors.

David and his managers believe that the gains that can be achieved from UTC's process disciplines are never-ending because its own R&D—in which it

STRATEGY IN ACTION (*continued*)

invests more than $2.5 billion a year—is constantly producing product innovations that can help all its businesses. Recognizing that its skills in creating process improvements are specific to manufacturing companies, UTC's strategy is to only acquire companies that make products that can benefit from the use of its ACE program—hence its Chubb acquisition. At the same time, David invests only in companies that have the potential to remain leading companies in their industries and can, therefore, charge above-average prices. His acquisitions strengthen the competencies of UTC's existing businesses. For example, he acquired a company called Sundstrand, a leading aerospace and industrial systems company, and combined it with UTC's Hamilton Aerospace Division to create Hamilton Sundstrand, which is now a major supplier to Boeing and makes products that command premium prices. In October 2011, UTC acquired Goodrich, a major supplier of airline components for over $22 billion to strengthen it aircraft division.

Source: utc.com, 2011

Related to strategic management skills is the ability of the top managers of a diversified company to identify inefficient and poorly managed companies in other industries and then to acquire and restructure them to improve their performance—and thus the profitability of the total corporation. There are several ways to improve the performance of the acquired company. First, the top managers of the acquired company are replaced with a more aggressive top management team. Second, the new top management team sells off expensive assets, such as underperforming divisions, executive jets, and elaborate corporate headquarters; it also terminates managers and employees to reduce the cost structure. Third, the new management team works to devise new strategies to improve the performance of the operations of the acquired business and improve its efficiency, quality, innovativeness, and customer responsiveness.

Fourth, to motivate the new top management team and the other employees of the acquired company to work toward such goals, a company-wide pay-for-performance bonus system linked to profitability is introduced to reward employees at all levels for their hard work. Fifth, the acquiring company often establishes "stretch" goals for employees at all levels; these are challenging, hard-to-obtain goals that force employees at all levels to work to increase the company's efficiency and effectiveness. Finally, the new top management team clearly understands that if they fail to increase their division's performance and meet these stretch goals within some agreed-upon amount of time, they will be replaced. In sum, the system of rewards and sanctions that corporate managers of the acquiring company establish provide the new top managers of the acquired unit with strong incentive to develop strategies to improve their unit's operating performance.

Two Types of Diversification

The last section discussed five principal ways in which companies can use diversification to transfer and implant their business models and strategies into other industries and so increase their long-term profitability. The two corporate strategies of *related diversification* and *unrelated diversification* can be distinguished by how they attempt to realize these five profit-enhancing benefits of diversification.[13]

Related Diversification

Related diversification is a corporate-level strategy that is based on the goal of establishing a business unit (division) in a new industry that is *related* to a company's existing business units by some form of commonality or linkage between the value-chain functions of the existing and new business units. As you might expect, the goal of this strategy is to obtain the benefits from transferring competencies, leveraging competencies, sharing resources, and bundling products that are discussed above.

The multibusiness model of related diversification is based on taking advantage of strong technological, manufacturing, marketing, and sales commonalities between new and existing business units that can be successfully "tweaked" or modified to increase the competitive advantage of one or more business units. Figure 10.3 illustrates the commonalities or linkages possible among the different functions of three different business units or divisions. The greater the number of linkages that can be formed among business units, the greater the potential to realize the profit-enhancing benefits of the five reasons to diversify discussed previously.

One more advantage of related diversification is that it can also allow a company to use any general organizational competency it possesses to increase the overall performance of *all* its different industry divisions—such as the different product brands within VF Corp. For example, strategic managers may strive to create a structure and culture that encourages entrepreneurship across divisions as VF, Apple, and 3M have done; beyond these general competences, these companies all have a set of distinctive competences that can be shared among their different business units and which they continuously strive to improve.

> **Related diversification**
>
> A corporate-level strategy that is based on the goal of establishing a business unit in a new industry that is related to a company's existing business units by some form of commonality or linkage between their value-chain functions.

Figure 10.3 Commonalities between the Value Chains of Three Business Units

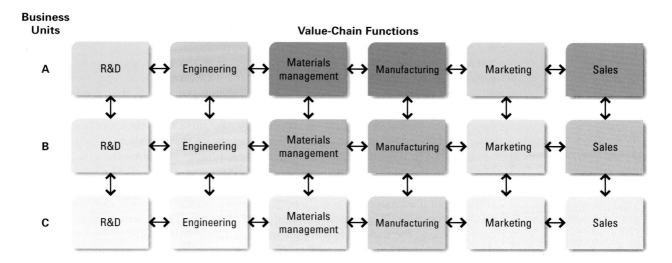

Unrelated Diversification

Unrelated diversification is a corporate-level strategy based on a multibusiness model with a goal to increase profitability through the use of general organizational competencies and increase the performance of *all* the company's business units. Companies pursuing this strategy are often called *conglomerates,* business organizations that operate in many diverse industries. Companies pursuing a strategy of unrelated diversification have *no* intention of transferring or leveraging competencies between business units or sharing resources. The only goal of strategic managers is to use their company's general organizational competencies to strengthen the business models of each of its individual business units or divisions. If the strategic managers of conglomerates have the special skills needed to manage many companies in diverse industries, the strategy can result in superior performance and profitability; often they do not have these skills, as is discussed later in the chapter. Some companies, such as UTC, discussed in Strategy in Action 10.1, have top managers who do possess these special skills.

The Limits and Disadvantages of Diversification

Many companies such as 3M, Samsung, UTC, and Cisco have achieved the benefits of pursuing either or both of the two diversification strategies just discussed, and they have managed to sustain their profitability over time. On the other hand, companies such as GM, Textron, and Philips that pursued diversification failed miserably and became unprofitable. There are three principal reasons why a business model based on diversification may lead to a loss of competitive advantage: (1) changes in the industry or inside a company that occur over time, (2) diversification pursued for the wrong reasons, and (3) excessive diversification that results in increasing bureaucratic costs.

Changes in the Industry or Company

Diversification is a complex strategy. To pursue diversification, top managers must have the ability to recognize profitable opportunities to enter new industries and to implement the strategies necessary to make diversification profitable. Over time, a company's top management team often changes; sometimes its most able executives join other companies and become their CEOs, sometimes successful CEOs decide to retire or step down. When the managers who possess the hard-to-define skills leave, they often take their visions with them. A company's new leaders may lack the competency or commitment necessary to pursue diversification successfully over time; thus, the cost structure of the diversified company increases and eliminates any gains the strategy may have produced.

In addition, the environment often changes rapidly and unpredictably over time. When new technology blurs industry boundaries, it can destroy the source of a company's competitive advantage; for example, by 2011, it was clear that Apple's iPhone and iPad had become a direct competitor with Nintendo's and Sony's mobile gaming consoles. When such a major technological change occurs in a company's core business, the benefits it has previously achieved from transferring or leveraging distinctive competencies disappear. The company is then saddled with a collection of businesses that have all become poor performers in their respective industries because they are not based on the new technology—something that has happened to Sony. Thus, a major problem with diversification is that the future success of a

Unrelated diversification

A corporate-level strategy based on a multibusiness model that uses general organizational competencies to increase the performance of all the company's business units.

business is hard to predict when this strategy is used. For a company to profit from it over time, managers must be as willing to divest business units as they are to acquire them. Research suggests managers do not behave in this way, however.

Diversification for the Wrong Reasons

As we have discussed, when managers decide to pursue diversification, they must have a clear vision of how their entry into new industries will allow them to create new products that provide more value for customers and increase their company's profitability. Over time, however, a diversification strategy may result in falling profitability for reasons noted earlier, but managers often refuse to recognize that their strategy is failing. Although they know they should divest unprofitable businesses, managers "make up" reasons why they should keep their collection of businesses together.

In the past, for example, one widely used (and false) justification for diversification was that the strategy would allow a company to obtain the benefits of risk pooling. The idea behind risk pooling is that a company can reduce the risk of its revenues and profits rising and falling sharply (something that sharply lowers its stock price) if it acquires and operates companies in several industries that have different business cycles. The business cycle is the tendency for the revenues and profits of companies in an industry to rise and fall over time because of "predictable" changes in customer demand. For example, even in a recession, people still need to eat; the profits earned by supermarket chains will be relatively stable; sales at Safeway, Kroger, and also at "dollar stores" actually rise as shoppers attempt to get more value for their dollars. At the same time, a recession can cause the demand for cars and luxury goods to plunge. Many CEOs argue that diversifying into industries that have different business cycles, would allow the sales and revenues of some of their divisions to rise, while sales and revenues in other divisions would fall. A more stable stream of revenue and profits is the net result over time. An example of risk pooling occurred when U.S. Steel diversified into the oil and gas industry in an attempt to offset the adverse effects of cyclical downturns in the steel industry.

This argument ignores two important facts. First, stockholders can eliminate the risk inherent in holding an individual stock by diversifying their *own* portfolios, and they can do so at a much lower cost than a company can. Thus, attempts to pool risks through diversification represent an unproductive use of resources; instead, profits should be returned to shareholders in the form of increased dividends. Second, research suggests that corporate diversification is not an effective way to pool risks because the business cycles of different industries are *inherently difficult to predict,* so it is likely that a diversified company will find that an economic downturn affects *all* its industries simultaneously. If this happens, the company's profitability plunges.[14]

When a company's core business is in trouble, another mistaken justification for diversification is that entry into new industries will rescue the core business and lead to long-term growth and profitability. An example of a company that made this mistake is Kodak. In the 1980s, increased competition from low-cost Japanese competitors, such as Fuji, combined with the beginnings of the digital revolution, soon led its revenues and profits to plateau and then fall. Its managers should have done all they could to reduce its cost structure; instead they took its huge free cash flow and spent tens of billions of dollars to enter new industries, such as health care, biotechnology, and computer hardware, in a desperate and mistaken attempt to find ways to increase profitability.

This was a disaster because every industry Kodak entered was populated by strong companies such as 3M, Canon, and Xerox. Also, Kodak's corporate managers lacked any general competencies to give their new business units a competitive advantage. Moreover, the more industries Kodak entered, the greater the range of threats they encountered, and the more time they had to spend dealing with these threats. As a result, they could spend much less time improving the performance of their core film business that continued to decline.

In reality, Kodak's diversification was just for growth itself, but *growth does not create value for stockholders*; growth is just the byproduct, not the objective, of a diversification strategy. However, in desperation, companies diversify for reasons of growth alone rather than to gain any well-thought-out strategic advantage.[15] In fact, many studies suggest that too much diversification may reduce rather than improve company profitability.[16] That is, the diversification strategies many companies pursue may *reduce* value instead of creating it.[17]

The Bureaucratic Costs of Diversification

A major reason why diversification often fails to boost profitability is that very often the *bureaucratic costs* of diversification exceed the benefits created by the strategy (that is, the increased profit that results when a company makes and sells a wider range of differentiated products and/or lowers its cost structure). As we mention in the previous chapter, **bureaucratic costs** are the costs associated with solving the transaction difficulties that arise between a company's business units and between business units and corporate headquarters, as the company attempts to obtain the benefits from transferring, sharing, and leveraging competencies. They also include the costs associated with using general organizational competencies to solve managerial and functional inefficiencies. The level of bureaucratic costs in a diversified organization is a function of two factors: (1) the number of business units in a company's portfolio and (2) the degree to which coordination is required between these different business units to realize the advantages of diversification.

Number of Businesses   The greater the number of business units in a company's portfolio, the more difficult it is for corporate managers to remain informed about the complexities of each business. Managers simply do not have the time to assess the business model of each unit. This problem occurred at GE in the 1970s when its growth-hungry CEO Reg Jones acquired many new businesses, as he commented:

> I tried to review each plan [of each business unit] in great detail. This effort took untold hours and placed a tremendous burden on the corporate executive office. After a while I began to realize that no matter how hard we would work, we could not achieve the necessary in-depth understanding of the 40-odd business unit plans.[18]

The inability of top managers in extensively diversified companies to maintain control over their multibusiness model over time often leads managers to base important resource allocation decisions only on the most superficial analysis of each business unit's competitive position. For example, a promising business unit may be starved of investment funds, while other business units receive far more cash than they can profitably reinvest in their operations. Furthermore, because they are distant from the day-to-day operations of the business units, corporate managers may find that business unit managers try to hide information on poor performance to save their own jobs. For example, business unit managers might blame poor performance on difficult competitive conditions, even when it is the result of their inability to craft a successful business model. As such organizational problems increase, top managers must spend an enormous amount of time and effort to solve these problems. This

Bureaucratic costs

The costs associated with solving the transaction difficulties between business units and corporate headquarters as a company obtains the benefits from transferring, sharing, and leveraging competencies.

increases bureaucratic costs and cancels out the profit-enhancing advantages of pursuing diversification, such as those obtained from sharing or leveraging competencies.

Coordination Among Businesses   The amount of coordination required to realize value from a diversification strategy based on transferring, sharing, or leveraging competencies is a major source of bureaucratic costs. The bureaucratic mechanisms needed to oversee and manage this coordination and handoffs between units, such as cross-business-unit teams and management committees, are a major source of these costs. A second source of bureaucratic costs arises because of the enormous amount of managerial time and effort required to accurately measure the performance and unique profit contribution of a business unit that is transferring or sharing resources with another. Consider a company that has two business units, one making household products (such as liquid soap and laundry detergent) and another making packaged food products. The products of both units are sold through supermarkets. To lower the cost structure, the parent company decides to pool the marketing and sales functions of each business unit, using an organizational structure similar to that illustrated in Figure 10.4. The company is organized into three divisions: a household products division, a food products division, and a marketing division.

Although such an arrangement may significantly lower operating costs, it can also give rise to substantial control problems, and hence bureaucratic costs. For example, if the performance of the household products business begins to slip, identifying who is to be held accountable—managers in the household products division or managers in the marketing division—may prove difficult. Indeed, each may blame the other for poor performance. Although these kinds of problems can be resolved if corporate management performs an in-depth audit of both divisions, the bureaucratic costs (managers' time and effort) involved in doing so may once again cancel out any value achieved from diversification. The need to reduce bureaucratic costs is evident from the experience of Pfizer discussed in Strategy in Action 10.2.

Figure 10.4   Coordination among Related Business Units

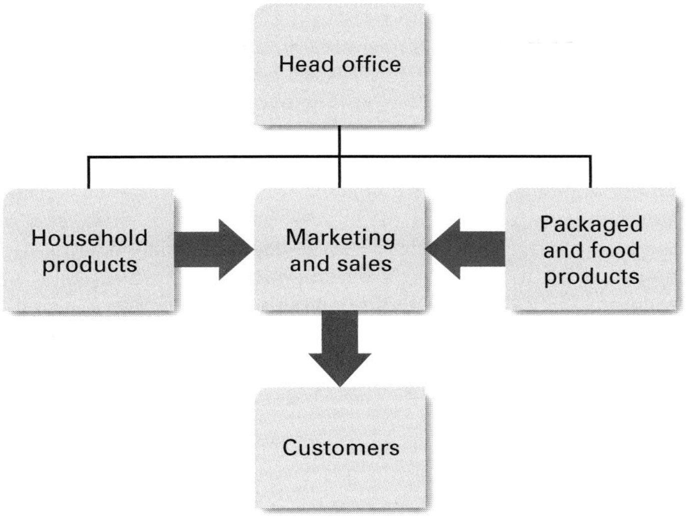

STRATEGY IN ACTION

How Bureaucratic Costs Rose Then Fell at Pfizer

Pfizer is the largest global pharmaceuticals company with sales of almost $50 billion in 2011. Its research scientists have innovated some of the most successful and profitable drugs in the world, such as the first cholesterol reducer, Lipitor. In the 2000s, however, Pfizer encountered major problems in its attempt to innovate new blockbuster drugs while its blockbuster drugs, such as Lipitor, lost their patent protection. While Lipitor once earned a $13 billion per year profit, its sales were now fast declining. Pfizer desperately needed to find ways to make its product development pipeline work—and one manager, Martin Mackay, believed he knew how to do it.

When Pfizer's R&D chief retired, Mackay, his deputy, made it clear to CEO Jeffrey Kindler that he wanted the job. Kindler made it equally clear he thought the company could use some new talent and fresh ideas to solve its problems. Mackay realized he had to quickly devise a convincing plan to change the way Pfizer's scientists worked to develop new drugs, gain Kindler's support, and get the top job. Mackay created a detailed plan for changing the way Pfizer's thousands of researchers made decisions, ensuring that the company's resources and its talent and funds, would be best put to use. After Kindler reviewed the plan, he was so impressed he promoted Mackay to the top R&D position. What was Mackay's plan?

As Pfizer had grown over time as a result of mergers with two other large pharmaceutical companies, Warner Lambert and Pharmacia, Mackay noted how decision-making problems and conflict between the managers of Pfizer's different drug divisions had increased. As it grew, Pfizer's organizational structure had become taller and taller and the size of its headquarters staff grew. With more managers and levels in the company's hierarchy there was a greater need for committees to integrate across activities.

However, in these meetings, different groups of managers fought to promote the development of the drugs they had the most interest in, and managers increasingly came into conflict with one another in order to ensure they got the resources needed to develop these drugs. In short, Mackay felt that too many managers and committees resulted in too much conflict between those who were actively lobbying the managers and the CEO to promote the interests of their own product groups—and the company's performance was suffering as a result. In addition, although Pfizer's success depended upon innovation, this growing conflict had resulted in a bureaucratic culture that reduced the quality of decision making, creating more difficulty when identifying promising new drugs—and increasing bureaucratic costs.

Mackay's bold plan to reduce conflict and bureaucratic costs involved slashing the number of management layers between top managers and scientists from 14 to 7, which resulted in the layoff of thousands of Pfizer's managers. He also abolished the product development committees whose wrangling he believed was slowing down the process of transforming innovative ideas into blockbuster drugs. After streamlining the hierarchy, he focused on reducing the number of bureaucratic rules scientists had to follow, many of which were unnecessary and had promoted conflict. He and his team eliminated every kind of written report that was slowing the innovation process. For example, scientists had been in the habit of submitting quarterly and monthly reports to top managers explaining each drug's progress; Mackay told them to choose which report they wanted to keep, and the other would be eliminated.

As you can imagine, Mackay's efforts caused enormous upheaval in the company as managers fought to keep their positions, and scientists fought to protect the drugs they had in development. However, Mackay was resolute and pushed his agenda through with the support of the CEO, who defended his efforts to create a new R&D product development process that empowered Pfizer's scientists and promoted innovation and entrepreneurship. Pfizer's scientists reported that they felt "liberated" by the new work flow; the level of conflict decreased, and new drugs were manufactured more quickly. By 2011, Pfizer had secured FDA approval for a major new antibacterial drug, and Mackay announced that several potential new blockbuster drugs in its development were on track. Finding ways to control and reduce bureaucratic costs is a vital element of managing corporate-level strategy.

Source: www.pfizer.com, 2011.

In sum, while diversification can be a highly profitable strategy to pursue, it is also the most complex and difficult strategy to manage because it is based on a complex multibusiness model. Even when a company has pursued this strategy successfully in the past, changing conditions both in the industry environment and inside a company may quickly reduce the profit-creating advantages of pursuing this strategy. For example, such changes may result in one or more business units losing their competitive advantage, as happened to Sony. Or, changes may cause the bureaucratic costs associated with pursuing diversification to rise sharply and cancel out its advantages. Thus, the existence of bureaucratic costs places a limit on the amount of diversification that a company can profitably pursue. It makes sense for a company to diversify only when the profit-enhancing advantages of this strategy *exceed* the bureaucratic costs of managing the increasing number of business units required when a company expands and enters new industries.

Choosing a Strategy

Related versus Unrelated Diversification

Because related diversification involves more sharing of competencies, one might think it can boost profitability in more ways than unrelated diversification and is, therefore, the better diversification strategy. However, some companies can create as much or more value from pursuing unrelated diversification, so this strategy must also have some substantial benefits. An unrelated company does *not* need to achieve coordination between business units; it has to cope only with the bureaucratic costs that arise from the number of businesses in its portfolio. In contrast, a related company must achieve coordination *among* business units if it is to realize the gains that come from utilizing its distinctive competencies. Consequently, it has to cope with the bureaucratic costs that arise *both* from the number of business units in its portfolio *and* from coordination among business units. Although it is true that related diversified companies can create value and profit in more ways than unrelated companies, they also have to bear higher bureaucratic costs to do so. These higher costs may cancel out the higher benefits, making the strategy no more profitable than one of unrelated diversification.

How, then, does a company choose between these strategies? The choice depends upon a comparison of the benefits of each strategy against the bureaucratic costs of pursuing it. It pays a company to pursue related diversification when (1) the company's competencies can be applied across a greater number of industries and (2) the company has superior strategic capabilities that allow it to keep bureaucratic costs under close control—perhaps by encouraging entrepreneurship or by developing a value-creating organizational culture.

Using the same logic, it pays a company to pursue unrelated diversification when (1) each business unit's functional competencies have few useful applications across industries, but the company's top managers are skilled at raising the profitability of poorly run businesses and (2) the company's managers use their superior strategic management competencies to improve the competitive advantage of their business units and keep bureaucratic costs under control. Some well-managed companies, such as UTC, discussed in Strategy in Action 10.1, have managers who can successfully pursue unrelated diversification and reap its rewards.

The Web of Corporate-Level Strategy

Finally, it is important to note that while some companies may choose to pursue a strategy of related or unrelated diversification, there is nothing that stops them from pursuing both strategies at the same time—*as well as all the other corporate-level strategies we have discussed.* The purpose of corporate-level strategy is to increase long-term profitability. A company should pursue any and all strategies as long as strategic managers have weighed the advantages and disadvantages of those strategies and arrived at a multibusiness model that justifies them. Figure 10.5 illustrates how Sony developed a Web of corporate strategies to compete in many industries—a program that proved a mistake and has actually *reduced* its differentiation advantage and increased its cost structure in the 2000s.

First, Sony's core business is its electronic consumer products business, and in the past, it has been well known for its innovative products that have made it a leading global brand. To protect the quality of its electronic products, Sony decided to manufacture a high percentage of the component parts for its televisions, DVD players, and other units and pursued a strategy of backward vertical integration. Sony also engaged in forward vertical integration: for example, it acquired Columbia Pictures and MGM to enter the movie or "entertainment software" industry, and it opened a chain of Sony stores in shopping malls (to compete with Apple). Sony also shared and leveraged its distinctive competencies by developing its own business units to

Figure 10.5 Sony's Web of Corporate-Level Strategy

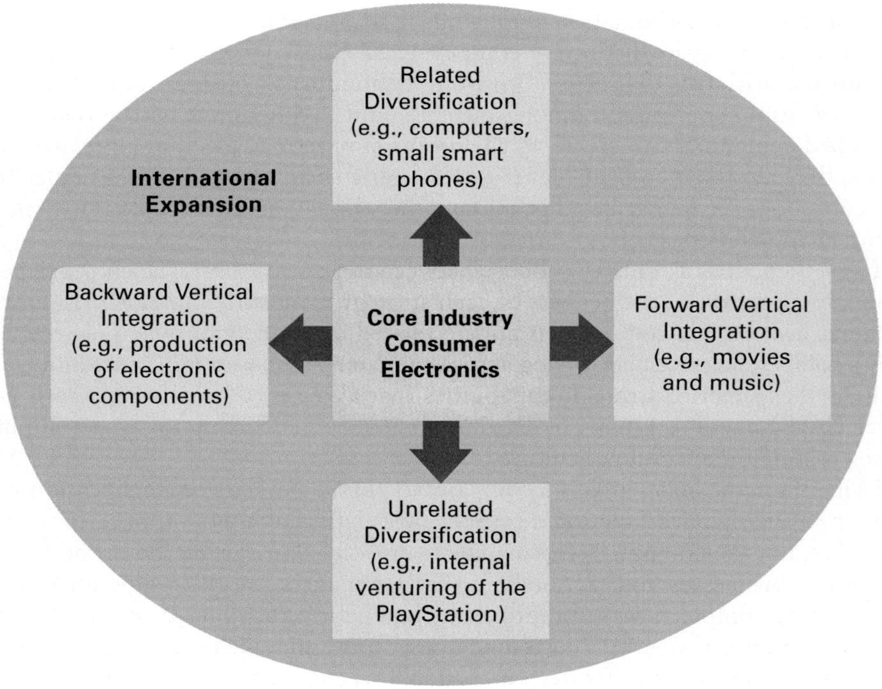

operate in the computer and smartphone industries, a strategy of related diversification. Finally, when it decided to enter the home video game industry and develop its PlayStation to compete with Nintendo, it was pursuing a strategy of unrelated diversification. In the 2000s, this division contributed more to Sony's profits than its core electronics business, but the company has not been doing well, as Strategy in Action 10.3 suggests.

STRATEGY IN ACTION

Sony's "Gaijin" CEO is Changing the Company's Strategies

Sony was renowned in the 1990s for using its engineering prowess to develop blockbuster new products such as the Walkman, Trinitron TV, and PlayStation. Its engineers churned out an average of four new product ideas every day, something attributed to its culture, called the "Sony Way," which emphasized communication, cooperation, and harmony among its company-wide product engineering teams. Sony's engineers were empowered to pursue their own ideas, and the leaders of its different divisions, and hundreds of product teams were allowed to pursue their own innovations—no matter what the cost. While this approach to leadership worked so long as Sony could churn out blockbuster products, it did not work in the 2000s as agile global competitors from Taiwan, Korea, and the United States innovated new technologies and products that began to beat Sony at its own game.

Companies such as LG, Samsung (see Closing case), and Apple innovated new technologies including advanced LCD flat-screens, flash memory, touch-screen commands, mobile digital music, video, and GPS positioning devices, and 3D displays that made many of Sony's technologies (such as its Trinitron TV and Walkman) obsolete. For example, products such as Apple's iPod and iPhone and Nintendo's Wii game console better met customer needs than Sony's out of date and expensive products. Why did Sony lose its leading competitive position?

One reason was that Sony's corporate-level strategies no longer worked in its favor; the leaders of its different product divisions had developed business-level strategies to pursue their own divisions' goals and not those of the whole company. Also, Sony's top managers had been slow to recognize the speed at which technology was changing and as each division's performance fell, competition between corporate and divisional managers increased. The result was slower decision making and increased operating costs as each division competed to obtain the funding necessary to develop successful new products.

By 2005, Sony was in big trouble, and at this crucial point in their company's history, Sony's top managers turned to a *gaijin*, or non-Japanese, executive to lead their company. Their choice was Welshman Sir Howard Stringer, who, as the head of Sony's U.S. operations, had been instrumental in cutting costs and increasing profits. Stringer was closely involved in all U.S. top management decisions, but, nevertheless, he still gave his top executives the authority to develop successful strategies to implement these decisions.

When he became Sony's CEO in 2005, Stringer faced the immediate problem of reducing operating costs that were *double* those of its competitors because divisional managers had seized control of Sony's top level decision-making authority. Stringer recognized how the extensive power struggles among Sony's different product division managers were hurting the company. So, he made it clear they needed to work quickly to reduce costs and cooperate, sharing resources and competencies to speed product development across divisions.

By 2008, it was clear that many of Sony's most important divisional leaders were still pursuing their own goals, so Stringer replaced all the divisional leaders who resisted his orders. Then, he downsized Sony's bloated corporate headquarters staff and replaced the top functional managers who had pursued strategies favoring their interests. He promoted younger managers to develop new strategies for its divisions and functions—managers who would obey his orders and focus on creating commonalities between the company's different businesses.

But, Sony's performance continued to decline, and in 2009, Stringer announced that he would assume more control over the divisions' business-level strategies, taking charge of the core electronics division, and continuing to reorganize and streamline Sony's divisions

STRATEGY IN ACTION (*continued*)

to increase differentiation and reduce costs. He also told managers to prioritize new products and invest only in those with the greatest chance of success in order to reduce out-of-control R&D costs. By 2010, Sony's financial results suggested that Stringer's initiatives were finally paying off; his strategies to reduce costs had stemmed Sony's huge losses and its new digital products were selling better.

In January 2011, Stringer announced that Sony's performance had increased so much that it would be profitable in the second half of 2011. Then, within months, hackers had invaded Sony's PlayStation Website and

stolen the private information of millions of its users. Sony was forced to shut down the Website for weeks and compensate users, which eventually cost it hundreds of millions of dollars. In addition, it also became clear that customers were not buying Sony's expensive new 3D flatscreen TVs and that its revenues from other consumer products would be lower than expected because of intense competition from companies like Samsung. Stringer reported that he expected Sony to make a record loss in 2011 and his turnaround efforts have been foiled as the company desperately strived to meet challenges from Apple and Samsung.

Source: www.sony.com, press releases, 2011.

As this discussion suggests, Sony's profitability has fallen dramatically because its multibusiness model led the company to diversify into too many industries, in each of which the focus was upon innovating high-quality products—as a result its cost structure increased so much it swallowed up all the profits its businesses were generating. Sony's strategy of individual business unit autonomy also resulted in each unit pursuing its own goals at the expense of the company's multibusiness model—which escalated bureaucratic costs and drained its profitability. In particular, because its different divisions did not share their knowledge and expertise, this incongruence allowed competitors such as Samsung to supersede Sony, especially with smartphones and flatscreen LCD TV products. Whether or not the changes Stringer has made will help Sony better manage its Web of corporate strategies to improve its profitability remains to be seen as competitors like Apple and Samsung attack it on all fronts.

Entering New Industries: Internal New Ventures

We have discussed all the corporate-level strategies managers use to formulate the multibusiness model. From this point, we can examine the three main methods managers employ to enter new industries: internal new ventures, acquisitions, and joint ventures. In this section, we consider the pros and cons of using internal new ventures. In the following sections, we look at acquisitions and joint ventures.

The Attractions of Internal New Venturing

Internal new venturing

The process of transferring resources to and creating a new business unit or division in a new industry to innovate new kinds of products.

Internal new venturing is typically used to implement corporate-level strategies when a company possesses one or more distinctive competencies in its core business model that can be leveraged or recombined to enter a new industry. **Internal new venturing** is the process of transferring resources to and creating a new business unit or division in a new industry. Internal venturing is used most by companies that have a business model based upon using their technology to innovate new kinds of products and enter related markets or industries. Thus, technology-based companies that pursue related diversification, like DuPont, which has created new markets with products such as cellophane, nylon, Freon, and Teflon, are most likely to use internal new venturing. 3M has a near-legendary knack for creating new or improved products from internally generated ideas, and then establishing new business units to create the business model that enables it to dominate a new market. Similarly, HP entered into the computer and printer industries by using internal new venturing.

A company may also use internal venturing to enter a newly emerging or embryonic industry—one in which no company has yet developed the competencies or business model to give it a dominant position in that industry. This was Monsanto's situation in 1979 when it contemplated entering the biotechnology field to produce herbicides and pest-resistant crop seeds. The biotechnology field was young at that time, and there were no incumbent companies focused on applying biotechnology to agricultural products. Accordingly, Monsanto internally ventured a new division to develop the required competencies necessary to enter and establish a strong competitive position in this newly emerging industry.

Pitfalls of New Ventures

Despite the popularity of internal new venturing, there is a high risk of failure. Research suggests that somewhere between 33% and 60% of all new products that reach the marketplace do not generate an adequate economic return[19] and that most of these products were the result of internal new ventures. Three reasons are often put forward to explain the relatively high failure rate of internal new ventures: (1) market entry on too small a scale, (2) poor commercialization of the new-venture product, and (3) poor corporate management of the new venture division.[20]

Scale of Entry   Research suggests that large-scale entry into a new industry is often a critical precondition for the success of a new venture. In the short run, this means that a substantial capital investment must be made to support large-scale entry; thus, there is a risk of major losses if the new venture fails. But, in the long run, which can be as long as 5–12 years (depending on the industry), such a large investment results in far greater returns than if a company chooses to enter on a small scale to limit its investment and reduce potential losses.[21] Large-scale entrants can more rapidly realize scale economies, build brand loyalty, and gain access to distribution channels in the new industry, all of which increase the probability of a new venture's success. In contrast, small-scale entrants may find themselves handicapped by high costs due to a lack of scale economies, and a lack of market presence limits the entrant's ability to build brand loyalty and gain access to distribution channels. These scale effects are particularly significant when a company is entering an *established* industry in which incumbent companies possess scale economies, brand loyalty, and access to distribution channels. In that case, the new entrant must make a major investment to succeed.

Figure 10.6 plots the relationship between scale of entry and profitability over time for successful small-scale and large-scale ventures. The figure shows that successful small-scale entry is associated with lower initial losses, but in the long term, large-scale entry generates greater returns. However, because of the high costs and risks associated with large-scale entry, many companies make the mistake of choosing a small-scale entry strategy, which often means they fail to build the market share necessary for long-term success.

Figure 10.6 Scale of Entry and Profitability

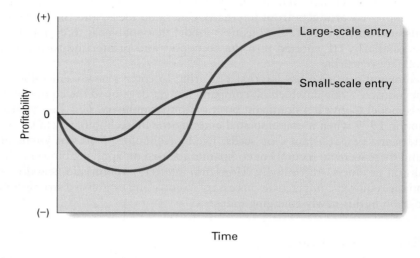

Commercialization Many internal new ventures are driven by the opportunity to use a new or advanced technology to make better products for customers and outperform competitors. But, to be commercially successful, the products under development must be tailored to meet the needs of customers. Many internal new ventures fail when a company ignores the needs of customers in a market. Its managers become so focused on the technological possibilities of a new product that customer requirements are forgotten.[22] Thus, a new venture may fail because it is marketing a product based on a technology for which there is no demand, or the company fails to correctly position or differentiate the product in the market at attract customers.

For example, consider the desktop PC marketed by NeXT, the company we discussed in Chapter 5, which was started by the founder of Apple, Steve Jobs. The NeXT system failed to gain market share because the PC incorporated an array of expensive technologies that consumers simply did not want, such as optical disk drives and hi-fidelity sound. The optical disk drives, in particular, turned off customers because it was difficult to move work from PCs with floppy drives to NeXT machines with optical drives. In other words, NeXT failed because its founder was so dazzled by leading-edge technology that he ignored customer needs. However, Jobs redeemed himself and was named "CEO of the Decade" by Fortune magazine in 2010, after he successfully commercialized Apple's iPod that dominates the deckling MP3 player market. Also, the iPhone set the standard in the smartphone market and the iPad dominated the tablet computer market in 2011—although Amazon.com announced its new Kindle Fire in October 2011.

Poor Implementation Managing the new-venture process, and controlling the new venture division, creates many difficult managerial and organizational problems.[23] For example, one common mistake some companies make to try to increase their chances of making successful products is to establish *too many* different internal new-venture divisions at the same time. Managers attempt to spread the risks of failure by having many divisions, but this places enormous demands upon a company's cash flow. Sometimes, companies are forced to reduce the funding each division receives to keep the entire company profitable, and this can result in the most promising ventures being starved of the cash they need to succeed.[24] Another common mistake is when corporate managers fail to do the extensive advanced planning necessary to ensure that the new venture's business model is sound and contains all the elements that will be needed later if it is to succeed. Sometimes corporate managers leave this process to the scientists and engineers championing the new technology. Focused on the new technology, managers may innovate new products that have little strategic or commercial value. Corporate managers and scientists must work together to clarify how and why a new venture will lead to a product that has a competitive advantage and jointly establish strategic objectives and a timetable to manage the venture until the product reaches the market.

The failure to anticipate the time and costs involved in the new-venture process constitutes a further mistake. Many companies have unrealistic expectations regarding the time frame and expect profits to flow in quickly. Research suggests that some companies operate with a philosophy of killing new businesses if they do not turn a profit by the end of the third year, which is unrealistic given that it can take 5 years or more before a new venture generates substantial profits.

Guidelines for Successful Internal New Venturing

To avoid these pitfalls, a company should adopt a well-thought-out, structured approach to manage internal new venturing. New venturing is based on R&D. It begins with the *exploratory research* necessary to advance basic science and technology (the "R" in R&D) and *development research* to identify, develop, and perfect the commercial applications of a new technology (the "D" in R&D). Companies with strong track records of success at internal new venturing excel at both kinds of R&D; they help to advance basic science and discover important commercial applications for it.[25] To advance basic science, it is important for companies to have strong links with universities where much of the scientific knowledge that underlies new technologies is discovered. It is also important to make sure that research funds are being controlled by scientists who understand the importance of both "R" and "D" research. If the "D" is lacking, a company will probably generate few successful commercial ventures no matter how well it does basic research. Companies can take a number of steps to ensure that good science ends up with good, commercially viable products.

First, many companies must place the funding for research into the hands of business unit managers who have the skill or know-how to narrow down and then select the best set of research projects—those that have the best chance of a significant commercial payoff. Second, to make effective use of its R&D competency, a company's top managers must work with its R&D scientists to continually develop and improve the business model and strategies that guide their efforts and make sure *all* its scientists and engineers understand what they have to do to make it succeed.[26]

Third, a company must also foster close links between R&D and marketing to increase the probability that a new product will be a commercial success in the future. When marketing works to identify the most important customer requirements for a new product and then communicates these requirements to scientists, it ensures that research projects meet the needs of their intended customers. Fourth, a company should also foster close links between R&D and manufacturing to ensure that it has the ability to make a proposed new product in a cost-effective way. Many companies successfully integrate the activities of the different functions by creating cross-functional project teams to oversee the development of new products from their inception to market introduction. This approach can significantly reduce the time it takes to bring a new product to market. For example, while R&D is working on design, manufacturing is setting up facilities, and marketing is developing a campaign to show customers how much the new product will benefit them.

Finally, because large-scale entry often leads to greater long-term profits, a company can promote the success of internal new venturing by "thinking big." A company should construct efficient-scale manufacturing facilities and give marketing a large budget to develop a future product campaign that will build market presence and brand loyalty quickly, and well in advance of that product's introduction. And, corporate managers should not panic when customers are slow to adopt the new product; they need to accept the fact there will be initial losses and recognize that as long as market share is expanding, the product will eventually succeed.

Entering New Industries: Acquisitions

In Chapter 9, we explained that *acquisitions* are the main vehicle that companies use to implement a horizontal integration strategy. Acquisitions are also a principal way companies enter new industries to pursue vertical integration and diversification, so it is necessary to understand both the benefits and risks associated with using acquisitions to implement a corporate-level strategy.

The Attraction of Acquisitions

In general, acquisitions are used to pursue vertical integration or diversification when a company lacks the distinctive competencies necessary to compete in a new industry, so it uses its financial resources to purchase an established company that has those competencies. A company is particularly likely to use acquisitions when it needs to move fast to establish a presence in an industry, commonly an embryonic or growth industry. Entering a new industry through internal venturing is a relatively slow process; acquisition is a much quicker way for a company to establish a significant market presence. A company can purchase a leading company with a strong competitive position in months, rather than waiting years to build a market leadership position by engaging in internal venturing. Thus, when speed is particularly important, acquisition is the favored entry mode. Intel, for example, used acquisitions to build its communications chip business because it sensed that the market was developing very quickly, and that it would take too long to develop the required competencies.

In addition, acquisitions are often perceived as being less risky than internal new ventures because they involve less commercial uncertainty. Because of the risks of failure associated with internal new venturing, it is difficult to predict its future success and profitability. By contrast, when a company makes an acquisition, it acquires a company with an already established reputation, and it knows the magnitude of the company's market share and profitability.

Finally, acquisitions are an attractive way to enter an industry that is protected by high barriers to entry. Recall from Chapter 2 that barriers to entry arise from factors such as product differentiation, which leads to brand loyalty and high market share that leads to economies of scale. When entry barriers are high, it may be very difficult for a company to enter an industry through internal new venturing because it will have to construct large-scale manufacturing facilities and invest in a massive advertising campaign to establish brand loyalty—difficult goals that require huge capital expenditures. In contrast, if a company acquires another company already established in the industry, possibly the market leader, it can circumvent most entry barriers because that company has already achieved economies of scale and obtained brand loyalty. In general, the higher the barriers to entry, the more likely it is that acquisitions will be the method used to enter the industry.

Acquisition Pitfalls

For these reasons, acquisitions have long been the most common method that companies use to pursue diversification. However, as we mentioned earlier, research suggests that many acquisitions fail to increase the profitability of the acquiring company and may result in losses. For example, a study of 700 large acquisitions found that although 30% of these resulted in higher profits, 31% led to losses and the remainder had little impact.[27] Research suggests that many acquisitions fail to realize their anticipated benefits.[28] One study of the post acquisition performance of acquired companies found that the profitability and market share of an acquired company often declines afterward, suggesting that many acquisitions destroy rather than create value.[29]

Acquisitions may fail to raise the performance of the acquiring companies for four reasons: (1) companies frequently experience management problems when they attempt to integrate a different company's organizational structure and culture into their own; (2) companies often overestimate the potential economic benefits from an acquisition; (3) acquisitions tend to be so expensive that they do not increase future profitability; and (4) companies are often negligent in screening their acquisition targets and fail to recognize important problems with their business models.

Integrating the Acquired Company Once an acquisition has been made, the acquiring company has to integrate the acquired company and combine it with its own organizational structure and culture. Integration involves the adoption of common management and financial control systems, the joining together of operations from the acquired and the acquiring company, the establishment of bureaucratic mechanisms to share information and personnel, and the need to create a common culture. Experience has shown that many problems can occur as companies attempt to integrate their activities.

After an acquisition, many acquired companies experience high management turnover because their employees do not like the acquiring company's way of operating—its structure and culture.[30] Research suggests that the loss of management talent and expertise, and the damage from constant tension between the businesses, can materially harm the performance of the acquired unit.[31] Moreover, companies often must take on an enormous amount of debt to fund an acquisition, and they are frequently unable to pay it once these management problems (and sometimes the weaknesses) of the acquired company's business model become clear.

Overestimating Economic Benefits Even when companies find it easy to integrate their activities, they often overestimate by how much combining the different businesses can increase future profitability. Managers often overestimate the competitive advantages that will derive from the acquisition and so pay more for the acquired company than it is worth. One reason is that top managers typically overestimate their own personal general competencies to create valuable new products from an acquisition. Why? The very fact that they have risen to the top of a company gives managers an exaggerated sense of their own capabilities, and a self-importance that distorts their strategic decision making.[32] Coca-Cola's acquisition of a number of medium-sized wine-making companies illustrates this. Reasoning that a beverage is a beverage, Coca-Cola's then-CEO decided he would be able to mobilize his company's talented marketing managers to develop the strategies needed to dominate the U.S. wine industry. After purchasing 3 wine companies and enduring 7 years of marginal profits because of failed marketing campaigns, he subsequently decided that wine and soft drinks are very different products; in particular they have different kinds of appeal, pricing systems, and distribution networks. He eventually sold the wine operations to Joseph E. Seagram and took a substantial loss.[33]

The Expense of Acquisitions Perhaps the most important reason for the failure of acquisitions is that acquiring a company with stock that is publicly traded tends to be very expensive—and the expense of the acquisition can more than wipe out the value of the stream of future profits that are expected from the acquisition. One reason is that the top managers of a company that is "targeted" for acquisition are likely to resist any takeover attempt unless the acquiring company agrees to pay a substantial premium above its current market value. These premiums are often 30%–50% above the usual value of a company's stock. Similarly, the stockholders of the target company are unlikely to sell their stock unless they are paid major premiums over market value prior to a takeover bid. To pay such high premiums, the acquiring company must be certain it can use its acquisition to generate the stream of future profits that justifies the high price of the target company. This is frequently a difficult thing to do given how fast the industry environment can change and the other problems discussed earlier, such as integrating the acquired company. This is a major reason why acquisitions are frequently unprofitable for the acquiring company.

The reason why the acquiring company must pay such a high premium is that the stock price of the acquisition target increases enormously during the acquisition process as investors speculate on the final price the acquiring company will pay to capture it. In the case of a contested bidding contest, where two or more companies simultaneously bid to acquire the target company, its stock price may surge. Also, when many acquisitions are occurring in one particular industry, investors speculate that the value of the remaining industry companies that have *not* been acquired has increased, and that a bid for these companies will be made at some future point. This also drives up their stock price and increases the cost of making acquisitions. This happened in the telecommunications sector when, to make sure they could meet the needs of customers who were demanding leading-edge equipment, many large companies went on acquisition "binges." Nortel and Alcatel-Lucent engaged in a race to purchase smaller, innovative companies that were developing new telecommunications equipment. The result was that the stock prices for these companies were bid up by investors, and they were purchased at a hugely inflated price. When the telecommunications boom turned to bust, the acquiring companies found that they had vastly overpaid for their acquisitions and had to take enormous accounting write-downs; Nortel was forced to declare bankruptcy and sold off all its assets, and the value of Alcatel-Lucent's stock plunged almost 90%, although by 2011, there were signs it may be recovering.

Inadequate Preacquisition Screening As the problems of these companies suggest, top managers often do a poor job of preacquisition screening, that is, evaluating how much a potential acquisition may increase future profitability. Researchers have discovered that one important reason for the failure of an acquisition is that managers make the decision to acquire other companies without thoroughly analyzing potential benefits and costs.[34] In many cases, after an acquisition has been completed, many acquiring companies discover that instead of buying a well-managed business with a strong business model, they have purchased a troubled organization. Obviously, the managers of the target company may manipulate company information or the balance sheet to make their financial condition look much better than it is. The acquiring company must remain aware and complete extensive research. In 2009, IBM was in negotiations to purchase chip maker Sun Microsystems. After spending one week examining its books, IBM reduced its offer price by 10% when its negotiators found its customer base was not as solid as they had expected. Sun Microsystems was eventually sold to Oracle in 2010, and so far the acquisition has not proven a success as Sun Microsystems's server sales fell in 2011.

Guidelines for Successful Acquisition

To avoid these pitfalls and make successful acquisitions, companies need to follow an approach to targeting and evaluating potential acquisitions that is based on four main steps: (1) target identification and preacquisition screening, (2) bidding strategy, (3) integration, and (4) learning from experience.[35]

Identification and Screening Thorough preacquisition screening increases a company's knowledge about a potential takeover target and lessens the risk of purchasing a problem company—one with a weak business model. It also leads to a more realistic assessment of the problems involved in executing a particular acquisition so that a company can plan how to integrate the new business and blend organizational structures and cultures. The screening process should begin with a detailed assessment of the strategic rationale for making the acquisition, an identification of the kind of company that would make an ideal acquisition candidate, and an extensive analysis of the strengths and weaknesses of the prospective company's business model compared to other possible acquisition targets.

Indeed, an acquiring company should select a set of top potential acquisition targets and evaluate each company using a set of criteria that focus on revealing (1) its financial position, (2) its distinctive competencies and competitive advantage, (3) changing industry boundaries, (4) its management capabilities, and (5) its corporate culture. Such an evaluation helps the acquiring company perform a detailed SWOT analysis that identifies the best target, for example, by measuring the potential economies of scale and scope that can be achieved between the acquiring company and each target company. This analysis also helps reveal the potential integration problems that might exist when it is necessary to integrate the corporate cultures of the acquiring and acquired companies. For example, Microsoft and SAP, the world's leading provider of Enterprise Resource Planning software, sat down together to discuss a possible acquisition by Microsoft. Both companies decided that despite the strong strategic rationale for a merger— together they could dominate the software computing market, satisfying the need of large global companies, they would have challenges to overcome. The difficulties of creating an organizational structure that could successfully integrate their hundreds of thousands of employees throughout the world, and blend two very different cultures, were insurmountable.

Once a company has reduced the list of potential acquisition candidates to the most favored one or two, it needs to contact expert third parties, such as investment bankers like Goldman Sachs and Merrill Lynch. These companies' business models are based on providing valuable insights about the attractiveness of a potential acquisition, current industry competitive conditions, and handling the many other issues surrounding an acquisition, such as how to select the optimal bidding strategy for acquiring the target company's stock and keep the purchase price as low as possible.

Bidding Strategy   The objective of the bidding strategy is to reduce the price that a company must pay for the target company. The most effective way a company can acquire another is to make a friendly takeover bid, which means the two companies decide upon an amicable way to merge the two companies, satisfying the needs of each company's stockholders and top managers. A friendly takeover prevents speculators from bidding up stock prices. By contrast, in a hostile bidding environment, such as between Oracle and PeopleSoft, and Microsoft and Yahoo!, the price of the target company often gets bid up by speculators who expect that the offer price will be raised by the acquirer or by another company that might have a higher counteroffer.

Another essential element of a good bidding strategy is timing. For example, Hanson PLC, one of the most successful companies to pursue unrelated diversification, searched for sound companies suffering from short-term problems because of the business cycle or because its performance was being seriously impacted by one underperforming division. Such companies are often undervalued by the stock market, so they can be acquired without paying a high stock premium. With good timing, a company can make a bargain purchase.

Integration   Despite good screening and bidding, an acquisition will fail unless the acquiring company possesses the essential organizational design skills needed to integrate the acquired company into its operations, and quickly develop a viable multibusiness model. Integration should center upon the source of the potential strategic advantages of the acquisition, for instance, opportunities to share marketing, manufacturing, R&D, financial, or management resources. Integration should also involve steps to eliminate any duplication of facilities or functions. In addition, any unwanted business units of the acquired company should be divested.

Learning from Experience   Research suggests companies that acquire many companies over time become expert in this process, and can generate significant value from their experience of the acquisition process.[36] Their past experience enables them to develop a "playbook," a clever plan that they can follow to execute an acquisition most efficiently and effectively. One successful company, Tyco International, never made hostile acquisitions; it audited the accounts of the target company in detail, acquired companies to help it achieve a critical mass in an industry, moved quickly to realize cost savings after an acquisition, promoted managers one or two layers down to lead the newly acquired entity, and introduced profit-based incentive pay systems in the acquired unit.[37] This is what VF is also seeking to achieve with its acquisition of Timberland.

Entering New Industries: Joint Ventures

Joint ventures, where two or more companies agree to pool their resources to create new business, are most commonly used to enter an embryonic or growth industry. Suppose a company is contemplating creating a new venture division in an embryonic industry, such a move involves substantial risks and costs because the company must make the huge investment necessary to develop the set of value-chain activities required to make and sell products in the new industry. On the other hand, an acquisition can be a dangerous proposition because there is rarely an established leading company in an emerging industry; even if there is it will be extremely expensive to purchase.

In this situation, a joint venture frequently becomes the most appropriate method to enter a new industry because it allows a company to share the risks and costs associated with establishing a business unit in the new industry with another company. This is especially true when the companies share *complementary* skills or distinctive competencies because this increases the probability of a joint venture's success. Consider the 50/50 equity joint venture formed between UTC and Dow Chemical to build plastic-based composite parts for the aerospace industry. UTC was already involved in the aerospace industry (it builds Sikorsky helicopters), and Dow Chemical had skills in the development and manufacture of plastic-based composites. The alliance called for UTC to contribute its advanced aerospace skills and Dow to contribute its skills in developing and manufacturing plastic-based composites. Through the joint venture, both companies became involved in new product markets. They were able to realize the benefits associated with related diversification without having to merge their activities into one company or bear the costs and risks of developing new products on their own. Thus, both companies enjoyed the profit-enhancing advantages of entering new markets without having to bear the increased bureaucratic costs.

Although joint ventures usually benefit both partner companies, under some conditions they may result in problems. First, while a joint venture allows companies to share the risks and costs of developing a new business, it also requires that they share in the profits if it succeeds. So, if one partner's skills are more important than the other partner's skills, the partner with more valuable skills will have to "give away" profits to the other party because of the 50/50 agreement. This can create conflict and sour the working relationship as time passes. Second, the joint venture partners may have different business models or time horizons, and problems can arise if they start to come into conflict about how to run the joint venture; these kinds of problems can disintegrate a business and result in failure. Third, a company that enters into a joint venture runs the risk of giving away important company-specific knowledge to its partner, which might then use the new knowledge to compete with its other partner in the future. For example, having gained access to Dow's expertise in plastic-based composites, UTC might have dissolved the alliance and produced these materials on its own. As the previous chapter discussed, this risk can be minimized if Dow gets a *credible commitment* from UTC, which is what Dow did. UTC had to make an expensive asset-specific investment to make the products the joint venture was formed to create.

Restructuring

Many companies expand into new industries to increase profitability. Sometimes, however, companies need to exit industries to increase their profitability and split their existing businesses into separate, independent companies. **Restructuring** is the process of reorganizing and divesting business units and exiting industries to refocus upon a company's core business and rebuild its distinctive competencies.[38] Why are so many companies restructuring and how do they do it?

Why Restructure?

One main reason that diversified companies have restructured in recent years is that the stock market has valued their stock at a *diversification discount*, meaning that the stock of highly diversified companies is valued lower, relative to their earnings, than the stock of less-diversified companies.[39] Investors see highly diversified companies as less attractive investments for four reasons. First, as we discussed earlier, investors often feel these companies no longer have multibusiness models that justify their participation in many different industries. Second, the complexity of the financial statements of highly diversified enterprises disguises the performance of its individual business units; thus, investors cannot identify if their multibusiness models are succeeding. The result is that investors perceive the company as being riskier than companies that operate in one industry, whose competitive advantage and financial statements are more easily understood. Given this situation, restructuring can be seen as an attempt to boost the returns to shareholders by splitting up a multibusiness company into separate and independent parts.

The third reason for the diversification discount is that many investors have learned from experience that managers often have a tendency to pursue too much diversification or do it for the wrong reasons: their attempts to diversify *reduce* profitability.[40] For example, some CEOs pursue growth for its own sake; they are empire builders who expand the scope of their companies to the point where fast-increasing bureaucratic costs become greater than the additional value that their diversification strategy creates. Restructuring thus becomes a response to declining financial performance brought about by over-diversification.

A final factor leading to restructuring is that innovations in strategic management have diminished the advantages of vertical integration or diversification. For example, a few decades ago, there was little understanding of how long-term cooperative relationships or strategic alliances between a company and its suppliers could be a viable alternative to vertical integration. Most companies considered only two alternatives for managing the supply chain: vertical integration or competitive bidding. As we discuss in Chapter 9, in many situations, long-term cooperative relationships can create the most value, especially because they avoid the need to incur bureaucratic costs or dispense with market discipline. As this strategic innovation has spread throughout global business, the relative advantages of vertical integration have declined.

Ethical Dilemma

Recently, many top managers have been convicted of illegally altering their company's financial statements or providing false information to hide the poor performance of their company from stockholders—or simply for personal gain. You have been charged with the task of creating a control system for your company to ensure managers behave ethically and legally when reporting the performance of their business. To help develop the control system, you identify the five main ways managers use diversification to increase profitability—transferring and leveraging competences, sharing resources, product bundling, and the use of general managerial competencies.

How might these five methods be associated with unethical behavior? Can you determine rules or procedures that could prevent managers from behaving in an unethical way?

Summary of Chapter

1. Strategic managers often pursue diversification when their companies are generating free cash flow, that is, financial resources they do not need to maintain a competitive advantage in the company's core industry that can be used to fund profitable new business ventures.

2. A diversified company can create value by (a) transferring competencies among existing businesses, (b) leveraging competencies to create new businesses, (c) sharing resources to realize economies of scope, (d) using product bundling, and (e) taking advantage of general organizational competencies that enhance the performance of all business units within a diversified company. The bureaucratic costs of diversification rise as a function of the number of independent business units within a company and the extent to which managers must coordinate the transfer of resources between those business units.

3. Diversification motivated by a desire to pool risks or achieve greater growth often results in falling profitability.

4. There are three methods companies use to enter new industries: internal new venturing, acquisition, and joint ventures.

5. Internal new venturing is used to enter a new industry when a company has a set of valuable competencies in its existing businesses that can be leveraged or recombined to enter a new business or industry.

6. Many internal ventures fail because of entry on too small a scale, poor commercialization, and poor corporate management of the internal venture process. Guarding against failure involves a carefully planned approach toward project selection and management, integration of R&D and marketing to improve the chance new products will be commercially successful, and entry on a scale large enough to result in competitive advantage.

7. Acquisitions are often the best way to enter a new industry when a company lacks the competencies required to compete in a new industry, and it can purchase a company that does have those competencies at a reasonable price. Acquisitions are also

the method chosen to enter new industries when there are high barriers to entry and a company is unwilling to accept the time frame, development costs, and risks associated with pursuing internal new venturing.

8. Acquisitions are unprofitable when strategic managers (a) underestimate the problems associated with integrating an acquired company, (b) overestimate the profit that can be created from an acquisition, (c) pay too much for the acquired company, and (d) perform inadequate preacquisition screening to ensure the acquired company will increase the profitability of the whole company. Guarding against acquisition failure requires careful preacquisition screening, a carefully selected bidding strategy, effective organizational design to successfully integrate the operations of the acquired company into the whole company, and managers who develop a general managerial competency by learning from their experience of past acquisitions.

9. Joint ventures are used to enter a new industry when (a) the risks and costs associated with setting up a new business unit are more than a company is willing to assume on its own and (b) a company can increase the probability that its entry into a new industry will result in a successful new business by teaming up with another company that has skills and assets that complement its own.

10. Restructuring is often required to correct the problems that result from (a) a business model that no longer creates competitive advantage, (b) the inability of investors to assess the competitive advantage of a highly diversified company from its financial statements, (c) excessive diversification because top managers who desire to pursue empire building that results in growth without profitability, and (d) innovations in strategic management such as strategic alliances and outsourcing that reduce the advantages of vertical integration and diversification.

Discussion Questions

1. Identify Honeywell's (www.honeywell.com) portfolio of businesses that can be found by exploring its Website. In how many different industries is Honeywell involved? Would you describe Honeywell as a related or unrelated diversification company? Has Honeywell's diversification strategy increased profitability over time?

2. Imagine that IBM has decided to diversify into the telecommunications business to provide online "cloud computing" data services and broadband access for businesses and individuals. What method would you recommend that IBM pursue to enter this industry? Why?

3. Under which conditions are joint ventures a useful way to enter new industries?

4. What factors make it most likely that (a) acquisitions or (b) internal new venturing will be the preferred method to enter a new industry?

5. When is a company likely to choose (a) related diversification and (b) unrelated diversification?

Practicing Strategic Management

 Small Group Exercises

Small-Group Exercise: Visiting General Electric

Break up into groups of 3–5, and explore GE's Website (www.ge.com) to answer the following questions. Then appoint one member of the group as spokesperson who will communicate the group's findings to the class.

1. Review GE's portfolio of major businesses. Upon what multibusiness model is this portfolio of business based? How profitable has that model been in past?
2. Has GE's multibusiness model been changing? Has its CEO, Jeffrey Immelt, announced any new strategic initiatives?
3. What kinds of changes would you make to its multibusiness model to boost its profitability?

Strategy Sign-On

Article File 10

Find an example of a diversified company that made an acquisition that apparently failed to create any value. Identify and critically evaluate the rationale that top management used to justify the acquisition when it was made. Explain why the acquisition subsequently failed.

Strategic Management Project

Developing Your Portfolio: Module 10 This module requires you to assess your company's use of acquisitions, internal new ventures, and joint ventures as ways to enter a new business or restructure its portfolio of businesses.

A. Your Company Has Entered a New Industry During the Past Decade

1. Pick one new industry that your company has entered during the past 10 years.
2. Identify the rationale for entering this industry.
3. Identify the strategy used to enter this industry.
4. Evaluate the rationale for using this particular entry strategy. Do you think that this was the best entry strategy to use? Why?
5. Do you think that the addition of this business unit to the company increased or reduced profitability? Why?

B. Your Company Has Restructured its Corporate Portfolio During the Past Decade

1. Identify the rationale for pursuing a restructuring strategy.
2. Pick one industry from which your company has exited during the past 10 years.
3. Identify the strategy used to exit from this particular industry. Do you think that this was the best exit strategy to use? Why or why not?
4. In general, do you think that exiting from this industry has been in the company's best interest?

CLOSING CASE
Samsung Electronics

In the 2000s, Samsung Electronics (SE), based in Seoul, Korea, became the second-most profitable global technology company after Microsoft. SE accomplished this when its pioneering CEO Lee Kun-hee decided to develop and build distinctive competences first in low-cost manufacturing, second in R&D, and then in new production in new industries.

SE's core industry is the consumer electronics industry. In the 1990s, its engineers studied how Japanese companies, Sony and Panasonic, innovated new products. Then, SE's engineers copied Japanese technology and used their low-cost skills to make low-priced versions of the products that they could sell at lower prices than the Japanese companies. For example, SE decided to enter the cell phone industry and make lower-cost phones than companies such as Nokia and Motorola. SE also entered the semiconductor industry in which it worked to make the lowest-cost memory chips; soon it became the global cost leader. SE also entered other digital-product markets such as cameras, printers, and storage devices.

In essence, Samsung was pursuing the corporate-level strategy of related diversification. Its goals were to create value and increase its profitability by transferring and leveraging its distinctive competencies in product development, and manufacturing by entering new industries and producing new products. SE's strategy was successful and profitable, but it was not playing in the same league as Sony, for example. Sony could charge premium prices for its leading electronics and continuously reinvest profits into the R&D needed to make more advanced state-of-the-art electronics. CEO Kun-hee decided to adopt new strategies that would allow his company to compete head-to-head with Japanese and European electronics companies and make it a global technology leader. SE's goal was not to copy technology innovated by Sony, Matsushita, Philips, and Nokia, but for SE's engineers to develop the research and engineering skills necessary to rapidly innovate leading-edge technologies, such as LCD displays, and create products more advanced than its competitors.

Within a decade, SE became the leading supplier of advanced flash memory chips and LCD screens, premium-priced products that it sold to other global electronics makers, including Japanese flat screen TV makers. Samsung also made the development of a new competence in global marketing an important part of its business model. For example, while Nokia was the leading cell phone innovator, Samsung was the first to realize customers wanted color screens for their phones to allow them to play games, and built-in cameras to send photographs to their friends. Both of these incremental advances allowed Samsung to dramatically increase its share of the cell phone market. In 2009, it was the second-largest cell phone maker after Nokia.

By 2007, Samsung had become one of the most innovative global electronics makers with its four research divisions: semiconductors, telecommunications, digital media, and flat screen LCD displays. Because many of its products require components developed by all four divisions, to pursue its strategy of related diversification, SE teams up researchers, designers, engineers, and marketers from all its divisions at its research facility outside Seoul. In this way, they can spur the economies of scope and leveraging of competencies that its strategy of related diversification permits. At the same time, it also can transfer its manufacturing competence between its divisions and make electronic products at lower cost than competitors.

In 2008, however, SE, like most other electronics companies, was forced to restructure its business divisions because of the global recession. The problem facing SE and other global electronics companies, such as Sony, was how to pursue related diversification while simultaneously reducing its cost structure and increasing its technological edge. In 2009, Samsung's new CEO Yoon-Woo Lee announced a major restructuring that would consolidate its four divisions into two and reduce costs but still speed product development. SE's semiconductor and LCD display businesses were combined into a new Device Solutions Division, and its televisions, mobile phones, and other consumer electronics, such as printers and computers, were placed in the Digital Media and Communications Division. Because all of SE's products use in-house chips and LCD displays, this means that while SE is pursuing related diversification, it is also using its low-cost skills to benefit from vertical integration.

In addition, it is important to note that SE is only one division of the Samsung Corporation, which is a huge conglomerate that also pursues unrelated diversification. The parent Samsung Corporation has dozens of divisions that are involved in industries such as shipbuilding, construction, life insurance, leisure, and so on—in fact, the Samsung empire accounts for 20% of South Korea's total exports.

Case Discussion Questions

1. In what ways has Samsung's multibusiness model changed over time? Why did its top managers make these changes?

2. How is Samsung currently performing? What kinds of changes is it making to its multibusiness model?

Notes

[1] www.vfc.com, 2011.

[2] Ibid.

[3] www.timberland.com, 2011

[4] Ibid.

[5] This resource-based view of diversification can be traced to Edith Penrose's seminal book, *The Theory of the Growth of the Firm* (Oxford: Oxford University Press, 1959).

[6] D. J. Teece, "Economies of Scope and the Scope of the Enterprise," *Journal of Economic Behavior and Organization* 3 (1980): 223–247. For recent empirical work on this topic, see C. H. St. John and J. S. Harrison, "Manufacturing Based Relatedness, Synergy and Coordination," *Strategic Management Journal* 20 (1999): 129–145.

[7] Teece, "Economies of Scope." For recent empirical work on this topic, see St. John and Harrison, "Manufacturing Based Relatedness, Synergy and Coordination."

[8] For a detailed discussion, see C. W. L. Hill and R. E. Hoskisson, "Strategy and Structure in the Multiproduct Firm," *Academy of Management Review* 12 (1987): 331–341.

[9] See, for example, G. R. Jones and C. W. L. Hill, "A Transaction Cost Analysis of Strategy Structure Choice," *Strategic Management Journal* 2 (1988): 159–172; and O. E. Williamson, *Markets and Hierarchies, Analysis and Antitrust Implications* (New York: Free Press, 1975), 132–175.

[10] R. Buderi, *Engines of Tomorrow* (New York: Simon & Schuster, 2000).

[11] See, for example, Jones and Hill, "A Transaction Cost Analysis"; Williamson, *Markets and Hierarchies*; and Hill, "The Role of Headquarters in the Multidivisional Firm."

[12] www.utc.com, 2011.

[13] The distinction goes back to R. P. Rumelt, *Strategy, Structure and Economic Performance* (Cambridge: Harvard Business School Press, 1974).

[14] For evidence, see C. W. L. Hill, "Conglomerate Performance over the Economic Cycle," *Journal of Industrial Economics* 32 (1983): 197–212; and D. T. C. Mueller, "The Effects of Conglomerate Mergers," *Journal of Banking and Finance* 1 (1977): 315–347.

[15] For reviews of the evidence, see V. Ramanujam and P. Varadarajan, "Research on Corporate Diversification: A Synthesis," *Strategic Management Journal* 10 (1989): 523–551; G. Dess, J. F. Hennart, C. W. L. Hill, and A. Gupta, "Research Issues in Strategic Management," *Journal of Management* 21 (1995): 357–392; and D. C. Hyland and J. D. Diltz, "Why Companies Diversify: An Empirical Examination," *Financial Management* 31 (Spring 2002): 51–81.

[16] M. E. Porter, "From Competitive Advantage to Corporate Strategy," *Harvard Business Review* (May–June 1987): 43–59.

[17] For reviews of the evidence, see Ramanujam and Varadarajan, "Research on Corporate Diversification"; Dess, Hennart, Hill, and Gupta, "Research Issues in Strategic Management"; and Hyland and Diltz, "Why Companies Diversify."

[18] C. R. Christensen et al., *Business Policy Text and Cases* (Homewood: Irwin, 1987), 778.

[19] See Booz, Allen, and Hamilton, *New Products Management for the 1980s* (privately published, 1982); A. L. Page, "PDMA's New Product Development Practices Survey: Performance and Best Practices" (presented at the PDMA 15th Annual International Conference, Boston, October 16, 1991); and E. Mansfield, "How Economists See R&D," *Harvard Business Review* (November–December 1981): 98–106.

[20] See R. Biggadike, "The Risky Business of Diversification," *Harvard Business Review* (May–June 1979): 103–111; R. A. Burgelman,

"A Process Model of Internal Corporate Venturing in the Diversified Major Firm," *Administrative Science Quarterly* 28 (1983): 223–244; and Z. Block and I. C. MacMillan, *Corporate Venturing* (Boston: Harvard Business School Press, 1993).

[21] Biggadike, "The Risky Business of Diversification"; Block and Macmillan, *Corporate Venturing*.

[22] Buderi, *Engines of Tomorrow*.

[23] I. C. MacMillan and R. George, "Corporate Venturing: Challenges for Senior Managers," *Journal of Business Strategy* 5 (1985): 34–43.

[24] See R. A. Burgelman, M. M. Maidique, and S. C. Wheelwright, *Strategic Management of Technology and Innovation* (Chicago: Irwin, 1996), 493–507. See also Buderi, *Engines of Tomorrow*.

[25] Buderi, *Engines of Tomorrow*.

[26] See Block and Macmillan, Corporate Venturing; and Burgelman, Maidique, and Wheelwright, Strategic Management of Technology and Innovation; Buderi, *Engines of Tomorrow*. See Block and Macmillan, *Corporate Venturing*; and Burgelman, Maidique, and Wheelwright, *Strategic Management of Technology and Innovation*.

[27] For evidence on acquisitions and performance, see R. E. Caves, "Mergers, Takeovers, and Economic Efficiency," *International Journal of Industrial Organization* 7 (1989): 151–174; M. C. Jensen and R. S. Ruback, "The Market for Corporate Control: The Scientific Evidence," *Journal of Financial Economics* 11 (1983): 5–50; R. Roll, "Empirical Evidence on Takeover Activity and Shareholder Wealth," in J. C. Coffee, L. Lowenstein, and S. Rose (eds.), *Knights, Raiders and Targets* (Oxford: Oxford University Press, 1989): 112–127; A. Schleifer and R. W. Vishny, "Takeovers in the 60s and 80s: Evidence and Implications," *Strategic Management Journal* 12 (Special Issue, Winter 1991): 51–60; T. H. Brush, "Predicted Changes in Operational Synergy and Post Acquisition Performance of Acquired Businesses," Strategic Management Journal 17 (1996): 1–24; and T. Loughran and A. M. Vijh, "Do Long Term Shareholders Benefit from Corporate Acquisitions?" *Journal of Finance* 5 (1997): 1765–1787.

[28] Ibid

[29] D. J. Ravenscraft and F. M. Scherer, *Mergers, Sell-offs, and Economic Efficiency* (Washington: Brookings Institution, 1987).

[30] See J. P. Walsh, "Top Management Turnover Following Mergers and Acquisitions," *Strategic Management Journal* 9 (1988): 173–183.

[31] See A. A. Cannella and D. C. Hambrick, "Executive Departure and Acquisition Performance," *Strategic Management Journal* 14 (1993): 137–152.

[32] R. Roll, "The Hubris Hypothesis of Corporate Takeovers," *Journal of Business* 59 (1986): 197–216.

[33] "Coca-Cola: A Sobering Lesson from Its Journey into Wine," *Business Week* (June 3, 1985): 96–98.

[34] P. Haspeslagh and D. Jemison, *Managing Acquisitions* (New York: Free Press, 1991).

[35] For views on this issue, see L. L. Fray, D. H. Gaylin, and J. W. Down, "Successful Acquisition Planning," *Journal of Business Strategy* 5 (1984): 46–55; C. W. L. Hill, "Profile of a Conglomerate Takeover: BTR and Thomas Tilling," *Journal of General Management* 10 (1984): 34–50; D. R. Willensky, "Making It Happen: How to Execute an Acquisition," *Business Horizons* (March–April 1985): 38–45; Haspeslagh and Jemison, *Managing Acquisitions*; and P. L. Anslinger and T. E. Copeland, "Growth Through Acquisition: A Fresh Look," *Harvard Business Review* (January–February 1996): 126–135.

[36] M. L. A. Hayward, "When Do Firms Learn from Their Acquisition Experience? Evidence from 1990–1995," *Strategic Management Journal* 23 (2002): 21–39; K. G. Ahuja, "Technological Acquisitions and the Innovation Performance of Acquiring Firms: A Longitudinal Study," *Strategic Management Journal* 23 (2001): 197–220; H. G. Barkema and F. Vermeulen, "International Expansion Through Startup or Acquisition," *Academy of Management Journal* 41 (1998): 7–26.

[37] Hayward, "When Do Firms Learn from Their Acquisition Experience?"

[38] For a review of the evidence and some contrary empirical evidence, see D. E. Hatfield, J. P. Liebskind, and T. C. Opler, "The Effects of Corporate Restructuring on Aggregate Industry Specialization," *Strategic Management Journal* 17 (1996): 55–72.

[39] A. Lamont and C. Polk, "The Diversification Discount: Cash Flows versus Returns," *Journal of Finance* 56 (October 2001): 1693–1721; R. Raju, H. Servaes, and L. Zingales, "The Cost of Diversity: The Diversification Discount and Inefficient Investment," *Journal of Finance* 55 (2000): 35–80.

[40] For example, see Schleifer and Vishny, "Takeovers in the '60s and '80s."

11 Corporate Performance, Governance, and Business Ethics

erei.photography/istockphoto.com

Did Goldman Sachs Commit Fraud?

In the mid-2000s, when housing prices in the United States were surging, hedge fund manager John Paulson approached Goldman Sachs. Paulson believed that housing prices had risen too much. There was, he felt, a speculative bubble in housing. In his view, the bubble had been fueled by cheap money from banks. The banks were enticing people to purchase homes with adjustable rate mortgages with very low interest rates for the first 1–3 years. Many of the borrowers, however, could probably not afford their monthly payments once higher rates would later begin. Paulson thought that homeowners would start to default on their mortgage payments in large numbers. When that happened, the housing market would be flooded with distressed sales and house prices would collapse. Paulson wanted to find a way to make money from this situation.

Goldman Sachs devised an investment vehicle that would allow Paulson to do just this. During the early-2000s, mortgage originators had started to pool thousands of individual mortgages together into bonds know as collateralized debt obligations, or CDOs. They then sold the bonds to institutional investors. The underlying idea was simple; the pool of mortgage payments generated income for the bondholders. As long as people continued to make their mortgage payments, the CDOs would generate good income and their price would be stable. Many of these bonds were given favorable ratings from the two main rating agencies,

LEARNING OBJECTIVES

After reading this chapter you should be able to:

- Understand the relationship between stakeholder management and corporate performance
- Explain why maximizing returns to stockholders is often viewed as the preeminent goal in many corporations
- Describe the various governance mechanisms that are used to align the interest of stockholders and managers
- Explain why these governance mechanisms do not always work as intended
- Identify the main ethical issues that arise in business and the causes of unethical behavior
- Identify what managers can do to improve the ethical climate of their organization, and to make sure that business decisions do not violate good ethical principles

Moody's and Standard & Poor's, suggesting that they were safe investments. At the time, institutional investors were snapping up CDOs. Paulson, however, took a very different view. He believed that the rating agencies were wrong and that many CDOs were far more risky than investors thought. He believed that when people started to default on their mortgage payments, the price of these CDOs would collapse.

Goldman Sachs decided to offer bonds for sale to institutional investors that were a collection of 90 or so CDOs. These bonds were referred to as *synthetic CDOs*. They asked Paulson to identify the CDOs that he thought were very risky and grouped them together into *synthetic CDOs*. Goldman then sold these very same bonds to institutional investors—many were long time Goldman Sachs clients. Goldman did not tell investors that Paulson had helped to pick the CDOs that were pooled into the bonds, nor did they tell investors that the underlying CDOs might be a lot more risky than the rating agencies thought. Paulson then took a short position in these synthetic CDOs. Short selling is a technique where the investor will make money if the price of the asset goes down over time. Paulson was effectively betting against the synthetic CDOs, a fact that Goldman knew, while he was actively marketing these bonds to institutions.

Shortly thereafter, Paulson was proved correct. People did start to default on their housing payments, the price of houses did fall, and the value of CDOs and the synthetic CDOs that Goldman had created, plunged. Paulson made an estimated $3.7 billion in 2007 alone from this event. Goldman Sachs, too, made over $1 billion by betting against the very same bonds that they had been selling.

The Securities and Exchange Commission (SEC) soon started to investigate the transactions. Some at the SEC believed that Goldman had knowingly committed fraud by failing to inform buyers that Paulson had selected the CDOs. The SEC's case was strengthened by internal Goldman e-mails. In one, a senior executive described the synthetic CDOs it was selling as "one shitty deal." In another, a colleague applauded the deal for making "lemonade from some big old lemons."

In April 2010, the SEC formally charged Goldman Sachs with civil fraud, arguing that the company had knowingly mislead investors about the risk and value of the synthetic CDOs, and failed to inform them of John Paulson's involvement in selecting the underlying CDOs. Goldman provided a vigorous defense. They argued that a market maker like Goldman Sachs owes no fiduciary duty to clients and offers no warranties—it is up to clients to make their own assessment of the value of a security. However, faced with a barrage of negative publicity, Goldman opted to settle the case out of court and pay a $550 million fine. In doing so, Goldman admitted no legal wrongdoing, but they did say that the company had made a "mistake" in not disclosing Paulson's role and they vowed to raise their standards forwarding the future.[1]

Ron Sachs/CNP/Corbis

Overview

The story of Goldman Sachs told in the Opening Case highlights some of the issues that we will discuss in this chapter. Goldman knowingly sold bonds to investors that were much riskier than they appeared. Goldman failed to inform investors that a well-known short seller, John Paulson, had selected the assets that underlay the bonds and had picked assets he thought were of a very poor quality. Goldman, in other words, was knowingly selling what Paulson thought of as "junk" to investors, but it failed to inform investors of the risks. Indeed, Goldman marketed the bonds as a solid investment. The SEC accused Goldman of civil fraud. The case was settled out of court. Goldman admitted no legal wrong doing, although the bank did pay a $550 million fine. While Goldman's actions may have been legal (although that is a subject for debate) many thought that they were not ethical. Goldman seems to have been deliberately misleading its clients. Goldman, too, seems to have recognized that these actions damaged the firm's reputation and could hurt its business going forward, because clients would be less willing to trust the bank. Goldman has recently raised their standards to ensure full disclosure to clients.

One of the key topics that we discuss in this chapter is business ethics, and the relationship between unethical behavior and business performance. While Goldman may have profited in the short run from behavior that many perceived as unethical, it certainly damaged the bank's reputation, and without corrective action, it may have resulted in lost business in the long term.

We open this chapter with a close look at the governance mechanisms that shareholders implement to ensure that managers are acting in the company's interest and are pursuing strategies that maximize shareholder value. We also discuss how managers need to pay attention to other stakeholders as well, such as employees, suppliers, and customers. Balancing the needs of different stakeholder groups is in the long-term interests of the company's owners, its shareholders. Good governance mechanisms recognize this truth. In addition, we will spend some time reviewing the ethical implications of strategic decisions, and we will discuss how managers can make sure that their strategic decisions are founded upon strong ethical principles, something that Goldman Sachs (arguably) failed to do.

Stakeholders and Corporate Performance

A company's **stakeholders** are individuals or groups with an interest, claim, or stake in the company, in what it does, and in how well it performs.[2] They include stockholders, creditors, employees, customers, the communities in which the company does business, and the general public. Stakeholders can be divided into two groups: internal stakeholders and external stakeholders (see Figure 11.1). **Internal stakeholders** are stockholders and employees, including executive officers, other managers, and board members. **External stakeholders** are all other individuals and groups that have some claim on the company. Typically, this group comprises customers, suppliers, creditors (including banks and bondholders), governments, unions, local communities, and the general public.

All stakeholders are in an exchange relationship with their company. Each of the stakeholder groups listed in Figure 11.1 supplies the organization with important

Stakeholders

Individuals or groups with an interest, claim, or stake in the company, in what it does, and in how well it performs.

Internal stakeholders

Stockholders and employees, including executive officers, other managers, and board members.

External stakeholders

All other individuals and groups that have some claim on the company.

Figure 11.1 Stakeholders and the Enterprise

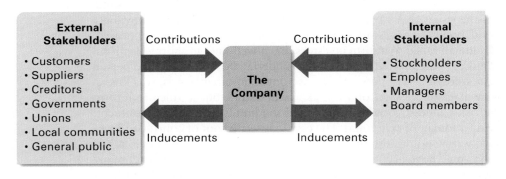

© Cengage Learning 2013

resources (or contributions), and in exchange, each expects its interests to be satisfied (by inducements).[3] Stockholders provide the enterprise with risk capital and in exchange expect management to attempt to maximize the return on their investment. Creditors, and particularly bondholders, also provide the company with capital in the form of debt, and they expect to be repaid on time, with interest. Employees provide labor and skills and in exchange expect commensurate income, job satisfaction, job security, and good working conditions. Customers provide a company with its revenues, and in exchange want high-quality, reliable products that represent value for money. Suppliers provide a company with inputs and in exchange seek revenues and dependable buyers. Governments provide a company with rules and regulations that govern business practice and maintain fair competition. In exchange they want companies that adhere to these rules. Unions help to provide a company with productive employees, and in exchange they want benefits for their members in proportion to their contributions to the company. Local communities provide companies with local infrastructure and in exchange want companies that are responsible citizens. The general public provides companies with national infrastructure and in exchange seeks some assurance that the quality of life will be improved as a result of the company's existence.

A company must take these claims into account when formulating its strategies, or else stakeholders may withdraw their support. For example, stockholders may sell their shares, bondholders may demand higher interest payments on new bonds, employees may leave their jobs, and customers may buy elsewhere. Suppliers may seek more dependable buyers, and unions may engage in disruptive labor disputes. Government may take civil or criminal action against the company and its top officers, imposing fines and, in some cases, jail terms. Communities may oppose the company's attempts to locate its facilities in their area, and the general public may form pressure groups, demanding action against companies that impair the quality of life. Any of these reactions can have a damaging impact on an enterprise.

Stakeholder Impact Analysis

A company cannot always satisfy the claims of all stakeholders. The goals of different groups may conflict, and in practice, few organizations have the resources to manage all stakeholders.[4] For example, union claims for higher wages can conflict with consumer demands for reasonable prices and stockholder demands for acceptable returns. Often the company must make choices. To do so, it must identify the most important stakeholders and give highest priority to pursuing strategies that satisfy their needs. Stakeholder impact analysis can provide such identification. Typically, stakeholder impact analysis follows these steps:

1. Identify stakeholders.
2. Identify stakeholders' interests and concerns.
3. As a result, identify what claims stakeholders are likely to make on the organization.
4. Identify the stakeholders who are most important from the organization's perspective.
5. Identify the resulting strategic challenges.[5]

Such an analysis enables a company to identify the stakeholders most critical to its survival and to make sure that the satisfaction of their needs is paramount. Most companies that have gone through this process quickly come to the conclusion that three stakeholder groups must be satisfied above all others if a company is to survive and prosper: customers, employees, and stockholders.

The Unique Role of Stockholders

A company's stockholders are usually put in a different class from other stakeholder groups, and for good reason. Stockholders are legal owners and the providers of **risk capital**, a major source of the capital resources that allow a company to operate its business. The capital that stockholders provide to a company is seen as risk capital because there is no guarantee that stockholders will ever recoup their investment and/or earn a decent return.

Recent history demonstrates all too clearly the nature of risk capital. For example, many investors who bought shares in Washington Mutual, the large Seattle-based bank and home loan lender, believed that they were making a low risk investment. The company had been around for decades and paid a solid dividend, which it increased every year. It had a large branch network and billions in deposits. However, during the 2000s, Washington Mutual was also making increasingly risky mortgage loans, reportedly giving mortgages to people without ever properly verifying if they had the funds to pay back those loans on time. By 2008, many of the borrowers were beginning to default on their loans and Washington Mutual had to take multibillion dollar write-downs on the value of its loan portfolio, effectively destroying its once strong balance sheet. The losses were so large that people with deposits at the bank started to worry about its stability, and they withdrew nearly $16 billion in November 2008 from accounts at Washington Mutual. The stock price collapsed from around $40 at the start of 2008, to under $2 a share, and with the bank teetering on the brink of collapse, the Federal government intervened, seized the bank's assets, and engineered a sale to JP Morgan. What did Washington Mutual's shareholders get? Absolutely nothing! They were wiped out.

Over the past decade, maximizing returns to stockholders has taken on significant importance as an increasing number of employees have become stockholders in the company for which they work through an employee stock ownership plan (ESOP). At Walmart, for example, all employees who have served for more than 1 year are eligible for the company's ESOP. Under an ESOP, employees are given the opportunity to purchase stock in their company, sometimes at a discount or less than the market value of the stock. The company may also contribute to a certain portion

Risk capital

Capital that cannot be recovered if a company fails and goes bankrupt.

of the purchase price to the ESOP. By making employees stockholders, ESOPs tend to increase the already strong emphasis on maximizing returns to stockholders, for they now help to satisfy two key stakeholder groups: stockholders and employees.

Profitability, Profit Growth, and Stakeholder Claims

Because of the unique position assigned to stockholders, managers normally seek to pursue strategies that maximize the returns that stockholders receive from holding shares in the company. As we noted in Chapter 1, stockholders receive a return on their investment in a company's stock in two ways: from dividend payments and from capital appreciation in the market value of a share (that is, by increases in stock market prices). The best way for managers to generate the funds for future dividend payments and keep the stock price appreciating is to pursue strategies that maximize the company's long-term profitability (as measured by the return on invested capital or ROIC) and grow the profits of the company over time.[6]

As we saw in Chapter 3, ROIC is an excellent measure of the profitability of a company. It tells managers how efficiently they are using the capital resources of the company (including the risk capital provided by stockholders) to generate profits. A company that is generating a positive ROIC is covering all of its ongoing expenses and has money left over, which is then added to shareholders' equity, thereby increasing the value of a company and thus the value of a share of stock in the company. The value of each share will increase further if a company can grow its profits over time, because then the profit that is attributable to every share (that is, the company's earnings per share) will also grow. As we have seen in this book, to grow profits, companies must be doing one or more of the following: (a) participating in a market that is growing, (b) taking market share from competitors, (c) consolidating the industry through horizontal integration, and (d) developing new markets through international expansion, vertical integration, or diversification.

While managers should strive for profit growth if they are trying to maximize shareholder value, the relationship between profitability and profit growth is a complex one because attaining future profit growth may require investments that reduce the current rate of profitability. The task of managers is to find the right balance between profitability and profit growth.[7] Too much emphasis on current profitability at the expense of future profitability and profit growth can make an enterprise less attractive to shareholders. Too much emphasis on profit growth can reduce the profitability of the enterprise and have the same effect. In an uncertain world where the future is unknowable, finding the right balance between profitability and profit growth is as much art as it is science, but it is something that managers must try to do.

In addition to maximizing returns to stockholders, boosting a company's profitability and profit growth rate is also consistent with satisfying the claims of several other key stakeholder groups. When a company is profitable and its profits are continuing to grow, it can pay higher salaries to productive employees and can also afford benefits such as health insurance coverage, all of which help to satisfy employees. In addition, companies with a high level of profitability and profit growth have no problem meeting their debt commitments, which provides creditors, including bondholders, with a measure of security. More profitable companies are also better able to undertake philanthropic investments, which can help to satisfy some of the claims that local communities and the general public place on a company. Pursuing strategies that maximize the long-term profitability and profit growth of the company is therefore generally consistent with satisfying the claims of various stakeholder groups.

There is an important cause-and-effect relationship here: pursuing strategies to maximize profitability and profit growth helps a company to better satisfy the demands that several stakeholder groups place on the company, not the other way around. The company that overpays its employees in the current period, for example, may have very happy employees for a short while, but such action will raise the company's cost structure and limit its ability to attain a competitive advantage in the marketplace, thereby depressing its long-term profitability and hurting its ability to award future pay increases. As far as employees are concerned, the way many companies deal with this situation is to make future pay raises contingent upon improvements in labor productivity. If labor productivity increases, labor costs as a percentage of revenues will fall, profitability will rise, and the company can afford to pay its employees more and offer greater benefits.

Of course, not all stakeholder groups want the company to maximize its long-run profitability and profit growth. Suppliers are more comfortable about selling goods and services to profitable companies because they can be assured that the company will have the funds to pay for those products. Similarly, customers may be more willing to purchase from profitable companies because they can be assured that those companies will be around in the long term to provide after-sales services and support. But neither suppliers nor customers want the company to maximize its profitability at their expense. Rather, they would like to capture some of these profits from the company in the form of higher prices for their goods and services (in the case of suppliers), or lower prices for the products they purchase from the company (in the case of customers). Thus, the company is in a bargaining relationship with some of its stakeholders, which was a phenomenon we discussed in Chapter 2.

Moreover, despite the argument that maximizing long-term profitability and profit growth is the best way to satisfy the claims of several key stakeholder groups, it should be noted that a company must do so within the limits set by the law and in a manner consistent with societal expectations. The unfettered pursuit of profit can lead to behaviors that are outlawed by government regulations, opposed by important public constituencies, or simply unethical. Governments have enacted a wide range of regulations to govern business behavior, including antitrust laws, environmental laws, and laws pertaining to health and safety in the workplace. It is incumbent on managers to make sure that the company is in compliance with these laws when pursuing strategies.

Unfortunately, there is plenty of evidence that managers can be tempted to cross the line between the legal and illegal in their pursuit of greater profitability and profit growth. For example, in mid-2003 the Air Force stripped Boeing of $1 billion in contracts to launch satellites when it was discovered that Boeing had obtained thousands of pages of proprietary information from rival Lockheed Martin. Boeing had used that information to prepare its winning bid for the satellite contract. This was followed by the revelation that Boeing's CFO, Mike Sears, had offered a government official, Darleen Druyun, a lucrative job at Boeing while Druyun was still involved in evaluating whether Boeing should be awarded a $17 billion contract to build tankers for the Air Force. Boeing won the contract against strong competition from Airbus, and Boeing hired Druyun. It was clear that the job offer may have had an impact on the Air Force decision. Boeing fired Druyun and the CFO, and shortly thereafter, Boeing CEO Phil Condit resigned in a tacit acknowledgment that he bore responsibility for the ethics violations that had occurred at Boeing during his tenure as leader.[8] In another case, the chief executive of Archer Daniels Midland, one of the world's largest producers of agricultural products, was sent to jail after an FBI investigation revealed that the company had systematically tried to fix the price for lysine by colluding with other manufacturers in the global marketplace. In another example of price fixing, the 76-year-old chairman of Sotheby's auction house was sentenced to a jail term and the former CEO to house arrest for fixing prices with rival auction house Christie's over a 6-year period (see Strategy in Action 11.1).

Examples such as these beg the question of why managers would engage in such risky behavior. A body of academic work collectively known as agency theory provides an explanation for why managers might engage in behavior that is either illegal or, at the very least, not in the interest of the company's shareholders.

Agency Theory

Agency theory looks at the problems that can arise in a business relationship when one person delegates decision-making authority to another. It offers a way of understanding why managers do not always act in the best interests of stakeholders and

STRATEGY IN ACTION

Price Fixing at Sotheby's and Christie's

Sotheby's and Christie's are the two largest fine art auction houses in the world. In the mid-1990s, the two companies controlled 90% of the fine art auction market, which at the time was worth approximately $4 billion per year. Traditionally, auction houses make their profit by the commission they charge on auction sales. In good times, these commissions can be as high as 10% on some items, but in the early-1990s, the auction business was in a slump, with the supply of art for auction shriveling. With Sotheby's and Christie's desperate for works of art, sellers played the two houses against each other, driving commissions down to 2%, or sometimes lower.

To try to control this situation, Sotheby's CEO, Dede Brooks, met with her opposite number at Christie's, Christopher Davidge, in a series of clandestine meetings held in car parking lots that began in 1993. Brooks claims that she was acting on behalf of her boss, Alfred Taubman, the chairman and controlling shareholder of Sotheby's. According to Brooks, Taubman had agreed with the chairman of Christie's, Anthony Tennant, to work together in the weak auction market and limit price competition. In their meetings, Brooks and Davidge agreed to a fixed and nonnegotiable commission structure. Based on a sliding scale, the commission structure would range from 10% on a $100,000 item to 2% on a $5 million item. In effect,

Brooks and Davidge were agreeing to eliminate price competition between them, thereby guaranteeing both auction houses higher profits. The price-fixing agreement started in 1993 and continued unabated for 6 years until federal investigators uncovered the arrangement and brought charges against Sotheby's and Christie's.

With the deal out in the open, lawyers filed several class action lawsuits on behalf of the sellers that Sotheby's and Christie's had defrauded. Ultimately, at least 100,000 sellers signed on to the class action lawsuits, which the auction houses settled with a $512 million payment. The auction houses also pleaded guilty to price fixing and paid $45 million in fines to U.S. antitrust authorities. As for the key players, the chairman of Christie's, as a British subject, was able to avoid prosecution in the United States (price fixing is not an offense for which someone can be extradited). Christie's CEO, Davidge, struck a deal with prosecutors, and in return for amnesty turned incriminating documents in to the authorities. Brooks also cooperated with federal prosecutors and avoided jail (in April 2002 she was sentenced to 3 years probation, 6 months home detention, 1,000 hours of community service, and a $350,000 fine). Taubman, ultimately isolated by all his former co-conspirators, was sentenced to 1 year in jail and fined $7.5 million.

Source: S. Tully, "A House Divided," *Fortune,* December 18, 2000, pp. 264–275; J. Chaffin, "Sotheby's Ex CEO Spared Jail Sentence," *Financial Times,* April 30, 2002, p. 10; T. Thorncroft, "A Courtroom Battle of the Vanities," *Financial Times,* November 3, 2001, p. 3.

why they might sometimes behave unethically, and, perhaps, also illegally.[9] Although agency theory was originally formulated to capture the relationship between management and stockholders, the basic principles have also been extended to cover the relationship with other key stakeholders, such as employees, as well as relationships between different layers of management within a corporation.[10] While the focus of attention in this section is on the relationship between senior management and stockholders, some of the same language can be applied to the relationship between other stakeholders and top managers and between top management and lower levels of management.

Principal-Agent Relationships

The basic propositions of agency theory are relatively straightforward. First, an agency relationship is held to arise whenever one party delegates decision-making authority or control over resources to another. The principal is the person delegating authority, and the agent is the person to whom authority is delegated. The relationship between stockholders and senior managers is the classic example of an agency relationship. Stockholders, who are the principals, provide the company with risk capital but delegate control over that capital to senior managers, and particularly to the CEO, who, as their agent, is expected to use that capital in a manner that is consistent with the best interests of stockholders. As we have seen, this means using that capital to maximize the company's long-term profitability and profit growth rate.

The agency relationship continues down the hierarchy within the company. For example, in the large, complex, multibusiness company, top managers cannot possibly make all the important decisions, therefore, they delegate some decision-making authority and control over capital resources to business unit (divisional) managers. Thus, just as senior managers—such as the CEO—are the agents of stockholders, business unit managers are the agents of the CEO (and in this context, the CEO is the principal). The CEO entrusts business unit managers to use the resources over which they have control in the most effective manner in order to maximize the performance of their units. This helps the CEO ensure that he or she maximizes the performance of the entire company, thereby discharging agency obligation to stockholders. More generally, whenever managers delegate authority to managers below them in the hierarchy and give them the right to control resources, an agency relation is established.

The Agency Problem

While agency relationships often work well, problems may arise if agents and principals have different goals and if agents take actions that are not in the best interests of their principals. Agents may be able to do this because there is an **information asymmetry** between the principal and the agent: agents almost always have more information about the resources they are managing than the principal does. Unscrupulous agents can take advantage of any information asymmetry to mislead principals and maximize their own interests at the expense of principals.

In the case of stockholders, the information asymmetry arises because they delegate decision-making authority to the CEO, their agent, who, by virtue of his or her position inside the company, is likely to know far more than stockholders do about the company's operations. Indeed, there may be certain information about the company that the CEO is unwilling to share with stockholders because that information

Information asymmetry

A situation where an agent has more information about resources they are managing than the principal has.

would also help competitors. In such a case, withholding some information from stockholders may be in the best interest of all. More generally, the CEO, involved in the day-to-day running of the company, is bound to have an information advantage over stockholders, just as the CEO's subordinates may have an information advantage over the CEO with regard to the resources under their control.

The information asymmetry between principals and agents is not necessarily a bad thing, but it can make it difficult for principals to measure how well an agent is performing and thus hold the agent accountable for how well he or she is using the entrusted resources. There is a certain amount of performance ambiguity inherent in the relationship between a principal and agent: principals cannot know for sure if the agent is acting in his or her best interests. They cannot know for sure if the agent is using the resources to which he or she has been entrusted as effectively and efficiently as possible. To an extent, principals must trust the agent to do the right thing.

Of course, this trust is not blind: principals do put mechanisms in place with the purpose of monitoring agents, evaluating their performance, and if necessary, taking corrective action. As we shall see shortly, the board of directors is one such mechanism, for, in part, the board exists to monitor and evaluate senior managers on behalf of stockholders. Other mechanisms serve a similar purpose. In the United States, publicly owned companies must regularly file detailed financial statements with the SEC that are in accordance with generally agreed-upon accounting principles (GAAP). This requirement exists to give stockholders consistent and detailed information about how well management is using the capital with which it has been entrusted. Similarly, internal control systems within a company are there to help the CEO ensure that subordinates are using the resources with which they have been entrusted as efficiently and effectively as possible.

Despite the existence of governance mechanisms and comprehensive measurement and control systems, a degree of information asymmetry will always remain between principals and agents, and there is always an element of trust involved in the relationship. Unfortunately, not all agents are worthy of this trust. A minority will deliberately mislead principals for personal gain, sometimes behaving unethically or breaking laws in the process. The interests of principals and agents are not always the same; they diverge, and some agents may take advantage of information asymmetries to maximize their own interests at the expense of principals and to engage in behaviors that the principals would never condone.

For example, some authors have argued that, like many other people, senior managers are motivated by desires for status, power, job security, and income.[11] By virtue of their position within the company, certain managers, such as the CEO, can use their authority and control over corporate funds to satisfy these desires at the cost of returns to stockholders. CEOs might use their position to invest corporate funds in various perks that enhance their status—executive jets, lavish offices, and expense-paid trips to exotic locations—rather than investing those funds in ways that increase stockholder returns. Economists have termed such behavior **on-the-job consumption**.[12]

Aside from engaging in on-the-job consumption, CEOs, along with other senior managers, might satisfy their desires for greater income by using their influence or control over the board of directors to persuade the compensation committee of the board to grant pay increases. Critics of U.S. industry claim that extraordinary pay has now become an endemic problem and that senior managers are enriching themselves at the expense of stockholders and other employees. They point out that CEO pay has been increasing far more rapidly than the pay of average workers, primarily because of very liberal stock option grants that enable a CEO to earn huge pay bonuses in a rising stock market, even if the company underperforms the market and

On-the-job consumption

A term used by Economists to describe the behavior of company funds by senior management to acquire perks (such as lavish offices, jets, etc.) that will enhance their status, instead of investing it to increase stockholder returns.

competitors.[13] In 1980, the average CEO in *Business Week's* survey of CEO's of the largest 500 American companies earned 42 times what the average blue collar-worker earned. By 1990, this figure had increased to 85 times. Today, the average CEO in the survey earns more than 350 times the pay of the average blue-collar worker.[14]

What rankles critics is the size of some CEO pay packages and their apparent lack of relationship to company performance.[15] For example, in 2006, shareholders of Home Depot complained bitterly about the compensation package for CEO Bob Nardelli at the company's annual meeting. Nardelli, who was appointed in 2000, had received $124 million in compensation, despite mediocre financial performance at Home Depot and a 12% decline in the company's stock price since he joined. When unexercised stock options were included, his compensation exceeded $250 million.[16] Critics feel that the size of pay awards such as these is disproportionate to the achievement of the CEOs. If so, this represents a clear example of the agency problem.

A further concern is that in trying to satisfy a desire for status, security, power, and income, a CEO might engage in empire building—buying many new businesses in an attempt to increase the size of the company through diversification.[17] Although such growth may depress the company's long-term profitability and thus stockholder returns, it increases the size of the empire under the CEO's control and, by extension, the CEO's status, power, security, and income (there is a strong relationship between company size and CEO pay). Instead of trying to maximize stockholder returns by seeking the right balance between profitability and profit growth, some senior managers may trade long-term profitability for greater company growth via new business purchases. Figure 11.2 graphs long-term profitability against the rate of growth in company revenues. A company that does not grow is likely missing out on some

Figure 11.2 The Tradeoff Between Profitability and Revenue Growth Rates

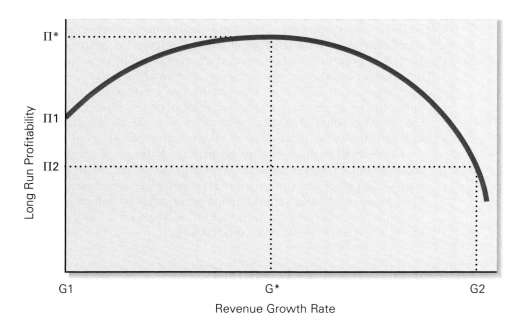

profitable opportunities.[18] A moderate revenue growth rate of G^* allows a company to maximize long-term profitability, generating a return of π^*. Thus, a growth rate of $G1$ in Figure 11.2 is not consistent with maximizing profitability ($\pi 1 < \pi^*$). By the same token, however, attaining growth in excess of $G2$ requires diversification into areas that the company knows little about. Consequently, it can be achieved only by sacrificing profitability; that is, past G^*, the investment required to finance further growth does not produce an adequate return, and the company's profitability declines. Yet $G2$ may be the growth rate favored by an empire-building CEO, for it will increase his or her power, status, and income. At this growth rate, profitability is equal only to $\pi 2$. Because $\pi^* > \pi 2$, a company growing at this rate is clearly not maximizing its long-run profitability or the wealth of its stockholders.

The magnitude of agency problems was emphasized in the early-2000s when a series of scandals swept through the corporate world, many of which could be attributed to self-interest-seeking senior executives and a failure of corporate governance mechanisms to hold the largess of those executives in check. Between 2001 and 2004, accounting scandals unfolded at a number of major corporations, including Enron, WorldCom, Tyco, Computer Associates, HealthSouth, Adelphia Communications, Dynegy, Royal Dutch Shell, and the major Italian food company, Parmalat. At Enron, $27 billion in debt was hidden from shareholders, employees, and regulators in special partnerships that were removed from the balance sheet. At Parmalat, managers apparently "invented" $8–$12 billion in assets to shore up the company's balance sheet—assets that never existed. In the case of Royal Dutch Shell, senior managers knowingly inflated the value of the company's oil reserves by 1/5, which amounted to 4 billion barrels of oil that never existed, making the company appear much more valuable than it actually was. At the other companies, earnings were systematically overstated, often by hundreds of millions of dollars, or even billions of dollars in the case of Tyco and WorldCom, which understated its expenses by $3 billion in 2001. In all of these cases, the prime motivation seems to have been an effort to present a more favorable view of corporate affairs to shareholders than was actually the case, thereby securing senior executives significantly higher pay packets.[19] Strategy in Action 11.2 specifically discusses accounting fraud at Computer Associates.

It is important to remember that the agency problem is not confined to the relationship between senior managers and stockholders. It can also bedevil the relationship between the CEO and subordinates and between them and their subordinates. Subordinates might use control over information to distort the true performance of their unit in order to enhance their pay, increase their job security, or make sure their unit gets more than its fair share of company resources.

Confronted with agency problems, the challenge for principals is to (1) shape the behavior of agents so that they act in accordance with the goals set by principals, (2) reduce the information asymmetry between agents and principals, and (3) develop mechanisms for removing agents who do not act in accordance with the goals of principals and mislead them. Principals try to deal with these challenges through a series of governance mechanisms.

Governance Mechanisms

Governance mechanisms are mechanisms that principals put in place to align incentives between principals and agents and to monitor and control agents. The purpose of governance mechanisms is to reduce the scope and frequency of the agency

STRATEGY IN ACTION

Self-Dealing at Computer Associates

Computer Associates is one of the world's largest software companies (company recently changed its name to CA Technologies). During the 1990s, its stock price appreciated at a rapid rate, driven primarily by surging revenues and a commensurate rise in profits. Because its revenues were growing more rapidly than those of rivals during the late-1990s, investors assumed that the company was gaining market share and that high profitability would follow, so they bid up the price of the company's stock. The senior managers of Computer Associates were major beneficiaries of this process.

Under a generous incentive program that the board of directors gave to the company's three top managers—Charles Wang, then CEO and chairman of the board; Sanjay Kumar, the chief operating officer; and Russell Artzt, the chief technology officer—if the stock price stayed above $53.13 for 60 days, they would receive a special incentive stock award amounting to some 20 million shares. In May 1998, Kumar announced that Computer Associates had "record" revenues and earnings for the quarter. The stock price surged beyond $53.13 and lingered long enough for all three managers to receive the special incentive stock award—then valued at $1.1 billion.

In late-July 1998, after all three managers had received the stock award, Kumar announced that the effect of Asian economic turmoil and the Y2K bug "leads us to believe that our revenue and earnings growth will slow over the next few quarters." The stock price promptly fell from the high $50s to under $40 a share. Immediately thereafter, a series of class action lawsuits, undertaken on behalf of stockholders, claimed that management had misled stockholders to enrich their own assets. As a result of the lawsuits, Wang, Kumar, and Artzt were compelled to give back some of their gains, and the size of the stock award was reduced to 4.5 million shares. Wang stepped down as CEO, although he retained his position as chairman of the board, and Kumar became the CEO.

This was not the end of matters, however; Computer Associates had attracted the attention of both the Justice Department and the SEC, which launched a joint investigation into the company's accounting practices. By 2002, they were reportedly focusing on a little-noticed action the company had taken in May 2000 to reduce its revenues by 10%, or $1.76 billion, below what it had previously reported for the 3 fiscal years that ended March 2000. The downward

revisions, detailed in the company's 10-K filings with the SEC, retroactively took hundreds of millions of dollars away from the top line in the 14 months preceding the May 1998 stock award to senior managers, including some $513 million for the year ending March 1998. According to the company, earnings were unaffected by the revision because the lost revenue was offset by a commensurate downward revision of expenses. The downward revision reportedly came at the urging of auditor KPMG, which replaced Ernst & Young as the company's accountant in June 1999.

Some observers implied that Computer Associates deliberately overstated its revenues in the period prior to May 1998 in order to enrich the three top managers. The losers in this process were stockholders, who purchased shares at the inflated price, and longer-term shareholders, who saw the value of their holdings diluted by the stock awarded to Wang, Kumar, and Artzt. In a statement issued after a report of the ongoing investigation was published in the *Wall Street Journal,* Computer Associates stated that it changed how it classified revenue and expenses at the advice of its auditors. "We continue to believe CA has acted appropriately," the company said. "This change in presentation had no impact on reported earnings, earnings per share, or cash flows."

By 2004, it was clear that Computer Associates had been doing business inappropriately. According to the SEC investigation, between 1998 and 2000, the company adopted a policy of backdating contracts to boost revenues. For example, in January 2000, Computer Associates negotiated a $300 million contract with a customer but backdated the contract so that the revenues appeared in 1999. Although initially this may have been done to help secure the $1.1 billion special stock award, by the mid 2000 the practice represented an increasingly desperate attempt to meet financial projects that the company was routinely missing. Under increasing pressure, Charles Wang stepped down as chairman in 2002, and in 2004, Kumar was forced to resign as CEO by the board of Computer Associates, which had belatedly come to recognize that the company's financial statements were fraudulent. In late 2004, in a deal with federal regulators, the company admitted to $2.2 billion in fraud. As part of the deal, Kumar was indicted by federal prosecutors on charges of obstruction of justice and securities fraud. In November 2006, Kumar was sentenced to 12 years in jail for his part in the fraud.

Source: J. Guidera, "Probe of Computer Associates Centers on Firm's Revenues," *Wall Street Journal* (2002): pp. A3, 15; Ronna Abramson, "Computer Associates Probe Focus on 1998, 1999 Revenue," *The Street.Com,* May 20, 2002; C. Forelle, M. Maremont, and G. Fields, "U.S. Indicts Sanjay Kumar for Fraud, Lies," *Wall Street Journal* (2004): p. A1. N. Varchaver, "Long Island Confidential," *Fortune* (2006): pp. 172–178.

problem: to help ensure that agents act in a manner that is consistent with the best interests of their principals. In this section, the primary focus is on the governance mechanisms that exist to align the interests of senior managers (as agents) with their principals, stockholders. It should not be forgotten, however, that governance mechanisms also exist to align the interests of business unit managers with those of their superiors, and likewise down the hierarchy within the organization.

Here we look at four main types of governance mechanisms for aligning stockholder and management interests: the board of directors, stock-based compensation, financial statements, and the takeover constraint. The section closes with a discussion of governance mechanisms within a company to align the interest of senior and lower-level managers.

The Board of Directors

The board of directors is the centerpiece of the corporate governance system. Board members are directly elected by stockholders, and under corporate law, they represent the stockholders' interests in the company. Hence, the board can be held legally accountable for the company's actions. Its position at the apex of decision making within the company allows it to monitor corporate strategy decisions and ensure that they are consistent with stockholder interests. If the board believes that corporate strategies are not in the best interest of stockholders, it can apply sanctions, such as voting against management nominations to the board of directors or submitting its own nominees. In addition, the board has the legal authority to hire, fire, and compensate corporate employees, including, most importantly, the CEO.[20] The board is also responsible for making sure that audited financial statements of the company present a true picture of its financial situation. Thus, the board exists to reduce the information asymmetry between stockholders and managers and to monitor and control management actions on behalf of stockholders.

The typical board of directors is composed of a mix of inside and outside directors. **Inside directors** are senior employees of the company, such as the CEO. They are required on the board because they have valuable information about the company's activities. Without such information, the board cannot adequately perform its monitoring function. But because insiders are full-time employees of the company, their interests tend to be aligned with those of management. Hence, outside directors are needed to bring objectivity to the monitoring and evaluation processes. **Outside directors** are not full-time employees of the company. Many of them are full-time professional directors who hold positions on the boards of several companies. The need to maintain a reputation as competent outside directors gives them an incentive to perform their tasks as objectively and effectively as possible.[21]

There is little doubt that many boards perform their assigned functions admirably. For example, when the board of Sotheby's discovered that the company had been engaged in price fixing with Christie's, board members moved quickly to oust both the CEO and the chairman of the company (see Strategy in Action 11.1). But not all boards perform as well as they should. The board of now bankrupt energy company Enron approved the company's audited financial statements, which were later discovered as grossly misleading.

Critics of the existing governance system charge that inside directors often dominate the outsiders on the board. Insiders can use their position within the management hierarchy to exercise control over what kind of company-specific information the board receives. Consequently, they can present information in a way that puts

Inside directors
Senior employees of the company, such as the CEO.

Outside directors
Directors who are not full-time employees of the company, needed to provide objectivity to the monitoring and evaluation of processes.

them in a favorable light. In addition, because insiders have intimate knowledge of the company's operations and because superior knowledge and control over information are sources of power, they may be better positioned than outsiders to influence boardroom decision making. The board may become the captive of insiders and merely rubber-stamp management decisions instead of guarding stockholder interests.

Some observers contend that many boards are dominated by the company CEO, particularly when the CEO is also the chairman of the board.[22] To support this view, they point out that both inside and outside directors are often the personal nominees of the CEO. The typical inside director is subordinate to the CEO in the company's hierarchy and therefore unlikely to criticize the boss. Because outside directors are frequently the CEO's nominees as well, they can hardly be expected to evaluate the CEO objectively. Thus, the loyalty of the board may be biased toward the CEO, not the stockholders. Moreover, a CEO who is also chairman of the board may be able to control the agenda of board discussions in such a manner as to deflect any criticisms of his or her leadership.

In the aftermath of a wave of corporate scandals that hit the corporate world in the early-2000s, there are clear signs that many corporate boards are moving away from merely rubber-stamping top management decisions and are beginning to play a much more active role in corporate governance. In part, they have been prompted by new legislation, such as the 2002 Sarbanes-Oxley Act in the United States, which tightened rules regulating corporate reporting and corporate governance. A growing trend on the part of the courts to hold directors liable for corporate misstatements has also been important. Powerful institutional investors such as pension funds have also been more aggressive in exerting their power, often pushing for more outside representation on the board of directors and for a separation between the roles of chairman and CEO—the chairman role going to an outsider. Partly as a result, over 50% of big companies had outside directors in the chairman's role by the late-2000s, up from less than half of that number in 1990. Separating the role of chairman and CEO limits the ability of corporate insiders, and particularly of the CEO, to exercise control over the board. Regardless, it must be recognized that boards of directors do not work as well as they should in theory, and other mechanisms are needed to align the interests of stockholders and managers.

Stock-Based Compensation

According to agency theory, one of the best ways to reduce the scope of the agency problem is for principals to establish incentives for agents to behave in the company's best interest through pay-for-performance systems. In the case of stockholders and top managers, stockholders can encourage top managers to pursue strategies that maximize a company's long-term profitability and profit growth, and thus the gains from holding its stock, by linking the pay of those managers to the performance of the stock price.

Giving managers **stock options** has been the most common pay-for-performance system: the right to purchase the company's shares at a predetermined (strike) price at some point in the future, usually within 10 years of the grant date. Typically, the strike price is the price at which the stock was trading when the option was originally granted. Ideally, stock options will motivate managers to adopt strategies that increase the share price of the company, for in doing so managers will also increase the value of their own stock options. Granting managers stock if they attain predetermined performance targets is another stock based pay-for-performance system.

Stock options

The right to purchase company stock at a predetermined price at some point in the future, usually within 10 years of the grant date.

Several academic studies suggest that stock-based compensation schemes for executives, such as stock options and stock grants, can align management and stockholder interests. For instance, one study found that managers were more likely to consider the effects of their acquisition decisions on stockholder returns if they were significant shareholders.[23] According to another study, managers who were significant stockholders were less likely to pursue strategies that would maximize the size of the company rather than its profitability.[24] More generally, it is difficult to argue with the proposition that the chance to get rich from exercising stock options is the primary reason for the 14-hour days and 6-day workweeks that many employees of fast-growing companies experience.

However, the practice of granting stock options has become increasingly controversial. Many top managers often earn huge bonuses from exercising stock options that were granted several years prior. Critics claim that these options are often too generous, but do not deny that they motivate managers to improve company performance. A particular cause for concern is that stock options are often granted at such low strike prices that the CEO can hardly fail to make a significant amount of money by exercising them, even if the company underperforms in the stock market by a significant margin. A serious example of the agency problem emerged in 2005 and 2006 when the SEC started to investigate a number of companies that had granted stock options to senior executives and apparently "backdated" the stock to a time when the price was lower, enabling executives to earn more money than if those options had simply been dated on the day they were granted.[25] By late-2006, the SEC was investigating nearly 130 companies for possible fraud related to stock option dating. Major corporations such as Apple, Jabil Circuit, United Healthcare, and Home Depot were included in the list.[26]

Other critics of stock options, including the famous investor Warren Buffett, complain that huge stock option grants increase the outstanding number of shares in a company and therefore dilute the equity of stockholders; accordingly, they should be shown in company accounts as an expense against profits. Under accounting regulations that were enforced until 2005, stock options, unlike wages and salaries, were not expensed. However, this has since changed, and as a result, many companies are beginning to reduce their use of options. Microsoft, for example, which had long given generous stock option grants to high performing employees, replaced stock options with stock grants in 2005.

Financial Statements and Auditors

Publicly trading companies in the United States are required to file quarterly and annual reports with the SEC that are prepared according to GAAP. The purpose of this requirement is to give consistent, detailed, and accurate information about how efficiently and effectively the agents of stockholders—the managers—are running the company. To make sure that managers do not misrepresent this financial information, the SEC also requires that the accounts be audited by an independent and accredited accounting firm. Similar regulations exist in most other developed nations. If the system works as intended, stockholders can have a lot of faith that the information contained in financial statements accurately reflects the state of affairs at a company. Among other things, such information can enable a stockholder to calculate the profitability (ROIC) of a company in which he or she invests and to compare its ROIC against that of competitors.

Unfortunately, this system has not always worked as intended in the United States. Despite that the vast majority of companies do file accurate information in their financial statements, and although most auditors review that information accurately, there is substantial evidence that a minority of companies have abused the system, aided in part by the compliance of auditors. This was clearly an issue at bankrupt energy trader Enron, where the CFO and others misrepresented the true financial state of the company to investors by creating off-balance-sheet partnerships that hid the true state of Enron's indebtedness from public view. Enron's auditor, Arthur Andersen, was complicit with this deception and in direct violation of its fiduciary duty. Arthur Anderson also had lucrative consulting contracts with Enron that it did not want to jeopardize by questioning the accuracy of the company's financial statements. The losers in this mutual deception were shareholders, who relied only upon inaccurate information to make their investment decisions.

There have been numerous examples in recent years of managers' gaming financial statements to present a distorted picture of their company's finances to investors. The typical motive has been to inflate the earnings or revenues of a company, thereby generating investor enthusiasm and propelling the stock price higher, which gives managers an opportunity to cash in stock option grants for huge personal gain, obviously at the expense of stockholders, who have been mislead by the reports (see Strategy in Action 11.2 for an example).

The gaming of financial statements by companies such as Enron and Computer Associates raises serious questions about the accuracy of the information contained in audited financial statements. In response, the United States passed the Sarbanes-Oxley Act in 2002, representing the biggest overhaul of accounting rules and corporate governance procedures since the 1930s. Among other things, Sarbanes-Oxley set up a new oversight board for accounting firms, required CEOs and CFOs to endorse their company's financial statements, and barred companies from hiring the same accounting firm for auditing and consulting services.

The Takeover Constraint

Given the imperfections in corporate governance mechanisms, it is clear that the agency problem may still exist at some companies. However, stockholders still have some residual power—they can always sell their shares. If stockholders sell in large numbers, the price of the company's shares will decline. If the share price falls far enough, the company might be worth less on the stock market than the actual value of its assets. At this point, the company may become an attractive acquisition target and runs the risk of being purchased by another enterprise, against the wishes of the target company's management.

The risk of being acquired by another company is known as the **takeover constraint**. The takeover constraint limits the extent to which managers can pursue strategies and take actions that put their own interests above those of stockholders. If they ignore stockholder interests and the company is acquired, senior managers typically lose their independence, and likely their jobs as well. Therefore, the threat of takeover can constrain management action and limit the worst excesses of the agency problem.

During the 1980s and early-1990s, the threat of takeover was often enforced by corporate raiders: individuals or corporations that purchase large blocks of shares in companies that appear to be pursuing strategies inconsistent with maximizing stockholder wealth. Corporate raiders argue that if these underperforming companies pursued different strategies, they could create more wealth for stockholders. Raiders purchase stock in a company either to take over the business and run it more efficiently, or to precipitate a change in the top management, replacing the existing team with one more

Takeover constraint
The risk of being acquired by another company.

likely to maximize stockholder returns. Raiders are motivated not by altruism but by gain. If they succeed in their takeover bid, they can institute strategies that create value for stockholders, including themselves. Even if a takeover bid fails, raiders can still earn millions, for their stockholdings will typically be bought out by the defending company for a hefty premium. Called **greenmail**, this source of gain stirred much controversy and debate about its benefits. While some claim that the threat posed by raiders has had a salutary effect on enterprise performance by pushing corporate management to run their companies better, others claim there is little evidence of this.[27]

Although the incidence of hostile takeover bids has fallen off significantly since the early-1990s, this should not imply that the takeover constraint has ceased to operate. Unique circumstances existed in the early-2000s that have made it more difficult to execute hostile takeovers. The boom years of the 1990s left many corporations with excessive debt (corporate America entered the new century with record levels of debt on its balance sheets), limiting the ability to finance acquisitions, particularly hostile acquisitions, which are often particularly expensive. In addition, the market valuations of many companies became maligned with underlying fundamentals during the stock market bubble of the 1990s, and after a substantial fall in certain segments of the stock market, such as the technology sector, valuations are still high relative to historic norms—making the hostile acquisition of even poorly run and unprofitable companies expensive. However, takeovers tend to occur in cycles, and it seems likely that once excesses are worked out of the stock market and off corporate balance sheets, the takeover constraint will begin to reassert again. It should be remembered that the takeover constraint is the governance mechanism of last resort and is often invoked only when other governance mechanisms have failed.

Governance Mechanisms Inside a Company

Thus far, this text has focused on the governance mechanisms designed to reduce the agency problem that potentially exists between stockholders and managers. Agency relationships also exist within a company, and the agency problem can arise between levels of management. In this section, we explore how the agency problem can be reduced within a company by using two complementary governance mechanisms to align the incentives and behavior of employees with those of upper-level management: strategic control systems and incentive systems.

Strategic Control Systems Strategic control systems are the primary governance mechanisms established within a company to reduce the scope of the agency problem between levels of management. These systems are the formal target setting, measurement, and feedback systems that allow managers to evaluate whether a company is executing the strategies necessary to maximize its long-term profitability and, in particular, whether the company is achieving superior efficiency, quality, innovation, and customer responsiveness. They are discussed in more detail in subsequent chapters.

The purpose of strategic control systems is to (1) establish standards and targets against which performance can be measured, (2) create systems for measuring and monitoring performance on a regular basis, (3) compare actual performance against the established targets, and (4) evaluate results and take corrective action if necessary. In governance terms, their purpose is to ensure that lower-level managers, as the agents of top managers, are acting in a way that is consistent with top managers' goals, which should be to maximize the wealth of stockholders, subject to legal and ethical constraints.

Greenmail

A source of gaining wealth by corporate raiders who benefit by pushing companies to either change their corporate strategy to one that will benefit stockholders, or by charging a premium for these stock when the company wants to buy them back.

One increasingly influential model that guides managers through the process of creating the right kind of strategic control systems to enhance organizational performance is the balanced scorecard model.[28] According to the balanced scorecard model, traditionally managers have primarily used financial measures of performance such as ROIC to measure and evaluate organizational performance. Financial information is extremely important, but it is not enough alone. If managers are to obtain a true picture of organizational performance, financial information must be supplemented with performance measures that indicate how well an organization has been achieving the four building blocks of competitive advantage: efficiency, quality, innovation, and responsiveness to customers. This is because financial results simply inform strategic managers about the results of decisions they have already taken; the other measures balance this picture of performance by informing managers about how accurately the organization has in place the building blocks that drive future performance.[29]

One version of the way the balanced scorecard operates is presented in Figure 11.3. Based on an organization's mission and goals, strategic managers develop a set of strategies to build competitive advantage to achieve these goals. They then establish an organizational structure to use resources to obtain a competitive advantage.[30] To evaluate how well the strategy and structure are working, managers develop specific performance measures that assess how well the four building blocks of competitive advantage are being achieved:

- *Efficiency* can be measured by the level of production costs, the productivity of labor (such as the employee hours needed to make a product), the productivity of capital (such as revenues per dollar invested in property, plant, and equipment), and the cost of raw materials.
- *Quality* can be measured by the number of rejects, the number of defective products returned from customers, and the level of product reliability over time.
- *Innovation* can be measured by the number of new products introduced, the percentage of revenues generated from new products in a defined period, the time

Figure 11.3 A Balanced Scorecard Approach

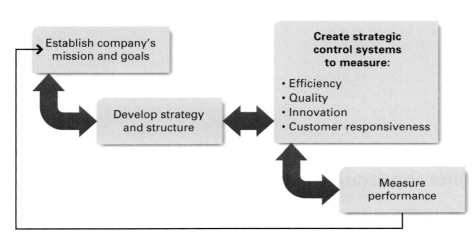

taken to develop the next generation of new products versus the competition, and the productivity of R&D (how much R&D spending is required to produce a successful product).

- *Responsiveness to customers* can be measured by the number of repeat customers, customer defection rates, level of on-time delivery to customers, and level of customer service.

As Kaplan and Norton, the developers of this approach, suggest, "Think of the balanced scorecard as the dials and indicators in an airplane cockpit. For the complex task of navigating and flying an airplane, pilots need detailed information about many aspects of the flight. They need information on fuel, air speed, altitude, learning, destination, and other indicators that summarize the current and predicted environment. Reliance on one instrument can be fatal. Similarly, the complexity of managing an organization today requires that managers be able to view performance in several areas simultaneously."[31]

The way in which managers' ability to build a competitive advantage translates into organizational performance is then assessed using financial measures such as the ROIC, the return on sales, and the capital turnover ratio (see Chapter 3). Based on an evaluation of the complete set of measures in the balanced scorecard, strategic managers are in a good position to reevaluate the company's mission and goals and take corrective action to rectify problems, limit the agency problem, or exploit new opportunities by changing the organization's strategy and structure—which is the purpose of strategic control.

Employee Incentives   Control systems alone may not be sufficient to align incentives between stockholders, senior management, and the rest of the organization. To help do this, positive incentive systems are often put into place to motivate employees to work toward goals that are central to maximizing long-term profitability. As already noted, ESOPs are one form of positive incentive, as are stock option grants. In the 1990s, ESOPs and stock ownership grants were pushed down deep within many organizations. The logic behind such systems is straightforward: recognizing that the stock price, and therefore their own wealth, is dependent upon the profitability of the company, employees will work toward maximizing profitability.

In addition to stock-based compensation systems, employee compensation can also be tied to goals that are linked to the attainment of superior efficiency, quality, innovation, and customer responsiveness. For example, the bonus pay of a manufacturing employee might depend upon attaining quality and productivity targets, which, if reached, will lower the costs of the company, increase customer satisfaction, and boost profitability. Similarly, a salesperson's bonus pay might be dependent upon surpassing sales targets, and an R&D employee's bonus pay upon the success of new products he or she had worked on developing.

Ethics and Strategy

Ethics

Accepted principles of right or wrong that govern the conduct of a person, the members of a profession, or the actions of an organization.

Business ethics

Accepted principles of right or wrong governing the conduct of businesspeople.

The term **ethics** refers to accepted principles of right or wrong that govern the conduct of a person, the members of a profession, or the actions of an organization. **Business ethics** are the accepted principles of right or wrong governing the conduct of businesspeople. Ethical decisions are in accordance with those accepted principles, whereas unethical decisions violate accepted principles. This is not as straightforward as it sounds. Managers may be confronted with **ethical dilemmas**, which are situations where there is no agreement over exactly what the accepted principles of right and wrong are, or where none of the available alternatives seems ethically acceptable.

In our society, many accepted principles of right and wrong are not only universally recognized but also codified into law. In the business arena there are laws governing product liability (tort laws), contracts and breaches of contract (contract law), the protection of intellectual property (intellectual property law), competitive behavior (antitrust law), and the selling of securities (securities law). Not only is it unethical to break these laws, it is illegal.

In this book we argue that the preeminent goal of managers in a business should be to pursue strategies that maximize the long-term profitability and profit growth of the enterprise, thereby boosting returns to stockholders. Strategies, of course, must be consistent with the laws that govern business behavior: managers must act legally while seeking to maximize the long-term profitability of the enterprise. Unfortunately, as we have already seen in this chapter, managers do break laws. Moreover, managers may take advantage of ambiguities and gray areas in the law, of which there are many in our common law system, to pursue actions that are at best legally suspect and, in any event, clearly unethical. It is important to realize, however, that behaving ethically surpasses staying within the bounds of the law. In the opening case, we discussed how Goldman Sachs sold bonds to investors that were deliberately structured to increase the risk of failure, and that it did so without informing clients. While the legality of this action is unclear (although Goldman did pay a fine, it admitted to no wrongdoing), it pushes the boundaries of ethical behavior.

For another example, see Strategy in Action 11.3, which discusses Nike's use of "sweatshop labor" in developing nations to make sneakers for consumers in the developed world. While Nike was not breaking any laws by using inexpensive labor that worked long hours for poor pay in poor working conditions, and neither were its subcontractors, many considered it unethical to use subcontractors who by Western standards clearly exploited their work force. In this section, we take a closer look at the ethical issues that managers may confront when developing strategy, and at the steps managers can take to ensure that strategic decisions are not only legal, but also ethical.

Ethical Issues in Strategy

The ethical issues that strategic managers confront cover many topics, but most are due to a potential conflict between the goals of the enterprise, or the goals of individual managers, and the fundamental rights of important stakeholders, including stockholders, customers, employees, suppliers, competitors, communities, and the general public. Stakeholders have basic rights that should be respected, and it is unethical to violate those rights.

Stockholders have the right to timely and accurate information about their investment (in accounting statements), and it is unethical to violate that right. Customers have the right to be fully informed about the products and services they purchase, including the right to information about how those products might cause them harm, and it is unethical to restrict their access to such information. Employees have the right to safe working conditions, fair compensation for the work they perform,

Ethical dilemmas

Situations where there is no agreement over exactly what the accepted principles of right and wrong are, or where none of the available alternatives seems ethically acceptable.

STRATEGY IN ACTION

Nike–the Sweatshop Debate

Nike is in many ways the quintessential global corporation. Established in 1972 by former University of Oregon track star Phil Knight, Nike is today one of the leading marketers of athletic shoes and apparel in the world, with sales in 140 countries. Nike does not do any manufacturing, rather, it designs and markets its products and contracts for their manufacture from a global network of 600 factories owned by subcontractors scattered around the globe, that together employ nearly 550,000 people. This huge corporation has made founder Phil Knight one of the richest people in America. Nike's marketing phrase: "Just Do It!" has become as recognizable in popular culture as its "swoosh" logo, or the faces of its celebrity sponsors, such as Tiger Woods.

For years the company was dogged by repeated and persistent accusations that its products are made in "sweatshops" where workers, many of them children, slaving away in hazardous conditions for wages below subsistence level. Nike's wealth, its detractors claim, has been built upon the backs of the world's poor. Many critics paint the Nike symbol as a sign of the evils of globalization: a rich Western corporation exploiting the world's poor to provide expensive shoes and apparel to the pampered consumers of the developed world. Nike's "Niketown" stores have become standard targets for anti-globalization protestors. Several nongovernmental organizations, such as San Francisco–based Global Exchange, a human rights organization dedicated to promoting environmental, political, and social justice around the world, targeted Nike for repeated criticism and protests. News organizations such as CBS's 48 Hours, hosted by Dan Rather, ran exposés on working conditions in foreign factories that supply Nike. Students on the campuses of several major U.S. universities, with which Nike entertains lucrative sponsorship deals, have protested against those deals, citing Nike's use of sweatshop labor.

Typical of the allegations were those detailed in the CBS news program 48 Hours in 1996. The report painted a picture of young women at a Vietnamese subcontractor who worked 6 days per week, in poor working conditions with toxic materials, for only $0.20 per hour. The report also stated that a living wage in Vietnam was at least $3 per day, an income that could not be achieved without working substantial overtime. Nike was not breaking any

laws, and nor were its subcontractors, but this report and others like it raised questions about the ethics of using "sweatshop labor" to make what were essentially fashion accessories. These actions may have been legal and may have helped the company to increase its profitability, but was it ethical to use subcontractors who, by Western standards, clearly exploited their work force? Nike's critics thought not, and the company found itself at the focus of a wave of demonstrations and consumer boycotts.

Adding fuel to the fire, in November 1997, Global Exchange obtained and leaked a confidential report by Ernst & Young of an audit that Nike had commissioned of a Vietnam factory owned by a Nike subcontractor. The factory had 9,200 workers and made 400,000 pairs of shoes per month. The Ernst & Young report painted a dismal picture of thousands of young women, most under age 25, laboring 10 and 1/2 hours per day, 6 days a week, in excessive heat and noise and foul air, for slightly more than $10 a week. The report also found that workers with skin or breathing problems had not been transferred to departments free of chemicals. More than half the workers who dealt with dangerous chemicals did not wear protective masks or gloves. The report stated that, in parts of the plant, workers were exposed to carcinogens that exceeded local legal standards by 177 times and that 77% of the employees suffered from respiratory problems.

These exposés surrounding Nike's use of subcontractors forced the company to reexamine its policies. Realizing that its subcontracting policies were perceived as unethical, Nike's management took a number of steps. They established a code of conduct for Nike subcontractors and set up a system whereby independent auditors would annually monitor all subcontractors. Nike's code of conduct required that all employees at footwear factories be at least 18 years old and that exposure to potentially toxic materials would not exceed the permissible exposure limits established by the U.S. Occupational Safety and Health Administration for workers in the United States. In short, Nike concluded that behaving ethically required going beyond the requirements of the law. It required the establishment and enforcement of rules that adhere to accepted moral principles of right and wrong.

Sources : "Boycott Nike," CBS News *48 Hours,* October 17, 1996; D. Jones, "Critics Tie Sweatshop Sneakers to 'Air Jordan'" *USA Today,* June 6, 1996, p. 1B; "Global Exchange Special Report: Nike Just Don't Do It," available at www.globalexchange.org/education/publications/ newsltr6.97p2.html#nike; S. Greenhouse, "Nike Shoeplant in Vietnam Is Called Unsafe for Workers," *New York Times,* November 8, 1997; V. Dobnik, "Chinese Workers Abused Making Nikes, Reeboks," *Seattle Times,* September 21, 1997, p. A4.

and just treatment by managers. Suppliers have the right to expect contracts to be respected, and the company should not take advantage of a power disparity between it and a supplier to opportunistically rewrite a contract. Competitors have the right to expect that the firm will abide by the rules of competition and not violate the basic principles of antitrust laws. Communities and the general public, including their political representatives in government, have the right to expect that a firm will not violate the basic expectations that society places on enterprises: for example, by dumping toxic pollutants into the environment, or overcharging for work performed on government contracts.

Those who take the stakeholder view of business ethics often argue that it is in the enlightened self-interest of managers to behave in an ethical manner that recognizes and respects the fundamental rights of stakeholders, because doing so will ensure the support of stakeholders and, ultimately, benefit the firm and its managers. Others go beyond this instrumental approach to ethics and argue that, in many cases, acting ethically is simply the right thing to do. They argue that businesses need to recognize their *noblesse oblige*, a French term that refers to honorable and benevolent behavior that is considered the responsibility of people of high (noble) birth, and give something back to the society that made their success possible. In a business setting, it is understood that benevolent behavior is the moral responsibility of successful enterprises.

Unethical behavior often arises in a corporate setting when managers decide to put the attainment of their own personal goals, or the goals of the enterprise, above the fundamental rights of one or more stakeholder groups (in other words, unethical behavior may arise from agency problems). The most common examples of such behavior involve self-dealing, information manipulation, anticompetitive behavior, opportunistic exploitation of other players in the value chain in which the firm is embedded (including suppliers, complement providers, and distributors), the maintenance of substandard working conditions, environmental degradation, and corruption.

Self-dealing occurs when managers find a way to feather their own nests with corporate monies, as we have already discussed in several examples in this chapter (such as Computer Associates). **Information manipulation** occurs when managers use their control over corporate data to distort or hide information in order to enhance their own financial situation or the competitive position of the firm. As we have seen, many accounting scandals have involved the deliberate manipulation of financial information. Information manipulation can also occur with nonfinancial data. An example of this is when managers at the tobacco companies suppressed internal research that linked smoking to health problems, violating the rights of consumers to accurate information about the dangers of smoking. When this evidence came to light, lawyers filed class action suits against the tobacco companies, claiming that they had intentionally caused harm to smokers: they had broken tort law by promoting a product that they knew was seriously harmful to consumers. In 1999, the tobacco companies settled a lawsuit brought by the states who sought to recover health care costs associated with tobacco-related illnesses; the total payout to the states was $260 billion.

Anticompetitive behavior covers a range of actions aimed at harming actual or potential competitors, most often by using monopoly power, and thereby enhancing the long-run prospects of the firm. For example, in the 1990s, the Justice Department claimed that Microsoft used its monopoly in operating systems to force PC makers to bundle Microsoft's Web browser, Internet Explorer, with the Windows Operating

Self-dealing

Managers using company funds for their own personal consumption, as done by Enron and Computer Associates in previous years.

Information manipulation

Managers use their control over corporate data to distort or hide information in order to enhance their own financial situation or the competitive position of the firm.

Anticompetitive behavior

A range of actions aimed at harming actual or potential competitors, most often by using monopoly power, and thereby enhancing the long-run prospects of the firm.

System, and to display Internet Explorer prominently on the computer desktop. Microsoft reportedly told PC makers that it would not supply them with Windows unless they did this. Since the PC makers needed Windows to sell their machines, this was a powerful threat. The alleged aim of the action, which exemplifies "tie-in-sales," which is illegal under antitrust laws, was to drive a competing browser maker, Netscape, out of business. The courts ruled that Microsoft was indeed abusing its monopoly power in this case, and under a 2001 consent decree, the company was forced to cease this practice.

Legality aside, the actions Microsoft managers allegedly engaged in are unethical on at least three counts; first, by violating the rights of end-users by unfairly limiting their choice; second, by violating the rights of downstream participants in the industry value chain, in this case PC makers, by forcing them to incorporate a particular product in their design; and third, by violating the rights of competitors to free and fair competition.

Opportunistic exploitation of other players in the value chain in which the firm is embedded is another example of unethical behavior. Exploitation of this kind typically occurs when the managers of a firm seek to unilaterally rewrite the terms of a contract with suppliers, buyers, or complement providers in a way that is more favorable to the firm, often using their power to force a revision to the contract. For example, in the late-1990s, Boeing entered into a $2 billion contract with Titanium Metals Corporation to purchase certain amounts of titanium annually for 10 years. In 2000, after Titanium Metals had already spent $100 million to expand its production capacity to fulfill the contract, Boeing demanded that the contract be renegotiated, asking for lower prices and an end to minimum purchase agreements. As a major purchaser of titanium, managers at Boeing probably thought they had the power to push this contract revision through, and Titanium's investment meant that it would be unlikely that the company walk away from the deal. Titanium promptly sued Boeing for breach of contract. The dispute was settled out of court, and under a revised agreement, Boeing agreed to pay monetary damages to Titanium Metals (reported to be in the $60 million range) and entered into an amended contract to purchase titanium.[32] This action was arguably unethical because it violated the supplier's rights to have buyers do business in a fair and open way, regardless of any legality.

Substandard working conditions arise when managers under-invest in working conditions, or pay employees below-market rates, in order to reduce their production costs. The most extreme examples of such behavior occur when a firm establishes operations in countries that lack the workplace regulations found in developed nations such as the United States. The example of Nike, mentioned earlier, falls into this category. In another example, The Ohio Art Company ran into an ethical storm when newspaper reports alleged that it had moved production of its popular Etch A Sketch toy from Ohio to a supplier in Shenzhen Province where employees—mostly teenagers—work long hours for $0.24 per hour, below the legal minimum wage of $0.33 per hour. Moreover, production reportedly started at 7:30 a.m. and continued until 10 p.m., with breaks only for lunch and dinner; Saturdays and Sundays were treated as normal workdays, meaning that employees worked 12 hours per day, 7 days per week, or 84 hours per week—well above the standard 40-hour week authorities set in Shenzhen. Working conditions such as these clearly violate employees' rights in China, as specified by local regulations (which are poorly enforced). Is it ethical for the The Ohio Art Company to use such a supplier? Many would say not.[33]

Opportunistic exploitation

Unethical behavior sometimes used by managers to unilaterally rewrite the terms of a contract with suppliers, buyers, or complement providers in a way that is more favorable to the firm.

Substandard working conditions

Arise when managers under-invest in working conditions, or pay employees below-market rates, in order to reduce their production costs.

Environmental degradation occurs when a company's actions directly or indirectly result in pollution or other forms of environmental harm. Environmental degradation can violate the rights of local communities and the general public for things such as clean air and water, land that is free from pollution by toxic chemicals, and properly managed forests.

Finally, **corruption** can arise in a business context when managers pay bribes to gain access to lucrative business contracts. For example, it was alleged that Halliburton was part of a consortium that paid nearly $180 million in bribes to win a lucrative contract to build a natural gas plant in Nigeria.[34] Corruption is clearly unethical because it violates many rights, including the right of competitors to a level playing field when bidding for contracts, and, when government officials are involved, the right of citizens to expect that government officials will act in the best interest of the local community (or nation) and not in response to corrupt payments that feather their own nests.

The Roots of Unethical Behavior

Why do some managers behave unethically? What motivates managers to engage in actions that violate accepted principals of right and wrong, trample on the rights of one or more stakeholder groups, or simply break the law? While there is no simple answer to this question, a few generalizations can be made.[35] First, it is important to recognize that business ethics are not divorced from **personal ethics**, which are the generally accepted principles of right and wrong governing the conduct of individuals. As individuals we are taught that it is wrong to lie and cheat and that it is right to behave with integrity and honor and to stand up for what we believe to be right and true. The personal ethical code that guides behavior comes from a number of sources, including parents, schools, religion, and the media. A personal ethical code will exert a profound influence on the way individuals behave as businesspeople. An individual with a strong sense of personal ethics is less likely to behave in an unethical manner in a business setting; in particular, he or she is less likely to engage in self-dealing and more likely to behave with integrity.

Second, many studies of unethical behavior in a business setting have come to the conclusion that businesspeople sometimes do not realize that they are behaving unethically, primarily because they simply fail to ask the relevant question: Is this decision or action ethical? Instead, they apply straightforward business calculus to what they perceive to be a business decision, forgetting that the decision may also have an important ethical dimension.[36] The fault here is within the processes that do not incorporate ethical considerations into business decision-making. This may have been the case at Nike when managers originally made subcontracting decisions (see the Strategy in Action 11.3). Those decisions were probably made on the basis of good economic logic. Subcontractors were probably chosen on the basis of business variables such as cost, delivery, and product quality, and key managers simply failed to ask: "How does this subcontractor treat its work force?" If managers pondered this question at all, they probably reasoned that it was the subcontractor's concern, not the company's.

Unfortunately, the climate in some businesses does not encourage people to think through the ethical consequences of business decisions. This brings us to the third cause of unethical behavior in businesses: an organizational culture that de-emphasizes business ethics and considers all decisions to be purely economic ones. A related fourth cause of unethical behavior may be pressure from top management to meet performance goals that are unrealistic and can only be attained by cutting corners or acting in an unethical manner.

Environmental degradation

Occurs when a company's actions directly or indirectly result in pollution or other forms of environmental harm.

Corruption

Can arise in a business context when managers pay bribes to gain access to lucrative business contracts.

Personal ethics

Generally accepted principles of right and wrong governing the conduct of individuals.

An organizational culture can "legitimize" behavior that society would judge as unethical, particularly when this is mixed with a focus upon unrealistic performance goals, such as maximizing short-term economic performance regardless of the costs. In such circumstances, there is a greater-than-average probability that managers will violate their own personal ethics and engage in behavior that is unethical. By the same token, an organization's culture can do just the opposite and reinforce the need for ethical behavior. At HP, for example, Bill Hewlett and David Packard, the company's founders, propagated a set of values known as "The HP Way." These values, which shape the way business is conducted both within and by the corporation, have an important ethical component. Among other things, they stress the need for confidence in and respect for people, open communication, and concern for the individual employee.

This brings us to a fifth root cause of unethical behavior: *unethical leadership*. Leaders help to establish the culture of an organization, and they set the example that others follow. Other employees in a business often take their cues from business leaders, and if those leaders do not behave in an ethical manner, employees may not either. It is not what leaders say that matters, but what they do. A good example is Ken Lay, the former CEO of the failed energy company Enron. While constantly referring to Enron's code of ethics in public statements, Lay simultaneously engaged in behavior that was ethically suspect. Among other things, he failed to discipline subordinates who had inflated earnings by engaging in corrupt energy trading schemes. Such behavior sent a very clear message to Enron's employees—unethical behavior would be tolerated if it could boost earnings.

Behaving Ethically

What is the best way for managers to ensure that ethical considerations are taken into account? In many cases, there is no easy answer to this question, for many of the most vexing ethical problems involve very real dilemmas and suggest no obvious right course of action. Nevertheless, managers can and should do at least 7 things to ensure that basic ethical principles are adhered to and that ethical issues are routinely considered when making business decisions. They can (1) favor hiring and promoting people with a well-grounded sense of personal ethics, (2) build an organizational culture that places a high value on ethical behavior, (3) make sure that leaders within the business not only articulate the rhetoric of ethical behavior but also act in a manner that is consistent with that rhetoric, (4) put decision-making processes in place that require people to consider the ethical dimension of business decisions, (5) use ethics officers, (6) put strong governance processes in place, and (7) act with moral courage.

Hiring and Promotion It seems obvious that businesses should strive to hire people who have a strong sense of personal ethics and would not engage in unethical or illegal behavior. Similarly, you would rightly expect a business to not promote people, and perhaps fire people, whose behavior does not match generally accepted ethical standards. But doing this is actually very difficult. How do you know if someone has a poor sense of personal ethics? In this society, if someone lacks personal ethics, he or she may hide this fact to retain people's trust.

Is there anything that businesses can do to ensure they do not hire people who have poor personal ethics, particularly given that people have an incentive to hide this from public view (indeed, unethical people may well lie about their nature)? Businesses can give potential employees psychological tests to try to discern their ethical predisposition, and they can check with prior employees regarding someone's reputation, such as by asking for letters of reference and talking to people who have worked with the prospective employee. The latter approach is certainly not uncommon and does influence the hiring process. Promoting people who have displayed poor ethics should not occur in a company where the organization's culture values ethical behavior and where leaders act accordingly.

Organization Culture and Leadership To foster ethical behavior, businesses must build an organization culture that places a high value on ethical behavior. Three actions are particularly important. First, businesses must explicitly articulate values that place a strong emphasis on ethical behavior. Many companies now do this by drafting a **code of ethics**, a formal statement of the ethical priorities to which a business adheres. Others have incorporated ethical statements into documents that articulate the values or mission of the business. For example, the food and consumer products giant Unilever's code of ethics includes the following points: "We will not use any form of forced, compulsory or child labor" and "No employee may offer, give or receive any gift or payment which is, or may be construed as being, a bribe. Any demand for, or offer of, a bribe must be rejected immediately and reported to management."[37] Unilever's principles send a very clear message to managers and employees within the organization. The Focus on Dell feature also shows, as you can see, that Dell has a well-established code of ethics, like Unilever.

Having articulated values in a code of ethics or some other document, it is important that leaders in the business give life and meaning to those words by repeatedly emphasizing their importance and then acting on them. This means using every relevant opportunity to stress the importance of business ethics and making sure that key business decisions not only make good economic sense—but also are ethical. Many companies have gone a step further and hired independent firms to audit them and make sure that they are behaving in a manner consistent with their ethical code. Nike, for example, has in recent years hired independent auditors to make sure that its subcontractors are adhering to Nike's code of conduct.

Finally, building an organization culture that places a high value on ethical behavior requires incentive and reward systems, including promotional systems that reward people who engage in ethical behavior and sanction those who do not.

Decision-Making Processes In addition to establishing the right kind of ethical culture in an organization, businesspeople must be able to think through the ethical implications of decisions in a systematic way. To do this, they need a moral compass, and both rights theories and Rawls's theory of justice help to provide such a compass. Beyond these theories, some experts on ethics have proposed a straightforward practical guide, or ethical algorithm, to determine whether a decision is ethical. A decision is acceptable on ethical grounds if a businessperson can answer "yes" to each of these questions:

1. Does my decision fall within the accepted values or standards that typically apply in the organizational environment (as articulated in a code of ethics or some other corporate statement)?
2. Am I willing to see the decision communicated to all stakeholders affected by it—for example, by having it reported in newspapers or on television?
3. Would the people with whom I have a significant personal relationship, such as family members, friends, or even managers in other businesses, approve of the decision?

Code of ethics

Formal statement of the ethical priorities to which a business adheres.

FOCUS ON D∕LL

Dell's Code of Ethics

Michael Dell has long put his name to a comprehensive code of ethics at Dell, Inc. The code specifies with great precision what Dell requires of its employees. Dell states that the success of the company is built upon "a foundation of personal and professional integrity" and that company's employees must hold themselves to standards of ethical behavior that "go well beyond legal minimums."

A set of values is at the center of the code of conduct that Michael Dell characterizes as "the Soul of Dell":

Trust - Our word is good. We keep our commitments to each other and to our stakeholders.

Integrity - We do the right thing without compromise. We avoid even the appearance of impropriety.

Honesty - What we say is true and forthcoming—not just technically correct. We are open and transparent in our communications with each other and about business performance.

Judgment - We think before we act and consider the consequences of our actions.

Respect -We treat people with dignity and value their contributions. We maintain fairness in all relationships.

Courage - We speak up for what is right. We report wrongdoing when we see it.

Responsibility - We accept the consequences of our actions. We admit our mistakes and quickly correct them. We do not retaliate against those who report violations of law or policy.

The code goes beyond these general statements, however, to detail what Dell employees cannot do. For example, with regard to bribes and gifts, the code states that "as a Dell employee you must never accept or give a bribe." The code also prohibits the receipt of any gifts with a nominal value of over $50 that may "compromise your judgment."

Dell has established a Global Ethics Officer, a Global Ethics Council, and Regional Ethics Committees to make sure that the company's ethics policy is enforced. Employees can report ethics violations directly to the Officer and associated committees, or via an anonymous ethics hotline.

Source: Dell Computer, "Code of Conduct: Winning with Integrity," Accessed from Dell's corporate Website.

Ethics Officers   To make sure that a business behaves in an ethical manner, a number of firms now have ethics officers. These individuals are responsible for making sure that all employees are trained to be ethically aware, that ethical considerations enter the business decision-making process, and that they adhere to the company's code of ethics. Ethics officers may also be responsible for auditing decisions to ensure that they are consistent with this code. In many businesses, ethics officers act as an internal ombudsperson with responsibility for handling confidential inquiries from employees, investigating complaints from employees or others, reporting findings, and making recommendations for change.

United Technologies, a large aerospace company with worldwide revenues of over $28 billion, has had a formal code of ethics since 1990. There are now some 160 "business practice officers" within United Technologies (this is the company's name for ethics officers) who are responsible for making sure that employees adhere to the code. United Technologies also established an ombudsperson program in 1986 that allows employees to inquire anonymously about ethics issues. The program has received approximately 56,000 inquiries since 1986, and 8,000 cases have been handled by an ombudsperson.[38]

Strong Corporate Governance   Strong corporate governance procedures are needed to ensure that managers adhere to ethical norms, in particular, that senior managers do not engage in self-dealing or information manipulation. Strong corporate governance procedures require an independent board of directors that is willing to hold top managers accountable for self-dealing and is capable of verifying the information managers provide them. If companies like Tyco, WorldCom, and Enron had had a strong board of directors, it is unlikely that these companies would have experienced accounting scandals, or that top managers would have been able to access the funds of these corporations as personal treasuries.

There are five cornerstones of strong governance. The first is a board of directors that is composed of a majority of outside directors who have no management responsibilities in the firm, who are willing and able to hold top managers accountable, and who do not have business ties with important insiders. Outside directors should be individuals of high integrity whose reputation is based on their ability to act independently. The second cornerstone is a board where the positions of CEO and chairman are held by separate individuals and the chairman is an outside director. When the CEO is also chairman of the board of directors, he or she can control the agenda, thereby furthering his or her own personal agenda (which may include self-dealing) or limiting criticism against current corporate policies. The third cornerstone is a compensation committee formed by the board that is composed entirely of outside directors. It is the compensation committee that sets the level of pay for top managers, including stock option grants and additional benefits. The scope of self-dealing is reduced by making sure that the compensation committee is independent of managers. Fourth, the audit committee of the board, which reviews the financial statements of the firm, should also be composed of outsiders, thereby encouraging vigorous independent questioning of the firm's financial statements. Finally, the board should use outside auditors who are truly independent and do not have a conflict of interest. This was not the case in many recent accounting scandals, where outside auditors were also consultants to the corporation and therefore less likely to ask management hard questions for fear that doing so would jeopardize lucrative consulting contracts.

Moral Courage   It is important to recognize that sometimes managers and others need significant moral courage. It is moral courage that enables managers to walk away from a decision that is profitable but unethical, that gives employees the strength to say no to superiors who instruct them to behave unethically, and that gives employees the integrity to go to the media and blow the whistle on persistent unethical behavior in a company. Moral courage does not come easily; there are well-known cases where individuals have lost their jobs because they blew the whistle on unethical corporate behaviors.

Companies can strengthen the moral courage of employees by making a commitment to refuse retribution on employees that exercise moral courage, say no to superiors, or otherwise complain about unethical actions. For example, Unilever's code of ethics includes the following:

> *Any breaches of the Code must be reported in accordance with the procedures specified by the Joint Secretaries. The Board of Unilever will not criticize management for any loss of business resulting from adherence to these principles and other mandatory policies and instructions. The Board of Unilever expects employees to bring to their attention, or to that of senior management, any breach or suspected breach of these principles. Provision has been made for employees to be able to report in confidence and no employee will suffer as a consequence of doing so.*

This statement gives "permission" to employees to exercise moral courage. Companies can also set up ethics hotlines that allow employees to anonymously register a complaint with a corporate ethics officer.

Final Words The steps discussed here can help to ensure that, when managers make business decisions, they are fully cognizant of the ethical implications and do not violate basic ethical prescripts. At the same time, not all ethical dilemmas have a clean and obvious solution—that is why they are dilemmas. At the end of the day, there are things that a business should not do, and there are things that a business should do, but there are also actions that present managers with true dilemmas. In these cases a premium is placed upon the ability of managers to make sense out of complex, messy situations and to make balanced decisions that are as just as possible.

Ethical Dilemma

You work for a U.S.-based textile company that is having trouble competing with overseas competitors that have access to low cost labor. While you pay your factory workers $14 an hour plus benefits, you know that a similar textile mill in Vietnam is paying its employees around $0.50 an hour, and the mill does not have to comply with the same costly safety and environmental regulations that your company does. After transportation costs have been taken into account, the Vietnamese factory still has a clear cost advantage. Your CEO says that it is time to shut down the mill, lay off employees, and move production to a country in Central America or South East Asia where labor and compliance costs are much, much lower. The U.S. mill is the only large employer in this small community. Many of the employees have been working at the mill their entire working lives. The mill is marginally profitable.

What appears to be the right action to take for stockholders? What is the most ethical course of action? Is there a conflict in this situation?

Summary of Chapter

1. Stakeholders are individuals or groups that have an interest, claim, or stake in the company, in what it does, and in how well it performs.

2. Stakeholders are in an exchange relationship with the company. They supply the organization with important resources (or contributions) and in exchange expect their interests to be satisfied (by inducements).

3. A company cannot always satisfy the claims of all stakeholders. The goals of different groups may conflict. The company must identify the most important stakeholders and give highest priority to pursuing strategies that satisfy their needs.

4. A company's stockholders are its legal owners and the providers of risk capital, a major source of the capital resources that allow a company to oper-

ate its business. As such, they have a unique role among stakeholder groups.

5. Maximizing long-term profitability and profit growth is the route to maximizing returns to stockholders, and it is also consistent with satisfying the claims of several other key stakeholder groups.

6. When pursuing strategies that maximize profitability, a company has the obligation to do so within the limits set by the law and in a manner consistent with societal expectations.

7. An agency relationship is held to arise whenever one party delegates decision-making authority or control over resources to another.

8. The essence of the agency problem is that the interests of principals and agents are not always the same, and some agents may take advantage of information asymmetries to maximize their own interests at the expense of principals.

9. A number of governance mechanisms serve to limit the agency problem between stockholders and managers. These include the board of directors, stock-based compensation schemes, financial statements and auditors, and the threat of a takeover.

10. The term ethics refers to accepted principles of right or wrong that govern the conduct of a person, the members of a profession, or the actions of an organization. Business ethics are the accepted principles of right or wrong governing the conduct of businesspeople, and an ethical strategy is one that does not violate these accepted principles.

11. Unethical behavior is rooted in poor personal ethics; the inability to recognize that ethical issues are at stake, as when there are psychological and geographical distances between a foreign subsidiary and the home office; failure to incorporate ethical issues into strategic and operational decision making; a dysfunctional culture; and failure of leaders to act in an ethical manner.

12. To make sure that ethical issues are considered in business decisions, managers should (a) favor hiring and promoting people with a well-grounded sense of personal ethics, (b) build an organizational culture that places a high value on ethical behavior, (c) ensure that leaders within the business not only articulate the rhetoric of ethical behavior but also act in a manner that is consistent with that rhetoric, (d) put decision-making processes in place that require people to consider the ethical dimension of business decisions, (e) use ethics officers, (f) have strong corporate governance procedures, and (g) be morally courageous and encourage others to be the same.

Discussion Questions

1. In a public corporation, should the CEO of the company also be allowed to be the chairman of the board (as allowed for by the current law)? What problems might this give rise to?

2. Is it ethical for a firm faced with a shortage of labor to employ illegal immigrants as labor?

3. How prevalent has the agency problem been in corporate America during the last decade? During the late-1990s there was a boom in initial public offerings of Internet companies (dot. com companies). The boom was supported by sky high valuations often assigned to Internet startups that had no revenues or earnings. The boom came to an abrupt end in 2001, when the NASDAQ stock market collapsed, losing almost 80% of its value. Who do you think benefited most from this boom: investors (stockholders) in those companies, managers, or investment bankers?

4. Why is maximizing ROIC consistent with maximizing returns to stockholders?

5. How might a company configure its strategy-making processes to reduce the probability that managers will pursue their own self-interest at the expense of stockholders?

6. Under what conditions is it ethically defensible to outsource production to producers in the developing world who have much lower labor costs when such actions involve laying off long-term employees in the firm's home country?

Practicing Strategic Management

Small Group Exercises

Small-Group Exercise: Evaluating Stakeholder Claims

Break up into groups of 3–5 people, and appoint one group member as a spokesperson who will communicate your findings to the class when called on by the instructor. Discuss the following:

1. Identify the key stakeholders of your educational institution. What claims do they place on the institution?
2. Strategically, how is the institution responding to those claims? Do you think the institution is pursuing the correct strategies in view of those claims? What might it do differently, if anything?
3. Prioritize the stakeholders in order of their importance for the survival and health of the institution. Do the claims of different stakeholder groups conflict with each other? If the claims do conflict, whose claim should be tackled first?

Strategy Sign-On

Article File 11

Find an example of a company that ran into trouble because it failed to take into account the rights of one of its stakeholder groups when making an important strategic decision.

Strategic Management Project

Developing Your Portfolio: Module 11 This module deals with the relationships your company has with its major stakeholder groups. With the information you have at your disposal, perform the tasks and answer the questions that follow:

1. Identify the main stakeholder groups in your company. What claims do they place on the company? How is the company trying to satisfy those claims?
2. Evaluate the performance of the CEO of your company from the perspective of (a) stockholders, (b) employees, (c) customers, and (d) suppliers. What does this evaluation tell you about the ability of the CEO and the priorities that he or she is committed to?
3. Try to establish whether the governance mechanisms that operate in your company do a good job of aligning the interests of top managers with those of stockholders.
4. Pick a major strategic decision made by your company in recent years, and try to think through the ethical implications of that decision. In the light of your review, do you think that the company acted correctly?

CLOSING CASE
The Fall of John Thain

When the new CEO, John Thain, arrived at the beleaguered investment bank Merrill Lynch in November 2007, he was viewed as a potential savior. Merrill Lynch had been staggering under enormous losses related to America's mortgage crisis. The company had a large portfolio of CDOs, or complex financial derivatives created to insure bonds backed by home mortgages against the possibility of default. The former CEO, Stan O'Neal, had taken Merrill Lynch into the CDOs business when trading these instruments was very profitable. But as real estate prices collapsed in America and mortgage defaults soared, the value of these CDOs could not be accurately determined, they could not be resold, and companies like Merrill Lynch had to write billions off their balance sheets. Stan O'Neal was fired from Merrill Lynch by the board of directors and replaced by John Thain.

Thain was recruited from the New York Stock Exchange, which he had lead since 2004. At the NYSE, Thain followed hot on the heels of Richard Grasso, who had been dismissed from the NYSE in a scandal over excessive executive compensation (in 1 year Grasso had received over $130 million in pay). Under Thain's, leadership, the NYSE prospered, its stock price rose 600% between 2004 and 2007, and Thain's reputation followed.

At Merrill Lynch, Thain found himself confronted by enormous challenges. He was able to raise additional capital for Merrill, helping to stave off bankruptcy. He also cut costs, laying off thousands of employees, and exiting several businesses. To the employees that remained, he preached the virtues of tight cost control, telling them that miscellaneous personal expenses had to be reduced to a minimum. Ultimately, however, Thain recognized that Merrill Lynch could not survive as an independent entity. Although the Federal Government had already committed $10 billion in additional capital to the company as part of its financial rescues package for the banking sector, Merrill Lynch still needed more. In the fall of 2008, and Thain

engineered the company's sale to Bank of America. The acquisition was set to close in early 2009; Thain received overwhelmingly positive press. Under the acquisition agreement, Thain would continue working at Bank of America, reporting directly to CEO Ken Lewis. It was at this point that things started to go very wrong for him.

First, it was revealed that when he was cutting jobs and preaching the virtues of cost controls, Thain was at the same time personally authorizing $1.2 million to redecorate his office at Merrill Lynch. He spent $800,000 to hire a well-known designer, $87,000 on an area rug, four pairs of curtains for $28,000, a pair of guest chairs for $87,000, and more. If this wasn't bad enough, it was soon discovered that he had accelerated 2008 bonus payments at Merrill Lynch by several weeks, thereby allowing executives to collect bonuses *before* the acquisition by Bank of American closed. Many wondered why Merrill Lynch was granting any bonuses, when the firm was booking large losses, the stock had lost over 80% of its value, and the government was lending $10 billion to the troubled company. Compensation and benefits at Merrill Lynch totaled $15 billion in 2008, including $2 billion in bonuses! The total compensation was down just 6% from the prior year. How, some asked, could this possibly be justified given the enormous destruction of stockholder wealth at Merrill Lynch? Moreover, newspapers were reporting that Thain had personally lobbied the board of directors' compensation committee at the company for a multimillion dollar bonus for 2008, arguing that he had effectively saved the company by engineering a sale and should be rewarded for it. When this information became public, an embarrassed Thain quickly changed his position and stated that he would take no bonus for the year 2008.

Things came to a head in December 2008, when Thain revealed to Ken Lewis that Merrill's losses in the fourth quarter would be much larger than previously thought, totaling nearly

$15.3 billion. Lewis, who was reportedly furious at being mislead, almost scuttled the buy out, but was pressured to proceed by the Federal Government, which had already loaned money to Bank of America, and now committed another $20 billion in capital to help it with Merrill Lynch's losses. Three weeks after the deal closed, however, Bank of America announced that Thain would leave the company. Effectively, he had been fired.[39]

Case Discussion Questions

1. If you put the issues related to bonuses and personal perks to one side, how would you judge the effectiveness of John Thain as the leader of an organization deep in crisis?

2. Where the actions that John Thain took on personal perks and bonuses legal? Were they ethical? What does this case teach you about the difference between staying within the bounds of the law and behaving ethically?

3. Why do you think John Thain pushed for such high bonuses in 2008 given that Merrill was in a deep financial crisis? What might his motivations have been?

4. What might John Thain have done differently? If he had pursued a different set of actions with regard to personal perks and bonuses, what might the outcome have been for him and for Merrill Lynch?

5. At the end of 2008, the financial markets were in the middle of the deepest crisis since the great depression. Losses were increasing in financial institutions by the hour as the value of their holdings of mortgage-backed securities plummeted. Given this situation, shouldn't Ken Lewis have expected higher losses at Merrill Lynch? Was Thain really misleading him? Why might he have been mislead?

Notes

[1] L. Story and G. Morgenson, "SEC accuses Goldman of Fraud in Housing Deal," *New York Times*, April 16, 2010; J. Stempel and S. Eder, "Goldman Sachs Charged with Fraud by SEC," *Reuters*, April 16, 2010; "Sachs and the Shitty," *The Economist*, May 1, 2010.

[2] E. Freeman, *Strategic Management: A Stakeholder Approach* (Boston: Pitman Press, 1984).

[3] C. W. L. Hill and T. M. Jones, "Stakeholder-Agency Theory," *Journal of Management Studies* 29 (1992): 131–154; J. G. March and H. A. Simon, *Organizations* (New York: Wiley, 1958).

[4] Hill and Jones, "Stakeholder-Agency Theory"; C. Eesley and M.J. Lenox, "Firm Responses to Secondary Stakeholder Action," *Strategic Management Journal* 27 (2006): pp. 13–24.

[5] I. C. Macmillan and P. E. Jones, *Strategy Formulation: Power and Politics* (St. Paul: West, 1986).

[6] Tom Copeland, Tim Koller, and Jack Murrin, *Valuation: Measuring and Managing the Value of Companies* (New York: Wiley, 1996).

[7] R. S. Kaplan and D. P. Norton, *Strategy Maps* (Boston: Harvard Business School Press, 2004).

[8] A. L. Velocci, D. A. Fulghum, and R. Wall, "Damage Control," *Aviation Week*, December 1, 2003, pp. 26–27.

[9] M. C. Jensen and W. H. Meckling, "Theory of the Firm: Managerial Behavior, Agency Costs and Ownership Structure," *Journal of Financial Economics* 3 (1976): 305–360; E. F. Fama, "Agency Problems and the Theory of the Firm," *Journal of Political Economy* 88 (1980): pp. 375–390.

[10] Hill and Jones, "Stakeholder-Agency Theory."

[11] For example, see R. Marris, *The Economic Theory of Managerial Capitalism* (London: Macmillan, 1964); J. K. Galbraith, *The New Industrial State* (Boston: Houghton Mifflin, 1970).

[12] Fama, "Agency Problems and the Theory of the Firm."

[13] A. Rappaport, "New Thinking on How to Link Executive Pay with Performance," *Harvard Business Review,* March–April 1999, pp. 91–105.

[14] D Henry and D. Stead, "Worker vs CEO: Room to Run," *Business Week*, October 30, 2006, p. 13.

[15] For academic studies that look at the determinants of CEO pay, see M. C. Jensen and K. J. Murphy, "Performance Pay and Top Management Incentives," *Journal of Political Economy* 98 (1990): pp. 225–264; Charles W. L. Hill and Phillip Phan, "CEO Tenure as a Determinant of CEO Pay," *Academy of Management Journal* 34 (1991): pp. 707–717; H. L. Tosi and L. R. Gomez-Mejia, "CEO Compensation Monitoring and Firm Performance," *Academy of Management Journal* 37 (1994): pp. 1002–1016; and Joseph F. Porac, James B. Wade, and Timothy G. Pollock, "Industry Categories and the Politics of the Comparable Firm in CEO Compensation," *Administrative Science Quarterly* 44 (1999): pp. 112–144.

[16] Andrew Ward, "Home Depot Investors Stage a Revolt," *Financial Times*, May 26, 2006, p. 20.

[17] For research on this issue, see Peter J. lane, A. A. Cannella, and M. H. Lubatkin, "Agency Problems as Antecedents to Unrelated Mergers and Diversification: Amihud and Lev Reconsidered," *Strategic Management Journal* 19 (1998): pp. 555–578.

[18] E. T. Penrose, *The Theory of the Growth of the Firm* (London: Macmillan, 1958).

[19] G. Edmondson and L. Cohn, "How Parmalat Went Sour," *Business Week*, January 12, 2004, pp. 46–50; "Another Enron? Royal Dutch Shell." *Economist,* March 13, 2004, p. 71.

[20] O. E. Williamson, *The Economic Institutions of Capitalism* (New York: Free Press, 1985).

[21] Fama, "Agency Problems and the Theory of the Firm."

[22] S. Finkelstein and R. D'Aveni, "CEO Duality as a Double Edged Sword," *Academy of Management Journal* 37 (1994): pp. 1079–1108; B. Ram Baliga and R. C. Moyer, "CEO Duality and Firm Performance," *Strategic Management Journal* 17 (1996): pp. 41–53; M. L. Mace, *Directors: Myth and Reality* (Cambridge: Harvard University Press, 1971); S. C. Vance, *Corporate Leadership: Boards of Directors and Strategy* (New York: McGraw-Hill, 1983).

[23] W. G. Lewellen, C. Eoderer, and A. Rosenfeld, "Merger Decisions and Executive Stock Ownership in Acquiring Firms," *Journal of Accounting and Economics* 7 (1985): pp. 209–231.

[24] C. W. L. Hill and S. A. Snell, "External Control, Corporate Strategy, and Firm Performance," *Strategic Management Journal* 9 (1988): pp. 577–590.

[25] The phenomenon of back dating stock options was uncovered by academic research, and then picked up by the SEC. See Erik Lie, "On the Timing of CEO Stock Option Awards," *Management Science*, 51 (2005) pp. 802–812.

[26] G. Colvin, "A Study in CEO Greed," *Fortune*, June 12, 2006, pp. 53–55.

[27] J. P. Walsh and R. D. Kosnik, "Corporate Raiders and Their Disciplinary Role in the Market for Corporate Control," *Academy of Management Journal* 36 (1993): pp. 671–700.

[28] R. S. Kaplan and D. P. Norton, "The Balanced Scorecard—Measures That Drive Performance," *Harvard Business Review,* January–February 1992, pp. 71–79; Kaplan and Norton, *Strategy Maps* (Boston: Harvard Business School Press, 2004).

[29] R. S. Kaplan and D. P. Norton, "Using the Balanced Scorecard as a Strategic Management System," *Harvard Business Review,* January–February 1996, pp. 75–85; Kaplan and Norton, *Strategy Maps.*

[30] R. S. Kaplan and D. P. Norton, "Putting the Balanced Scorecard to Work," *Harvard Business Review,* September–October 1993, pp. 134–147; Kaplan and Norton, *Strategy Maps.*

[31] Kaplan and Norton, "The Balanced Scorecard," p. 72.

[32] Anonymous, "Timet, Boeing Settle Lawsuit," *Metal Center News,* June 2001, vol. 41, pp. 38–39.

[33] Joseph Kahn, "Ruse in Toyland: Chinese Workers Hidden Woe," *New York Times,* December 7, 2003, pp. A1, A8.

[34] N. King, "Halliburton Tells the Pentagon Workers Took Iraq Deal Kickbacks," *Wall Street Journal,* (2004): p. A1; Anonymous, "Whistleblowers Say Company Routinely Overcharged," *Reuters,* February 12, 2004; R. Gold and J. R. Wilke. "Data Sought in Halliburton Inquiry," *Wall Street Journal* (2004): p. A6.

[35] Saul W. Gellerman, "Why Good Managers Make Bad Ethical Choices," *Ethics in Practice: Managing the Moral Corporation,* ed. Kenneth R. Andrews (Harvard Business School Press, 1989).

[36] Ibid.

[37] Can be found on Unilever's Web site at www.unilever.com/company/ourprinciples/

[38] Taken from United Technologies Website

[39] D. Fitzpatrick, "Thain Ousted in Clash at Bank of America," *Wall Street Journal* 2009; G. Farrell, "BofA had role in Merrill Bonuses," *Financial Times*, January 25, 2009; C. Gasparino, "John Thain's $87,000 Rug," *The Daily Beast*, January 22, 2009.

Alan Mulally Transforms Ford's Structure and Culture

After a loss of more than $13 billion in 2006, William Ford III, who had been Ford Motor's CEO for 5 years, decided he was not the right person to turnaround the company's performance.[1] In fact, it became apparent that he was a part of Ford's management problems because he and other top managers at Ford tried to build and protect their own corporate empires, and none would ever admit that mistakes had occurred over the years. As a result, the entire company's performance had suffered; its future was in doubt. Deciding they needed an outsider to change the way the company operated, Ford recruited Alan Mulally from Boeing to become the new CEO.

After arriving at Ford, Mulally attended hundreds of executive meetings with his new managers. At one meeting, he became confused why one top division manager, who obviously did not know the answer to one of Mulally's questions concerning the performance of his car division, rambled on for several minutes trying

to disguise his ignorance. Mulally turned to his second-in-command Mark Fields and asked him why the manager had done that. Fields explained that "at Ford you never admit when you don't know something." He also told Mulally that when he arrived as a middle manager at Ford and wanted to ask his boss to lunch to gain information about divisional operations, he was told: "What rank are you at Ford? Don't you know that a subordinate never asks a superior to lunch?"[2]

Mulally discovered that over the years Ford had developed a tall hierarchy composed of managers whose primary goal was to protect their turf and avoid any direct blame for its plunging car sales. When asked why car sales were falling, they did not admit to bad design and poor quality issues in their divisions; instead they hid in the details. Managers brought thick notebooks and binders to meetings, using the high prices of components and labor costs to explain why their own particular car models were not selling well—or why they had to be sold at a loss. Why, Mulally wondered, did Ford's top executives have this inward-looking, destructive mind-set? How could he change Ford's organizational structure and culture to reduce costs and speed product development to build the kinds of vehicles customers wanted?

First, Mulally decided he needed to change Ford's structure, and that a major reorganization of the company's hierarchy was necessary. He decided to flatten Ford's structure and recentralize control at the top so that all top divisional managers reported to him. But, at the same time, he emphasized that teamwork and the development of a cross-divisional approach to manage the enormous value-chain challenges that confronted Ford in its search for ways to reduce its cost structure. He eliminated two levels in the top management hierarchy and clearly defined each top manager's role in the turn-around process so the company could begin to act as a whole instead of as separate divisions in which managers pursued their own interests.[3]

Mulally also realized, however, that simply changing Ford's structure was not enough to change the way it operated, its other major organizational problem was that the values and norms in Ford's culture that had developed over time hindered cooperation and teamwork. These values and norms promoted secrecy and ambiguity; they emphasized status and rank so managers could protect their information—the best way managers of its different divisions and functions believed to maintain jobs and status was to hoard, rather than share, information. The reason only the boss could ask a subordinate to lunch was to allow superiors to protect their information and positions!

What could Mulally do? He issued a direct order that the managers of every division share with every other Ford division a detailed statement of the costs they incurred to build each of its vehicles. He insisted that each of Ford's divisional presidents should attend a weekly (rather than a monthly) meeting to openly share and discuss the problems all the company's divisions faced. He also told managers they should bring a different subordinate with them to each meeting so every manager in the hierarchy would learn of the problems that had been kept hidden.

Essentially, Mulally's goal was to demolish the dysfunctional values and norms of Ford's culture that focused managers' attention on their own empires at the expense of the entire company. Mulally's goal was to create new values

Bradley C. Bower/Bloomberg via Getty Images

and norms that encouraged employees to admit mistakes, share information about all aspects of model design and costs, and, of course, find ways to speed development and reduce costs. He also wanted to change Ford's culture to allow norms of cooperation to develop both within and across divisions to allow its new structure to work effectively and improve company performance.

By 2011, it was clear that Mulally's attempts to change Ford's structure and culture had succeeded. The company reported a profit in the spring of 2010, for which Mulally received over $17 million in salary and other bonuses, and by 2011 it was reporting record profits as the sales of its vehicles soared.[4] In 2011, Mulally had reached 65, the normal retirement age for Ford's top managers, but in a press conference announcing Ford's record results, William Ford joked that he hoped Mulally would still be in charge of the transformed company in 2025.

Overview

As the story of Ford's recovery suggests, organizational structure and culture can have a direct effect upon a company's profits. This chapter examines how managers can best implement their strategies through their organization's structure and culture to achieve a competitive advantage and superior performance. A well-thought-out business model becomes profitable only if it can be implemented successfully. In practice, however, implementing strategy through structure and culture is a difficult, challenging, and never-ending task. Managers cannot create an organizing framework for a company's value-chain activities and assume it will keep working efficiently and effectively over time—just as they cannot select strategies and assume that these strategies will still be effective in the future–in a changing competitive environment.

We begin by discussing the primary elements of organizational design and the way these elements work together to create an organizing framework that allows a company to implement its chosen strategy. We also discuss how strategic managers can use structure, control, and culture to pursue functional-level strategies that create and build distinctive competencies. We will also discuss the implementation issues facing managers in a single industry at the industry level. The next chapter examines strategy implementation across industries and countries—that is—corporate and global strategy. By the end of this chapter and the next, you will understand why the fortunes of a company often rest on its managers' ability to design and manage its structure, control systems, and culture to best implement its business model.

Implementing Strategy through Organizational Design

Strategy implementation involves the use of **organizational design**, the process of deciding how a company should create, use, and combine organizational structure, control systems, and culture to pursue a business model successfully. **Organizational structure**

Organizational design

The process of deciding how a company should create, use, and combine organizational structure, control systems, and culture to pursue a business model successfully.

Organizational structure

The means through which a company assigns employees to specific tasks and roles and specifies how these tasks and roles are to be linked together to increase efficiency, quality, innovation, and responsiveness to customers.

assigns employees to specific value creation tasks and roles and specifies how these tasks and roles are to work together in a way that increases efficiency, quality, innovation, and responsiveness to customers—the distinctive competencies that build competitive advantage. The purpose of organizational structure is to *coordinate and integrate* the efforts of employees at all levels—corporate, business, and functional—and across a company's functions and business units so that all levels work together in a way that will allow the company to achieve the specific set of strategies in its business model.

Organizational structure does not, by itself, provide the set of incentives through which people can be *motivated* to make the company work. Hence, there is a need for control systems. The purpose of a **control system** is to provide managers with (1) a set of incentives to motivate employees to work toward increasing efficiency, quality, innovation, and responsiveness to customers and (2) specific feedback on how well an organization and its members are performing and building competitive advantage so that managers can continuously take action to strengthen a company's business model. Structure provides an organization with a skeleton; control gives it the muscles, sinews, nerves, and sensations that allow managers to regulate and govern its activities.

Organizational culture, the third element of organizational design, is the specific collection of values, norms, beliefs, and attitudes that are shared by people and groups in an organization and that control the way they interact with each other and with stakeholders outside the organization.[5] Organizational culture is a company's way of doing something: it describes the characteristic ways—"this is the way we do it around here"—in which members of an organization get the job done. Top managers, because they can influence which kinds of beliefs and values develop in an organization, are an important determinant of how organizational members will work toward achieving organizational goals, as we discuss later.[6]

Figure 12.1 sums up what has been discussed in this chapter. Organizational structure, control, and culture are the means by which an organization motivates and coordinates its members to work toward achieving the building blocks of competitive advantage.

Control system

Provides managers with incentives for employees as well as feedback on how the company performs.

Organizational culture

The specific collection of values, norms, beliefs, and attitudes that are shared by people and groups in an organization and that control the way they interact with each other and with stakeholders outside the organization.

Figure 12.1 Implementing Strategy through Organizational Design

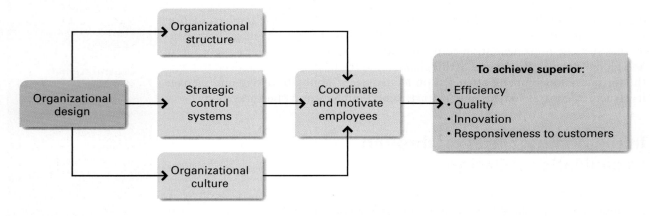

Top managers who wish to find out why it takes a long time for people to make decisions in a company, why there is a lack of cooperation between sales and manufacturing, or why product innovations are few and far between, need to understand how the design of a company's structure and control system, and the values and norms in its culture, affect employee motivation and behavior. *Organizational structure, control, and culture shape people's behaviors, values, and attitudes and determine how they will implement an organization's business model and strategies.*[7] On the basis of such an analysis, top managers can devise a plan to reorganize or change their company's structure, control systems, and culture to improve coordination and motivation. Effective organizational design allows a company to obtain a competitive advantage and achieve above-average profitability.

Building Blocks of Organizational Structure

After formulating a company's business model and strategies, managers must make designing an organizational structure their next priority. The value creation activities of organizational members are meaningless unless some type of structure is used to assign people to tasks and connect the activities of different people and functions.[8] Managers must make three basic choices:

1. How best to group tasks into functions and to group functions into business units or divisions to create distinctive competencies and pursue a particular strategy.
2. How to allocate authority and responsibility to these functions and divisions.
3. How to increase the level of coordination or integration between functions and divisions as a structure evolves and becomes more complex.

We first discuss basic issues and then revisit them when considering appropriate choices of structure at different levels of strategy.

Grouping Tasks, Functions, and Divisions

Because an organization's tasks are, to a large degree, a function of its strategy, the dominant view is that companies choose a form of structure to match their organizational strategy. Perhaps the first person to address this issue formally was the Harvard business historian Alfred D. Chandler.[9] After studying the organizational problems experienced in large U.S. corporations such as DuPont and GM as they grew in the early decades of the 20th century, Chandler reached two conclusions: (1) in principle, organizational structure follows the range and variety of tasks that the organization chooses to pursue and (2) structures of U.S. companies' structures change as their strategy changes in a predictable way over time.[10] In general, this means that most companies first group people and tasks into functions and then functions into divisions.[11]

As we discussed earlier, a *function* is a collection of people who work together and perform the same types of tasks or hold similar positions in an organization.[12] For example, the salespeople in a car dealership belong to the sales function. Together, car sales, car repair, car parts, and accounting are the set of functions that allow a car dealership to sell and maintain cars.

As organizations grow and produce a wider range of products, the amount and complexity of the *handoffs*, that is, the work exchanges or transfers among people, functions, and subunits, increase. The communications and measurement problems and the managerial inefficiencies surrounding these transfers or handoffs are a major source of *bureaucratic costs*, which we discussed in Chapter 10. Recall that these are the costs associated with monitoring and managing the functional exchanges necessary to add value to a product as it flows along a company's value chain to the final customer.[13] We discuss why bureaucratic costs increase as companies pursue more complex strategies later in the chapter.

For now, it is important to note that managers first group tasks into functions, and second, group functions into a business unit or division, to reduce bureaucratic costs. A *division* is a way of grouping functions to allow an organization to better produce and transfer its goods and services to customers such as the way Ford's vehicles are made in different divisions. In developing an organizational structure, managers must decide how to group an organization's activities by function and division in a way that achieves organizational goals effectively.[14]

Top managers can choose from among many kinds of structures to group their activities. The choice is made on the basis of the structure's ability to successfully implement the company's business models and strategies.

Allocating Authority and Responsibility

As organizations grow and produce a wider range of goods and services, the size and number of their functions and divisions increase. The number of handoffs, or transfers, between employees also increases. To economize on bureaucratic costs and effectively coordinate the activities of people, functions, and divisions, managers must develop a clear and unambiguous **hierarchy of authority**, or chain of command, which defines each manager's relative authority beginning with the CEO, continuing through middle managers and first-line managers, and then to the employees who directly make goods or provide services.[15] Every manager, at every level of the hierarchy, supervises one or more subordinates. The term **span of control** refers to the number of subordinates who report directly to a manager. When managers know exactly what their authority and responsibilities are, information distortion problems that promote managerial inefficiencies are kept to a minimum, and handoffs or transfers can be negotiated and monitored to economize on bureaucratic costs. For example, managers are less likely to risk invading another manager's turf and can avoid the costly conflicts that inevitably result from such encroachments.

Tall and Flat Organizations   Companies choose the number of hierarchical levels they need on the basis of their strategy and the functional tasks necessary to create distinctive competencies.[16] As an organization grows in size or complexity (measured by the number of its employees, functions, and divisions), its hierarchy of authority typically lengthens, making the organizational structure "taller." A *tall structure* has many levels of authority relative to company size; a *flat structure* has fewer levels relative to company size (see Figure 12.2). As the hierarchy becomes taller, problems that make the organization's structure less flexible and slow managers' response to changes in the competitive environment may result. It is vital that managers understand how these problems arise so they know how to change a company's structure to respond accordingly.

First, communication problems may arise. When an organization has many levels in the hierarchy, it can take a long time for the decisions and orders of top managers to reach other managers in the hierarchy, and it can take a long time for top managers

Hierarchy of authority

The clear and unambiguous chain of command that defines each manager's relative authority from the CEO down through top, middle, to first-line managers.

Span of control

The number of subordinates who report directly to a particular manager.

Figure 12.2 Tall and Flat Structures

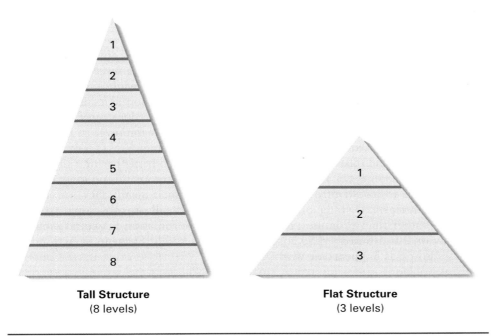

Tall Structure
(8 levels)

Flat Structure
(3 levels)

© Cengage Learning 2013

to learn how well the actions based upon their decisions work. Feeling out of touch, top managers may want to verify that lower-level managers are following orders and may require written confirmation from them. Lower-level managers, who know they will be held strictly accountable for their actions, start devoting more time to the process of making decisions to improve their chances of being right. They might even try to avoid responsibility by making top managers decide what actions to take.

A second communication problem that can result is the distortion of commands and orders as they are transmitted up and down the hierarchy, which causes managers at different levels to interpret what is happening in their own unique way. Accidental distortion of orders and messages occurs when different managers interpret messages from their own narrow functional perspectives. Intentional distortion can occur when managers lower in the hierarchy decide to interpret information in a way that increases their own personal advantage.

Tall hierarchies usually indicate that an organization is employing too many expensive managers, creating a third problem. Managerial salaries, benefits, offices, and secretaries are a huge expense for organizations. Large companies such as IBM, Ford, and Google pay their managers billions of dollars per year. In the recent recession, millions of middle and lower managers were laid off as companies strived to survive by reorganizing and simplifying their structures, and downsizing their workforce to reduce their cost structure.

The Minimum Chain of Command To avoid the problems that result when an organization becomes too tall and employs too many managers, top managers need to ascertain whether they are employing the right number of top, middle, and first-line managers, and see whether they can redesign their hierarchies to reduce the number of managers. Top managers might follow a basic organizing principle: the **principle of the minimum chain of command,** which states that a company should choose the hierarchy with the *fewest* levels of authority necessary to use organizational resources efficiently and effectively.

Effective managers constantly scrutinize their hierarchies to see whether the number of levels can be reduced—for example, by eliminating one level and giving the responsibilities of managers at that level to managers above, while empowering employees below. This practice has become increasingly common as companies battle with low-cost overseas competitors and search for ways to reduce costs. Many well-known managers such as Alan Mulally continually strive to empower employees and keep the hierarchy as flat as possible; their message is that employees should feel free to go above and beyond their prescribed roles to find ways to better perform their roles.

When companies become too tall, and the chain of command too long, strategic managers tend to lose control over the hierarchy, which means they lose control over their strategies. Disaster often follows because a tall organizational structure decreases, rather than promotes, motivation and coordination between employees and functions, and bureaucratic costs escalate as a result. Strategy in Action 12.1 discusses how this happened at Walt Disney.

Centralization or Decentralization? One important way to reduce the problems associated with too-tall hierarchies and reduce bureaucratic costs is to *decentralize*

Principle of the minimum chain of command

The principal that a company should design its hierarchy with the fewest levels of authority necessary to use organizational resources effectively.

STRATEGY IN ACTION

Bob Iger Flattens Walt Disney

When Bob Iger, who had been COO of Disney under its then-CEO Michael Eisner, took control of the troubled Walt Disney company, he decided to immediately act upon a problem he had observed with the way the company was operating. For several years, Disney had been plagued by slow decision making and analysts claimed it had made many mistakes in putting its new strategies into action. Disney stores were losing money, its Internet properties were not getting many "hits," and even its theme parks seemed to have lost their luster as few new rides or attractions had been introduced.

Iger believed that one of the main reasons for Disney's declining performance was that it had become too tall and bureaucratic, and its top managers were following financial rules that did not lead to innovative strategies. To turn around the performance of the poorly performing company, one of Iger's first decisions was to dismantle Disney's central strategic planning office. In this office,

several levels of managers were responsible for sifting through all the new ideas and innovations suggested by Disney's different business divisions (such as theme parks, movies, gaming) and then deciding which ideas to present to the CEO. Iger saw the strategic planning office as a bureaucratic bottleneck that actually reduced the number of ideas coming from below. He dissolved the office and reassigned its managers to Disney's different business units.

More new ideas are being generated by the different business units as a result of eliminating this unnecessary layer in Disney's hierarchy. The level of innovation has also increased because managers are more willing to speak out and champion ideas when they know they are working directly with the CEO and a top management team searching for innovative new ways to improve performance rather than a layer of strategic planning "bureaucrats" only concerned for the bottom line.

Source: www.waltdisney.com, 2011.

authority—that is, vest authority in managers at lower levels in the hierarchy as well as at the top. Authority is *centralized* when managers at the upper levels of a company's hierarchy retain the authority to make the most important decisions. When authority is decentralized, it is delegated to divisions, functions, and employees at lower levels in the company. Delegating authority in this fashion reduces bureaucratic costs because it avoids the communication and coordination problems that arise when information is sent up the hierarchy, sometimes to the top of the organization, and then back down again in order for decisions to be made. There are three advantages to decentralization.

First, when top managers delegate operational decision-making responsibility to middle- and first-level managers, they reduce information overload and are able to spend more time on competitively positioning the company and strengthening its business model. Second, when managers in the bottom layers of the company become responsible for implementing strategies to suit local conditions, their motivation and accountability increase. The result is that decentralization promotes flexibility and reduces bureaucratic costs because lower-level managers are authorized to make on-the-spot decisions; handoffs are not needed. The third advantage is that when lower-level employees are given the right to make important decisions, fewer managers are needed to oversee their activities and tell them what to do—a company can flatten its hierarchy.

If decentralization is so effective, why don't all companies decentralize decision making and avoid the problems of tall hierarchies? The answer is that centralization has its advantages, too. Centralized decision making allows for easier coordination of the organizational activities needed to pursue a company's strategy. If managers at all levels can make their own decisions, overall planning becomes extremely difficult, and the company may lose control of its decision making.

Centralization also means that decisions fit an organization's broad objectives. When its branch operations managers were getting out of control, for example, Merrill Lynch increased centralization by installing more information systems to give corporate managers greater control over branch activities. Similarly, HP centralized R&D responsibility at the corporate level to provide a more directed corporate strategy. Furthermore, in times of crisis, centralization of authority permits strong leadership because authority is focused upon one person or group. This focus allows for speedy decision making and a concerted response by the whole organization. How to choose the right level of centralization for a particular strategy is discussed later. Strategy in Action 12.2, however, discusses one company that benefits from centralizing authority and one company that benefits from decentralizing authority.

Integration and Integrating Mechanisms

Much coordination takes place among people, functions, and divisions through the hierarchy of authority. Often, however, as a structure becomes complex, this is not enough, and top managers need to use various **integrating mechanisms** to increase communication and coordination among functions and divisions. The greater the complexity of an organization's structure, the greater is the need for coordination among people, functions, and divisions to make the organizational structure work efficiently.[17] We discuss three kinds of integrating mechanisms that illustrate the kinds of issues involved.[18] Once again, these mechanisms are employed to economize on the information distortion problems that commonly arise when managing the handoffs or transfers among the ideas and activities of different people, functions, and divisions.

Integrating mechanisms

Ways to increase communication and coordination among functions and divisions.

STRATEGY IN ACTION

Important Choices at Union Pacific and Yahoo!

Union Pacific (UP), one of the biggest railroad freight carriers in the United States, faced a crisis when an economic boom in the early-2000s led to a record increase in the amount of freight the railroad had to transport. At the same time, the railroad was experiencing record delays in moving this freight. UP's customers complained bitterly about the problem, and the delivery delays cost the company tens of millions of dollars in penalty payments. Why the problem? UP's top managers decided to centralize authority high in the organization and to standardize operations to reduce operating costs. All scheduling and route planning were handled centrally at headquarters to increase efficiency. The job of regional managers was largely to ensure the smooth flow of freight through their regions.

Recognizing that efficiency had to be balanced by the need to be responsive to customers, UP announced a sweeping reorganization. Regional managers would have the authority to make everyday operational decisions; they could alter scheduling and routing to accommodate customer requests even if it raised costs. UP's goal was to "return to excellent performance by simplifying our processes and becoming easier to deal with." In deciding to decentralize authority, UP was following the lead of its competitors that had already decentralized their operations. Its managers would continue to "decentralize decision making into the field, while fostering improved customer responsiveness, operational excellence, and personal accountability." The result has been continued success for the company; in fact, in 2011 several large companies recognized UP as the top railroad in on-time service performance and customer service.

Yahoo! has been forced by circumstances to pursue a different approach to decentralization. In 2009, after Microsoft failed to take over Yahoo! because of the resistance of Jerry Wang, a company founder, the company's stock price plunged. Wang, who had come under intense criticism for preventing the merger, resigned as CEO and was replaced by Carol Bartz, a manager with a long history of success in managing online companies. Bartz moved quickly to find ways to reduce Yahoo!'s cost structure and simplify its operations to maintain its strong online brand identity. Intense competition from the growing popularity of online companies such as Google, Facebook, and Twitter also threatened its popularity.

Bartz decided the best way to restructure Yahoo! was to recentralize authority. To gain more control over its different business units and reduce operating costs, she decided to centralize functions that had previously been performed by Yahoo!'s different business units, such as product development and marketing activities. For example, all the company's publishing and advertising functions were centralized and placed under the control of a single executive. Yahoo!'s European, Asian, and emerging markets divisions were centralized, and another top executive took control. Bartz's goal was to find out how she could make the company's resources perform better. While she was centralizing authority, she was also holding many "town hall" meetings asking Yahoo! employees from all functions, "What would you do if you were me?" Even as she centralized authority to help Yahoo! recover its dominant industry position, she was looking for the input of employees at every level in the hierarchy.

Nevertheless, in 2011, Yahoo! was still in a precarious position. It had signed a search agreement with Microsoft to use the latter's search technology, Bing; Bartz had focused on selling off Yahoo!'s noncore business assets to reduce costs and gain the money for strategic acquisitions. But the company was still in an intense battle with other dot-coms that had more resources, such as Google and Facebook, and in September 2011 Bartz was fired by Yahoo!'s board of directors. In October 2011, both Microsoft and Google were reportedly planning to acquire the troubled company for around $20 billion—obviously Yahoo! is still for sale—at the right price.

Source: www.ups.com, 2011; www.yahoo.com, 2011.

Direct Contact   Direct contact among managers creates a context within which managers from different functions or divisions can work together to solve mutual problems. However, several problems are associated with establishing this contact. Managers from different functions may have different views about what must be done to achieve organizational goals. But if the managers have equal authority (as functional managers typically do), the only manager who can tell them what to do is the CEO. If functional managers cannot reach agreement, no mechanism exists to resolve the conflict apart from the authority of the boss. In fact, one sign of a poorly performing organizational structure is the number of problems sent up the hierarchy for top managers to solve. The need to solve everyday conflicts and handoff or transfer problems raises bureaucratic costs. To reduce such conflicts and solve transfer problems, top managers use more complex integrating mechanisms to increase coordination among functions and divisions.

Liaison Roles Managers can increase coordination among functions and divisions by establishing liaison roles. When the volume of contacts between two functions increases, one way to improve coordination is to give one manager in each function or division the responsibility for coordinating with the other. These managers may meet daily, weekly, monthly, or as needed to solve handoff issues and transfer problems. The responsibility for coordination is part of the liaison's full-time job, and usually an informal relationship forms between the people involved, greatly easing strains between functions. Furthermore, liaison roles provide a way of transmitting information across an organization, which is important in large organizations where employees may know no one outside their immediate function or division.

Teams When more than two functions or divisions share many common problems, direct contact and liaison roles may not provide sufficient coordination. In these cases, a more complex integrating mechanism, the **team**, may be appropriate. One manager from each relevant function or division is assigned to a team that meets to solve a specific mutual problem; team members are responsible for reporting back to their subunits on the issues addressed and the solutions recommended. Teams are increasingly being used at all organizational levels.

Strategic Control Systems

Strategic managers choose the organizational strategies and structure they hope will allow the organization to use its resources most effectively to pursue its business model and create value and profit. Then they create **strategic control systems**, tools that allow them to monitor and evaluate whether, in fact, their strategy and structure are working as intended, how they could be improved, and how they should be changed if they are not working.

Strategic control is not only about monitoring how well an organization and its members are currently performing, or about how well the firm is using its existing resources. It is also about how to create the incentives to keep employees motivated and focused on the important problems that may confront an organization in the future so that the employees work together and find solutions that can help an organization perform better over time.[19] To understand the vital importance of strategic control, consider how it helps managers obtain superior efficiency, quality, innovation, and responsiveness to customers—the four basic building blocks of competitive advantage:

1. *Control and efficiency.* To determine how *efficiently* they are using organizational resources, managers must be able to accurately measure how many units of inputs (raw materials, human resources, and so on) are being used to produce a unit of output. They must also be able to measure the number of units of outputs (goods and services) they produce. A control system contains the measures or yardsticks that allow managers to assess how efficiently they are producing goods and services.

Team

Formation of a group that represents each division or department facing a common problem, with the goal of finding a solution to the problem.

Strategic control systems

The mechanism that allows managers to monitor and evaluate whether their business model is working as intended and how it could be improved.

Moreover, if managers experiment to find a more efficient way to produce goods and services, these measures tell managers how successful they have been. Without a control system in place, managers have no idea how well their organizations are performing nor how to perform better in the future—something that is becoming increasingly important in today's highly competitive environment.[20]

2. *Control and quality.* Today, competition often revolves around increasing the *quality* of goods and services. In the car industry, for example, within each price range, cars compete against one another over features, design, and reliability. Whether a customer buys a Ford 500, a GM Impala, a Chrysler 300, a Toyota Camry, or a Honda Accord depends significantly upon the quality of each company's product. Strategic control is important in determining the quality of goods and services because it gives managers feedback on product quality. If managers consistently measure the number of customers' complaints and the number of new cars returned for repairs, they have a good indication of how much quality they have built into their product.

3. *Control and innovation.* Strategic control can help to raise the level of *innovation* in an organization. Successful innovation takes place when managers create an organizational setting in which employees feel empowered to be creative and in which authority is decentralized to employees so that they feel free to experiment and take risks, such as at Apple, 3M, and NVIDIA. Deciding upon the appropriate control systems to encourage risk taking is an important management challenge. As discussed later in the chapter, an organization's culture becomes important in this regard.

4. *Control and responsiveness to customers.* Finally, strategic managers can help make their organizations more *responsive to customers* if they develop a control system that allows them to evaluate how well employees with customer contact are performing their jobs. Monitoring employees' behavior can help managers find ways to help increase employees' performance level, perhaps by revealing areas in which skills training can help employees, or by finding new procedures that allow employees to perform their jobs more efficiently. When employees know their behaviors are being monitored, they may have more incentive to be helpful and consistent in the way they act toward customers.

Strategic control systems are the formal target-setting, measurement, and feedback systems that allow strategic managers to evaluate whether a company is achieving superior efficiency, quality, innovation, and customer responsiveness and implementing its strategy successfully. An effective control system should have three characteristics. It should be *flexible* enough to allow managers to respond as necessary to unexpected events; it should provide *accurate information*, thus giving a true picture of organizational performance; and it should supply managers with the information in a *timely manner* because making decisions on the basis of outdated information is a recipe for failure.[21] As Figure 12.3 shows, designing an effective strategic control system requires four steps: establishing standards and targets, creating measuring and monitoring systems, comparing performance against targets, and evaluating results.

Levels of Strategic Control

Strategic control systems are developed to measure performance at four levels in a company: corporate, divisional, functional, and individual. Managers at all levels must develop the most appropriate set of measures to evaluate corporate-, business-,

Figure 12.3 Steps in Designing an Effective Strategic Control System

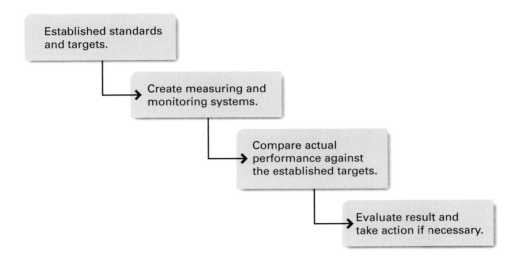

and functional-level performance. As the balanced scorecard approach discussed in Chapter 11 suggests, these measures should be tied as closely as possibly to the goals of developing distinctive competencies in efficiency, quality, innovativeness, and responsiveness to customers. Care must be taken, however, to ensure that the standards used at each level do not cause problems at the other levels—for example, that a division's attempts to improve its performance do not conflict with corporate performance. Furthermore, controls at each level should provide the basis upon which managers at lower levels design their control systems. Figure 12.4 illustrates these relationships.

Types of Strategic Control Systems

In Chapter 11, the balanced scorecard approach was discussed as a way to ensure that managers complement the use of ROIC with other kinds of strategic controls to ensure they are pursuing strategies that maximize long-run profitability. In this chapter, we consider three more types of control systems: *personal control, output control*, and *behavior control*.

Personal Control **Personal control** is the desire to shape and influence the behavior of a person in a *face-to-face interaction* in the pursuit of a company's goals. The most obvious kind of personal control is direct supervision from a manager farther up in the hierarchy. The personal approach is useful because managers can question subordinates about problems or new issues they are facing to get a better understanding of the situation and to ensure that subordinates are performing their work effectively and that they are not hiding any information that could cause additional problems later. Personal control also can come from a group of peers, such as when people work in teams. Once again, personal control at the group level means that there is more possibility for learning to occur and competencies to develop, as well as greater opportunities to prevent free-riding or shirking.

Personal control

The way one managers shapes and influences the behavior of another in a face-to-face interaction in the pursuit of a company's goals.

Figure 12.4   Levels of Organizational Control

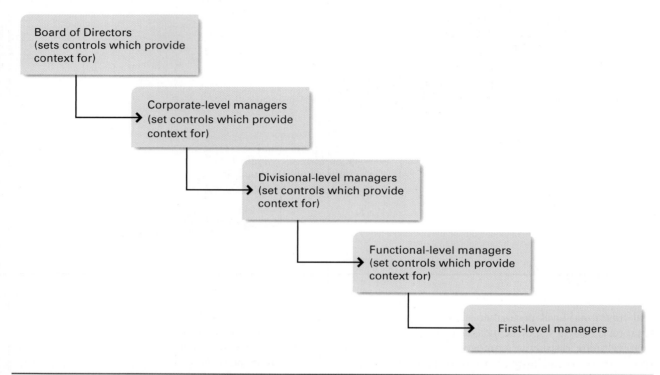

Output Control   **Output control** is a system in which strategic managers estimate or forecast appropriate performance goals for each division, department, and employee, and then measure actual performance relative to these goals. Often a company's reward system is linked to performance on these goals, so output control also provides an incentive structure for motivating employees at all levels in the organization. Goals keep managers informed about how well their strategies are creating a competitive advantage and building the distinctive competencies that lead to future success. Goals exist at all levels in an organization.

Divisional goals state corporate managers' expectations for each division concerning performance on dimensions such as efficiency, quality, innovation, and responsiveness to customers. Generally, corporate managers set challenging divisional goals to encourage divisional managers to create more effective strategies and structures in the future. At Ford, for example, Alan Mulally gives the top managers of each division clear performance goals to achieve, and they have considerable autonomy to formulate a strategy to meet these goals—as long as they cooperate with other divisions to find ways to speed innovation or increase quality.

Output control at the functional and individual levels is a continuation of control at the divisional level. Divisional managers set goals for functional managers that will allow the division to achieve its goals. As at the divisional level, functional goals are established to encourage the development of generic competencies that provide the company with a competitive advantage, and functional performance is evaluated

Output control

The control system managers use to establish appropriate performance goals for each division, department, and employee and then measure actual performance relative to these goals.

by how well a function develops a competency. In the sales function, for example, goals related to efficiency (such as cost of sales), quality (such as number of returns), and customer responsiveness (such as the time necessary to respond to customer needs) can be established for the whole function.

Finally, functional managers establish goals that individual employees are expected to achieve to allow the function to achieve its goals. Sales personnel, for example, can be given specific goals (related to functional goals) that they are required to achieve. Functions and individuals are then evaluated based on whether or not they are achieving their goals; in sales, compensation is commonly anchored by achievement. The achievement of goals is a sign that the company's strategy is working and meeting the organization's wider objectives.

The inappropriate use of output control can promote conflict among divisions. In general, setting across-the-board output targets, such as ROIC targets for divisions, can lead to destructive results if divisions single-mindedly try to maximize divisional ROIC at the expense of corporate ROIC. Moreover, to reach output targets, divisions may start to distort the numbers and engage in strategic manipulation of the figures to make their divisions look good—which increases bureaucratic costs.[22]

Behavior Control **Behavior control** is control through the establishment of a comprehensive system of rules and procedures to direct the actions or behavior of divisions, functions, and individuals.[23] The intent of behavior controls is not to specify the g*oals* but to standardize the *way or means* of reaching them. Rules standardize behavior and make outcomes predictable. If employees follow the rules, then actions are performed and decisions are handled the same way time and time again. The result is predictability and accuracy, the aim of all control systems. The primary kinds of behavior controls are operating budgets, standardization, and rules and procedures.

Once managers at each level have been given a goal to achieve, they establish operating budgets that regulate how managers and workers are to attain those goals. An **operating budget** is a blueprint that outlines how managers intend to use organizational resources to most efficiently achieve organizational goals. Most commonly, managers at one level allocate to managers at a lower level a specific amount of resources to use in the production of goods and services. Once a budget is determined, lower-level managers must decide how they will allocate finances for different organizational activities. Managers are then evaluated on the basis of their ability to stay within the budget and make the best use of it. For example, managers at GE's washing machine division might have a budget of $50 million to develop and sell a new line of washing machines; they must decide how much money to allocate to R&D, engineering, sales, and so on, to ensure that the division generates the most revenue possible, and hence makes the biggest profit. Most commonly, large companies treat each division as a stand-alone profit center, and corporate managers evaluate each division's performance by its relative contribution to corporate profitability, something discussed in detail in the next chapter.

Standardization refers to the degree to which a company specifies how decisions are to be made so that employees' behavior becomes predictable.[24] In practice, there are three things an organization can standardize: *inputs, conversion activities*, and *outputs*.

When managers standardize, they screen *inputs* according to preestablished criteria, or standards that determine which inputs to allow into the organization. If employees are the input, for example, then one way of standardizing them is to

Behavior control

Control achieved through the establishment of a comprehensive system of rules and procedures that specify the appropriate behavior of divisions, functions, and people.

Operating budget

A blueprint that states how managers intend to use organizational resources to most efficiently achieve organizational goals.

Standardization

The degree to which a company specifies how decisions are to be made so that employees' behavior become measurable and predictable.

specify which qualities and skills they must possess, and only selecting applicants who possess those qualities. If the inputs are raw materials or component parts, the same considerations apply. The Japanese are renowned for the high quality and precise tolerances they demand from component parts to minimize problems with the product at the manufacturing stage. JIT inventory systems also help standardize the flow of inputs.

The aim of standardizing *conversion activities* is to program work activities so that they can be done the same way time and time again; the goal is predictability. Behavior controls, such as rules and procedures, are among the chief means by which companies can standardize throughputs. Fast-food restaurants such as McDonald's and Burger King standardize all aspects of their restaurant operations; the result is consistent fast food.

The goal of standardizing *outputs* is to specify what the performance characteristics of the final product or service should be—the dimensions or tolerances the product should conform to, for example. To ensure that their products are standardized, companies apply quality control and use various criteria to measure this standardization. One criterion might be the number of goods returned from customers, or the number of customers' complaints. On production lines, periodic sampling of products can indicate whether they are meeting performance characteristics.

As with other kinds of controls, the use of behavior control is accompanied by potential pitfalls that must be managed if the organization is to avoid strategic problems. Top management must be careful to monitor and evaluate the usefulness of behavior controls over time. Rules constrain people and lead to standardized, predictable behavior. However, rules are always easier to establish than to get rid of, and over time the number of rules an organization uses tends to increase. As new developments lead to additional rules, often the old rules are not discarded, and the company becomes overly bureaucratized. Consequently, the organization and the people within it become inflexible and are slow to react to changing or unusual circumstances. Such inflexibility can reduce a company's competitive advantage by lowering the pace of innovation and reducing its responsiveness to customers.

Using Information Technology

Information technology (IT) is playing an increasing role in strategy implementation at all organizational levels. In fact, IT is making it much easier for organizations to cost-effectively develop output and behavior controls that give strategic managers much more and much better information to monitor the aspects of their strategies and respond appropriately. IT, which provides a way of standardizing behavior through the use of a consistent, often cross-functional software platform, is a form of behavior control. IT is also a form of output control; when all employees or functions use the same software platform to provide up-to-date information on their activities, it codifies and standardizes organizational knowledge, making it easier to monitor progress toward strategic objectives. IT is also a kind of integrating mechanism; it provides people at all levels in the hierarchy and across all functions with more of the information and knowledge they need to effectively perform their roles. For example, today functional-level employees are able to easily access information from other functions using cross-functional software systems that keep all employees informed about changes in product design, engineering, manufacturing schedules, and marketing plans that may have an impact on their activities. IT overlays, improves, and facilitates the arrangement of tasks and roles that is an organization's structure.

As an example of how IT can help a company quickly respond to changing industry conditions, consider the fast-moving semiconductor business organizational in which Cypress Semiconductor CEO T. J. Rodgers was facing a problem. How could he exert effective control over his 2,000 employees without developing a bureaucratic management hierarchy? Rodgers' belief is that a tall hierarchy hinders the ability of an organization to adapt to changing conditions. He is committed to maintaining a flat and decentralized organizational structure with a minimum of management layers. At the same time, he wants to control his employees to ensure that they perform in a manner consistent with company goals. The solution Rodgers adopted was to implement an IT information system allowing him to monitor what every employee and team is doing in his decentralized organization. Each employee maintains a list of 10 to 15 goals, such as "Meet with marketing for new product launch" or "Make sure to check with customer X." Notes are also made when each goal is agreed upon, to track the goal's progress, and indicate when the goal is completed. Rodgers can use IT to review all employees' goals in merely hours, and he does this each week. He can achieve the goals because he "manages by exception." He looks only for employees who appear to be falling behind, contacts them, not to scold, but to ask if there is anything he can do to help get the job done. Rodgers' control system allows him to maintain his organization without resorting to the expensive layers of a management hierarchy.[25]

Strategic Reward Systems

Organizations strive to control employees' behavior by linking reward systems to their control systems.[26] Based on a company's strategy (cost leadership or differentiation, for example), strategic managers must decide which behaviors to reward. They then create a control system to measure these behaviors and link the reward structure to them. Determining how to relate rewards to performance is a crucial strategic decision because it determines the incentive structure that affects the way managers and employees behave at all levels in the organization. As Chapter 11 pointed out, top managers can be encouraged to work on behalf of shareholders' interests when rewarded with stock options linked to a company's long-term performance. Companies such as Kodak and GM require managers to purchase company stock. When managers become shareholders, they are more motivated to pursue long-term rather than short-term goals. Similarly, in designing a pay system for salespeople, the choice is whether to motivate them through salary alone, or salary plus a bonus based on how much they sell. Neiman Marcus, the luxury retailer, pays employees only salary because it wants to encourage high-quality service and discourage a hard-sell approach. Thus, there are no incentives based on quantities sold. On the other hand, the pay system for rewarding car salespeople encourages high-pressure selling; it typically contains a large bonus based on the number and price of cars sold.

Organizational Culture

The third element of successful strategy implementation is managing *organizational culture*, the specific collection of values and norms shared by people and groups in an organization.[27] Organizational values are beliefs and ideas about what kinds of goals the members of an organization should pursue and about the appropriate kinds or standards of behavior organizational members should use to achieve these goals. Bill

Gates is famous for the set of organizational values that he created for Microsoft: entrepreneurship, ownership, creativity, honesty, frankness, and open communication. By stressing entrepreneurship and ownership, he strives to get his employees to feel that Microsoft is not one big bureaucracy but a collection of smaller and very adaptive companies run by the members. Gates emphasizes that lower-level managers should be given autonomy and encouraged to take risks—to act like entrepreneurs, not corporate bureaucrats.[28]

From organizational values develop organizational norms, guidelines, or expectations that prescribe appropriate kinds of behavior by employees in particular situations and control the behavior of organizational members toward one another. Behavioral norms for software programmers at Microsoft include working long hours and weekends, wearing whatever clothing is comfortable (but never a suit and tie), consuming junk food, and communicating with other employees by e-mail and the company's state-of-the-art intranet.

Organizational culture functions as a kind of control because strategic managers can influence the kind of values and norms that develop in an organization—values and norms that specify appropriate and inappropriate behaviors, and that shape and influence the way its members behave.[29] Strategic managers such as Gates deliberately cultivate values that tell their subordinates how they should perform their roles; at Microsoft and Nokia, innovation and creativity are stressed. These companies establish and support norms that tell employees they should be innovative and entrepreneurial and should experiment even if there is a significant chance of failure.

Other managers might cultivate values that tell employees they should always be conservative and cautious in their dealings with others, consult with their superiors before they make important decisions, and record their actions in writing so they can be held accountable for what happens. Managers of organizations such as chemical and oil companies, financial institutions, and insurance companies—any organization in which great caution is needed—may encourage a conservative, vigilant approach to decision making.[30] In a bank or mutual fund, for example, the risk of losing investors' money makes a cautious approach to investing highly appropriate. Thus, we might expect that managers of different kinds of organizations will deliberately attempt to cultivate and develop the organizational values and norms that are best suited to their strategy and structure.

Organizational socialization is the term used to describe how people learn organizational culture. Through socialization, people internalize and learn the norms and values of the culture so that they become organizational members.[31] Control through culture is so powerful that once these values have been internalized, they become part of the individual's values, and the individual follows organizational values without thinking about them.[32] Often the values and norms of an organization's culture are transmitted to its members through the stories, myths, and language that people in the organization use, as well as by other means.

Culture and Strategic Leadership

Strategic leadership is also provided by an organization's founder and top managers who help create its organizational culture. The organization's founder is particularly important in determining culture because the founder imprints his or her values and management style on the organization. Walt Disney's conservative influence on the company he established continued well after his death. Managers were afraid to experiment with new forms of entertainment because they were afraid "Walt Disney wouldn't like it." It wasn't until the installation of a new management team under Michael Eisner that the company turned around its fortunes, which allowed it to deal with the realities of the new entertainment industry.

The founder's leadership style established is transmitted to the company's managers; as the company grows, it typically attracts new managers and employees who share the same values. Moreover, members of the organization typically recruit and select only those who share their values. Thus, a company's culture becomes more distinct as its members become more similar. The virtue of these shared values and common culture is that they *increase integration and improve coordination among organizational members*. For example, the common language that typically emerges in an organization when people share the same beliefs and values facilitates cooperation among managers. Similarly, rules and procedures and direct supervision are less important when shared norms and values control behavior and motivate employees. When organizational members buy into cultural norms and values, they feel a bond with the organization and are more committed to finding new ways to help it succeed. Strategy in Action 12.3 profiles the way in which Walmart's founder Sam Walton built a strong culture.

Strategic leadership also affects organizational culture through the way managers design organizational structure, that is, the way they delegate authority and divide task relationships. Thus, the way an organization designs its structure affects the cultural norms and values that develop within the organization. Managers need to be aware of this fact when implementing their strategies. Michael Dell, for example, has always kept his company's structure as flat as possible. He has decentralized authority to lower-level managers and employees to make them responsible to get as close to the customer as possible. As a result, he has created a cost-conscious customer service culture at Dell and employees strive to provide high-quality customer service.

Traits of Strong and Adaptive Corporate Cultures

Few environments are stable for a prolonged period of time. If an organization is to survive, managers must take actions that enable it to adapt to environmental changes. If they do not take such action, they may find themselves faced with declining demand for their products.

Managers can try to create an **adaptive culture**, one that is innovative and that encourages and rewards middle- and lower-level managers for taking initiative.[33] Managers in organizations with adaptive cultures are able to introduce changes in the way the organization operates, including changes in its strategy and structure that allow it to adapt to changes in the external environment. Organizations with adaptive cultures are more likely to survive in a changing environment and should have higher performance than organizations with inert cultures.

Several scholars have tried to uncover the common traits that strong, adaptive corporate cultures share, to find out whether there is a particular set of values that dominates adaptive cultures not present in weak or inert ones. An early but still influential attempt is T. J. Peters and R. H. Waterman's account of the values and norms characteristic of successful organizations and their cultures.[34] They argue that adaptive organizations show three common value sets. First, successful companies have values promoting a *bias for action*. The emphasis is on autonomy and entrepreneurship, and employees are encouraged to take risks—for example, to create new products—despite that there is no assurance that these products will be popular. Managers are closely involved in the day-to-day operations of the company and do

Adaptive culture

A culture that is innovative and encourages and rewards middle- and lower-level managers for taking the initiative to achieve organizational goals.

STRATEGY IN ACTION

How Sam Walton Created Walmart's Culture

Walmart, headquartered in Bentonville, Arkansas, is the largest retailer in the world. In 2009, it sold more than $700 billion worth of products. A large part of Walmart's success is due to the nature of the culture that its founder, the late Sam Walton, established for the company. Walton wanted all his managers and workers to take a hands-on approach to their jobs and be committed to Walmart's primary goal, which he defined as total customer satisfaction. To motivate his employees, Walton created a culture that gave all employees, called "associates," continuous feedback about their performance and the company's performance.

To involve his associates in the business and encourage them to develop work behaviors focused on providing quality customer service, Walton established strong cultural values and norms for his company. One of the norms associates are expected to follow is the "10-foot attitude." This norm encourages associates, in Walton's words, to "promise that whenever you come within 10 feet of a customer, you will look him in the eye, greet him, and ask him if you can help him." The "sundown rule" states that employees should strive to answer customer requests by sundown of the day they are made. The Walmart cheer ("Give me a W, give me an A," and so on) is used in all its stores.

The strong customer-oriented values that Walton has created are exemplified in the stories Walmart members tell one another about associates' concern for customers. They include stories such as the one about Sheila, who risked her own safety when she jumped in front of a car to prevent a little boy from being struck; about Phyllis, who administered CPR to a customer who had suffered a heart attack in her store; and about Annette, who gave up the Power Ranger she had on layaway for her own son

to fulfill the birthday wish of a customer's son. The strong Walmart culture helps to control and motivate employees to achieve the stringent output and financial targets the company sets.

A notable way Walmart builds its culture is through its annual stockholders' meeting, its extravagant ceremony celebrating the company's success. Every year, Walmart flies thousands of its highest performing associates to an annual meeting at its corporate headquarters in Arkansas for entertainment featuring famous singers, rock bands, and comedians. Walmart feels that expensive entertainment is a reward its employees deserve and that the event reinforces the company's high-performance values and culture. The proceedings are also broadcast live to all Walmart stores so that all employees can celebrate the company's achievements together.

Since Sam Walton's death, public attention to Walmart, which has more than 1 million employees, has revealed the "hidden side" of its culture. Critics claim that few Walmart employees receive reasonably priced health care or other benefits, and the company pays employees at little above the minimum wage. They also contend that employees do not question these policies because managers have convinced them into believing that this has to be the case—that the only way Walmart can keep its prices low is by keeping their pay and benefits low. However, in the 2010s Walmart has been forced to respond to these lawsuits and to public pressure. Not only has it paid billions of dollars of fines to satisfy the claims of employees who have been discriminated against, it has also been forced to offer many of its employees increased health benefits: Although it is constantly searching for ways to reduce these benefits of make its employees pay a higher share of their costs.

Source: www.walmart.com, 2012.

not simply make strategic decisions isolated in some ivory tower. Employees have a hands-on, value-driven approach.

The second set of values stems from the *nature of the organization's mission.* The company must continue to do what it does best and develop a business model focused on its mission. A company can easily divert and pursue activities outside its area of expertise because other options seem to promise a quick return. Management should cultivate values so that a company "sticks to its knitting," which means strengthening its business model. A company must also establish close relationships with customers as a way of improving its competitive position. After all, who knows more about a company's performance than those who use its products or services? By emphasizing customer-oriented values, organizations are able to identify customer needs and improve their ability to develop products and services that customers desire. All of these management values are strongly represented in companies such as McDonald's, Walmart, and Toyota, which are sure of their mission and continually take steps to maintain it.

The third set of values determines *how to operate the organization*. A company should attempt to establish an organizational design that will motivate employees to perform best. Inherent in this set of values is the belief that productivity is obtained through people and that respect for the individual is the primary means by which a company can create the right atmosphere for productive behavior. An emphasis on entrepreneurship and respect for the employee leads to the establishment of a structure that gives employees the latitude to make decisions and motivates them to succeed. Because a simple structure and a lean staff best fit this situation, the organization should be designed with only the number of managers and hierarchical levels that are necessary to get the job done. The organization should also be sufficiently decentralized to permit employees' participation but centralized enough for management to ensure that the company pursues its strategic mission and that cultural values are followed.

In summary, these three primary sets of values are at the center of an organization's culture, and management transmits and maintains these values through strategic leadership. Strategy implementation continues as managers build strategic control systems that help perpetuate a strong adaptive culture, further the development of distinctive competencies, and provide employees with the incentive to build a company's competitive advantage. Finally, organizational structure contributes to the implementation process by providing the framework of tasks and roles that reduces transaction difficulties and allows employees to think and behave in ways that enable a company to achieve superior performance.

Building Distinctive Competencies at the Functional Level

In this section, we discuss the issue of creating specific kinds of structures, control systems, and cultures to implement a company's business model. The first level of strategy to examine is the functional level because, as Chapters 3 and 4 discussed, a company's business model is implemented through the functional strategies managers adopt to develop the distinctive competencies that allow a company to pursue a particular business model.[35] What is the best kind of structure to use to group people and tasks to build competencies? The answer for most companies is to group them by function and create a functional structure.

Functional Structure: Grouping by Function

In the quest to deliver a final product to the customer, two related value chain management problems increase. First, the range of value chain activities that must be performed expands, and it quickly becomes clear that a company lacks the expertise needed to perform these activities effectively. For example, in a new company, the expertise necessary to effectively perform activities is lacking. It becomes apparent, perhaps, that the services of a professional accountant, a production manager, or a marketing expert are needed to take control of specialized tasks as sales increase. Second, it also becomes clear that a single person cannot successfully perform more than one value-chain activity without becoming overloaded. The new company's founder, for instance, who may have been performing many value chain activities simultaneously, realizes that he or she can no longer make and sell the product. As most entrepreneurs discover, they must decide how to group new employees to perform the various value chain activities most efficiently. Most choose the functional structure.

Functional structures group people on the basis of their common expertise and experience or because they use the same resources.[36] For example, engineers are grouped in a function because they perform the same tasks and use the same skills or equipment. Figure 12.5 shows a typical functional structure. Each of the rectangles represents a different functional specialization—R&D, sales and marketing, manufacturing, and so on—and each function concentrates upon its own specialized task.[37]

Functional structures have several advantages. First, if people who perform similar tasks are grouped together, they can learn from one another and become more specialized and productive at what they do. This can create capabilities and competencies in each function. Second, they can monitor each other to make sure that all are performing their tasks effectively and not shirking their responsibilities. As a result, the work process becomes more efficient by reducing manufacturing costs and increasing operational flexibility. A third important advantage of functional structures is that they give managers greater control of organizational activities. As already noted, many difficulties arise when the number of levels in the hierarchy increases. If people are grouped into different functions, each with their own managers, then *several different hierarchies are created*, and the company can avoid becoming too tall. There will be one hierarchy in manufacturing, for example, and another in accounting and finance. Managing a business is much easier when different groups specialize in different organizational tasks and are managed separately.

Functional structure

Grouping of employees on the basis of their common expertise and experience or because they use the same resources.

The Role of Strategic Control

An important element of strategic control is to design a system that sets ambitious goals and targets for all managers and employees and then develops performance measures that *stretch and encourage managers and employees* to excel in their quest to raise performance. A functional structure promotes this goal because it increases

Figure 12.5   Functional Structure

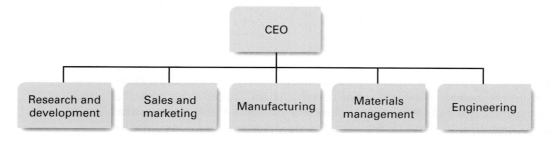

the ability of managers and employees to monitor and make constant improvements to operating procedures. The structure also encourages organizational learning because managers, working closely with subordinates, can mentor them and help develop their technical skills.

Grouping by function also makes it easier to apply output control. Measurement criteria can be developed to suit the needs of each function to encourage members to stretch themselves. Each function knows how well it is contributing to overall performance and the part it plays in reducing the cost of goods sold or the gross margin. Managers can look closely to see if they are following the principle of the minimum chain of command and whether or not they need several levels of middle managers. Perhaps, instead of using middle managers, they could practice **management by objectives**, a system in which employees are encouraged to help set their own goals so that managers, such as Cypress' Rodgers, *manage by exception*, intervening only when they sense something is not going right. Given this increase in control, a functional structure also makes it possible to institute an effective strategic reward system in which pay can be closely linked to performance, and managers can accurately assess the value of each person's contributions.

Developing Culture at the Functional Level

Often functional structures offer the easiest way for managers to build a strong, cohesive culture. We discussed earlier how Sam Walton worked hard to create values and norms that are shared by Walmart's employees. To understand how structure, control, and culture can help create distinctive competencies, think about how they affect the way these three functions operate: manufacturing, R&D, and sales.

Manufacturing In manufacturing, functional strategy usually centers upon improving efficiency and quality. A company must create an organizational setting in which managers can learn how to economize on costs and lower the cost structure. Many companies today follow the lead of Japanese companies such as Toyota and Honda, which have strong capabilities in manufacturing because they pursue TQM and flexible manufacturing systems (see Chapter 4).

Pursuing TQM, the inputs and involvement of all employees in the decision-making process are necessary to improve production efficiency and quality. Thus, it becomes necessary to decentralize authority to motivate employees to improve the production process. In TQM, work teams are created, and workers are given the responsibility and authority to discover and implement improved work procedures. Managers assume the role of coach and facilitator, and team members jointly take on the supervisory burdens. Work teams are often given the responsibility to control and discipline their own members and also decide who should work in their team. Frequently, work teams develop strong norms and values, and work-group culture becomes an important means of control; this type of control matches the new decentralized team approach. Quality control circles are created to exchange information and suggestions about problems and work procedures. A bonus system or employee stock ownership plan is frequently established to motivate workers and to allow them to share in the increased value that TQM often produces.

Nevertheless, to move down the experience curve quickly, most companies still exercise tight control over work activities and create behavior and output controls that standardize the manufacturing process. For example, human inputs are standardized through the recruitment and training of skilled personnel; the work process is programmed, often by computers; and quality control is used to make sure that outputs are being produced correctly. In addition, managers use output controls such as operating budgets to continuously monitor costs and quality. The extensive use of output controls and the continuous measurement of efficiency and quality ensure that the work team's activities meet the goals set for the function by management. Efficiency and quality increase as new and improved work rules and procedures are developed to raise the level of standardization. The aim is to find the match between structure and control and a TQM approach so that manufacturing develops the distinctive competency that leads to superior efficiency and quality.

R&D   The functional strategy for an R&D department is to develop distinctive competencies in innovation and quality as excellence that result in products that fit customers' needs. Consequently, the R&D department's structure, control, and culture should provide the coordination necessary for scientists and engineers to bring high-quality products quickly to market. Moreover, these systems should motivate R&D scientists to develop innovative products.

In practice, R&D departments typically have a flat, decentralized structure that gives their members the freedom and autonomy to experiment and be innovative. Scientists and engineers are also grouped into teams because their performance can typically be judged only over the long term (it may take several years for a project to be completed). Consequently, extensive supervision by managers and the use of behavior control are a waste of managerial time and effort.[38] Managers avoid the information distortion problems that cause bureaucratic costs by letting teams manage their own transfer and handoff issues rather than using managers and the hierarchy of authority to coordinate work activities. Strategic managers take advantage of scientists' ability to work jointly to solve problems and enhance each other's performance. In small teams, too, the professional values and norms that highly trained employees bring to the situation promote coordination. A culture for innovation frequently emerges to control employees' behavior, as it did at Nokia, Intel, and Microsoft, where the race to be first energizes the R&D teams. To create an innovative culture and speed product development, Intel uses a team structure in its R&D function. Intel has many work teams that operate side by side to develop the next generation of chips. When the company makes mistakes, as it has recently, it can act quickly to join each team's innovations together to make a state-of-the-art chip that meets customer needs, such as multimedia chips. At the same time, to sustain its leading-edge technology, the company creates healthy competition between teams to encourage its scientists and engineers to champion new product innovations that will allow Intel to control the technology of tomorrow.[39]

To spur teams to work effectively, the reward system should be linked to the performance of the team and company. If scientists, individually or in a team, do not share in the profits a company obtains from its new products, they may have little motivation to contribute wholeheartedly to the team. To prevent the departure of their key employees and encourage high motivation, companies such as Merck, Intel, and Microsoft give their researchers stock options, stock, and other rewards that are tied to their individual performance, their team's performance, and the company's performance.

Sales   Salespeople work directly with customers, and when they are dispersed in the field, these employees are especially difficult to monitor. The cost-effective way to monitor their behavior and encourage high responsiveness to customers is usually to develop sophisticated output and behavior controls. Output controls, such as specific sales goals or goals for increasing responsiveness to customers, can be easily established and monitored by sales managers. These controls can then be linked to a bonus reward system to motivate salespeople. Behavioral controls, such as detailed reports that salespeople file describing their interactions with customers, can also be used to standardize behavior and make it easier for supervisors to review performance.[40]

Usually, few managers are needed to monitor salespeople's activities, and a sales director and regional sales managers can oversee large sales forces because outputs and behavior controls are employed. Frequently, however, and especially when salespeople deal with complex products, such as pharmaceutical drugs or even luxury clothing, it becomes important to develop shared employee values and norms about the importance of patient safety or high-quality customer service; managers spend considerable time training and educating employees to create such norms.

Similar considerations apply to the other functions, such as accounting, finance, engineering, and human resource management. Managers must implement functional strategy through the combination of structure, control, and culture to allow each function to create the competencies that lead to superior efficiency, quality, innovation, and responsiveness to customers. Strategic managers must also develop the incentive systems that motivate and align employees' interests with those of their companies.

Functional Structure and Bureaucratic Costs

No matter how complex their strategies become, most companies always retain a functional orientation because of its many advantages. Whenever different functions work together, however, bureaucratic costs inevitably arise because of information distortions that lead to the communications and measurement problems discussed in Chapter 10. These problems often arise from the transfers or handoffs across different functions that are necessary to deliver the final product to the customer.[41] The need to economize on the bureaucratic costs of solving such problems leads managers to adopt new organizational arrangements that reduce the scope of information distortions. Usually, companies divide their activities according to more complex plans to match their business models and strategies in discriminating ways. These more complex structures are discussed later in the chapter. First, we review five areas in which information distortions can arise: communications, measurement, customers, location, and strategy.

Communication Problems As separate functional hierarchies evolve, functions can grow more remote from one another, and it becomes increasingly difficult to communicate across functions and coordinate their activities. This communication problem stems from *differences in goal orientations*—the various functions develop distinct outlooks or understandings of the strategic issues facing a company.[42] For example, the pursuit of different competencies can often lead to different time or goal orientations. Some functions, such as manufacturing, have a short time frame and concentrate on achieving short-term goals, such as reducing manufacturing costs. Others, such as R&D, have a long-term point of view; their product development goals may have a time horizon of several years. These factors may cause each function to develop a different view of the strategic issues facing the company. Manufacturing, for example, may see the strategic issue as the need to reduce costs, sales may see it as the need to increase customer responsiveness, and R&D may see it as the need to create new products. These communication and coordination problems among functions increase bureaucratic costs.

Measurement Problems   Often a company's product range widens as it develops new competencies and enters new market segments. When this happens, a company may find it difficult to gauge or measure the contribution of a product or a group of products to its overall profitability. Consequently, the company may turn out some unprofitable products without realizing it and may also make poor decisions about resource allocation. This means that the company's measurement systems are not complex enough to serve its needs.

Customer Problems   As the range and quality of an organization's goods and services increase, often more and different kinds of customers are attracted to its products. Servicing the needs of more customer groups and tailoring products to suit new kinds of customers result in increasing handoff problems among functions. It becomes increasingly difficult to coordinate the activities of value chain functions across the growing product range. Also, functions such as production, marketing, and sales have little opportunity to differentiate products and increase value for customers by specializing in the needs of particular customer groups. Instead, they are responsible for servicing the complete product range. Thus, the ability to identify and satisfy customer needs may fall short in a functional structure.

Location Problems   Being in a particular location or geographical region may also hamper coordination and control. Suppose a growing company in the Northeast begins to expand and sell its products in many different regional areas. A functional structure will not be able to provide the flexibility needed for managers to respond to the different customer needs or preferences in the various regions.

Strategic Problems   The combined effect of all these factors results in long-term strategic considerations that are frequently ignored because managers are preoccupied with solving communication and coordination problems. The result is that a company may lose direction and fail to take advantage of new strategic opportunities–thus bureaucratic costs escalate.

Experiencing one or more of these problems is a sign that bureaucratic costs are increasing. If this is the case, managers must change and adapt their organization's structure, control systems, and culture to economize on bureaucratic costs, build new distinctive competencies, and strengthen the company's business model. These problems indicate that the company has outgrown its structure and that managers need to develop a more complex structure that can meet the needs of their competitive strategy. An alternative, however, is to reduce these problems by adopting the outsourcing option.

The Outsourcing Option

Rather than move to a more complex, expensive structure, companies are increasingly turning to the outsourcing option (discussed in Chapter 9) and solving the organizational design problem by contracting with other companies to perform specific functional tasks. Obviously, it does not make sense to outsource activities in which a company has a distinctive competency, because this would lessen its competitive advantage; but it does make sense to outsource and contract with companies to perform particular value chain activities in which they specialize and therefore have a competitive advantage.

Thus, one way of avoiding the kinds of communication and measurement problems that arise when a company's product line becomes complex is to reduce the number of functional value chain activities it performs. This allows a company to focus on those competencies that are at the heart of its competitive advantage and to economize on bureaucratic costs. Today, responsibility for activities such as a company's marketing, pension and health benefits, materials management, and information systems is being increasingly outsourced to companies that specialize in the needs of a company in a particular industry. More outsourcing options, such as using a global network structure, are considered in Chapter 13.

Implementing Strategy in a Single Industry

Building capabilities in organizational design that allow a company to develop a competitive advantage begins at the functional level. However, to pursue its business model successfully, managers must find the right combination of structure, control, and culture that *links and combines* the competencies in a company's value chain functions so that it enhances its ability to differentiate products or lower the cost structure. Therefore, it is important to coordinate and integrate across functions and business units or divisions. In organizational design, managers must consider two important issues: one concerns the revenue portion of the profit equation and the other concerns the cost portion, as Figure 12.6 illustrates.

Figure 12.6 How Organizational Design Increases Profitability

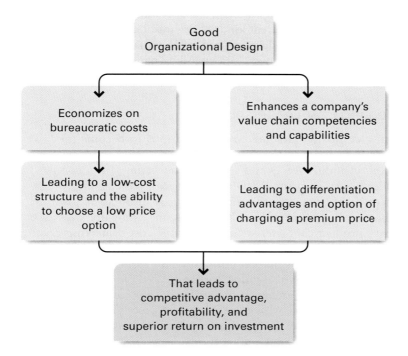

First, effective organizational design improves the way in which people and groups choose the business-level strategies that lead to increasing differentiation, more value for customers, and the opportunity to charge a premium price. For example, capabilities in managing its structure and culture allow a company to more rapidly and effectively combine its distinctive competencies or transfer or leverage competencies across business units to create new and improved, differentiated products.

Second, effective organizational design reduces the bureaucratic costs associated with solving the measurement and communications problems that derive from factors such as transferring a product in progress between functions or a lack of cooperation between marketing and manufacturing or between business units. A poorly designed or inappropriate choice of structure or control system or a slow-moving bureaucratic culture (e.g., a structure that is too centralized, an incentive system that causes functions to compete instead of cooperate, or a culture in which value and norms have little impact on employees) can cause the motivation, communication, measurement, and coordination problems that lead to high bureaucratic costs.

Effective organizational design often means moving to a more complex structure that economizes on bureaucratic costs. A more-complex structure will cost more to operate because additional, experienced, and more highly paid managers will be needed; a more expensive IT system will be required; there may be a need for extra offices and buildings; and so on. However, these are simply costs of doing business, and a company will happily bear this extra expense provided its new structure leads to increased revenues from product differentiation and/or new ways to lower its *overall* cost structure by obtaining economies of scale or scope from its expanded operations.

In the following sections, we first examine the implementation and organizational design issues involved in pursuing a cost-leadership or differentiation business model. Then we describe different kinds of organizational structures that allow companies to pursue business models oriented at (1) managing a wide range of products, (2) being responsive to customers, (3) expanding nationally, (4) competing in a fast-changing, high-tech environment, and (5) focusing on a narrow product line.

Implementing Cost Leadership

The aim of a company pursuing cost leadership is to become the lowest-cost producer in the industry, and this involves reducing costs across *all* functions in the organization, including R&D and sales and marketing.[43] If a company is pursuing a cost-leadership strategy, its R&D efforts probably focus on product and process development rather than on the more expensive product innovation, which carries no guarantee of success. In other words, the company stresses competencies that improve product characteristics or lower the cost of making existing products. Similarly, a company tries to decrease the cost of sales and marketing by offering a standard product to a mass market rather than different products aimed at different market segments, which is also more expensive.[44]

To implement cost leadership, a company chooses a combination of structure, control, and culture compatible with lowering its cost structure while preserving its ability to attract customers. In practice, the functional structure is the most suitable provided that care is taken to select integrating mechanisms that will reduce communication and measurement problems. For example, a TQM program can be effectively implemented when a functional structure is overlaid with cross-functional teams because team members can now search for ways to improve operating rules and procedures that lower the cost structure or standardize and raise product quality.[45]

Cost leadership also requires that managers continuously monitor their structures and control systems to find ways to restructure or streamline them so that they operate more effectively. For example, managers need to be alert to ways of using IT to standardize operations and lower costs. To reduce costs further, cost leaders use the cheapest and easiest forms of control available: output controls. For each function, a cost leader adopts output controls that allow it to closely monitor and evaluate functional performance. In the manufacturing function, for example, the company imposes tight controls and stresses meeting budgets based on production, cost, or quality targets.[46] In R&D, the emphasis also falls on the bottom line; to demonstrate their contribution to cost savings, R&D teams focus on improving process technology. Cost leaders are likely to reward employees through generous incentive and bonus plans to encourage high performance. Their culture is often based on values that emphasize the bottom line, such as those of Walmart, McDonald's, and Dell profiled in the Focus on Dell feature.

Implementing Differentiation

Effective strategy implementation can improve a company's ability to add value and to differentiate its products. To make its product unique in the eyes of the customer, for example, a differentiated company must design its structure, control, and culture around the *particular source* of its competitive advantage.[47] Specifically, differentiators need to design their structures around the source of their distinctive competencies, the differentiated qualities of their product, and the customer groups they serve. Commonly, in pursuing differentiation, a company starts to produce a wider range of products to serve more market segments, which means it must customize its products for different groups of customers. These factors make it more difficult to standardize activities and usually increase the bureaucratic costs associated with managing the handoffs or transfers between functions. Integration becomes much more of a problem; communications, measurement, location, and strategic problems increasingly arise; and the demands upon functional managers increase.

To respond to these problems, strategic managers develop more sophisticated control systems, increasingly make use of IT, focus on developing cultural norms and values that overcome problems associated with differences in functional orientations and focus on cross-functional objectives. The control systems used to match the structure should be aligned to a company's distinctive competencies. For successful differentiation, it is important that the various functions do not pull in different directions; indeed, cooperation among the functions is vital for cross-functional integration. However, when functions work together, output controls become much harder to use. In general, it is much more difficult to measure the performance of people in different functions when they are engaged in cooperative efforts. Consequently, a differentiator must rely more upon behavior controls and shared norms and values.

This explains why companies pursuing differentiation often have a markedly different kind of culture from those pursuing cost leadership. Because human resources—scientists, designers, or marketing employees—are often the source of differentiation, these organizations have a culture based on professionalism or collegiality that emphasizes the distinctiveness of the human resources rather than the high pressure of the bottom line.[48] HP, Motorola, and Coca-Cola, all of

FOCUS ON D≪LL

Strategy Implementation at Dell

Dell was one of the fastest-growing companies of the 1990s, and its stock price increased at the rate of 100% per year, delighting its stockholders. Achieving this high return has been a constant challenge for Michael Dell. One of his biggest battles has been to manage and change Dell's organizational structure, control systems, and culture as his company grows.

Michael Dell was 19 in 1984, when he took $1,000 and spent it on the computer parts he assembled into PCs that he sold over the phone. Increasing demand for his PCs meant that within a few weeks, he needed to hire people to help him. Soon he found himself supervising three employees who worked together around a 6-foot table to assemble computers while two more employees took orders over the phone.[49]

By 1993, Dell employed 4,500 workers and was hiring more than 100 new workers each week to keep pace with the demand for the computers. When Dell found himself working 18-hour days managing the company, he realized that he could not lead it single-handedly. The company's growth had to be managed, and he knew that he had to recruit and hire strategic managers who had experience in managing different functional areas, such as marketing, finance, and manufacturing. He recruited executives from IBM and Compaq. With their help, he created a functional structure, one in which employees were grouped by their common skills or tasks they performed, such as sales or manufacturing, to organize the value chain activities necessary to deliver his PCs to customers. As a part of this organizing process, Dell's structure also became taller, with more levels in the management hierarchy, to ensure that he and his managers had sufficient control over the different activities of his growing business. Dell delegated authority to control the company's functional value chain activities to his managers, which gave him the time he needed to perform his entrepreneurial task of finding new opportunities for the company.

Dell's functional structure worked well and, under its new management team, the company's growth continued to soar. Moreover, Dell's new structure had given functional managers the control they needed to squeeze out costs, and Dell had become the lowest-cost PC maker. Analysts also reported that Dell had developed a lean organizational culture, meaning that employees had developed norms and values that emphasized the importance of working hard to help each other find innovative new ways of making products to keep costs low and increase their reliability. Dell rose to the top of the customer satisfaction rankings for PC makers because few customers complained about its products. Its employees became known for the excellent customer service they gave to PC buyers who were experiencing problems with setting up their computers.

However, Michael Dell realized that new and different kinds of problems were arising. Dell was now selling huge numbers of computers to different kinds of customers, for example, home, business, and educational customers and different branches of government. Because customers were demanding computers with different features or more computing power, the company's product line broadened rapidly. It became more difficult for employees to meet the needs of these customers efficiently because each employee needed information about all product features or all of Dell's thousands of different sales offers across its product range.

By the late-1990s, Michael Dell moved to change his company and split the sales function into different departments each of which now was organized to serve the needs of a particular type of customer, for example, home buyers, business users, and government or academic customers. In each department, teams of sales employees specialized in servicing the needs of one of these customer groups. This change in structure also allowed each department to develop a unique subculture that suited its tasks, and employees were able to obtain in-depth knowledge that allowed them to respond better to the particular customers they served. Because this change in structure and culture was so successful, Dell's revenues and profits soared and it soon became the biggest PC maker globally.

Michael Dell has continued to change his company's structure in the 2000s to respond to changing customer needs and increasing competitive challenges from Apple and HP. For example, Michael Dell realized that he could leverage his company's strengths in materials management, manufacturing, and Internet sales over a wider range of computer hardware products. He decided to begin assembling servers, workstations, and storage devices to compete with IBM, Sun, and HP. The increasing importance of the Internet also led him to pay more attention to more specialized groups of customers and find the best way to customize its approach to best meet each group's specific needs over the Internet. Today, for example, Dell can offer large and small

FOCUS ON D**⊘**LL *(continued)*

companies and private buyers a complete range of computers, workstations, and storage devices that can be customized to their needs.

To help coordinate its growing activities, Dell is increasingly making use of its corporate Intranet to standardize activities across divisions and integrate its activities across functions to reduce costs. Dell's hierarchy is shrinking as managers increasingly delegate decision making to employees who use its advanced IT to access the information they

need to provide excellent customer service. To reduce costs, Dell has also outsourced most of its customer service function to India.[50] As a result of these moves, Dell's smaller U.S. workforce has become even more committed to maintaining a low-cost advantage. Its cost-conscious culture is now an important factor affecting its competitive advantage, which has been threatened by the many cost-saving moves made by competitors (such as Apple and HP) that have imitated and even improved upon its cost-saving strategies.[51]

which emphasize some kind of distinctive competency, exemplify companies with professional cultures.

In practice, the implementation decisions that confront managers who must simultaneously strive for differentiation and a low cost structure are dealt with together as strategic managers move to implement new, more complex kinds of organizational structure. As a company's business model and strategies evolve, strategic managers usually start to *superimpose* a more complex divisional grouping of activities on its functional structure to better coordinate value chain activities. This is especially true of companies seeking to become *broad differentiators*—companies that have the ability to simultaneously increase differentiation and lower their cost structures. These companies are the most profitable in their industry, and they have to be especially adept at organizational design—a major source of a differentiation and cost advantage (see Figure 12.6). No matter what the business model, however, more complex structures cost more to operate than a simple functional structure. Managers are willing to bear this extra cost, however, as long as the new structure makes better use of functional competencies, increases revenues, and lowers the overall cost structure.

Product Structure: Implementing a Wide Product Line

The structure that organizations most commonly adopt to solve the control problems that result from producing many different kinds of products for many different market segments is the *product structure*. The intent is to break up a company's growing product line into a number of smaller, more manageable subunits to reduce bureaucratic costs due to communication, measurement, and other problems. Nokia moved to a product structure as it grew in size; its structure is shown in Figure 12.7.

An organization that chooses a **product structure** first divides its overall product line into product groups or categories (see Figure 12.7). Each product group focuses on satisfying the needs of a particular customer group and is managed by its own team of managers. Second, to keep costs as low as possible, value chain support functions such as basic R&D, marketing, materials, and finance are centralized at the top of the organization, and the different product groups share their services. Each support function, in turn, is divided into product-oriented teams of functional specialists who focus on the needs of one particular product group. This arrangement

Product structure

A way of grouping employees into separate product groups or units so that each product group can focus on the best ways to increase the effectiveness of the product.

Figure 12.7 Nokia's Product Structure

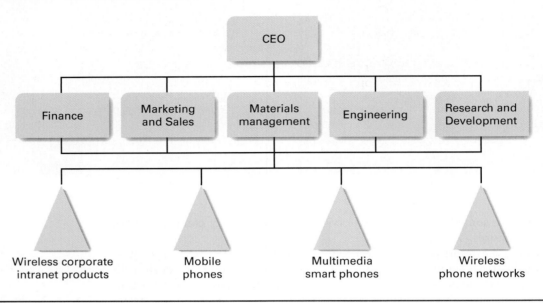

allows each team to specialize and become expert in managing the needs of its product group. Because all of the R&D teams belong to the same centralized function, however, they can share knowledge and information with each other and build their competence over time.

Strategic control systems can now be developed to measure the performance of each product group separately from the others. Thus, the performance of each product group is easy to monitor and evaluate, and corporate managers at the center can move more quickly to intervene if necessary. Also, the strategic reward system can be linked more closely to the performance of each product group, although top managers can still decide to make rewards based on corporate performance an important part of the incentive system. Doing so will encourage the different product groups to share ideas and knowledge and promote the development of a corporate culture, as well as the product group culture that naturally develops inside each product group. A product structure is commonly used by food processors, furniture makers, personal and health products companies, and large electronics companies such as Nokia.

Market Structure: Increasing Responsiveness to Customer Groups

> **Market structure**
>
> A way of grouping employees into separate customer groups so that each group can focus on satisfying the needs of a particular customer group in the most effective way.

Suppose the source of competitive advantage in an industry depends upon the ability to meet the needs of distinct and important sets of customers or different customer groups. What is the best way of implementing strategy now? Many companies develop a **market structure** that is conceptually quite similar to the product structure except that the focus is on customer groups instead of product groups.

For a company pursuing a strategy based on increasing responsiveness to customers, it is vital that the nature and needs of each different customer group be identified. Then, employees and functions are grouped by customer or market segment. A different set of managers becomes responsible for developing the products that each group of customers wants and tailoring or customizing products to the needs of each particular customer group. In other words, to promote superior responsiveness to customers, a company will design a structure around its customers, and a market structure is adopted. A typical market structure is shown in Figure 12.8.

A market structure brings customer group managers and employees closer to specific groups of customers. These people can then take their detailed knowledge and feed it back to the support functions, which are kept centralized to reduce costs. For example, information about changes in customer preferences can be quickly fed back to R&D and product design so that a company can protect its competitive advantage by supplying a constant stream of improved products for its installed customer base. This is especially important when a company serves well-identified customer groups such as Fortune 500 companies or small businesses.

Geographic Structure: Expanding By Location

Suppose a company begins to expand locally, regionally, or nationally through internal expansion or by engaging in horizontal integration and merging with other companies to expand its geographical reach. A company pursuing this competitive approach frequently moves to a **geographic structure** in which geographic regions become the basis for the grouping of organizational activities (see Figure 12.9). A company may divide its manufacturing operations and establish manufacturing plants in different regions of the country, for example. This allows the company to be responsive to the needs of regional customers and reduces transportation costs. Similarly, as a service organization such as a store chain or bank expands beyond one geographic area, it may begin to organize sales and marketing activities on a regional level to better serve the needs of customers in different regions.

> **Geographic structure**
>
> A way of grouping employees into different geographic regions to best satisfy the needs of customers within different regions of a state or country.

A geographic structure provides more coordination and control than a functional structure does because several regional hierarchies are created to take over the work, as in a product structure, where several product group hierarchies are created.

Figure 12.8 Market Structure

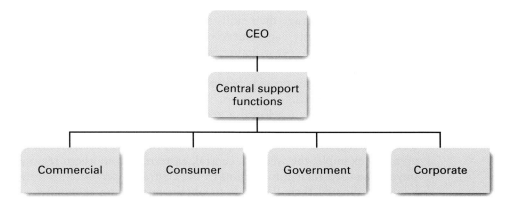

Figure 12.9 Geographic Structure

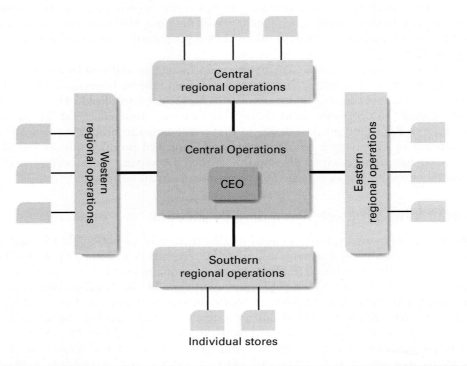

© Cengage Learning 2013

A company such as FedEx clearly needs to operate a geographic structure to fulfill its corporate goal: next-day delivery. Large merchandising organizations, such as Neiman Marcus, Dillard's Department Stores, and Walmart, also moved to a geographic structure as they started building stores across the country. With this type of structure, different regional clothing needs (e.g., sunwear in the South, down coats in the Midwest) can be handled as required. At the same time, because the information systems, purchasing, distribution, and marketing functions remain centralized, companies can leverage their skills across all the regions. When using a geographic structure, a company can achieve economies of scale in buying, distributing, and selling and lower its cost structure, while simultaneously being more responsive (differentiated) to customer needs. One organization that moved from a geographic to a market structure to provide better quality service and reduce costs is discussed in Strategy in Action 12.4.

Neiman Marcus developed a geographic structure similar to the one shown in Figure 12.9 to manage its nationwide chain of stores. In each region, it established a team of regional buyers to respond to the needs of customers in each geographic area, for example, the western, central, eastern, and southern regions. The regional buyers then fed their information to the central buyers at corporate headquarters, who coordinated their demands to obtain purchasing economies and ensure that Neiman Marcus's high-quality standards, upon which its differentiation advantage depends, were maintained nationally.

STRATEGY IN ACTION

The HISD Moves from a Geographic to a Market Structure

Like all organizations, state and city government agencies such as school districts may become too tall and bureaucratic over time and, as they grow, develop ineffective and inefficient organizational structures. This happened to the Houston Independent School District (HISD) when the explosive growth of the city during the last decades added over one million new students to schools. As Houston expanded many miles in every direction to become the 4th largest U.S. city, successive HISD superintendents adopted a geographic structure to coordinate and control all the teaching functions involved in creating high-performing elementary, middle, and high schools. The HISD eventually created five different geographic regions or regional school districts. And over time each regional district sought to control more of its own functional activities and became increasingly critical of HISD's central administration. The result was a slowdown in decision making, infighting between districts, an increasingly ineffectual team of district administrators, and falling student academic test scores across the city.

In 2010, a new HISD superintendent was appointed who, working on the suggestions of HISD's top managers, decided to reorganize HISD into a market structure. HISD's new organizational structure is now grouped by the needs of its customers—its students—and three "chief officers" oversee all of Houston's high schools, middle schools, and elementary schools, respectively. The focus will now be upon the needs of its 3 types of students, not on the needs of the former 5 regional managers. Over 270 positions were eliminated in this restructuring, saving over $8 million per year, and many observers hope to see more cost savings ahead.

Many important support functions were recentralized to HISD's headquarters office to eliminate redundancies and reduce costs, including teacher professional development. Also, a new support function called school improvement was formed with managers charged to share ideas and information between schools and oversee their performance on many dimensions to improve service and student performance. HISD administrators also hope that eliminating the regional geographic structure will encourage schools to share best practices and cooperate so student education and test scores will improve over time.

By 2011, major cost savings had been achieved, but a huge budget deficit forced the HISD to close 12 middle and elementary schools and relocate students to new facilities in which class sizes would be higher. The result is a streamlined, integrated divisional structure that HISD hopes will increase performance—student scores—in the years ahead, but at a lower cost.

Matrix and Product-Team Structures: Competing in Fast-Changing, High-Tech Environments

The communication and measurement problems that lead to bureaucratic costs escalate quickly when technology is rapidly changing and industry boundaries are blurring. Frequently, competitive success depends upon rapid mobilization of a company's skills and resources, and managers face complex strategy implementation issues. A new grouping of people and resources becomes necessary, often one that is based on fostering a company's distinctive competencies in R&D. Managers need to make structure, control, and culture choices around the R&D function. At the same time, they need to ensure that implementation will result in new products that cost-effectively meet customer needs and will not result in products so expensive that customers will not wish to buy them.

Matrix Structure   To address these problems, many companies choose a matrix structure.[52] In a **matrix structure**, value chain activities are grouped in two ways (see Figure 12.10). First, activities are grouped vertically by *function* so that there is a

> **Matrix structure**
>
> A way of grouping employees in two ways simultaneously by function and by product or project to maximize the rate at which different kinds of products can be developed.

Figure 12.10 Matrix Structure

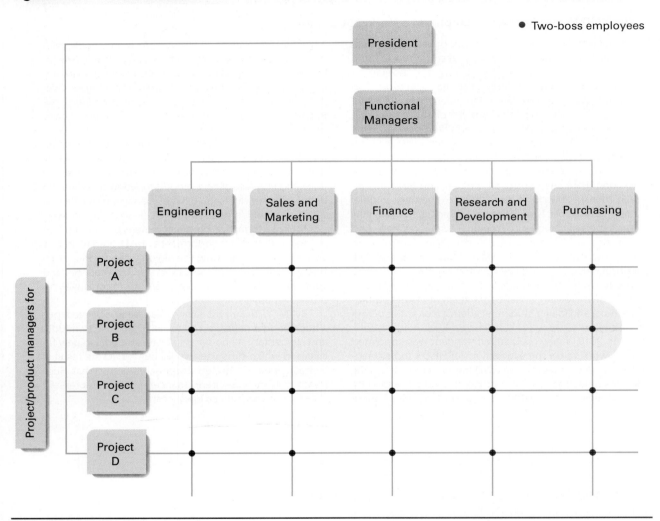

• Two-boss employees

© Cengage Learning 2013

familiar differentiation of tasks into functions such as engineering, sales and marketing, and R&D. In addition, superimposed upon this vertical pattern is a horizontal pattern based on grouping by *product or project* in which people and resources are grouped to meet ongoing product development needs. The resulting network of reporting relationships among projects and functions is designed to make R&D the focus of attention.

Matrix structures are flat and decentralized, and employees inside a matrix have two bosses: a *functional boss*, who is the head of a function, and a *product or project boss*, who is responsible for managing the individual projects. Employees work on a project team with specialists from other functions and report to the project boss on project matters and the functional boss on matters relating to functional issues. All employees who work on a project team are called **two-boss employees** and are

Two-boss employees

Employees who report both to a project boss and who report to a functional boss.

responsible for managing coordination and communication among the functions and projects.

Implementing a matrix structure promotes innovation and speeds product development because this type of structure permits intensive cross-functional integration. Integrating mechanisms such as teams help transfer knowledge among functions and are designed around the R&D function. Sales, marketing, and production targets are geared to R&D goals, marketing devises advertising programs that focus upon technological possibilities, and salespeople are evaluated on their understanding of new-product characteristics and their ability to inform potential customers about these new products.

Matrix structures were first developed by companies in high-technology industries such as aerospace and electronics, for example, TRW and Hughes. These companies were developing radically new products in uncertain, competitive environments, and the speed of product development was the crucial consideration. They needed a structure that could respond to this need, but the functional structure was too inflexible to allow the complex role and task interactions necessary to meet new-product development requirements. Moreover, employees in these companies tend to be highly qualified and professional and perform best in autonomous, flexible working conditions. The matrix structure provides such conditions.

This structure requires a minimum of direct hierarchical control by supervisors. Team members control their own behavior, and participation in project teams allows them to monitor other team members and to learn from each other. Furthermore, as the project goes through its different phases, different specialists from various functions are required. For example, at the first stage, the services of R&D specialists may be called for; at the next stage, engineers and marketing specialists may be needed to make cost and marketing projections. As the demand for the type of specialist changes, team members can be moved to other projects that require their services. Thus, the matrix structure can make maximum use of employees' skills as existing projects are completed and new ones come into existence. The freedom given by the matrix not only provides the autonomy to motivate employees but also leaves top management free to concentrate upon strategic issues because they do not have to become involved in operating matters. For all these reasons, the matrix is an excellent tool for creating the flexibility necessary for quick reactions to competitive conditions.

In terms of strategic control and culture, the development of norms and values based on innovation and product excellence is vital if a matrix structure is to work effectively.[53] The constant movement of employees around the matrix means that time and money are spent establishing new team relationships and getting the project running. The two-boss employee's role, as it balances the interests of the project with the function, means that cooperation among employees is problematic, and conflict between different functions and between functions and projects is possible and must be managed. Furthermore, changing product teams, the ambiguity arising from having two bosses, and the greater difficulty of monitoring and evaluating the work of teams increase the problems of coordinating task activities. A strong and cohesive culture with unifying norms and values can mitigate these problems, as can a strategic reward system based on a group- and organizational-level reward system.

Product-Team Structure A major structural innovation in recent years has been the *product-team structure*. Its advantages are similar to those of a matrix structure, but it is much easier and far less costly to operate because of the way people are organized into permanent cross-functional teams, as Figure 12.11 illustrates. In the **product-team structure**, as in the matrix structure, tasks are divided along product or project lines. However, instead of being assigned only *temporarily* to different projects, as in the matrix structure, functional specialists become part of a *permanent* cross-functional team that focuses on the development of one particular range of products, such as luxury cars or computer workstations. As a result, the problems associated with coordinating cross-functional transfers or handoffs are much lower than in a matrix structure, in which tasks and reporting relationships change rapidly. Moreover, cross-functional teams are formed at the beginning of the product development process so that any difficulties that arise can be ironed out early, before they lead to major redesign problems. When all functions have direct input from the beginning, design costs and subsequent manufacturing costs can be kept low. Moreover, the use of cross-functional teams speeds innovation and customer responsiveness because, when authority is decentralized, team decisions can be made more quickly.

A product-team structure groups tasks by product, and each product group is managed by a cross-functional product team that has all the support services necessary to bring the product to market. This is why it is different from the product structure, in which support functions remain centralized. The role of the product team is to protect and enhance a company's differentiation advantage and at the same time coordinate with manufacturing to lower costs.

Focusing on a Narrow Product Line

As Chapter 5 discussed, a focused company concentrates on developing a narrow range of products aimed at one or two market segments, which may be defined by type of customer or location. As a result, a focuser tends to have a higher cost

> **Product-team structure**
>
> A way of grouping employees by product or project line but employees focus on the development of only one particular type of product.

Figure 12.11   Product-Team Structure

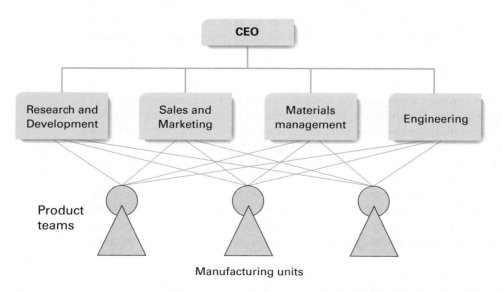

structure than a cost leader or differentiator, because output levels are lower, making it harder to obtain substantial scale economies. For this reason, a focused company must exercise cost control. On the other hand, some attribute of its product gives the focuser its distinctive competency—possibly its ability to provide customers with high-quality, personalized service. For both reasons, the structure and control system adopted by a focused company has to be inexpensive to operate but flexible enough to allow a distinctive competency to emerge.

A company using a focus strategy normally adopts a functional structure to meet these needs. This structure is appropriate because it is complex enough to manage the activities necessary to make and sell a narrow range of products for one or a few market segments. At the same time, the handoff problems are likely to be relatively easy to solve because a focuser remains small and specialized. Thus, a functional structure can provide all the integration necessary, provided that the focused firm has a strong, adaptive culture, which is vital to the development of some kind of distinctive competency.[54] Additionally, because such a company's competitive advantage is often based on personalized service, the flexibility of this kind of structure allows the company to respond quickly to customers' needs and change its products in response to customers' requests.

Restructuring and Reengineering

To improve performance, a single business company often employs restructuring and reengineering. **Restructuring** a company involves two steps: (1) streamlining the hierarchy of authority and reducing the number of levels in the hierarchy to a minimum and (2) reducing the number of employees to lower operating costs. Restructuring and downsizing become necessary for many reasons.[55] Sometimes a change in the business environment occurs that could not have been foreseen; perhaps a shift in technology made the company's products obsolete. Sometimes an organization has excess capacity because customers no longer want the goods and services it provides; perhaps the goods and services are outdated or offer poor value for the money. Sometimes organizations downsize because they have grown too tall and inflexible and bureaucratic costs have become much too high. Sometimes they restructure even when they are in a strong position simply to build and improve their competitive advantage and stay ahead of competitors.

All too often, however, companies are forced to downsize and lay off employees because they fail to monitor and control their basic business operations and have not made the incremental changes to their strategies and structures over time that allow them to adjust to changing conditions. Advances in management, such as the development of new models for organizing work activities, or IT advances, offer strategic managers the opportunity to implement their strategies in more effective ways.

A company may operate more effectively using **reengineering**, which involves the "fundamental rethinking and radical redesign of business processes to achieve dramatic improvements in critical, contemporary measures of performance, such as cost, quality, service, and speed."[56] As this definition suggests, strategic managers who use reengineering must completely rethink how they organize their value chain activities. Instead of focusing on how a company's *functions* operate, strategic managers make business *processes* the focus of attention.

A *business process* is any activity that is vital to delivering goods and services to customers quickly or that promotes high quality or low costs (such as IT, materials

Restructuring

The process by which a company streamlines its hierarchy of authority and reduces the number of levels in its hierarchy to a minimum to lower operating costs.

Reengineering

The process of redesigning business processes to achieve dramatic improvements in performance such as cost, quality, service, and speed.

management, or product development). It is not the responsibility of any one function but *cuts across functions*. Because reengineering focuses on business processes, not on functions, a company that reengineers always has to adopt a different approach to organizing its activities. Companies that take up reengineering deliberately ignore the existing arrangement of tasks, roles, and work activities. They start the reengineering process with the customer (not the product or service) and ask: "How can we reorganize the way we do our work—our business processes—to provide the best quality and the lowest-cost goods and services to the customer?"

Frequently, when managers ask this question, they realize that there are more effective ways to organize their value chain activities. For example, a business process that encompasses members of 10 different functions working sequentially to provide goods and services might be performed by one person or a few people at a fraction of the cost. Often individual jobs become increasingly complex, and people are grouped into cross-functional teams as business processes are reengineered to reduce costs and increase quality.

Hallmark Cards, for example, reengineered its card design process with great success. Before the reengineering effort, artists, writers, and editors worked separately in different functions to produce all kinds of cards. After reengineering, these same artists, writers, and editors were put on cross-functional teams, each of which now works on a specific type of card, such as birthday, Christmas, or Mother's Day. The result is that the production time to bring a new card to market decreased from years to months, and Hallmark's performance increased dramatically.

Reengineering and TQM, discussed in Chapter 4, are highly interrelated and complementary. After reengineering has taken place and value-chain activities have been altered to speed the product to the final customer, TQM takes over, with its focus on how to continue to improve and refine the new process and find better ways of managing task and role relationships. Successful organizations examine both issues simultaneously and continuously attempt to identify new and better processes for meeting the goals of increased efficiency, quality, and customer responsiveness. Thus, companies are always seeking to improve their visions of their desired future.

Another example of reengineering is the change program that took place at IBM Credit, a wholly owned division of IBM, that manages the financing and leasing of IBM computers—particularly mainframes—to IBM's customers. Before reengineering took place, a financing request arrived at the division's headquarters in Old Greenwich, Connecticut, and completed a 5-step approval process that involved the activities of 5 different functions. First, the IBM salesperson called the credit department, which logged the request and recorded details about the potential customer. Second, this information was taken to the credit-checking department, where a credit check on the potential customer was done. Third, when the credit check was complete, the request was taken to the contracts department, which wrote the contract. Fourth, from the contracts department, it went to the pricing department, which determined the actual financial details of the loan, such as the interest rate and the term of the loan. Finally, the whole package of information was assembled by the dispatching department and delivered to the sales representative, who presented it to the customer.

This series of cross-functional activities took an average of 7 days to complete, and sales representatives constantly complained that the delay resulted in a low level of customer responsiveness that reduced customer satisfaction. Also, potential customers were tempted to shop around for financing and look at competitors' machines in the process. The delay in closing the deal caused uncertainty for all involved.

The change process began when two senior IBM credit managers reviewed the finance approval process. They found that the time different specialists spent on the different functions processing a loan application was only 90 minutes. The 7-day approval process was caused by the delay in transmitting information and requests between departments. Managers also learned that the activities taking place in each department were not complex; each department had its own computer system containing its own work procedures, but the work done in each department was routine.

Armed with this information, IBM managers realized that the approval process could be reengineered into one overarching process handled by one person with a computer system containing all the necessary information and work procedures to perform the 5 loan-processing activities. If the application were complex, a team of experts stood ready to help process it, but IBM found that, after the reengineering effort, a typical application could be done in 4 hours rather than the previous 7 days. A sales representative could speak with the customer the same day to close the deal, and all the uncertainty surrounding the transaction would be removed.

As reengineering consultants Hammer and Champy note, this dramatic performance increase was instigated by a radical change to the whole process. Change through reengineering requires managers to assess the most basic level, and look at each step in the work process to identify a better way to coordinate and integrate the activities necessary to provide customers with goods and services. As this example makes clear, the introduction of new IT is an integral aspect of reengineering. IT also allows a company to restructure its hierarchy because it provides more and better-quality information. IT today is an integral part of the strategy implementation process.

Ethical Dilemma

Suppose a poorly performing organization has decided to terminate hundreds of middle managers. Top managers making the termination decisions might choose to keep subordinates that they like rather than the best performers or terminate the most highly paid subordinates even if they are top performers. Remembering that organizational structure and culture affects all company stakeholders, which ethical principles about equality, fairness, and justice would you use to redesign the organization hierarchy? Keep in mind that some employees may feel to have as strong a claim on the organization as some of its stockholders, even claiming to "own" their jobs from contributions to past successes.

Do you think this is an ethical claim? How would it factor into your design?

Summary of Chapter

1. Implementing a company's business model and strategies successfully depends upon organizational design, the process of selecting the right combination of organizational structure, control systems, and culture. Companies must monitor and oversee the organizational design process to achieve superior profitability.

2. Effective organizational design can increase profitability in two ways. First, it economizes on bureaucratic costs and helps a company lower its cost structure. Second, it enhances the ability of a company's value creation functions to achieve superior efficiency, quality, innovativeness, and customer responsiveness and obtain the advantages of differentiation.

3. The main issues in designing organizational structure are how to group tasks, functions, and divisions; how to allocate authority and responsibility (whether to have a tall or flat organization or to have a centralized or decentralized structure); and how to use integrating mechanisms to improve coordination between functions (such as direct contacts, liaison roles, and teams).

4. Strategic control provides the monitoring and incentive systems necessary to make an organizational structure work as intended and extends corporate governance down to all levels inside the company. The main kinds of strategic control systems are personal control, output control, and behavior control. IT is an aid to output and behavior

control, and reward systems are linked to every control system.

5. Organizational culture is the set of values, norms, beliefs, and attitudes that help to energize and motivate employees and control their behavior. Culture is a way of doing something, and a company's founder and top managers help determine which kinds of values emerge in an organization.

6. At the functional level, each function requires a different combination of structure and control system to achieve its functional objectives.

7. To successfully implement a company's business model, structure, control, and culture must be combined in ways that increase the relationships among all functions to build distinctive competencies.

8. Cost leadership and differentiation each require a structure and control system that strengthens the business model that is the source of their competitive advantage. Managers must use organizational design in a way that balances pressures to increase differentiation against pressures to lower the cost structure.

9. Other specialized kinds of structures include the product, market, geographic, matrix, and product-team structures. Each has a specialized use and is implemented as a company's strategy warrants.

10. Restructuring and reengineering are two ways of implementing a company's business model more effectively.

Discussion Questions

1. When would a company choose a matrix structure? What are the problems associated with managing this structure, and why might a product-team structure be preferable?

2. For each of the structures discussed in the chapter, outline the most suitable control systems.

3. What is the relationship among organizational structure, control, and culture? Give some examples of when and under what conditions a mismatch among these components might arise.

4. What kind of structure, controls, and culture would you be likely to find in (a) a small manufacturing company, (b) a chain store, (c) a high-tech company, and (d) a Big Four accounting firm?

5. What kind of structure best describes the way your (a) business school and (b) university operate? Why is the structure appropriate? Would another structure fit better?

Practicing Strategic Management

Small Group Exercises

Small-Group Exercise: Deciding on an Organizational Structure

Break up into groups of 3–5 people and discuss the following scenario. You are a group of managers of a major soft drink company that is going head-to-head with Coca-Cola to increase market share. Your business model is based on increasing your product range to offer a soft drink in every segment of the market to attract customers. Currently you have a functional structure. What you are trying to work out now is how best to implement your business model to launch your new products. Should you move to a more complex kind of product structure and, if so, which one? Alternatively, should you establish new-venture divisions and spin off each kind of new soft drink into its own company so that it can focus its resources on its market niche? Thinking strategically, debate the pros and cons of the possible organizational structures and decide which structure you will implement.

Strategy Sign-On

Article File 12

Find an example of a company that competes in one industry and has recently changed the way it implements its business model and strategies. What changes did it make? Why did it make these changes? What effect did these changes have on the behavior of people and functions?

Strategic Management Project

Developing Your Portfolio: Module 12 This module asks you to identify how your company implements its business model and strategy. For this part of your project, you need to obtain information about your company's structure, control systems, and culture. This information may be hard to obtain unless you can interview managers directly. But you can make many inferences about the company's structure from the nature of its activities, and if you write to the company, it may provide you with an organizational chart and other information. Also, published information, such as compensation for top management, is available in the company's annual reports or 10-K reports. If your company is well known, magazines such as *Fortune* and *Business Week* frequently report on corporate culture or control issues. Nevertheless, you may be forced to make some bold assumptions to complete this part of the project.

1. How large is the company as measured by the number of its employees? How many levels in the hierarchy does it have from the top to the bottom? Based on these two measures and any other

information you may have, would you say your company operates with a relatively tall or flat structure? Does your company have a centralized or decentralized approach to decision making?

2. What changes (if any) would you make to the way the company allocates authority and responsibility?

3. Draw an organizational chart showing the primary way in which your company groups its activities. Based on this chart, decide what kind of structure (functional, product, or divisional) your company is using.

4. Why did your company choose this structure? In what ways is it appropriate for its business model? In what ways is it inappropriate?

5. What kind of integration or integration mechanisms does your company use?

6. What are the primary kinds of control systems your company is using? What kinds of behaviors is the organization trying to (a) shape and (b) motivate through the use of these control systems?

7. What role does the top management team play in creating the culture of your organization? Can you identify the characteristic norms and values that describe the way people behave in your organization? How does the design of the organization's structure affect its culture?

8. What are the sources of your company's distinctive competencies? Which functions are most important to it? How does your company design its structure, control, and culture to enhance its (a) efficiency, (b) quality, (c) innovativeness, and (d) responsiveness to customers?

9. How does it design its structure and control systems to strengthen its business model? For example, what steps does it take to further cross-functional integration? Does it have a functional, product, or matrix structure?

10. How does your company's culture support its business model? Can you determine any ways in which its top management team influences its culture?

11. Based on this analysis, would you say your company is coordinating and motivating its people and subunits effectively? Why or why not? What changes (if any) would you make to the way your company's structure operates? What use could it make of restructuring or reengineering?

CLOSING CASE

A New Look for Liz Claiborne

Liz Claiborne, like other well-known apparel makers, embarked on a major product expansion strategy in the 1990s when it acquired many smaller clothing and accessory companies, and internally ventured new brands of its own.

The company's goal was to achieve greater operating efficiencies so that rising sales would also result in rising profits. By 2005, it had grown to 36 different brands, but while revenues had soared from $2 billion to more than $5 billion, its profits had not kept pace. In fact, profits were falling because costs were rising due to the enormous complexity and expense involved in managing so many

brands. Also, in the 2000s, clothing retailers such as Walmart, Macy's, and Target were increasingly offering their own private-label brands; this put pressure on apparel makers to reduce their prices if they wished to keep selling their brands in these store chains.[57]

Liz Claiborne recruited a new CEO, William McComb, to turn around the troubled company. Within months, he decided to reverse course, shrink the company, and move to a new form of organizational structure that would reduce the problems associated with managing its 36 different brands, and once again allow it to grow—but this time with increasing profitability. McComb believed the company had developed a "culture of complexity" that had gotten out of control. The core merchandising culture that had made Liz Claiborne so successful had been lost because of its rapid growth and overly complex organizational structure.

Liz Claiborne's former top managers had created 5 different apparel divisions to manage its 36 brands; brands were grouped into different divisions according to the style of clothing or accessories they made. For example, luxury designer lines such as Ellen Tracy were grouped into one division; clothes for working women, such as its signature Liz Claiborne and Dana Buchman brands, were in a second division; trendy, hip clothing directed at young customers such as its Juicy Couture line were in a third division; and so on. A separate management team controlled each division, and each division performed all the functional activities that marketing and design needed to support its brands. The problem was that over time it had become increasingly difficult to differentiate between apparel brands in *each* division, as well as between the brands of *different* divisions, because fashion styles change quickly in response to changing customer tastes. Also, costs were rising because of the duplication of activities between divisions, and, as noted earlier, increasing industry competition was pressuring the company to lower prices to retail stores to protect its sales.

McComb decided to streamline and change Liz Claiborne's organizational structure to meet the changing needs of customers and the increasing competition in the retailing industry. First, he decided the company would either sell, license, or close down 16 of its 36 brands and focus on the remaining 20 brands that had the highest chance of generating good future profits.[58] To better manage these 20 brands, he reorganized the company's structure and reduced its 5 divisions to only 2. This eliminated an entire level of top management. It also eliminated the duplication in marketing, distribution, and retail functions across the original 5 divisions. The result was a huge drop in operating costs and a simpler organization to manage.

The 2 remaining divisions were now its retail division called "direct brands," and its wholesale division called "partnered brands." The company's new structure was intended to bring focus, energy, and clarity to the way each division operated. The retail division, for example, was responsible for the brands that were sold primarily through Liz Claiborne's retail store chains, such as its Kate Spade, Lucky Brand Jeans, and Juicy Couture chains. Grouping together the fastest growing brands would allow divisional managers to make better marketing and distribution decisions to differentiate its products and attract more customers.[59] The problem in the wholesale division, which sells branded apparel lines such as Liz Claiborne and Dana Buchman directly to department stores and other retailers, is how to reduce costs to slow down the growing threat from private labels. For example, sales of Macy's private labels increased from 15% in 2005 to 18% in 2007. If managers of the wholesale division could find ways to reduce costs by turning inventory over more quickly, sharing marketing costs, and so forth, it could offer stores such as Macy's lower prices for its clothing and encourage the stores to stick with its brands and still make higher profits.

McComb realized that to reduce complexity and allow each division to build the right merchandising culture, it was necessary to change Liz Claiborne's organizational structure. He changed from grouping clothing brands into divisions according to their quality or price, to two divisions in which clothing brands were grouped according to the needs of each division's customers—either the people in its stores or the retail chains that purchase its clothes to resell to individual customers. The real problem is that each division faces a quite different set of strategic and operational problems; with its new structure, managers in each division can focus upon solving a specific set of problems to achieve the best performance from their particular brands. McComb's hope is that the company's sales will grow rapidly, but this time its new structure will lead to rising profitability.

Unfortunately this did not happen and the company has struggled since. In fact In 2011 it was forced to sell-off its signature Liz Claiborne brand to J.C. Penney. What went wrong?

Case Discussion Questions

1. In what ways did McComb change Liz Claiborne's structure and control systems over time?
2. Why did he make these changes? Did they improve its performance? Search the Internet to find out what has happened to Liz Claiborne since these changes were made.

Notes

[1] www.ford.com, 2011.

[2] D. Kiley, "The New Heat on Ford," www.businessweek.com, June 4, 2007.

[3] B. Koenig, "Ford Reorganizes Executives Under New Chief Mulally," www.bloomberg.com, December 14, 2006.

[4] www.ford.com, 2011.

[5] L. Smircich, "Concepts of Culture and Organizational Analysis," *Administrative Science Quarterly* 28 (1983): 339–358.

[6] G. R. Jones and J. M. George, "The Experience and Evolution of Trust: Implications for Cooperation and Teamwork," *Academy of Management Review* 3 (1998): 531–546.

[7] Ibid.

[8] J. R. Galbraith, *Designing Complex Organizations* (Reading: Addison-Wesley, 1973).

[9] A. D. Chandler, *Strategy and Structure* (Cambridge: MIT Press, 1962).

[10] The discussion draws heavily on Chandler, *Strategy and Structure* and B. R. Scott, *Stages of Corporate Development* (Cambridge: Intercollegiate Clearing House, Harvard Business School, 1971).

[11] R. L. Daft, *Organizational Theory and Design*, 3rd ed. (St. Paul: West, 1986), 215.

[12] J. Child, *Organization 9: A Guide for Managers and Administrators* (New York: Harper & Row, 1977), 52–70.

[13] G. R. Jones and J. Butler, "Costs, Revenues, and Business Level Strategy," *Academy of Management Review* 13 (1988): 202–213; G. R. Jones and C. W. L. Hill, "Transaction Cost Analysis of Strategy-Structure Choice," *Strategic Management Journal* 9 (1988): 159–172.

[14] G. R. Jones, *Organizational Theory, Design, and Change: Text and Cases* (Englewood Cliffs: Pearson, 2011).

[15] Blau, "A Formal Theory of Differentiation in Organizations," *American Sociological Review* 35 (1970): 684–695.

[16] G. R. Jones, "Organization-Client Transactions and Organizational Governance Structures," *Academy of Management Journal* 30 (1987): 197–218.

[17] P. R. Lawrence and J. Lorsch, *Organization and Environment* (Boston: Division of Research, Harvard Business School, 1967), 50–55.

[18] Galbraith, *Designing Complex Organizations*, Chapter 1; J. R. Galbraith and R. K. Kazanjian, *Strategy Implementation: Structure System and Process*, 2nd ed. (St. Paul: West, 1986), Chapter 7.

[19] R. Simmons, "Strategic Orientation and Top Management Attention to Control Systems," *Strategic Management Journal* 12 (1991): 49–62.

[20] R. Simmons, "How New Top Managers Use Control Systems as Levers of Strategic Renewal," *Strategic Management Journal* 15 (1994): 169–189.

[21] W. G. Ouchi, "The Transmission of Control through Organizational Hierarchy," *Academy of Management Journal* 21 (1978): 173–192; W. H. Newman, *Constructive Control* (Englewood Cliffs: Prentice-Hall, 1975).

[22] E. Flamholtz, "Organizational Control Systems as a Managerial Tool," *California Management Review* (Winter 1979): 50–58.

[23] O. E. Williamson, *Markets and Hierarchies: Analysis and Antitrust Implications* (New York: Free Press, 1975); W. G. Ouchi, "Markets, Bureaucracies, and Clans," *Administrative Science Quarterly* 25 (1980): 129–141.

[24] H. Mintzberg, *The Structuring of Organizations* (Englewood Cliffs: Prentice-Hall, 1979), 5–9.

[25] www.cypress.com, 2011.

[26] E. E. Lawler III, *Motivation in Work Organizations* (Monterey: Brooks/Cole, 1973); Galbraith and Kazanjian, *Strategy Implementation*, Chapter 6.

[27] Smircich, "Concepts of Culture and Organizational Analysis."

[28] www.microsoft.com, 2011.

[29] Ouchi, "Markets, Bureaucracies, and Clans," 130.

[30] Jones, *Organizational Theory, Design, and Change*.

[31] J. Van Maanen and E. H. Schein, "Towards a Theory of Organizational Socialization," in B. M. Staw (ed.), *Research in Organizational Behavior* 1 (Greenwich: JAI Press, 1979), 209–264.

[32] G. R. Jones, "Socialization Tactics, Self-Efficacy, and Newcomers' Adjustments to Organizations," *Academy of Management Journal* 29 (1986): 262–279.

[33] J. P. Kotter and J. L. Heskett, *Corporate Culture and Performance*.

[34] T. J. Peters and R. H. Waterman, *In Search of Excellence: Lessons from America's Best-Run Companies* (New York: Harper & Row, 1982).

[35] G. Hamel and C. K. Prahalad, "Strategic Intent," *Harvard Business Review* (May–June 1989): 64.

[36] Galbraith and Kazanjian, *Strategy Implementation*; Child, *Organization*; R. Duncan, "What Is the Right Organization Structure?" *Organizational Dynamics* (Winter 1979): 59–80.

[37] J. Pettet, "Walmart Yesterday and Today," *Discount Merchandiser* (December 1995): 66–67; M. Reid, "Stores of Value," *Economist* (March 4, 1995): ss5–ss7; M. Troy, "The Culture Remains the Constant," *Discount Store News* (June 8, 1998): 95–98; www.walmart.com, 2011.

[38] W. G. Ouchi, "The Relationship between Organizational Structure and Organizational Control," *Administrative Science Quarterly* 22 (1977): 95–113.

[39] R. Bunderi, "Intel Researchers Aim to Think Big While Staying Close to Development," *Research-Technology Management* (March–April 1998): 3–4.

[40] K. M. Eisenhardt, "Control: Organizational and Economic Approaches," *Management Science* 16 (1985): 134–148.

[41] Williamson, *Markets and Hierarchies*.

[42] P. R. Lawrence and J. W. Lorsch, *Organization and Environment* (Boston: Graduate School of Business Administration, Harvard University, 1967).

[43] M. E. Porter, *Competitive Strategy: Techniques for Analyzing Industries and Competitors* (New York: Free Press, 1980); D. Miller, "Configurations of Strategy and Structure," *Strategic Management Journal* 7 (1986): 233–249.

[44] D. Miller and P. H. Freisen, *Organizations: A Quantum View* (Englewood Cliffs: Prentice-Hall, 1984).

[45] J. Woodward, *Industrial Organization: Theory and Practice* (London: Oxford University Press, 1965); Lawrence and Lorsch, *Organization and Environment*.

[46] R. E. White, "Generic Business Strategies, Organizational Context and Performance: An Empirical Investigation," *Strategic Management Journal* 7 (1986): 217–231.

[47] G. Rivlin, "He Naps. He Sings. And He Isn't Michael Dell," *New York Times,* September 11, 2005, 31.

[48] Porter, *Competitive Strategy;* Miller, "Configurations of Strategy and Structure."

[49] E. Deal and A. A. Kennedy, *Corporate Cultures* (Reading: Addison-Wesley, 1985); "Corporate Culture," *Business Week,* October 27, 1980, 148–160.

[50] www.dell.com, 2011.

[51] Ibid.

[52] S. M. Davis and R. R. Lawrence, *Matrix* (Reading: Addison-Wesley, 1977); J. R. Galbraith, "Matrix Organization Designs: How to Combine Functional and Project Forms," *Business Horizons* 14 (1971): 29–40.

[53] Duncan, "What Is the Right Organizational Structure?"; Davis and Lawrence, *Matrix*.

[54] D. Miller, "Configurations of Strategy and Structure," in R. E. Miles and C. C. Snow (eds.), *Organizational Strategy, Structure, and Process* (New York: McGraw-Hill, 1978).

[55] G. D. Bruton, J. K. Keels, and C. L. Shook, "Downsizing the Firm: Answering the Strategic Questions," *Academy of Management Executive* (May 1996): 38–45.

[56] M. Hammer and J. Champy, *Reengineering the Corporation* (New York: HarperCollins, 1993).

[57] www.lizclaiborne.com, 2011.

[58] R. Dodes, "Claiborne Seeks to Shed 16 Apparel Brands," www.businessweek.com, July 11, 2007.

[59] www.lizclaiborne.com, 2011.

13 Implementing Strategy in Companies that Compete Across Industries and Countries

erei photography/istockphoto.com

Nokia Expands its Organizational Structure Around the Globe

Nokia is still the world's largest mobile phone maker, although it has been fighting to maintain its lead as the popularity of smartphones has soared and companies like Apple, Samsung, and Google are competing to dominate the lucrative smartphone market. While these other companies outsource their cellphone production to Asian companies, Nokia does not. One reason for Nokia's continuing dominance in the cellphone market is its skills in global supply chain management, which allow it to provide low-cost phones that are tailored to the needs of customers in different world regions. To achieve its global strategy, Nokia designs its global organizational structure to manufacture its phones in the different world regions in which they will be sold. So, Nokia has opened new global divisions and built state-of-the-art factories in Germany, Brazil, China, and India, and in 2008 it created a new Romanian division to make phones for the expanding eastern European and Russian market.

A major reason for establishing an operating division in Romania is that it has low labor

LEARNING OBJECTIVES

After reading this chapter, you should be able to:

- Discuss the reasons why companies pursuing different corporate strategies need to implement these strategies using different combinations of organizational structure, control, and culture
- Describe the advantages and disadvantages of a multidivisional structure
- Explain why companies that pursue different kinds of global expansion strategies choose different kinds of global structures and control systems to implement these strategies
- Discuss the strategy implementation problems associated with the three primary methods used to enter new industries: internal new venturing, joint ventures, and mergers
- Identify the ways in which advanced Information Technology (IT) may reduce bureaucratic costs and allow a company to more effectively implement its business model

costs. Skilled Romanian engineers can be hired for 1/4 of what they would earn in Finland or Germany; similarly production line employees can expect to earn about $450 a month—a fraction of what Nokia's German employees earn. In fact, once Nokia's Romanian division was opened, Nokia closed down its operations in Bochum, Germany in 2008 because its cost structure was too expensive to operate—given the highly competitive global environment.

Opening a new division and factories in a new country is a complex process; to increase the chances its new global divisions will operate efficiently, Nokia's managers adopt several ways to organize its employees. First, managers worked to create a culture in its new manufacturing facilities that is attractive to its new Romanian employees so they will be motivated to learn the skills required to make it operate more efficiently over time and remain with the company. For example, the factory's cafeteria offers free food and there are gyms, sports facilities, and a Finnish sauna. In addition, although managers from other countries run the plant at present, Nokia hopes that within a few years most of the factory's managers and supervisors will be Romanian. Its goal is to create a career ladder that will motivate employees to perform at a high level and be promoted.

At the same time, Nokia is hardheaded about how efficiently it expects its Romanian factory to operate because all its factories are required to operate at the same level of efficiency that its *most* efficient global factory has achieved—in this way it will reduce its global cost structure. In order to do this, Nokia has created a compensation plan for all its global division managers based on the collective performance of all its factories worldwide. All the managers of its global operating facilities will see their bonuses reduced if only one factory in any country performs below expectations. This is a tough approach, but its purpose is to encourage all managers to develop a global view and quickly adopt more efficient manufacturing techniques; any ways to reduce costs or increase quality that have been discovered in one of its global plants must be shared with all its other plants around the world if managers are to obtain their bonuses. Nokia's goal is that efficiency and quality will continuously improve as managers are motivated to find better ways to operate and share this knowledge throughout the company.

Just 6 months after it opened in June 2008, the Romanian plant reached a milestone and produced the 1 millionth handset. The plant's efficiency has exceeded Nokia's expectations—so much so that Nokia opened a new cell phone accessory factory next to the plant and has hired hundreds of new workers who all received a 9% salary increase in 2010 because of their high productivity. Nokia contemplated opening a new plant in Argentina to serve the booming South American market, but it eventually decided to outsource cellphone manufacturing to an Argentinean supplier, and open its newest plant in Brazil, the largest market in South America—and one in which the demand for smartphones is rapidly growing.[1]

Overview

The way in which Nokia has been working to expand its global organizational structure to effectively compete in countries around the world suggests that strategic thinking becomes very complex at the corporate level. Managers must continuously examine and improve the way they implement their business and multibusiness models to increase their long-term profitability–otherwise the result can be a disaster. In 2011, while Nokia's global organizational structure worked efficiently, it was lagging behind Apple in its attempt to develop advanced smartphones that had the features and speed its global customers wanted. This chapter begins where the last one ends; it examines how to implement strategy when a company decides to enter and compete in new industries or in new countries when it expands globally. The strategy implementation issue remains the same, however: deciding how to use organizational design and combine organizational structure, control, and culture to strengthen a company's multibusiness model and increase its profitability.

Once a company decides to compete across industries and countries, it confronts a new set of problems; some of them are continuations of the organizational problems we discussed in Chapter 12, and some of them are a direct consequence of the decision to enter and compete in overseas markets and new industries. As a result, strategic managers must make a new series of organizational design decisions to successfully implement their company's new global multibusiness model. By the end of the chapter, you will appreciate the many complex issues that confront global multibusiness companies and understand why effective strategy implementation is an integral part of achieving competitive advantage and superior performance.

Managing Corporate Strategy through the Multidivisional Structure

As Chapters 10 and 11 discuss, there are many ways in which corporate-level strategies such as vertical integration or diversification can be used to strengthen a company's business model and improve its competitive position. However, important implementation problems also arise when a company enters new industries, often due to the increasing bureaucratic costs associated with managing a collection of business units that operate in different industries. Bureaucratic costs are especially high when a company seeks to gain the differentiation and low-cost advantages of transferring, sharing, or leveraging its distinctive competencies across its business units in different industries—something that Nokia is doing. Companies that pursue a multibusiness model based on related diversification, for example, face many problems and costs in managing the handoffs or transfers between the value chain functions of its business units in different industries or around the world to boost profitability. The need to economize on these costs propels strategic managers to search for improved ways to implement the corporate-level strategies necessary to pursue a multibusiness model—as Nokia is trying to do by linking managers' bonuses to the efficiency of its global manufacturing operations.

As a company begins to enter new industries and produce different kinds of products, such as cars, fast food, and mobile computing devices, the structures described in Chapter 12, such as the functional and product structures, are not up to the task. These structures cannot provide the level of coordination between managers, functions, and business units necessary to implement a multibusiness model effectively. As a result, the control problems that give rise to bureaucratic costs, such as those related to measurement, customers, location, or strategy, escalate.

Experiencing these problems is a sign that a company has once again outgrown its structure. Strategic managers need to invest additional resources to develop a more complex structure—one that allows it to implement its multibusiness model and strategies successfully. The answer for most large, complex companies is to move to a multidivisional structure, design a cross-industry control system, and fashion a global corporate culture to reduce these problems and economize on bureaucratic costs.

A **multidivisional structure** has two organizational design advantages over a functional or product structure that allow a company to grow and diversify while it also reduces the coordination and control problems that inevitably arise as it enters and competes in new industries. First, in each industry in which a company operates, strategic managers group all its different business operations in that industry into one division or subunit. Each industry division contains all the value chain functions it needs to pursue its industry business model and is thus called a **self-contained division**. For example, GE competes in more than 150 different industries, and all of its 150 divisions are self-contained and perform all the value creation functions necessary to give each of them a competitive advantage.

Second, the office of *corporate headquarters staff* is created to monitor divisional activities and exercise financial control over each division.[2] This staff contains the corporate-level managers who oversee the activities of divisional managers. Hence, the organizational hierarchy is taller in a multidivisional structure than in a product or functional structure. An important function of the new level of corporate management is to develop strategic control systems that lower a company's overall cost structure, including finding ways to economize on the costs of controlling the handoffs and transfers between divisions, as in Nokia's case. The extra cost of these corporate managers is more than justified if their actions lower the cost structure of the operating divisions or increase their ability to differentiate their products—both of which boost total company profitability.

In the multidivisional structure, the day-to-day operations of each division are the responsibility of divisional management; that is, divisional managers have *operating responsibility*. The **corporate headquarters staff**, which includes top executives as well as their support staff, is responsible for overseeing the company's long-term multibusiness model and providing guidance for increasing the value created by interdivisional projects. These executives have *strategic responsibility*. Such an organizational grouping of self-contained divisions with centralized corporate management results in an organizational structure that provides the extra coordination and control necessary to compete in new industries or world regions successfully.

Figure 13.1 illustrates a typical multidivisional structure found in a large chemical company such as DuPont. Although this company has at least 20 different divisions, only three—the oil, pharmaceuticals, and plastics divisions—are represented in this figure. Each division possesses the value chain functions it needs to pursue its own industry business model. Each division is treated by corporate managers as an independent profit center, and measures of profitability such as ROIC are used to monitor and evaluate each division's individual performance.[3] The use of this kind of output control makes it easier for corporate managers to identify high-performing and underperforming divisions and to take corrective action as necessary.

Multidivisional structure

A complex organizational design that allows a company to grow and diversify while it also reduces coordination and control problems because it uses self-contained divisions and has a separate corporate headquarters staff.

Self-contained division

An independent business unit or division that contains all the value chain functions it needs to pursue its business model successfully.

Corporate headquarters staff

The team of top executives, as well as their support staff, who are responsible for overseeing a company's long-term multibusiness model and providing guidance to increase the value created by the company's self-contained divisions.

Figure 13.1   Multidivisional Structure

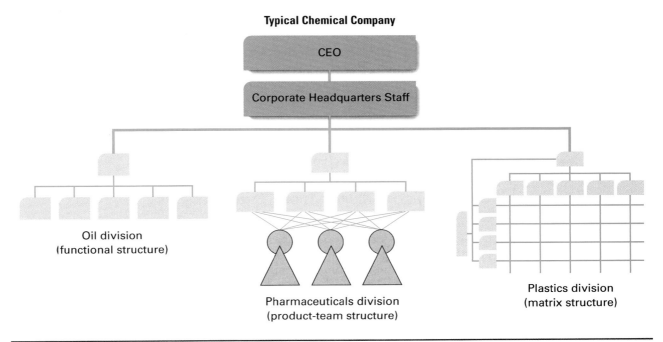

Because each division operates independently, the divisional managers in charge of each individual division can choose which organizational structure (e.g., a product, matrix, or market structure), control systems, and culture to adopt to implement its business model and strategies most effectively. Figure 13.1 illustrates how this process works. It shows that managers of the oil division have chosen a functional structure (the one that is the least costly to operate) to pursue a cost-leadership strategy. The pharmaceuticals division has adopted a product-team structure that allows each separate product-development team to focus their efforts on the speedy development of new drugs. And, managers of the plastics division have chosen to implement a matrix structure that promotes cooperation between teams and functions and allows for the continuous innovation of improved plastic products that suit the changing needs of customers. These two divisions are pursuing differentiation based on a distinctive competence in innovation.

The CEO famous for employing the multidivisional structure to great advantage was Alfred Sloan, GM's first CEO, who implemented a multidivisional structure in 1921, noting that GM "needs to find a principle for coordination without losing the advantages of decentralization." Sloan placed each of GM's different car brands in a self-contained division so it possessed its own functions—sales, production, engineering, and finance. Each division was treated as a profit center and evaluated upon its return on investment. Sloan was clear about the main advantage of decentralization: it made it much easier to evaluate the performance of each division. And, Sloan observed, it: (1) "increases the morale of the organization by placing each operation on its own foundation ... assuming its own responsibility and contributing its share to the final result"; (2) "develops statistics correctly reflecting … the true measure of efficiency"; and (3) "enables the corporation to direct the placing of additional capital where it will result in the greatest benefit to the corporation as a whole."[4]

Sloan recommended that exchanges or handoffs between divisions be set by a *transfer-pricing system* based on the cost of making a product plus some agreed-upon rate of return. He recognized the risks that internal suppliers might become inefficient and raise the cost structure, and he recommended that GM should benchmark competitors to determine the fair price for a component. He established a centralized headquarters management staff to perform these calculations. Corporate management's primary role was to audit divisional performance and plan strategy for the entire organization. Divisional managers were to be responsible for all competitive product-related decisions.

Advantages of a Multidivisional Structure

When managed effectively at both the corporate and the divisional levels, a multidivisional structure offers several strategic advantages. Together, they can raise corporate profitability to a new peak because they allow a company to more effectively implement its multibusiness model and strategies.

Enhanced Corporate Financial Control   The profitability of different business divisions is clearly visible in the multidivisional structure.[5] Because each division is its own **profit center**, financial controls can be applied to each business on the basis of profitability criteria such as ROIC. Corporate managers establish performance goals for each division, monitor their performance on a regular basis, and intervene selectively if a division starts to underperform. They can then use this information to identify the divisions in which investment of the company's financial resources will yield the greatest long-term ROIC. As a result, they can allocate the company's funds among competing divisions in an optimal way, that is, a way that will maximize the profitability of the *whole* company. Essentially, managers at corporate headquarters act as "internal investors" who channel funds to high-performing divisions in which they will produce the most profits.

Enhanced Strategic Control   The multidivisional structure makes divisional managers responsible for developing each division's business model and strategies; this allows corporate managers to focus on developing the multibusiness model, which is their main responsibility. The structure gives corporate managers the time they need to contemplate wider long-term strategic issues and develop a coordinated response to competitive changes, such as quickly changing industry boundaries. Teams of managers at corporate headquarters can also be created to collect and process crucial information that leads to improved functional performance at the divisional level. These managers also perform long-term strategic and scenario planning to find new ways to increase the performance of the entire company, such as evaluating which of the industries they compete in will likely be the most profitable in the future. Then managers can decide which industries they should expand into and which they should exit.

Profitable Long-Term Growth   The division of responsibilities between corporate and divisional managers in the multidivisional structure allows a company to overcome

Profit center

When each self-contained division is treated as a separate financial unit and financial controls are used to establish performance goals for each division and measure profitability.

organizational problems, such as communication problems and information overload. Divisional managers work to enhance their divisions' profitability; teams of managers at corporate headquarters devote their time to finding opportunities to expand or diversify its existing businesses so that the entire company enjoys profitable growth. Communication problems are also reduced because corporate managers use the same set of standardized accounting and financial output controls to evaluate all divisions. Also, from a behavior control perspective, corporate managers can implement a policy of management by exception, which means that they intervene only when problems arise.

Stronger Pursuit of Internal Efficiency As a single-business company grows, it often becomes difficult for top managers to accurately assess the profit contribution of each functional activity because their activities are so interdependent. This means that it is often difficult for top managers to evaluate how well their company is performing relative to others in its industry—and to identify or pinpoint the specific source of the problem. As a result, inside one company, considerable degrees of **organizational slack**—that is, the unproductive use of functional resources—can go undetected. For example, the head of the finance function might employ a larger staff than is required for efficiency to reduce work pressures inside the department and to bring the manager higher status. In a multidivisional structure, however, corporate managers can compare the performance of one division's cost structure, sales, and the profit it generates against another. The corporate office is, therefore, in a better position to identify the managerial inefficiencies that result in bureaucratic costs; divisional managers have no excuses for poor performance.

Problems in Implementing a Multidivisional Structure

Although research suggests large companies that adopt multidivisional structures outperform those that retain functional structures, multidivisional structures have their disadvantages as well.[6] Good management can eliminate some of these disadvantages, but some problems are inherent in the structure. Corporate managers must continually pay attention to the way they operate and detect problems.

Establishing the Divisional-Corporate Authority Relationship The authority relationship between corporate headquarters and the subordinate divisions must be correctly established. The multidivisional structure introduces a new level in the management hierarchy: the corporate level. Corporate managers face the problem of deciding how much authority and control to delegate to divisional managers, and how much authority to retain at corporate headquarters to increase long-term profitability. Sloan encountered this problem when he implemented GM's multidivisional structure.[7] He found that when corporate managers retained too much power and authority, the managers of its business divisions lacked the autonomy required to change its business model to meet rapidly changing competitive conditions; the need to gain approval from corporate managers slowed down decision making. On the other hand, when too much authority is delegated to divisions, managers may start to pursue strategies that benefit their own divisions, but add little to the whole company's profitability. Strategy in Action 13.1 describes the problems Andrea Jung experienced as Avon recentralized control over its functional operations to U.S. corporate managers from overseas divisional managers under order to overcome this problem.

> **Organizational slack**
>
> The unproductive use of functional resources by divisional managers that can go undetected unless corporate managers monitor their activities.

STRATEGY IN ACTION

Why Avon Needed to Change the Balance Between Centralization and Decentralization

After a decade of profitable growth, Avon suddenly began to experience falling global sales in the mid-2000s, both at home and in developing markets abroad. After spending several months visiting the managers of its worldwide divisions, Andrea Jung, Avon's CEO, decided that Avon had lost the balance between centralization and decentralization of authority. Managers abroad had gained so much authority to control operations in their respective countries and world regions that they had made decisions to benefit their own divisions, and these decisions had hurt the performance of the whole company. Specifically, Avon's operating costs were out of control, and it was losing both low-cost and differentiation advantages. Avon's country-level managers from Poland to Mexico ran their own factories, made their own product development decisions, and spearheaded their own advertising campaigns. These decisions were often based on poor marketing knowledge and with little concern for operating costs because the goal was to increase sales as rapidly as possible.

Also, when too much authority is decentralized to managers lower in an organization's hierarchy, these managers often recruit more and more managers to help them build their country "empires." The result was that Avon's global hierarchy had exploded—it had risen from 7 levels to 15 levels of managers in a decade as tens of thousands of additional managers were hired around the globe! Because Avon's profits were rising fast, Jung and her top management team had not paid enough attention to the way Avon's organizational structure was becoming taller and taller—and how this was taking away its competitive advantage.

Once Jung recognized this problem she had to confront the need to lay off thousands of managers and restructure the hierarchy. She embarked on a program to take away the authority of Avon's country-level managers and to transfer authority to regional and corporate headquarters managers to streamline decision making and reduce costs. She cut out 7 levels of management and laid off 25% of Avon's global managers in its 114 worldwide markets. Then, using teams of expert managers from corporate headquarters, she embarked on a detailed examination of all Avon's functional activities, country by country, to find out why its costs had risen so quickly, and what could be done to bring them under control. The duplication of marketing efforts in countries around the world was one source of these high costs. In Mexico, one team found that country managers' desire to expand their empires led to the development of a staggering 13,000 different products! Not only had this caused product development costs to soar, it had led to major marketing problems, for how could Avon's Mexican sales reps learn about the differences between 13,000 products—and then find an easy way to tell customers about them?

In Avon's new structure the focus is now upon centralizing all new major product development; Avon develops over 1,000 new products per year, but in the future, the input from different country managers would be used to customize products to country needs including fragrance, packaging and so on, and R&D would be performed in the United States. Similarly, the future goal is to develop marketing campaigns targeted at the average "global" customer, but that can also be easily customized to any country. Using the appropriate language, or changing the nationality of the models used to market the products, for example, could be used in these campaigns. Other initiatives have been to increase the money spent on global marketing and a major push to increase the number of Avon representatives in developing nations in order to attract more customers. By 2011, Avon recruited another 400,000 reps in China alone!

Country-level managers now are responsible for managing this army of Avon reps and for ensuring that marketing dollars are being directed to the right channels for maximum impact. However, they no longer have any authority to engage in major product development or build new manufacturing capacity—or to hire new managers without the agreement of regional- or corporate-level managers. The balance of control has changed at Avon, and Jung and all her managers are now firmly focused on making operational decisions that lower its costs or increase its differentiation advantage in ways that serve the best interests of the whole company—and not only the country in which its cosmetics are sold.

Source: www.avon.com, 2011.

As this example suggests, the most important issue in managing a multidivisional structure is how much authority should be *centralized* at corporate headquarters and how much should be *decentralized* to the divisions—in different industries or countries. Corporate managers must consider how their company's multibusiness model and strategies will be affected by the way they make this decision now and in the future. There is no easy answer because every company is different. In addition, as the environment changes or a company alters its multibusiness model, the optimal balance between centralization and decentralization of authority will also change.

Restrictive Financial Controls Lead to Short-Run Focus Suppose corporate managers place too much emphasis on each division's *individual* profitability, for example, by establishing very high and stringent ROIC targets for each division. Divisional managers may engage in **information distortion**, that is, they manipulate the facts they supply to corporate managers to hide declining divisional performance, or start to pursue strategies that increase short-term profitability but reduce future profitability. For example, divisional managers may attempt to make the ROIC of their division look better by cutting investments in R&D, product development, or marketing—all of which increase ROIC in the short run. In the long term, however, cutting back on the investments and expenditures necessary to maintain the division's performance, particularly the crucial R&D investments that lead a stream of innovative products, will reduce its long-term profitability. Hence, corporate managers must carefully control their interactions with divisional managers to ensure that both the short- and long-term goals of the business are being met. In sum, a problem can stem from the use of financial controls that are too restrictive; Chapter 11 discusses the "balanced scorecard" approach that helps solve it.

Competition for Resources The third problem of managing a multidivisional structure is that when the divisions compete among themselves for scarce resources, this rivalry can make it difficult—or sometimes impossible—to obtain the gains from transferring, sharing, or leveraging distinctive competencies across business units. For example, every year the funds available to corporate managers to allocate or distribute to their divisions is fixed, and, usually, the divisions that have obtained the highest ROIC proportionally receive more of these funds. In turn, because managers have more money to invest in their business, this usually will raise the company's performance the next year so strong divisions grow ever stronger. This is what leads to competition for resources and reduces interdivisional coordination; there are many recorded instances in which one divisional manager tells another: "You want our new technology? Well you have to pay us $2 billion to get it." When divisions battle over transfer prices, the potential gains from pursuing a multibusiness model are lost.

Transfer Pricing As just noted, competition among divisions may lead to battles over **transfer pricing**, that is, conflicts over establishing the fair or "competitive" price of a resource or skill developed in one division that is to be transferred and sold to other divisions that require it. As Chapter 9 discusses, a major source of bureaucratic costs are the problems that arise from handoffs or transfers between divisions to obtain the benefits of the multibusiness models when pursuing a vertical integration or related diversification strategy. Setting prices for resource transfers between divisions is a major source of these problems, because every supplying division has the incentive to set the highest possible transfer price for its products or resources to maximize its *own* profitability. The "purchasing" divisions realize the supplying divisions' attempts to charge high prices will reduce their profitability; the result is competition between divisions that undermines cooperation and coordination. Such competition can completely destroy the corporate culture and turn a company into a battleground; if unresolved, the benefits of the multibusiness model will not be achieved. Hence, corporate managers must be sensitive to this problem and work hard with

Information distortion

The manipulation of facts supplied to corporate managers to hide declining divisional performance.

Transfer pricing

The problem of establishing the fair or "competitive" price of a resource or skill developed in one division that is to be transferred and sold to another division.

the divisions to design incentive and control systems to make the multidivisional structure work. Indeed, managing transfer pricing is one of corporate managers' most important tasks.

Duplication of Functional Resources Because each division has its own set of value chain functions, functional resources are duplicated across divisions; thus, multidivisional structures are expensive to operate. R&D and marketing are especially costly functional activities; to reduce their cost structure, some companies centralize most of the activities of these two functions at the corporate level in which they service the needs of all divisions. The expense involved in duplicating functional resources does not result in major problems if the differentiation advantages that result from the use of separate sets of specialist functions are substantial. Corporate managers must decide whether the duplication of functions is financially justified. In addition, they should always be on the lookout for ways to centralize or outsource functional activities to reduce a company's cost structure and increase long-run profitability.

In sum, the advantages of divisional structures must be balanced against the problems of implementing them, but an observant, professional set of corporate (and divisional) managers who are sensitive to the complexities involved can respond to and manage these problems. Indeed, advances in IT have made strategy implementation easier, as we will discuss later in this chapter.

Structure, Control, Culture, and Corporate-Level Strategy

Once corporate managers select a multidivisional structure, they must then make choices about what kind of integrating mechanisms and control systems necessary to make the structure work efficiently. Such choices depend upon whether a company chooses to pursue a multibusiness model based on a strategy of unrelated diversification, vertical integration, or related diversification.

As Chapter 9 discusses, many possible differentiation and cost advantages derive from vertical integration. A company can coordinate resource transfers between divisions operating in adjacent industries to reduce manufacturing costs and improve quality, for example.[8] This might mean locating a rolling mill next to a steel furnace to save on costs to reheat steel ingots, making it easier to control the quality of the final steel product.

The principal benefits from related diversification also derive from transferring, sharing, or leveraging functional competencies across divisions, such as sharing distribution and sales networks to increase differentiation, or lowering the overall cost structure. With both strategies, the benefits to the company result from some *exchange* of distinctive competencies among divisions. To secure these benefits, managers must coordinate the activities of the various divisions, so an organization's structure and control systems must be designed to manage the handoffs or transfers among divisions.

In the case of unrelated diversification, the multibusiness model is based on using general strategic management capabilities, for example, in corporate finance or organizational design. Corporate managers' ability to create a culture that supports entrepreneurial behavior that leads to rapid product development, or to restructure an underperforming company and establish an effective set of financial controls, can result in substantial increases in profitability. With this strategy, however, there are *no* exchanges among divisions; each division operates separately and independently. The only exchanges that need to be coordinated are those between the divisions and corporate headquarters. Structure and control must therefore be designed to allow each division to operate independently, while making it easy for corporate managers to monitor divisional performance and intervene if necessary.

The choice of structure and control mechanisms depends upon the degree to which a company using a multidivisional structure needs to control the handoffs and interactions among divisions. The more *interdependent are divisions*—that is, the more they depend on each other for skills, resources, and competencies—the greater the bureaucratic costs associated with obtaining the potential benefits from a particular corporate-level strategy.[9] Table 13.1 illustrates what forms of structure and control companies should adopt to economize on the bureaucratic costs associated with the three corporate strategies of unrelated diversification, vertical integration, and related diversification.[10] We examine these strategies in detail in the next sections.

Unrelated Diversification　　Because there are *no exchanges or linkages* among divisions, unrelated diversification is the easiest and cheapest strategy to manage; it is associated with the lowest level of bureaucratic costs. The primary advantage of the structure and control system is that it allows corporate managers to evaluate divisional performance accurately. Thus, companies use multidivisional structures, and each division is evaluated by output controls such as ROIC. A company also uses an IT-based system of financial controls to allow corporate managers to obtain information quickly from the divisions and compare their performance on many dimensions. UTC, Tyco, and Textron are companies well-known for their use of sophisticated financial controls to manage their structures and track divisional performance on a daily basis.

Divisions usually have considerable autonomy *unless* they fail to reach their ROIC goals, in which case corporate managers will intervene in the operations of a division to help solve problems. As problems arise, corporate managers step in and take corrective action, such as replacing managers or providing additional funding, depending on the reason for the problem. If they see no possibility of a turnaround, they may decide to divest the division. The multidivisional structure allows the unrelated company to operate its businesses as a portfolio of investments that can be bought and

Table 13.1 Corporate Strategy, Structure, and Control

Corporate Strategy	Appropriate Structure	Need for Integration	Type of Control		
			Financial Control	Behavior Control	Organizational Culture
Unrelated Diversification	Multidivisional	Low (no exchanges between divisions)	Great use (e.g., ROIC)	Some use (e.g., budgets)	Little use
Vertical Integration	Multidivisional	Medium (scheduling resource transfers)	Great use (e.g., ROIC, transfer pricing)	Great use (e.g., standardization, budgets)	Some use (e.g., shared norms and values)
Related Diversification	Multidivisional	High (achieving synergies between divisions by integrating roles)	Little use	Great use (e.g., rules, budgets)	Great use (e.g., norms, values, common language)

© Cengage Learning 2013

sold as business conditions change. Typically, managers in the various divisions do not know one another; they may not even know what other companies are represented in the corporate portfolio. Hence, the idea of a corporate-wide culture is meaningless.

The use of financial controls to manage a company means that no integration among divisions is necessary. This is why the bureaucratic costs of managing an unrelated company are low. The biggest problem facing corporate managers is to make capital allocations decisions between divisions to maximize the overall profitability of the portfolio and monitor divisional performance to ensure they are meeting ROIC targets.

Alco Standard, once one of the largest U.S. office supply companies provides an example of how to operate a successful strategy of unrelated diversification. Alco's corporate management believed that authority and control should be completely decentralized to the managers of each of the company's 50 divisions. Each division was then left to make its own manufacturing or purchasing decisions, despite that the potential benefits to be obtained from corporate-wide purchasing or marketing were lost. Corporate managers pursued this nonintervention policy because they judged that the gains from allowing divisional managers to act in an entrepreneurial way exceeded potential cost savings that might result from attempts to coordinate interdivisional activities. Alco believed that a decentralized operating system would allow a big company to act as a small company and avoid the problems that arise when companies become bureaucratic and difficult to change.

Vertical Integration   Vertical integration is a more expensive strategy to manage than unrelated diversification because *sequential resource flows* from one division to the next must be coordinated. Once again, the multidivisional structure economizes on the bureaucratic costs associated with achieving such coordination because it provides the centralized control necessary for a vertically integrated company to benefit from resource transfers. Corporate managers are responsible for devising financial output and behavior controls that solve the problems of transferring resources from one division to the next; for example, they solve transfer pricing problems. Also, rules and procedures are created that specify how resource exchanges are made to solve potential handoff problems; complex resource exchanges may lead to conflict among divisions; and corporate managers must try to prevent this.

The way to distribute authority between corporate and divisional managers must be considered carefully in vertically integrated companies. The involvement of corporate managers in operating issues at the divisional level risks that divisional managers feel they have no autonomy, so their performance suffers. These companies must strike the appropriate balance of centralized control at corporate headquarters and decentralized control at the divisional level if they are to implement this strategy successfully.

Because the interests of their divisions are at stake, divisional managers need to be involved in decisions concerning scheduling and resource transfers. For example, the plastics division in a chemical company has a vital interest in the activities of the oil division because the quality of the products it receives from the oil division determines the quality of its products. Integrating mechanisms must be created between divisions that encourage their managers to freely exchange or transfer information and skills.[11] To facilitate communication among divisions, corporate managers create teams composed of both corporate and divisional managers, **integrating roles** whereby an experienced corporate manager assumes the responsibility for managing complex transfers between two or more divisions. The use of integrating roles to coordinate divisions is common in high-tech and chemical companies, for example.

Integrating roles

Managers who work in full-time positions established specifically to improve communication between divisions.

Thus, a strategy of vertical integration is managed through a combination of corporate and divisional controls. As a result, the organizational structure and control systems used to economize upon the bureaucratic costs of managing this strategy are more complex and difficult to implement than those used for unrelated diversification. However, as long as the benefits that derive from vertical integration are realized, the extra expense in implementing this strategy can be justified.

Related Diversification   In the case of related diversification, the gains from pursuing this multibusiness model derive from the transfer, sharing, and leveraging of R&D knowledge, industry information, customer bases, and so on, across divisions. Also, with this structure, the high level of divisional resource sharing and the exchange of functional competencies makes it difficult for corporate managers to evaluate the performance of each individual division.[12] Thus, bureaucratic costs are substantial. The multidivisional structure helps to economize on these costs because it provides some of the extra coordination and control that is required. However, if a related company is to obtain the potential benefits from using its competencies efficiently and effectively, it has to adopt more complicated forms of integration and control at the divisional level to make the structure work.

First, output control is difficult to use because divisions share resources, so it is not easy to measure the performance of an individual division. Therefore, a company needs to develop a corporate culture that stresses cooperation among divisions and the corporate team rather than focusing purely on divisional goals. Second, corporate managers must establish sophisticated integrating devices to ensure coordination among divisions. Integrating roles and integrating teams of corporate and divisional managers are essential because these teams provide the forum in which managers can meet, exchange information, and develop a common vision of corporate goals. An organization with a multidivisional structure must have the right mix of incentives and rewards for cooperation if it is to achieve gains from sharing skills and resources among divisions.[13] With unrelated diversification, divisions operate autonomously, and the company can easily reward managers based upon their division's individual performance. With related diversification, however, rewarding divisions is more difficult because the divisions are engaged in so many shared activities; corporate managers must be alert to the need to achieve equity in the rewards the different divisions receive. The goal is always to design a company's structure and control systems to maximize the benefits from pursuing a particular strategy while economizing on the bureaucratic costs of implementing it.

The Role of Information Technology

The expanding use of IT is increasing the advantages and reducing the problems associated with effectively implementing a multibusiness model because IT facilitates output control, behavior control, and integration between divisions and among divisions and corporate headquarters.

IT provides a common software platform that can make it much less problematic for divisions to share information and knowledge and obtain the benefits from leveraging their competencies. IT facilitates output and financial control, making it easier for corporate headquarters to monitor divisional performance and selectively decide when to intervene. It also helps corporate managers better use their strategic and implementation skills because managers can react more quickly when they access higher-quality, more timely information from the use of a sophisticated, cross-organizational IT infrastructure.

In addition, IT makes it easier to manage the problems that can occur when implementing a multidivisional structure. Because it provides both corporate and divisional managers with more and better information, IT makes it easier for corporate managers to decentralize control to divisional managers and yet react quickly, if the need arises. IT can also make it more difficult to distort information because divisional managers must provide standardized information that can be compared across divisions. Finally, IT eases the transfer pricing problem because divisional managers have access to detailed, up-to-date information about how much certain resources or skills would cost to purchase in the external marketplace. Thus, a fair transfer price is easier to determine. The way in which SAP's Enterprise Resource Planning (ERP) software helps to integrate the activities of divisions in a multidivisional structure is discussed in Strategy in Action 13.2.

STRATEGY IN ACTION

SAP's ERP System

SAP is the world's leading supplier of ERP software; it introduced the world's first ERP system in 1973. The demand for its software was so great that SAP had to train thousands of IT consultants from companies such as IBM, HP, Accenture, and Cap Gemini to install and customize it to meet the needs of companies around the globe. SAP's ERP system is popular because it manages functional activities at all stages of a company's value chain, as well as resource transfers among a company's different divisions.

First, SAP's software has modules specifically designed to manage each core functional activity. Each module contains the set of best practices that SAP's IT engineers have found to work in building competencies in efficiency, quality, innovation, and responsiveness to customers. Each function inputs its data into a functional module in the way specified by SAP. For example, sales input all the information about customer needs required by SAP's sales module, and materials management inputs information about the product specifications it requires from suppliers into SAP's materials-management module. Each SAP module functions as an *expert system* that can reason through the information that functional managers put into it. It then provides managers with real-time feedback about the current state of vital functional operations and gives recommendations that allow managers to improve them. However, the magic of ERP does not stop there. SAP's ERP software connects across functions inside each division. This means that managers in all functions of a division

have access to other functions' expert systems; SAP's software is designed to alert managers when their functional operations are affected by changes taking place in another function. *Thus, SAP's ERP software allows managers throughout a division to better coordinate their activities,* which is a major source of competitive advantage.

Moreover, SAP software, running on corporate mainframe computers, takes the information from all the different expert systems in the divisions and creates a company-wide ERP system that provides corporate managers with an overview of the operations of all a company's divisions. In essence, SAP's ERP system creates a sophisticated corporate-level expert system that can reason through the huge volume of information being provided by all its divisions and functions. The ERP system can then recognize and diagnose common issues and problems, and recommend organization-wide solutions, such as suggesting new ways to leverage, transfer, and share competencies and resources. Top managers, armed with the knowledge that their ERP software provides, can also use it to adjust their business model with the changing environment. The result, SAP claims, is that when a multidivisional company implements its corporate-wide ERP software, it can achieve productivity gains of 30% to 50%, which amounts to billions of dollars of savings for large multinational companies like Nestlé and Exxon. In 2011, SAP was the biggest supplier of ERP software to the world's largest companies; clearly it pays to use the competences of this industry leader.

Source: www.sap.com, 2011.

Implementing Strategy Across Countries

Global strategy can play a crucial role in strengthening the business model of both single-business and multibusiness companies. Indeed, few large companies that have expanded into new industries have not already expanded globally and replicated their business model in new countries to grow their profits. Companies can use four basic strategies as they begin to market their products and establish production facilities abroad:

1. A *localization strategy* is oriented toward local responsiveness, and a company decentralizes control to subsidiaries and divisions in each country in which it operates to produce and customize products to local markets.
2. An *international strategy* is based on R&D and marketing being centralized at home and all the other value creation functions being decentralized to national units.
3. A *global standardization strategy* is oriented toward cost reduction, with all the principal value creation functions centralized at the optimal global location.
4. A *transnational strategy* is focused so that it can achieve local responsiveness and cost reduction. Some functions are centralized; others are decentralized at the global location best suited to achieving these objectives.

The need to coordinate and integrate global value-chain activities increases as a company moves from a localization to an international, to a global standardization, and then to a transnational strategy. To obtain the benefits of pursuing a transnational strategy, a company must transfer its distinctive competencies to the global location where it can create the most value and establish a global network to coordinate its divisions at home and abroad. The objective of such coordination is to obtain the benefits from transferring or leveraging competencies across a company's global business units. Thus, the bureaucratic costs associated with solving the communication and measurement problems that arise in managing handoffs or transfers across countries are much higher for companies pursuing a transnational strategy than for those pursuing the other strategies. The localization strategy does not require coordinating activities on a global level because value creation activities are handled locally, by country or world region. The international and global standardization strategies fit between the other two strategies although products have to be sold and marketed globally; hence, global product transfers must be managed, and there is less need to coordinate skill and resource transfers when using an international strategy than when using a transnational strategy.

The implication is that, as companies change from localization to international, global standardization, or transnational strategies, they require more complex structures, control systems, and cultures to coordinate the value creation activities associated with implementing those strategies. More complex structures economize on bureaucratic costs. In general, the choice of structure and control systems for managing a global business is a function of three factors:

1. The decision about how to distribute and allocate responsibility and authority between managers at home and abroad so that effective control over a company's global operations is maintained
2. he selection of the organizational structure that groups divisions both at home and abroad in a way that allows the best use of resources and serves the needs of foreign customers most effectively

3. he selection of the right kinds of integration and control mechanisms and organizational culture to make the overall global structure function effectively

Table 13.2 summarizes the appropriate design choices for companies pursuing each of these strategies.

Implementing a Localization Strategy

When a company pursues a localization strategy, it generally operates with a global-area structure (see Figure 13.2). When using this structure, a company duplicates all value creation activities and establishes overseas divisions in every country or world area in which it operates. Authority is decentralized to managers in each overseas division, and these managers devise the appropriate strategy for responding to the needs of the local environment. Managers at global headquarters use market and output controls such as ROIC, growth in market share, and changes in operating costs to evaluate the performance of overseas divisions. On the basis of such global comparisons, they can make decisions about capital allocation and orchestrate the transfer of new knowledge among divisions.

A company that makes and sells the same products in many different countries often groups its overseas divisions into world regions to simplify the coordination of products across countries. Europe might be one region, the Pacific Rim another, and the Middle East a third. Grouping allows the same set of output and behavior controls to be applied across all divisions inside a region. Thus, global companies can reduce communications and transfer problems because information can be transmitted

Table 13.2 Global Strategy/Structure Relationships

	Localization Strategy	International Strategy	Global Standardization Strategy	Transnational Strategy
	Low	**Need for Coordination Bureaucratic Costs**		**High**
Centralization of Authority	Decentralized to national unit	Core competencies centralized; others decentralized to national units	Centralized at optimal global location	Simultaneously centralized and decentralized
Horizontal Differentiation	Global-area structure	Global-division structure	Global product-group structure	Global-matrix-structure, matrix-in-the mind
Need for Complex Integrating Mechanisms	Low	Medium	High	Very high
Organizational Culture	Not important	Quite important	Important	Very important

Figure 13.2 Global-Area Structure

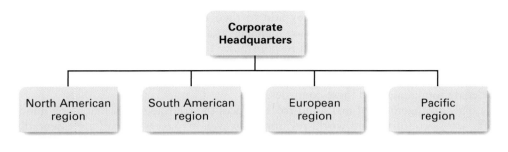

© Cengage Learning 2013

more easily across countries with broadly similar cultures. For example, consumers' preferences regarding product design and marketing are likely to be more similar among countries in one world region than among countries in different world regions.

Because the overseas divisions themselves have little or no contact with others in different regions, no integrating mechanisms are needed. Nor does a global organizational culture develop because there are no transfers of skills or resources or transfer of managerial personnel among the various world regions. Historically, car companies such as GM and Ford used global-area structures to manage their overseas operations. Ford of Europe, for example, had little or no contact with its U.S. parent; capital was the principal resource exchanged.

One problem with a global-area structure and a localization strategy is that the duplication of specialist activities across countries raises a company's overall cost structure. Moreover, the company is not taking advantage of opportunities to transfer, share, or leverage its competencies and capabilities on a global basis; for example, it cannot apply the low-cost manufacturing expertise that it has developed in one world region to another. Thus, localization companies lose the many benefits of operating globally. As Chapter 8 discusses, the popularity of this strategic orientation has decreased.

Implementing an International Strategy

A company pursuing an international strategy adopts a different route to global expansion. Normally, a company shifts to this strategy when it decides to sell domestically made products in markets abroad. Until the 1990s, for example, companies such as Mercedes-Benz and Jaguar made no attempt to produce in foreign markets; instead, they distributed and sold their domestically produced cars internationally. Such companies usually just add a *foreign sales organization* to their existing structure and continue to use the same control system. If a company is using a functional structure, this department has to coordinate manufacturing, sales, and R&D activities with the needs of the foreign market. Efforts at customization are minimal. In overseas countries, a company usually establishes a subsidiary to handle local sales and distribution. For example, the Mercedes-Benz overseas subsidiaries allocate dealerships, organize supplies of spare parts, and, of course, sell cars. A system of behavior controls is then established to keep the home office informed of changes in sales, spare parts requirements, and so on.

A company with many different products or businesses operating from a multi-divisional structure has the challenging problem of coordinating the flow of different products across different countries. To manage these transfers, many companies create *global divisions*, which they add to their existing divisional structures (see Figure 13.3).[14] Global operations are managed as a separate divisional business, with managers given the authority and responsibility for coordinating domestic product divisions with overseas markets. The global division also monitors and controls the overseas subsidiaries that market the products and decides how much authority to delegate to managers in these countries.

This arrangement of tasks and roles reduces the transaction of managing hand-offs across countries and world regions. However, managers abroad are essentially under the control of managers in the global division, and if domestic and overseas managers compete for control of strategy making, conflict and lack of cooperation may result. Companies such as IBM, Citibank, and DaimlerAG have experienced this problem. Very often, significant strategic control has been decentralized to overseas divisions. When cost pressures force corporate managers to reassess their strategy and they decide to intervene, such intervention frequently provokes resistance, much of it due to differences in culture—not just corporate but also country differences.

Implementing a Global Standardization Strategy

When a company embarks on a global standardization strategy today, it locates its manufacturing and other value-chain activities at the global location that will allow it to increase efficiency, quality, and innovation. In doing so, it has to solve the problems of coordinating and integrating its global value-chain activities. It has to find a structure that lowers the bureaucratic costs associated with resource transfers between corporate headquarters and its overseas divisions and provides the centralized

Figure 13.3   Global Division Structure

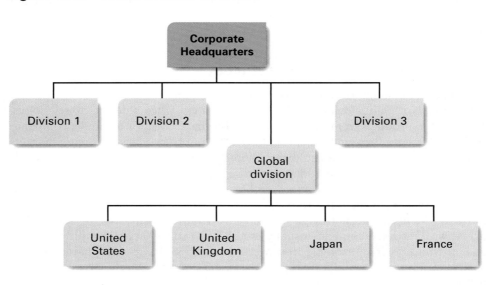

control that a global standardization strategy requires. The answer for many companies is a *global product-group structure* (see Figure 13.4).

In this structure, a product-group headquarters is created to coordinate the activities of a company's home and overseas operations. The managers at each product group's headquarters decide where to locate the different functions at the optimal global location for performing that activity. For example, Philips has one product group responsible for global R&D, manufacturing, marketing, and sales of its light bulbs; another for medical equipment; and so on. The headquarters of the medical division and its R&D is located in Bothell, Washington; manufacturing is done in Taiwan; and the products are sold by sales subsidiaries in each local market.

The product-group structure allows managers to decide how best to pursue a global standardization strategy, for example, to decide which value-chain activities, such as manufacturing or product design, should be performed in which country to increase efficiency. Increasingly, American and Japanese companies are moving manufacturing to low-cost countries such as China but establishing product design centers in Europe or the United States to take advantage of foreign skills and capabilities and thus obtain the benefits from this strategy.

For example, retailing giant Walmart has been aggressively expanding globally in recent years to boost its profitability. After moving into Mexico and Europe and establishing two global product groups in these regions, its managers turned their focus to Japan, where the supermarket business is extremely lucrative. Walmart's focus is on developing a sophisticated global supply chain to lower the costs of its purchasing, shipping, and sales activities to make the company the most efficient global discount retailer and grocer and give it a competitive advantage over rivals in the countries in which it competes.

Implementing a Transnational Strategy

The main failing of the global product-group structure is that, although it allows a company to achieve superior efficiency and quality, it is weak when it comes to responsiveness to customers because the focus is still on centralized control to reduce

Figure 13.4 Global Product-Group Structure

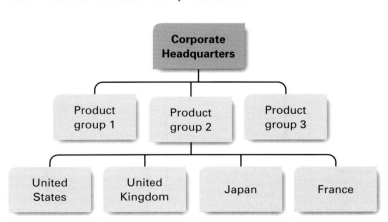

costs. Moreover, this structure makes it difficult for the different product divisions to trade information and knowledge and obtain the benefits from transferring, sharing, and leveraging their competencies. Sometimes the potential gains from sharing product, marketing, or R&D knowledge among product groups are high, but so too are the bureaucratic costs associated with achieving these gains. Is there a structure that can simultaneously economize on these costs and provide the coordination necessary to obtain these benefits?

In the 1990s, many companies implemented a *global-matrix structure* to simultaneously lower their global cost structures *and* differentiate their activities through superior innovation and responsiveness to customers globally. Figure 13.5 shows such a structure that might be used by a company such as Ford, HP, or SAP. On the vertical axis, instead of functions, are the company's product *groups*. These groups provide specialist services such as R&D, product design, and marketing information to its overseas divisions, which are often grouped by world region. They might be the petroleum, plastics, pharmaceuticals, or fertilizer product groups. On the horizontal axis are the company's *overseas divisions* in the various countries or world regions in which it operates. Managers at the regional or country level control local operations. Through a system of output and behavior controls, they then report to managers in product-group headquarters in the United States and ultimately to the CEO. Managers for world regions or countries are also responsible for working with U.S. product-group managers to develop the control and reward systems that will promote transfer, sharing, or leveraging of competencies.

Implementing a matrix structure thus decentralizes control to overseas managers and provides them with considerable flexibility for managing local issues, but it can still give product-group and top corporate executives in the United States the

Figure 13.5 Global-Matrix Structure

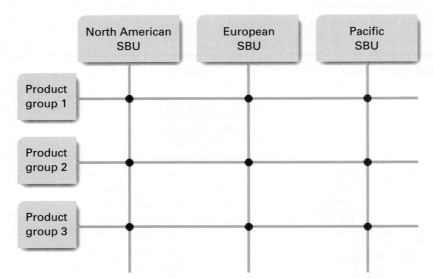

● Individual operating companies

centralized control they need to coordinate company activities on a global level. The matrix structure can allow knowledge and experience to be transferred among divisions in both product groups and geographic regions because it offers many opportunities for face-to-face contact between managers at home and abroad. The matrix also facilitates the transmission of a company's norms and values and, hence, the development of a global corporate culture. This is especially important for a company with far-flung global operations for which lines of communication are longer. Club Med, for instance, uses a matrix to standardize high-quality customer service across its global vacation villages. Nestlé's experience with the global-matrix structure is profiled in Strategy in Action 13.3.

Nestlé is not the only company to find the task of integrating and controlling a global-matrix structure a difficult task. Some, such as ABB, Motorola, and Ford have dismantled their matrix structures and moved to a simplified global product-group approach using IT to integrate across countries. If a matrix is chosen, however, other possible ways of making it work effectively include developing a strong global organizational culture to facilitate communication and coordination among country-based managers. For example, many companies transfer managers between their domestic and overseas operations, so they can implant their domestic culture in their new global division.

Toyota has made great efforts to understand how to manage car plants in overseas locations and how to transplant its culture into those plants. Every Toyota plant, for example, is under the control of Japanese managers, and managers from Toyota's Japanese headquarters monitor their performance and work to transfer and implant Toyota's latest R&D innovations into its next car models. At the same time, Toyota has established major new design and quality control operations facilities in the United States to help customize vehicles to the needs of U.S. customers.

Entry Mode and Implementation

As we discuss in Chapter 10, many organizations today are altering their business models and strategies and entering or leaving industries to find better ways to use their resources and capabilities to create value. This section focuses on the implementation issues that arise when companies use internal new venturing, joint ventures, and/or acquisitions to enter new industries.

Internal New Venturing

Chapter 10 discusses how companies enter new industries by using internal new venturing to transfer and leverage their existing competencies to create the set of value-chain activities necessary to compete effectively in a new industry. How can managers create a setting in which employees are encouraged to think about how to apply their functional competencies in new industries? In particular, how can structure, control, and culture be used to increase the success of the new-venturing process?

Corporate managers must treat the internal new-venturing process as a form of entrepreneurship and the managers who are to pioneer new ventures as **intrapreneurs**, that is, as inside or internal entrepreneurs. This means that organizational structure, control, and culture must be designed to encourage creativity and give new-venture managers real autonomy to develop and champion new products. At the same time, corporate managers want to make sure that their investment in a new market or

Intrapreneurs
Managers who pioneer and lead new venture projects or divisions and act as inside or internal entrepreneurs.

STRATEGY IN ACTION

Nestlé's Global Matrix Structure

Nestlé, based in Vevey, Switzerland, is the world's largest food company, with global sales in excess of $85 billion in 2011. The company has been pursuing an ambitious program of global expansion by acquiring many famous companies, for example, Perrier, the French mineral water producer, and Rowntree, the British candy maker. In the United States, Nestlé bought Carnation, Stouffer's, Contadina, Ralston Purina, and Dreyer's Grand Ice Cream.

In the past, Nestlé pursued a localization strategy and managed its operating companies through a global-area structure. In each country, its individual divisions (such as its Carnation division) were responsible for managing business-level strategy. For example, they had the authority to make all product development, marketing, and manufacturing decisions. Nestlé's corporate managers at its Vevey headquarters made the vital acquisition, expansion, and corporate resource decisions, such as how best to invest its capital; the size of the corporate staff had also increased dramatically to manage its rapid global expansion.

In the 1990s, Nestlé realized it had major problems. Corporate managers had become remote from the divisional managers in its thousands of operating divisions. They did not understand the problems divisions faced, and because authority was centralized, Nestlé was often slow to respond to the fast-changing food products industry. Moreover, the way the company operated made it impossible to obtain the potential benefits from sharing and leveraging its distinctive competencies in food product development and marketing, both among divisions in a product group and among product groups and world regions. Because each product group operated separately, corporate executives could not integrate product-group activities around the world. To raise corporate performance, Nestlé's managers had to find a new way to organize its activities.

Its CEO at the time, Helmut Maucher, started restructuring Nestlé from the top down. He stripped away the power of corporate managers by decentralizing authority to the managers of seven global product groups that he created to oversee the company's major product lines (e.g., coffee, milk, and candy). Each global product group was to integrate the activities of all the operating divisions in its group to transfer and leverage distinctive competencies to increase profitability. After the change, managers in the candy product group, for instance, began orchestrating the marketing and sale of Rowntree candy products, such as After Eight Mints and Smarties throughout Europe and the United States, and sales climbed by 60%.

Maucher then grouped all divisions within a country or world region into one national or regional strategic business unit (SBU) and created a team of SBU managers to link, coordinate, and oversee their activities. When the different divisions started to share joint purchasing, marketing, and sales activities, major cost savings resulted. In the United States, the SBU management team reduced the number of sales offices nationwide from 115 to 22 and the number of suppliers of packaging materials from 43 to 3.

Finally, Maucher decided to use a matrix structure to integrate the activities of the seven global-product groups with the operations of Nestlé's country-based SBUs. The goal of this matrix structure is to allow the company to pursue a transnational strategy and obtain the benefits of differentiation from global learning and from cost reductions from higher cooperation among divisions inside each product group. For example, regional SBU managers spend considerable time in Vevey with product-group executives discussing ways to take advantage of transferring and sharing the resources of the company on a global basis and inside each product group.

To further increase integration, Nestlé signed a $300 million contract with SAP to install and maintain a company-wide ERP system to integrate across *all* its global operations. Nestlé's top managers use their ERP system to provide them with the information they need to centralize control over the far-flung operations that they found the matrix structure did not alone provide. Using the ERP system, for example, provides managers with real-time information about the way Nestlé's global divisions are performing. They no longer need to rely solely upon divisional managers for this information, and can intervene on a global level as necessary.

Source: www.nestle.com, 2011.

industry will be profitable because commonalities exist between the new industry and its core industry so that the potential benefits of transferring or leveraging competencies will be obtained.[15] Apple, 3M, and Google are examples of companies that carefully select the right mix of structure, control, and culture to create a work context that facilitates the new-venturing process and promotes product innovation. For example, 3M's goal is that at least 30% of its growth in sales each year should come from new products developed within the past 5 years. To meet this challenging goal, 3M designed a sophisticated control and incentive system that provides its employees with the freedom and motivation to experiment and take risks.

Another approach to internal new venturing is championed by managers who believe that the best way to encourage new-product development is to separate the new venture unit from the rest of the organization. To provide the new-venture's managers with the autonomy to experiment and take risks, a company establishes a **new-venture division**, that is, a separate and independent division to develop a new product. If a new venture's managers work within a company's existing structure under the scrutiny of its corporate managers, they will not have the autonomy they need to pursue exciting new product ideas. In a separate unit in a new location, however, new venture managers will be able to act as external entrepreneurs as they work to create a new product and develop a business model to bring it to market successfully.

The new-venture unit or division uses controls that reinforce its entrepreneurial spirit. Strict output controls are inappropriate because they may promote short-term thinking and inhibit risk taking. Instead, stock options are often used to create a culture for entrepreneurship. Another issue is how to deal with corporate managers. The upfront R&D costs of new venturing are high, and its success is uncertain. After spending millions of dollars, corporate managers often become concerned about how successful the new-venture division will be. As a result, they might attempt to introduce strict output controls, including restrictive budgets to make the managers of the new venture more accountable—but which at the same time harm its entrepreneurial culture.[16] Corporate managers may believe it is important to use output and behavior controls to limit the new venture manager's autonomy; otherwise, they might make costly mistakes and waste resources on frivolous ideas.

Recently, there have been some indications that 3M's internal approach may be superior to the use of external new-venture divisions. It appears that many new-venture divisions have failed to bring successful new products to market. And even if they do, the new-venture division eventually begins to operate like other divisions and the entire company's cost structure increases because of the duplication of value-chain activities. Another issue is that scientists lack the formal training necessary to develop successful business models. Just as many medical doctors are earning MBAs today to understand the many strategic issues they must confront when they decide to become hospital managers, so scientists need to be able to think strategically. If strategic thinking is lacking in a new-venture division, the result is failure.

Joint Ventures

Joint ventures are a second method used by large, established companies to maintain momentum and grow their profits by entering new markets and industries.[17] A joint venture occurs when two companies agree to pool resources and capabilities and establish a new business unit to develop a new product and a business model that will allow it bring the new product to market successfully. These companies believe that through collaboration, by sharing their technology or marketing skills to develop an improved product for example, they will be able to create more value and profit in the new industry than if they decide to "go it alone." Both companies transfer competent managers, who have a proven track record of success, to manage the

New-venture division

A separate and independent division established to give its managers the autonomy to develop a new product.

new subunit that they both own. Sometimes they take an equal "50/50" ownership stake, but sometimes one company insists on having a 51% share or more, giving it the ability to buy out the other party at some point in the future should problems emerge. The way a joint venture is organized and controlled becomes an important issue in this context.

Allocating authority and responsibility is the first major implementation issue upon which companies must decide. Both companies need to be able to monitor the progress of the joint venture so that they can learn from its activities and benefit from their investment in it. Some companies insist on 51% ownership stakes because only then do they have the authority and control over the new ventures. Future problems could arise, such as what to do if the new venture performs poorly, or how to proceed if conflict develops between the parent companies over time—because one partner feels "cheated." For example, what will happen in the future is unknown, and frequently one parent company benefits much more from the product innovations the new company develops; if the other company demands "compensation," they come into conflict.[18] As was discussed in Chapter 8, a company also risks losing control of its core technology or competence when it enters into a strategic alliance. One parent company might believe this is taking place and feel threatened by the other. A joint venture can also be dangerous not only because one parent might decide to take the new technology and then "go it alone" in the development process, but also because its partner might be acquired by a competitor. For example, Compaq shared its proprietary server technology with a company in the computer storage industry to promote joint product development. Then, it watched helplessly as that company was acquired by Sun Microsystems, which consequently obtained Compaq's technology.

The implementation issues are strongly dependent upon whether the purpose of the joint venture is to share and develop technology, jointly distribute and market products and brands, or share access to customers. Sometimes companies can simply realize the joint benefits from collaboration without having to form a new company. For example, Nestlé and Coca-Cola announced a 10-year joint venture called Beverage Partners Worldwide through which Coca-Cola will distribute and sell Nestlé's Nestea iced tea, Nescafé, and other brands throughout the globe.[19] Similarly, Starbucks' Frappuccino is distributed by Pepsi. In these kinds of joint ventures, both companies can gain from sharing and pooling different competencies so that both realize value that would not otherwise be possible. Issues of ownership and control in these examples are less important.

Once the ownership issue has been settled, one company appoints the CEO who becomes responsible for creating a cohesive top management team out of the managers transferred from the parent companies. The job of the top management team is to develop a successful business model. These managers then need to choose an organizational structure, such as the functional or product team, that will make the best use of the resources and skills they receive from the parent companies. The need to create an effective organizational design that integrates people and functions is of paramount importance to ensure that the best use is made of limited resources. The need to build a new culture that unites managers who used to work in companies with different cultures is equally as important.

Managing these implementation issues is difficult, expensive, and time-consuming, so it is not surprising that when a lot is at stake and the future is uncertain, many companies decide they would be better to acquire another company and integrate it into their operations. This is Microsoft's favored strategy when it decides to enter new industries in the computer sector. Usually, it takes a 51% stake in an emerging company, which gives it the right to buy out the company and integrate its technology into its existing software divisions—should it prove to have some competency vital to Microsoft's future interests. First, however, Microsoft shares its resources and expertise with the new company to spur the development of its R&D competence. If the risks are lower, however, and it is easier to forecast the future, as in the venture between Coca-Cola and Nestlé, then to reduce bureaucratic costs, a strategic alliance (which does not require the creation of a new subunit), may be capable of managing the transfers of complementary resources and skills between companies.

Mergers and Acquisitions

Mergers and acquisitions are the third method companies use to enter new industries or countries.[20] How to implement structure, control systems, and culture to manage a new acquisition is important because many acquisitions are unsuccessful. One of the primary reasons acquisitions perform poorly is that many companies do not anticipate the difficulties associated with merging or integrating new companies into their existing operations.[21]

At the level of organizational structure, managers of both the acquiring and acquired companies must confront the problem of how to establish new lines of authority and responsibility that will allow them to make the best use of both companies' competencies. The massive merger between HP and Compaq illustrates these issues. Before the merger, the top management teams of both companies spent thousands of hours analyzing the range of both companies' activities and performing a value-chain analysis to determine how cost and differentiation advantages might be achieved. Based on this analysis, they merged all of both company's divisions into four main product groups.

Imagine the problems deciding who would control which group and which operating division, and to whom these divisions would report! To counter fears that infighting would prevent the benefits of the merger from being realized, the CEOs of HP and Compaq were careful to announce in press releases that the process of merging divisions was going smoothly and that battles over responsibilities and control of resources would be resolved. One problem with a mishandled merger is that skilled managers who feel they have been demoted will leave the company, and if many leave, the loss of their skills may prevent the benefits of the merger from being realized. This is why Google, for example, is committed to giving the software experts in the companies it acquires a major role in its current product development efforts, and why it encourages the development of strong cooperative values while working to maintain its innovative organizational culture.

Once managers have established clear lines of authority, they must decide how to coordinate and streamline the operations of both merged companies to reduce costs and leverage and share competencies. For large companies like HP, the answer is to choose the multidivisional structure, but important control issues still must be resolved. In general, the more similar or related are the acquired companies' products and markets, the easier it is to integrate their operations. If the acquiring company has an efficient control system, it can be adapted to the new company to standardize the way its activities are monitored and measured. Alternatively, managers can work hard to combine the best elements of each company's control systems and cultures or introduce a new IT system to integrate their operations.

If managers make unrelated acquisitions, however, and then attempt to interfere with a company's strategy in an industry they know little about, or apply inappropriate structure and controls to manage the new business, then major strategy implementation problems can arise. For example, if managers try to integrate unrelated companies with related companies, apply the wrong kinds of controls at the divisional level, or interfere in business-level strategy in the search for some elusive benefits, corporate performance can suffer as bureaucratic costs skyrocket. These mistakes explain why related acquisitions are sometimes more successful than unrelated ones.[22]

Even with examples of related diversification, the business processes of each company are frequently different, and their computer systems may be incompatible. The merged company faces the issue of how to use output and behavior controls to standardize business processes and reduce the cost of handing off and transferring resources. After Nestlé installed SAP's ERP software, for example, managers discovered that each of Nestlé's 150 different U.S. divisions was buying its own supply of vanilla from the same set of suppliers. However, the divisions were not sharing information about these purchases, and vanilla suppliers, dealing with each Nestlé division separately, tried to charge each division as much as they could![23] Each division paid a different price for the same input, and ach division used a different code for its independent purchase. Managers at U.S. headquarters did not have the means to discover this discrepancy until SAP's software provided the information.

Finally, even when acquiring a company in a closely related industry, managers must realize that each company has unique norms, values, and culture. Such idiosyncrasies must be understood to effectively integrate the operations of the merged company. Indeed, such idiosyncrasies are likely to be especially important when companies from different countries merge. Over time, top managers can change the culture and alter the internal workings of the company, but this is a difficult implementation task.

In sum, corporate managers' capabilities in organizational design are vital in ensuring the success of a merger or acquisition. Their ability to integrate and connect divisions to leverage competencies ultimately determines how well the newly merged company will perform.[24] The path to merger and acquisition is fraught with danger, which is why some companies claim that internal new venturing is the safest path and that it is best to grow organically from within. Yet with industry boundaries blurring and new global competitors emerging, companies often do not have the time or resources to go it alone. Choosing how to enter a new industry or country is a complex implementation issue that requires thorough strategic analysis.

Information Technology, the Internet, and Outsourcing

The many ways in which advances in IT affect strategy implementation is an important issue today. Evidence that managerial capabilities in managing IT can be a source of competitive advantage is growing; companies that do not adopt leading-edge information systems are likely to be at a competitive disadvantage. IT includes the many different varieties of computer software platforms and databases and the computer hardware on which they run, such as mainframes and servers. IT also encompasses a broad array of communication media and devices that link people including e-mail, video-teleconferencing, groupware and corporate intranets, smartphones, tablet computers, and similar devices.[25]

Information Technology and Strategy Implementation

At the level of organizational structure, control, and culture, advanced IT drastically increases the number of ways in which strategic managers can effectively implement their strategies. First, IT is an important factor that promotes the development of functional competencies and capabilities. Indeed, a company's IT capabilities are often a major source of competitive advantage because they are embedded in a company and are difficult to imitate. Walmart, for example, takes steps to legally protect its core competency in IT by blocking the movement of some of its key programmers to dot-coms like Amazon or Target. A company's ability to pursue a cost-leadership or differentiation business model depends upon its possession of distinctive competencies in efficiency, quality, innovation, and customer responsiveness—and IT is a major facilitator of these sources of competitive advantage.[26]

Second, IT enables a company to transfer its knowledge and expertise across functional groups and integrate that knowledge into a function's operations, so it can deliver new and improved products to customers. The way in which Citibank implemented an organization-wide IT system to increase responsiveness to customers is instructive. After studying its business model, Citibank's managers found that the primary customer complaint was the amount of time needed to wait for a response to a banking question, so they set out to solve this problem. Teams of managers examined the way Citibank's current IT system worked and then redesigned it to reduce the handoffs between people and functions necessary to provide customers with answers. Employees were then given extensive training in operating the new IT system. These changes resulted in significant time and cost savings, as well as an increase in the level of personalized service offered to clients, therefore increasing customer satisfaction and, in turn, the number of customers served.[27]

IT also has important effects on a company's ability to innovate and perform R&D. It improves the knowledge base that employees draw upon when they engage in problem solving and decision making. IT also provides a mechanism to promote collaboration and information sharing both inside and across a company's functions and business units that helps speed product development. However, the availability of knowledge alone is not enough to promote innovation; organizational members' ability to creatively use knowledge is the key to promoting innovation and creating competitive advantage.[28] IT allows new ideas to be transmitted easily and quickly to the product team, function, or divisions that can use it to add value to products and boost profitability. The project-based work that is characteristic of matrix structures provides a vivid example of this process.

As a project progresses, the need for particular team members waxes and wanes. Some employees will be part of a project from beginning to end, but others only participate at key times when their expertise is required. IT provides managers with the real-time capability to monitor project progress and needs, to allocate each expert's time accordingly, and to increase the value each employee can add to a product. Traditionally, product design has involved sequential processing across functions, with handoffs as each stage of the process is completed (see Chapter 4). Using advanced IT, this linear process has been replaced by parallel engineering that allows employees in different functions to work simultaneously and interact in real time to share information about design improvements, opportunities to reduce costs, and so on. This also promotes innovation.

IT has major effects on other aspects of a company's structure and control systems. The increasing use of IT has allowed managers to flatten the organizational hierarchy and reduce the number of management levels necessary to coordinate the work process. Because it provides managers with so much more useful, quality, and timely information, IT also permits greater decentralization of authority while simultaneously increasing integration within organizations. E-mail systems, the development of organization-wide corporate intranets, and, of course, ERP systems have smoothed communication between functions and divisions. The result has been improved performance.[29] To facilitate the use of IT and make organizational structure work, however, a company must create a control and incentive structure to motivate people and subunits.

Some companies are taking full advantage of IT's ability to help integrate their activities to respond better to customer needs. These companies make the most cost-effective use of their employees' skills by using a virtual organizational structure. The **virtual organization** is composed of people who are linked by laptops, smartphones, computer-aided design (CAD) systems, and global video teleconferencing and who may rarely, if ever, see one another face-to-face. People join and leave a project team as their services are needed, much as in a matrix structure. In virtual organizations, consultants connect through their laptops to a company's centralized **knowledge management system**, the company-specific information system that systematizes the knowledge of its employees and provides them with access to other employees who have the expertise to solve the problems that they encounter. For example, software experts and management consultants pool their knowledge to create a comprehensive internal database that all of an organization's members can easily access externally through the Internet. IBM and Accenture take advantage of the way IT creates virtual organizations, as Strategy in Action 13.4 discusses.

Strategic Outsourcing and Network Structure

IT has also affected a company's ability to pursue strategic outsourcing to strengthen its business model. As Chapter 9 discusses, strategic outsourcing is rapidly increasing because companies recognize the many opportunities it offers to promote differentiation, reduce costs, and increase flexibility. Recall that outsourcing occurs as companies use short- and long-term contracts and strategic alliances to form relationships with other companies. IT increases the efficiency of these relationships. For example, it allows for the more efficient movement of raw materials and component parts between a company and its suppliers and distributors. It also promotes the transfer, sharing, and leveraging of competencies between companies that have formed a strategic alliance that can lead to design and engineering improvements, increasing differentiation and lowering costs.

As a consequence, there has been growing interest in electronic **business-to-business (B2B)** networks in which companies in adjacent industries, for example, carmakers and car component makers, use the same software platform to link to each other and negotiate over prices, quality specifications, and delivery terms. The purchasing companies list the quantity and specifications of the inputs they require and invite bids from the thousands of component suppliers around the world. Because suppliers use the same software platform, electronic bidding, auctions, and transactions are conducted more efficiently between buyers and sellers around the world. The goal is to achieve joint gains for buyers and suppliers, and help drive down costs while raising quality at the industry level. Strategy in Action 13.5, which describes the role of Li & Fung in managing the global supply chain for companies in Southeast Asia, illustrates how this process works.

To effectively implement outsourcing, strategic managers must decide what organizational arrangements to adopt. Increasingly, a **network structure**—the set of

---

Virtual organization

A collection of employees linked by laptops, smartphones, and global video teleconferencing who may rarely meet face-to-face, but who join and leave project teams as their skills are needed.

Knowledge management system

The company-specific information system that systematizes the knowledge of all its employees and provides access to employees who have the expertise needed to solve problems as they arise.

Business-to-business (B2B)

Marketplace An industry-specific trading network established to connect buyers and sellers through the Internet to lower costs.

Network structure

A cluster of different companies whose actions are coordinated by contracts and outsourcing agreements rather than by a formal hierarchy of authority.

13.4 STRATEGY IN ACTION

IBM and Accenture Use IT to Create Virtual Organizations

Accenture, a global management consulting company, has been a pioneer in using IT to revolutionize its organizational structure. Its managing partners realized that because only its consultants in the field could diagnose and solve clients' problems, the company should design a structure that facilitated creative, on-the-spot decision making. To accomplish this, Accenture decided to replace its tall hierarchy of authority with a sophisticated IT system and create a virtual organization. First, it flattened the organizational hierarchy, eliminating many managerial levels, and established a shared, organization-wide IT system that provides each of Accenture's consultants with the information necessary to solve client problems. If the consultant still lacks the specific knowledge needed to solve a client's problem, they can use the system to request expert help from Accenture's thousands of consultants around the globe.

To implement the change, Accenture equipped all its consultants with state-of-the-art laptops and smartphones that can connect to its sophisticated corporate intranet and tap into Accenture's immense databases that contain volumes of potentially relevant information. The consultants can also communicate directly using their smartphones and use teleconferencing to help speed problem solving. For example, if a project involves installing a particular kind of IT system, a consultant has quick access to consultants around the globe who know how to install the system. Accenture has found that its virtual organization has increased the creativity of its consultants and enhanced their performance. By providing employees with more information and enabling them to easily confer with others, electronic communication has made consultants more autonomous and willing to make their own decisions, which led to high performance and made Accenture one of the best-known of all global consulting companies.

Similarly, IBM had been experiencing tough competition in the 2000s and has recently been searching for ways to better utilize its talented workforce to lower costs and offer customers specialized kinds of services its competitors cannot. IBM has also used IT to develop virtual teams of consultants to accomplish this.

IBM has created "competency centers" around the globe that are staffed by consultants who share the same specific IT skill; its competency centers are located in the countries in which IBM has the most clients and does the most business. To use its consultants most effectively, IBM used its own IT expertise to develop sophisticated software, allowing it to create self-managed teams of IBM consultants who have the skills to solve a client's particular problems. To form these teams, IBM's software engineers first analyzed the skills and experience of its consultants and entered the results into the software program. Then, they analyzed and coded the nature of a client's specific problem. Using this information, IBM's program matches each specific client problem to the skills of IBM's consultants and identifies a list of "best fit" employees. One of IBM's senior managers reviews this list and decides on the consultants who will form the self-managed team.

Once selected, team members assemble as quickly as possible in the client's home country and work to develop the software necessary to solve or manage the client's problem. This new IT allows IBM to create an ever-changing set of global, self-managed teams capable of solving the problems of its global clients. In addition, because each team enters learned knowledge about its activities into IBM's intranet, as at Accenture, consultants and teams can learn from one another, increasing problem-solving skills over time.

Source: T. Davenport and L. Prusak, *Information Ecology* (London: Oxford University Press, 1997); www.accenture.com, 2011; www.ibm.com, 2011.

virtual strategic alliances an organization forms with suppliers, manufacturers, and distributors to produce and market a product—is becoming the structure of choice to implement outsourcing. An example of a network structure is the series of strategic alliances that Japanese carmakers, such as Toyota and Honda, have formed with their parts suppliers. All members of the network work together on a long-term basis to find new ways to reduce costs and increase car component quality. Moreover, developing a network structure allows an organization to avoid the high bureaucratic costs of operating a complex organizational structure. Finally, a network structure allows a company to form strategic alliances with foreign suppliers, which gives managers access to low-cost foreign sources of inputs. The way Nike uses a global network structure to produce and market its sports, casual, and dress shoes is instructive.

STRATEGY IN ACTION

Li & Fung's Global Supply-Chain Management

Identifying the overseas suppliers that offer the lowest-priced and highest-quality products is an important but difficult task for strategic managers because the suppliers are located in thousands of cities in many countries around the world. To help them, global companies use the services of foreign intermediaries, or brokers, located near these suppliers to find the one that will best suit their purchasing needs. Li & Fung, run by brothers Victor and William Fung, is one of the brokerage companies that have helped hundreds of global companies identify suitable foreign suppliers, especially suppliers in mainland China.

In the 2000s, managing global companies' supply chains became an even more complicated task because overseas suppliers were increasingly specializing in just one part of the task of producing a product in their search for ways to reduce costs. In the past, a company such as Target might have negotiated with a supplier to manufacture one million units of a shirt at a certain cost per unit. But with specialization, Target might find it can reduce the costs of making shirts even more by splitting the operations involved in producing the shirt and negotiating with different suppliers, often in different countries, to perform each separate operation. For example, to reduce the unit cost of a shirt, Target might first negotiate with a yarn manufacturer in Vietnam to

make the yarn, ship the yarn to a Chinese supplier to weave it into cloth, and ship the cloth to several different factories in Malaysia and the Philippines to cut the cloth and sew the pieces into shirts. Another company might take responsibility for packaging and shipping the shirts to wherever in the world they are required. Because a company like Target has thousands of different clothing products in production, and these products change all the time, there are enormous problems associated with managing a global supply chain to obtain the most potential cost savings.

This is the opportunity upon which Li & Fung capitalized. Realizing that many global companies do not have the time or expertise to find such specialized low-price suppliers, they moved quickly to provide this service. Li & Fung employs 3,600 agents who travel across 37 countries to find new suppliers and inspect existing suppliers to find new ways to help their clients—global companies—get lower prices or higher-quality products. Global companies are happy to outsource their supply-chain management to Li & Fung because they realize significant cost savings. And although companies pay a hefty fee to Li & Fung, they avoid the costs of employing their own agents. As the complexity of supply-chain management continues to increase, more companies like Li & Fung will be appearing.

Source: www.li&fung.com. 2011.

Nike, located in Beaverton, Oregon, is the largest and most profitable sports shoemaker in the world. The key to Nike's success is the network structure that Philip Knight, its founder and CEO, created to allow his company to design and market its shoes. Today, the most successful companies simultaneously pursue a low-cost and a differentiation strategy. Knight realized this early in his company's development and created the network structure to allow his company to achieve this goal.

By far, the largest function at Nike's headquarters in Beaverton is the design function, which is staffed by talented designers who pioneer the innovations in sports shoe design that have made Nike so successful. Designers use CAD to innovate new shoe models, and all new-product information, including manufacturing instructions, is stored electronically. When the designers have completed their work, they relay the blueprints for the new products via the Internet to its network of suppliers and manufacturers throughout Southeast Asia with which Nike has formed contracts and alliances. Instructions for a new sole, for example, may be sent to a supplier in Taiwan, and instructions for leather uppers may be sent to a supplier in Malaysia. These suppliers produce the component shoe parts that are then sent for final assembly to a contract manufacturer in China. From China, a shipping company that has also partnered with Nike, will ship its shoes to wholesalers and distributors throughout the world. Of the 100 million pairs of shoes Nike makes each year, 99% are made in Southeast Asia.

There are three main advantages to this network structure for Nike (and other companies). First, Nike can lower its cost structure because wages in Southeast Asia are a fraction of what they are in the United States. Second, Nike can respond to changes in sports shoe fashion very quickly. Using its global IT system, it can, literally overnight, change the instructions it gives to each of its suppliers so that within a few weeks contract manufacturers abroad can produce the new models of shoes. Any alliance partners that fail to meet Nike's standards are replaced with new partners, so Nike has great control over its network structure. In fact, the company works closely with its suppliers to take advantage of any new developments in technology that can help it reduce costs and increase quality. Third, the ability to outsource all its manufacturing abroad allows Nike to keep its U.S. structure fluid and flexible. Nike uses a functional structure to organize its activities and decentralize control of the design process, assigning teams to develop each of the new kinds of sports shoes for which it is known.

In conclusion, the implications of IT for strategy implementation are still evolving and will continue to evolve as new software and hardware reshape a company's business model and strategies. IT is changing the nature of value-chain activities both inside and among organizations, affecting all four building blocks of competitive advantage. For the multibusiness company (as for the single-business company) the need to be alert to such changes to strengthen its position in its core business has become vital. The success of companies such as Nike, Toyota, and Walmart, compared to the failure of others like GM and Kmart, can be traced, in part, to their success in developing the IT capabilities that lead to sustained competitive advantage.

Ethical Dilemma

"sweatshop" conditions abroad and turning a blind eye on contract manufacturers' abusive behavior toward workers.

Unethical and illegal behavior is prevalent in global business. For example, while bribery is considered "acceptable" in some countries, multinational companies are often found guilty of allowing overseas executives to bribe government officials. Many countries, like the United States, have laws and severe penalties to discourage payouts on bribes. In addition to bribery, many U.S. companies have been accused of perpetuating unethical

As a manager, if asked to improve your company's structure to prevent unethical and illegal behavior, what kind of control system could you use? In what ways could you develop a global organizational culture that reduces the likelihood of such behavior? What is the best way to decide upon the balance between centralization and decentralization to reduce these problems?

Summary of Chapter

1. A company uses organizational design to combine structure, control systems, and culture in ways that allow it to successfully implement its multibusiness model.

2. As a company grows and diversifies, it adopts a multidivisional structure. Although this structure costs more to operate than a functional or product structure, it economizes on the bureaucratic costs associated with operating through a functional structure and enables a company to handle its value creation activities more effectively.

3. As companies change their corporate strategies over time, they must change their structures because different strategies are managed in different ways. In particular, the move from unrelated diversification to vertical integration to related diversification increases the bureaucratic costs associated with managing a multibusiness model. Each requires a different combination of structure, control, and culture to economize on those costs.

4. As a company moves from a localization to an international, global standardization, and transnational strategy, it also needs to switch to a more complex structure that allows it to coordinate increasingly complex resource transfers. Similarly, it needs to adopt a more complex integration and control system that facilitates resource sharing

and the leveraging of competencies around the globe. When the gains are substantial, companies frequently adopt a global-matrix structure to share knowledge and expertise or implement their control systems and culture.

5. o encourage internal new venturing, companies must design internal venturing processes that give new-venture managers the autonomy they need to develop new products. Similarly, when establishing a joint venture with another company, managers need to carefully design the new unit's structure and control systems to maximize its chance of success.

6. he profitability of mergers and acquisitions depends upon the structure and control systems that companies adopt to manage them and the way a company integrates them into its existing operating structure. IT has increasingly important effects upon the way multibusiness companies implement their strategies. Not only does IT help improve the efficiency with which the multidivisional structure operates, it also allows for better control of complex value-chain activities. The growth of outsourcing has also been promoted by IT, and some companies have developed network structures to coordinate their global value-chain activities.

Discussion Questions

1. What prompts a company to change from a global standardization to a transnational strategy, and what new implementation problems arise as it does so?

2. When would a company decide to change from a functional to a multidivisional structure?

3. What are the problems associated with implementing a strategy of related diversification through acquisitions?

4. If a related company begins to purchase unrelated businesses, in what ways should it change its structure or control mechanisms to manage the acquisitions?

5. How would you design a structure and control system to encourage entrepreneurship in a large, established corporation?

Practicing Strategic Management

Small Group Exercises

Deciding on an Organizational Structure

This small-group exercise is a continuation of the small-group exercise in Chapter 12. Break into the same groups that you used in Chapter 12, reread the scenario in that chapter, and recall your group's debate about the appropriate organizational structure for your soft drink company. Because it is your intention to compete with Coca-Cola for market share worldwide, your strategy should also have a global dimension, and you must consider the best structure globally as well as domestically. Debate the pros and cons of the types of global structures and decide which is most appropriate and which will best fit your domestic structure.

Strategy Sign-On

Article File 13

Find an example of a company pursuing a multibusiness model that has changed its structure and control systems to manage its strategy better. What were the problems with the way it formerly implemented its strategy? What changes did it make to its structure and control systems? What effects does it expect these changes will have on performance?

Strategic Management Project

Developing Your Portfolio: Module 13 Take the information that you collected in the strategic management project from Chapter 12 on strategy implementation and link it to the multibusiness model. You should collect information to determine if your company competes across industries or countries, and also to see what role IT plays in allowing your company to implement its business model. If your company *does* operate across countries or industries, answer the following questions:

1. Does your company use a multidivisional structure? Why or why not? What crucial implementation problems must your company tackle to implement its strategy effectively? For example, what kind of integration mechanisms does it employ?
2. What are your company's corporate-level strategies? How do they affect the way it uses organizational structure, control, and culture?
3. What kind of international strategy does your company pursue? How does it control its global activities? What kind of structure does it use? Why?

4. Can you suggest ways of altering the company's structure or control systems to strengthen its business model? Would these changes increase or decrease bureaucratic costs?
5. Does your company have a particular entry mode that it has used to implement its strategy?
6. In what ways does your company use IT to coordinate its value-chain activities?
7. Assess how well your company has implemented its multibusiness (or business) model.

CLOSING CASE

Cisco Systems Develops a Collaborative Approach to Organizing

Cisco Systems is famous for developing the routers and switches on which the Internet is built. In 2010, Cisco still made most of its $10 billion yearly revenue by selling its Internet routers and switches to large companies and Internet service providers. But the boom years of Internet building that allowed Cisco to make enormous profits are over. Its CEO, John Chambers, who has led the company from the beginning, has had to reexamine his organizing approach in order to improve the way his company's different teams and divisions work together.

Chambers admits that until the mid-2000s, he had a "control and command" approach to organizing. He and the company's 10 top corporate managers would work together to plan the company's new product development strategies; they then sent their orders down the hierarchy to team and divisional managers who worked to implement these strategies. Top managers monitored how quickly these new products were developed and how well they sold, and intervened as necessary to take corrective action. Chambers and Cisco's approach was largely mechanistic.

Chambers was forced to reevaluate his approach when Cisco's market value shrunk by $400 billion after the dot.com crisis. Now that the Internet was established, how could he develop the new products to allow Cisco to continue growing? After listening to his top managers, he realized he needed Cisco's organizing approach and developed a "collaborative approach," meaning that he and his top managers would focus on listening carefully to the ideas of lower-level managers and involve these managers in top-level decision making. In other words, the goal of Cisco's new collaborative approach was to move toward a more organic structure that would allow Cisco's different teams and divisions to plan long-term strategies, work together to achieve them, develop new products, and share technology across the organization.

To facilitate collaboration, Chambers created cross-functional teams of managers from its different divisions who were excited to work together to develop promising new kinds of products. Within 1 year, 15% of his top managers who could not handle its new organic approach resigned. At the same time, Chambers insisted that cross-functional teams set measurable goals, such as time required for product development, and time to bring a product to market, to force these teams to think about short-term goals, long-term goals, and speed product development. The top managers of Cisco's divisions who once competed for power and resources would share responsibility for one another's success in the new collaborative, organic approach—their collective goal to get more products to market faster. Cisco's network of cross-functional councils, boards, and groups empowered to launch new businesses has reduced the time needed to plan successful new product launches from years to months. Chambers now believes Cisco's new organic approach will allow the company to develop the new products that will make Cisco the global leader in both communications technology and Internet-linked IT hardware in the 2010s, as it finds ways to bring innovative products to the market more quickly than its competitors.

Case Discussion Questions

1. How has Cisco changed its structure and control systems?
2. Relate Cisco's changes to its control and evaluation systems to the stages of growth in Greiner's model.
3. Use the Internet to investigate how Cisco's new approach has worked. How is the company continuing to change its structure and control systems to solve its ongoing problems?

Notes

[1] www.nokia.com, 2011.

[2] A. D. Chandler, *Strategy and Structure* (Cambridge: MIT Press, 1962); O. E. Williamson, *Markets and Hierarchies* (New York: Free Press, 1975); L. Wrigley, "Divisional Autonomy and Diversification" (Ph.D. Diss., Harvard Business School, 1970).

[3] R. P. Rumelt, *Strategy, Structure, and Economic Performance* (Boston: Division of Research, Harvard Business School, 1974); B. R. Scott, *Stages of Corporate Development* (Cambridge: Intercollegiate Clearing House, Harvard Business School, 1971); Williamson, *Markets and Hierarchies*.

[4] A. P. Sloan, *My Years at General Motors* (Garden City: Doubleday, 1946); A. Taylor III, "Can GM Remodel Itself?" *Fortune*, January 13 (1992): 26–34; W. Hampton and J. Norman, "General Motors: What Went Wrong?" *Business Week*, March 16 (1987): 102–110; www.gm.com (2002). The quotations are on 46 and 50 in Sloan, *My Years at General Motors*.

[5] The discussion draws on each of the sources cited in endnotes 20–27 and on G. R. Jones and C. W. L. Hill, "Transaction Cost Analysis of Strategy-Structure Choice," *Strategic Management Journal* 9 (1988): 159–172.

[6] H. O. Armour and D. J. Teece, "Organizational Structure and Economic Performance: A Test of the Multidivisional Hypothesis," *Bell Journal of Economics* 9 (1978): 106–122.

[7] Sloan, *My Years at General Motors*.

[8] Jones and Hill, "Transaction Cost Analysis of Strategy-Structure Choice," *Strategic Management Journal* 9 (1988): 159–172.

[9] Ibid.

[10] R. A. D'Aveni and D. J. Ravenscraft, "Economies of Integration versus Bureaucracy Costs: Does Vertical Integration Improve Performance?" *Academy of Management Journal* 5 (1994): 1167–1206.

[11] P. R. Lawrence and J. Lorsch, *Organization and Environment* (Boston: Division of Research, Harvard Business School, 1967); J. R. Galbraith, *Designing Complex Organizations* (Reading: Addison-Wesley, 1973); M. Porter, *Competitive Advantage: Creating and Sustaining Superior Performance* (New York: Free Press, 1985).

[12] P. R. Nayyar, "Performance Effects of Information Asymmetry and Economies of Scope in Diversified Service Firm," *Academy of Management Journal* 36 (1993): 28–57.

[13] L. R. Gomez-Mejia, "Structure and Process of Diversification, Compensation Strategy, and Performance," *Strategic Management Journal* 13 (1992): 381–397.

[14] J. Stopford and L. Wells, *Managing the Multinational Enterprise* (London: Longman, 1972).

[15] R. A. Burgelman, "Managing the New Venture Division: Research Findings and the Implications for Strategic Management," *Strategic Management Journal* 6 (1985): 39–54.

[16] Burgelman, "Managing the New Venture Division."

[17] R. A. Burgelman, "Corporate Entrepreneurship and Strategic Management: Insights from a Process Study," *Management Science* 29 (1983): 1349–1364.

[18] G. R. Jones, "Towards a Positive Interpretation of Transaction Cost Theory: The Central Role of Entrepreneurship and Trust," in M. Hitt, R. E. Freeman, and J. S. Harrison (eds.), *Handbook of Strategic Management* (London: Blackwell, 2001), 208–228.

[19] www.nestle.com, 2011; www.cocacola.com, 2011.

[20] M. S. Salter and W. A. Weinhold, *Diversification through Acquisition* (New York: Free Press, 1979).

[21] F. T. Paine and D. J. Power, "Merger Strategy: An Examination of Drucker's Five Rules for Successful Acquisitions," *Strategic Management Journal* 5 (1984): 99–110.

[22] H. Singh and C. A. Montgomery, "Corporate Acquisitions and Economic Performance," (unpublished manuscript, 1984).

[23] B. Worthen, "Nestlé's ERP Odyssey," *CIO* (2002): 1–5.

[24] G. D. Bruton, B. M. Oviatt, and M. A. White, "Performance of Acquisitions of Distressed Firms," *Academy of Management Journal* 4 (1994): 972–989.

[25] T. Dewett and G. R. Jones, "The Role of Information Technology in the Organization: A Review, Model, and Assessment," *Journal of Management* 27 (2001): 313–346.

[26] M. E. Porter, *Competitive Strategy* (New York: Free Press, 1980).

[27] M. Hammer and J. Champy, *Reengineering the Corporation* (New York: Harper Collins, 1993).

[28] G. Hamel and C. K. Prahalad, *Competing for the Future* (Boston: Harvard Business School Press, 1994).

[29] Ibid.

Cases

Analyzing a Case Study and Writing a Case Study Analysis

What is Case Study Analysis?

Case study analysis is an integral part of a course in strategic management. The purpose of a case study is to provide students with experience of the strategic management problems that actual organizations face. A case study presents an account of what happened to a business or industry over a number of years. It chronicles the events that managers had to deal with, such as changes in the competitive environment, and charts the managers' response, which usually involved changing the business- or corporate-level strategy. The cases in this book cover a wide range of issues and problems that managers have had to confront. Some cases are about finding the right business-level strategy to compete in changing conditions. Some are about companies that grew by acquisition, with little concern for the rationale behind their growth, and how growth by acquisition affected their future profitability. Each case is different because each organization is different. The underlying thread in all cases, however, is the use of strategic management techniques to solve business problems.

Cases prove valuable in a strategic management course for several reasons. First, cases provide you, the student, with experience of organizational problems that you probably have not had the opportunity to experience firsthand. In a relatively short period of time, you will have the chance to appreciate and analyze the problems faced by many different companies and to understand how managers tried to deal with them.

Second, cases illustrate the theory and content of strategic management. The meaning and implications of this information are made clearer when they are applied to case studies. The theory and concepts help reveal what is going on in the companies studied and allow you to evaluate the solutions that specific companies adopted to deal with their problems. Consequently, when you analyze cases, you will be like a detective who, with a set of conceptual tools, probes what happened and what or who was responsible and then marshals the evidence that provides the solution. Top managers enjoy the thrill of testing their problem-solving abilities in the real world. It is important to remember that no one knows what the right answer is. All that managers can do is to make the best guess. In fact, managers say repeatedly that they are happy if they are right only half the time in solving strategic problems. Strategic management is an uncertain game, and using cases to see how theory can be put into practice is one way of improving your skills of diagnostic investigation.

Third, case studies provide you with the opportunity to participate in class and to gain experience in presenting your ideas to others. Instructors may sometimes call on students as a group to identify what is going on in a case, and through classroom discussion the issues in and solutions to the case problem will reveal themselves. In such a situation, you will have to organize your views and conclusions so that you can present them to the class. Your classmates may have analyzed the issues differently from you, and they will want you to argue your points before they will accept your conclusions, so be prepared for debate. This mode of discussion is an example of the dialectical approach to decision making. This is how decisions are made in the actual business world.

Instructors also may assign an individual, but more commonly a group, to analyze the case before the whole class. The individual or group probably will be responsible for a thirty- to forty-minute presentation of the case to the class. That presentation must cover the issues posed, the problems facing the company, and a series of recommendations for resolving the problems. The discussion then will be thrown open to the class, and you will have to defend your ideas. Through such discussions and presentations, you will experience how to convey your ideas effectively to others. Remember that a great deal of managers' time is spent in these kinds of situations: presenting their ideas and engaging in discussion with other managers who have their own views about what is going on. Thus, you will experience in the classroom the actual process of strategic management, and this will serve you well in your future career.

If you work in groups to analyze case studies, you also will learn about the group process involved in working as a team. When people work in groups, it is often difficult to schedule time and allocate responsibility for the case analysis. There are always group members who shirk their responsibilities and group members who are so sure of their own ideas that they try to dominate the group's analysis. Most of the strategic management takes place in groups, however, and it is best if you learn about these problems now.

Analyzing a Case Study

The purpose of the case study is to let you apply the concepts of strategic management when you analyze the issues facing a specific company. To analyze a case study, therefore, you must examine closely the issues confronting the company. Most often you will need to read the case several times—once to grasp the overall picture of what is happening to the company and then several times more to discover and grasp the specific problems.

Generally, detailed analysis of a case study should include eight areas:

1. The history, development, and growth of the company over time

2. The identification of the company's internal strengths and weaknesses

3. The nature of the external environment surrounding the company

4. A SWOT analysis

5. The kind of corporate-level strategy that the company is pursuing

6. The nature of the company's business-level strategy

7. The company's structure and control systems and how they match its strategy

8. Recommendations

To analyze a case, you need to apply the concepts taught in this course to each of these areas. To help you further, we next offer a summary of the steps you can take to analyze the case material for each of the eight points we just noted:

1. *Analyze the company's history, development, and growth*. A convenient way to investigate how a company's past strategy and structure affect it in the present is to chart the critical incidents in its history—that is, the events that were the most unusual or the most essential for its development into the company it is today. Some of the events have to do with its founding, its initial products, how it makes new-product market decisions, and how it developed and chose functional competencies to pursue. Its entry into new businesses and shifts in its main lines of business are also important milestones to consider.

2. *Identify the company's internal strengths and weaknesses*. Once the historical profile is completed, you can begin the SWOT analysis. Use all the incidents you have charted to develop an account of the company's strengths and weaknesses as they have emerged historically. Examine each of the value creation functions of the company, and identify the functions in which the company is currently strong and currently weak. Some companies might be weak in marketing; some might be strong in research and development. Make lists of these strengths and weaknesses. The SWOT Checklist (Table 1) gives examples of what might go in these lists.

3. *Analyze the external environment*. To identify environmental opportunities and threats, apply all the concepts on industry and macroenvironments to analyze the environment the company is confronting. Of particular importance at the industry level are the Competitive Forces Model, adapted from Porter's Five Forces Model and the stage of the life-cycle model. Which factors in the macroenvironment will appear salient depends on the specific company being analyzed. Use each factor in turn (for instance, demographic factors) to see whether it is relevant for the company in question.

   Having done this analysis, you will have generated both an analysis of the company's environment and a list of opportunities and threats. The SWOT

Table 1   A SWOT Checklist

Potential Internal Strengths	Potential Internal Weaknesses
Many product lines?	Obsolete, narrow product lines?
Broad market coverage?	Rising manufacturing costs?
Manufacturing competence?	Decline in R&D innovations?
Good marketing skills?	Poor marketing plan?
Good materials management systems?	Poor material management systems?
R&D skills and leadership?	Loss of customer good will?
Information system competencies?	Inadequate human resources?
Human resource competencies?	Inadequate information systems?
Brand name reputation?	Loss of brand name capital?
Portfolio management skills?	Growth without direction?
Cost of differentiation advantage?	Bad portfolio management?
New-venture management expertise?	Loss of corporate direction?
Appropriate management style?	Infighting among divisions?
Appropriate organizational structure?	Loss of corporate control?
Appropriate control systems?	Inappropriate organizational
Ability to manage strategic change?	structure and control systems?
Well-developed corporate strategy?	High conflict and politics?
Good financial management?	Poor financial management?
Others?	Others?

Table 1   (*continued*)

Potential Environmental Opportunities	Potential Environmental Threats
Expand core business(es)?	Attacks on core business(es)?
Exploit new market segments?	Increases in domestic competition?
Widen product range?	Increase in foreign competition?
Extend cost or differentiation advantage?	Change in consumer tastes?
Diversify into new growth businesses?	Fall in barriers to entry?
Expand into foreign markets?	Rise in new or substitute products?
Apply R&D skills in new areas?	Increase in industry rivalry?
Enter new related businesses?	New forms of industry competition?
Vertically integrate forward?	Potential for takeover?
Vertically integrate backward?	Existence of corporate raiders?
Enlarge corporate portfolio?	Increase in regional competition?
Overcome barriers to entry?	Changes in demographic factors?
Reduce rivalry among competitors?	Changes in economic factors?
Make profitable new acquisitions?	Downturn in economy?
Apply brand name capital in new areas?	Rising labor costs?
Seek fast market growth?	Slower market growth?
Others?	Others?

Checklist table also lists some common environmental opportunities and threats that you may look for, but the list you generate will be specific to your company.

4. *Evaluate the SWOT analysis.* Having identified the company's external opportunities and threats as well as its internal strengths and weaknesses, consider what your findings mean. You need to balance strengths and weaknesses against opportunities and threats. Is the company in an overall strong competitive position? Can it continue to pursue its current business- or corporate-level strategy profitably? What can the company do to turn weaknesses into strengths and threats into opportunities? Can it develop new functional, business, or corporate strategies to accomplish this change? *Never merely generate the SWOT analysis and then put it aside.* Because it provides a succinct summary of the company's condition, a good SWOT analysis is the key to all the analyses that follow.

5. *Analyze corporate-level strategy.* To analyze corporate-level strategy, you first need to define the company's mission and goals. Sometimes the mission and goals are stated explicitly in the case; at other times, you will have to infer them from available information. The information you need to collect to find out the company's corporate strategy includes such factors as its lines of business and the nature of its subsidiaries and acquisitions. It is important to analyze the relationship among the company's businesses. Do they trade or exchange resources? Are there gains to be achieved from synergy? Alternatively, is the company just running a portfolio of investments? This analysis should enable you to define the corporate strategy that the company is pursuing (for example, related or unrelated diversification, or a combination of both) and to conclude whether the company operates in just one core business. Then, using your SWOT analysis, debate the merits of this strategy. Is it appropriate given the environment the company is in? Could a change in corporate strategy provide the company with new opportunities or transform a weakness into a strength? For example, should the company diversify from its core business into new businesses?

    Other issues should be considered as well. How and why has the company's strategy changed over time? What is the claimed rationale for any changes? Often, it is a good idea to analyze the company's businesses or products to assess its situation and identify which divisions contribute the most to or detract from its competitive advantage. It is also useful to explore how the company has built its portfolio over time. Did it acquire new businesses, or did it internally venture its own? All of these factors provide clues about the company and indicate ways of improving its future performance.

6. *Analyze business-level strategy.* Once you know the company's corporate-level strategy and have done the SWOT analysis, the next step is to identify the company's business-level strategy. If the company is a single-business company, its business-level strategy is identical to its corporate-level strategy. If the company is in many businesses, each business will have its own business-level strategy. You will need to identify the company's generic competitive

strategy—differentiation, low-cost, or focus—and its investment strategy, given its relative competitive position and the stage of the life cycle. The company also may market different products using different business-level strategies. For example, it may offer a low-cost product range and a line of differentiated products. Be sure to give a full account of a company's business-level strategy to show how it competes.

Identifying the functional strategies that a company pursues to build competitive advantage through superior efficiency, quality, innovation, and customer responsiveness and to achieve its business-level strategy is very important. The SWOT analysis will have provided you with information on the company's functional competencies. You should investigate its production, marketing, or research and development strategy further to gain a picture of where the company is going. For example, pursuing a low-cost or a differentiation strategy successfully requires very different sets of competencies. Has the company developed the right ones? If it has, how can it exploit them further? Can it pursue both a low-cost and a differentiation strategy simultaneously?

The SWOT analysis is especially important at this point if the industry analysis, particularly Porter's model, has revealed threats to the company from the environment. Can the company deal with these threats? How should it change its business-level strategy to counter them? To evaluate the potential of a company's business-level strategy, you must first perform a thorough SWOT analysis that captures the essence of its problems.

Once you complete this analysis, you will have a full picture of the way the company is operating and be in a position to evaluate the potential of its strategy. Thus, you will be able to make recommendations concerning the pattern of its future actions. However, first you need to consider strategy implementation, or the way the company tries to achieve its strategy.

7. *Analyze structure and control systems.* The aim of this analysis is to identify what structure and control systems the company is using to implement its strategy and to evaluate whether that structure is the appropriate one for the company. Different corporate and business strategies require different structures. You need to determine the *degree of fit between the company's strategy and structure.* For example, does the company have the right level of vertical differentiation (e.g., does it have the appropriate number of levels in the hierarchy or decentralized control?) or horizontal differentiation (does it use a functional structure when it should be using a product structure?)? Similarly, is the company using the right integration or control systems to manage its operations? Are managers being appropriately rewarded? Are the right rewards in place for encouraging cooperation among divisions? These are all issues to consider.

In some cases, there will be little information on these issues, whereas in others there will be a lot. In analyzing each case, you should gear the analysis toward its most salient issues. For example, organizational conflict, power, and politics will be important issues for some companies. Try to analyze why problems in these areas are occurring. Do they occur because of bad strategy formulation or because of bad strategy implementation?

Organizational change is an issue in many cases because the companies are attempting to alter their strategies or structures to solve strategic problems. Thus, as part of the analysis, you might suggest an action plan that the company in question could use to achieve its goals. For example, you might list in a logical sequence the steps the company would need to follow to alter its business-level strategy from differentiation to focus.

8. *Make recommendations.* The quality of your recommendations is a direct result of the thoroughness with which you prepared the case analysis. Recommendations are directed at solving whatever strategic problem the company is facing and increasing its future profitability. Your recommendations should be in line with your analysis; that is, they should follow logically from the previous discussion. For example, your recommendation generally will center on the specific ways of changing functional, business, and corporate strategies and organizational structure and control to improve business performance. The set of recommendations will be specific to each case, and so it is difficult to discuss these recommendations here. Such recommendations might include an increase in spending on specific research and development projects, the divesting of certain businesses, a change from a strategy of unrelated to related diversification, an increase in the level of integration among divisions by using task forces and teams, or a move to a different kind of structure to implement a new business-level strategy. Make sure your recommendations are mutually consistent and written in the form of an action plan. The plan might contain a timetable that sequences the actions for changing the company's strategy and a description of how changes at the corporate level will necessitate changes at the business level and subsequently at the functional level.

After following all these stages, you will have performed a thorough analysis of the case and will be in a position to join in class discussion or present your ideas to the class, depending on the format used by your professor. Remember that you must tailor your analysis to suit the specific issue discussed in your case. In some cases, you might completely omit one of the steps in the analysis because it is not relevant to the situation you are considering. You must be sensitive to the needs of the case and not apply the framework we have discussed in this section blindly. The framework is meant only as a guide, not as an outline.

Writing a Case Study Analysis

Often, as part of your course requirements, you will need to present a written case analysis. This may be an individual or a group report. Whatever the situation, there are certain guidelines to follow in writing a case analysis that will improve the evaluation your work will receive from your instructor. Before we discuss these guidelines and before you use them, make sure that they do not conflict with any directions your instructor has given you.

The structure of your written report is critical. Generally, if you follow the steps for analysis discussed in the previous section, *you already will have a good structure for your written discussion.* All reports begin with an *introduction* to the case. In it, outline briefly what the company does, how it developed historically, what problems it is experiencing, and how you are going to approach the issues in the case write-up. Do this sequentially by writing, for example, "First, we discuss the environment of Company X. . . . Third, we discuss Company X's business-level strategy. . . . Last, we provide recommendations for turning around Company X's business."

In the second part of the case write-up, the *strategic analysis* section, do the SWOT analysis, analyze and discuss the nature and problems of the company's business-level and corporate strategies, and then analyze its structure and control systems. Make sure you use plenty of headings and subheadings to structure your analysis. For example, have separate sections on any important conceptual tool you use. Thus, you might have a section on the Competitive Forces Model as part of your analysis of the environment. You might offer a separate section on portfolio techniques when analyzing a company's corporate strategy. Tailor the sections and subsections to the specific issues of importance in the case.

In the third part of the case write-up, present your *solutions and recommendations.* Be comprehensive, and make sure they are in line with the previous analysis so that the recommendations fit together and move logically from one to the next. The recommendations section is very revealing because your instructor will have a good idea of how much work you put into the case from the quality of your recommendations.

Following this framework will provide a good structure for most written reports, though it must be shaped to fit the individual case being considered. Some cases are about excellent companies experiencing no problems. In such instances, it is hard to write recommendations. Instead, you can focus on analyzing why the company is doing so well, using that analysis to structure the discussion. Following are some minor suggestions that can help make a good analysis even better:

1. Do not repeat in summary form large pieces of factual information from the case. The instructor has read the case and knows what is going on. Rather, use the information in the case to illustrate your statements, defend your arguments, or make salient points. Beyond the brief introduction to the company, you must avoid being *descriptive*; instead, you must be *analytical.*

2. Make sure the sections and subsections of your discussion flow logically and smoothly from one to the next. That is, try to build on what has gone before so that the analysis of the case study moves toward a climax. This is particularly important for group analysis, because there is a tendency for people in a group to split up the work and say, "I'll do the beginning, you take the middle, and I'll do the end." The result is a choppy, stilted analysis; the parts do not flow from one to the next, and it is obvious to the instructor that no real group work has been done.

3. Avoid grammatical and spelling errors. They make your work look sloppy.

4. In some instances, cases dealing with well-known companies end in 1998 or 1999 because no later information was available when the case was written. If possible, do a search for more information on what has happened to the company in subsequent years.

   Many libraries now have comprehensive Web-based electronic data search facilities that offer such sources as *ABI/Inform*, *The Wall Street Journal Index*, the *F&S Index*, and the *Nexis-Lexis* databases. These enable you to identify any article that has been written in the business press on the company of your choice within the past few years. A number of nonelectronic data sources are also useful. For example, *F&S Predicasts* publishes an annual list of articles relating to major companies that appeared in the national and international business press. *S&P Industry Surveys* is a great source for basic industry data, and *Value Line Ratings and Reports* can contain good summaries of a firm's financial position and future prospects. You will also want to collect full financial information on the company. Again, this can be accessed from Web-based electronic databases such as the *Edgar* database, which archives all forms that publicly quoted companies have to file with the Securities and Exchange Commission (SEC; e.g., 10-K filings can be accessed from the SEC's *Edgar* database). Most SEC forms for public companies can now be accessed from Internet-based financial sites, such as Yahoo's finance site (http://finance.yahoo.com/).

5. Sometimes instructors hand out questions for each case to help you in your analysis. Use these as a guide for writing the case analysis. They often illuminate the important issues that have to be covered in the discussion.

If you follow the guidelines in this section, you should be able to write a thorough and effective evaluation.

The Role of Financial Analysis in Case Study Analysis

An important aspect of analyzing a case study and writing a case study analysis is the role and use of financial information. A careful analysis of the company's financial condition immensely improves a case write-up. After all, financial data represent the concrete results of the company's strategy and structure. Although analyzing financial statements can be quite complex, a general idea of a company's financial position can be determined through the use of ratio analysis. Financial performance ratios can be calculated from the balance sheet and income statement. These ratios can be classified into five subgroups: profit ratios, liquidity ratios, activity ratios, leverage ratios, and shareholder-return ratios. These ratios should be compared with the industry average or the company's prior years of performance. It should be noted, however, that deviation from the average is not necessarily bad; it simply warrants further investigation. For example, young companies will have purchased assets at a different price and will likely have a different capital structure than older companies do. In addition to ratio analysis, a company's cash flow position is of critical importance and should be assessed. Cash flow shows how much actual cash a company possesses.

Profit Ratios

Profit ratios measure the efficiency with which the company uses its resources. The more efficient the company, the greater is its profitability. It is useful to compare a company's profitability against that of its major competitors in its industry to determine whether the company is operating more or less efficiently than its rivals. In addition, the change in a company's profit ratios over time tells whether its performance is improving or declining.

A number of different profit ratios can be used, and each of them measures a different aspect of a company's performance. Here, we look at the most commonly used profit ratios.

Return on Invested Capital (ROIC)   This ratio measures the profit earned on the capital invested in the company. It is defined as follows:

$$\text{Return on invested capital (ROIC)} = \frac{\text{Net profit}}{\text{Invested capital}}$$

Net profit is calculated by subtracting the total costs of operating the company away from its total revenues (total revenues – total costs). Total costs are the (1) costs of goods sold, (2) sales, general, and administrative expenses, (3) R&D expenses, and (4) other expenses. Net profit can be calculated before or after taxes, although many financial analysts prefer the before-tax figure. Invested capital is the amount that is invested in the operations of a company—that is, in property, plant, equipment, inventories, and other assets. Invested capital comes from two main sources: interest-bearing debt and shareholders' equity. Interest-bearing debt is money the company borrows from banks and from those who purchase its bonds. Shareholders' equity is the money raised from selling shares to the public, *plus* earnings that have been retained by the company in prior years and are available to fund current investments. ROIC measures the effectiveness with which a company is using the capital funds that it has available for investment. As such, it is recognized to be an excellent measure of the value a company is creating.[1] Remember that a company's ROIC can be decomposed into its constituent parts.

Return on Total Assets (ROA)   This ratio measures the profit earned on the employment of assets. It is defined as follows:

$$\text{Return on total assests} = \frac{\text{Net profit}}{\text{Total assets}}$$

Return on Stockholders' Equity (ROE)   This ratio measures the percentage of profit earned on common stockholders' investment in the company. It is defined as follows:

$$\text{Return on stockholders equity} = \frac{\text{Net profit}}{\text{Stockholders equity}}$$

If a company has no debt, this will be the same as ROIC.

Liquidity Ratios

A company's liquidity is a measure of its ability to meet short-term obligations. An asset is deemed liquid if it can be readily converted into cash. Liquid assets are current assets such as cash, marketable securities, accounts receivable, and so on. Two liquidity ratios are commonly used.

Current Ratio   The current ratio measures the extent to which the claims of short-term creditors are covered by assets that can be quickly converted into cash. Most companies should have a ratio of at least 1, because failure to meet these commitments can lead to bankruptcy. The ratio is defined as follows:

$$\text{Current ratio} = \frac{\text{Current assets}}{\text{Current liabilities}}$$

Quick Ratio   The quick ratio measures a company's ability to pay off the claims of short-term creditors without relying on selling its inventories. This is a valuable measure since in practice the sale of inventories is often difficult. It is defined as follows:

$$\text{Quick ratio} = \frac{\text{Current assets} - \text{inventory}}{\text{Current liabilities}}$$

Activity Ratios

Activity ratios indicate how effectively a company is managing its assets. Two ratios are particularly useful.

Inventory Turnover   This measures the number of times inventory is turned over. It is useful in determining whether a firm is carrying excess stock in inventory. It is defined as follows:

$$\text{Inventory turnover} = \frac{\text{Cost of goods sold}}{\text{Inventory}}$$

Cost of goods sold is a better measure of turnover than sales because it is the cost of the inventory items. Inventory is taken at the balance sheet date. Some companies choose to compute an average inventory, beginning inventory, and ending inventory, but for simplicity, use the inventory at the balance sheet date.

Days Sales Outstanding (DSO) or Average Collection Period   This ratio is the average time a company has to wait to receive its cash after making a sale. It measures how effective the company's credit, billing, and collection procedures are. It is defined as follows:

$$\text{DSO} = \frac{\text{Accounts receivable}}{\text{Total sales/360}}$$

Accounts receivable is divided by average daily sales. The use of 360 is the standard number of days for most financial analysis.

Leverage Ratios

A company is said to be highly leveraged if it uses more debt than equity, including stock and retained earnings. The balance between debt and equity is called the *capital structure*. The optimal capital structure is determined by the individual company. Debt has a lower cost because creditors take less risk; they know they will get their interest and principal. However, debt can be risky to the firm because if enough profit is not made to cover the interest and principal payments, bankruptcy can result. Three leverage ratios are commonly used.

Debt-to-Assets Ratio   The debt-to-assets ratio is the most direct measure of the extent to which borrowed funds have been used to finance a company's investments. It is defined as follows:

$$\text{Debt-to-assets ratio} = \frac{\text{Total debt}}{\text{Total assets}}$$

Total debt is the sum of a company's current liabilities and its long-term debt, and total assets are the sum of fixed assets and current assets.

Debt-to-Equity Ratio   The debt-to-equity ratio indicates the balance between debt and equity in a company's capital structure. This is perhaps the most widely used measure of a company's leverage. It is defined as follows:

$$\text{Debt-to-equity ratio} = \frac{\text{Total debt}}{\text{Total equity}}$$

Times-Covered Ratio   The times-covered ratio measures the extent to which a company's gross profit covers its annual interest payments. If this ratio declines to less than 1, the company is unable to meet its interest costs and is technically insolvent. The ratio is defined as follows:

$$\text{Times-covered ratio} = \frac{\text{Profit before interest and tax}}{\text{Total interest charges}}$$

Shareholder-Return Ratios

Shareholder-return ratios measure the return that shareholders earn from holding stock in the company. Given the goal of maximizing stockholders' wealth, providing shareholders with an adequate rate of return is a primary objective of most companies. As with profit ratios, it can be helpful to compare a company's shareholder returns against those of similar companies as a yardstick for determining how well the company is satisfying the demands of this particularly important group of organizational constituents. Four ratios are commonly used.

Total Shareholder Returns   Total shareholder returns measure the returns earned by time $t + 1$ on an investment in a company's stock made at time t. (Time t is the time at which the initial investment is made.) Total shareholder returns include both dividend payments and appreciation in the value of the stock (adjusted for stock splits) and are defined as follows:

$$\text{Total shareholder returns} = \frac{\substack{\text{Stock price } (t + 1) - \text{stock price } (t) \\ + \text{ sum of annual dividends per share}}}{\text{Stock price } (t)}$$

If a shareholder invests $2 at time t and at time $t + 1$ the share is worth $3, while the sum of annual dividends for the period t to $t + 1$ has amounted to $0.20, total shareholder returns are equal to $(3 - 2 + 0.2)/2 = 0.6$, which is a 60 percent return on an initial investment of $2 made at time t.

Price-Earnings Ratio   The price-earnings ratio measures the amount investors are willing to pay per dollar of profit. It is defined as follows:

$$\text{Price-earnings ratio} = \frac{\text{Market price per share}}{\text{Earnings per share}}$$

Market-to-Book Value   Market-to-book value measures a company's expected future growth prospects. It is defined as follows:

$$\text{Market-to-book value} = \frac{\text{Market price per share}}{\text{Earnings per share}}$$

Dividend Yield The dividend yield measures the return to shareholders received in the form of dividends. It is defined as follows:

$$\text{Dividend} = \frac{\text{Dividend per share}}{\text{Market price per share}}$$

Market price per share can be calculated for the first of the year, in which case the dividend yield refers to the return on an investment made at the beginning of the year. Alternatively, the average share price over the year may be used. A company must decide how much of its profits to pay to stockholders and how much to reinvest in the company. Companies with strong growth prospects should have a lower dividend payout ratio than mature companies. The rationale is that shareholders can invest the money elsewhere if the company is not growing. The optimal ratio depends on the individual firm, but the key decider is whether the company can produce better returns than the investor can earn elsewhere.

Cash Flow

Cash flow position is cash received minus cash distributed. The net cash flow can be taken from a company's statement of cash flows. Cash flow is important for what it reveals about a company's financing needs. A strong positive cash flow enables a company to fund future investments without having to borrow money from bankers or investors. This is desirable because the company avoids paying out interest or dividends. A weak or negative cash flow means that a company has to turn to external sources to fund future investments. Generally, companies in strong-growth industries often find themselves in a poor cash flow position (because their investment needs are substantial), whereas successful companies based in mature industries generally find themselves in a strong cash flow position.

A company's internally generated cash flow is calculated by adding back its depreciation provision to profits after interest, taxes, and dividend payments. If this figure is insufficient to cover proposed new investments, the company has little choice but to borrow funds to make up the shortfall or to curtail investments. If this figure exceeds proposed new investments, the company can use the excess to build up its liquidity (that is, through investments in financial assets) or repay existing loans ahead of schedule.

Conclusion

When evaluating a case, it is important to be *systematic*. Analyze the case in a logical fashion, beginning with the identification of operating and financial strengths and weaknesses and environmental opportunities and threats. Move on to assess the value of a company's current strategies only when you are fully conversant with the SWOT analysis of the company. Ask yourself whether the company's current strategies make sense given its SWOT analysis. If they do not, what changes need to be made? What are your recommendations? Above all, link any strategic recommendations you may make to the SWOT analysis. State explicitly how the strategies you identify take advantage of the company's strengths to exploit environmental opportunities, how they rectify the company's weaknesses, and how they counter environmental threats. Also, do not forget to outline what needs to be done to implement your recommendations.

Endnote

1 Tom Copeland, Tim Koller, and Jack Murrin, *Valuation: Measuring and Managing the Value of Companies* (New York: Wiley, 1996).

The Home Video Game Industry, 1968–2010

An Industry is Born

In 1968, Nolan Bushell, the 24-year-old son of a Utah cement contractor, graduated from the University of Utah with a degree in engineering.[1] Bushnell then moved to California, where he worked briefly in the computer graphics division of Ampex. At home, Bushnell turned his daughter's bedroom into a laboratory (she was relegated to the couch). There, he created a simpler version of Space War, a computer game that had been invented in 1962 by an MIT graduate student, Steve Russell. Bushnell's version of Russell's game, which he called Computer Space, was made of integrated circuits connected to a 19-inch black-and-white television screen. Unlike a computer, Bushnell's invention could do nothing but play the game, which meant that, unlike a computer, it could be cheaply produced.

Bushnell envisioned video games like his standing next to pinball machines in arcades. With hopes of having his invention put into production, Bushnell left Ampex to work for a small pinball company that manufactured 1,500 copies of his video game. The game never sold, primarily because the player had to read a full page of directions before he or she could play the game—way too complex for an arcade game. Bushnell left the pinball company and with a friend, Ted Dabney, put up $500 to start a company that would develop a simpler video game. They wanted to call the company Syzygy, but the name was already taken, so they settled on Atari, a Japanese word that was the equivalent of "check in the go."

In his home laboratory, Bushnell built the simplest game he could devise. People knew the rules immediately, and it could be played with one hand. The game was modeled on table tennis, and players batted a ball back and forth with paddles that could be moved up and down the sides of a court by twisting knobs. He named the game "Pong" after the sonar-like sound that was emitted every time the ball connected with a paddle.

In the fall of 1972, Bushnell installed his prototype for Pong in Andy Capp's tavern in Sunnyvale, California. The only instructions were "avoid missing the ball for a high score." In the first week, 1,200 quarters were deposited in the casserole dish that served for a coin box in Bushnell's prototype. Bushnell was ecstatic; his simple game had brought in $300 in a week. The pinball machine that stood next to it averaged $35 a week.

Lacking the capital to mass-produce the game, Bushnell approached established amusement game companies, only to be repeatedly shown the door. Down, but hardly out, Bushnell cut his hair, put on a suit, and talked his way into a $50,000 line of credit from a local bank. He set up a production line in an abandoned roller skating rink and he hired people to assemble machines, while Led Zeppelin and The Rolling Stones were played at full volume over the speaker system of the rink. Among his first batch of employees was a skinny 17-year-old named Steve Jobs, who would later found Apple Computer (now Apple) and NeXT. Like others, Jobs had been attracted by a classified ad that read "Have Fun and Make Money."

In no time at all, Bushnell was selling all the machines that his small staff could make—about 10 per day—but to grow, he needed additional capital. While the ambience at the rink, with its mix of rock music and marijuana fumes, put off most potential investors, Don Valentine, one of the country's most astute and credible venture capitalists, was impressed with

---

This case was prepared by Charles W. L. Hill, University of Washington.

Copyright © Charles W.L. Hill, 2011

This case is intended to be used as a basis for class discussion rather than as an illustration of either effective or ineffective handling of the situation. Reprinted by permission of Charles W. L. Hill.

the growth story. Armed with Valentine's money, Atari began to increase production and expand their range of games. New games included "Tank" and "Breakout"; the latter was designed by Jobs and a friend of his, Steve Wozniak, who had left Hewlett Packard to work at Atari.

By 1974, 100,000 Pong-like games were sold worldwide. Although Atari manufactured only 10% of the games, the company still made $3.2 million that year. With the Pong clones coming on strong, Bushnell decided to make a Pong system for the home. In fact, Magnavox had been marketing a similar game for the home since 1972, although sales had been modest.[2] Bushnell's team managed to compress Atari's coin-operated Pong game down to a few inexpensive circuits that were contained in the game console. Atari's Pong had a sharper picture and more sensitive controllers than Magnavox's machine. It also cost less. Bushnell then went on a road show, demonstrating Pong to toy buyers, but he received an indifferent response and no sales. A dejected Bushnell returned to Atari with no idea of what to do next. Then, the buyer for the sporting goods department at Sears came to see Bushnell, reviewed the machine, and offered to buy every home Pong game Atari could make. With Sears' backing, Bushnell boosted production. Sears ran a major television ad campaign to sell home Pong, and Atari's sales soared, hitting $450 million in 1975. The home video game had arrived.

Boom and Bust

Nothing attracts competitors like success, and by 1976 about 20 different companies were crowding into the home video game market, including National Semiconductor, RCA, Coleco, and Fairchild. Recognizing the limitations of existing home video game designs, Fairchild came out in 1976 with a home video game system capable of playing multiple games. The Fairchild system consisted of three components—a console, controllers, and cartridges. The console was a small computer optimized for graphics processing capabilities. It was designed to receive information from the controllers, process it, and send signals to a television monitor. The controllers were hand-held devices used to direct on-screen action. The cartridges contained chips encoding the instructions for a game.

The cartridges were designed to be inserted into the console.

In 1976, Bushnell sold Atari to Warner Communications for $28 million; Bushnell stayed on to run Atari. Backed by Warner's capital, in 1977 Atari developed and bought its own cartridge-based system, the Atari 2600. The 2600 system was sold for $200, and associated cartridges retailed for $25–$30. Sales surged during the 1977 Christmas season. However, a lack of manufacturing capacity on behalf of market leader Atari, and a very cautious approach to inventory by Fairchild led to shortages and kept sales significantly below what they could have been. Fairchild's cautious approach was the result of prior experience in consumer electronics. A year earlier it had increased demand for its digital watches, only to accumulate a buildup of excess inventory that had caused the company to take a $24.5 million write-off.[3]

After the 1977 Christmas season, Atari claimed to have sold about 400,000 units of the 2600 VCA, about 50% of all cartridge-based systems in American homes. Atari had also earned more than $100 million in sales of game cartridges. By this point, second-place Fairchild sold around 250,000 units of its system. Cartridge sales for the year totaled about 1.2 million units, with an average selling price of around $20. Fresh from this success and fortified by market forecasts predicting sales of 33 million cartridges and an installed base of 16 million machines by 1980, Bushnell committed Atari to manufacturing 1 million units of the 2600 for the 1978 Christmas season. Atari estimated that total demand would reach 2 million units. Bushnell was also encouraged by signals from Fairchild that it would again be limiting production to around 200,000 units. At this point, Atari had a library of 9 games. Fairchild had 17.[4]

Atari was not the only company to be excited by the growth forecasts. In 1978, a host of other companies, including Coleco, National Semiconductor, Magnavox, General Instrument, and a dozen other companies, entered the market with incompatible cartridge-based home systems. The multitude of choices did not seem to entice consumers, however, and the 1978 Christmas season brought unexpectedly low sales. Only Atari and Coleco survived an industry shakeout. Atari lost Bushnell, who was ousted by Warner executives. (Bushnell went on to start Chuck E. Cheese Pizza Time Theater, a restaurant chain that had 278 outlets by 1981.) Bushnell later stated that part of the problem was a disagreement over strategy. Bushnell wanted Atari to price the 2600 at cost and make money on sales of software; Warner wanted to continue making profits on hardware sales.[5]

Several important developments occurred in 1979. First, several game producers and programmers defected from Atari to set up their own firm, Activision, and to make games compatible with the Atari 2600. Their success encouraged others to follow suit. Second, Coleco developed an expansion module that allowed its machine to play Atari games. Atari and Mattel (which entered the market in 1979) did likewise. Third, the year 1979 saw the introduction of three new games to the home market—Space Invaders, Asteroids, and Pac-Man. All three were adapted from popular arcade games and all three helped drive demand for players.

Demand strongly recovered in late-1979 and kept growing for the next 3 years. In 1981, U.S. sales of home video games and cartridges hit $1 billion. In 1982, they surged to $3 billion, with Atari accounting for half of this amount. It seemed as if Atari could do no wrong; the 2600 was everywhere. About 20 million units were sold, and by late-1982, a large number of independent companies, including Activision, Imagic, and Epyx, were now producing hundreds of games for the 2600. Second-place Coleco was also doing well, partly because of a popular arcade game, Donkey Kong, which it had licensed from a Japanese company called Nintendo.

Atari was also in contact with Nintendo. In 1982, the company very nearly licensed the rights to Nintendo's Famicom, a cartridge-based video game system machine that was a big hit in Japan. Atari's successor to the 2600, the 5200, was not selling well, and the Famicom seemed like a good substitute. The negotiations broke down, however, when Atari discovered that Nintendo had extended its Donkey Kong license to Coleco. This allowed Coleco to port a version of the game to its home computer, which was a direct competitor to Atari's 800 home computer.[6]

After a strong 1982 season, the industry hoped for continued growth in 1983. Then, the bottom dropped out of the market. Sales of home video games plunged to $100 million. Atari lost $500 million in the first 9 months of the year, causing the stock of parent company Warner Communications to drop by half. Part of the blame for the collapse was laid at the feet of an enormous inventory overhang of unsold games. About 1–20 million surplus game cartridges were left over from the 1982 Christmas season (in 1981, there were none). On top of this, around 500 new games hit the market in 1993. The average price of a cartridge plunged from $30 in 1979 to $16 in 1982, and then to $4 in 1983. As sales slowed, retailers cut back on the shelf space allocated to video games. It proved difficult for new games to make a splash in a crowded market. Atari had to dispose of 6 million "ET: The Extraterrestrial" games. Meanwhile, big hits from previous years, such as Pac-Man, were bundled with game players and given away free to try to encourage system sales.[7]

Surveying the rubble, commentators claimed that the video game industry was dead. The era of dedicated game machines was over, they claimed. Personal computers were taking their place.[8] It seemed to be true. Mattel sold off its game business, Fairchild moved on to other things, Coleco folded, and Warner decided to break up Atari and sell its constituent pieces—at least, those pieces for which it could find a buyer. No one in America seemed to want to have anything to do with the home video game business; no one, that is, except for Minoru Arakawa, the head of Nintendo's U.S. subsidiary, Nintendo of America (NOA). Picking through the rubble of the industry, Arakawa noticed that there were people who still packed video arcades, bringing in $7 billion a year, more money than the entire movie industry. Perhaps it was not a lack of interest in home video games that had killed the industry. Perhaps it was bad business practice.

The Nintendo Monopoly

Nintendo was a century-old Japanese company that had built up a profitable business making playing cards before diversifying into the video game business. Based in Kyoto and still run by the founding Yamauchi family, the company started to diversify into the video game business in the late-1970s. The first step was to license video game technology from Magnavox. In 1977, Nintendo introduced a home video game system in Japan based on this technology that played a variation of Pong. In 1978, the company began to sell coin-operated video games. It had its first hit with "Donkey Kong," designed by Sigeru Miyamoto.

The Famicom

In the early-1980s, the company's boss, Hiroshi Yamauchi, decided that Nintendo had to develop its own video game machine. He pushed the company's engineers to develop a machine that combined superior graphics-processing capabilities and low cost. Yamauchi wanted a machine that could sell for $75, less than half the price of competing machines at the time. He dubbed the machine the Family Computer, or Famicom. The machine that his engineers designed was based on the controller, console, and plug in the cartridge format pioneered by Fairchild. It contained two custom chips—an 8-bit central processing unit and a graphics-processing unit. Both chips had been scaled down to perform only essential functions. A 16-bit processor was available at the time, but to keep costs down, Yamauchi refused to use it.

Nintendo approached Ricoh, the electronics giant, which had spare semiconductor capacity. Employees at Ricoh said that the chips had to cost no more that 2,000 yen. Ricoh thought that the 2,000-yen price point was absurd. Yamauchi's response was to guarantee Ricoh a 3-million-chip order within 2 years. Because the leading companies in Japan were selling, at most, 30,000 video games per year at the time, many within the company viewed this as an outrageous commitment, but Ricoh went for it.[9]

Another feature of the machine was its memory—2,000 bytes of random access memory (RAM), compared to the 256 bytes of RAM in the Atari machine. The result was a machine with superior graphics-processing capabilities and faster action that could handle far more complex games than Atari games. Nintendo's engineers also built a new set of chips into the game cartridges. In addition to chips that held the game program, Nintendo developed memory map controller (MMC) chips that took over some of the graphics-processing work from the chips in the console and enabled the system to handle more complex games. With the addition of the MMC chips, the potential for more-sophisticated and more complex games had arrived. Over time, Nintendo's engineers developed more powerful MMC chips, enabling the basic 8-bit system to do things that originally seemed out of reach. The engineers also figured out a way to include a battery backup system in cartridges that allowed some games to store information independently—to keep track of where a player had left off or to track high scores.

The Games

Yamauchi recognized that great hardware that would not sell itself. The key to the market, he reasoned, was great games. Yamauchi had instructed the engineers, when they were developing the hardware, to make sure that "it was appreciated by software engineers." Nintendo decided that it would become a haven for game designers. "An ordinary man," Yamauchi said, "cannot develop good games no matter how hard he tries. A handful of people in this world can develop games that everyone wants. Those are the people we want at Nintendo."[10]

Yamauchi had an advantage in the person of Sigeru Miyamoto. Miyamoto had joined Nintendo at the age of 24. Yamauchi had hired Miyamoto, a graduate of Kanazawa Munici College of Industrial Arts, as a favor to his father and an old friend, although he had little idea what he would do with an artist. For 3 years, Miyamoto worked as Nintendo's staff artist. Then, in 1980, Yamauchi called Miyamoto into his office. Nintendo had started selling coin-operated video games, but one of the new games, Radarscope, was a disaster. Could Miyamoto come up with a new game? Miyamoto was delighted. He had always spent a lot of time drawing cartoons, and as a student, he had played video games constantly. Miyamoto believed that video games could be used to bring cartoons to life.[11]

The game Miyamoto developed was nothing short of a revelation. At a time when most coin-operated video games lacked characters or depth, Miyamoto created a game around a story that had both. Most games involved battles with space invaders or heroes shooting lasers at aliens; Miyamoto's game did neither. Based loosely on *Beauty and the Beast* and *King Kong*, Miyamoto's game involved a pet ape who runs off with his master's beautiful girlfriend. His master is an ordinary carpenter called Mario, who has a bulbous nose, a bushy mustache, a pair of large pathetic eyes, and a red cap (which Miyamoto added because he was not good at hairstyles). Mario does not carry a laser gun. The ape runs off with the girlfriend to get back at his master, who was not especially nice to the beast. The man, of course, has to get his girlfriend back by running up ramps, climbing ladders, jumping off elevators, and the like, while the ape throws objects at the hapless carpenter. Since the main character is an ape, Miyamoto called him Kong; because the main character is as stubborn as a donkey, he called the game "Donkey Kong."

Released in 1981, Donkey Kong was a sensation in the world of coin-operated video arcades and a smash hit for Nintendo. In 1984, Yamauchi again summoned Miyamoto to his office. He needed more games, this time for Famicom. Miyamoto was made the head of a new research and development (R&D) group and told to come up with the most imaginative video games ever.

Miyamoto began with Mario from Donkey Kong. A colleague had told him that Mario looked more like a plumber than a carpenter, so a plumber he became. Miyamoto gave Mario a brother, Luigi, who was as tall and thin as Mario was short and fat. They became the Super Mario Brothers. Since plumbers spend their time working on pipes, large green sewer pipes became obstacles and doorways into secret worlds. Mario and Luigi's task was to search for the captive Princess Toadstool. Mario and Luigi are endearing bumblers, unequal to their tasks yet surviving. They shoot, squash, or evade their enemies—a potpourri of inventions that include flying turtles and stinging fish, man-eating flowers and fire-breathing dragons—while they collect gold coins, blow air bubbles, and climb vines into smiling clouds.[12]

"Super Mario Brothers" was introduced in 1985. For Miyamoto, this was just the beginning. Between 1985 and 1991, Miyamoto produced 8 Mario games. About 60–70 million were sold worldwide, making Miyamoto the most successful game designer in the world. After adapting Donkey Kong for Famicom, he also went on to create other top-selling games, including another classic, "The Legend of Zelda." While Miyamoto drew freely from folklore, literature, and pop culture, the main source for his ideas was his own experience. The memory of being lost among a maze of sliding doors in his family's home was re-created in the labyrinths of the Zelda games. The dog that attacked him when he was a child attacks Mario in Super Mario. As a child, Miyamoto had once climbed a tree to catch a view of far-off mountains and had become stuck; Mario gets himself in a similar fix. Once Miyamoto went hiking without a map and was surprised to stumble across a lake. In the Legend of Zelda, part of the adventure is in walking into new places without a map and being confronted by surprises.

Nintendo in Japan

Nintendo introduced Famicom into the Japanese market in May 1983. Famicom was priced at $100, more than Yamauchi wanted, but significantly less than the products of competitors. When he introduced the machine, Yamauchi urged retailers to forgo profits on the hardware because it was just a tool to sell software, and that is where they would make their money. Backed by an extensive advertising campaign, 500,000 units of Famicom were sold in the first 2 months. Within a year, the figure stood at 1 million, and sales were still rapidly expanding. With the hardware quickly finding its way into Japanese homes, Nintendo was besieged with calls from desperate retailers frantically demanding more games.

At this point, Yamauchi told Miyamoto to come up with the most imaginative games ever. However, Yamauchi also realized that Nintendo alone could not satisfy the growing thirst for new games, so he initiated a licensing program. To become a Nintendo licensee, companies had to agree to an unprecedented series of restrictions. Licensees could issue only 5 Nintendo games per year, and they could not write those titles for other platforms. The licensing fee was set at 20% of the wholesale price of each cartridge sold (game cartridges wholesaled for around $30). It typically cost $500,000 to develop a game and took around 6 months. Nintendo insisted that games not contain any excessively violent or sexually suggestive material and that they review every game before allowing it to be produced.[13]

Despite these restrictions, 6 companies (Bandai, Capcom, Konami, Namco, Taito, and Hudson) agreed to become Nintendo licensees, not least because millions of customers were now clamoring for games. Bandai was Japan's largest toy company. The others already made either coin-operated video games or computer software games. Because of these licensing agreements, they saw their sales and earnings surge. For example, Konami's earnings went from $10 million in 1987 to $300 million in 1991.

After the 6 licensees began selling games, reports of defective games began to reach Yamauchi. The original 6 licensees were allowed to manufacture their own game cartridges. Realizing that he had given away the ability to control the quality of the cartridges, Yamauchi decided to change the contract for future licensees. Future licensees were required to submit all manufacturing orders for cartridges to Nintendo. Nintendo charged licensees $14 per cartridge, required that they place a minimum order for 10,000 units (later the minimum order was raised to 30,000), and insisted on cash payment in full when the order was placed. Nintendo outsourced all manufacturing to other companies, using the volume of its orders to get rock bottom prices. The cartridges were estimated to cost Nintendo between $6 and $8 each. The licensees then picked up the cartridges from Nintendo's loading dock and were responsible for distribution. In 1985, there were 17 licensees. By 1987, there were 50. By this point, 90% of the home video game systems sold in Japan were Nintendo systems.

Nintendo in America

In 1980, Nintendo established a subsidiary in America to sell its coin-operated video games. Yamauchi's American-educated son-in-law, Minoru Arakawa, headed the subsidiary. All of the other essential employees were Americans, including Ron Judy and Al Stone. For its first 2 years, Nintendo of America (NOA), originally based in Seattle, struggled to sell second-rate games such as Radarscope. The subsidiary seemed on the brink of closing. NOA could not even make the rent payment on the warehouse. Then they received a large shipment from Japan: 2,000 units of a new coin-operated video game. Opening the box, they discovered Donkey Kong. After playing the game briefly, Judy proclaimed it a disaster. Stone walked out of the building, declaring "it's over."[14] The managers were appalled. They could not imagine a game less likely to sell in video arcades. The only promising sign was that a 20-year employee, Howard Philips, rapidly became enthralled with the machine.

Arakawa, however, knew he had little choice but to try to sell the machine. Judy persuaded the owner of the Spot Tavern near Nintendo's office to take one of the machines on a trial basis. After one night, Judy discovered $30 in the coin box, a phenomenal amount. The next night there was $35, and $36 the night after that. NOA had a hit on its hands.

By the end of 1982, NOA had sold over 60,000 copies of Donkey Kong and had booked sales in excess of $100 million. The subsidiary had outgrown

its Seattle location. They moved to a new site in Redmond, a Seattle suburb, where they located next to a small but fast-growing software company run by an old school acquaintance of Howard Philips, Bill Gates.

By 1984, NOA was riding a wave of success in the coin-operated video game market. Arakawa, however, was interested in the possibilities of selling Nintendo's new Famicom system in the United States. Throughout 1984, Arakawa, Judy, and Stone met with numerous toy and department store representatives to discuss the possibilities, only to be repeatedly rebuffed. Still smarting from the 1983 debacle, the representatives wanted nothing to do with the home video game business. They also met with former managers from Atari and Coleco to gain their insights. The most common response they received was that the market collapsed because the last generation of games was awful.

Arakawa and his team decided that if they were going to sell Famicom in the United States, they would have to find a new distribution channel. The obvious choice was consumer electronics stores. Thus, Arakawa asked the R&D team in Kyoto to redesign Famicom for the U.S. market so that it looked less like a toy (Famicom was encased in red and white plastic), and more like a consumer electronics device. The redesigned machine was renamed the Nintendo Entertainment System (NES).

Arakawa's big fear was that illegal, low-quality Taiwanese games would flood the U.S. market if NES was successful. To stop counterfeit games being played on NES, Arakawa asked Nintendo's Japanese engineers to design a security system into the U.S. version of Famicom so that only Nintendo-approved games could be played on NES. The Japanese engineers responded by designing a security chip to be embedded in the game cartridges. NES would not work unless the security chips in the cartridges unlocked, or shook hands with, a chip in NES. Since the code embedded in the security chip was proprietary, the implication of this system was that no one could manufacture games for NES without Nintendo's specific approval.

To overcome the skepticism and reluctance of retailers to stock a home video game system, Arakawa decided in late-1985 to make an extraordinary commitment. Nintendo would stock stores and set up displays and windows. Retailers would not have to pay for anything they stocked for 90 days. After that, retailers could pay Nintendo for what they sold and return the rest. NES was bundled with Nintendo's best-selling game in Japan, Super Mario Brothers. It was essentially a risk-free proposition for retailers, but even with this, most were skeptical. Ultimately, 30 Nintendo personnel descended on the New York area. Referred to as the Nintendo SWAT team, they persuaded some stores to stock NES after an extraordinary blitz that involved 18-hour days. To support the New York product launch, Nintendo also committed itself to a $5 million advertising campaign aimed at the 7- to 14-year-old boys who seemed to be Nintendo's likely core audience.

By December 1985, between 500 and 600 stores in the New York area were stocking Nintendo systems. Sales were moderate, and only about half of the 100,000 NES machines shipped from Japan were sold, but it was enough to justify going forward. The SWAT team then moved first to Los Angeles, then to Chicago, then to Dallas. As in New York, sales started at a moderate pace, but by late-1986 they started to accelerate rapidly, and Nintendo went national with NES.

In 1986, around 1 million NES units were sold in the United States. In 1987, the figure increased to 3 million. In 1988, it jumped to over 7 million. In the same year, 33 million game cartridges were sold. Nintendo mania had arrived in the United States. To expand the supply of games, Nintendo licensed the rights to produce up to 5 games per year to 31 American software companies. Nintendo continued to use a restrictive licensing agreement that gave it exclusive rights to any games, required licensees to place their orders through Nintendo, and insisted on a 30,000-unit minimum order.[15]

By 1990, the home video game market was worth $5 billion worldwide. Nintendo dominated the industry, with a 90% share of the market for game equipment. The parent company was, by some measures, now the most profitable company in Japan. By 1992, it was netting over $1 billion in gross profit annually, or more than $1.5 million for each employee in Japan. The company's stock market value exceeded that of Sony, Japan's premier consumer electronics firm. Indeed, the company's net profit exceeded that of all the American movie studios combined. Nintendo games, it seemed, were bigger than the movies.

As of 1991, there were over 100 licensees for Nintendo, and over 450 titles were available for NES. In the United States, Nintendo products were distributed through toy stores (30% of volume), mass

merchandisers (40% of volume), and department stores (10% of volume). Nintendo tightly controlled the number of game titles and games that could be sold, quickly withdrawing titles as soon as interest appeared to decline. In 1988, retailers requested 110 million cartridges from Nintendo. Market surveys suggested that perhaps 45 million could have been sold, but Nintendo allowed only 33 million to be shipped.[16] Nintendo claimed that the shortage of games was, in part, due to a worldwide shortage of semiconductor chips.

Several companies had tried to reverse-engineer the code embedded in Nintendo's security chip, which competitors characterized as a lockout chip. Nintendo successfully sued them. The most notable was Atari Games, one of the successors of the original Atari, which sued Nintendo of America in 1987 for anticompetitive behavior. Atari claimed that the purpose of the security chip was to monopolize the market. At the same time, Atari announced that it had found a way around Nintendo's security chip and would begin to sell unlicensed games.[17] NOA responded with a countersuit. In a March 1991 ruling, Atari was found to have obtained Nintendo's security code illegally and was ordered to stop selling NES-compatible games. However, Nintendo did not always have it all its own way. In 1990, under pressure from Congress, the Department of Justice, and several lawsuits, Nintendo rescinded its exclusivity requirements, freeing up developers to write games for other platforms. However, developers faced a real problem: what platform could they write for?

Sega's Sonic Boom

In 1954, David Rosen, a 20-year-old American, left the U.S. Air Force after a tour of duty in Tokyo.[18] Rosen had noticed that Japanese people needed lots of photographs for ID cards, but that local photo studios were slow and expensive. He formed a company, Rosen Enterprises, and went into the photo-booth business, which was a big success. By 1957, Rosen had established a successful nationwide chain. At this point, the Japanese economy was booming, so Rosen decided it was time to get into another business—entertainment. As his vehicle, he chose arcade games, which were unknown in Japan at the time. He picked up used games on the cheap from America and set up arcades in the same Japanese department stores and theaters that typically housed his photo booths. Within a few years, Rosen had 200 arcades nationwide. His only competition came from another American-owned firm, Service Games (SeGa), whose original business was jukeboxes and fruit machines.

By the early-1960s, the Japanese arcade market had caught up with the U.S. market. The problem was that game makers had run out of exciting new games to offer. Rosen decided that he would have to get into the business of designing and manufacturing games, but to do that he needed manufacturing facilities. SeGa manufactured its own games, so in 1965 Rosen approached the company and suggested a merger. The result was Sega Enterprise, a Japanese company with Rosen as its CEO.

Rosen himself designed Sega's first game, "Periscope," in which the objective was to sink chain-mounted cardboard ships by firing torpedoes, represented by lines of colored lights. Periscope was a big success not only in Japan, but also in the United States and Europe, and it allowed Sega to build up a respectable export business. Over the years, the company continued to invest heavily in game development, always using the latest electronic technology.

Gulf and Western, a U.S. conglomerate, acquired Sega in 1969, and Rosen ran the subsidiary. In 1975, Gulf and Western (G&W) took Sega public in the United States, but left Sega Japan as a G&W subsidiary; Hayao Nakayama, a former Sega distributor, was drafted as president. In the early-1980s, Nakayama pushed G&W to invest more in Sega Japan so that the company could enter the then-booming home video game market. When G&W refused, Nakayama suggested a management buyout. G&W agreed, and in 1984, for the price of just $38 million, Sega became a Japanese company once more. (Sega's Japanese revenues were around $700 million, but by now the company was barely profitable.)

Sega was caught off guard by the huge success of Nintendo's Famicom. Although it released its own 8-bit system in 1986, the machine never commanded more than 5% of the Japanese market. Nakayama, however, was not about to give up. From years in the arcade business, he understood that great games drove sales. Nevertheless, he also understood that more powerful technology gave game developers the tools to develop more appealing games. This philosophy underlay Nakayama's decision to develop a 16-bit game system, Genesis.

Sega took the design of its 16-bit arcade machine and adapted it for Genesis. Compared to Nintendo's 8-bit machine, the 16-bit machine featured an array of superior technological features, including high-definition graphics and animation, a full spectrum of colors, two independent scrolling backgrounds that created an impressive depth of field, and near CD quality sound. The design strategy also made it easy to port Sega's catalog of arcade hits to Genesis.

Genesis was launched in Japan in 1989, and in the United States in 1990. In the United States, the machine was priced at $199. The company hoped that sales would be boosted by the popularity of its arcade games, such as the graphically violent Altered Beast. Sega also licensed other companies to develop games for the Genesis platform. In an effort to recruit licensees, Sega asked for lower royalty rates than Nintendo, and it gave licensees the right to manufacture their own cartridges. Independent game developers were slow to on board, however, and the $200 price tag for the player held back sales.

One of the first independent game developers to sign up with Sega was Electronic Arts. Established by Trip Hawkins, Electronic Arts had focused on designing games for personal computers and consequently had missed the Nintendo 8-bit era. Now Hawkins was determined to get a presence in the home video game market, and aligning his company's wagon with Sega seemed to be the best option. The Nintendo playing field was already crowded, and Sega offered a far less restrictive licensing deal than Nintendo. Electronic Arts subsequently wrote several popular games for Genesis, including John Madden football and several gory combat games.[19]

Nintendo had not been ignoring the potential of the 16-bit system. Nintendo's own 16-bit system, Super NES, was ready for market introduction in 1989—at the same time as Sega's Genesis. Nintendo introduced Super NES in Japan in 1990, where it quickly established a strong market presence and beat Sega's Genesis. In the United States, however, the company decided to hold back longer to reap the full benefits of the dominance it enjoyed with the 8-bit NES system. Yamauchi was also worried about the lack of backward compatibility between Nintendo's 8-bit and 16-bit systems. (The company had tried to make the 16-bit system so that it could play 8-bit games but concluded that the cost of doing so was prohibitive.) These concerns may have led the company to delay market introduction until the 8-bit market was saturated.

Meanwhile, in the United States, the Sega bandwagon was beginning to gain momentum. One development that gave Genesis a push was the introduction of a new Sega game, "Sonic the Hedgehog." Developed by an independent team that was contracted to Sega, the game featured a cute hedgehog that impatiently tapped his paw when the player took too long to act. Impatience was Sonic's central feature—he had places to go, and quickly. He zipped along, collecting brass rings when he could find them, before rolling into a ball and flying down slides with loops and underground tunnels. Sonic was Sega's Mario.

In mid-1991, in an attempt to jump-start slow sales, Tom Kalinske, head of Sega's American subsidiary, decided to bundle Sonic the Hedgehog with the game player. He also reduced the price for the bundled unit to $150, and he relaunched the system with an aggressive advertising campaign aimed at teenagers. The campaign was built around the slogan "Genesis does what Nintendon't." The shift in strategy worked, and sales accelerated sharply.

Sega's success prompted Nintendo to launch its own 16-bit system. Nintendo's Super NES was introduced at $200. However, Sega now had a 2-year head start in games. By the end of 1991, about 125 game titles were available for Genesis, compared to 25 for Super NES. In May 1992, Nintendo reduced the price of Super NES to $150. At this time Sega was claiming a 63% share of the 16-bit market in the United States, and Nintendo claimed a 60% share. By now, Sega was cool. It began to take more chances with mass media–defined morality. When Acclaim Entertainment released its bloody "Mortal Kombat" game in September 1992, the Sega version let players rip off heads and tear out hearts. Reflecting Nintendo's image of their core market, its version was sanitized. The Sega version outsold Nintendo's 2:1.[20] Therefore, the momentum continued to run in Sega's favor. By January 1993, there were 320 titles available for Sega Genesis, and 130 for Super NES. In early-1994, independent estimates suggested that Sega had 60% of the U.S. market and Nintendo had 40%, figures Nintendo disputed.

3DO

Trip Hawkins, whose first big success was Electronic Arts, founded 3DO in 1991.[21] Hawkins' vision for 3DO was to shift the home video game business away from the existing cartridge-based format and toward a CD-ROM-based platform. The original partners in 3DO were Electronic Arts, Matsushita, Time Warner, AT&T, and the venture capital firm Kleiner Perkins. Collectively, they invested over $17 million in 3DO, making it the richest start-up in the history of the home video game industry. 3DO went public in May 1993 at $15 per share. By October of that year, the stock had risen to $48 per share, making 3DO worth $1 billion—not bad for a company that had yet to generate a single dollar in revenues.

The basis for 3DO's $1 billion market cap was patented computer system architecture and a copyrighted operating system that allowed for much richer graphics and audio capabilities. The system was built around a 32-bit RISC microprocessor and proprietary graphics processor chips. Instead of a cartridge, the 3DO system stored games on a CD-ROM that was capable of holding up to 600 megabytes of content, sharply up from the 10 megabytes of content found in the typical game cartridge of the time. The slower access time of a CD-ROM compared to a cartridge was alleviated somewhat by the use of a double-speed CD-ROM drive.[22]

The belief at 3DO—a belief apparently shared by many investors—was that the superior storage and graphics-processing capabilities of the 3DO system would prove very attractive to game developers, allowing them to be far more creative. In turn, better games would attract customers away from Nintendo and Sega. Developing games that used the capabilities of a CD-ROM system altered the economics of game development. Estimates suggested that it would cost approximately $2 million to produce a game for the 3DO system and could take as long as 24 months to develop. However, at $2 per disc, a CD-ROM cost substantially less to produce than a cartridge.

The centerpiece of 3DO's strategy was to license its hardware technology for free. Game developers paid a royalty of $3 per disc for access to the 3DO operating code. Discs typically retailed for $40 each.

Matsushita introduced the first 3DO machine into the U.S. market in October 1993. Priced at $700, the machine was sold through electronic retailers that carried Panasonic high-end electronics products. Sega's Tom Kalinsky noted, "It's a noble effort. Some people will buy 3DO, and they'll have a wonderful experience. It's impressive, but it's a niche. We've done the research. It does not become a large market until you go below $500. At $300, it starts to get interesting. We make no money on hardware. It's a cutthroat business. I hope Matsushita understands that."[23] CD-ROM discs for the 3DO machine retailed for around $75. The machine came bundled with "Crash'n Burn," a high-speed combat racing game. However, only 18 3DO titles were available by the crucial Christmas period, although reports suggested that 150 titles were under development.[24]

Sales of the hardware were slow, reaching only 30,000 by January 1994.[25] In the same month, AT&T and Sanyo both announced that they would begin to manufacture the 3DO machine. In March, faced with continuing sluggish sales, 3DO announced that it would give hardware manufacturers two shares of 3DO stock for every unit sold at or below a certain retail price. Matsushita dropped the price of its machine to $500. About the same time, Toshiba, LG, and Samsung all announced that they would start to produce 3DO machines.

By June 1994, cumulative sales of 3DO machines in the United States stood at 40,000 units. Matsushita announced plans to expand distribution beyond the current 3,500 outlets to include the toy and mass merchandise channels. Hawkins and his partners announced that they would invest another $37 million in 3DO. By July, there were 750 3DO software licensees, but only 40 titles were available for the format. Despite these moves, sales continued at a very sluggish pace and the supply of new software titles started to dry up.[26]

In September 1996, 3DO announced that it would either sell its hardware system business or move it into a joint venture.[27] The company announced that about 150 people, 1/3 of the work force, would probably lose their jobs in the restructuring. According to Trip Hawkins, 3DO would now focus on developing software for online gaming. Hawkins stated that the Internet and Internet entertainment constituted a huge opportunity for 3DO. The stock dropped $1.375 to $6.75.

Sony's Playstation

In the fall of 1995, Sony entered the fray with the introduction of the Sony PlayStation.[28] PlayStation used a 32-bit RISC microprocessor running at 33 MHz and using a double-speed CD-ROM drive. PlayStation cost an estimated $500 million to develop. The machine had actually been under development since 1991, when Sony decided that the home video game industry was getting too big to ignore. Initially, Sony was in an alliance with Nintendo to develop the machine. Nintendo walked away from the alliance in 1992, however, after a disagreement over who owned the rights to any future CD-ROM games, Sony went alone.[29]

From the start, Sony felt that it could leverage its presence in the film and music business to build a strong position in the home video game industry. A consumer electronics giant with a position in the Hollywood movie business and the music industry (Sony owned Columbia Pictures and the Columbia record label), Sony believed that it had access to significant intellectual property that could form the basis of many popular games.

In 1991, Sony established a division in New York: Sony Electronic Publishing. The division was to serve as an umbrella organization for Sony's multimedia offerings. Headed by Iceland native Olaf Olafsson, then just 28 years old, this organization ultimately took the lead role in both the market launch of PlayStation and in developing game titles.[30] In 1993, as part of this effort, Sony purchased a well-respected British game developer, Psygnosis. By the fall of 1995, this unit had 20 games ready to complement PlayStation: "The Haldeman Diaries," "Mickey Mania" (developed in collaboration with Disney), and "Johnny Mnemonic," based on the William Gibson short story. To entice independent game developers such as Electronic Arts, Namco, and Acclaim Entertainment, Olafsson used the promise of low royalty rates. The standard royalty rate was set at $9 per disc, although developers that signed on early enough were given a lower royalty rate. Sony also provided approximately 4,000 game development tools to licensees in an effort to help them speed games to market.[31]

To distribute PlayStation, Sony set up a retail channel separate from Sony's consumer electronics sales force. It marketed the PlayStation as a hip and powerful alternative to the outdated Nintendo and Sega cartridge-based systems. Sony worked closely with retailers before the launch to find out how it could help them sell the PlayStation. To jump-start demand, Sony set up in-store displays to allow potential consumers to try the equipment. Just before the launch, Sony had lined up an impressive 12,000 retail outlets in the United States.[32]

Sony targeted its advertising for PlayStation at males in the 18- to 35-year age range. The targeting was evident in the content of many of the games. One of the big hits for PlayStation was Tomb Raider, whose central character, Lara Croft, combined sex appeal with savviness and helped to recruit an older generation to PlayStation.[33] PlayStation was initially priced at $299, and games retailed for as much as $60. Sony's Tokyo-based executives had reportedly been insisting on a $350–$400 price for PlayStation, but Olafsson pushed hard for the lower price. Because of the fallout from this internal battle, in January 1996, Olafsson resigned from Sony. By then, however, Sony was following Olafsson's script.[34]

Sony's prelaunch work was rewarded with strong early sales. By January 1996, more than 800,000 PlayStation systems had been sold in the United States, plus another 4 million games. In May 1996, with 1.2 million PlayStations shipped, Sony reduced the price of PlayStation to $199. Sega responded with a similar price cut for its Saturn. The prices on some of Sony's initial games were also reduced to $29.99. The weekend after the price cuts, retailers reported that PlayStation sales were up by between 350% and 1,000% over the prior week.[35] The sales surge continued through 1996. By the end of the year, sales of PlayStation and associated software amounted to $1.3 billion, out of a total for U.S. sales at $2.2 billion for all video game hardware and software. In March 1997, Sony cut the price of PlayStation again, this time to $149. It also reduced its suggested retail price for games by $10 to $49.99. By this point, Sony had sold 3.4 million units of PlayStation in the United States, compared to Saturn's 1.6 million units.[36] Worldwide, PlayStation had outsold Saturn by 13 million to 7.8 million units, and Saturn sales were slowing.[37] The momentum was clearly running in Sony's favor, but the company now had a new challenge to deal with: Nintendo's latest generation game machine, the N64.

Nintendo Strikes Back

In July 1996, Nintendo launched Nintendo 64 (N64) in the Japanese market. This release was followed by a late-fall introduction in the United States. N64 is a 64-bit machine developed in conjunction with Silicon Graphics. Originally targeted for introduction a year earlier, N64 had been under development

since 1993. The machine used a plug-in cartridge format rather than a CD-ROM drive. According to Nintendo, cartridges allow for faster access time and are far more durable than CD-ROMs (an important consideration with children).[38]

The most-striking feature of the N64 machine, however, was its 3D graphics capability. N64 provides fully rounded figures that can turn on their heels and rotate through 180 degrees. Advanced ray tracing techniques, borrowed from military simulators and engineering workstations, added to the sense of realism by providing proper highlighting, reflections, and shadows.

N64 was targeted at children and young teenagers. It was priced at $200 and launched with just 4 games. Despite the lack of games, initial sales were very strong. Indeed, 1997 turned out to be a banner year for both Sony and Nintendo. The overall U.S. market was strong, with sales of hardware and software combined reaching a record $5.5 billion. Estimates suggest that PlayStation accounted for 49% of machines and games by value. N64 captured a 41% share, leaving Sega trailing badly with less than 10% of the market. During the year, the average price for game machines had fallen to $150. By year-end there were 300 titles available for PlayStation, compared to 40 for N64. Games for PlayStation retailed for $40, on average, compared to over $60 for N64.[39]

By late-1998, PlayStation was widening its lead over N64. In the crucial North American market, PlayStation was reported to be outselling N64 by a 2:1 margin, although Nintendo retained a lead in the under-twelve category. At this point, there were 115 games available for N64 versus 431 for PlayStation.[40] Worldwide, Sony had now sold close to 55 million PlayStations. The success of PlayStation had a major impact on Sony's bottom line. In fiscal 1998, PlayStation business generated revenues of $5.5 billion for Sony, 10% of its worldwide revenues, but accounted for $886 million, or 22.5%, of the company's operating income.[41]

The 128-Bit ERA

When Nintendo launched its 64-bit machine in 1996, Sony and Sega didn't follow, preferring instead to focus on the development of even more powerful 128-bit machines.

Sega was the first to market a 128-bit video game console, which it launched in Japan in late-1998 and in the United States in late-1999. The Dreamcast came equipped with a 56-kilobit modem to allow for online gaming over the Internet. By late-2000, Sega had sold around 6 million Dreamcasts worldwide, accounting for about 15% of console sales since its launch. Sega nurtured Dreamcast sales by courting outside software developers who helped develop new games, including Crazy Taxi, Resident Evil, and Quake III Arena. The company had a goal of shipping 10 million units by March 2001, a goal it never reached.[42]

Despite its position as first mover with a 128-bit machine, and despite solid technical reviews, by late-2000 the company was struggling. Sega was handicapped first by product shortages due to constraints on the supply of component parts and then by a lack of demand as consumers waited to see whether Sony's 128 bit offering, the much anticipated PlayStation 2 (PS2), would be a more attractive machine. In September 2000, Sega responded to the impending U.S. launch of Sony's PS2 by cutting the price for its console from $199 to $149. Then in late-October, Sega announced that, due to this price cut, it would probably lose over $200 million for the fiscal year ending March 2001.[43]

Sony's PlayStation 2

PlayStation 2 was launched in Japan in mid-2000 and in the United States at the end of October 2000. Initially priced at $299, PlayStation 2 is a powerful machine. At its core was a 300-megahertz graphics processing chip that was jointly developed with Toshiba and consumed about $1.3 billion in R&D. Referred to as the Emotion Engine processor, the chip allows the machine to display stunning graphic images previously found only on supercomputers. The chip made the PlayStation 2 the most powerful video game machine yet.

The machine was set up to play different CD and DVD formats, as well as proprietary game titles. As is true with the original PlayStation, PlayStation 2 could play audio CDs. The system was also compatible with the original PlayStation: any PlayStation title could be played on the PlayStation 2. To help justify the initial price tag, the unit doubled as a DVD player with picture quality as good as current players. The PlayStation 2 did not come equipped with a modem,

but it did have networking capabilities and a modem could be attached using one of two USB ports.[44]

Nintendo GameCube

Nintendo had garnered a solid position in the industry with its N64 machine by focusing on its core demographic, 7- to 12-year-olds. In 1999, Nintendo took 33% of the hardware market and 28% of the game market. Nintendo's next generation video game machine, GameCube, packed a modem and a powerful 400-megahertz, 128-bit processor made by IBM into a compact cube. GameCube marked a shift away from Nintendo's traditional approach of using proprietary cartridges to hold game software. Instead, software for the new player came on 8-cm compact disks, which are smaller than music compact disks. The disks held 1.5 gigabytes of data each, far greater storage capacity than the old game cartridges. Players could control GameCube using wireless controllers.[45]

Nintendo tried to make the GameCube easy for developers to work with rather than focusing on raw peak performance. While developers no doubt appreciated this, by the time GameCube hits store shelves in late-2001, PlayStation 2 had been on the market for eighteen months and boasted a solid library of games. Despite its strong brand and instantly recognized intellectual property which included Donkey Kong, Super Mario Brothers, and the Pokemon characters, Nintendo was playing catch up to Sony. Moreover, another new entrant into the industry launched its 128-bit offering at around the same time; Microsoft.

Microsoft's Xbox

Microsoft was first rumored to be developing a video game console in late-1999. In March 2000, Bill Gates made it official when he announced that Microsoft would enter the home video game market in fall 2001 with a console code named Xbox. In terms of sheer computing power, the 128-bit Xbox had the edge over competitors. Xbox had a 733-megahertz Pentium III processor, a high-powered graphics chip from NVIDIA Corp, a built-in broadband cable modem to allow for online game playing and high-speed Internet browsing, 64 megabytes of memory, CD and DVD drives, and an internal hard disk drive. The operating system was a stripped-down version of its popular Windows system optimized for graphics-processing capabilities. Microsoft claimed that because the Xbox was based on familiar PC technology, it would be much easier for software developers to write games for, and it would be relatively easy to convert games from the PC to run on the Xbox.[46]

Although Microsoft was a new entrant to the video game industry, it was no stranger to games. Microsoft had long participated in the PC gaming industry and was one of the largest publishers of PC games, with hits such as "Microsoft Flight Simulator" and "Age of Empires I" and "II" to its credits. Sales of Microsoft's PC games have increased 5% annually between 1998 and 2001, and the company controlled about 10% of the PC game market in 2001. Microsoft had also offered online gaming for some time, including its popular MSN Gaming Zone site. Started in 1996, by 2001 the Website had become the largest online PC gaming hub on the Internet with nearly 12 million subscribers pay $9.95 a month to play premium games such as Asheron's Call or Fighter Ace. Nor is Microsoft new to hardware; its joysticks and game pads outsell all other brands and it has an important mouse business.

To build the Xbox, Microsoft chose Flextronics, a contract manufacturer that already made computer mice for Microsoft. Realizing that it would probably have to cut Xbox prices over time, Microsoft guaranteed Flextronics a profit margin, effectively agreeing to subsidize Flextronics if selling prices fell below a specified amount. By 2003, Microsoft was thought to be losing $100 on every Xbox sold. To make that back and turn a profit, Microsoft reportedly had to sell between 6 and 9 video games per Xbox.[47]

Analysts speculated that Microsoft's entry into the home video game market was a response to a potential threat from Sony. Microsoft was worried that Internet-ready consoles like PlayStation 2 might take over many Web-browsing functions from the personal computer. Some in the company described Internet-enabled video game terminals as Trojan horses in the living room. In Microsoft's calculation, it made sense to get in the market to try and keep Sony and others in check. With annual revenues in excess of $20 billion worldwide, the home video game market is huge and an important source of potential growth for Microsoft. Still, by moving away from its core market, Microsoft was taking a big risk, particularly given the scale of investments

required to develop the Xbox, reported to run as high as $1.5 billion.

Mortal Combat: Microsoft versus Sony

The launch of Xbox and Game Cube helped propel sales of video game hardware and software to a record $9.4 billion in 2001, up from $6.58 billion in 2000. Although both Xbox and Nintendo initially racked up strong sales, the momentum started to slow significantly in 2002. Microsoft in particular, found it very difficult to penetrate the Japanese market. By September 2002, Sony had sold 11.2 million units of PS2 in the United States, versus 2.2 million units of Xbox, and 2.7 million units of Nintendo's game Cube. Unable to hold onto market share in the wake of the new competition, Sega withdrew from the console market, announcing that henceforth, it would focus just on developing games for other platforms.

In June 2002, Sony responded to the new entry by cutting the price for PS2 from $299 to $199. Microsoft quickly followed, cutting the price for Xbox from $299 to $199, while Nintendo cut its price from $299 to $149.[48] A year later, Sony cut prices again, this time to $179 a console. Again, Microsoft followed with a similar price cut, and in March 2004 it took the lead, cutting Xbox prices to $149. Sony followed suit two months later.[49]

Microsoft's strategy, however, involved far more than just cutting prices. In November 2002, Microsoft announced that it would introduce a new service for gamers, Xbox Live. For $50 a year, Xbox Live subscribers with broadband connections would be able to play online enabled versions of Xbox games with other online subscribers. To support Xbox Live, Microsoft invested some $500 million in its own data centers to host online game playing.

Online game playing was clearly a strategic priority from the outset. Unlike the PS2 and Game Cube, Xbox came with a built in broadband capability. The decision to make the Xbox broadband capable was made back in 1999, when less than 5% of U.S. homes were linked to the Internet with a broadband connection. Explaining the decision to build broadband capabilities into the Xbox at a time when rivals lacked them, the head of Xbox, Jay Allard, noted that "my attitude has always been to bet on the future, not against it."[50] While Sony's PS2 can be hooked up to the Internet via a broadband connection, doing so requires purchase of a special network adapter for $40.

By mid-2003 Xbox Live had some 500,000 subscribers, versus 80,000 who had registered to play PlayStation 2 games online. By this point, there were 28 online games for Xbox, and 18 for PS2. By January 2004, the comparative figures stood at 50 for Microsoft and 32 for Sony. By mid-2004, Xbox live reportedly had over one million subscribers, with Sony claiming a similar number of online players.[51] In May 2004, Microsoft struck a deal with Electronic Arts, the world's largest video game publisher, to bring EA games, including its best selling Madden Football, to the Xbox live platform. Until this point, EA had only produced live games for Sony's platform.

In spite of all these strategic moves, by late-2004 Xbox was still a distant second of PS2 in the video game market having sold 14 million consoles against Sony's 70 million (Nintendo had sold 13 million Game Cube consoles by this point). While Sony was making good money from the business, Microsoft was registering significant losses. In fiscal 2004, Microsoft's home & entertainment division, of which Xbox is the major component registered $2.45 billion in revenues, but lost $1.135 billion. By way of contrast, Sony's game division had $7.5 billion of sales in fiscal 2004 and generated operating profits of $640 million.

Microsoft, however, indicated that it was in the business for the long term. In late-2004, the company got a boost from the release of "Halo 2," the sequel to Halo, one of its best selling games. As first day sales for Halo 2 were totaled up, executives at Sony had to be worried. Microsoft announced that Halo 2 had sales of $125 million in its first 24-hours on the market in the United States and Canada, an industry record. These figures represented sales of 2.38 million units, and put Halo 2 firmly on track to be one of the biggest video games ever with a shot at surpassing Nintendo's "Super Mario 64," which had sold $308 million in the U.S. since its September 1996 debut. Moreover, the company was rumored to be ahead of Sony by as much as a year to bring the next generation video game console to market. In late-2004, reports suggest that Xbox 2 would be on the market in time for the 2005 Christmas season, probably a full year ahead of Sony's PlayStation 3. Sony was rumored to be running into technical problems as it tries to develop PlayStation 3.[52]

The Next Generation

As the battle between PS2 and Xbox drew to a close, it was clear that clear that Sony was the big winner. From 2001 through the Fall of 2006, when Play Station 3 (PS3) hit the market, Sony had sold around 110 million PS2 consoles, versus 25 million for Microsoft's Xbox and 21 million for Nintendo's Game Cube.[53] Sony's advantage is installed base translated into a huge lead in number of games sold—some 1.08 billion for PS2 by mid-2006, versus 200 million for the Xbox.[54] With the console companies reportedly making an average royalty on third party software of $8 per game sold, the financial implications of Sony's lead with PS2 are obvious.[55] Indeed, in 2005, Sony's games division contributed to 6.24% of the company's total revenue, but 38% of operating profit. In contrast, Microsoft's home and entertainment division lost $4 billion between the launch of Xbox and mid-2006.

However, by 2006 this was all history. In November 2005, Microsoft introduced its next generation machine, Xbox 360, beating Sony and Nintendo to the market by a solid year. The Xbox 360 represented a big technological advance over the original Xbox. To deliver improved picture quality, the Xbox 360 could execute 500 million polygons/sec—a four-fold increase over the Xbox. The main microprocessor was 13 times faster than the chip in the Xbox. Xbox 360 had 512 megabytes of memory, an 8-fold increase, and a 20 gigabyte hard drive, 2.5 times bigger than that found on the Xbox. Xbox 360 is of course, enabled for a broadband connection to the Internet.

Flextronics and Wistron two contract manufacturers (a third started production after launch) made the machine. Priced at $299, Xbox 360 was sold at a loss. The cost for making Xbox 360 was estimated to be as high as $500 at launch, falling to $350 by late-2006. Microsoft's goal was to ultimately break even on sales of the hardware as manufacturing efficiencies drove down unit costs.

To seed the market with games, Microsoft took a number of steps. Taking a page out of its Windows business, Microsoft provided game developers with tools designed to automate many of the key software programming tasks and reduce development time and costs. The company had also expanded its own in-house game studios, in part by purchasing several independent game developers including Bungie Studios, makers of Halo. This strategy enabled

Microsoft to offer exclusive content for the Xbox 360, something that third party developers were reluctant to do.

With the costs of game development increasing to between $10–15 million for more complex games, and development time stretching out to between 24 and 36 months, Microsoft also had to provide and inducement to get third party developers onboard. Although details of royalty terms are kept private, it is believed that Microsoft offered very low royalty rates, and perhaps even zero royalties, for a specified period of times to game developers who committed early to Xbox 360. One of those to commit early was Electronic Arts, the leading independent game development company, which reportedly budgeted as much as $200 million to develop some 25 versions of its best selling games, such as its sports games, for Xbox 360. Microsoft itself budgeted a similar amount to develop its own games.[56]

In the event, some 18 games were available for the November 2005 launch of Xbox 360, and by the end of 2006, this figure had increased to around 160. "Halo 3," which was expected to be one of the biggest games for Xbox 360, was released in September 2007. Exclusive to the Xbox 360, Halo 3 racked in first day sales of $170 million, which was an industry record. "Grand Theft Auto 4," the most popular franchise on PS2, was also launched simultaneously for both Xbox 360 and PS3 in 2007—a major coup for Microsoft.

The initial launch of Xbox 360 was marred by shortages of key components, which limited the number of machines that Microsoft could bring to market. Had Sony been on time with its launch of PS3, this could have been a serious error, but Sony delayed its launch of PS3, first until Spring of 2006, and then to November 2006. By the time Sony launched PS3 in November 2006, some 6 million Xbox 360 consoles had been sold, and Microsoft was predicting sales of 10 million by the end of 2006.

As with Xbox, Microsoft is pushing Xbox Live with Xbox 360. The company invested as much as $1 billion in Live from its inception. By late-2006, Microsoft was claiming that some 60% of Xbox 360 customers had also signed on for Xbox Live and that the service 4 million subscribers. By early-2008 there were over 10 million subscribers. Xbox Live allows games to play against each other online, and to download digital content from Xbox Live

Marketplace. Looking forward, there is little doubt that Microsoft sees Xbox Live as a critical element of its strategy, enabling Xbox owners to download any digital content—games, film, music—onto their consoles, which could become the hub of a home digital entertainment system.

The business model for Xbox 360 depends upon the number of games sold per console, the percentage of console owners who sign up for Xbox Live, sales of hardware accessories (e.g., controllers, an HD-DVD drive, wireless networking adapter), and the console itself achieving break even production costs. Reports suggest that Microsoft will breakeven if each console owners buys 6–7 games, 2–3 accessories, and if some 10 million sign on to Xbox Live (Microsoft splits Xbox Live revenues with game developers). By the end of 2006, it was estimated that some 33 million games had been sold for Xbox 360.[57]

Sony finally introduced PS3 on November 11 in Japan, and on November 17 in the United States. The delay in the launch of PS3 was due to Sony; decision to bundle a Blu-ray drive with PS3, and problems developing the "cell" processor that sits at the core of the PS3. Blu-ray is Sony's proprietary high definition DVD format. The company is currently locked in a format war with Toshiba, which is pushing its rival HD-DVD format (which can be purchased as an accessory for the Xbox 360). Sony has argued that the combination of its cell processor and Blu-ray DVD drive will give PS3 a substantial performance edge over Xbox 360. While this is true in a technical sense (the Blu-ray discs have 5 times the storage capacity of the DVD discs for Xbox 360), few reviewers have noticed much in the way of difference from a game playing perspective—perhaps because few games were initially available that showed the true power of the PS3.

What is certain is that incorporating Blu-ray drives in the PS3 has significantly raised the costs of the PS3. Sony is selling its stand alone Blu-ray drives for $999, which suggests that the PS3, initially priced at between $500 and $600 depending upon configuration, is in a sense a subsidized Blu-ray player. Shortages of blue diodes, a critical component in high definition DVD drives, also limited supply of the PS3 after its launch. Only 93,000 PS3 players were available for the Japanese launch. At launch, there were some 20 games available for the PS3. Sony also announced its own Live offering to compete with Xbox Live and stated that it would be free to PS3 users.

Nintendo also joined the fray again. In November 2006, it launched its own next generation offering, Wii. When developing the Wii, Nintendo made a number of interesting strategic decisions. First, they decided not to compete with Microsoft and Sony on graphics processing power. Instead of developing a high powered machine crammed full of expensive custom built components, they used off-the-shelf components to assemble a much cheaper machine that could be sold at a much lower price point (the initial price was $250). While this machine did not offer the graphics processing capabilities of Xbox 360 or PS3, the games where cheaper to develop, around $5 million each as opposed to as much as $20 million for the PS3. Second, Nintendo decided to target a new demographic, indifferent people who had no interest in video games, as opposed to the stereotypical game player. Nintendo already had some evidence that this market could be tapped and that it was extremely lucrative. In 2004, Nintendo had introduced a game for its handheld player, the DS, that was aimed not at its core 7- to 12-year old demographic, but at much wider market. The game, "Brain Age," based on a brain training regime developed by a Japanese neuroscientist, was a huge hit in Japan, with sales of more than 12 million units. It made the DS a hit in such unlikely places as nursing homes. Third, rather than processing power, Nintendo decided to focus on developing a motion sensitive wireless controller that could detect arm and hand motions and transfer them to the screen. This enabled the development of interactive games, with players physically controlling the action on screen by moving their arms, whether by swinging an imaginary bat, driving a go kart, or slashing a sword through the air.[58]

By early-2007, it was clear that the Wii was turning into a surprise hit. The combination of low price, innovative design, and a portfolio of recognizable games based on Nintendo's long established franchises, such as Mario Brothers and Pokémon, helped to drive sales forward. Moreover, as planned, the Wii seemed to have appeal to a broad range of age groups and to both genders. Soon articles started to appear explaining how retirement homes were buying the Wii so that residents could play virtual baseball with their visiting grandchildren and sales stated to accelerate.

The Industry in 2010

As 2010 drew to a close, it was clear that the Wii had been the major success story of this generation of gaming consoles. Since their respective launches, the Wii had sold 74.5 million units, compared to 43.8 million for Xbox 360 and 38.7 million of PlayStation 3. Nintendo also had a strong lead in the popular handheld market, with 135 million units sold worldwide, compared to 60.5 million for the PSP, Sony's hand held game player (Microsoft did not have a hand held player).[59] On the other hand, a key to the success of a console is the number of games sold per box, and on this measure Xbox 360 had the best performance. After each console had been on the market for 29 months, Xbox had sold 7.5 games per box, compared to 6.5 for PlayStation and 6.2 for Nintendo. By October 2010, the ratio had risen to around 9.0 games per box for Xbox 360 (these figures are for the U.S. only).[60]

Total industry sales in the United States peaked in 2008 at $22.11 billion, before declining to $20.2 billion as the recession cut into demand (worldwide sales were $54 billion in 2008). Despite the recession, all three players in the market were profitable on an operating basis in 2009 and 2010. Worldwide sales are expected to exceed $60 billion in 2012. Both Microsoft and Sony had shot themselves in the foot with quality problems and component shortages early in the product cycle (Microsoft had to take a $1.05 billion write off in 2007 for replacing poor quality consoles), but were now performing well. Microsoft is predicting that this generation of console will last about 10 years, making it the longest generation ever.

Looking forward, and number of factors may change the industry. In November 2010 Microsoft released its response to Nintendo's motion sensor with a device known as Kinect. Kinect may fundamentally alter the way users interact with digital content. Kinect combines technologies such as body movement detection, facial recognition, and voice recognition, to let gamers use natural motions and voice to control games. The input device is a camera and depth sensor mounted on top of the TV. In essence, Kinect is a potentially revolutionary step forward in human machine interface design that could have implication that go way beyond video games. To start, Microsoft will use Kinect to go after the casual gamers with which Nintendo's Wii has been so successful.

As always with a new game technology, the success of Kinect will hinge crucially upon the quality of the games available. While it will take some time until games utilize the full power of Kinect, the early sales figures bode well for the device. Between launch and the start of March, 2011, Microsoft sold over 10 million Kinect devices, making it the fastest selling consumer electronics device of all time.[61]

Online gaming is also continuing to gain traction. Xbox Live has turned into a big hit for Microsoft and now has some 25 million subscribers who use it for everything from playing multiplayer games to streaming movies from Netflix and browsing Facebook. It is estimated that about 50% of Xbox Live subscribers are paying Gold Member subscribers. In fiscal 2009 (which ended June 30, 2010) Microsoft generated over $1.2 billion in revenues of Xbox Live subscriptions and services. This seems to be a growth engine going forward. Microsoft has announced the Xbox Live will be fully integrated into Windows 8, the next version of its Windows operating system now under development.

Interestingly enough, the largest multiplayer online game, however, has no connection with any of the console platforms. The "World of Warcraft," the massive multiplayer online game with 12 million paying subscribers and annual revenues in excess of $1.2 billion, making it the best-selling game of all time.

Endnotes

1 A good account of the early history of Bushnell and Atari can be found in S. Cohen, *Zap! The Rise and Fall of Atari* (New York: McGraw-Hill, 1984).

2 R. Isaacs, "Video Games Race to Catch a Changing Market," *Business Week,* December 26, 1977, 44B.

3 P. Pagnano, "Atari's Game Plan to Overwhelm Its Competitors," *Business Week,* May 8, 1978, 50F.

4 R. Isaacs, "Video Games Race to Catch a Changing Market," *Business Week,* December 26, 1977, 44B.

5 P. Pagnano, "Atari's Game Plan to Overwhelm Its Competitors," *Business Week,* May 8, 1978; D. Sheff, *Game Over* (New York: Random House, 1993).

6 S. Cohen, *Zap! The Rise and Fall of Atari* (New York: McGraw-Hill, 1984).

7 L. Kehoe, "Atari Seeks Way out of Video Game Woes," *Financial Times,* December 14, 1983, 23.

8 M. Schrage, "The High Tech Dinosaurs: Video Games, Once Ascendant, Are Making Way," *Washington Post,* July 31, 1983, F1.

9 D. Sheff, *Game Over* (New York: Random House, 1993).

10 Ibid.

11 Ibid.

12 D. Golden, "In Search of Princess Toadstool," *Boston Globe,* November 20, 1988, 18.

13 N. Gross and G. Lewis, "Here Come the Super Mario Bros.," *Business Week,* November 9, 1987, 138.

14 D. Sheff, *Game Over* (New York: Random House, 1993).

15 D. Golden, "In Search of Princess Toadstool," *Boston Globe,* November 20, 1988, 18.

16 Staff Reporter, "Marketer of the Year," *Adweek,* November 27, 1989, 15.

17 C. Lazzareschi, "No Mere Child's Play," *Los Angeles Times,* December 16, 1988, 1.

18 For a good summary of the early history of Sega, see J. Battle and B. Johnstone, "The Next Level: Sega's Plans for World Domination," *Wired,* Release 1.06, December 1993.

19 D. Sheff, *Game Over* (New York: Random House, 1993).

20 J. Battle and B. Johnstone, "The Next Level: Sega's Plans for World Domination," *Wired,* Release 1.06, December 1993.

21 For background details, see J. Flower, "3DO: Hip or Hype?" *Wired,* Release 1.02, May/June 1993.

22 R. Brandt, "3DO's New Game Player: Awesome or Another Betamax?" *Business Week,* January 11, 1993, 38.

23 J. Flower, "3DO: Hip or Hype?" *Wired,* Release 1.02, May/June 1993.

24 S. Jacobs, "Third Time's a Charm (They Hope)," *Wired,* Release 2.01, January 1994.

25 A. Dunkin, "Video Games: The Next Generation," *Business Week,* January 31, 1994, 80.

26 J. Greenstein, "No Clear Winners, Though Some Losers; The Video Game Industry in 1995," *Business Week,* December 22, 1995, 42.

27 Staff Reporter, "3DO Says 'I Do' on Major Shift of Its Game Strategy," *Los Angeles Times,* September 17, 1996, 2.

28 S. Taves, "Meet Your New Playmate," *Wired,* Release 3.09, September 1995.

29 I. Kunni, "The Games Sony Plays," *Business Week,* June 15, 1998, 128.

30 C. Platt, "WordNerd," *Wired,* Release 3.10, October 1995.

31 I. Kunni, "The Games Sony Plays," *Business Week,* June 15, 1998, 128.

32 J.A. Trachtenberg, "Race Quits Sony Just Before U.S. Rollout of Its PlayStation Video-Game System," *Wall Street Journal,* August 8, 1995, B3.

33 S. Beenstock, "Market Raider: How Sony Won the Console Game," *Marketing,* September 10, 1998, 26.

34 J.A. Trachtenberg, "Olafsson Calls It Quits as Chairman of Sony's Technology Strategy Group," *Wall Street Journal,* January 23, 1996, B6.

35 J. Greenstein, "Price Cuts Boost Saturn, Playstation Hardware Sales," *Video Business,* May 31, 1996, 1.

36 J. Greenstein, "Sony Cuts Prices of Playstation Hardware," *Video Business,* March 10, 1997, 1.

37 D. Hamilton, "Sega Suddenly Finds Itself Embattled," *Wall Street Journal,* March 31, 1997, A10.

38 Staff Reporter, "Nintendo Wakes Up," *The Economist,* August 3, 1996, 55–56.

39 D. Takahashi, "Game Plan: Video Game Makers See Soaring Sales Now—And Lots of Trouble Ahead," *Wall Street Journal,* June 15, 1998, R10.

40 D. Takahashi, "Sony and Nintendo Battle for Kids Under 13," *Wall Street Journal,* September 24, 1998, B4.

41 I. Kunni, "The Games Sony Plays," *Business Week,* June 15, 1998, 128.

42 R.A. Guth, "Sega Cites Dreamcast Price Cuts for Loss Amid Crucial Time for Survival of Firm," *Wall Street Journal,* October 30, 2000, A22.

43 Ibid.

44 T. Oxford and S. Steinberg, "Ultimate Game Machine Sony's PlayStation 2 Is Due on Shelves Oct. 26. It Brims with Potential—But at This Point Sega's Dreamcast Appears a Tough Competitor," *Atlanta Journal/Atlanta Constitution,* October 1, 2000, P1.

45 R.A. Guth, "New Players from Nintendo Will Link to Web," *Wall Street Journal,* August 25, 2000, B1.

46 D. Takahashi, "Microsoft's X-Box Impresses Game Developers," *Wall Street Journal,* March 13, 2000, B12.

47 K. Powers, "Showdown," *Forbes,* August 11, 2003, 86–87.

48 *The Economist,* "Console Wars," *The Economist,* June 22, 2002, 71.

49 R.A. Guth, "Game Gambit: Microsoft to Cut Xbox Price," *Wall Street Journal,* March 19, 2004, B1.

50 K. Powers, "Showdown," *Forbes,* August 11, 2003, 86–87.

51 E. Taub, "No Longer a Solitary Pursuit: Video Games Move Online," *New York Times,* July 5, 2004, C4.

52 J. Greene and C. Edwards, "Microsoft Plays Video Leapfrog," *Business Week,* May 10, 2004, 44–45.

53 "Playing a Long Game," *The Economist,* November 18, 2006, 63–65.

54 B. Thill, "Micrsoft: Gat Game? Update on Vista, Xbox and the Tender," *Citigroup Capital Markets,* August 30, 2006.

55 Ibid.

56 D. Takahashi, "The Xbox 360 Uncloaked," *Spider Works,* 2006.

57 B. Thill, "Micrsoft: Gat Game? Update on Vista, Xbox and the Tender," *Citigroup Capital Markets,* August 30, 2006.

58 J.M. O'Brian and C. Tkaczyk, "Wii Will Rock You," *Fortune,* June 11, 2007, 82–92.

59 D. Takahashi, "The Video Game Console War Could End in a Three-Way Tie," June 9, 2010, Venturebeat.com.

60 M. Matthews, "Console Tie Rations Reveal Market Dynamics," April 22, 2009, http://www.gamasutra.com

61 S. Kessler, "Microsoft Kinect Sales Top 10 Million," *Mashable,* March 9, 2011.

CASE 2

How SAP's Business Model and Strategies Made it the Global Business Software Leader—Part 1

Gareth R. Jones
Texas A&M University

In 1972, after the project they were working on for IBM's German subsidiary was abandoned, 5 German IBM computer analysts left the company and founded Systems Applications and Products in Data Processing, known today as SAP. These analysts had been involved in the provisional design of a software program that would allow information about cross-functional and cross-divisional financial transactions in a company's value chain to be coordinated and processed centrally—resulting in enormous savings in time and expense. They observed that other software companies were also developing software designed to integrate across value-chain activities and subunits. Using borrowed money and equipment, the 5 analysts worked day and night to create an accounting software platform that could integrate across all the parts of an entire corporation. In 1973, SAP unveiled an instantaneous accounting transaction processing program called R/1, one of the earliest examples of what is now called an enterprise resource planning (ERP) system.

Today, ERP is an industry term for the multimodule applications software that allows a company to manage the set of activities and transactions necessary to manage the business processes for moving a product from the input stage, along the value chain, and to the final customer. As such, ERP systems can recognize, monitor, measure, and evaluate all the transactions involved in business processes such as product planning, the purchasing of inputs from suppliers, the manufacturing process, inventory and order processing, and customer service. Essentially, a fully developed ERP system provides a company with a standardized information technology (IT) platform that provides managers with complete information about all aspects of its business processes and cost structure across all functions and divisions. This allows managers at all levels to (1) continually search for ways to perform these processes more efficiently and lower its cost structure, and (2) improve and service its products and raise their value to customers. For example, ERP systems provide information that allows for the redesign of products to better match customer needs and that result in superior responsiveness to customers.

To give one example, Nestlé installed SAP's newest ERP software across its more than 150 U.S. food divisions in the 2000s. Using its new IT platform, corporate managers discovered that each division was paying a different price for the same flavoring—vanilla. The same small set of vanilla suppliers was charging each individual division as much as they could, and different divisions paid prices that varied widely depending upon their bargaining power with the supplier. Before the SAP system was installed, corporate managers had no idea this was happening because their old IT system could not compare and measure the same transaction—purchasing vanilla—across divisions. SAP's standardized cross-company software platform revealed this problem, and hundreds of thousands of dollars in cost savings were achieved by solving this one transaction difficulty alone. This is why ERP systems can save large companies hundreds of millions and billions of dollars over time, and explains why SAP's ERP became so popular.

Focus on Large Multinationals

SAP first focused its R/1 software on the largest multinational companies with revenues of at least $2.5 billion because they would reap the biggest cost savings there. Although relatively few in number, these companies, mostly large global product manufacturers stood to gain the most benefit from ERP, and they were willing to pay SAP a premium price for its product. Its focus on this influential niche of companies helped SAP develop a global base of leading companies. Its goal, as it had been from the beginning, was to create the global industry standard for ERP by providing the best business applications software infrastructure—and it succeeded in 2011—it still has the largest installed base of the world's most well-known companies.

ERP and Consulting

In its first years, SAP not only developed ERP software, but it also used its own internal consultants to physically install it on-site at its customers' corporate IT centers, manufacturing operations, and similar locations. Determined to increase its customer base quickly, however, SAP switched strategies in the 1980s. It decided to focus primarily upon the development of its ERP software and to outsource (to external consultants), more and more of the highly complex implementation consulting services needed to install and service its software on-site in a particular company. It formed a series of strategic alliances with major global consulting companies such as IBM, Accenture, and Cap Gemini to install its R/1 system in its growing base of global customers.

ERP installation can often be a long and complicated process. A company cannot simply adapt its information systems to fit SAP's software; it must rework the way it performs its value-chain activities so that its business processes—and the IT system that measures and evaluates these business processes—can become compatible with SAP's software. SAP's claim to fame was that by modeling its business processes on its ERP platform, which contains the solutions needed to achieve best industry practices across its operations, a large company could expect a substantial increase—often 10% or more in performance. However, the more a particular company's managers wanted to customize the SAP platform to

fit their own internal business processes, the more difficult and expensive the implementation process would become—and the harder it would, in turn, become for companies to realize the potential gains from cost savings and value added to the product by SAP's software.

SAP's outsourcing consulting strategy allowed it to penetrate global markets quickly and eliminated the huge capital investment needed to employ the thousands of consultants required to provide this service on a global basis. On the other hand, for consulting companies, the installation of SAP's popular software became a major money-spinner and they earned billions by learning how to install its ERP system. Consequently, SAP did not enjoy the huge revenue streams associated with providing software consulting services, such as the design, installation, and maintenance of an ERP platform on an ongoing basis. It earned only a small amount of revenue by training external consultants in the intricacies of how to install, customize, and maintain its ERP systems within its customer base. This was a major error because revenues from consulting over time are often as great as that those that can be earned from selling complex software applications. By focusing on ERP software development, SAP could forfeit high consulting profits and also become dependent upon consulting companies that were now the experts in the installation/customization arena—such as Accenture and IBM.

The Changing Global Landscape

This decision had unfortunate long-term consequences because SAP began to lose first-hand knowledge of its customers' emerging problems and an understanding of the changing needs of its customers—something especially important as growing global competition, outsourcing, and the increasing use of the Internet to facilitate cross-company commerce had become major competitive factors changing the ERP industry and software applications market. For a company with a goal to provide a standardized platform across functions and divisions, this outsourcing consulting strategy seemed like a major error to many analysts. SAP's failure to work quickly to expand its own consulting operations to run parallel to those of external consultants, rather than providing a training service to these consultants to keep them informed about its constantly changing ERP software, left the door open for IBM and Accenture to dominate the software consulting industry—and they still do today.

To some degree, SAPs decision to focus upon software development and outsource more than 80% of installation was a consequence of its German founders' "engineering" mindset. Founded by computer program engineers, SAP's culture was built upon values and norms that emphasized technical innovation, and the development of leading-edge ERP software algorithms and best practices. SAP's managers poured most of its profits into research and development (R&D) to fund new projects that would increase its ERP platform's capabilities; they had little desire to spend money on developing its consulting services. Essentially, SAP became a *product-focused*, not a customer–focused company since it believed R&D would produce the technical advances that would be the source of its competitive advantage and allow it to charge its customers a premium price for its ERP platform. By 1990, SAP spent more than 30% of gross sales on R&D.

Global Sales and Marketing Problems

SAP's top managers, who had focused on developing its technical competency, had another unfortunate consequence. They underestimated the enormous problems involved in developing and implementing its global marketing and sales competency to increase its large customer base—and to attract new kinds of customers—especially smaller companies. The need to build an efficient global structure and control system to effectively manage its own operations was largely ignored because managers believed the ERP platform would sell itself! Indeed, SAP's focus on R&D and neglect of its other functions made its sales, marketing, and internal consultants and training experts feel as if they were second-class citizens—despite the fact that they brought in new business and were the people responsible maintaining good relationships with SAP's growing customer base.

The classic problem of managing a growing business from the entrepreneurial to the professional management phase was emerging in SAP and its revenues and profits were slowing as a result. SAP's top managers were not experienced business managers

who understood the problems of implementing a rapidly growing company's strategy on a global basis; the need to develop a sound corporate infrastructure was being shoved aside—something that had cost it billions of dollars in lost profits over the decades.

The Second Generation R/2 ERP Platform

In 1981, SAP introduced its second-generation ERP software, R/2. Not only did it contain many more value-chain/business process software modules, but it also linked its ERP software seamlessly to the existing or legacy databases and communication systems used on a company's mainframe computers. This allowed for greater connectivity and ease of use of ERP throughout a company at all levels and across all subunits. The R/1 platform had largely been a cross-organizational accounting/financial software module; the new software modules could handle procurement, product development, and inventory and order tracking. Of course, these additional components needed to be compatible with one another so that they could be seamlessly integrated together on-site, at a customer's operations, and with its existing or legacy IT system.

SAP did not develop its own database management software package; its system was designed to be compatible with Oracle's database management software, the global leader in this segment of the software applications industry. Once again, this would have repercussions later, when Oracle began to rapidly develop its own ERP software platform during the 2000s, essentially moving from database software into ERP and other kinds of business software applications. As part of its push to make its R/2 software the global industry standard for the next decades, SAP also developed new "middleware" software that will allow the hardware and software made by different global computer companies to work seamlessly together on any particular company's IT system. This is also an industry in which Oracle competes.

Recognizing that the way value-chain activities and business processes are performed differs *from industry to industry* because of differences in manufacturing and other business processes. SAP also spent a lot of time and money customizing its basic

ERP platform to accommodate the needs of companies in different kinds of industries. Increasingly, over time, ERP companies recognized that their long-term competitive advantage depended upon being able to provide the ERP software solutions that must be customized by industry to perform most effectively. Its push to become the ERP leader across industries, across all large global companies, and across all value-chain business processes required a huge R&D investment.

SAP Becomes a Global Leader

In 1988, SAP went public on the Frankfurt stock exchange to raise the necessary cash to fund its growing global operations, and by 1990, it had become a global leader of business applications software as its market capitalization soared. SAP now dominated ERP software sales in the high-tech and electronics, engineering and construction, consumer products, chemical, and retail industries. Its product was increasingly being recognized as superior to the other ERP software being developed by companies such as PeopleSoft, S. D. Edwards, and Oracle. The main reason for SAP's increasing competitive advantage was that it was the only company that could offer a potential customer a broad, standardized, state-of-the-art solution that spanned a wide variety of value-chain activities spread around the globe. By contrast, its competitors, like PeopleSoft, offered more-focused solutions aimed at one business process, such as human resources management.

SAP Introduces the R/3 Solution

SAP's continuing massive investment in developing new ERP software resulted in the introduction of its R/3, or third-generation, ERP solution in 1992. Essentially, the R/3 platform expanded upon its previous solutions; it offered seamless, real-time integration for over 80% of a company's business processes. It had also embedded in the platform hundreds, and then thousands, of industry best practice solutions, or templates, that customers could use to improve their operations and processes. The R/3 system was initially composed of seven different modules corresponding to the most common business processes: production planning, materials management, financial accounting, asset management, human resources management, project systems, and sales and distribution. R/3 was designed to meet the diverse demands of its previous global clients. It could operate in multiple languages, convert exchange rates, and additional functions, on a real-time basis.

By the 1990s, however, as it now dominated the ERP market for large companies, SAP realized that for its sales to expand quickly it also needed to address the needs of small- and medium-sized businesses (SMBs). Recognizing the huge potential revenues to be earned from SMB customers, SAP's engineers designed the R/3 platform so that it could be configured for smaller customers as well as customized to suit the needs of a broader range of industries in which they competed. Furthermore, SAP designed R/3 to be "open architecturally," meaning that using its middleware, the R/3 could operate with whatever kind of computer hardware or software (the legacy system) a SMB was presently using.

Finally, in response to customer concerns that SAP's standardized system meant huge implementation problems in changing their business processes to match SAP's standardized solution, SAP introduced some limited customization opportunity into its software. Using specialized software from other companies, SAP claimed that up to 20% of R/3 could now be customized to work with the company's existing operating methods and thus would reduce the problems of learning and implementing the new system. However, the costs of doing this were extremely high and became a huge generator of fees for consulting companies. SAP used a variable-fee licensing system for its R/3 system; the cost to the customer was based upon the number of users within a company, upon the number of different R/3 modules that were installed, and upon the degree to which users utilized these modules in the business planning process.

SAP's R/3 far outperformed its competitors' products in a technical sense and once again allowed it to charge a premium price for its new software. Believing that competitors would take at least 2 years to catch up, SAP's goal was to get its current customers to switch to its new product and then rapidly build its customer base to penetrate the growing ERP market. In doing so, it was also seeking to establish R/3 as the new ERP market standard in order to lock in customers before competitors could offer viable alternatives. This strategy was vital to its future success because, because of the way an ERP system changes the nature of a customer's business processes once it is installed and running; there are high switching costs involved in moving to another ERP product, costs that customers want to avoid.

SAP's Growing Global Implementation Problems

R/3's growing popularity led SAP to decentralize more and more control of the marketing, sale, and installation of its software on a global basis to its overseas subsidiaries. While its R&D and software development remained centralized in Germany, it began to open wholly-owned subsidiaries in most major country's markets. By 1995, it had 18 national subsidiaries; today, it has over 50. In 1995, SAP established a U.S. subsidiary to drive sales in the huge and most profitable market—the U.S. market. Its German top managers set the subsidiary a goal of achieving $1 billion in revenues within 5 years. To implement this aggressive growth strategy, and given that R/3 software needs to be installed and customized to suit the needs of particular companies and industries, several different regional SAP divisions were created to manage the needs of companies and industries in different U.S. regions. Also, the regional divisions became responsible for training an army of both internal and external consultants on how to install and customize the R/3 software. For every internal lead SAP consultant, there were soon about 9–10 external consultants working with SAP's customers to install and modify the software—which again boosted IBM and Accenture's profits.

Problems with its U.S. Operations

The problems with its policy of decentralization soon caught up with SAP, however. Because SAP was growing so fast, and demand for its product was increasing so rapidly, it was hard to provide the thorough training consultants needed to perform the installation of its software. Often, once SAP had trained an internal consultant, that consultant would leave to join the company for which he or she was performing the work, or even to start an industry-specific SAP consulting practice! The result was that

SAP customers' needs were being poorly served and the number of complaints about the cost and difficulty of installing its ERP software was increasing. Since large external consulting companies made their money based upon the time it took their consultants to install a particular SAP system, many customers complained that consultants were deliberately taking too long to implement the new software to maximize their earnings and were even pushing inappropriate or unnecessary R/3 modules. For example, Chevron spent over $100 million and 2 years installing and getting its R/3 system operating effectively. In one well-publicized case, FoxMeyer Drug blamed SAP software for the supply chain problems that led to its bankruptcy and the company's major creditors, and sued SAP alleging that the company had promised R/3 would do more than it could. SAP responded that the problem was not the software but the way the company had installed it, but SAP's reputation was harmed nevertheless.

SAP's policy of decentralization was also somewhat paradoxical because the company's mission was to supply software that linked functions and divisions rather than separated them, and the characteristic problems of too much decentralization of authority soon became evident throughout SAP. In its U.S. subsidiary, each regional SAP division started developing its own procedures for pricing SAP software, offering discounts, dealing with customer complaints, and even rewarding its employees and consultants. There was a complete lack of standardization and integration inside SAP America and between SAP's many foreign subsidiaries and their headquarters in Germany. This meant that little learning was taking place between divisions or consultants, there was no monitoring or coordination mechanism in place to share SAP's *own* best practices between its consultants and divisions, and organizing by region in the U. S. was doing little to build core competences. For example, analysts were asking: "If R/3 has to be customized to suit the needs of a particular industry, why didn't SAP use a market structure and divide its activities by the needs of customers based in different industries?" These problems slowed down the process of implementing SAP software and prevented quick and effective responses to the needs of potential customers.

SAP's R/3 was also criticized as being too standardized because it forced all companies to adapt to what SAP had decided were best industry practices.

When consultants reconfigured the software to suit a particular company's needs, this process often took a long time, and sometimes the system did not perform as well as had been expected. Many companies felt that the software should be configured to suit their business processes and not the other way around, but again SAP argued that such a setup would not lead to an optimal outcome. For example, SAP's retail R/3 system could not handle Home Depot's policy of allowing each of its stores to order directly from suppliers, based upon centrally negotiated contracts between Home Depot and those suppliers. SAP's customers also found that supporting their new ERP platform was expensive and that ongoing support cost 3–5 times as much as the actual purchase of the software, although the benefits they received from its R/3 system usually substantially exceeded these costs.

The Changing Industry Environment

Although the United States had become SAP's biggest market, the explosive growth in demand for SAP's software had begun to slump by 1995. Competitors such as Oracle, Baan, PeopleSoft, and Marcum were catching up technically, often because they were focusing their resources on the needs of one or a few industries, or on a particular kind of ERP module (for example, PeopleSoft's focus on the human resources management module). Indeed SAP had to play catch-up in the HRM area and develop its own to offer a full suite of integrated business solutions. Oracle, the second largest software maker after Microsoft, was becoming a particular threat as it expanded its ERP offerings outward from its leading database knowledge systems and began to offer more and more of an Internet-based ERP platform. As new aggressive competitors emerged and changed the environment, SAP found it needed to change as well.

Competitors were increasing their market share by exploiting weaknesses in SAP's software. They began to offer SAP's existing and potential customers ERP modules that could be customized more easily to their situation and that were less expensive than SAP's. SAP's managers were forced to reevaluate their business model, and their strategies and the ways in which they implemented this model.

New Implementation Problems

To a large degree, SAP's decision to decentralize control of its marketing, sales, and installation to its subsidiaries was due to the way the company had operated from its beginnings. Its German founders had emphasized the importance of excellence in innovation as the root value of its culture, and SAP's culture was often described as "organized chaos." Its top managers had operated from the beginning by creating as flat a hierarchy as possible to create an internal environment where people could take risks and try new ideas of their own choosing. If mistakes occurred or projects didn't work out, employees were given the freedom to try a different approach. Hard work, teamwork, openness, and speed were the norms of their culture. Required meetings were rare and offices were frequently empty because most of the employees were concentrating on research and development. The pressure was on software developers to create superior products. In fact, the company was proud of the fact that it was product driven, not service oriented. It wanted to be the world's leading innovator of software, not a service company that installed it.

Increasing competition led SAP's managers to realize that they were not capitalizing on its main strength—its human resources. In 1997, it established a human resources management (HRM) department and gave it the responsibility to build a more formal organizational structure. Previously it had outsourced its own HRM. HRM managers started to develop job descriptions and job titles, and put in place a career structure that would motivate employees and keep them loyal to the company. They also put in place a reward system, which included stock options, to increase the loyalty of their technicians, who were being attracted away by competitors or were starting their own businesses because SAP did not then offer a future: a career path. For example, SAP sued Siebel Systems, a niche rival in the customer relationship software business, in 2000 for enticing 12 of its senior employees, who it said took trade secrets with them. SAP's top managers realized that they had to plan long term and that innovation by itself was not enough to make SAP a dominant global company with a sustainable competitive advantage.

At the same time that it started to operate more formally, it also became more centralized to encourage organizational learning and to promote the sharing of its own best implementation practices across divisions and subsidiaries. Its goal was to standardize the way each subsidiary or division operated across the company, thus making it easier to transfer people and knowledge where they were needed most. Not only would this facilitate cooperation, it would also reduce overhead costs, which were spiraling because of the need to recruit trained personnel as the company grew quickly and the need to alter and adapt its software to suit changing industry conditions. For example, increasing customer demands for additional customization of its software made it imperative that different teams of engineers pool their knowledge to reduce development costs, and that consultants should not only share their best practices, but also cooperate with engineers so that the latter could understand the problems facing customers in the field.

The need to adopt a more standardized and hierarchical approach was also being driven by SAP's growing recognition that it needed more of the stream of income it could get from both the training and installation sector of the software business. It began to increase the number of its consultants. By having its consultants work with SAP's software developers they became the acknowledged experts and leaders when it came to specific software installations and could command a high price. SAP also developed a large global training function to provide the extensive ERP training that consultants needed and charged both individuals and consulting companies high fees for attending these courses so that they would be able to work with the SAP platform. SAP's U.S. subsidiary also moved from a regional to a more market-based focus by re-aligning its divisions, not by geography, but by their focus on a particular sector or industry, for example, chemicals, electronics, pharmaceuticals, consumer products, and engineering.

Once again, however, the lines of authority between the new industry divisions and the software development, sales, installation, and training functions were not structured well enough, and the hoped-for gains from increased coordination and cooperation were slow to be realized. Globally, too, SAP was still highly decentralized and remained a product-focused company, thus allowing its subsidiaries to form their own sales, training, and installation policies. Its subsidiaries continued to form strategic alliances with global consulting companies,

allowing them to obtain the majority of revenues from servicing SAP's growing base of R/3 installations. SAP's top managers, with their engineering mindset, did not appreciate the difficulties involved in changing a company's structure and culture, either at the subsidiary or the global level. They were disappointed in the slow pace of change because their cost structure remained high, although their revenues were increasing.

New Strategic Problems

By the mid-1990s, despite its problems in implementing its strategy, SAP was the clear market leader in the ERP software industry and the 4th largest global software company because of its recognized competencies in the production of state-of-the-art ERP software. Several emerging problems posed major threats to its business model, however. First, it was becoming increasingly obvious that the development of the Internet and broadband technology would become important forces in shaping a company's business model and processes in the future. SAP's R/3 systems were specifically designed to integrate information about all of a company's value-chain activities, across its functions and divisions, and to provide real-time feedback on its ongoing performance. However, ERP systems focused principally on a company's internal business processes; they were not designed to focus and provide feedback on cross-company and industry-level transactions and processes on a real-time basis. The Internet was changing the way in which companies viewed their boundaries; the emergence of global e-commerce and online cross-company transactions was changing the nature of a company's business processes both at the input and output sides.

At the input side, the Internet was changing the way a company managed its relationships with its parts and raw materials suppliers. Internet-based commerce offered the opportunity of locating new, low-cost suppliers. Developing Web software was also making it much easier for a company to cooperate with suppliers and manufacturing companies and to outsource activities to specialists who could perform the activities at lower cost. A company that previously made its own inputs or manufactured its own products could now outsource these value-chain activities, which changed the nature of the ERP systems it needed to manage such transactions. In general, the changing nature of transactions across the company's boundaries could affect its ERP system in thousands of ways. Companies like Commerce One and Ariba, which offered this supply-chain management (SCM) software, were rapidly growing and posing a major threat to SAP's "closed" ERP software.

At the output side, the emergence of the Internet also radically altered the relationship between a company and its customers. Not only did the Internet make possible new ways to sell to wholesalers, its largest customers, or directly to individual customers, it also changed the whole nature of the company—customer interface. For example, using new customer relationship management (CRM) software from software developers like Siebel Systems, a company could offer its customers access to much more information about its products so that customers could make more-informed purchase decisions. A company could also understand customers' changing needs so it could develop improved or advanced products to meet those needs; and a company could offer a whole new way to manage after-sales service and help solve customers' problems with learning about, operating, and even repairing their new purchases. The CRM market was starting to boom.

In essence, the Internet was changing both industry- and company-level business processes and providing companies and entire industries with many more avenues for altering their business processes at a company or industry level, so that they could lower their cost structure or increasingly differentiate their products. Clearly, the hundreds of industry best practices that SAP had embedded in its R/3 software would become outdated and redundant as e-commerce increased in scope and depth, and offered improved industry solutions. SAP's R/3 system would become a dinosaur within a decade unless it could move quickly to develop or obtain competencies in the software skills needed to develop Web-based software.

These developments posed a severe shock to SAP's management, who had been proud of the fact that, until now, SAP had developed all its software internally. They were not alone in their predicament. The largest software companies, Microsoft and Oracle, had been caught unaware by the quickly growing implications of Web-based computing. The introduction of Netscape's Web browser had led to a collapse in Microsoft's stock price because investors saw Web-based computing, not PC-based computing, as the choice of the future. SAP's stock price also began to reflect the beliefs of many people that expensive, rigid, standardized ERP systems would not become the software choice as the Web developed. One source of SAP's competitive advantage was based on the high switching costs of moving from one ERP platform to another. However, if new Web-based platforms allowed both internal and external integration of a company's business processes, and new platforms could be more easily customized to answer a particular company's needs, these switching costs might disappear. SAP was at a critical point in its development.

The other side of the equation was that the emergence of new Web-based software technology allowed hundreds of new software industry start-ups, founded by technical experts equally as qualified as those at SAP and Microsoft, to enter the industry and compete for the wide-open Web-computing market. The race was on to determine which standards would apply in the new Web-computing arena, and who would control them. The large software makers like Microsoft, Oracle, IBM, SAP, Netscape, Sun Microsystems, and Computer Associates had to decide how to compete in this totally changed industry environment. Most of their customers, companies large and small, were still watching developments before deciding how and where to commit their IT budgets. Hundreds of billions of dollars in future software sales were at stake, and it was not clear which company had the competitive advantage in this changing environment.

Rivalry among major software makers in the new Web-based software market became intense. Rivalry between the major players and new players, like Netscape, Siebel Systems, Marcum, I2 Technology, and SSA, also intensified. The major software makers, each of which was a market leader in one or more segments of the software industry, such as SAP in ERP, Microsoft in PC software, and Oracle in database management software, sought to showcase their strengths to make their software compatible with Web-based technology. Thus, Microsoft strove to develop its Windows NT network-based platform and its Internet Explorer Web browser to compete with Netscape's Internet browser and Sun Microsystems' open-standard Java Web software programming language, which was compatible with any company's proprietary software, unlike Microsoft's NT.

SAP also had to deal with competition from large and small software companies that were breaking into the new Web-based ERP environment. In 1995, SAP teamed with Microsoft, Netscape, and Sun Microsystems to make its R/3 software Internet-compatible with any of their competing systems. Within one year, it introduced its R/3 Release 3.1 Internet-compatible system, which was most easily configured, however, when using Sun's Java Web-programming language. SAP raised new funds on the stock market to undertake new rounds of the huge investment necessary to keep its Web-based R/3 system up to date with the dramatic innovations in Web software development, and to broaden its product range to offer new, continually emerging Web-based applications, for example, applications such as the corporate intranets, business-to-business (B2B) and business-to customer (B2C) networks, Website development and hosting, security and systems management, and streaming audio and video teleconferencing.

Because SAP had no developed competency in Web software development, its competitors started to catch up. Oracle emerged as its major competitor; it had taken its core database management software, which was used by thousands of large companies, and overlaid it with Web-based operating and applications software. Oracle could now offer its huge customer base a growing suite of Web software, all seamlessly integrated. The suite of software also allowed them to perform Internet-based ERP value chain business processes. While Oracle's system was nowhere near as comprehensive as SAP's R/3 system, it allowed for cross-industry networking at both the input and output sides, it was cheaper and easier to quickly implement, and it was easier to customize to the needs of a particular customer. Oracle began to take market share away from SAP.

New companies like Siebel Systems, Commerce One, Ariba, and Marcum, which began as niche players in some software applications such as SCM, CRM, intranet, or Website development and hosting, also began to build and expand their product offerings so that they now possessed ERP modules that competed with some of SAP's most lucrative R/3 modules. Commerce One and Ariba, for example, emerged as the main players in the rapidly expanding B2B industry SCM market. B2B is an industry-level ERP solution that creates an organized market and thus brings together industry buyers and suppliers electronically, and provides the software to write and enforce contracts for the future development and supply of an industry's inputs. Although these niche players could not provide the full range of services that SAP could provide, they had become increasingly able to offer attractive alternatives to customers seeking specific aspects of an ERP system. Also, companies like Siebel, Marcum, and I2 claimed that they had the ability to customize their low-price systems, and prices for ERP systems began to fall.

In the new software environment, SAP's large customers started to purchase software on a "best of breed" basis, meaning that customers purchased the best software applications for their specific needs from different, leading-edge companies rather than purchasing all of their software products from one company as a package—such as SAP offered. Sun Microsystems began to promote a free Java computer language as the industry "open architecture" standard, which meant that as long as each company used Java to craft their specific Web-based software programs, they would all work seamlessly together, and there would no longer be an advantage to using a single dominant platform like Microsoft's Windows or SAP's R/3. Sun Microsystems was (and still is) trying to break Microsoft's hold over the operating system industry standard, Windows. Sun Microsystems wanted each company's software to succeed because it was "best of breed," not because it locked customers in and created enormous switching costs for them should they contemplate a move to a competitor's product.

All these different factors caused enormous problems for SAP's top managers. What strategies should they use to protect their competitive position? Should they forge ahead and offer their customers a broad, proprietary, Web-based ERP solution and try to lock them in to continue to charge a premium price? Should they move to an open standard and make their R/3 ERP Internet-enabled modules compatible with solutions from other companies, and forge alliances with those companies to ensure that the software seamlessly operated together? Since SAP's managers still believed they had the best ERP software and the capabilities to lead in the Web software arena, was this the best long-run competitive solution? Should SAP focus on making its ERP software more customizable to its customers' needs, and make it easier for them to buy selected modules to reduce the cost of SAP software? This alternative might also make it easier for them to develop ERP modules that could be scaled back to suit the needs of medium and small firms, which were increasingly becoming the targets of its new software competitors. Once these new firms established toeholds in the market, it would only be a matter of time before they improved their products and began to compete for SAP's installed customer base. SAP realized that it had to refocus its business model, especially because rivals were rapidly buying niche players and, at the same time, filling gaps in their product lines to be able to compete with SAP.

Protecting its Competitive Position

In 1997, SAP sought a quick fix to its problems by releasing new R/3 solutions for ERP Internet-enabled SCM and CRM solutions, which converted its internal ERP system into an externally based network platform. SCM, now known as the "back end" of the business, integrates the business processes necessary to manage the flow of goods, from the raw material stage to the finished product. SCM programs forecast future needs, and plan and manage a company's operations, especially its manufacturing operations. CRM, known as the "front-end" of the business, provides companies with solutions and support for business processes directed at improving sales, marketing, customer service, and field service operations. CRM programs are rapidly growing in popularity because they lead to better customer retention and satisfaction and higher revenues. In 1998, SAP followed with industry solution maps, business technology maps, and service maps, all of which were aimed at making its R/3 system dynamic and responsive to changes in industry conditions.

Also in 1998, recognizing that its future rested on its ability to protect its share of the U.S. market, SAP listed itself on the New York Stock Exchange and began to expand the scope of its U.S. operations, both to encourage internal "organic growth," meaning growth through internal new venturing, and to allow it to develop a U.S. top management team that could develop the strategies and business model necessary to allow it to respond to the growing competition it was facing. As with all growing businesses, the need to manage the fit between its strategy and structure had become its major priority—SAP's R&D culture was hurting it in its battle with agile competitors, and had to be changed.

Endnotes

www.sap.com, 1988–2011.
SAP Annual Reports and 10K Reports, 1989–2011.
SAP 10K Reports, 1989–2011.

SAP and the Evolving Global Business Software Industry in 2011—Part 2

Gareth R. Jones
Texas A&M University

As Part 1 discusses, by 1997, SAP realized the need to release new Internet-enabled ERP R/3 solutions, which converted its internal ERP system into an externally-based network platform, to satisfy customers needs for SCM and CRM. Recall that SAP's Supply Chain Management (SCM) integrates the business processes necessary to manage the flow of goods from the raw material stage to the finished product—it is a set of supply value-chain solutions designed to control costs and increase differentiation over the product life-cycle. By, for example, forecasting future product developments, and then devising solutions to more effectively manage a company's value-chain operations, especially its manufacturing operations, to increase performance. Customer Relationship Management (CRM), at the front-end of the value chain, provides companies with solutions and support for business processes directed at improving sales, marketing, customer service, and field service operations. By 2000, CRM programs were rapidly growing in popularity because they lead to better customer retention and satisfaction and higher revenues and profits for the companies that make them part of their IT system.

The mySAP.com Initiative

Like most software applications companies, SAP had been slow to recognize the enormous potential of the Internet to build a company's global competitive advantage in so many different ways. In 1999, however, SAP's realization of the growing importance of the Internet was made apparent by major changes to its business model and strategies when it introduced its mySAP.com (mySAP) initiative. The strategy behind mySAP was to allow the company to regain leadership of the Internet Web-based ERP, SCM, and CRM markets, and to promote its ability to develop new Internet-based software applications as they have evolved over time. In essence, the mySAP initiative was a comprehensive ebusiness platform designed to promote internal collaboration inside a client company, and collaboration with other companies in its supply chain. mySAP demonstrated several elements of top managers changing strategic thinking for how to succeed in the 2000s.

First, to meet its customers' needs in a new electronic environment, SAP used the mySAP platform to change itself from a vendor of ERP components to a provider of ebusiness solutions. The platform would be the online portal through which customers could view and understand the way its Internet-enabled R/3 modules could match their evolving needs. Customers wanted to be able to leverage new ebusiness technologies to improve basic business goals like increasing profitability, improving customer satisfaction, and lowering overhead costs. In addition, customers wanted total solutions that could help them manage their relationships and supply chains.

mySAP would offer a total solutions ERP package, including SCM and CRM applications that would no longer force customers to adapt to SAP's standardized architecture. Rather, mySAP software was designed to help facilitate a client company's transition into ebusiness and provide them with the advantages offered by the Internet. Of course, mySAP solutions would also create value for clients by building on

SAP's established core competencies, including its industry best practices. In addition, mySAP solutions would also allow a client company to leverage its own core competencies and build its competitive advantage from within, SAP created a full range of front- and back-end ERP products available through its mySAP.com portal that were specific to different industries and manufacturing technologies. These changes meant that it could compete in niche markets and make it easier to customize a particular application to an individual company's needs. mySAP showed it was offering customers not product-based solutions but customer-based solutions. Its mySAP ebusiness platform solutions are designed to be a scalable and flexible architecture that supports databases, software applications, operating systems, and hardware platforms from almost every major vendor.

Second, mySAP provided the evolving IT platform that would allow SAP's own product offerings—software applications—to expand and broaden over time, something especially important because Web-based applications software was evolving in ever more varied and unexpected ways as new high-tech software companies recognized a new niche in the market and were striving to develop software applications that companies would want to buy and use. In essence, SAP had begun to pursue related diversification, and other major software applications makers, such as rivals Oracle and Microsoft, were, too. All these competitors were branching out into more segments of the software industry to capitalize on higher-growth emerging software segments, and to fill the niches to keep potential competitors from invading their core software markets and stealing away their customers.

Third, SAP realized that price was becoming a more important issue because both large software companies and new software startups competition were increasingly offering companies lower-priced software solutions and solutions to persuade these companies to shift their loyalties and abandon SAP's software platform. Major rivals, Oracle and Microsoft had begun to offer good deals to companies to build their market share; they offered their software at discount prices or packed their ERP software with their other software such as database or PC software to generate demand for their product. SAP focused on making mySAP more affordable by breaking up its modules and business solutions into smaller, separate products. Customers could now choose which

particular solutions best met their specific needs; they no longer had to buy the whole package. At the same time, all mySAP offerings were fully compatible with the total R/3 system so that customers could easily expand their use of SAP's products. SAP was working across its entire product range to make its system easier and cheaper to use. SAP realized that repeat business is much more important than a 1-time transaction, so they began to focus on seeking out and developing new, related solutions for their customers to keep them coming back and purchasing more products and upgrades.

Fourth, SAP was announcing that in the future, its mySAP solutions would be designed to fit and support the needs of large, medium, and small companies, and it intended to compete in all market segments. SAP would broaden its mySAP ebusiness solution packages so it would target not only large corporations, but also small- and medium-sized business enterprises (SMEs). mySAP allowed SAP to provide several simpler and cheaper versions of its application software, such as low-cost ERP solutions that could be scaled down to suit the needs of smaller firms. Also, for SMEs that lacked the internal resources to maintain their own business applications on-site, mySAP offered hosting for data centers, networks, and applications. Small businesses could greatly benefit from the increased speed of installation and reduced cost possible through outsourcing and by paying a fee to use mySAP in lieu of purchasing SAP's expensive software modules. SAP also focused on making its R/3 mySAP offerings easier to install and use, and reduced implementation times and consulting costs in turn reduced the costs of supporting the SAP platform for both small and large organizations.

To support its mySAP initiative, SAP had continued to build in-house training and consulting capabilities to increase its share of revenues from the services side of its business. SAP's increasing Web-based software efforts paid off because the company was now better able to recognize the problems experienced by customers. This result led SAP to recognize both the needs for greater responsiveness to customers, and customization of its products to make their installation easier. Its growing customer awareness had also led it to redefine its mission as a developer of business solutions, the approach embedded in mySAP, rather than as a provider of software products.

To improve the cost effectiveness of mySAP installations, SAP sought a better way to manage its relationships with consulting companies. It moved to a parallel sourcing policy, in which several consulting firms competed for a customer's business, and it made sure an internal SAP consultant was always involved in the installation and service effort to monitor external consultants' performance. This helped keep service costs under control for its customers. Because customer needs changed so quickly in this fast-paced market and SAP continually improved its products with incremental innovations and additional capabilities, it also insisted that consultants undertake continual training to update their skills, training for which it charged high fees. In 2000, SAP adopted a stock option program to retain valuable employees after losing many key employees—programmers and consultants—to competitors like IBM.

Indeed, strategic alliances and acquisitions became increasingly important parts of its strategy to reduce its cost structure, enhance the functionality of its products, and build its customer base. Because of the sheer size and expense of many Web-based software endeavors, intense competition, and the fast-paced dynamics of this industry, SAP's top managers began to realize they could not go it alone and produce everything in-house. SAP's overhead costs had rocketed in the 1990s, as it pumped money into building its mySAP initiative. Intense competition seemed to indicate that continuing massive expenditures would be necessary. SAP's stock price had decreased because higher overhead costs meant falling profits despite increasing revenues. SAP had never seemed to be able to enjoy sustained high profitability because changing technology and competition had not allowed it to capitalize on its acknowledged position as the ERP industry leader.

Given existing resource constraints and time pressures and the need to create a more profitable business model, in the 2000s, SAP's managers realized that they needed to partner with companies that had developed the "best of breed" software applications in various niches of the Web software market. Now SAP could avoid the high R&D outlays necessary to develop new software itself. In addition, synergies with its software partners might make it possible to bring new mySAP products to the market more quickly and efficiently.

SAP also began to use acquisitions to speed its entry into crucial new segments of the Web software market. For example, SAP acquired Top Tier Software Inc. in 2001 to gain access to its iView technology. This technology allows seamless integration between the Web software of different companies and is critical for SAP because it lets customers drag-and-drop and mix information and applications from both SAP and non-SAP platform-based systems. Top Tier was also an enterprise portal software maker, and in 2001, SAP used these competencies to create a new U.S. subsidiary called SAP Portals, which would deliver state-of-the-art enterprise portal products that would result in greater business efficiency and attract more customers. It also opened SAP hosting to provide hosting and Web maintenance services to its new portal customers.

By 2002, SAP believed that its alliances and acquisitions had given it a competitive advantage it could use to sustain its position as the dominant business applications software company. Its alliances with other software makers promoted mySAP as the industry standard and the dominant player in the ERP Web software market. SAP's managers were therefore shocked when it became clear that Microsoft, which also recognized the enormous potential of Web software ERP sales, particularly in the SME segment of the market, was also planning to compete in this fast-growing market segment. In 2002, Microsoft had bought two companies that competed in the SME segment to bolster its own Web software offerings such as its suite of office products including email, word processing and other important applications that it could now bundle with its ERP offerings to SMEs. Microsoft's goal was clearly to become a formidable competitor for SAP, and with its competencies in a wide area of software products and huge resources, it could quickly and easily develop an ERP system with Web-based solutions that integrated with its other applications software.

SAP's number of global software installations and customers increased steadily between 1998 and 2002 when SAP was still the industry leader with a worldwide market share of over 30%. Oracle was next with a 16% share of the market, and Microsoft had around 7%. SAP claimed that it had 10 million users and 50,000 SAP installations in 18,000 companies in 120 countries in 2002, and that 1/2 of the world's top 500 companies used its software.

Implementing mySAP

SAP's problems were not just in the strategy area, however. Its mySAP initiative had increased its overhead costs dramatically, and it still could not find the appropriate organizational structure to make the best use of its resources and competencies. It continued to search for the right structure for servicing the growing range of its products and the increasing breadth of the companies, in terms of size, industry, and global location, it was now serving.

Recall that in the mid-1990s, SAP had begun to centralize authority and control to standardize its own business processes and effectively manage knowledge across its organizational subunits. While this reorganization helped reduce costs, unfortunately it also lengthened the time it took SAP to respond to the fast-changing Web software ERP environment. To quickly respond to changing customer needs, the needs for product customization, and the actions of its rivals, SAP now moved to decentralize control to teams of software engineers who were experts in a business process or in a particular industry, and who now worked with its local salesforce to manage customer problems where and when they arose. SAP's managers felt that in a market dominated by high rivalry among ERP vendors and in which customers had more bargaining power to obtain software and services cheaper and easier to use, it was important to get close to the customer. SAP had now put into place its own applications software to integrate across its operating divisions and subsidiaries and allow them to share best practices and new developments. Thus, it hoped to avoid the problems it had experienced in the past when it had decentralized too much authority.

SAP also changed the way its three German engineering groups worked with the different mySAP products groups. Henceforth, a significant part of the engineering development effort would take place inside each mySAP product engineering group so that the software engineers, who write and improve the specific new mySAP software applications, were joined with the sales force for that group. Now they could integrate their activities and provide better customized solutions. The software engineers at its German headquarters, besides conducting basic R&D, would be responsible for coordinating the efforts of the different mySAP engineering groups, sharing new software developments among groups, providing expert solutions, and ensuring all the different mySAP applications seamlessly worked together.

Each mySAP product group is now composed of a collection of cross-functional product development teams focused on their target markets. Teams are given incentives to meet their specific sales growth targets and to increase operating effectiveness, including reducing the length of installation time. The purposes of the new product group/team approach was to decentralize control, make SAP more responsive to the needs of customers and to changing technical developments, and still give SAP centralized control of development efforts. To ensure that its broadening range of software was customizable to the needs of different kinds of companies and industries, SAP enlisted some of its key customers as "development partners" and as members of these teams. Customers from large, mid-sized, and small companies were used to test new concepts and ideas. Within every mySAP product group, cross-functional teams focused upon customizing its products for specific customers or industries.

At the global level, SAP grouped is national subsidiaries into 3 main world regions: Europe, the Americas, and Asia/Pacific. This grouping made it easier to transfer knowledge and information between countries and serve the specific demands of national markets inside each region. Also, this global structure made it easier to manage relationships with consulting companies and to coordinate regional marketing and training efforts, both under the jurisdiction of the centralized marketing and training operations.

Thus, in the 2000s, SAP had begun to operate with a loose form of matrix structure. To increase internal flexibility and responsiveness to customers while at the same time boosting efficiency and market penetration, the world regions, the national subsidiaries, and the salespeople and consultants within them constitute one side of the matrix. The centralized engineering, marketing, and training functions and the 20 or so different mySAP product groups compose the other side. The problem facing SAP is to coordinate all these distinct subunits so they will lead to rapid acceptance of SAP's new mySAP platform across all the national markets in which it operates.

In practice, a salesperson in any particular country will work directly with a client to determine what type of ERP system he or she needs. Once it is determined which system will be used, a project manager from the regional subsidiary or from one of the mySAP groups is appointed to assemble an installation team from members of the different product groups that have the expertise required to implement the new client's system. Given SAP's broad range of evolving products, the matrix structure allows SAP to provide those products that fit the customer's needs in a fast, coordinated way. SAP's policy of decentralizing authority and placing it in the hands of its employees enables the matrix system to work. SAP prides itself on its talented and professional staff that can learn and adapt to many different situations and networks across the globe.

Developments in the Early-2000s

In April 2002, SAP announced that its revenues had climbed 9.2%, but its first-quarter profit fell 40% because of a larger-than-expected drop in license revenue from the sale of new software. Many customers had been reluctant to invest in the huge cost of moving to the mySAP system and the 2000 economic recession reduced IT expenditures. SAP announced it had several orders for mySAP in the works, however, and that it believed the 18,000 companies around the world using its flagship R/3 software would soon move to mySAP once their own revenues and profits recovered. In the meantime, SAP announced that it would introduce a product called R/3 Enterprise that would be targeted at large R/3 customers to show them what mySAP can accomplish once it is up and running in their companies.

SAP's managers believed these initiatives would allow the company to jump from being the third largest global software company to being the second, ahead of main competitor Oracle. They also wondered if they could use its mySAP open system architecture to overcome Microsoft's stranglehold on the software market and bypass the powerful Windows standard. Microsoft is the largest global software company.

Pursuing this idea, SAP put considerable resources into developing a new business computing solution called SAP NetWeaver that is a Web-based, open integration and middleware application platform that serves as the foundation for enterprise service-oriented architecture (Enterprise SOA) and allows the integration and alignment of people,

information, and business processes across business and technology boundaries. Enterprise SOA utilizes *open standards* to enable the integration of the software applications of most different software companies no matter upon what particular technology, for example, JAVA or LINUX, it is based. SAP NetWeaver is now the foundation for all Enterprise SOA SAP applications and mySAP Business Suite solutions; it also powers SAP's partners' solutions and custom-built applications. Also NetWeaver integrates business processes across various systems, databases, and sources—from any business software supplier—and is marketed to large companies as a service-oriented application and integration platform. NetWeaver's development was a major strategic move by SAP to drive companies to run all their business software using a single SAP platform.

Although SAP was developing and upgrading its products at a fast pace throughout the early-2000s, the continuing worldwide recession continued to limit or reduce the company's IT expenditures. SAP, like all other computer hardware and software companies, suffered as its revenues fell and SAP's stock price plunged in 2002 from $40 to almost $10 as the stock market crashed. However, while SAP's revenues fell by 5% in 2003 because of lower ERP and consulting sales, its profit doubled because it had finally brought its global cost structure under control and was making better use of its resources. Strict new controls on expenses had been implemented, a hiring freeze imposed, and the company was focusing its German programmers to work on urgent problems. Consequently, its stock was back up to $35 by the end of 2003 as its future growth prospects looked good.

As a part of its major push to reduce costs, SAP began to outsource the enormous amount of routine programming involved in improving and creating advanced applications to low-cost countries overseas, such as India. In 2003, SAP recruited 750 software programmers in India, this number grew to 1,500 in 2004, and 5,000 in 2006. SAP used its growing army of low-cost Indian programmers to work the bugs out of its mySAP modules and to increase their reliability when they were installed in a new company. This prevented embarrassing blows-ups that sometimes arose when a company implemented SAP's ERP for the first time. Fewer bugs also made it easier to install its modules in a new company, which reduced the need for consulting and lowered costs, leading to more satisfied customers. Increasingly,

SAP also began to use the advanced skills of its Indian research center programmers to cooperate in the development of new mySAP ERP modules to serve new customers in an increasing number of industries or "vertical markets." By 2006, SAP's Indian research group was bigger than its research group in Waldorf, Germany and has been growing ever since. Outsourcing has saved the company billions in development costs and had continuously contributed to its rising profitability in the 2000s.

The Growing Small- and Medium-Enterprise Market

In 2003, SAP changed the name of its software from mySAP.com to mySAP Business Suite because more customers were now licensing its software suite rather than purchasing it. Part of this change occurred because of the many upgrades SAP was continuously releasing, and in a licensing arrangement, its clients could expect continual free upgrades as it improved its ERP modules as a part of their contract. However, while SAP continued to attract new, large business customers, the market was becoming increasingly saturated; it already had around 50% of the global large business market by 2003. To promote growth and increase sales revenues, SAP began a major push to increase its share of the SME market segment of the ERP industry.

The small size of these companies, and so the limited amount of money they had to spend on business software, was a major challenge for SAP, which had primarily worked with multinational companies that had huge IT budgets. Also, there were major competitors in this market segment that had specialized in meeting the needs of SMEs to avoid direct competition with SAP—and they had locked up a significant share of business in this ERP segment. By focusing primarily on large companies, SAP had left a gap in the SME market. Other large software companies, such as Oracle and Microsoft, but also newcomers such as Siebel, PeopleSoft, and salesforce.com, rushed to develop their own SME ERP products and services to compete for revenues in the fast-growing SME market segment—worth billions of dollars.

To attract SME customers as quickly as possible, SAP decided to develop two primary product offerings customized to their needs: SAP All-in-One and SAP Business One. SAP All-in-One is a streamlined version of its R/3 mySAP Business Suite; it is much easier to install and maintain and much more affordable for SMEs. To develop All-in-One, SAP's software engineers took its mySAP Business Suite modules designed for large companies and scaled them down for users of small companies. All-in-One is a reduced version of SAP's total range of products such as SAP Customer Relationship Management, SAP ERP modules, SAP Product Lifecycle Management, SAP Supply Chain Management, and SAP Supplier Relationship Management. Despite its reduced size, it is still a complex business solution and one that requires a major commitment of IT resources for a SME.

Recognizing the need to provide a much simpler, limited, and affordable ERP solution for smaller companies, SAP decided to also create a second SME ERP solution. SAP decided not to begin anew to develop a software package based on its R/3 platform, as it did with its All-in-One solution. Rather, it took a new path and bought an Israeli software company called TopManage Financial Solutions in 2002, and rebranded its system as SAP Business One. SAP Business One would be a much more limited ERP software package that integrates CRM with financial and logistic modules to meet a specific customer's basic needs. However, it still provides a powerful, flexible SME solution and is designed to be easy to use and affordable. Business One works in real time, the software suite manages and records the ongoing transactions involved in a business such as cost of goods received, through inventory, processing and sale, and delivery to customers, and automatically records transactions in a debit and credit account. In 2005, SAP began reporting revenues from the SME market segment separately from revenues for its larger customers, one way of showing its commitment to SME customers.

The Changing Competitive Environment

By 2004, achieving rapid growth by increasing the number of new large business customers was becoming more and more difficult, simply because SAP's share of the global ERP market had now grown to 58%—one of the major reasons it entered the SME ERP market. SAP reported that because of slowing ERP sales it expected single digit growth in the next few years—growth worth billions in revenues, but still growth that would not fuel a rapid rise in its stock price.

However, competition in the SME market was also increasing as its business software rivals watched SAP develop and introduce its All-in-One and Business One solutions. SAP's rapid growth in this segment led to increasing competition and to a wave of consolidation in the ERP industry. In 2003, PeopleSoft, the leader in the HRM software module segment, bought J. D. Edwards & Son, a leader in SCM, to enlarge its product offerings and strengthen its market share against growing competition from SAP and Oracle. However, Oracle, the leading database software management company also realized the stakes ahead in the rapidly consolidating business applications software market.

Essentially, the problem was that all the major competitors needed to be able to offer potential customers—large or small—a broad range of business software applications so that it could bundle them together and offer them at a reduced price. For example, most large companies already were using Oracle's database software, if it could provide them with an ERP solution to meet their needs at a lower cost than SAP or Microsoft, it could grow its market share. While SAP had never made billion-dollar acquisitions, preferring "organic growth" from the inside or small acquisitions, the opposite was the case with Oracle.

Its CEO Larry Ellison decided that to compete with SAP in the ERP market, Oracle would have to make major acquisitions to rapidly expand Oracle's range of business modules to complement the suite of ERP modules it had been internally developing, and gain market share. Only through acquisitions could it quickly develop an ERP suite with the breadth of SAP's to meet the needs of SMEs. Also, Ellison decided it could use its new competencies, combined with its existing database competences to attack SAP in the large company segment that Oracle now also regarded as a major growth opportunity.

In 2004, Oracle had begun a hostile takeover of PeopleSoft, which had also acquired several other ERP companies to build its competitive advantage. PeopleSoft's top managers battled to prevent the takeover, but Oracle offered PeopleSoft's customers special low-cost licensing deals on Oracle database software and guaranteed them the changeover to its software would be smooth. It finally acquired PeopleSoft—and the resources and customers necessary to gain a large market share in the SME segment at the expense of SAP and Microsoft—in 2005.

Oracle kept up the pressure. Between January 2005 and June 2007 it acquired 25 more business software companies in a huge acquisition drive to build its distinctive competencies and market share in ERP software. PeopleSoft brought Oracle expertise in HRM solutions, and J. D. Edwards' expertise in SCM solutions. Then in a major acquisition of Siebel Systems, Oracle bought a leading CRM software developer. These acquisitions allowed Oracle to dramatically increase its range of ERP offerings and build market share with small- and medium-sized businesses. Before purchasing Seibel, for example, Oracle had a 6.8% share of this market; now it could add Seibel's 11% market share to become one of the top 3 CRM suppliers—alongside SAP and Salesforce.com.

Oracle, already a major supplier of middleware, also wanted to be able to offer companies middleware that allowed them to seamlessly connect different ERP software packages from different companies. In turn, it developed a new ebusiness suite called Oracle Fusion middleware that would allow companies to leverage their existing investments in the software applications of other companies, including SAP, so that they work seamlessly with Oracle's new ERP modules. Fusion is Oracle's answer to SAP's NetWeaver because it gives SME customers no incentive to move to SAP's All-in-One or Business One suite. Indeed, Fusion became a threat to SAP because many of oracle's ERP modules such as its CRM and HRM solutions often better fit the needs of SMEs than SAP's. Thus, many companies decide to keep their existing PeopleSoft installations and then choose more offerings from Oracle's growing array business applications.

The third leading SME ERP supplier, Microsoft, is also keeping up the pressure. Using the competencies from its acquisition of Great Plains and Navision, it released a business package called Microsoft Dynamics NAV, ERP software that can be customized to the needs of SME users, to their industries, and scaled to their size. Microsoft's advantage lies in the compatibility of its ERP offerings with the Windows platform, which is still used by more than 85% of SMEs, especially as it can offer substantial discounts when customers choose both types of software. Also, as Microsoft continues to introduce new versions of its Windows and Office software, such as Windows 8, it can use low-cost pricing to convince its customers to upgrade to its new ERP software.

SAP has worked hard to develop strategic alliances with all kinds of software companies to respond to the challenge from Oracle and Microsoft. By 2007, it had formed contracts with over 1,000 independent software vendors (ISVs) that have helped it expand its offerings, and it has jointly developed 300 new ERP solutions for the 25 industries it now serves, and all these applications are all powered by SAP NetWeaver. An important alliance was announced with IBM in 2006, IBM would invest $40 million over the next 5 years to develop the capabilities necessary to install SAP's new software. Also, SAP will integrate NetWeaver with IBM's new cloud computing data storage offerings for large companies.

SAP also made many small acquisitions to improve its competitive position in various industries and to develop Web-based products to help companies utilize the Internet more effectively. For example, in the retail software industry, it acquired companies like Triversity and Khimetrics. Triversity provides point of sales, store inventory, customer relations and service solutions for retail companies, and Khimetrics helps retailers price and position products to manage demand, improve margins, and predict sales and income. It also acquired TomorrowNow, that specialized in providing maintenance and support services for PeopleSoft and J. D. Edwards & Company customers (that were now Oracle clients). SAP also created "safe passage programs" designed to help companies switch to SAP solutions from software applications now owned by Oracle. SAP also planned to develop a variety of new-generation products, including new SAP industry solutions, and more applications for SMEs—in a direct challenge to Oracle's Fusion software.

Strategic Moves 2006–2008

In 2006, SAP's CEO Henning Kagermann announced 4 major priorities for the next decade—to increase market share, especially in SME; to increase profitability by improving productivity and efficiency; to better serve SAP users with new software applications products and expand to new industries; and to help customers transition to and gain benefits from the rapidly developing software on-demand or software as a service (SaaS) segment of the Web-based applications segment.

SAP's need to focus upon the on-demand applications segment reflected its rapid rise in importance by the mid-2000s. New Internet companies, such as salesforce.com (which had become a major software as a service (SaaS) competitor to SAP by 2011), were offering SMEs the ability to license ERP modules services, especially CRM modules, and then access these modules online and store their databases on the Internet hosting company's Website. This was a game changing move for large ERP companies because it signaled to SMEs that on-demand Internet providers such as salesforce.com could offer much lower prices—even if they were less customized. SAP's answer was to introduce a SaaS platform available to customers through on-demand and hosted delivery—and since 2007, SAP had been expanding the number of ERP modules it had offered through its "Business by Design" software suite, that by 2011, had become a part of its cloud computing services. Its SaaS service that will use its NetWeaver middleware also allowed customers to seamlessly integrate the software of different vendors and make possible real-time upgrades and improvements.

In 2007, Henning Kagermann, who was now partnered at the top by deputy CEO Leo Apotheker, now embarked upon a major change in strategy. As noted earlier, SAP was proud of its "organic growth" or internal R&D to develop new software products. However, in March 2007, Oracle announced it would acquire Hyperion Solutions, a global provider of business intelligence software that provided performance-enhancing solutions for $3.3 billion. In doing so, it was entering a new segment of the applications software market—one that might prove to be disruptive. The growing power of mathematical algorithms to offer radical changes to a company's strategy to enhance performance seemed to fit well with the products of an ERP company that was continuously trying to improve best practices. SAP thought this might be a disruptive game-changing move by Oracle, and determined to respond quickly, it was forced to acquire the leading company in the Business Intelligence segment, Business Objects, for $6.8 billion. Today, SAP Business Objects has become the fastest growing of SAP's different software businesses, business intelligence (BI) and the industry leader—outcompeting Oracle's BI applications obtained through its acquisition of Hyperion. Oracle does not have the complementary skills needed to push the boundaries in BI. While BI generated only 7% of SAP's revenues in 2007, it is expected to generate over 15% in 2011. SAP has leveraged all its existing competences and applied them to Business Objects—and vice-versa—to increase the value of its BI services to customers. In addition, in 2010 SAP Business Objects announced a revolutionary new "in-memory computing solution" that speeds the processing of real-time information in ways that lead to new solutions and practices that can dramatically increase performance. SAP claims that this is a disruptive technology and one that will change the BI and ERP markets and give it a competitive advantage over its rivals.

Apotheker is Replaced by Two Co-CEOs

In 2008, Leo Apotheker became CEO of SAP, and because of the new global recession, he presided over the first annual drop in revenue at SAP since 2003, as customers refrained from purchasing new software. Moreover, SAP's global cost structure had soared as its workforce increased and it entered new markets like Business Intelligence. At the same time, Oracle had, since 2005, spent more than $42 billion to acquire additional ERP and business applications software, and claimed it was winning market share at the expense of SAP, by becoming a one-stop shop for customers—beginning with the PeopleSoft acquisition. Microsoft was also claiming gains in market share in the SME segment, and so were smaller players such as salesforce.com in CRM, and Sage another niche player in the growing global ERP market. Oracle's sales almost doubled to $23.3 billion between 2005 to 2009, while SAP's sales rose 42%.

SAP's board of directors decided that change was necessary; in 2010, he was replaced by dual CEOs, Bill McDermott, who took control of SAP global field operations, and Jim Hagemann Snabe, who took control of business solutions and technology. Their dual roles reflect SAP's continuing need to coordinate its global matrix structure to manage its growth across world regions, countries, and the large and SME customer's segments, while providing the business applications package best tailored to the needs of different customers in different countries.

By 2010, it had become clear that three major strategic priorities were now facing all ERP companies. First, the need to provide the best-customized suite of business solutions to companies, especially large companies, that wanted to install and implement SAP's software applications "on premise" meaning that the software installation was maintained and upgraded across a company's global facilities. Second, the need to provide a suite of software applications, especially CRM solutions that could be obtained on-demand, the SaaS solution that allowed SMEs to lease an SAP business solution package and use it to process and store their data on the Internet or in the cloud, as described earlier. And, third, to provide SAP solution's "on device," meaning that SAP's customers could access its solution from their laptops, smartphones, and other mobile devices.

The last "on device" method of delivering SAP's services was most problematic since it lacked advanced capabilities in mobile software applications. In 2010, co-CEOs, McDermott and Snabe decided that a major new acquisition was necessary if SAP was to keep up with Oracle and Microsoft, which already had their own mobile platforms up and running. In 2010, they decided to acquire Sybase, a leader in the kind of software that helps corporate customers run applications on mobile devices for $5.8 billion, which would allow its corporate customers to run SAP applications, and link into their company's database on mobile devices from anywhere in the world. SAP will use the purchase to cater to customers that want employees to use tablets and smartphones while working: "This will literally connect the shop floor to the corner office," CEO McDermott announced. Also, Sybase is strong in the telecom and financial sectors where SAP is weak, so that it will be able to expand its existing client base. Sybase CEO John Chen will continue to run Sybase as an independent unit complementing all of SAP's other software services. SAP Sybase is expected to contribute significantly to SAP Business Objects' revenues and profits over time, and give it one more competitive advantage over Oracle, which was fighting to develop a major presence in mobile computing applications in 2011. Sybase can work with Microsoft's mobile platform as well as Apple's iPhone and Google's Android systems.

Competitive Advantage in 2011

In 2011, SAP was working closely with customers and partners worldwide, to develop a product and services strategy that would enable customers to use its enterprise application software wherever and whenever they need it–on premise, on demand, or on device. SAP's NetWeaver technology platform will serve as the foundation for all its SAP Business Suite applications.

SAP "Business Suite" that contains a complete set of software solutions aimed at large customers; SAP "All in One Suite" that can be tailored to the needs of companies with 100–2500 employees; and SAP "Business One" and "Business By Design" that essentially offer a cost-effective package of on-demand business solutions that can be hosted on SAP's remote cloud computing network.

SAP is also working to be able to offer all its customers the advantage of cloud computing as it advances, and as it becomes more reliable and secure. SAP Business Objects solutions are continually being upgraded and developed to help companies optimize business processes on premise, on demand, and on device.

SAP believes that it is has developed a competitive position in these three areas, and developed a suite of software applications suited to the needs of different sized companies that will allow it to compete effectively against Oracle, now it major rival, in the next decade. However, many analysts believe that its share of the large and SME segments, particularly in CRM, may decline by 2–5% in the next 2–3 years; it is expected to more than double its share of the growing BI market. If it can develop and leverage its competencies in BI solutions and its Sybase mobile platform applications across market segments—and develop first-rate cloud computing solutions—it may be able to gain 2–5% market share.

SAP's ability to retain and grow its market share is critical because this determines how well its stock price will perform in the 2010s. The higher its stock price rises, the more existing and new global customers will be attracted to use its growing business software applications; stock increases show it has achieved sustainable competitive advantage. In July 2011, SAP announced record revenues for the quarter and that it would exceed its profit forecast for the year as its software and service licenses soared.

It also announced that its profits would exceed its previous forecast as it was taking market share away from Oracle as its second-quarter software license sales grew 26%, compared to Oracle that reported a 19%. Its stock price also soared as investors now believed SAP was developing the right business model and strategies to beat Oracle and maintain its dominance as the biggest global business software maker.

SAP's Co-CEOs Bill McDermott and Jim Hagemann Snabe announced that their goal was to increase SAP's profits by 10% per year, driven by increases in its mobile products, on-demand services, and its new real-time business solution analytics technology "Hana." "The pipeline for Hana is the biggest in the history of SAP," McDermott proudly announced, "The Hana in-memory product, or High-Performance Analytic Appliance, is designed to speed up analysis of business data. It comes on servers from companies such as Hewlett-Packard Co., International Business Machines Corp., Dell, and Cisco Systems Inc." McDermott also said SAP was benefiting from the use of Apple's iPad tablet among executives, who can use the device to take advantage of SAP's software that provides them with mobile access to real-time business analytics. "By 2014, 6.5 billion workers worldwide will be on mobile devices. What you are seeing is a generational change," he announced.

Indeed, SAP provides the software for the order fulfillment process behind Apple's iTunes download system and Apple, and other large companies are experimenting with its Hana in-memory technology. SAP formed alliances with major companies such as Verizon, Dell, and Amazon.com, to sell its mobile products, Hana, and its SOA software as a service. McDermott also announced that unlike Oracle, SAP's future focus would be on organic growth from internal new venturing across its software divisions. Clearly, that battle in the business software industry is escalating. In July 2011, Oracle also announced many improvements to its software suite for businesses of all sizes, and niche players such as salesforce.com continue to grow their sales.

Endnotes

www.sap.com, 1998–2011.
SAP Annual Reports and 10K Reports, 1998–2011.
SAP 10K Reports, 1998–2011.

Internet Search and the Growth of Google

Charles W.L. Hill
University of Washington

Introduction

In the early-2000s, many Internet users started to gravitate toward a new search engine. It was called Google, and it delivered remarkable results. Put in a keyword, and in a blink of an eye the search engine would return a list of links, with the most relevant links appearing at the top of the page. People quickly realized that Google was an amazing tool, enabling users to quickly find almost anything they wanted on the Web—to effortlessly sort through the vast sea of information contained in billions of Web pages and retrieve the precise information they desired. It seemed like magic. Before long, "to Google" became a verb (in June 2006, the verb Google was added to the Oxford English Dictionary). To find out more about a person, you would "Google them." To find out more about a subject, you would "Google it." Enter a key word in Google, and a list of relevant links would be returned in an instant. For many users, Google quickly became the "go to" page every time they wanted information about anything.

What captured the attention of the business community, however, was Google's ability to monetize its search results. Google's core business model was the essence of simplicity. The company auctioned off the keywords used in searches to advertisers. The highest bidders would have links to their sites placed on the right hand side of a page returning search results. The advertisers would then pay Google every time someone clicked on a link and was directed to their site. Thus, when bidding for a keyword, advertisers would bid for the price per click. Interestingly, Google did not necessarily place the advertiser who bid the highest amount per click at the top of the page. Rather, the top spot was determined by the amount per click multiplied by Google's statistical estimate of the likelihood that someone would actually click on the advertisement. This refinement maximized the revenue that Google got from its valuable real estate.

By May 2011, some 65.5% all U.S. Internet searches were conducted through Google sites.[1] Yahoo! (15.9% share), Microsoft (14.1% share), and Ask Network (2.9% share) were Behind Google. Google had been gaining ground; 5 years earlier its share had stood at 45%.[2] In an effort to catch up to Google, Microsoft and Yahoo! had joined forces. Yahoo! had agreed to use Microsoft's Bing search engine (or *decision engine* as Microsoft preferred to call it). In late-2010, Bing powered searching was implemented throughout Yahoo! properties, making Bing's share 30% in May 2011. The belief at Microsoft was that adding Yahoo! search queries to the mix would enable Bing to gain scale economies and boost revenues per search.

As more users gravitated to Google's site, more advertisers were attracted to it, and Google's revenues and profits took off. From a standing start in 2001, by 2010 revenues had grown to $29.3 billion and net income to $8.5 billion. Google had become the gorilla in the online advertising space. In 2001, Google garnered 18.4% of total US search ad spending. By 2005, its share had increased to 48.5% and according to the research firm eMarketer, 75% of all U.S. search-advertising dollars went to Google in 2007.[3] Moreover, the future looks bright. In 2010, Internet advertising spending looked set to exceed $25 billion, up from $16.9 billion in 2006, and accounting for 15.1% of all media spending in the U.S.[4] Google was reportedly accounting for well over 70% of *worldwide* search marketing spending. Forecasts called for Google's revenues to hit $36 billion by 2012, as ever more advertisers moved from traditional media to the Web.[5]

Flushed by this success, Google introduced a wave of new products, including mapping services (Google Maps and Google Earth), an e-mail service (gmail), Google Desktop (which enables users to search files on their own computers), Google Apps, which includes free online word processing and spread sheet programs that have much of the look, feel, and functionality of Microsoft's Word and Excel offerings, its own Web browser, Chrome, and its smartphone operating system, Android. These products fueled speculation that Google's ambitions extended outside search capabilities and that the company was trying to position itself as a platform company supported by an ecosystem that would rival that fostered by Microsoft, the long-dominant player in the software industry.

Search Engines[6]

A search engine connects the keywords that users enter (queries) to a database it has created of Web pages (an index). It then produces a list of links to pages (and summaries of content) that it believes are most relevant to a query.

Search engines consist of four main components—a Web crawler, an index, a runtime index, and a query processor (the interface that connects users to the index). The Web crawler is a piece of software that goes from link to link on the Web, collecting the pages it finds and sending them back to the index. Once in the index, Web pages are analyzed by sophisticated algorithms that look for statistical patterns. Google's page rank algorithm, for example, looks at the links on a page, the text around those links, and the popularity of the pages that link to that page, to determine how relevant a page is to a particular query (in fact, Google's algorithm looks at more than 100 factors to determine a page's relevance to a query term).

Once analyzed, pages are tagged. The tag contains information about the pages, for example, whether it is porn, or spam, written in a certain language, or updated infrequently. Tagged pages are then dumped into a runtime index, which is a database that is ready to serve users. The runtime index forms a bridge between the back end of an engine, the Web crawler and index, and the front end, the query processor and user interface. The query processor takes a keyword inputted by a user, transports it to the runtime index, where an algorithm matches the keyword to pages, ranking them by relevance, and then transports the results back to the user, where they are displayed on the user interface.

The computing and data storage infrastructure required to support a search engine is significant. It must scale with the continued growth of the Web and with demands on the search engine. In 2007, Google had $2.7 billion in information technology assets on its balance sheet, had close to 400,000 computers configured in large scale clusters dedicated to the job of running its search engine, and spent around $600 million on maintaining its system.[7]

The Early Days of Search

Search did not begin with Google. The first Internet search engine was Archie. Created in 1990, before the World Wide Web had burst onto the scene, Archie connected users through queries to the machines on which documents they wanted were stored. The users then had to dig through the public files on those machines to find what they wanted. The next search engine, Veronica, improved upon Archie, as it allowed searchers to connect directly to the document they had queried.

The Web started to take off after 1993, with the number of Websites expanding from 130 to more than 600,000 by 1996. As this expansion occurred, the problem of finding the information you wanted on the Web became more difficult. The first Web-based search engine was the WWW Wanderer, developed by Matthew Gray at MIT. This was soon surpassed by Web Crawler, which was a search engine developed by Brian Pinkerton of the University of Washington. Web Crawler was the first search engine to index the full text of Web pages, rather than just the title. Web Crawler was sold to AOL for $1 million in 1995. This marked the first time anyone had ascribed an economic value to a search engine.

In December 1995, the next search engine appeared on the scene, Alta Vista. Developed by an employee at Digital Equipment Corporation (DEC), Louis Monier, like Web Crawler, Alta Vista indexed the entire text of a Web page. Unlike Web Crawler, however, Alta Vista sent out thousands of Web crawlers, which enabled it to build the most complete index of the Web to date. Avid Web users soon came to value the service, but the search engine was handicapped by two things. First, it was very much a step child within DEC, which was seen as a hardware-driven business and didn't really know what to do with Alta Vista. Second, there was no obvious way for Alta Vista to make much money, which meant that it was difficult for Monier to get the resources required for Alta Vista to keep up with the rapid growth of the Web. Ultimately, DEC was acquired by Compaq. Compaq then sold Alta Vista and related Internet properties to a high-flying Internet firm, CMGI, at the height of the Internet boom in 1999, for $2.3 billion in CMGI stock. CMGI did have plans to spin off Alta Vista in an Initial Public Offering, but it never happened. The NASDAQ stock market collapsed in 2000, taking CMGI's stock down with it, and the market had no appetite for another dot.com IPO.

Around the same time that Alta Vista was gaining traffic, two other companies introduced search engines, Lycos and Excite. Both search engines represented further incremental improvement. Lycos was the first search engine to use algorithms to try and determine the relevance of a Web page for a search query. Excite utilized similar algorithms. However, neither company developed a way of making money directly from search. Instead they saw themselves as portal companies, like Yahoo!, AOL and MSN. Search was just a tool to increase the value of their portal as a destination site, enabling them to capture revenues from banner ads, ecommerce transactions, and the like. Both Lycos and Excite went public and then squandered much of the capital raised on acquiring other Internet properties, before seeing their value implode as the Internet bubble burst in 2000–2001.

Another company that tried to make sense out of the Web for users was Yahoo!, but Yahoo! did not use a search engine. Instead it created a hierarchical directory of Web pages. This helped drive traffic to its site. Other content kept users coming back, enabling Yahoo! to emerge as one of the most popular portals on the Web. In contrast to many of its smaller competitors, Yahoo!'s industry leading scale allowed it to make good money from advertising on its site. Yahoo! did add a search engine to its offering, but until 2003 it always did so through a partner. At one time, Alta Vista powered Yahoo!'s search function, then Inktomi, and ultimately Google. Yahoo!'s managers did consider developing their own search engine, but they saw it as too capital intensive—search required a lot of computing power, storage and bandwidth. Besides, there was no business model for monetizing search. That, however, was all about to change, and it wasn't Google that pioneered the way, it was a serial entrepreneur called Bill Gross.

GoTo.com: A Business Model Emerges[8]

Bill Gross made his first million with Knowledge Adventure, which developed software to help kids learn. After he sold Knowledge Adventure to Cendant for $100 million, Gross created IdeaLab, a business incubator that subsequently generated a number of Internet startups including GoTo.com.

GoTo.com was born of Gross' concern that a growing wave of spam was detracting from the value of search engines such as Alta Vista. Spam arose because publishers of Websites realized that they could drive traffic to their sites by including commonly used search key words such as "used cars" or "airfares" on their sites. Often the words were in the same color as the background of the Website (e.g., black words on a black background) so that they could not be seen by Web users, who would suddenly wonder why their search for used cars had directed them to a porn site.

Gross also wanted a tool that would help drive good traffic to the Websites of a number of Internet businesses being developed by IdeaLab. In Gross' view, much of the traffic arriving at Websites was undifferentiated—people who had come to a site because of spam, bad portal real estate deals, or poor search engine results. Gross established GoTo.com to build a better search engine, one that would defeat spam, produce highly relevant results, and eliminate bad traffic.

Gross concluded that a way to limit spam was to charge for search. He realized that it was unworkable to charge the Internet user, so why not charge the advertiser? This led to his key insight—the keywords that Internet users typed into a search engine were inherently valuable to the owners of Websites. They drove traffic to their sites, and many sites made money from that traffic, so why not charge for the keywords? Moreover, Gross realized that if a search engine directed higher quality traffic to a site, it would be possible to charge more for relevant keywords.

By this time, GoTo.com had decided to license search engine technology from Inktomi and focus its efforts on developing the paid search model. However, GoTo.com faced a classic chicken and egg problem—to launch a service the company needed both audience and advertisers, but it had neither.

To attract advertisers GoTo.com adopted two strategies.[9] First, GoTo.com would only charge advertisers when somebody clicked on a link and was directed to their Website. To Gross' way thinking, for merchants this pay-per-click model would be more efficient than advertising through traditional media, or through banner ads on Web pages. Second, GoTo.com initially priced keywords low—as low as $0.01 a click (although they could, of course, be sold for more).

To capture an audience, a Website alone would not be enough. GoTo.com needed to tap into the traffic already visiting established Websites. One approach was to pay the owners of high-traffic Websites to place banner ads that would direct traffic to GoTo.com's Website. A second approach, which ultimately became the core of GoTo.com's business, was to syndicate its service, allowing affiliates to place a co-branded GoTo.com search box on their site, or to use GoTo.com's search engine and identify the results as "partner results." GoTo.com would then split the revenues from search with them. GoTo.com had to pay an upfront fee to significant affiliates, who viewed their Websites as valuable real estate. For example, in late-2000 GoTo.com paid AOL $50 million to syndicate GoTo.com's listings on its sites, which included AOL, CompuServe, and Netscape.

To finance its expansion, GoTo.com raised some $53 million in venture capital funding—a relatively easy proposition in the heady days of the dot.com boom. In June 1999, GoTo.com raised another $90 million through an initial public offering.[10]

GoTo.com launched its service in June 1998 with just 15 advertisers. Initially GoTo.com was paying more to acquire traffic than it was earning from click-through-ad revenue. According to its initial IPO filing, in its first year of operation, GoTo.com was paying $0.055 a click to acquire traffic from Microsoft's MSN sites and around $0.04 a click to acquire traffic from Netscape. The average yield from this traffic, however, was still less than the cost of acquisition, resulting in red ink—not an unusual situation for a dot.com in the 1990s.

However, the momentum was beginning to shift toward the company. As traffic volumes grew, and as advertisers began to understand the value of keywords, yields improved. By early-1999, the price of popular keywords was starting to rise. The highest bidder for the keyword "software" was $0.59 a click, "books" was $0.38 a click, "vacations" $0.36 a click, and "porn," the source of so much spam, $0.28 a click.[11]

The turning point was the AOL syndication deal signed in September 2000. Prior to signing with AOL,

GoTo.com was reaching 24 million users through its affiliates. After the deal, it was reaching 60 million unique users, or some 75% of the United States Internet audience (AOL itself had 23 million subscribers, CompuServe 3 million, and Netscape—which was owned by AOL—another 31 million registered users).[12] With over 50,000 advertisers now in its network and a large audience pool, both keyword prices and click-through rates increased. GoTo.com turned profitable shortly after the AOL deal was put into effect. In 2001, the company earned net profits of $20.2 million on revenues of $288 million. In 2002, it earned $73.1 million on revenues of $667.7 million, making it one of the few dot.com companies to break into profitability.

In 2001, GoTo.com changed its name to Overture Services. The name change reflected the results of a strategic shift. By 2001, the bulk of revenues were coming from affiliate sites, with the GoTo.com Website only garnering 5% of the company's total traffic.[13] Still, because GoTo.com had its own Website, it was in effect competing with traffic going to affiliates and creating potential channel conflict. Many in the company feared that channel conflict might induce key affiliates, such as AOL, to switch their allegiance. After much internal debate, the company decided to phase out the GoTo.com Website, focusing all of its attention on the syndication network.

Around the same time, Bill Gross apparently talked to the founders of another fast growing search engine, Google, about whether they would be interested in merging the two companies. At the time Google had no business model. Gross was paying attention to the fast growth of traffic going to Google's Website. He saw a merger as an opportunity to join a superior search engine with Overture's advertising and syndication network (the company was still using Inktomi's search engine). The talks stalled, however, reportedly because Google's founders stated that they would never be associated with a company that mixed paid advertising with organic results.[14]

Within months, however, Google had introduced its own advertising service using a pay-for-click model that looked very similar in conception to Overture's. Overture promptly sued Google for patent infringement. To make maters worse, in 2002 AOL declined to renew its deal with Overture, and instead switched to Google for search services.

By 2003, it was clear that although still growing and profitable, Overture was losing traction to

Google (Overture's revenues were on track to hit $1 billion in 2003 and the company had 80,000 advertisers in its network)[15]. Moreover, Overture was invisible to many of its users, who saw the service as a part of the offering of affiliates, many of whom were powerful brands in their own right, including Yahoo! and Microsoft's MSN. Yahoo! and Microsoft were also waking up to the threat posed by Google. Realizing that paid search was becoming a highly profitable market, both began to eye Overture to jump start their own paid search services. While Microsoft apparently decided to build its own search engine and ad service from scratch, Yahoo! decided to bid for Overture. In June 2003, a deal was announced, and Overture was sold to Yahoo! for $1.63 billion in cash. The payday was a bittersweet one for Bill Gross. IdeaLab had done very well out of Overture, but Gross couldn't help but feel that a bigger opportunity had slipped through his fingers and into the palms of Google's founders.

As for the patent case, this settled in 2004 when Google agreed to hand over 2.7 million shares to Yahoo!. This represented about 1% of the outstanding stock, which at the time was valued at $330. Today the value of those shares is closer to $1 billion.[16]

Google Rising

Google started as a research project undertaken by Larry Page while he was a computer science PhD student at Stanford in 1996. Called BackRub, the goal of the project was to document the link structure of the Web. Page had observed that while it was easy to follow links from one page to another, it was much more difficult to discover links *back*. Put differently, just by looking at a page, it was impossible to know who was linking to that page. Page reasoned that this might be very important information. Specifically, one might be able to rank to value of a Web page by discovering which pages were linking to it and if those pages were linked to many other pages.

To rank pages, Page knew that he would have to send out a Web crawler to index pages and archive links. At this point, another PhD student, Sergey Brin became involved in the project. Brin, a gifted mathematician, was able to develop an algorithm that ranked Web pages according not only to the number of links into that site, but also the number of links into each of the linking sites. This methodology had

the virtue of discounting links from pages that had few if any links into them.

Brin and Page noticed that the search results generated by this algorithm were superior to those returned by Alta Vista and Excite, both of which often returned irrelevant results, including a fair share of spam. They had stumbled onto the key ingredient for a better search engine—rank search results according to their relevance using a back link methodology. Moreover, they realized that the bigger the Web, the better the results would be.

Brin and Page released the basic details of what was now a search engine on the Stanford Website in August 1996. They christened their new search engine "Google" after googol, the term for the number 1 followed by 100 zeros. Early on Brin and Page talked to several companies about the possibility of licensing Google. Executives at Excite took a look but passed, as did executives at Infoseek and Yahoo!. Many of these companies were embroiled in the portal wars—and portals were all about acquiring traffic, not about sending it away via search. Search just didn't seem central to their mission.

By late-1998, Google was serving some 10,000 queries per day and was rapidly outgrowing the computing resources available at Stanford. Brin and Page realized that to get the resources required to keep scaling Google they needed capital, and that meant starting a company. Here Stanford's deep links into Silicon Valley came in useful. Before long they found themselves sitting together with Andy Bechtolsheim, one of the founders of another Stanford startup, Sun Microsystems. Bechtolsheim watched a demo of Google and wrote a check on the spot for $100,000.

Google was formally incorporated on September 7, 1998 with Page as CEO and Brin as President. From this point on, things began to rapidly accelerate. Traffic was growing by nearly 50 % a month, enough to attract the attention of several angle investors (including Amazon founder Jeff Bezos), who collectively put in another million. That was not enough; search engines have a voracious appetite for computing resources. To run its search engine, Brin and Page had custom designed a low-cost, Linux based server architecture that was modular and could be rapidly scaled. But to keep up with the growth of the Web and return answers to search queries in a fraction of a second, they needed ever more machines (by late-2005, the company was reportedly using over 250,000 Linux servers to handle more than 3,000 searches a second).[17]

To finance growth of their search engine, in early-1999 Brin and Page started to look for venture capital funding. It was the height of the dot.com boom and money was cheap. Never mind that there was no business model, Google's growth was enough to attract considerable interest. By June 1999, the company had closed its first round of venture capital financing, raising $25 million from two of the premier firms in Silicon Valley, Sequoia Capital and Kleiner Perkins Caufield & Byers. Just as importantly perhaps, the legendary John Doerr, one of Silicon Valley's most successful investors and a Kleiner Perkins partner, took a seat on Google's board.

By late-1999, Google had grown to around 40 employees, and it was serving some 3.5 million searches a day. However, the company was burning through $500,000 a month, and there was still no business model. They had some licensing deals with companies that used Google as their search technology, but they were not bringing in enough money to stem the flow of red ink. At this point, Google started to experiment with ads, but they were not yet pay-per-click ads. Rather, Google began selling text-based ads to clients that were interested in certain keywords. The ads would then appear on the page returning search results, but not in the list of relevant sites. For example, if someone typed in "Toyota Corolla," an ad would appear at the top of the page, above the list of links for Toyota Corolla cars. These ads were sold on a "cost per thousand impressions" basis, or CPM (the M being the Roman numeral for thousand). In other words, the cost of an ad was determined by how many people were estimated to have viewed it—not how many clicked on it. It didn't work very well.

The management team also started to ponder placing banner ads on Google's Website as a way of generating additional revenue, but before they made that decision the dot.com boom imploded, the NASDAQ crashed, and the volume of online advertising dropped precipitously. Google clearly needed to figure out a different way to make money.

Google Gets a Business Model

Brin and Page now looked closely at the one search company that seemed to be making good money, GoTo.com. They could see the value of the pay-per-click model, and of auctioning off keywords, but

there were things about GoTo.com that they did not like. GoTo.com would give guarantees that Websites would be included more frequently in Web crawls, making sure they were updated, provided that the owners were prepared to pay more. Moreover, the purity of GoTo.com's search results was biased by the desire to make money from advertisers, with those who paid the most being ranked highest. Brin and Page were ideologically attached to the idea of serving up the best possible search results to users, uncorrupted by commercial considerations. At the same time, they needed to make money.

Although Bill Gross pitched the idea of GoTo.com teaming up with Google, Brin and Page decided to go it alone. They believed they could do as good a job as GoTo.com, so why share revenues with the company?[18]

The approach that Google ultimately settled on combined the innovations of GotTo.com with Google's superior relevance based search engine. Brin and Page had always believed that Google's Web page should be kept as clean and elegant as possible—something that seemed to appeal to users. Moreover, they knew that users valued the fact that Google served up relevant search results that were unbiased by commercial considerations. The last thing they wanted to do was alienate their rapidly growing user base. So they decided to place text-based ads on the right hand side of a page, clearly separated from search results by a thin line.

Like GoTo.com, they decided to adopt a pay-per-click model. Unlike GoTo.com, Brin and Page decided that in addition to the price an advertiser had paid for a keyword, ads should also be ranked according to relevance. Relevance was measured by how frequently users clicked on ads. More popular ads rose to the top of the list, less popular ones fell. In other word's, Google allowed their users to rank ads. This had a nice economic advantage for Google, since an ad that is generating $1.00 a click, but is being clicked on three times as much as an ad generating $1.50 a click would make significantly more money for Google. It also motivated advertisers to make sure that their ads were appealing.

The system that Google used to auction off keywords was also different in detail from that used by GoTo.com. Google used a *Vickery second price auction* methodology. Under this system, the winner pays only $0.01 more than the bidder below them. Thus, if there are bids of $1, $0.50 and $0.25

for a keyword, the winner of the top place pays just $0.51 not $1, the winner of the second place $0.26, and so on. The auction is nonstop, with the price for a keyword rising or falling depending upon bids at each moment in time. Although the minimum bid for a keyword was set at $0.05, most were above that, and the range was wide. One of the most expensive search terms was reputed to be "mesothelioma," a type of cancer caused by exposure to asbestos. Bids were around $30 per click! They came from lawyers vying for a chance to earn lucrative fees by representing clients in suits against asbestos producers.[19]

While developing this service, Google continued to grow like wildfire. In mid-2000, the service was dealing with 18 million search queries per day and the index surpassed one billion documents, making it by far the largest search engine on the Web. By late-2000, when Google introduced the first version of its new service, which it called "AdWords," the company was serving up 60 million search queries a day—giving it a scale that GoTo.com never came close to achieving. In February 2002, Google introduced a new version of AdWords that included for the first time the full set of pay-per-click advertising, keyword auctions, and advertising links ranked by relevance. Sales immediately started to accelerate. Google had hit on the business model that would propel the company into the big league.

In 2003, Google introduced a second product, AdSense. AdSense allowed third party publishers large and small to access Google's massive network of advertisers on a self-service basis. Publishers could sign up for AdSense in a matter of minutes. AdSense would then scan the publisher's site for content and place contextually relevant ads next to that content. As with AdWords, this is a pay-per-click service, but AdSense splits the revenues with the publishers. In addition to large publishers, such as online news sites, AdSense has been particularly appealing to many small publishers, such as Web Bloggers. Small publishers found that by adding a few lines of code to their site, they could suddenly monetize their content. However, many advertisers feel that AdSense is not as effective as AdWords in driving traffic to their sites. Google allowed advertisers to opt out of AdSense in 2004. Despite this, AdSense has also grown into a respectable business, accounting for 15% of Google's revenues in 2005, or close to $1 billion.

Google Grows Up

Between 2001 and 2010, Google changed in a number of ways. First, in mid-2001 the company hired a new CEO to replace Larry Page, Eric Schmidt. Schmidt had been the Chief Technology Officer of Sun Microsystems, and then CEO of Novell. Schmidt was brought on to help manage the company's growth with the explicit blessing of Brin and Page. Both Brin and Page were still in their 20s, and the board felt they needed a "grown up" who had run a large company to help Google transition to the next stage (Google turned a profit the month after Schmidt joined). Brin and Page became the Presidents of Technology and Products, respectively. When Schmidt was hired, Google had over 200 employees and was handling over 100 million searches a day.

According to knowledgeable observers, Schmidt, Brin and Page acted as a triumvirate, with Brin and Page continuing to exercise a very strong influence over strategies and policies at Google. Schmidt may have been CEO, but Google was still very much Brin and Page's company.[20] Working closely together, the three drove the development of a set of values and an organization that would come to define Google's unique way of doing things. In January 2011, Schmidt retired from the CEO position, passing the reins back to Larry Page. Schmidt remained Chairman.

Vision and Values

As Google's growth started to accelerate, there was concern that rapid hiring would quickly dilute the vision, values and principles of the founders. In mid-2001, Brin and Page gathered a core group of early employees and asked them to come up with a policy for ensuring that the company's culture did not fracture as the company added employees. From this group, and subsequent discussions, emerged a vision and list of values that have continued to shape the evolution of the company. These were not new, rather, they represented the formalization of principles to which Brin and Page felt they had always adhered.

The central vision of Google is to *organize the world's information and make it universally acceptable and useful.*[21] The team also articulated a set of 10 core philosophies (values), which are now listed on its Website.[22] Perhaps the most significant and certainly the most discussed of these values is captured by the phrase "*don't be evil.*" The central message underlying this phrase was that Google should never compromise the integrity of its search results. Google would never let commercial considerations bias its rankings. Don't be evil, however, has become more than that at Google; it has become a central organizing principle of the company, albeit one that is far from easy to implement. Google got positive press from libertarians when it refused to share its search data with the U.S. government, which wanted the data to help fight child porn. However, the same constituency reacted with dismay when the company caved into the Chinese government and removed from its Chinese service offending results for search terms such as "human rights" and "democracy"! Brin justified the Chinese decision by saying that "it will be better for Chinese Web users, because ultimately they will get more information, though not quite all of it."[23]

Another core value at Google is "*focus on the user, and all else will follow.*" In many ways, this value captures what Brin and Page initially developed. They focused on giving the user the best possible search experience—highly relevant results, delivered with lightening speed to an uncultured and elegant interface. The value also reflects a belief at Google that it is okay to deliver value to users first and then figure out the business model for monetizing that value. This belief seems to reflect Google's own early experience.

Yet another key principle, although it is not one that is written down anywhere, is captured by the phrase "*launch early and often.*" This seems to underpin Google's approach to product development. Google has introduced a rash of new products over the last few years, not all of which are initially that compelling, but through rapid upgrades, it has subsequently improved the efficacy of those products.

Google also prides itself on being a company where decisions are *data driven*. Opinions are said to count for nothing unless they are backed up by hard data. It is not the loudest voice that wins the day in arguments over strategy, it is the data. In some meetings, people are not allowed to say "I think . . ." but instead "The data suggests. . . ."[24]

Finally, Google devotes considerable resources to making sure that its employees are working in a supportive and stimulating environment. To quote from the company's Website:

Google Inc. puts employees first when it comes to daily life in our Googleplex headquarters. There is an emphasis on team achievements and pride in individual accomplishments that contribute to the company's overall success. Ideas are traded, tested, and put into practice with an alacrity that can be dizzying. Meetings that would take hours elsewhere are frequently little more than a conversation in line for lunch and few walls separate those who write the code from those who write the checks. This highly communicative environment fosters a productivity and camaraderie fueled by the realization that millions of people rely on Google results. Give the proper tools to a group of people who like to make a difference, and they will.[25]

Organization

By all accounts, Google has a flat organization. In November 2005, Google had 1 manager for every 20 line employees. At times, the ratio has been as high as 1:40. For a while—one manager had 180 direct reports.[26] The structure is reportedly based on teams. Big projects are broken down and allocated to small, tightly focused teams. Hundreds of projects may be going on at the same time. Teams often release new software in 6 weeks or less and look at how users respond hours later. Google can try a new user interface, or some other tweak, with just 0.1% of its users and get massive feedback very quickly, letting it decide a project's fate in weeks.[27]

One aspect of Google's organization that has garnered considerable attention is the company's approach toward product development. Employees are expected to spend 20% of their time on something that interests them, away from their main jobs. Seemingly based on 3M's famous 15% rule, Google's 20% rule is designed to encourage creativity. The company has set up forums on its internal network where anyone can post ideas, discuss them, and solicit help from other employees. As a natural part of this process, talent tends to gravitate to those projects that seem most promising, giving those who post the most interesting ideas the ability to select a talented team to take them to the next level.

Like 3M, Google has set up a process by which projects coming out of 20% time can be evaluated, receive feedback from peers, and ultimately garner funding. Marissa Myer, one of Google's early employees, acts as a gatekeeper, helping to decide when projects are ready to be pitched to senior management (and that typically means Brin and Page). Once in front of the founders, advocates have 20 minutes, and no more, to make their pitch.[28] Myer has also articulated a number of other principals that guide product development at Google.[29] These include:

1. Ideas come from everywhere: Set up a system where good ideas rise to the top.
2. Focus on users, not money: Money follows consumers. Advertisers follow consumers. If you amass a lot of consumers you will find ways to monetize your ideas.
3. Innovation, not instant perfection: Put products on the market, learn and iterate.
4. Don't kill projects, morph them: If an idea has managed to make its way out of the door, there is usually some kernel of truth to it. Don't walk away from ideas, think of ways to replace or rejuvenate them.

One of the early products to come out 20% time was Google News, which returns news articles ranked by relevance in response to a key word query. Put the term "oil prices" into Google News, for example, and the search will return news dealing with changes in oil prices, with the most relevant at the top of the list. A sophisticated algorithm determines relevance on a real-time basis by looking at the quality of the news source (e.g., *The New York Times* rates higher than local news papers), publishing date, the number of other people who click on that source, and numerous other factors. Krishna Bharat, a software engineer from India, initiated the project, who, in response to the events of September 11, 2001, had a desire to learn what was being written and said around the world. Two other employees worked with Bharat to construct a demo that was released within Google. Positive reaction soon got Bharat in front of Brin and Page, who were impressed and gave the project a green light; Bharat started to work on the project full time.[30]

Another feature of Google's organization is its hiring strategy. Like Microsoft, Google has made a virtue out of hiring people with a high IQ. The hiring process is very rigorous. Each prospect has to take an "exam" to test their conceptual abilities. This is followed by interviews with 8 or more people, each of who rate the applicant on a 1–4 scale (4 being "I would hire this person"). Applicants also undergo detailed background checks to find out their work-

ing styles. Reportedly, some brilliant prospects don't get hired when background checks find state they are difficult to work with. In essence, all hiring at Google is by committee, and while this can take considerable time, the company insists that the effort yields dividends.

While accounts of Google's organization and culture tend to emphasize their positive aspects, not everyone has such a sanguine view. Brain Reid, who was recruited into senior management at Google in 2002 and fired 2 years later, told author John Battelle "Google is a monarchy with two kings, Larry and Sergey. Eric is a puppet. Larry and Sergey are arbitrary, whimsical people . . . they run the company with an iron hand . . . Nobody at Google from what I could tell had any authority to do anything of consequence except Larry and Sergey."[31] According to Battelle, several other former employees made similar statements.

Other former employees have noted that in practice 20% time turns out to be 120% time, because people still have their regular work load. There are also complaints that the culture is one of long work days and 7-day work weeks, with little consideration for family issues. Several employees have complained that Google's organization is not scaling that well and that with nearly 14,000 employees on the books, the firm's personnel department is "collapsing" and that "absolute chaos reigns." One former employee noted that when she was hired, nobody knew when or where she was supposed to work.[32]

Many of the early employees, who are now financially wealthy, are starting to leave. As a result, employee turnover is increasing. At the same time, there are reports that the company's free wheeling culture has led to a rather anarchic resource allocation process, and extensive duplication, with multiple teams working on the same project.[33]

The IPO

As Google's growth started to accelerate, the question of if and when to undertake an IPO became more pressing. There were two obvious reasons for doing an IPO—gaining access to capital and providing liquidity for early backers and the large number of employees who had equity positions. On the other hand, from 2001 onward, the company was profitable, generating significant cash flows, and could internally fund its expansion. Moreover, management felt that the longer they could keep the details of what was turning out to be an extraordinarily successful business model private, the better. In the end, the company's hand was forced by an obscure SEC regulation that required companies that give stock options to employees to report as if they were public company by as early as April 2004. Realizing that the cat would be out of the bag anyway, Google told its employees in early-2004 that it would go public.

True to form, Google flouted Wall Street tradition in the way it structured its IPO. The company decided to auction off shares directly to the public using an untested and modified version of a Dutch auction, which starts by asking for a high price and then lowers it until someone accepts. Two classes of shares were created, Class A and B; Class B's shares had 10 times the votes of Class A shares. Only Class A shares were auctioned. Brin, Page and Schmidt were holders of Class B shares. Consequently, although they would own 1/3 of the company after the IPO, they would control 80% of the votes. Google also announced that it would not provide regular financial guidance to Wall Street financial analysts. In effect, Google had thumbed its nose at Wall Street.

The controversial nature of the IPO, however, was overshadowed by the first public glimpse of Google's financials, which were contained in the offering document. They were jaw dropping. The company had generated revenues of $1.47 billion in 2003, an increase of 230% over 2002. Google earned net profits of $106 million in 2003, but accountants soon figured out that the number was depressed by certain one time accounting items and that cash flow in 2003 had been over $500 million!

Google went public on August 19, 2004 at $85 a share. The company's first quarterly report showed sales doubling over the prior year, and by November the price was $200.

In September 2005, with the stock close to $300 a share, Google undertook a secondary offering, selling 14 million shares to raise $4.18 billion. With positive cash flow adding to this, by June 2008 Google was sitting on $12.8 billion in cash and short-term investments, prompting speculation as to the company's strategic intentions.

Strategy

Since 2001, Google has endeavored to keep enhancing the efficacy of its search engine, continually im-

proving the search algorithms and investing heavily in computing resources. The company has branched out from a text-based search engine. One strategic thrust has been to extend search to as many digital devices as possible. Google started out on PCs, but can now be accessed through PDAs and cell phones. A second strategy has been to widen the scope of search to include different sorts of information. Google has pushed beyond text into indexing and offering up searches of images, news reports, books, maps, scholarly papers, a blog search, a shopping network (Froogle), and videos. Google Desktop, which searches files on a user's personal computer, also fits in with this schema. However, not all of these new search formats have advertising attached to them (e.g., images and scholarly papers do not include sponsored links, while map and book searching does).

Not all of this has gone smoothly. Book publishers have been angered by Google's book project, which seeks to create the world's largest searchable digital library of books by systematically scanning books from the libraries of major universities (e.g., Stanford). The publishers have argued that Google has no right to do this without first getting permission from the publishers and is violating copyright by doing so. Several publishers have filed a complaint with the U.S. District Court in New York. Google has responded that users will not be able to download entire books and that in any event creating an easy to use index of books is fair use under copyright law and will increase the awareness and sales of books, directly benefiting copyright holders. On another front, the World Association of Newspaper Publishers has formed a task force to examine the exploitation of content by search engines.[34]

Over the last 6 years Google has introduced a rash of product offerings, not all of which have a strong affinity with the company's search mission. Many of these products grew out of the company's new product development process. They have include free e-mail (gmail) and online chat programs, a calendar, a blog site (Blogger), a social networking site (Orkut), a finance site (Google Money), a service for finding, editing and sharing photos (Picasa), and plans to offer citywide free WiFi networks.

Google has introduced several Web-based applications that seem squarely aimed at Microsoft's Office franchise, collectively known as Google Apps. In March of 2006, the company acquired a word processing program, Writely. This was quickly followed by the introduction of a spreadsheet program, Google Spreadsheets. These products have the look and feel of Microsoft Word and Excel, respectively. Both products are designed for online collaboration. They can save files in formats used by Microsoft products, although they lack the full feature set of Microsoft's offerings. Google states that the company is not trying to match the features of office and that "90% of users don't necessarily need 90% of the functions that are in there."[35] For an annual licensing fee of $50, Google provides corporate customers with an Apps service that includes gmail and its Office-like products.

In July 2006, Google introduced a product to compete with PayPal, a Web-based payment system owned by the online auction giant, eBay. Google's product, known as "Checkout," offers secure online payment functionality for both merchants and consumers. For merchants, the fee for using Checkout is being priced below PayPal's. Moreover, Checkout is being integrated into Google's AdWords product, so merchants who participate will be highlighted in Google's search results. In addition, merchants who purchase Google's search advertising will get a discount on processing fees. According to one analysis, a merchant with monthly sales of $100,000 who uses Checkout and AdWords stands to reduce their transaction costs by 28%, or $8,400 a year. If they use just Checkout, they will reduce their transaction costs by 4%, or $1,200 a year.[36] However, with 105 million accounts in mid-2006, PayPal will be difficult to challenge.

In late-2007, Google announced another new product, this time a suite of software for smartphones that include an operating system, Android, and applications that work with it. Android is squarely aimed at Apple's iPhone and Research In Motion's BlackBerry, which are the two runaway successes in the smartphone space. The attraction for Google is that advertising is increasingly being inserted into content viewed on mobile handsets. By one estimate, worldwide spending on mobile advertising will rise to $19 billion in 2012, up from $2.7 billion in 2007.[37] Google gives away Android for free, and aims to make money through mobile search.

By 2011, Android was gaining strong traction, with a number of equipment manufacturers including HTC, Motorola, Samsung, and LG offering Android powered smartphones. In January 2011, Android powered phones led the U.S. smartphone market with a 31.2% share, followed by RIM with a 30.4% share, and Apple with a 24.7% share.[38] Phones powered by a Microsoft operating system had only an 8% share. Android was gaining share at the expense of all other players except Apple—its share had increased from 13% in May 2010. In October 2010, Google reported that its mobile advertising revenues were growing strongly and had hit an annualized run rate of $1 billion.[39]

Some analysts have questioned the logic behind Google's new product efforts, noting that their track record on new product offerings has been mixed. One noted that: "Google has product ADD. They don't know why they are getting into all of these products. They have fantastic cash flow, but terrible discipline on products."[40] Another has accused Google of having an insular culture and argued that "Neither Froogle or Google's travel efforts has gained any traction, at least partly because of Google's tendency to provide insufficient support to its ecosystem partners and its habit of acting in an independent, secretive manner."[41] However, others argue that Google has been successful in upgrading the quality of its new offerings and that several products that were once laggards, such as Google News, are now the best in breed.[42] Moreover, it is very difficult to argue with the success of Android.

On the acquisition front, Google stuck to purchasing small technology firms until 2006. This changed in October 2006 when Google announced that it would purchase YouTube for $1.64 billion in stock. YouTube is a simple, fun Website to which anybody can upload video clips in order to share them. In October 2006 some 65,000 video clips were being uploaded every day and 100 million were being watched. Like Google in its early days, YouTube had no business model. Google thought it would find ways to sell advertising that is linked to video clips on YouTube.[43]

Over the next 4 years, YouTube continued to grow at a rapid pace. By May 2011, YouTube ranked as the top U.S. online video site with 147 million unique viewers, followed by Vevo, the fast growing music video site, which had 60.4 million unique viewers. Yahoo! sites were next with 55.5 million, followed by Facebook sites with 48.2 million.[44] Although detailed figures are not available, it appears that Google is starting to make significant money from YouTube by selling display ads, and through a service where advertisers pay Google whenever a user clicks on and watches one of their ads.

Another notable Google acquisition was its $3.1 billion purchase of DoubleClick in 2007. DoubleClick is an online display advertising specialist, using formats such as banner ads that are targeted at building brand awareness. Internet publishers pay DoubleClick to insert display ads on their Websites as users visit their Websites. While display advertising has not grown as rapidly as search-based advertising, it is a big business accounting for around 1/4 of all Internet advertising revenue with significant upside potential as companies begin to apply demographic technology to increase the effectiveness of Internet display ads.[45] The DoubleClick deal was criticized by Google's rivals, including Microsoft, on antitrust grounds, but regulators in the United States and the EU approved the deal, which closed in 2008. By the end of 2010, Google was reporting that annualized revenues for display ads were running at around $2.5 billion.

Critics argue that as Google moves into these additional areas, its profit margins will be compressed. Henry Blodget of Cherry Hill Research notes that in its core business, Google makes profit margins of about 60%. In its more recent business of placing advertisements on Web pages belonging to other people, such as bloggers, its profit margins are 10–20%, because it is harder to make the advertisements as relevant to the audience and it must share the resulting revenues. Display advertising also offers lower returns. Google, not surprisingly, does not see things this way. The company argues that since its costs are mostly fixed, and incremental revenue is profit, it makes good sense to push into other markets, even if its average revenue per viewer is only $0.01 (compared with $0.50 for each click on the Web).[46]

The Online Advertising Market in 2010

There is an old adage in advertising that half of all the money spent on advertising is wasted—advertisers just don't know which half. Estimates suggest that around 1/2 of the $500 billion worldwide advertising spent is wasted because the wrong message is sent to the wrong audience.[47] The problem is that traditional media advertising is indiscriminate. Consider a 30 second ad spot on broadcast TV. Advertisers pay a rate for such a spot called CPM (costs per thousand). The CPM is based on estimates of how many people are watching a show. There are numerous problems with this system. The estimates of audience numbers are only approximations at best. The owners of the TV may have left the room while the commercials are airing. They may channel surf during the commercial break, be napping, or talking on the telephone. The viewer may not be among the intended audience—a Viagra commercial might be wasted on a teenage girl, for example. Or the household might be using a TiVo or a similar digital video recorder that skips commercials.

By contrast, new advertising models based on pay-per-click are more discriminating. Rather than sending out ads to a large audience, only a few of whom will be interested in the products being advertised, consumers select in to search based ads. They do this twice, first, by entering a key word in a search engine, and second, by scanning the search results as well as the sponsored links, and clicking on a link. In effect, potential purchasers pull the ads toward them through the search process. Advertisers only pay when someone clicks on their ad. Consequently, the conversion rate for search-based ads is far higher than the conversion rate for traditional media advertising.

Moreover, traditional advertising is so wasteful that most firms only advertise 5%–10% of their products in the mass media, hoping that other products will benefit from a halo effect. In contrast, the targeted nature of search-based advertising makes it cost effective to advertise products that only sell in small quantities. In effect, search based Internet advertising allows producers to exploit the economics of the long tail. Pay-per-click models also make it economical for small merchants to advertise their wares on the Web.

The Growth Story

Powered by the rapid growth of search based pay-per-click advertising, and the increasing amount of time people spend online, total advertising spending on the Internet is expected to account for 15.1% of all global advertising spending in 2011, up from 13.9% in 2010 and 10.2% in 2008.[48] This structural growth trend is likely to continue for some time, since consumers in many developed nations are now spending over 25% of their media time online.[49] In terms of the mix of advertising online, search-based advertising dominates accounting for 47.2% of U.S. online advertising spending in 2010, followed by display advertising with a 36.1% share (classifieds and lead generation makes up most of the balance).[50]

Google has been the main beneficiary of this trend. In mid-2011 Google was the dominant search engine in America with a 65.5% share of all searches, up from 45% in 2006, followed by Yahoo! (15.9%) and Microsoft (14.1%). Google's share of total U.S. paid search advertising is larger still at around 75%. In the world's second largest market for search advertising, Europe, Google is estimated to command a staggering 97% of advertising spent.[51]

Google's rise is reflected in its increased share of all Internet traffic. In mid-2006 Google's Websites had the fourth largest unique audience on the Web, close behind the longer established portal sites maintained by Microsoft (MSN), Yahoo! and Time Warner (AOL) respectively. By mid-2010 Google's We sites were tied with Yahoo! sites for the number 1 spot, followed by Microsoft, Facebook, and AOL. In no small part, the addition of YouTube has helped to propel Google to the top of the traffic rankings.[52]

Google's Competitors

Google's most significant competitors are Yahoo! and Microsoft. As paid search has grown, all three have increased their investment in search.[53] Both Yahoo! and Microsoft spent several years and hundreds of millions in R&D spending trying to improve their search engine technology and gain market share at the expense of Google. Yahoo! failed, and their share has declined, while Microsoft recorded small market share gains of around 2% after it launched its Bing search engine in 2008. However, Microsoft has never made any money in the online search arena—in fact, it has lost billions. In fiscal 2010, its annualized run rate losses in this business were projected to be around $2.3 billion. Put differently, absent of any financial improvement, if Microsoft closed its search business tomorrow, this would boost the company's earnings per share by about $0.26, which at a price-to-earnings ratio of 15 represents a $3.90 increase in the share price. CEO Steve Ballmer, however, has indicated that search is a key strategic business for the company and exiting the business does not seem to be an option.

In February 2008, Microsoft launched an unsolicited takeover bid for Yahoo!. Microsoft offered $44.6 billion, or $31 a share, for Yahoo!, representing a 62% premium over the closing share price before the takeover announcement. Microsoft's rationalization for the takeover rested on the assumption that the combined entity would be able to realize substantial scale economies, with its expanded Web properties offering a more attractive value proposition to advertisers. In addition, Microsoft argued that it would be able to reduce costs by $1 billion per year by combining some assets, such as data centers.

After several months of difficult negotiations, during which Microsoft raised its bid to $33 a share and also threatened to fight a proxy battle to replace Yahoo!'s board with one favorable to the bid, Microsoft eventually withdrew its offer to acquire Yahoo!. In rationalizing its decision, Microsoft argued that Yahoo!'s continuing market share erosion during the months of negotiations had made the acquisition far less compelling. Yahoo!'s managers continued to argue that Microsoft was not offering enough.

Yahoo!, however, continued to lose market share. After some top management changes at Yahoo!, in June 2009, Microsoft and Yahoo! announced a broad based partnership in the search area. Under the terms of the agreement, Bing will be the exclusive search platform at Yahoo!. Yahoo! will be the exclusive seller to both companies' Premium Search advertisers, while Microsoft's AdCenter will handle self-service advertising. Each company will continue to manage their own display advertising business. Yahoo! also has the option to use Bing on their mobile properties.

The partnership received regulatory approval in mid-2010, and both companies began to implement the agreement in late-2010. To succeed, the partnership must (a) increase search query volume and (b) drive greater revenues per search. In 2009, estimates suggest that Google was generating $36.37 of revenue per thousand search queries, Yahoo! $17.06, and Microsoft $14.31.

Search query volume could increase if the greater traffic improves the relevance of search results generated by Bing and if consumers and advertisers notice this. Revenues per search could increase if advertisers are willing to bid more for keywords on Bing given the greater traffic volume of the search engine.

Another significant strategic partner for Microsoft is Facebook, the leading social network site with over 750 million registered users. Microsoft invested $240 million in Facebook in 2007 for a 1.6% stake. Since then, the two companies have worked together to introduce advertisements on Facebook. In October 2010, the two companies announced an extended deal that will incorporate Facebook data into Bing search results. Bing results will now include a Facebook module offering users the likes, images, comments, and other public data from their network of friends. Thus, when searching for restaurants, you can see if any of your friends liked or recommended a restaurant. There is no question that the evolving partnership between Microsoft and Facebook is in part a response to their common rival, Google.

Looking Forward

With online advertising predicted to grow strongly, Google seems to be in the driver's seat. It has the largest market share in search, the greatest name recognition, and is capturing a proportionately greater share of search based advertising than its rivals.

However, despite market share losses, Microsoft and Yahoo! cannot be dismissed. As their partnership in search progresses, will they be able to leverage their substantial assets and capabilities to gain ground of Google? As for Google, what is its long-term game plan? Recent strategic moves suggest that it is attempting to expand beyond search, but where will this take the company, and what does that mean for other Internet companies?

Endnotes

1 comScore Releases May 2011 Search Engine Rankings, comScore Press Release, June 10, 2011.

2 Nielsen/Net Ratings, "Google Accounts for Half of all U.S. Searches," May 25, 2006.

3 Dadid Hallerman, "Search Marketing: Players and Problems," *eMarketer,* April 2006; "Search Marketing Still Dominates Online Advertising," *eMarketer Press R elease,* January 29, 2008.

4 Citigroup Global Markets, "The Microhoo Search Transaction," May 23, 2010.

5 Citigroup Global markets, "Google Inc.," September 26, 2010.

6 This section draws heavily upon the excellent description of search given by John Battelle. See John Battelle, *The Search* (Penguin Portfolio, New York, 2005).

7 Google 10K for 2007.

8 The basic story of GoTo.com is related in John Battelle, *The Search* (Penguin Portfolio, New York, 2005).

9 Karl Greenberg, "Pay-for-placement Search Services Offer Ad Alternatives," *Adweek,* September 25, 2000, 60.

10 M. Gannon, "GoTo.com Inc," *Venture Capital Journal,* August 1, 1999, 1.

11 Tim Jackson, "Cash is the Key to a True Portal," *Financial Times,* February 2, 1999, 16.

12 Karl Greenberg, "Pay-for-placement Search Services Offer Ad Alternatives," *Adweek,* September 25, 2000, 60.

13 Sarah Heim, "GoTo.com Changes to Overture Services, Launches Campaign," *Adweek,* September 10, 2001, 7.

14 This little gem comes from John Battelle, *The Search* (Penguin Portfolio, New York, 2005). There is no independent confirmation of the story.

15 Anonymous, "Yahoo! to Acquire Overture Services for 2.44 Times Revenues," *Weekly Corporate Growth Service,* July 21, 2003, 8.

16 Richard Waters, "Google Settles Yahoo! Case with Shares," *Financial Times,* August 19, 2004, 29.

17 Fred Vogelstein, "Gates vs Google: Search and Destroy," *Fortune,* May 2, 2005, 72–82.

18 This is according to David A. Vise, *The Google Story* (Random House, New York, 2004).

19 David A. Vise, *The Google Story* (Random House, New York, 2004).

20 John Battelle, *The Search* (Penguin Portfolio, New York, 2005). There is no independent confirmation of the story.

21 http://www.google.com/corporate/index.html

22 http://www.google.com/corporate/tenthings.html

23 Andy Kessler, "Sellout.com," *Wall Street Journal,* January 31, 2006, A14.

24 Quentin Hardy, "Google Thinks Small," *Fortune,* November 14, 2005, 198–199.

25 http://www.google.com/corporate/tenthings.html

26 Quentin Hardy, "Google Thinks Small," *Fortune,* November 14, 2005, 198–199.

27 Quentin Hardy, "Google Thinks Small," *Fortune,* November 14, 2005, 198–199.

28 Ben Elgin, "Managing Google's Idea Factory," *Business Week,* October 3, 2005, 88–90.

29 Michael Krauss, "Google's Mayer Tells How Innovation Gets Done," *Marketing News,* April 1, 2007, 7–8.

30 David A. Vise, *The Google Story* (Random House, New York, 2004).

31 John Battelle, *The Search* (Penguin Portfolio, New York, 2005), 233.

32 *The Economist,* "Inside the Googleplex," September 1, 2007, 53–56.

33 B. Lashinsky and Y.W. Yen, "Where does Google go Next?" *Fortune,* May 26, 2008, 104–110.

34 Jacqueline Doherty, "In the Drink," *Barrons*, February 13, 2006, 31–36.

35 K.J. Delaney and R.A. Guth, "Google's Free Web Services Will Vie with Microsoft Office," *Wall Street Journal*, October 11, 2006, B1.

36 Mark Mahany, "Building Out the Option Value of Google," *Citigroup Portfolio Strategist*, July 13, 2006.

37 *eMarketer*, "Mobile Ad Spending to Soar," eMarketer Press Release, August 20, 2008.

38 *comScore*, "comScore Reports January 2011 Mobile Subscriber Market Share," ComScore Press release, March 7, 2011.

39 Citigroup Global Markets, "Google Inc.," October 14, 2010.

40 Ben Elgin, "So Much Fanfare, So Few Hits," *Business Week*, July 10, 2006, 27.

41 David Card, "Understanding Google," *Jupiter Research*, March 10, 2006.

42 Mark Mahany, "Building Out the Option Value of Google," *Citigroup Portfolio Strategist*, July 13, 2006.

43 *The Economist*, "Two Kings Get Together; Google and YouTube," October 14, 2006, 82–83.

44 *comScore*, "May 2011 Online Video Rankings," comScore Press Release, June 17, 2011.

45 R. Hof, "Ad Wars: Google's Green Light," *Business Week*, March 3, 2008, 22.

46 *The Economist*, "Inside the Googleplex," September 1, 2007, 53–56.

47 *The Economist*, "The Ultimate Marketing Machine," July 8, 2006, 61–64; K.J. Delaney, "Google Push to Sell Ads on YouTube Hits Snag," *Wall Street Journal*, July 9, 2008, A1.

48 Emily Fredrix, "Firm Boosts This Year's Advertising Forecasts," *The Canadian Press*, October 18, 2010.

49 *The Economist*, "The Ultimate Marketing Machine," July 8, 2006, 61–64.

50 Citigroup Global Markets, "The Microhoo Search Transaction," May 23, 2010.

51 Citigroup Global Markets, "The Microhoo Search Transaction," May 23, 2010.

52 Nielsen/Net Ratings Press Release, "U.S. Broadband Composition Reaches 72% at Home," June 21, 2006; comScore, "comScore Media Matrix Ranks top 50 US Web Properties for August 2010," comScore Press Release, September 23, 2010.

53 David Hallerman, "Search Marketing, Players and Problems," *eMarketer*, April 2006.

CASE 5

Ecomagination: Driving Sustainable Growth for GE

"GE should be commended for a bold approach to climate issues. However, the company has a long way to go before it can legitimately claim to be an environmentally progressive company."[1]
—Jeff Jones, Communications Director, Environmental Advocates of New York,[2] in 2009.

Green Can Be Green!

On June 24, 2009, US-based technology giant General Electric Company (GE), surpassed its target of investing US$5 billion in research and development in its environmental initiative, Ecomagination. GE had earlier set 2010 as the target for achieving this goal but reached it a year ahead of schedule.[3] The company planned to invest an additional US$10 billion in R&D by 2015. It was also on its way to achieving the US$20 billion mark in revenues from Ecomagination products, having generated US$18 billion in 2009, an increase of 6%. GE expected the Ecomagination revenue to grow at twice the rate of the total company revenue by 2015, which would give Ecomagination an even larger share of the total company sales. According to Steve M. Fludder (Fludder), vice president, Ecomagination, "We have grown Ecomagination revenue and research and development every year, even in challenging economic times. Given our success, we are committing to do more. The vision of a cleaner, affordable, secure, and globally accessible energy infrastructure inspires and motivates us."[4]

Established in 1892, GE is a diversified conglomerate with products and services ranging from aircraft engines and power generation to business and consumer financial services, healthcare, and television programming. Started in 2005, Ecomagination embodied GE's commitment to building innovative clean energy technologies and meeting customers' demands for more energy-efficient products and bringing reliable growth for the company. The main objectives of this green initiative were to reduce greenhouse gas (GHG) emissions, increase energy efficiency of GE operations, improve water use, double the investment in R&D for cleaner technologies, and keep the public informed about its Ecomagination efforts.

Through Ecomagination, GE developed products and services with lower environmental impact, such as energy-efficient engines, appliances, locomotives, and wind turbines. According to some analysts, Ecomagination was a business opportunity for GE to increase revenues by introducing energy-efficient products to customers.

However, some critics felt that Ecomagination was just a business savvy move by the company, aimed at resurrecting its image as an environment friendly company. Behind the façade of environmental sustainability and green technologies was GE's corporate goal of increasing profits, they alleged. Critics felt that the initiative was over-hyped and that GE was pursuing profits in the name of clean technologies. According to Kavita Prakash Mani, vice president of SustainAbility,[5] "GE has invested billions of dollars in Ecomagination, but it hasn't really changed the rest of its business. It's made out to be bigger than it actually is."[6] Executives from GE, however, maintained that Ecomagination was not a brand building exercise; it was a good business opportunity for GE to make money while at the same time contributing to environmental sustainability. "It's not an advertising ploy or marketing gimmick. GE wants to do this because it is right, but also we plan to make money while we do so,"[7] said Peter O'Toole (O'Toole), director of public relations at GE.

*This case was written by **Syeda Maseeha Qumer**, under the direction of **Debapratim Purkayastha**, IBS Center for Management Research. It was compiled from published sources, and is intended to be used as a basis for class discussion rather than to illustrate either effective or ineffective handling of a management situation.*

About GE

GE was formed in 1892 by the merger of the Edison General Electric Company (EGEC) and the Thomas-Houston Electric Company[8] (TEC). By the 1950s, GE had grown into a large industrial conglomerate with interests in diverse businesses. In the late 1960s, GE had 46 Strategic Business Units (SBUs) within the company and also diversified into other new businesses like computers, nuclear power, and aircraft engines. In 1977, GE's earnings crossed the US$1 billion mark.

In 1981, an important phase began in GE's history when Jack Welch (Welch) was appointed as CEO. One of Welch's core strategies was the Number One Number Two strategy.[9] In 1995, GE's market value exceeded US$100 billion. In 1996, GE completed 100 years on the Dow Jones Industrial Average,[10] the only company remaining from the original list of 12 stocks, first published on May 26, 1896.

In mid-2001, Jeffrey R. Immelt (Immelt) succeeded Welch as the Chairman and CEO of GE. Within days of his taking over, the September 11, 2001 terrorist attacks occurred. As a result, GE too was affected by the changes in the business environment. Immelt then brought in several changes at the company in order to win investor confidence. The company was listed on the Dow Jones Sustainability Index in late 2004.[11] In the fiscal year ended December 2005, GE posted revenues of more than US$149 billion.

In 2009, *Forbes* ranked GE as the world's largest company with over 300,000 employees in its various business units. At the end of 2009, GE had six core business units and was the biggest manufacturer of power plants, jet engines, locomotives, and medical equipment worldwide[12] (Refer Exhibit I). GE Global Research consisted of more than 3,000 employees working in four state-of-the-art facilities at Niskayuna (New York), Bangalore (India), Shanghai (China), and Munich (Germany). In 2009, despite the tough economic climate, GE reported earnings of US$11.2 billion (Refer Exhibit II and III). In 2010, GE was ranked among *Fortune's* 'Most Admired Companies in the World' for the 5th consecutive year. In the second quarter ended June 2010, the company's revenues fell by 4% to US$37.4 billion. Industrial sales were US$24.4 billion, down 6% compared to corresponding period of the previous year.

Winds of Change at GE

According to some analysts, GE had not been known over the years as a particularly environment-friendly company. In fact, it was considered for a long time as one of the biggest corporate polluters in the US. Though the company delivered outstanding returns to shareholders, it lagged behind on the social responsibility front. GE was criticized on several occasions for its lack of social responsibility. However, the company chose to ignore its critics and gave precedence to profitability and financial goals rather than social and environmental objectives, added experts.

During the 1980s and 1990s, GE stonewalled and delayed most of its environmental initiatives, and this led to significant negative equity among many in the environmental community. One of the biggest environmental controversies involving GE was related to the pollution of the Hudson and Housatonic rivers in the US. In the early-1980s, GE was indicted for dumping several million of pounds of polychlorinated biphenyls (PCBs)[13] into stretches of the two rivers from its factories located along their banks. In 1977, after the US Congress passed the Clean Water Act,[14] the US Environment Protection Agency (EPA)[15] banned the production of PCB. Since most of GE's PCB dumping had been done before 1972, when the substance was not banned by law, the company argued that it was not responsible for the sediments already present in the rivers. But environmentalists argued that the dangerous nature of PCBs had been well known even before the law had been passed, and that GE had acted irresponsibly in dumping the chemicals in the rivers.

Between 1991 and 1996, EPA charged GE with 23 violations when toxic releases from its plants went unreported. In March 1992, the Nuclear Regulatory Commission (NRC)[16] slapped a fine of US$20,000 on GE for violating regulations at its fuel fabrication plant in Wilmington, North Carolina. It was reported that workers at the plant had accidentally moved about 320 pounds of uranium to a waste treatment tank, which could have led to a nuclear accident. Later, the NRC found that the mistake had been made because of lax safety controls at the plant. Again in March 1998, GE was fined US$92,000 for violations of environmental reporting requirements for toxic releases at its silicone manufacturing plant in Waterford, New York.

Though GE gave more significance to profitability than to social responsibility, the business environment prevailing in the early-2000s made companies look beyond financial goals. Sustainability became critical for business success as climate change, water scarcity, and poverty were seen as profound challenges for the global economy. During this time, the Kyoto Protocol[17] was a much discussed subject, and at global forums like the G8[18] and WTO[19] meetings, environmental sustainability became a hot topic. Moreover, as consumers and investors became more environmentally conscious than before, it became more important for companies to consider environmental sustainability in their operations.

In 2001, when Immelt succeeded Welch, the company started to focus more on addressing environmental challenges. Immelt felt that sustainability was a profitable business opportunity rather than a cost and hence seized on the idea of greening GE's technology and turning it into a corporate-wide strategy for growth. He felt that with creativity and imagination, it was possible to solve some of the world's most difficult environmental problems and make money while doing it. Immelt's new slogan was "green is green," meaning that green business equaled green money.

Immelt wanted GE to support climate change and invest in creating new markets for cleaner fuels and technologies as they offered opportunities for product innovation. He consulted executives from other companies who had launched environmental programs such as DuPont[20] Chairman and CEO, Charles Holliday Jr. They advised him to solve the company's earlier environmental problems and then go ahead with green product ideas.

In 2002, a large team of executives from GE attended a training session on CSR at Crotonville. As part of the training, the executives visited several companies that dealt with social and environmental issues such as IBM,[21] Eli Lilly,[22] BP,[23] and Nike.[24] They also interacted with regulators, activists, and investors, who had an interest in CSR. During the course of their training, the executives found that though GE was well known for its management quality and operations, it ranked low on the social responsibility aspect. They felt that for GE to maintain its position in the global economy, immediate steps had to be taken to build its image as an environmentally-friendly company.

In 2002, Christine Todd Whitman, the then EPA Administrator, issued a ruling related to the Hudson river clean-up that gave GE two options—to agree to an out of court settlement, or pay fines of up to US$2 billion.[25] In 2005, GE entered into an agreement with the EPA and the US Department of Justice to carry out a two stage clean-up of the Hudson River at an estimated cost of around US$750 million.[26]

In the early 2000s, GE launched several global initiatives in order to make the company more socially responsible. For instance, it started conducting audits on its suppliers to ensure that they were complying with globally accepted labor, environmental, health, and safety standards in their operations. In 2002, Immelt appointed Bob Corcoran, a long-time GE employee, as the company's first vice president for corporate citizenship. Immelt also restructured GE's business portfolio to include more companies operating in emerging industries and acquired companies such as Enron Wind Corp.,[27] Ionics Inc.,[28] Osmonics Inc.,[29] and AstroPower Inc.[30] The company began to invest in new technologies. For instance, in 2004, GE invested in a new coal technology called Integrated Gasification Combined-Cycle (IGCC), which filtered out GHG and pollutants when coal was burned for energy.[31]

As part of the green drive, Immelt began delegating preliminary tasks to various teams within the company like researching greenhouse legislation, formulating metrics, conducting customer surveys, prototyping new products, formulating cross-company guidelines, etc. The company's marketing team identified a B2B[32] market opportunity for green products and outlined the monetary benefits of these products to its customers.

In late 2004, a senior-level brainstorming session at GE set the stage for the companywide environmental initiative, Ecomagination. The initiative was initially greeted with skepticism by a majority of the senior level management as they felt that it would require huge investments. Senior executives posed questions such as "Do we want to attract attention?" and "Will this create problems around the Hudson River [issue]?" during internal discussions. Instead of stepping back, Immelt drew on the trust and support he had earned from his team and went ahead with the proposal. Since GE comprised many businesses, convincing the heads of each business unit was one of the toughest parts of the execution process. According to O'Toole, "Ecomagination had to enable our business leaders to work better with their customers. It couldn't be an 'unfunded mandate' from corporate. So there had to be give-and-take with our top leaders to ensure we were helping our customers."[33]

Some environmentalists too supported the initiative as it addressed environmental challenges such as global warming and climate change. According to Eileen Claussen, president of the Pew Center for Climate Change,[34] "We are still quite politically polarized on the issue of climate change in this country. The fact that a company that size wants to take a very public position to talk about their products in terms of climate change and then, most important of all, to say they want to be part of the policy dialogue, which is very difficult in the United States at this moment, is an act of courage."[35]

The Launch of Ecomagination

On May 9, 2005, Immelt announced the launch of the US$ 150 billion environmental initiative. According to GE's Ecomagination Website, Ecomagination is "a business initiative to help meet customers' demand for cleaner and more energy-efficient products and to drive reliable growth for GE."[36] Commenting on the initiative, Immelt said, "It's no longer a zero-sum game—things that are good for the environment are also good for business. We are launching Ecomagination not because it is trendy or moral, but because it will accelerate our growth and make us more competitive."[37]

The name 'Ecomagination', which was derived from GE's "Imagination at Work" slogan, addressed challenges such as the need for cleaner and more efficient sources of energy, reduced emissions, and new sources of clean water. Through Ecomagination, GE aimed to focus on its energy, technology, manufacturing, and infrastructure capabilities to develop new sustainable solutions and invest in technologies such as solar energy, hybrid locomotives, wind power generation, fuel cells, lower emission aircraft engines, efficient lighting, and water purification technologies and appliances.

Through Ecomagination, GE planned to invest in technologies such as biomimicry, nanotechnology, and other emerging clean technologies. Experts were of the view that at a time when most other companies were cutting back on R&D funding for projects that lacked clear market application with customers, GE, through the initiative, had created options to develop radical technologies which would take longer to develop but deliver results with large payoffs. According to Lorraine Bolsinger (Bolsinger), president and CEO of GE Aviation Systems LLC, "Ecomagination is for us, above everything else, a

growth strategy. It is a business strategy based on the idea that by investing in technologies to help customers solve these big megatrends that we're seeing, to help them grow sustainably in this world—where there is more regulation, more scarcity, higher energy costs—that we can grow sustainably as well."[38]

As part of the initiative, GE committed itself to doubling its annual research investment in cleaner technologies, from US$700 million in 2004 to US$1.5 billion in 2010.[39] During the same period, GE aimed to double its revenue from Ecomagination products and services to US$20 billion annually and expected more than half of its product revenue to come from such products by 2015. GE set a target to reduce GHG emissions from its factory operations by 1% by 2012 from a 2004 baseline and to improve energy efficiency by 30% by the end of 2012.[40]

GE promoted Ecomagination widely through advertisements and other promotion campaigns, as part of its 'keeping the public informed' objective. It launched an integrated advertising campaign in the television, print, and online media to make consumers aware of the company's energy-efficient products available in the market. Besides advertisements, GE also launched an exclusive Website and several short online films. In October 2005, GE partnered with Dow Jones to launch a US$50,000 prize competition called "ECOnomics: The Environmental Business Plan Challenge" which invited entrepreneurs, executives, and students to submit eco-friendly business ideas. In September 2006, GE in association with MtvU[41] rolled out the "MtvU GE Ecomagination Challenge" wherein college students across the US were asked to submit innovative ideas for projects that would make their institutions more environmentally responsible. In 2008, GE launched a comprehensive campaign to promote its Smart Grid technology. According to Jeff Renaud, Director of GE's Ecomagination program, "Looking at GE's overall advertising and digital media efforts, it's clear that Ecomagination is a core element . . . We also believe that Ecomagination has had and will continue to have a positive impact on GE's overall brand value."[42]

Ecomagination at Work

One of the vital components of GE's Ecomagination program was to build strategic partnerships with corporations and governments around the world, universities, and research institutions to solve energy needs.

In 2005, GE Energy Financial Services entered into a partnership with AES Corporation[43] to develop a venture called Greenhouse Gas Services[44] in the US. The goal of the partnership was to offset the equivalent of an annual production volume of 10 million metric tons (MMT) of carbon dioxide gas by 2010 through the reduction of methane emissions from landfill gas, coal mines, and agricultural waste. In 2008, Greenhouse Gas Services joined with Google, Inc.[45] to codevelop a GHG reduction project[46] at a landfill in Caldwell County, North Carolina.

According to GE's 2005 Ecomagination Report, in 2004 and 2005, the company had undertaken nearly 500 global energy conservation projects which had led to substantial energy cost savings and a reduction of more than 250,000 tons of GHG emissions, equivalent to keeping nearly 50,000 cars off the road.[47] Between 2005 and 2009, GE financed and invested in 247 megawatts of solar projects, including one of the world's largest, the 11-megawatt Serpa solar plant in Portugal. The company focused not only on individual projects but also invested capital in other companies that were developing solar power around the world. For instance, GE Oil & Gas Ecomagination technology played a vital role in the development of Asia's natural gas pipeline infrastructure to supply gas from Uzbekistan and Kazakhstan to China for meeting China's rising energy demands.

In May 2006, GE launched Ecomagination in China followed by its launch in Australia five months later. According to GE, China Ecomagination products brought significant growth to GE's business in China. In the first three quarters of 2009, GE's Ecomagination revenues in China reached US$656 million, an increase of 50% compared to the previous year. In 2009, GE signed 20 memorandums of under standing (MOUs) with central and local government bodies and 10 MOUs with state-owned-enterprises and Chinese universities to develop energy-efficient solutions in areas such as biogas solutions, wind power, clean coal technology, industrial emissions reduction, aircraft engines, locomotives, etc.[48]

In February 2007, GE Aviation signed an MOU with Air India,[49] to make Air India's operations more sustainable by providing the airline's fleet with fuel-efficient engines. By using these engines, the airline was expected to save US$150 million over the next 15 years while establishing itself as an environmentally friendly service. In 2007, to combat severe potable water shortages in countries in Southeast Asia, Africa, and Latin America, GE provided solar energy modules and water filtration technologies to rural areas in these regions. In Africa, GE partnered with the Algerian government and the Algerian Energy Company to build the continent's largest desalination plant at Hamma.

GE also collaborated with end users and external partners to identify energy-saving lighting projects. In 2007, Wal-Mart[50] fitted refrigerated display cases with GE's light emitting diodes (LEDs) to reduce energy consumption in more than 500 of its retail stores. The same year, oil giant BP also formed a global alliance with GE to develop about 15 hydrogen power projects in order to cut GHG emissions from electricity generation.[51] Besides big companies, GE also partnered with non-profit organizations such as the World Resources Institute[52] and the Pew Center on Global Climate Change to check GHG emissions. According to Beth Comstock (Comstock), Chief Marketing Officer of GE, "Ecomagination has been strengthened by input from a variety of partners . . . When you're teamed with a partner who shares a common vision and commitment and complementary capabilities, a new kind of energy is created."[53]

As part of the Ecomagination initiative, GE rolled out several energy efficient and renewable energy technologies at its facilities too, including products such as solar panels and advanced lighting systems which it manufactured itself. Within the company, GE began engaging employees to see where energy savings could be achieved. It implemented initiatives such as turning off the lights when a factory was idle, installing LED lights on factory floors, recycling water at nuclear facilities, etc. GE installed solar panels on many buildings, including its headquarters, and energy efficient light bulbs in many of its factories. "Leading by example is the essence of Ecomagination. If we are proposing that customers and enterprises around the world use GE solutions to reduce their emissions, then we should do the same,"[54] said Fludder.

To reduce energy usage and GHG reductions, GE made use of the "Energy Treasure Hunts"[55] developed by Toyota.[56] GE carried out regular treasure hunt sessions from 2005 to identify energy-efficiency savings at a specific manufacturing site. For instance, at its, locomotive operations in Erie, Pennsylvania, GE switched to natural-gas fired power from oil, saving money and cutting emissions in the manufacture of locomotive engines. As of July 2010, GE had conducted 200 internal treasure hunts, which helped the company save more than US$130 million annually and contributed to reductions in excess of 250,000 metric tons of CO_2.[57]

In 2007, GE Transportation partnered with Union Pacific,[58] to launch hybrid locomotives capable of re-cycling thermal energy as stored power in on-board batteries. The energy stored in the batteries could reduce fuel consumption and emissions by as much as 10% compared to ordinary freight locomotives. In the automotive sector, GE Energy Financial Services[59] invested in the battery company, A123 Systems Inc.,[60] to develop the next generation of battery technology for hybrid and plug-in hybrid electrics. For instance, GE made an investment to help A123Systems roll out batteries for Norwegian electric car manufacturer Think Global.[61] Besides providing capital, GE, through GE Global Research, offered system design expertise and supported A123's power product development for electric grid applications, and designed battery system components for A123's automotive programs.

In May 2007, GE's media arm, NBC Universal[62] (NBCU), announced its "Green is Universal" initiative to bring about environmental awareness and educate consumers about environmental sustainability. NBCU aimed to reduce its GHG emissions at least 1% by 2012. As part of this effort, NBCU aired environmentally themed content through its on-air networks and online platforms during its Green Week (in November) and Earth Week (in April). In November 2009, NBCU's "Make Green Count" campaign was launched. This campaign encouraged audiences to make one small green change to their daily lives such as turning the lights off or walking to work.

Ecomagination Products

To ensure that Ecomagination products and services improved environmental performance, GE employed a rigorous review and qualification procedure known as the Ecomagination Product Review (EPR) process to assess which products and services should be included in the Ecomagination portfolio. The EPR process was carried out by the Ecomagination team comprising environmental health and safety counsel product marketing teams from the GE business units and corporate legal counsel. The evaluation process was audited by a third party. Product characteristics considered during the EPR process included environmental factors such as energy consumption, GHG emissions, and water usage, in addition to the financial benefits of the product to customers.

For products to be included in the Ecomagination portfolio they had to be better in terms of operating as

well as environmental performance, support growth of new technologies, and drive a more sustainable form of development. Talking about the product verification process, Bolsinger said, "If we got this great green technology, but it's totally unaffordable, we say no, that's not ready to be an ecoproduct. It has to be better, in terms of operating performance for the customer—to give them some economic return—as well as the environmental piece of it."[63]

As part of the EPR process, GE analyzed the environmental attributes of its products relative to benchmarks such as competitors' products, regulatory standards, and historical performance. It ensured that all Ecomagination products met the required criteria and that the product marketing was clear and substantiated. To provide independent, quantitative environmental analysis and verification of GE's product claims, GE partnered with GreenOrder.[64] The firm verified the product information and advised GE on the associated marketing claims of the products. For this purpose, GreenOrder developed a scorecard system for evaluating Ecomagination products and technologies. For each product, an extensive scorecard was created quantifying the product's environmental attributes, impact, and benefits relative to comparable products. The scorecards were then used to create product marketing claims. "This process is flexible enough to cover incredibly diverse industries, since Ecomagination creates, compares, measures, and launches products as small as a light bulb or as big as a jet engine,"[65] said Comstock.

As of June 2010, GE was marketing 90 Ecomagination certified products ranging from compact fluorescent lighting, smart grid components, and wind turbines, to smart appliances, aircraft engines, and water treatment technologies (Refer to Exhibit IV). Products developed under the Ecomagination umbrella were not limited to GE's manufacturing businesses alone but was also extended to the company's financial business. Once a product became a part of the Ecomagination portfolio it was reviewed regularly to ensure that performance claims were based on the latest relevant information and reflected any changes to the product itself or its market. R&D funding for Ecomagination products was provided by GE's four Global Research Centers and some major businesses of the company.

Between 2002 and 2005, GE invested more than US$350 million to develop high efficiency appliance products and to meet the ENERGY STAR[66] qualification for as many of its Consumer & Industrial products as possible. In 2005, GE invested more than US$60 million to develop 164 new ENERGY STAR qualified appliances. Again in 2007, the company invested approximately US$47 million to create 215 new ENERGY STAR qualified appliance models. In recognition of GE's commitment to developing high-efficiency appliance products, the US Department of Energy and the EPA awarded GE the ENERGY STAR Partner of the Year "Sustained Excellence" award for three consecutive years (2006–2008).[67]

In May 2007, GE launched 11 new Ecomagination products and services including a hybrid locomotive[68] and a carbon offset company. In July 2007, GE Money[69] launched the first-ever US credit card with a reward program known as GE Money Earth Rewards.[70] The program offered cardholders an easy way to offset their carbon impact and reduce carbon emissions by contributing up to 1% of their net spend to buy carbon offsets. On May 24, 2007, the GE and Masco Contractor Services[71] (MCS) Environments for Living division announced the Ecomagination Homebuilder Program to help residential developers and builders design homes which were are not only comfortable, but also more efficient in their energy consumption and indoor water consumption. Homes built under this program resulted in at least 20% saving in household energy, water consumption, and emissions compared to industry accepted new homes. In 2008, for the first time, GE Healthcare products joined the Ecomagination portfolio. These products not only provided outstanding clinical performance, but also offered significant savings. In 2010, GE launched two new products in the Ecomagination portfolio—the WattStation electric vehicle charger[72] and the Nucleus,[73] a real-time home energy monitor.

On July 13, 2010, GE launched a US$200 million global innovation challenge called the GE Ecomagination Challenge: Powering the Grid to create and adopt more efficient and economically sustainable electric grid technologies. The challenge invited technologists, entrepreneurs, and startups to design innovative business models, technologies, and processes that would bring clean, usable energy to the market through renewable energy, power grid efficiency, and eco homes. Co-funded by four venture capital firms,[74] the challenge aimed to leverage on GE's technical expertise and bring new ideas to market quickly. Until September 30, 2010, participants could submit proposals in three general

categories—Renewable Energy, Grid Efficiency, and EcoBuildings/Homes. Each of the five innovation challenge award winners would receive US$100,000 in cash and bag a partnership deal with GE to develop and distribute the technology.

Results

According to analysts, Ecomagination was a turning point for the company, which had been grappling with the problem of an inconsistent green image. Since its launch in 2005, the initiative paid off in a big way as it helped GE to evolve as a sustainable enterprise and contributed to the rise in its brand value, they said. Talking about the success of the program, Immelt said, "Ecomagination is one of the most successful cross-company business initiatives in our recent history. It is a clear amplifier of our strong reputation for innovation and execution, harnessing the strength of every GE business to maximize returns for GE investors while minimizing our own energy use and greenhouse gas emissions."[75]

In 2005, revenues from the sale of Ecomagination products and services reached US$10.1 billion compared to US$6.2 billion in 2004.[76] Orders and commitments doubled to about US$17 billion. In 2006, revenues from the Ecomagination portfolio of products and services surged past US$12 billion, up 20% from 2005, while the order backlog increased to US$50 billion.[77] In 2007, Ecomagination revenues crossed US$14 billion, an increase of 15% from 2006.[78] For the first time, GE's investment in cleaner technology R&D crossed US$1 billion in 2007. In 2008, GE's revenues from Ecomagination grew by 21% to US$17 billion.[79] The company increased its investment in R&D of clean tech solutions by 27% to US$ 1.4 billion, up from US$750 million in 2005. In 2008, GE reduced GHG intensity by 41%, surpassing its goal of reducing it by 30%.

In the year 2009, which marked the fifth anniversary of the Ecomagination program, revenues from Ecomagination products and services grew by 6% to cross US$18 billion despite the global economic recession.[80] In 2009, GE invested US$1.5 billion on Ecomagination R&D. In 2009 GE's GHG emissions were 22% below its 2004 baseline and water consumption reduced by 30% compared to a 2006 baseline, surpassing the original goal of 20% by 2012. According to GE statistics, since the inception of Ecomagination, the company had invested a total of US$5 billion in its R&D investment and generated a total of US$70 billion in revenues through the end of 2009.[81] "Ecomagination is one of our most successful cross-company business initiatives. If counted separately, 2009 Ecomagination revenues would equal that of a Fortune 130 company and Ecomagination revenue growth equals almost two times the company average,"[82] said Immelt.

The Other View

Despite the positive aspects of this green initiative, some experts felt that GE could not call itself an eco-friendly company because of its history of pollution, particularly the dumping of PCBs in the Hudson River and the delay in cleaning it up. Some analysts charged that despite making tall claims about its products being environmental friendly, GE continued to sell coal-fired steam turbines and was involved in oil and gas extraction.

Some analysts accused GE of greenwashing as they felt that the Ecomagination initiative was meant to divert people's attention from the company's negligent stance toward environmental matters. Ecomagination was an attempt to cover up GE's poor environmental image and its continuing obsession with profit at the expense of the environment, they charged. According to Chris Ballantyn, director of the Hudson River Program, "Actions speak louder than words. When you scratch beneath the public relations surface, I'm afraid they have unfinished business in terms of environmental protection."[83]

Moreover, GE's annual US$1 million investment in marketing Ecomagination was criticized as an expensive branding exercise which amounted to greenwashing. Some experts were of the view that Ecomagination did not address all of the company's environmental problems and was risky as companies were generally reluctant to play up their products' environmental benefits fearing that their green claims would not able to match the company's overall environmental footprint. They observed that sustainability as a corporate strategy worked only if it was made a company-wide initiative. If it remained restricted to a few products, its impact would be limited. "Even at $20 billion, Ecomagination is only about 10 percent of GE. It's a very creative way to drive and differentiate the company, but it's not

going to make, break, or save GE,"[84] said William Rothschild, a Consultant at Rothschild Strategies Unlimited.[85]

According to some experts, Ecomagination products and technologies focused on large scale, centralized solutions and were mostly capital-intensive applications based on existing business models. Little attention was paid to small-scale standalone applications that might address distinct market needs and customers, they said. Industry observers felt that Ecomagination products mostly served the needs of customers at the top of the economic pyramid[86] and ignored the requirements of customers at the base of the pyramid who lacked reliable and affordable solutions related to energy, transportation, water, materials, and financial services.

Commenting on the criticism related to the initiative, Bolsinger said, "I think the skepticism piece was never a big deal for me because (Ecomagination) was never based on "we're doing this for philanthropy" or "we're doing this to make the world safe." We're glad to be doing that as a result of making money. It's a different lens that informs your decisions about where to spend money and what resources you're going to invest."[87]

Looking Ahead

According to GE, Ecomagination was not a short-term proposition and the company planned to make it a part of its identity and market the brand aggressively to the world. GE planned to increase revenues from Ecomagination products and services to at least US$25 billion by the end of 2010.[88] GE committed itself to reducing its GHG emissions by 1% by 2012 and to improving energy efficiency by 30% by the end of 2012 compared to the 2004 baseline. GE aimed to achieve its commitment to double annual investment in clean tech R&D to US$ 1.5 billion by 2010.[89] It also planned to invest an additional US$10 billion in Ecomagination R&D by 2015, particularly in the development of low-carbon products.

The company committed itself to ensuring that by 2015, Ecomagination revenue would grow at twice the rate of total company revenue and planned to improve the energy intensity of its operations by 50% and reduce its absolute GHG emissions by 25%, both against the 2004 baseline.[90] The company also altered its goal of reducing freshwater consumption by 20% by 2012 from the 2006 baseline to 25% by 2015. As part of its public awareness, GE planned to increase its interactions with the public and revamp its Website to enable people to put forward their questions and queries.

In the future, under the Ecomagination program, GE planned to build a massive battery plant in New York and a US$2 billion wind project in Oregon and to launch a series of high-end energy-efficient front-load washers and dryers. In June 2010, GE Energy Financial Services entered into an agreement with a Spanish renewable energy company Abengoa,[91] to develop the largest cogeneration[92] power plant in Mexico. The companies were to invest US$180 million in the project expected to be commercially operational by 2012. The 300 megawatt plant was to supply electricity and steam over the next 20 years and help the Mexican government meet its energy efficiency targets by reducing GHG emissions by 50% in comparison with 2002 by 2050. GE identified China and South Korea as countries where the company expected green technology to thrive in the future.[93]

GE said while it would continue to invest in products like energy efficient turbines, green locomotives, and sodium batteries in the future, it would also focus on bringing more intelligence and networking to its existing product categories. For instance, it planned to roll out software applications for monitoring flight paths, take-offs, and landings for airplanes in order to reduce the time that planes had to spend circling airports. This would help cut fuel consumption. "It is a cost savings to the airlines and it is a huge comfort factor for customers. These are the kind of IT-enabled solutions we will invest in,"[94] said Fludder.

According to industry observers, Ecomagination was a good platform for GE to make investments in new technologies while making money at the same time. They felt that the initiative had huge scope for expansion in the future as more green technologies would be able to address new problems, create new markets, and reach underserved customers. While there were some discordant notes as well, the company said it was committed to taking this initiative forward. According to Comstock, "With Ecomagination, we've learned that sustainability is as much a change-management challenge as it is a business or scientific challenge . . . Change happens when others see opportunity—and change their behavior, join in, and make it their own. Ecomagination's mantra is no longer just GE's. And that's just fine with us."[95]

Exhibit I GE-Business Groups

Energy
• Digital Energy
• Electrical Distribution
• Energy
• Oil & Gas
• Sensing & Inspection
• Water & Process Technologies
Technology Infrastructure
• Aviation
• Healthcare
• Transportation
GE Capital
• Commercial Lending & Leasing
• Consumer Financing
• Energy Financial Services
• GE Capital Aviation Services
• Real Estate Financing
• Worldwide GE Capital Locations
NBC Universal
• Cable
• Film
• Networks
• Parks & Resorts
GE Home & Business Solutions
• Appliances
• Consumer Electronics
• Intelligent Platforms
• Lighting

Source: http://www.ge.com/products_services/directory/by_business.html

Exhibit II General Electric Company-Consolidated Statement of Earnings
For the years ended December 31
Dollar amounts and share amounts in millions; per-share amounts in dollars

	2009	2008	2007
Revenues			
Sales of goods	65,068	69,100	60, 670
Sales of services	38,709	43,669	38,856
Other income	1,006	1,586	3,019
GECS earnings from continuing operations	—	—	—
GECS revenues from services	52,000	68,160	69,943
Total Revenues	156,783	182,515	172,488
Costs and expenses			
Cost of goods sold	50,580	54,602	47,309
Cost of services sold	25,341	29,170	25,816
Interest and other financial charges	18,769	26,209	23,762
Investment contracts, insurance losses and insurance annuity benefits	3,017	3,213	3,469
Provision for losses on financing receivables	10,928	7,518	4,431
Other costs and expenses	37,804	42,021	40,173
Total costs and expenses	146,439	162,733	144,960
Earnings (loss) from continuing operations before income taxes	10,344	19,782	27,528
Benefit (provision) for income taxes	1,090	(1,052)	(4,155)
Earnings from continuing operations	11,434	18,730	23,373
Loss from discontinued operations, net of taxes	(193)	(679)	(249)
Net earnings	11,241	18,051	23,124
Less net earnings (loss) attributable to non controlling interests	216	641	916
Net earnings attributable to the Company	11,025	17,410	22,208
Preferred stock dividends declared	(300)	(75)	—
Net earnings attributable to GE common shareowners	10,725	17,335	22,208
Amounts attributable to the Company:			
Earnings from continuing operations	11,218	18,089	22,457
Loss from discontinued operations, net of taxes	(193)	(679)	(249)
Net earnings attributable to the Company	11,025	17,410	22,208
Per-share amounts—net earnings			
Diluted earnings per share	1.01	1.72	2.17
Basic earnings per share	1.01	1.72	2.18
Dividends declared per common share	0.61	1.24	1.15

Source: GE 2009 Annual Report

Exhibit III Top 10 in Fortune's Ranking of America's Largest Corporations (2010)

Rank	Company	Revenues (US$ millions)	Profits (US$ millions)
1	Wal-Mart Stores	408,214.0	14,335.0
2	Exxon Mobil	284,650.0	19,280.0
3	Chevron	163,527.0	10,483.0
4	General Electric	156,779.0	11,025.0
5	Bank of America Corp.	150,450.0	6,276.0
6	ConocoPhillips	139,515.0	4,858.0
7	AT&T	123,018.0	12,535.0
8	Ford Motor	118,308.0	2,717.0
9	J.P. Morgan Chase & Co.	115,632.0	11,728.0
10	Hewlett-Packard	114,552.0	7,660.0

Adapted from http://money. cnn.com/magazines/fortune/fortune500/2010/full_list/

Exhibit IV Ecomagination Statistics

	Total Products	Investment in R&D	Greenhouse Gas (GHG) emissions	Revenues
2005	GE has increased its Ecomagination pipeline by 75% over the last year—from 17 products to 30.	GE invested US$700 million in cleaner technologies in 2005.	GHG emissions from operations remained relatively flat in 2005 compared to 2004, while GHG intensity was reduced by 10% and energy intensity was reduced by 11%.	GE's revenues from Ecomagination products and services reached US$10.1 billion. Orders and commitments nearly doubled to US$17 billion. Revenues for 2005 were at US$10.1 billion; orders went up 93% from 2004, nearly doubling to US$17 billion.
2006	GE has increased its Ecomagination pipeline by 50% over the last year—from 30 products to 45.	GE invested US$900 million in cleaner technologies in 2006.	GHG emissions in 2006 from operations have been reduced by about 4% from the 2004 baseline. GHG and energy intensity have been reduced by 21% and 22% respectively compared to 2004.	In 2006—GE's revenues grew from US$10 billion in 2005 to US$12 billion, delivering a 20% increase in revenue. 2006 revenues at US$12 billion; orders and commitments have increased to US$50 billion.

	Total Products	Investment in R&D	Greenhouse Gas (GHG) emissions	Revenues
2007	GE increased the number of Ecomagination-certified products by 38 percent over last year—from 45 to 62 products.	It invested US$1.1 billion in cleaner technology research and development.	It reduced its greenhouse gas (GHG) emissions by about 8% in 2007 from the 2004 baseline, while reducing GHG and energy intensity by 34% and 33% respectively.	It increased its revenues from Ecomagination products with US$14 billion in revenues from Ecomagination products and services in 2007.
2008	GE increased its Ecomagination portfolio—from 17 products in 2005 to more than 80 products today.	GE invested US$1.4 billion in cleaner technology research and development in 2008, up from US$750 million in 2005.	GHG emissions from operations reduced by about 13% from the 2004 baseline. GHG and energy intensity reduced by 41% and 37%, respectively, compared to 2004.	GE reported US$17 billion in revenues from Ecomagination products and services in 2008, an increase of 21% over the previous year.
2009	Products grew to 90.	It invested US$1.5 billion in cleaner technologies, achieving its 2010 goal one year ahead of schedule.	Reduced greenhouse gas emissions from operations approximately 22% from the 2004 baseline. GHG and energy intensity reduced by 39% and 34% respectively.	Revenues grew by 6% to US$18 billion.

Compiled from various sources

References:

1. Ariel Schwartz, "GE Boosts Ecomagination Initiative with an Extra $10 Billion," www.fastcompany.com, June 25, 2010.
2. Candace Lombardi, "GE to Invest $10 billion in Ecomagination Initiative," http://news.cnet.com, June 24, 2010.
3. "Ecomagination at 5: Unleashing Action & Measurement," www.gereports.com, June 24, 2010.
4. "GE Surpassed $5 Billion in Research & Development Investment in Ecomagination Technology," www.genewscenter.com, June 24, 2010.
5. Michael Kaneloss, "GE Looks to Smart Grids for Airports, Railroads in Ecomagination 2.0," www.greentechmedia.com, June 24, 2010.
6. "GE's Ecomagination Business in China Records 50% Growth," www.reliableplant.com, 2010.
7. Caylena Cahill, "Problems in Green Marketing," fuse.ithaca.edu, December 2009.
8. James Murray, "GE Talks up Ecomagination Success," www.businessgreen.com, May 28, 2009.
9. "GE's Ecomagination Team Unveils its Annual Scorecard," www.gereports.com, May 27, 2009.
10. "GE Ecomagination Revenue Grows 21% to $17B," www.environmentalleader.com, May 27, 2009.
11. GE 2009 Annual Report.
12. GE 2009 Ecomagination Report.
13. Lisa Roner, "GE: Runaway Ecomagination is Not Enough," www.climatechangecorp.com, June 4, 2008.
14. "GE's_Ecomagination' Business Grows to $14 billion; Revenue Target Raised to $25 billion as Orders Top $70 billion," www.domain-b.com, May 29, 2008.
15. "GE's_ecomagination' business grows to $14 billion; revenue target raised to $25 billion as orders top $70 billion news," www.domain-b.com, May 28, 2008.
16. Martin LaMonica, "GE to Lower Water Use, Raise Ecomagination Target," http://news.cnet.com, May 28, 2008.
17. Douglas MacMillan, "The Analysis: In Immelt We Trust," www.businessweek.com, March 4, 2008.
18. GE 2008 Ecomagination Report.

19. Lucy Aitken, "Wiping out _Greenwash," www .guardian.co.uk, November 19, 2007.

20. Martin LaMonica, "Stirring GE's Ecomagination," http://news.cnet.com, October 26, 2007.

21. "GE's Jeff Renaud Discusses Ecomagination and Transparency," www.environmentalleader.com, August 22, 2007.

22. Mary Milliken, "GE "Green" Ecomagination Unit Gaining Ground: CEO," http://uk.reuters.com, May 24, 2007.

23. GE 2007 Ecomagination Report.

24. Amanda Griscom Little, "GE's Green Gamble," Vanity Fair, July 12, 2006.

25. GE 2006 Ecomagination Report.

26. Elizabeth M. Whelan, "Public Health Absurdities," The Washington Times, December 30, 2005.

27. Brett Clark, "General Electric's Ecomagination: New Veneer, Same Propaganda," http://mrzine.monthlyreview .org, August 2, 2005.

28. Ron Irwin, "GE Imagines a Greener Future," www .brandchannel.com, July 11, 2005.

29. Greg Schneider, "GE Determined to Show More_ Ecomagination," www.washingtonpost.com, May 10, 2005.

30. "Global Environmental Challenges," www.ge.com, May 9, 2005.

31. Joel Makeower, "Ecomagination: Inside GE's Power Play," www.worldchanging.com, May 8, 2005.

32. GE 2005 Ecomagination Report.

33. www.ecomagination.com

34. www.ge.com.

35. www.hoovers.com

Endnotes

1. Caylena Cahill, "Problems in Green Marketing," www .fuse.ithaca.edu, December 2009.

2. Environmental Advocates of New York is a watchdog group on environmental issues affecting New York.

3. "GE Surpassed $5 Billion in Research & Development Investment in Ecomagination Technology," www .genewscenter.com, June 24, 2010.

4. Ibid.

5. SustainAbility is an independent think tank and strategy consultancy.

6. Lucy Aitken, "Wiping out 'Greenwash'," www.guardian .co.uk, November 19, 2007.

7. Ron Irwin, "GE Imagines a Greener Future," www .brandchannel.com, July 11, 2005.

8. The Thomas-Houston Electric Company was founded in 1879. It was a competitor to EGEC until the merger of the two companies.

9. As per the 'Number One Number Two' strategy GE had to be either the number one or number two player in every segment it operated. If any business failed to meet this criterion, it was shut down or sold off.

10. The Dow Jones Industrial Average (DJIA) is the average value of 30 large, industrial stocks. These market averages help investors know how companies traded on the stock market are performing in general.

11. Launched in 1999, the Dow Jones Sustainability Indexes are a group of indexes which track the financial performance of companies that fulfill criteria for environmental, social, and financial sustainability.

12. Amanda Griscom Little, "GE's Green Gamble," Vanity Fair, July 12, 2006.

13. PCBs are chemical compounds with low water solubility and environmental degradability, and studies have shown that people exposed to them could suffer several adverse effects.

14. Established in 1972, The Clean Water Act is a primary federal law in the US governing water pollution.

15. EPA is an agency of the US federal government responsible for protecting human health and safeguarding the natural environment.

16. Formed in 1975, NRC is a US government agency responsible for overseeing the civilian use of nuclear materials in the US.

17. The Kyoto Protocol is an agreement made under the UN Framework Convention on Climate Change concerning issues related to global warming. The countries that ratify the protocol commit themselves to reducing their emissions of carbon dioxide and five other greenhouse gases, or to engage in emissions trading if they maintain or increase emissions of these gases. The treaty was negotiated in December 1997 and came into force on February 16, 2005. As of July 2010, there were 192 signatories to the treaty.

18. The G8 or the Group of Eight is an annual political summit meeting of the heads of government of eight of the most powerful countries in the world. The members are: Canada, France, Germany, Italy, Japan, Russia, the UK, and the US.

19. Headquartered in Geneva, Switzerland, the WTO (World Trade Organization) is an international, multilateral organization, which sets the rules for the global trading system and resolves disputes between its member states.

20. Founded in 1802, DuPont is a science-based products and services company operating in 80 countries worldwide.

21. IBM Corporation is a multinational computer, technology, and IT consulting company headquartered in Armonk, New York.

22. Headquartered in Indianapolis, Eli Lilly and Company is a global pharmaceutical company.

23. Headquartered in London, UK, BP Plc is one of the largest oil and gas companies in the world with operations in over 100 countries.

24 Nike, Inc is a leading US-based sportswear and equipment manufacturer and supplier.

25 Ibid

26 Elizabeth M. Whelan, "Public Health Absurdities," *The Washington Times*, December 30, 2005.

27 Enron Wind Corp was a global supplier of wind turbine generators.

28 Ionics, Inc provided water and water treatment equipment through the use of proprietary separation technologies and systems.

29 Osmonics, Inc designed, manufactured, and marketed a wide range of products used in the filtration, separation, and processing of fluids.

30 AstroPower Inc was one of the biggest manufacturers of solar energy equipment in the US.

31 Ibid

32 The Business-to-Business (B2B) market involves transactions between businesses, such as between a manufacturer and a wholesaler, or between a wholesaler and a retailer.

33 Douglas MacMillan, "The Analysis: In Immelt We Trust," www.businessweek.com, March 4, 2008.

34 Established in 1998, The Pew Center on Global Climate Change is a nonprofit, independent organization dedicated to providing credible information and solutions related to global climate change.

35 Greg Schneider, "GE Determined to Show More 'Ecomagination'," www.washingtonpost.com, May 10, 2005.

36 www.ge.com/in/company/factsheet_in.html.

37 "Global Environmental Challenges," www.ge.com, May 9, 2005.

38 Martin LaMonica, "Stirring GE's Ecomagination," http://news.cnet.com, October 26, 2007.

39 GE 2005 Ecomagination Report.

40 "GE's 'Ecomagination' Business Grows to $14 billion; Revenue Target Raised to $25 billion as Orders Top $70 billion," www.domain-b.com, May 29, 2008.

41 MtvU is MTV Networks' 24-hour television network just for college students in the US. It is broadcast to more than 750 college campuses and 700 college communities in the US.

42 "GE's Jeff Renaud Discusses Ecomagination and Transparency," www.environmentalleader.com, August 22, 2007.

43 Headquartered in Arlington, Virginia, AES Corporation is a global power company involved in generation and distribution of electric power.

44 Greenhouse Gas Services builds a portfolio of projects that reduce, avoid, or destroy gases that directly contribute to global warming.

45 Google Inc. is a global technology company that provides a Web-based search engine through its Website. The company offers a wide range of search options, including Web, image, groups, directory, and news searches.

46 Through the project, Greenhouse Gas Services would capture and destroy methane gas emitted from the landfill to generate about an estimated 110,000 tons of carbon credits over a ten-year timeframe. Google would use a percentage of the credits to achieve carbon neutrality.

47 Ibid

48 "GE's Ecomagination Business in China Records 50% Growth" www.reliableplant.com, 2010.

49 Air India is the state owned domestic airline of India.

50 Wal-Mart Stores, Inc. is a US based chain of large retail discount department stores.

51 Mary Milliken, "GE "Green" Ecomagination Unit Gaining Ground: CEO," http://uk.reuters.com, May 24, 2007.

52 Based in Washington, The World Resources Institute (WRI) is an environmental think tank which protects the earth and improves people's lives.

53 "Ecomagination at 5: Unleashing Action & Measurement," www.gereports.com, June 24, 2010.

54 "GE's Ecomagination Team Unveils its Annual Scorecard," www.gereports.com, May 27, 2009.

55 The Energy Treasure Hunt process created by Toyota Motor Manufacturing North America identifies projects that drive energy efficiency.

56 Headquartered in Japan, Toyota Motor Corporation is one of the largest automakers in the world.

57 GE 2009 Ecomagination Report

58 Union Pacific Corporation is one of the leading transportation companies and the operator of one of the largest railroads in North America.

59 GE Energy Financial Services, a division of GE, provides financial and technological investment in energy infrastructure projects around the world. In renewable energy, GE Energy Financial Services is growing its portfolio of more than US$4 billion in assets in wind, solar, biomass, hydro, and geothermal power.

60 Founded in 2001, A123Systems develops and manufactures advanced lithium-ion batteries and battery systems for the transportation, electric grid services, and portable power markets.

61 Founded in 1991, Think Global is a Norwegian electric car company which manufactures cars under the TH!NK brand.

62 NBC Universal is one of the world's leading media and entertainment companies involved in the development, production, and marketing of entertainment, news, and information.

63 Ibid

64 Established in 2000, GreenOrder is a US-based sustainability strategy consulting firm.

65 Ibid

66 ENERGY STAR, a joint program of the U.S. Environmental Protection Agency and the US Department of Energy, is an international standard for energy efficient consumer products. It was created in 1992 as a US government program and was subsequently adopted by Australia, Canada, Japan, New Zealand, Taiwan, and the European Union.

67 The Sustained Excellence award recognizes GE's achievement in developing high-performance household appliance and lighting products, which help reduce energy spending and protect the environment.

68 GE engineers designed a hybrid diesel electric locomotive that captures the energy dissipated during braking and stores it in a series of batteries which can be used by the crew on demand. The electric locomotive reduces fuel consumption by as much as 15% and emissions by about 50% compared to normal freight locomotives.

69 Headquartered in London, GE Money is part of GE Capital operating division of GE.

70 Under the GE Money Earth Rewards program, cardholders were able to automatically contribute up to 1% of their purchases to buy carbon offsets. The credit card rewards accrued over the course of the year and could be redeemed for emissions credit on each Earth Day (April 22).

71 Based in Florida, Masco Contractor Services provides products and installation services for residential and commercial builders.

72 Named the GE WattStation, the electric-vehicle charging station was designed to charge an electric vehicle in four to six hours. The charging station, as tall as a bar stool. featured a sleek silver column equipped with a retractable cord. The electric vehicle charger not only significantly decreased the time needed for charging, but its smart grid technology let utilities manage the impact on local and regional grids.

73 Nucleus is an in-home energy consumption tracking device that communicates with GE appliances and allows consumers to track their energy usage through a display or Website.

74 The venture capital firms included Emerald Technology Ventures, Foundation Capital, Kleiner Perkins Caufield & Byer and RockPort Capital.

75 Martin LaMonica, "GE to Lower Water Use, Raise Ecomagination Target," http://news.cnet.com, May 28, 2008.

76 Ibid

77 GE 2006 Ecomagination Report.

78 Ibid

79 GE 2008 Ecomagination Report.

80 Ibid

81 Candace Lombardi, "GE to Invest $10 billion in Ecomagination Initiative," http://news.cnet.com, June 24, 2010.

82 Ibid

83 Ibid

84 Lisa Roner, "GE: Runaway Ecomagination is Not Enough," www.climatechangecorp.com, June 4, 2008.

85 Rothschild Strategies Unlimited, is a US-based consulting firm specializing in strategy development, review and human resources.

86 An economic pyramid depicts the distribution of wealth among the world's population. The bottom rung of the economic pyramid comprises low income group people whereas high earners are placed at the top of the pyramid.

87 Martin LaMonica, "Stirring GE's Ecomagination," http://news.cnet.com, October 26, 2007.

88 Ibid

89 Ibid

90 Ibid

91 Abengoa SA is a technology company that applies innovative solutions to sustainable development in the infrastructures, environment, and energy sectors.

92 Cogeneration involves simultaneous production of electricity and heat using a single fuel source such as natural gas. This can result in higher thermal efficiency and can reduce carbon dioxide emissions substantially.

93 Ibid

94 Michael Kaneloss, "GE Looks to Smart Grids for Airports, Railroads in Ecomagination 2.0," www.greentechmedia.com, June 24, 2010.

95 Ibid

Nike: Sweatshops and Business Ethics

Charles W.L. Hill, University of Washington

Introduction

Nike is in many ways the quintessential global corporation. Established in 1972 by former University of Oregon track star Phil Knight, Nike is now one of the leading marketers of athletic shoes and apparel on the planet. The company has $10 billion in annual revenues and sells its products in some 140 countries. Nike does not do any manufacturing. Rather, it designs and markets its products, while contracting for their manufacture from a global network of 600 factories scattered around the globe that employ nearly 550,000 people.[1] This huge corporation has made founder Phil Knight one of the richest people in America. Nike's marketing phrase "Just do it!" and "swoosh" logo have become as recognizable in popular culture as the faces of its celebrity sponsors, such as Michael Jordan and Tiger Woods.

For all of its successes, the company has been dogged for more than a decade by repeated and persistent accusations that its products are made in "sweatshops" where workers, many of them children, slave away in hazardous conditions for below-subsistence wages. Nike's wealth, its detractors claim, has been built upon the backs of the world's poor. To many, Nike has become a symbol of the evils of globalization: a rich Western corporation exploiting the world's poor to provide expensive shoes and apparel to the pampered consumers of the developed world. Nike's Niketown stores have become standard targets for anti-globalization protestors. Nike has been the target of repeated criticism and protests from several nongovernmental organizations, such as San Fransisco–based Global Exchange, a human-rights organization dedicated to promoting environmental, political, and social justice around the world.[2] News media have run exposés on working conditions in foreign factories that supply Nike. Students on the campuses of several major U.S. universities with which Nike has lucrative sponsorship deals have protested against the ties, citing Nike's use of sweatshop labor.

For its part, Nike has taken many steps to counter the protests. Yes, it admits, there have been problems in some overseas factories. But the company has signaled a commitment to improving working conditions. It requires that foreign subcontractors meet minimum thresholds for working conditions and pay. It has arranged for factories to be examined by independent auditors and terminated contracts with factories that do not comply with its standards. But for all this effort, the company continues to be a target of protests.

The Case Against Nike

CBS 48 Hours aired a news report on October 17, 1996 depicting a typical exposé against Nike.[3] Reporter Roberta Basin visited a Nike factory in Vietnam. With a shot of the factory, her commentary began:

> The signs are everywhere of an American invasion in search of cheap labor. Millions of people who are literate, disciplined, and desperate for jobs. This is Niketown near what used to be called Saigon, one of 4 factories Nike doesn't own but subcontracts to make a million shoes a month. It takes 25,000 workers, mostly young women, to "Just Do It."
>
> But the workers here don't share in Nike's huge profits. They work 6 days a week for only $40 a month, just $0.20 an hour.

Baskin interviews one of the workers in the factory, a young woman named Lap. Baskin tells the listener:

> Her basic wage, even as a sewing team leader, still doesn't amount to the minimum wage. . . . She's down to 85 lbs. Like most of the young women who make shoes, she has little choice but to accept the low wages and long hours. Nike says that it requires all subcontractors to obey local laws; but Lap has already put in much more overtime than the annual legal limit: 200 hours.

This case is intended to be used as a basis for class discussion rather than as an illustration of either effective or ineffective handling of the situation. Reprinted by permission of Charles W. L. Hill.

Baskin then asks Lap what would happen if she wanted to leave, if she was sick or had to take care of a sick relative: could she leave the factory? Through a translator, Lap replies:

> It is not possible if you haven't made enough shoes. You have to meet the quota before you can go home.

The clear implication of the story was that Nike was at fault for allowing such working conditions to persist in the Vietnamese factory (which, incidentally, was owned by a Korean company).

Another example of an attack on Nike's subcontracting practices occurred in June 1996. It was launched by USA, a foundation largely financed by labor unions and domestic-apparel manufacturers that oppose free trade with low-wage countries. According to Joel Joseph, chairman of the foundation, a popular line of high-priced Nike sneakers, the "Air Jordans," were put together by 11-year-olds in Indonesia making $0.14 per hour. A Nike spokeswoman, Donna Gibbs, countered that this was false. According to Gibbs, the average worker made 240,000 *rupiah* ($103) a month working a maximum 54-hour week, or about $0.45 per hour. Moreover, Gibbs noted, Nike had staff members in each factory monitoring conditions to make sure that they obeyed local minimum-wage and child-labor laws.[4]

Another example of the criticism against Nike is the following extracts from a newsletter published by Global Exchange:[5]

During the 1970s, most Nike shoes were made in South Korea and Taiwan. When workers there gained new freedom to organize and wages began to rise, Nike looked for "greener pastures." It found them in Indonesia and China, where Nike started producing in the 1980s, and most recently in Vietnam.

The majority of Nike shoes are made in Indonesia and China, countries with governments that prohibit independent unions and set the minimum wage at rock bottom. The Indonesian government admits that the minimum wage there does not provide enough to supply the basic needs of one person, let alone a family. In early-1997, the entry-level wage was a miserable $2.46 a day. Labor groups estimate that a livable wage in Indonesia is about $4.00 a day.

In Vietnam the pay is even less—$0.20 an hour, or a mere $1.60 a day. But in urban Vietnam, 3 simple meals cost about $2.10 a day, and then of course there is rent, transportation, clothing, health care, and much more. According to Thuyen Nguyen of Vietnam Labor Watch, a living wage in Vietnam is at least $3 a day.

In another attack on Nike's practices, Global Exchange published a report in September 1997 on working conditions in 4 Nike and Reebok subcontractor's factories in southern China.[6] Global Exchange, in conjunction with two Hong Kong human-rights groups, had interviewed workers at the factories in 1995, and again in 1997. According to Global Exchange, in one factory, a Korean-owned subcontractor for Nike, workers as young as 13 earned as little as $0.10 an hour and toiled up to 17 hours daily in enforced silence. Talking during work was not allowed, and violators were fined $1.20 to $3.60, according to the report. The practices were in violation of Chinese labor law, which states that no child under 16 may work in a factory, and the Chinese minimum-wage requirement of $1.90 for an 8-hour day. Nike condemned the study as "erroneous," charging that it incorrectly stated the wages of workers and made irresponsible accusations.

Global Exchange, however, continued to be a major thorn in Nike's side. In November 1997, the organization obtained and then leaked a confidential report by Ernst & Young of an audit that Nike had commissioned of a factory in Vietnam owned by a Nike subcontractor.[7] The factory had 9,200 workers and made 400,000 pairs of shoes per month. The Ernst & Young report painted a dismal picture of thousands of young women, most under age 25, laboring 10 1/2 hours a day, 6 days a week, in excessive heat, noise, and foul air, for slightly more than $10 a week. The report also found that workers with skin or breathing problems had not been transferred to departments free of chemicals, and that more than half the workers who dealt with dangerous chemicals did not wear protective masks or gloves. It claimed workers were exposed to carcinogens that exceeded local legal standards by 177 times in parts of the plant, and that 77% of the employees suffered from respiratory problems.

Put on the defensive yet again, Nike called a news conference and pointed out that it had commissioned the report, and had acted on it.[8] The company stated that it had formulated an action plan to deal with the problems cited in the report, and had slashed overtime, improved safety and ventilation, and reduced the use of toxic chemicals. The company also asserted that the report showed that Nike's internal monitoring system had performed exactly as it should have. According to one spokesman:

> "This shows our system of monitoring works. . . . We have uncovered these issues clearly before anyone else, and we have moved fairly expeditiously to correct them."

Nike's Responses

Unaccustomed to playing defense, Nike formulated a number of strategies and tactics over the years to deal with the problems of working conditions and pay in subcontractor facilities. In 1996, Nike hired one-time U.S. ambassador to the United Nations, representative, and former Atlanta mayor Andrew Young to assess working conditions in subcontractors' plants around the world. The following year, after a 2-week tour of 3 countries that included inspections of 15 factories, Young released a mildly critical report. He informed Nike it was doing a good job in its treatment of workers, though it should do better. According to Young, he did not see: "sweatshops, or hostile conditions. . . . I saw crowded dorms . . . but the workers were eating at least 2 meals a day on the job and making what I was told were subsistence wages in those cultures."[9]

Young was widely criticized by human-rights and labor groups for not taking his own translators and for doing slipshod inspections, an assertion he repeatedly denied.

In 1996, Nike joined a presidential task force designed to find a way of banishing sweatshops in the shoe and clothing industries. The task force included industry leaders, representatives from human-rights groups, and labor leaders. In April 1997, they announced an agreement for workers' rights that U.S. companies could agree to when manufacturing abroad. The accord limited the work week to 60 hours, and called for paying at least the local minimum wage in foreign factories. The task force also agreed to establish an independent monitoring association—later named the Fair Labor Association (FLA)—to assess whether companies were abiding by the code.[10]

The FLA now includes among its members the Lawyers Committee for Human Rights, the National Council of Churches, the International Labor Rights Fund, 135 universities (universities have extensive licensing agreements with sports-apparel companies), and companies such as Nike, Reebok, and Levi Strauss.

In early 1997, Nike also began to commission independent organizations such as Ernst & Young to audit the factories of its subcontractors. In September 1997, Nike tried to show its critics that it was involved in more than just a public-relations exercise when it terminated its relationship with 4 Indonesian subcontractors, stating that they had refused to comply with the company's standards for wage levels and working conditions. Nike identified one of the subcontractors, Seyon, which manufactured specialty sports gloves for Nike, saying that Seyon refused to meet a 10.7% increase in the monthly wage, to $70.30, required by the Indonesian government in April 1997.[11]

On May 12, 1998, in a speech given at the National Press Club, Phil Knight spelled out in detail a series of initiatives designed to improve working conditions for the 500,000 people that make products for Nike at subcontractor facilities.[12] Among the initiatives Knight highlighted were the following:

We have effectively changed our minimum age limits from the ILO (International Labor Organization) standards of 15 in most countries and 14 in developing countries to 18 in all footwear manufacturing and 16 in all other types of manufacturing (apparel, accessories and equipment). Existing workers legally employed under the former limits were grandfathered into the new requirements.

During the past 13 months we have moved to a 100 percent factory audit scheme, where every Nike contract factory will receive an annual check by PricewaterhouseCoopers teams who are specially trained on our Code of Conduct Owner's Manual and audit/monitoring procedures. To date they have performed about 300 such monitoring visits. In a few instances in apparel factories they have found workers under our age standards. Those factories have been required to raise their standards to 17 years of age, to require 3 documents certifying age, and to redouble their efforts to ensure workers meet those standards through interviews and records checks.

Our goal was to ensure workers around the globe are protected by requiring factories to have no workers exposed to levels above those mandated by the permissible exposure limits (PELs) for chemicals prescribed in the OSHA indoor air quality standards.[13]

These moves were applauded in the business press, but they were greeted with a skeptical response from Nike's long-term adversaries in the debate over the use of foreign labor. While conceding that Nike's policies were an improvement, one critic writing in the *New York Times* noted that:

Mr. Knight's child labor initiative is . . . a smokescreen. Child labor has not been a big problem with Nike, and Philip Knight knows that better than anyone. But public relations is public relations. So he announces that he's not going to let the factories hire kids, and suddenly that's the headline.

Mr. Knight is like a 3-card monte player. You have to keep a close eye on him at all times.

The biggest problem with Nike is that its overseas workers make wretched, below-subsistence wages. It's not the minimum age that needs raising, it's the minimum wage. Most of the workers in Nike *factories in China and Vietnam make less than $2 a day, well below the subsistence levels in those countries. In Indonesia the pay is less than $1 a day.*

The company's current strategy is to reshape its public image while doing as little as possible for the workers. Does anyone think it was an accident that Nike set up shop in human rights sinkholes, where labor organizing was viewed as a criminal activity and deeply impoverished workers were willing, even eager, to take their places on assembly lines and work for next to nothing?[14]

Other critics question the quality of Nike's auditors, PricewaterhouseCoopers (PwC). Dara O'Rourke, an assistant professor at MIT, followed the PwC auditors around several factories in China, Korea, and Vietnam. He concluded that although the auditors found minor violations of labor laws and codes of conduct, they missed major labor-practice issues, including hazardous working conditions, violations of overtime laws, and violation of wage laws. The problem, according to O'Rourke, was that the auditors had limited training and relied on factory managers for data and for setting up interviews with workers, all of which were performed in the factories. The auditors, in other words, were getting an incomplete and somewhat sanitized view of conditions in the factory.[15]

Continued Controversy

Fueled perhaps by the unforgiving criticisms of Nike that continued after Phil Knight's May 1998 speech, a wave of protests against Nike occurred on many university campuses from 1998 to 2001. The moving force behind the protests was the United Students Against Sweatshops (USAS). The USAS argued that the Fair Labor Association (FLA), which grew out of the presidential task force on sweatshops, was an industry tool, and not a truly independent auditor of foreign factories. The USAS set up an alternative independent auditing organization, the Workers Rights Consortium (WRC), which they charged with auditing factories that produce products under collegiate licensing programs (under which Nike is a high-profile supplier of products). The WRC is backed, and partly funded, by labor unions and refuses to cooperate with companies, arguing that doing so would jeopardize its independence.

By mid-2000, the WRC had persuaded some 48 universities to join, including all 9 campuses of the University of California systems, the University of Michigan, and the University of Oregon, Phil Knight's alma mater. When Knight heard that the University of Oregon would join the WRC, as opposed to the FLA, he withdrew a planned $30 million donation to the university.[16] Despite this, in November 2000 another major northwest university, the University of Washington, announced that it too would join the WRC, although it would also retain its membership in the FLA.[17]

Nike continued to push forward with its own initiatives, updating progress on its Website. In April 2000, in response to accusations that it was still hiding conditions, it announced that it would release the complete reports of all independent audits of its subcontractors' plants. Global Exchange continued to criticize the company, arguing in mid-2001 that the company was not living up to Phil Knight's 1998 promises and that it was intimidating workers from speaking out about abuses.[18]

Endnotes

1 From Nike's corporate Website at www.nikebiz.com.
2 www.globalexchange.org.
3 "Boycott Nike," *CBS News 48 Hours,* October 17, 1996.
4 D. Jones, "Critics Tie Sweatshop Sneakers to 'Air Jordan,'" *USA Today,* June 6, 1996, 1B.
5 Global Exchange Special Report: Nike Just Don't Do It. www.globalexchange.org/education/publications/newsltr6.97p2.html#nike.
6 V. Dobnik, "Chinese Workers Abused Making Nikes, Reeboks," *Seattle Times,* September 21, 1997, A4.
7 S. Greenhouse, "Nike Shoeplant in Vietnam is Called Unsafe for Workers," *New York Times,* November 8, 1997.
8 Ibid.
9 Quoted in: V. Dobnik, "Chinese Workers Abused Making Nikes, Reeboks," *Seattle Times,* September 21, 1997, A4.
10 W. Bounds and H. Stout, "Sweatshop Pact: Good Fit or Threadbare?" *Wall Street Journal,* April 10, 1997, A2.
11 Associated Press Reporter, "Nike Gives Four Factories the Boot," *Los Angeles Times,* September 23, 1997, 20.
12 Archived at www.nikebiz.com/labor/speech_trans.shtml.
13 OSHA is the United States Occupational Safety and Health Agency.
14 B. Herbert, "Nike Blinks," *New York Times,* May 21, 1998.
15 Dara O'Rourke, Monitoring the Monitors: A critique of the Pricewaterhousecoopers (PwC) Labor Monitoring. Department of Urban Studies and Planning, Mit.
16 L. Lee and A. Bernstein, "Who Says Student Protests Don't Matter?" *Business Week,* June 12, 2000, 94–96.
17 R. Dee, "UW to Join Anti-sweatshop Group," *Seattle Post Intelligencer,* November 20, 2000, B2.
18 Anonymous, "Rights Group Says Nike Isn't Fulfilling Promises," *Wall Street Journal,* May 16, 2001.

eBay and the Online Auction and Retail Sales Industry in 2011

Gareth R. Jones
Texas A&M University

With almost 18,000 employees, eBay, headquartered in San Jose, California, manages and hosts the well-known global online auction and shopping Website that people all around the world visit to buy and sell goods and services. In 2010, eBay generated $9.5 billion in revenue, up from $4.5 billion in 2005, but it generated only $3.5 billion in earnings (measured by EBITDA) compared to $2.1 billion in 2005. Prior to 2007, eBay had been a stellar performer on the stock exchange under the guidance of Meg Whitman, its first CEO; the company's stock market valuation was $46 billion in 2007, making investors extremely happy. But since 2007, eBay has experienced increasing competition and so many problems that its stock price has dramatically fallen—so much so that in July 2011, its market valuation had dropped to $43 billion. Why? Investors became worried its business model would not be so profitable in the future because the online auction market was becoming mature and opportunities for growth were declining. In addition, the nature of competition in online retailing was changing and Amazon.com had emerged as the top online retail portal. Its stock plunged in value as it seemed likely that eBay's business model had run out of steam. But to understand the sources of eBay's success and the current challenges it faces, it is necessary to explore the way eBay's business model and strategies have changed over time.

eBay's Beginnings

Until the 1990s, the auction business was largely fragmented; thousands of small city-based auction houses offered a wide range of merchandise to local buyers. And a few famous global houses, such as Sotheby's and Christie's, offered carefully chosen selections of high-priced antiques and collectibles to limited numbers of dealers and wealthy collectors. However, the auction market was not very efficient, for there was often a shortage of sellers and buyers, and so it was difficult to determine the fair price of a product. Dealers were often able to influence auction prices and obtain bargains at the expense of sellers. Typically, dealers were able to buy at low prices and then charge buyers high prices in the bricks-and-mortar (B&M) antique stores that are found in every town and city around the world; they reaped high profits. The auction business was changed forever in 1995, when Pierre Omidyar developed innovative software that allowed buyers around the world to bid online against each other to determine the fair price for a seller's product.

Omidyar founded his online auction site in San Jose on September 4, 1995, under the name "Auction Web." A computer programmer, Omidyar had previously worked for Microsoft, but he left that company when he realized the potential opportunity to develop new software that provided an online platform to connect Internet buyers and sellers. The entrepreneurial Omidyar changed his company's name to eBay in September 1997, and the first item sold on eBay was Omidyar's broken laser pointer for $13.83. A frequently repeated story that eBay was founded to help Omidyar's fiancée trade PEZ Candy dispensers was fabricated by an eBay public relations manager in 1997 to interest the media. Apparently the story worked, for eBay's popularity grew quickly by word of mouth, and the company did not need to advertise until the early-2000s. Omidyar had tapped into a huge unmet buyer need and people flocked to use auction software platform. Another major reason eBay did not advertise in its early years was that its growing global popularity had put major pressure on its internal computer information systems, both its hardware and software. In particular, the technology behind its search engine—which was not developed by Omidyar but furnished by independent specialist software companies–could not keep pace with the hundreds of millions of search requests that eBay's users generated each day. eBay was also installing powerful servers as quickly as it could to manage its fast-growing global database, and it was recruiting computer programmers and IT managers to run its systems at a rapid rate.

To finance eBay's rapid growth, Omidyar turned to venture capitalists to supply the hundreds of millions of dollars his company required to build its online IT infrastructure. Seeing the success of his business model, he was quickly able to find willing investors. As part of the loan agreement, however, the venture capitalists insisted that Omidyar give control of the running of his company to an experienced dot.com top manager. They were very aware that founding entrepreneurs often have problems in building and implementing a successful business model over time. They recommended that Meg Whitman, an executive who had had great success as a manager of several software start-up companies, be recruited to become eBay's CEO, while Omidyar would assume the role of chairman of the company.

eBay's Evolving Business Model

From the beginning, eBay's business model and strategies were based on developing and refining Omidyar's auction software to create an easy-to-use online market platform that would allow buyers and sellers to meet and transact easily and inexpensively. eBay's software was created to make it easy for sellers to list and describe their products, and easy for buyers to search for, compare, and bid on the products they wanted to purchase. The magic of eBay's software is that the company simply provides the electronic conduit between buyers and sellers; it never takes physical possession of the products that are listed, and their shipping is the responsibility of sellers and payment the responsibility of buyers.

Thus, eBay does not need to develop all the high-cost functional activities like inventory, shipping, and purchasing to deliver products to customers, unlike Amazon.com, for example. So, eBay operates with a low cost structure given the huge volume of products it sells and sales revenues it generates—hence the high revenues and profits it earned before until 2007, as mentioned earlier. Also, word of mouth enabled eBay to avoid paying high advertising costs, an especially important consideration early on because these are a major expense for many online portals seeking to gain a reputation. And, as far as buyers are concerned, eBay is also low cost, for under current U.S. law, sellers located outside a buyer's state do not have to collect sales tax on a purchase. This allows buyers to avoid paying state taxes on expensive items such as jewelry and computers, which can save them tens or even hundreds of dollars, and makes purchasing on eBay more attractive.

To make transactions between anonymous Internet buyers and sellers possible, however, Omidyar's software had to reduce the risks facing buyers and sellers. In particular, it had to convince buyers that they would receive what they paid for, and that sellers would accurately describe their products online. Also, sellers had to be convinced that buyers would pay for the products they committed to purchase on eBay, although of course they were able to wait for the money to arrive in the mail, so their risk was lower; however, many buyers do not pay or pay extremely late. To minimize the ever-present possibility of fraud from sellers misrepresenting their products, or from buyers unethically bidding for pleasure and then not paying, eBay's software contains a method for building and establishing trust between buyers and sellers—building a reputation over time.

After every transaction, buyers and sellers can leave online feedback about their view of the other's behavior and the value of the transaction they have completed. They can fill in an online comment form, which is then published on the Web for each seller and buyer. When sellers and buyers consistently act in an honest way in more and more transactions over time, they are able to build an increasingly stronger positive feedback score that provides them with a good reputation for honesty. More buyers are attracted to a reputable seller, so the seller obtains higher prices for their products. Sellers can also decide if they are dealing with a reputable buyer—one who pays promptly, for example. Over time, this became more difficult because new "unknown" buyers come into the market continuously, so eBay developed online mechanisms so sellers can refuse to deal with any new or existing buyer if they wish, and can remove that buyer's bid from an auction.

eBay generates the revenues that allow it to operate and profit from its electronic auction platform by charging a number of fees to sellers (buyers pay no specific fees). In the original eBay model, sellers paid a fee to list a product on eBay's site and paid a fee if the product was sold by the end of the auction. As its platform's popularity increased and the number of buyers grew, eBay increased the fees it charged sellers. The eBay fee system is quite complex, but in the United States in 2006, eBay took between $0.20 and $80 per listing, and 2%–8% of the final price, depending on the particular product being sold, and the format in which the product sold. In addition, eBay acquired the PayPal payment system that charges substantial fees of its own; this is discussed in detail below.

This core auction business model worked well for the first years of eBay's existence. Using this basic software platform, every day tens of millions of products such as antiques and collectibles, cars, computers, furniture, clothing, books, DVDs and a myriad of other items are listed by sellers all around the world on eBay and bought by the highest bidders. The incredible variety of items sold on eBay suggests why eBay's business model has been so successful—the same set of auction platform programs, constantly improved and refined over time from Omidyar's original programs, can be used to sell almost every kind of product, from low-priced books and magazines costing only cents, to cars and antiques costing tens or hundreds of thousands of dollars. Some of the most expensive items sold include a Frank Mulder 4 Yacht Gigayacht ($85 million), a Grumman Gulfstream II jet ($4.9 million), and a 1993 San Lorenzo 80 Motor Yacht (just under $2 million). One of the largest items ever sold was a World War II submarine that had been auctioned off by a small town in New England that decided it did not need the historical relic anymore.

Meg Whitman's biggest problem was to find search engine software that could keep pace with the increasing volume of buyers' inquiries. Initially, small independent suppliers provided this software; then IBM provided this service. But as search technology advanced in the 2000s, eBay recruited its own search experts from other companies such as Yahoo! and Google. Today, it has its own in-house search technology teams who continually refine and improve its own proprietary search engine software to make it more appealing to its sellers and buyers—and to keep up with competitors. CEO Whitman looked for new ways to improve eBay's business model, while the most pressing concerns were keeping the eBay Website up and running 24 hours per day, and keeping its online storefront meeting the needs of its rapidly increasing number of buyers and sellers.

First, to take advantage of the capabilities of eBay's software, the company began to expand the range and categories of the products it offered for sale to increase revenue. Second, it increased the number of retail or "selling" formats used to bring sellers and buyers together. For example, its original retail format was the 7-day auction format, where the last bidder within this time period "won" the auction, provided the bid met the seller's reserve or minimum price. Then, it introduced the "buy-it-now" format where a buyer could make an instant purchase at the seller's specified price, and later a real-time auction format in which online bidders, and bidders at a B&M auction site, compete against each other in real time to purchase the product up for bid. In this format, a live auctioneer, not the eBay auction clock, decides when to close an auction.

Beyond introducing new kinds of retail formats, over time eBay continuously strived to improve the range and sophistication of the information services it provides its users—to make it easier for sellers to list, describe, present, and ship their products, and for buyers to make better purchasing decisions. For example, software was developed to make it easier for sellers to list their products for sale and upload photographs and add or change information to the listing—however eBay began to charge more for these services. Buyers were also able to take advantage of the new services offered in what is called My eBay; buyers can now keep a list of "watched" items so that over the life of a particular auction they can see how the price of a product has changed and how many bidders are interested in it. This is a useful service for buyers because frequently bidders for many items enter in the last few minutes to try to "snipe" an item or obtain it at the lowest possible cost. As the price of an item becomes higher, this often encourages more buyers to bid on it, so there is value to buyers (although not sellers, who want the highest prices possible) to wait or just bid a minimal amount so they can easily track the item.

By creating and then continually improving its easy-to-use retail platform for sellers and buyers, eBay revolutionized the auction market, bringing together international buyers and sellers in a huge, never-ending yard sale. eBay became the means of cleaning out the "closets of the world" with its user-friendly platform.

New Types of Sellers

Over time, eBay also encouraged the entry of new kinds of sellers into its electronic auction platform. Initially, it focused on individual, small-scale sellers; however, it then sought to attract larger-scale sellers using its eBay Stores selling platform, which allows sellers to list not only products up for auction but also all the items they have available for sale, perhaps in a B&M antique store or warehouse. Store sellers then pay eBay a fee for these "buy it now" sales. Hundreds of thousands of eBay stores became established in the 2000s, greatly adding to eBay's revenues.

Also, during the 2000s, small specialized online stores and large international manufacturers and retailers such as Sears, IBM, and Dell began to open their own online stores on eBay to sell their products using competitive auctions for "clearance goods" and fixed-priced buy-it-now storefronts to sell their latest products. By using eBay, these companies established a new delivery channel for their products, and they were able to bypass wholesalers such as discount stores or warehouses that take a much larger share of the profit than eBay does through its selling fees.

Software advances arrived faster and faster in the 2000s, in part due to eBay's new Developers Program that allowed independent software developers to create new specialized applications that seamlessly integrate with eBay's electronic platform. By 2005, there were over 15,000 members in the eBay Developers Program, comprising a broad range of companies creating software applications to support specialized eBay sellers and buyers, as well as eBay Affiliates. All this progress helped speed and smooth transactions between buyers and sellers and drove up eBay's revenues and profits, something that resulted in a huge increase in the value of its stock.

Competition in the Retail Auction Industry

eBay's growing popularity and growing user or customer base made it increasingly difficult for the hundreds of other online auction houses that had also come online to compete effectively against it. Indeed, its competitive advantage was increasing because both sellers and buyers discovered that they were more likely to find what they wanted and get the best prices from a bigger auction Website's user base or market. And, from the beginning, eBay controlled the biggest market of buyers and sellers, and new users became increasingly loyal over time. So even when large, well-known online companies such as Yahoo! and AOL attempted to enter the online auction business, and even when they offered buyers and sellers *no-fee* auction transactions, they found it was impossible to grow their user bases and establish themselves in this market. From network effects, eBay had obtained a first-mover advantage and was benefiting from this.

The first-mover advantage eBay gained from Pierre Omidyar's auction software created an unassailable business model that effectively gave eBay a monopoly position in the global online auction market. Even today, there are few online or B&M substitutes for the auction service that eBay provides. For example, sellers can list their items for sale on any kind of Website or bulletin board, and specialist kinds of Websites exist to sell highly specialized kinds of products like heavy machinery or large sailboats, but for most products, the sheer reach of eBay guarantees it a dominant position in the marketplace. Because there has been little new entry into the online auction business, the fees eBay charges to sellers steadily increased as it grew, and skimmed off ever more of the profit in the auction value chain. eBay decided it did not have to worry about the power of buyers or sellers to complain about fee increases because it has access to millions of individual buyers and sellers. Sellers would only be a threat to eBay if they could band together and demand reductions in eBay's fees and charges.

This happened first during the early-2000s. Meg Whitman, desperate to keep eBay's revenues growing to protect its stock price, started to continuously increase the fees charged to eBay stores to list their items on eBay. Store sellers rebelled and used the eBay community bulletin boards and chat rooms to register their complaints. eBay realized there was a limit to how much it could charge sellers. It would have to find new ways to attract more buyers to the sellers' products, and get them better prices, if was going to be able to increase the fees it charged sellers. Or it would have to find new ways to extract profit from the auction value chain.

New Ways to Grow eBay's Value Chain

Meg Whitman always preached to eBay's employees that to maintain and increase the value of its stock (and many employees own stock options in the company), eBay must (1) continually attract more buyers and sellers to its auction site, and (2) search for ways to generate more revenue from these buyers and sellers. To create more value from its auction business model, eBay has adopted many other kinds of strategies to grow profitability over time.

International Expansion

Online, buyers from any country in the world can bid on an auction, and so it became clear early on that one way to grow eBay's business would be to replicate its business model in different countries around the world. Accordingly, eBay quickly moved to establish storefronts around the world customized to the needs and language of a particular country's citizens. Globally, eBay established its own online presence in countries like the United Kingdom and Australia, but in other countries, particularly non-English-speaking countries, it often acquired the national start-up online auction company that had stolen the first-mover advantage in a particular country. In 1999, for example, eBay acquired the German auction house Alando for $43 million and changed it into eBay Germany. In 2001, eBay acquired MercadoLibre, Lokau, and iBazar, Latin American auction sites, and established eBay Latin America. In 2003, eBay acquired

EachNet, a leading e-commerce company in China, for $150 million to enter the Chinese market. And, in 2004, it bought Baazee.com, an Indian auction site, and took a large stake in Korean rival Internet Auction Co. In 2006, eBay acquired Tradera.com, Sweden's leading online auction-style marketplace, for $48 million, in 2009 it acquired Gmarket, Korea's leading online marketplace.

All these global acquisitions helped eBay to retain its dominant presence in the global online auction business to facilitate transactions both inside countries and between countries to build up revenue. Once eBay was up and running in a particular country, network dynamics took effect, and it became difficult for a new auction start-up to establish a strong foothold in its domestic online auction market. But, eBay has faced serious competition in countries such as Japan and Hong Kong, where Yahoo! gained a head start over eBay and thus gained the first-mover advantage in these countries; in China, too, eBay has run into major opposition. Thus, by 2011, significant global expansion was difficult because the cost of overseas online auctions sites had become extremely expensive and eBay's goal was to protect its market share around the world.

Expanding its Value Chain Activities

Providing more kinds of value-chain services that add value and create revenue and profit at different stages of the online auction and retail value chain is a second way in which eBay has grown the revenues from its auction model. This strategy emerged gradually as it sought new sources of revenues to bolster its bottom line.

eBay Drop-Off Stores

One service it created in the early-2000s to encourage more business from individuals who want to sell their goods online—but lacked the computer skills to do so—was eBay Drop Off. eBay licenses reputable eBay sellers that have consistently sold hundreds of items using its platform to open B&M consignment stores in cities where anybody can "drop off" the products they want to sell. The owner of the

Drop-Off Store describes, photographs, and lists the item on eBay and then handles all the payment and shipping activities involved in the auction process. The store owner receives a commission, often 15% or more of the final selling price (not including eBay's commission) for providing this service. These stores have proved highly profitable for their owners and thousands have sprung up across the United States and the world (a search request on eBay's site allows buyers to identify the closest eBay Drop-Off Store). The advantage for eBay is that this drop-off service gives it access to the millions of people who have no experience in posting photographs online, organizing payment, or opening an eBay account and learning how to list an item, and so eBay gains from increased listing fees.

Increased Advertising

To promote the millions of products it has for sale on its site, eBay increased its use of advertising—on television, newspapers, and on popular Websites—to expand its user base in the 2000s. Its goal was to make eBay *the* preferred place to shop online by demonstrating two things: first, the incredible diversity of products available for purchase on its site, and second, the fact that its products generally cost less than buyers would pay in B&M stores—or even on other online stores. New and used DVDs, books, designer clothing, electronics and computers are some of the multitude of products that can be obtained at a steep discount on eBay. Thus, while the range of the products eBay sells provides it with a differentiation advantage, the low prices that buyers can often obtain gives it a low-price advantage too—provided buyers are prepared to wait a few days to receive their newly purchased products.

PayPal Payment Service

Meg Whitman was also working to find ways to make transactions easier for eBay buyers and sellers to increase the ease, security, and volume of online sales. One way to do this was to get involved in an extremely profitable part of any company's value chain activity—the payment system involved in managing the financial transactions necessary to complete online transactions—to both purchase and sell products online. The effective management of financial transactions is vital in online transactions for this poses the greatest risks to buyers, who may be taken advantage of by unscrupulous or fraudulent sellers who take money and then fail to deliver the expected product. Sellers also faced problems. When eBay first started, sellers usually demanded money orders or bank cashiers' checks as secure forms of payment from buyers, or insisted that ordinary checks had to be cleared through their accounts before mailing the product to customers. This increased the length of time and effort involved in a transaction for sellers and buyers and led to lost sales—customers don't like to wait a long time to receive their purchases.

By the early-2000s, online companies like PayPal and Billpoint had emerged that offered secure online electronic payment services that greatly facilitated online commerce. To work efficiently, these services require sellers and buyers to register and enter a valid bank account number, and usually a credit card number, to authenticate the sellers' and buyers' identities and their ability to pay for the items purchased. Now payment became instantaneous; the money was taken directly from the buyer's bank account or paid for by credit card. Buyers could now purchase on credit, while sellers could immediately send off the product to the buyer. When buyers paid sellers, the online payment company collected a 3% commission, which was taken from the seller's proceeds—a very profitable source of revenue.

eBay recognized this was highly profitable value-chain activity because by becoming involved in online payment services it would increase its share of the fees involved in eBay transactions. But, eBay also realized that ownership of a secure online payment system would reinforce its attempts to increase the reputation of both buyers and sellers to encourage the growth of online sales by preventing fraud. Major synergies between selling and payment activities were possible. Since it was late to enter this business and would take a long time to develop its own payment service from scratch, eBay acquired the online payment service Billpoint and worked to get eBay buyers and sellers to register with Billpoint. However, eBay found itself running up against a brick wall; just as eBay had gained the first-mover advantage in the auction business, so PayPal had gained it in the online payment business. Millions of eBay users were already signed up with PayPal. After failing to make Billpoint the market leader, in 2002 eBay acquired PayPal for $1.5 billion in stock—a great return for PayPal's stockholders. Then, to reduce costs, eBay switched all Billpoint customers to PayPal and shut down Billpoint. This purchase has been very profitable for eBay, for it now owns the world's leading online payment system. The PayPal acquisition has paid for itself many times over, as discussed below.

More Retail Formats

eBay also began to make many acquisitions to facilitate its entry into new kinds of specialized retail and auction formats to increase its market reach—and its revenues and profits. In 1999, it acquired the well-known auction house Butterfield & Butterfield to facilitate its entry into the auctioning of high-priced antiques and collectibles and compete with upper-end auction houses such as Sotheby's and Christie's. However, eBay's managers discovered that a lot more involvement was needed to correctly identify, price, list, and then auction rare, high-priced antiques, and it exited the upper-end auction niche in 2002 when it sold Butterfield & Butterfield to Bonhams, an upscale auction house that wanted to develop a much bigger online presence.

To further its expansion into the highly profitable motor vehicle segment of the market, in 2003 eBay acquired CARad.com, an auction management service for car dealers, to strengthen eBay Motors. Now eBay controls the auctions in which vehicle dealers bid on cars that they then resell to individual buyers, often on eBay Motors. In another move to enter a new retail market in 2004, eBay acquired Rent.com for $415 million. This online site offers a completely free rental and roommate search service; it offers to pay users who have signed a new lease at a property found on its Website $100 when they inform Rent.com. Once again, the "sellers" of the rentals on its Websites are charged the fees; the online roommate search is free. Rent.com has millions of up-to-date rental listings, with thousands added every day; listings include a property's address and phone number, a detailed description, photos, floor plans, and so on, which makes it easier for prospective renters to research and select a rental.

In 2000, eBay acquired Half.com for $318 million. Half.com is an online retail platform that specializes in the sale of new and used fixed-price consumer products such as books, movies, video games, DVDs, and so on that are offered at a fixed price and sold on a first-come-first-served basis, not by auction. eBay's "Buy It Now" feature is similar, although sellers are allowed to set a lower start price than the buy-it-now price, and the selling process can develop into an auction if bidders start to compete for the product. In the 2000s, the popularity of fixed-price online retailing led to a significant expansion in eBay's activities in this segment of the retail market. In 2006, eBay opened its new eBay Express site, which was designed to work like a standard Internet shopping site to consumers with U.S. addresses. Select eBay items are mirrored on eBay Express, where buyers use a shopping cart to purchase products from multiple sellers. A UK version of eBay Express is also in development.

In 2005, eBay acquired Shopping.com, an online price-comparison shopping site, for $635 million. With millions of products, thousands of merchants, and millions of reviews from the Epinions community, Shopping.com empowers consumers to make informed choices and, as a result, encourages more buyers to purchase products. Information provided by Shopping.com also facilitates eBay sellers' pricing knowledge about their online competitors and helps them price their products competitively so that they can sell them more quickly. The site also allows customers to purchase products from various eBay retail formats.

In the 2000s, online local classifieds have become an increasingly popular way for people to sell their unwanted products, especially because there are usually no fees associated with them. Local classifieds are very popular for bulky products like furniture, appliances, exercise equipment, and so on, where high transportation costs represent a significant percentage of the purchase price. In 2004, to ensure its foothold in this online retail segment, eBay bought a 25% stake in the popular free online classifieds Website Craigslist by buying the stock of one of Craigslist's founders.

These free local classified services have been hurting newspapers whose classified sales have sharply decreased. It remains to be seen in the future whether these classified services will remain free or whether they will also be charging fees. Clearly, eBay would like to charge a fee if it owned a controlling stake in Craigslist. Perhaps preparing for the future when money will be made from online classifieds, in 2004, eBay acquired Marktplaats, a Dutch competitor that had achieved an 80% market share in the Netherlands by focusing on small fixed-price ads, not auctions. Then, in 2005, eBay acquired Gumtree, a network of UK local city classifieds sites; the Spanish classifieds site, Loquo; and the German language classifieds site, Opus Forum. In 2005 eBay launched Kijiji, a local classifieds site it made available in nearly a dozen countries to try to dominate this growing retailing market.

The Skype Acquisition

Perhaps going furthest away from its core business, in 2005, eBay acquired Skype, the dominant Voice-Over-Internet-Provider (VOIP) telephone company, for $2.6 billion. Meg Whitman's rationale for this expensive purchase was that Skype would provide eBay with the ability to perform an important service for its users, specifically, to give them a quick, inexpensive way to communicate and exchange the information required to complete online transactions. Skype's software allows users to make free calls from their computers over the Internet to anyone, anywhere in the world. Skype boasts superior call quality and the ability to allow users not just to make phone calls but also to send instant messages, transfer big files, chat, and make video conference calls. It is a full-scale online communications company.

According to Whitman, Skype would help eBay sellers build their online businesses. Using Skype, buyers can contact sellers anytime on their Skype phone number. Sellers can also call regular phone numbers anywhere in the world using SkypeOut at very low rates, and with a SkypeIn phone number, buyers can call a regular telephone number wherever the seller is in the world. Also, in the case of large sellers, Skype allows continuous contact between all the members of the store with SkypeIn numbers and Skype Voicemail. For buyers, Skype allows them to get all the product information they need to buy with confidence and to get answers immediately, without waiting for e-mail.

Many analysts believed it was questionable whether eBay needed to buy a VOIP company given that so many alternative methods of instant communication were offered by so many online companies as AOL, MSN, Yahoo!, Google, and so on. Nevertheless, eBay quickly developed strategies to get sellers to integrate Skype into their storefronts and to find new ways to include it in the regular transaction process just as it was doing with its PayPal service.

eBay ProStores

Another strategy eBay has used to grow its revenues was to create a new online retail consulting service called ProStores in 2005 that allows potential sellers to utilize eBay's functional competencies in online retailing to create their own online storefront using eBay's software—for a fee of course. ProStores offers sellers a fully featured Web store that can be customized specifically for each online seller and that is then maintained and hosted by eBay. Sellers using the ProStores service might be specialist B&M stores searching for a quick and easy way to establish an online presence, or any entrepreneur who wishes to start an online store. The difference between eBay ProStores and regular eBay Stores is that ProStores sites are accessed through a URL unique to each seller and are not required to carry eBay branding. ProStores sellers are responsible for driving their own store traffic. While items on ProStores sites sell at fixed prices only, they can be simultaneously listed on the eBay marketplace in either the auction or fixed-price formats.

ProStores provides all software needed to build a storefront and then create the listing, promotion, and payment systems needed to make it work. ProStores uses templates and wizards that allow users to quickly and easily build an attractive, feature-rich store with no technical or design skills whatsoever. In return, eBay charges two basic fees to all sellers who purchase a ProStores Web store: (1) a monthly subscription fee and (2) a monthly successful transaction fee calculated as a percentage of the sales price of items sold in the store. The subscription fee ranges from $6.95 to $249.95, depending on the size of the store. The successful transaction fee varies between 1.5 and 2.5%.

eBay Express

Finally, reacting to growing buyer demand for a discounted, fixed-price retail format, in 2006, eBay established eBay Express, where a vast inventory of brand-new, brand-name, and hard-to-find products are offered at fixed prices by top eBay sellers. Buyers are able to obtain the products they want with no bidding and no waiting; they can fill their shopping carts from multiple eBay merchants and pay for everything, including shipping, in a single, secure payment using PayPal. eBay is touting that every transaction is safe, secure, and fully covered by free buyer protection from PayPal. eBay Express was eBay's first major move to react to the growing threat it was facing from Amazon.com, whose rapid growth was based on the growing popularity among online customers for fixed-price retailing. As discussed below, eBay was too late to enter fixed-price retailing because Amazon.com had now gained the first mover advantage and this has resulted in growing problems, as discussed next.

New Problems for eBay

Despite adopting all these new strategies to strengthen its business model, in the 12 months ending August 2006, eBay's stock declined 30% from its lofty height, while the stock market had risen about 8%. Why? The first major problem facing eBay was that while the number of its global users was increasing, it was increasing at a decreasing rate—even after all its promotional and advertising efforts and its emphasis on introducing new site features, functionality, retail formats and international expansion. Similarly, although the number of items listed on eBay's retail platforms was increasing (by 45% in 2004 and 33% in 2005), growth was also slowing. In fact, in eBay's U.S. retail segment, net transaction revenues increased only 31% in 2005 and 30% in 2004, compared to 43% in 2003, while gross merchandise volume increased 19% in 2005 and 27% in 2004, compared to 41% in 2003. eBay's revenue growth was slowing, and it seemed clear to investors that despite all its new strategies and entry into online payment and communications activities would not be able to sustain its future growth—and so justify its lofty stock price.

A second major problem was its failure to recognize the potential of online advertising revenues. By 2006, it was clear that leading Internet companies like Yahoo!, Microsoft, and eBay were all facing a major threat from Google, which was perfecting its incredibly lucrative online search and advertising model. Google was now the "new eBay" in terms of stock appreciation because of the way it was able to implant its advertising search software into its own

and any other Internet Website willing to share advertising revenues with Google. In fact, because eBay is one of the world's biggest buyers of Web search terms, it is one of Google's largest customers. eBay manages a portfolio of 15 million keywords on different search sites, such as Google, Yahoo!, and AOL. These searches are aimed at attracting bidders to one of eBay's retail formats, which is why eBay, or one of its subsidiaries, often comes up first on a search inquiry.

All the large Internet companies realized they had underestimated the enormous potential revenues to be earned from Internet advertising and were anxious to get a bigger share of the pie and copy Google's approach. eBay, which had not placed ads on its pages in the past to allow its users to focus on the products for sale, now began to have banner ads, pop-ups, and the other obtrusive and annoying ways of advertising developed by software advertising engineers. By 2007, it had placed several ads on each page in its desperate hurry to increase revenues. eBay became concerned Google would start to drain away even more of its revenues and customers, and it searched for ways to counter Google's threat. However, analysts noted that eBay could not abandon its "friendly" relationship with Google because Google is the most popular search engine on which eBay promotes its retail storefronts.

Third, in another controversial move, in the spring of 2006, eBay decided to sharply increase the fees it charged its fixed-cost storefronts to advertise on its site. By 2006, sales of fixed-price products, which carried smaller margins than auction products, had grown to over 80% of total retail sales. In charging higher fees, eBay risked alienating large fixed-cost sellers, which would be forced to pass on these increases to customers, and of alienating customers who now could choose a popular shopping comparison tool like eBay, MSN, or Google's shopping-specific Websites, all of which attempt to locate the lowest-priced products. They could also go and shop at Amazon.com. Analysts questioned if this strategy would backfire—and it did as discussed below.

A 2007 Turnaround?

In 2007, eBay announced some impressive financial results that provided a lift to its stock price that had fallen from $60 in 2005 to a low of $25 in 2006. Shares of eBay jumped by 8% in February 2007 when eBay reported a fourth-quarter profit that climbed 24% as sales rose more than expected, helped by a surge in its PayPal electronic payments business and higher prices for the items eBay sells online. Net income for the fourth quarter rose to $346 million, or $0.25 a share, from $279 million, or $0.20, a year earlier. Revenue from eBay's PayPal payments business rose 37% to $417 million, or 1/4 of the company's total, while sales in its online marketplace business rose 24%. These results suggested that eBay's decision to raise its charges to list items in eBay stores to some of its highest-volume sellers had paid off, the quality of the listing had improved, and more of these sellers had been encouraged to use the higher fee-paying auction method. eBay's stock price climbed to $40 by October 2007, and that once again seemed to suggest to investors that its competitive advantage was secure, even in the face of challenges from Google and Amazon.com. However, the turnaround was short-lived.

A New CEO and New Problems and Strategies

When eBay reported results in the next two quarters, however, it was clear that all was not well as its core auction business experienced sequential declines in listings. It was becoming clear that the company's growth was still slowing despite all of Meg Whitman's efforts to expand its sales and retail channels, payment services, and communication through Skype. When the company's stock had dropped back to $26 by March 2008, Whitman decided to resign and a new CEO, John Donahoe, who had been president of eBay Marketplaces and its retail channels, was named to succeed her.

In one of his first press conferences as CEO, Donahoe announced that eBay's biggest problem was that it was lagging behind in its attempts to develop an advanced search engine that would let users find the products they want: "Today our buyers tell us that we know you have unmatched selection, but we can't always find what we want and find values as fast as we want," Donahoe said. Donahoe's new goal for eBay's retail channels was to use its massive database on seller and buyer transactions to provide the most relevant search experience possible, Donahoe

also proposed to develop a much clearer way of combining fixed-price listings, which are appropriate for new current-model products, and auctions, which are the best way to find prices for unique, older and used merchandise. In 2008, buyers could purchase fixed-price goods on the main eBay site, as well as on its eBay Express site and Shopping.com site. In the future, Donahoe wants all these different options to be presented on a single page of search results from eBay's main site. This was an ambitious goal as the changes eBay's software designers had been making over time were often not well received by buyers or sellers, who had not liked the changes eBay had been making to its search engine. However, eBay was now increasingly under attack from Google and Amazon.com, that had been developing much more advanced search engines and were attracting more customers as a result.

Donahoe also noted that an increasing percentage of eBay's revenues and profits were coming from its PayPal operations and that one of his major priorities would be to promote the use and scale of PayPal's financial operations. On the other hand, he also noted that the Skype acquisition was not increasing the profitability of eBay's value-chain operations, and that he would look at the pros and cons of divesting it to free up working capital to be invested in eBay's Marketplaces retail channels.

Donahoe also announced that eBay would be creating a new fee structure for sellers that would reduce the initial cost of listing an item, including the cost of putting photographs on the listing, and shifting the burden to an increased percentage of the final sale price. He claimed that, as Amazon.com was doing, sellers prefer this model that only charges a fee when a sale is made because it involves less risk to them. However, as he said: "There definitely will be those that are concerned or upset about these changes, our clear belief is what's good for buyers is good for sellers, and is good for eBay." Little did he know what was in store for eBay.

eBay's Seller's Revolt

As noted earlier, since its founding, eBay has sought to cultivate good relationships with the millions of sellers that advertise their goods on its Website. But, at the same time, to increase its revenues and profits it steadily increased the fees it charges sellers to list and promote their products on its sites, to use its PayPal payment service, and so on. This had caused some grumbling and problems with sellers in the past because it reduced their profit margins. However, eBay had been increasing its advertising and developing new retail channels to attract millions more buyers to its Websites so sellers would receive better prices and this would offset their higher costs. As a result, sellers tolerated eBay's fee structure.

This all changed in February 2008 when Donohue's new fee structure took effect. For its small-scale sellers that already had thin profit margins the fee hikes that increased back-end commissions on completed sales and payments were painful. In addition, in the future, eBay announced it would block sellers from leaving negative feedback about buyers—feedback such as buyers who didn't pay for the goods they purchased or took too long to do so. Donohue's claimed this change was to improve the buyer's experience because many buyers had complained that if they left negative feedback for a seller—the seller would then leave negative feedback for the buyer!

Together, however, these changes resulted in a blaze of conflict between eBay and its millions of sellers who thought they were being harmed by these changes, that they had lost their prestige and standing at eBay, and their bad feelings resulted in a revolt. Blogs and forums across the Internet were filled with messages expressing feelings that eBay had abandoned its smaller sellers and was pushing them out of business in favor of high-volume "powersellers" who contributed more to eBay's profits. eBay and Donohue received millions of hostile e-mails and sellers threatened they would move their business elsewhere, such as onto Amazon.com. Sellers even organized a 1-week boycott of eBay during which they would list no items with the company to express their hostility. Many sellers did shut down their eBay online storefronts and moved to Amazon.com, which claimed in 2009 that for the first time its network of retail sites had overtaken eBay in monthly unique viewers or "hits." One informal survey found that while over 50% of buyers thought Amazon.com was an excellent sales channel, only 23% regarded Bay as being excellent.

Realizing his changes had backfired, Donohue reversed course in 2009 and eliminated several of eBay's fee increases and revamped its feedback system so that buyers and sellers can now respond to one another's comments in a fairer way. These moves did smooth over the bad feeling between sellers and eBay, but the old "community relationship" it had enjoyed with sellers largely disappeared.

Improving Retail Channels and Product Search

Clearly, Donahoe would not be able to significantly increase eBay's revenues by increasing fees to sellers in the future, so his focus now was on expanding and improving its retail channels and product search capabilities to increase revenues. In 2007, eBay had acquired StubHub, the world's largest online ticket marketplace, and Donahoe worked to increase its market share and profits, once again by increasing fees, but also by improving its search software capabilities. eBay has also launched its Kijiji classified sites in 200 U.S. cities during 2007, but had not had the success it expected. In 2010, eBay relaunched its Kijiji classifieds site as eBayClassifieds.com with major software enhancements that it claimed would create industry-leading standards in trust and safety, customer service and user experience. In 2008, eBay Marketplaces introduced gift cards to capitalize on the growing popularity of "private" credit cards.

In 2009, eBay introduced "Daily Deals" to compete with Groupon and Living Social, backed by Amazon.com. This new online coupon retail channel connects buyers with sellers faster than ever, and its popularity has exploded. In 2011, eBay launched a new home page design that offers more deals and personalization—especially for fixed-price goods the latest step in Donahoe's attempts to improve its search engine capabilities. Also, in 2011, it acquired local product search company, Milo.com, to enhance its daily deal channel offerings.

New Moves with PayPal

Over the last several years, PayPal was contributing more and more to eBay's profits as the number of its active users, compared to eBay users, and the volume and value of PayPal's transactions increased (See Exhibit 1).

eBay has been working hard to make PayPal a financial powerhouse, and a leading conduit through which buyers and sellers can transact internationally,

Exhibit 1 Changes in eBay and PayPal Users and PayPal Payments 2006–2010

	2006	2007	2008	2009	2010
Number of Active Global eBay Users (in millions)	82	85	88	90	94
Number of Active Global PayPal Users (in millions)	49	57	70	81	94
Total PayPal Payment Volume (in billions)	$366	$486	$606	$726	$926

© Cengage Learning 2013

something that often involves high fees for buyers and sellers. PayPal also issues eBay credit cards and it has become another important means to reassure buyers that sellers are honest and reputable. During the last decade complaints about fraud on eBay have received increasing publicity as the scams practiced by unethical sellers have been revealed. PayPal allows eBay to offers buyers who use PayPal to pay for their products free product insurance protection in the event that their purchases are either fraudulent or misrepresented. It also reassures sellers that they can trust buyers. Through PayPal, eBay can police sellers and buyers and suspend their accounts if necessary to increase the reliability and quality of its performance. Today, the eBay Buyer Protection program offered through PayPal is the most comprehensive online consumer protection provided by a global retailer.

eBay has also been working to expand PayPal's appeal in many other ways to make it the leading online payment company. In 2005, PayPal launched its Merchant Services division that allows sellers of all sizes to easily and securely accept payments across the Internet. In 2006, PayPal launched a mobile application that allows PayPal users to send money via their mobile phones. By 2008, 8% of all e-commerce worldwide was transacted via PayPal. In 2009, PayPal acquired Israel's Fraud Sciences Ltd. to enhance its security and fraud management systems. Also in 2009, eBay launched its iPhone application, giving millions of buyers mobile access to eBay so that they could buy their items and then pay for them online. To allow its customers more credit facilities, eBay also acquired "Bill Me Later," a leading online-oriented payments brand and began to offer Bill Me Later as an option to customers during checkout.

In 2009, PayPal also opened its platform, PayPal X to become the first major global payments company that was open to third-party development so other companies could link in directly to the PayPal system and customize their payment approach. For example, in 2010

Facebook users became able to use PayPal to pay for Facebook Ads through the company's online advertising tool and for gaming services such as Zynga's Cityville and Farmville. In 2011, PayPal launched a new service that lets digital-game players pay for digital goods without leaving the content site—and it has already processed $3.4 billion in digital-goods payments.

Given the growing importance of secure mobile payments in the 2010s as Apple and Google also began offering their own mobile online payments system, in 2011 eBay acquired privately-held Zong Inc. for $240 million to strengthen PayPal's position in the fast-growing mobile payments and digital goods market. Zong allows consumers to pay for purchases from their mobile phones (or direct-carrier billing) on the Internet and offers a secure connection to more than 250 mobile operators in 45 countries. PayPal President Scott Thompson said that eBay expects that "Zong will strengthen PayPal's value by helping us reach the more than 4 billion people who have mobile phones, giving them more choice and security when they pay."

The Skype Divestiture

Meg Whitman's strategy that Skype, by providing easy and free global communication, would speed information flow between sellers and buyers and drive eBay's global sales and revenues was not realized—most eBay users stayed with their own e-mail or SMS providers. Consequently, in 2009 announced that it would sell about 70% of Skype to a group of private investors for $2.75 billion, which it bought for about $3.1 billion in 2005. While this seemed to be a poor return on eBay's investment, it received a pleasant surprise in 2011 when Microsoft announced that it was acquiring Skype for $8.5 billion; that gave eBay a quick $1.4 billion profit on its remaining 30% stake.

A 2011 Turnaround?

After all these strategic changes to its business model, by October 2010, Donahoe's turnaround plan for eBay was showing signs of success; 2009 revenues were $8.7 million, or 14% higher than before Donahoe took over in 2008, and in 2010, revenues were $9.5 billion while profit had also increased fueled by the Skype sale, growth in PayPal and growth in revenues from increased sales from its online retail channels." CEO John Donahoe announced that he was pleased with the progress that buyers and sellers were noticing, but also that there was still a lot of work to do. eBay's biggest challenge is still how to manage the threats posed by Amazon.com and Google, which have also been changing their business models to outcompete eBay.

One strategy eBay announced in July 2011 was that it was going to start rolling out a fulfillment service for its merchants, similar to Amazon.com's Marketplace service, and this will handle the storage and shipping of inventory of the merchants who sell their products on its Websites. Merchants who use Amazon.com's value-chain services benefit enormously from its huge supply chain and the economies of scale that come with it, such as not having to handle inventory, and fast and often free shipping. In the past, eBay appeared to have a stronger business model than Amazon.com's because, unlike Amazon.com, it did not have to bear the costs of warehouses, inventory, and shipping. It provided the marketplace for buyers and sellers to meet, and then, of course, also provided the profitable PayPal payment service that has allowed it to take a greater percentage of the revenues from online transactions on its Website. However, Amazon.com, has shown that by using IT to manage the huge supply chain infrastructure of warehouses necessary to control transactions along the value chain it can provide a better experience for merchants and customers—driving merchants to sell through Amazon.com instead of eBay. Recall, that in the late-1990s Amazon.com tried to take on eBay in auctions and failed. Now eBay is playing catch-up to Amazon.com in the fixed-price product market and is establishing its own physical value chain. Will this work? In 2011, more and more of eBay's profits were coming from expanding its PayPal financial services and analysts worried that this was not a good strategy to increase the profitability of its business model.

Endnotes

www.ebay.com, press releases 1997–2011.

eBay Annual and 10K Reports, 1997–2011.

Belbin, David, *The eBay Book: Essential Tips for Buying and Selling on eBay.co.uk*, (London: Harriman House Publishing, 2004).

Cihlar, Christopher, *The Grilled Cheese Madonna and 99 Other of the Weirdest, Wackiest, Most Famous eBay Auctions Ever*, (New York: Random House, 2006).

Cohen, Adam, *The Perfect Store: Inside eBay*, (Boston: Little, Brown & Company, 2002)

Jackson, Eric M., *The PayPal Wars: Battles with eBay, the Media, the Mafia, and the Rest of Planet Earth*, (Los Angeles: World Ahead Publishing, 2004).

Nissanoff, Daniel, *FutureShop: How the New Auction Culture Will Revolutionize the Way We Buy, Sell and Get the Things We Really Want*, London: The Penguin Press, 2006).

Spencer, Christopher Matthew, *The eBay Entrepreneur*, New York: Kaplan Publishing 2006).

CASE 8

The Evolution of the Small Package Express Delivery Industry, 1973–2010

Charles W.L. Hill
University of Washington

Introduction

The small package express delivery industry is the segment of the broader postal and cargo industries that specializes in rapid (normally 1–3 days) delivery of small packages (small packages are defined as those weighing less than 150 lbs. or having less than 165 inches in combined length and girth). It is generally agreed that the modern express delivery industry in the United States began with Fred Smith's vision for Federal Express Company (now FedEx), which started operations in 1973. FedEx transformed the structure of the existing air cargo industry and paved the way for rapid growth in the overnight package segment of that industry. A further impetus to the industry's development was the 1977 deregulation of the U.S. air cargo industry. This deregulation allowed FedEx (and its emerging competitors) to buy large jets for the first time. The story of the industry during the 1980s was one of rapid growth and new entry. Between 1982 and 1989, small package express cargo shipments by air in the United States grew at an annual average rate of 31%. In contrast, shipments of airfreight and air mail grew at an annual rate of only 2.7%.[1] This rapid growth attracted new entrants such as United Parcel Service (UPS) and Airborne Freight (which operated under the name Airborne Express). The entry of UPS triggered severe price cutting, which ultimately drove some of the weaker competitors out of the market and touched off a wave of consolidation in the industry.

By the mid-1990s, the industry structure had stabilized with four organizations —FedEx, UPS, Airborne Express and the United States Postal Service (USPS)—accounting for the vast majority U.S. express shipments. During the first half of the 1990s, the small package express industry continued to grow at a healthy rate, with shipments expanding by slightly more than 16% per annum.[2] Despite this growth, the industry was hit by repeated rounds of price cutting as the three big private firms battled to capture major accounts. In addition to price cutting, the big three also competed vigorously on the basis of technology, service offerings, and the global reach of their operations. By the late-1990s and early-2000s, the intensity of price competition in the industry had moderated, with a degree of pricing discipline being maintained, despite the fact that the growth rate for the industry slowed down. Between 1995 and 2000, the industry had grown at 9.8% per year. In 2001, the volume of express parcels shipped by air fell by 5.9%, partly due to an economic slowdown, and partly due to the aftereffects of the September 11 terrorist attack on the United States.[3] Growth picked up again in 2002. Estimates suggest that the global market for small package express delivery should continue to grow by a little over 6% per annum between 2005 and 2025. Most of that growth, however, is forecasted to take place outside of the now mature North American market. Within the United States, the annual growth rate is predicted to match the growth in United States GDP.[4]

In North America, the biggest change to take place in the 2000s was the 2003 entry of DHL with the acquisition of Airborne Express for $1 billion. DHL is owned by Deutsche Post World Net, formally the German post office, which since privatization has been rapidly transforming itself into a global express mail and logistics operation. Prior to 2003, DHL lacked a strong presence in the all-important

United States market. The acquisition of Airborne gave DHL a foothold in the United States. DHL subsequently spent $1.5 billion trying to upgrade Airborne's delivery network in a quest for market share. Despite heavy investments, DHL failed to gain traction and after 5 years of losses, in 2009 it exited the United States market. With the exit of DHL, the United States market looks increasingly like a duopoly. In 2010, FedEx held onto 54% of the $14 billion overnight express market, UPS accounted for 41% and the USPS held 6% (although they actually contracted out its express deliveries to FedEx). UPS dominated the $34 billion ground market in 2010, with a 61% share, followed by FedEx with 22% and the USPS with 16%.[5]

The Industry Before FedEx

In 1973, roughly 1.5 billion tons of freight were shipped in the United States. Most of this freight was carried by surface transport, with airfreight accounting for less than 2% of the total.[6] While shipment by airfreight was often quicker than shipment by surface freight, the high cost of airfreight had kept down demand. The typical users of airfreight at this time were suppliers of time-sensitive, high-priced goods, such as computer parts and medical instruments, which were needed at dispersed locations but which were too expensive for their customers to hold as inventory.

The main cargo carriers in 1973 were major passenger airlines, which operated several all-cargo planes and carried additional cargo in their passenger planes, along with a handful of all-cargo airlines such as Flying Tigers. From 1973 onward, the passenger airlines moved steadily away from all-cargo planes and began to concentrate cargo freight in passenger planes. This change was a response to increases in fuel costs, which made the operation of many older cargo jets uneconomical.

With regard to distribution of cargo to and from airports, in 1973 about 20% of all airfreight was delivered to airports by the shipper and/or picked up by the consignee. The bulk of the remaining 80% was accounted for by three major intermediaries: (1) Air Cargo Incorporated, (2) freight forwarders, and (3) the U.S. Postal Service. Air Cargo Incorporated was a trucking service, wholly owned by 26 airlines, which performed pickup and delivery service for the airlines' direct customers. Freight forwarders were trucking carriers who consolidated cargo going to the airlines. They purchased cargo space from the airlines and retailed this space in small amounts. They dealt primarily with small customers, providing pickup and delivery services in most cities, either in their own trucks or through contract agents. The U.S. Postal Service used air service for transportation of long-distance letter mail and air parcel post.[7]

The Federal Express Concept

Founded by Fred Smith, Jr., Federal Express was incorporated in 1971 and began operations in 1973. At that time, a significant portion of small-package airfreight flew on commercial passenger flights. Smith believed that there were major differences between packages and passengers, and he was convinced that the two had to be treated differently. Most passengers moved between major cities and wanted the convenience of daytime flights. Cargo shippers preferred nighttime service to coincide with late-afternoon pickups and next-day delivery. Because small-package airfreight was subservient to the requirements of passengers' flight schedules, it was often difficult for the major airlines to achieve next-day delivery of airfreight.

Smith's aim was to build a system that could achieve next-day delivery of small-package airfreight (less than 70 lbs.). He set up Federal Express with his $8 million family inheritance and $90 million in venture capital (the company's name was changed to FedEx in 1998). Federal Express established a hub-and-spoke route system, the first airline to do so. The hub of the system was Memphis, chosen for its good weather conditions, central location, and the fact that it was Smith's hometown. The spokes were regular routes between Memphis and shipping facilities at public airports in the cities serviced by Federal Express. Every weeknight, aircraft would leave their home cities with a load of packages and fly down the spokes to Memphis (often with one or two stops on the way). At Memphis, all packages were unloaded, sorted by destination, and reloaded. The aircraft then returned back to their home cities in the early hours of the morning. Packages were ferried to and from airports by Federal Express couriers driving the company's vans and working to a tight schedule. Thus, from door to door, the package was in Federal Express' hands. This system guaranteed that a package picked up from a customer in New York at 5 p.m. would reach its final destination in Los Angeles (or any other major city) by noon the following day. It enabled Federal Express to realize economies in sorting and to utilize its air cargo capacity efficiently. Federal Express also pioneered the use of standard packaging with an upper weight limit of 70 lbs. and a maximum length plus girth of 108 inches. This standard helped Federal Express to gain further efficiencies from mechanized sorting at its Memphis hub. Later entrants into the industry copied Federal Express' package standards and hub-and-spoke operating system.

To accomplish overnight delivery, Federal Express had to operate its own planes. Restrictive regulations enforced by the Civil Aeronautics Board (CAB), however, prohibited the company from buying large jet aircraft. To get around this restriction, Federal Express bought a fleet of twin-engine executive jets, which it converted to mini-freighters. These planes had a cargo capacity of 6,200 lbs., which enabled Federal Express to get a license as an air-taxi operator.

After 1973, Federal Express quickly built up volume. By 1976, it had an average daily volume of 19,000 packages, a fleet of 32 aircraft, 500 delivery vans, and 2,000 employees, and it had initiated service in 75 cities. After 3 years of posting losses, the company turned in a profit of $3.7 million on revenues of $75 million.[8] However, volume had grown so much that Federal Express desperately needed to use larger planes to maintain operating efficiencies. As a result, Smith's voice was added to those calling for Congress to deregulate the airline industry and allow greater competition.

Deregulation And Its Aftermath

In November 1977, Congress relaxed regulations controlling competition in the air cargo industry, one year before passenger services were deregulated. This involved a drastic loosening of standards for entry into the industry. The old CAB authority of naming the carriers that could operate on the various routes was changed to the relatively simple authority of deciding which candidate carriers was fit, willing, and able to operate an all-cargo route. In addition, CAB controls over pricing were significantly reduced. The immediate effect was an increase in rates for shipments, particularly minimum- and high-weight

categories, suggesting that prices had been held artificially low by regulation. As a result, the average yield (revenue per ton-mile) on domestic airfreight increased 10.6% in 1978 and 11.3% in 1979.[9]

Freed from the constraints of regulation, Federal Express immediately began to purchase larger jets and quickly established itself as a major carrier of small-package airfreight. Despite the increase in yields, however, new entry into the air cargo industry was limited, at least initially. This was mainly due to the high capital requirements involved in establishing an all-cargo carrier. Indeed, by the end of 1978, there were only 4 major all-cargo carriers serving the domestic market: Airlift International, Federal Express, Flying Tigers, and Seaboard World Airlines. While all of these all-cargo carriers had increased their route structure following deregulation, only Federal Express specialized in next-day delivery for small packages. Demand for a next-day delivery service continued to boom. Industry estimates suggest that the small-package priority market had grown to about 82 million pieces in 1979, up from 43 million in 1974.[10]

At the same time, in response to increasing competition from the all-cargo carriers, the passenger airlines continued their retreat from the all-cargo business (originally begun in 1973 as a response to high fuel prices). Between 1973 and 1978, there was a 45% decline in the mileage of all-cargo flights by the airlines. This decrease was followed by a 14% decline between 1978 and 1979. Instead of all-cargo flights, the airlines concentrated their attentions on carrying cargo in passenger flights. This practice hurt the freight forwarders badly. The freight forwarders had long relied on the all-cargo flights of major airlines to achieve next-day delivery. Now the freight forwarders were being squeezed out of this segment by a lack of available lift at the time needed to ensure next-day delivery.

This problem led to one of the major post-deregulation developments in the industry: the acquisition and operation by freight forwarders of their own fleets of aircraft. Between 1979 and 1981, 5 of the 6 largest freight forwarders became involved in this activity. The two largest were Emery Worldwide and Airborne Express. Emery operated a fleet of 66 aircraft at the end of 1979, the majority of which were leased from other carriers. In mid-1980, this fleet was providing service to approximately 129 cities, carrying both large-volume shipments and small-package express.

Airborne Express acquired its own fleet of aircraft in April 1980 with the purchase of Midwest Express, an Ohio-based all-cargo airline. In 1981, Airborne opened a new hub in Ohio, which became the center of its small-package express operation. This enabled Airborne to provide next-day delivery for small packages to 125 cities in the United States.[11] Other freight forwarders that moved into the overnight mail market included Purolator Courier and Gelco Courier, and both offered overnight delivery by air on a limited geographic scale.

Industry Evolution, 1980–1986

New Products and Industry Growth

In 1981, Federal Express expanded its role in the overnight market with the introduction of an overnight letter service, with a limit of two ounces. This guaranteed overnight delivery service was set up in direct competition with the USPS's Priority Mail. The demand for such a service was illustrated by its expansion to about 17,000 letters per day within its first 3 months of operation.

More generally, the focus of the air express industry was changing from being predominantly a conduit for goods to being a distributor of information—particularly company documents, letters, contracts, drawings, and the like. As a result of the growth in demand for information distribution, new product offerings such as the overnight letter, and Federal Express' own marketing efforts, the air express industry enjoyed high growth during the early-1980s, averaging more than 30% per year.[12] Indeed, many observers attribute most of the growth in the overnight delivery business at this time to Federal Express' marketing efforts. According to one industry participant, "Federal Express pulled off one of the greatest marketing scams in the industry by making people believe they absolutely, positively, had to have something right away."[13]

Increasing Price Competition

Despite rapid growth in demand, competitive intensity in the industry increased sharply in 1982 following the entry of UPS into the overnight-delivery market. UPS was already by far the largest private package transporter in the United States, with an enormous ground-oriented distribution network and revenues in excess of $4 billion per year. In addition, for a long time, UPS had offered a second-day air service for priority packages, primarily by using the planes of all-cargo and passenger airlines. In 1982, UPS acquired a fleet of 24 used Boeing 727–100s and added four DC-8 freighters from Flying Tigers. These purchases allowed UPS to introduce next-day air service in September 1982—at roughly half the price Federal Express was charging.[14]

Federal Express countered almost immediately by announcing that it would institute 10:30 a.m. priority overnight delivery (at a cost to the company of $18 million). None of the other carriers followed suit, however, reasoning that most of their customers are usually busy or in meetings during the morning hours, so delivery before noon was not really that important. Instead, by March 1983, most of the major carriers in the market (including Federal Express) were offering their high-volume customers contract rates that matched the UPS price structure. Then, three new services introduced by Purolator, Emery, and Gelco Courier pushed prices even lower. A competitive free-for-all followed, with constant price changes and volume discounts being offered by all industry participants. These developments hit the profit margins of the express carriers. Between 1983 and 1984, Federal Express saw its average revenue per package fall nearly 14%, while Emery saw a 15% decline in its yield on small shipments.[15]

Beginning around this time, customers began to group together and negotiate for lower prices. For example, Xerox set up accounts with Purolator and Emery that covered not only Xerox's express packages but also those of 50 other companies, including Mayflower Corp., the moving company, and the Chicago Board of Trade. By negotiating as a group, these companies could achieve prices as much as 60% lower than those they could get on their own.[16]

The main beneficiary of the price war was UPS, which by 1985 had gained the number 2 spot in the industry, with 15% of the market. Federal Express, meanwhile, had seen its market share slip to 37% from about 45% two years earlier. The other 4 major players in the industry at this time were Emery Air Freight (14% of market share), Purolator (10% of market share), Airborne Express (8% of market share), and the U.S. Postal Service (8% of market share).[17] The survival of all four of these carriers in the air express business was in question by 1986. Emery, Purolator, and the U.S. Postal Service were all reporting losses on their air express business, while Airborne had seen its profits slump 66% in the first quarter of 1986 and now had razor-thin margins.

Industry Evolution, 1987–1996

Industry Consolidation

A slowdown in the growth rate of the air express business due to increasing geographic saturation and inroads made by electronic transmission (primarily fax machines) stimulated further price discounting in 1987 and early-1988. Predictably, this discounting created problems for the weakest companies in the industry. The first to go was Purolator Courier, which had lost $65 million during 1985 and 1986. Purolator's problems stemmed from a failure to install an adequate computer system. The company was unable to track shipments, a crucial asset in this industry, and some of Purolator's best corporate customers were billed 120 days late.[18] In 1987, Purolator agreed to be acquired by Emery. Emery was unable to effect a satisfactory integration of Purolator, and it sustained large losses in 1988 and early-1989.

Consolidated Freightways was a major trucking company and parent of CF Air Freight, the third largest heavy shipment specialist in the United States. In April 1989, Consolidated Freightways acquired Emery for $478 million. However, its shipment specialist, CF Air Freight, soon found itself struggling to cope with Emery's problems. In its first 11 months with CF, Emery lost $100 million. One of the main problems was Emery's billing and tracking system, described as a "rat's nest" of conflicting tariff schedules, which caused overbilling of customers and made tracking packages en route a major chore. In addition, CF enraged corporate customers by trying to add a "fuel surcharge" of 4–7% to prices in early-1989. Competitors held the line on prices and picked up business from CF/Emery.[19]

As a result of the decline of the CF/Emery/Purolator combination, the other firms in the industry were able to pick up market share. By 1994, industry estimates suggested that Federal Express accounted for 35% of domestic airfreight and air express industry revenues, UPS had 26%, Airborne Express was third with 9%, and Emery and the U.S.

Postal Service each held onto 4% of the market. The remainder of the market was split among numerous small cargo carriers and several combination carriers, such as Evergreen International and Atlas Air. (Combination carriers specialize mostly in heavy freight, but do carry some express mail.)[20]

The other major acquisition in the industry during this time was the purchase of Flying Tigers by Federal Express for $880 million in December 1988. Although Flying Tigers had some air express operations in the United States, its primary strength was as a heavy cargo carrier with a global route structure. The acquisition was part of Federal Express' goal of becoming a major player in the international air express market. However, the acquisition had its problems. Many of Flying Tigers' biggest customers, including UPS and Airborne Express, were Federal Express' competitors in the domestic market. These companies had long paid Flying Tigers to carry packages to those countries where they had no landing rights. It seemed unlikely that these companies would continue to give international business to their biggest domestic competitor. Additional problems arose in the process of trying to integrate the two operations. These problems included the scheduling of aircraft and pilots, the servicing of Flying Tigers' fleet, and the merging of Federal's nonunionized pilots with Flying Tigers' unionized pilots.[21]

During the late-1980s and early-1990s, there were also hints of further consolidations. TNT Ltd., a large Australian-based air cargo operation with a global network, made an unsuccessful attempt to acquire Airborne Express in 1986. TNT's bid was frustrated by opposition from Airborne and by the difficulties inherent in getting around U.S. law, which limited foreign firms from having more than a 25% stake in U.S. airlines. In addition, DHL Airways, the U.S. subsidiary of DHL International, was reportedly attempting to enlarge its presence in the United States and was on the lookout for an acquisition.[22]

Pricing Trends

In October 1988, UPS offered new discounts to high-volume customers in domestic markets. For the first time since 1983, competitors declined to match the cuts. Then, in January 1989, UPS announced a price increase of 5% for next-day air service, its first price increase in nearly 6 years. Federal Express, Airborne, and Consolidated Freightways all followed suit with moderate increases. UPS announced additional rate increases of 5.9% on next-day air letters in February 1990. Federal Express followed suit in April, and Airborne also implemented selective price hikes on noncontract business of 5%, or $0.50 per package on packages up to 20 lbs.

Just as prices were stabilizing, however, the 1990–1991 recession came along. For the first time in the history of the U.S. air express industry, there was a decline in year-on-year shipments, with express freight falling from 4,455 million ton-miles in 1989 to 4,403 million ton-miles in 1990. This decline triggered another round of competitive price cuts and yields plummeted. Although demand strongly rebounded, repeated attempts to raise prices in 1992, 1993, and 1994 simply did not stick.[23]

Much of the price cutting was focused on large corporate accounts, which by this time accounted for 75% by volume of express mail shipments. For example, as a result of deep price discounting in 1994, UPS was able to lure home shopping programmer QVC and computer mail-order company Gateway 2000 away from Federal Express. At about the same time, however, Federal Express used discounting to capture retailer Williams-Sonoma away from UPS.[24] This prolonged period of price discounting depressed profit margins and contributed to losses at all three major carriers during the early-1990s. Bolstered by a strong economy, prices finally began to stabilize during late-1995, when price increases announced by UPS were followed by similar announcements at Federal Express and Airborne.[25]

Product Trends

Second-Day Delivery Having seen a slowdown in the growth rate of the next-day document delivery business during the early-1990s, the major operators in the air express business began to look for new product opportunities to sustain their growth and margins. One trend was a move into the second-day delivery market, or deferred services, as it is called in the industry. Airborne Express started the move toward second-day delivery in 1991, and that was soon imitated by its major competitors. Second-day delivery commands a substantially lower price point than next-day delivery. In 1994, Federal Express made an average of $9.23 on second-day deliveries, compared to $16.37 on priority overnight service. The express mail operators saw deferred services as a

way to utilize excess capacity at the margin, thereby boosting revenues and profits. Since many second-day packages could be shipped on the ground, the cost of second-day delivery could more than compensate for the lower price.

In some ways, however, the service has been almost too successful. During the mid-1990s, the growth rate for deferred services was significantly higher than for priority overnight mail because many corporations came to the realization that they could live with a second-day service. At Airborne Express, for example, second-day delivery accounted for 42% of total volume in 1996, up from 37% in 1995.[26]

Premium Services Another development was a move toward a premium service. In 1994, UPS introduced its Early AM service, which guaranteed delivery of packages and letters by 8:30 a.m. in select cities. UPS tailored Early AM toward a range of businesses that needed documents or materials before the start of the business day, including hospitals, which expect to use the service to ship critical drugs and medical devices; architects, who need to have their blueprints sent to a construction site; and salespeople. Although demand for the service is predicted to be light, the premium price makes for high profit margins. In 1994, UPS' price for a letter delivered at 10:30 a.m. was $10.75, while it charged $40 for an equivalent Early AM delivery. UPS believed that it could provide the service at little extra cost because most of its planes arrived in their destination cities by 7:30 a.m. Federal Express and Airborne initially declined to follow UPS' lead.[27]

Logistics Services Another development of some note was the move by all major operators into third-party logistics services. Since the latter half of the 1980s, more and more companies have been relying on air express operations as part of their just-in-time inventory control systems. As a result, the content of packages carried by air express operators has been moving away from letters and documents and toward high-value, low-weight products. By 1994, less than 20% of Federal Express' revenues came from documents.[28] To take advantage of this trend, all of the major operators have been moving into logistics services designed to assist business customers in their warehousing, distribution, and assembly operations. The emphasis of this business is on helping their customers reduce the time involved in their production cycles and gain distribution efficiencies.

In the late-1980s, Federal Express set up a Business Logistics Services (BLS) division. The new division evolved from Federal Express' Parts Bank. The Parts Bank stores critical inventory for clients, who are mostly based in the high-tech electronics and medical industries. On request, Federal Express ships this inventory to its client's customers. The service saves clients from having to invest in their own distribution systems. It also allows their clients to achieve economies of scale by making large production runs and then storing the inventory at the Parts Bank.

The BLS division has expanded this service to include some assembly operations and customs brokerage and to assist in achieving just-in-time manufacturing. Thus, for example, one U.S. computer company relies on BLS to deliver electronic subassemblies from the Far East as a key part of its just-in-time system. Federal Express brings the products to the United States on its aircraft, clears them through customs with the help of a broker, and manages truck transportation to the customer's dock.

UPS moved into the logistics business in 1993 when it established UPS Worldwide Logistics, which it positioned as a third-party provider of global supply chain management solutions, including transportation management, warehouse operations, inventory management, documentation for import and export, network optimization, and reverse logistics. UPS based its logistics business at its Louisville, Kentucky, hub. In 1995, the company announced that it would invest $75 million to expand the scope of this facility, bringing total employment in the facility to 2,200 by the end of 1998.[29]

Airborne Express also made a significant push into this business. Several of Airborne's corporate accounts utilized a warehousing service called Stock Exchange. As with Federal Express' Parts Bank, clients warehouse critical inventory at Airborne's hub in Wilmington, Ohio, and then ship those items on request to their customers. In addition, Airborne set up a commerce park on 1,000 acres around its Wilmington hub. The park was geared toward companies that wanted to outsource logistics to Airborne and could gain special advantages by locating at the company's hub. The ability to make shipping decisions as late as 2 a.m. Eastern time was one of these advantages.

Information Systems

Since the late-1980s, the major U.S. air express carriers have devoted more and more attention to competing on the basis of information technology. The ability to track a package as it moves through an operator's delivery network has always been an important aspect of competition in an industry where reliability is so highly valued. Thus, all the major players in the industry have heavily invested in barcode technology, scanners, and computerized tracking systems. UPS, Federal Express, and Airborne have also all invested in Internet-based technology that allows customers to schedule pickups, print shipping labels, and track deliveries online.

Globalization

Perhaps the most important development for the long-run future of the industry has been the increasing globalization of the airfreight industry. The combination of a healthy U.S. economy, strong and expanding East Asian economies, and the move toward closer economic integration in Western Europe all offer opportunities for growth in the international air cargo business. The increasing globalization of companies in a whole range of industries from electronics to autos, and from fast food to clothing, is beginning to dictate that the air express operators follow suit.

Global manufacturers want to keep inventories at a minimum and deliver just-in-time as a way of keeping down costs and fine-tuning production—which requires speedy supply routes. Thus, some electronics companies will manufacture key components in one location, ship them by air to another for final assembly, and then deliver them by air to a third location for sale. This setup is particularly convenient for industries producing small high-value items (for example, electronics, medical equipment, and computer software) that can be economically transported by air and for whom just-in-time inventory systems are crucial for keeping down costs. It is also true in the fashion industry, where timing is crucial. For example, the clothing chain The Limited manufactures clothes in Hong Kong and then ships them by air to the United States to keep from missing out on fashion trends.[30] In addition, an increasing number of wholesalers are beginning to turn to international air express as a way of meeting delivery deadlines.

The emergence of integrated global corporations is also increasing the demand for the global shipment of contracts, confidential papers, computer printouts, and other documents that are too confidential for Internet transmission or that require real signatures. Major U.S. corporations are increasingly demanding the same kind of service that they receive from air express operators within the United States for their far-flung global operations.

As a consequence of these trends, rapid growth is predicted in the global arena. According to forecasts, the market for international air express is expected to grow at approximately 18% annually from 1996 to 2016.[31] Faced with an increasingly mature market at home, the race is on among the major air cargo operators to build global air and ground transportation networks that will enable them to deliver goods and documents between any two points on the globe within 48 hours.

The company with the most extensive international operations by the mid-1990s was DHL. In 1995, DHL enjoyed a 44% share of the worldwide market for international air express services (see Exhibit 1).[32] Started in California in 1969 and now based in Brussels, DHL is smaller than many of its rivals, but it has managed to capture as much as an 80% share in some markets, such as documents leaving Japan, by concentrating solely on international air express. The strength of DHL was enhanced in mid-1992 when Lufthansa, Japan Airlines, and the Japanese trading company Nissho Iwai announced that they intended to invest as much as $500 million for a 57.5% stake in DHL. Although Lufthansa and

Japan Airlines are primarily known for their passenger flights, they are also among the top five airfreight haulers in the world, both because they carry cargo in the holds of their passenger flights, and because they each have a fleet of all-cargo aircraft.[33]

TNT Ltd., a $6 billion Australian conglomerate, is another big player in the international air express market, with courier services from 184 countries as well as package express and mail services. In 1995, its share of the international air express market was 12%, down from 18% in 1990.[34]

Among U.S. carriers, Federal Express was first in the race to build a global air express network. Between 1984 and 1989, Federal Express purchased 17 other companies worldwide in an attempt to build its global distribution capabilities, culminating in the $880 million purchase of Flying Tigers. The main asset of Flying Tigers was not so much its aircraft, but its landing rights overseas. The Flying Tigers acquisition gave Federal Express service to 103 countries, a combined fleet of 328 aircraft, and revenues of $5.2 billion in fiscal year 1989.[35]

However, Federal Express has had to suffer through years of losses in its international operations. Start-up costs were heavy, due in part to the enormous capital investments required to build an integrated air and ground network worldwide. Between 1985 and 1992, Federal Express spent $2.5 billion to build an international presence. Faced also with heavy competition, Federal Express found it difficult to generate the international volume required to fly its planes above the break-even point on many international routes. Because the demand for outbound service from the United States is greater than the demand for inbound service, planes that left New York full often returned half empty.

Trade barriers have also proved very damaging to the bottom line. Customs regulations require a great deal of expensive and time-consuming labor, such as checking paperwork and rating package contents for duties. These regulations obviously inhibit the ability of international air cargo carriers to effect express delivery. Federal Express has been particularly irritated by Japanese requirements that each inbound envelope be opened and searched for pornography, a practice that seems designed to slow down the company's growth rate in the Japanese market.

Federal Express has also found it extremely difficult to get landing rights in many markets. For example, it took 3 years to get permission from

Exhibit 1   International Air Express Market Shares, 1995

Company	Market Share
DHL International	44%
Federal Express	21%
UPS	12%
TNT	12%
Others	11%

Source: Standard & Poor's, "Aerospace and Air Transport," *Industry Survey*, February 1996.

Japan to make 4 flights per week from Memphis to Tokyo, a key link in the overseas system. Then, in 1988, just 3 days before the service was due to begin, the Japanese notified Federal Express that no packages weighing more than 70 lbs. could pass through Tokyo. To make matters worse, until 1995 Japan limited Federal Express' ability to fly on from Tokyo and Osaka to other locations in Asia. The Japanese claimed, with some justification, that due to government regulations, the U.S. air traffic market is difficult for foreign carriers to enter, so they see no urgency to help Federal Express build a market presence in Japan and elsewhere in Asia.[36]

After heavy financial losses, Federal Express abruptly shifted its international strategy in 1992, selling off its expensive European ground network to local carriers to concentrate on intercontinental deliveries. Under the strategy, Federal Express relies on a network of local partners to deliver its packages. Also, Federal Express entered into an alliance with TNT to share space on Federal Express' daily trans-Atlantic flights. Under the agreement, TNT flies packages from its hub in Cologne, Germany, to Britain, where they are loaded onto Federal Express' daily New York flight.[37]

UPS has also built up an international presence. In 1988, UPS bought 8 smaller European airfreight companies and Hong Kong's Asian Courier Service, and it announced air service and ground delivery in 175 countries and territories. However, it has not been all smooth sailing for UPS either. UPS had been using Flying Tigers for its Pacific shipments. The acquisition of Flying Tigers by Federal Express left UPS in the difficult situation of shipping its parcels on a competitor's plane. UPS was concerned that its shipments would be pushed to the back of the aircraft. Since there were few alternative carriers, UPS pushed for authority to run an all-cargo route to Tokyo, but approval was slow in coming. "Beyond rights," to carry cargo from Tokyo to further destinations (such as Singapore and Hong Kong), were also difficult to gain.

In March 1996, UPS sidestepped years of frustrations associated with building an Asian hub in Tokyo by announcing that it would invest $400 million in a Taiwan hub, which would henceforth be the central node in its Asian network. The decision to invest in an Asian hub followed closely on the heels of a 1995 decision by UPS to invest $1.1 billion to build a ground network in Europe. In September 1996, UPS went one step further toward building an international air express service when it announced that it would start a pan-European next-day delivery service for small packages. UPS hoped that these moves would push the international operations of the carrier into the black after 8 years of losses.[38]

Industry Evolution, 1997–2010

Pricing Trends

The industry continued to grow at a solid rate through 2000, which helped to establish a stable pricing environment. In 2001, things took a turn for the worse. Recessionary conditions in the United States triggered a 7.6% decline in the number of domestic packages shipped by air. Even though the economy started to rebound in 2002, growth remained sluggish by historic comparison, averaging only 4% per annum.[39] Despite this, pricing discipline remained solid. Unlike the recession in 1990–1991, there was no price war in 2001–2002. In early 2002, UPS pushed through a 3.5% increase in prices, which was quickly followed by the other carriers. The carriers were able to continue to raise prices, at least in line with inflation, through to 2008. They were also successful in tacking on a fuel surcharge to the cost of packages to make up for sharply higher fuel costs.[40] During the 2002–2006, the average revenue per package at both UPS and FedEx increased as more customers opted for expedited shipments and as both carriers shipped a high proportion of heavier packages.[41] The global financial crisis of 2008–2009 and the recession that it ushered in did lead to a slump in volume, a shift to deferred shipping, and more pricing pressures. At FedEx for example, the average revenue per overnight package fell from $18.42 in 2008 to $16.04 in 2010. However, volume and pricing trends improved in 2011 along with the economy, and revenue per package at FedEx rose to $18.08 by the 4th quarter of 2010.[42]

Continuing Growth of Logistics

During 1997–2010 all players continued to build their logistics services. During the 2000s, UPS was much more aggressive in this area than FedEx.

By 2010, UPS' logistics business had revenues of $8.7 billion. UPS was reportedly stealing share from FedEx in this area. FedEx reportedly decided to stay more focused on the small package delivery business (although it continues to have a logistics business). Most analysts expected logistics services to continue to be a growth area. Outside of the North American market, DHL emerged as the world's largest provider of logistics services, particularly following its 2006 acquisition of Britain's Exel, a large global logistics business.

Despite the push of DHL and UPS into the global logistics business, the market remains very fragmented. According to one estimate, DHL, now the world's largest logistics company, has a 5.5% share of the global market in contract logistics, UPS has a 3% share and TNT has a 2.2% share.[43] The total global market for contract logistics was estimated to be worth over $200 billion in 2005. In 2006, TNT sold its logistics business to Apollo Management L.P. for $1.88 billion so that it could focus more on its small package delivery business.

Expanding Ground Network

In the late-1990s and early-2000s all the main carriers supplementing their air networks with extensive ground networks and ground hubs to ship packages overnight. With more customers moving from overnight mail to deferred services, such as second-day delivery, this shift in emphasis has become a necessity. Demand for deferred services help up reasonably well during 2001, even as demand for overnight packages slumped. Prices for deferred and ground services are considerably lower than are prices for air services, but so are the costs.

UPS has been the most aggressive in building ground delivery capabilities (of course, it already had extensive ground capabilities before its move into the air). In 1999, UPS decided to integrate overnight delivery into its huge ground transportation network. The company spent about $700 million to strengthen its ground delivery network by setting up regional ground hubs. By doing so, it found it could ship packages overnight on the ground within a 500-mile radius. Because ground shipments are cheaper than air shipments, the result was a significant cost savings for UPS. The company also deferred delivery of about 123 aircraft that were on

order, reasoning that they would not be needed as quickly because more of UPS' overnight business was moved to the ground.[44]

FedEx entered the ground transportation market in 1998 with its acquisition of Caliber Systems for $500 million. This was followed by further acquisitions in 2001 and 2006 of significant U.S. trucking companies, including the 2006 acquisition of Watkins Motor Lines, a provider of long haul trucking services in the U.S. with sales of around $1 billion. Watkins was re-branded as FedEx National LTL. By 2002, FedEx was able to provide ground service to all U.S. homes, giving it a similar capability to UPS.

In addition, FedEx struck a deal in 2001 with the U.S. Postal Service (USPS), under which FedEx agreed to provide airport-to-airport transportation for 250,000 lbs. of USPS Express Mail packages nightly and about 3 million lbs. of USPS Priority Mail packages. The Priority Mail was to be moved on FedEx planes that normally sit idle during the day. The deal was reportedly worth $7 billion in additional revenues to FedEx over the 7-year term of the agreement. In addition, FedEx reaped cost savings from the better utilization of its lift capacity.[45] As of 2010, FedEx and the USPS still cooperated with each other.

Bundling

Another industry wide trend has moved toward selling various product offerings—including air delivery, ground package offerings, and logistics services—to business customers as a bundle. The basic idea behind bundling is to offer complementary products at a bundled price that is less than if each item had been purchased separately. Yet again, UPS has been the most aggressive in offering bundled services to corporate clients. UPS is clearly aiming to set itself up as a one-stop shop offering a broad array of transportation solutions to customers. FedEx has also made moves in this area. Airborne Express started to bundle its product offerings in mid-2001.[46]

Retail Presence

In 2001, UPS purchased Mail Boxes Etc. for $185 million. Mail Boxes Etc. had 4,300 franchisees, most in the United States, who operated small retail packaging, printing and copying stores. At the time, Mail Boxes Etc. was shipping some 40 million packages per year, around 12 million of which were via UPS. UPS stated that it would continue to allow the Mail Boxes stores to ship packages for other carriers. In 2003, the stores were re-branded as the UPS Store. While some franchisees objected to this move, the vast majority ultimately switched to the new brand.[47] In addition to the franchise stores, UPS has also begun to open wholly owned UPS stores, not just in the United States, but also internationally, and by 2006 had 5,600 outlets. In addition to The UPS Store, the company put UPS Centers in office supplies stores, such as Office Depot, and by 2006 it had some 2,200 of these.

In 2004, FedEx followed UPS by purchasing Kinko's for $2.4 billion. Kinko's, which had 1,200 retail locations, 90% in the United States, focused on providing photocopying, printing and other office services to individuals and small businesses. FedEx has plans to increase the network of Kinko's stores (now called FedEx Office) to 4,000. In addition to providing printing, photocopying, and package services, FedEx is also experimenting using FedEx Office stores as mini warehouses to store high value goods, such as medical equipment, for its supply chain management division.[48]

The Entry and Exit of DHL

In the late-1990s, DHL was acquired by Deutsche Post. Deutsche Post also spent approximately $5 billion to acquire several companies in the logistics business between 1997 and 1999. In November 2000, Deutsche Post went private with an initial public offering that raised $5.5 billion and announced its intention to build an integrated global delivery and logistics network. Many believed it was only a matter of time before the company entered the United States. Thus, few were surprised when in 2003 DHL acquired Airborne Express. Under the terms of their agreement, Airborne Express sold its truck delivery system to DHL for $1.05 billion. Airborne's fleet of planes were moved into an independent company called ABX Air, owned by Airborne's shareholders, and which continues to serve DHL Worldwide Express under a long-term contract. This arrangement overcame the U.S. law that prohibits foreign control of more than 25% of a domestic airline. In the meantime, DHL spun its own fleet of U.S.-based planes into a U.S.-owned company called Astar,

to also escape the charge that its U.S. airline was foreign owned. Between 2003 and 2005 DHL reportedly invested some $1.2 billion to upgrade the capabilities of assets acquired from Airborne.[49]

The DHL acquisition created 3 major competitors in both the U.S. and global delivery markets. By the fall of 2003, DHL had launched an ad campaign aimed at UPS and FedEx customers promoting the service and cost advantages that they would benefit from because of its merger with Airborne. DHL targeted specific zip code areas in its advertising promoting its claim to be the number one in international markets, something important to many companies given the increasing importance of global commerce. In its ads, DHL reported that "current Airborne customers will be connected to DHL's extensive international delivery system in more than 200 countries."[50]

DHL's stated goal was to become a powerhouse in the U.S. delivery market. While its share of the U.S. small package express market remained small after the acquisition at around 10%, many thought that DHL would benefit from ownership by Deutsche Post and from its own extensive ex-U.S. operations. When it first acquired Airborne, Deutsche Post stated that the U.S. operation would be profitable by the end of 2006.

However, the company ran into "integration problems" and suffered from reports of poor customer services and missed delivery deadlines. In 2006, DHL management stated that they now did not see the North American unit turning profitable until 2009. DHL lost some $500 million in the U.S. in 2006.[51] In 2007, they lost close to $1 billion. With corporate customers leaving for rivals, and market share sliding, in late-2008, DHL announced that it would exit the U.S. market. DHL shut down its air and ground hubs, laid off 9,600 employees, and took a charge against earnings of some $3.9 billion. In explaining the exit decision, DHL management stated that they underestimated just how tough it would be to gain share against FedEx and UPS.[52]

Continued Globalization

Between 1997 and 2010, UPS and FedEx continued to build out their global infrastructure. By 2010, UPS delivered to more than 200 countries. Much of the within country delivery is handled by local enterprises. The company has 5 main hubs. In addition to its main U.S. hub in Louisville, Kentucky, it has hubs in Cologne, Taipei, Miami (serving Latin American traffic), and the Philippines. In 2002, UPS launched an intra-Asian express delivery network from its Philippines hub. In 2004, it acquired Menio World wide Forwarding, a global freight forwarder, to boost its global logistics business. In the same year, it also acquired complete ownership of its Japanese delivery operation (which was formally a joint venture with Yamato Transport Company). In 2005, UPS acquired operators of local ground networks in the UK and Poland, and it is pushing into mainland China, which it sees as a major growth opportunity.

Like UPS, FedEx serves more than 200 countries around the world, although also like UPS, most of the local ground delivery is in the hands of local partners. FedEx has recently been focusing upon building a presence in both China and India. The company has announced the development of a new Asian Pacific hub in Guangzhou China. This will be FedEx's 4th international hub. The others are in Paris (handling intra-European express), the Philippines (handling intra-Asian express), and Alaska (which handles packages flowing between Asia, North America, and Europe). In 2006, FedEx signaled its commitment to the Chinese market by buying out its joint venture partner, Tianjin Datian W. Group, for $400 million. The acquisition gave FedEx control of 90 parcel handling facilities and a 3,000 strong work force in China.[53]

While UPS and FedEx dominate the U.S. market for small package express delivery services, in Europe DHL and TNT lead with 23% and 11% respectively (TNT, formally an Australian enterprise, was acquired by the Royal Netherlands Post Office in 1996). In the intercontinental market, DHL leads with a 36% share, while in intra-Asian traffic Asia Yamato of Japan is the leader with a 20% share followed by Sagawa with 16%. The fragmented nature of the European and intra-Asia Pacific markets suggest that much is still at stake in this increasingly global business.

The U.S. and Global Markets in 2010

With DHL out of the picture in the United States, FedEx and UPS tightened their hold on the market. The USPS held onto a small share of the overnight express market and a somewhat bigger share of the

ground market (see Exhibit 2). Despite challenging economic conditions, UPS and FedEx were both able to push through list rate increases of around 4–5% during the late-2000s, although after negotiations with large corporations, those increases were often reduced to 2–3%. They were also able to add fuel surcharges to prices, which helped given the high price of oil in the late-2000s.

Domestic volume continued to expand at a moderate pace and tended to match the growth in U.S. GDP. Most of the domestic volume growth was in the ground network. International volume growth was correlated to the growth in international trade and was generally higher than domestic growth. The volume of international trade had slumped in 2009, but rebounded strongly in 2010 and 2011. While the volume of document shipments was declining due to electronic transmission, the slack was being picked up by increased shipment of goods purchased online, and growth of low weight high value inventory, such as electronic components. The globalization of supply chains and moves toward just-in-time inventory was helping both companies.[54]

By 2010, UPS was shipping some 15 million packages a day through its network, while FedEx was moving between 6 and 7 million. Peak volumes were hitting 25 million for UPS and 16 million for FedEx.

Both FedEx and UPS were solidly profitable in 2010 (see Exhibit 3). Profit margins in the industry were leveraged to volume; higher volume meant significant margin expansion. Both FedEx and UPS were looking to a strong 2011 as volume expanded. The USPS, however, was deep in the red. In 2010, the

....

Exhibit 2: U.S. Market Share (%), 2010

	Overnight Express	Deferred Air	Ground
FedEx	54%	48%	22%
UPS	41%	52%	61%
USPS	6%	0%	16%
Market Size	$14 billion	$6 billion	$34 billion

Source: W.J. Greene et al, "Airfreight and Surface Transport: Parcel Industry Primer," *Morgan Stanley*, May 25, 2011.

Exhibit 3: Comparing FedEx and UPS in 2010

	FedEx	UPS
Revenue	$34.7 billion	$49.5 billion
Net Income	$1.12 billion	$3.49 billion
Cash Flow	$3.14 billion	$3.84 billion
Capital Expenditure	$2.82 billion	$1.39 billion
ROIC	7.41%	19.39%

Source: Company Reports

USPS lost $8 billion on total revenues of $67 billion. Traditional mail delivery was now a declining business as ever more mail was sent electronically. Some believed that the privatization of the USPS was inevitable.

Despite its exit from the U.S. market, DHL still was the largest operator globally in 2010 with $71 billion in revenues, and $2 billion in net income, followed by UPS and FedEx. TNT was in 4th place with $15 billion in revenues and $1 billion in net income.

Endnotes

1 Standard & Poor's, "Aerospace and Air Transport," *Industry Surveys,* February 1996.

2 Ibid.

3 Standard & Poor's, "Airlines," *Industry Surveys,* March 2002.

4 John Kartsonas, "United Parcel Service," *Citigroup Global Capital Markets,* November 13, 2006. W.J. Greene et al, "Airfreight and Surface Transport: Parcel Industry Primer," *Morgan Stanley,* May 25, 2011.

5 W.J. Greene et al, "Airfreight and Surface Transport: Parcel Industry Primer," *Morgan Stanley,* May 25, 2011.

6 C.H. Lovelock, "Federal Express (B)," Harvard Business School Case No. 579–040, 1978.

7 Standard & Poor's, "Aerospace and Air Transport," *Industry Surveys,* January 1981.

8 Lovelock, "Federal Express (B)."

9 Standard & Poor's, "Aerospace and Air Transport," *Industry Surveys,* January 1981.

10 Ibid.

11 Ibid.

12 Standard & Poor's, "Aerospace and Air Transport," *Industry Surveys*, January 1984.

13 C. Hall, "High Fliers," *Marketing and Media Decisions,* August 1986, p. 138.

14 Standard & Poor's, "Aerospace and Air Transport," *Industry Surveys,* January 1984.

15 Standard & Poor's, "Aerospace and Air Transport," *Industry Surveys,* December 1984.

16 B. Dumaine, "Turbulence Hits the Air Couriers," *Fortune,* July 21, 1986, pp. 101–106.

17 Ibid.

18 C. Hawkins, "Purolator: Still No Overnight Success," *BusinessWeek,* June 16, 1986, pp. 76–78.

19 J. O'C. Hamilton, "Emery Is One Heavy Load for Consolidated Freightways," *BusinessWeek,* March 26, 1990, pp. 62–64.

20 Standard & Poor's "Aerospace and Air Transport," *Industry Surveys,* February 1996.

21 "Hold That Tiger: FedEx Is Now World Heavyweight," *Purchasing,* September 14, 1989, pp. 41–42.

22 Standard & Poor's, "Aerospace and Air Transport," *Industry Surveys*, April 1988.

23 Standard & Poor's, "Aerospace and Air Transport," *Industry Surveys,* February 1996.

24 D. Greising, "Watch Out for Flying Packages," *BusinessWeek,* November 1994, p. 40.

25 Staff Reporter, "UPS to Raise its Rates for Packages," *Wall Street Journal,* January 9, 1995, p. C22.

26 M. Royce, "Airborne Freight," *Value Line Investment Survey,* September 20, 1996.

27 R. Frank, "UPS Planning Earlier Delivery," *Wall Street Journal,* September 29, 1994, p. A4.

28 Frank, "Federal Express Grapples with Changes in U.S. Market."

29 Company Press Releases (http://www.ups.com/news/).

30 J. M. Feldman, "The Coming of Age of International Air Freight," *Air Transport World,* June 1989, pp. 31–33.

31 Standard & Poor's, "Aerospace and Air Transport," *Industry Surveys,* February 1996.

32 Ibid.

33 P. Greiff, "Lufthansa, JAL, and a Trading Firm Acquire a Majority Stake in DHL," *Wall Street Journal,* August 24, 1992, p. A5.

34 Standard & Poor's, "Aerospace and Air Transport," *Industry Surveys,* February 1996.

35 "Hold That Tiger: FedEx Is Now a World Heavyweight."

36 D. Blackmon, "FedEx Swings from Confidence Abroad to a Tightrope," *Wall Street Journal,* March 15, 1996, p. B4.

37 D. Pearl, "Federal Express Plans to Trim Assets in Europe," *Wall Street Journal,* March 17, 1992, p. A3.

38 Company Press Releases (http://www.ups.com/news/).

39 C. Haddad and M. Arndt, "Saying No Thanks to Overnight Air," *Business Week,* April 1, 2002, p. 74.

40 Salomon Smith Barney Research, Wrap It Up—Bundling and the Air Express Sector, May 3, 2002. J. Kartsonas,

"United Parcel Service," *Citigroup Global Capital Markets*, November 13, 2006.

41 J. Kartsonas, "FedEx Corp," *Citigroup Global Capital Markets*, November 13, 2006.

42 W.J. Greene and A. Longson, "FedEx Corporation" *Morgan Stanley Research*, June 22, 2011.

43 Data from Deutsche Post World Net, 2005 Annual Report.

44 C. Haddad and M. Arndt, "Saying No Thanks to Overnight Air," *Business Week*, April 1, 2002, p. 74.

45 E. Walsh, "Package Deal," *Logistics*, February 2001, pp. 19–20.

46 Salomon Smith Barney Research, Wrap It Up—Bundling and the Air Express Sector, May 3, 2002.

47 R. Gibson, "Package Deal: UPS' Purchase of Mail Boxes Etc. Looked Great on Paper," *Wall Street Journal*, May 8, 2006, p. R13.

48 A. Ward, "Kinko's Plans to Push the Envelope Further," *Financial Times*, August 7, 2006, p. 22.

49 J.D. Schultz, "DHL Crashes the Party," *Logistics*, August 2005, pp. 59–63.

50 P. Needham, "Coming to America," *Journal of Commerce*, April 22, 2002, p. 12.

51 B. Barnard, "Logistics Spurs Deutsche Post," *Journal of Commerce*, November 8, 2006, p. 1.

52 A. Roth and M. Esterl, "DHL Beats a Retreat from the U.S.," *Wall Street Journal*, November 11, 2008, p. B1.

53 A. Ward, "A Dogfight for Courier Service Dominance," *Financial Times*, February 15, 2006, p. 10.

54 W.J. Greene et al, "Airfreight and Surface Transport: Parcel Industry Primer," *Morgan Stanley*, May 25, 2011.

How Amazon.com Became the Leading Online Retailer by 2011

Gareth R. Jones
Texas A&M University

Since its founding in 1995, Amazon.com (Amazon) has grown from an online bookseller to a virtual retail supercenter selling products as diverse as books, toys, food, and electronics for which it is best known today. On Amazon's main storefront, customers can discover anything they might want to buy online and it endeavors to offer customers the lowest possible prices. However, its less well-known that by 2010 it had become the world's biggest provider of service oriented software (SOA), combined with cloud computing solutions that can be accessed by all kinds of customers including individuals, small- and medium-sized businesses, and large corporations— just one more kind of online retail storefront for virtual products such as data processing and storage. In 2011, its business mission states that its goal is to be "Earth's most customer-centric company" for three primary customer groups: consumer customers, seller customers, and developer customers.

In many ways, the last decade has been a wild ride for Amazon as its revenues, profits, and stock price initially soared and then plunged as a result of the dot-com boom and then bust of the early-2000s. But, since hitting a low of $8 in 2001, in the last decade—and especially in the last 3 years—its stock has soared. It was over $210 in July 2011— an incredible increase. It has also been a wild ride for Amazon's founder, Jeff Bezos, who through all the turmoil in its performance, consistently championed his company and claimed investors had to look long term to measure the success of Amazon's business model. He originally said he did not expect his company to become profitable for several years, and his forecast turned out to be correct. But, his claims are correct, and every year in his annual letter to shareholders, he includes his 2007 letter that stated why its business model would succeed (see his 2010 letter on the Amazon.com investors' Webpages).

Amazon's Beginnings: The Online Bookstore Business

In 1994, Jeffrey Bezos, a computer science and electrical engineering graduate from Princeton University, was growing weary of working for a Wall Street investment bank. Seeking to take advantage of his computer science background, he saw an entrepreneurial opportunity as he observed that Internet usage was enormously growing every year as tens of millions of new users were becoming aware of its potential uses. Bezos decided the bookselling market offered an excellent opportunity for him to take advantage of his IT skills in the new electronic, virtual marketplace. His vision was an online bookstore that could offer millions more books to millions more customers than a typical brick-and-mortar (B&M) bookstore. To act upon his vision, he packed up his belongings and headed for the West Coast to found his new dot-com start-up. On route, he had a hunch that Seattle, the hometown of Microsoft and Starbucks, was a place where first-rate software developers could be easily found. His trip ended there, and he began to flesh out the business model for his new venture.

What was the vision for his new venture? To build an online bookstore that would be customer-friendly, easy to navigate, provide buying advice, and offer the broadest possible selection of books at low prices.

Bezos' original mission was to use the Internet to offer books "that would educate, inform and inspire." From the beginning, Bezos realized that, compared to a physical B&M bookstore, an online bookstore could offer customers a much larger and much more diverse selection of books. There are about 1.5 million books in print, but most B&M bookstores stock only around 10,000 books; the largest stores in major cities might stock 40,000 to 60,000. Moreover, online customers would be able to easily search for any book in print using computerized catalogs. There was also scope for an online company to find ways to tempt customers to browse books in different subject areas, read reviews of books, and even ask other shoppers for online recommendations— all of which would encourage people to buy more books. One of Amazon's popular features is the users' ability to submit product reviews on its Website. As part of their reviews, users rate the products on a scale from 1 to 5 stars and then provide detailed information that helps other users decide whether to purchase the products. In turn, the users of these ratings can then rate the usefulness of the reviews, so the best reviews are those that rise to the top and are read first in the future!

Operating from his garage in Seattle with a handful of employees, Bezos launched his online venture in 1995 with $7 million in borrowed capital. Because Amazon was one of the first major Internet or dot-com retailers, it received an enormous amount of free national publicity, and the new venture quickly attracted an increasing number of book buyers. Book sales quickly picked up as satisfied Internet customers spread the good word and Amazon became a model for other dot-com retailers to follow. Within weeks, Bezos was forced to relocate to larger premises, a 2,000-square-foot warehouse, and hire new employees to receive books from book publishers and fill and mail customer orders as book sales soared. Within 6 months, he was once again searching for additional capital to fund his growing venture; he raised another $7 million from venture capitalists, which he used to move to a 17,000-square-foot warehouse that was now required to handle increasing book sales. As book sales continued to soar month by month over the next 2 years, Bezos decided that the best way to raise more capital would be to take his company public and issue stock. This, of course, would reward him as the founder and the venture capitalists who had funded Amazon because

they would all receive significant percentages of the company's stock. In May 1997, Amazon.com's stock began trading on the NASDAQ stock exchange.

Building Up Amazon's Value Chain

Amazon's rapid growth continued to put enormous pressure on the company's physical warehousing and distribution capabilities. The costs of operating an online Website, for example, continuously improving the capabilities of the Website's software, and maintaining and hosting the computer hardware and Internet bandwidth connections necessary to serve customers, are relatively low given the hundreds of millions of visits to its Website and the millions of sales that are completed. However, Bezos soon found out that the costs of developing and maintaining the physical B&M infrastructure necessary to obtain and stock supplies of books and then package and ship the books to customers, were much higher than he had anticipated—as was the cost of the employees required to perform these activities.

Soon, developing and maintaining the physical B&M side of Amazon's value chain became the source of the greatest proportion of its operating costs, and these high costs were draining its profitability—given the low prices at which it was selling its books. Also, price competition was also heating up because of new competition from B&M booksellers such as Barnes & Noble and Borders, that had been late to recognize the potential of the Internet and now opened their own online bookstores to compete with Amazon. In fact, in 1997, as it passed the 1-million-different-customers-served point, Amazon was forced to open up a new 200,000-square-foot warehouse and distribution center and expand its old one to keep pace with demand.

Bezos then sought ways to increase the motivation of his employees across all the company. Working to quickly fill customer orders is vital to an online company; minimizing the wait time for a product like a book to arrive is a key success factor in building customer loyalty. On the other hand, motivating Amazon's rapidly expanding army of software engineers to develop innovative customer-oriented software, such as its patented 1-Click (SM) Internet ordering and payment software, was also vital to sustaining its competitive advantage. To ensure good responsiveness to customers, Bezos implemented a policy of decentralizing significant decision-making authority to employees and empowered them to find ways to meet customer needs quickly. Because Amazon.com employed a relatively small number of people—about 2,500 worldwide in 2000—Bezos also empowered employees to recruit and train new employees to quickly learn their new jobs. And to motivate employees, Bezos decided to give all employees stock in the company. Amazon employees own over 10% of their company, a factor behind Amazon.com's rapid growth.

In fact, Jeff Bezos is a firm believer in the power of using teams of employees to spur innovation. At Amazon, teams are given considerable autonomy to develop their ideas and experiment without interference from managers. Teams are kept deliberately small, and, according to Bezos, no team should need more than "two pizzas to feed its members"; if more pizza is needed, the team is too large. Amazon's "pizza teams," which usually have no more than about 5–7 members, have come up with many innovations that have made its site so user-friendly. For example, one team developed the "Gold Box" icon that customers can click on to receive special offers that expire within an hour of opening the treasure chest; another developed "Bottom of the Page Deals," low-priced offers for products such as batteries and power bars, and one more team developed the "Search Inside the Book" feature discussed later. These teams have helped Amazon expand into many different retail storefronts and provide the wide range of IT services it does today. Indeed, Bezos and his top managers believe th Amazon is a *technology company* first and foremost, and its mission is to use and develop its technological expertise to sell more and more goods and services in ways that satisfy customers and keep its profit growing. Hence, the enormous buildup of its DA software services and on-demand cloud computing services as discussed below.

Since the beginning, Bezos has personally played a very important part in energizing employees and representing his company to customers. He is a hands-on, articulate, forward-looking executive who puts in long hours and works closely with employees to find innovative and cost-saving solutions to problems. Moreover, Bezos has consistently acted as a figurehead for his company and become a national

media celebrity as he worked to further Amazon's visibility with customers. He spends a great deal of time flying around the world to publicize his company and its activities, and he has succeeded because Amazon is in the top five of the best recognized dot-com companies.

The Amazon Associates program, created in 1996 to attract new customers to its retail storefront and grow sales, is another important strategy. Any person or small business that operates a Website can become affiliated to Amazon by putting an official Amazon hyperlink to Amazon's Website on its own Website. If a referral results in a sale, the Associate receives a commission from Amazon. By 2004, Amazon had signed up over 1 million Associates and by 2007, about 40% of Amazon's revenues were generated from the sales of its Associates, who pay a commission to Amazon to advertise and sell their products on its Website.

By 1998, Amazon could claim that 45% of its business was repeat business, which translated into lower marketing, sales, and operating expenses, and higher profit margins. By using all his energies to act on the online bookselling opportunity, Bezos had given his company a first-mover advantage over rivals, which has been an important contributor to its strong position in the marketplace. Nevertheless, Amazon still had yet to make a profit, just as Bezos had predicted.

The Bookselling Industry Environment

The book distribution and bookselling industry was changed forever in July 1995 when Jeff Bezos brought virtual bookseller Amazon.com online. His new company changed the entire nature of the environment. Previously, book publishers had indirectly sold their books to book wholesalers that supplied small bookstores, directly to large book chains like Barnes & Noble or Borders, or to book-of-the month clubs. There were so many book publishers and so many individual booksellers that the industry was relatively stable, with both large and small bookstores enjoying a comfortable, nonprice competitive niche in the market. In this stable environment, competition was relatively low, and all companies enjoyed good revenues and profits.

Amazon.com's Web-based approach to buying and selling books changed all this. First, since it was able to offer customers quick access to all of the 1.5 million plus books in print and discount the prices of its books, a higher level of industry competition immediately developed. Second, it also negotiated directly with the large book publishers over price and supply because it wanted to quickly get books to its customers; the industry value chain and Amazon, therefore, gained more power over publishers because it is a powerful buyer. All players—book publishers, wholesalers and bookstore chains had to rethink their strategies. Third, as a result of these factors and continuing improvements in IT and the speed of the Internet, the competitive forces in the bookselling business began to rapidly change and lower prices became a major priority.

As the first in the online bookselling business, Amazon was able to capture customers' attention and establish a first-mover advantage. Its entry into the bookselling industry using its new IT posed a major threat for B&M bookstores, and Barnes & Noble, the largest U.S. bookseller, and Borders, the second largest bookseller, realized that with its competitive prices, Amazon would be able to siphon off a significant percentage of industry revenues. These B&M bookstores decided to launch their own online ventures to meet Amazon's challenge and to convince book buyers that they, not Amazon, were still the best places to shop for books. However, being first to market with a new way to deliver books to customers resulted in satisfied customers who became loyal customers. Once a customer had signed up as an Amazon customer, it was often difficult to get that person to register again at a competing Website.

Amazon's early success also made it difficult for the hundreds of new "unknown" online booksellers who entered the market to survive because they faced the major hurdle of attracting customers to their Websites rather than to Amazon.com's. Even the major B&M competitors such as Barnes & Noble and Borders that now imitated Amazon's online business model faced major problems in developing a major online presence let alone attracting away Amazon's customer base.

If large B&M bookstores had problems attracting customers, small specialized B&M bookstores were in desperate trouble. Their competitive advantage has been based on providing customers with hard-to-find books, a convenient location, and good customer service. Now they were faced with competition from an online bookstore that could offer customers all 1.5 million books in print at significantly lower prices. Thousands of small, specialized B&M bookstores closed their doors nationwide in the 2000s, as the large B&M bookstores struggled to compete.

Competition increased by 2000 as large B&M bookstores began a price war with Amazon that resulted in falling book prices; this squeezed Amazon's profit margins and put more pressure on it to contain its increasing operating costs. Amazon and its largest competitors, Barnes & Noble and Borders, announced a 50% discount off the price of new best-selling books to defend their market shares; they were locked in a fierce battle to see which company would dominate the bookselling industry in the new millennium. Barnes & Noble did manage to establish an online presence and its storefront has continued to exist into the 2010s, although it has never regained market share from Amazon. Border's online bookstore was a complete failure, and in 2002, it announced all referrals to its online storefront would be referred to Amazon, for which it would receive a commission. This arrangement was a disaster for now Border's had given up on online retailing, as a B&M bookstore. Its performance continued to decline, its agreement with Amazon was ended in 2008, and in 2011, Border's liquidated and its stores were closed. By 2011, the value of Barnes & Noble also suffering heavily from competition from Amazon, had dropped to $1 billion from over $30 billion, and many analysts wondered how long it would survive as Amazon became the online portal of choice for most major book publishers as the digital download book business became the way of the future as discussed below.

From Online Bookstore to Internet Retailer

Although Bezos initially focused on selling books, he soon realized that Amazon's rapidly developing IT competences could be used to sell many other kinds of products online. But he was cautious because he also now understood how high were the value-chain costs involved in stocking and delivering a wide range of different products customers. However, Amazon's slowing growth the late-1990s led many of its stockholders to complain that the company was not on track to becoming profitable fast enough, so Bezos began to search for other products that could profitably be sold over the Internet. One growing on-line business was music CDs, and he realized CDs were a good fit with books, so in 1999, Amazon announced its intention to become the "earth's big-gest book and music store." The company used its IT competences to widen its product line by selling music CDs on its retail Website. The strategy of sell-ing CDs also seemed like a good move because the leading Internet music retailers at this time, such as CDNow, were struggling—they had also discovered the high physical costs associated with delivering products bought online to customers. Amazon now had built up its skills in this area, and its online re-tail competencies were working to its advantage; for example, its IT now allowed it to constantly alter the mix of products it offered on its storefront to keep up-to-date with changing customer needs.

Amazon also took many more steps to increase the usefulness of its retail sites to attract more cus-tomers and get its established customers to spend more. For example, to entice customers to send books and CDs as presents at important celebration and holiday shopping times such as birthdays, Christ-mas, and New Year's, Amazon opened a holiday gift store. Customers could take advantage of a gift-wrapping service as well as using a free greeting card e-mail service to announce the arrival of the Amazon gift. Amazon began to explore other kinds of online retail ventures; for example, recognizing the grow-ing popularity of online auctions pioneered by eBay, Bezos moved into this market by purchasing Live-bid.com, the Internet's only provider of live online auctions at that time. Also in 1999, it entered into an agreement with Sotheby's, the famous auction house, to enter the high end of the online auction business. In making these moves, it was attempting to compete in eBay's auction segment of the market—a move that not only failed because eBay had the first mover advantage, but also because, fixed-price sales were becoming the most popular segment of the market, as discussed later.

Nevertheless, starting in 2000, Amazon's stock price fell sharply as investors believed that intense competition from Barnes & Noble and other online retailers like eBay might keep its operating margins low into the foreseeable future. Despite his com-pany's moves into CDs and the auction business,

Bezos was being increasingly criticized as much too slow to take advantage of Amazon's brand name and core skills and to use them to sell other kinds of products online—much like a general B&M retailer sells many different kinds of products in the same store. Bezos responded that he had to make sure his company's business model would successfully work in book retailing before he could commit his com-pany to a widespread expansion into new kinds of retail ventures. However, Amazon's plunging stock price forced him into action, and from 2000 for-ward, it expanded its storefronts and began to sell a wider range of electronic and digital products, such as cameras, DVD players, and MP3 players. To achieve a competitive advantage in these new prod-uct categories, Amazon used its expertise in retailing software to provide customers with more in-depth information about the nature of the products they were buying and to offer users better ways to review, rank, and comment on the products they bought on its Website. Customers were increasingly seeing the utility of Amazon's service—especially because of its low prices.

Bezos pushed Amazon and its "pizza teams" to find new ways to use its core skills to expand into different kinds of retail segments, and by 2003, it had developed 23 different storefronts. By 2006, Amazon had 35 storefronts selling products as var-ied as books, CDs, DVDs, software, consumer elec-tronics, kitchen items, tools, lawn and garden items, toys and games, baby products, apparel, sporting goods, gourmet food, jewelry, watches, health and personal-care items, beauty products, musical in-struments, and industrial and scientific supplies. Increasingly consumers came to see Amazon as the low-price retailer for many products. Customers be-gan to visit B&M retail stores to view the physical product, but then they would go online to buy from Amazon. Customers can avoid paying state sales tax when they buy online, and for high-ticket items, this is an important savings, often amounting to a 10% price advantage (although sometimes there are ship-ping costs).

New Problems

As time went on, however, customers increasingly be-gan to compare the prices charged by different online retail Websites to locate the lowest priced product, and many dot-coms, desperate to survive in a highly competitive online retail environment, undercut Amazon's prices and put more pressure on its profit margins. To strengthen Amazon's competitive position and make it the preferred online retailer, Bezos moved aggressively to find ways to attract customers, such as by offering them free shipping or "deals of the day." To make its service more convenient, Amazon also began to forge alliances with B&M companies like Toys"R"Us, Office Depot, Circuit City, Target, and many others. Now, customers could buy products online at Amazon's Website, but if they wanted their purchases immediately, they could pick them up from these retailers' local B&M stores. Amazon had to share its profits with these retailers, but it also avoided high product stocking and distribution costs. These alliances also helped Bezos quickly transform his company from "online bookseller" to "leading Internet product provider." His goal was for Amazon to become the leading online retailer across many market segments and drive out the weaker online competitors in those segments, consolidating many segments of the online retail industry. As it happened, he also drove out the weakest B&M retailers, such as Circuit City and Border's, which were giving up on online operations, and forced to liquidate.

Amazon's Online Retail SOA Software Platform

Small- and medium-sized businesses quickly discovered the high costs of operating the value chain functions necessary to deliver products to customers, which helped Bezos. Increasingly, Amazon began to offer its online services to these companies, such as Borders and Waldenbooks in the book business, but also to Sears and Target; as noted above, these booksellers were also eventually forced to close down their B&M operations. Weaker companies became Amazon Associates and began directing Internet traffic from their Websites to Amazon's instead in return for sales commissions.

Amazon soon realized the important revenues associates could bring in, and began offering all kinds of small- and medium-sized companies the opportunity to establish storefronts on Amazon.com, and offer their products—many of which are often sold in direct competition with Amazon's own products as its service operations software brings up the offerings of all sellers for a particular product. However, this has proved to be a major advantage, and in 2011, 40% of Amazon's sales revenue was generated by the millions of associates who pay to establish storefronts on its Website and pay it fees when their products are sold on its Website. The Internet bubble burst in the early-2000s strengthened Amazon's competitive advantage; thousands of cut-price online retailers went out of business—because they had no source of competitive advantage. Despite that its own stock price plunged too, Amazon was now the strongest dot-com in the most important retail segment—the fixed-price segment.

Many well-known B&M retailers that had also established virtual storefronts found they could not make their online storefronts profitable in the 2000s because of high operating costs. The few that did succeed, such as Lands' End, did so because they already possessed well-developed catalog operations that were obviously suited to Internet retailing—paradoxically Sears, which had been the strongest in catalog sales, had shut down its operations by the 1990s when shopping malls and chain stores like Walmart had come to dominate U.S. retailing.

Over the 2000s, tens of thousands of other established B&M companies that found online retailing too complex and expensive also formed agreements with Amazon (or eBay) to operate their online stores. As noted earlier, Amazon seized this opportunity to get into the new business of using its proprietary retail IT to design, operate, and host other companies' online storefronts for them for a fee. By 2007, Amazon also had many online storefronts developed to sell its SOA retail solutions. Amazon had become an IT services company as well, and today its other Websites such as its major IT SAO service site (www.amazonservices.com) and its affiliates program (https://affiliate-program.amazon.com/), detail the enormous range of services that it offers to potential sellers, or "developers," as Amazon often calls them. A noted above, its SOA software services division has become a major source of its rapidly rising revenues and profits—and it continues to expand its retail IT activities as it moves to become a leader in cloud computing and storage.

Branching off into these new retail market segments also allowed Amazon to more fully utilize its expensive warehouse and distribution system; faster sales across product categories increased inventory turnover and reduced costs. Moreover, its alliances with retailers to sell their products on its Website allowed it to reduce the quantity of expensive merchandise it needed to purchase and warehouse until sold, which, in turn, helped its profit margins. In addition, by offering many different kinds of products for sale, customers could now "mix" purchases and add a book or CD to their electronic product order, and so on, which led to economies of scale and scope for Amazon. Essentially, Amazon was pursuing related diversification, by giving customers more and more reasons to visit its site, and hoped to drive business and sales across all its product categories, using its 1-Click system to make the transactions as easy as possible for consumers.

However, from the beginning, to keep its operating costs low, Amazon adopted a low-key approach to providing customer service; it did not reveal a customer service telephone number anywhere on its U.S. Website. However, as the complexity of its business has grown and fraud has increased, it recognized the need to provide some level of service, and in 2006, Amazon added to its Website an e-mail link. Using this link, customers provide their phone numbers, and Amazon customer service reps make outbound calls to provide whatever help is needed, for example, with parcel tracking information. Customer service is handled by datacenters in different countries all around the world and Amazon has outsourced most of this activity to minimize costs.

Amazon's venture into the online auction market failed in the early-2000s and was shut down, but now its top managers can focus all their energies on building its competences in the fixed-price retailing market, and by expanding into new kinds of retail formats. In 2001, Amazon added a new retail service that turned out to be highly profitable and important to maintaining its leadership position in online retailing. Amazon launched zShops, a fixed-price retail marketplace that became the foundation of its highly successful Amazon Marketplace Service. This retail service allows customers to sell their used books, CDs, DVDs, and other products alongside the identical brand-new products that Amazon offers on the product pages of its retail Website. This significantly added to its sales revenues, and Amazon has continually added to its offerings over the 2000s. Today, its marketplace services retail storefront is part of its amazonservices.com Website reflecting its move into related diversification by its continual effort to share and leverage its core IT competences across its different storefronts. eBay bought a company called half.com to compete with Amazon Marketplace, and today it is Amazon's main rival as both companies compete to provide a profitable fee-based service to sellers of used products.

In the 2000s, as Amazon became the acknowledged leader in Internet retailing, it took advantage of its skills to offer a SOA consulting service to virtual and B&M retailers and to create for them a unique, customer-friendly storefront using Amazon's proprietary IT. As discussed above, this consulting service has proved to be a very profitable business activity, especially because in the process of designing storefronts and SOA services for other companies, Amazon's software engineers found new opportunities to improve its own IT software services by learning from its "leading customers." However, to protect its competitive advantage and proprietary IT, Amazon also started lawsuits against other virtual or B&M companies that had started to imitate services such as its 1-Click checkout system and infringe other proprietary software it claims is protected by patents. By 2011, many high-tech companies had begun to launch lawsuits claiming others had infringed on their patents; this became a multibillion dollar issue by 2011 as Google, Apple, and Oracle fought to claim the ownership of touch-screen, mobile payment, and other kinds of software services.

Global Expansion

Since IT is not specialized to any one country or world region, a virtual company can use the Internet and WWW to sell to customers around the globe—providing, of course, that the products it sells meet the needs of overseas consumers. Bezos was quick to realize that Amazon's IT could be profitably transferred to other countries to sell books. However, the ability to enter new overseas markets was limited by one major factor: Amazon.com offered its customers the biggest selection of books written in the *English* language, so overseas customers had to be able to read English. Where to locate them?

An obvious first choice would be the United Kingdom, followed by other English-speaking nations such as Australia, New Zealand, India, and Germany (of any nation in the world, Germany has one of the highest proportion of English-as-a-second-language speakers because English is taught in all its schools). To speed entry into overseas markets, Amazon searched for Internet book retailers that had gained a strong foothold in their local domestic market and acquired them. In the UK, Amazon bought Bookpages.com in 1996, installed its proprietary IT, replicated its value creation functions, and renamed it Amazon.co.uk. In Germany, it acquired a new online venture, ABC Bücherdienst/Telebuch.de, and created Amazon.de in 1998. Amazon continued its path of global expansion, and by 2006, it also operated retail Websites in Canada, France, China, and Japan, and shipped its English language books to customers anywhere in the world. All these ventures have been tremendously successful and have significantly added to its revenues and profits.

To facilitate the growth of its global IT and distribution retail systems across all market segments, Amazon also established SOA software product and service development centers in England, Scotland, India, Germany, and France. Just as Amazon expanded the range of products/software services it sold on its U.S. Websites, it also increased the range of products/services it sold abroad as its warehouse and distribution systems became strong enough to sustain its expansion and its local managers selected the product mix best suited to the needs of local customers.

Developments in the 2000s

Amazon finally turned its first profit in the fourth quarter of 2002—a meager $5 million, just $0.01 per share on revenues of over $1 billion—but this was an important signal to investors. In fact, Amazon's stock price soared again in the early-2000s as investors believed its business model would enable it to become an online retail leader. Its stock price increased from $6 in 2001 to $60 by 2004. Amazon's net profits also increased to $35 million in 2003 and to $588 million in 2004, while its revenues more than doubled to $7 billion in the same period. Amazon's future looked bright as it became the largest Internet retailer and achieved a dominant position in many market segments.

New Acquisitions and Business Opportunities

To make better use of its resources and capabilities and to maintain its profit growth, Amazon began to acquire many small specialized retail and IT companies. Its strategy to acquire small IT companies was to strengthen its distinctive competencies in SOA IT and to develop more kinds of Web-based IT commercial services that it could sell to both B&M and online companies. Bezos has always preached that Amazon is first and foremost a *technology company* and that its core skills drive its retail mission. Its goal in buying small retail companies was to find new opportunities to increase sales of its existing retail storefronts and to allow it to establish storefronts in new segments of the retail market. Some acquisitions have been successful, and some have not.

For example, Amazon bought Internet Movie Database (www.IMDb.com), a company that hosts a comprehensive list of all movies in existence. Amazon transformed it into a commercial venture whose function is to help customers easily find and identify DVDs to purchase and to make related suggestions to encourage additional purchases on its Website. Similarly, Amazon acquired Exchange.com, which specialized in hard-to-find book titles at its Bibliofind.com Website, and hard-to-find music titles and memorabilia at MusicFile.com. The acquisition also helped Amazon develop user-friendly search engines to help customers identify and buy its products, once again using its 1-Click system.

Amazon bought PlanetAll.com, which operated a Web-based address book, calendar, and reminder service that had over 1 million registered users, and Junglee.com, an XML-based data-mining start-up that had technology for searching and tracking Internet users' Website visits based on their personal interests. As it purchased these companies, Amazon absorbed these technologies and employees into its IT operations to improve its retail software services. For example, PlanetAll's "relationship-building" software applications were folded into Amazon's Friends and Favorites area, and its new employees went on to build community-focused features for Amazon's Website including the Amazon.com Marketplace and Amazon.com Purchase Circles. Amazon was driven by the goal of developing superior Web-based techniques for attracting and keeping

Internet customers when rivalry with eBay, Apple, and Google increased because these companies started to enter each other's businesses. For example, the online download music business when Apple introduced its online music download iTunes store, and thus leapfrogged over Amazon to control this market—although Amazon still controls the online sales of music CDs.

Amazon started its own online music store in 2007 selling downloads in the MP3 format after securing agreements with the four major record companies, however, its music download service never obtained the success of Apple's iTunes, which has prospered because of its link to the iPod and now the iPhone. In another venture into entertainment content, Amazon launched a digital download video service called Amazon Unbox in 2007. This new download service offered customers thousands of television shows, movies, and other video content from more than 30 studio and network partners from Hollywood and around the world. Unbox claimed to be the only video download service to offer DVD-quality pictures, however, within weeks this new download service had generated negative comments from users; the number of movies downloaded was disappointingly few because the service's poor software caused many glitches and very slow—hours—of download time. Essentially, Amazon was too early to enter this vital Movie/TV Content Streaming Download Service. Even in 2011, it was still uncertain which company and which digital format would prevail, and customers were confused as competitors such as Google's YouTube, Netflix's streaming offerings, Hulu's content, and Apple's new video content services, were competing to be the next industry standard. In addition, many Websites still offered illegal downloading free of charge. The online entertainment streaming market segment is a complex one in which to compete, but also a vital one given the enormous growth in downloading using smartphones and tablet computers that has occurred in the 2010s.

Amazon also acquired several companies to enter and grow in the search engine market to find ways to track its customers across the WWW to personalize the retail service it could offer and, therefore, boost sales. However, it did not understand that Google's search engine business model was based on increasing online advertising revenues—not offering them

actual products—and its efforts failed. Customers do not like to be tracked across the WWW and efforts to prevent Web tracking have increased in the 2010s. Even Amazon's own efforts are considered invasive by many people as it stores personal information in order to offer customized product choices.

In the effort to keep its customers loyal, Amazon began providing a range of new customer services. In 2006 it launched Amazon Prime, a $79 per year service that allows users to get unlimited free two-day shipping for a year on all eligible items bought from its storefronts. Also, in 2006, it began its first cloud computing data storage product called Amazon S3 that allows users to store data for $0.15 per gigabyte per month—something that was soon rendered useless when Google began to offer its customers free online data storage that has expanded to hundreds of gigabytes. In 2007, Amazon entered the grocery delivery business when it launched Amazon Fresh, a new grocery storefront that sold a wide variety of nonperishable food and household items that, once ordered, can be reordered using Amazon's shopping-list software. To ensure competitive pricing with B&M grocery stores, customers receive free shipping on purchases of canned and packed food products over $25.

In the 2000s, Amazon continued to refine its SOA business software solutions to make it easier and faster for businesses to take advantage of its expanding array of services. By 2010, its increasing expertise made it simple for small or large businesses to use services such as Fulfillment by Amazon and WebStore by Amazon to manage many aspects of their value chains. Essentially, Amazon was offering companies a value-chain outsourcing service. For example, Fulfillment by Amazon allows small businesses to use Amazon's own order fulfillment and after-order customer services, and gives their customers the ability to benefit from Amazon's shipping offers. Fulfillment by Amazon performs the value chain activities that allow small online businesses to minimize the costs required to store, pick, pack, ship, and provide customer service for the products they sell online. After paying Amazon's service fee, small businesses ship their products to an Amazon fulfillment center that stores and sends those products to customers who order them on the small business' or Amazon's storefront. Amazon also manages post-order customer service such as customer returns and refunds for businesses that use Fulfillment by Amazon. Small businesses benefit from the cost savings that result when Amazon's service fees are lower than the costs of performing the value chain service themselves.

WebStore by Amazon allows businesses to create their own privately branded e-commerce Websites using Amazon technology. Businesses can choose from a variety of Website layout options and can customize their sites using their own photos and branding. For example, Seattle Gift Shop now has its own WebStore at www.seattlesgifts.com. WebStore by Amazon users pay a commission of 7% (price includes credit card processing fees and fraud protection) for each product purchased through their site and a monthly fee of $59.95. As one business owner commented, "Not only has WebStore increased my sales dramatically, but also its easy-to-use tools give me complete control of the look and feel of my site." WebStore allows small businesses to build their brand name while using Amazon's easy-to-use flexible "back-end" technology—including Amazon's 1-Click checkout system—and allows them to refer customers through the Amazon Associates program if they choose.

Amazon's Growing Dominance in the Retail Sector

All of Amazon's expenditures to develop the new IT platforms necessary to launch complex digital storefronts that sell books, music, and video, and build the SOA services side of its business increased its operating costs and reduced its profit margins in 2007. So, too, did Amazon's need to open enormous new warehouses or "fulfillment" centers in many different states during the late-2000s. In 2011, for example, it announced it would open a fourth 1.2 million square-foot facility in Phoenix, Arizona, bringing its total capacity in that state to over 4 million square feet. Rising costs, together with increasing competition from Apple, eBay, and especially Google led many analysts to wonder if Amazon could maintain its rapid growth—something that led to Bezos' 2007 letter to shareholders, pointing out that once again his company's strategy was to build the infrastructure that would lead to long-term growth and profits and that short term results were

meaningless (see Appendix). Proof that its business model was working, and one measure of Amazon's growing dominance, was the increase in the number of repeat customers—from 45% in 2005, to 59% in 2007, and to over 70% by 2010. Repeat business is a major indicator of a company's ability to grow its business and profit growth.

The Amazon's Kindle Reader Arrives

In 2007, Amazon pushed to dominate the online the online book-downloading business when it announced its new Kindle book reader. Its new $399 3G device with free Internet connection was based on technology developed by a company it had acquired in 2005. The Kindle allows customers to download digital versions of books in print and also allows Amazon to offer these digital books at greatly discounted prices—including new books and bestsellers. By 2008, Amazon announced that the Kindle had become its best selling product and that digital downloads were increasing rapidly; spurred by the acceptance of the Kindle, it offered a cheaper non-3G version. By 2011, its special offer Kindle was selling for $114 and $139, its free 3G version for $189, and its top-of-the-line DX version for $379. Why the fall in price? Apple's iPad tablet computer was overshadowing the Kindle's amazing popularity and growing dominance. The Kindle was a black and white reader optimized for reading print in all lighting conditions; the iPad was a full-color touch screen device that could access the Internet and download all kinds of digital applications, not just eBooks.

Nevertheless, many analysts claimed that Amazon realized too late that the money to be made was not in the hardware itself, but in the money it received from the digital content—books and magazines that users downloaded. In 2010, Amazon announced that for the first time its Kindle digital books sales exceeded that of its paper-based books. Some analysts wondered why Amazon was not giving away its reader free of charge, but there was speculation in 2011 that Amazon was planning to introduce a new advanced color version of the Kindle to rival the iPad. But in July 2011, Amazon announced that it would begin to allow students to rent textbooks in e-book format for its Kindle readers for as much as 80% off the list price, and that the three major textbook companies had signed up for this service.

A sign of Bezos' commitment to this product came in his 2010 letter to shareholders, where demonstrating the prowess of Amazon's software engineers, he announced a new Kindle application Whispersync, a "Kindle service designed to ensure that everywhere you go, no matter what devices you have with you, you can access your reading library and all of your highlights, notes, and bookmarks, all in sync across your Kindle devices and mobile apps. The technical challenge is making this a reality for millions of Kindle owners, with hundreds of millions of books, and hundreds of device types, living in over 100 countries around the world—at 24/7 reliability." To enlarge the content for its Kindle device, Amazon announced in 2011 that it had acquired The Book Depository, an online bookseller that offers 6 million specialized books for delivery worldwide.

More Moves in SOA and Cloud Computing

In March 2011, Amazon launched Cloud Drive, Amazon Cloud Player for the Web, and Amazon Cloud Player for Android. Together, these services enabled individual customers to securely store music in the cloud and play it on any Android phone, Android tablet, Mac or PC, and now iPad, wherever they are located. Customers can easily upload their music library to Amazon Cloud Drive and can save any new Amazon MP3 purchases directly to their Amazon Cloud Drive for free. In July 2011, Amazon announced three improvements to Amazon Cloud Drive and Cloud Player to better compete with Google and Apple's alternatives: storage plans that include unlimited space for music for $20 a year, free storage for all Amazon MP3 purchases and a Cloud Player iPad application. It also offered any customer 5GBs of free storage to encourage customers to try out its new services.

By 2010, Amazon's engineers had developed advances in data management, which led to new architectures and cloud storage and data management services that could be scaled to the needs of companies from small, to medium to large. It renamed its IT customer storefront Amazon Web Services (AWS) and analysts expect it to become its next billion dollar business. Of course, this also meant large expenditures on servers and datacenters to support AWS expansion, but this is completely in keeping with Bezos's 2007 letter to shareholders. Amazon believes revenues may reach $3 billion by 2015 as individuals and companies outsource more of their data center needs. The growing popularity of AWS is that it is "on-demand" software and services; business customers are charged a fee based on how much they use its SOA and there are no upfront costs to prevent potential customers from trying out its services.

Amazon's Future Prospects

Jeff Bezos and his top management team seem committed to leveraging Amazon's core competencies in whatever ways they can to find to realize the value of the company's assets. The range of possible services Amazon can offer appears endless. Today, Amazon is the leading fixed-price product Internet retailer. It has over 34,000 employees and in 2010 it earned $700 million on $10.7 billion revenues. This was a huge increase in profit from the year before, and its stock price soared in early-2011 as investors became convinced it would remain the industry leader. Only eBay was now a major competitor, but its failure to enter and capitalize on the fixed-price market sooner had resulted in a major decline in its stock price as the growth of the online auction market slowed in the 2000s. Customers today favor the fixed-price format as long as they are offered lower prices than they can get in B&M stores. Also, customers like the daily deal kind of online offers pioneered by Groupon and other companies such as LivingSocial that has Amazon as a major investor.

Record Sales in 2011

Finally, another sign that Amazon's business model and strategies are working came in July 2011 when Amazon reported its second quarter results. Its revenues had increased by 50% compared to the same quarter in 2010 as its product sales increased and its Kindle e-reader and digital-media services revenues soared. However, its profit also dropped by 8% because operating expenses rose by 54%. Why? Following its business model, Amazon has been spending billions to build its IT infrastructure to build its cloud computing and entertainment streaming services IT infrastructure to serve both individual and business customers. And, investing a billion more to build new state-of-the-art fulfillment centers to be able to distribute the products that it sells under its own name, and under the names of the millions of companies that now use its services to sell their products on its Website.

The Kindle Fire: Building New Opportunities and Threats

Then, at the end of September 2011 the long awaited new color Kindle download media device that would rival Apple's iPad was introduced by Bezos to wide acclaim. Amazon decided to sell the new Kindle Fire for $199, lower than it cost to produce, because Bezos believes that Amazon will make its profits from all the books, magazines, movies, music, and TV shows that users can now download to its new touch screen device. Amazon controls important

media content—much more so than Apple and the Market for tablets computers was weakening in late 2011 as customers were wondering exactly what they were buying as new much more powerful and lightweight laptops were being introduced.

Nevertheless, when on October 25th 2011 Amazon reported that its third quarter profit had plunged by 73% because of the high costs necessary to create the new Kindle Fire and the IT infrastructure to support it—plus its huge investment in IT cloud computing—investors immediately reacted be sending its stock price down by $30 or 15%. Throughout its history its stock price has soared or plunged as investors try to evaluate the future results of its strategy; but its CEO Jeff Bezos just seems to be having fun as he strives to create the most successful company he can—the one that adds the most value for its customers and stockholders.

What new strategies will Bezos pursue to take Amazon to the next level? Are any new mergers and acquisitions on the horizon? How many more B&M companies will Amazon drive out of business?

APPENDIX ADAPTED FROM AMAZON.COM 2007 LETTER TO SHAREHOLDERS

We believe that a fundamental measure of our success will be the shareholder value we create over the *long term*. This value will be a direct result of our ability to extend and solidify our current market leadership position. The stronger our market leadership, the more powerful our economic model. Market leadership can translate directly to higher revenue, higher profitability, greater capital velocity, and correspondingly stronger returns on invested capital.

Our decisions have consistently reflected this. We first measure ourselves in terms of the metrics most indicative of our market leadership: customer and revenue growth, the degree to which our customers continue to purchase from us on a repeat basis, and the strength of our brand. We have invested and will continue to invest aggressively to expand and leverage our customer base, brand, and infrastructure as we move to establish an enduring franchise. Because of our

emphasis on the long term, we may make decisions and weigh tradeoffs differently than some companies.

Accordingly, we want to share with you our fundamental management and decision-making approach so that you, our shareholders, may confirm that it is consistent with your investment philosophy:

- We will continue to focus relentlessly on our customers.
- We will continue to make investment decisions in light of long-term market leadership considerations rather than short-term profitability considerations or short-term Wall Street reactions.
- We will continue to measure our programs and the effectiveness of our investments analytically, to jettison those that do not provide acceptable returns, and to step up our investment in those that work best. We will continue to learn from both our successes and our failures.

- We will make bold rather than timid investment decisions where we see a sufficient probability of gaining market leadership advantages. Some of these investments will pay off, others will not, and we will have learned another valuable lesson in either case.
- When forced to choose between optimizing the appearance of our GAAP accounting and maximizing the present value of future cash flows, we'll take the cash flows.
- We will share our strategic thought processes with you when we make bold choices (to the extent competitive pressures allow), so that you may evaluate for yourselves whether we are making rational long-term leadership investments.
- We will work hard to spend wisely and maintain our lean culture. We understand the importance of continually reinforcing a cost-conscious culture, particularly in a business incurring net losses.
- We will balance our focus on growth with emphasis on long-term profitability and capital management. At this stage, we choose to prioritize growth because we believe that scale is central to achieving the potential of our business model.
- We will continue to focus on hiring and retaining versatile and talented employees, and continue to weight their compensation to stock options rather than cash. We know our success will be largely affected by our ability to attract and retain a motivated employee base, each of whom must think like, and therefore must actually be, an owner.

Selected Sources

www.amazon.com, 2011.
Amazon.com, Annual and 10K Reports, 1997–2011.

CASE 10

Whole Foods Markets: How to Grow in an Increasingly Competitive Market?

Patricia Harasta and Alan N. Hoffman
Rotterdam School of Management, Erasmus University and Bentley University

Reflecting back over his three decades of experience in the grocery business, John Mackey smiled to himself over his previous successes. His entrepreneurial history began with a single store which he has now grown to the nation's leading natural food chain. Whole Foods is not just a food retailer but instead represents a healthy, socially responsible lifestyle that customers can identify with. The Company has differentiated itself from competitors by focusing on quality as excellence and innovation that allows them to charge a premium price for premium products. This strategy has formed their success over the last 30 years but like any success story there are limits to how far it can go before a new direction is needed so that it remains successful for the next 30 years. While proud of the past, John had concerns about the future direction Whole Foods should head.

Company Background

Whole Foods carries both natural and organic food offering customers a wide variety of products. "Natural" refers to food that is free of growth hormones or antibiotics, where "certificated organic" food conforms to the standards, as defined by the U.S. Department of Agriculture (USDA) in October 2002. Whole Foods Market® is the world's leading retailer of natural and organic foods, with 193 stores in 31 states and Canada and the United Kingdom. John Mackey, current president and cofounder of Whole Foods, opened "Safer Way" natural grocery store in 1978. The store had limited success as it was a small location allowing only for a limited selection, focusing entirely on vegetarian foods. John joined forces with Craig Weller and Mark Skiles, founders of "Clarsville Natural Grocery" (founded in 1979), to create Whole Foods Market. This joint venture took place in Austin, Texas in 1980 resulting in a new company, a single natural food market with a staff of nineteen.

In addition to the supermarkets, Whole Foods owns and operates several subsidiaries. Allegro Coffee Company was formed in 1977 and purchased by Whole Foods Market in 1997 now acting as their coffee roasting and distribution center. Pigeon Cove is Whole Foods seafood processing facility, which was founded in 1985 and known as M & S Seafood until 1990. Whole Foods purchased Pigeon Cove in 1996, located in Gloucester, MA. The Company is now the only supermarket to own and operate a waterfront seafood facility. The last two subsidiaries are Produce Field Inspection Office and Select Fish, which is Whole Foods West Coast seafood processing facility acquired in 2003. In addition to the above, the Company has eight distribution centers, seven regional bake houses and four commissaries.

"Whole Foods Market remains uniquely mission driven: The Company is highly selective about what they sell, dedicated to stringent quality standards, and committed to sustainable agriculture. They believe in a virtuous circle entwining the food chain, human beings and Mother Earth: each is reliant upon the others through a beautiful and delicate symbiosis." The message of preservation and sustainability are followed while providing high quality good to customers and high profits to investors.

The authors would like to thank Will Hoffman, Christopher Ferrari, Robert Marshall, Julie Giles, Jennifer Powers and Gretchen Alper for their research and contributions to this case.

Please address all correspondence to: Dr. Alan N. Hoffman, Department of Management, Bentley University, 175 Forest Street, Waltham, MA 02452-4705, voice (781) 891-2287, ahoffman@bentley.edu, fax (781) 459-0335. Printed by permission of Dr. Alan N. Hoffman, Bentley University.

Whole Foods has grown over the years through mergers, acquisitions and new store openings. The $565 million acquisition of its lead competitor, Wild Oats, in 2007 firmly set Whole Foods as the leader in natural and organic food market and added 70 new stores. The Federal Trade Commission (FTC) focused their attention on the merger on antitrust grounds. The dispute was settled in 2009, with Whole Foods closing 32 Wild Oats stores and agreed to selling the Wild Oats Markets brand.

The organic grocer's stock plunged in 2008 as its sales staggered. Later that year the private equity firm Green Equity Investors invested $425 million in Whole Foods, thereby acquiring about a 17% stake in the chain. For the first time in its 29-year history, Whole Foods reported negative same-store sales in the quarter ended December 2008 as traffic in its stores fell.

Today Whole Foods is listed in the S & P 500 and ranked 284th in the Fortune 500. It is the world's leading natural and organic foods supermarket and is America's first national certified organic grocer. In 2009, it had sales of $8 billion and 289 stores; 273 stores in 38 states of the US and the District of Columbia, 6 stores in Canada, and 5 stores in the UK. The Company has grown from 19 original employees to more than 53,500 team members.[1]

While the majority of Whole Foods locations are in the U.S., European expansion provides enormous potential growth due to the large population and it holds "a more sophisticated organic-foods market than the U.S. in terms of suppliers and acceptance by the public." Whole Foods targets their locations specifically by an area's demographics. The Company targets locations where 40% or more of the residents have a college degree as they are more likely to be aware of nutritional issues.

Whole Foods Market's Philosophy

Their corporate Website defines the company philosophy as follows, "Whole Foods Market's vision of a sustainable future means our children and grandchildren will be living in a world that values human creativity, diversity, and individual choice. Businesses will harness human and material resources without devaluing the integrity of the individual or the planet's ecosystems. Companies, governments, and institutions will be held accountable for their actions.

People will better understand that all actions have repercussions and that planning and foresight coupled with hard work and flexibility can overcome almost any problem encountered. It will be a world that values education and a free exchange of ideas by an informed citizenry; where people are encouraged to discover, nurture, and share their life's passions."

While Whole Foods recognizes it is only a supermarket, they are working toward fulfilling their vision within the context of their industry. In addition to leading by example, they strive to conduct business in a manner consistent with their mission and vision. By offering minimally processed, high quality food, engaging in ethical business practices and providing a motivational, respectful work environment, the Company believes they are on the path to a sustainable future.

Whole Foods incorporate the best practices of each location back into the chain. This can be seen in the Company's store product expansion from dry goods to perishable produce, including meats, fish and prepared foods. The lessons learned at one location are absorbed by all, enabling the chain to maximize effectiveness and efficiency while offering a product line customers love. Whole Foods carries only natural and organic products. The best tasting and most nutritious food available is found in its purest state—unadulterated by artificial additives, sweeteners, colorings, and preservatives.

Whole Foods continually improves customer offerings, catering to its specific locations. Unlike business models for traditional grocery stores, Whole Foods products differ by geographic regions and local farm specialties.

Employee & Customer Relations

Whole Foods encourages a team based environment allowing each store to make independent decisions regarding its operations. Teams consist of up to eleven employees and a team leader. The team leaders typically head up one department or another. Each store employs anywhere from 72 to 391 team members. The manager is referred to as the "store team leader." The "store team leader" is compensated by an Economic Value Added (EVA) bonus and is also eligible to receive stock options.

Whole Foods tries to instill a sense of purpose among its employees and has been named for 13 consecutive years as one of the "100 Best Companies to

Work For" in America by Fortune magazine. In employee surveys, 90% of its team members stated that they always or frequently enjoy their job.

The company strives to take care of their customers, realizing they are the "lifeblood of our business," and the two are "interdependent on each other." Whole Foods' primary objective goes beyond 100% customer satisfaction with the goal to "delight" customers in every interaction.

Competitive Environment

At the time of Whole Foods' inception, there was almost no competition with less than six other natural food stores in the U.S. Today, the organic foods industry is growing and Whole Foods' finds itself competing hard to maintain its elite presence.

In the early- to mid-2000s, its biggest competitor was Wild Oats. In 2007, Whole Foods put a bid on Wild Oats for $670 million[2] and drew an anti-trust investigation from the FTC. The FTC felt that a merger of the two premium natural and organic supermarkets would create a monopoly situation, ultimately harming consumers. It was found that although Whole Foods and Wild Oats were the two key players in the premium natural and organic food market, they are not insulated from competition from conventional grocery store chains. With the decision coming down in favor of Whole Foods and Wild Oats, the transaction was completed. Although this eliminated Whole Foods most direct competitor, they still faces stiff competition in the general grocery market.

Whole Foods competes with all supermarkets. With more U.S. consumers focused on eating healthfully, environmental sustainability, and the green movement, the demand for organic and natural foods has increased. More traditional supermarkets are now introducing "lifestyle" stores and departments to compete directly with Whole Foods. This can be seen in the Wild Harvest section of Shaw's, or the "Lifestyle" stores opened by conventional grocery chain Safeway.

Whole Foods competitors now include big box and discount retailers who have made a foray into the grocery business. Currently, the U.S. largest grocer is Wal-Mart. Not only do they compete in the standard supermarket industry, but they have even begun offering natural and organic products its Supercenter stores. Other discount retailers now competing in the supermarket industry include Target, Sam's Club and Costco. All of these retailers offer grocery products, generally at a lower price than what one would find at Whole Foods.

Another of Whole Foods' key competitors is Los Angeles based Trader Joe's, a premium natural and organic food market. By expanding its presence and product offerings while maintaining high quality at low prices, Trade Joe's has found its competitive niche. It has 215 stores, primarily on the west and east coasts of the U.S., offering upscale grocery fare such as health foods, prepared meals, organic produce and nutritional supplements. A low cost structure allows Trader Joe's to offer competitive prices while still maintaining its margins. Trader Joe's stores have no service department and average just 10,000 square feet in store size.

Additional competition has arisen from grocery stores, such as Stop 'N Shop and Shaw's, which now incorporate natural foods sections in their conventional stores, placing them in direct competition with Whole Foods. Because larger grocery chains have more flexibility in their product offerings, they are more likely to promote products through sales, a strategy Whole Foods rarely practices.

A Different Shopping Experience

The setup of the organic grocery store is a key component to Whole Foods' success. The store's setup and its products are carefully researched to ensure that they are meeting the demands of the local community. Locations are primarily in cities and are chosen for their large space and heavy foot traffic. According to Whole Foods' 10K, "approximately 88% of our existing stores are located in the top 50 statistical metropolitan areas." The Company uses a specific formula to choose their store sites that is based upon several metrics, which include but are not limited to income levels, education, and population density.

Upon entering a Whole Foods supermarket, it becomes clear that the Company attempts to sell the consumer on the entire experience. Team members (employees) are well trained and the stores themselves are immaculate. There are in-store chefs to help with recipes, wine tasting and food sampling. There are "Take Action food centers" where customers can access information on the issues that affect their food such as legislation and environmental factors. Some stores offer extra services such as home delivery, cooking classes, massages and valet parking. Whole Foods goes out of their way to appeal to the above-average income earner.

Whole Foods uses price as a marketing tool in a few select areas, as demonstrated by the 365 Whole Foods brand name products, priced less than similar organic products that are carried within the store. However, the Company does not use price to differentiate itself from competitors. Rather, Whole Foods focuses on quality and service as a means of standing out from the competition.

Whole Foods spends much less than other supermarkets on advertising, approximately 0.4% of total sales in the fiscal year 2009. They rely heavily on word-of-mouth advertising from their customers to help market themselves in the local community. They are also promoted in several health conscious magazines, and each store budgets for in-store advertising each fiscal year.

Whole Foods also gains recognition via their charitable contributions and the awareness that they bring to the treatment of animals. The Company donates 5% of their after tax profits to not-for-profit charities. It is also very active in establishing systems to make sure that the animals used in their products are treated humanly.

The Green Movement

Whole Foods exists in a time where customers equate going green and being environmentally friendly with enthusiasm and respect. In recent years, people began to learn about food and the processes completed by many to produce it. Most of what they have discovered is disturbing. Whole Foods launched a nationwide effort to trigger awareness and action to remedy the problems facing the U.S. food system. It has decided to host 150 screenings of a 12 film series called "Let's Retake Our Plates," hoping to inspire change by encouraging and educating consumers to take charge of their food choices. Jumping on the band wagon of the "go green" movement, Whole Foods is trying to show its customers that it is dedicated to not only all natural foods, but to a green world and healthy people. As more and more people become educated, the Company hopes to capitalize on them as new customers.[3]

Beyond the green movement, Whole Foods has been able to tap into a demographic that appreciates the "trendy" theme of organic foods and all natural products. Since the store is associated with a type of affluence, many customers shop there to show they fit into this category of upscale, educated, new age people.

The Economic Recession

The uncertainty of today's market is a threat to Whole Foods. The expenditure income is low and "all natural foods" are automatically deemed as expensive. Because of people being laid off, having their salaries cut, or simply not being able to find a job, they now have to be more selective when purchasing things. While Whole Foods has been able to maintain profitability, its questionable how long they will last if the recession continues or worsens. The reputation of organic products being costly may be enough to motivate people to not ever enter through the doors of Whole Foods. In California, the chain is frequently dubbed "Whole Paycheck."[4]

However, the Company understood that it must change a few things if it were to survive the decrease in sales felt because customers were not willing to spend their money so easily. They have been working to correct this "pricey" image by expanding offerings of private label products through their "365 Everyday Value" and "365 Organic" product lines. Private label sales accounted for 11% of Whole Foods total sales in 2009, up from 10% in 2008. They have also instituted a policy that their 365 product lines must match prices of similar products at Trader Joe's.[5]

During the economic recession, restaurants had a severe impact. A survey conducted showed that adults were eating out 50% less than they were prior to the economic crash.[6] Whole Foods saw this as opportunity to enter a new area of business, the premade meals sector. They began selling premade dinners and lunches marketing towards those still on the go but interested in eating healthy and saving money. Offering the feed "4 for $15" deal, they were able to recapture some lost sales. In November of 2008, the stock fell to $7 dollars. After the premade meals were created, the stock increased to $28 dollars in September 2009.[7] If Whole Foods continues to come up with innovative ideas to still compete during a recession, there is much opportunity as the economy evolves and climbs up the economic life cycle into recovery, expansion, and boom states.

Organic Foods a Commodity

When Whole Foods first started in the natural foods industry in 1980 it was a relatively new concept and over the first decade Whole Foods enjoyed the benefits of offering a unique value proposition to consumers wanting to purchase high quality natural foods from a trusted retailer. Over the last few years, however, the natural and organic foods industry has attracted the attention of general food retailers that have started to offer foods labeled as natural or organic at reasonable prices.

As of 2007, the global demand for organic and natural foods far exceeded the supply. This is becoming a huge issue for Whole Foods, as more traditional supermarkets with higher purchasing power enter the premium natural and organic foods market. The supply of organic food has been significantly impacted by the entrance of Wal-Mart into the competitive arena. Due to the limited resources within the U.S., Wal-Mart begun importing natural and organic foods from China and Brazil, which led to it coming under scrutiny for passing off non-natural or organic products as the "real thing." Additionally, the quality of natural and organic foods throughout the entire market has been decreased due to constant pressure from Wal-Mart.

The distinction between what is truly organic and natural is difficult for the consumer to decipher as general supermarkets have taken to using terms such as "all natural," "free-range," "hormone free," confusing customers. Truly organic food sold in the U.S. bears the "USDA Organic" label and needs to have at least 95% of the ingredients organic before it can get this distinction.[8]

In May 2003 Whole Foods became America's first Certified Organic grocer by a federally recognized independent third-party certification organization. In July 2009, California Certified Organic Growers (CCOF), one of the oldest and largest USDA-accredited third-party organic certifiers, individually certified each store in the U.S., complying with stricter guidance on federal regulations. This voluntary certification tells customers that Whole Foods have gone the extra mile by not only following the USDA's Organic Rule, but opening their stores up to third-party inspectors and following a strict set of operating procedures designed to ensure that the products sold and labeled as organic are indeed organic–procedures that are not specifically required by the Organic Rule. This certification verifies the handling of organic goods according to stringent national guidelines, from receipt through repacking to final sale to customers. To receive certification, retailers must agree to adhere to a strict set of standards set forth by the USDA, submit documentation, and open their facilities to on-site inspections—all designed to assure customers that the chain of organic integrity is preserved.

Operations

Whole Foods purchases most of their products from regional and national suppliers. This allows the Company to leverage its size in order to receive deep discounts and favorable terms with their vendors. It still permits store to purchase from local producers to keep the stores aligned with local food trends and is seen as supporting the community. Whole Foods operates ten regional distribution centers to support its stores. It also operates two procurement centers, four seafood-processing and distribution centers, a specialty coffee and tea procurement and brewing operation, five regional kitchens, and eight bake house facilities. Whole Foods largest third-party supplier is United Natural Foods which accounted for 28% of total purchases in 2009, down from 32% in 2008.

Product categories at Whole Foods include, but are not limited to:

- Produce
- Seafood
- Grocery
- Meat and Poultry
- Bakery
- Prepared Foods and Catering
- Specialty (Beer, Wine and Cheese)
- Whole body (nutritional supplements, vitamins, body care and educational products such as books)
- Floral
- Pet Products
- Household Products[i]

While Whole Foods carries all the items that one would expect to find in a grocery store (and plenty that one would not), their ". . . heavy emphasis on perishable foods is designed to appeal to both natural foods and gourmet shoppers." Perishable foods now account for two-thirds of its sales. This is demonstrated by the Company's own statement that, "We believe it is our strength of execution in perishables that has attracted many of our most loyal shoppers."

Whole Foods also provides fully cooked frozen meal option through their private label Whole Kitchen, to satisfy the demands of working families. For example, The Whole Foods Market located Woodland Hills, CA that has redesigned its prepared foods section more than three times in response to a 40% growth in prepared foods sales.

Whole Foods doesn't take just any product and put it on their shelves. In order to make it into the Whole Foods grocery store, products have to under go a strict test to determine if they are "Whole Foods material." The quality standards that all potential Whole foods products must meet include:

- Foods that is free of preservatives and other additives
- Foods that is fresh, wholesome and safe to eat
- Promote organically grown foods
- Foods and products that promote a healthy life

Meat and poultry products must adhere to a higher standard:

- No antibiotics or added growth hormones
- An affidavit from each producer that outlines the whole process of production and how the animals are treated
- An annual inspection of all producers by Whole Foods Market
- Successful completion of a third-party audit to attest to these findings

Also, due to the lack of available nutritional brands with a national identity, Whole Foods decided to enter into the private label product business. They currently have three private label products with a fourth program called Authentic Food Artisan, which promotes distinctive products that are certified organic. The three private label products: (1) 365 Everyday Value: A well-recognized and trusted brand that meets the standards of Whole Foods and is less expensive then the regular product lines; (2) Whole Kids Organic: Healthy items that are directed at children; and (3) 365 Organic Everyday Value: All the benefits of organic food at reduced prices.

Whole Foods growth strategy is to expand primarily through new store openings. New stores are typically located on premier real estate sites, often in urban, high-population locales. They do not have a standard store design, instead each store's design is customized to fit the size and configuration of the site selected. They have traditionally opened stores in upper-income, more urban neighborhoods that typically have a high percentage of college graduates.[9]

The Company tracks what it calls the "Tender Period" which is the time between when it takes possession of the leased space for construction and other purposes and the time when the store is opened for business. **Exhibit 1** shows the time and cost involved can be significant with preopening expenses running between $2.5 and $3 million dollars and the time required ranging from 8.5 to 12.6 months. If Whole Foods opens 17 stores per year, this will consume $43 to $51 million dollars of its available cash each year.

When opening a new store, Whole Foods stocks it with almost $700,000 worth of initial inventory, which their vendors partially finance. Like most conventional grocery stores, the majority of Whole Foods inventory is turned over fairly quickly; this is especially true of produce. Fresh organic produce is central to Whole Foods existence and turns over on a faster basis than other products.

Financial Operations

Whole Foods Market focuses on earning a profit while providing job security to its workforce to lay the foundation for future growth. The company is determined not to let profits deter the Company from providing excellent service to its customers and quality work environment for its staff. Their mission statement defines their recipe for financial success.

Exhibit 1   Stores—Time & Cost

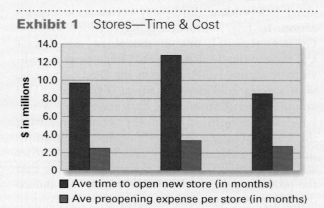

- Ave time to open new store (in months)
- Ave preopening expense per store (in months)

"Whole Foods, Whole People, Whole Planet-emphasizes that our vision reaches far beyond just being a food retailer. Our success in fulfilling our vision is measured by customer satisfaction, Team Member excellence and happiness, return on capital investment, improvement in the state of the environment, and local and larger community support."

Whole Foods also caps the salary of its executives at no more than fourteen times that of the average annual salary of a Whole Foods worker; this includes wages and incentive bonuses as well. The company also donates 5% of their after tax profits to non-profit organizations.

Over a period from September 2005 through January 2010, while total sales of Whole Foods have continued to increase, the operating margin has declined. With the acquisition of the Wild Oats the operating margin decreased significantly from 5.7% in 2006 to 3% in 2008 as Whole Foods struggled to handle the addition of 70+ new stores. The fiscal year 2009 has shown some improvement with the most recent operating margin back up to 3.9% on an annualized basis from the low point of 3.0% for the year ended September 2008. The operating margin has improved due to cost and efficiency improvements[10] (**Exhibit 2**).

Whole Foods strategy of expansion and acquisition has fueled growth in net income since the company's inception. The total number of stores has increased from 175 at September 2005 to 289 in January 2010. They managed to open only a total of ten new stores for the two years ended September 2009. This was a result of their integrating the stores from the Wild Oats acquisition in 2007 and conserving cash in order to pay down some of the debt taken on in that transaction. The Company did open five new stores in the first quarter of 2010 with a projection of an additional ten new stores for the remainder of the year. They forecast to open 17 new stores in each of the following two years (**Exhibit 3**).

Though new stores are being opened, average weekly same store sales have declined from $617,000 for the year ended September 2007 to $549,000 for the year ended September 2009 (**Exhibit 4**). The Company's sales have been impacted by the recession and resultant pullback in consumer spending as well as increased competition as more traditional grocery and discount chains expand their offerings of natural and organic products.[11]

Whole Foods has improved its balance sheet since the acquisition of the Wild Oats chain in 2007.

Long-Term debt has declined from $929 million at September 28, 2008 to $734 million as of January 17, 2010, a reduction of $195 million or 21%. Cash and Short-term Investment balances for the same periods increased from only $31 million to $482 million, an increase of $451 million (**Exhibit 5**). The Company's long- and short-term debt ratios are in line with industry averages and reflect a solid financial condition.[12] These improvements to the balance sheet were primarily the result of a preferred stock offering in late 2008 for approximately $413 million dollars which was subsequently called and converted into common stock. During the fourth quarter of 2008, they suspended the quarterly dividend on common shares for the foreseeable future.

Whole Foods has improved its accounts receivable and inventory levels as compared to sales. In 2005 and 2006, the combined percentage was 5.1%. This jumped dramatically to 8.5% in 2007 with the acquisition of Wild Oats. The Company has now brought this metric back to the historical norm of 5.1% as of January 2010 (**Exhibit 6**).

Whole Foods stock was outperforming the market and its industry based on the Company's growth and earnings prospects (**Exhibit 7**). The Wild Oats acquisition and the economic recession have impacted the stock, but it has subsequently recovered somewhat as Whole Foods has improved its efficiency and resumed its growth strategy through store expansion.

Struggling to Grow in An Increasingly Competitive Market

Whole Foods has historically grown by opening new stores or acquiring stores in affluent neighborhoods targeting the wealthier and more educated consumers. This strategy has worked in the past however the continued focus on growth has been impacting existing store sales. Average weekly sales per store have decreased over the last number of years despite the fact that overall sales have been increasing. It is likely that this trend will continue unless Whole Foods start to focus on growing sales within the stores they have and not just looking to increase overall sales by opening new stores. It is also increasingly difficult to find appropriate locations for new stores that are first are foremost in an area where there is limited competition and also to have the store in a location that is easily accessible by both consumers and the distribution network. Originally Whole Foods had forecast to open 29 new stores in 2010 but this has since been revised downward to 17.

Opening up new stores or the acquisition existing stores is also costly. The average cost to open a new store ranges from $2 to $3 million and it takes on average 8–12 months. A lot of this can be explained by the fact that Whole Foods custom build the stores which reduces the efficiencies that can be gained from the experience of having opened up many new stores previously. Opening new stores requires the company to adapt their distribution network, information management, supply and inventory management and adequately supply the new stores in a timely manner without impacting the supply to the existing stores. As the Company expands this task increases in complexity and magnitude.

The organic and natural foods industry overall has become a more concentrated market with few larger competitors having emerged from a more fragmented market composed of a large number of smaller companies. Future acquisitions will be more difficult for Whole Foods as the FTC will be monitoring the company closely to ensure that they do not violate any federal antitrust laws through the elimination of any substantial competition within this market.

Over the last number of years there has been an increasing demand by consumers for natural and organic foods. Sales of organic foods increased by 5.1% in 2009 despite the fact that U.S. food sales overall only grew by 1.6%.[13] This increase in demand and high margin availability on premium organic products had led to an increasing number of competitors moving into the organic foods industry. Conventional grocery chains such as Safeway have remodeled stores at a rapid pace and have attempted to narrow the gap with premium grocers like Whole Foods in terms of shopping experience, product quality, and selection of takeout foods. This increase in competition can lead to the introduction of price wars where profits are eroded for both existing competitors and new entrants alike.

Unlike low-price leaders such as Wal-Mart, Whole Foods dominates because of its brand image, which is trickier to manage and less impervious to competitive threats. As competitors start to focus on emphasizing organic and natural foods within their own stores, the power of the Whole Foods brand will gradually decline over time as it becomes more difficult for consumers to differentiate Whole Foods value proposition from that of their competitors.

Exhibit 2   Sales, Net Income and Operating Margin

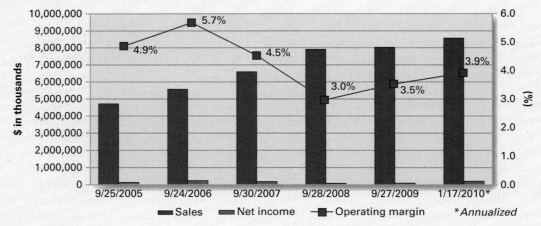

Exhibit 3 # Stores

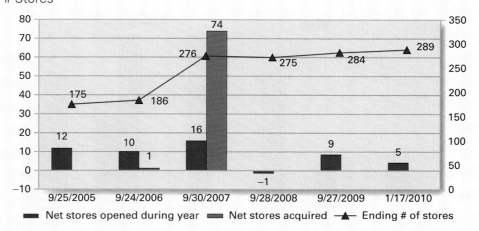

- Net stores opened during year
- Net stores acquired
- Ending # of stores

Exhibit 4 Average Weekly Sales per Stores

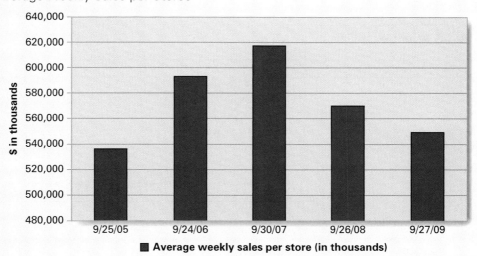

- Average weekly sales per store (in thousands)

Exhibit 5 Cash & Long-Term Debt

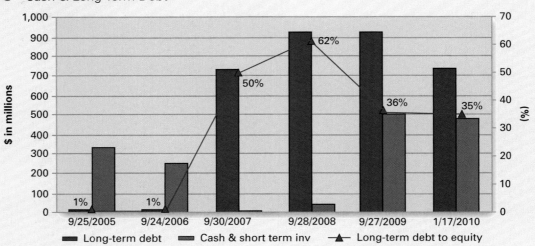

Exhibit 6 A/R & Inventory to Sales

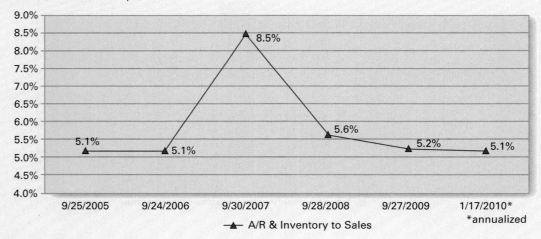

Exhibit 7 WFNI Daily

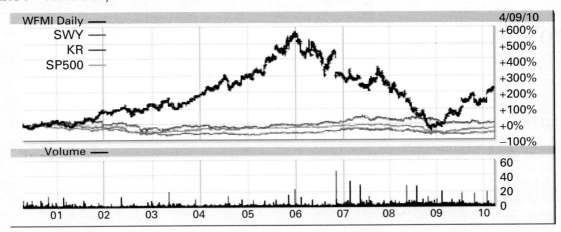

Endnotes

1 Hoover's Company Information, "Thomson Reuters Company in Context Report," Fast Company Magazine, December 2009

2 Lambert, Thomas A. "Four Lessons from the Whole Foods Case: The Antitrust Analysis of Mergers Should Be Reconsidered," Regulation. 31.1 (Spring 2008): 22(8). General Business File ASAP. Gale. Bentley College-Solomon R Baker Lib. 10 April, 2010

3 "Whole Foods Market; Whole Foods Market Challenge: Let's Retake Our Plates!" Food Business Week, 15 April, 2010

4 "Eating Too Fast At Whole Foods," Business Week (2005): Print.

5 "As Sales Slip, Whole Foods Tries Health Push," Katy McLaughlin, 8/15/2009, Wall Street Journal

6 Ziobro, Paul. "Whole Foods Highlights Its Eat-At-Home Values," Wall Street Journal 2009, Web. 10 April, 2010.

7 Ibid.

8 "Whole Foods Markets Organic China California Blend," YouTube, 10 April, 2010. http://www.youtube.com/watch?v=JQ31Ljd9T_Y

9 Whole Foods Market, Inc. SEC filing, Form 10-K dated 27 September, 2009

10 McLaughlin, Katy. "As Sales Slip, Whole Foods Tries Health Push," Wall Street Journal 2009.

11 Steverman, Ben. "Wal-Mart vs. Whole Foods," Business Week, 14 May, 2009

12 Market Edge Research Report, 12 April, 2010

13 Organic Trade Association http://www.organicnewsroom.com/2010/04/us_organic_product_sales_reach_1.html

TomTom: New Competition Everywhere!

Alan N. Hoffman
Bentley University and Rotterdam School of Management, Erasmus University

Synopsis

TomTom, an Amsterdam-based company that provides navigation services and devices, leads the navigation systems market in Europe and is second in the US. Its most popular products include TomTom Go and TomTom One for cars, TomTom Rider for bikes, TomTom Navigator (digital maps), and TomTom for iPhone—its most recent release.

The company attributes its market leadership to its technology, large customer base, distribution power, and prominent brand image. But as the US and European personal navigation device market gets saturated, TomTom's sales growth rate declines. The company also faces increasing competition from other platforms using GPS technology like cell phones and smart phones with a built-in navigation function. Legal and environmental restrictions on the digital navigation industry make TomTom's future even more uncertain. Whether TomTom can keep expanding may well depend on whether it can become the prime mover in creating digital maps and navigational services for developing countries.

TomTom: New Competition Everywhere!

TomTom is one of the largest producers of satellite navigation systems in the world, comprised of both stand alone devices and applications. It leads the navigation systems market in Europe while stands second in the United States. TomTom attributes its position as a market leader to the following factors: the size of its customer and technology base; its distribution power; and its prominent brand image and recognition.[19]

With the acquisition of Tele Atlas, TomTom has become vertically integrated and also controls the map creation process now. This has helped TomTom establish itself as an integrated content, service and technology business. The company is Dutch by origin and has its headquarters based in Amsterdam, Netherlands. In terms of geography, the company's operations span from Europe to Asia Pacific, covering North America, Middle East and Africa.[19]

TomTom is supported by a workforce of 3,300 employees from 40 countries. The diverse workforce enables the company to compete in international markets.[4] The company's revenues have grown from €8 million in 2002 to €1.674 billion in 2008. However, more recently, because of the Tele Atlas acquisition and the current economic downturn the company has become a cause of concern for investors. On 22nd July 2009, TomTom reported a fall of 61% in its net income at the end of 2nd quarter 2009.[3]

TomTom is in the business of navigation based information services and devices. The company has been investing structurally and strategically in Research and Development to bring new and better products and services to its customers. The company's belief in radical innovation has helped it remain at the cutting edge of innovation within the navigation industry.

The vision of TomTom is to improve people's lives by transforming navigation from a 'don't-get-lost solution' into a true travel companion that gets people from one place to another safer, faster, cheaper and better informed. This vision has helped the company to be a market leader in every market place in the satellite navigation information services market.[6]

The author would like to thank Will Hoffman, Mansi Asthana, Aakashi Ganveer, Hing Lin, Che Yii for their research. Please address all correspondence to Professor Alan N. Hoffman, Bentley University, 175 Forest Street, Waltham, MA 02452; ahoffman@bentley.edu. Printed by permission of Dr. Alan N. Hoffman.

The objectives of the company focus around radical advances in three key areas:

Better Maps: This objective is achieved by maintaining TomTom's high quality map data base that is continuously kept up to date by a large community of active users who provide corrections, verifications and updates to TomTom. This is supplemented by inputs from TomTom's extensive fleet of surveying vehicles.[6]

Better Routing: TomTom has the world's largest historical speed profile data base IQ Routes™ facilitated by TomTom HOME, the company's user portal.[6]

Better Traffic Information: TomTom possesses unique real time traffic information service TomTom HD traffic™ which provides users with high quality, real time traffic updates.[6] These three objectives form the base of satellite navigation, working in conjunction to help TomTom achieve its mission.

TomTom's Products

TomTom offers a wide variety of products ranging from portable navigation devices to software navigation applications and digital maps. The unique features in each of these products make them truly "the smart choice in personal navigation."[19] Some of these products are described below:

TomTom Go and TomTom One

These devices come with a LCD screen that makes it easy to use with fingertips while driving. They provide 1,000 Points of Interests (POI) that help in locating petrol stations, restaurants and places of importance. A number of other POIs can also be downloaded. Precise, up to minute traffic information, jam alerts and road condition alerts are provided by both these devices.[3]

TomTom Rider

These are portable models especially for bikers. The equipment consists of an integrated GPS receiver that can be mounted on any bike and a wireless headset inside the helmet. Similar to the car Portable Navigation Devices (PNDs), the TomTom Rider models have a number of POI applications. The interfaces used in TomTom Rider are user friendly and come in a variety of languages.[3]

TomTom Navigator and TomTom Mobile

These applications provide navigation software along with digital maps. Both of these applications are compatible with most mobiles and PDAs, provided by companies like Sony, Nokia, Acer, Dell and HP. These applications come with TomTom HOME which can be used to upgrade to the most recent digital maps and application versions.[3]

TomTom for iPhone

On August 17, 2009, TomTom released TomTom for the iPhone. "With TomTom for iPhone, millions of iPhone users can now benefit from the same easy-to-use and intuitive interface, turn-by-turn spoken navigation and unique routing technology that our 30 million portable navigation device users rely on every day," said Corinne Vigreux, Managing Director of TomTom. "As the world's leading provider of navigation solutions and digital maps, TomTom is the most natural fit for an advanced navigation application on the iPhone."[6]

The TomTom app for iPhone 3G and 3GS users includes a map of the US and Canada from Tele Atlas and is available for $99.99 USD.

The TomTom app for iPhone includes the exclusive IQ Routes™ technology. Instead of using travel time assumptions, IQ Routes bases its routes on the actual experience of millions of TomTom drivers to calculate the fastest route and generate the most accurate arrival times in the industry. TomTom IQ Routes empowers drivers to reach their destination faster up to 35% of the time.

Company Background

Company History

TomTom was founded as 'Palmtop' in 1991 by Peter-Frans Pauwels and Pieter Geelen, two graduates from Amsterdam University, Netherlands. Palmtop started out as a software development company and was involved in producing software for hand held computers, one of the most popular devices of the 90s. In the following few years the company diversified into producing commercial applications including software for personal finance, games, a dictionary and maps. In the year 1996, Corinne Vigreux joined Palmtop as the third partner. In the same year, the company announced the launch of Enroute and RouteFinder, the first navigation software titles. As more and more people using PCs adopted Microsoft's operating system, the company developed applications which were compatible with it. This helped the company increase its market share. The year 2001 marks the turning point in the history of TomTom. It was in this year that Harold Goddijn, the former Chief Executive of Psion joined the company as the fourth partner. Not only did Palmtop get renamed to TomTom, but it also entered the satellite navigation market. TomTom launched TomTom Navigator, the first mobile car satnav system. Since then, as can be seen in Exhibit 1, the company has celebrated the successful launch of at least a product each year.[3]

In 2002, the company generated revenue of €8 million by selling the first GPS-linked car navigator, the TomTom Navigator to PDAs. The upgraded version, Navigator 2 was released in early 2003. Meanwhile, the company made efforts to gain technical and marketing personnel. TomTom took strategic steps to grow its sales. The former CTO of Psion, Mark Gretton, led the hardware team while Alexander Ribbink, a former top marketing official looked after sales of new products introduced by the company.

TomTom Go, an all in one car navigation system, was the next major launch of the company. With its useful and easy-to-use features TomTom Go was included in the list of successful products of 2004. In the same year, the company launched TomTom Mobile, a navigation system which sat on top of smartphones.[3]

TomTom completed its IPO on the Amsterdam Stock Exchange in May 2005. It raised €469 million ($587 million) from this offer. The net worth of the company was nearly €2 billion after the IPO. A majority of the shares were with the four partners.[5] From the years 2006 to 2008, TomTom strengthened itself by making three key strategic acquisitions. Datafactory AG was acquired to power TomTom WORK through WEBfleet technology, while Applied Generics gave its technology for Mobility Solutions Services. However, the most prominent of these three was the acquisition of Tele Atlas.[5]

In July of 2007, TomTom bid for Tele Atlas, a company specializing in digital maps. The original bid price of €2 billion was countered by a €2.3 billion offer from Garmin, TomTom's biggest rival. With TomTom raising the bid price to €2.9 billion, the two companies had initiated a bidding war for Tele Atlas. Although there was speculation that Garmin would further increase its bid price, in the end they decided not to pursue Tele Atlas any further. Rather, Garmin struck a content agreement with Navteq. Finally, TomTom's shareholders approved the takeover in December, 2007.[13]

TomTom's Customers

TomTom is a company that has a wide array of customers each with their own individual needs and desires. TomTom has a variety of products to meet the requirements of a large and varied customer base. As an example, their navigational products range from $100–$500 in the United States, ranging from lower end products with fewer capabilities, to high end products with advanced features.

The first group is the individual consumers who buy stand alone portable navigation devices and services.   The second group is automobile manufacturers. TomTom has teamed up with companies such as Renault to develop built-in navigational units to install as an option in cars. A third group of customers is the aviation industry and pilots with personal planes. TomTom produces navigational devices for air travel at affordable prices. Another group of customers is business enterprises. Business enterprises refers to companies such as Wal-Mart, Target, or Home-Depot; huge companies with large mobile-workforces. To focus on these customers, TomTom formed a strategic partnership with a technology company called 'Advanced integrated solutions' to "optimize business fleet organization and itinerary planning on the TomTom pro series of navigation devices". This new advanced feature on PNDs offers ways for fleet managers and route dispatchers to organize, plan and optimize routes and to provide detailed mapping information about the final destination. "Every day, companies with mobile workforces are challenged to direct all their people to all the places they need to go. Our customers appreciate having a central web repository to hold and manage all their location and address information," says Scott Wyatt, CEO of Advanced Integrated Solutions.[7] TomTom's last group of customers is the coast guards. They are able to use Tom-Tom's marine navigational devices for their everyday responsibilities.

Mergers and Acquisitions

TomTom has made various mergers and acquisitions as well as partnerships that have positioned the company well. In 2008 TomTom acquired a digital mapping company called Tele Atlas. The acquisition has significantly improve TomTom customers' user experience and created other benefits for the customers and partners of both companies, including: more accurate navigation information, improved coverage, and new enhanced features such as map updates and IQ routes which will be discussed in the scarce/unique resource section of the paper. Commenting on the proposed Offer, Alain De Taeye, Co-founder and CEO of Tele Atlas said:

> ". . .the TomTom-Tele Atlas partnership signals a new era in the digital mapping industry. The combination of Tom-Tom's customer feedback tools and Tele Atlas' pioneering map production processes allows Tele Atlas to dramatically change the way digital maps are continuously updated and enhanced. The result will be a completely new level of quality', content and innovation that helps our partners deliver the best navigation products. This transaction is not only very attractive to our shareholders but demonstrates our longstanding commitment towards all of our partners and customers to deliver the best digital map products available."[1]

TomTom also formed a partnership with a company called Advanced Integrated Solutions, adding an itinerary planning and route guidance feature to the pro series of navigation devices to help businesses enterprises with large mobile-workforces. A few years ago they also partnered with Avis, adding their user-friendly navigation system to all Avis rental cars. This partnership began in Europe and recently the devices have made their way into Avis rental cars in North America as well many other countries where Avis operates. Harold Goddijn, chief executive officer of TomTom commented:

> "Any traveler can relate to the stress of arriving in a new and unfamiliar city and getting horribly lost, with the availability of the TomTom GO 700 we're bringing unbeatable, full feature car navigation straight into the hands of Avis customers."[2]

TomTom has acquired several patents for all of their different technologies. By having these patents for each of its ideas, the company has protected itself against its competition and other companies trying to enter into the market.

TomTom prides itself on being the innovator in its industry and always being a step ahead of the competition in terms of its technology. On their Website they say, "TomTom leads the navigation industry with the technological evolution of navigation products from static 'find-your-destination' devices into products and services that provide connected, dynamic 'find-the-optimal-route-to-your-destination', with time-accurate travel information. We are well positioned to maintain that leading position over the long-term because of the size of our customer and technology base, our distribution power, and our prominent brand image and recognition. By being vertically integrated and also control the map creation process TomTom is in a unique position to evolve into an integrated content, service and technology business."[6]

TomTom's has a strong brand name/image. TomTom has positioned itself well throughout the World as the leader in portable navigation devices. It markets its products through its very user-friendly online Website and also through large companies such as Best Buy and Wal-Mart. Recently TomTom teamed up with Locutio Voice Technologies and Twentieth Century Fox Licensing & Merchandising to bring the original voice of Homer Simpson to all TomTom devices via download. "Let Homer Simpson be your TomTom co-pilot" is just one of the many interesting way's TomTom markets its products and its name to its consumers.[9]

TomTom's Resources and Capabilities

The company believes that there are three fundamentals to a navigation system—digital mapping, routing technology and dynamic information. Based on these requirements three key resources can be identified that really distinguished TomTom from its competition.

The first of these resources is their in-house *routing algorithms*. These algorithms enable them to introduce technologies like—IQ Routes, that provides "community based information database." IQ Routes calculate your routes based on the real average speeds measured on roads at that particular time. Their Website says, "The smartest route hour-by-hour, day-by-day, saving you time, money and fuel."[5]

The second unique resource identified was Tele-Atlas and the *digital mapping technology* that the TomTom group specializes in. Having the technology and knowledge in mapping that the company brought to TomTom, has allowed them to introduce many unique features to their customers. Firstly, TomTom recently came out with a map update feature. The company recognizes that roads around the world are constantly changing and because of this they used the technology to come out with four new maps each year, one per business quarter. This allows their customers to always have the latest routes to incorporate into their everyday travel. A second feature they recently introduced is their MapShare program. The idea behind this is that customers of TomTom who notice mistakes in a certain map are able to go in and request a change be made. The change is then verified and checked directly by TomTom and is shared with the rest of their global user community. "One and a half million map corrections have been submitted since the launch of TomTom Map Share™ in the summer of 2007."[5]

The third unique resource identified was *automotive partnerships* with two companies in particular; Renault and Avis. At the end of 2008, TomTom reached a deal with Renault to offer its navigation devices installed in their cars as an option. An article in Auto-week magazine said the following about the deal. "Renault developed its new low-cost system in partnership with Amsterdam-based technology company TomTom, the European leader in portable navigation systems. The system will be an alternative to the existing satellite navigation devices in Renault's upper-end cars."[8] The catch here is the new price of the built in navigation units. The cost of a navigation device installed in Renault's cars before TomTom was €1,500. Now with TomTom system it costs only €500. As talked about earlier in the paper, TomTom also partnered with Avis back in 2005 to offer its navigation devices, specifically the model GO700 in all Avis rental cars, first starting in Europe and expanding into other countries where Avis operates.

Competition Facing TomTom

Traditional Competition

TomTom faces competition from two main companies. The first of these is Garmin which holds 45% of the market share, by far the largest and dou-

ble Tom-Tom's market share (24%). Garmin was founded in 1989 by Gary Burrell and Min H. Kao. The company is known for their on-the-go directions since its introduction into GPS navigation in 1989. At the end of 2008, Garmin reported annual sales of $3493.1 million. Last year Garmin competed head-to-head with TomTom in trying to acquire Tele-Atlas for their mapmaking. Garmin withdrew their bid when it became evident that it was becoming too expense to own Tele-Atlas. Garmin executives made a decision that it was cheaper to work out a long-term deal with its current supplier than to try to buy out a competitor. Garmin's current supplier for map services is Navteq which was also acquired by Nokia in 2008.

The second direct competitor is Magellan, which holds 15% of the market share. Magellan is part of a privately held company under the name of MiTac Digital Corporation. Similar to Garmin, Magellan products use Navteq based maps. Magellan was the creator of Magellan NAV 100 that was the world's first commercial handheld GPS receiver which was created in 1989. The company is also well known for their award-winning RoadMate and Maestro series portable car navigation systems.

Together these three dominant players account for about 85% of the total market. Other competitors in the personal navigation device market are: Navigon, Nextar, and Nokia. Navigon and Nextar compete in the personal navigation devices with TomTom, Magellan, and Garmin who are the top three in the industry. But Navigon competes in the high-end segment which retails for more than any of the competitors but offer a few extra features in their PNDs. Nextar compete in the low-end market and its strategy is low cost. Finally, Nokia is mention as a competitor in this industry because they recently acquired Navteq who is a major supplier of map services in this industry. Along with that, Nokia has a big market share in the cell phone industry and plans on incorporating GPS technology in every phone making them a potential key player to look at for in the GPS navigation industry.

New Competition

Cell Phones Cell phones are a widely used technology by people all around the world. With the 2005 FCC mandate that requires the location of any cell phone used to call 911, phone manufacturers have now included GPS receiver in almost every cell phone.

Due to this mandate, cell phone manufacturers and cellular services are now able to offer a GPS navigation services through the cell phone for a fee.

ATT Navigator GPS Navigation with AT&T Navigator and AT&T Navigator Global Edition feature real-time GPS enabled turn-by-turn navigation on AT&T mobile Smartphones (iPhone and Blackberry) or static navigation and Local Search on a non-GPS AT&T mobile Smartphone.

ATT Navigator features Global GPS turn-by-turn navigation—Mapping and Point of Interest content for three continents, including North America (U.S., Canada, and Mexico), Western Europe, and China where wireless coverage is available from AT&T or its roaming providers. The ATT Navigator is sold as a subscription service and costs $9.99 per month.

Online Navigation Applications Online navigation Websites that are still popular amongst many users for driving directions and maps are MapQuest, Google Maps, and Yahoo Maps. Users are able to use this free site to get detail directions on how to get to their next destination. In today's economic downturn many people are looking for cheap, or if possible free solutions to solve their problems. These online Websites offer the use free mapping and navigation information that will allow them to get what they need at no additional costs. However, there are down-sides to these programs, "such as they are not portable and may have poor visualization designs (such as vague image, or text-based)."[12]

Built-In Car Navigation Devices In car navigation device first came about in more luxury, high-end vehicles. In today's market it has become more mainstream and now being offered in mid to lower tier vehicles. These built-in car navigation devices offer similar features to the personal navigation device but don't have the portability so you won't have to carry multiple devices but come with a hefty cost. Some examples of these are Kenwood, Pioneer, and Eclipse units all installed into your car. These units tend to be expensive and over-priced because of the fact that they are brand name products and require physical installation. For example, the top of the line Pioneer unit is $1,000 for the monitor and then another $500 for the navigation device plus the physical labor. When buying such products, a customer is spending a huge amount of money on a product that is almost identical to a product TomTom offers at significantly lower prices.

Physical Maps Physical maps have been the primary option for navigating for decades until technology came around. Physical maps provide detail road information to help a person get from point A to point B. Although cumbersome to use than some of the modern technology alternatives, it is an alternative for people who are not technically savvy or for whom navigation device is an unnecessary luxury that they do not feel the need to spend money on.

Potential Adverse Legislation and Restrictions

In the legal and political realm, TomTom is facing two issues that are not critical now, but may have significant ramifications to not only TomTom in the future, but also the entire portable navigation device industry. TomTom's reactions to each of these issues will determine whether or not there is an opportunity for gain or a threat of a significant loss will occur.

The most important issue deals with the possible legislative banning of all navigational devices from automobiles. In Australia, there is growing concern over the distraction caused by PNDs and the legislature has taken the steps toward banning these devices entirely from automobiles.[26] There is a similar sentiment in Ontario, Canada where a law that is currently under review would ban all PNDs that were not mounted either to the dashboard or to the windshield itself.[27]

With the increase in legislation adding to the restrictions placed on PND devices, the threat that the PND market in the future will be severely limited cannot be ignored. All of the companies within the PND industry, not just TomTom, must create a coordinated and united effort to stem this tidal wave of restrictions as well as provide reassurance to the public that they are also concerned with the safe use of their products. An example of this opportunity comes from the toy industry where safety regulations are fast and furious at times. Many companies within the toy industry have combined to form the International Council of Toy Industries[23] to be proactive in regards to safety regulations as well as lobby governments on behalf the toy industry against laws that may unfairly threaten the toy industry[23].

The other issue within the legal and political spectrum that TomTom must focus on is the growing use of GPS devices as tracking devices. Currently, law enforcement agents are allowed to use their own GPS devices to track the movements and locations of individuals they deem to be suspicious, but how long will it be before budget cuts reduce the access to these GPS devices and then the simple solution will be to use the PND devices already installed in many automobiles?

This issue also requires the industry as whole to proactively work with the consumers and the government to come to an amicable resolution. The threat of having every consumer's GPS information at the finger tips of either the government or surveillance company will most certainly stunt or even completely halt any growth within the PND industry and that is why the industry must be on the offensive and not become a reactor.

Another alarming trend is the rise in PND thefts around the country[22]. With the prices for PNDs at a relatively high level, thieves are targeting vehicles that have visible docking stations for PNDs either on the dashboard or windshield. The onus will be on TomTom to create new designs that will help not only hide PNDs from would-be thieves but also deter them from ever trying to steal one. Consumers who are scared to purchase PNDs because of this rise in crime will become an issue if this problem is not resolved.

There is also a trend currently that is labeled the GREEN movement,[29] that aims to reduce any activities that will endanger the environment. This movement is a great opportunity for TomTom to tout its technology as the smarter and more environmentally safe tool if driving is an absolute necessity. Not only can individuals tout this improved efficiency, but more importantly on a larger scale, businesses that require large amounts of materials to be transported across long stretches can show activists that they too are working to becoming a green company.

It is ironic that the core technology used in TomTom's navigation system, the GPS system, is proliferating into other electronic devices at such a rapid pace that it is causing serious competition to the PND industry. GPS functionality is virtually a requirement for all new smartphones that enter the market and soon will become a basic functionality in regular cellular phones. TomTom will be hard pressed to compete with these multifunctional devices unless they can improve upon their designs and transform themselves into just a single focused device.

Another concern not only for TomTom, but for every company that relies heavily on GPS technology, is the aging satellites that support the GPS system. Analysts predict that these satellites will be either replaced or fixed before there are any issues, but this issue is unsettling due to the fact that TomTom has no control over it[24]. TomTom will have to devise contingency plans in case of catastrophic failure of the GPS system much like what happened to Research in Motion when malfunctioning satellites caused disruption in their service.

Currently TomTom is one of the leading companies in the PND markets in both Europe and the United States. Although they are the leader in Europe, that market is showing signs of becoming saturated, and even though the U.S. market is currently growing, TomTom should not wait for the inevitable signs of that market's slowdown as well. TomTom needs to be proactive to the next big market instead of using its large resources to become a *fast follower*.

The two main opportunities for TomTom to expand, creating digital maps for developing countries and creating navigational services can either be piggybacked one on top of each other or can be taken in independent paths. The first-mover advantage for these opportunities will erect a high barrier of entry for any companies that do not have large amounts of resources to invest in the developing country. TomTom is already playing catch-up to Garmin and their already established service in India. Being proactive is an important and valuable opportunity that TomTom should take advantage of.

Globalization of any company's products does not come without a certain set of issues. For TomTom, the main threat brought on by foreign countries is two fold. The first threat which may be an isolated instance, but could also be repeated in many other countries is the restriction of certain capabilities for all of TomTom's products. Due to security and terrorism concerns, GPS devices are not allowed in Egypt since 2003[28]. In these times of global terrorism TomTom must be vigilant of the growing trend for countries to become overly protective of foreign companies and their technologies.

Internal Environment

Finance

TomTom's current financial objectives are to diversify and become a broader revenue based company. The company not only seeks to increase the revenue base in terms of geographical expansion but also wants to diversify its product and service portfolio. Additionally, another important goal the company strives to achieve is to reduce its operating expenses.

Sales Revenue and Net Income In Exhibit 2 it can be observed that from 2005 to 2007 there is a consistent growth in sales revenue and a corresponding increase in net income too. However, year 2008 is an exception to this trend. In this year sales revenue decreased by 3.7% and the net income decreased by 136%. In fact, in the first quarter the net income is actually negative totaling -€37 million. The decrease in sales can be accounted by the downturn in the economy. Actually, according to their 2008 annual report, the sales are in line with their expectations from the market. However, the net income plummeted much more than the decrease in sales. This was actually triggered by its acquisition of a digital mapping company—Tele Atlas, which was funded by both cash assets and debt.

1. **Quarterly sales**—In second quarter of 2009 TomTom received sales revenue of €368 million compared to €213 million in first quarter and €453 million in the same quarter last year. (Exhibit 3) By evaluating quarterly sales for a three year period from 2007 till present, it is apparent that the sales do follow a seasonal trend in TomTom. With highest sales in last quarter and lowest in the first quarter. However, focusing on just the first and second quarter for three years one can infer that the sales revenue as a whole is also going down year after year. To investigate further on the causes of this scenario we will have to delve deeper into its revenue base. TomTom's sources of revenue can be broadly grouped into two categories—market segment and geographic location.

   Revenue per segment: TomTom's per segment revenue stream can be divided into PNDs and others, where others consist of services and content. Evaluating first quarter of 2008 against that of 2009 and last quarter of 2008, TomTom experienced steep decline of 40% and 68%.(Exhibit 4) This could be a consequence of compounded effect of the following—Firstly, the number of devices (PNDs) decreased by a similar amount both the time periods. And secondly, the average selling price of PNDs has also been decreasing consistently. In a technology company a decrease in average selling price is a part and parcel of doing business in a highly competitive and dynamic market place. Nevertheless, the revenue stream from business units other than PNDs has seen a steady increase in both the scenarios.

   Revenue per region: TomTom's per region revenue stream can be further divided into Europe, North America and the rest of the world. Comparing first quarter of 2009 against 2008 it can be seen that, revenue from both Europe and North America are on decline, with a decrease of 22% and 52% respectively (Exhibit 5). At the same time, revenue from rest of the world has seen a huge increase of 90%. Both of these analyses support TomTom's current objective to increase their revenue base and is aligned with their long-term strategy of being a leader in navigation industry.

2. **Long term debt**—In 2005 TomTom was cash-rich company but the recent acquisition of Tele Atlas which amounted to €2.9 billion and was funded by cash, release of new shares as well as long term debt, which is in this case a borrowing of €1.2 billion. Currently, TomTom's debt is €1,006 million.

3. **Operating Margin**—TomTom saw a consistent increase in operating margin till 2006 (exhibit 7). But since 2007 operating margin has been decreasing for the firm. In fact, by the end of 2008 it came down to 13% compared to 26% in 2006.

Marketing

Traditionally high quality and ease of use of solutions have been of utmost importance to TomTom. In 2006, in an interview, TomTom's Marketing Head Anne Louise Hanstad, could not have emphasized more on the importance of simplicity and ease of use of their devices. (Hanstad) This underlines the TomTom's belief that—"People prefer fit for purpose devices that are developed and designed to do one specific thing very well." At that time both of these were core to the TomTom's strategy as their targeted customers were *early adopters*, but now as navigation industry has moved from embryonic to a growth industry TomTom's current customers are *early majority*, and hence, simplicity and ease alone could no longer provide it with competitive advantage.

Recently, to be in line with its immediate goal of diversifying into different market segment, TomTom is more focused on strengthening its brand name. In December 2008, TomTom's CEO stated—". . .we are constantly striving to increase awareness of our brand and strengthen our reputation for providing smart, easy-to-use, high-quality portable navigation products and services."[19]

Along with Tele Atlas the group has gained the depth and breadth of expertise over the last 30 years, and this makes it a trusted brand. Three out of four people are aware of the brand of the TomTom business across the markets. The Tom-Tom group has always been committed to three fundamentals of navigation—mapping, routing algorithm and dynamic information. Tele Atlas' core competency is the digital mapping database and TomTom's is routing algorithms and guidance services using dynamic information, and the group together create synergies that enable them to introduce products almost every year advancing on one or a combination of these three elements. Acquiring their long time supplier of digital maps, Tele Atlas, in 2008 gives them an edge with in-house digital mapping technology.

TomTom provides a range of PND devices like—TomTom One, TomTom XL and TomTom Go Series. Periodically, it tries to enhance those devices with new features and services, that they build based on the feedback from customers. Examples of services are—IQ routes and LIVE services. While IQ routes provides drivers with the most efficient route planning; accounting for situations as precise as speed bumps and traffic lights, LIVE services forms a range of information services delivered directly to the LIVE devices. The LIVE services bundle includes Map Share and HD Traffic—that is bringing the content collected from vast driving community directly to the end user.

These products and services accentuate effective designs and unique features, and require TomTom to work along with its customers to share precise updates and also get feedback for future improvements. Hence, effective customer interaction becomes essential to its long term goal of innovation. In 2008, J.D. Power associates recognized TomTom for providing outstanding customer service experience.[18] Although, it awarded TomTom for customer service satisfaction, J.D. Power and associates ranked Garmin highest in overall customer satisfaction. Tom-Tom followed Garmin in the ranking, performing well in the routing, speed of system and voice direction factors.[16]

As mentioned previously, when the navigation industry was still in its embryonic stages—Features, ease of use and high quality of its solutions gave TomTom products a competitive edge. Eventually, the competition increased in the navigation industry and even substitutes pose substantial threat to market share now. Currently, TomTom offers PNDs in different price ranges, broadly classified into—high-range and mid-range PNDs, with an average selling price of €99. There are entry-level options that allow a savvy shopper to put navigation in his/her car for just over $100. Higher-end models add advanced features and services previously described.

TomTom sells its PNDs to consumers through retailers and distributors. After acquiring Tele Atlas it is strategically placed to gain the first mover advantage created by its rapid expansion of geographical coverage.[19] This is of key importance when it comes to increasing the global market share.

TomTom directs its marketing expenditure towards B2B advertising that is direct to retailers and distributors. TomTom also invested in an official blog Website as well as search optimization which places it in premium results in online searches. This has enabled TomTom to do effective word-of-mouth promotion while keeping flexible marketing spending, in accordance to changes in the macroeconomic environment or seasonal trends[19]. Although, this approach gives it spending flexibility, it lacks a direct B2C approach. Currently only 21% US adults own PNDs while 65% US adults neither own nor use navigation[14]. By not spending on B2C marketing TomTom is discounting on the opportunity both to attract first-tier noncustomers and glean an insight of needs of second-tier noncustomers.[17]

Operations

The focus of operations has always been on innovation. More recently, TomTom's operational objective is to channel all the resources and core capabilities to create economies of scale so as to be aligned with their long term strategy. TomTom aims to focus and centralize R&D resources to create scale economies to continue to lead the industry in terms of innovation.[19]

Implementation of this strategy is well underway and the changes are visible. By second quarter of 2009 mid-range PNDs were introduced with capabilities from high-range devices, 50% of PNDs were sold with IQ Routes Technology, first in-dash product was also launched in alliance with Renault and TomTom iPhone application was also announced[19].

After aquiring Tele Atlas, to better support the broader navigation solutions and content and services, the group underwent restructuring. New organization structure consists of four business units, that have clear focus on a specific customer group and are supported by two shared development centers.

TomTom's supply chain and distribution model is outsourced. This increases TomTom's ability to scale up or down the supply chain, while limiting capital expenditure risks. But, at the same time, it depends on a limited number of third parties and in certain instances sole suppliers, for component supply and manufacturing, which increases its dependency on these suppliers.

TomTom's dynamic content sharing model uses high quality digital maps along with the connected services, like HD Traffic, Local Search with Google and weather information, provides our customers with relevant real-time information at the moment they need it, and this is helping them deliver the benefits of innovative technology directly to the end user and that to now at affordable prices. Although, the network externalities previously mentioned are one of the advantages of TomTom's LIVE, it has also increased TomTom's dependency on the network of the connected driving community. Bigger the network will be, the more effective would be the information from the guidance services.

Furthermore, in order to reduce operating expenses and strengthen the balance sheet, undue emphasis has been placed on the cost cutting program. Currently the cost reductions are made up of—Reduction of staff, Restructuring and integration of Tele Atlas, Reduced discretionary spending and Reduction in the number of contractors and Marketing spenditures. However, if not exceuted wisely it could hamper TomTom's long term objective of being a market leader. For example one of the core capabilities of any technology company is its staff; reducing it can hinder future innovative projects. Likewise, reducing the marketing expenditures in a market which still holds rich prospects of high growth. There are still 65% of US adults who don't own any kind of navigation system either a device, or in-car, or that of phone.[14]

Human Resources

Like any other technology company success of individual employees is very important to TomTom. Additionaly, TomTom has a vision that success for TomTom as a business should also mean success for the individual employee. Therefore, at TomTom, employee competency is taken very seriously and talent development programs are built around it. There is a personal navigation plan that provides employees with a selection of courses based on competencies in their profile. In 2008 TomTom completed its Young Talent Development Program which was aimed at broadening the participants' knowledge, while improving their technical and personal skills.

TOMTOM GROUP	TOMTOM	TELE ATLAS	WORK	AUTOMOTIVE
	B2C	B2B	B2B	B2B
→	→ Consumers	→ PND → Automotive → Mobile → Internet → GIS	→ Commercial fleets	→ Car industry → Car industry suppliers
	DYNAMIC CONTENT & PUBLISHING			
	SHARED TECHNOLOGIES			

TomTom's motto is to do business efficiently, profitably as well as responsibly. This underlines its corporate social responsibility. TomTom's headquarters is one of the most energy efficient buildings in Amsterdam. As mentioned before, earlier navigation was oriented towards making the drivers arrive their their destintion without getting lost. TomTom was the pioneer in introducing different technology that actually helps drivers to make their journeys safer and more economical. This shows their commitment to their customer base as well as to the community as a whole.

Issues of Concern for TomTom

First, TomTom is facing increasing competition from other platforms using GPS technology. Two main areas that come to mind are cell phones and smartphones. In the cell phone industry, Nokia is leading the charge in combing cell phone technology with GPS technology. They have a plan to put GPS technology in all their phones. Around the same time TomTom acquired Tele Atlas, Nokia also purchased Navteq, a competitor to Tele Atlas. With the acquisition of Navteq, Nokia hopes to shape the cell phone industry by merging cell phone, internet, and GPS technology together.

As we see the Smartphone industry emerging with the IPhone and the Palm Pre, we also see a shift in how people are able to utilize these technologies as a navigation tool. A big trend in smartphones these days are applications. Because of the ease of developing software on platforms for smartphones, more and more competitors are coming to the forefront and developing GPS navigation application.

For TomTom, both of these sectors might signal major change is in the horizon and that there is no longer a need for hardware for GPS navigation devices. And that we're heading towards a culture where consumers want an all-in-one device such as cell phone or Smartphone that will do everything they need including a GPS navigation services. In a recent study done by Charles Golvin for Forrester, he believes that by 2013 phone-based navigation will dominate the industry. And the reason is due to Gen Y and Gen X customers who are increasingly reliant on their mobile phone and who will demand social networking and other connected services integrated into their navigation experience[14].

The other problem TomTom is facing is a mature US & European personal navigation device market. After 3 years of steady growth in the PND market, TomTom has seen decreasing growth rate for PND sales. There could be many factors that are causing this such as the world wide recession but we felt that base on sales figure we're seeing the same trend in the US market as we have seen in the European market for TomTom. Initially entering the European market 12 months before entering the US market, TomTom has seen 21% dip in sales for the European market. Although, TomTom experiences some growth in the US market for 2008, they are noticing the growth rate has not been as good as the prior years.

Exhibit 1 Company history

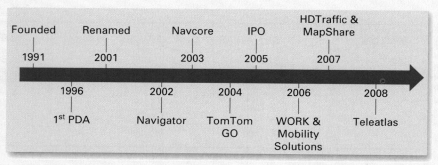

Exhibit 1 *(continued)*

Year	Historical Event
1991	Palmtop founded by Harold Goddijn, Peter-Frans Pauwels and Pieter Geelen.
1994	Corinne Vigreux joined the Company to sell Palmtop applications in Europe.
1996	First navigation software for PDAs, EnRoute and RouteFinder launched.
2001	Palmtop renamed TomTom. Harold Goddijn joins TomTom as CEO. Number of employees 30.
2002	First GPS-linked car navigation product for PDAs, TomTom NAVIGATOR shipped. €8 million revenue.
2003	NavCore Software Architecture developed, on which all TomTom products are still based. Number of employees 90.
2004	First portable navigation device shipped, the TomTom GO. 248,000 PND units sold.
2005	TomTom listed on Euronext Amsterdam. €720 million revenue.
2006	TomTom WORK and TomTom Mobility Solutions launched. Number of employees 818.
2007	TomTom makes offer for Tele Atlas. TomTom HD Traffic and TomTom Map Share launched. 9.6 million PND units sold.
2008	TomTom acquired Tele Atlas.

Source: http://investors.tomtom.com/overview.cfm

Exhibit 2 Sales Revenue and Net Income (€)

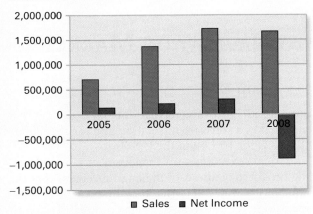

Exhibit 3 Quarterly sales (in millions €)

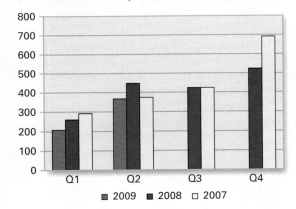

Exhibit 4 Revenue per segment

(in € millions)	Q1'09	Q1'08	y.o.y	Q4'08	q.o.q
Revenue	172	264	−35%	473	−64%
PNDs	141	234	−40%	444	−68%
Others	31	29	5%	29	5%
# of PNDs sold (in thousands)	1,419	1,997	−29%	4,443	−68%
Average selling price (€)	99	117	−15%	100	−1%

Exhibit 5 Revenue per region

(in € millions)	Q1'08	Q1'09	Difference
Europe	178,114	146,549	−22%
North America	84,641	55,558	−52%
Rest of world	1,087	10,976	90%
Total	263,842	213,083	−24%

Exhibit 6 Cash versus Long term debt (in thousand €)

	12/31/2005	12/31/2006	12/31/2007	12/31/2008	6/30/2009
Long Term Debt	301	338	377	4,749	4,811
Cash Assets	178,377	437,801	463,339	321,039	422,530
Borrowings	0	0	0	1,241,900	1,195,715

Exhibit 7 Operating Margin

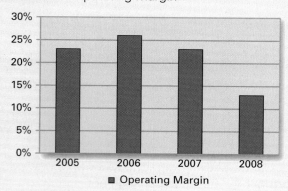

APPENDIX: GOOGLE DRIVES INTO NAVIGATION MARKET
RUETERS
Wed Oct 28, 2009 11:30 am EDT

SAN FRANCISCO (Reuters)—Google Inc. is adding Garmin Ltd and TomTom to its growing list of rivals as the Internet search giant weaves technology for driving directions into new versions of its smartphone software.

Google said its new Google Maps Navigation product will provide real-time, turn-by-turn directions directly within cell phones that are based on the new version of its Android software.

The navigation product, which features speech recognition and a visual display that incorporates Google's online archive of street photographs, marks the latest step by Google to challenge Apple Inc's iPhone and Microsoft Corp's Windows Mobile software with its Android smartphone software.

It also represents a direct competitive threat to companies like Garmin and TomTom which sell specialized hardware navigation devices. TomTom also makes a software navigation app for the iPhone that sells for $99.99 in the U.S.

Google executives told reporters at a press briefing on Tuesday ahead of the announcement that the company decided to offer turn-by-turn driving directions in its four-year-old maps product because it was the most requested feature by users.

CEO Eric Schmidt said that expanding into a new market with new competitors was not a part of Google's motivation.

"Those are tactical problems that occur after the strategic goal which is to offer something which is sort of magical on mobile devices using the cloud," Schmidt said.

The new navigation service will work with Google's forthcoming Android 2.0 software, the next version of the smartphone operating system developed by Google. The company announced development tools for Android 2.0 on Tuesday, but a spokeswoman said specific details about when Android 2.0 will be available should be directed to phone-makers and wireless carriers.

Google said the product, which will initially be limited to driving directions in the U.S., will be free for consumers.

Reporting by Alexei Oreskovic; Editing Bernard Orr © Thomson Reuters 2009 All rights reserved.

Bibliography

1. TeleAtlas Press Release. <http://www.teleatlas.com/WhyTeleAtlas/Pressroom/PressReleases/TA_CT015133>.
2. TomTom press release. TomTom and Avis Announce the First Pan-European Deal to Provide TomTom GO.
3. Compare GPS Sat Nav Systems. <http://www.satellitenavigation.org.uk/gps-manufacturers/tomtom/>; Daniel, Robert. TomTom Net Fell 61%, Revenue Off 19%. <http://www.foxbusiness.com/story/markets/industries/telecom/tomtom-net-fell—revenue/>.
4. TomTom Challenge. <http://www.tomtomchallenge.nl/resources/AMGATE_400083_1_TICH_R76719135691/>.
5. TomTom NV. <http://www.answers.com/topic/tomtom-n-v>.
6. TomTom. TomTom, portable GPS car navigation systems. <http://investors.tomtom.com/overview.cfm>.
7. Advanced Integrated Solutions. TomTom and Advantage Integrated Solutions Partner to Deliver an Intelligent Fleet Routing Solution for Businesses. March 2009. <http://www.highbeam.com/doc/1G1-196311252.html>.
8. Auto-Week Article. Renault, TomTom promise cheap navigation. <http://www.autoweek.com/article/20080929/free/809299989#ixzz0MQ8bKdYo>.
9. Boston Business Article. <http://www.boston.com/business/ticker/2009/06/let_homer_simps.html)>.
10. Garmin Website. <http://www8.garmin.com/about Garmin/>.
11. Gis Development Article. <http://www.gisdevelopment.net/technology/lbs/techlbs008.htm>.
12. Magellan Website. <http://www.magellangps.com/about/>.
13. Thomson Reuters. TomTom launches 2.9 bln euro bid for Tele Atlas. 19 November 2007. <http://www.reuters.com/article/technology-media-telco-SP/idUSL1839698320071119>.
14. Forrestor Research. "Phone-Based Navigation Will Dominate By 2013." 27 March 2009.
15. Hanstad, L. Anne. TomTom VP of Marketing Fletch. 27 September 2006.
16. J.D. Power and Associates. Garmin Ranks Highest in Customer Satisfaction with Portable Navigation Devices. 23 October 2008. <http://www.jdpower.com/corporate/news/releases/pressrelease.aspx?ID=2008221>.
17. Kim, W. Chan and Mauborgne. Blue Ocean Strategy. Boston: Harvard Business School Press, 2005.
18. Reuters. TomTom Inc. Recognized for Call Center Customer Satisfaction Excellence by J.D. Power. 7 January 2008. <http://www.reuters.com/article/pressRelease/idUS141391+07-Jan-2008+PRN20080107>.
19. TomTom AR-08. "TomTom Annual Report 2008." TomTom Annual Report 2008. December 2008.
20. TomTom Q2 2009. "Investor relations." TomTom Website. <http://investors.tomtom.com/reports.cfm?year=2009>.
21. Foley, Ryan. Chicago Tribune. 7 May 2009. 29 July 2009 <http://archives.chicagotribune.com/2009/may/07/news/chi-ap-wi-gps-police>.
22. GPS Magazine. GPS Magazine. 23 September 2007. 29 July 2009 <http://gpsmagazine.com/2007/09/gps_thefts_rise.php>.
23. ICTI. ICTI. 2009. 29 July 2009 <http://www.toy-icti.org/>.
24. Jones, Nick. Garnter. 5 January 2009. 29 July 2009 <http://www.gartner.com/resources/168400/168438/findings_risks_of_gps_perfor_168438.pdf>.
25. PriceGrabber.com. Price Grabber. April 2007. 29 July 2009 <https://mr.pricegrabber.com/2007_GPS_Pricing_Trends_Report.pdf>.
26. Richards, David. Smarthouse. 17 June 2009. 29 July 2009 <http://www.smarthouse.com.au/Automotive/Navigation/P4P3H9J8>.
27. Talaga, Tanya and Rob Ferguson. TheStar.com. 28 Oct 2008. 29 July 2009 <http://www.thestar.com/News/Ontario/article/525697>.
28. US News. US News. 14 October 2008. 29 July 2009 <http://usnews.rankingsandreviews.com/cars-trucks/daily-news/081014-GPS-Devices-Banned-in-Egypt/>.
29. Webist Media. Web Ecoist. 17 August 2008. 29 July 2009 <http://webecoist.com/2008/08/17/a-brief-history-of-the-modern-green-movement/>.

Viacom is Successful in 2011

Gareth R. Jones
Texas A&M University

CBS Broadcasting established Viacom as an independent company in 1970 to comply with regulations set forth by the U.S. Federal Communications Commission (FCC) barring television networks from owning cable TV systems, or from syndicating their own programs in the United States. The increasing spread of cable television and the continuing possibility of conflicts of interest between television networks and cable television companies made the spinoff necessary, and Viacom formally separated from CBS in 1971, when Viacom's stock was distributed to CBS shareholders.

Viacom quickly became one of the largest cable operators in the United States, with over 90,000 cable subscribers. It also owned the syndication rights to a large number of popular, previously run CBS television series that it made available for syndication to cable TV stations. In 1976, to take advantage of Viacom's experience in syndicating programming to cable TV stations, its managers decided to establish the Showtime movie network to directly compete with HBO, the leading outlet for films on cable television. In 1977, Viacom earned $5.5 million on sales of $58.5 million. Most of its earnings represented revenues from the syndication of its television series, but they also reflected growth of its own cable TV systems, which at this time had about 350,000 subscribers. Recognizing that both producing and syndicating television programming could earn greater profits, Viacom's managers decided to produce their own television programs in the late-1970s and early-1980s. Their efforts produced only mixed results, however, no hit series resulted from their work, and the Big Three television networks of ABC, NBC, and CBS continued to dominate the airwaves.

During the early-1980s, the push to expand the cable television side of its business was Viacom's managers' priority, and it rapidly grew its subscriber base. Viacom's managers, however, believed that its core cable operations were not a strong enough engine for future growth. Cable TV prices were regulated at this time, so cable companies had limited ability to increase prices, but its managers believed that real profit growth would come from providing the *content* of cable programming—television programs—not from just cable television service. Given that Viacom had failed to make its own successful new TV programs, its managers sought to acquire companies that made entertainment programs—the content. In 1981, Viacom started in a small way by buying a stake in Cable Health Network, a new advertiser-supported television network. Then, in September 1985, in a stroke of fortune, it made the acquisition that would totally change the company's future. Viacom purchased the MTV Networks from a competitor, Warner Bros., that desperately needed cash to invest in its own cable TV system to keep it viable. As it turned out, Warner Bros. had sold the jewel in its crown.

The MTV Networks included MTV, a new popular music video channel geared toward the 14–24 age groups; Nickelodeon, a channel geared toward children; and VH-1, a music video channel geared toward an older 25–44 age audience. MTV was the most popular property in the MTV Network. Its quick pace and flashy graphics attracted young television viewers who were a major target for large advertising companies, and the popularity of a TV station's programming determines how much a broadcast network can charge for advertising—which is why Super Bowl ads cost millions. MTV was performing well, but Nickelodeon had been less successful and had not achieved much of a following among young TV viewers, which limited its advertising revenues. Viacom's managers moved quickly to revamp Nickelodeon and give it the slick, flashy look of MTV. They developed unique programming to appeal to children—programming a very different aesthetic than *The Mickey Mouse Show*, which competitors like the Disney Channel offered. In the next few years, Nickelodeon went from being the least popular children's cable TV channel to being the most popular! Viacom's managers were confident that they had the foundation of a new content programming strategy to complement its cable TV interests to increase the company's profit growth.

Enter Sumner Redstone

Viacom's hopes were shattered when its Showtime channel lost 300,000 subscribers by 1986 because of intense competition from HBO, which, under its CEO Frank Biondi, had become the dominant subscriber movie channel. Viacom's cash flow plunged, it reported a loss in 1986, and, weakened by the $2 billion debt incurred to fund its growth, it became a takeover target.

After a 6-month battle to acquire the company Sumner M. Redstone bought Viacom for $3.4 billion in 1986. Redstone was the owner of National Amusements Inc. that owned and operated 675 movie theatres. Redstone had built NAI from 50 drive-in movie theaters to a modern theater chain and is credited with pioneering the multiplex movie theater concept. However, running a chain of movie theaters is very different from running a debt-laden media company like Viacom. Many analysts believed Redstone had overpaid for Viacom—but he saw a great potential for growth.

Aside from its cable television systems and syndication rights, which now included the popular TV series *The Cosby Show*, Redstone recognized the potential of its MTV and Nickelodeon channels. Also, Viacom had acquired 5 television and 8 radio stations in major markets that were also valuable properties. Redstone quickly moved to solve Viacom's problems and with his "hands-on," directive management style, he fired Viacom's top managers and searched for more capable managers who would be loyal to him. To turn Showtime around, he hired Frank Biondi, who had made HBO the major pay movie channel, as CEO of Viacom.

Viacom Speeds Up

Redstone bought Viacom because he believed that cable TV programming would become the main channel to deliver customers with entertainment content in the future. Redstone believed Viacom's MTV and Nickelodeon networks were its "crown jewels," they provided half the company's revenues and profits, which came both from subscribers (the cable companies that bought the programming) and from advertisers (who advertised on these channels). To strengthen these networks and build their brand name, Redstone hired a more aggressive advertising and sales management team, and against the expectations of industry analysts MTV and Nickelodeon experienced continuing growth and profitability. In 1989, for example, the MTV Networks won 15% of all dollars spent on TV cable advertising. Also, MTV was rapidly expanding throughout the world—broadcasting to Western Europe, Japan, Australia, large portions of Latin America, and eventually to countries in Asia.

Viacom in the 1990s

The problem facing Redstone and Biondi was how to position Viacom for profitable growth in the 1990s. Both executives felt that developing and expanding Viacom's strengths in developing entertainment content was the key to its future success, although this is a very expensive process. They believed that the message or content that is sent is what really mattered, not the distribution channel carrying it. As Biondi put it, "In the end, a pipe is just a pipe. The customer doesn't care how the information is obtained; all that matters is "the message." To build its entertainment programming strengths, Biondi worked hard to expand the success of Viacom's MTV channels. His goal was to promote the MTV networks as global brands that were perceived as having something unique to offer. Since MTV's viewers dominate the record-buying audience, Biondi sought to negotiate exclusive contracts that gave MTV the first crack at playing most major record companies' music videos—thus making it unique. At the same time, MTV went from being a purely music video channel to a channel that championed new kinds of innovative programming to appeal to a younger audiences, such as *Beavis and Butthead,* and *Road Stories,* that were interspersed with music videos.

In developing its programming strategy, however, Viacom's interest was not in promoting certain specific programs or stars—all of which may have short-lived popularity of fame—but in building its networks as unique brands. For example, on the MTV channel, the goal was to attract viewers because of what the channel as a whole personified—an appeal to youth. Soon, MTV reached 250 million households in 74 countries. Viacom began to perform much better: in 1992 it made profits of $48 million on sales of $1.86 billion, and in 1993 it made profits of $70 million on sales of $2 billion. While the development of innovative programming was one reason for Viacom's return to profitability, a second reason was Redstone's emphasis on keeping costs under control. Redstone is well known for his frugal way of doing business. He runs Viacom in a cost-conscious manner and this is evident throughout the organization. For example, costs soared in Hollywood studios and television networks as movie stars, writers, and production companies demanded ever increasing prices for their services. At Viacom, Redstone demanded that its own programming should be made by using low-cost, homegrown talent. An example of this is in the production of its MTV shows—most of its homegrown hosts are paid little compared to employees at well-known networks that are often paid millions of dollars per year.

Changes in the Media and Entertainment Industry

Although focused on building Viacom's programming strengths, Redstone and Biondi realized the entertainment industry was rapidly changing and that it was not at all clear how entertainment programming would be delivered, that is, through which distribution channels, in the future. In the 1990s, the U.S. cable television industry was in a state of flux as emerging technologies such as wireless satellite TV and Internet broadband threatened to bypass traditional cable systems—making Viacom's investment in wired cable much less valuable. Also, pressures were building to deregulate the industry so that by the end of the 1990s, companies in different industries—cable companies, telephone companies,

Internet service providers (ISPs), radio stations, and others, were allowed to enter each other's markets. These changes led to industry consolidation and the emergence of new giants such as Time Warner, News Corp., Comcast, and Disney, companies that were now all competing to offer the best selection of entertainment content or programming "software" as well as the best way to distribute this content through channels such as cable, wireless, or the Internet, the "hardware" side of the business.

Viacom's business model was based on the premise that to prosper in the fast-changing entertainment industry, a company needed to be the provider of the entertainment to all the different distribution channels. In other words, the most successful entertainment companies would be those that could offer programming suitable for any channel, and be the primary software providers—not the hardware providers that provided the infrastructure to bring entertainment into peoples' homes. With its well-known channels such as MTV, Nickelodeon, Showtime, and its syndicated programming, Viacom should base its strategy on forming alliances with the companies that provided the "hardware" channels into peoples' homes. Viacom's revenues would come both from the fees it charged to the hardware providers for its entertainment channels and most importantly, from the huge revenues it would obtain from selling advertising spots on its many popular TV shows, revenues that are determined by the size of the viewing audience. However, the issue was how to obtain high-quality programming at a price lower than the revenues to be earned from advertising and distributing its programs to maximize profits in an industry in which the value of entertainment and media companies was rocketing as stock prices increased.

The Paramount and Blockbuster Acquisitions

Viacom's new mission was to become an entertainment software-driven company with the goal to drive its entertainment content through every distribution channel possible, and to every world region to maximize revenues and profits. To achieve this mission, Viacom needed to acquire companies that could produce unique entertainment programming content for worldwide distribution. In particular, Viacom needed an entertainment company that had an established film/TV studio and library that could round out Viacom's current programming portfolio by supplying old feature films and TV shows to its television channels. Paramount Pictures provided an opportunity for this when it became an acquisition target in 1993.

Paramount's many businesses included entertainment including the production, financing, and distribution of motion pictures, television programming, the operation of movie theaters, independent television stations, regional theme parks, and Madison Square Garden. Paramount also owned a large library of movies. Redstone and Biondi began to picture the extensive synergies that a merger with Paramount would provide Viacom in the future. As Redstone told reporters, "This merger is not about two plus two equaling four, but six, or eight, or ten." Together Viacom and Paramount would be a much more efficient and profitable organization because, for example, Paramount could make films that featured MTV characters like Beavis and Butthead and new cable TV channels supported by Paramount's library of 1,800 films and 6,100 television programs. In 1993, after behind-the-scene talks between Redstone and Paramount executives, Paramount announced an $8.2 billion merger with Viacom. However, a bidding war for Paramount started when Barry Diller, CEO of QVC Network Inc., another large entertainment company, announced a hostile bid for Paramount. On September 20, 1993, QVC announced an $80 per share or $9.5 billion bid for Paramount, and the battle between Viacom and QVC for ownership of Paramount Communications Inc. had begun.

This unwelcome bid from QVS was a major problem for Redstone because Viacom still had a substantial debt due to the original 1987 acquisition of Viacom, and the expenses incurred to rapidly develop its own TV programming. Redstone could not afford to counter QVS's bid unless he obtained other sources of financing and cash flow. At the same time, Blockbuster Video's energetic CEO, Wayne Huizinga, who had made it the largest chain of video stores in the nation, was also on the market. Blockbuster was cash rich because of its rapid growth, but Huizinga recognized the growing threat that digital electronic entertainment channels, such as pay-per-view, wireless cable, and the

Internet, could pose to the sale and rental of movies and games in the future was looking for a buyer for Blockbuster. Redstone also knew that Blockbuster's future was in doubt because of the development of new digital entertainment distribution technologies, but now Redstone was in a war with Diller to acquire Paramount, and offers for the company soared. In January 1994, Viacom announced an $8.4 billion merger with Blockbuster; it also announced a higher bid for Paramount of $105 a share—a huge premium price—but this bid allowed Viacom to acquire Paramount in July 1994. Redstone hailed the new Viacom as an "entertainment colossus" and "a massive global media company."

Explosive Growth

In a few short years, Redstone had gone from controlling several hundred movie theaters to controlling the properties and franchises of three *Fortune 500* companies—Viacom, Blockbuster, and Paramount. By engineering the 3-way merger of Viacom, Paramount, and Blockbuster Entertainment, Redstone created one of the three largest global media empires (the others were Disney/Capital Cities ABC, and AOL Time Warner) each with annual revenues in excess of $10 billion. This was a large jump from the $2 billion revenue that Viacom had generated just before its new acquisitions. It was clear that Redstone and Biondi faced several major challenges to manage Viacom's new entertainment empire to allow it to achieve profitable growth.

Engineering Synergies

To justify the expensive purchase of Paramount and Blockbuster, it was essential that CEO Biondi engineer synergies between Viacom's different entertainment properties, each of which was now organized as a separate business division. Efforts began immediately, Paramount executives were instructed to evaluate the potential of new shows developed by MTV and Nickelodeon to sell to television networks. Viacom launched a new TV channel, the United Paramount Network (UPN) in 1995 to take advantage of its new programming resources across its entertainment divisions. For example, MTV executives were instructed to quickly begin developing programming for UPN.

In another attempt to create synergies, Paramount executives were instructed to make their moviemaking skills available to the MTV Network, and to help it make inexpensive movies that could be distributed through Paramount. One result of this was a "Beavis and Butthead" movie produced by Paramount that proved very successful when it was launched in theatres in 1996. To keep costs low, Redstone's strategy was to boost the output of movies at Paramount, while at the same time keeping its budget under control and forcing its managers to find ways to make low-budget successful movies—not an easy task. Redstone and Biondi also searched for synergies between Blockbuster and Viacom's other divisions, hoping that Blockbuster could link its retail stores with Viacom's cable networks and Paramount's extensive film library. Perhaps Blockbuster could sell copies of Paramount's vast library of movies to encourage people to create their own DVD collections. Also, the release of a new Paramount movie on DVD could be timed to coincide with a major advertising campaign in Blockbuster stores to promote the launch. Finally, the launch of new movies could be timed to accompany a major advertising blitz on the MTV channel—something that happened when Paramount released *Mission Impossible* in 1996. Redstone claimed that: "Viacom through its new combination of assets is poised to participate in, and in many ways define, the entertainment and information explosion about to engulf the globe." As events turned out, however, few potential synergies emerged between Viacom's various divisions to help boost revenues and profits.

Media and Entertainment Industry Challenges

The fast-changing entertainment and media industry created many challenges for Redstone and Biondi especially because the major U.S. entertainment companies were all rapidly expanding and the industry was consolidating. Seven major studios dominated movie production and the "Big Three" networks—ABC, CBS, and NBC—had for years dominated the production of TV programming for the mass audience. The growing strength of Viacom spurred industry consolidation; in 1995 AOL Time Warner announced that it would merge with Turner Broadcasting; Disney announced that it would merge with Capital Cities/ABC; and News Corp. that had established the Fox channel and owned the 20th Century Fox was also buying new entertainment channels—especially online digital channels. As a result, the industry was now composed of four major players: Disney, AOL Time Warner, News Corp., and Viacom, which was the fourth biggest company.

A major threat by the mid-1990s was that the number of entertainment distribution channels was exploding as government regulations prevented broadcast networks from owning TV programming companies and so on were phased out. Viacom's strategy to develop a full line of movie and TV entertainment programming had also spurred changes in the competitive dynamics of the entertainment and media industry as many new small independent movie and TV studios, such as Pixar and DreamWorks, were established to provide attractive new programming that could be sold to movie distributors and cable TV providers.

The industry was also experiencing rapid globalization as U.S. movies, news, and TV shows were now being shown around the world. A major challenge facing Viacom was to obtain access to the global marketplace to increase revenues and profits, for example, there was a potential market of over a billion viewers in India and China. As one example of Viacom's global strategy in 1995, Viacom won a cable television license to launch its Nickelodeon and VH-1 channels in Germany, Europe's biggest and potentially most lucrative media market, to complement the MTV pop music network that had operated in Europe since 1987. However, all this global expansion was expensive and Viacom's cost structure increased, which resulted in lower profits.

New technology challenges also confronted Viacom and the media industry because advances in digital technology, including streaming audio and video over the Internet began to offer online companies viable new channels to distribute entertainment content. Just as the dominance of the Big Three networks had been eroded by the growth of companies like Viacom with its new programming networks, so now new channels to distribute content to consumers were now threatening major entertainment companies. Moreover, digital piracy had become a major threat to these companies, as Websites such as Napster and LimeWire were developed to exchange digital music and movie files. This was also a major threat to revenues and profits and by the 2000s digital piracy resulted in major entertainment companies losing billions in potential revenues—even new movie releases were often available illegally online for download just days after being introduced in movie theaters.

Major Problems for Viacom

Soon after Redstone's expensive decision to buy Paramount, its new movie *Forrest Gump* became a surprise hit that generated over $250 million for Viacom and silenced analysts who argued that he had spent far too much to purchase the movie studio. Viacom's managers began to feel like *Forrest Gump* with his philosophy that: "Life is like a box of chocolates: You never know what you're going to get." It seemed that Redstone and Viacom had been in the right place at the right time and had made a profitable acquisition. Just as Redstone had sensed the potential of MTV, he had also sensed the potential of Paramount and Blockbuster. By the end of 1995, however, the selection of chocolates in Viacom's box had gone downhill as many of the hoped-for synergies were not obtained. Before the merger, Redstone claimed that Blockbuster would be valuable to Viacom as a distributor of its creative programming—but few benefits of this kind were achieved. Analysts argued that Paramount had to cooperate more closely with Viacom's cable TV channels and Blockbuster to achieve synergies.

Most importantly, both the Paramount and Blockbuster divisions' performance had proved disappointing. The Gump smash hit was followed by a string of expensive failures that lost hundreds of millions, and Redstone began to realize that making hit movies is a highly risky business—past successes are no indication of future success. Paramount's share of box office revenues dropped by 5% during 1995, but the marketing and production costs to make its movies were rapidly increasing. Paramount's poor performance hurt Viacom's cash flow and ability to pay its huge debts.

Viacom's situation was made worse because Blockbuster was also not performing well. Redstone bought Blockbuster at the peak of its success—when its revenues were doubling every year and its free cash flow was a valuable asset. But after the acquisition, Blockbuster ran into increased competition from new rival video chains, such as Hollywood

Video, that were creating a price war in some markets, while pay-per-view and on demand television was spreading rapidly in large urban markets. Blockbuster's revenues were flat; its costs were increasing and the hoped-for growth in cash flow to service Viacom's debts did not occur.

Redstone fell out with the top management teams of Paramount and Blockbuster that he thought were doing a poor job; he forced the resignations of key executives and went in search of new leadership talent. Then, in 1996, he announced that he was firing his second-in-command Frank Biondi because Biondi did not have the "hands-on skills" needed to manage the kinds of problems that Viacom was facing. Redstone felt that Biondi's decentralized management style was out of place in a company actively searching for synergies and cost reductions. In place of Biondi he promoted his two lieutenants, Philippe Dauman and Tom Dooley, to orchestrate Viacom's strategy despite that they had little direct experience with the entertainment business.

Viacom's New Moves

In 1996, Redstone hired William Fields, a senior Walmart manager who had extensive experience using IT to run efficient retail operations, to be Blockbuster's new CEO. Redstone hoped he could find a way to transform the Blockbuster Video stores into broader based entertainment-software stores because video cassettes were being replaced by DVDs, and new wireless cable, DSL telephone, and direct broadcasting technologies, such as the DISH network, were rapidly expanding.

However, it was too late; in early-1996 Viacom's stock price plunged from $55 to $35 as investors fled the stock because of problems at Blockbuster and Paramount. By summer of that year, after a string of flops, Redstone announced plans to cut back the number of movies Paramount would make and to reduce its production costs as he searched for a new strategy. Chief among Viacom's problems was its huge debt that had to be pruned by selling its assets. Also, Viacom had to find ways to reduce rising operating costs as well new ways to leverage resources and competences across divisions to increase revenues and build cash flow. Flat revenues and soon-to-be losses at Blockbuster and Paramount were pulling down the performance of the whole corporation.

Blockbuster was now a growing liability, and Field's efforts were not bearing quick results.

In fact, Blockbuster's revenues were falling, and in 1997, Fields left and Redstone brought in a new CEO, John Antioco, and they streamlined Blockbuster's operations. (See the Blockbuster case for detailed information on its new strategy.) They also introduced the radical idea of video-rental revenue sharing with the movie studios, and within a few years, Blockbuster's revenue stream was increasing again.

On the revenue side, there were signs that some potential synergies were emerging. Paramount did produce successful *Beavis and Butthead* movies. Viacom's global presence was widening as its TV studios developed new and customized channels to meet the demands of customers in different countries around the world. In 1997, growing demand for its entertainment content led Viacom to buy the rest of Spelling Entertainment, with its *Star Trek* franchise, to help its struggling UPN network that was failing (it became part of CBS in 2006). Redstone integrated Spelling Entertainment into Paramount's TV operations to obtain economies of scale and scope in the production of new television programming—such as new *Star Trek* programming that has proved to be highly profitable.

Although Redstone was focused on creating long-term benefits from his entertainment empire, the poor performance of Viacom's stock was a continual embarrassment to him because he had not been able to realize the potential of Viacom's entertainment assets. However, Blockbuster enjoyed increasing revenues in 1999 because of its revenue sharing agreement, and this gave Redstone the opportunity he needed to dispose of this risky asset. Viacom announced that Blockbuster stock would be listed separately from Viacom's so its performance could be evaluated separately. Approximately 18% of Blockbuster's stock was sold at $16 to $18 a share, and this raised over $250 million that was used to pay off Viacom's debt.

Also in 1999, Redstone hired the experienced media and entertainment manager, and former head of CBS, Mel Karmazin, as Viacom's CEO to help solve its ongoing problems. Karmazin had made his reputation by selecting hit TV programming, and for his hands-on ability to find ways to leverage resources to increase profitability. He set to work to restructure Viacom's different entertainment assets to engineer cross-divisional synergies, create new programming content, and enhance its revenue and earnings.

Both Redstone and Karmazin understood that the most important source of profits from owning an entertainment empire was to achieve economies of scale and scope that arise when a company is able to offer large companies the opportunity to advertise their products across multiple channels that attract different kinds of viewers. In other words, a potential advertiser could produce one or more themed commercials to run across all of Viacom's different TV networks as well as its movies, theme parks, and other channels. Redstone noted that Disney merged with the Capital/ABC networks to provide it with important new distribution and advertising channels for the Disney franchise.

Since the majority of Viacom's future revenue stream would come from the success of its advertising, Redstone established a new unit, Viacom Plus, to provide a centralized advertising service to manage relationships with large companies and handle advertising for *all* of Viacom's divisions. For example, in 2001, Procter & Gamble (P&G) and Viacom Plus negotiated a new cross-channel deal whereby P&G would pay $300 million for advertising spread across 9 of Viacom's major divisions. This deal worked out so well for P&G it paid $350 million in 2002 for advertising spread across 14 of Viacom's divisions. P&G could obtain a much better deal than if it negotiated with each Viacom channel separately and Viacom Plus had reduced the costs of managing the vital advertising process across the company. Other companies followed P&G's lead to "scatter" their advertising dollars across Viacom's different channels and reach different demographic groups including children who watched Nickelodeon, teens who tuned into MTV, and different groups of adults who watched its different network programming. The future of the Viacom advertising platform looked bright indeed, perhaps it could provide the platform for giving the company the synergies it needed to boost revenues and profits.

The CBS Acquisition

To capitalize on advertising synergies, a new opportunity arose in 1999 when CBS was in trouble because of falling ratings, and its managers were interested in merging with another entertainment company. Redstone decided that CBS's entertainment assets would give Viacom access to a much larger number of channels to reach the greatest number of viewers and listeners (CBS-owned Infinity Radio Broadcasting) of any media enterprise, spanning all ages and demographics from "cradle to cane." This would allow Viacom to become the premier outlet for large companies around the world because it could offer them the opportunity to achieve huge economies of scale and scope when spending their advertising dollars. Advertising content could be driven and promoted across all media segments, including broadcast and cable television, radio, outdoor advertising and new digital media. Also, channels such as MTV, MTV2, VH-1, and CMT could now be broadcast over Trinity's radio stations and over the Internet, and CBS's high-quality content, such as its news and sports programming, could be broadcast over all Viacom's properties. After the merger, Viacom's bigger empire would also give it more bargaining power with programming suppliers (to reduce programming costs) and allow it to maximize the effectiveness of its advertising salesforce across all its divisions. Perhaps Viacom's problem was that it was simply not big enough to generate higher revenues and profits?

In 2000, Viacom and CBS Corp. began the process of merging the operations of the two companies to create the largest global media company, because they believed that "biggest is the best." The range of Viacom's properties was now staggering in its scope, especially because CBS had acquired radio station owner Infinity Broadcasting and King World productions that syndicated such programs as *Jeopardy* and the *Oprah Winfrey Show*. Karmazin now gave his full attention to structuring and managing Viacom's new assets to realize the gains from sharing and leveraging the competencies of its divisions across all its entertainment operations—not an easy thing to do given all the uncertainties involved in managing their different business models and a rapidly changing industry environment.

However, it began to appear that the CBS acquisition had given Viacom the critical mass it needed to achieve advertising synergies and cost savings. Karmazin integrated Paramount's and CBS' television groups, and the new division consisted of 35 television stations reaching 18 of the top 20 U.S. television markets. CBS would now function as a local as well as a national broadcaster, and it could

leverage its news, sports, and other programming across many more of Viacom's channels. Viacom's TV studios also formed a unit called MTV Films to produce movies for Paramount. Some of its low-budget movies made a profit including *The Rugrats* and *Beavis and Butthead Do America*.

In yet another move to make it the number 1 advertising platform in the world for advertisers with programming that appealed to every demographic category, in 2001, Viacom acquired Black Entertainment Television (BET) for $3 billion. The BET network reaches 63.4 million U.S. households, and its other channels, like BET on Jazz and BET International, reach 30 countries in Europe and 36 in Africa. Continuing its strategy of leveraging value from its properties, BET began to seek ways to integrate its activities with other Viacom properties, both by customizing various Viacom TV programming for BET's channels, and vice versa, such as its popular shows and also news and sports programming.

Karmazin instructed all of Viacom's networks to follow MTV's lead and develop a global strategy to locally produce content in each country in which they were broadcasting in order to increase the company's global viewing audience. MTV, for example, has a presence in most of the world's major markets; it reaches a billion households and generates crucial revenues for Viacom today. And, while it broadcasts its U.S. programming in countries abroad, it had also produced successful shows in countries abroad that are customized to local tastes; these have proved so popular that they have been successfully transferred to the United States and other countries.

Viacom's stock climbed in 2002 despite the huge fall in advertising revenues caused by the 2000 recession that caused the earnings of its broadcast networks to drop by 20%. Nevertheless, analysts believed that Viacom was the best-positioned media company to benefit from the upswing in advertising that was expected in the 2000s because of its combination of large-scale operations and leading brands. Reeling from the downturn in advertising revenues, Redstone and Karmazin continued to seek ways to counter future threats to the Viacom empire particularly because the threat from digital and broadband technology was directly impacting its Blockbuster unit, and would in the future, threaten Viacom's distribution channels.

Indeed, many analysts reported that Mel Karmazin and Redstone had locked heads on many occasions about emerging strategic issues having to do with digital and programming content. Karmazin was especially critical of Redstone's expensive acquisitions that increased debt, but had not yet realized the benefits that had been expected. Karmazin also argued that Viacom needed to increase its online presence as quickly as possible. However, in 2002, the increased revenues and profits resulting from the CBS and BET acquisitions suggested that Redstone's "growth-by-acquisition" strategy was working. Karmazin joked that their management styles were complementary, and that he was in no rush to assume leadership of Viacom, especially since the 79-year-old Redstone was "good for another 30–40 years—at least!" Redstone, however, joked that when Karmazin's contract expired in 2003, Karmazin "might want to retire." Karmazin's response? "Never, never, never."

New Problems for Viacom

In the early-2000s, Viacom made no significant acquisitions, Redstone felt his company has all the right pieces of entertainment property in place and the company still had a huge debt load. Redstone believed the primary strategic problem facing Karmazin was to manage Viacom's assets to realize the huge potential stream of advertising revenues and profits locked up in its entertainment assets. Operating revenues from its entertainment division, which included Paramount Pictures and theme parks, rose by 46% in 2003, and its operating income was up 15% to $66 million as a result of higher movie ticket sales and stronger sales of DVDs. Its Viacom Plus unit continued to aggressively market its "one-stop-shopping approach across all marketing channels," and as the economy picked up in 2003, advertising revenues rebounded. In 2004, Viacom announced its overall revenues were up 11% and half the increase was due to increased advertising revenues.

The Growing Use of the Internet

While national advertising revenues on Viacom's many cable channels rebounded, however, local advertising revenues from its TV stations, including the CBS network, and from its radio stations were falling and hurting the company's performance; fewer and fewer people were watching or listening to local channels—preferring to watch their favorite cable channels or to surf the Web. Slowly but steadily, the growing use of the Internet and new online digital media properties were taking away advertising revenues and Viacom was slow to realize the dangers the Internet posed as a major alternative entertainment channel. Competition began to increase as new Websites that offered specialist services, such as www.rottentomatoes.com (a movie review Website owned by News Corp.), video Websites such as YouTube, and a host of illegal Websites that offered free downloading of video content, had emerged. Viacom's revenues fell, but perhaps this was a temporary phenomenon because Redstone and Karmazin announced they expected major increases in revenues and profits in the future.

Problems at CBS

Another major problem for Viacom was that its acquisition of CBS was not generating the hoped for cost savings or synergies that drive revenue growth. When a company buys different kinds of media properties and channels, it also enters new industries and faces different sets of competitive opportunities and threats! Investors became increasingly wary of Viacom's stock because they no longer believed Redstone or Karmazin could manage its new assets—and they found it much more difficult to evaluate the real value of each of its many media properties and channels, especially its Blockbuster division.

Spinning off Blockbuster into a separate company would eliminate this source of uncertainty; in 2004, when Blockbuster's stock was trading at a recent new high of $20, Viacom announced it would divest its remaining shareholding in Blockbuster. By making the deal attractive to Viacom stockholders, Redstone was finally able to divest the unit which became an independent company headed by its CEO John Antioco. (See the Blockbuster case for what has happened since.)

Viacom's Failing Business Model: Bye Bye CBS

Viacom had failed to realize the importance of building strong online entertainment assets when they were cheap, and it now lagged behind major competitors like Disney and News Corp. At the same time, despite having spent 5 years developing strategies to realize the value from the 2000 CBS acquisition, it was clear that Redstone and Karmazin had failed. Adding TV and radio stations and a host of other media assets to Viacom's TV channel and movie programming empire had increased the strategic problems associated with managing its empire of media assets. Redstone learned the hard way that the different divisions of a company grow at different rates, and the performance of the weakest division pulls down the performance of the whole company—and Viacom's growth was slowing fast. Its CBS assets, like Blockbuster had before, could not meet Viacom's aggressive growth targets. Redstone was frustrated once again that Viacom's underperforming assets were dragging down its stock price, which by 2004, was almost half of its 2000 stock price! Karmazin had warned Redstone about this, and the personal relationship between Redstone and Karmazin now deteriorated fast. Redstone fired Karmazin (who was the CEO of SiriusXM Radio in 2011).

In 2005, to improve Viacom's future growth, Redstone announced that he would split the $60 billion conglomerate into two smaller, separately traded companies. CBS would be allocated Viacom's slow and steady growth properties and channels, such as CBS TV programming and TV and radio stations, Showtime, outdoor advertising, and so on. The future Viacom would be made up of high potential growth properties and channels such as MTV, Nickelodeon, BET Networks, and Paramount Studios—essentially the company's focus after it divested Viacom, and before it merged with CBS. CBS was also allocated slow-growth Paramount Parks, which it later sold to amusement park operator Cedar Fair in 2006. The split took effect at the beginning of 2006 and effectively retracted the Viacom/CBS merger.

The New Viacom Business Model

After a decade of growth by acquisition, Viacom, like other media conglomerates, such as Sony, Disney, and Time Warner, began to reconfigure its business model. These companies were now being pushed hard by new Internet technologies and changing customer viewing habits that had altered the channels on which they could hope to obtain maximum advertising revenues—still the main source of

revenues upon which most entertainment companies depended. By the 2000s, the cookie-cutter business model, whereby a media giant could simply add new media properties to its existing ones to increase profitability, had been shown to be a failure—at least in terms of generating consistent increases in a company's stock price.

As noted above, Redstone's focus upon fixing the ongoing problems with his media empire also delayed his recognition of the growing importance of the Internet as an entertainment distribution channel and the threat of competition from (illegal) digital video downloading and streaming media. In the mid-2000s, Viacom moved to acquire some small Internet media properties such as Neopets, a virtual pet Website, and Xfire, iFilm, Quizilla.com, Harmonix Music Systems, and Atom Entertainment, that served niche markets. However, these acquisitions didn't have the reach of News Corp.'s acquisition of the social networking company MySpace, which was valued at $3 billion (although it had been bought for only a few hundred million in 2004). Viacom was much slower than its rivals to react to the changes in digital and Internet technologies taking place, and its stock price continued to suffer. The entertainment company with the best digital strategy in the 2000s had been News Corp.

As the "unknown" names of its Internet acquisitions suggest, Viacom was failing in its attempt to develop a strong, coherent Internet strategy. This strategic failure hurt its stock price, which had risen to $45 after the 2005 split, but now plunged to $35 in 2006. Redstone, as usual, responded by firing Viacom's CEO, blaming him for the company's poor performance, and appointed Philippe Dauman as the new CEO of Viacom. Dauman had been one of Redstone's top strategists for decades, and a top Viacom executive from 1994 to 2000—he was now in charge of maximizing the value from Viacom's assets.

In his first public statement, Dauman claimed he had free reign to develop a new business model, and that he wasn't simply a pawn for Redstone to use and then discard. If Redstone attempted to micromanage or meddle in operational issues Dauman said, "I can push back." He also indicated he would work to create a new business model based on "creative excellence" and focus on strategic movie, TV channel and Internet internal ventures and acquisitions. Dauman claimed Viacom still had an enormous potential for achieving internal "organic growth," meaning that it could innovate new entertainment products internally and increase the value from its first-class set of entertainment properties and channels. He noted that BET and Comedy Central had a huge future potential and that even established brands such as MTV and Nickelodeon could be developed to offer a much wider range of programming to attract different kinds of customers. As a result, Viacom would be able to increase its advertising revenues by offering large companies the opportunity to reach the mass audience, and targeted marketing toward specific customer groups, which was becoming increasingly important in the 2000s. Once again, a division similar to Viacom's centralized marketing division, which had been closed down, was reactivated to focus on increasing advertising revenues. If this failed, then further divestitures seemed likely because the new Viacom had to realize the value from its assets in order to pay down its huge debt.

In late-2006, Viacom reported a 16% fall in third-quarter profit as weakness at the box office from unprofitable movies offset strength in cable and higher advertising revenues. Viacom's recovering share price plunged; as usual, Redstone fired someone, this time its chief financial officer, and he said that Viacom would now "move rapidly to the forefront of emerging digital markets, keeping us on the path to outstanding long-term financial performance and free cash flow generation." Clearly, even managing a smaller, more focused media company to achieve profitable growth is a difficult task—especially when each of its different divisions face complex problems and agile competitors.

Dauman's Creates a Successful Business Model for Viacom

In 2007, CEO Dauman faced difficult choices in deciding upon the right corporate and business strategies to pursue to create a profitable future business model for the company. Having an 83-year-old owner in charge was probably not the best thing for Dauman, or for Viacom's shareholders, apart from Redstone himself, of course. Dauman set to work after observing the reasons for the failures and firings of its several last CEOs. Since 2007, Dauman has made few acquisitions, although it bought

RateMyProfessors.com in 2007, and acquired the global franchise for *Teenage Mutant Ninja Turtles* in 2009. He did however, form several strategic alliances to increase the value of Viacom's assets such as several joint ventures with Indian companies to expand its presence in a country with almost a billion viewers, and with U.S. media companies to find better ways to make use of their resources. He also sold some of its little-known online assets such as Harmonix Music Systems and Famous Music to Sony to exit the music business.

His new focus was upon finding ways to use Viacom's assets in creative ways. For example, he created a new specialty movie division called Paramount Vantage, and Paramount decided to take control of distributing its own movies in the 15 major markets outside the United States. Also, a major rebranding of its TV networks took place as the company developed increasing numbers of TV channels to further segment its network viewing audience to directly target specific customer groups. For example, its Nickelodeon network now includes channels such as Nickelodeon, Nick at Night, Nick.com, Nick Jr., Teen Nick, Nickelodeon Kids, Nick Toons, Nickelodeon Virtual Worlds, and Family Games! The costs of such increased differentiation and market segmentation has been spurred by the development of digital technologies that dramatically reduce the costs involved in creating new channels. At the same time, differentiation provides a way to attract advertisers, who wish to focus on a specific market segment and are willing to pay for it. It has made the same kinds of changes to its global MTV networks that today allow for increasing customization of programming, both between and within countries, and new ideas are quickly transferred around the world and have resulted in several hit new shows.

Most importantly, Dauman recruited a top management team of media experts to develop hit new shows for its networks, shows that could be made at relatively low costs, such as reality programming. In the last 5 years, Viacom has excelled at creating new shows that have resulted in major increases in its advertising revenues and profits. At the same time, Dauman has been vigilant to protect the value of Viacom's digital content, and in 2009, it sued Google because it claimed its YouTube channel was allowing the streaming of thousands of its TV shows and movies. It lost the suit, but Google has been forced to more closely monitor the content being uploaded onto YouTube. In addition, realizing it was too late to establish its own online entertainment distribution channels, Dauman has been increasingly working to form strategic alliances with distribution companies such as Netflix and Hulu and license the rights to show its programming content in return for a share of the revenues. Given that once the programming has been made and shown on its own networks, where it receives advertising revenues to cover the costs of production and make a profit, almost all the revenues it makes from online streaming agreements translate into profits. This is also true of streaming its Paramount movies through other distribution channels, where it can at least obtain some revenue by attracting customers that dislike illegal downloading, and are willing to pay a modest fee to obtain Viacom's content in a safe and legal manner. Every dollar Viacom obtains from licensing its content results in 90% profit because the costs of making its content available to Internet distributors are extremely low.

Viacom in 2011

How well has Dauman's new business strategy succeeded? Perhaps the best way to evaluate this is to look at Viacom's financial results released in August 2011, and the new business model behind the company. Viacom announced that its third-quarter earnings grew 37% because its portfolio of entertainment properties resulted in growing advertising sales and higher fees from cable TV companies that wish to show its programming, and by online companies, such as Netflix, that want to stream its content. The media company earned $574 million, or $0.97 per share, up 37% from $420 million (or $0.69 per share) a year earlier.

Advertising and programming revenues grew because of the success of its new movies, TV networks and its new TV shows such as "Jersey Shore" and "16 and Pregnant." CEO Dauman said the "breadth of hit programming found across Viacom's media network portfolio was the major contributor to its strong advertising growth. In a press release, Dauman said: "Our media networks are creating hit after hit, sought after by both audiences and advertisers, and Paramount Pictures is putting together a truly unprecedented year of box office success." Viacom said revenue from its media or TV networks division that includes MTV, Nickelodeon and other channels grew 16%; revenues from its Paramount film division increased by 13%, thanks to gains in DVD sales and TV license revenue. At the same time, global advertising revenue grew by 14%, which was more than in the previous quarter—a sign that the global advertising market was improving.

In addition, Viacom's efforts to secure more revenues from the cable and wireless TV providers, and online digital providers that want to show its entertainment content, also increased by 19%. This includes revenues from Viacom's older TV shows such as "SpongeBob SquarePants," and especially from new shows such as "Jersey Shore" and Comedy Central's "The Sarah Silverman Show." Its agreement with Hulu and Netflix significantly boosted revenues. Its blockbuster film *Transformers: Dark of the Moon* was released too late to contribute to its reported profits, so it expects a continuing improvement in revenues through 2011.

In 2011, it seemed that Dauman had been able to realize the value in Viacom's assets, and had been able to develop new potential sources of revenue. He had also kept the company's cost structure under control while pursuing new low-cost digital avenues to expand its revenues. How well has Viacom performed compared to its competitors over the last 5 years? In August 2011, while its stock price had increased by 150%, Disney's had increased by 20%, while News Corp. had fallen by 16%, and Time Warner's had fallen by 38%. Under Dauman, Viacom finally appears to be managing its entertainment assets and channels to add value to the company; if its good performance continues, it will be able to reduce its debt and develop new entertainment content that will provide new sources of revenue and profit for the future.

Endnotes

www.amazon.com, 1997–2011.
Amazon.com, Annual and 10K Reports, 1997–2011.

CASE 13

The Apollo Group

Charles W.L. Hill
University of Washington

Introduction

Which is the largest university system in the United States? After some thought, you might be tempted to answer that it is giant the University of California system with its 11 campuses and 208,000 students. You would be wrong. The largest provider of high education in the United States is the University of Phoenix, which has over 400,000 students, and operates around 200 campuses and learning centers in 39 states. The University of Phoenix is the flagship subsidiary of the Apollo Group, which also runs Western International University, the Institute for Professional Development and the College for Financial Planning. In total, the Apollo Group served some 470,000 students in 2010.

The Apollo Group has been a very successful enterprise. Between 1996 and 2010, its revenues expanded from $214 million to $4.9 billion and net profits increased from $21.4 million to $553 million. The University of Phoenix accounts for about 90% of the revenues of the Apollo Group. Apollo's return on invested capital, a key measure of profitability, averaged around 30% over this period, well above its cost of capital, which has been calculated to be around 10%.[1]

The Apollo Group is also a controversial enterprise. Founded by John Sperling, a former economic history professor and one time union organizer at San Jose State University, the University of Phoenix has been depicted by defenders of the educational establishment as a low quality "diploma mill" that has commoditized education and which is willing to sacrifice educational standards for the opportunity to make profits. Scott Rice, a San Jose State University English Professor who has become a vocal critic of for-profit education, summarizes this view when he states that "John Sperling's vision of education is entirely mercenary. It's merely one more opportunity to turn a buck. When education becomes one more product, we obey the unspoken rule of business: to

give consumers as little as they will accept in exchange for as much as they will pay. Sperling is a terrible influence on American education."[2]

Sperling, who was still chairman in 2010 despite being 90 years old, certainly does not see things this way. In his view, the University of Phoenix serves a niche that the educational establishment has long ignored, working adults who need a practical education in order to further their careers, and cannot afford the commitment associated with full-time education. Some high powered academics agree. The Nobel Prize winning economist Milton Friedman regard the triumph of the for-profit sector as inevitable, because traditional universities are run "by faculty, and the faculty is interested in its own welfare."[3]

Some analysts suggest that the for-profit sector still has significant growth opportunities ahead of it. The postsecondary education market in the United States is estimated to be worth over $430 billion, with only $20–$25 billion of that currently captured by for-profit enterprises. Looking forward, analysts expect enrollment at for-profit schools to grow as they gain share from traditional higher educational institutions. Supporting this thesis are estimates that 37% of all students (more than 6 million) are older than 24, a large portion of whom are likely to be working and will be attracted to the flexibility that the for-profit sector provides.[4]

On the other hand, the traditional educational establishment is not blind to this opportunity. Many long established public and private not-for-profit universities are now offering part-time degree programs and online degrees aimed at working adults. Some believe that this emerging threat, coupled with the brand advantage enjoyed by big name universities, will limit enrollment growth going forward at the University of Phoenix and similar institutions.

The outlook for the for-profit sector was further clouded in the late-2000s when the sector was attacked in the media, and in Congress, for aggressive recruiting practices and high drop-out rates. More than 80% of the revenue of for-profit institutions comes from government financial aid. Critics claim that companies in this sector targeted low-income students who were most likely to receive student aid, but who may be ill prepared for course work. Those who do graduate often default their loans, leaving the taxpayer to pick up the bill. In June 2011, the Department of Education issued new regulations that were designed to limit such practices.

John Sperling and the Birth of the University of Phoenix

University of Phoenix founder John Sperling was born in rural Missouri in 1921, in a cabin that already housed a family of six.[5] His mother was overbearing, his father habitually beat him. When his father died, Sperling recalled that he could hardly contain his joy. Sperling barely graduated from high school and went off to join the merchant marine—as far away from Missouri as he could get. There he started his real education, reading through the books of his shipmates, many of whom were socialists. Sperling emerged from this experience an unabashed liberal with a penchant for challenging the status quo—something that he still delights in (among other things, Sperling is a regular financial contributor to ballot initiatives aimed at legalizing marijuana).

After two years in the merchant marine, Sperling went to Reed College in Oregon. This was followed by a Master's at Berkeley and a PhD in Economic History at the University of Cambridge. A conventional academic seemed the logical next step for Sperling. By the 1960s, he was a tenured professor of Economic History at San Jose State University. Always the activist, he joined the American Federation of Teachers (AFT) and rose to state and national positions in the union. In his leadership role at the AFT, he persuaded professors at San Jose State to mount a walkout to support striking professors at San Francisco State University. The strike was a failure and almost resulted in the mass firing of 100 professors. Sperling lost his credibility on campus. He was widely reviled and lost his position as head of the United Professors of California, a union that he had built almost single handedly. But Sperling claims that the humiliating defeat taught him an important

lesson: "It didn't make a goddamn but of difference what people thought of me. Without that psychological immunity, it would have been impossible to create and protect the University of Phoenix from hostility, legal assaults, and attempts to legislate us out of existence."[6]

By the early-1970s, Sperling's academic career was going nowhere—but that was all about to change. As part of a federal project to fight juvenile delinquency, San Jose State University arranged a series of courses for the police and school teachers who had to deal with the youngsters. Sperling, who had been experimenting with novel approaches to delivering education, was to run the workshops. He devised a curriculum, divided the classes into small groups, brought in teachers who were expert practitioners in their field to lead each group (none of whom were professors), and challenged each group to complete a project that addressed the problem of juvenile delinquency.

The student feedback was very favorable. More than that, the enthusiastic participants lobbied him to create a degree program. Sperling sketched out a curriculum for working adults in the criminal justice area and pitched the idea to the Academic Vice President at San Jose State. In Sperling's words, the VP was impressed and sympathetic but utterly discouraging. He told Sperling that the University had its hands full with regular students, and saw no need to create part-time programs for working adults. Moreover, to gain approval, such a program would have to navigate its way through the academic bureaucracy at San Jose, a process that could take several years, and at the end of the day what emerged might significantly differ from Sperling's original proposal due to the input of other faculty members.

Unperturbed by the rejection, Sperling started to cast around for other schools who might want to run the program. He contacted the vice president of development at Stanford University, Frank Newman, who told Sperling that educational bureaucracies were inherently inert and would only innovate if they were in financial trouble. Newman advised Sperling to find a school in financial trouble and persuaded them that the program would make a profit.

The former union organizer immediately saw the value in Newman's suggestion. Left wing he might have been, but Sperling was eager to try out his ideas in the marketplace. He formed a private organization, the Institute for Professional Development, with the mission of making higher education available to the working community. Sperling approached the University of San Francisco, a financially troubled Jesuit school. USF agreed to sponsor the IPD program, using its accreditation to validate the degree. The program was an immediate financial success. Before long, Sperling was contracting with other schools for similar programs. The educational establishment, however, reacted with open hostility to Sperling's for-profit venture. For the first time, but not the last, Sperling was accused of devaluing education and producing a diploma mill. Sperling's sin, in his view, was that his model cut the professors out of the educational equation, and they were not about to let that happen.

Although he had been an academic for years, Sperling had up to this point paid little attention to the process of accrediting institutions and degree programs. What he quickly discovered was legitimacy required that the sponsoring institution for a degree program be accredited by recognized accreditation agencies. In the case of USF, this was the Western Association of Schools and Colleges (WASC) which had jurisdiction over California, along with the California State Department of Education. For the first time, but not for the last, Sperling discovered that these regulatory agencies had enormous power and could destroy the legitimacy of his programs by refusing to grant accreditation to the sponsoring institutions. In Sperling's own words:

> "We had no idea the extent to which education is a highly politicized and regulated activity, not the extent to which innovators were to be searched out and destroyed as quickly as possible by the academics who controlled the institutions and by their allies in regulatory agencies."[7]

What followed was a bitter 5-year battle with Sperling trying to get and maintain accreditation for his programs in California, and politicians, professors, and accreditation agencies blocking him every step of the way. Ultimately, Sperling decided that it would be impossible to fully develop his concepts of education for working adults within the confines of an existing institution. He decided to establish a university of his own. Sperling gave up and moved to Phoenix Arizona, where he though regulators would be more open to his ideas. They weren't. The established state institutions were openly hostile to Sperling's venture. It took more campaigning, which

included an all out media campaign's intensive lobbying of the States legislature, and vitriolic debates in the committee rooms of higher education regulators, before Arizona accredited Sperling's venture in 1978, now named the University of Phoenix. Sperling learned the lesson well—today the Apollo Group maintains a staff of 40 or so political lobbyists whose job it is to get and maintain accreditation.

University of Phoenix Business Model[8]

The University of Phoenix (UOP) is designed to cater to the needs of working adults, who make up 95% of its students. The average age is 36, and until recently the minimum age was 23. The emphasis is on practical subjects, such as business, information technology, teaching, criminal justice, and nursing. In addition to undergraduate degrees, UOP offers several graduate degrees, including Master's degrees in business (MBA), counseling, and nursing. Today some 43% of students at the UOP are enrolled in undergraduate courses, 15% are in Master's programs, 42% are taking 2-year Associate degrees and 1.6% are doctoral students.

The UOP views the student as the customer, and the customer is king. Classes are offered at times that fit the busy schedules of the fully employed—often in the evening. The schedule is year round—there are no extended breaks for summer vacation. Steps are taken to make sure that it is as easy as possible for students to get to classes—one of the golden rules is that there should be plenty of parking, and that students should be able to get from their cars to the classroom in 5 minutes.

UOP campuses lack many of the facilities found in traditional universities. There are no dormitories, student unions, athletic facilities, gymnasiums, research laboratories, extensive network of libraries, and the support staff required for all of these facilities. Instead, the typical campus comprises a handful of utilitarian buildings sited close to major roads.

In designing a university for working adults, Sperling introduced several key innovations. The classes are small with 10–15 students each and are run as seminars. Students usually take just one class at a time. Classes generally meet once or twice a week for 5–9 weeks. The faculty is expected to act as discussion leaders and facilitators, rather than lecturers. They are there to help guide students through the curriculum, and to provide feedback and grading. In addition to classes, students are assigned to 3–5 people groups, called "Learning Teams," which work together on group projects and studying.

Since the mid-1990s, UOP has been relying heavily upon online resources to deliver much of the course content. A typical 5-week undergraduate course with a significant online component would go something like this: students would attend class on campus for 4 hours the first week, giving them a chance to meet the instructor and be introduced to their learning teams and coursework. Weeks 2–4 are completed over the Internet, with homework assignments and participation requirements to be fulfilled. Students return to campus in week 5 for presentations.[9]

Sperling hired working professionals who were looking for part-time employment to teach. In 2005, only 400 of the 21,000 faculty at UOP were full-time. Part-time faculty must have a Master's degree or higher and have had 5 years of professional experience in an area related to the subject they teach. New faculty are subject to peer review by other faculty members, are given training in grading and instructing students, and a teaching mentorship with more experienced faculty members. There is no such thing as academic tenure at the UOP and no research requirements for faculty, full-time or part-time.

Third, the UOP established "ownership" over the curriculum taught in classrooms. In traditional universities, it is the faculty that develops and "owns" the curriculum. This can lead to significant variation in the content offered for the same class when taught by different professors in the same university. The decentralized nature of curriculum development in traditional universities makes it very difficult for the central administration to mandate changes to the curriculum. Moreover, in traditional universities significant curriculum change can take a significant amount of time and energy, involving faculty committees, and in the case of new programs, approval from central administration. In contrast, at the UOP content experts, typically the small number of full time faculty, develop the curriculum. Part-time teachers are then expected to deliver this standardized curriculum. This centralization allows UOP to have a uniform curriculum and to rapidly include new material in a curriculum and roll it out system

wide if the need arises. When designing the curriculum, the UOP solicits input from students 2 years after graduation and from employers who hire UOP graduates.

The centralization of curriculum has also enabled UOP to challenge the publishers of traditional textbooks. The UOP contacts authors directly and contracts with them to develop course materials exactly to their specifications, cutting textbook publishers out of the loop. The goal is for all UOP programs to use customized materials that exist entirely in digital form. Today, nearly all UOP students get course materials and resources digitally through the company's resource Internet portal. This eliminates the need for textbooks and is a source of added profit for the UOP. The cost to the student is roughly $60 a course (for undergraduates), while the cost to UOP is about $20.[10]

The contrast between UOP and traditional not-for-profit universities is stark. At the undergraduate level, traditional universities focus on 18–25 year olds who are engaged in full-time education. They have high labor costs due to the employment of full-time faculty, the majority of who have Doctoral degrees. Newly minted professors straight out of a doctoral program often command high starting salaries—as much as $120,000 a year plus benefits in some disciplines such as business. Faculty members are given low teaching loads to allow them to focus on research, which is the currency of the realm in academia. Research output is required for tenure in the "publish or perish" model of academia adopted by traditional universities.

Although the knowledge produced by research faculty can be and often is socially and economically valuable, the research culture of these knowledge factories translates into a high cost of instruction. At the University of Washington, for example, one of the nation's premier research institutions, 3,900 full-time faculty educated 40,000 students in 2005. The average faculty salary was $76,951 for the 9 months of the academic year, which translated into an instructional cost of around $300 million. In contrast, the part-time faculty at the UOP are inexpensive. In 2005, the 21,000 faculty at the Apollo Group were paid $195 million, or roughly $9,200 each—and this to instruct 307,400 students. In addition, student, faculty, and research facilities dramatically increase the capital intensity of traditional universities, while their attendant staff increases the labor costs.

As a consequence of these factors, the total costs of running a traditional university are much higher than at the UOP. At the University of Washington, for example, total operating expenses in 2004–2005 were $2.7 billion, compared to $1.53 billion at the Apollo Group.[11] According to one estimate, the average *cost to the institution* of educating an undergraduate student for 2 semesters at a public university is around 2 1/2 times greater than that at a for-profit institution such as the UOP. At a private institution, it is more than 3 times greater.[12] It is the inherently low cost structure of the UOP that allows the Apollo Group to make its high profits.

Naturally, such comparisons ignore the fact that the mission of many traditional universities such as the University of Washington is fundamentally different from that of the University of Phoenix. The UOP produces zero new knowledge, whereas the nation's research universities have been and will continue to be major producers of the knowledge that underlies technological progress and economic growth.

On the revenue side, estimates suggest that in 2005 it cost around $22,500 to get an Associate degree at UOP, $51,000 for a Bachelor's degree, and $22,932 for a Master's degree (costs vary by program).[13] Students attending the UOP rely heavily upon Federal Assistance Programs to help pay for their college education. Some 85% of students at the UOP in 2010 received financial aid under Title IV programs from the U.S. Department of Education. To be eligible for Title IV funding, a student has to be registered at an institution that is accredited by an agency recognized by the Department of Education and enrolled in a program with at least 30 weeks of instructional time and 24 credit hours.

In addition to Title IV financial aid programs, some 45% of UOP students had some form of tuition assistance from their employer. The IRS code allows an employee to exclude some $5,250 a year in tuition assistance from taxable income.

Accreditation

Accreditation by a respected agency is critical for any university. Accreditation verifies that a proper college education, consistent with the institution's mission, and meeting or exceeding thresholds of approved standards of education quality, is attainable at an institution.[14] Accreditation is an important element of the brand equity of an institution, is valued by employers who want to know the worth of their degrees earned by their employees, allows students to transfer credits to another institution, and is a pre-request for Title IV financial aid. In addition, most employees will only offer tuition assistance if the student is enrolled at an accredited institution.

The UOP is accredited by the Higher Learning Commission. Accreditation was first granted in 1978, and reaffirmed 5 times since. The next comprehensive review will take place in 2012. The Higher Learning Commission is one of 6 regional institutional accreditation agencies in the United States and is recognized by the Department of Higher Education. Regional accreditation is recognized nationally. In some states it is sufficient authorization to operate a degree granting institution, but in most states, the UOP must also get authorization from state authorities.

In addition to the Higher Learning Commission, the Bachelor and Master of Science programs in nursing are accredited by the Commission on Collegiate Nursing Education, and the Masters' program in Community Counseling is accredited by the Council for Accreditation of Counseling and Related Educational Programs. However, the Bachelors' and Masters' degree programs in business at UOP are not accredited by the Association to Advance Collegiate Schools of Business (AACSB). The AACSB is the largest and most influential accrediting organization for undergraduate, Master's, and Doctoral degree programs in business schools around the world, having granted international accreditation to more than 500 business schools in 30 countries.

Throughout its history, the UOP has found gaining accreditation an uphill battle. For example, the UOP reentered California in 1980. After initially receiving a license to operate based on its accreditation by North Central, a regional accreditation agency recognized by the U.S. Department of Education, the UOP was informed in 1981 that due to a change in California law, North Central accreditation was not sufficient for the UOP to operate in California. Instead, accreditation was required from the Western Association of Schools and Colleges WASC. The WASC was run by an old critic of Sperling, and there was zero chance that it would accredit the UOP, leaving the institution with a stranded investment in California. It took another three years for the UOP to resolve the issue, which it did by extensive political lobbying, ultimately getting a political ally to sponsor a bill in the California legislature that resulted in a change in the law, making WASC accreditation unnecessary for out of state institutions.

The hostility the UOP encountered in California was repeated in many other states, and the UOP was not always successful at countering it. Illinois for example, refused to grant a license to the UOP after existing institutions argued that there were already too many colleges in the state and that the UOP was unnecessary since other institutions already offered similar programs.

In Sperling's views, the persistent hostility to his company reflects the cultural biases of higher education, which are opposed to the idea of a for-profit university. To quote: "The whole regulatory structure of higher education is designed to favor non-profit and public colleges and universities, which it does by placing added regulatory burdens on those institutions organized for profit."[15] One of these burdens is that regulations grant Title IV eligibility to non-profit and public institutions that have achieved candidate for accreditation status, but only grant Title IV eligibility after they have achieved full accreditation.

Apollo's Growth Strategy

The company's strategy has been to grow by opening more campuses and learning centers in new states, by increasing enrollment at existing campuses and learning centers, and by product extensions, including online course offerings and expanding its Associate degree offerings through Axia College.

UOP Expansion

The basic UOP business model has proved to be very scalable. In addition to centrally developed curriculum, UOP has developed customized computer programs that are used for student tracking, marketing, faculty recruitment and training, and academic quality management. These computer programs are intended to provide uniformity among University of Phoenix's campuses and learning centers. In turn, this enhances University of Phoenix's ability to expand rapidly into new markets.

To attract more students, UOP invests heavily in marketing and sales. Selling and promotional costs accounted 22.6% of total revenues in 2010, or $1.12 billion, which is a much higher percentage than at traditional 4-year colleges.

UOP's aggressive marketing has troubled the U.S. Department of Education. In 2004, the Department issued a report that was highly critical of how UOP compensated its enrollment advisors. According to the Department, enrollment advisors at UOP soon found out that UOP based their salaries solely on the number of students they recruit—a practice that is prohibited by Federal Law. One recruiter who started out at $28,000 was bumped up to $85,000 after recruiting 151 students in 6 months. Another who started out at the same level got just a $4,000 raise after signing up 79 students. This report could have ultimately led to UOP being barred from Federal loan programs, which would have been very damaging. Although an Apollo spokesman called the report "very misleading and full of inaccuracies," the company agreed to change its compensation practices and pay $9.8 million fine without admitting guilt.[16]

Online Education

One of the big engines of growth at UOP has been online education. UOP was an early mover in this area. In 1989, Sperling purchased as defunct distance learning company and instructed a team of technicians to come up with a viable, portable electronic education system. By the time the idea of Web-based distance education was discussed among traditional universities, they found that UOP was already there. By 2006, Apollo had more than 160,000 students enrolled in online programs and had become the global leader in online education.[17]

Online classes are conducted in groups of 10–12 students. Prior to the beginning of each class, students pay a fee to access eResource, the online delivery method for course materials. Online there are a series of 8 newsgroups. The main newsgroup is designated for class discussion. There is an assignments newsgroup to which students submit their assignments, a chat newsgroup for students to discuss noncontent related topics, a course materials newsgroup that houses the syllabus and lectures for the class, and 4 newsgroups which function as forums for the Learning Team assignments. Each week, the instructor posts a lecture to the classroom course materials newsgroup. Students log on and read the lecture or print the lecture to read at their convenience. Throughout the week, students participate in class discussions, based on the class content for that week, which is actively facilitated by the instructor. Both the instructor and students are expected to engage in content discussions 5 out of 7 days each class week. In addition to the class participation requirement, students are also expected to complete individual assignments and to work within a small group of 3–5 students on a specific Learning Team assignment.

The online approach appeals to students who work irregular hours, or who struggle to balance the demands of work, family, and education. Flexibility, not cost, is the prime selling point. The cost of an online MBA program at UOP is about $30,000, similar to online education program fees at traditional universities who are moving into this space. The cost of a getting a Bachelors degree online at UOP is about $475 per semester credit hour, which compares to an average of $398 for an online degree at a selection of state institutions, and $446 at private schools.[18]

Axia College

Another major thrust at the Apollo Group has been to expand it 2-year Associate degree offerings. In the last few years, this has been done through Axia College, which initially was part of Apollo's Western International University. Today, Axia is part of the UOP. The demographic strategy at Axia is very different from that at UOP. Axia targets 18–24 year old students with zero to little college education. The revenue per student is lower, but this is balanced by larger class sizes (30–40), fewer dropouts, and lower student acquisition costs, which translates into slightly higher profit margins. The goal is for Axia to become a feeder for the UOP, with students who gain an Associate degree at Axia transferring to UOP to obtain a Bachelor's, either immediately upon graduation or at some time in the future. Due to the rapid growth of Axia, most of which is online, Associate degrees have grown from about 3.9% of Apollo's student base in 2004 to about 42% in 2010. The growth of Axia has hurt Apollo's revenue per student numbers, and the stock price, although many analysts see this as a good long-term strategy.[19]

The Competitive Landscape

The postsecondary education industry in the United States is estimated to be worth around $430 billion, with the for-profit sector capturing about $25 billion of that total in 2010. The industry will continue to grow, fueled by favorable demographics and tuition hikes, which have historically outpaced inflation by a wide margin. The U.S. Department of Education (DOE) expects postsecondary enrollment to grow at 2% per annum. Analysts estimate that the for-profit sector could grow enrollments by 5–6% per annum as it gains share, and increase tuition at 4–5% per annum.[20] To back up these forecasts, they point to DOE figures which suggest that only 26% of Americans 25 and older have a Bachelor's degree or higher.

Although UOP pioneering the for-profit university model, and remains by far the largest institution, it is not alone in the space. Competition has increased and may continue to do so. By 2006, there were around 850 for-profit institutions offering degrees in the United States, up from around 600 in 1996. Most of these institutions, however, are quite small. The largest competitors to the UOP are Corinthian College, with 66,000 students in 2005, ITT Educational Services, with 43,000 students, and Career Education.

Corinthian College focuses primarily on diploma or certificate courses designed for students with little or no college experience who are looking for entry level jobs. As such, it is not a strong direct competitor to UOP. Florida Metropolitan University, the largest school operated by Corinthian College, is currently being investigated for marketing and advertising practices by the Florida Attorney General. ITT Educational Services has traditionally focused on Associate degrees, but has been expanding its offerings of Bachelor's degrees. ITT's niche is technical degrees, although like UOP it also offers business degrees. Career Education is the holding company for a number of for-profit establishments, including Colorado Technical University and American Inter-Continental University. Currently Career Education is mired in legal and accreditation issues that have constrained its ability to expand.

Analysts' estimates suggest that among for-profit universities, UOP has the premium brand, but prices its offerings competitively, which constitutes a compelling value proposition for students (see Exhibit 1).

In addition to other non-profits, UOP faces increased competition from traditional not-for-profit universities. In recent years, both private and public institutions have expanded their part-time and online offerings to adults, particularly in areas like businesses administration. Executive MBA programs have become major revenue generators at many state and private universities. To take one example, at the University of Washington business school the number of students enrolled in part-time evening or executive MBA programs has expanded from around 40 a decade ago to over 300 today. These students pay "market based" fees, and the programs are run as profit centers that contribute earnings to support the operations of the business school. The programs are structured to minimize the demands on working adults (classes are held in the evening or on weekends) and make heavy use of "learning teams" to facilitate the educational process.

Some traditional universities are also getting into the business of online education, although their success has been decidedly mixed so far. One of the leaders, the University of Massachusetts, had 9,200 students taking online courses in 2006. Most were working adults between 25 and 50, and 30% were from out of state. At UMass, online applicants undergo the same admission process as candidates for campus slots. Tuition is slightly higher than that for on-campus students, since Web-based courses are not subsidized by the state. At another state institution, Pennsylvania State University, there are some 6,000 students taking online courses, and demand is growing rapidly. The University of Maryland University College, the open enrollment arm of the state university, had 51,405 online students in 2005, up from 9,696 in 1998. Nearly 40% of these were American military personnel around the world—a market that the UOP also targets.[21]

On the other hand, many top schools have been reluctant to offer online courses, believing that doing so might compromise quality. Underlying this view is a belief that much of the value in education comes from face-to-face interaction with professors, and with other students in a classroom setting. This perspective is backed by empirical and anecdotal evidence. In one recent survey, employers overwhelmingly preferred traditional Bachelor's degrees when hiring over credentials even partially completed online. Two professors asked 270 small- and medium-sized companies in 8 cities about their attitudes toward online credentials. The companies sought entry level employees or managers in engineering, business and information technology. 96 % said they would choose traditional candidates over those with an online degree.[22]

In response to a journalist's question about the value of online degrees, a spokesman at Texas Instruments stated that: "We do not hire people with online degrees. We primarily hire engineers, and we target very well-established engineering degree programs. The chance for someone with an online degree program to get in is not very likely."[23] On the other hand, several employers told the same journalist that an online degree did not limit options so long as it was from an accredited institution. These organizations included Northrop Grumman, United Parcel Service, Boeing and Discovery Communications.

Regulatory Issues: 2006–2011

Between 2006 and 2011 the industry continued to be the target of criticisms and attacks from critics in the media, in traditional higher education, and from Government Agencies. An investigation by the Department of Education in 2010 found practices such as overly aggressive recruiting, in which school representatives barraged potential students with phone calls, gave false information about a college's accreditation, potential, salary and job opportunities after graduation, and doctored federal aid forms. Other investigations found that for-profit recruiters heavily targeted low income and minority students, veterans, and people whose parents have never gone to college.[24]

The same investigations suggest that public investment in educating some students at some for-profit institutions isn't a good deal for taxpayers or for many students. According to the Department of Education, for-profit colleges educated around 1 in 10 students in 2008, but these students took out nearly 1/4 of all federal student financial aid dollars, about $24 billion of taxpayer money. They also accounted for almost 1/2 of all loan defaulters. For many of the larger for-profit schools, such as UOP, federal dollars account for 80–90% of their revenues.

An investigation by the Senate Committee on Health, Education, Labor and Pensions highlighted one of the smaller institutions, Bridgepoint, which enrolled about 8,000 students in Associate degree programs in

2008. By 2010, 85% had withdrawn, and only about 1% had received a degree. The Committee found that dropout rates at most for-profit schools investigated were hovering at around 66%. Compared to 55% at public colleges and 48% at private non-profit schools.[25]

In June 2011, the U.S. Department of Education issued new regulations designed to curb some of the aggressive practices in the for-profit sector.[26] In order to gain access to Federal Funds, schools had to demonstrate that loan repayment rates by students exceeded 45%. In addition, under what is known as the "gainful employment" rules, access to Federal funds required that students' debt payment to income after graduation should not amount to more than 30% of their discretionary income, and annual loan payments must not exceed 12% of their total earnings. The Government will be collecting this data going forward. Although the rules will go into effect in June 2012, the Government gave for-profit colleges until 2015 to comply with them. The new rules join an existing regulation under which schools' lose access to Federal dollars if more than 90% of their revenue comes from such sources.

The Apollo Group was anticipating these changes by the late-2000s and making moves to get ahead of them. In 2010, Apollo changed its compensation system for admissions personnel to eliminate any tie between compensation and enrollment volume. Apollo also introduced a 3-week program called University Orientation for students with limited college experience. The students are not charged fees during this period, but are introduced to curriculum and teaching practices. The idea is to help students determine if enrolling on a program at the UOP is right for them *before* they take on any debt. In 2010, Apollo's revenue from Federal dollars stood at 88% and was approaching the 90% limit. The company recognized that staying below this limit may constrain growth going forward. The UOP was also only 1% over the required 45% loan repayment rate, although the company believed that the University Orientation Program would change this going forward.

Despite the negative publicity, in 2008 and 2009 Apollo registered strong enrollment growth. The major reason for this seems to have been the weak national economy. With unemployment rates pushing over 9%, people were going back to school in larger numbers in order to try and strengthen their position in a tough job market.

Exhibit 1   Graduate Salary and Tuition for Bachelor's Degrees

School	Mean Graduate Salary	Mean Total Tuition
University of Phoenix	$52,597	$51,000
American InterContinental University	$44,363	$43,863
Florida Metropolitan University	$35,019	$50,400
ITT Technical Institute	$39,726	$69,480

Source: Data taken from Paul Bealand, "What's a degree worth?" *Citigroup Equity Research*, February 17, 2006.

Endnotes

1 Standard & Poor's Stock Report, Apollo Group Inc., October 14, 2006.

2 Quoted in B. Breen, "The Hard Life and Restless Mind of America's Educational Billionaire," *Fast Company*, March 2003, 80–86.

3 Quoted in Anonymous, "Survey: Higher Ed Inc," *The Economist*, September 10, 2005, 19–21.

4 Paul Bealand, "What's a Degree Worth?" *Citigroup Equity Research*, February 17, 2006.

5 Sperling describes his life in is autobiography, John Sperling, *Rebel with a Cause*, New York: John Wiley, 2006.

6 Quoted in B. Breen, "The Hard Life and Restless Mind of America's Educational Billionaire," *Fast Company*, March 2003, 80–86.

7   J. Sperling, *Rebel with a Cause*, New York: John Wiley, 2006, 78.

8   Much of the material in this section is drawn from the 2010 10K Reports of the Apollo Group filed with the Securities and Exchange Commission.

9   S. Baltes, "Phoenix Builds Presence Amid Turmoil," *Des Moines Business Record*, September 20, 2004, 14.

10 P. Bealand, "What's a Degree Worth?" *Citigroup Equity Research*, February 17, 2006.

11 University of Washington data is taken from the UW Fact book which can be accessed online at: http://www.washington.edu/admin/factbook/.

12 R.S. Ruch, *Higher Ed Inc: The Rise of the For Profit University*, Baltimore: John Hopkins University Press, 2001.

13 P. Bealand, "What's a Degree Worth?" *Citigroup Equity Research*, February 17, 2006.

14 R.S. Ruch, *Higher Ed Inc: The Rise of the For Profit University*, Baltimore: John Hopkins University Press, 2001.

15 J. Sperling, *Rebel with a Cause*, New York: John Wiley, 2006, 105.

16 W. C. Symonds, "Back to Earth for Apollo Group?" *Business Week*, January 31, 2005, 50.

17 D. Golden, "Degrees@StateU.edu," *Wall Street Journal*, May 9, 2006, B1.

18 P. Bealand, "What's a Degree Worth?" *Citigroup Equity Research*, February 17, 2006.

19 K. Rowland, "Apollo Group A," *Morning Star Research Report*, October 19, 2006.

20 P. Bealand, "What's a Degree Worth?" *Citigroup Equity Research*, February 17, 2006.

21 D. Golden, "Degrees@StateU.edu," *Wall Street Journal*, May 9, 2006, B1.

22 A. Wellen, "Degrees of Acceptance," *Wall Street Journal*, July 30, 2006, A26.

23 Ibid.

24 D. Lipperman and L. Mulvany, "Class Act or Just a Course to Failure?" *Chicago Tribune*, June 21, 2011, 4.

25 Ibid.

26 M. Alva, "Fed's Let For-Profit Colleges off the Regulatory Hook, a Bit," *Investor's Business Daily*, June 21, 2011, A7.

CASE 14

Is Yahoo!'s Business Model Working in 2011?

Gareth R. Jones
Texas A&M University

In 2006, Yahoo! was the world's most-visited interactive Web portal or entryway into the World Wide Web (WWW). It averaged over 144 million page views per day, earned $2 billion on revenues of $6.4 billion in 2006, and its stock price was around $30 (down from its all time high of $100 before the 2000 dot.com bust led its stock price to plunge in value to $4.40!). By 2010, Yahoo! was still the third most-visited Web portal, despite that both Google and Facebook surpassed it in their numbers of daily page views. Moreover, its share of the search engine market had dramatically plummeted from over 30% to around 12% while Google search increased its share to a whopping 65%. The result of these changes was that in 2011, Yahoo!'s stock price averaged around only $15—it had lost over half its value in the last 5 years. What went wrong? Why had Yahoo!'s business model been performing so poorly; why were its strategies not working in the rapidly evolving Internet content provider industry?

Yahoo!'s Beginnings

The Yahoo! portal has its origins in the Website directory created as a hobby by its two founders, David Filo and Jerry Yang. Filo and Yang, two Ph.D. candidates in electrical engineering at Stanford University. They wanted a quick and easy way to remember and revisit the Websites they had identified as the best and most useful from the hundreds of thousands of sites that were quickly appearing on the WWW in the early-1990s. They soon realized that as the list of their favorite Websites grew longer and longer, the list began to lose its usefulness, as they had to wade through a longer and longer list of URLs (Website addresses) to find the specific site they wanted. So to reduce their search time Filo and Yang decided to divide their list of Websites into smaller and more manageable categories according to each one's specific content or subject matter, such as sports, business, politics, or culture. In 1994, they published their Website directory online calling it "Jerry's Guide to the WWW" for their friends to use. Soon, hundreds—then thousands—of people located and clicked on their Website because it saved them time and effort to identify the most useful sites— their Website went viral.

As they continued to develop their directory, Filo and Yang found that each of the directory's subject categories were also quickly becoming large and unwieldy to search, so they further divided them into subcategories. Now, their directory organized Websites into a hierarchy, rather than a searchable index of pages, so they renamed their directory "Yahoo!" supposedly short for "Yet Another Hierarchical Officious Oracle," and the Yahoo! search engine was born. However, Filo and Yang insisted they selected the name because they liked the word's general meaning as originated by Jonathan Swift in *Gulliver's Travels* as someone or something that is "rude, unsophisticated, and uncouth"; their goals was, after all, to continuously improve the site over time. As their directory grew, they realized they could not possibly identify all the best Websites that were appearing in the WWW, so they recruited human volunteers to help them improve, expand, and refine their directory and make it a more useful, laborsaving search device.

By 1994, hundreds of thousands of users were visiting Yahoo! every day; it had quickly become the primary search portal of choice for people surfing the Web to help them find the sites that provided the most useful, interesting and entertaining content.

By 1995, Yahoo! recorded over a million "hits" or user visits per day as word kept spreading about the utility of their search engine. The increasing size of their search engine had outgrown the limited hosting capacity of their Stanford University account so they arranged to borrow server capacity from nearby Netscape, which had developed the first Web browser. Yang and Filo decided to put their graduate studies on hold and turn their attention and skills to work on building Yahoo! into a business.

When they created their directory, Filo and Yang had no idea they had a potential gold mine at their fingertips. They enjoyed surfing the Web and were interested in making it easier for ordinary people to do so as well. But, by 1994, it became clear that they could make major money from their directory if they allowed companies to advertise their products on the site in order to attract more sales. Of course, all along, the Internet had been rapidly expanding, and Filo and Yang realized they had to move quickly to capitalize on Yahoo!'s popularity—in any market there are always several other entrepreneurs who are pursuing a similar idea, and the race is on to become the first to successfully develop a new product and make it a success. Although their search engine was the first of its kind to be up and running, they knew it could be imitated. Indeed, competitive Web-crawling search engine companies like AltaVista that used mathematical algorithms to detect the most relevant Websites had already emerged. At this time, Yahoo!'s advantage was that it was a human-powered search engine where real people did the legwork for ordinary Internet surfers, and listed sites handpicked for their usefulness. The new mathematical algorithms being developed at this time could not match Yahoo!'s ability to select relevant results for specific user inquiries—however, technology quickly improved, and Filo and Yang's human-powered search engine was already on the way to becoming a dinosaur because of the incredible growth of the Internet and WWW that would occur in the next decade.

Nevertheless, as visits to Yahoo!'s hits continued to increase, so did requests by companies to advertise on its Web portal, and its advertising revenues rapidly increased, which paid for the rocketing costs of hosting their online directory on computer servers. With a hot new business on their hands, Yang and Filo's business model was to generate revenues by renting advertising space on the rapidly expanding Web pages of their search engine. When a user clicked on an ad, this "click impression" became a charge to the advertiser's account, and the greater the number of impressions the greater the advertising fees. As their fledgling company grew and the number of user visits soared, Filo and Yang realized they needed to find new sources of funding to develop a sophisticated IT infrastructure to support their portal's growth. Searching for backing from venture capitalists, they soon struck a deal with Sequoia Capital, a Silicon Valley firm that had supported Apple and Oracle among other high-tech companies. Using the $2 million seed capital to build their company's IT systems, their portal continued to soar in popularity, and in 1996, this success led to Yahoo!'s initial public stock offering that raised $338 million by selling 2.6 million shares at $13 each, to allow it to fund future growth.

Sequoia Capital understood the problems facing new startups and entrepreneurs and insisted that Filo and Yang, who had no business background, should hire experienced executives to develop Yahoo!'s business model. Sequoia's partners had learned that the skills needed to be a successful manager often diverge from those necessary to develop successful business strategies, especially if entrepreneurs are driven by their technical or scientific background and do not understand the realities of industry competition. Filo and Yang hired Tim Koogle, an experienced ex-Motorola executive with an engineering background to be Yahoo!'s new CEO. Filo and Yang became joint co-chairmen of Yahoo! with the title of "Chief Yahoo!".

Developing Yahoo!'s Business Model

Koogle started to build Yahoo!'s business model by focusing on recruiting marketing experts and increasing the company's advertising function to strengthen Yahoo!'s core competences and increase ad revenues to fund the company's further growth. At the same time, Koogle decided revenue growth should be driven by increasing the number of site users, and so the need to continuously improve Yahoo!'s search engine—and find new ways to attract visitors—was vital.

Filo and Yang took responsibility for improving the search engine but now hired many experts such as Srinija Srinivasan or "Ontological Yahoo!" as she became known in the company's early days because of her crucial role in refining and developing the classification system that was the hallmark of Yahoo!'s search engine. She helped Filo and Yang hire hundreds more software engineers to broaden and increase the reach and usefulness of Yahoo!'s search engine, and to manage its fast-growing IT infrastructure that was being continuously upgraded to handle the tens of millions of daily user requests the company was now receiving. By 1996, Yahoo! listed over 200,000 individual Websites in over 20,000 different categories. Hundreds of companies had signed up with Yahoo! to advertise their products on its portal to reach its millions of users.

Another strategy Koogle developed was to take Yahoo!'s business model and replicate it around the world—to increase global advertising revenue. By the end of 1996, there were 18 Yahoo! portals using 12 languages operating outside the United States. In each country, Yahoo!'s portal and Web directory was customized to the tastes and needs of local users. However, there was considerable overlap between countries in terms of popular global news, politics, media, and entertainment Websites, which also helped Yahoo! to find new attractive Websites and strengthen its U.S. search engine. This, of course, led to the development of new Web pages that helped increasing its advertising revenues.

Yahoo!'s success with its growing global Internet search operations convinced Koogle to craft a new vision and business model for Yahoo!. The company would no longer operate only as a search engine, but would now develop new media and entertainment services to allow it become the dominant global communication, media entertainment, and retail company. Yahoo! would become a portal that could be used to enable anyone to connect with anything or anybody on the Internet.

In the vision its top executives crafted, Yahoo! would not only continue to generate increasing revenues from the sale of advertising space on its search engine pages, it would also earn significant revenues from engaging in e-commerce transactions—buying and selling between Internet users—and take a percentage of the value of each transaction executed using its portal as its fee. Of course, other companies such as eBay and Amazon.com were also quickly developing this kind of Website service. In 1998, Yahoo! acquired the Internet shopping portals Viaweb and Yoyodyne to create its new retail-shopping platform, Yahoo! Stores. Its new online services would enable new and existing businesses to quickly create and manage secure online stores to market and sell their products. After launching their store, these merchants were also included in searches on Yahoo! Shopping, one of the increasingly popular shopping portals that provided potential customers with price comparisons of the products in which they are interested, and so helped to determine the online store from which they would purchase.

To build brand awareness and make it the portal of choice for all kinds of Internet-based services Yahoo! spent heavily on advertising, using radio and television ads targeted at mainstream America. To make its portal more useful, Koogle pioneered Yahoo!'s strategy of expanding the range of content and services of the Internet communication services it provided to its users to make the portal more useful to them. Over the next decade, Yahoo! continuously developed its technology and made many (expensive) acquisitions that allowed users to access services such as e-mail, instant and text messaging, news, stock alerts, personals, and job placement services. Moreover, it made these services available over a rapidly expanding array of digital and computing devices or channels from desktop PCs to wireless laptops, and eventually to mobile computing devices such as PalmPilots and smartphones.

Yahoo! also began to work with media and entertainment content providers to help them build and improve their own online content and ability to work on Yahoo!'s digital platform. This increased the value of Yahoo!'s portal to users who could access any content or merchants they needed through Yahoo!. Its goal was to become the portal of choice—the place where Internet users would routinely visit to enjoy and complete online transactions.

At the same time, these moves made Yahoo! increasingly valuable to companies anxious to advertise on the Internet to grow their business. Each specific new online service Yahoo! offered allowed advertisers to better target their advertising message to specific demographic groups, for example, sports fans, teens, game players, or investors. Online brokers such as E*Trade and Ameritrade started to heavily advertise on Yahoo!'s popular financial pages; similarly, sports magazines, eBay, and Blockbuster focused on the best way to spend their ad dollars on its shopping and news pages. Targeted advertising increased the rate at which a user clicks on ads, which translated into more completed online transactions, therefore increasing the yield (or return) of online advertising to merchants. (This is something Google understood much better than Yahoo! and the reason why Google is the leader in online advertising today.)

The result of Koogle's new business model and strategies was spectacular. By the end of 1998, the company had 50 million unique users, up from 26 million in the prior year; 35 million of these were now registered Yahoo! users who had created e-mail, gaming, and other kinds of accounts with the company. Moreover, 3,800 companies were advertising on Yahoo!'s pages up from 2,600 in 1997, and 700 in 1996. By 1999, 5000 merchants were selling products on the Yahoo! Shopping page up from 3,500 in 1998, and the company's revenues had grown from $21.5 million in 1996 to $203 million in 1998!

Building a Stronger Business Model: More Content and Channels

To keep Yahoo!'s profits growing, it was necessary to drive an increasing number of users to its portal, and Koogle's new strategies revolved around making Yahoo! a "megabrand" by "becoming the most useful and well-known Web portal on the Internet." His entire focus was to create compelling news, media, shopping, and entertainment content by adding additional Yahoo! channels, which had more services and features to increase its value to users, and encourage them to become regular registered users. The ability to attract and retain customers is a major metric used by investors to evaluate a company's value, not only Internet content providers but also cable TV providers, wireless phone providers, and so on. Yahoo!'s goal was to lock in users and increase their switching costs of turning to a new portal.

To facilitate this process, Yahoo! provided features that made it possible for users to customize Yahoo!'s Web pages and services to better meet their specific needs. For example, Yahoo!'s registered users could customize its popular news service to show the specific news sections they were the most interested in, such as technology or entertainment, or users could input their personal portfolios into its

financial Web page and track their portfolio's value over time. The financial Webpage also provided links to message boards where individual investors can jointly discuss a company's prospects. The ability to create a high level of customization created major switching costs for customers. Once users created their portfolios, personal pages, shopping lists, and other profiles, they would be much less likely to want to repeat this process by signing up at another Web portal—unless it offered some other "killer application," or compelling content, which of course is what Google and Facebook have been able to offer in the 2000s.

Yahoo! worked hard to remain the Web portal of choice by continuing to introduce additional kinds of online services as soon new startup Internet companies had showed their services were popular among online users. It developed a strategy of acquiring the leading Internet company in a particular online area, for example, online dating, to extend its portfolio of services, and keep its leadership as an online portal, thereby increasing its value to its users. In 1999, for example, it made three important acquisitions, RocketMail, an e-mail service provider that became the basis for Yahoo! Mail; GeoCities that provided a free Web-hosting service to registered users, which allowed them to publish their own personal homepages (containing material of their own choice) and to share it with friends and any other interested parties. Lastly, it bought Broadcast.com, an early leader in online streaming digital audio and video programming that allowed Yahoo! to broadcast audio and video content on all its channels to users. Yahoo!'s goal was to make its services even more valuable to its users—and thus to its advertisers as well—so that these acquisitions would result in increasing advertising revenues. Then, in 2000, Yahoo! acquired eGroups, a free social group/mailing list hosting service that allowed registered users to set up any kind of online group of their choice, and use it as a forum to attract other Internet users that shared their interests; soon hundreds of thousands of specialized groups had been established. Yahoo! integrated eGroups into its successful Yahoo! Groups service to develop and strengthen its services, and today it has millions of registered groups of users and is a popular mailing list service for all kinds of social networking purposes. Yahoo! paid billions to acquire these companies, however, because this was the time of the dot.com bubble;

afterwards the value of these acquisitions plunged—as did Yahoo!'s stock.

In addition to the services just mentioned, Yahoo! also now provided services such as Yahoo! Messenger, an instant messaging client that allowed for online chat; Yahoo! Games, a successful game-playing service; and various specialized online retail sites, including an online auction service it had started to compete with highly-profitable eBay. Its original search engine had, by this time, become just one of the many services it provided. As it turned out, Koogle's (and Filo and Yang's) failure to realize the central importance of Internet searching was a major factor that led to Yahoo!'s later problems—just as this same error hurt Microsoft, AOL, and all the other major search portals. Google was the exception, as it was focusing its efforts on search capabilities, although its reasons were not obvious until the early-2000s.

Nevertheless, as Koogle hoped, as the range of services Yahoo! offered expanded, its popularity increased as it became a "one-stop shop" that could cater to most kinds of services that Internet users' needed—information, entertainment, and retail, for example. Its expanding business model seemed to be working. Most of its services were provided free to Yahoo! users because the advertising revenues it earned from the ads on the millions of Web pages on its portal were the primary source of revenues in its profitable business model. In addition, it earned some revenues from the fees it charged sellers and buyers on its shopping and specialized retail sites. Also, Yahoo! charged for specialized services such as its personals dating service, a streaming stock quotes service, a job hunting service, and various premium e-mail and Web storage options that provided users with more kinds of value-added solutions. This also helped to increase revenues and earnings.

The success of its strategy of bundling online services to attract ever-greater numbers of users became clear as Yahoo!'s user base exploded. By the end of the 1990s, 15 million people a day were visiting Yahoo! and it had become the most visited portal on the WWW. Its business model, based on the idea that the more services it offered, the greater the number of Internet users it would attract, (and the higher would be the advertising fees it could charge companies) seemed to be working. In 2000, Yahoo!'s stock price reached the astronomical height of $237, its market value was $220 billion!

Big Problems Face Yahoo!

Just 2 years later, however, Yahoo!'s stock had plummeted to just $9 a share, which valued the company at less than $10 billion. Why? Because the dot.com bust sent thousands of Internet companies into bankruptcy and caused an across-the-board plunge in their stock prices. However, Yahoo! was still regarded as a dot.com powerhouse and many analysts put some of the blame for the fall in its stock price (eBay's did not fall greatly) on managerial mistakes at the top of the company—in particular on the way Yahoo!'s business model had developed over time.

CEO Tim Koogle had staked Yahoo!'s continuing success on its ability to develop an increasing range of compelling Web content and services to drive increased visits to its portal and generate more advertising and e-commerce revenues. The problem with this business model was that it made Yahoo!'s profitability (and stock price) totally dependent upon how fast advertising revenues increased—or how fast they fell. The dot.com bust and the economic recession that followed in the early-2000s led to a huge fall in the amount large and small companies were willing to spend on Internet advertising. As its advertising revenues plunged, Yahoo!'s stock price plummeted, and its investors' hopes of increasing revenue growth disappeared. Moreover, it turned out that Koogle had spend far too much money—billions too much—to pay for acquisitions such as GeoCities and eGroups (especially given that these companies profits were also highly dependent on Internet advertising!). Had these companies remained independent, they would now be valued at a fraction of the price Yahoo! paid for them.

Advances in Internet and Digital Technologies

At the same time, Internet and digital technologies were continually advancing and improving, and that lowered the value of the acquired companies' distinctive competencies, and therefore their competitive advantage in providing a specific online service—the primary reason why Yahoo! acquired them. Technological advances had made it easier for entrepreneurs to start new dot.coms that could provide similar kinds of specialized Internet services that Yahoo! offered—but which also had a new twist or killer application that was better than Google's. Thus in the 2000s, competitors like Monster.com, MySpace, and YouTube emerged offering digital services that proved so attractive they also became leading Web portals in providing a particular kind of online application: job hunting, social networking, and online video, respectively. These portals became major threats to Yahoo! because they siphoned off its users, and reduced its advertising revenues, which at that time were mainly based on the number of users visiting a Website. Now, Yahoo! lacked the resources to buy these portals, it had spent its cash and its stock price was low.

Search Engine's Become More Powerful: The Growing Threat from Google

On the search engine front as well, the search information service that had been the key to Yahoo!'s rise and its original distinctive competence was also experiencing a new threat. Yahoo! was experiencing increased competition because of the growing popularity of Google, a small, relatively unknown search engine company in 2000. By the early-2000s, however, it became obvious to Web watchers that Google was pioneering advances in WWW search technology that was making Yahoo!'s hierarchical directory classification obsolete! Yahoo!, like other major Web portals such as Microsoft's MSN and AOL had failed to realize how the search function would increase so much in importance as the breadth and depth of information on the WWW increased. It had become increasingly difficult for Internet users to locate the specific information they needed. The search engine that can find the specific information users want in the fastest time is the one that wins the search engine war, and Google's proprietary technology was attracting more and more users by word of mouth— just as Yahoo!'s directory had grown in popularity so fast in the 1990s. Yahoo! had been providing more and more kinds of online services but in the process had forgotten—or lost—the reason for its original success. Perhaps a professional manager at the helm was not such a good idea in the first place. Or, perhaps Filo and Yang were simply enjoying their newfound wealth and had not worked to improve

Yahoo!'s search engine technology because it had become a portal providing so many different kinds of information services.

The Web Portal Industry

To appreciate the problems Yahoo! was now facing, it is necessary to understand how the incredible growth in the 1990s of the Internet and WWW, and rapid advances in Internet hardware and software, changed the function of Web portals dramatically over the 2000s.

Internet Service Provider Portals

The first commercial portals were entry or access portals called Internet Service Providers (ISPs) that provided people with a way to log on to the Internet. For example, companies such as CompuServe, MSN, and AOL offered customers e-mail service and access to the WWW for time-related fees. Slow dial-up connections meant high monthly fees, and early on, ISPs charged users for each individual e-mail they sent! Moreover, once on the WWW, users were hampered by the fact that there was no Internet Web browser available to help them easily find and navigate to the thousands (and then millions) of Web pages and Websites that were emerging. Yahoo!'s directory, and then Netscape's Internet browser (introduced in 1994), changed all this. So did the growth in the number of search engines, including early leaders such as AltaVista, Inktomi, and Infoseek, that were all available to help users surf the Web. Typically, a user would connect to the Web through an access portal, and then go to their specific search engine of choice to identify Websites of interest, which they could then bookmark as favorites using Netscape's Web browser.

Product Bundling Portals

When Yahoo! became the leading search engine, this began the second phase of portal development, the product bundling or aggregation phase. Dot.coms such as Yahoo!, AOL, MSN, and hundreds of other now defunct Web portals were competing to attract Internet users and become the main portal of choice—to obtain advertising revenues. Now differences in the business models of different portals became increasingly clear, for example, portals like Yahoo! focused on offering users the widest possible selection of free Internet services to create switching costs and develop brand loyalty. Others, like AOL and MSN, adopted the fee-paying model, in which users paid to access the Web through a dial-up connection their portals provided, then they could use the range of services they offered free or for a charge for a premium service, like personals.

Competition between these combined access/aggregation portals increased as they strived to attract the tens of millions of new Internet users who were coming online at this time. The bigger their user base, the higher the potential fees and advertising revenues they could collect, so the price of Internet service quickly fell. By the mid-1990s, AOL made a major decision to offer its users unlimited Internet connection time for $19.95 a month. In the U.S., this attracted millions of new customers, and AOL became the leading access and aggregation portal with over 30 million users at its height, followed by MSN, and many other smaller ISPs.

The competitive problem these ISP/aggregated service portals like AOL faced from the beginning was that once their users were online, they would search out the "best of breed" Web portal that could provide them with the particular kind of information service they most wanted. So, millions of AOL subscribers, for example, used the portal to get online, but then used the myriad of services available on Yahoo! and other portals. The business model used by AOL, MSN, and others was to improve their content to keep subscribers on their portals in order to obtain the vital advertising and e-commerce revenues that Yahoo! was enjoying.

The problem soon facing the ISP/aggregation portals was that new companies started to offer lower-priced Internet access service, and, especially, that developing broadband technology had started to rapidly grow in popularity because of the speed it offered in using and downloading the WWW services or content that users wanted. This worked in favor of free portals like Yahoo! that did not generate revenues from getting users online. But, it began to hurt fee-based portals such as AOL and MSN that soon experienced falling revenues as new and existing Internet users chose faster broadband ISP connections, and users continued to gravitate to portals such as Yahoo!, eBay, Amazon.com, MySpace, YouTube, and other similar sites.

Customized Portals

In fact, the next major development in Web portals arrived when some Web portals started to specialize in developing "deeper" relationships with their users. Their goal was to offer their users an increasingly customized online experience that set out to help users make better or more informed choices when buying goods or services. Internet book-selling Amazon.com was one of the first portals to pioneer the development of the personalized or customized shopping experience. Amazon.com's software focused upon providing more information to users by, for example, allowing people who had bought books to provide detailed feedback to users about a particular book—and subsequently all kinds of products that it sold. Similarly, one of Amazon.com's central goals became to track its users around its site to help them find other products that they might be attracted to. Amazon.com's database recorded each user's buying preferences to help them make better buying decisions, and in the 2000s, its tracking technology became so invasive it developed software to track its users as they surfed the Web on other sites to find new products to offer them. Not surprisingly, many of its users thought this was an invasion of their privacy, but in the last decade these new tracking technologies have proliferated, and few ordinary Internet users today are aware of how much information is being collected about them by tracking companies that can sell this information to advertising companies.

All the major portals began to realize the importance of offering users a customized online experience, to increase their switching costs, and to keep them loyal, repeat users so their purchases and use could be tracked. Yahoo!, for example, uses "beacons" that allow it to follow its users around the WWW unless they choose to turn off this feature to increase their privacy. All the major portals began to make the "My" personal preferences choices on their portals a more important part of their service such as "MyAOL and MyYahoo! in order to be able to increasingly target advertising toward specific customer groups and make their portals easier to use by, for example, offering easy online payment checkout services.

However, it became increasingly apparent that the "best of breed" or leading category Web portals were quickly developing a first-mover advantage and strong brand loyalty. Amazon.com's stock price had also plunged after the dot.com bust, but it still pursued its business model to develop the online software that would attract the most customers and allow it to become the leader in Internet retailing. It succeeded, and was able to withstand the challenge from the thousands of other shopping portals that had sprung up in the 2000s, but Amazon.com also crushed the shopping channels of leading portals such as Yahoo! and AOL. Similarly, Yahoo!'s online auction service, despite that it was *free* to its registered users, could not compete with online auction leader eBay because eBay had gained the first-mover advantage, and its popularity allowed it to offer buyers and sellers a much larger market (and therefore a much better selection and higher prices).

Yahoo! Problems Increase throughout the 2000s

In the 2000s, it became clear that the two biggest sources of revenue and profit for Web portals were those gained from e-commerce, for example, from online retail and auction sales, which has been the source of Amazon.com's success in the 2010s; and to the generation of and sale of online advertising revenues. In the search engine segment of the market, the search engine company that could quickly provide online customers with the specific information necessary for them to make the best purchase possible, attracted the most advertisers, and could charge higher advertising rates. Google's strategy to continuously increase its competencies to provide fast, relevant information has, of course, been the business model behind its huge success, and the failure of most other search engine companies, including Yahoo! and MSN. However, customized portals like Facebook that provide specialist services such as social networking, could also earn high advertising and e-commerce revenues. Facebook's software platform and huge user base has allowed it to collect detailed information about its users that it can sell to generate targeted advertising revenues. In addition, its online games, such as CityVille, provided by Zynga, allow it to generate revenues from the fees it can charge game providers, retail providers, and others.

Many analysts argued that when Yahoo!'s stock price was at its peak, it should have purchased other e-commerce companies that were generating revenue by other means than advertising—such as eBay—so that it could have broadened the source of its revenues and reduced its dependency on advertising revenues. If advertising revenues decreased, Yahoo!'s profitability and stock price would plunge. In the early-2000s, Yahoo!'s stock price plummeted as the dot.com bust led to a huge fall in advertising revenues, and investors began to realize the weaknesses associated with its business model.

Yahoo!'s disastrous performance convinced its board of directors that new leadership was needed, and Tim Koogle was replaced as CEO by Terry Semel, an experienced Hollywood media executive who had once controlled Warner Brothers. To change Yahoo!'s business model, especially as it could no longer afford to acquire specialized Web portals, Semel adopted new strategies to generate increased online revenues.

First and foremost, Yahoo! needed to improve its search engine technology, a major portal attraction, to generate more users and advertising revenues. As time went on, and the success of Google's business model became increasingly obvious, Yahoo! focused upon improving its search software to beat Google at its own game and develop the ability to offer high-quality targeted advertising. Also, Semel decided to pursue a new content-driven strategy, and Yahoo! internally developed new kinds of services, and acquired small specialist Internet companies that could provide it with the new competencies it needed to compete in new emerging online information and media market segments. For example, Yahoo! acquired HotJobs, a leading Internet job hunting and placement company, and it began to expand its global news and media services operations.

Recognizing the growing importance of digital communications media to generate advertising revenues, it established a new Media Group function to develop advanced imaging and video news content to take advantage of increasing broadband Internet access. Yahoo! launched its own video search engine service in 2005, and revamped the Yahoo! Music download service; it also acquired Flickr, a leading photograph hosting and sharing site. All these strategies were designed to become a part of its new social networking strategy in order to compete with MySpace, YouTube, and Facebook. In fact, Yahoo! lost its battle to acquire YouTube to Google in 2006, and, of course, the fast growth of Facebook destroyed its chances to develop a popular social networking site, as Facebook overpowered MySpace, which had been purchased by News Corp. The fast-changing fortunes of Web portals is shown by the change in MySpace's fortunes; in 2005 it was valued at $3 billion, but its owner New Corp. was happy to divest it in 2011 for $100 million.

Semel continued to try to make new acquisitions to revitalize the appeal of Yahoo!'s hundreds of different online content and media services to create a more customized, social network-like appeal to its users. Yahoo! launched a personalized blogging and social networking service Yahoo! 360°, revamped its MyWeb personal Web hosting service, created a new PhotoMail service, and purchased online social event calendar company Upcoming .org to compete with Google's new online calendar service. Continuing its push to strengthen its social networking services. Yahoo! acquired blo.gs, a service based on RSS feed aggregation and del.icio.us, which allows registered users to create a scrapbook or notebook of information they wish to keep from the Websites they visit, similar to Google's notebook service.

Semel's content-driven strategy was to make Yahoo!'s media and entertainment services so useful and attractive to online customers that they would be willing to pay for them—in the form of once-and-for-all or monthly fees for services. For example, monthly fees for personal ads in its dating site, or ads to sell or rent merchandise like cars or homes, and fees that provided premium services in areas such as e-mail, data storage, photo sharing, e-commerce, message boards, and similar services. Also, it followed Amazon.com's initiative and worked to provide online software to generate fees from small businesses that wished to link to its Web portal and use Yahoo!'s specialist services to create, host, and manage their retail stores. Through these moves, Yahoo! kept its position as the most popular portal; its revenue more than tripled from 2003 to 2006 to over $6 billion, and its stock price recovered somewhat in the first half of 2006.

New Problems with a Content-Driven Strategy

By the summer of 2006, things were not so rosy, and major questions were surfacing about how Yahoo!'s content-driven strategy could continue to drive its revenues in the future as competition, especially as Google's and Facebook's popularity increased. Yahoo!'s stock fell 25% in the last half of 2006, and analysts worried that these popular search engine and social networking portals were stealing away its users, and that advertising revenues and user fees would fall in the future. For example, Google was now offering an ever-increasing number of free online services such as e-mail, chat, storage, and word processing software to compete with MSN as well as Yahoo!

In an internal e-mail leaked to the media, one of Yahoo!'s top managers expressed concern that many of its new investments in content and services were too expensive, unlikely to generate much profit, and it would not be able to keep up with agile new specialist portals; Google was becoming an Internet Giant. In the "Peanut Butter" memo, senior executive Brad Garlinghouse described Yahoo! as a company in search of a successful business model and strategies: "I've heard our strategy described as spreading peanut butter across the myriad opportunities that continue to evolve in the online world. The result: a thin layer of investment spread across everything we do and thus we focus on nothing in particular. I hate peanut butter. We all should." He had good reasons for his concern because the new specialist portals were more popular than Yahoo!'s own instant messaging and e-mail service, and, especially, in online imaging and video that had become increasingly important to Internet users. For example, Google drew further ahead of Yahoo! after its purchase of YouTube in 2006.

Nevertheless, Yahoo! still had impressive content covering sports, entertainment and finance, in particular. Also, it had embarked upon a major push to enhance the mobile delivery of all its services to better meet the needs of people on the go as the number of people using mobile-computing devices such as smartphones soared through the end of the 2000s, and is still growing in 2011. By 2008, for example, mobile video was a killer application, and to compete with Google, Yahoo! had heavily invested to upgrade this service—but eventually Yahoo! was forced to shut down its video service to cut costs.

The problem for Yahoo! was that its cost structure was increasing and it had lost its first-mover advantage to its new rivals—not a good position in the fast-changing online world.

The Search Engine Dilemma

A discussed earlier, for online digital media companies it had become essential to improve their search engine capabilities. Only Google had understood the crucial strategic relationship between providing users with fast, accurate search results, and the search engine provider that gives the ability to generate increasing advertising revenues. Google's business model was based upon providing better search capabilities and then providing an increasing number of free online services to attract more users and develop brand loyalty. To achieve significant revenue and profit growth, Semel recognized that Yahoo! also had to increase the capabilities of its search engine and generate the high volume of user visits that lead to increased revenues from online advertising and facilitating e-commerce transactions. Semel began to look for acquisitions to strengthen and improve Yahoo!'s search engine, and it bought several search companies such as Inktomi and Overture to improve its search competences. However, Google was unbeatable; its share of the search engine market was double that of Yahoo!'s—49% compared to Yahoo!'s 24% in 2006—and Microsoft's own search engine also plunged in popularity.

To meet Google's challenge, Semel combined the distinctive competencies of Inktomi and Overture, with its own in-house technology, to develop an improved search engine that would allow Yahoo! to offer a much more targeted online advertising program to compete with Google's—*Project Panama*. This huge, expensive project soon fell behind schedule, the company failed to launch it according to schedule, and Yahoo!'s stock price continued to plunge as it played catch up to Google and the other specialized Web portals. In fact, in 2005, Yahoo! and Google were neck-and-neck and each had about 18% of total online advertising revenues. By the end of 2006, Google's revenue had grown to 25% and Yahoo!'s had dropped to less than 14%.

In 2007, Semel reorganized Yahoo!'s management structure to allow it to better implement its business model and compete with its rivals—a shakeup sparked by the peanut butter memo. The new streamlined organizational structure grouped Yahoo!'s services into three primary product divisions, one focused upon satisfying the needs of its Website users, one upon finding better ways to service the needs of its advertisers, and one upon developing new technology. Semel hoped the reorganization would make Yahoo! more proficient at delivering online services and ads to capture the attention of online users. In 2007, Yahoo! rolled out its new targeted advertising system and announced that it expected major improvements in advertising revenues by the summer. Revenue per search query may grow by 10% or more in the second half of the year, and Semel said, "We believe this will deliver more relevant text ads to users, which in turn should create more high-quality leads. By the time we get to 2008 and beyond, this is a very, very, significant amount of additional profit and I'm pleased with the tangible progress we have made. I'm convinced we're on the right path." Yahoo!'s stock increased by over 10% as investors bet that this would be a turnaround moment in Yahoo!'s battle with Google.

Jerry Yang Takes Over as CEO

Semel and Yahoo! Investors were wrong. The number of users, including registered Yahoo! users, of Google's advanced search engine and other services, and the rapid development of popular specialized portals such as YouTube, and social networking Websites like Facebook, continued to siphon off millions of visits to Yahoo!'s Website. At the same time, the number of Yahoo! employees needed to provide the new advanced media services it was trying to offer soared, and so did its R&D costs; its cost structure increased. Also, at the same time, Microsoft recognized it had been slow to develop its search competencies and it began to pour billions into developing an advanced search engine called "Bing" that emerged at the end of the 2000s.

Investors lost confidence in Semel, who was forced out in 2008, and Yahoo!'s new CEO was now one of its original founders Jerry Yang. Yang spent the next 8 months streamlining Yahoo!'s business model, prioritizing the importance of its vast array of online services, and improving its search and advertising competences, while reducing its workforce to cut costs. But the Google Juggernaut was roaring ahead, and the value of Yahoo!'s stock continued to fall, so much so that in late-2008, Microsoft announced that it wanted to acquire Yahoo! for $40 billion, a huge premium over its stock price, before the bid and Yahoo!'s stock soared in value. Microsoft's logic was that its new search engine technology was now mature enough to replace Yahoo!'s and that in combining their search engines and online advertising functions, the merger would reap billions of dollars in cost savings. Furthermore, the merger would allow it to combine its MSN online service with Yahoo!'s so its registered customer base would soar, as would the number of users of its new combined Web portal. $40 billion was a lot of money, however.

After the bid, CEO Yang announced that Microsoft's offer to buy Yahoo! was a "galvanizing" event for his beleaguered company. However, he also made it clear that he was not interested in the takeover bid, and that he would meet with its board of directors to defend against what he expected would turn into a hostile bid. The battle raged for months during which Yang said he was holding out for a higher offer than the current bid that substantially undervalued Yahoo!'s assets. However, many analysts claimed that Yang was dreaming, and that the company's founder was not the right person to be in charge of making such an important decision.

Yang was supported by the board, and continued to reject repeated buyout and search-ad deal offers from Microsoft throughout 2008; eventually Microsoft announced it was withdrawing its bid for the company—upon which the value of the company's stock plunged and irate stockholders demanded that Yang be replaced. During this crucial year, Yang had been distracted by the takeover bid from streamlining the company's business model, so its performance had continued to fall! An exhausted Yang, whose resistance to the merger had personally cost him billions of dollars, decided that his future as CEO looked bleak and he handed over the reins to former Autodesk CEO Carol Bartz who became Yahoo! CEO in January 2009.

Bartz Reorganizes Yahoo!

Bartz has a long history of success in managing online companies and she moved quickly to find ways to reduce Yahoo!'s cost structure and simplify its operations to maintain its strong online brand identity. Bartz decided that the best way to restructure Yahoo! to gain more control over its business units and reduce operating costs was to centralize functions that had previously been performed by Yahoo!'s different business units, such as product development and marketing activities. For example, all the company's online publishing and advertising functions were centralized and put under the control of a single executive. Yahoo!'s European, Asian, and emerging markets divisions were combined and centralized under the control of another top executive. Bartz was astonished to find that Yahoo!'s talented programmers and engineers, who worked in different business units, didn't talk to each other, and she brought them all under the centralized control of a new executive in charge of product development, Chief Technology Officer Ari Balogh.

Bartz' cost-cutting efforts helped Yahoo! satisfy investors when, in the Spring of 2009, she announced plans to cut 5% more of Yahoo! staff, on top of 1,600 job cuts that had been made in December 2008. However, the way she would grow its revenues was not clear, especially as she assumed control when the financial crisis and recession had begun in 2009, and online advertising revenues plunged. Bartz said brand marketers put the brakes on ad spending, especially on display ads; the pictorial banners that were Yahoo!'s chief source of business and revenues fell 13% in 2009. Also, Yahoo!'s search engine advertising business fell 3% after having made progress in the last few years—Google kept powering ahead. Nevertheless, she had reduced operating expenses by 4% and had not cut employees in key functions such as product development and marketing. Yahoo!'s stock price rose 5% in the middle of 2009.

Although Yang had refused to sell the company he founded, Bartz made it clear that the company was still for sale—at the right price. Microsoft, however, was no longer interested in a takeover as the power of specialized portals such as Facebook, YouTube, and Amazon.com had by now become apparent—being a generalist and offering all things to all users was no longer possible. Nevertheless, the possibility of a major strategic alliance between the companies, so both could enjoy cost savings from economies of scale and scope in combining their search engine and online-targeted advertising functions, still existed. Essentially, Microsoft sought to obtain many of the advantages it had sought to achieve from acquiring Yahoo! by forming a strategic alliance. Now, Yahoo!'s position was considerably weaker as Bartz had to find ways to reduce costs given that Yahoo!'s revenues were stagnant or declining in many areas. She needed to keep up the company's stock price, in part, to still make it an attractive acquisition despite the fact that its market value had now plunged below $30 billion—over $10 billion less than Microsoft had offered for the company. In addition, Bartz announced that when the economy turned around, Yahoo!'s strategy for restoring growth would capitalize upon its online brand name and large size, and focus on "creating kick-ass products" to drive its growth.

The Agreement with Microsoft

In 2009, Yahoo! and Microsoft announced they had formed a strategic alliance that would benefit both companies in their battle with Google and Facebook. Yahoo! agreed to outsource its back-end search functions such as Web crawling, indexing and ranking to Microsoft to save money and use its Bing search engine to enhance its competitive position. In exchange, Yahoo! agreed to pay Microsoft a commission for paid search ads sold on Yahoo! and Yahoo! partner sites. Yahoo! estimated that this alliance would boost its annual operating income by about $500 million and reduce costs by about $200 million. Nevertheless, Bartz noted that "Search is a very valuable business for Yahoo!; we need to retain some stake in search to help it target display ads better. Search is important to our users and search is important to our advertisers."

At the same time, Bartz continued to prune Yahoo!'s unprofitable online services to reduce costs and focus its efforts upon the fastest growing, most profitable ad display markets. Yahoo! also announced continuing job cuts throughout 2009 and 2010 to reduce its workforce to under 14,000 and bring costs back under control.

Yahoo! in 2011

In June 2011, Yahoo! announced some disappointing results, in the most recent quarter its revenues had dropped by 23% compared to a year ago while Google announced that its revenues had increased by 32%. In the past year, Yahoo!'s 14,000 employees had generated $5.6 billion in revenues and $1.2 billion in

profit, while Google's 29,000 employees had generated $33 billion in revenues and $9 billion in profit. Why?

First, Yahoo! had not obtained the potential benefits it had expected to receive from its deal with Microsoft; although it was guaranteed a minimum payment of $450 million per year, the alliance had not generated a major increase in the number of visits to its search engine. However, Bartz said she expected revenues to substantially increase by the end of 2011 as the Bing search engine used by Yahoo! was increasing in popularity.

Second, Yahoo!'s targeted display advertising business had not performed as well as expected and profits had significantly fallen. However, Bartz announced that the costs of upgrading Yahoo!'s advertising platform and making it consistent across its global Websites was the main reason for this. With its new systems in place, Yahoo! would be able to deliver targeted advertising faster across all its different online services globally, and to provide companies with more effective advertising. Also, Yahoo! could now deliver its content and ads on all kinds of mobile computing devices, not just desktops, and Bartz stressed Yahoo!'s leading position in the U.S. and abroad in important content channels such as news and finance. However, Yahoo! has faced increasing competition from Facebook and Google, and investors worried if it could recover revenue in this highly lucrative market segment.

Yahoo!'s stock fell after this report, especially because it also announced lower revenue guidelines for the rest of 2011. But, its stock also took a major hit in June 2011 when it was announced that Alibaba, a huge Chinese Web portal, in which Yahoo! owns a 40% stake, had spun off its Alipay online payment service into a new company—without securing agreement from Yahoo!. Alibaba is worth many billions to Yahoo!, so this seemed to wipe off billions more of its market value and its stock plunged again. In August 2011, Bartz announced that Yahoo! would receive between $2 and $6 billion if and when the Alipay service was eventually spun off in an initial public offering, but this further reduced the value of its Alibaba investment and damaged Bartz' position. In August 2011, Yahoo!'s market value was about $18 billion, and 2/3 of that value was made up of its Asian assets valued at $9 billion, its $3 billion in cash; what was left was Yahoo!'s global online assets, now valued at around $6 billion. Microsoft had offered to pay $40 billion for its assets just a few years ago!

Thus, in August 2011, Yahoo! analysts could not decide if Yahoo! was undervalued because its online properties still offered the possibility of generating substantial revenue from search and advertising. Or, if its value might decline further in the future because it now had given up its online search expertise to Microsoft? It could not counter the strategies of Google and Facebook, and there was still no pipeline of innovative products to attract new users. Bartz' turnaround plan for Yahoo! had kept the company profitable because it had reduced costs, but what was its future vision and mission?

Yahoo! Fires Bartz

In September 2011, Yahoo!'s board of directors decided to fire Bartz—over the phone—claiming she had not found the right strategies to turn around the company. Yahoo! was in disarray in October 2011 as no new strategic leadership had emerged to orchestrate the company's turnaround and a stunned Bartz tweeted through her iPad that "Yahoo has. . . . me over." It seems that Yahoo!'s dysfunctional board is desperately trying to find a buyer for the company in order to provide stockholders with the most value for their investment.

In October, Microsoft, Google, and private investment funds had all been suggested as potential buyers for the company at a price around $20 billion—half of Microsoft's original offer. The company was still for sale—but the billion dollar question is at what price? The longer it takes to find a new buyer the less valuable Yahoo! is likely to be in the future—unless it can find some visionary CEO that can provide the company with a new vision and mission.

Endnotes

www.yahoo.com, 1990–2011.
Yahoo! 10K Reports, 1990–2011.

CASE 15

Boeing Commercial Aircraft in 2011

Charles W.L. Hill
University of Washington

Introduction

The first decade of the 20th century was one of ups and downs for Boeing Commercial Airplane, the commercial aircraft division of the world's largest aerospace company. In the late-1990s and early-2000s, Boeing had struggled with a number of ethics scandals and production problems that had tarnished the reputation of the company and led to sub-par financial performance. To make maters worse, its global rival, Airbus, had been gaining market share. Between 2001 and 2005, the European company regularly garnered more new orders than Boeing.

The tide started to turn Boeing's way in 2003, when it formally launched its next generation jet, the 787. Built largely out of carbon-fiber composites, the wide-bodied 787 was billed as the most fuel-efficient large jetliner in the world. The 787 was forecasted to consume 20% less fuel than Boeing's older wide-bodied jet, the 767. By 2006, the 787 was logging significant orders. This, together with strong interest in Boeing's best-selling narrow bodied jet, the 737, helped the company to recapture the lead in new commercial jet aircraft orders. Moreover, in 2006 Boeing's rival, Airbus, was struggling with significant production problems and weak orders for its new aircraft, the A380 super-jumbo. Airbus was also late to market with a rival for the 787, the wide-bodied Airbus A350, which would also be built largely out of carbon-fiber. While the 787 was scheduled to enter service in 2008, the A350 would not appear until 2012, giving Boeing a significant lead.

Over the next few years, Boeing encountered a number of production problems and technical design issues with the 787 that resulted in the introduction of the 787 being delayed 5 times. The 787 is now scheduled to enter service in late-2011, more than 3 years later than planned. Despite this, Boeing has a very healthy backlog for the 787, with 827 jets ordered as of mid-2011, compared to 567 for the rival A350. Airbus has also encountered some production problems of its own with the A350, and delivery of that aircraft model has now slipped into 2013.

Looking forward, Boeing now has some important decisions to make regarding its venerable narrow-bodied 737 aircraft family, which accounts for some 60% of Boeing's total aircraft deliveries. The main competitor for the 737 has long been Airbus' A320. In late-2010, Airbus announced that it would build a new version of the A320, designed to use advanced engines from Pratt & Whitney, and estimated to be 10–15% more efficient than existing engines. Know as the A320NEO (NEO stands for "new engine option"), by August 2011, the aircraft had garnered an impressive 1,029 orders. Airbus' success here forced Boeing's hand. Boeing, too, has stated that they will offer a version of the 737 using new engines (this will require some redesign of the 737, driving up Boeing's R&D costs). However, the company still must decide whether to totally redesign the 737, taking advantage of knowledge gained during the process of developing the 787, to build an all-new 737 out of composites that would also be designed with more efficient engines.

To complicate matters, for the first time in a generation there are several new entrants on the horizon. The Canadian regional jet manufacturer, Bombardier, is starting to gain orders for the 110–130 seat narrow bodied CSeries jet, which would place it in direct competition with the smallest of the 737 and A320 families. In addition, the Commercial Aircraft Corporation of China (Comac) has announced that it will build a 170–190 seat narrow-bodied jet.

The Competitive Environment

By the 2000s, the market for large commercial jet aircraft was dominated by just two companies, Boeing and Airbus. A third player in the industry, McDonnell Douglas, had been historically significant, but had lost share during the 1980s and 1990s. In 1997, Boeing acquired McDonnell Douglas, primarily for its strong military business, because in the mid-1990s Airbus has been gaining orders at Boeing's expense. By the mid-2000s, Boeing and Airbus were splitting the market.

Both Boeing and Airbus have a full range of aircraft. Boeing offers 5 aircraft "families" that range in size from 100 to over 500 seats. They are the narrow bodied 737 and the wide bodied 747, 767, 777 and 787 families. Each family comes in various forms. For example, there are currently 4 main variants of the 737 aircraft. They vary in size from 110 to 215 seats, and in range from 2,000 to over 5,000 miles. List prices vary from $47 million for the smallest member of the 737 family, the 737–600, to $282 million for the largest Boeing aircraft, the 747–8. The newest member of the Boeing family, the 787, lists for between $138 million and $188 million depending upon the model.[1]

Similarly, Airbus offers 5 "families," the narrow bodied A320 family, and the wide bodied A300/310, A330/340, A350 and A380 families. These aircraft vary in size from 100 to 550 seats. The range of list prices is similar to Boeing's. The A380 super-jumbo lists for between $282 million to $302 million, while the smaller A320 lists for between $62 million and $66.5 million.[2] Both companies also offer freighter versions of their wide bodied aircraft.

Airbus was a relatively recent entrant into the market. Airbus began its life as a consortium between a French company and Germany company in 1970. Later, a British and Spanish company joined the consortium. Initially, few people gave Airbus much chance for success, but the consortium gained ground by innovating. It was the first aircraft maker to build planes that "flew by wire," made extensive use of composites, had only two flight crew members (most had three), and used a common cockpit layout across models. It also gained sales by being the first company to offer a wide bodied twin-engine jet, the A300, that was positioned between smaller single aisle planes like the 737 and large aircraft such as the Boeing 747.

In 2001, Airbus became a fully integrated company. The European Defense and Space Company (EADS), formed by a merger between French, German and Spanish interests, acquired 80% of the shares in EADS, and BAE Systems, a British company, took a 20% stake.

Development and Production

The economics of development and production in the industry are characterized by a number of facts. First, the R&D and tooling costs associated with developing a new airliner are very high. Boeing spent some $5 billion to develop the 777. Its latest aircraft, the 787, was initially expected to cost $8 billion to develop, but delays have increased that to at least $12 billion. Development costs for Airbus' A380 super-jumbo reportedly exceeded $15 billion.

Second, given the high upfront costs, in order to break even a company must capture a significant share of projected world demand. The breakeven point for the Airbus super-jumbo, for example, is estimated to be between 250 and 270 aircraft. Estimates of the total potential market for this aircraft vary widely. Boeing has suggested that the total world market will be for no more than 320 aircraft over the next 20 years—Airbus believes that there will be demand for some 1,250 aircraft of this size. It may take 5–10 years of production before Airbus breaks even on the A380–on top of years of negative cash flow during development.[3]

Third, there are significant learning effects in aircraft production.[4] On average, unit costs fall by about 20% each time *cumulative* output of a specific model is doubled. The phenomenon occurs because managers and shop floor workers learn over time how to assemble a particular model of plane more efficiently, reducing assembly time, boosting productivity, and lowering the marginal costs of producing subsequent aircraft.

Fourth, the assembly of aircraft is an enormously complex process. Modern planes have over 1 million component parts that have to be designed to fit with each other, and then produced and brought together at the right time in order to assemble the engine. At several times in the history of the industry, problems with the supply of critical components have held up production schedules and resulted in losses. In 1997, Boeing took a charge of $1.6 billion against earnings when it had to halt the production of its 737 and 747 models due to a lack of component parts. In 2008, Boeing had to delay production of the 787 due to a shortage of fasteners.

Historically, airline manufacturers tried to manage the supply process through vertical integration, by making many of the component parts that went into an aircraft (engines were long the exception to this). Over the last two decades, however, there has been a trend to contract out production of components and even entire sub-assemblies to independent suppliers. On the 777, for example, Boeing outsourced about 65% of the aircraft production, by value, excluding the engines.[5] While helping to reduce costs, contracting out has placed enormous onus on airline manufacturers to work closely with its suppliers to coordinate the entire production process.

Finally, all new aircraft are now designed digitally, and assembled virtually before a single component is produced. Boeing was the first to do this with its 777 in the early-1990s, and with its new version of the 737 in the late-1990s.

Customers

Demand for commercial jet aircraft is very volatile and tends to reflect the financial health of the commercial airline industry, which is prone to boom and bust cycles (see Exhibits 1, 2 and 3). The airline industry has long been characterized by excess capacity, intense price competition, and a perception

Exhibit 1 Commercial Aircraft Orders 1990–2010

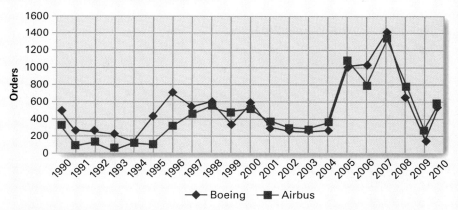

Source: Boeing and Airbus Websites http://www.boeing.com/
http://www.airbus.com/

Exhibit 2 World Airline Industry Revenues

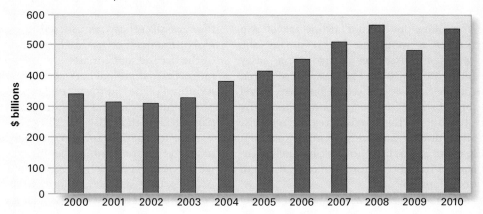

Source: IATA Data.

Exhibit 3 World Airline Industry Net Profit ($ billions) 2001–2010

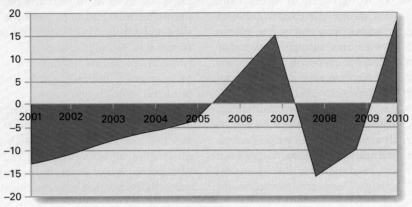

Source: IATA Data.

Exhibit 4 Jet Fuel Prices July 2001–June 2011

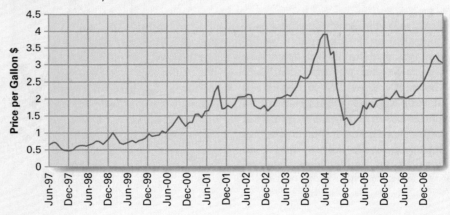

Source: www.iata.org

among the travelling public that airline travel is a commodity. After a moderate boom during the 1990s, the airline industry went through a nasty downturn during 2001–2005. The downturn started in early-2001 due to a slowdown in business travel after the boom of the 1990s. It was compounded by a dramatic slump in airline travel after the terrorist attacks on the United States in September of 2001. Between 2001 and 2005, the entire global airline industry lost some $40 billion, more money than it had made since its inception.[6]

The industry recovered in 2006 and 2007, only to rack up big losses again in 2008 and 2009 due to the recession that was ushered in by the 2008–2009 global financial crisis. High fuel prices during much of the decade made matters worse (prices for jet fuel more than doubled between 2004 and 2006—see Exhibit 4). The bill for jet fuel represented over 25% of the industry's total operating costs in 2006, compared to less than 10% in 2001.[7]

During the 2001–2005 period, losses were particularly severe among the big six airlines in the world's largest market, the United States (American Airlines, United, Delta, Continental, US Airways and Northwest). Three of these airlines (United, Delta and Northwest) were forced to seek Chapter 11 bankruptcy protections. Despite that demand and profits plummeted at the big six airlines, some carriers continued to make profits during 2001–2005, most notably the budget airline Southwest. In addition, other newer budget airlines including AirTran and JetBlue (which was started in 2000), gained market share during this period. Indeed, between 2000 and 2003, the budget airlines in the United States expanded capacity by 44% even as the majors slashed their carrying capacity and parked unused planes in the desert. In 1998, the budget airlines held a 16% share of U.S. market; by mid-2004 their share had risen to 29%.[8]

The key to the success of the budget airlines is a strategy which gives them a 30–50% cost advantage over traditional airlines. The budget airlines all follow the same basic script–they purchase just one type of aircraft (some standardize on Boeing 737s, others on Airbus 320s). They hire nonunion labor and cross-train employees to perform multiple jobs (e.g. to help meet turnaround times, the pilots might help check tickets at the gate). As a result of flexible work rules, Southwest needs only 80 employees to support and fly an aircraft, compared to 115 at the big six airlines. The budget airlines also favor flying "point-to-point," rather than through hubs, and often use cheap secondary airports, rather than major hubs. They focus on large markets with lots of traffic (e.g. up and down the East coast). There are no frills on the flights, no in flight meals . and prices are set low to fill up seats.

In contrast, the operations of major airlines are based on the network or "hub and spoke" system. Under this system, the network airlines route their flights through major hubs. Often, a single airline will dominate a hub (for example, United dominates Chicago's O'Hare airport). This system was developed for good reason—it was a way of efficiently using airline capacity when there wasn't enough demand to fill a plane flying point-to-point. By using a hub and spoke system, the major network airlines have been able to serve some 38,000 city pairs, some of which generate fewer than 50 passengers per day. But by focusing a few hundred city pairs where there is sufficient demand to fill their planes, and flying directly between them (point-to-point) the budget airlines seem to have found a way around this constraint. The network carriers also suffer from a higher cost structure due to their legacy of a unionized workforce. In addition, their costs are higher by their superior in flight service. In good times, the network carriers can recoup their costs by charging higher prices than the discount airlines, particularly for business travelers, who pay more to book late, and to fly business or first class. In the competitive environment of the 2000s, however, this was no longer the case. Between 2000 and 2010, the price of an average round trip domestic ticket in the U.S. increased from $317 to $338, an increase of 6.7% over the decade, while the consumer price index increased 26.6% (i.e. in real terms prices fell).[9]

Due to the effect of increased competition, the real yield that U.S. airlines got from passengers fell from $0.087 cents per mile in 1980 to 6.37 cents per mile in 1990, $0.0512 cents per mile in 2000, and $0.04 cents per mile in 2005 (these figures are expressed in constant 1978 cents).[10] Real yields are also declining elsewhere. With real yields declining, the only way that airlines can become profitable is to reduce their operating costs.

Outside of the United States, competition has intensified as deregulation has allowed low cost airlines to enter local markets and capture share from long established national airlines that have utilized the hub and spoke model. In Europe, for example, Ryanair and easyJet have adopted the business model of Southwest, and used it to grow aggressively.

By the mid-2000s, large airlines in the U.S. were starting to improve their operating efficiency, helped by growing traffic volumes, higher load factors and reductions in operating costs, particularly labor costs. Load factors refers to the percentage of a plane that is full on average, which hit a record 86% in mid-2006 in the United States, and 81% in international markets. Load factors have remained reasonably high since then, moving between 75% and 85% on a monthly basis between 2006 and 2010.

Demand Projections

Both Boeing and Airbus issue annual projects of likely future demand for commercial jet aircraft. These projections are based upon assumptions about future global economic growth, the resulting growth in demand for air travel, and the financial health of the world's airlines.

In its 2011 report, Boeing assumed that the world economy would grow by 3.3% per annum over the next 20 years, which should generate growth in passenger traffic of 5.1% per annum, and growth in cargo traffic of 5.6% per year. On this basis, Boeing forecast demand for some 33,500 new aircraft valued at more than $4 trillion over the next 20 years. Of this, some 15,370 aircraft will be replacement for aircraft retired from service, and the remaining aircraft will satisfy an expanded market. In 2030, Boeing estimates that the total global fleet of aircraft will be 39,530 up from 17,330 in 2005. Boeing believes that North America will account for 22% of all new orders, Asia Pacific for 34% and Europe for 23%. Passenger traffic is projected to grow at 7% per annum in Asia, versus 2.3% in North America and 4% in Europe.[11]

Regarding the mix of orders, Boeing believes that 70% of all orders by units will be for narrow bodied aircraft such as the 737 and A320, 22% will be for wide-bodied twin aisle jets such as the 787 and 747, and 3% for large aircraft such as the 747 and A380.

The latest Airbus forecast covers 2010–2029. Over that period, Airbus forecasts world passenger traffic to grow by 4.8% per annum, and predicts demand for 25,850 new aircraft worth $3.2 trillion. (Note that Airbus excludes regional jets from its forecast, there are some 2,000 regional jet deliveries included in Boeing's forecasts). Airbus believes that demand for very large aircraft will be robust, amounting to 1,740 large passenger aircraft and freighters in the 747 range and above, or 18% of the total value of aircraft delivered.[12]

The difference in the mix of orders projected by Boeing and Airbus reflect different views of how future demand will evolve. Airbus believes that hubs will continue to play an important role in airline travel, particularly international travel, and that very large jets will be required to transport people between hubs. Airbus bases this assumption partly on an analysis of data over the last 20 years, which shows that traffic between major airline hubs has grown faster than traffic between other city pairs. Airbus also assumes that urban concentrations will continue to grow. Airbus states that demand is simply a function of where people want to go, and most people want to travel between major urban centers. The company notes, for example, that 90% of travelers from the United States to China go to 3 major cities. Fifty other cities make up the remaining 10%, and Airbus believes that very few of these cities will have demand large enough to justify a nonstop service from North America or Europe. Based on this assumption, Airbus sees robust demand for very large aircraft, and particularly its A380 offering.

Boeing has a different view of the future. The company has theorized that hubs will become increasingly congested, and that many travelers will seek to avoid them. Boeing thinks that passengers prefer frequent nonstop service between the cities they wish to visit. Boeing also sees growth in travel between city pairs as being large enough to support an increasing number of direct long-haul flights. The company notes that continued liberalization of regulations governing airline routes around the world will allow for the establishment of more direct flights between city pairs. As in the United States, the company believes that long haul low-cost airlines that focus on serving city pairs and avoid hubs will emerge.

In sum, Boeing believes that airline travelers will demand more frequent nonstop flights, not larger aircraft.[13] To support this, the company has data showing that all of the growth in airline travel since 1995 has been met by the introduction of new nonstop flights between city pairs, and by an increased frequency of flights between city pairs, and not by an increase in airplane size. For example, Boeing notes that following the introduction of the 767, airlines introduced more flights between city pairs in North America and Europe, and more frequent departures. In 1984, 63% of all flights across the North Atlantic were in the 747. By 2004, the figure had declined to 13%, with smaller wide bodied aircraft such as the 767 and 777 dominating traffic. Following the introduction of the 777, which can fly nonstop across the Pacific, and is smaller than the 747, the same process occurred in the North Pacific. In 2006, there were 72 daily flights serving 26 city pairs in North America and Asia.

Boeing's History[14]

William Boeing established the Boeing Company in 1916 in Seattle. In the early-1950s, Boeing took an enormous gamble when it decided to build a large jet aircraft that could be sold both to the military as a tanker, and to commercial airlines as a passenger plane. Known as the "Dash 80," the plane had swept back wings and 4 jet engines. Boeing invested $16 million to develop the Dash 80, 2/3 of the company's entire profits during the post war years. The Dash 80 was the basis for 2 aircraft—the KC-135

Air Force tanker and the Boeing 707. Introduced into service in 1957, the 707 was the world's first commercially successful passenger jet aircraft. Boeing went on to sell some 856 Boeing 707s along with 820 KC-135s. The final 707, a freighter, rolled off the production line in 1994 (production of passenger planes ended in 1978). The closest rival to the 707 was the Douglas DC8, of which some 556 were ultimately sold.

The 707 was followed by a number of other successful jetliners including the 727 (which entered service in 1962), the 737 (which entered service in 1967), and the 747 (which entered service in 1970). The single aisle 737 went on to become the workhorse of many airlines. In the 2000s, a completely redesigned version of the 737 that could seat between 110 and 180 passengers was still selling strong. Cumulative sales of the 737 totaled 6,500 by mid-2006, making it by far the most popular commercial jet aircraft ever sold.

It was the 747 "jumbo jet," however, that probably best defined Boeing. In 1966, when Boeing's board made the decision to develop the 747, they were widely viewed as betting the entire company on the jet. The 747 was born out of the desire of Pan Am, then America's largest airline, for a 400 seat passenger aircraft that could fly 5,000 miles. Pan Am believed that the aircraft would be ideal for the growing volume of trans-continental traffic. However, beyond Pan Am, which committed to purchasing 25 aircraft, demand was very uncertain. Moreover, the estimated $400 million in development and tooling costs placed a heavy burden on Boeing's financial resources. To make a return on its investment, the company estimated it would need to sell close to 400 aircraft. To complicate matters further, Boeing's principal competitors, Lockheed and McDonnell Douglas, were each developing 250 seat jumbo jets.

Boeing's big bet turned out to be auspicious. Pan Am's competitors feared being left behind, and by the end of 1970, almost 200 orders for the aircraft had been placed. Successive models of the 747 extended the range of the aircraft. The 747–400, introduced in 1989, had a range of 8,000 miles and a maximum seating capacity of 550 (although most configurations seated around 400 passengers). By this time, both Douglas and Lockheed had exited the market giving Boeing a lucrative monopoly in the very large commercial jet category. By 2005, the company had

sold nearly 1,430 747s, and was actively selling its latest version of the 747 family, the 747–8 which was scheduled to enter service in 2008.

By the mid-1970s Boeing was beyond the break even point on all of its models (707, 727, 737 and 747). The positive cash flow helped to fund investment in two new aircraft, the narrow bodied 757 and the wide bodied 767. The 757 was designed as a replacement to the aging 727, while the 767 was a response to a similar aircraft from Airbus. These were the first Boeing aircraft to be designed with two person cockpits, rather than three. Indeed, the cockpit layout was identical, allowing crew to shift from one aircraft to the other. The 767 was also the first aircraft for which Boeing subcontracted a significant amount of work to a trio of three Japanese manufacturers—Mitsubishi, Kawasaki, and Fuji—who supplied about 15% of the airframe. Introduced in 1981, both aircraft were successful. Some 1049 757s were sold during the life of the program (which ended in 2003). By 2006, over 950 767s had been sold, and the program was still ongoing.

The next Boeing plane was the 777. A two-engine wide bodied aircraft with seating capacity of up to 400 and a range of almost 8,000 miles, the 777, was initiated in 1990. The 777 was seen as a response to Airbus' successful A330 and A340 wide bodied aircraft. Development costs were estimated at some $5 billion. The 777 was the first wide bodied long-haul jet to have only two engines. It was also the first to be designed entirely on computer. To develop the 777, for the first time Boeing used cross-functional teams composed of engineering and production employees. It also bought major suppliers and customers into the development process. As with the 767, a significant amount of work was outsourced to foreign manufacturers including the Japanese trio of Mitsubishi, Kawasaki, and Fuji who supplied 20% of the 777 airframe. In total, some 60% of parts for the 777 were outsourced. The 777 proved to be another successful venture—by mid-2006, 850 777s had been ordered, far greater than the 200 or so required to break even.

In December 1996, Boeing stunned the aerospace industry by announcing it would merge with long-time rival McDonnell Douglas in a deal estimated to be worth $13.3 billion. The merger was driven by Boeing's desire to strengthen its presence in the defense and space side of the aerospace business, areas in which McDonnell Douglas was traditionally strong. On the commercial side of the aerospace business, Douglas had been losing market share since the 1970s. By 1996, Douglas accounted for less than 10% of production in the large commercial jet aircraft market and only 3% of new orders placed that year. The dearth of new orders meant the long-term outlook for Douglas's commercial business was increasingly murky. With or without the merger, many analysts felt that it was only a matter of time before McDonnell Douglas would be forced to exit from the commercial jet aircraft business. In their view, the merger with Boeing merely accelerated that process.

The merger transformed Boeing into a broad-based aerospace business within which commercial aerospace accounted for 40–60% of total revenue, depending upon the stage of the commercial production cycle. In 2001, for example, the commercial aircraft group accounted for $35 billion in revenues out of a corporate total of $58 billion, or 60%. In 2005, with the delivery cycle at a low point (but the order cycle rebounding), the commercial airplane group accounted for $22.7 billion out of a total of $54.8 billion, or 41%. A wide range of military aircraft, weapons and defense systems, and space systems comprised the balance of their revenue.

In the early-2000s, in a highly symbolic act, Boeing moved its corporate headquarters from Seattle to Chicago. The move was an attempt to put some distance between top corporate officers and the commercial aerospace business, the headquarters of which remained in Seattle. The move was also intended to signal to the investment community that Boeing was far more than its commercial businesses.

To some extent, the move to Chicago may have been driven by a number of production missteps in the late-1990s that occurred at a time when the company should have been enjoying financial success. During the mid-1990s orders had boomed as Boeing cut prices in an aggressive move to gain share from Airbus. However, delivering these aircraft meant that Boeing had to more than double its production schedule between 1996 and 1997. As it attempted to do this, the company ran into some server production bottlenecks.[15] The company scrambled to hire and train some 41,000 workers, recruiting many from suppliers, a move it came to regret when many of the suppliers could not meet Boeing's demands, and shipments of parts were delayed. In the Fall of 1997, things got so bad that Boeing shut down its 747 and 737 production lines so that workers could

catch up with out of sequence work, and wait for backordered parts to arrive. Ultimately, the company had to take a $1.6 billion charge against earnings to account for higher costs and penalties paid to airlines for the late delivery of jets. As a result, Boeing made very little money out of its mid-1990s order boom. The head of Boeing's commercial aerospace business was fired, and the company committed itself to a major acceleration of its attempt to overhaul its production system, elements of which dated back half a century.

Boeing in the 2000s

In the 2000s, 3 things dominated the development of Boeing Commercial Aerospace. First, the company accelerated a decade-long project aimed at improving the company's production methods by adopting the lean production systems initially developed by Toyota and applying them to the manufacture of large jet aircraft. Second, the company considered, and then rejected, the idea of building a successor to the 747. Third, Boeing decided to develop a new wide bodied long haul jetliner, the 787.

Lean Production at Boeing

Boeing's attempt to revolutionize the way planes could be built began in the early-1990s. Beginning in 1990, the company started to send teams of executives to Japan to study the production systems of Japan's leading manufacturers, particularly Toyota. Toyota had pioneered a new way of assembling automobiles, known as lean production (in contrast to conventional mass production).

Toyota's lean production system was developed by one of the company's engineers, Ohno Taiichi.[16] After working at Toyota for 5 years and visiting Ford's U.S. plants, Ohno became convinced that the mass production philosophy for making cars was flawed. He saw numerous problems, including 3 major drawbacks. First, long production runs created massive inventories, which had to be stored in large warehouses. This was expensive because of the cost of warehousing and because inventories tied up capital in unproductive uses. Second, if the initial machine settings were wrong, long production runs resulted in the production of a large number of defects (that is, waste). And third, the mass production system was unable to accommodate consumer preferences for product diversity.

In looking for ways to make shorter production runs economical, Ohno developed a number of techniques designed to reduce setup times for production equipment, a major source of fixed costs. By using a system of levers and pulleys, he was able to reduce the time required to change dies on stamping equipment from a full day in 1950 to 3 minutes by 1971. This advance made small production runs economical, which allowed Toyota to respond better to consumer demands for product diversity. Small production runs also eliminated the need to hold large inventories, thereby reducing warehousing costs. Furthermore, small product runs and the lack of inventory meant that defective parts were produced only in small numbers and entered the assembly process immediately. This reduced waste and made it easier to trace defects to their source and fix the problem. In sum, Ohno's innovations enabled Toyota to produce a more diverse product range at a lower unit cost than was possible with conventional mass production.

Impressed with what Toyota had done, in the mid-1990s, Boeing started to experiment with applying Toyota-like lean production methods to the production of aircraft. Production at Boeing was formerly focused upon producing parts in high volumes, and then storing them in warehouses until they were ready to be used in the assembly process. After visiting Toyota, engineers realized that Boeing was drowning in inventory. A huge amount of space and capital was tied up in things that didn't add value. Moreover, expensive specialized machines often took up a lot of space, and were frequently idle for long stretches of time.

Like Ohno at Toyota, the company engineers started to think about how they could modify equipment and processes at Boeing to reduce waste. Boeing set aside space and time for teams of creative plant employees—design engineers, maintenance technicians, electricians, machinists and operators—to start experimenting with machinery. They called these teams "moonshiners." The term "moonshine" was coined by Japanese executives who visited the United States after World War II. They were impressed by two things in the U.S.—supermarkets, and the stills built by people in the Appalachian hills. They noticed that people built these stills with no money. They would use salvaged parts to make small stills that produced alcohol that they sold for money. The Japanese took this philosophy back home with them, and applied it to industrial machinery—which is where Boeing executives saw the concept in operation in the 1990s. With the help of Japanese consultants, they decided to apply the moonshine creative philosophy at Boeing—to produce new "right-sized" machines with very little money that could be used to make money.

The moonshine teams were trained in lean production techniques, given a small budget, and then set loose. Initially, many of the moonshine teams focused on redesigning equipment to produce parts. Underlying this choice was a Boeing study, which showed that more than 80% of the parts manufactured for aircraft are less than 12 inches long, and yet the metal working machinery is huge, inflexible, and could only economically produce parts in large lots.[17]

Soon, empowered moonshine teams were designing their own equipment—small-scale machines with wheels on that could be moved around the plant, and that took up little space. One team replaced a large stamping machine that cost 6-figures and was used to produce L-shaped metal parts in batches of 1,000 with a miniature stamping machine powered by a small hydraulic motor that could be wheeled around the plant. With the small machine, that cost a couple of thousand dollars, parts could be produced very quickly in small lots, eliminating the need for inventory. They also made a sanding machine and a parts cleaner of equal size. Now the entire process—from stamping the raw material to the finished part—is completed in minutes (instead of hours or days) just by configuring these machines into a small cell and having them serviced by a single person. The small scale and quick turnaround now made it possible to produce these parts just-in-time, eliminating the need to produce and store inventory.[18]

Another example of a moonshine innovation concerns the process for loading seats onto a plane during assembly. Historically, this was a cumbersome process. After the seats would arrive at Boeing from a supplier, wheels were attached to each seat, and then the seats were delivered to the factory floor in a large container. An overhead crane lifted the container up to the level of the aircraft door. Then, the seats were unloaded and rolled into the aircraft, before being installed. The process was repeated until all of the seats had been loaded. For a single aisle plane this could take 12 hours. For a wide bodied jet, it would take much longer. A moonshine team adapted a hay elevator to perform the same job. It cost a lot less, delivered seats quickly through the passenger door, and took just 2 hours, while eliminating the need for cranes.[19]

Multiply the examples given here, and soon there would be a very significant impact on production costs. A drill machine was built for 5% of the cost of a full scale machine from Ingersoll-Rand; portable routers were built for 0.2% of the cost of a large fixed router; one process that took 2,000 minutes for a 100 part order (20 minutes per part because of setup, machining and transit) now takes 100 minutes (one minute per part); employees building 737 floor beams reduced labor hours by 74%, increased inventory turns from 2 to 18 per year, and reduced manufacturing space by 50%; employees building the 777 tail cut lead time by 70% and reduced space and work in progress by 50%; production of parts for landing gear support used to take 32 moves from machine to machine, and required 10 months—production now takes 3 moves and 25 days.[20]

In general, Boeing found that it was able to produce smaller lots of parts economically, often from machines that it built itself, which were smaller and cost less than the machines available from outside vendors. In turn, these innovations enabled Boeing to switch to just-in-time inventory systems and reduce waste. Boeing was also able to save on space. By eliminating large production machinery at its Auburn facility, replacing much of it with smaller more flexible machines, Boeing was able to free up 1.3 million square feet of space, and sold 7 buildings.[21]

In addition to moonshine teams, Boeing also adopted other process improvement methodologies, using them when deemed appropriate. Six Sigma quality improvement processes are widely used within Boeing. The most wide reaching process change, however, was the decision to switch from a static assembly line to a moving line. In traditional aircraft manufacture, planes are docked in angled stalls. Ramps surround each plane, and workers go in and out to find parts and install them. Moving a plane to the next work station was a complex process. The aircraft had to be lowered from its work station, a powered cart was brought in, the aircraft was towed to the next station, and then it was lifted again. This could take two shifts. A lot of time was wasted bringing parts to a stall, and moving a plane from one stall to the next.

In 2001, Boeing introduced a moving assembly line into its Renton plant near Seattle, which manufactures the 737. With a moving line, each aircraft is attached to a "sled" that rides a magnetic strip embedded in the factory floor, pulling the aircraft at a rate of 2 inches per minute, moving past a series of stations where tools and parts arrive at the moment need, allowing workers to install the proper assemblies. The setup can eliminate wandering for tools and parts, as well as expensive tug pulls or crane lifts (only having tools delivered to workstations, rather than having workers fetch them, was found to save 20–45 minutes on every shift). Preassembly tasks can be performed on feeder lines. For example, inboard and outboard flaps can be assembled on the wing before it will arrive for joining to the fuselage.[22]

Like a Toyota assembly line, the moving line can be stopped if a problem arises. Lights indicate the state of the line. A green light will indicate a normal work flow, the first sign of a stoppage brings a yellow warning light, and if the problem isn't solved within 15 minutes, a purple light will indicate that the line has stopped. Each work area and feeder line has will require its own lights, so there is no doubt where the problem may occur.[23]

The cumulative effects of these process innovations have been significant. By 2005, assembly time for the 737 had been cut from 22 days to just 11 days. In addition, work in process inventory had been reduced by 55% and stored inventory by 59%.[24] By 2006, all of Boeing's production lines, except for the 747, had shifted from static bays to a moving line. The 747 is scheduled to shift to moving line when Boeing starts production of the 747–8.

The Super-Jumbo Decisions

In the early-1990s Boeing and Airbus started to contemplate new aircraft to replace Boeing's aging 747. The success of the 747 had given Boeing a monopoly in the market for very large jet aircraft, making the plane one of the most profitable in the jet age, but the basic design dated back to the 1960s, and some believed there might be sufficient demand for a super-jumbo aircraft with as many as 900 seats.

Initially, the two companies considered establishing a joint venture to share the costs and risks associated with a developing a super-jumbo aircraft, but Boeing withdrew in 1995 citing costs and uncertain demand prospects. Airbus subsequently concluded that Boeing was never serious about the joint venture, and the discussions were nothing more than a ploy to keep Airbus from developing its own plane.[25]

After Boeing withdrew, Airbus started to talk about offering a competitor to the 747 in 1995. The plane, then dubbed the A3XX, was to be a super-jumbo with capacity for over 500 passengers. Indeed, Airbus stated that some versions of the plane might carry as many as 900 passengers. Airbus initially estimated that there would be demand for some 1,400 planes of this size over 20 years, and that development costs would total around $9 billion (estimates ultimately increased to some $15 billion). Boeing's latest 747 offering—the 747–400—could carry around 416 passengers in 3 classes.

Boeing responded by drafting plans to develop new versions of the 747 family. The 747–500X and the 747–600X. The 747–600X was to have a new (larger) wing, a fuselage almost 50 feet longer than the 747–400, would carry 550 passengers in 3 classes and have a range of 7,700 miles. The smaller 747–500X would have carried 460 passengers in 3 classes and had a range of 8,700 miles.

After taking a close look at the market for a super-jumbo replacement to the 747, in early-1997 Boeing announced that it would not proceed with the program. The reasons given for this decision included the limited market and high development costs, which at the time, were estimated to be $7 billion. There were also fears that the wider wing span of the new planes would mean that airports would have to redesign some of their gates to take the aircraft. Boeing, McDonnell Douglas (prior to the merger with Boeing) and the major manufacturers of jet engines all forecast demand for about 500–750 such aircraft over the next 20 years. Airbus alone forecasts demand has high as 1,400 aircraft. Boeing stated that the fragmentation of the market due to the rise of "point-to-point" flights across oceans would limit demand for a super-jumbo. Instead of focusing on the super-jumbo category, Boeing stated that it would develop new versions of the 767 and 777 aircraft that could fly up to 9,000 miles and carry as many as 400 passengers.

Airbus, however, continued to push forward with planes to develop the A3XX. In December 2000, with more than 50 orders in hand, the board of EADS, Airbus' parent company, approved development of the plane, which was now dubbed the A380. Development costs at this point were pegged at $12 billion, and the plane was forecasted to enter service in 2006 with Singapore Airlines. The A380 would have 2 passenger decks, more space per seat and wider aisles. It would carry 555 passengers in great comfort, something that passengers would appreciate on long transoceanic flights. According to Airbus, the plane would carry up to 35% more passengers than the most popular 747–400 configuration, yet cost per seat would be 15–20% lower due to operating efficiencies. Concerns were raised about turnaround time at airport gates for such a large plane, but Airbus stated that dual boarding bridges and wider aisles meant that turnaround times would be no more than those for the 747–400.

Airbus also stated that the A380 was also designed to operate on exiting runways and within existing gates. However, London's Heathrow airport found that it had to spend some $450 million to accommodate the A380, widening taxiways and building a baggage reclaim area for the plane. Similarly, 18 U.S. airports had reportedly spent some $1 billion just to accommodate the A380.[26]

The 787

While Airbus pushed forward with the A380, in March 2001, Boeing announced the development of a radically new aircraft. Dubbed the sonic cruiser, the plane would carry 250 passengers 9,000 miles and fly just below the speed of sound, cutting 1 hour of transatlantic flights and 3 hours of transpacific flights. To keep down operating costs, the sonic cruiser would be built out of low weight carbon-fiber "composites." Although the announcement created considerable interest in the aviation community, in the wake of the recession that hit the airline industry after September 11, 2001, both Boeing and the airlines became considerably less enthusiastic. In March 2002, the program was cancelled. Instead, Boeing said that it would develop a more conventional aircraft using composite technology. The plane was initially known as the 7E7 with the "E" standing for "Efficient" (the plane was renamed the 787 in early-2005).

In April 2004, the 7E7 program was formally launched with an order for 50 aircraft worth $6 billion from All Nippon Airlines of Japan. It was the largest launch order in Boeing's history. The 7E7 was a twin-aisle wide bodied, two-engine plane designed to carry 200–300 passengers up to 8,500 miles, making the 7E7 well suited for long haul point-to-point flights. The range exceeded all but the longest range plane in the 777 family, and the 7E7 could fly 750 miles more than Airbus' closest competitor, the mid-sized A330–200. With a fuselage built entirely out of composites, the aircraft was lighter and would use 20% less fuel than existing aircraft of comparable size.

The plane was also designed with passenger comfort in mind. The seats would be wider, as would the aisles, and the windows would be larger than in existing aircraft. The plane would be pressurized at 6,000 feet altitude, as opposed to 8,000 feet, which is standard industry practice. Airline cabin humidity was typically kept at 10% to avoid moisture buildup and corrosion—but composites don't corrode, so humidity would be closer to 20–30%.[27]

Initial estimates suggested that the jet would cost some $7–8 billion to develop and enter service in 2008. Boeing decided to outsource more work for the 787 than on any other aircraft to date. Boeing would build some 35% of the plane's fuselage and wing structure. The trio of Japanese companies that worked on the 767 and 777, Mitsubishi Heavy Industries, Kawasaki Heavy Industries, and Fuji Heavy Industries, would build another 35%, and some 26% would be built by Italian companies, particularly Alenia.[28] For the first time, Boeing asked its major suppliers to bear some of the development costs for the aircraft.

The plane was to be assembled at Boeing's wide bodied plant in Everett, Washington State. Large subassemblies were to be built by major suppliers, and then shipped to Everett for final assembly. The idea was to "snap together" the parts in Everett in 3 days, cutting down on total assembly time. To speed up transportation, Boeing would adopt air freight as its major transportation method for many components.

Airbus' initial response was to dismiss Boeing's claims of cost savings as inconsequential. They pointed out that even if the 787 used less fuel than the A330, that amount was equivalent to just 4% of total operating costs.[29] However, even by Airbus' calculations, as fuel prices were starting to accelerate, the magnitude of the savings rose. Moreover, Boeing quickly started to snag some significant orders for the 787. In 2004, Boeing booked 56 orders for the

787, and in 2005 some 232 orders. Another 85 orders were booked in the first 9 months of 2006 for a running total of 373–well beyond break even point.

In December 2004, Airbus announced that it would develop a new model, the A350, to compete directly with the 787. The planes were to be long haul twin-aisle jets, seating 200–300 passengers, and constructed of composites. The order flow, however, was slow, with airlines complaining that the A350 did not match the Boeing 787 on operating efficiency, range or passenger comfort. Airbus went back to the drawing board and in mid-2006, it announced a new version of the A350, the A350 XWB for "Extra Wide Body." Airbus estimated that the A350 XWB would cost $10 billion to develop and enter service in 2012, several years behind the 787. The two-engine A350 XWB will carry between 250 and 375 passengers and fly up to 8,500 miles. The largest versions of the A350 XWB will be competing directly with the Boeing 777, not the 787. Like the 787, the A350 XWB it will be built primarily of composite materials. The "Extra Wide Body" is designed to enhance passenger comfort. To finance the A350 XWB, Airbus stated that it would seek launch aid from Germany, France, Spain and the UK, all countries where major parts of Airbus are based.[30]

Trade Tensions

It is impossible to discuss the global aerospace industry without touching on trade issues. Over the last 3 decades, both Boeing and Airbus have charged that their competitor benefited unfairly from government subsidies. Until 2001, Airbus functioned as a consortium of 4 European aircraft manufacturers: one British (20.0% ownership stake), one French (37.9% ownership), one German (37.9% ownership), and one Spanish (4.2% ownership). In the 1980s and early-1990s, Boeing maintained that subsidies from these nations allow Airbus to set unrealistically low prices, to offer concessions and attractive financing terms to airlines, to write off development costs, and to use state-owned airlines to obtain orders. According to a study by the United States Department of Commerce, Airbus received more than $13.5 billion in government subsidies between 1970 and 1990 ($25.9 billion if commercial interest rates are applied). Most of these subsidies were in the form of loans at below-market interest rates and tax breaks.

The subsidies financed research and development and provided attractive financing terms for Airbus's customers. Airbus responded by pointing out that both Boeing had benefited for years from hidden US government subsidies, and particularly Pentagon R&D grants.

In 1992, the 2 sides appeared to reach an agreement that put to rest their long-standing trade dispute. The 1992 pact, which was negotiated by the European Union on behalf of the four member states, limited direct government subsidies to 33% of the total costs of developing a new aircraft and specified that and such subsidies had to be repaid with interest within 17 years. The agreement also limited indirect subsidies, such as government supported military research that has applications to commercial aircraft, to 3% of a country's annual total commercial aerospace revenues, or 4% of commercial aircraft revenues of any single company on that country. Although Airbus officials stated that the controversy had now been resolved, Boeing officials argued that they would still be competing for years against subsidized products.

The trade dispute heated up again in 2004 when Airbus announced the first version of the A350 to compete against Boeing's 787. What raised a red flag for the U.S. government was signs from Airbus that it would apply for $1.7 billion in launch aid to help fund the development of the A350. As far as the United States was concerned, this was too much. In late-2004, U.S. Trade Representative Robert Zoellick issued a statement formally renouncing the 1992 agreement and calling for an end to launch subsidies. According to Zoellick: "since its creation 35 years ago, some Europeans have justified subsidies to Airbus as necessary to support an infant industry. If that rationalization were ever valid, its time has long passed. Airbus now sells more large civil aircraft than Boeing." Zoellick went on to claim that Airbus has received some $3.7 billion in launch aid for the A380 plus another $2.8 billion in indirect subsidies including $1.7 billion in tax payer funded infrastructure improvements for a total of $6.5 billion.

Airbus shot back that Boeing, too, continued to enjoy lavish subsidies, and that the company had received some $12 billion from NASA to development technology, much of which has found its way into commercial jet aircraft. The Europeans also contended that Boeing would receive as much as $3.2 billion in tax breaks from Washington State, where the 787 is to be assembled, and more than $1 billion in loans from the Japanese government to 3 Japanese suppliers, who will build over 1/3 of the 787. Moreover, Airbus was quick to point out that a trade war would not benefit either side, and that Airbus purchased some $6 billion a year in supplies from companies in the United States.

In January 2005, both the U.S. and EU agreed to freeze direct subsidies to the 2 aircraft makers while talks continued. However, in May 2005, news reports suggested (and Airbus confirmed), that the jet maker had applied to 4 EU governments for launch aid for the A350, and that the British government would announce some $700 million in aid at the Paris Air Show in mid-2005. Simultaneously, the EU offered to cut launch aid for the A350 by 30%. Dissatisfied, the U.S. side decided that the talks were going nowhere, and on May 31 the United States formally filed a request with the World Trade Organization (WTO) for the establishment of a dispute resolution panel to resolve the issues. The EU quickly responded by filing a countersuit with the WTO claiming that U.S. aid to Boeing exceeded the terms set out in the 1992 agreement.[31]

In early-2011, the WTO ruled on the complaint by Boeing, and on Airbus's counterclaim. The WTO stated that Airbus had indeed benefitted from some $15 billion in improper launch aid subsidies over the prior 40 years, and that this practice must stop. Boeing, however, had little time to celebrate. In a separate ruling, the WTO stated that Boeing, too, had benefited from improper subsidies, including $5.3 billion from the United States Government to develop the 787 (the WTO stated that most of these subsidies were in the form of payments from NASA to development space technology that subsequently had commercial applications. Both sides in the dispute are engaged in the process of appealing these rulings, which could drag out for years.[32]

The Next Chapter

Huge financial bets have been placed on very different visions of the future of airline travel—Airbus with the A380 and Boeing with the 787. By mid-2011, Airbus had delivered 51 A380s and had a backlog of 236 on order. The rate of new orders had been slow, however; Boeing orders of 827 787s have had a backlog. Airbus also hedged its bets by announcing the A350 XWB, and after a slow start the aircraft has amassed some 567 orders.

Both companies have had substantial production problems and faced significant delays. In mid-2006, Airbus announced that deliveries for the A380 would be delayed by 6 months while the company dealt with "production issues" arising from problems installing the wiring bundles in the A380. Estimates suggest that the delay would cost Airbus some $2.6 billion over 4 years.[33] Within months, Airbus had revised the expected delay to 18 months, and stated that the number of A380s it now needed to sell in order to break even had increased from 250 to 420 aircraft. The company also stated that due to production problems, it would only be able to deliver 84 A380 planes by 2010, compared to an original estimate of 420 (in fact it delivered only half of this amount).[34]

Boeing ran into a number of production and design problems with the 787 that resulted in 5 delay announcements, pushing out the first deliveries more than 3 years. For the 787, Boeing outsourced an unprecedented amount of work to suppliers. This was seen at the time as a risky move, particularly given the amount of new technology incorporated into the 787. As it turns out, several suppliers had problems meeting Boeing's quality specification, supplying substandard parts that had to be reworked or redesigned. The issues included a shortage of fasteners, a misalignment between the cockpit section and the fuselage, and microscopic wrinkles in the fuselage skin. In addition, Boeing found that it had to redesign parts of the section where the wing meets the fuselage. Boeing executives complained that their engineers were often fixing problems "that should not have come to us in the first place."[35]

Some company sources suggest that Boeing erred by not managing its supplier relationships as well as it should have. In particular, there may have been a lack of ongoing communication between Boeing and key suppliers. Boeing tended to throw design specifications "over the wall" to suppliers, and then was surprised when they failed to comply fully with the company's expectations. In addition, Boeing's dependency on single suppliers for key components meant that a problem in any one of those suppliers could create a bottleneck that would hold up production.

In an attempt to fix some of the supply chain issues, in 2009, Boeing purchased a Vought Industries

Aircraft plant for $580 million. Vought had been in a joint venture with the Italian company, Alenia Aeronautical, to make fuselage parts for the 787. Vought had not been able to keep up with the demands of the program and Boeing's acquisition has seen it as a move to exert more control over the production process, and inject capital into Vought.

In another development, Boeing quietly launched the 747–8 program in November 2005. This plane is a completely redesigned version of the 747 and incorporates many of the technological advances developed for the 787, including significant use of composites. It will be offered in both a freighter and intercontinental passenger configuration that will carry 467 passengers in a 3-seat configuration and have a range of 8,000 miles (the 747–400 can carry 416 passengers). The 747–8 will also use the fuel efficient engines developed for the 787, and will have the same cockpit configuration as the 737, 777 and 787. Development costs are estimated to be around $4 billion. By July 2011, Boeing had orders for 78 747–8 freighters and 36 passenger planes. The first deliveries occurred in late-2011.

Looking forward, the primary issue confronting both Airbus and Boeing is what to do about their aging narrow bodies planes, the A320 and the 737 respectively? These aircraft are the workhorses of many airlines comprising some 70% of all units produced by the 2 manufacturers. Strong demand is expected for this category in the future. Boeing estimates that over the next 20 years, airlines will buy 23,000 single aisle jets worth some $1.95 trillion. Ideally, both Boeing and Airbus would probably prefer to wait for a few more years before bearing the R&D costs associated with new product development. The argument often made is that this will give time for new technologies to mature, and make for a better aircraft at the end of the day. However, events have conspired to force their hands.

First, new engine technologies developed by Pratt & Whitney reportedly increases fuel efficiency by 10–15%. Airlines want these new engines on their aircraft, but doing so requires some redesign of the A320 and 737. The wings of the 737 in particular, are too low slung to take the new engines, so Boeing would be required to do some major redesign work.

Second, there are several potential new entrants into the narrow body segment of the market. The Canadian regional jet manufacturer, Bombardier, is developing a 110–150 seat aircraft that makes extensive use of composites to reduce weight. This will reduce operating costs by about 15% compared to the older 737 and A320 models. Known as the CSeries, as of June 2011, Bombardier had 133 firm orders for this aircraft plus options for an additional 129. The first CSeries aircraft are expected to enter service in 2013.

In addition, the Commercial Aircraft Corporation of China (Comac) has announced that it will build a 170–190 seat narrow-bodied jet. Scheduled for introduction in 2016, this will compete with the larger 737 and A320 models. The European low cost airline, Ryanair, has entered into a co-development agreement with Comac and has talked about a 200+ plane order that could be as high as 400. Formerly, Ryanair had been a Boeing customer. Boeing must decide how to confront these growing threats.

Responding to these threats, Airbus in late-2010 announced that it would introduce a redesigned version of the A320 that utilizes the Pratt & Whitney engine. Known as the A320NEO (New Engine Option), the offering has garnered strong interest from airlines, racking up over 1,000 orders by August of 2011.

These developments have presented Boeing with a major strategic dilemma. Should they continue to evaluate what to do with the 737, perhaps waiting a few more years before making the heavy investment associated with redesign. This would allow them to design a high technology successor to the 737 that would incorporate many of the technologies developed for the 787. Alternatively, should they jump into the fray now, and offer a redesigned version of the 737 that can utilize new engine technology?

In a sign of how Boeing's hand may be forced, in July 2011, Boeing announced a large new order from American Airlines for 200 narrow-bodied aircraft. Boeing agreed to fit half of these aircraft with new engine technology, a requirement that will necessitate substantially higher R&D spending. At the same time, American Airlines announced that it would buy 260 A320 aircraft from Airbus, half of which will be A320NEOs. This will be the first order from American Airlines for Airbus since the 1980s.[36]

Endnotes

1   Boeing Website.

2   Airbus Website.

3   J. Palmer, "Big Bird," *Barron's*, December 19, 2005, 25–29; www.yeald.com/Yeald/a/33941/both_a380_and_787_have_bright_futures.html

4   G.J. Steven, "The Learning Curve; From Aircraft to Space Craft," *Management Accounting*, May 1999, 64–66.

5   D. Gates, "Boeing 7E7 Watch: Familiar Suppliers Make Short List," *Seattle Times*.

6   The figures are from the International Airline Travelers Association (IATA).

7   IATA, "2006 Loss Forecast Drops to US$1.7 billion," Press Release, August 31, 2006.

8   "Turbulent Skies: Low Cost Airlines," *The Economist,* July 10, 2004, 68–72; "Silver Linings, Darkening Clouds," *The Economist,* March 27, 2004, 90–92.

9   Air Transport Association, *The Economic Climb Out for U.S. Airlines*, ATA Economics, August 3, 2011 (accessed on ATA Website).

10   Data from the Air Transport Association at www.airlines.org.

11   Boeing, Current Market Outlook, 2011. Archived on Boeing's Website.

12   Airbus' Website. www.airbus.com/en/myairbus/global_market_forcast.html.

13   Presentation by Randy Baseler, Vice President of Boeing Commercial Airplanes, given at the Farnborough Air show, July 2006. Archived at www.boeing.com/nosearch/exec_pres/CMO.pdf.

14   This material is drawn from an earlier version of the Boeing case written by Charles W.L. Hill. See C.W.L. Hill, "The Boeing Corporation: Commercial Aircraft Operations," in C.W.L. Hill and G.R. Jones, *Strategic Management*, third edition (Boston: Houghton Mifflin, 1995). Much of Boeing's history is described in R.J. Sterling, *Legend and Legacy* (St Martin's Press, New York, 1992).

15   S. Browder, "A Fierce Downdraft at Boeing," *Business Week*, January 26, 1988, 34.

16   M.A. Cusumano, *The Japanese Automobile Industry* (Cambridge, Mass.: Harvard University Press, 1989); Ohno Taiichi, *Toyota Production System* (Cambridge, Mass.: Productivity Press, (1990); J. P. Womack, D. T. Jones, and D. Roos, *The Machine That Changed the World* (New York: Rawson Associates, 1990).

17   J. Gillie, "Lean Manufacturing Could Save Boeing's Auburn Washington Plant," *Knight Ridder Tribune Business News*, May 6, 2002, 1.

18   P.V. Arnold, "Boeing Knows Lean," *MRO Today*, February 2002.

19   Boeing, "Converted Farm Machine Improves Production Process," Press Release, July 1, 2003.

20   P.V. Arnold, "Boeing Knows Lean," *MRO Today*, February 2002. Also "Build in Lean: Manufacturing for the Future," on Boeing's Website www.boeing.com/aboutus/environment/create_build.htm.; J.Gillie, "Lean Manufacturing Could Save Boeing's Auburn, Washington Plant," *Knight Ridder Tribune Business News*, May 6, 2002, 1.

21 J. Gillie, "Lean Manufacturing Could Save Boeing's Auburn Washington Plant," *Knight Ridder Tribune Business News*, May 6, 2002, 1.

22 P.V. Arnold, "Boeing Knows Lean," *MRO Today*, February 2002.

23 M. Mecham, "The Lean, Green Line," *Aviation Week*, July 19, 2004, 144–148.

24 Boeing, "Boeing Reduces 737 Airplane's Final Assembly Time by 50 Percent," Press Release, January 27, 2005.

25 *The Economist*, "A Phony War," May 5, 2001, 56–57.

26 J.D. Boyd, "Building Room for Growth," *Traffic World*, August 7, 2006, 1.

27 W. Sweetman, "Boeing, Boeing, Gone," *Popular Science*, June 2004, 97.

28 Anonymous, "Who Will Supply the Parts?", *Seattle Times*, June 15, 2003.

29 W. Sweetman, "Boeing, Boeing, Gone," *Popular Science*, June 2004, 97.

30 D. Michaels and J.L. Lunsford, "Airbus Chief Reveals Plans for New Family of Jetliners," *Wall Street Journal*, July 18, 2006, A3.

31 J. Reppert-Bismarck and W. Echikson, "EU Countersues over U.S. Aid to Boeing," *Wall Street Journal*, June 1, 2005, A2; United States Trade Representative Press Release, "United States Takes Next Steps in Airbus WTO Litigation," May 30, 2005.

32 N. Clark, "WTO Rules U.S. Subsidies for Boeing Unfair," *New York Times*, March 31, 2011.

33 Anonymous, "Airbus Agonistes," *Wall Street Journal*, September 6, 2006, A20.

34 Anonymous, "Forecast Dimmer for Profit on Airbus' A380," *Seattle Times*, October 20, 2006, Web Edition.

35 J. Weber, "Boeing to Rein in Dreamliner Outsourcing," *Bloomberg Business Week*, January 16, 2009.

36 Staff Reporter, "American Airlines Orders 200 Boeing 737s, 260 More from Airbus," *Associated Press*, July 19, 2011.

CASE 16

Alarm Ringing: Nokia in 2010

"[...]Nokia's problems are still fixable but the window is closing. I am not optimistic that they will be fixed in 2010 because there isn't much time left, and if they aren't fixed in 2011, Nokia will be in big trouble."[1]

—Nick Jones, vice president, Gartner, Inc.[2] in 2010.

Market Leader In Trouble

In September 2010, Stephen Elop (Elop) joined Nokia Corporations (Nokia) as the President and CEO. Elop, former head of Microsoft's Business Division[3] (MBD), was brought in to fix the numerous problems faced by the world's leading mobile phone company. His tasks included the onerous job of reversing not only Nokia's eroding market share in the high-end smartphone segment but also its slumping profits. "My role, as the leader of Nokia, is to lead this team through this period of change, take the organization through a period of disruption. My job is to create an environment where those opportunities are properly captured, to ultimately ensure we are meeting the needs of our customers, while delivering superior financial result,"[4] said Elop.

The Finland-based Nokia had a presence in over 160 countries as of 2010. Though it was the world's largest mobile phone maker with a market share of 35% in the first quarter of 2010, Nokia had been losing market share consistently in the high-end mobile phone market. According to analysts, problems began for the company with the increase in the global demand for smartphones, a segment in which Nokia was unable to find its footing compared to rivals like Research In Motion[5] (RIM) and Apple.[6] Nokia was not only slow in launching smartphones with the latest version of its Symbian[7] operating system (OS), but also in catching up with the touch-screen technology, they said. Nokia's major problems were development of new software services, hardware design, and North American distribution. The plunging market share price and dwindling investor confidence

ultimately led to Elop replacing Olli-Pekka Kallasvuo (Kallasvuo), who had been CEO since mid-2006. Experts opined that under Kallasvuo, Nokia had struggled to keep up with rivals in the smartphone segment, the most profitable and fastest-growing segment in the global mobile phone market.

Analysts felt that Elop had a tough road ahead as he had to establish the company's presence in the smartphone segment and increase its profits. Moreover, he would have to revitalize the Nokia brand and stand up against the competition. What made the assignment even more challenging for Elop was the deeply-entrenched culture at Nokia. Being a Canadian, who had spent most of his time managing the affairs of US-based companies, he was expected to face resistance from the management team with a strong Finnish cultural bias. Elop's appointment elicited mixed reactions from analysts. However, they were unanimous in their view that the decisions he took would determine whether Nokia would be able to regain its past glory or whether it would capitulate to the fast emerging competition.

About Nokia

As of 2010, Nokia employed about 123,553 employees and operated under three business segments—Devices & Services, NAVTEQ (a leader in comprehensive digital mapping and navigation services), and Nokia Siemens Networks. It operated 15 manufacturing facilities in nine countries and maintained R&D facilities in 12 countries. Nokia had been market leader in the mobile phone market since 1998.

In the new millennium, though the company developed expensive high-end handsets based on 3G technology to capture a substantial share of the high-end phone market, its greatest strength was in the lower end of the market. In countries such as China, Brazil, and India there was a huge demand for low-priced mobile phones. The early-2000s saw a major erosion in the company's brand value. In particular, 2004, saw a huge drop in the company's market share as well as brand value, as younger buyers opted for the trendier mobile phones offered by rivals such as Motorola,[8] Samsung,[9] and Sony Ericsson.[10] In 2004, its market share declined to less than 30% from around 40% in 2003.[11] Analysts felt that the company had also failed to foresee how popular clamshell mobile phones would become. While its rivals were offering such models, it continued to churn out the single-piece design popularly called 'Candy Bar.' Some analysts felt the brand was losing its sheen and that it was counted among the world's top ten brands more because of its size than for its ability to form a meaningful relationship with its customers.

In 2005, Nokia put renewed emphasis on new product development and branding and moving beyond the umbrella branding that it had been zealously following. Analysts felt that the two sub-brands, the Nseries and the Eseries, had helped Nokia in capturing the new market for high-end multimedia mobile phones and business-oriented mobile phones respectively. In addition, Nokia entered the Internet services space with the 'Ovi' brand on August 29, 2007. 'Ovi' was an umbrella brand for a range of Internet services offered by Nokia—such as an online music store, an online navigation service, and an online games store. These initiatives led to some improvements. However, some analysts felt the emerging markets of India and China were largely responsible for Nokia's revival in the mid-2000s and the company could expect more growth in these markets as the consumers upgraded to more expensive models. For instance, for 2006, the Average Selling Price (ASP) of Nokia in the Asia-Pacific region including India, rose by 4.1 percent to €77, while in China it rose by 3.8 percent to €81.[12]

Meanwhile, in June 2006, Jorma Ollila (Ollila), who had been CEO of Nokia since 1991, made way for Kallasvuo, the head of the handset division. Ollila himself became chairman. In the same month, Nokia merged its networks business with the carrier-related operations of Siemens AG[13] to form a new unit called Nokia Siemens Networks which provided equipment, services, and solutions for communications networks globally. On July 10, 2008, Nokia acquired NAVTEQ Corporation.[14]

In 2009, Nokia's net sales decreased by 19% to €40,984 million (€50,710 million in 2008). Net sales of Devices & Services for 2009 decreased by 21% to €27,853 million (€35,099 million). In 2009, Europe accounted for 36% of Nokia's net sales, Asia-Pacific 22%, Greater China 16%, the Middle East & Africa 14%, Latin America 7%, and North America 5% (Refer Exhibits I, II, and III).

Nokia's Problems

Drop in Smartphone Market Share

Though Nokia remained the largest mobile phone maker by units, with a global market share of about 35% (Q1 2010), the company struggled to keep pace with rivals such as Apple, Google,[15] and RIM in the high-end smartphone market[16] (Refer Exhibit IV). It had lost a significant market share in the smartphone segment as it was slow in launching premium handsets and failed to foresee the boom in the smartphone market, analysts felt. In the first quarter of 2010, Nokia's global market share in smartphones fell to 44.3% from 48.8% a year earlier.[17]

According to analysts, since the launch of the iPhone in 2007, Nokia began to lose share in the smartphone market as it was unsuccessful in releasing a compelling touchscreen model that could compete with the iPhone. Nokia's only successful high-end phone was the N95,[18] unveiled in 2006. The N95 smartphone launched in December 2008 failed to make an impact in the market. As a result, consumers' loyalty shifted to the iPhone. It was reported that since 2007, Nokia's share price had fallen by almost two-thirds, thereby eliminating about €60 billion of the company's market capitalization. "The high-end user they've lost to the iPhone has signed up for iTunes and put their information on Apple; Nokia won't get them back or not without an enormous amount of pain,"[19] said Stuart O'Gorman, co-head of UK-based investment management firm, Henderson Global Investors.

Nokia also postponed the launch of its latest flagship smartphone, the touchscreen equipped Nokia

N8. The N8, based on the Symbian 3 OS, was slated for release in April 2010, but the release was postponed to the year-end owing to software problems. According to industry insiders, the delay generated a lot of negative attention for the company and led to a drop in its stock price. In the second quarter of 2010, Nokia's market share in the smartphone market dropped to 38.1% from 40.3% in the corresponding period of the previous year[20] (Refer Exhibit V).

In the smartphone OS market, competitors were quickly catching up with Nokia's Symbian platform. As the Symbian OS was not optimized for touch-screen devices, users were turning to the Android, Blackberry OS, and Apple's iOS. While Nokia's new Linux-based mobile OS MeeGo, developed in association with Intel[21] to power high-end smartphones, was yet to be released, its Symbian began to lose market share to rivals like Android and iOS. Its market share fell to 44.3% in Q1 2010, compared to 48.8% in Q1 2009.[22] Analysts said Symbian's market share was expected to further drop to 34% in 2011.

Besides, Nokia's limited presence and minimum brand recognition in the US smartphone market also led to a drop in its worldwide market share, said analysts. The major problem for Nokia was its inability to break into the US market, considered the fastest growing market for smartphones in the world. In March 2002, Nokia's market share in the US was 35%. This dropped to 10% in 2008. By June 2009, Nokia's share in the US was just 7%.[23] Experts said Nokia had failed to build long-term partnerships with any of the major wireless carriers in the US such as Sprint Nextel, AT&T, Verizon Wireless, and Vodafone Group which sold more than 90% of all mobile phones in the US. As a result, Nokia's smartphones were not offered with subsidies on these carrier networks. While wireless subscribers could get an iPhone for US$199 they had to pay full retail price for a Nokia smartphone. "Despite holding 38 percent market share of the smartphone market, Nokia's failure to compete with the iPhone and high-tier Android devices, combined with its lack of progress in gaining significant traction in the United States, has led to press and investor dissatisfaction,"[24] said Pete Cunningham, an analyst at technology research firm Canalys.

Some analysts said that over the past few years, Nokia had begun developing new services such as Ovi instead of building phones and mobile applications and concentrating on important markets like North America. But these services were not picking up as expected and Nokia had to had shut down certain services.[25] According to analysts, the company's digital mapping service Navteq too was not a big success. Nokia Siemens Networks was also struggling with falling revenues due to reduced operator investments and tough competition. Experts said Nokia's loss of focus had affected its market share significantly, leaving it struggling to catch up with its competitors.

In a brand-ranking study released in May 2010 by Millward Brown Optimor,[26] Nokia ranked 43rd, tumbling 30 places compared to the previous year. As per the study, the company lost 58% of its brand value.[27] According to Allen Nogee (Nogee), principal analyst at In-Stat, "Nokia has a huge market in the low-end part of the market, which in some ways could present a negative image among people who want state-of-the-art smartphones."[28]

Competition

Nokia was facing increasing competition from Apple and Google's Android OS for smartphones which hit the market in 2010. It was reported that the adoption of Android was growing faster as more leading smartphone makers such as Samsung, Motorola, LG, and Sony Ericsson were backing it. Analysts predicted that by end 2010, Android would become the top mobile OS in the US. Talking about Nokia's problems, Tony Cripps (Cripps), principal analyst at UK-based consultancy firm, Ovum, said, "Nokia's well reported problems competing in the high-end handset market against Apple are being further compounded by the inroads smartphones based on Google's Android platform are making far down into the traditional mid-range. Add in the lowering wholesale prices of mass market handsets and even Nokia's massive global shipments of low cost phones are struggling to compensate."[29]

Analysts were of the view that Nokia had been edged out by rivals in the smartphone market, who had launched new, better products. In the third quarter of 2009, Apple emerged as the world's most profitable phone-maker, generating US$1.6 billion in profit on the iPhone in the quarter compared to Nokia's US$ 1.1 billion.[30] Experts said though Nokia had spent almost six times as much as Apple on R&D in 2009, it had failed to develop a device with the same appeal as the iPhone.[31]

In order to hold on to its global market share, Nokia cut the prices of its handsets and shipped more low-priced models, resulting in a drop in profits. The ASP of Nokia handsets was low compared to that of other manufacturers. For instance, in the third quarter of 2009, the ASP for a Nokia handset was €62 compared to €72 in the corresponding quarter of the previous year. For a smartphone, Nokia charged €155 in the first quarter of 2010, down from €190 in the last quarter of 2009. In the second quarter 2010, Nokia's ASP was €143 compared to €181 in the second quarter 2009.[32] Experts felt the reduced ASP per device had brought down Nokia's profits. In 2009, Nokia sold about 40% of the world's cell phones, with strong business in Europe and in India and China. Despite selling several times more devices than its rivals, Nokia made lower profits as most of the devices it sold were lower-priced models with limited profit margins. Nokia's competitors, on the other hand, were shipping fewer handsets but making more profit per handset sold.

Dwindling Sales

In Q2 2010, Nokia's net income dropped by 40% to €227 million, down from €380 million a year earlier.[33] Analysts attributed the drop to the company's falling sales in the smartphone market. Analysts said Nokia's sales increased by only 0.9% to €10 billion in Q2 despite its shipping more than 111 million mobile devices, an increase of 8% compared to the corresponding quarter of the previous year. Devices & Services net sales increased 3% to €6.8 billion, compared with €6.6 billion in the second quarter of 2009 (Refer Exhibit 6). Shipments in North America declined by 19% year-on-year and 4% quarter-on-quarter, to 2.6 million. According to experts, factors such as the competitive environment, shifts in product mix toward lower gross margin products, the depreciation of the Euro, operating expenses, and global pricing strategies negatively impacted Nokia's business in the second quarter. Some analysts predicted that with global shipments and profits set to decline further, Nokia might even lose its market leadership in the future.

Since the company reported its first quarter earnings in March 2010, its share price dropped about 20% in the two weeks, wiping out €8.2 billion (US$10.5 billion) in market value. As of May 2010, Nokia's market capitalization was €34 billion (US$44 billion) compared to Apple's US$230 billion.[34] Nokia announced that in 2010, its volume market share in the mobile device segment would be lower than in 2009.

Management Issues

According to experts, at Nokia, decisions were not based on product vision. Besides, potential ideas were either delayed or ignored by top management. The management was not innovative enough and there were too many silos in the company working independently without any communication with other departments. According to Juhani Risku (Risku), former senior Executive of Nokia, "I would say that the highest abstraction level of the problem is that there are incompetent people managing, ordering, or directing things. When incompetent people are managing the chain, they have the mandate but don't have that courage. Even when we bring something to market, we're always developing versions from 1.0 to 1.2, but not to version 3 or 4."[35]

Analysts said investors were expecting challenging products from the company that had once had the innovative edge in the industry. But that had not happened since Kallasvuo took over as the CEO in 2006. Though Kallasvuo promised to tackle problems and establish the company's presence in North America, he had failed to do so and had only seen the market share decline from 20% in 2006 to 7% as of June 2010.[36] Some experts opined that Nokia's top management had failed to bring innovative products to market, despite a rich R&D base and had also made some wrong strategic decisions.

In 2009, when Nokia reported the first third quarter loss of €559 million (US$ 834 million) since it began reporting quarterly in 1996,[37] the company shuffled its management. In October 2009, Nokia's CFO Rick Simonson was replaced by Timo Ihamuotila, who had been head of global sales. Simonson was put in charge of the low-end mobile-phone unit in the devices division. Later, in the first quarter of 2010, when Nokia again reported lower than expected earnings, the top management was reshuffled again to revive its core business units. In July 2010, marketing chief Anssi Vanjoki was appointed head of the smartphone unit which included the company's smartphones and services operations, while Mary McDowell took over Nokia's key mobile phones unit from Simonson. According to some analysts,

Nokia's multiple reshuffle of the top management did not, however, get the expected results.

In early 2010, Nokia's management was under increasing pressure from analysts and shareholders as the company's share price was consistently falling. The company had 156,000 shareholders at the end of 2009, with 38% of shares owned in the US. Reports showed that between 2007 and 2010, Nokia's share plummeted 67% and the company lost almost €60 billion (US$77 billion) in market value (Refer Exhibit VII). Investors called for management changes and Kallasuvo came in for severe criticism.

Analysts opined that Kallasvuo had failed to understand the company's problems and had not done anything right to fix them. He could have reclaimed the company's share in the smartphone market as it had the opportunity to acquire Palm's WebOS,[38] which would have provided it with not just a good OS to compete with rivals but also a strong presence in the US, they said. During the last three years of Kallasuvo's tenure, Nokia lost 75% of its market capitalization, plunging from US$40 per share in 2007 to less than US$10 in 2010. In April 2010, investors were further disappointed when Kallasvuo announced a delay in the release of the updated Symbian software until later in 2010.

In May 2010, Ollila confirmed that the board was looking at a replacement and that the search for a new CEO had started after a review of the company's strategy. It was rumored that Nokia had auditioned heads of several US-based technology companies but that some of them had rejected the offer because Nokia wanted the new CEO to move to Finland. However, some analysts were not sure that merely changing the CEO would change Nokia's fortunes. "While CEO Olli-Pekka Kalasvuo is the man who must take ultimate responsibility for Nokia's falling profitability, the problem is unlikely to go away simply by replacing him at the helm,"[39] said Cripps.

Elop Joins Nokia

On September 10, 2010, Nokia's Board of Directors replaced Kallasvuo with Elop. Elop had earlier been president of MBD, which makes the Office suite of applications. His tenure at Microsoft was marked by the successful launch of Microsoft's Office 2010 suite. Before joining Microsoft in January 2008,

he had served as CEO of Juniper Networks[40] for a year. Prior to that, in 2005, Elop was CEO of graphics software developer at Macromedia[41] and later became president of worldwide field operations at Adobe Systems[42] after Adobe acquired Macromedia. He also worked as a CIO at Boston Chicken.[43] Elop held a degree in computer engineering and management from McMaster University in Hamilton, Canada, his home country.

Analysts felt the appointment of Elop was an unusual move and a major shift for Nokia as he would be the first non-Finn CEO to run the company in its long history. According to Ollila, Elop was the right candidate to drive both innovation and efficient execution of the company strategy.[44] According to the company, Elop had adequate exposure to the inner workings of Nokia as he had represented Microsoft when the two companies had partnered to develop software for Nokia phones. Industry observers said Elop was as a well-traveled executive with a very broad software experience and deep knowledge of the North American market. However, just after the announcement was made, Vanjoki, who had been considered the prospective candidate for the CEO position, decided to quit the company.

Elop's appointment evoked mixed reactions. Some analysts felt that having worked closely with Microsoft and Macromedia, Elop had adequate software knowledge and experience. Elop's experience of working in the US market and knowledge of the US corporate culture in the highly competitive field of technology would be a big advantage for Nokia as it would help the company regain its share in the North American mobile phone market, they added. "He's worked at the biggest software firm in the world. This is very important for Nokia, which is trying to go from being a Finnish box maker to being a player in the U.S.-centric software and Internet-services business,"[45] said Lee Simpson, an analyst at Jefferies International.[46] Analysts were of the view that Elop would be able to chalk out a strategy wherein the company would be able to take advantage of both the Symbian and MeeGo platforms.[47]

Some analysts said Elop was an aggressive leader. As CEO of Macromedia, he had focused on Flash Internet software instead of bigger product lines and organized the company's US$3.4 billion sale to Adobe Systems in 2005. "Macromedia bore the brunt when the dot-com bubble burst, and Elop was there. He had a lot of challenges he rode through. I tell you, there were lots of CEOs who didn't make it through those tumultuous years. That tells you something about Elop's professionalism, his ability to execute,"[48] said Chris Swenson of NPD Group.[49] At Microsoft, Elop revamped the Office software and was responsible for making MBD profitable. It was reported that MBD was one of Microsoft's biggest and most profitable units. In fiscal year 2009, MBD generated US$18.6 billion in sales—about 30% of the company's total sales.[50]

However, some critics felt Elop was not the right candidate for the job as he did not have the hardcore experience in the mobile phone industry required for the strong strategy overhaul that Nokia would need in the future to be a global smartphone competitor. He was involved more in networking and enterprise software and not mobile phones, they said. "We think Elop ticks most but not all of the right boxes . . . However, it remains to be seen how well he will do on hardware devices,"[51] said Mawston of Strategy Analytics. They said he could be a good manager but not a consumer product visionary, which was what Nokia needed. "He comes from a software background, which is good, but he also comes from a company that's had the same issues as Nokia in terms of adapting to a new world,"[52] said Carolina Milanesi, research director, mobile device and consumer-services practice, Gartner. Moreover, analysts pointed out, barring Microsoft, Elop had never run a business as large as Nokia. According to Jones, "Nokia's board has made a safe choice when they should have made a courageous choice. In the current state of the market when the two main competitors, Google and Apple, are very much headed by recognizable visionaries, you need someone who is charismatic and can explain how you're driving the industry forward in new directions."[53]

Challenges Galore

Elop's biggest challenge would be to manage a quick turnaround of the company and reassert Nokia's place as the largest mobile maker in the world. His other tasks included focusing on the smartphone market, addressing loss in earnings, and establishing the company's business in the US. "Elop faces a daunting task. Nokia has lost its leadership in high-tier phones and has struggled with the rise of Inter-net-led services,"[54] said Ben Wood, head of research at UK-based telecoms analyst firm CCS Insight.

According to experts, one of the most important tasks for Elop would be to develop a challenger to iPhone as the smartphone market was expected to expand and occupy about 40% of the total device market by 2013. Smartphones accounted for 17.3% of all mobile handset sales in the first quarter of 2010, up from 13.6% in the same period in 2009 (Refer Exhibit VIII). Experts pointed out that Apple and RIM, which had had just about 3% market share in the mobile devices as of 2009, had over 50% share in industry profits which proved the high profitability of the smartphones. Analyst Kevin Restivo from IDC said, "Lower smartphone average selling prices, increased consumer interest, and aggressive expansion plans on the part of key suppliers will keep the device type growing above market growth rate."[55]

Elop would have to steer Nokia in a new and innovative direction and build up the brand image of the company. He had to plan a new strategy for the company and build an efficient OS that lived up to the competition in the smartphone market. Some experts were of the view that Elop needed to drop the Symbian and adopt the Android OS to regain Nokia's footing in the smartphone market. But for Elop, Nokia's transition to the Android would be difficult as the company had already made a huge investment in Symbian and had several Symbian-based devices.

Establishing Nokia's presence in North America was another daunting challenge for Elop who needed to strike major deals with US cell phone carriers and work closely with them. "Hiring Elop is an indication of reinvigorated commitment to the U.S. market at the highest levels in the company. But Elop's background seems more focused on business rather than consumer products where the real need is, and he does not seem to have any prior background working with operators who really control the U.S. market,"[56] noted Satish Menon, senior analyst at Forward Concepts, a US-based market research firm. Moreover, he would have to develop and design an interface that suited the US market as the typefaces, screen layouts, and hardware designs of Nokia phones reflected European sensibility, according to some experts.

Adjusting to Nokia's corporate culture would also be a challenge for Elop, the first non-Finnish CEO of the company. According to Risku, "Nokia is so Finnish. We have so many Americans, they're very good but arrogance and aggression is not the Finnish way of working."[57] They noted that Nokia's product creation right from concept to design was very Finnish, usually characterized by long approval processes and lack of leadership. Moreover, they expected Elop to face problems playing a strong leadership role, as he would be stuck between a very powerful chairman Ollila and a long standing management team with a strong cultural bias. Rod Hall, an analyst at investment management firm JPMorgan, said, "Nokia's business culture tends to be very consensus oriented versus the star system more prevalent within N. American tech companies."[58] Moreover, Nokia's choice of a Canadian CEO did not go down well with the Finnish press.

According to Dan Frommer of *Business Insider,* "Nokia's board just hired another CEO who is a seasoned manager, but not a consumer product visionary. So unless Stephen Elop, Nokia's new boss, has hidden talents, he may represent more of the same for Nokia—which would be a disaster."[59]

Road Ahead

Some analysts were optimistic that Nokia, under Elop, would overcome its problems and retain its position as the largest mobile maker in the world. Though Nokia was not doing well in the smartphone market, it was still strong at the entry-level with a global manufacturing and distribution base. It was also a major player in the emerging markets like China and India that would contribute to Nokia's growth in the future, they said. However, others felt the company would have to invest heavily in its strategy for developed markets as well. They felt transforming Nokia would by no means be an easy task. It would require Elop to bring about a change in its corporate culture. "That Finnish mindset of caution has to be overturned,"[60] said Simpson. Moreover, he would have to change the perception that Nokia was a conservative business with a Finnish mindset. It would be interesting to watch how Elop brought about the change in a big company like Nokia and balanced short-term results with long-term goals for Nokia, analysts said.

However, as rivals continued to grab market share, some analysts were skeptical about whether Elop would be able to solve Nokia's problems and restore it to its past glory. Time was fast running out for Nokia, they said. Jeff Kagan, of *E-Commerce Times,* noted: "Will Stephen Elop, the new Nokia CEO, be able to turn the company around? That is the question. It all depends on what he does—this is a big job. He has to focus on transforming not only the technology, but also the brand. He has to reinvent Nokia's image in the mind of the customer. Will it work? Will Nokia be able to re-energize with new leadership, or is it in the process of passing the torch to the next generation of competitors?"[61]

Exhibit I   Nokia's Consolidated Income Statement

(in € millions except per share data)	2009	2008	2007
Net Sales	40,984	50,710	51,058
Cost of Sales	27,720	33,337	33,781
Gross profit	13,264	17,373	17,277
Research and development expenses	5,909	5,968	5,636
Selling and marketing expenses	3,933	4,380	4,379
Administrative and general expenses	1,145	1,284	1,165
Impairment of goodwill	908	—	—
Other income	338	420	2,312
Other expenses	510	1,195	424

Exhibit I (*continued*)

(in € millions except per share data)	2009	2008	2007
Operating profit	1,197	4,966	7,985
Share of results of associated companies	30	6	44
Financial income and expenses	265	2	239
Profit before tax	962	4,970	8,268
Tax	702	1,081	1,522
Profit	260	3,889	6,746
Profit attributable to equity holders of the parent	891	3,988	7,205
Loss attributable to minority interests	631	99	459
Earnings per share			
Basic	0.24	1.07	1.85
Diluted	0.24	1.05	1.83
Average number of shares (1000's)			
Basic	3,705,116	3,743,622	3,885,408
Diluted	3,721,072	3,780,363	3,932,008

Source: www.nokia.com/about-nokia/financials/key-data/reportable-segments

Exhibit II　Nokia's Balance Sheet

(in € millions)	2009	2008
Assets		
Fixed assets and other noncurrent assets		
Intangible assets		
Capitalized development costs	13	21
Intangible rights	46	52
Other intangible assets	418	152
	477	228
Tangible assets		
Investments		
Investments in subsidiaries	12109	12084
Investments in associated companies	30	10
Long-term loan receivables from Group companies	10	8
Other non-current assets		
		(*continued*)

Exhibit II (*continued*)

(in € millions)	2009	2008
Current assets		
Inventories and work in progress		
Raw materials and supplies	45	84
Work in progress	86	100
Finished goods	86	70
Receivables		
Deferred tax assets	1	—
Trade debtors from Group companies	1080	899
Trade debtors from other companies	713	913
Short-term loan receivables from Group companies	3472	12039
Short-term loan receivables from other companies	—	1
Prepaid expenses and accrued income from Group companies	15	65
Prepaid expenses and accrued income from other companies	1858	2179
	7139	16096
Short-term investments	35	2
Bank and cash	70	197
Total	20161	28920
Shareholders' Equity and Liabilities		
Shareholders' equity		
Share capital	246	246
Treasury shares	−685	−1885
Reserve for invested nonrestricted equity	3154	3291
Retained earnings	3788	4489
Net profit for the year	767	1749
Liabilities		
Long-term liabilities		
Long-term finance liabilities to other companies	3255	—

Exhibit II (*continued*)

(in € millions)	2009	2008
Short-term liabilities		
Current finance liabilities from Group companies	3380	13345
Current finance liabilities from other companies	473	2598
Advance payments from other companies	217	182
Trade creditors to Group companies	3280	2377
Trade creditors to other companies	531	695
Accrued expenses and prepaid income to Group companies	73	217
Accrued expenses and prepaid income to other companies	1682	1616
Total liabilities	9636	21030
Total	12891	21030

Source: Nokia_in_2009.pdf

Exhibit III Nokia's Ten Major Markets Based on Net Sales

	(in € millions)	
	2009	2008
China	5 990	5 916
India	2 809	3 719
UK	1 916	2 382
Germany	1 733	2 294
USA	1 731	1 907
Russia	1 528	2 083
Indonesia	1 458	2 046
Spain	1 408	1 497
Brazil	1 333	1 902
Italy	1 252	1 774

Source: www.nokia.com/about-nokia/financials/key-data/markets

Exhibit IV   Worldwide Mobile Phone Sales (Units)

	Q2 2010 (millions)	Share Q2 2010 (%)	Q2 2009 (millions)	Share Q2 2009 (%)
Nokia	111.5	34.2	105.4	36.8
Samsung	65.3	20.1	55.4	19.3
LG	29.4	9.0	30.5	10.7
RIM	11.2	3.4	7.7	2.7
Sony Ericsson	11.0	3.4	13.6	4.7
Motorola	9.1	2.8	15.9	5.6
Apple	8.7	2.7	5.4	1.9
HTC	5.9	1.8	2.5	0.9
ZTE	5.5	1.7	3.7	1.3
GFive	5.2	1.6	—	—
Others	62.6	19.3	46.0	16.1
Total	325.6	100.0	286.1	100.0

Source: www.bloomberg.com

Exhibit V   Worldwide Smartphone Sales by Platform

	Units Q2 2010 (millions)	Share Q2 2010 (%)	Units Q2 2009 (millions)	Units Q2 2009 (%)
Symbian	25.4	41.2	20.9	51.0
RIM	11.2	18.2	7.8	19.0
Android	10.6	17.2	0.8	1.8
iPhone OS	8.7	14.2	5.3	13.0
Windows Mobile	3.1	5.0	3.8	9.3
Linux	1.5	2.4	1.9	4.6
Others	1.1	1.8	0.5	1.2
Total	61.6	100.0	41.0	100.0

Source: www.bloomberg.com

Exhibit VI   Nokia: Reported Second Quarter Results

(in € millions)	Q2/2010	Q2/2009	YoY Change	Q1/2010
Net sales	10 003	9 912	1%	9 522
Devices & Services	6 799	6 586	3%	6 663
NAVTEQ	252	147	71%	189
Nokia Siemens Networks	3 039	3 199	−5%	2 718
Operating profit	295	427	−31%	488
Devices & Services	643	763	−16%	831
NAVTEQ	−81	−100		−77
Nokia Siemens Networks	−179	−188		−226
Operating margin	2.9%	4.3%		5.1%
Devices & Services	9.5%	11.6%%		12.5%
NAVTEQ	−32.1%	−68.0%		−40.7%
Nokia Siemens Networks	−5.9%	−5.9%		−8.3%
EPS, EUR Diluted	0.06	0.10	−40%	0.09

Source: www.nokia.com/about-nokia/financials/quarterly-and-annual-information/q2-2010

Exhibit VII   Nokia's Three-year Stock Price Chart

Source: http://bigcharts.marketwatch.com

Exhibit VIII   Global Smartphone Share

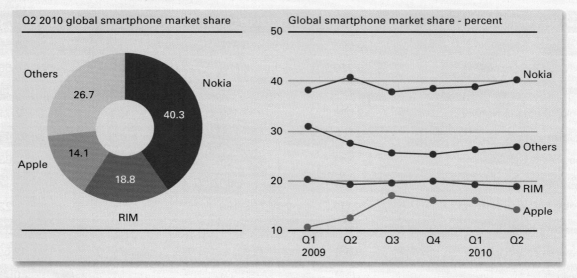

Q2 2010 global smartphone market share

Global smartphone market share - percent

Others 26.7
Nokia 40.3
Apple 14.1
RIM 18.8

Source: www.reuters.com

References & Suggested Readings:

1. Diana ben-Aaron, "Nokia Investors Left without Buzz, Increasing Pressure on Elop," www.bloomberg.com, September 16, 2010.
2. Jeff Kagan, "The Mountain Elop has to Climb to Keep Nokia on Top," www.ecommercetimes.com, September 16, 2010.
3. Kerri Shannon, "Will Nokia's CEO Change be the Catalyst to Boost Its Share in the Smartphone Market?" www.dailymarkets.com, September 13, 2010.
4. Christopher Lawton and Joann S. Lublin, "Nokia Replaces CEO with Microsoft Boss," http://online.wsj.com, September 11, 2010.
5. "Nokia Turns to Microsoft for New Chief," http://economictimes.indiatimes.com, September 11, 2010.
6. Aude Lagorce, "Nokia Corp. Names Microsoft Executive as New CEO," www.marketwatch.com, September 10, 2010.
7. Ben Popper, "The Wrong Guy: Nokia's New CEO, Stephen Elop, Lacks Smartphone Smarts," www.bnet.com, September 10, 2010.
8. Dan Frommer, "Nokia Makes the Same Mistake Again: Hires a Manager, Not a Product Visionary," www.businessinsider.com, September 10, 2010.
9. Diana ben-Aaron, "Nokia Hires Microsoft's Elop as CEO to Reverse Losses to Apple," www.bloomberg.com, September 10, 2010.
10. Erika Morphy, "Nokia's New CEO May Whip up Savvier Smartphone Strategy," www.ecommercetimes.com, September 10, 2010.
11. "How Microsoft's Elop Could Turn Nokia Around," http://blogs.forbes.com, September 10, 2010.
12. Kevin J. O'Brien, "Nokia Chooses a Microsoft Officer as Its New Chief Executive," www.nytimes.com, September 10, 2010.
13. "Nokia Appoints Stephen Elop to President and CEO as of September 21, 2010," http://investors.nokia.com, September 10, 2010.
14. Rick Meritt, "Analyst: Five Challenges for New Nokia CEO," www.eetimes.com, September 10, 2010.
15. Tarmo Virki and Georgina Prodhan, "Nokia Brings in Microsoft Exec to Replace CEO," www.reuters.com, September 10, 2010.
16. Surojit Chatterjee, "Nokia Appoints Microsoft Top Exec as New CEO, Market Hopeful but Challenges Remain," http://uk.ibtimes.com, September 10, 2010.
17. Rafe Blandford, "Stephen Elop Replaces Olli-Pekka Kallasvuo as Nokia's CEO," www.allaboutmeego.com, September 10, 2010.
18. "Replacing CEO Won't Solve Nokia's Problems," http://about.datamonitor.com, July 30, 2010.
19. "Mobile Phone Demand Expands 14.5% as Market Fragments; Top 5 Pressured by Challengers, Says IDC," www.businesswire.com, July 29, 2010.
20. Andrew Orlowski, "Rescuing Nokia? A Former Exec has a Radical Plan," www.theregister.co.uk, July 22, 2010.
21. "Nokia's Fall from Grace: The Background Story," www.mobileindustryreview.com, July 22, 2010.
22. Diana ben-Aaron, "Nokia Board Faces Call for Change on $77 Billion Lost Value," www.bloomberg.com, July 16, 2010.
23. Mikael Ricknäs, "Nokia on Long Comeback Trail after Smartphone Misses," www.macworld.com, July 2, 2010.

24. Kit Eaton, "Nokia Profit Warning: It's Been Outmaneu-vered by Apple," www.fastcompany.com, June 16, 2010.

25. Steve Goldstein and Aude Lagorce, "Nokia Issues Profit Warning at Handset Division," www.marketwatch.com, June 16, 2010.

26. "Nokia Shares Fall on Profit Warning Talk-Traders," http://uk.reuters.com, June 9, 2010.

27. Gabriel Perna, "Nokia's Top Position Erodes," www.ibtimes.com, June 7, 2010.

28. "Gartner: Worldwide Smarphone Sales Grew 49% in Q1 2010," http://smartphone.biz-news.com, May 20, 2010.

29. Chad Berndtson, "Google Android, RIM Lead Big Smartphone Sale Gains in Q1," www.crn.com, May 19, 2010.

30. "Gartner Says Worldwide Mobile Phone Sales Grew 17 Per Cent in First Quarter 2010," www.gartner.com, May 19, 2010.

31. Diana ben-Aaron, "Nokia Investors Lose Patience 3 Years after IPhone (Update2)," www.businessweek.com, May 6, 2010.

32. "Apple Becomes Top Phone Maker by Profits-Research," www.reuters.com, November 10, 2009.

33. Kevin J. O'Brien, "Nokia Tries to Undo Blunders in U.S.," www.nytimes.com, October 18, 2009.

34. Diana ben-Aaron and Marcel van de Hoef, "Nokia CFO Simonson Moved to New Post after Loss (Update4)," www.bloomberg.com, October 16, 2009.

35. Eric Lai, "How will Stephen Elop Fare at Microsoft?" http://blogs.computerworld.com, January 11, 2008.

36. www.nokia.com

37. Nokia Annual Reports

38. http://bigcharts.marketwatch.com

39. www.reuters.com

40. www.bloomberg.com

Endnotes

1 Mikael Ricknäs, "Nokia on Long Comeback Trail after Smartphone Misses," www.macworld.com, July 2, 2010.

2 Gartner, Inc. is an IT research and advisory firm.

3 The Microsoft Business Division develops Microsoft's line of Office software that includes Microsoft Office Applications.

4 Rafe Blandford, "Stephen Elop Replaces Olli-Pekka Kallasvuo as Nokia's CEO," www.allaboutmeego.com, September 10, 2010.

5 Founded in 1984, Research In Motion Limited is a Canadian telecommunication and wireless device company, best known as the developer of the Black-Berry smartphone. The company's revenues for fiscal 2010 second quarter were US$ 4.62 billion.

6 Apple Inc. designs, manufactures, and markets personal computers and related personal computing and mobile communication devices along with a variety of related software and services. In the third quarter ended June 26, 2010, Apple posted revenues of US$15.7 billion and a net quarterly profit of US$3.25 billion.

7 Symbian OS is Nokia's mobile operating system for mobile devices and smartphones.

8 Based in Schaumburg, Illinois, Motorola Inc. is a manu-facturer of wireless telephone handsets and network infrastructure equipment such as cellular transmission base stations and signal amplifiers.

9 Samsung Electronics Co. Ltd., headquartered in Seoul, South Korea, is one of the world's largest electronics companies. Its revenues for the fiscal year 2005 were US$78.99 billion.

10 Sony Ericsson Mobile Communications AB is a mobile phone company formed in 2001 as a joint venture between one of the leading consumer electronics com-panies Sony Corporation (Sony) of Japan and a lead-ing mobile phone company Ericsson AB (Ericsson) of Sweden. It was the world's fourth largest mobile phone company as of July 2007. Its revenues for the fiscal year 2006 were €10,959 million.

11 "Nokia: Nseries Leads Nokia Brand Revival," www.brandrepublic.com, January 25, 2007.

12 Juho Erkheikki, "Nokia Owes Revival to Emerging Markets," www.iht.com, July 17, 2007.

13 Headquartered in Berlin and Munich, Siemens is one of the world's largest electrical engineering and electronics companies. The company offers innovative technologies to customers in over 190 countries.

14 NAVTEQ Corporation developed and delivered digital map, traffic, and location data for navigation and location-based platforms.

15 Google Inc. is a global technology company that provides a Web-based search engine through its Website. The Company offers a wide range of search options, includ-ing Web, image, groups, directory, and news searches. In the second quarter ended June 30, 2010, Google's revenues were US$5.1 billion.

16 "Gartner Says Worldwide Mobile Phone Sales Grew 17 Per Cent in First Quarter 2010," www.gartner.com, May 19, 2010.

17 Gabriel Perna, "Nokia's Top Position Erodes," www.ibtimes.com, June 7, 2010.

18 The N95 was Nokia's first handset with GPS navigation. When the N95 was introduced in 2006, it sold more than 10 million units and increased the operating mar-gin in devices to more than 21% that year.

19 Diana ben-Aaron, "Nokia Investors Lose Patience 3 Years after IPhone (Update2)," www.businessweek.com, May 6, 2010.

20 Surojit Chatterjee, "Nokia Appoints Microsoft Top Exec as New CEO, Market Hopeful but Challenges Remain," http://uk.ibtimes.com, September 10, 2010.

21 Intel Corporation is a US-based technology company, and one of the largest semiconductor chip makers in the world.

22 Chad Berndtson, "Google Android, RIM Lead Big Smartphone Sale Gains in Q1," www.crn.com, May 19, 2010.

23 Kevin J. O'Brien, "Nokia Tries to Undo Blunders in U.S.," www.nytimes.com, October 18, 2009.

24 "Nokia Turns to Microsoft for New Chief," http://economictimes.indiatimes.com, September 11, 2010.

25 Nokia was to shut its cloud-based file-sharing service known as Ovi File, from October 1, 2010. It also dropped its "share on Ovi" media-sharing site in 2009. The company also planned to discontinue its N-Gage gaming service later in 2010.

26 Millward Brown Optimor is the brand finance and ROI arm of leading market research and consultancy firm Millward Brown.

27 Diana ben-Aaron, "Nokia Investors Lose Patience 3 Years after IPhone (Update2)," www.businessweek.com, May 6, 2010.

28 Erika Morphy, "Nokia's New CEO May Whip up Savvier Smartphone Strategy," www.ecommercetimes.com, September 10, 2010.

29 "Replacing CEO Won't Solve Nokia's Problems," http://about.datamonitor.com/media/archives/4563, July 30, 2010.

30 "Apple Becomes Top Phone Maker by Profits -Research," www.reuters.com, November 10, 2009.

31 Diana ben-Aaron, "Nokia Investors Lose Patience 3 Years after IPhone (Update2)," www.businessweek.com, May 6, 2010.

32 www.nokia.com/about-nokia/financials/quarterly-and-annual-information/q2-2010.

33 www.nokia.com/about-nokia/financials/quarterly-and-annual-information/q2-2010.

34 Diana ben-Aaron, "Nokia Investors Lose Patience 3 Years after IPhone (Update2)," www.businessweek.com, May 6, 2010.

35 By Andrew Orlowski, "Rescuing Nokia? A Former Exec has a Radical Plan," www.theregister.co.uk, July 22, 2010.

36 Surojit Chatterjee, "Nokia Appoints Microsoft Top Exec as New CEO, Market Hopeful but Challenges Remain," http://uk.ibtimes.com, September 10, 2010.

37 Diana ben-Aaron and Marcel van de Hoef, "Nokia CFO Simonson Moved to New Post after Loss (Update4)," www.bloomberg.com, October 16, 2009.

38 Palm webOS is proprietary mobile operating system of Palm Inc., a smartphone manufacturer based in Sunnyvale, California. According to analysts, Palm's OS failed because of Palm's poor sales and marketing strategy. While Nokia could have solved Palm's sales and distribution problems with its massive global channels, Palm, on its part, could have given Nokia a strong presence in the Silicon Valley and the North American market.

39 "Replacing CEO Won't Solve Nokia's Problems," http://about.datamonitor.com/media/archives/4563, July 30, 2010.

40 Founded in 1996, Juniper Networks, Inc. is an information technology and computer networking products company. It is headquartered in Sunnyvale, California.

41 Macromedia Inc. is a US-based graphics and Web-development software company which developed the Flash video and Dreamweaver software. In December 2005, Macromedia was acquired by Adobe Systems, for US$ 3.4 billion in 2005.

42 Founded in 1982, Adobe Systems Inc. is a leading provider of graphic design, publishing, and imaging software for Web and print production. The company is headquartered in San Jose, California.

43 Boston Market, known as Boston Chicken until 1995, is a chain of American fast casual restaurants.

44 "Nokia Appoints Stephen Elop to President and CEO as of September 21, 2010," http://investors.nokia.com, September 10, 2010.

45 Aude Lagorce, "Nokia Corp. Names Microsoft Executive as New CEO," www.marketwatch.com, September 10, 2010.

46 Based in the UK, Jefferies International Limited offers asset management services including convertible bonds and securities.

47 Erika Morphy, "Nokia's New CEO May Whip up Savvier Smartphone Strategy," www.ecommercetimes.com, September 10, 2010.

48 Eric Lai, "How will Stephen Elop Fare at Microsoft?" http://blogs.computerworld.com, January 11, 2008.

49 NPD group is a global provider of consumer and retail market research information.

50 Tarmo Virki and Georgina Prodhan, "Nokia Replaces CEO Kallasvuo with Microsoft's Elop," http://in.reuters.com, September 10, 2010.

51 Surojit Chatterjee, "Nokia Appoints Microsoft Top Exec as New CEO, Market Hopeful but Challenges Remain," http://uk.ibtimes.com, September 10, 2010.

52 Aude Lagorce, "Nokia Corp. Names Microsoft Executive as New CEO," www.marketwatch.com, September 10, 2010.

53 Diana ben-Aaron "Nokia Hires Microsoft's Elop as CEO to Reverse Losses to Apple," www.bloomberg.com, September 10, 2010.

54 Tarmo Virki and Georgina Prodhan, "Nokia Brings in Microsoft Exec to Replace CEO," www.reuters.com, September 10, 2010.

55 "Mobile Phone Demand Expands 14.5% as Market Fragments; Top 5 Pressured by Challengers, Says IDC," www.businesswire.com, July 29, 2010.

56 RickMeritt, "Analyst: Five Challenges for New Nokia CEO," www.eetimes.com, September 10, 2010.

57 Andrew Orlowski, "Rescuing Nokia? A Former Exec has a Radical Plan," www.theregister.co.uk, July 22, 2010.

58 Diana ben-Aaron "Nokia Hires Microsoft's Elop as CEO to Reverse Losses to Apple," www.bloomberg.com, September 10, 2010.

59 Dan Frommer, "Nokia Makes the Same Mistake Again: Hires a Manager, Not a Product Visionary," www.businessinsider.com, September 10, 2010.

60 Surojit Chatterjee, "Nokia Appoints Microsoft Top Exec as New CEO, Market Hopeful but Challenges Remain," http://uk.ibtimes.com, September 10, 2010.

61 Jeff Kagan, "The Mountain Elop Has to Climb to Keep Nokia on Top," www.ecommercetimes.com, September 16, 2010.

CASE 17

KCI Technologies:
Engineering the Future, One Employee at a Time*[1]

Vera L. Street, PhD
Perdue School of Business, Salisbury University

Christy Weer, PhD
Perdue School of Business, Salisbury University

Frank Shipper, PhD
Perdue School of Business, Salisbury University

To an outsider, KCI Technologies may appear to be a typical, run of the mill engineering firm. However, once introduced, prospective clients soon understand why KCI was recently ranked 83rd on the *Engineering News-Record's* list of the top 500 Engineering Firms in the country, 7th on its list of Top 20 Telecommunications Firms, and 55th out of the Top 100 "Pure" Designers. With a focus on providing the highest quality service through a commitment to innovation and employee development, KCI is clearly positioning itself for the future.

KCI Technologies is currently the largest employee-owned, multidisciplined engineering firm in Maryland. Providing consulting, engineering, and environmental construction management services, KCI had revenues of approximately $131 million in 2009 and serves clients in the Northeast, Southeast and Mid-Atlantic regions of the US. The more than 900 employee owners of KCI operate out of offices in 12 states—Delaware, Florida, Georgia, Indiana, Maryland, New York, North Carolina, Ohio, Pennsylvania, Tennessee, Virginia and West Virginia, as well as the District of Columbia.

KCI has undergone incredible changes over the last several decades. From a basement dream, to a multimillion dollar employee owned organization, KCI is poised to face the future. However, with an uncertain economy and reduced governmental and private-sector spending, will the loyalty and commitment of the employee-owners be enough for KCI to continue building the impressive set of awards and recognition for which the company has become accustomed?

Background

The company now known as KCI was founded in Baltimore County, Maryland in 1955 in the basement of one of its cofounders. In 1977, the company was purchased by industrial products conglomerate Walter Kidde & Company and was subsequently merged with three other architectural and engineering firms into an engineering subsidiary that came to be known as Kidde Consultants Inc., or KCI. In 1987, Kidde was purchased by Hanson Trust PLC, a British manufacturing company with diversified holdings worldwide.

Although Hanson favored some of the Kidde businesses, there was a lack of fit between KCI and its new parent company. In particular, being a service-driven firm, as opposed to a product-oriented manufacturing company, KCI's measures of profitability were not consistent with Hanson's expectations. As an example, Terry Neimeyer, KCI's CEO explained:

> They had a term called, "Return on Capital Employed," . . . and they expected any company that worked for them to have an ROCE of 80 percent. . . . We said, "Well, look, we are an engineering company,

Sources: Vera Street, Salisbury University; Christy Weer, Salisbury University, Frank Shipper, Salisbury University. The research on this company was partially supported by the Foundation for Enterprise Development and the ESOP Association. Used by kind permission of the authors.

Keywords: ESOP, Shared leadership, Intellectual capital, Organizational culture

*An earlier version of this case was published in the Journal of Business Case Studies, 2011, Vol. 7, No. 1, pp. 57–68.

we're lucky to do 5 or 6 percent and we think we're doing well at 5 or 6 percent." And they said, "Look, our number's 80 percent."

Even beyond the inconsistencies with respect to financial expectations, the corporate cultures of Hanson and KCI differed drastically. KCI was used to having autonomy in decision making and authority. Hanson on the other hand, took a much more centralized, top-down approach to management. For example, as Neimeyer remembers, "if you wanted to buy a computer, you would have to go to London and make a presentation."

It was no secret that Hanson's business strategy was to enter the U.S., buy a conglomerate, keep what they viewed to be their profitable assets—assets that would be returning 80 percent—and then divest the unprofitable assets. Thus, aware that Hanson would likely want to sooner rather than later divest of KCI, senior managers had an idea. Driven largely by self-preservation, but also with a touch of optimism, the top management team thought, "Hey, let's see what we can do to buy ourselves." And why not? Who knew what would happen if KCI were to be taken over by another company? Indeed, there was a level of excitement over the potential of being a part of, and perhaps even leading, an employee owned company.

Unfortunately, Hanson was not at all receptive to the idea. As Neimeyer remembers, Hanson's view on selling KCI to its employees was;

> Absolutely not. We do not sell to people. We do not sell to former employees. It's just not what we do. We'd like to sell and rid ourselves of this [company] and it's over . . . and we don't do it [sell to former employees].

However, by this time, the KCI senior management team was actively seeking a strategy to make a buy-out happen. Having determined that alone the senior managers could not come up with enough equity to leverage a deal, they sought the buy-in of the 800 KCI employees. An existing Kidde profit sharing plan, which had accumulated some significant funds, laid the foundation for employee contributions. According to Neimeyer,

> We said, let's look at doing this where we'll ask people [employees] if they'd like to do it. We'll put out perspectives; we'll do a whole pro forma, which we did. And then people [employees] would have the option of contributing whatever they wanted. They could contribute 0 percent, they could contribute

100 percent, they could contribute anywhere in between. So, [based on our calculations as to the value of the company at that time], we basically had the scenario where ballpark figures it was 80 percent employee owned, with 20 percent held by these managers.

However, Hanson refused the offer. They were just not interested in selling the company to former employees.

Disappointed, but ever cognizant of the potential harsh consequences of being purchased by another organization, senior management at KCI went back to the drawing board. They knew the risks of upping the offer, but they also had confidence in their organization and, perhaps even more importantly, in their employees. Ultimately, they presented an increased, leveraged offer Hanson could not refuse. Shortly thereafter, KCI initiated an employee buyout and became a majority employee-owned company on December 15, 1988. On January 1, 1990, KCI established a qualified retirement program for the stock of KCI Technologies, Inc., to be held in trust by an Employee Stock Ownership Plan (ESOP). The ESOP initially owned approximately 82% of KCI stock, however, in June 1998, the company bought all of the management shares (non-ESOP shares) and became 100% employee-owned. Terry Neimeyer is the current Chief Executive Officer and Chairman of the Board of KCI; Nathan Beil is the President.

Operations and Quality Management

Although most people know an engineer or have at least met one, many may not know exactly what engineers do. To help better understand the nature of KCI, Harvey Floyd, a Senior Vice President and Chief Client Services Officer, offered the following as an explanation of KCI's businesses to outsiders:

> You know what architects do, you know what lawyers do, you know what doctors do, but you have no idea what engineers do . . . you know when you get up in the morning and you turn the lights on; How do you think that light comes on? It's from the generators that were built by engineers, the power plants, the transmission lines, everything built by, everything was designed by engineers. [To clarify] Not built, but designed by engineers. Then, you walked over and turned the water on, and out came

water. Well, where do you think the water came from? From the reservoirs, the towers, the pumps, the pumping stations, all designed by engineers. You flush the toilet. Where do you think it all goes? Pipes, the treatments plants, all designed by engineers. You drove across a road to get here. Where do you think the road came from? The bridge you drove over . . . who designed the bridges?

In other words, KCI is in the business of designing and coordinating facility and infrastructure projects and improvements for both the public and private sectors. Much of their work, approximately 80%, involves public sector work from various Departments of Transportation (e.g., MD DOT, Georgia DOT, PennDOT). Examples of work KCI may become involved with in the private sector include projects at research parks and universities for contractors and developers. Figure 1 provides examples of recent projects undertaken by KCI.

The competitive environment facing KCI, as well as the need for precision in the nature of the projects undertaken, drives a quality-focused culture at KCI. In part, there is the recognition that repeat business is critical, and to get that repeat business, projects must be completed to precision. When things do not

go as well as expected, it is not uncommon for KCI employees to get out in the field to figure out what could be improved upon for future projects.

Quality is important on both the business side as well as the technical side of the work done at KCI. On the business side there are quality issues with, for example determining project scope, understanding and negotiating client needs, and understanding regulations. On the technical side, the quality of designs, calculations, and reports and plans must be regulated. Because there are no set products that are being produced, as every project is different, these are challenging tasks.

Obtaining and maintaining ISO certification (verification by the International Organization on Standardization that relevant business standards are met) has been an important quality initiative at KCI. However, obtaining this certification has not been without its challenges. To begin, the standard was initially developed for manufacturing firms. Thus, as a service firm, KCI has had to adopt very broad interpretations of various components of the standard. Additionally, as a requirement, KCI had to explicitly write down their business processes. This proved to be somewhat of a hurdle, because, as Floyd put it, ". . . a lot of these

Figure 1   Example KCI Projects*

Project	Discipline	Location	Description
St. Mary's County Courthouse	Construction	Leonardtown, MD	Construction management over renovation and expansion of historic courthouse.
Clarice Smith Stormwater Management Pond	Environment	College Park, MD	Designed changes to stormwater management pond.
Capitol West Refrigeration Plant Expansion	Land Development	Washington, DC	Survey and layout services for plant expansion.
Gettysburg Interchange	Transportation	Cumberland County, PA	Team lead for highway interchange project.
Bonita Springs Tower	Telecommunications	Bonita Springs, FL	Worked on repair of tower damaged by hurricane.
Verizon	Telecommunications	Varies	On-call to provide engineering services to Verizon.
Suwannee Pedestrian Bridge	Transportation	Suwanee, GA	Engineering services for bridge and Boardwalk.

*Adapted From KCI Website

things are "that's just the way we do it"." Another issue was getting people to exert the extra effort required to obtain the certification. Senior management tried to make this as painless as possible, and they were quick to point out that, although some extra effort was necessary, often times this effort resulted in not only a step toward certification, but also in making business processes easier than they were before.

Logically, they began slowly, just focusing on part of the company. Then as the benefits were seen, it was decided to begin certification for the whole company in order to take the quality of their processes to the next level. The requisite codification of best business and quality control practices has helped to impose a level of discipline in the company's processes that may not have been present prior to the certification. And, although it is not necessarily required by all clients, it is looked upon very favorably and helps to win business. At this time, not all of KCI businesses have been certified however, they are actively seeking how to do so.

Marketing

Given that KCI is an engineering services firm, marketing is different than in a traditional manufacturing company and is even different from many other types of service firms. Marketing is primarily done through the preparation of proposals and statements of qualification for potential clients. Ultimately, work is secured because of the "expertise and experience of the technical staff at KCI." According to Deborah Boyd, Director of Proposal Preparation;

> I would say that 90 percent of our marketing falls within developing project descriptions of work that we've done in the past, employee resumes. Our marketing is very technical in nature, where it revolves around the projects and the staff team qualifications and the qualifications of our sub-consultants.

The process begins by finding potential clients who have jobs that need to be done. This primarily happens in two ways. The first, more conventional route is done by searching for client advertisements. This is usually done by the marketing staff searching online and/or looking in trade publications. A second, perhaps more fruitful route is done by a type of networking. Here, the Business Development staff, as well as other employees working on various projects, keeps in contact with current and past clients to see

what other projects they have in the pipeline. Other consultants that KCI has worked with also often prove to be a good source of leads. The marketing staff track these potential projects. Then, a qualified technical lead is brought in to work on the proposal that will be drawn up for the potential client.

The business development staff meets with the potential clients to ascertain information that will help in the proposal writing process. They try to determine what exactly the potential client is looking for, e.g. a probable price range, or any "hot buttons." Whereas general advertisements by these clients can be fairly generic and don't always contain everything the client is looking for, the Business Developers play a critical role in information gathering. The marketing staff then pulls together this information, matches it with the qualifications of KCI and prepares a package to submit to the potential client.

A key to this process is to get shortlisted. This is an area in which KCI may be able to improve. As Boyd put it,

> So either we're not qualified to do the job or we're qualified and we didn't show it very well. And if we're qualified and we didn't show it very well, that's a reflection on me because that means my proposal didn't answer the questions in the RFP.

An important part of the marketing effort is building project descriptions on prior work and maintaining a database of these descriptions. The project descriptions are like a project "resume." They contain information about the project, including the qualifications of the team that worked on it, and qualifications of any subconsultants.

Additionally, there are efforts aimed at increasing potential clients' awareness of KCI. One way that KCI attempts to build awareness is by standardizing their proposals. Consistency in fonts and colors is maintained so that potential clients can recognize a KCI proposal at a glance. Another example of how KCI attempts to increase awareness is through their corporate website. The website is continually updated to highlight successful projects they are currently working on or have completed. Other corporate communications are also available to interested parties. They produce folders of information including descriptions of successful projects they have completed, indications of awards they've won, and lists of where they are operating. Additionally, presentations at conferences and seminars help to promote the employees of KCI as experts in their respective fields.

HR and Intellectual Capital Development

Clearly, in such a technically focused, service oriented organization, employee knowledge and expertise are key elements for success, and this is not taken for granted at KCI. There are many ways in which intellectual capital is developed, starting right from the beginning; every attempt is made to hire the right people!

With a focus on shared leadership, hiring managers have a hand in developing realistic job descriptions. Openings are first posted internally, allowing current employees the opportunity to investigate and pursue available positions. After five days, the openings are posted externally. Often, department managers are involved in the entire hiring process, from creating job descriptions to prescreening applicants, to interviewing and making final hiring decisions. Although talent is hard to come by, Tammy Jones, a Vice President and HR Director, feels that KCI gets high quality applicants due to the company's reputation for doing great work in high profile projects—projects of which employees are proud to be a part.

Once hired, employees have the option to become involved in a year-long formal mentoring program at KCI. This program, launched about three years ago, was established, in large part, in an attempt to keep the intellectual capital developed at KCI from moving to competitor firms. New hires are paired with more senior employees and move through a 12-month formal mentoring regime. Most senior managers mentor two or three new hires each year and the program appears to be paying off. As indicated by Jones;

> When I came to KCI, which has been almost five years ago, previous employee surveys, and as well as our turnover reports indicated that we were losing employees at two to three years. So thus launched the formal mentoring program. Actually, I was reviewing those statistics recently and we're retaining about 33 percent more than we did prior [to the mentoring program].

Beyond the mentoring program, formal training and development programs are a cornerstone of intellectual capital development at KCI. Perhaps most notably is an extensive set of leadership development programs for which employees at various levels of the organization can be nominated. The series includes three programs: Emerging Leaders, Professional Leaders, and The Advanced Leadership Program.

The Emerging Leaders Program typically consists of 40–60 individuals who have been with the company for fewer than five years. Designed by an outside consultant, employees are nominated and accepted into the Emerging Leaders program based on their leadership potential as noted by their immediate manager. Participants meet every other month for 24 months and have a culminating project focusing on the development of a KCI initiative.

According to Beil;

> On the Emerging Leaders, for example, you have the team building piece as well as training on interpersonal skills, basic management, priority management, conflict management or resolution, stress management, positive reinforcement, and motivation. Sometimes it's hard to motivate even yourself, so expressing yourself in the proper way. And, we actually have a graduation program for these folks . . .

The Professional Leaders program is more selective and is typically limited to 20 employees. This program was also designed with the help of an outside consultant and is continuously customized based on survey feedback from KCI middle managers. The program runs for one year—in Spring and Fall "semesters"—and focuses on topics such as motivating others, coaching and developing others, and relationship management. Participants complete a number of self-assessments, which allow them to better understand themselves and their roles within the organization. With a variety of "credits" to choose from, the program culminates in a three-day off site Foundations of Leadership Program offered by the University of Maryland.

The third and final component, the Advanced Leadership Program is facilitated by an outside consultant. This intimate, high-level, high-touch component is composed of only those nominated employees who are deemed as potential Vice Presidents of KCI. The Advanced Leadership component is an intense development program consisting of deep level soft skills training. This program has not been offered at KCI in a while.

Another development program is the Project Management Academy. This is a one day, annual event during which participants become deeply involved in project and quality management issues. There are three levels for the program, all focused on project scope, scheduling, and budgeting, but at the highest level the soft skills of management are also honed. Participants in this program are typically those at the project management level or above.

Other types of development are available or supported as well. For instance, there is support for CAD training, safety training, LEED certification, and various software training. KCI hires and supports interns. Additionally, there is a licensure management system to help everyone stay on top of their licenses. And all of this is not to mention the informal training that occurs at KCI on a daily basis. As one can imagine, KCI earmarks significant resources for these training and development programs. Senior management at KCI feels that these career-development initiatives are a necessity to recruit and retain the high-quality talent for which KCI is known.

KCI also offers generous benefits to its employees. These vary from a 401K with a company match, to a floating holiday. One benefit that employees find particularly beneficial is tuition assistance. KCI pays 100% after an individual has been with the company for more than five years and 80% if not. Many employees feel that it is an excellent program. As one employee who recently completed a graduate program put it,

> Excellent, excellent program. I mean, I wouldn't have been able to pay for it had it not been for KCI. So to me, that's another huge benefit. I feel like I owe them [KCI] something because of the benefit. I mean, it's huge.

Tuition assistance also enriches the firm by increasing KCI's intellectual capital and qualifications needed to successfully bid on additional projects.

Finance

Given the recent economic downturn, most firms have been faced with financial difficulties. KCI is no exception. This is exhibited by a considerable drop in revenue in recent years. In 2007, total revenues were $142 million, in 2008 revenues stayed constant at $142 million; however, in 2009, revenues dropped to $131 million. Despite this decline, Neimeyer is optimistic, "dealing with this economy—this is my fourth recession, you know—this will pass. I know that it will."

Neimeyer has reason to be optimistic. According to a recent Business Week article, one way to help a company overcome an economic downturn is to practice open book management. Open book management is when a company shares its financial and other data with its employees and often times helps these employees to understand how this data relates to their work. And, KCI does just this. The financials for the company are open. Employees can ask to see most anything regarding the financial health of the organization. This is important to employees as a portion of their compensation is based on the financial well-being of the company. KCI makes an ESOP contribution based on a percentage of an employee's salary, currently 6.5%, which vests in five years. Despite its ups and downs, the ESOP share price is impressive. At inception, one share was worth $1,000, now it is valued at almost 10 times that amount. (see Figure 2).

Figure 2 KCI Stock Value

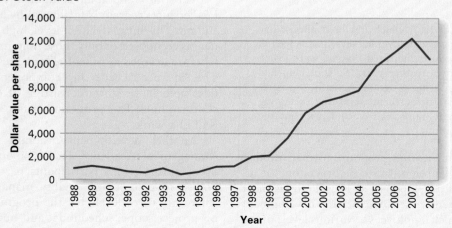

As one employee commented,

> It was amazing to see over the years how much the ESOP continued to make money over time. One of my coworkers who has been here 12 years now, he has thousands of dollars in this ESOP that he's never had to put any money aside.

To get continued employee buy-in, ESOP education is constant. The company has several events during the year that promote awareness about the program, such as a contest where employees guess the exact value of the stock. Interestingly, and a good sign, many employees' guesses are not too far from the true value. ESOP bingo is another exciting event where employees—even those out in the field -have a chance to play and learn ESOP definitions and terminology.

Sharing in the ESOP is truly that—equal sharing. The largest stock holder is only so because he has been with the company for the longest length of time. No one receives extra perks to make their percentage of stock ownership particularly high, and unlike cash flow issues that can sometime arise when employees leave an employee-owned company, KCI has not had issue with cashing people out. So they know the money from the ESOP is real and truly is the employees'.

Since in service organizations employee compensation is typically such a huge part of the financial outlay, it is worth noting other forms of compensation here. Aside from the ESOP and regular wages or salaries, top earners at KCI have an "at risk" compensation incentive. A portion, typically 5–30% of their compensation is based on the profitability of the business for which they are involved. Additionally, the top 20 earners have a deferred compensation plan. This plan is designed to make the compensation of top employees a bit more competitive with that at rival partnership firms.

The Competitive Marketplace

Considering such a large portion of KCI's projects are public sector projects, it is important to consider this marketplace. There are opposing forces at work here. On one hand, the aging infrastructure in the US could create great demand for the services of firms like KCI. On the other hand, there are potentially severe budget constraints that could limit the number and profitability of projects requiring those services.

That being said, KCI faces fierce competition. Because they are a multidisciplined (e.g., construction, environmental, transportation) engineering firm, the competitors that they meet for a given project depend upon the business line(s) needed for that project. Some of their competitors are regional, employee-owned firms of about the same size, like JMT. Others are large, international publically traded firms like Michael Baker Corporation. Additionally, there are many partnerships in the mix, like RK&K, LLP. But, it's important to note that in this field, the competition is not always the competition. Often times firms will be competing with each other for one project and be partners on another. That is, when there is considerable overlap in the skills between two firms, they may compete with one another for a project. However, sometimes the firms will have complementary skills needed to best meet the demands of a potential client, so they will partner with one another.

Two keys to successful competition in this arena are having the proper qualifications for a potential client's project and having relationships built with clients and partners. A company must have the talent available to meet the needs of a potential client's project. This means having available employees with the proper education, experience, and certifications. But just having this talent is not quite enough. As previously mentioned, the company must be able to expertly demonstrate the fit between the company's expertise and the client's needs. Proper coordination of talent and being able to show the fit to the project can be challenging.

Having strong relationships with potential clients and partners is critical to get a leg up on the competition. These relationships are used to both learn about new projects and to find out more detail about potential projects. The earlier a company can start working on a proposal for a potential project and the more specific the proposal is, the more likely they are to beat the competition.

An additional significant area of competition is the competition not for clients, but rather for employees. In the US, the engineering population is "graying." That is, there is a great shortage of new talent, so firms have to fight over the talent that's out there. According to Beil, KCI relies on their challenging work environment and open culture to capture great talent. Beil also mentioned that they had hoped that the ESOP would be a great recruitment tool, but this has not turned out to be the case. Today's applicant pool is really looking for a job for a couple of years, rather than a career with an organization. As such, they would not be as likely to see the benefits of the ESOP. But that is not to say it is without its recruitment merits. When one employee was asked what brought her to KCI, she commented, "The things I really liked about KCI, besides the staff—we have a great staff here. They had a really good benefits package. The ESOP was very appealing to me . . ."

At the upper management level, a different scenario plays out. Many of KCI's competitors are partnerships, and partnerships allow the partners to have a higher earning potential than that expected of the top executives in an ESOP. As such, it could be difficult to recruit into these positions. But, at least recently, according to Beil, finding upper managers has not been an issue. He believes this due in part to the nature of financial risk differences in the two types of organizations. The financial risk facing the upper managers in an ESOP firm tends to be less than that which faces partners in a partnership.

Shared Leadership

Leadership is about integrity and credibility. Accordingly, Beil feels that letting people know where things stand is important, and never promising more than you feel you can deliver gets real buy in. It's not at all about 'just barking orders to employees." The KCI leaders see their role as articulating a vision that resonates with employees.

This mentality is largely derived from the culture at KCI, but it is also a result of being employee owned. Employee involvement resonates through the organization, and it is clear that the employees play a large role in the overall direction of the organization. For instance, an employee designee serves on the board of directors. According to Beil,

> So our employees actually have a popular election where they elect a member to the Board of Directors . . . They go out and they have to get ballots and they have to get 35 shareholders sign [the ballot] to say the employee is "OK." And then there's this popular election . . .

Now the true power in any ESOP organization is in its trustees, as trustees control the voting of the stock on all things with the exception of mergers and acquisitions and major changes to corporate bylaws. Interestingly, two nonmanagement employee members are also on the Board of Trustees at KCI—one elected employee member and one appointed. Having an employee representative involved in governing and approving major decisions for the organization is a true example of shared leadership.

In addition to having formal representation on the Board of Directors and the Board of Trustees, it is clear that there are many avenues for open communication that allow ideas to filter from the lower ranks of the organization to the upper echelons. Niemeyer commented,

> One thing about it, and it may be our management style, is that our people have a tendency to speak up. And when they do speak up, they speak up without fear of repercussion. So it's not as if they're worried about saying something in a meeting or to me or to the president and all of a sudden seeing the Grim Reaper come and fire them.

Others in the organization have echoed the idea that there is open and easy communication up the organizational ladder. Indeed, the leaders at KCI provide many avenues through which employees can bring up issues, comment on processes, and make other suggestions to management. As an example, The Companywide Employee Committee was formed whereby 36 members, representing each department, meet on a regular basis to discuss issues that are raised from members of their respective departments. In essence, this committee, for which membership rotates on a yearly basis, acts as a sounding board for employee concerns.

In addition, anonymous survey boxes are located in the cafeteria, and an annual survey provides an outlet for employees to provide feedback on a wide range of topics including job satisfaction, human resource issues, compensation, supervisors, and coworkers. Moreover, a blog, to which employees may anonymously post, will soon be available as another mechanism for employee feedback. Townhall meetings, though in practice are primarily a top-down information dissemination tool, provide an additional venue where employees could voice their ideas. Moreover, senior management pride themselves on their availability and openness through an open-door policy.

It is not unusual to hear that organizations are "employee friendly" or have "open door communication"; however, sometimes these espoused views are simply not enacted. However, at KCI, what they preach is exactly what they practice. Employee suggestions do not go unheeded. One key example is the creation of one of KCI's business lines, the Geographic Information Systems (GIS) group. According to Neimeyer,

> The GIS group idea really came up through the organization by some computer folks who weren't in the engineering field, but said, "Look, I think there is going be a business line in geographic information systems. And it's something that we can really deal with the engineering or the planning sector even though it's not typical engineering." And, so one gent came and said, "Hey look, let me take this on. I think I can create a business on this and make a business line." And, that's an example of an idea that came up [through the ranks] and spawned a business.

Another initiative generated from the employees is a technology refresh program, where technology updating is based on technological advancements rather than on a fixed time interval. Neimeyer jokes, "It's not like I come up with all these ideas. I've been here 32 years. My new ideas are limited." These examples make apparent the notion that employee ideas get heard and implemented.

The idea of open lines of communication and continuous implementation of employee ideas is not only an upper echelon perception. Employees do indeed feel like their ideas are respected and welcomed. As one employee put it, "the culture is one where everyone, from the leaders at the top to the newest nonmanagement employees, is in it together."

Information Sharing

Communication of information is critical in any organization, however, in an ESOP, employees have more of a vested interest in understanding, retaining, and utilizing information disseminated to them. Neimeyer and Beil have similar views,

> . . . on the ESOP side [as compared to a partnership], communication skills probably have to be a step up. I think your ability to have a vision, and articulate it, then lead the company through it, has to be a step up.

Employees' echo this sentiment. For instance, an employee offered,

> I've worked for a partnership before. I had no idea how I was doing on a project, how much money we were making, how much money the company was making, whether my project was a success or not because the profits all went to the partners. In an ESOP culture, we're all owners. We all know what's going on, and because of that, we push information down to our employees.

Another employee added,

> We try really hard to communicate what's going on. We have town meetings once a month. The managers are very open to talking to employees. I mean, they'll tell you, "I can't tell you; it's not for discussion right now," and they're honest.

KCI has formal approaches to getting important and worthwhile information out to employees. As mentioned above, Townhall meetings play an important role in information sharing. These open meetings are held by the President once per month at headquarters with those in remote locations tele-, video-, or web-conferencing in. The meetings are also recorded and shared on the company intranet. During these meetings the status of the company is shared, company-wide issues are addressed, like changes to benefits or austerity measures, and exciting new projects are announced. Financial results are also shared quarterly.

In addition to Townhall meetings, departmental managers hold monthly meetings with the hope that the information shared will be funneled down through the company ranks. To help facilitate this process, minutes from the meetings are sent out to second tier management.

Beyond these formal approaches, more informal channels of communication exist as well. Even the CEO takes a hands-on approach to information sharing. For example, he attempts to reach out and visit branch offices. On his visit he says his approach is to, "just sit with the people and you ask them how things are going and have a little staff meeting and tell them what's going on." Regarding information sharing in general, he comments,

> And again, we try and continue to do it. It's a never ending cycle. You can never do enough of it. And in our company we get critiqued for not doing enough of it. No matter what we do, we still have to do more.

Growth and Change through Innovation and Initiatives

It is well understood that KCI cannot simply rest on its laurels and continue to do business as it has always done. Innovation is key to continued growth and development and KCI has been involved in some innovation, forward thinking projects. For instance, Floyd recalls one innovation done to mitigate the impact of a bridge on the environment:

> There were just a number of things that were blocking fish passages, so the fish couldn't go back up the river to spawn, they hadn't for years. So as part of the mitigation effort, the State Highway Administration agreed to create these natural fish passages. They didn't want fish ladders. They didn't want pipes. They wanted natural. Well, this is something that we haven't necessarily done on the East coast, but they're doing it in the West. So some of our guys went out to the West and studied what was being done out there by literature searches, talking with people, and going out visiting.
>
> We saw what they were doing, but what they were doing they were doing in a rural area. We had to do this in an urban area, so our environmental scientists and our hydrologic people actually developed the design method to take that technology and apply it in an urban environment. What they did was they built these natural fish passages in the bottom of the streams, so depending on what type of fish you had, it would determine how strong the fish—what current the fish could swim up, how strong the current could be, and how long they could (swim against) it, their endurance. So what they had to do was they had to design these rock ladders, basically, these fish ladders so that the fish could make it up through the current, and then they had to space boulders to form these little resting areas for the fish so they could get up the stream . . . you would never know that it was a manmade thing. It just looks like it's natural, but in actuality, they were purposely built and constructed so the fish could get up over the natural blockages. We won a lot of awards for that because that was very innovative.

Providing environmental-friendly solutions to client problems comes natural to KCI, perhaps because the company and its employee owners are invested in sustainability themselves. KCI's headquarters, one of Maryland's newest green buildings, has recently been awarded the US Green Building Council's (USGBC) Leadership in Energy and Environmental Design (LEED) gold certification. The 120,000 square foot building features a white solar reflective roof, which reflects sunlight in the summertime reducing the air-conditioning requirements, a stormwater management pond, and high-performance climate control plumbing and electrical systems, all designed by KCI engineers and LEED specialists. According to Neimeyer, the facility uses resources more efficiently than traditional office buildings and offers employees a healthier and more comfortable work environment.

Indeed, KCI has a forward-thinking mindset. Not being afraid to take on new initiative is another hallmark of KCI's continued growth. In a typical year, 15–20% of profits are used to fund new corporate initiatives—those that are funded at the corporate level because they tend to be too expensive for an individual division. Usually, an initiative runs upward of $250,000. A prime example is the aforementioned GIS division. This began as a corporate initiative and was funded as such until it reached a critical mass of clients. It now operates on its own with 22 employees. This is not to say that all initiatives work. If an initiative is not on target at year three, funding will be reallocated to other projects, and the initiative will be discontinued. But, one cannot expect rewards without taking some risks.

The Reorganization

KCI is in the process of reorganizing. This is a step they have been considering since the mid-1990s. For the most part, KCI has taken a geographic approach to their structure. Now, they are moving to a discipline-based approach. This includes such disciplines as transportation facilities, site management, telecom, and urban planning and development surveys. The headquarters has been somewhat organized by discipline, but the remainder of company has not. The geographic regions were initially established to help promote geographic expansion, and to aid in succession planning at KCI. Unfortunately, particularly during downtimes in the economy, regions would be very protective of their resources and be out for themselves—not for the good of the whole company. It is expected that the new discipline based approach will be more integrated and less territorial.

The President has vested a great deal of time and effort into trying to facilitate a smooth transition. He has discussed the expectations for the reorganization with individuals, small groups, and large groups. Employee survey data indicate that employees are generally favorably disposed toward the reorganization; however there are employees who feel that they aren't really affected and that it's mostly a management reorganization. Some believe that people will not quite understand what is happening and why until the official reorganization has taken place and until results start coming in. Additionally, there is some sentiment that the reorganization will be quite challenging because, although senior management realizes that role definition will be important, the lines of authority in the organization may not be as clear after the reorganization. It is expected that there will be more shared and collaborative leadership.

References

1. http://www.businessweek.com/small-business/
2. http://www.kci.com

Endnotes

1   The authors would like to thank the employee-owners of KCI Technologies who graciously shared their knowledge, experiences, and perspectives about the company. Their viewpoints were invaluable in ensuring that this

Looking Forward

With the current economic uncertainty, KCI faces an all too common challenge among businesses—securing enough business to keep their highly talented and committed employees working. According to Beil,

> We don't hire for a job and then we fire them later. That's really not our efforts. . . . right now, we're just maintaining it [the firm], finding enough work so that we don't have to tell a good person to find work elsewhere is probably what keeps me awake at night the most.

This is not to say that KCI is not constantly looking for good talent. When asked about the future of the organization, Beil, was quick to mention,

> Our challenge will always be finding highly competent people. We're laying people off in a certain sector, but there are other sectors that are strong where we're looking to hire people. And finding talented people is a marathon struggle for us.

3. http://www.iso.org/iso/support/faqs/faqs conformity assessment and certification.htm
4. http://www.nceo.org/main/article.php/id/28/

case provides a true representation of the culture and practices of the company. In addition, the authors would like to thank the Beyster Institute and the Foundation for Enterprise Development for their support of this work.

CASE 18

Airborne Express: The Underdog

Charles W.L. Hill
University of Washington

Introduction

Airborne Inc., which operated under the name Airborne Express, was an air-express transportation company, providing express and second-day delivery of small packages (less than 70 lbs.) and documents throughout the United States and to and from many foreign countries. The company owned and operated an airline and a fleet of ground-transportation vehicles to provide complete door-to-door service. It was also an airfreight forwarder, moving shipments of any size worldwide. In 2003, Airborne Express held third place in the U.S. air express industry, with 9% of the market for small package deliveries. Its main domestic competitors were Federal Express, which had 26% of the market; United Parcel Service (UPS), which had 53% of the market. There were several smaller players in the market at the time, including DHL Airways, Consolidated Freightways and the U.S. Postal Service, each of which held under 5% of the market share.[1] DHL however, had a huge presence outside of North America and was in fact the largest small package delivery company in the world. In 2003, after years of struggling to survive in the fiercely competitive small package express delivery industry, Airborne was acquired by DHL, which was owned by Deutsche Post, the large German postal, express package, and logistics company.

The evolution of the air express industry and the current state of competition in the industry were discussed in a companion case to this one, "The Evolution of the Air Express Industry, 1973–2010." The current case focuses on the operating structure, competitive strategy, organizational structure, and cultures of Airborne Express, from its inception until it was acquired by DHL in 2003. It also deals with the aftermath of the DHL acquisition.

History of Airborne Express

Airborne Express was originally known as Pacific Air Freight when it was founded in Seattle at the close of World War II by Holt W. Webster, a former Army Air Corps officer. (See Table 1 for a listing of major milestones in the history of Airborne Express.) The company was merged with Airborne Freight Corporation of California in 1968, taking the name of the California company, but retaining management direction by the former officers of Pacific Air Freight. Airborne was initially an exclusive airfreight forwarder. Freight forwarders such as Airborne arrange for the transportation of air cargo between any two destinations. They purchase cargo space from the airlines and retail this in small amounts. They deal primarily with small customers, providing pickup and delivery services in most cities, either in their own trucks or through contract agents.

Following the 1977 deregulation of the airline industry, Airborne entered the air express industry by leasing the airplanes and pilots of Midwest Charter, a small airline operating out of its own airport in Wilmington, Ohio. However, Airborne quickly became dissatisfied with the limited amount of control they were able to exercise over Midwest,

This case was made possible by the generous assistance of Airborne Express. The information given in this case was provided by Airborne Express. Unless otherwise indicated, Airborne Express and Securities and Exchange Commission's 10–K filings are the sources of all information contained within this case. The case is based on an earlier case, which was prepared with the assistance of Daniel Bodnar, Laurie Martinelli, Brian McMullen, Lisa Mutty, and Stephen Schmidt.

Table 1 Major Milestones at Airborne Express[2]

1946: Airborne Flower Traffic Association of California is founded to fly fresh flowers from Hawaii to the mainland.

1968: Airborne of California and Pacific Air Freight of Seattle merge to form Airborne Freight Corporation. Headquarters are in Seattle, Washington.

1979–81: Airborne Express is born. After purchasing Midwest Air Charter, Airborne buys Clinton County Air Force Base in Wilmington, Ohio, becoming the only carrier to own and operate an airport. The package sort center opens, creating the "hub" for the hub-and-spoke system.

1984–86: Airborne is the first carrier to establish a privately operated Foreign Trade Zone in an air industrial park.

1987: Airborne opens the Airborne Stock Exchange, a third-party inventory management and distribution service. In the same year, service begins to and from more than 8,000 Canadian locations.

1988: Airborne becomes the first air express carrier to provide same-day delivery, through its purchase of Sky Courier.

1990: The International Cargo Forum and Exposition names Airborne the carrier with the most outstanding integrated cargo system over the previous two years.

1991: A trio of accolades: Airborne is the first transportation company to receive Volvo-Flyg Motors' Excellent Performance Award. Computerworld ranks us the "most effective user of information systems in the U.S. transportation industry." In addition, we receive the "Spread the Word!" Electronic Data Interchange (EDI) award for having the largest number of EDI users worldwide in the air express and freight forwarding industry.

1992: Airborne introduces Flight-ReadySM—the first prepaid Express Letters and Packs.

1993: Airborne introduces Airborne Logistics Services (ALS), a new subsidiary providing outsourced warehousing and distribution services. IBM consolidates its international shipping operation with Airborne.

1994: Airborne opens its Ocean Service Division, becoming the first express carrier to introduce ocean shipping services. Airborne Logistics Services (ALS) establishes the first new film distribution program for the movie industry in 50 years. We also become the first company to provide on-line communication to Vietnam.

1995: Airborne Alliance Group, a consortium of transportation, logistics, third-party customer service operations and high-tech companies providing value-added services, is formed. Airborne opens a second runway at its hub, which is now the United States' largest privately owned airport. We also expand our fleet, acquiring Boeing 767–200 aircraft.

1996: Airborne Express celebrates 50 years of providing value-added distribution solutions to business.

1997: Airborne Express has its best year ever, with net earnings increasing three-and-a-half-fold over the previous year. Airborne's stock triples, leading to a two-for-one stock split in February, 1998.

1998: Airborne posts record profits and enters the Fortune 500. The first of 30 Boeing 767s is introduced to our fleet. The Business Consumer Guide rates Airborne as the Best Air Express Carrier for the 4th consecutive year.

1999: Airborne@home, a unique alliance with the United States Postal Service, is introduced. It enables e-tailers, catalog companies and similar businesses to ship quickly and economically to the residential marketplace. Optical Village is created. Part of Airborne Logistics Services, this new division brings together some of the biggest competitors in the optical industry to share many costs and a single location for their assembly, storage, inventory, logistics, and delivery options.

(continued)

Table 1   (*continued*)

2000: Airborne announces several changes in senior management, including a new President and Chief Operating Officer, Carl Donaway. Several new business initiatives are announced, most notably a ground service scheduled to begin April 1, 2001. Airborne also wins the Brand Keys Customer Loyalty Award, edging out our competition for the second consecutive year.

2001: Airborne launches Ground Delivery Service and 10:30 A.M. Service, giving Airborne a comprehensive, full-service industry competitive capability. Airborne.com launches its Small Business Center, as well as a variety of enhancements to help all business customers speed and simplify the shipping process. We also release the Corporate Exchange shipping application, simplifying desktop shipping for customers while giving them greater control. Advanced tracking features are added to airborne.com and Airborne eCourier is released, enabling customers to send confidential, signed documents electronically.

2003: Airborne's ground operations acquired by DHL for $1.1 billion.

© Cengage Learning 2013

which made it very difficult to achieve the kind of tight coordination and control of logistics that was necessary to become a successful air express operator. Instead of continuing to lease Midwest's planes and facility, in 1980 Airborne decided to buy "the entire bucket of slop; company, planes, pilots, airport and all."

Among other things, the Midwest acquisition put Airborne in the position of being the only industry participant to own an airport. Airborne immediately began the job of developing a hub-and-spoke system capable of supporting a nationwide distribution system. An efficient sorting facility was established at the Wilmington hub. Airborne upgraded Midwest's fleet of prop and propjet aircraft, building a modern fleet of DC-8s, DC-9s, and YS-11 aircraft. These planes left major cities every evening, flying down the spokes carrying letters and packages to the central sort facility in Wilmington, Ohio. There the letters and packages were unloaded, sorted according to their final destination, and then reloaded and flown to their final destination for delivery before noon the next day.

During the late-1970s and early-1980s, dramatic growth in the industry attracted many competitors. As a consequence, the high-growth rate price competition became intense, forcing a number of companies to the sidelines by the late-1980s. Between 1984 and 1990 average revenues per domestic shipment at Airborne fell from around $30 to under $15 (in 2003 they were just under $9).

Airborne was able to survive this period by pursuing a number of strategies that increased productivity and drove costs down to the lowest levels in the industry. Airborne's operating costs per shipment fell from $28 in 1984 to around $14 by 1990, and to $9.79 by 2001. As a consequence, by the late-1980s Airborne had pulled away from a pack of struggling competitors to become one of the top three companies in the industry, a position it still held when acquired by DHL in 2003.

Air Express Operations

The Domestic Delivery Network

As of 2002, its last full year as an independent enterprise, Airborne Express had 305 ground stations within the United States. The stations were the ends of the spokes in Airborne's hub-and-spoke system and the distribution of stations allows Airborne to reach all major population centers in the country. In each station there were about 50–55 drivers plus staff. About 80% of Airborne's 115,300 full-time and 7,200 part-time employees were found at this level. The stations were the basic units in Airborne's delivery organization. Their primary task was to ferry packages between clients and the local air terminal. Airborne utilized approximately 14,900 radio-dispatch delivery vans and trucks to transport packages, of which 6,000 were owned by the company. Independent contractors provided the balance of the company's pickup and delivery services.

Airborne's drivers made their last round of major clients at 5 P.M. The drivers either collected packages directly from clients or from one of the company's 15,300 plus drop boxes. The drop boxes were placed at strategic locations, such as in the lobbies of major commercial buildings. To give clients a little more time, in most major cities there were also a few central drop boxes emptied at 6 P.M. If a client needed still more time, so long as the package could be delivered to the airport by 7 P.M., it would make the evening flight.

When a driver picked up a package, he or she read a bar code attached to the package with a handheld scanner. This information was fed directly into Airborne's proprietary FOCUS (Freight, On-Line Control and Update System) computer system. The FOCUS system, which had global coverage, records shipment status at key points in the life cycle of a shipment. FOCUS allowed a customer direct access to shipment information through the Internet. All a customer needed to do is access Airborne's Website and key the code number assigned to a package, and the FOCUS system would tell the customer where in Airborne's system the package was.

When a driver completed a pickup route, she or he took the truck to Airborne's loading docks at the local airport. (Airborne served all 99 major metropolitan airports in the United States.) There the packages were loaded into C-containers (discussed later in this case study). C-containers were then towed by hand (or by tractor) to a waiting aircraft, where they were loaded onto a conveyor belt and moved through the passenger door of the aircraft. Before long the aircraft was loaded and departed. It would either fly directly to the company's hub at Wilmington, or make one or two stops along the way to pick up more packages.

Sometime between midnight and 2 A.M., most of the aircraft would have landed at Wilmington. An old strategic air command base, Wilmington's location places it within a 600-mile radius (an overnight drive or 1-hour flying time) of 60% of the U.S. population. Wilmington has the advantage of a good-weather record. In all the years that Airborne operated at Wilmington, air operations were "fogged out" on only a handful of days. In 1995, Airborne opened a second runway at Wilmington. Developed at a cost of $60 million, the second runway made Wilmington the largest privately owned airport in the country. The runway expansion was part of a $120 million upgrade of the Wilmington sort facility.

After arrival at Wilmington, the plane taxed down the runway and parked alongside a group of aircraft that were already disgorging their load of C-containers. Within minutes, the C-containers were unloaded from the plane down a conveyor belt and towed to the sort facility by a tractor. The sort facility had the capacity to handle 1.2 million packages per night. At the end of 2001, the facility handled an average of 1 million packages per night. The bar codes on the packages were read, and then the packages were directed through a labyrinth of conveyor belts and sorted according to final destination. The sorting was partly done by hand and partly by automation. At the end of this process, packages were grouped together by final destination and loaded into a C-container. An aircraft bound for the final destination was then loaded with C-containers, and by 5 A.M. most aircraft had departed.

Upon arrival at the final destination, the plane was unloaded and the packages sorted according to their delivery points within the surrounding area. Airborne couriers then took the packages on the final leg of their journey. Packages had a 75% probability of being delivered to clients by 10:30 A.M., and a 98% probability of being delivered by noon.

Regional Trucking Hubs

Although about 71% of packages were transported by air and passed through Wilmington, Airborne also established 10 regional trucking hubs to deal with the remaining 29% of the company's domestic volume. These hubs sorted shipments that originated and had a destination within approximately a 300-mile radius. The first one opened was in Allentown, Pennsylvania, centrally located on the East Coast. This hub handled packages transported between points within the Washington, D.C., and Boston areas. Instead of transporting packages by air, packages to be transported within this area were sorted by the drivers at pickup and delivered from the driver's home station by scheduled truck runs to the Allentown hub. There they were sorted according to destination and taken to the appropriate station on another scheduled truck run for final delivery.

One advantage of ground-based transportation through trucking hubs is that operating costs are much lower than for air transportation. The average cost of a package transported by air is more than 5 times greater than the cost of a package transported on the ground. However, this cost differential is transparent to the customer, who assumes that all packages are flown. Thus, Airborne could charge the same price for ground-transported packages as for air-transported packages, but the former yielded a much higher return. The trucking hubs also had the advantage of taking some of the load of the Wilmington sorting facility, which was operating at about 90% capacity by 2003.

International Operations

In addition to its domestic express operations, Airborne was also an international company providing service to more than 200 countries worldwide. International operations accounted for about 11% of total revenues in 2002. Airborne offered two international products: freight products and express products. Freight products were commercial-sized, larger-unit shipments. This service provides door-to-airport service. Goods were picked up domestically from the customer and then shipped to the destination airport. A consignee or an agent of the consignee got the paperwork and cleared the shipment through customs. Express packages are small packages, documents, and letters. This was a door-to-door service, and all shipments were cleared through customs by Airborne. Most of Airborne's international revenues come from freight products.

Airborne did not fly any of its own aircraft overseas. Rather, it contracted for space on all-cargo airlines or in the cargo holds of passenger airlines. Airborne owned facilities overseas in Japan, Taiwan, Hong Kong, Singapore, Australia, New Zealand, and London. These functioned in a manner similar to Airborne's domestic stations. (That is, they had their own trucks and drivers and were hooked into the FOCUS tracking system.) The majority of foreign distribution, however, was carried out by foreign agents. Foreign agents were large, local, well-established surface delivery companies. Airborne entered into a number of exclusive strategic alliances with large foreign agents. It had alliances in Japan, Thailand, Malaysia, and South Africa. The rationale for entering strategic alliances, along with Airborne's approach to global expansion, is discussed in greater detail later in this case.

Another aspect of Airborne's international operations was the creation at its Wilmington hub, the only privately certified Foreign Trade Zone (FTZ) in the United States. While in an FTZ, no taxes are to be paid and no customs duty is required until merchandise leaves. Thus, a foreign-based company could store critical inventory in the FTZ and have Airborne deliver it just-in-time to U.S. customers. This allowed the foreign company to hold inventory in the United States without having to pay customs duty on it until necessary.

Aircraft Purchase and Maintenance

As of 2002, Airborne Express owned a fleet of 118 aircraft, including 24 DC-8s, 74 DC-9s, and twenty Boeing 767s. In addition, approximately 70 smaller aircraft were chartered nightly to connect smaller cities with company aircraft that then operate to and from the Wilmington hub. To keep down capital expenditures, Airborne preferred to purchase used planes. Airborne converted the planes to suit its specifications at a maintenance facility in its Wilmington hub. Once it got a plane, Airborne typically gutted the interior and installed state-of-the-art electronics and avionics equipment. The company's philosophy was to get all of the upgrades that it could into an aircraft. Although this can cost a lot up front, there is a payback in terms of increased aircraft reliability and a reduction in service downtime. Airborne also standardized cockpits as much as possible. This made it easier for crews to switch from one aircraft to another if necessary. According to the company, in the early-1990s, the total purchase and modification of a secondhand DC-9 cost about $10 million, compared with an equivalent new plane cost of $40 million. An additional factor reducing operating costs was that Airborne's DC-9 aircraft only required a 2-person cockpit crew, as opposed to the 3-person crews required in most FedEx and UPS aircraft at that time.

After conversion, Airborne strove to keep aircraft maintenance costs down by carrying out virtually all of its own fleet repairs. (It was the only all-cargo carrier to do so.) The Wilmington maintenance facility could handle everything except major engine repairs and had the capability to machine critical aircraft parts, if needed. The company saw this in-house facility as a major source of cost savings. It estimated that maintenance labor costs were 50–60% below the costs of having the same work performed outside.

In December 1995, Airborne announced a deal to purchase 12 used Boeing 767–200 aircraft between the years 1997 and 2000, and it announced plans to purchase a further 10–15 used 767–200s between the years 2000 and 2004. These were the first wide-bodied aircraft in Airborne's fleet. The cost of introducing the first 12 aircraft was about $290 million, and the additional aircraft would cost another $360 million. The shift to wide-bodied aircraft was promoted by an internal study, which concluded that with growing volume, wide-bodied aircraft would lead to greater operating efficiencies.

During 2001, Airborne was using about 66.6% of its lift capacity on a typical business day. This compared with 76.7% capacity utilization in 1997, and 70% utilization in 2000. In late-2001, Airborne reduced its total lift capacity by some 100,000 lbs. to about 4 million lbs. per day. It did this to try and reduce excess capacity of certain routes and better match supply with demand conditions.

C-Containers

C-containers are uniquely shaped 60-cubic-foot containers, developed by Airborne Express in 1985 at a cost of $3.5 million. They are designed to fit through the passenger doors of DC-8 and DC-9 aircraft. They replaced the much larger A-containers widely used in the air cargo business. At 6 times the size of a C-container, A-containers can only be loaded through specially built cargo doors and require specialized loading equipment. The loading equipment required for C-containers is a modified belt loader, similar to that used for loading baggage onto a plane, and about 80% less expensive than the equipment needed to load A-containers. The use of C-containers meant that Airborne did not have to bear the $1 million per plane cost required to install cargo doors that would take A-containers. The C-containers are shaped to allow maximum utilization of the planes' interior loading space. Fifty of the containers fit into a converted DC-9, and about 83 fit into a DC-8-62. Moreover, a C-container filled with packages can be moved by a single person, making them easy to load and unload. Airborne Express took out a patent on the design of the C-containers.

Information Systems

Airborne utilized three information systems to help it boost productivity and improve customer service. The first of these systems was the LIBRA II system. LIBRA II equipment, which included a metering device and PC computer software, was installed in the mailroom of clients. With minimum data entry, the metering device weighed the package, calculated the shipping charges, generated the shipping labels, and provided a daily shipping report. By 2002, the system was in use at approximately 9,900 domestic customer locations. The use of LIBRA II not only benefited customers, but also lowered Airborne's operating costs since LIBRA II shipment data were transferred into Airborne's FOCUS shipment tracking system automatically, thereby avoiding duplicate data entry.

FOCUS was the second of Airborne's three main information systems. As discussed earlier, the FOCUS system was a worldwide tracking system. The bar codes on each package were read at various points (for example, at pickup, at sorting in Wilmington, at arrival, and so forth) using handheld scanners, this information was fed into Airborne's computer system. Using FOCUS, Airborne could track the progress of a shipment through its national and international logistics system. The major benefit was increased customer service. Through an Internet link, Airborne's customers could track their own shipment through Airborne's system on a 24-hour basis.

For its highest-volume corporate customers, Airborne developed Customer Linkage, an electronic data interchange (EDI) program and the third information system. The EDI system was designed to eliminate the flow of paperwork between Airborne and its major clients. The EDI system allowed customers to create shipping documentation at the same time they were entering orders for their goods. At the end of each day, shipping activities were transmitted electronically to Airborne's FOCUS system and captured for shipment tracking and billing. Customer Linkage benefited the customer by eliminating repetitive data entry and paperwork. It also lowered the company's operating costs by eliminating manual data entry. (In essence, both LIBRA II and Customer Linkage reallocated a lot of the data-entry work into the hands of customers.) The EDI system also included electronic invoicing and payment remittance processing. Airborne also offered its customers a program known as Quicklink, which significantly reduced the programming time required by customers to take advantage of linkage benefits.

Strategy

Market Positioning

In the early-1980s, Airborne Express tried hard to compete head-to-head with FedEx. This included an attempt to establish broad market coverage, including both frequent and infrequent users. Frequent users are those that generate more than $20,000 of business per month, or more than 1,000 shipments per month. Infrequent users generate less than $20,000 per month, or less than 1,000 shipments per month.

To build broad market coverage, Airborne followed FedEx' lead of funding a television advertising campaign designed to build consumer awareness. However, by the mid-1980s, Airborne decided that this was an expensive way of building market share. The advertising campaign bought recognition but little penetration. One of the principal problems was that it was expensive to serve infrequent users. Infrequent users demanded the same level of service as frequent users, but Airborne would typically only get one shipment per pickup with an infrequent user, compared with 10 or more shipments per pickup with a frequent user, so far more pickups were required to generate the same volume of business. Given the extremely competitive nature of the industry at this time, such an inefficient utilization of capacity was of great concern to Airborne.

Consequently, in the mid-1980s Airborne decided to become a niche player in the industry and focus on serving the needs of high-volume corporate accounts. The company slashed its advertising expenditure, pulling the plug on its TV ad campaign, and invested more resources in building a direct sales force, which grew to be 460 strong. By focusing upon high-volume corporate accounts, Airborne was able to establish scheduled pickup routes and

use its ground capacity more efficiently. This enabled the company to achieve significant reductions in its unit cost structure. Partly due to this factor, Airborne executives reckoned that their cost structure was as much as $3 per shipment less than that of FedEx. Another estimate suggested that Airborne's strategy reduced labor costs by 20% per unit for pickup, and 10% for delivery.

Of course, there was a downside to this strategy. High-volume corporate customers have a great deal more bargaining power than infrequent users, so they can and do demand substantial discounts. For example, in March 1987, Airborne achieved a major coup when it won an exclusive 3-year contract to handle all of IBM's express packages weighing less than 150 lbs. However, to win the IBM account, Airborne had to offer rates up to 84% below FedEx's list prices! Nevertheless, the strategy does seem to have worked. As of 1995 approximately 80% of Airborne's revenues came from corporate accounts, most of them secured through competitive bidding. The concentrated volume that this business represents helped Airborne to drive down costs.

Delivery Time, Reliability, and Flexibility

A further feature of Airborne's strategy was the decision not to try to compete with Federal Express on delivery time. FedEx and UPS have long guaranteed delivery by 10:30 A.M. Airborne guaranteed delivery by midday, although it offered a 10:30 guarantee to some very large corporate customers. Guaranteeing delivery by 10:30 A.M. would mean stretching Airborne's already tight scheduling system to the limit. To meet its 10:30 A.M. deadline, FedEx has to operate with a deadline for previous days' pickups of 6:30 P.M. Airborne could afford to be a little more flexible and arrange pickups at 6:00 P.M. if that suited a corporate client's particular needs. Later pickups clearly benefit the shipper, who is, after all, the paying party.

In addition, Airborne executives felt that a guaranteed 10:30 A.M. delivery was unnecessary. They argued that the extra hour and a half would not make a great deal of difference to most clients, and they are willing to accept the extra time in exchange for lower prices. In addition, Airborne stressed the reliability of its delivery schedules. As one executive put it, "a package delivered consistently at 11:15 A.M.

is as good as delivery at 10:30 A.M." This reliability was enhanced by Airborne's ability to provide shipment tracking through its FOCUS system.

Deferred Services

With a slowdown in the growth rate of the express mail market toward the end of the 1980s, in 1990 Airborne decided to enter the deferred-delivery business with its Select Delivery Service (SDS) product. The SDS service provides for next-afternoon or second-day delivery. Packages weighing 5 lbs. or less are generally delivered on a next-afternoon basis, with packages of more than 5 lbs. being delivered on a second-day basis. SDS shipment comprised approximately 42% of total domestic shipments in 1995. They were priced lower than overnight express products, reflecting the less time-sensitive nature of these deliveries. The company utilized any spare capacity on its express flights to carry SDS shipments. In addition, Airborne used other carriers, such as passenger carriers with spare cargo capacity in the bellies of their planes, to carry less urgent SDS shipments.

Early in 1996 Airborne began to phase in two new services to replace its SDS service. Next Afternoon Service was available for shipments weighing 5 lbs. or less, and Second Day Service was offered for shipments of all weights. By 2001, deferred shipments accounted for 46% of total domestic shipments.

Ground Delivery Service

In April 2001, Airborne launched a Ground Delivery Service (GDS) in response to similar offerings from FedEx and UPS. Airborne came to the conclusion that it was very important to offer this service in order to retain parity with its principle competitors, and to be able to offer bundled services to its principle customers (that is, to offer them air, ground, and logistics services for a single bundled price). Airborne also felt that they could add the service with a relatively minor initial investment, $30 million, since it leveraged existing assets, including trucks, tracking systems, and regional ground hubs and sorting facilities.

The new service had initially been introduced on a limited basis, and targeted large corporate customers. GDS was priced less than deferred services, reflecting the less time sensitive nature of the

GDS offering. GDS accounted for 1.5% of domestic shipments in 2001, and 4% in the fourth quarter of 2001.

Logistics Services

Although small-package express mail remained Airborne's main business, through its Advanced Logistics Services Corp. (ALS) subsidiary, the company increasingly promoted a range of third-party logistics services. These services provided customers with the ability to maintain inventories in a 1-million-square-foot "stock exchange" facility located at Airborne's Wilmington hub, or at 60 smaller "stock exchange" facilities located around the country. The inventory could be managed either by the company or by the customer's personnel. Inventory stored at Wilmington could be delivered utilizing either Airborne's airline system or, if required, commercial airlines on a next-flight-out basis. ALS' central print computer program allowed information on inventories to be sent electronically to customers' computers located at Wilmington, where Airborne's personnel monitored printed output and shipped inventories according to customers' instructions.

For example, consider the case of Data Products Corp., a producer of computer printers. Data Products takes advantage of low labor costs to carry out significant assembly operations in Hong Kong. Many of the primary component parts for its printers, however, such as microprocessors, are manufactured in the United States and have to be shipped to Hong Kong. The finished product is then shipped back to the United States for sale. In setting up a global manufacturing system, Data Products had a decision to make: either consolidate the parts from its hundreds of suppliers in-house and then arrange for shipment to Hong Kong, or contract out to a company that could handle the entire logistics process. Data Products decided to contract out, and they picked Airborne Express to consolidate the component parts and arrange for shipments.

Airborne controlled the consolidation and movement of component parts from the component part suppliers through to the Hong Kong assembly operation in such a way as to minimize inventory-holding costs. The key feature of Airborne's service was that all of Data Products' materials were collected at Airborne's facility at Los Angeles International Airport. Data Products' Hong Kong assembly plants could then tell Airborne what parts to ship by air as and when they are needed. Airborne was thus able to provide inventory control for Data Products. In addition, by scheduling deliveries so that year-round traffic between Los Angeles and Hong Kong could be guaranteed, Airborne was able to negotiate a better air rate from Japan Air Lines (JAL) for the transportation of component parts.

International Strategy

One of the major strategic challenges that Airborne faced (along with the other express mail carriers) was how best to establish an international service that is comparable to their domestic service. Many of Airborne's major corporate clients were becoming ever more global in their own strategic orientation. As this occurred, they were increasingly demanding a compatible express mail service. In addition, the rise of companies with globally dispersed manufacturing operations that relied upon just-in-time delivery systems to keep inventory holding costs down created a demand for global air express services that could transport critical inventory between operations located in different areas of the globe (consider the example of Data Products discussed earlier in this case study).

The initial response of FedEx and UPS to this challenge was to undertake massive capital investments to establish international airlift capability and international ground operations based upon the U.S. model. Their rationale was that a wholly owned global delivery network was necessary to establish the tight control, coordination, and scheduling required for a successful air express operation. In the 1990s, however, FedEx pulled out of its European ground operations, while continuing to fly its own aircraft overseas.

Airborne decided upon a quite different strategy. In part born of financial necessity (Airborne lacks the capital necessary to imitate FedEx and UPS), Airborne decided to pursue what they referred to as a *variable cost strategy*. This involved two main elements: (1) the utilization of international airlift on existing air cargo operators and passenger aircraft to get their packages overseas and (2) entry into strategic alliances with foreign companies that already had established ground delivery networks. In these two ways, Airborne hoped to be able to establish

global coverage without having to undertake the kind of capital investments that Federal Express and UPS have borne.

Airborne executives defend their decision to continue to purchase space on international flights rather than fly their own aircraft overseas by making a number of points. First, they pointed out that Airborne's international business was 70% outbound and 30% inbound. If Airborne were to fly its own aircraft overseas, this would mean flying them back half-empty. Second, on many routes Airborne simply didn't have the volume necessary to justify flying its own planes. Third, national air carriers were giving Airborne good prices. If Airborne began to fly directly overseas, the company would be seen as a competitor and may no longer be given price breaks. Fourth, getting international airlift space was not a problem. While space can be limited in the third and fourth quarters of the year, Airborne was such a big customer that it usually had few problems getting lift.

On the other hand, the long-term viability of this strategy was questionable given the rapid evolution in the international air express business. Flying Tigers was once one of Airborne's major providers of international lift. However, following the purchase of Flying Tigers by FedEx, Airborne had reduced its business with Flying Tigers. Airborne worried that its packages would be "pushed to the back of the plane" when Flying Tigers had problems of capacity overload.

With regard to strategic alliances, Airborne had joint venture operations is Japan, Thailand, Malaysia, and South Africa. The alliance with Mitsui was announced in December 1989. Mitsui is one of the world's leading trading companies. Together with Tonami Transportation Co., Mitsui owns Panther Express, one of the top-five express carriers in Japan, and a company with a substantial ground network. The deal called for the establishment of a joint venture between Airborne, Mitsui, and Tonami. To be known as Airborne Express Japan, the joint venture combined Airborne's existing Japanese operations with Panther Express. Airborne handled all of the shipments to and from Japan. The joint venture was 40% owned by Airborne, 40% by Mitsui, and 20% by Tonami. The agreement specified that board decisions had to be made by consensus between the three partners. A majority of two could not outvote the third. In addition, the deal called for Mitsui to invest $40 million in Airborne Express through the purchase of a new issue of nonvoting 6.9% cumulative convertible preferred stock and a commitment to Airborne from Mitsui of up to $100 million for aircraft financing. There is no doubt that Airborne executives saw the Mitsui deal as a major coup, both financially and in terms of market penetration into the Japanese market. Airborne executives claimed that the primary advantage of expanding via strategic alliances is that the company got an established ground-based delivery network overseas without having to make capital investments.

Organization

In 2001, Carl Donaway became CEO, replacing the long time top management team of Robert Cline, the CEO, and Robert Brazier, the president and COO, both of whom had been with the company since the early-1960s. Prior to becoming CEO, Donaway was responsible for the airline operations, included managing the Wilmington hub, the package sorting facility, and all aircraft and flight maintenance operations. The philosophy at Airborne was to keep the organizational structure as flat as possible, to shorten lines of communication and allow for a free flow of ideas within the managerial hierarchy. The top managers generally felt that they were open to ideas suggested by lower-level managers. At the same time, the decision-making process was fairly centralized. The view was that interdependence between functions made centralized decision making necessary. To quote one executive, "Coordination is the essence of this business. We need centralized decision making in order to achieve this."

Control at Airborne Express was geared toward boosting productivity, lowering costs, and maintaining a reliable high-quality service. This was achieved through a combination of budgetary controls, pay-for-performance incentive systems, and a corporate culture that continually stressed key values.

For example, consider the procedure used to control stations (which contained about 80% of all employees). Station operations were reviewed on a quarterly basis using a budgetary process. Control and evaluation of station effectiveness stressed four categories. The first was service, measured by the time between pickup and delivery. The goal was to achieve 95–97% of all deliveries before noon. The second category was productivity, measured by total shipments per employee hour. The third category was controllable cost, and the fourth station profitability. Goals for each of these categories were determined each quarter in a bottom-up procedure that involved station managers in the goal-setting process. These goals are then linked to an incentive pay system whereby station managers can earn up to 10% of their quarterly salary just by meeting their goals with no maximum on the upside if they go over the goals.

The direct sales force also had an incentive pay system. The target pay structure for the sales organization was 70% base pay and a 30% commission. There was, however, no cap on the commissions for salespeople. So in theory, there was no limit to what a salesperson could earn. There were also contests that are designed to boost performance. For example, there was a so-called Top Gun competition for the sales force, in which the top salesperson for each quarter won a $20,000 prize.

Incentive pay systems apart, however, Airborne is not known as a high payer. The company's approach is not to be the compensation leader. Rather, the company tries to set its salary structure to position it in the middle of the labor market. Thus, according to a senior human resource executive, "We target our pay philosophy (total package—compensation plus benefits) to be right at the 50th percentile plus or minus 5%."

A degree of self-control was also achieved by trying to establish a corporate culture that focused employees' attention upon the key values required to maintain a competitive edge in the air express industry. The values continually stressed by top managers at Airborne and communicated throughout the organization by the company's newspaper and a quarterly video, emphasized serving customers' needs, maintaining quality, doing it right the first time around, and excellent service. There was also a companywide emphasis on productivity and cost control. One executive, when describing the company's attitude to expenditures, said, "We challenge everything. . . . We're the toughest sons of bitches on the block." Another noted that "among managers I feel that there is a universal agreement on the need to control costs. This is a very tough business, and our people are aware of that. Airborne has an underdog mentality—a desire to be a survivor."

The DHL Acquisition and its Aftermath

By 2002 Airborne Express faced a number of key strategic opportunities and threats. These included (1) the rapid globalization of the air express industry, (2) the development of logistics services based on rapid air transportation, (3) the growth potential for deferred services and ground-based delivery services, (4) lower margins associated with the new GDS offering, (5) the superior scale and scope of its two main competitors, FedEx and UPS, (6) an economic slowdown in the United States, and (7) persistently high fuel costs (oil prices rose from $18 a barrel in mid-1995 to $25 a barrel in 2002). The company's financial performance, which had always been volatile, was poor during 2001, when the company lost $12 million on revenues of $3.2 billion. In 2002, Airborne earned $58 million on revenues of $3.3 billion, even though average revenue per shipment declined to $8.46 from $8.79 a year earlier. Management attributed the improved performance to strong employee productivity, which improved 9.4% over the prior year. In their guidance for 2003, management stated that they would be able to further improve operating performance—then in March 2003 DHL made its takeover bid for the company. Under the terms of the deal, which was finalized in 2003, DHL acquired the ground assets of Airborne Express, while the airline continued as an independent entity.

In the late-1990s, DHL had been acquired by Deutsche Post, the German postal service. Deutsche Post had been privatized some years earlier. Deutsche Post spent approximately $5 billion to acquire several companies in the logistics business between 1997 and 1999. In November 2000, Deutsche Post went private with an initial public offering that raised $5.5 billion and announced its intention to build an integrated global delivery and logistics network.

DHL's goal with the Airborne acquisition was to expand its presence in the United States, where it had long been a marginal player. In 2004–2005 DHL spent some $1.5 billion upgrading Airborne's network to handle higher volumes. The company also embarked upon an aggressive media advertising campaign, presenting itself as a viable alternative to FedEx and UPS. In doing this, DHL seemed to be departing from Airborne's highly focused niche strategy.

The results were disappointing. The company reportedly ran into significant "integration problems" and suffered from reports of poor customer services and missed delivery deadlines. In 2006, DHL management stated that they did not see the North American unit turning profitable until 2009. DHL lost some $500 million in the U.S. in 2006.[3] In 2007, they lost close to $1 billion. With corporate customers leaving for rivals, and market share sliding, in November 2008, DHL announced that it would exit the U.S. market. DHL shut down its air and ground hubs, laid off 9,600 employees, and took a charge against earnings of some $3.9 billion. In explaining the exit decision, DHL management stated that they underestimated just how tough it would be to gain share against FedEx and UPS.[4]

Endnotes

1 Standard & Poor's Industry Survey, Airlines, March, 2002.
2 Source: www.airborne.com/Company/History.asp?nav=AboutAirborne/CompanyInfo/History
3 B. Barnard, "Logistics Spurs Deutsche Post," *Journal of Commerce*, November 8, 2006, 1.
4 A. Roth and M. Esterl, "DHL Beats a Retreat from the U.S.," *Wall Street Journal*, November 11, 2008, B1.

CASE 19

American Airlines Since Deregulation

Isaac Cohen
San Jose State University

Since the passage of the Airline Deregulation Act in 1978, eight major U.S. air carriers filed for bankruptcy. All were old, established carriers flying domestic as well as international routes. Three of the major carriers—Pan American Airways, Eastern Airlines, and Trans World Airways (TWA)—were eventually liquidated and their assets were sold to rival carriers. Two others—Continental Airlines and U.S. Air—filed for bankruptcy protection at least twice. And the remaining three—United, Delta, and Northwest Airlines—were operating in 2005–2006 under Chapter 11 of the Bankruptcy Code. Alone among all U.S. international majors, American Airlines (AA) had never filed for bankruptcy protection.

American's financial position was stronger than that of its competitors all through the era of deregulation. During the first two decades of the new era, Robert Crandall ran AA, first as President (1980–1985), and then as CEO (1985–1998). An executive widely regarded as the industry's most innovative strategist, Crandall introduced the frequent-flier program and the two-tier wage system, expanded American globally, formed alliances with other carriers, and established a successful regional airline affiliated with AA.

As Crandall retired in 1998, Donald Carty was selected CEO. An insider whose tenure was overshadowed by the terrorist attack of September 11, 2001, Carty was a lackluster leader, and his career ended in a public scandal that led to his replacement by Gerald Arpey in April 2003. Arpey needed to act quickly. Following the unprecedented losses incurred by American as a result of the September 11 attack—a loss of over $5 billion dollars during 2001 and 2002, and an additional loss of over $1 billion in the first quarter of 2003—American Airlines was on the brink of bankruptcy.

What should Arpey do?

Should Arpey follow the strategies undertaken by Crandall to cut operating cost, improve AA's financial position, and turn the carrier profitable? Should Arpey, rather, reject some of the policies introduced by his predecessor? Or should he, instead, introduce brand new innovative strategies applicable to the airline industry in the 21st century?

To assess Arpey's strategic choices, this case looks back at the experience of his legendary predecessor. How precisely did Robert Crandall manage to turn American around?

The Airline Industry

The airline industry dates back to the Air Mail Service of 1918–1925. Using its own planes and pilots, the Post Office Department directly operated scheduled flights to ship mail. With the passage of the Air Mail Act (Kelly Act) of 1925, the Post Office subcontracted air mail transport to private companies and thereby laid the foundation of a national air transport system. The Post Office paid contractors substantial sums and encouraged them to extend their routes, buy larger planes, and expand their services.

The formative period of the private airline industry was the Great Depression. The five or six years following Charles Lindbergh's 1927 flight across the Atlantic were years of mergers and acquisitions in which every major carrier came into existence, mostly through the acquisition of smaller lines. American,

This case was presented in the October 2006 Meeting of the North American Case Research Association at San Diego California. Copyright Isaac Cohen and NACRA. I am grateful to the San Jose State University College of Business for its support.

United, Delta, Northwest, Continental and Eastern Airlines were all formed during this period. The increase in passenger transport during the 1930s led, in turn, to growing competition, price cutting, bankruptcies, and serious safety problems. It convinced the architects of the New Deal that the entire transport system—not just the air mail—required federal regulation. The outcome was the passage of the Civil Aeronautics Act (CAA) of 1938.[1]

The CAA had two major provisions. First, it prohibited price competition among carriers, and second, it effectively closed the industry to newcomers. The Civil Aeronautics Board (CAB) required that all air carriers flying certain routes charge the same fares for the same class of passengers. Similarly, the CAB required all applicants wishing to enter the industry to show that they were "fit, willing and able" to do so and that their service was "required by the public convenience and necessity." Typically, between 1950 and 1975 the board denied all 79 applications it had received from carriers asking to enter the domestic, scheduled airline industry.[2] The number of scheduled air carriers was reduced from 16 in 1938 to just 10 in the 1970s, following mergers, consolidations, and route transfers among carriers.[3]

By the mid-1970s, the airline industry had experienced serious financial troubles. Rising fuel prices, an economic recession, and the introduction of expensive wide-body aircraft (Boeing 747s, Lockheed L-1011s, and McDonnell Douglas DC-10s) led to climbing costs, higher fares, reduced traffic, falling revenues, and a growing public demand for opening up the airline industry to competition. As a result, in 1975, a Senate subcommittee chaired by Edward Kennedy held hearings on the airlines. Working closely with Kennedy was a Harvard law professor named Stephen Breyer, who later became a U.S. Supreme Court Justice. A specialist in regulation, the author of *Regulation and Reform*, and the Staff Director of the Kennedy hearings, Breyer helped Kennedy build up a strong case against airline regulation.

Together, Breyer and Kennedy contrasted intrastate air service—which had never been regulated by the CAB—with interstate service—which had been regulated since 1938. The figures were astounding. Air fares charged by an interstate carrier flying the New York-Boston route (191 miles) were almost double the fares charged by an intrastate carrier (Southwest Airlines) flying the Houston-San Antonio route (also 191 miles), and air fares charged

by an interstate airline servicing the Chicago-Minneapolis city pair market (339 miles) were more than double those charged by an intrastate airline (Pacific Southwest Airlines) serving the Los Angeles-San Francisco market (338 miles). The experience of Southwest Airlines in Texas—like that of Pacific Southwest Airlines in California—Breyer and Kennedy concluded, demonstrated the efficiency of the free market and the urgent need for deregulation.[4] Three years later, in 1978, Congress deregulated the airline industry.

Company Background

The early history of American Airlines dates back to 1929 when dozens of small airline companies merged together to form American Airways, a subsidiary of an aircraft manufacturing /airline service conglomerate called the Aviation Corporation (AVCO). From the outset, American Airlines shipped mail along the Southern sub-continental route from Los Angeles to Atlanta via Dallas. With the passage of the Air Mail Act of 1934, Congress prohibited aircraft manufacturing firms from owning airline companies and redistributed existing airmail contracts on a new, competitive bidding basis. To bid successfully on the new contracts, American Airways changed its name to American Airlines, and reorganized itself as stand alone company, independent of AVCO. Winning back its original government contracts, AA resumed its airmail operations and moved aggressively to expand its nascent passenger service.[5]

For the next 35 years, 1934–1968, a single CEO—Cyrus Rowlett Smith—ran American Airlines. A Texan, C. R. Smith managed to improve AA performance in the 1930s and led the company to sustained growth during the following three decades. He paid particular attention to two critical aspects of airline management, namely, aircraft technology and labor relations.

Smith played a key role in the introduction of the DC-3 aircraft in 1936, a well-designed, and efficient plane with two piston engines. The first commercially viable passenger aircraft ever produced, the DC-3 dominated the world's airways until after WWII. Because AA operated the largest fleet of DC-3s in the industry, it soon became the industry leader, carrying about 30% of the domestic passenger traffic in the late 1930s.[6]

Working together with Donald Douglas on the design and development of the DC-3, C. R. Smith lay the foundations for long lasting relations between AA and the Douglas (since 1967, McDonnell Douglas) Corporation. Not until 1955 did Smith select a Boeing model over a Douglas one [AA ordered its first jet—the B-707—from Boeing),[7] but soon thereafter American Airlines resumed its customer relations with Douglas. The two companies continued cooperating for decades. In 2005, long after C.R. Smith had retired, and nearly a decade after the Boeing Company bought the McDonnell Douglas Corporation, American Airlines' fleet was made up of 327 MD-80 McDonnell Douglas planes, and 320 Boeing planes (the B-737, 757, 767, and 777 models), a 46/45% mix which reflected AA's traditional ties with the McDonnell Douglas Corporation.[8]

C. R. Smith, in addition, played a central role in shaping AA's labor relations. AA employees, like the employees of virtually all other major airlines, had become highly unionized by the late 1940s, and subsequently, the company experienced growing labor troubles. Responding to two large-scale pilot strikes that shut down American airlines in 1954 and 1958, C. R. Smith proposed the establishment of a cooperative arrangement among air carriers known as the Mutual Aid Pact (MAP). Thinking in terms of the entire industry, Smith saw the pact as a self-protecting measure designed to check the rising power of unions. Originally established in 1958 by American and five other carriers (United, TWA, Pan American, Eastern, and Capital), the pact authorized airlines benefiting from a strike that shut down one or more carriers to transfer their strike-generated revenues to the struck carrier(s), an arrangement which reduced the financial losses of the struck carrier(s) and thereby increased management bargaining power across the industry. In its several different forms, the MAP survived for twenty years, providing AA and its rival carriers with a measure of protection against lengthy strikes.[9]

Smith's last four years at American Airlines, 1964–67, were AA's most profitable. In 1968, he retired, and was succeeded by George Spater, a corporate lawyer whose tenure at American was marred by recession and scandal. Spater not only failed to improve AA's performance during the recession of the early 1970s, but he also admitted making illegal corporate contributions to President Nixon's re-election campaign. As a result, the AA board forced Spater to resign in 1973 and invited C.R. Smith to rejoin American as a caretaker for a short transitional period. Smith served just seven months until the board recruited Albert Casey, a media executive, to head the company.[10]

Casey's early years at American coincided with the political debate over airline deregulation. On the one side, AA financial results during these years were impressive: Casey turned a loss of $34 million in 1975 to a record profit of $122 million in 1978, and raised AA's cash position from $115 million in 1974 to $537 million in 1978. But on the other, Casey opposed deregulation. Casey's management team believed that airline deregulation would promote competition with low-cost carriers and shift passenger traffic away from transcontinental and semi-transcontinental routes—AA's most profitable ones—to short and medium haul routes. "We opposed [deregulation] all the way," Casey recalled years later. "We had the wrong route structure. We had the wrong aircraft . . . We weren't equipped right. [And w]e had very unfavorable union contracts."[11]

Notwithstanding his opposition to deregulation, Casey expected Congress to pass the deregulation act. To prepare for the passage of the act, Casey undertook two early initiatives which later contributed to AA's eventual success under deregulation. First, he established a major hub airport at Dallas/Fort Worth (D/FW) and moved the company's headquarters from New York to Dallas. Second, he promoted Robert Crandall to the presidency of American Airlines.

The Crandall Era, 1980–1998

Crandall's management style was distinctly different from that of Casey. Casey had a personable, relaxed, and jolly manner. Crandall was famous for his charismatic, intense, and combative style. Casey was diplomatic. Crandall was forthright, temperamental, and impatient. "The [airline] business is intensely, vigorously, bitterly, savagely competitive,"[12] Crandall once said, adding, "I want to crush all my competition. That is what competition is about."[13]

Crandall served as AA President for five years, and as CEO for 13 years. During the early period of 1980–1985, Casey turned over to Crandall the day-to-day operation of the company, and focused his attention on American's financial performance.[14]

During the later period, Crandall assumed full responsibility for AA's financial performance, becoming one of the industry's longest serving chief executives. As both President and CEO, Crandall developed a large body of corporate level strategies which helped American gain a competitive advantage over it rivals.

Developing the Hub and Spoke System

The hub and spoke system was the product of airline deregulation. During the regulatory era, government rules restricted the entry of carriers into new travel markets. With the coming of deregulation, such restrictions were removed, and airlines were free to establish their own connecting hubs for the purpose of transferring passengers from incoming to outgoing flights. Utilizing the hub-and-spoke system, carriers were able to cut costs in at least two ways. First, centralizing aircraft maintenance in hubs reduced the fleet's maintenance costs, and second, increasing the carriers' load factor and bringing it close to capacity resulted in a more efficient operation. In addition, the hub-and-spoke system resulted in greater flight frequency for passengers—a service benefit valued especially by business travelers.[15]

Throughout the first two years of his presidency, 1981–1982, Crandall added 17 new domestic cities to AA's D/FW hub, and seven new international destinations (in Mexico as well as the Caribbean). The sheer number of daily flights AA operated in D/FW climbed from 100 to 300 in 1981 alone. Building its central hub in D/FW, American shifted passenger traffic away from other carriers serving Dallas's outlaying cities, subjecting these carriers to relentless competitive pressure. Braniff International Airways is a case in point. The leading carrier serving the D/FW airport in the 1970s, Braniff filed bankruptcy and suspended operation in 1982 largely as a result of the cutthroat competition it was subject to by American Airlines in the Dallas area.[16]

Under Crandall's direction, AA expanded its hub and spoke operations in the 1980s, establishing major hubs in Chicago, Miami, and San Juan, Puerto Rico, and focusing on long-haul fights, the most profitable segment of the industry. By the mid 1990s, these new hubs—together with the D/FW one— had all become major international airports serving passengers flying to destinations in Europe, South America, Central America, and the Caribbean.[17]

Introducing the Two-Tier Wage System

Dubbed "the father of the two-tier pay scale," Crandall had little to do with the origins of the two-tier plan. The idea grew out of management's endless discussions of the need to achieve low cost growth. Rejecting employee concessions as an insufficient means to attain a low cost operation, Crandall nurtured the two-tier idea and transformed it from an abstract notion into a concrete policy—practical, consistent, and effective.[18]

The two-tier wage system distinguished between two types of employees: current employees paid by an A-scale and newly-hired employees paid by a B-scale. Initially, under the system established by Crandall at American, the two scales were not intended to merge at all; in other words, the top pay received by B-scale employees was expected to be significantly lower than the top pay received by A-scale employees. To persuade AA's labor unions to accept the two-tier plan, Crandall offered employees job security, job expanding opportunities, higher wages and benefits, and profit sharing. He also threatened to shrink the carrier unless the unions accepted the two-tier deal. Believing that lay-offs were eminent, American unionized employees agreed to the new wage structure, and in 1983, AA signed the industry's first two-tier contracts with its principal unions, the Allied Pilots Association (APA, representing the pilots), the Transport Workers Union (TWU, representing the machinists and other ground workers), and the Association of Professional Flight Attendants (APFA, representing the flight attendants). AA's major competitors—United, Delta, U.S. Air, and others—negotiated similar labor agreements. Consequently, the number of two-tier union contracts signed in the airline industry jumped from eight in 1983, to 35 in 1984, and then to 62 in 1985.[19]

AA's two-tier wage plan resulted in a significant pay gap between old and new employees. A newly-hired B-727 captain with a five year experience earned $68 an hour or less than half the $140 paid to his/her veteran counterpart. Such a wage gap led to substantial cost savings: between 1984 and 1989 American Airlines' labor cost fell from 37% to 34% of the carrier's total expenses.[20]

Creating a Holding Company

In 1982, Crandall oversaw the formation of the AMR Corporation—a holding company created "to provide [American] with access to sources of financing that otherwise might be unavailable."[21] AMR owned American Airlines together with several other non-airline subsidiaries, an arrangement which gave management greater flexibility in shifting assets among airline and non-airline subsidiaries, and in identifying new profit sources. Equally important was the protection AMR gave the airline from the swings of the business cycle: profits generated by AMR's nonairline units were expected to mitigate the impact of the industry's periodic downturns.

Consider the following example. During the downturn of 1990–1993, Crandall devised a "transition plan" that called for shifting assets from AMR's unprofitable airline operation to its profitable nonairline businesses. He even suggested leaving the airline business altogether. As AA's losses were mounting—and profits generated from AMR's non-airline units were increasing—Crandall threatened to sell AA and keep instead AMR's nonairline subsidiaries only.[22]

AMR's principal subsidiary—apart from AA—was the Sabre computer reservation system. Owned by AMR, Sabre (Semi Automatic Business Research Environment) had become AMR's most profitable unit during the 1990s, generating far higher returns on sales than the airline itself. In 1995, for instance, Sabre recorded total sales of $1.5 billion, or 9% of AMR revenues, and an operating profit of 19%.[23]

Building a Regional Airline

Another subsidiary of AMR was American Eagle. American Eagle was established in 1984 as AA's regional affiliate. Operating under the affiliate name, several small regional airlines were franchised by AA to supply connecting flights to American air services. From the start, American Eagle offered customers "seamless service," that is, assigned seats, boarding passes, and frequent flyer mileage. In 1987, AMR began acquiring American Eagle's franchised carriers, and in 1990, it consolidated these carriers into six airline systems that served the D/FW, Nashville, New York City, Chicago, Raleigh/Durham and San Juan regional markets. To better coordinate planning, operation, schedules, training, and marketing of commuter services, AMR sought further consolidation. Accordingly, in 1998, it merged the six regional airlines into a single entity carrier, the America Eagle Airlines, creating the world's largest regional airline system. Operating 1,450 daily flights to 125

destinations in the U.S., Canada, and the Caribbean; employing 10,000; and generating $1 billion in revenue, American Eagle was named "Airline of the Year" by *Commuter World* magazine in 1998.[24]

American Eagle's growth helped improve AMR's financial results. Originally, American Eagle operated as a regional carrier feeding passengers to American Airlines flights. But by the mid-1990s, Crandall had replaced a growing number of routes flown by AA pilots with routes flown by American Eagle pilots, a move which resulted in substantial labor cost savings, given the higher pay received by American than Eagle pilots (in 1997 AA pilots earned an average yearly pay of $120,000 and Eagle pilots $35,000).[25]

Upgrading the Computer Reservation System (CRS)

The Sabre computer reservation system was born in 1962, following a decade-long research effort carried out jointly by American Airlines engineers and IBM technicians. Initially, Sabre lagged behind comparable CRS systems used by its competitors, namely, United's Apollo, TWA's PARS, and Eastern Airlines' System One. But by the mid-1970s, with the appointment of Crandall to the position of AA's Vice President for Marketing, Sabre received a new lease of life. As marketing chief, Crandall controlled the company's budget for technology research and development. He recruited a strong team of Sabre computer engineers, and supplied the team with ample funding. At the same time, he launched a campaign to build an industry-wide CRS owned jointly by the major airlines, and used by travel agents. Confident that its own CRS was ahead of its competitors, United declined to join the industry-wide project, and instead, decided to sell its Apollo system's services directly to travel agents. Crandall reacted quickly. Implementing a carefully crafted back-up plan, he sent hundreds of sales people and technicians to travel agents all across the country, offering them a variety of Sabre services. Caught unprepared, United was unable to deliver its own computer reservation system's services until months later. The result was a swift victory of American over United in the race to wire travel agents.[26]

Sabre provided American Airlines with several information technology services. First, it calculated the yield of each American flight, setting and resetting the price of every seat sold. Second, it managed an inventory of close to one billion spare parts used by American's fleet in its maintenance facilities. Third, it directed the routing and tracking of all baggage and freight. And fourth, it supplied American with ongoing data on aircraft fuel requirements, take off weight, and flight plan.[27]

More important were Sabre's travel services. Sabre provided travel agents around the world with fares and schedules for flights offered by hundreds of carriers, not only American and American Eagle. In 1997, Sabre signed a comprehensive 25-year agreement to manage the information technology infrastructure of U.S. Air, and in addition, it renewed a five-year contract with Southwest Airlines to operate the carrier's reservation and inventory systems. Sabre and Canadian Airlines International signed a similar agreement in 1994.

Sabre's clients, it should be noted, were not limited to the airline industry. Both the London Underground and the French National Railway were Sabre's customers in the 1990s, the first contracted Sabre to manage its train and crew scheduling, the second, to design its computer reservation system. Under Crandall's leadership, furthermore, Sabre signed agreements with both Dollar Rent-a-Car and Thrifty Rent-a-Car to manage each company's reservation system.[28]

Under Crandall's leadership, Sabre had become the U.S. largest computer reservation system with a 40% share of all travel agent bookings in 1996. Nearly 30,000 travel agent offices in 70 countries subscribed to Sabre, and more than 2.5 million individual passengers subscribed to Travelocity, Sabre's Internet service. In 1995, the total value of travel-related products and services reserved through Sabre was estimated at $40 billion.[29]

Promoting Yield Management

Developing a revenue maximizing process called yield management was impossible without enhanced computer capabilities. To fill all empty seats on a given flight, American Airlines needed to obtain information pertaining to the desirable number of seats that could be sold at full versus discount fares, and the optimal mix of fares that could maximize the yield of a given flight. Obtaining such information required complex computer calculations based on the carrier's past performance. Hence the key role played by Sabre. Sabre could track any passenger on

any seat traveling any distance at any time. It could find out how early business travelers booked their flights, how far in advance coach passengers did so, and how sensitive each of these two groups was to fare price changes. With Sabre's growing computer capabilities, American began offering a large variety of discounted fares, as Don Reed, author of *Bob Crandall and American Airlines*, explained:

> Instead of offering first-class, coach, and one level of discount fares, American began offering several layers of discounts. The bigger the savings off full-fare prices, the more restrictions the tickets had. The more modest the savings, the fewer restrictions. So fourteen-day and seven-day advance purchase discount fares cost more than twenty-one-day fares, but they were less restricted. Because of this sliding scale of discounts, American could juggle the percentage of seats on any airplane allocated to one fare type or another. . . . By the late 1980s American would be able to, and often did, juggle the mix of fares right up until the moment of departure.[30]

Sabre's yield management system gave American a clear competitive advantage over its rivals. On any given flight, AA was able to offer a variety of discounted fares using projections based on past experience. Sabre's technology permitted Crandall to match or undercut the cheaper fares offered by competitors by simply lowering American's own discount prices for some seats and/or increase the number of seats available at the lowest price category. There was no need to reduce fares on all seats. While competitors lacking American's technology were unable to match AA's price flexibility, they soon introduced their own yield management systems; nevertheless, American Airlines managed to retain its leadership position in the field for decades.

Pioneering the Frequent-Flyer Program

Just as Sabre promoted the development of AA's yield management system, so did it facilitate the introduction of American's AAdvantage frequent flyer program, an innovation that allowed regular passengers to earn free tickets on miles traveled with American. And just as the hub-and spoke system was the outgrowth of deregulation, so was the frequent flyer program. While deregulation promoted competition, the frequent flyer program protected carriers from the competitive market forces by creating brand loyalty among travelers.

Crandall introduced the AAdvantage program—the first in the industry—in 1981, a year after he became president. Managed by Sabre, the frequent flyer innovation was an effective marketing program which lowered the advertising costs by targeting individuals AAdvantage card-holders reachable through mailing and/or email distribution lists. Sabre had been gathering information on passengers early on. As Mike Gunn, AA's Vice President for Marketing under Crandall noted: "one reason we were able to seize the competitive edge was that we already knew who many of our best customers were and how to reach them quickly. As other airlines struggled to match our initiative and identify their base of frequent-flyers, we were already placing AAdvantage cards and welcome letters in the hands of our best customers."[31]

More than one million passengers joined AAdvantage before the end of 1981, and another million joined the frequent flyer programs introduced by other airlines in 1981 in response to AAdvantage. Ten years later, 28 million travelers were card-carrying members of at least one frequent flyer program, and they held, on average, membership in 3.5 programs. American Airlines' program was the industry's largest. In 1991, American's frequent flier program had one million members more than that of its closest competitor, United, and four million more than Delta, the nation's third largest carrier.[32]

At the time Crandall left office in 1998, the frequent flyer program had become an airline industry standard feature. It impacted other industries as well and generated both revenues and profits for the airlines. American sold miles to a variety of companies which awarded, in turn, AA miles to loyal customers as an incentive. In 1998, over 2,500 companies awarded miles to customers using the AAdvantage Incentive Miles program, most of which were retail stores and food serving establishments.[33]

Expanding Internationally

Before the passage of the airline regulation act in 1978, American Airlines had virtually no international presence. The dominant U.S. international carriers at the time were TWA and Pan America World Airways, and neither United nor Delta Airlines served any foreign destinations.[34] The Deregulation Act removed government restrictions on entry into new travel markets, promoted the development of hub-and-spoke systems, and as such, prompted the leading domestic airlines—United, American, and Delta—to begin serving a growing number of international destinations.

From the outset, AA's domestic hub system supported international expansion, helping the carrier fill empty seats on overseas flights. In the early 1980s, Crandall extended AA's route network to Mexico and the Caribbean, but not until 1990 did he launch a massive drive at global expansion, adding many more overseas destinations in Europe and Latin America.

Crandall's decision to extend AA's international route network was informed by air-traffic projections. Over the ten-year period 1990–2000, U.S. air traffic was expected to grow at a modest rate of 3%-4% a year while transatlantic air traffic, as well as traffic between the U.S. and Latin America's destinations, was projected to increase at an annual rate of 6%-7%. To take advantage of these projections, Crandall committed $11 billion, or half of AA's investment budget, to global expansion over the five year period, 1990–1995. He also made two important acquisitions, both in 1989–1991. He first bought TWA's Chicago-London route in 1989, and six more TWA-London routes in 1991. He next acquired Eastern Airline's Latin America route system in 1990. In the Latin American market, AA used its strong Miami hub to handle traffic from 20 cities in 15 South and Central American countries. In the European market, Crandall embarked on what he called a "fragmentation strategy," namely, the break-up of the traditional route system linking one international city to another, for example, New York—London (and flying large commercial aircraft such as the 400-seat Boeing B-747), and replacing it with a route system that linked less congested cites like Chicago and Brussels or Chicago and Glasgow (and flying smaller 200-seat aircraft such as the Boeing B-767).[35]

Five years later, Crandall's plan achieved its main goals. By the mid-1990s, AA had become the dominant U.S. carrier serving Latin America, and the number two U.S. carrier serving Europe, closely behind Delta. In Latin America, AA carried 58% of all U.S. airline traffic to and from the region, served 27 nations, and opened two new U.S. gateway hubs, one in New York, the other in Dallas/Fort Worth, in addition to its principal one in Miami. In the transatlantic travel market, AA's share accounted for 23% of all airline traffic. In 1995, American derived 14%-15% of its airline revenues from the Latin America market, and 13% from the European market. As expected, both international markets were quite profitable: in 1996, AA generated an operating profit margin of 10% in Latin America, and 8% in Europe.[36]

Forming Alliances

Signing code-sharing agreements with foreign carriers was another growth strategy undertaken by Crandall. Code-sharing allowed American to assign its two letter code—AA—to flights operated by another carrier, thereby offering passengers flights to destinations not served by American. Enhanced by shared computer reservation systems and joint frequent-flyer programs, such agreements enabled American to increase its passenger traffic without extending its own route network, hence saving the carrier the expensive and risky cost of starting new international services.

American signed its first code-sharing agreement with Canadian Airlines International (CAI) in 1995. The agreement extended AA's route network to dozens of Canadian cities served by CAI and linked CAI route system to dozens of U.S. destinations served by AA. Seeking to extend AA's route structure to Asia, Crandall signed another code-sharing agreement with CAI in 1997. The 1997 agreement offered AA passengers trans-Pacific service on flights operated by CAI between Vancouver and Taipei. To further increase its Asia-bound traffic, American formed an alliance with China Eastern Airlines in 1998—the first code-sharing agreement between a U.S. carrier and an airline based in the People Republic of China. Under the agreement's provisions, American placed its code on fights operated by China Eastern from Los Angeles and San Francisco to both Shanghai and Beijing, thereby offering passengers from destinations as distant as Latin America full service to Mainland China. Finally, in September 1998, a few months after Crandall stepped down, American Airlines announced the formation of OneWorld Alliance, a code-sharing agreement signed by five international carriers: American Airlines, British Airways, Canadian Airlines International, Qantas Airway (Australia), and Cathy Pacific Airlines (Hong Kong).[37]

Escalating the War with the Unions, 1990–1998

AA's labor relations under Crandall may be divided into two, distinctly different, periods: 1980–1989 and 1990–1998. In the 1980s, relations between labor and management at American were, for the most part, cooperative and peaceful. Crandall, as discussed, managed to convince the leadership of the pilots', flight attendants', and machinists' unions to negotiate and sign two-tier labor agreements which allowed management to place newly hired employees on a lower, B-type wage scale.

In the 1990s, by contrast, labor relations at American were stormy and contentious. Contract negotiations were long and difficult to conclude, and labor disputes triggered strikes, strike threats, and repeated instances of federal intervention to avert strikes. As a consequence, labor disputes were costly, resulting in revenue and income losses.

One major cause of the 1990s labor troubles was the lingering dissatisfaction—expressed by AA employees—with the two-tier wage system. For any unionized job, B-scale employees were paid much lower wages than their veteran counterparts, and over the years, these lower paid employees had turned extremely resentful toward management. As Crandall hired a growing number of B-scale recruits in the 1980s and 1990s, the "B-scalers" had eventually become the majority of all AA's unionized employees.

Two labor disputes at American during the 1990s stand out. The first involved a strike staged by the Professional Association of Fight Attendants. In 1993, 21,000 fight attendants struck American airlines during Thanksgiving Day weekend, crippling the carrier and ruining whatever prospects management had of posting profits that year (AA ended the year with a small loss of $110 million on $15.8 billion in revenues). Union leaders pointed out that Crandall's unwillingness to bend during negotiations precipitated the strike. Industry analysts agreed, noting Crandall's compulsion to keep labor cost-low. As the strike entered its fifth day, President Clinton intervened and pressured both sides to accept binding arbitration. The dispute was later settled, but the flight attendants remained disgruntled.[38]

A pilots' strike-threat underlay the second labor dispute. In November 1996, the Allied Pilots

Association's board of directors approved a tentative pilots' contract, and presented it to the union membership for ratification. Persuaded by a dissident group of grassroots union activists made largely of B-scale pilots, the membership rejected the contract by a margin of almost two to one. The union leadership, in turn, hardened it position, and threatened to strike the carrier. As the strike deadline approached, President Clinton intervened, invoking a rarely used provision of the 1926 Railway Act which empowered him to appoint a three-member emergency board to help settle the dispute. In the meantime American's losses were mounting. By April 1997, AA lost at least $100 million in advanced bookings, as passengers avoided flying an airline facing impending walkout days. The contract was eventually ratified, but here again, the pilots remained embittered, and they continued resenting Crandall's heavy-handed management methods.[39]

Improving Financial Results, 1985–1997

AA's financial performance under Crandall needs to be analyzed in conjunction with Crandall's evolving strategy. Serving as CEO for 13 years, Crandall shaped and reshaped his strategy, paying close attention to changes in the business cycle. In the 1980s, Crandall undertook a growth strategy that resulted in a rapid expansion of American Airlines' fleet, as well as workforce. The larger AA grew, the lower were its costs, the higher its revenues, and the larger its profits. In the early 1990s, as the air travel market slid into a protracted recession, and AA experienced four years of losses, Crandall embarked on a retrenchment strategy, laying off employees, grounding old planes, exiting unprofitable markets, and outsourcing selected services. Following the recession of 1990–1993, the industry expanded once again, and Crandall introduced a second growth plan. His renewed efforts at increasing revenues and improving profits were sustained by AA's industry-leading yield management system, its formidable AAdvantage frequent flyer program, and its extensive global route network. Notwithstanding the labor troubles of 1996–1997, the carrier had become profitable again, posting a net income of over $1 billion in 1996, close to $1 billion in 1997, and $1.3 billion in 1998, as Exhibit 1 shows, and reducing its debt as a percentage of capitalization from 83% in 1994 to 66% at the end of 1996.[40]

Exhibit 1 Robert Crandall's American Airlines Highlights of Financial Data, 1985–1998

	Revenues ($Mil.)	Net Income ($Mil.)	Income as % of Revenues
1985	6.131	346	5.6%
1986	6.018	279	4.6%
1987	7,198	198	2.8%
1988	8,824	477	5.4%
1989	10,480	455	4.3%
1990	11,120	(40)	—
1991	12,887	(240)	—
1992	14,396	(935)	—
1993	15,816	(110)	—
1994	16,137	228	—
1995	16,910	167	1.0%
1996	17,753	1,067	5.7%
1997	18,570	985	5.3%
1998	19,205	1,314	6.8%

Sources: "AMR Corporation," *Hoover's Handbook of American Business*, 1992, p. 110, 2002, p. 165.

Donald Carty and the September 11, 2001 Terrorist Attack

Donald Carty served as American Airlines CEO for five years. An AA's career executive, he was hand picked by Crandall to lead the carrier, first as President, and then, following Crandall's retirement in 1998, as CEO. Carty's five year tenure was marred by labor troubles, recession, and terrorism, and ended in a public scandal: as a result of the September 11, 2001 attack, American Airlines was losing several million dollars a day, yet in Spring 2003, at the time the carrier was inching towards bankruptcy, AA's senior executives—including Carty—received undisclosed bonuses and pension guarantees worth millions of dollars.

Carty's labor problems began early on. In 1999, he convinced the AMR board to acquire a small low-cost commuter airline called Reno Air. The proposed acquisition evoked a staunch opposition on the part of American pilots. Believing that Carty planed to replace them with low-paid Reno pilots, members of the Allied Pilots Association staged an 11 days sickout which forced American to cancel 6,700 fights, left 600,000 passengers stranded, and cost the carrier $225 million in lost earnings. Also in 1999, AA flight attendants rejected a tentative contract offer and threatened to strike the carrier. In 2001, AA's flight attendants agreed to accept a contract agreement only after exhaustive negotiations that ended hours before a strike deadline.[41]

Notwithstanding these labor differences, Carty moved to expand the airline by merger, purchasing TWA—a trunk-line carrier experiencing serious financial problems. Approved in April 2001, AA's merger with TWA created the nation's largest airline, adding 188 commercial airplanes to American's fleet (TWA's 104 McDonnell Douglas MD-80 jets fit nicely into AA's fleet), and providing American with a central hub at St. Louis. The cost of the transaction was just $742 million—a modest sum by any industry standards—and more important, the merger was supported by all major unions. Backed by the unionized employees of both carriers, Carty managed to integrate the two companies smoothly, earning the praise of industry analysts.[42]

Yet the TWA acquisition was untimely. The merger was approved at the time the entire airline industry was moving rapidly into a recession. Following the merger's approval in Spring 2001, business travel dropped precipitously, leisure travel fell too, and fuel prices were rising. As a result, AA lost $550 million during the first half of 2001.[43] Less than three months later, the 9/11 terrorist attack erupted, destroying two AA passenger jets at mid air, and shutting down all airline travel in the U.S. for two days.

The impact of the 9/11 attack on American's financial performance was long lasting. As shown in Exhibit 2, AA lost $1.8 billion in 2001, and a record $3.5 billion in 2002. In April 2003, following another loss of a billion dollar during the first quarter of the year, American Airlines was nearly bankrupt.

To avoid filing bankruptcy under Chapter 11, Carty asked the three unions representing the majority of AA employees to agree to major wage and benefit concessions. The leadership of each union accepted management's demand for a concessional contract and put the issue before the membership for a vote. Within two weeks, AA employees ratified a collective bargaining agreement that gave the carrier back a total of $1.8 billion, or 20% of the carrier's annual payroll.[44]

A day later the deal began to unravel. Following the contract ratification, union leaders, as well as members, learned from news reports that the AMR corporation awarded Cary and five other executives bonuses that equaled twice their annual salaries, and set aside a $41 million trust that was intended to protect the pensions of 45 executives in the event of bankruptcy. As it turned out, the carrier delayed filing a report detailing these executive compensation plans with the Security and Exchange Commission until after the contract vote was completed.[45]

The belated disclosure angered the employees and prompted two of the three unions to call for another contract vote. Carty, in turn, sent a letter to

Exhibit 2 Donald Carty's American Airlines Highlights of Financial Data, 1998–2002

	Revenues	Net Income	Income as	Stock Prices
	($Mil.)	($Mil.)	% of Revenues	FY Close
1998	19,205	1,314	6.8%	$26.54
1999	17,730	985	5.3%	29.95
2000	19,703	813	5.7%	39.19
2001	18,963	(1,762)	—	22.30
2002	17,299	(3,511)	—	6.60

Source: "AMR Corporation," *Hoover's Handbook of American Business*, 2005, p. 88.

AA employees apologizing for his conduct, and announcing the cancellation of the proposed bonuses: "My mistake was failing to explicitly describe these retention benefits . . . Please know that it was never my intention to mislead you."[46] The disclosure, in addition, surprised several members of the AMR board who felt misled by top management, believing that Carty had discussed the executive compensation package with the union leaderships prior to the contract vote. In response to the mounting public outcry over the disclosure, AMR board of directors sought Carty's resignation. Pressured by the board, Carty promptly stepped down, and the directors moved at once to elect a new CEO.[47]

The Future: Gerard Arpey's American Airlines, 2003—

A few board members suggested rehiring Robert Crandall. Others rejected Crandall's choice and sought instead a candidate that was likely to create a sense of management continuity in AA and act quickly to save the company from filing bankruptcy. Such a candidate, the majority of directors agreed, was American Airlines President Gerard Arpey. Elected by the board to replace Carty, Arpey had 24 hours to save the carrier. Crafting a revised labor management agreement that included the essential $1.8 billion cuts in wages and benefits, and offered the employees a number of additional nonmonetary gains, Arpey managed to convince the union leaderships to approve the new labor agreement and thereby save the carrier from filing for bankruptcy protection. Passing his first test as a chief executive, Arpey outlined a key management objective he would strive to accomplish throughout his tenure as AA CEO: "There is a definite need to rebuild trust [between management and labor} within the company. I hear that loud and clear. . .and I commit myself to earning everybody's trust."[48]

Gerard Arpey spent his entire career at American Airlines, joining the company as a financial analyst in 1982. Before accepting the top job, the 46 year old Arpey sought, and received, the approval of AA's union leaders: "He said he wouldn't take the position unless . . . he had our support, " John Darrah, President of the Allied Pilots Association recalled, adding, "I have a great deal of respect

for Mr. Arpey . . . I can honestly [say] there's not a person I have more respect for or trust in."[49]

Arpey's turnaround plan was based on several elements. First, Arpey believed that in order to compete successfully in the post 9/11 world, American Airlines needed to shift its strategic focus from revenue growth to cost reduction. To achieve this goal, he introduced a cooperative labor management scheme, a continuous improvement program, and other labor cost cutting-measures. Second, Arpey realized that American could take advantage of its global positioning to expand profitable international operation and curtail unprofitable domestic services. To achieve this goal, he sought to form closer alliances with foreign carriers. Altogether, Arpey embarked on four distinct strategies in his efforts to turn American around:

International Expansion. Referring to his plan to expand AA's international operation, Arpey explained:

> One of the things that we can capitalize on is the depth and breath of our network. Its one of the ways that we can compete more effectively with low-cost carriers that operate primarily in the domestic market . . . We have very aggressive plans internationally . . . Our strengths include a very broad network that spans the globe. . . the [industry's] largest frequent-flyer program, Admiral airport clubs, and a great first-class product. . . [W]e get more revenue per passenger than the low cost carrier[s and] . . . we can sustain a revenue premium.[50]

Arpey expected AA's international service to grow from over 30% of capacity in 2005 to 40% by the end of the decade. He planned to expand, above all, trans-Pacific travel service. In 2005, American introduced two nonstop services to Japan, operating flights between Chicago and Nagoya, and between Dallas and Osaka. Similarly, in 2005, AA started a nonstop service to India, flying the 7,500-mile route between Chicago and New Delhi, American's longest, in 14–15 hours. American also competed aggressively over the contested rights to serve China, planning to introduce a Chicago-Shanghai nonstop service as early as approval by the Chinese government was granted. Additionally, AA formed alliances with Aloha Airlines and Mexicana Airlines, on the one side, and consolidated its code sharing agreement with British airways, on the other.[51]

Labor-Management Cooperation. To improve his relations with the unions, Arpey instituted an open door policy. During his first two years in office, Arpey spent more time meeting union leaders than the time spent for this purpose by any other chief executive in the company's 75 years history. "You demonstrate commitment by where you put your time," he told a *Financial Times* reporter in 2005. "We are trying to make our unions our business partners."[52] Unlike Crandall and Carty, Arpey constantly highlighted the importance of getting AA employees involved in the business of airline management. Once elected CEO, he traveled widely, visited AA operations in one city after another, conducted town-hall meetings with AA employees, and solicited employee suggestions. "I try to spend as much time as I can [with the employees] when I travel," Arpey explained in a 2004 interview, "going to break rooms, talking to agents at the gate, talking to flight attendants on board [of] the airplane, riding jump seats, and . . . answering all the e-mail[s I] get."[53]

Still, Arpey was unable to change AA's climate of labor-relations single-handedly. He needed external help. To improve labor management relations at American, Arpey hired an employee-relations consultancy called the Overland Resource Group in Summer 2003. Instrumental in improving labor-relations at Boeing, Ford, and the Goodyear Corporation, the Overland group instructed AA managers to follow three fundamental principles, or maxims, in their relations with AA's employees: "Involve before Deciding," "Discuss before Implementing," and "Share before Announcing." More important, the Overland group created a Joint Leadership Team (JLT) chaired by Arpey and the national presidents of AA's three main unions (representing the pilots, flight attendants, and mechanics and ground workers), and attended by the company CFO as well as four vice presidents, on management side, and three representatives of each union, on labor side. The team met once a month to discuss issues ranging from AA's corporate-level strategies to union demands and grievances. The team also reviewed AA's financial data on a quarterly basis, an arrangement that helped senior union officials understand the airline business.[54] To help team members communicate, two Overland consultants attended all JLT meetings, acting as the dialogue facilitators. To ensure an honest, open, and free-flowing discussion with no fear of reprisal, each JLT participant signed a nondisclosure agreement.[55]

In addition to the team headed by Arpey and the union presidents, Overland facilitated the formation of seven regional JLTs located in different airports and maintenance bases throughout AA network. A local JLT met once a month to review the region's financial performance and to evaluate employee cost-saving ideas.[56]

Overland presence at AA enhanced employee motivation and morale. The higher level of employee motivation was reflected, first and foremost, in the growing number of cost savings suggestions initiated by employees. While AA management routinely ignored employee suggestions in the past [one union leader observed], Overland consultants now encouraged the adoption of such suggestions. And while Arpey's management team was actively soliciting employee ideas, no employee whose ideas were adopted received any compensation; on the contrary, helping the company was the employee's sole motivation.[57]

As a result of implementing employee-identified cost-saving ideas, AA saved about $100 million in 2004.[58] The overall decline in labor cost was larger. Partly as a consequence of introducing cost-saving ideas, and partly as a result of implementing the landmark concessional contract of April 2003, AA unit labor cost under Arpey declined by more than 20% in two years, as shown in Exhibit 3.

Exhibit 3   Labor Cost of U.S. Network Carriers, 4th Quarter 2002 and 4th Quarter 2004, Cents Per Available Seat-Mile (CASM)

Network	4Q-02 CASM	4Q-04 CASM
American	3.93	3.12
Continental	3.10	30.2
Delta	4.01	3.67
Northwest	3.98	3.82
United	4.51	3.25
U.S. Airways	4.15	3.11
Network	4.01	3.34

Sources: Eclat Consulting, *Aviation Daily,* May 4, 2004, p. 7, and May 26, 2005, p. 7

Continuous improvement

The Continuous Improvement (CI) program was implemented across all AA's maintenance facilities. During 2001–2004, United Airlines, Northwest Airlines, and U.S. Airways closed several of their maintenance bases, and sought instead to outsource heavy maintenance to outside contractors.[59] American Airlines, by contrast, kept maintenance work in house, and launch a massive drive at efficiency, seeking productivity gains in the shop floor.

The Continuous Improvement program had three main goals: the elimination of waste in any form, the standardization of maintenance work, and the optimal utilization of "human talent." The idea—and practice—of CI was based on the assumption that workers, not managers, were the real experts, and that employee empowerment was critical for building effective work teams. The CI program addressed a variety of issues ranging from shop floor reorganization to engine-overhaul turnover time reduction. To achieve these objectives, a "5S" technique ("sort, strengthen, standardize, shine, sustain") was introduced throughout AA's maintenance facilities. At American's largest maintenance base in Tulsa, Oklahoma, for example, Continuous Improvement teams in the avionic shop used the 5S technique to free nearly 12,000 sq. ft. of floor space and thereby save the company $1.5 million in inventory cost.[60]

Employee-identified CI ideas included new ways to reduce the cost of replacing aircraft parts and components. On the McDonnell Douglas MD-80 model, for instance, the cargo door torque (spring) tube needed to be replaced once a year. To do so, the company bought new tubes at a cost of $660 per tube. The CI team investigated the issue and ascertained that repairing broken tubes at a cost of only $134 per unit saved the company a total of $250,000 a year. On the Boeing 737, similarly, AA economized by replacing passenger light bulbs and cabin windows only when needed. In the past, AA replaced all light bulbs and cabin windows at the same time regardless of whether the bulbs were burned out or the windows worn out. The selective replacement of light bulbs and cabin windows saved AA $100,000 per year.[61]

American used CI teams to reduce engine overhaul times as well. One team of engine mechanics drafted a series of diagrams showing the most efficient way to disassemble a jet engine. Another devised a "point-of-use tool box" which contained all the tools necessary for an engine's assembly and dis-

assembly. Together, the two teams helped AA cut an engine's overhaul turnaround time from 53 days in 2003 to 40 days in 2004, an improvement of 25% in a single year.[62]

Continuous Improvement teams helped AA cut costs in still other ways. To service American Airlines fleet, company mechanics used thousands of drill bits monthly at a cost of $20 to $200 a piece. Two AA mechanics invented a drill bit-sharpening tool which refurbished bits for reuse at a cost saving of $300,000–400,000 a year. And in 2004, a CI team came up with the idea of reusing parts of obsolete DC-10 coffee makers on other AA airplanes, generating a one-time savings of $675,000.[63]

Taken together, all these improvements helped AA reduce its maintenance cost by 34% in two years (2002–2004). A comparison between American's maintenance cost reduction and that of five other U.S.-based network carriers shows that AA led the way, exceeding the industry average by 13 percentage points, and well ahead of any of its competitors (Exhibit 4).

Other Cost Cutting Measures. "Simplification and standardization drives efficiency,"[64] Arpey said in 2004, and he moved quickly to both simplify and standardize AA's fleet of aircraft. To simplify the fleet, Arpey reduced the number of aircraft types flown by American from 14 to 6, retiring many old models. The move reduced American spending on spare parts as well as crew training, especially pilots and

Exhibit 4   Maintenance Cost of U.S. Network Carriers, 4th Quarter 2002 and 4th Quarter 2004, Cents Per Available Swat Mile (CASM)

Network	4Q02 CASM	4Q04 CASM	% CASM
American	1.65	1.09	34%
Continental	0.96	0.93	3%
Delta	0.98	0.92	6%
Northwest	1.43	1.08	24%
United	1.41	1.24	12%
U.S. Airways	1.67	1.30	22%
Network	1.36	1.08	21%

Source: Eclat Consulting, *Aviation Daily*, May 4, 2004, p.7, and May 26, 2005, p.7

mechanics training. In addition, Arpey standardized aircraft seating, arranging all seats on a given aircraft type in a single configuration, as the two following examples suggest. Under Carty's leadership, the MD-80 fleet had two seating configurations, one designed to serve AA's business routes, the other to serve AA's low fare routes. Under Carty likewise, the B-777 had two seating configurations, one aimed at flights over the Pacific, the other at flights over the Atlantic. In an effort to simplify both aircraft maintenance and flight schedules, Arpey standardized all seating on the MD-80 and B-777 models in a single arrangement, a reconfiguration that resulted in substantial cost savings.[65]

Arpey reversed two other Carty's initiatives, first, the creation of more legroom for passengers, and second, the transformation of TWA's St. Louis hub into a major AA hub. In 2000, Carty launched the "More Room in Coach" marketing campaign in an attempt to increase revenues. AA, accordingly, removed more than 7,000 economy seats from its fleet, reducing the fleet's seating capacity by 6.4%. Carty's initiative, however, failed to generate the expected revenues, and therefore Arpey decided to undo it. In 2004, AA added two rows of seats to its fleet of 140 B-757s and 34 A-300s, and used both models to serve low-fare leisure markets. In 2005, AA added six more seats to its B-737 fleet, seven more to its fleet of MD-80s and B-767s, and nine more seats to its fleet of B-777s. The change in seating capacity was projected to generate a revenue increase of over $100 million a year.[66]

Lastly, Arpey announced early on his decision to scale back significantly AA's St. Louis operation. Expecting TWA's central hub in St. Louis to fit nicely into American route system, Carty, as noted, purchased TWA in 2001. Arpey, however, did not share Carty's vision. To improve AA's financial performance, Arpey shifted flights from routes out of the St. Louis hub to more profitable routes out of AA's Chicago and Dallas hubs. As a result, AA laid off more than 2,000 employees at the St. Louis airport in 2003 alone.[67]

Future Prospects and Concerns

One result of the successful implementation of Arpey's turnaround strategy was the deep decline in AA's operating costs. As shown in Exhibit 5, by 2005, American operating costs were lower than those of

Exhibit 5 Operating Cost of U.S. Network Carriers, 1st Quarter 2005, Cents in Available Seat Mile (CASM)

Network	1Q05 CASM
American	9.9
Continental	9.9
United	10.4
U.S. Air	10.7
Northwest	11.2
Delta	12.2

Source: Back-Aviation Solutions in Micheline Maynard and Jeremy Peters, "Circling a Decision," *New York Times,* August 18, 2005.

any other network carriers save Continental. American's stock prices too performed well. Following a sharp drop in AMR stock price during the post 9/11 years, AMR's stock more than doubled in value in 2005, rising 101% and outperforming the share prices of all major U.S. carriers, including Southwest Airlines. AA's cash position, furthermore, was stronger than that of other network carriers. AA managed to increase its cash surplus from $3 billion in 2004 to $4.3 billion in 2005, a margin sufficiently comfortable to give the carrier a greater staying power in the industry than its rivals.[68]

Nevertheless, American Airlines still faced a number of daunting challenges. First and most important was the need to achieve profitability. During Arpey's first three years in office, AMR continued to post large losses that amounted to $1.2 billion in 2003, $0.8 billion in 2004, and $0.9 billion in 2005. While analysts were impressed by AA's cost-cutting measures (as well as its collaborative labor management relations, strong cash position, rising fares, and trimmed capacity), and while AA stock doubled in value in 2005 in anticipation of profits in 2006, the continual increase in fuel costs during 2006 clouded AA's recovery prospects.[69]

Another concern pertained to labor relations. AA employees resented a stock-related bonus paid to American managers in 2006. The payout was authorized by an 18 year old "Long Term Incentive Program" which tied executive pay to AA's stock performance. Because AA's stock prices outperformed the stock prices of its five competitors (United, Delta, Continental, U.S. Air, Northwest) in 2005, American's top 1,000 mangers were eligible to share $80 million in cash. The payout, however, was viewed by American's unionized employees as extra compensation for managers not shared by other AA employees. A letter sent by top management to members of the Allied Pilots Association congratulating the pilots on saving $80 million in fuel cost in 2005—an amount equivalent to management's bonus—angered the pilots further, and threatened to undermine the cooperative labor relations at American.[70]

A final concern stemmed from AA's pension crisis. In 2005, American's pension plans were underfunded by about $2.7 billion. To be sure, AA's funding deficit was smaller than that of Delta ($5.3 billion) and Northwest ($3.8 billion), yet unlike Delta and Northwest, American's commitment to protecting its employees' pensions was embedded in a collective bargaining agreement: a key union demand incorporated into the 2003 labor agreement that saved AA from bankruptcy was the preservation of the carrier's pension plan intact. In 2006, Delta, Northwest, United, and other network carriers were all engaged in a process of converting their pension plans from defined benefit plans (plans that paid employees lifetime retirement pensions funded by the employer) to the less expensive defined contribution plans (plans that operated like retirement saving accounts funded by both the employee and the employer). American Airlines, accordingly, experienced a growing competitive pressure to convert its pension plans too, but such a move was likely to jeopardize the longstanding industrial peace at American which Arpey had worked so hard to craft and preserve.[71]

Endnotes

1 Henry Ladd Smith, *Airways: the History of Commercial Aviation in the United States* (1942, reprinted, New York: Russell and Russell, 1964).

2 Stephen Breyer, *Regulation and Its Reform* (Cambridge Mass.: Harvard University Press, 1982), p. 205.

3 Thomas K. McCraw, *Prophets of Regulations* (Cambridge Mass.: Harvard University Press, 1984), p. 3.

4 McCraw, *Prophets of Regulations*. pp. 266–67; Breyer, *Regulation and Its Reform*, pp. 204–5.

5 Smith, *Airways*, Chapters 12, 16, 22.

6 "AMR Corporation," *Hoover's Handbook of American Business 1992* (Austin: Hoovers Business Press, 1992), p. 110, "AMR Corporation," *International Directory of Company Histories* (Detroit: St. James Press, 1999). p. 23.

7 Robert Serling, *Eagle: The Story of American Airlines* (New York: At. Martin, 1985), p. 280.

8 "Carrier Profile," *Aviation Daily*, April 5, 2005.

9 Mark Kahn, "Airlines," in Gerald Somers, ed., *Collective Bargaining: Contemporary American Experience* (Bloomingdale, Illinois: Industrial Relations Research Association Series, 1980), pp. 354–58; Serling, *Eagle*, pp. 270–73, 304–306.

10 Dan Reed, *The American Eagle: The Ascent of Bob Crandall and American Airlines* (New York: St. Martin, 1993), Chapter 2.

11 Dan Reed, *American Eagle*, pp. 100–2. The quotation is on page 101.

12 Cited in Stewart Toy and Seth Payne, "The Airline Mess," *Business Week*, July 6, 1992, p. 50.

13 Cited in, "American Airlines Loses its Pilot," *Economist*, April 18, 1998, p. 58.

14 Reed, *American Eagle*, p. 207.

15 Steven Morrison and Clifford Winston, *The Evolution of the Airline Industry* (Washington D.C.: The Brooking Institution, 1995), pp. 44–45.

16 Reed, *American Eagle*, pp. 158–164, 174–175.

17 AA, in addition, established secondary hubs in Nashville, Tennessee, Raleigh/Durham, North Carolina, and San Jose, California, but following the recession of the early 1990s, American closed these three hubs, withdrawing from unprofitable short-hall travel markets. See Suzanne Loeffelholz, "Competitive Anger," *Financial World*, January 10, 1989, p. 31; and Perry Flint and Danna Henderson, "American at Bay," *Air Transport World*, March 1997. Online. ABI database, Start Page 28.

18 Dan Reed, *American Eagle*, pp. 204–205.

19 Seth Rosen, "A Union Perspective," in Jean McKelvey, Ed. *Cleared for Takeoff: Airline Labor Relations Since Deregulation* (Ithaca, New York: ILR Press, 1988), p. 22; Robert Crandall, "The Airlines: On Track or Off Course," in McKelvey, Ed. *Clear for Takeoff*, p. 352; Dan Reed, *American Eagle*, p. 202–204.

20 *Financial World*, January 10. 1989, pp. 29–30.

21 According to the company's annual report cited in "AMR Corporation," *International Directory of Company Histories*, p. 24.

22 Don Bedwell, *Silverbird: The American Airlines Story* (Sandpoint Idaho; Airway International Inc. 1999), pp. 137, 244.

23 Perry Flint, "Sabre Unlimited," *Air Transport World*, November 1996, p. 95.

24 Bedwell, *Silverbird*, p. 132, and Chapter 20.

25 Ronald Lieber, "Bob Crandall's BOO-BOOS," *Fortune*, April 28, 1997, p. 368; Don Lee and Jennifer Oldham,

"American Woos Wary Travelers," *Los Angeles Times*, Feb. 16, 1997.

26 Reed, *American Eagle*, Chapter 5; Bedwell, *Silverbird*, pp. 130–131, 250–251.

27 Kenneth Labich, "The Computer Network that Keeps American Flying," *Fortune*, September 24, 1990, p. 46.

28 Bedwell, *Silverbird*, p. 248.

29 *Air Transport World*, November 1996, p. 95.

30 Reed, *American Eagle*, p. 184.

31 Cited in Bedwell, *Silverbird*, p. 161.

32 Reed, *American Eagle*, pp. 176–177; Morrison and Winston, *The Evolution of the Airline Industry*, p. 59.

33 Bedwell, *Silverbird*, p. 161.

34 Seth Rosen, "Corporate Restructuring," in Peter Cappelli, ed., *Airline Labor Relations in the Global Era* (Ithaca, New York: ILR press, 1995). p. 33.

35 Kenneth Labich, "American Takes on the World," *Fortune*, September 24, 1990, pp. 41–42, Read, *American Eagle*, pp. 249, 251, 269, and "AMR Corporation," *International Directory of Company Histories*, p. 24.

36 *Air Transport World*, March 1997. Online. ABI Data Base. Start page 28.

37 Bedwell, *Silverbird*, pp. 233–236; "AMR Corporation," *International Directory of Company Histories*, p. 25.

38 Jeri Clausing, "Crandall's Hard-Ball Style Legendary," *Seattle Times*, November 25, 1993; James Peltz, "A 'Mellower' AMR Chief?" *Los Angeles Times*, Feb. 14, 1997.

39 *Fortune*, April 28, 1997, p. 368; *Los Angeles Times*, Feb. 14, 1997; Scott McCartney, "The Deal Breakers," *Wall Street Journal*, Feb. 11, 1997; "American Airlines Loses its Pilot," *Economist* April 18, 1998, p. 58.

40 *Air Transport World*, March 1997, Start page 28.

41 Peter Elkind, "Flying for Fun & Profits," *Fortune*, Oct. 25, 1999, pp. 36–37; James Peltz, "Carty Has Been Forced to Guide AMR Through Turbulent Times," *Los Angeles Times*, Nov. 14, 2001; John Helyar, "American Airlines: A Wing and a Prayer," *Fortune*, Dec. 10, 2001, p. 182.

42 *Los Angeles Times*, Nov. 14, 2001; "American, TWA Deal Approved," *Aviation Daily*, April 10, 2001; and U.S. Senate. *TWA/American Airlines Workforce Integration*. Hearing before the Committee on Health, Education, and Pensions. 108thCong., 1st Sess., June 12, 2003, p. 24.

43 *Los Angeles Times*, Nov. 14, 2001.

44 Scott McCarthney, "At American, 48 Hours of Drama Help Airline Avert Bankruptcy, *Wall Street Journal*, April 28, 2003.

45 Brad Foss, "How It All Went Wrong," *Chicago Sun Times*, April 27, 2003.

46 Cited in *Chicago Sun Times*, April 27, 2003.

47 *Wall Street Journal*, April 28, 2003; and Edward Wong and Micheline Maynard, "A Taut, Last-minute Stretch to Save an Airline," *New York Times*, April 27, 2003.

48 Cited in the *Wall Street Journal*, April 28, 2003; but see also *New York Times*, April 27, 2003.

49 Cited in Eve Tahmincioglu, "Back from the Brink," *Workforce Management*, Dec. 2004. Online. ABI Data Base. Start page 32. See also Sara Goo, "Key Union Accepts Cuts at American," *Washington Post*, April 26, 2003.

50 Cited in Melanie Trottman, "Boss Talk," *Wall Street Journal*, Dec. 30, 2004.

51 David Field, "The American Way," *Airline Business*, Dec. 2004, p. 31; "American Enters India," *Aviation Daily*, July 13, 2005.

52 Cited in Caroline Daniel, "A Top Flight Employee Strategy," *Financial Times*, April 4, 2005.

53 Cited in the *Wall Street Journal*, Dec. 30, 2004.

54 *Financial Times*, April 4, 2005; *Workforce Management*, Dec. 2004, Start page 32.

55 *Workforce Management*, Dec. 2004, Start page 32.

56 *Financial Times*, April 4, 2005.

57 *Workforce Management*, Dec. 2004, Start page 32.

58 *Workforce Management*, Dec. 2004, Start page 32.

59 Perry Flint, "Rewired for Success: American Embraces Continuous Improvement," *Air Transport World*, August 2004, 39.

60 *Air Transport World*, August 2004, 39.

61 *Air Transport World*, August 2004, 39.

62 *Air Transport World*, August 2004, 39.

63 *Workforce Management*, Dec. 2004, Start page 32.

64 Cited in *Airline Business*, Dec. 2004, p. 31.

65 *Wall Street Journal*, Dec. 30, 2004; Michael Maynard, "No Longer on the Brink, American Air is Still in Peril," *New York Times*, March 18, 2004; Scott McCartney, "Low Cost Rivals Prompt American Airlines to Try Flying Like One of Them," *Wall Street Journal*, June 8, 2004; *Airline Business*, Dec. 2004, p. 31.

66 *Airline Business*, Dec. 2004, p. 33; Edward Wong, "American Air is Adding Seats," *New York Times*, May 22, 2003; "American Looks to Counteract $1.4 Billion Fuel Cost Increase," *Aviation Daily*, March 13, 2005.

67 *Wall Street Journal*, June 8, 2004; Edward Wong, "In a Sign of Stronger Finances, American Reports a Profit," *New York Times*, Oct. 23, 2003.

68 Melanie Trottman, "AMR Investors Bet on Clearer Skies Ahead," *Wall Street Journal*, Feb. 16, 2006; Caroline Daniel, "In Hard Times, Saving Dollars Makes Sense," *Financial Times*, March 15, 2005.

69 "AMR Company Records, Financials," *Hoovers*. Online. ABI Data Base. *Wall Street Journal*, Feb. 16, 2006.

70 Scott McCartney, "Airline Discord May Hurt Travelers," *Wall Street Journal*, Feb. 7, 2006.

71 Brad Foss, American Path Less Traveled," *Seattle Times*, June 11, 2005.

CASE 20

CEMEX's Acquisition Strategy—The Acquisition of Rinker Group

"The lessons CEMEX has learned in the crisis means it has a lighter, more flexible, and dynamic operating base that will allow its eventual recovery . . . multiplying its profitability not only in the United States but in the majority of its subsidiaries."[1]

—Carlos Hermosillo, Analyst, Vector Brokerage, in January 2010.

"CEMEX is in a much stronger financial position to regain our financial flexibility and, eventually, our investment-grade capital structure."[2]

—Lorenzo Zambrano, Chief Executive Officer, CEMEX, in August 2009.

Introduction

On January 27, 2010, Mexico-based cement company CEMEX S.A.B de C.V (CEMEX) announced that its net sales for the fourth quarter ended December 31, 2009, had dropped by 17% to US$ 3.42 billion. Moreover, the company reported that its annual net sales in fiscal 2009 had dropped by 28% to US$ 14.5 billion as compared to the net sales reported in fiscal 2008. In 2009, the company reported a fall of 35% in its earnings before interest, depreciation, taxes, and amortization (EBIDTA) to US$ 2.7 billion. CEMEX had been facing problems like lower net sales and high debt since mid-2007 since its acquisition of Australia-based major cement company, the Rinker Group (Rinker).

As of early 2010, CEMEX was the largest cement company in the world in terms of production capacity. It was one of the companies based in an emerging nation like Mexico that had grown to become one of the top multinational companies in the global cement industry. Most of CEMEX's expansion in the domestic market as well as abroad came through acquisitions. Over the decades, it had developed strong expertise in successfully integrating acquired companies and reaping significant benefits. The company also relied on technology to optimize its operational efficiency, which placed it among the most profitable cement companies in the world.

CEMEX, which was known for its post-merger integration skills, also managed its cash flows well and used the free cash flows to amortize and eventually pay off the debt it had incurred for an acquisition. However, in mid-2007, CEMEX completed its largest acquisition ever by paying US$ 14.2 billion for acquiring Rinker. CEMEX financed the Rinker acquisition completely through a debt from a syndicate of banks. It estimated that Rinker's operations would result in strong cash flows and that, along with its own cash flows, it would be able to successfully service the huge debt burden. The company had set ambitious targets of achieving within 24 months leverage ratios similar to the ones that had existed prior to Rinker's acquisition. However, the US, which after acquisition was CEMEX's largest market, faced an economic slowdown due to the subprime crisis[3] that emerged in late 2007.

CEMEX, which derived a major portion of its revenues from the US, had to deal with low demand for its products since late 2007. The huge debt it had incurred for Rinker's acquisition added to the company's woes. The deficit in its anticipated free cash flows forced it to refinance its debts, sell assets, and take several cost-cutting measures like job cuts. The subprime crisis affected many of the financial institutions including commercial banks and investment banks which resulted in cautious lending from banks. CEMEX's debt credit rating was downgraded

*This case was written by **A. Harish**, under the direction of **Vivek Gupta**, IBS Center for Management Research. It was compiled from published sources and is intended to be used as a basis for class discussion rather than to illustrate either effective or ineffective handling of a management situation.*

by several credit rating agencies, which dented its credibility. With low credibility, CEMEX's cost of capital increased as it had to pay higher interest on the debt raised by the company.

By early 2010, analysts were predicting that the US markets would recover from the economic crisis and that the construction activity in the country would pick up. They also said that the stimulus packages announced by the US government in 2008 and 2009 would be used for infrastructure projects which would also add to the demand for building materials. CEMEX Vice president for Finance and Legal, Hector Medina, said, "While we are seeing a bottoming out in some of our markets as evidenced by some leading indicators, we expect first quarter 2010 to continue to be weak and that most of the expected growth in EBITDA will occur in the second half of the year."[4]

Background Note

CEMEX had its roots in a cement company called Cementos Hidalgo which was founded way back to 1906 in Monterrey, Northern Mexico. Cementos Hidalgo had a production capacity of 5,000 metric tons (MT) of cement per annum. In 1920, Lorenzo Zambrano established Cementos Portland Monterrey with a production capacity of 20,000 MT of cement per annum near Monterrey. In 1931, Cementos Hidalgo and Cementos Portland Monterrey merged to form Cementos Mexicanos. By 1959, Cementos Mexicanos had expanded its production capacity to produce over 230,420 MT of gray cement and 14,692 tons of white cement. Till the late 1960s, the company operated as a local company in Monterrey. In the late 1960s, the company started expanding to other parts of the country like Southern and Central Mexico through acquisitions and also by opening new plants.

In 1976, Cementos Mexicanos went public and got its shares listed on the Mexico stock exchange. It also became the largest cement producer in the same year after acquiring three plants of Cementos Guadalajara. By the mid-1980s, Cementos Mexicanos' annual cement production capacity had crossed 15 million MT. The mid-1980s, however, brought a major challenge for Cementos Mexicanos, which had been thriving in Mexico since its inception. Mexico started relaxing its protectionist policies and allowed multinational companies to operate in the country.

In 1985, Lorenzo Zambrano (Zambrano)[5], grandson of Cementos Mexicanos founder Lorenzo

Zambrano, was made the Chairman and CEO of Cementos Mexicanos. With a strong academic background[6] and experience in working with Cementos Mexicanos since 1968, Zambrano embarked on an aggressive expansion plan. He also focused on improving operational efficiency and customer satisfaction. Till the mid-1980s, the practice in the cement industry in Mexico was to provide its customers with an expected delivery time which usually ranged between 3 and 5 hours. Cementos Mexicanos also followed the same practice before Zambrano became Chairman and CEO.

CEMEX did not have an Information Technology (IT) department and scheduling delivery trucks and plant operations was done manually. This was operationally inefficient. Zambrano created an IT department which observed customer interaction and delivery methods implemented at several companies like FedEx, Exxon and City of Houston's 911 emergency system. In 1989, CEMEX implemented a satellite communication system called CEMEXnet which connected all the plants of CEMEX via satellite. A central office was opened to coordinate operational activities at several plants. This helped the plants to have information relating to supply and demand.

In 1988, Cementos Mexicanos was renamed as CEMEX S.A.B de C.V. During the late 1980s, CEMEX acquired several small cement plants in Mexico including Cementos Anahuac[7] in 1987 and Cementos Tolteca[8], its biggest domestic competitor, in 1989. By the year 1990, CEMEX had acquired a 65% market share in Mexico and was one of the ten largest companies in the world. In 1992, CEMEX expanded internationally by acquiring Valenciana and Sanson, Spain's two largest cement companies, for US$ 1.84 billion. CEMEX's investors expressed concerns on the rapid pace at which it was going ahead with its expansion plans and the amount of debt the company had taken for funding these acquisitions. To address these concerns, CEMEX paid off a large portion of its debts by selling the nonstrategic assets of the Spanish companies it had acquired.

In 1994, CEMEX acquired a 60% equity stake in Vencemos, Venezuela's largest cement manufacturer at that time, for US$ 550 million. Its other acquisitions during the year included Cemento Bayano in Panama and Balcones in the US. In 1995, CEMEX acquired Cementos Nacionales, a leading cement company in the Dominican Republic. In 1996, CEMEX emerged as the third largest cement company in the world after acquiring Colombia's

Cementos Diamante[9] and Samper. In 1997, CEMEX started its Asian operations by acquiring Rizal Cement in the Philippines. In 1999, CEMEX's acquisitions included APO Cements in the Philippines, Assiut Cement Company in Egypt, and Dementos del Pacifico of Costa Rica. In 1999, CEMEX's shares were listed on the New York Stock Exchange.

In 2000, CEMEX became North America's largest cement company by acquiring Houston-based Southdown[10], then the second largest cement producer in the US, for US$ 2.63 billion. This was the largest acquisition made by CEMEX till that time. In the same year, CEMEX launched the CEMEX Way, an initiative to identify, incorporate, and execute standardized best practices in different functional areas like logistics, finance, human resources, and planning throughout the organization.

In 2001, CEMEX acquired the Saraburi Cement Company in Thailand. In the same year, it launched an online customer service initiative where customers could place orders, purchase products, and access other services and information electronically. As most of CEMEX's growth came from acquisitions, the company had developed strong post-merger integration (PMI) expertise. After completing an acquisition, it usually deployed a post-merger integration team that analyzed the operations of the acquired company to identify the areas where costs could be cut, reduce headcount, and upgrade technical and management systems to fall in-line with what were being followed at CEMEX. This expertise helped CEMEX in turning around several ailing companies it had acquired by cutting down on costs and improving operational efficiency.

In the early 2000s, CEMEX concentrated on expanding its presence in developing markets like the Philippines, Indonesia, and Thailand. The company's profitability was higher than its major international rivals—Holcim and Lafarge—because of its concentration on developing nations where profit margins were higher. Developing nations also offered CEMEX's businesses a longer term growth potential. In 2003, CEMEX launched a company-wide procurement process and global sourcing office to consolidate its international sourcing operations and realize the benefits of economies of scale.

In 2005, CEMEX acquired the UK-based RMC Group[11] for US$ 5.8 billion. The acquisition made the company a worldwide leader in the ready-mix concrete market and increased its exposure to the European markets significantly. It also doubled the size of CEMEX's operations, taking its total annual cement production capacity to 97 million MT. CEMEX ended the year 2006 with revenues of US$ 18.2 billion and a net profit of US$ 2.3 billion (Refer to Exhibit I, II and III for Financial Statements of CEMEX).

CEMEX had a three-point acquisition strategy—the acquired company must provide risk adjusted returns in excess of the company's weighted average cost of capital, it must enhance the company's geographical presence, and it must contribute to CEMEX's capital structure[12].

The Acquisition Integration Process

CEMEX had learnt in the course of its business that implementing the technical and management standards it followed in its existing plants was not sufficient to ensure the smooth integration of an acquired company. The company realized that it had to learn the processes already implemented in the acquired company, compare it with the corresponding processes it followed, and retain the better of the two. CEMEX then made efforts to implement the best practices learned from the acquired company across its worldwide operations. This acquisition integration process was later named as the 'CEMEX Way.'

The 'CEMEX Way' was an internal benchmarking process which resulted in a core set of best business practices based on which CEMEX conducted business across the globe. It was driven by five guidelines developed by the company (Refer to Table I for CEMEX Way Guidelines).

After acquiring a target company, CEMEX deployed multinational standardization teams

Table I CEMEX Way Guidelines

Efficiently manage the global knowledge base
Identify and disseminate the best practices
Standardize business processes
Implement key information and Internet-based technologies
Foster innovation

Source: www.cemex.com.

comprising experts from various functional areas like Finance, HR, and IT. The work was overseen by an executive at the Vice-president level. The PMI team studied the processes of the acquired company. Typically, 20% of the processes of an acquired company were retained. The remaining 80% processes were stored in a centralized database, and were compared with internal and external processes. If deemed to be superior to the existing processes, they were then implemented in all other plants. According to industry experts, around 70% of the processes followed in CEMEX operations were actually adopted from the acquired companies.

The teams for each PMI operation were selected on an ad hoc basis. Functional level managers, typically middle level managers, were selected from different plants of CEMEX. These managers were responsible for understanding the existing processes of the acquired company and identifying those processes which were superior to the processes that were being followed at CEMEX. Since these managers had gained expertise of working on a particular process at CEMEX, they taught the managers at the acquired company about the processes at CEMEX. Also, they were experienced in the functional departments of CEMEX,

and so were able to judge better whether the corresponding processes in the acquired company would be able to positively contribute to CEMEX's operations.

Acquisition of Rinker

On October 30, 2006, CEMEX made an offer to buy all issued and outstanding shares of Rinker for US$ 12.8 billion. The offer was at a 27% premium over Rinker's share closing price as on October 27, 2006, and at a 26.2% premium over Rinker's three-month volume weighted average price.[13] CEMEX expected to derive annual cost synergies of US$ 130 million from the second year after completing the acquisition.

Rinker had generated approximately 50% of its revenues from the commercial and civil construction sector in the fiscal 2005. Its product portfolio was diversified and included aggregates, concrete, cement pipes, cement, gypsum wallboard supply, concrete block, and asphalt. The acquisition of Rinker significantly enhanced the position of CEMEX in the ready-mix and aggregates sector though the impact on cement production capacity was not much (Refer to Table II for Global Cement Industry Rankings in 2005).

Table II   Global Cement Industry Rankings (2005)

Cement (In million metric tons)		Ready-Mix (In million cubic meters)		Aggregates (In million metric tons)	
Company	Capacity	Company	Sales Volume	Company	Sales Volume
Holcim	183	CEMEX+Rinker	97	CEMEX+Rinker	284
Lafarge	155	CEMEX	76	CRH	253
CEMEX+Rinker	97	Holcim	40	Lafarge	240
CEMEX	94	Lafarge	39	Hanson	240
Heidelberg	86	Heidelberg	28	Vulcan	236
Italcementi	64	Italcementi	21	Martin Marietta	184
Anhui Conch	62	Rinker	21	CEMEX	175
Taiheiyo	46	Hanson	20	Holcim	174
Buzzi	34	CRH	19	Rinker	118
Eurocement	31	Tarmac	8	Colas	101
Rinker	3	Vicat / Cimpor	7	Heidelberg	98
Others	~1,750	Others	~2,900	Others	~18,000

Source: www.cemex.com.

Rinker was the market leader in some of the key markets in the US like Florida, Arizona, and had a wide presence in Australia. It was one of the top three companies in the ready mix business, among the top five in aggregates[14] in the US, and among the top three in building materials in Australia. Rinker had huge reserves of aggregates, around 3.6 billion MT, in the US and Australia which were estimated to last for 30 years of production in the US and 43 years of production in Australia.

Rinker provided CEMEX with an opportunity to diversify geographically and increase its presence in Australia. In the fiscal 2005, CEMEX generated the highest amount of EBIDTA from its Mexican operations followed by the US. Rinker's acquisition brought down CEMEX's significant reliance on the Mexican markets. However, the acquisition increased CEMEX's reliance on the US markets (Refer to Figure I for Geographical Contribution of CE-MEX and CEMEX + Rinker EBIDTA in 2005).

CEMEX announced that the markets in the US where Rinker held most of its assets and operations were complementary to its operations in the US and would enhance its position in the country. The company expected that the demand for building materials in the US would be robust in the long term. In addition to geographical diversification, Rinker's acquisition also offered it an opportunity to change the product- wise contribution to the CEMEX's EBIDTA (Refer to Figure II for Product Wise contribution to CEMEX and CEMEX+ Rinker EBIDTA in 2005).

Following the announcement of acquisition by CEMEX, Rinker's share price increased and traded over CEMEX's bid price of A\$ 17,[15] implying that CEMEX had to increase its bid in order to get shareholders' approval for the acquisition (**Refer to Exhibit IV for Rinker's Stock Price Chart**). Rinker's board rejected CEMEX's initial bid.

After failing to convince Rinker's board and shareholders to approve the deal, CEMEX increased its offer to A\$ 19.41 in April 2007. Rinker's board approved the deal. The upward revision saw the total acquisition bid of CEMEX amounting to US\$ 14.2 billion after adjusting for the exchange rate fluctuations between the Australian and the US dollar during the intervening period. (Refer to Exhibits V and VI **for Rinker's Financial Statements**).

In order to convince Rinker's retail shareholders in Australia, CEMEX took the help of Georgeson, one of Australia's leading proxy solicitation and shareholder communications firms. With the help of Georgeson, in April 2007, CEMEX conducted a three-phase canvassing campaign, where it contacted Rinker's shareholders in Australia to deliver key messages and to motivate them by communicating the benefits of accepting its offer within a given time frame (Refer to Table III **for the reasons communicated to Rinker's shareholders to accept the offer**).

On April 05, 2007, CEMEX also got approval from the Department of Justice (DoJ) in the US for Rinker's acquisition after agreeing to sell 39 ready mix concrete, concrete block, and aggregate facilities in the country. The DoJ required CEMEX to

Figure I Geographical Contribution of CEMEX and CEMEX + Rinker EBIDTA (2005)

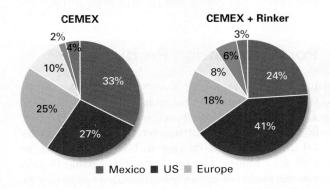

Adapted from data available in www.cemex.com

Figure II Product Wise Contribution to CEMEX and CEMEX + Rinker EBIDT A (2005)

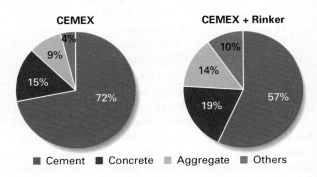

Adapted from data available in www.cemex.com

Table III   Reasons Communicated to Rinker's Shareholders to Accept the Offer

1. All Rinker directors recommended that you accept CEMEX's offer and have decided to accept the offer in respect of their own Rinker's shares.

2. Rinker's major shareholder, Perpetual, who held approximately 10% of Rinker has accepted CEMEX's offer.

3. You will receive a 45% premium and full value for your Rinker's shares.

4. You will receive the announced Rinker dividend of A$ 0.25 regardless of when you accept the offer.

5. CEMEX's offer is within the independent expert's valuation range.

6. There is no reason to delay your acceptance, the offer had been declared final and cannot legally be increased.

7. If CEMEX acquired over 50% but less than 100% of Rinker and you do not accept, then you will become a minority shareholder in Rinker. Changes under CEMEX management may include a lowering of Rinker's dividend payout ratio.

8. If the CEMEX Offer does not succeed, Rinker's share price is likely to fall.

Source: www.sec.gov

Table IV   CEMEX Payment Options

Option 1: US$ 15.85 for each of their Rinker shares converted into and paid in A$.

Option 2: A$ 19.50 per share for their first 2,000 Rinker shares (or for all of their shares if they held 2,000 Rinker shares or less) and US$ 15.85 for each of their remaining shares (if any) converted into and paid in A$.

Option 3: US$ 15.85 for each of their Rinker shares paid in US$.

Option 4: A$ 19.50 per share for their first 2,000 Rinker shares (or for all of their shares if they held 2,000 Rinker shares or less) and US$ 15.85 for each of their remaining shares (if any) paid in US$.

Source: www.ato.gov.au

According to the company sources, if a shareholder did not elect an option before the deadline, then CEMEX would pay them using Option 1, in case the shareholder's registered address with Rinker was in Australia, and Option 3, if the shareholder's registered address with Rinker was outside Australia.

By the end of December 2007, CEMEX reported that its PMI team had been able to complete the core postmerger integration process at Rinker. The company said it had identified the best practices and would capitalize US$ 400 million resulting from synergies in fiscal 2008 and 2009, US$ 270 million above what it had estimated before completing the acquisition. Typically, CEMEX relied on the free cash flows to pay off the debts it had raised for any acquisition. In the case of Rinker's acquisition, CEMEX expected to generate enough free cash flows right from the first year to pay off its annual debt obligations.

Post-Acquisition Problems

In January 2008, CEMEX announced its financial results for the financial year ended December 31, 2007. The company reported net sales of US$ 21.7 billion, 19% higher than the net sales reported in fiscal 2006. Its net profit rose to US$ 2.9 billion from US$ 2.37 billion. The results included Rinker's sales and net profit for the six months ended December 31, 2007. CEMEX ended the fiscal 2007 with a debt of

sell some of its plants in Tampa, St. Petersburg, Fort Walton Beach, Panama City, Pensacola, Jacksonville, Orlando, Fort Myers, and Naples where the competition would significantly reduce after CEMEX's acquisition of Rinker. Later, in December 2007, CEMEX sold some of these assets.

On July 10, 2007, CEMEX announced that it had acquired a 90% equity stake in Rinker and would compulsorily acquire the rest of the shares. Under Australian law, a company could compulsorily acquire the remaining shares once it had acquired a minimum of 90% equity stake. CEMEX offered Rinker's remaining shareholders four payment options from which they had to select one and confirm it by July 16, 2007 (Refer to Table IV for CEMEX Payment Options).

US$ 19.9 billion[16] as against a debt of US$ 5.81 billion at the end of fiscal 2006. Its net-debt-to-EBIDTA ratio went up to 3.6 by the end of 2007, from 1.4 at the end of fiscal 2006. CEMEX's interest coverage ratio fell to 5.7 at the end of fiscal 2007 from 8.4 at the end of fiscal 2006 mainly due to the additional debt it had raised for financing Rinker's acquisition. CEMEX said that its target was to bring down the net-debt-EBIDTA ratio to 2.7 and to maintain its interest coverage ratio at above 4.5 by mid-2009. However, CEMEX failed to achieve these financial targets due to a significant fall in cement demand in its major markets including the US in fiscal 2008 and 2009 (Refer to Exhibit VII for Note on Cement Industry in US) and the huge debt burden post Rinker's acquisition.

Fall In Cement Demand

In late 2007, the subprime crisis in the US resulted in a significant slowdown in the growth of residential mortgage markets in the US. Prices in the real-estate sector started falling sharply. The demand for housing properties began to decline. The crisis eventually spread to other sectors as a number of financial institutions who reported significant losses, tightened their lending norms. The construction industry which was highly capital-intensive and relied heavily on external funding for executing projects was adversely impacted. The demand for residential and commercial properties plunged deeply in the US beginning late 2007. One of the industries that was adversely affected by the slowdown in the residential and commercial real estate industry was the building materials industry.

CEMEX was one of the major players in the building materials industry in the US which saw its net sales and sales volumes falling sharply in the fiscal 2007 and 2008. The crisis which originated in the US spread to other major world economies and resulted in a global economic slowdown in 2008 (Refer to Table V and Table VI for Country Wise Volume Growth of CEMEX Products in fiscal 2007 and 2008).

Huge Debt Burden

CEMEX had financed Rinker's acquisition by raising short-term and long-term debts from a syndicate of banks including the Royal Bank of Scotland, HSBC, Banco Santander, BNP Paribas, and Citibank. The

Table V   Country Wise Volume Growth (%) of CEMEX Products (2007)

Product/Country	Cement	Ready Mix	Aggregates
Mexico	4	8	NA
US	(8)	13	75
Spain	(5)	(4)	N
United Kingdom	12	(2)	2
Germany	(6)	NA	NA
France	NA	5	2
South/Central America and Caribbean	8	NA	NA
Africa and Middle East	8	NA	NA
Asia and Australia	7	NA	NA
Australia	NA	5	7
Philippines	12	NA	NA

Source: CEMEX Annual Report 2007.
*NA- not available in the annual reports.

Table VI Country Wise Volume Growth (%) of CEMEX Products (2008)

Product/Country	Cement	Ready Mix	Aggregates
Mexico	(4)	(6)	
US	(14)	(13)	(3)
Spain	(30)	(26)	
United Kingdom	(16)	(21)	(11)
Germany	4	NA	
France	NA	0	(5)
South/Central America and Caribbean	(13)	NA	NA
Africa and Middle East	8	NA	NA
Asia and Australia	(1)	NA	NA
Australia	NA	6	5
Philippines	(2)	NA	NA

Source: CEMEX Annual Report 2008.
*NA- not available in the annual report.

Table VII CEMEX Debt Issuances (2006–2007)

Nominal Amount (In Million)	Issue Date	Repurchase Option	Interest Rate (%)
€ 730	May 2007	Tenth Anniversary	6.3
US$ 730	February 2007	Eighth Anniversary	6.6
US$ 750	December 2006	Fifth Anniversary	6.2
US$ 900	December 2006	Tenth Anniversary	6.7

Source: CEMEX Annual Report, 2007.

debt instruments involved had maturities starting from 2009 till 2011.

In late 2006 and 2007, CEMEX issued several debt instruments the proceeds of which were predominantly targeted at paying off its existing debts as well as the debt it had incurred for acquiring Rinker (**Refer to Table VII for CEMEX's debt issuances in late 2006 and 2007**).

In 2008, CEMEX could not raise new capital from the financial markets as they had witnessed a significant downturn. In February 2008, CEMEX

decided to sell assets worth around US$ 2 billion to reduce some of its debt load. However, analysts opined that CEMEX needed to sell around US$ 2.7 billion worth of assets in order to meet its debt obligations. A Mexico-based analyst said, "CEMEX is likely to need to sell more than they say. The debt issue is a big challenge."[17]

In March 2008, CEMEX sold its 9.5% equity stake in Mexican telecom company Axtel for US$ 257 million. By mid-2008, another of CEMEX's key markets, Spain, started facing an economic slowdown, due to the impact of the recession on American and European countries. Economists also predicted that the slowdown in the US would impact Mexico, its #2 trade partner. In July 2008, CEMEX sold its subsidiaries in Austria and Hungary to Austria-based construction company, Strabag, for around € 310 million (Refer to Exhibit VIII for CEMEX Contractual Obligations for year 2008).

In October 2008, the credit rating agency Standard & Poor's[18] (S&P) lowered its credit rating on the long-term corporate credit and senior unsecured debt ratings of CEMEX to 'BBB-' from BBB and said that its outlook on the company was negative. Juan Pablo Becerra, Analyst at S&P, said, "The rating actions reflect our expectations that CEMEX's financial performance for the rest of 2008 and into 2009 will fall short of our previous expectations, given the weakening of economic growth prospects in its principal markets and around the globe. In addition, CEMEX faces important debt maturities (US$ 5.7 billion) at the end of 2009 (particularly in December when US$ 3.7 billion related to its acquisition of Rinker Group Limited are due), which pose a significant challenge to the company in light of current market conditions. The negative outlook reflects the risk of further deterioration in the company's financial condition due to the weakness in the global economy. In particular, a downgrade is likely if CEMEX fails to improve its FFO-to-total net adjusted debt ratio to a low 20% by 2010 and if it is unable to refinance its 2009 maturities well in advance."[19] Soon after the ratings were lowered, CEMEX decided to cut 6000 jobs worldwide as a cost-cutting measure. In the same month, Fitch Ratings,[20] another credit rating agency, downgraded the credit rating of CEMEX to below investment grade standard.

In November 2008, CEMEX announced that it had sold its operations in Canary Islands to a Spanish Investment holding company, Cimpor Inversiones, for US$ 211 million. On December 11, 2008, CEMEX reported that it had been successful in refinancing US$ 72 million debt mostly due in December 2008 and January 2009. These debt obligations would now be due in September 2011. However, the amount refinanced was just 17% of the total US$ 418 million debt CEMEX had actually planned to refinance. Failure to refinance this debt completely led to CEMEX's stock price falling by 19% on the same day to close at US$ 8.3 (Refer to Exhibit IX for CEMEX Stock Price Chart).

CEMEX reported net sales of US$ 21.7 billion in the fiscal 2008, which was almost flat compared to the corresponding figures of fiscal 2007. CEMEX's cost of sales as a percent of total sales increased from 66.6% to 68.3%. The company reported a 5% drop in EBIDTA at US$ 4.5 billion as compared to 2007. Its interest coverage ratio in fiscal 2008 came down to 4.9 from 5.7 in fiscal 2007. The Mexican peso which depreciated vis-à-vis the US dollar in 2008 resulted in foreign exchange losses of US$ 386 million (Refer to Exhibit X for Mexican Peso VS American Dollar Chart). CEMEX lost US$ 1.35 billion on financial instruments like currency swaps of which most was attributed to the depreciation of the peso against the US dollar. The company reported a free cash flow of US$ 2.6 billion in 2008 (Refer to Exhibit XI for CEMEX Cash Flow Statement of 2008) of which US$ 1.56 billion went into capital expenditure for capacity expansion and the rest for reducing debt. CEMEX had a net debt of US$ 17.91 billion and its net-debt-to-EBDITA rose to 4 in 2008.

In January 2009, CEMEX announced that it would close down the operations of its Davenport plant and lay off 125 employees to align its operations with weakened demand. S&P had downgraded CEMEX's rating to BB+, a notch below investment grade status BBB-. On March 05, 2009, CEMEX announced that it would delay its proposed plan to sell bonds to raise US$ 500 million that was to fund its repayment of the US$ 4.24 billion of debt that was maturing between the second quarter and fourth quarter of fiscal 2009. CEMEX decided to delay the US$ 500 million bond sale as not enough investors showed an interest in subscribing to the issue despite its extensive road shows in London and New York. Following its failure to raise capital, credit rating agencies downgraded the rating on CEMEX again. S&P downgraded CEMEX's rating by 5 notches to B- from BB+.

In April 2009, CEMEX announced very disappointing results for the first quarter of 2009. The company reported a 99.36% drop in its net profits to US$ 3 million as compared to US$ 470 million in the corresponding quarter in 2008. During the same period, its revenues fell by 32% to US$ 3.7 billion. CEMEX's free cash flows, which were important for repaying its debt, fell by 76% in the same period to US$ 118 million. CEMEX's management assured the investors that it was progressing well in the debt restructuring talks with its lenders. It said that the depreciation of the peso against the US dollar and weak sales in its major markets like the US and Spain were the main reasons for its poor financial performance. CEMEX received a large chunk of its revenues in Mexican pesos whereas most of its debt was in US dollars. The peso's depreciation against the US dollar exacerbated its debt obligations. CEMEX said that it had stopped most of its capital-intensive expansion projects to save cash for repaying its debt.

In June 2009, CEMEX announced that it would be selling the Australian operations of Rinker to its rival Holcim for US$ 1.6 billion. According to industry analysts, the price at which CEMEX sold the Australian operations was almost half of what it had paid for acquiring them from Rinker in 2007. They opined that the poor demand for cement in CEMEX's major markets coupled with huge debt liabilities had forced it to exit one of the lucrative markets for cement production.

Future Tense?

In July 2009, CEMEX lowered its free cash flow forecasts for the fiscal year 2009 to US$ 1.6 billion as against the previous forecast of US$ 2.05 billion. This led to worries among the company's shareholders and lenders. In August 2009, CEMEX announced that all its creditors had agreed to support its proposal for refinancing a debt of US$ 15 billion maturing over the next two years. According to the new plan, the debt that was to mature between 2009 and 2011 would have extended maturities till 2014.

However, in spite of refinancing approvals from the lenders, credit rating agencies did not upgrade the rating of CEMEX to investment grade as there were uncertainties in the economic scenario. Also, they were not certain about CEMEX's ability to generate sufficient cash flows in the years through 2014 to repay its debt obligations. Juan Pablo Becerra, Credit Analyst at S&P, said, "For an improvement in the rating, we would have to see a more stable macroeconomic environment, a refinancing not just of 2009 debt but also of that in 2010 and 2011 and a cut in company debt levels."[21]

According to financial experts, the cost of refinancing would add to CEMEX's annual interest burden, estimated to be an additional US$ 2 billion. Moreover, they opined that CEMEX may require additional refinancing in future, given the uncertainty

in demand for its products in its major markets. The fresh refinancing terms limited the company's ability to invest in expansion projects or to go in for new acquisitions.

In its effort to raise capital, in September 2009, CEMEX issued 1.3 billion Ordinary Participatory Notes (OPOs) in the form of American Depository Shares (ADS). Each ADS comprised 10 OPOs. Each ADS was priced at US$ 12.5 and OPOs were priced at MXP 16.64825.[22] Of the issued 1.3 billion, 325 million CPOs were sold in Mexico and the rest in other countries in the form of ADS. CEMEX raised US$ 1.8 billion from this issue.

In December 2009, CEMEX also raised US$ 1.25 billion through the issue of notes maturing in seven years and carried an annual coupon rate of 9.5% and € 350 million in eight year notes carrying an annual coupon rate of 9.625%. Financial analysts expressed concern over CEMEX's strategy to raise capital by issuing fresh bonds to repay a portion of its earlier debts. According to Gonzalo Fernandez of Santander brokerage, "We are still somewhat concerned that CEMEX continues refinancing banking debt with bonds, and that it is not effectively reducing debt."[23]

Industry analysts remained skeptical about CEMEX's ability to significantly improve its financial performance in the near future. They opined that after Rinker's acquisition, CEMEX could not generate enough free cash flows to repay the debt like it had done in the case of earlier acquisitions.

In early 2010, CEMEX's problems continued. On January 26, 2010, the company announced disappointing results for the fiscal year 2009. The company generated revenues of US$ 14.5 billion, about 28% lower as compared to fiscal 2008. During the same period, the company's EBIDTA decreased by 35% to US$ 2.7 billion. The free cash flows after maintenance capital expenditure was also down by 53% to US$ 1.2 billion.

Industry analysts opined that CEMEX needed to expand its operations in major cement consuming markets like China and India. However, until it had repaid a significant part of the debt, the company's creditors would not allow CEMEX to expand its operations in these countries. Moreover, analysts pointed out that after selling several assets globally, CEMEX's reliance on the US markets had further increased Hence, the company's future success relied heavily on the economic recovery in the US.

Exhibit I CEMEX—Income Statements (2004–08) (In US$ millions)

	2004	2005	2006	2007	2008
Net Sales	8,149.36	15,320.96	18,249.36	21,672.99	21,688.53
Cost of Sales	(4,586.35)	(9,271.20)	(11,648.47)	(14,441.03)	(14,822.86)
Gross Profit	3,563.01	6,049.76	6,600.89	7,231.96	6,865.68
Selling, General and Administrative Expenses	(1,711.33)	(3,563.10)	(3,655.06)	(4,260.50)	(4,379.01)
Operating Income	1,851.68	2,486.66	2,945.83	2,971.46	2,486.67
Other Expenses, Net	(513.50)	(316.43)	(49.86)	(300.52)	(1,916.96)
Operating Income After Other Expenses, Net	1,338.18	2,170.23	2,895.97	2,670.94	569.71
Financial Expenses	(372.23)	(526.17)	(493.91)	(806.64)	(911.65)
Financial Income	23.42	39.26	45.71	78.96	51.63
Exchange Gain (Loss), Net	(23.56)	(78.82)	20.30	(22.24)	(385.91)
Monetary Position Gain (Loss)	385.87	418.83	409.44	630.92	37.24
Gain (Loss) on Financial Instruments	119.84	386.20	(13.68)	218.56	(1,353.05)
Total Comprehensive Financing Cost (Income)	133.34	239.31	(32.14)	99.56	(2,561.75)
Net income Before Income Taxes	1,501.15	2,408.48	2,879.51	2,770.50	(1,992.04)
Income Tax	(183.45)	(330.26)	(497.30)	(439.20)	2,101.24
Net income Before Participation of Uncons. Subs	1,288.07	2,079.28	2,366.52	2,331.30	109.20
Participation in Unconsolidated Subsidiaries	40.06	87.35	121.69	136.20	97.90
Consolidated Net Income	1,328.13	2,166.63	2,488.21	2,467.50	207.10
Net Income Attributable to Minority Interest	20.93	55.04	110.28	76.67	3.98
Majority Interest Net Income	1,307.20	2,111.59	2,377.93	2,390.83	203.13
Earnings per ADS (NYSE:CX)	3.93	6.10	3.31	3.22	0.27
EBITDA*	2,538.26	3,557.10	4,137.68	4,586.11	4,343.11
Free Cash Flow*	1,478.00	2,013.00	1,943.00	1,144.00	1,040.00

Source: www.cemex.com.

Exhibit II CEMEX Quarterly Income Statements (2009) (In US$ Millions)

	1Q	2Q	3Q	4Q
Net Sales	3,660.12	4,188.11	4,217.08	3,443.80
Cost of Sales	(2,614.98)	(2,906.51)	(2,897.06)	(2,532.49)
				(continued)

Exhibit II (*continued*)

	1Q	2Q	3Q	4Q
Gross Profit	1,045.14	1,281.60	1,320.02	911.31
Selling, General and Administrative Expenses	(719.48)	(870.62)	(909.02)	(813.00)
Operating Income	325.66	410.98	411.01	98.31
Other Expenses, Net	(37.87)	(100.55)	(61.85)	(219.84)
Operating Income After Other Expenses, Net	287.79	310.43	349.16	(121.53)
Financial Expenses	(205.08)	(210.47)	(275.08)	(315.94)
Financial Income	7.14	5.84	10.82	8.69
Exchange Gain (Loss), Net	(138.22)	80.75	15.99	50.18
Monetary Position Gain (Loss)	5.28	7.53	9.98	7.96
Gain (Loss) on Financial Instruments	(138.72)	(5.01)	(23.02)	20.72
Total Comprehensive Financing Cost (Income)	(469.60)	(121.35)	(261.30)	(228.40)
Net income Before Income Taxes	(181.81)	189.08	87.85	(349.93)
Income Tax	189.78	(4.41)	25.56	613.20
Net income Before Participation of Uncons. Subs	7.96	184.67	113.42	263.28
Participation in Unconsolidated Subsidiaries	(2.19)	7.34	20.37	1.78
Consolidated Net Income	5.78	192.01	133.79	(213.15)
Net Income Attributable to Minority Interest	2.98	5.45	12.84	(3.70)
Majority Interest Net Income	2.79	186.56	120.95	(209.45)
Earnings per ADS (2)	0.00	0.24	0.14	(0.22)
EBITDA*	712.22	811.59	805.56	473.69

Source: www.cemex.com.

Exhibit III   CEMEX Balance Sheets (2006–08) (In Mexican Pesos millions)

Balance Sheet	2008	2007	2006
Assets			
Current Assets			
Cash and investments	13,604	8,670	18,494
Trade receivables less allowance for doubtful accounts	18,276	20,719	16,525
Other accounts receivable	9,945	9,830	9,206
Inventories,net	22,358	19,631	13,974
Other current assets	4,012	2,394	2,255
Total current assets	68,195	61,244	60,454

Exhibit III (*continued*)

Balance Sheet	2008	2007	2006
Non-current Assets			
Investment in associates	14,200	10,220	8,712
Other investments and non-current accounts receivable	24,633	11,339	9,966
Property, machinery and equipment, net	281,858	262,189	201,425
Goodwill, intangible assets and deferred charges, net	234,736	197,322	70,526
Total non-current assets	555,427	481,070	290,629
Total assets	623,622	542,314	351,083
Liabilities and stockholders' equity			
Current liabilities			
Short-term debt including current maturities of long-term debt	95,270	36,257	14,657
other financial obligations	3,462		
Trade payables	22,543	23,660	20,110
Other accounts payable and accrued expenses	31,462	23,471	17,203
Total current liabilities	152,737	83,388	51,970
Non-current Liabilities			
Long-term debt	162,824	180,654	73,674
other financial obligations	1,823	0	0
Employee benefits	6,788	7,650	7,484
Deferred income tax liability	38,439	50,307	30,119
other non-current liabilities	23,744	16,162	14,725
Total non-current liabilities	233,618	254,773	126,002
Total liabilities	386,355	338,161	177,972
Shareholder's Equity			
Majority interest:			
Common Stock	4,117	4,115	4,113
Additional Paid-in capital	70,171	63,379	56,982
Other equity reserves	28,730	(104,574)	(91,244)
Retained earnings	85,396	174,140	152,921
Net income	2,278	26,108	27,855
Total majority interest	190,692	163,168	150,627
Minority interest and perpetual debentures	46,575	40,985	22,484
Total stockholders' equity	237,267	204,153	173,111
Total liabilities and stockholder's equity	623,622	542,314	351,083

Source: CEMEX Annual Reports 2007–08.

Exhibit IV   Rinker Stock Price Chart (April 2006—October 2006)

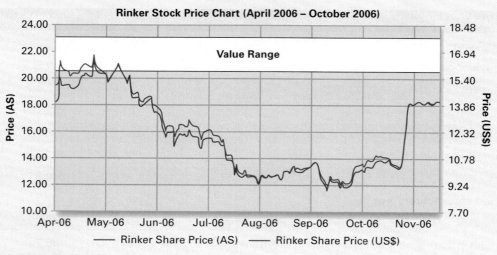

Source: www.sec.gov.

Exhibit V   Income Statements of Rinker (2006–07) (In US$ millions)

Year ended March 31	2007	2006
Trading revenue	5,337.30	5108.40
Cost of sales	(2,744.00)	(2,666.30)
Warehouse and distribution costs	(1,058.60)	(1,015.20)
Selling, general and administrative costs		
-general	(366.30)	(373.80)
-takeover defence costs	(14.50)	
Share of profits from investments accounted for using the equity method	25.30	32.60
Other income	44.50	68.40
Other expenses	(5.80)	(8.50)
Profit before finance and income tax expense	1,217.90	1,145.60
Interest Income	15.90	21.7
Finance Costs	(57.30)	(41.8)
Profit before income tax	1,176.50	1,125.50
Income tax	(390.10)	(381.9)
Net profit	786.40	743.6

Source: Rinker Annual Report 2007.

Exhibit VI Balance Sheets of Rinker (2006–2007)

Year ended March 31	2007	2006
Current Assets		
Cash and cash equivalents	185.9	289.1
Receivables	671.4	672.3
Inventories	373.7	330.9
Other current assets	23.1	20.7
Current Assets	1,254.10	1,313.00
Non-current assets		
Receivables	22.3	45.2
Inventories	9.8	8.6
Investments accounted for using the equity method	148	132.9
Other financial assets	40.3	32.6
Property, plant and equipment	2,233.10	1,963.40
Intangibles, including goodwill	937.1	901.7
Other non-current assets	59.6	59.8
Non-current assets	3,450.20	3,144.20
Total Assets	4,704.30	4,457.20
Current liabilities		
Payables	511.8	542.2
Borrowings	9.4	5.4
Income tax liabilities	49.1	62.4
Provisions	77.4	76.2
Current liabilities	647.7	686.2
Non-current Liabilities		
Payables	88.8	94.1
Borrowings	1,092.30	645.2
Net deferred income tax liabilities	218	205.8
Provisions	144.5	138.6
Non-current Liabilities	1,543.60	1,083.70
Total Liabilities	2,191.30	1,769.90
Net Assets	2,513.00	2,687.30
Equity		
Contributed equity(a)	636	1,138.70
Shares held in trust	−52.3	−44.2
Reserves	286.5	182.4
Retained profits	1,632.70	1,401.30
Equity attributable to members of Rinker Group Limited	2,502.90	2,678.20
Minority interests	10.1	9.1
Total equity	2,513.00	2,687.30

Source: Rinker Annual Report 2007.

Exhibit VII   A Note on Cement Industry in the US (2005–2009)

Cement has been one of the most commonly used construction materials in the world. The construction boom in the US in early 2000s through mid-2006 fueled the demand for cement from both the domestic cement producers as well as imports from foreign cement producers. In response to the increasing demand, several cement companies in the US invested in the latest technology to improve the efficiency of their plants as well as increasing their production capacities significantly. The cement production touched a record high of 99.319 million MT in 2005. The production contracted marginally for the years 2006 and 2007 before contracting by 25% from the peak to reach 75 million MT in 2009. The annual production of 75 million MT was the lowest in the US since the mid-1990s (Refer to Table A for Cement Production, Trade and Consumption in the US between 1995 and 2009).

Table A   Cement Production, Trade, and Consumption in*US (In million MT except year)

Year	Production	Imports	Exports	Aggregate Consumption
1995	76.906	10.969	0.759	86.003
1996	79.266	11.565	0.803	90.355
1997	82.582	14.523	0.791	96.018
1998	83.931	19.878	0.743	103.457
1999	85.952	24.578	0.694	108.862
2000	87.846	24.561	0.738	110.470
2001	88.900	23.694	0.746	112.810
2002	89.732	22.198	0.834	110.020
2003	92.843	21.015	0.837	114.091
2004	97.434	25.396	0.749	121.981
2005	99.319	30.403	0.766	128.276
2006	98.167	32.141	0.723	127.595
2007	95.464	21.496	0.885	116.695
2008	87.700	11.000	0.950	98.610
2009	75.000	10.000	0.900	84.000

Adapted from data available with US Geological Survey, January 2010.

The share of cement imports in the US domestic consumption peaked in 2006 when it hit 25.2%. That share had come down drastically to 11.90% by 2009. In absolute terms, the cement imports in the US fell from the peak of 32.141 million MT in 2006 to 10 million MT in 2009. However, the exports increased from 0.723 million MT per annum in 2006 to 0.9 million MT in 2009 as many global companies including CEMEX diverted their local production to other countries.

Despite a significant reduction in production volumes in 2008 and 2009, the average production volumes remained at around 91.13 million MT per annum over the five-year period ending 2009. The average figure was about the same as compared to the average production volume of 91.35 million MT per annum over the five-year period ending 2004. However, the average annual cement industry revenue was recorded at around US$ 10.2 billion per annum over the five years ending 2009 as compared to US$ 9.2 billion per annum over the five years ending 2004. The higher realization was due to the uptrend in the average prices of cement and related products since the mid-2000s. The cement industry's EBITDA also decreased from 54.5% of revenue in 2006 to 46% of revenue in 2009.

Exhibit VII (*continued*)

Housing starts, which represented new construction activity in the housing sector in the US, reflected the demand for cement from the housing sector. The starts fell to 550,000 in 2009 from a cyclical peak of 2,068,300 in 2005. On an average, around 21 MT of cement was consumed to construct a single family house with an average size of 2,500 square feet. In the year 2009, the cement consumption in the US fell to 84 million MT while the domestic production was at 75 million MT. In the same year, the industry reported revenue of US$ 8.25 billion, a fall of 14.8 percent as compared to 2008 revenues (Refer to Table B for Cement Industry Revenue in US between 1995 and 2009).

Table B Cement Industry Revenue in the US (1995–2009)

Year	Industry Revenue (In US$ Million)	Growth (%)
1995	7,230.10	8.9
1996	7,727.80	6.9
1997	8,533.40	10.4
1998	9,024.10	5.8
1999	8,955.20	−0.8
2000	8,927.40	−0.3
2001	9,215.40	3.2
2002	9,862.70	7
2003	9,113.50	−7.6
2004	9,930.80	9
2005	10,756.60	8.3
2006	11,522.00	7.1
2007	11,000.00	−4.5
2008	10,000.00	−9.1
2009	8,525.00	−14.8

Adapted from data available with US Geological Survey, January 2010.

Though the new construction activity and prices in the housing sector declined because of the subprime crisis, construction activity in the nonhousing sector helped the cement industry to a certain extent. The nonhousing sector, including industrial buildings, bridges, roads, and other infrastructure projects, was provided financial support by the US administration through various stimulus packages to revive the sagging economy.

Though the years 2008 and 2009 had been tough for the cement industry, analysts expected the future for the industry in the US to be better. They estimated that the cement industry would record a strong cyclical growth in revenues at an average annual growth rate of 4.5% over the next five years till 2014. They expected the average annual production to be around 80.8 million MT during this period. Some analysts expected that domestic companies would resume running their facilities at full capacity to improve their productivity and combat low cost imports from the Asian countries. The cement imports were expected to rebound to 22.5 million MT by 2014.

A significant 77.5% market share in the US cement industry was controlled by the top five players. As of 2009, CEMEX was the leading player with a 25% market share followed by Holcim Inc (17.5%), HeidelbergCement AG (15%), Lafarge North America (15%), and Texas Industries Inc (5%).

Compiled from various sources.

Exhibit VIII   CEMEX–Contractual Obligations as of December 31, 2008 (In US$ Million)

Maturing	Less than 1 year	1–3 years	3–5 years	More than 5 years	2008 Total	2007 Total
Long-term debt	4,161	8,565	1,396	1,876	15,998	18,100
Capital Lease Obligation	14	10	3	—	27	51
Total debt	4,175	8,575	1,393	1,876	16,025	18,151
Operating Leases	214	339	228	179	960	841
Interest Payments on Debt	357	566	213	136	1,272	2,624
Interest rate derivatives	9	53	5	25	92	407
Pension plans and other benefits	164	309	311	825	1,609	1,925
Inactive derivative financial instruments	252	30	95	8	385	—
Total Contractual obligations	71,050	135,641	30,929	41,893	279,513	261,513

Source: CEMEX Annual Report 2008.

Exhibit IX   CEMEX Stock Price Chart

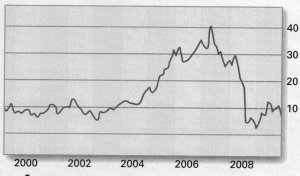

Cemex Stock Price Chart

Source: www.reuters.com.

Exhibit X Mexican Peso vs US$ Chart

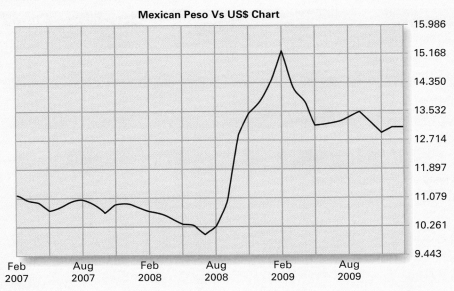

Mexican Peso Vs US$ Chart

Source: www. forexdirectory. net
*X-axis= US$ value in Mexican Pesos
Y-axis= Time Period

Exhibit XI CEMEX Cash Flow Statement (2008) (In US$ millions)

	2008
Operating Activities	
Consolidated Net income	2,278
Non-Cash Items:	
Depreciation and amortization of assets	20,864
Impairment of assets	21,125
Equity in income of associates	(1,098)
Other expenses, net	(4,727)
Comprehensive financing result	28,725
Income taxes paid in cash	(23,562)
Change in working capital, excluding financial expenses and income taxes	1,243
Net cash flows provided by operating activities before comprehensive financing results and income taxes	44,848
Financial expenses paid in cash	(9,951)
Income taxes paid in cash	(3,625)
Net cash flows provided by operating activities before comprehensive financing results and income taxes	31,272
	(continued)

Exhibit XI *(continued)*

	2008
Investing activities	
Property, machinery and equipment, net	(21,248)
Disposal of subsidiaries and associates, net	10,845
Investment derivatives	2,856
Intangible assets and other deferred charges	(1,975)
Long-term assets, net	(2,838)
Others, net	586
Net cash flows used in investing activities	(11,774)
Financing Activities	
Issuance of common stock	6,794
Financing Derivatives	(12,765)
Dividends paid	(7,009)
Repayment of debt, net	(3,710)
Issuance of perpetual debentures, net of interest paid	(1,801)
Noncurrent liabilities, net	1,897
Net cash flows used in financing activities	(16,594)
Cash and investments conversion effect	2,030
Increase in cash and investments	4,934
Cash and investments at beginning of the year	8,670
Cash and investments at the end of year	13,604

Source: CEMEX Annual Report 2008.

Suggested Readings and References:

1. CRH Buying CEMEX Cement Assets, www.domain-b.com, 18 September 2007.
2. William Patalon III, Global Cement Giant CEMEX Looks to Cut Costs, Debt After Rinker Buyout, http://moneymorning.com, December 14, 2007.
3. Fitch: CEMEX Results in Line; Expect Further U.S. Slowdown, www.bnamericas.com, January 30, 2008.
4. Robin Emmott, **Mexico's CEMEX Starts Big Asset Sale to Pay Debt**, w.reuters.com, April 01, 2008.
5. Michael Tian, CEMEX Faces an Uncertain Future, http://quicktake.morningstar.com, October 10, 2008.
6. **S&P Cuts CEMEX CCR To 'BBB-', Outlook** Still Negative, http://uk.reuters.com, October 14, 2008.
7. Neil Gerrard, CEMEX To Cut 6,000 Jobs Worldwide; UK Sales Drop 19%, www.contractjournal.com, October 17, 2008.
8. CEMEX Sells Plant In Canary Islands To Reduce Debt From Rinker Acquisition, www.domain-b.com, 11 November 2008.
9. Shanna McCord, CEMEX Will Shut Down For Six Months, Lay Off More Than 100, www.mercurynews.com, January 09, 2009.
10. CEMEX In Trouble, http://concreteconstruction.net, March 06, 2009.
11. Robin Emmott and Andrea Ricci, No CEMEX Upgrade Soon Even After Debt Refinanced- S&P, www.reuters.com, March 11, 2009.
12. David Lee Smith, **CEMEX's Financial Bungee Jumping**, http://www.fool.com, May 01, 2009.
13. CEMEX to sell Australian operations to Holcim Group, www.domain-b.com, June 15, 2009.
14. Robin Emmott, CEMEX Sell Assets Cheap, Tries To Refinance, www.reuters.com, June 15, 2009.
15. Laura Mandaro, CEMEX Could Sell Stock To Relieve Debt Squeeze, www.marketwatch.com, June 18, 2009.
16. Robin Emmott, **CEMEX's 2nd-qtr** Profit Falls On US Housing Impact, www.reuters.com, July 22, 2008.

17. Robin Emmott and Chris Aspin, CEMEX Sees Worsening U.S. Housing Market, www.reuters.com, July 23, 2008.

18. Robin Emmott, CEMEX Creditors Back Debt Plan; Sales View Bleak, www.reuters.com, July 29, 2009.

19. Robin Emmott, Buy Or Sell-**Mexico's** CEMEX Fate Hangs On Debt Talks, www.reuters.com, July 30, 2009.

20. Gabriela Lopez, **Mexico's CEMEX Wins Time On $1.2 Bln Debt,** www.reuters.com, July 31, 2009.

21. Gabriela Lopez, **Mexico's CEMEX Says All Creditors Support Debt Deal,** www.reuters.com, August 10, 2009.

22. Robert Campbell, CEMEX Gains On Debt News, But Questions Remain, www.reuters.com, August 11, 2009.

23. Anthony Harrup, CEMEX Given Rinker Debt Lifeline, www.theaustralian.com.au, August 12, 2009.

24. Thomas Black, CEMEX Extends Payments on $15 Billion in Debt to 2014, www.bloomberg.com, August 14, 2009.

25. Patricia Oey, CEMEX Completes Debt Restructuring, www.morningstar.com, August 14, 2009.

26. Chris Sleight, CEMEX to Launch US $1.8 Billion Share Issue, www.khl.com, September 09, 2009.

27. CEMEX Reports Third Quarter 2009 Results, http://news.moneycentral.msn.com, October 27, 2009.

28. Thomas Black, **CEMEX Should Have Financed 'More Conservatively': Week Ahead,** www.bloomberg.com, November 02, 2009.

29. Kejal Vyas, CEMEX Raises $1.25B, EUR350M In Bond Offer As Buyers Step Up, http://online.wsj.com, December 09, 2009.

30. Robin Emmott, **Mexico's CEMEX Sells Nearly $1.8 bn in Bonds,** www.reuters.com, December 09, 2009.

31. Veronica Navarro Espinosa, CEMEX Prices $500 Million of 2016 Bonds in Re-Opening, www.businessweek.com, January 13, 2010.

32. Gabriela Lopez, CEMEX Juggles Debt But US Still a Worry, ww.forexyard.com, January 19, 2010.

33. Thomas Black, CEMEX Falls as 2010 EBITDA Forecast Trails Estimates, www.bloomberg.com, January 27, 2010.

34. **Mexico's CEMEX Reports $265 Million Profit For 4q,** www.businessweek.com.

35. www.cio.com.

36. www.sec.gov.

37. www.cemex.com.

Endnotes

1 Gabriela Lopez, "CEMEX Juggles Debt But U.S.Still a Worry," ww.forexyard.com, January 19, 2010.

2 Thomas Black, "CEMEX Extends Payments on $15 Billion in Debt to 2014," www.bloomberg.com, August 14, 2009.

3 The sub-prime crisis that emerged in the US in late 2007 led to a crash in the prices of several asset classes. Investments of several financial institutions and individuals incurred deep losses. Several industries eliminated thousands of jobs resulting in an economic slowdown and a global financial crisis.

4 Thomas Black, Cemex Falls as 2010 EBITDA Forecast Trails Estimates, www.bloomberg.com, January 27, 2010.

5 Both the founder and his grandson, who eventually became the CEO of Cementos Mexicano, were given the same name, Lorenzo Zambrano.

6 Lorenzo Zambrano spent his teenage years in Missouri Military Academy in Mexico. He earned an engineering graduate degree from the Institute Tecnologico in Monterrey and an MBA degree from Stanford University.

7 Cementos Anahuac was a cement company in Mexico with two plants and total capacity of 4 million MT per year.

8 Cementos Tolteca was a cement company in Mexico with seven plants and total capacity of 6.8 million MT per year.

9 Founded in 1927, Cementos Diamante was a Colombia-based company engaged in the production, sale, and distribution of cement and ready-made concrete.

10 Founded in 1930, Southdown was a Houston, Texas-based cement and ready-mix concrete manufacturing company.

11 The RMC Group, formerly known as Ready Mix Concrete PLC, was founded in 1930 and was based in Egham.

12 One of the important criteria in CEMEX's acquisition strategy was that the acquisition should contribute to its capital structure. By that, the company meant that

it should manage its investment grade rating even after acquiring the target company. 'BBB-' and above rating awarded by Standard & Poor's rating services company are considered as investment grade rating in the US.

13 Volume weighted average price is the ratio of value traded to the total volume over a particular period of time. Value traded is the summation of the product of share volume and traded price of each transaction and volume is the total volume of shares traded during a particular period. VWAP = X (number of shares bought X share price)/Total number of shares.

14 Aggregates are inert granular materials such as sand, gravel, or crushed stone that along with water and cement are an essential ingredient for concrete.

15 On February 22, 2010, US$ 1= A$ 1.10965.

16 The US$ 19.9 billion debt included Rinker's US$ 1.1 billion outstanding debt at the time of acquisition.

17 Robin Emmott, "Mexico's Cemex Starts Big Asset Sale to Pay Debt," www.reuters.com, April 01, 2008.

18 Standard & Poor's is one of the leading credit rating agencies based in the US. It is a division of McGraw Hill and publishes financial research reports on different types of financial securities. It was founded in 1860.

19 "S&P Cuts Cemex CCR to 'BBB-', Outlook Still Negative," http://uk.reuters.com, October 14, 2008.

20 Founded in 1913, Fitch Ratings is one of the leading credit rating agencies dual head quartered at London and New York.

21 Robin Emmott and Andrea Ricci, "No Cemex Upgrade Soon Even After Debt Refinanced- S&P," www.reuters.com, March 11, 2009.

22 On February 22, 2010, US$ 1= MXP 12.8087.

23 Gabriela Lopez, "CEMEX Juggles Debt But US Still a Worry," ww.forexyard.com, January 19, 2010.

3M: The Second Century

Charles W.L. Hill
University of Washington

Established in 1902, 3M was one of the largest technology driven enterprises in the United States with annual sales of $26 billion, (63% of which were outside the United States) by 2010. The company was solidly profitable, earning $4.09 billion in net income in 2010, and generating a return on invested capital of 20.53%. Throughout its history, 3M's researchers had driven much of the company's growth. In 2010, the company sold some 55,000 products, including Post-it Notes, Flexible Circuits, Scotch Tape, abrasives, specialty chemicals, Thinsulate insulation products, Nexcare bandage, optical films, fiber optic connectors, drug delivery systems and much more. Around 7,350 of the company's 80,000 employees were technical employees. 3M's annual R&D budget exceeded $1.4 billion. The company had garnered over 8,000 patents since 1990, with 589 new patents awarded in 2010 alone. 3M was organized into 35 different business units grouped together into 6 main areas; consumer and office products; display and graphics; electronics and telecommunications; health care; industrial and transportation; safety, security and protection services (see Exhibit 1 for details).

The company's 100-year anniversary in 2002 was a time for celebration, but also one for strategic reflection. During the prior decade, 3M had grown profits and sales by 6–7% per annum, a respectable figure, but one that lagged behind the growth rates achieved by some other technology-based enterprises and diversified industrial enterprises like General Electric. In 2001, 3M took a step away from its past when the company hired James McNerney Jr. as CEO, the first outsider to hold this position. McNerney, who joined 3M after heading up GE's fast growing medical equipment business (and losing out in the race to replace legendary GE CEO, Jack Welch), was quick to signal that he wanted 3M to accelerate its growth rate. McNerney set an ambitious target for 3M–to grow sales by 11% per annum

and profits by 12% per annum. Many wondered if McNerney could achieve this without damaging the innovation engine that had propelled 3M to its current stature. The question remained unanswered, as McNerney left to run the Boeing Company in 2005. His successor, however, George Buckley, another outsider, seemed committed to continuing on the course McNerney had set for the company.

The History of 3M: Building Innovative Capabilities

The 3M story begins in 1902 when 5 Minnesota business men established the Minnesota Mining and Manufacturing company to mine a mineral that they thought was corundum, which is ideal for making sandpaper. The mineral, however, turned out to be low-grade anorthosite, nowhere near as suitable for making sandpaper, and the company nearly failed. To try and salvage the business, 3M turned to making the sandpaper using materials purchased from another source.

In 1907, 3M hired a 20-year old business student, William McKnight, as assistant bookkeeper. This turned out to be a pivotal move in the history of the company. The hardworking McKnight soon made his mark. By 1929, he was CEO of the company, and in 1949 he became chairman of 3M's board of directors, a position that he held until 1966.

From Sandpaper to Post-it Notes

It was McKnight, then 3M's president, who hired the company's first scientist, Richard Carlton, in 1921. Around the same time, McKnight's interest had been peaked by an odd request from a Philadelphian printer named Francis Okie for samples of every sandpaper grit size that 3M made. McKnight dispatched

Exhibit 1 Financial Facts—Year-End 2010

3M is one of 30 companies in the Dow Jones Industrial Average and also is a component of the Standard & Poor's 500 Index.

Sales	
Worldwide	$26.66 billion
International	$17.45 billion
65 percent of company's total	
Net Income	
Net Income	$4.085 billion
Percent to sales	15.3 percent
Earnings per share—diluted	$5.63
Taxes	
Income tax expense	$1.592 billion
Dividends	
(Paid every quarter since 1916) Cash dividends per share	$2.10
One original share, if held, is now	3,072 shares
R&D and Related Expenditures	
For 2010	$1.434 billion
Total for last five years	$6.055 billion
Capital Spending	
For 2010	$1.091 billion
Total for last five years	$6.055 billion
Employees	
Worldwide	80,057
United States	32,955
International	47,102

Organization

- More than 35 business units, organized into six businesses: Consumer and Office; Display and Graphics; Electro and Communications; Health Care; Industrial and Transportation; Safety, Security and Protection Services

- Operations in more than 65 countries—38 international companies with manufacturing operations, 35 with laboratories

- In the United States, operations in 28 states

Patents	
U.S. patents awarded in 2010	589

Source: 3M Website http://phx.corporate-ir.net/phoenix.zhtml?c=80574&p=irol-irhome

3M's East coast sales manager to find out why Okie wanted the samples. The sales manager discovered that Okie had invented a new kind of sandpaper that he had patented. It was waterproof sandpaper that could be used with water or oil to reduce dust and decrease the friction that marred auto finishes. In addition, the lack of dust reduced the poisoning associated with inhaling the dust of paint that had a high lead content. Okie had a problem though; he had no financial backers to commercialize the sandpaper. 3M quickly stepped in to the breach, purchasing the rights to Okie's Wetordry waterproof sandpaper, and hiring the young printer to come and join Richard Carlton in 3M's lab. Wetordry sandpaper revolutionized the sandpaper industry, and was the driver of significant growth at 3M.

Another key player in the company's history, Richard Drew, also joined 3M in 1921. Hired straight out of the University of Minnesota, Drew would round out the trio of scientists, Carlton, Okie and Drew, who under McKnight's leadership would do much to shape 3M's innovative organization.

McKnight charged the newly hired Drew with developing a stronger adhesive to better bind the grit for sandpaper to paper backing. While experimenting with adhesives, Drew accidentally developed a weak adhesive that had an interest quality—if placed on the back of a strip of paper and stuck to a surface, the strip of paper could be peeled off the surface it was adhered to without leaving any adhesive residue on that surface. This discovery gave Drew an epiphany. He had been visiting auto-body paint shops to see how 3M's Wetordry sand paper was used, and he noticed that there was a problem with paint running. His epiphany was to cover the back of a strip of paper with his weak adhesive, and use it as "masking tape" to cover parts of the auto's body that were not to be painted. An excited Drew took his idea to McKnight, and explained how masking tape might create an entirely new business for 3M. McKnight reminded Drew that he had been hired to fix a specific problem, and pointedly suggested that he concentrate only on doing that.

Chastised, Dew went back to his lab, but he could not get the idea out of his mind, so he continued to work on it at night, long after everyone else had gone home. Drew succeeded in perfecting the masking tape product, and then went to visit several auto-body shops to show them his innovation. He quickly received several commitments for orders. Drew then went to see McKnight again. He told him that he had continued to work on the masking tape idea on his own time, had perfected the product, and got several customers interested in purchasing it. This time it was McKnight's turn to be chastised. Realizing that he had almost killed a good business idea, McKnight reversed his original position, and gave Drew the go ahead to pursue the idea.[1]

Introduced into the market in 1925, Drew's invention of masking tape represented the first significant product diversification at 3M. Company legend has it that this incident was also the genesis for 3M's famous 15% rule. Reflecting on Drew's work, both McKnight and Carlton both agreed that technical people could disagree with management, and should be allowed to do some experimentation on their own. The company then established a norm that technical people could spend up to 15% of their own workweek on projects that might benefit the consumer, without having to justify the project to their manager.

Drew himself was not finished. In the late-1920s, he was working with cellophane, a product that had been invented by DuPont, when lightning struck for a second time. Why, Drew wondered, couldn't cellophane be coated with an adhesive and used as a sealing tape? The result was Scotch Cellophane Tape. The first batch was delivered to a customer in September 1930, and Scotch Tape went on to become one of 3M's best selling products. Years later, Drew noted: "Would there have been any masking or cellophane tape if it hadn't been for earlier 3M research on adhesive binders for 3M™ Wetordry™ Abrasive Paper? Probably not!"[2]

Over the years, other scientists followed Drew's footsteps at 3M, creating a wide range of innovative products by leveraging existing technology and applying it to new areas. Two famous examples illustrate how many of these innovations occurred—the invention of Scotch Guard, and the development of the ubiquitous "Post-it Notes."

The genesis of Scotchgard was in 1953, when a 3M scientist named Patsy Sherman was working on a new kind of rubber for jet aircraft fuel lines. Some of the latex mixture splashed onto a pair of canvas tennis shoes. Over time, the spot stayed clean while the rest of the canvas soiled. Sherman enlisted the help of fellow chemist Sam Smith. Together they began to investigate polymers, and it didn't take long for them to realize that they were on to something. They discovered an oil and water repellant substance, based on the fluorocarbon fluid used in air conditioners, which had enormous potential for protecting fabrics from stains. It took several years before the team perfected a way to apply the treatment using water as the carrier, thereby making it economically feasible for use as a finish in textile plants.

Three years after the accidental spill, the first rain and stain repellent for use on wool was announced. Experience and time revealed that one product could not, however, effectively protect all fabrics, so 3M continued working, producing a wide range of Scotchgard products that could be used to protect all kinds of fabrics.[3]

The story of Post-it Notes began with Spencer Silver, a senior scientist studying adhesives.[4] In 1968, Silver had developed an adhesive with properties like no other; it was a pressure sensitive adhesive that would adhere to a surface, but was weak enough to easily peel off the surface and leave no residue. Silver spent several years shopping his adhesive around 3M, to no avail. It was a classic case of a technology is search of a product. Then, one day in 1973, Art Fry, a new product development researcher who had attended one of Silver's seminars, was singing in his church choir. He was frustrated that his bookmarks kept falling out of his hymn book, when he had a "Eureka" moment. Fry realized that Silver's adhesive could be used to make a wonderfully reliable bookmark.

Fry went to work the next day, and using his 15% time, started to develop the bookmark. When he started using the sample to write notes to his boss, Fry suddenly realized that he had stumbled on a much bigger potential use for the product. Before the product could be commercialized, however, Fry had to solve a host of technical and manufacturing problems. With the support of his boss, Fry persisted and after 18 months the product development effort moved from 15% time to a formal development effort funded by 3M's own seed capital.

The first Post-it Notes were test marketed in 1977 in 4 major cities, but customers were lukewarm at best. This did not support the experience within 3M, where people in Fry's division were using samples all the time to write messages to each other. Further research revealed that the test marketing effort, which focused on ads and brochures, didn't resonate well with consumers, who didn't seem to value Post-it Notes until they had the actual product in their hands. In 1978, 3M tried again, this time

descending on Boise, Idaho, where they handed out samples. Follow up research revealed that 90% of consumers who tried the product said they would buy it. Armed with this knowledge, 3M rolled out the national launch of Post-it Notes in 1980. The product subsequently became a best seller.

Institutionalizing Innovation

Early on, McKnight set an ambitious target for 3M–a 10% annual increase in sales and 25% profit target. He also indicated how he thought that should be achieved—with a commitment to plow 5% of sales back into R&D every year. The question, however, was how to ensure that 3M would continue to produce new products?

The answer was not apparent all at once, but rather evolved over the years from experience. A prime example was the 15% rule, which developed after McKnight's experience with Drew. In addition to the 15% rule and the continued commitment to push money back into R&D, a number of other mechanisms evolved at 3M to spur innovation.

Initially, research took place in the business units that made and sold products, but by the 1930s, 3M had already diversified into several different fields, thanks in large part to the efforts of Drew and others. McKnight and Carlton realized that there was a need for a central research function. In 1937 they established a central research laboratory which was charged with supplementing the work of product divisions and undertaking long-term basic research. From the outset, the researchers at the lab were multidisciplinary, with people from different scientific disciplines often working next to each other on research benches.

As the company continued to grow, it became clear that there was a need for some mechanism to knit together the company's increasingly diverse business operations. This led to the establishment of the 3M Technical Forum in 1951. The goal of Technical Forum was to foster idea sharing, discussion, and problem solving between technical employees located in different divisions and the central research laboratory. The Technical Forum sponsored "problem solving sessions" at which businesses would present their most recent technical nightmares in the hope that somebody might be able to suggest a solution—and that often was the case. The forum also established an annual event in which each division put up a booth to show off its latest technologies. Chapters were also created to focus on specific disciplines, such as polymer chemistry or coating processes.

During the 1970s, the Technical Forum cloned itself, establishing forums in Australia and England. By 2001, the forum had grown to 9,500 members in 8 U.S. locations and 19 other countries, becoming an international network of researchers who could share ideas, solve problems, and leverage technology.

According to Marylee Paulson, who coordinated the Technical Forum from 1979 to 1992, the great virtue of the Technical Forum is to cross-pollinate ideas:

> 3M has lots of polymer chemists. They may be in tape; they may be medical or several other divisions. The forum pulls them across 3M to share what they know. It's a simple but amazingly effective way to bring like minds together.[5]

In 1999, 3M created another unit within the company, 3M Innovative Properties (3M, IPC) to leverage technical know-how. 3M IPC is explicitly charged with protecting and leveraging 3M's intellectual property around the world. At 3M there had been a long tradition that while divisions "own" their products, the company has a whole "owns" the underlying technology, or intellectual property. One task of 3M IPC is to find ways in which 3M technology can be applied across business units to produce unique marketable products. Historically, the company has been remarkably successful at leveraging company technology to produce new product ideas (see Exhibit 2 for some examples).

Another key to institutionalizing innovation at 3M has been the principle of "patient money." The basic idea is that producing revolutionary new products requires substantial long-term investments, and often repeated failures, before a major payoff occurs.

Exhibit 2   Examples of Leveraging Technology at 3M[6]

Richard Miller, a corporate scientist in 3M Pharmaceuticals, began experimental development of an antiherpes medicinal cream in 1982. After several years of development, his research team found that the interferon-based materials they were working with could be applied to any skin-based virus. The innovative chemistry they were working with was applied topically and was more effective than other compounds on the market. They found that the cream was particularly effective to inhibiting the growth mechanism of genital warts. Competitive materials on the market at the time were caustic and tended to be painful. Miller's team obtained FDA approval for its Aldara (imiquimod) line of topical patient-applied creams in 1997.

Miller then applied the same Aldara-based chemical mechanism to basal cell carcinomas and found that, here too, it was particularly effective to restricting the growth of the skin cancer. "The patient benefit is quite remarkable," says Miller. New results in efficacy have been presented for treating skin cancers. His team recently completed phase III clinical testing and expects to apply later this year for FDA approval for this disease preventative. This material is already FDA approved for use in the treatment of genital warts. Doctors are free to choose to use it to treat those patients with skin cancers.

Andrew Ouderkirk is a corporate scientist in 3M's Film & Light Management Technology Center. 3M has been working in light management materials applied to polymer-based films since the 1930s, according to Ouderkirk. Every decade since then, 3M has introduced some unique thin-film structure for a specific customer application from high-performance safety reflectors for street signs, to polarized lighting products. Every decade, 3Ms technology base has become more specialized and more sophisticated. Their technology has now reached the point at which they can produce multiple-layer interference films, each to 100-nm thicknesses, and hold the tolerances on each layer to within +/− 3 nm. "Our laminated films are now starting to compete with vacuum-coated films in some applications," says Ouderkirk.

Rick Weiss is technical director of 3M's Microreplication Technology Center, one of 3M's 12 core technology centers. The basic microreplication technology was discovered In the early-1960s, when 3M researchers were developing the fresnel lenses for overhead projectors. 3M scientists have expanded upon this technology to use it on a wide variety of applications including optical reflectors for solar collectors, and adhesive coatings with air bleed ribs that allow large area films to be applied without allowing the characteristic "bubbles" appear. Weiss is currently working on development of dimensionally precise barrier ribs that can be applied to separate the individual "gas" cells on the new high resolution large screen commercial plasma displays. Other applications include fluid management where capillary action can be used in biological testing systems to split a drop of blood into a large number of parts.

The principle can be traced back to 3M's early days. It took the company 12 years before its initial sandpaper business started to show a profit, a fact that drove home the importance of taking the long view. Throughout the company's history, similar examples can be found. Scotchlite reflective sheeting, now widely used on road signs, didn't show much profit for 10 years. The same was true of flurochemicals and duplicating products. Patent money doesn't mean substantial funding for long periods of time, however. Rather, it might imply that a small group of 5 researchers is supported for 10 years while they work on a technology.

More generally, if a researcher creates a new technology or idea, they can begin working on it using 15% of their time. If the idea shows promise, they may request seed capital from their business unit managers to develop it further. If that funding is denied, which can occur, they are free to take the idea to any other 3M business unit. Unlike many other companies, requests for seed capital do not require that researchers draft detailed business plans that are reviewed by top management; that comes later in the process. As one former senior technology manager has noted:

> In the early stages of a new product or technology, it shouldn't be overly managed. If we start asking for business plans too early and insist on tight financial evaluations, we'll kill an idea or surely slow it down.[7]

Explaining the patent money philosophy, Ron Baukol, a former Executive Vice President of 3M's international operations, and a manager who started as a researcher, has noted that:

> You just know that some things are going to be worth working on, and that requires technological patience ... you don't put too much money into the investigation, but you keep one to five people working on it for twenty years if you have to. You do that because you know that, once you have cracked the code, it's going to be big.[8]

An internal review of 3M's innovation process in the early-1980s concluded that despite the liberal process for funding new product ideas, some promising ideas did not receive funding from business units, or the central research budget. This led to the establishment of Genesis Grants, which provide up to $100,000 in seed capital for projects that do not get funded through 3M's regular channels, in 1985.

About a dozen of these grants will be given every year. One of the recipients of these grants, a project that focused on creating a multilayered reflective film, has subsequently produced a break though reflective technology that may have applications in a wide range of businesses, from better reflective strips on road signs to computer displays and the reflective linings in light fixtures. Company estimates in 2002 suggested that the commercialization of this technology might ultimately generate $1 billion in sales for 3M.

Underlying the patient money philosophy is recognition that innovation is a very risky business. 3M has long acknowledged that failure is an accepted and essential part of the new product development process. As former 3M CEO Lew Lehr once noted:

> We estimate that 60% of our formal new product development programs never make it. When this happens, the important thing is to not punish the people involved.[9]

In an effort to reduce the probability of failure, in the 1960s, 3M started to establish a process for auditing the product development efforts ongoing in the company's business units. The idea has been to provide a peer review, or technical audit, of major development projects taking place in the company. A typical technical audit team is composed of 10–15 business and technical people, including technical directors and senior scientists from other divisions. The audit team will look at the strengths and weaknesses of a development program, and its probability of success, both from a technical standpoint and a business standpoint. The team then will make non-binding recommendations, but are normally taken very seriously by the managers of a project. For example, if an audit team concludes that a project has enormous potential, but is terribly underfunded, managers of the unit would often increase the funding level. Of course, the converse can also happen, and in many instances, the audit team can provide useful feedback and technical ideas that can help a development team to improve their project's chance of success.

By the 1990s, the continuing growth of 3M had produced a company that was simultaneously pursuing a vast array of new product ideas. This was a natural outcome of 3M's decentralized and bottom up approach to innovation, but it was problematic in one crucial respect, the company's R&D resources were being spread too thinly over a wide range of opportunities, resulting in potentially major projects being under funded. To try and channel R&D resources into projects that had blockbuster potential, 3M introduced what was known as the Pacing Plus Program in 1994.

The program asked businesses to select a small number of programs that would receive priority funding, but 3M's senior executives made the final decision on which programs were to be selected for the Pacing Plus Program. An earlier attempt to do this in 1990 had been met with limited success because each sector in 3M submitted as many as 200 programs. The Pacing Plus Program narrowed the list down to 25 key programs that, by 1996, were receiving some 20% of 3M's entire R&D funds (by the early-2000s the number of projects funded under the Pacing Plus Program had grown to 60). The focus was on "leapfrog technologies," revolutionary ideas that might change the basis of competition and lead to entirely new technology platforms that might in typical 3M fashion, spawn an entire range of new products.

To further foster a culture of entrepreneurial innovation and risk taking, 3M established a number of reward and recognition programs to honor employees who make significant contributions to the company. These include the Carton Society Award, which honors employees for outstanding career scientific achievements, and the Circle of Technical Excellence and Innovation Award, which recognizes people who have made exceptional contributions to 3M's technical capabilities, among others.

Another key component of 3M's innovative culture has been an emphasis on dual career tracks. Right for its early days, many of the key players in 3M's history, people like Richard Drew, chose to stay in research, turning down opportunities to go into the management side of the business. Over the years, this became formalized in a dual career path. Today, technical employees can choose to follow a technical career path or a management career path, with equal advancement opportunities. This can allow researchers to develop their technical professional interests, without being financially penalized for not going into management.

Although 3M's innovative culture emphasizes the role of technical employees in producing innovations, the company also has a strong tradition of emphasizing that new product ideas often come from watching customers at work. Richard Drew's original idea for masking tape, for example, came from watching workers use 3M Wetordry sandpaper

in auto body shops. As with much else at 3M, the tone was set by McKnight, who insisted that salespeople needed to "get behind the smokestacks" of 3M customers, going onto the factory floor, talking to workers, and finding out what problems they were experiencing. Over the years, this theme had become ingrained in 3M's culture, with salespeople often requesting time to watch customers work, and then brining their insights about customer problems back into their organization.

By the mid-1990s, McKnight's notion of getting behind the smokestacks had evolved into the idea that 3M could learn a tremendous amount from what were termed "lead users," who were customers working in very demanding conditions. Over the years, 3M had observed that in many cases, customers can be innovators, developing new products to solve problems that they face in their workplace. This was most likely to occur for customers working in very demanding conditions. To take advantage of this process, 3M has instituted a lead user process in the company in which cross-functional teams from a business unit observe how customers work in demanding situations.

For example, 3M now has a $100 million business selling surgical drapes, which are drapes backed with adhesives that are used to cover parts of a body during surgery and help prevent infection. As an aid to new product development, 3M's surgical drapes business had formed a cross-functional team that observed surgeons at work in very demanding situations–including on battlefields, in hospitals in developing nations, and in veterinarian's offices. The result was a new set of product ideas, including low-cost surgical drapes that were affordable in developing nations, and devices for coating a patient's skin and surgical instruments with antimicrobial substances that would reduce the chance of infection during surgery.[10]

Driving the entire innovation machine at 3M has been a series of stretch goals set by top managers. The goals date back to 3M's early days and McKnight's ambitious growth targets. In 1977, the company established "Challenge 81," which called for 25% of sales to come from products that had been on the market for less than 5 years by 1981. By the 1990s, the goal had been raised to the requirement that 30% of sales should come from products that had been on the market less than 4 years.

The flip side of these goals was that many products and businesses that had been 3M staples were phased out over the years. More than 20 of the businesses that were 3M mainstays in 1980, for example, had been phased out by 2000. Analysts estimate that sales from mature products at 3M generally fall by 3% to 4% per annum. The company has a long history of inventing businesses, leading the market for long periods of time, and then shutting those businesses down, or selling them off, when they can no longer meet 3M's own demanding growth targets. Notable examples include the duplicating business, a business 3M invented with Thermo-Fax copiers (which were ultimately made obsolete my Xerox's patented technology) and the video and audio magnetic tape business. The former division was sold off in 1985, and the latter in 1995. In both cases, the company exited these areas because they had become low growth commodity businesses, which could not generate the kind of top line growth for which 3M was looking.

Still, 3M was by no means invulnerable in the realm of innovation, and on occasion squandered huge opportunities, such as the document copying business. 3M invented this business in 1951 when it introduced the world's first commercially successful Thermo-Fax copier (which used specially coated 3M paper to copy original typed documents). 3M dominated the world copier business until 1970, when Xerox surpassed the company with its revolutionary xerographic technology that used plane paper to make copies. 3M anticipated Xerox' move, but rather than try and develop their own plain paper copier, the company invested funds in trying to improve its (increasingly obsolete) copying technology. It wasn't until 1975 that 3M introduced its own plain paper copier, and by then it was too late. Strangely, 3M turned down the chance to acquire Xerox' technology 20 years earlier, when the company's founders had approached 3M.

Building the Organization

McKnight, a strong believer in decentralization, organized the company into product divisions in 1948, making 3M one of the early adopters of this organizational form. Each division was set up as an individual profit center that had the power, autonomy and resources to run independently. At the same time, certain functions remained centralized, including significant R&D, human resources, and finance.

McKnight wanted to keep the divisions small enough that people had a chance to be entrepreneurial, and focused on the customer. A key philosophy of McKnight's was "divide and grow." Put simply, when a division became too big, some of its embryonic businesses were developed into a new division. Not only did this new division then typically attain higher growth rates, but the original division had to find new drivers of growth to offset the contribution of the businesses that had gained independence. This drove the search for further innovations.

At 3M, the process of organic diversification by splitting divisions became known as "renewal." The examples of renewal within 3M are legion. A copying machine project for Thermo-Fax copiers grew into the Office Products Division. When Magnetic Recording Materials was developed from the Electrical Products division, it had become its own division, and then in turn spawned a spate of divisions.

However, this organic process was not without its downside. By the early-1990s some of 3M's key customers were frustrated that they had to do business with a large number of different 3M divisions. In some cases, there could be representatives from 10–20 different 3M divisions calling on the same customer. To cope with this problem, 3M started to assign key account representatives to sell 3M products directly to major customers in 1992. These representatives typically worked across divisional lines. Implementing the strategy required many of 3M's general managers to give up some of their autonomy and power, but the solution seemed to work well, particularly for 3M's consumer and office divisions.

Underpinning the organization that McKnight put in place was his own management philosophy. As explained in a 1948 document, his basic management philosophy consisted of the following values:

As our business grows, it becomes increasingly necessary to delegate responsibility and to encourage men and women to exercise their initiative. This requires considerable tolerance. Those men and women to whom we delegate authority and responsibility, if they are good people, are going to want to do their jobs in their own way.

Mistakes will be made. But if a person is essentially right, the mistakes he or she makes are not as serious in the long run as the mistakes management will make if it undertakes to tell those in authority exactly how they must do their jobs.

Management that is destructively critical when mistakes are made kills initiative. And it's essential that we have many people with initiative if we are to continue to grow.[11]

At just 3% per annum, employee turnover rate at 3M has long been among the lowest in corporate America, a fact that is often attributed to the tolerant, empowering and family-like corporate culture that McKnight helped to establish. Reinforcing this culture has been a progressive approach toward employee compensation and retention. In the depths of the Great Depression, 3M was able to avoid laying off employees while many others didn't because the company's innovation engine was able to keep building new businesses even through the most difficult economic times.

In many ways, 3M was ahead of its time in management philosophy and human resource practices. The company introduced its first profit sharing plan in 1916, and McKnight instituted a pension plan in 1930 and an employee stock purchase plan in 1950. McKnight himself was convinced that people would be much more likely to be loyal in a company if they had a stake within it. 3M also developed a policy of promoting from within, and of giving its employees a plethora of career opportunities within the company.

Going International

The first steps abroad occurred in the 1920s. There were some limited sales of Wetordry sandpaper in Europe during the early-1920s. These increased after 1929 when 3M joined the Durex Corporation, a joint venture for international abrasive product sales in which 3M was involved, along with 8 other United States companies. In 1950, however, the Department of Justice alleged that the Durex Corporation was a mechanism for achieving collusion among U.S. abrasive manufacturers, and a judge ordered that the corporation be dissolved. After the Durex Corporation was dissolved in 1951, 3M was left with a sandpaper factory in Britain, a small plant in France, a sales office in Germany, and a tape factory in Brazil. International sales at this point amounted to no more than 5% of 3M's total revenues.

Although 3M opposed the dissolution of the Durex Corporation, in retrospect it turned out to be one of the most important events in the company's history, for it forced the corporation to build its own international operations. By 2010, international sales amounted to 63% of total revenues.

In 1952, Clarence Sampair was put in charge of 3M's international operations and was responsible for launching them. He was given considerable strategic and operational independence. Sampair and his successor, Maynard Patterson, worked hard to protect the international operations from getting caught in the red tape of a major corporation. For example, Patterson recounts how:

> I asked Em Monteiro to start a small company in Columbia. I told him to pick a key person he wanted to take with him "Go start a company," I said, "and no one from St Paul is going to visit you unless you ask for them. We'll stay out of your way, and if someone sticks his nose in your business you call me."[12]

The international businesses were grouped into an International Division that Sampair lead. From the beginning, the company insisted that foreign ventures pay their own way. In addition, 3M's international companies were expected to pay a 5% to 10% royalty to the corporate head office. Starved of working capital, 3M's International Division relied heavily upon local borrowing to fund local operations, a fact that forced those operations to quickly pay their own way.

The international growth at 3M typically occurred in stages. The company would start by exporting to a country and working through sales subsidiaries. In that way, it began to understand the country, the local marketplace, and the local business environment. Next, 3M established warehouses in each nation, and stocked those with goods paid for in local currency. The next phase involved converting products to the sizes and packaging forms that the local market conditions, customs and culture dictated. 3M would ship jumbo-sized rolls of products from the United States, which were then broken down and repackaged for each country. The next stage was designing and building plants, buying machinery and making the plants operational. Over the years, R&D functions were often added, and by the 1980s, considerable R&D was being done outside of the United States.

Both Sampair and Patterson set an innovative, entrepreneurial framework that according to the company, still guides 3M's International Operations today. The philosophy can be reduced to several key and simple commitments: (1) Get in early (within the company, the strategy is known as FIDO—"First in Defeats Others"); (2) Hire talented and motivated local people; (3) Become a good corporate citizen of the country; (4) Grow with the local economy; (5) American products are not one-size-fits-all around the world—tailor products to fit local needs; (6) Enforce patents in local countries.

As 3M stepped into the international market vacuum, foreign sales surged from less than 5% in 1951 to 42% by 1979. By the end of the 1970s, 3M was beginning to understand how important it was to integrate the international operations more closely with the U.S. operations, and to build innovative capabilities overseas. It expanded the company's international R&D presence (there are now more than 2,200 technical employees outside the U.S.), built closer ties between the U.S. and foreign research organizations, and started to transfer more managerial and technical employees between businesses in different countries.

In 1978, the company started the Pathfinder Program to encourage the innovation of new products and new business initiatives born outside the United States. By 1983, products developed under the initiative were generating sales of over $150 million a year. For example, 3M Brazil invented a low-cost, hot-melt adhesive from local raw materials, 3M Germany teamed up with Sumitomo 3M of Japan (a joint venture with Sumitomo) to develop electronic connectors with new features for the worldwide electronics industry, and 3M Philippines developed a Scotch-Brite cleaning pad shaped like a foot after learning that Filipinos polished floors with their feet. On the back of such developments, in 1992, international operations exceeded 50% for the first time in the company's history.

By the 1990s, 3M started to shift away from a country-by-country management structure to more regional management. Drivers behind this development included the fall of trade barriers, the rise of trading blocks such as the European Union and NAFTA, and the need to drive down costs in the face of intense global competition. The first European Business Center (EBC) was created in 1991 to manage 3M's chemical business across Europe. The EBC was responsible for product development, manufacturing, and sales and marketing for Europe, but also for paying attention to local country requirements. Other EBCs soon followed, such as EBCs for Disposable Products and Pharmaceuticals.

As the millennium ended, 3M was transforming its company into a transnational organization characterized by an integrated network of businesses that spanned the globe. The goal was to get the right mix of global scale to deal with competitive pressures, while at the same time maintain 3M's traditional focus on local market differences and decentralize R&D capabilities.

The New Era

The DeSimone Years

In 1991, Desi DeSimone had become CEO of 3M. A long time 3M employee, the Canadian born DeSimone was the epitome of a 21st century manager—he had made his name by building 3M's Brazilian business and spoke 5 languages fluently. Unlike most prior 3M CEOs, DeSimone came from the manufacturing side of the business, rather than the technical aide. He soon received praise for managing 3M through the recession of the early-1990s. By the late-1990s, however, his leadership had come under fire from both inside and outside the company.

In 1998 and 1999, the company missed its earnings targets, and the stock price fell as disappointed investors sold. Sales were flat, profit margins fell, and earnings slumped by 50%. The stock had underperformed the widely tracked S&P 500 Stock Index for most of the 1980s and 1990s.

One cause of the earnings slump in the late-1990s was 3M's sluggish response to the 1997 Asian crisis. During the Asian crisis, the value of several Asian currencies fell by as much as 80% against the U.S. dollar in a matter of months. 3M generated 1/4 of its sales from Asia, but it was slow to cut costs there in the face of slumping demand following the collapse of currency values. At the same time, a flood of cheap Asian products cut into 3M's market share in the United States and Europe as lower currency values made Asian products much cheaper.

Another problem was that for all of its vaunted innovative capabilities, 3M had not produced a new blockbuster product since Post-it Notes. Most of the new products produced during the 1990s were just improvements over existing products, not truly new products.

DeSimone was also blamed for not pushing 3M hard enough earlier in the decade to reduce costs. An example was the company's supply chain excellence program. Back in 1995, 3M's inventory was turning over just 3.5 times a year—sub-par for manufacturing. An internal study suggested that every half-point increase in inventory turnover could reduce 3M's working capital needs by $700 million, and boost its return on invested capital. But by 1998, 3M had made no progress on this front.[13]

By 1998, there was also evidence of internal concerns. Anonymous letters from 3M employees were sent to the board of directors, claiming that DeSimone was not as committed to research as he should have been. Some letters complained that DeSimone was not funding important projects for future growth, others that he had not moved boldly enough to cut costs, and still others that the company's dual career track was not being implemented well, and that technical people were underpaid. Critics argued that he was a slow and cautious decision maker in a time that required decisive strategic decisions. For example, in August 1998, DeSimone announced a restructuring plan that included a commitment to cut 4,500 jobs, but reports suggest that other senior managers wanted 10,000 job cuts, and DeSimone had watered down the proposals.[14]

Despite the criticism, 3M's board, which included 4 previous 3M CEOs among its members, stood behind DeSimone until he retired in 2001. However, the board began a search for a new top executive in February 2000 and signaled that it was looking for an outsider. In December 2000, the company announced that it had found the person they wanted, Jim McNerney, a 51-year old General Electric veteran who ran GE's medical equipment businesses, and before that GE's Asian operations. McNerney was one of the front runners in the race to succeed Jack Welsh as CEO of General Electric, but lost out to Jeffrey Immelt. One week after that announcement, 3M hired McNerney.

McNerney's Plan for 3M

In his first public statement days after being appointed, McNerney said that his focus would be upon getting to know 3M's people and culture and its diverse lines of business:

I think getting to know some of those businesses and bringing some of GE here to overlay on top of 3M's strong culture of innovation will be particularly important.[15]

It soon became apparent that McNerney's game plan was exactly that: to bring the GE play book to 3M and use it to try and boost 3M's results, while simultaneously not destroying the innovative culture that had produced the company's portfolio of 50,000 products.

The first move came in April 2001, when 3M announced that the company would cut 5,000 jobs, or about 7% of the workforce, in a restructuring effort that would zero in on struggling businesses. To cover

severance and other costs of restructuring, 3M announced that it would take a $600 million charge against earnings; the job cuts were expected to save $500 million a year. In another effort to save costs, the company streamlined its purchasing processes, for example, by reducing the number of packaging suppliers on a global basis from 50 to 5, saving another $100 million a year in the process.

Next, McNerney introduced the Six Sigma process, a rigorous statistically-based quality control process that was one of the drivers of process improvement and cost savings at General Electric. At heart, Six Sigma is a management philosophy, accompanied by a set of tools, that is rooted in identifying and prioritizing customers and their needs, reducing variation in all business processes, and selecting and grading all projects based upon their impact on financial results. Six Sigma breaks every task (process) in an organization down into increments to be measured against a perfect model.

McNerney called for Six Sigma to be rolled out across 3M's global operations. He also introduced a 3M-like performance evaluation system at 3M, under which managers were asked to rank every single employee who reported to them.

In addition to boosting performance from existing business, McNerney quickly signaled that he wanted to play a more active role in allocating resources between new business opportunities. At any given time, 3M has around 1,500 products in the development pipeline. McNerney stated that was too many, and he indicated that wanted to funnel more cash to the most promising ideas, those with a potential market of $100 million a year or more, while cutting funding to weaker looking development projects.

In the same vein, he signaled that he wanted to play a more active role in resource allocation than had traditionally been the case for a 3M CEO, using cash from mature businesses to fund growth opportunities elsewhere. He scrapped the requirement that each division get 30% of its sales from products introduced in the past 4 years, noting that:

To make that number, some managers were resorting to some rather dubious innovations, such as pink Post-it Notes. It became a game, what could you do to get a new SKU?[16]

Some long time 3M watchers, however, worried that by changing resource allocation practices McNerney might harm 3M's innovative culture. If the company's history proves anything, they say, it's that it is hard to tell which of today's tiny products will become tomorrow's home runs. No one predicted that Scotchgard or Post-it Notes would earn millions. They began as little experiments that evolved without planning into big hits. McNerney's innovations all sound fine in theory, they say, but there is a risk that he will transform 3M into "3E" and lose what is valuable in 3M in the process.

In general though, securities analysts greeted McNerney's moves favorably. One noted that "McNerney is all about speed," and that there will be "no more Tower of Babel-everyone speaks-one language." This "one company" vision was meant to replace the program under which 3M systematically placed successful new products into new business centers. The problem with this approach, according to the analyst, was that there was no leveraging of best practices across businesses.[17]

McNerney also signaled that he would reform 3M's regional management structure, replacing it with a global business unit structure that will be defined by either products or markets.

At a meeting for investment analysts, held on September 30, 2003, McNerney summarized a number of achievements.[18] At the time, the indications seemed to suggest that McNerney was helping to revitalize 3M. Profitability, measured by ROIC, had risen from 19.4% in 2001, and was projected to hit 25.5% in 2003. 3M's stock price had risen from $42 just before McNerney was hired, to $73 in October 2003 (see Exhibit 5 for details).

Like his former boss, Jack Welsh at GE, McNerney seemed to place significant value on internal executive education programs as a way of shifting to a performance-oriented culture. McNerney noted that some 20,000 employees had been through Six Sigma training by the third quarter of 2003. Almost 400 higher level managers had been through an Advanced Leadership Development Program setup by McNerney, and offered by 3M's own internal executive education institute. Some 40% of participants had been promoted upon graduating. All of the company's top managers had graduated from an Executive Leadership Program offered by 3M.

McNerney also emphasized the value of 5 initiatives that he put in place at 3M; indirect cost control, global sourcing, e-productivity, Six Sigma, and the 3M Acceleration program. With regard to indirect cost control, some $800 million had been taken out of 3M's cost structure since 2001, primarily by reducing employee numbers, introducing more efficient processes that boosted productivity, benchmarking operations internally and leveraging best practices. According to McNerney, internal benchmarking highlighted another $200–$400 million in potential cost savings over the next few years.

On global sourcing, McNerney noted that more than $500 million had been saved since 2000 by consolidating purchasing, reducing the number of suppliers, switching to lower cost suppliers in developing nations, and introducing dual sourcing policies to keep price increases under control.

The e-productivity program at 3M embraced the entire organization, and all functions. It involved the digitalization of a wide range of processes, from customer ordering and payment, through supply chain management and inventory control, to managing employee processes. The central goal was to boost productivity by using information technology to more effectively manage information within the company, and between the company and its customers and suppliers. McNerney cited some $100 million in annual cost savings from this process.

The Six Sigma program overlays the entire organization, and focuses upon improving processes to boost cash flow, lower costs (through productivity enhancements), and boost growth rates. By late-2003, there were some 7,000 Six Sigma projects in process at 3M. By using working capital more efficiently, Six Sigma programs had helped to generate some $800 million in cash, with the total expected to rise to $1.5 billion by the end of 2004. 3M has applied the Six Sigma process to the company's R&D process, enabling researchers to engage customer information in the initial stages of a design discussion, which according to Jay Inlenfeld, the VP of R&D, Six Sigma tools:

Allow us to be more closely connected to the market and give us a much higher probability of success in our new product designs.[19]

Finally, the 3M's Acceleration Program is aimed at boosting the growth rate from new products through better resource allocation, particularly by shifting resources from slower growing to faster growing markets. As McNerney noted:

3M has always had extremely strong competitive positions, but not in markets that are growing fast enough. The issue has been to shift emphasis into markets that are growing faster.[20]

Part of this program is a tool termed 2X/3X, 2X is an objective for 2 times the number of new products that were introduced in the past, and 3X is a business objective for 2 times as many winning products as there were in the past (see Exhibit 3). 2X focuses upon generating more "major" product initiatives, and 3X upon improving the commercialization of those initiatives. Exhibit 3 illustrates 3M's "stage gate" process, and each gate represents a major decision point in the development of a new product, from idea generation to post launch.

Other initiatives aimed at boosting 3M's organization growth rate through innovation include the Six Sigma process, leadership development programs, and technology leadership (see Exhibit 4). The purpose of these initiatives was to help implement the 2X/3X strategy.

As a further step in the Acceleration Program, 3M decided to centralize its corporate R&D effort. Prior to the arrival of McNerney, there were 12 technology centers staffed by 900 scientists that focused on core technology development. The company is now replacing these with one central research lab, staffed by 500 scientists, some 120 of whom will be located outside the United States. The remaining 400 scientists will be relocated to R&D centers in

the business units. The goal of this new corporate research lab is to focus on developing new technology that might fill high growth "white spaces," which are areas where the company currently has no presence, but where the long-term market potential will be great. Research on fuel cells, which is currently a big research project within 3M, provides a good example of this.

Responding to critics' charges that changes such as these might impact 3M's innovative culture, VP of R&D Inlenfeld noted that

> We are not going to change the basic culture of innovation at 3M. There is a lot of culture in 3M, but we are going to introduce more systematic, more productive tools that allow our researchers to be more successful.[23]

For example, Inlenfeld repeatedly emphasized that the company remains committed to basic 3M principles, such as the 15% rule and leveraging technology across businesses.

By late-2003, McNerney noted that some 600 new product ideas were under development and that collectively, they were expected to reach the market and generate some $5 billion in new revenues between 2003 and 2006, up from $3.5 billion

---

Exhibit 3 The New Product Development Process at 3M[21]

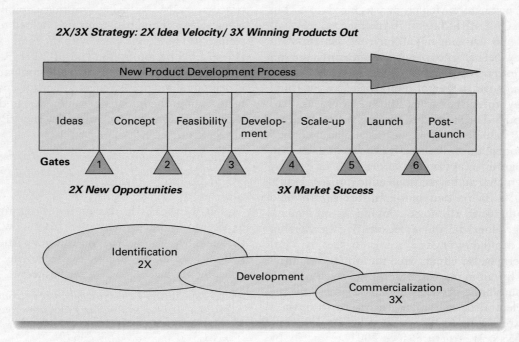

Exhibit 4   R&D's Role in Organic Growth[22]

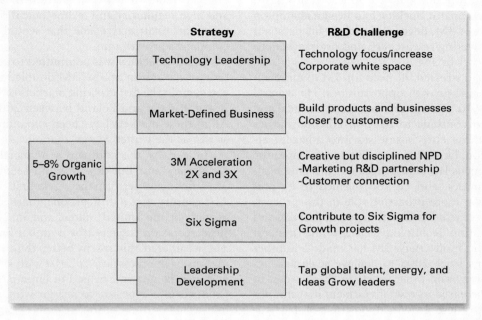

18 months earlier. Some $1 billion of these gains were expected to come in 2003.

George Buckley Takes Over

In mid-2005 McNerney announced that he would leave 3M to become CEO and Chairman of Boeing, a board on which he had served for some time. He was replaced in late-2005 by another outsider, George Buckley, who was Brunswick Industries highly regarded CEO. Buckley, a Brit with a Ph.D. in electrical engineering, described himself as a scientist at heart. Over the next year in several presentations, Buckley outlined his strategy for 3M, and it soon became apparent that he was sticking to the general course laid out by McNerney, albeit with some important corrections.[24]

Buckley did not see 3M as an enterprise that needed radical change. He saw 3M as a company with impressive internal strengths, but one that has been too cautious about pursuing growth opportunities.[25] Buckley's overall strategic vision for 3M included solving customer needs through the provision of innovative and differentiated products that increase the efficiency and competitiveness of customers. Consistent with long-term 3M strategy, he

believed this could be achieved by taking 3M's multiple technology platforms, and applying them to different market opportunities.

Controlling costs and boosting productivity through Six Sigma continued to be a major thrust under Buckley. This was hardly a surprise, since Buckley had pushed Six Sigma at Brunswick. By late-2006, some 55,000 3M employees had been trained in Six Sigma methodology, 20,000 projects had been completed, and some 15,000 more were under way. 3M was also adding techniques gleaned from Toyota's lean production methodology to its Six Sigma tool kit. As a result of Six Sigma and other cost control methods, between 2001 and 2005, productivity measured by sales per employee increased from $234 to $311, and some $750 million were taken out of overhead costs.

However, Buckley departed from McNerney's playbook in one significant way, he removed Six Sigma from the labs. The feeling of many at 3M was that Six Sigma's rules choked those working on innovation. As one 3M researcher noted: "It's really tough to schedule innovation."[26] When McNerney left 3M in 2005, the percentage of sales from new products introduced in the last 5 years had fallen to 21%, down from the company's long-term goal of

30%. By 2010, after 5 years of Buckley's leadership, the percentage was back up to 30%. According to many in the company, Buckley had been a champion of researchers at 3M, devoting much of his personal time to empowering researchers, and urging them to restore the luster of 3M.

Buckley had stressed the need for 3M to more aggressively pursue growth opportunities. He wanted the company to use its differentiated brands and technology to continue to develop core businesses and extend those core businesses into adjacent areas. In addition, like McNerney, Buckley wanted the company to focus R&D resources on emerging business opportunities, and he, too, seemed to be prepared to play a more proactive role in this process. Areas of focus included filtration systems, track and trace information technology, energy and mineral extraction, and food safety. 3M has made a number of acquisitions since 2005 to achieve scale and acquire technology and other assets in these areas. In addition, it increased its own investment in technologies related to these growth opportunities, particularly nanotechnology.

Buckley had made selective divestures of businesses not seen as core. Most notably, in November 2006, 3M reached an agreement to sell its pharmaceutical business for $2.1 billion. 3M took this step after deciding that a combination of slow growth, and high regulatory and technological risk, made the sector an unattractive one that would dampen the company's growth rate.

Finally, Buckley was committed to continuing internationalization at 3M. 3M doubled its capital investment in the fast growing markets of China, India, Brazil, Russia, and Poland between 2005 and 2010. All of these markets have been expanding 2–3 times as fast as the United States' market.

Judged by the company's financial results, the McNerney and Buckley eras did seem to improve 3M's financial performance. The first decade of the 21st century was a difficult one, marked by sluggish growth in the United States, and in 2008–2009, a steep recession triggered by a global financial crisis. 3M weathered this storm better than most, bouncing out of the recession in 2010 with strong revenue and income growth, helped in large part by its new products and exposure to fast growing international markets. For the decade, revenues expanded from $16 billion in 2001 to $26.66 billion in 2010, earnings per share expanded from $1.79 to $5.63, and ROIC increased from the mid-teens in the 1990s to the mid-20s for most of the decade.

Suggested Readings and References:

1. J. C. Collins and J. I. Porras, *Built to Last* (Harper Business, New York, 1994).
2. M. Conlin, "Too Much Doodle?" *Forbes,* October 19, 1998, 54–56.
3. M. Dickson, "Back to the Future," *Financial Times,* 1994, May 30, 7.
4. J. Hallinan, "3M's Next Chief Plans to Fortify Results with Discipline He Learned at GE Unit," *Wall Street Journal*, December 6, 2000, B17.
5. E. Von Hippel et al., "Creating Breakthroughs at 3M," *Harvard Business Review,* September-October 1999.
6. R. Mullin, "Analysts Rate 3M's New Culture," *Chemical Week,* September 26, 2001, 39–40.
7. 3M. A Century of Innovation, the 3M Story. 3M, 2002. Available at www.3m.com/about3m/century/index.jhtml.
8. 3M Investor Meeting, September 30, 2003, archived at www.corporate-ir.net/ireye/ir_site.zhtml?ticker=MMM&script=2100
9. T. Studt. "3M–Where Innovation Rules," *R&D Magazine,* April 2003, Vol 45, 20–24.
10. De'Ann Weimer, "3M: The Heat is on the Boss," *Business Week*, March 15, 1999, 82–83.
11. J. Useem. "(Tape) + (Light bulb) = ?", *Fortune,* August 12, 2002, 127–131.
12. M. Gunther, M. Adamo, and B. Feldman, "3M's Innovation Revival," *Fortune,* September 27, 2010, 73–76.

Endnotes

1 M. Dickson, "Back to the Future," *Financial Times*, May 30, 1994, 7. www.3m.com/profile/looking/mcknight.jhtml.
2 www.3m.com/about3M/pioneers/drew2.jhtml
3 www.3m.com/about3M/innovation/scotchgard50/index.jhtml
4 3M. A Century of Innovation, the 3M Story. 3M, 2002. Available at http://www.3m.com/about3m/century/index.jhtml
5 3M. A Century of Innovation, the 3M Story. 3M, 2002, page 33. Available at http://www.3m.com/about3m/century/index.jhtml
6 T. Studt, "3M–Where Innovation Rules," *R&D Magazine,* April 2003, Vol 45, 20–24.
7 3M. A Century of Innovation, the 3M Story. 3M, 2002, page 78. Available at http://www.3m.com/about3m/century/index.jhtml

8 3M. A Century of Innovation, the 3M Story. 3M, 2002, page 78. Available at http://www.3m.com/about3m/century/index.jhtml

9 3M. A Century of Innovation, the 3M Story. 3M, 2002, page 42. Available at http://www.3m.com/about3m/century/index.jhtml

10 E. Von Hippel et al., "Creating Breakthroughs at 3M," *Harvard Business Review,* September–October 1999.

11 From 3M Website at www.3m.com/about3M/history/mcknight.jhtml

12 3M. A Century of Innovation, the 3M Story. 3M, 2002, 143–144. Available at http://www.3m.com/about3m/century/index.jhtml

13 M. Conlin, "Too Much Doodle?", *Forbes,* October 19, 1998, 54–56.

14 De'Ann Weimer, "3M: The Heat is on the Boss," *Business Week,* March 15, 1999, 82–83.

15 J. Hallinan, "3M's Next Chief Plans to Fortify Results with Discipline He Learned at GE Unit," *Wall Street Journal,* December 6, 2000, B17.

16 J. Useem. "(Tape) + (Light bulb) = ?", *Fortune,* August 12, 2002, 127–131.

17 R. Mullin, "Analysts Rate 3M's New Culture," *Chemical Week*, September 26, 2001, 39–40.

18 3M Investor Meeting, September 30, 2003, archived at http://phx.corporate-ir.net/phoenix.zhtml?c=80574&p=irol-irhome

19 Tim Studt, "3M—Where Innovation Rules," *R&D Magazine,* April 2003, 22.

20 3M Investor Meeting, September 30, 2003, archived at http://phx.corporate-ir.net/phoenix.zhtml?c=80574&p=irol-irhome

21 Adapted from presentation by Jay Inlenfeld, 3M Investor Meeting, September 30, 2003, archived at http://phx.corporate-ir.net/phoenix.zhtml?c=80574&p=irol-irhome

22 Ibid.

23 Tim Studt, "3M—Where Innovation Rules," *R&D Magazine,* April 2003, 21.

24 Material here drawn from George Buckley's presentation to Prudential's investor conference on "Inside our Best Ideas," September 28, 2006. This and other relevant presentations are archived at http://phx.corporate-ir.net/phoenix.zhtml?c=80574&p=irol-irhome

25 J. Sprague, "MMM: Searching for Growth with New CEO Leading," *Citigroup Global Markets,* May 2, 2006.

26 M. Gunther, M. Adamo, and B. Feldman, "3M's Innovation Revival," *Fortune,* September 27, 2010, 74.

Merck, the FDA, and the Vioxx Recall[1]

Anne Lawrence, San Jose State University

In 2006, the pharmaceutical giant Merck faced major challenges. Vioxx, the company's once best-selling prescription painkiller, had been pulled off the market in September 2004 after Merck learned it increased the risk of heart attacks and strokes. When news of the recall broke, the company's stock price had plunged thirty percent to $33 a share, its lowest point in eight years, where it had hovered since. Standard & Poor's had downgraded the company's outlook from "stable" to "negative." In late 2004, the Justice Department had opened a criminal investigation into whether the company had "caused federal health programs to pay for the prescription drug when its use was not warranted."[2] The Securities and Exchange Commission was inquiring into whether Merck had misled investors. By late 2005, more than 6,000 lawsuits had been filed, alleging that Vioxx had caused death or disability. From many quarters, the company faced troubling questions about the development and marketing of Vioxx, new calls for regulatory reform, and concerns about its political influence on Capitol Hill. In the words of Senator Charles Grassley, chairman of a Congressional committee investigating the Vioxx case, "a blockbuster drug [had become] a blockbuster disaster."[3]

Merck, Inc.[4]

Merck, the company in the eye of this storm, was one of the world's leading pharmaceutical firms. As shown in Exhibit 1, in 2005 the company ranked fourth in sales, after Pfizer, Johnson & Johnson, and Glaxo-SmithKline. In assets and market value, it ranked fifth. However, Merck ranked first in profits, earning $7.33 billion on $30.78 billion in sales (24 percent).

Merck had long enjoyed a reputation as one of the most ethical and socially responsible of the major drug companies. For an unprecedented seven consecutive years (1987 to 1993), *Fortune* magazine had named Merck its "most admired" company. In 1987, Merck appeared on the cover of *Time* under the headline, "The Miracle Company." It had consistently appeared on lists of best companies to work for and in the portfolios of social investment funds. The company's philanthropy was legendary. In the 1940s, Merck had given its patent for streptomycin, a powerful antibiotic, to a university foundation. Merck was especially admired for its donation of Mectizan. Merck's scientists had originally developed this drug for veterinary use, but later discovered that it was an effective cure for river blindness, a debilitating parasitic disease afflicting some of the world's poorest people. When the company realized that the victims of river blindness could not afford the drug, it decided to give it away for free, in perpetuity.[5]

In 1950, George W. Merck, the company's long-time CEO, stated in a speech: "We try never to forget that medicine is for the people. It is not for the profits. The profits follow, and if we have remembered that, they never fail to appear. The better we have remembered that, the larger they have been."[6] This statement was often repeated in subsequent years as a touchstone of the company's core values.

Merck was renowned for its research labs, which had a decades-long record of achievement, turning out one innovation after another, including drugs for tuberculosis, cholesterol, hypertension, and AIDS. In the early 2000s, Merck spent around $3 billion annually on research. Some felt that the company's culture had been shaped by its research agenda. Commented the author of a history of Merck, the company was "intense, driven, loyal, scientifically brilliant, collegial, and arrogant."[7] In 2006, although Merck had several medicines in the pipeline—including vaccines for rotavirus and cervical cancer, and drugs for insomnia, lymphoma, and the effects of stroke—some analysts worried that the pace of research had slowed significantly.

Exhibit 1   The World's Top Pharmaceutical Companies, 2005

Company	Sales ($bil)	Profits ($bil)	Assets ($bil)	Market Value ($bil)
Pfizer	40.36	6.20	120.06	285.27
Johnson & Johnson	40.01	6.74	46.66	160.96
Merck	**30.78**	**7.33**	**42.59**	**108.76**
Novartis	26.77	5.40	46.92	116.43
Roche Group	25.18	2.48	45.77	95.38
GlaxoSmithKline	34.16	6.34	29.19	124.79
Aventis	21.66	2.29	31.06	62.98
Bristol-Myers Squibb	19.89	2.90	26.53	56.05
AstraZeneca	20.46	3.29	23.57	83.03
Abbott Labs	18.99	2.44	26.15	69.27

Source: Forbes 2000, available online at www.forbes.com. Listed in order of overall ranking in the Forbes 2000.

Estimating the company's financial liability from the Vioxx lawsuits was difficult. Some 84 million people had taken the drug worldwide over a five-year period from 1999 to 2004. In testimony before Congress, Dr. David Graham, a staff scientist at the Food and Drug Administration (FDA), estimated that as many as 139,000 people in the United States had had heart attacks or strokes as a result of taking Vioxx, and about 55,000 of these had died.[8] Merrill Lynch estimated the company's liability for compensatory damages alone in the range of $4 to $18 billion.[9] However, heart attacks and strokes were common, and they had multiple causes, including genetic predisposition, smoking, obesity, and a sedentary lifestyle. Determining the specific contribution of Vioxx to a particular cardiovascular event would be very difficult. The company vigorously maintained that it had done nothing wrong and vowed to defend every single case in court. By early 2006, only three cases had gone to trial, and the results had been a virtual draw—one decision for the plaintiff, one for Merck, and one hung jury.

Government Regulation of Prescription Drugs

In the United States, prescription medicines—like Vioxx—were regulated by the Food and Drug Administration (FDA).[10] Before a new drug could be sold to the public, its manufacturer had to carry out clinical trials to demonstrate both safety and effectiveness. Advisory panels of outside medical experts reviewed the results of these trials and recommended to the FDA's Office of Drug Safety whether or not to approve a new drug.[11] After a drug was on the market, the agency's Office of New Drugs continued to monitor it for safety, in a process known as post-market surveillance. These two offices both reported to the same boss, the FDA's director of the Center for Drug Evaluation and Research.

Once the FDA had approved a drug, physicians could prescribe it for any purpose, but the manufacturer could market it only for uses for which it had been approved. Therefore, companies had an incentive to continue to study approved drugs to provide data that they were safe and effective for the treatment of other conditions.

In the 1980s, the drug industry and some patient advocates had criticized the FDA for being too slow to approve new medicines. Patients were concerned that they were not getting new medicines fast enough, and drug companies were concerned that they were losing sales revenue. Each month an average drug spent under review represented $41.7 million in lost revenue, according to one study.[12]

In 1992, Congress passed the Prescription Drug User Fee Act (PDUFA). This law, which was supported by the industry, required pharmaceutical companies to pay "user fees" to the FDA to review proposed new medicines. Between 1993 and 2001, the FDA received around $825 million in such fees from drug makers seeking approval. (During this period, it also received $1.3 billion appropriated by Congress). This infusion of new revenue enabled the agency to hire 1,000 new employees and to shorten the approval time for new drugs from 27 months in 1993 to 14 months in 2001.[13]

Despite the benefits of PDUFA, some felt that industry-paid fees were a bad idea.

In an editorial published in December 2004, the *Journal of the American Medical Association (JAMA)* concluded: "It is unreasonable to expect that the same agency that was responsible for approval of drug licensing and labeling would also be committed to actively seek evidence to prove itself wrong (i.e., that the decision to approve the product was subsequently shown to be incorrect)." *JAMA* went on to recommend establishment of a separate agency to monitor drug safety.[14] Dr. David Kessler, a former FDA Commissioner, rejected this idea, responding that "strengthening post-marketing surveillance is certainly in order, but you don't want competing agencies."[15]

Some evidence suggested that the morale of FDA staff charged with evaluating the safety of new medicines had been hurt by relentless pressure to bring drugs to market quickly. In 2002, a survey of agency scientists found that only 13 percent were "completely confident" that the FDA's "final decisions adequately assess the safety of a drug." Thirty-one percent were "somewhat confident" and 5 percent lacked "any confidence." Two-thirds of those surveyed lacked confidence that the agency "adequately monitors the safety of prescription jobs once they are on the market." And nearly one in five said they had "been pressured to approve or recommend approval" for a drug "despite reservations about [its] safety, efficacy or quality."[16]

After the FDA shortened the approval time, the percentage of drugs recalled following approval increased from 1.56% for 1993–1996 to 5.35% for 1997–2001.[17] Vioxx was the ninth drug taken off the market in seven years.

Influence at the Top

The pharmaceutical industry's success in accelerating the approval of new drugs reflected its strong presence in Washington. The major drug companies, their trade association PhRMA (Pharmaceutical Research and Manufacturers of America), and their executives consistently donated large sums of money to both political parties and, through their political action committees, to various candidates. The industry's political contributions are shown in Exhibit 2.

Exhibit 2 Pharmaceutical/Health Products Industry: Political Contributions 1990–2006

Election Cycle	Total Contributions	Contributions from Individuals	Contributions from PACs	Soft Money Contributions	Percentage to Republicans
2006	$5,187,393	$1,753,159	$3,434,234	N/A	70%
2004	$18,181,045	$8,445,485	$9,735,560	N/A	66%
2002	$29,441,951	$3,332,040	$6,957,382	$19,152,529	74%
2000	$26,688,292	$5,660,457	$5,649,913	$15,377,922	69%
1998	$13,169,694	$2,673,845	$4,107,068	$6,388,781	64%
1996	$13,754,796	$3,413,516	$3,584,217	$6,757,063	66%
1994	$7,706,303	$1,935,150	$3,477,146	$2,294,007	56%
1992	$7,924,262	$2,389,370	$3,205,014	$2,329,878	56%
1990	$3,237,592	$771,621	$2,465,971	N/A	54%
Total	$125,291,328	$30,374,643	$42,616,505	$52,300,180	67%

Source: Center for Responsive Politics, online at www.opensecrets.org

Following the Congressional ban on soft money contributions in 2003, the industry shifted much of its contributions to so-called stealth PACs, nonprofit organizations which were permitted by law to take unlimited donations without revealing their source. These organizations could, in turn, make "substantial" political expenditures, providing political activity was not their primary purpose.[18]

In addition, the industry maintained a large corps of lobbyists active in the nation's capital. In 2003, for example, drug companies and their trade association spent $108 million on lobbying and hired 824 individual lobbyists, according to a report by Public Citizen.[19] Merck spent $40.7 million on lobbying between 1998 and 2004.[20] One of the industry's most effective techniques was to hire former elected officials or members of their staffs. For example, Billy Tauzin, formerly a Republican member of Congress from Louisiana and head of the powerful Committee on Energy and Commerce, which oversaw the drug industry, became president of PhRMA at a reported annual salary of $2 million in 2004.[21]

Over the years, the industry's representatives in Washington had established a highly successful record of promoting its political agenda on a range of issues. In addition to faster drug approvals, these had more recently included a Medicare prescription drug benefit, patent protections, and restrictions on drug imports from Canada.

The Blockbuster Model

In the 1990s, 80 percent of growth for the big pharmaceutical firms came from so-called blockbuster drugs.[22] Blockbusters have been defined by *Fortune* magazine as "medicines that serve vast swaths of the population and garner billions of dollars in annual revenue."[23] The ideal blockbuster, from the companies' view, was a medicine that could control chronic but usually nonfatal conditions that afflicted large numbers of people with health insurance. These might include, for example, daily maintenance drugs for high blood pressure or cholesterol, allergies, arthritis pain, or heartburn. Drugs that could actually cure a condition—and thus would not need to be taken for long periods—or were intended to treat diseases, like malaria or tuberculosis, that affected mainly the world's poor, were often less profitable.

Historically, drug companies focused most of their marketing efforts on prescribing physicians.

The industry hired tens of thousands of sales representatives—often, attractive young men and women—to make the rounds of doctors' offices to talk about new products and give out free samples.[24] Drug companies also offered doctors gifts—from free meals to tickets to sporting events—to cultivate their good will. They also routinely sponsored continuing education events for physicians, often featuring reports on their own medicines, and supported doctors financially with opportunities to consult and to conduct clinical trials.[25] In 2003 Merck spent $422 million to market Vioxx to doctors and hospitals.[26]

During the early 2000s, when Vioxx and Pfizer's Celebrex were competing head-to-head, sales representatives for the two firms were hard at work promoting their brand to doctors. Commented one rheumatologist of the competition between Merck and Pfizer at the time: "We were all aware that there was a great deal of marketing. Like a Coke-Pepsi war."[27] An internal Merck training manual for sales representatives, reported in *The Wall Street Journal,* was titled "Dodge Ball Vioxx." It explained how to "dodge" doctors' questions, such as "I am concerned about the cardiovascular effects of Vioxx." Merck later said that this document had been taken out of context and that sales representatives "were not trained to avoid physician's questions."[28]

Direct-to-Consumer Advertising

Although marketing to doctors and hospitals continued to be important, in the late 1990s the focus shifted somewhat. In 1997, the FDA for the first time allowed drug companies to advertise directly to consumers. The industry immediately seized this opportunity, placing numerous ads for drugs—from Viagra to Nexium—on television and in magazines and newspapers. In 2004, the industry spent over $4 billion on such direct-to-consumer, or DTC, advertising. For example, in one ad for Vioxx, Olympic figure skating champion Dorothy Hamill glided gracefully across an outdoor ice rink to the tune of "It's a Beautiful Morning" by the sixties pop group The Rascals, telling viewers that she would "not let arthritis stop me." In all, Merck spent more than $500 million advertising Vioxx.[29]

The industry's media blitz for Vioxx and other drugs was highly effective. According to research by the Harvard School of Public Heath, each dollar spent on DTC advertising yielded $4.25 in sales.

The drug companies defended DTC ads, saying they informed consumers of newly available therapies and encouraged people to seek medical treatment. In the age of the Internet, commented David Jones, an advertising executive whose firm included several major drug companies, "consumers are becoming much more empowered to make their own health care decisions."[30]

However, others criticized DTC advertising, saying that it put pressure on doctors to prescribe drugs that might not be best for the patient. "When a patient comes in and wants something, there is a desire to serve them," said David Wofsy, president of the American College of Rheumatology. "There is a desire on the part of physicians, as there is on anyone else who provides service, to keep the customer happy."[31] Even some industry executives expressed reservations. Said Hank McKinnell, CEO of Pfizer, "I'm beginning to think that direct-to-consumer ads are part of the problem. By having them on television without a very strong message that the doctor needs to determine safety, we've left this impression that all drugs are safe. In fact, no drug is safe."[32]

The Rise of Vioxx

Vioxx, the drug at the center of Merck's legal woes, was a known as "a selective COX-2 inhibitor." Scientists had long understood that an enzyme called cyclo-oxygenase, or COX for short, was associated with pain and inflammation. In the early 1990s, researchers learned that there were really two kinds of COX enzyme. COX-1, it was found, performed several beneficial functions, including protecting the stomach lining. COX-2, on the other hand, contributed to pain and inflammation. Existing anti-inflammatory drugs suppressed both forms of the enzyme, which is why drugs like ibuprofen (Advil) relieved pain, but also caused stomach irritation in some users.

A number of drug companies, including Merck, were intrigued by the possibility of developing a medicine that would block just the COX-2, leaving the stomach-protective COX-1 intact. Such a drug would offer distinctive benefits to some patients, such as arthritis sufferers who were at risk for ulcers (bleeding sores in the intestinal tract).[33] As many as 16,500 people died each year in the United States from this condition.[34]

In May 1999, after several years of research and testing by Merck scientists, the FDA approved Vioxx for the treatment of osteoarthritis, acute pain in adults, and menstrual symptoms. The drug was later approved for rheumatoid arthritis. Although Merck, like other drug companies, never revealed what it spent to develop specific new medicines, estimates of the cost to develop a major new drug ran as high as $800 million.[35]

Vioxx quickly became exactly what Merck had hoped: a blockbuster. At its peak in 2001, Vioxx generated $2.1 billion in sales in the United States alone, contributing almost 10 percent of Merck's total sales revenue worldwide, as shown in Exhibit 3.

Exhibit 3 Vioxx Sales in the United States, 1999–2004

	U.S. Prescriptions Dispensed	U.S. Sales	U.S. Sales of Vioxx as % of Total Merck Sales
1999	4,845,000	$372,697,000	2.2%
2000	20,630,000	$1,526,382,000	7.6%
2001	25,406,000	$2,084,736,000	9.8%
2002	22,044,000	$1,837,680,000	8.6%
2003	19,959,000	$1,813,391,000	8.1%
2004*	13,994,000	$1,342,236,000	5.9%

*Withdrawn from the market in September 2004.

Sources: Columns 1 and 2: IMS Health (www.imshealth.com); Column 3: Merck *Annual Reports* (www.merck.com).

The retail price of Vioxx was around $3.00 per pill, compared with pennies per pill for older anti-inflammatory drugs like aspirin and Advil. Of course, Vioxx was often covered, at least partially, under a user's health insurance, while over-the-counter drugs were not.

Safety Warnings

Even before the drug was approved, some evidence cast doubt on the safety of Vioxx. These clues were later confirmed in other studies.

Merck Research: Internal company e-mails suggested that Merck scientists might have been worried about the cardiovascular risks of Vioxx as early as its development phase. In a 1997 e-mail, reported in *The Wall Street Journal*, Dr. Alise Reicin, a Merck scientist, stated that "the possibility of CV (cardiovascular) events is of great concern." She added, apparently sarcastically, "I just can't wait to be the one to present those results to senior management!" A lawyer representing Merck said this e-mail had been taken out of context.[36]

VIGOR: A study code-named VIGOR, completed in 2000 after the drug was already on the market, compared rheumatoid arthritis patients taking Vioxx with another group taking naproxen (Aleve). Merck financed the research, which was designed to study gastrointestinal side effects. The study found—as the company had expected—that Vioxx was easier on the stomach than naproxen. But it also found that the Vioxx group had nearly five times as many heart attacks (7.3 per thousand person-years) as the naproxen group (1.7 per thousand person-years).[37] Publicly, Merck hypothesized that these findings were due to the heart-protective effect of naproxen, rather than to any defect inherent in Vioxx. Privately, however, the company seemed worried. In an internal e-mail dated March 9, 2000, under the subject line "Vigor," the company's research director, Dr. Edward Scolnick, said that cardiovascular events were "clearly there" and called them "a shame." But, he added, "there is always a hazard."[38] At that time, the company considered reformulating Vioxx by adding an agent to prevent blood clots (and reduce CV risk), but then dropped the project.

The FDA was sufficiently concerned by the VIGOR results that it required Merck to add additional warning language to its label. These changes appeared in April 2002, after lengthy negotiations between the agency and the company over their wording.[39]

Kaiser/Permanente: In August 2004, Dr. David Graham, a scientist at the FDA, reported the results of a study of the records of 1.4 million patients enrolled in the Kaiser health maintenance organization in California. He found that patients on high doses of Vioxx had three times the rate of heart attacks as patients on Celebrex, a competing COX-2 inhibitor made by Pfizer. Merck discounted this finding, saying that studies of patient records were less reliable than double blind clinical studies.[40] Dr. Graham later charged that his superiors at the FDA had "ostracized" him and subjected him to "veiled threats" if he did not qualify his criticism of Vioxx. The FDA called these charges "baloney."[41]

APPROVe: In order to examine the possibility that Vioxx posed a cardiovascular risk, Merck decided to monitor patients enrolled in a clinical trial called APPROVe to see if they those taking Vioxx had more heart attacks and strokes than those who were taking a placebo (sugar pill). This study had been designed to determine if Vioxx reduced the risk of recurrent colon polyps (a precursor to colon cancer); Merck hoped it would lead to FDA approval of the drug for this condition. The APPROVe study was planned before the VIGOR results were known.

Merck Recalls the Drug

On the evening of Thursday, September 23, 2004, Dr. Peter S. Kim, president of Merck Research Labs, received a phone call from scientists monitoring the colon polyp study. Researchers had found, the scientists told him, that after 18 months of continuous use individuals taking Vioxx were more than twice as likely to have a heart attack or stroke than those taking a placebo. The scientists recommended that the study be halted because of "unacceptable" risk.[42]

Dr. Kim later described to a reporter for *The New York Times* the urgent decision-making process that unfolded over the next hours and days as the company responded to this news.

> On Friday, I looked at the data with my team. The first thing you do is review the data. We did that. Second is you double-check the data, go through it and make sure that everything is O.K. [At that point] I knew that barring some big mistake in the analysis, we had an issue here. Around noon, I called [CEO] Ray Gilmartin and told him what was up.

He said, 'Figure out what was the best thing for patient safety.' We then spent Friday and the rest of the weekend going over the data and analyzing it in different ways and calling up medical experts to set up meetings where we would discuss the data and their interpretations and what to do.[43]

According to later interviews with some of the doctors consulted that weekend by Merck, the group was of mixed opinion. Some experts argued that Vioxx should stay on the market, with a strong warning label so that doctors and patients could judge the risk for themselves. But others thought the drug should be withdrawn because no one knew why the drug was apparently causing heart attacks. One expert commented that "Merck prides itself on its ethical approach. I couldn't see Merck saying we're going to market a drug with a safety problem."[44]

On Monday, Dr. Kim recommended to Gilmartin that Vioxx be withdrawn from the market. The CEO agreed. The following day, Gilmartin notified the board, and the company contacted the FDA.

On Thursday, September 30, Merck issued a press release, which stated in part:

> Merck & Co., Inc. announced today a voluntary withdrawal of VIOXX®. This decision is based on new data from a 3-year clinical study. In this study, there was an increased risk for cardiovascular (CV) events, such as heart attack and stroke, in patients taking VIOXX 25 mg compared to those taking placebo (sugar pill). While the incidence of CV events was low, there was an increased risk beginning after 18 months of treatment. The cause of the clinical study result is uncertain, but our commitment to our patients is clear . . . Merck is notifying physicians and pharmacists and has informed the Food and Drug Administration of this decision. We are taking this action because we believe it best serves the interests of patients. That is why we undertook this clinical trial to better understand the safety profile of VIOXX. And it's why we instituted this voluntary withdrawal upon learning about these data. Be assured that Merck will continue to do everything we can to maintain the safety of our medicines.

Endnotes

1 By Anne T. Lawrence, San Jose State University. Copyright © 2006 by the author. All rights reserved. An earlier version of this case was presented at the Western Casewriters Association Annual Meeting, Long Beach, California, March 30, 2006. This case was prepared from publicly available materials.

2 "Justice Dept. and SEC Investigating Merck Drug," *New York Times*, November 9, 2004.

3 "Opening Statement of U.S. Senator Chuck Grassley of Iowa," U.S. Senate Committee on Finance, Hearing—FDA, Merck, and Vioxx: Putting Patient Safety First?" November 18, 2004, online at http://finance.senate.gov.

4 A history of Merck may be found in Fran Hawthorne, *The Merck Druggernaut: The Inside Story of a Pharmaceutical Giant* (Hoboken, NJ: John Wiley & Sons, 2003).

5 Merck received the 1991 Business Enterprise Trust Award for this action. See Stephanie Weiss and Kirk O. Hanson, "Merck and Co., Inc.: Addressing Third World Needs" (Business Enterprise Trust, 1991).

6 Hawthorne, op. Cit., pp. 17–18.

7 Hawthorne, op. Cit., p. 38.

8 "FDA Failing in Drug Safety, Official Asserts," *New York Times*, November 19, 2004. The full transcript of the hearing of the U.S. Senate Committee on Finance, "FDA, Merck, and Vioxx: Putting Patient Safety First?" is available online at http://finance.senate.gov.

9 "Despite Warnings, Drug Giant Took Long Path to Vioxx Recall," *New York Times*, November 14, 2004.

10 A history of the FDA and of its relationship to business may be found in Philip J. Hilts, *Protecting America's Health: The FDA, Business, and One Hundred Years of Regulation* (New York: Alfred A. Knopf, 2003).

11 Marcia Angell, *The Trust About the Drug Companies* (New York: Random House, 2004), Ch. 2.

12 Merrill Lynch data reported in "A World of Hurt," *Fortune*, January 10, 2005, p. 18.

13 U.S. General Accounting Office, *Food and Drug Administration: Effect of User Fees on Drug Approval Times, Withdrawals, and Other Agency Activities*, September 2002.

14 "Postmarketing Surveillance—Lack of Vigilance, Lack of Trust," *Journal of the American Medical Association* 92(21), December 1, 2004, p. 2649.

15 "FDA Lax in Drug Safety, Journal Warns," *www.sfgate.com*, November 23, 2004.

16 2002 Survey of 846 FDA scientists conducted by the Office of the Inspector General of the Department of Health and Human Services, online at www.peer.org/FDAscientistsurvey.

17 "Postmarketing Surveillance," op. Cit.

18 "Big PhRMA's Stealth PACs: How the Drug Industry Uses 501(c) Non-Profit Groups to Influence Elections," *Congress Watch*, September 2004.

19 "Drug Industry and HMOs Deployed an Army of Nearly 1,000 Lobbyists to Push Medicare Bill, Report Finds," June 23, 2004, www.citizen.org.

20 Data available online at www.publicintegrity.org.

21 "Rep. Billy Tauzin Demonstrates that Washington's Revolving Door is Spinning Out of Control," *Public Citizen*, December 15, 2004, press release.

22 "The Waning of the Blockbuster," *Business Week*, October 18, 2004.

23 "A World of Hurt," *Fortune*, January 10, 2005, p.20.

24 In 2005, 90,000 sales representatives were employed by the pharmaceutical industry, about one for every eight doctors. The *New York Times* revealed in an investigative article ("Give Me an Rx! Cheerleaders Pep Up Drug Sales," November 28, 2005) that many companies made a point of hiring former college cheerleaders for this role.

25 The influence of the drug industry on the medical professional is documented in Katharine Greider, *The Big Fix: How the Pharmaceutical Industry Rips Off American Consumers* (New York: Public Affairs, 2003).

26 "Drug Pullout," *Modern Healthcare*, October 18, 2004.

27 "Marketing of Vioxx: How Merck Played Game of Catch-Up," *New York Times*, February 11, 2005.

28 "E-Mails Suggest Merck Knew Vioxx's Dangers at Early Stage," *Wall Street Journal*, November 1, 2004.

29 IMS Health estimate reported in: "Will Merck Survive Vioxx?" *Fortune*, November 1, 2004.

30 "With or Without Vioxx, Drug Ads Proliferate," *New York Times*, December 6, 2004.

31 "A 'Smart' Drug Fails the Safety Test," *Washington Post*, October 3, 2004.

32 "A World of Hurt," *Fortune*, January 10, 2005, p. 18.

33 "Medicine Fueled by Marketing Intensified Troubles for Pain Pills," *New York Times*, December 19, 2004.

34 "New Scrutiny of Drugs in Vioxx's Family," *New York Times*, October 4, 2004.

35 This estimate was hotly debated. See, for example, "How Much Does the Pharmaceutical Industry Really Spend on R&D?" Ch. 3 in Marcia Angell, op. Cit., and Merrill Goozner, *The $800 Million Pill: The Truth Behind the Cost of New Drugs* (Berkeley: University of California Press, 2004).

36 "E-Mails Suggest Merck Knew Vioxx's Dangers at Early Stage," *Wall Street Journal*, November 1, 2004.

37 "Comparison of Upper Gastrointestinal Toxicity of Rofecoxib and Naproxen in Patients with Rheumatoid Arthritis," *New England Journal of Medicine*, 2000: 323.

38 "E-Mails Suggest Merck Knew Vioxx's Dangers at Early Stage," *Wall Street Journal*, November 1, 2004.

39 At one of the early Vioxx trials, the plaintiff introduced a Merck internal memo that calculated that the company would make $229 million more in profits if it delayed changes to warning language on the label by four months (*New York Times*, August 20, 2005). The FDA did not have the authority to dictate label language; any changes had to be negotiated with the manufacturer.

40 "Study of Painkiller Suggests Heart Risk," *New York Times*, August 26, 2004.

41 "FDA Official Alleges Pressure to Suppress Vioxx Findings," *Washington Post*, October 8, 2004.

42 "Painful Withdrawal for Makers of Vioxx," *Washington Post*, October 18, 2004. Detailed data reported the following day in *The New York Times* showed that 30 of the 1287 patients taking Vioxx had suffered a heart attack, compared with 11 of 1299 taking a placebo; 15 on Vioxx had had a stroke or transient ischemic attack (minor stroke), compared with 7 taking a placebo.

43 "A Widely Used Arthritis Drug is Withdrawn," *New York Times*, October 1, 2004.

44 "Painful Withdrawal for Makers of Vioxx," *Washington Post*, October 18, 2004.

Glossary

absolute cost advantage a cost advantage that is enjoyed by incumbents in an industry and that new entrants cannot expect to match.

absorptive capacity the ability of an enterprise to identify, value, assimilate, and use new knowledge.

acquisition when a company uses its capital resources to purchase another company.

adaptive culture a culture that is innovative and encourages and rewards middle- and lowerlevel managers for taking the initiative to achieve organizational goals.

anticompetitive behavior a range of actions aimed at harming actual or potential competitors, most often by using monopoly power, and thereby enhancing the long-run prospects of the firm.

availability error a bias that arises from our predisposition to estimate the probability of an outcome based on how easy the outcome is to imagine.

barriers to imitation factors that make it difficult for a competitor to copy a company's distinctive competencies.

behavior control control achieved through the establishment of a comprehensive system of rules and procedures that specify the appropriate behavior of divisions, functions, and people.

brand loyalty preference of consumers for the products of established companies.

broad differentiators companies that have developed business-level strategies to better differentiate their products and lower their cost structures simultaneously to offer customers the most value.

bureaucratic costs the costs associated with solving the transaction difficulties between business units and corporate headquarters as a company obtains the benefits from transferring, sharing, and leveraging competencies.

business ethics accepted principles of right or wrong governing the conduct of businesspeople.

business model the conception of how strategies should work together as a whole to enable the company to achieve competitive advantage.

business unit a self-contained division that provides a product or service for a particular market.

business-tobusiness (B2B) marketplace An industryspecific trading network established to connect buyers and sellers through the Internet to lower costs.

capabilities a company's skills at coordinating its resources and putting them to productive use.

chaining a strategy designed to obtain the advantages of cost leadership by establishing a network of linked merchandising outlets interconnected by IT that functions as one large company.

code of ethics formal statement of the ethical priorities to which a business adheres.

cognitive biases systematic errors in human decision making that arise from the way people process information.

commonality some kind of skill or competency that when shared by two or more business units allows them to operate more effectively and create more value for customers.

competitive advantage the achieved advantage over rivals when a company's profitability is greater than the average profitability of firms in its industry.

corporate headquarters staff the team of top executives, as well as their support staff, who are responsible for overseeing a company's long-term multibusiness model and providing guidance to increase the value created by the company's selfcontained divisions.

corruption corruption can arise in a business context when managers pay bribes to gain access to lucrative business contracts.

cost-leadership a business model that pursues strategies that work to lower its cost structure so it can make and sell products at a lower cost than its competitors.

credible commitment a believable promise or pledge to support the development of a long-term relationship between companies.

customer defection rates (or churn rates) percentage of a company's customers who defect every year to competitors.

customer response time time that it takes for a good to be delivered or a service to be performed.

devil's advocacy a technique in which one member of a decisionmaking team identifies all the considerations that might make a proposal unacceptable.

dialectic inquiry the generation of a plan (a thesis) and a counterplan (an antithesis) that reflect plausible but conflicting courses of action.

differentiation a business model that pursues businesslevel strategies that allow it to create a unique product, one that customers perceive as different or distinct in some important way.

diseconomies of scale unit cost increases associated with a large scale of output.

distinctive competencies firm-specific strengths that allow a company to differentiate its products and/or achieve substantially lower costs to achieve a competitive advantage.

diversification the process of entering new industries, distinct from a company's core or original industry, to make new kinds of products for customers in new markets.

diversified company a company that makes and sells products in two or more different or distinct industries.

divestment strategy when a company decides to exit an industry by selling off its business assets to another company.

dominant design common set of features or design characteristics.

economies of scale reductions in unit costs attributed to a larger output.

economies of scope the synergies that arise when one or more of a diversified company's business units are able to lower costs or increase differentiation because they can more effectively pool, share, and utilize expensive resources or capabilities.

employee productivity the output produced per employee.

environmental degradation occurs when a company's actions directly or indirectly result in pollution or other forms of environmental harm.

escalating commitment a cognitive bias that occurs when decision makers, having already committed significant resources to a project, commit even more resources after receiving feedback that the project is failing.

ethical dilemmas situations where there is no agreement over exactly what the accepted principles of right and wrong are, or where none of the available alternatives seems ethically acceptable.

ethics accepted principles of right or wrong that govern the conduct of a person, the members of a profession, or the actions of an organization.

experience curve the systematic lowering of the cost structure, and consequent unit cost reductions, that have been observed to occur over the life of a product.

external stakeholders all other individuals and groups that have some claim on the company.

first-mover disadvantages competitive disadvantages associated with being first.

fixed costs costs that must be incurred to produce a product regardless of the level of output.

flexible production technology (or, lean production) a range of technologies designed to reduce setup times for complex equipment, increase the use of individual machines through better scheduling, and improve quality control at all stages of the manufacturing process.

focused cost leadership a business model based on using cost leadership to compete for customers by offering low-priced products to only one, or a few, market segments.

focused differentiation a business model based on using differentiation to focus on competing customers by making unique to customized products for only one, or a few, market segments.

format wars battles to control the source of differentiation, and thus the value that such differentiation can create for the customer.

fragmented industry an industry composed of a large number of small- and medium-sized companies.

franchising a strategy in which the franchisor grants to its franchisees the right to use the franchisor's name, reputation, and business model in return for a franchise fee and often a percentage of the profits.

functional managers managers responsible for supervising a particular function, that is, a task, activity, or operation, such as accounting, marketing, research and development (R&D), information technology, or logistics.

functional structure grouping of employees on the basis of their common expertise and experience or because they use the same resources.

functional-level strategies strategy aimed at improving the effectiveness of a company's operations and its ability to attain superior efficiency, quality, innovation, and customer responsiveness.

general managers managers who bear responsibility for the overall performance of the company or for one of its major self-contained subunits or divisions.

general organizational competencies competencies that result from the skills of a company's top managers that help every business unit within a company perform at a higher level than it could if it operated as a separate or independent company.

generic business level strategy a strategy that gives a company a specific form of competitive position and advantage vis-à-vis its rivals that results in aboveaverage profitability.

geographic structure a way of grouping employees into different geographic regions to best satisfy the needs of customers within different regions of a state or country.

global strategic alliances cooperative agreements between companies from different countries that are actual or potential competitors.

global standardization strategy a business model based on pursuing a low-cost strategy on a global scale.

greenmail a source of gaining wealth by corporate raiders who benefit by pushing companies to either change their corporate strategy to one that will benefit stockholders, or by charging a premium for these stock when the company wants to buy them back.

growth strategy a strategy designed to allow a company to maintain its relative competitive position in a rapidly expanding market and, if possible, to increase it.

harvest strategy when a company reduces to a minimum the assets it employs in a business to reduce its cost structure and extract or "milk" maximum profits from its investment.

hierarchy of authority the clear and unambiguous chain of command that defines each manager's relative authority from the CEO down through top, middle, to first-line managers.

hold-and-maintain strategy when a company expends resources to develop its distinctive competency to remain the market leader and ward off threats from other companies that are attempting to usurp its leading position.

holdup when a company is taken advantage of by another company it does business with after it has made an investment in expensive specialized assets to better meet the needs of the other company.

horizontal integration the process of acquiring or merging with industry competitors to achieve the competitive advantages that arise from a large size and scope of operations.

hostage taking a means of exchanging valuable resources to guarantee that each partner to an agreement will keep its side of the bargain.

illusion of control a cognitive bias rooted in the tendency to overestimate one's ability to control events.

information asymmetry a situation where an agent has more information about resources they are managing than the principal has.

information distortion the manipulation of facts supplied to corporate managers to hide declining divisional performance.

information manipulation managers use their control over corporate data to distort or hide information in order to enhance their own financial situation or the competitive position of the firm.

inside directors senior employees of the company, such as the CEO.

intangible resources nonphysical entities such as brand names, company reputation, experiential knowledge and intellectual property, including patents, copyrights, and trademarks.

integrating mechanisms ways to increase communication and coordination among functions and divisions.

integrating roles managers who work in full-time positions established specifically to improve communication between divisions.

internal new venturing the process of transferring resources to and creating a new business unit or division in a new industry to innovate new kinds of products.

internal stakeholders stockholders and employees, including executive officers, other managers, and board members.

intrapreneurs managers who pioneer and lead new venture projects or divisions and act as inside or internal entrepreneurs.

just-in-time system of economizing on inventory holding costs by scheduling components to arrive just in time to enter the production process or as stock is depleted.

killer applications applications or uses of a new technology or product that are so compelling that customers adopt them in droves, killing the competing formats.

knowledge management system the company-specific information system that systematizes the knowledge of all its employees and provides access to employees who have the expertise needed to solve problems as they arise.

leadership strategy when a company develops strategies to become the dominant player in a declining industry.

learning effects cost savings that come from learning by doing.

leveraging competencies the process of taking a distinctive competency developed by a business unit in one industry and using it to create a new business unit in a different industry.

localization strategy strategy focused on increasing profitability by customizing the company's goods or services so that the goods provide a favorable match to tastes and preferences in different national markets.

location economies the economic benefits that arise from performing a value creation activity in an optimal location.

market concentration when a company specializes in some way and adopts a focus business model to reduce investment needs and searches for a viable and sustainable competitive position.

market development when a company searches for new market segments for a company's existing products to increase sales.

market penetration when a company concentrates on expanding market share to strengthen its position in its existing product markets.

market segmentation the way a company decides to group customers based on important differences in their needs to gain a competitive advantage.

marketing strategy the position that a company takes with regard to pricing, promotion, advertising, product design, and distribution.

market structure a way of grouping employees into separate customer groups so that each group can focus on satisfying the needs of a particular customer group in the most effective way.

mass customization the use of flexible manufacturing technology to reconcile two goals that were once thought to be incompatible: low cost, and differentiation through product customization.

matrix structure a way of grouping employees in two ways simultaneously by function and by product or project to maximize the rate at which different kinds of products can be developed.

merger an agreement between two companies to pool their resources and operations and join together to better compete in a business or industry.

mission the purpose of the company, or a statement of what the company strives to do.

multidivisional company a company that competes in several different businesses and has created a separate self-contained division to manage each.

multidivisional structure a complex organizational design that allows a company to grow and diversify while it also reduces coordination and control problems because it uses self-contained divisions and has a separate corporate headquarters staff.

multinational company a company that does business in two or more national markets.

network effects the network of complementary products as a primary determinant of the demand for an industry's product.

network structure a cluster of different companies whose actions are coordinated by contracts and outsourcing agreements rather than by a formal hierarchy of authority.

new-venture division a separate and independent division established to give its managers the autonomy to develop a new product.

niche strategy when a company focuses on pockets of demand that are declining more slowly than the industry as a whole to maintain profitability.

nonprice competition the use of product differentiation strategies to deter potential entrants and manage rivalry within an industry.

on-the-job consumption a term used by Economists to describe the behavior of company funds by senior management to acquire perks (such as lavish offices, jets, etc.) that will enhance their status, instead of investing it to increase stockholder returns.

operating budget a blueprint that states how managers intend to use organizational resources to most efficiently achieve organizational goals.

opportunism seeking one's own selfinterest often through the use of guile.

opportunistic exploitation unethical behavior sometimes used by managers to unilaterally rewrite the terms of a contract with suppliers, buyers, or complement providers in a way that is more favorable to the firm.

opportunities elements and conditions in a company's environment that allow it to formulate and implement strategies that enable it to become more profitable.

organizational culture the specific collection of values, norms, beliefs, and attitudes that are shared by people and groups in an organization and that control the way they interact with each other and with stakeholders outside the organization.

organizational design the process of deciding how a company should create, use, and combine organizational structure, control systems, and culture to pursue a business model successfully.

organizational design skills the ability of the managers of a company to create a structure, culture, and control systems that motivate and coordinate employees to perform at a high level.

organizational slack the unproductive use of functional resources by divisional managers that can go undetected unless corporate managers monitor their activities.

organizational structure the means through which a company assigns employees to specific tasks and roles and specifies how these tasks and roles are to be linked together to increase efficiency, quality, innovation, and responsiveness to customers.

output control the control system managers use to establish appropriate performance goals for each division, department, and employee and then measure actual performance relative to these goals.

outside directors directors who are not full-time employees of the company, needed to provide objectivity to the monitoring and evaluation of processes.

outside view identification of past successful or failed strategic initiatives to determine whether those initiatives will work for project at hand.

parallel sourcing policy a policy in which a company enters into longterm contracts with at least two suppliers for the same component to prevent any problems of opportunism.

personal control the way one managers shapes and influences the behavior of another in a face-to-face interaction in the pursuit of a company's goals.

personal ethics generally accepted principles of right and wrong governing the conduct of individuals.

positioning strategy the specific set of options a company adopts for a product based upon four main dimensions of marketing: price, distribution, promotion and advertising, and product features.

price leadership when one company assumes the responsibility for determining the pricing strategy that maximizes industry profitability.

price signaling the process by which companies increase or decrease product prices to convey their intentions to other companies and influence the price of an industry's products.

primary activities activities related to the design, creation, and delivery of the product, its marketing, and its support and after-sales service.

principle of the minimum chain of command the principal that a company should design its hierarchy with the fewest levels of authority necessary to use organizational resources effectively.

prior hypothesis bias a cognitive bias that occurs when decision makers who have strong prior beliefs tend to make decisions on the basis of these beliefs, even when presented with evidence that their beliefs are wrong.

process innovation development of a new process for producing products and delivering them to customers.

product innovation development of products that are new to the world or have superior attributes to existing products.

product structure a way of grouping employees into separate product groups or units so that each product group can focus on the best ways to increase the effectiveness of the product.

product development the creation of new or improved products to replace existing products.

product differentiation the process of designing products to satisfy customers' needs.

product proliferation the strategy of "filling the niches," or catering to the needs of customers in all market segments to deter entry by competitors.

product-team structure a way of grouping employees by product or project line but employees focus on the development of only one particular type of product.

profit center when each self-contained division is treated as a separate financial unit and financial controls are used to establish performance goals for each division and measure profitability.

profit growth the increase in net profit over time.

profitability the return a company makes on the capital invested in the enterprise.

public domain government- or association- set standards of knowledge or technology that any company can freely incorporate into its product.

razor and blade strategy pricing the product low in order to stimulate demand and pricing complements high.

reasoning by analogy use of simple analogies to make sense out of complex problems.

reengineering the process of redesigning business processes to achieve dramatic improvements in performance such as cost, quality, service, and speed.

related diversification a corporate-level strategy that is based on the goal of establishing a business unit in a new industry that is related to a company's existing business units by some form of commonality or linkage between their value-chain functions.

representativeness a bias rooted in the tendency to generalize from a small sample or even a single vivid anecdote.

resources assets of a company.

restructuring the process by which a company streamlines its hierarchy of authority and reduces the number of levels in its hierarchy to a minimum to lower operating costs.

risk capital equity capital for which there is no guarantee that stockholders will ever recoup their investment or ear a decent return.

scenario planning formulating plans that are based upon "what-if" scenarios about the future.

self-contained division an independent business unit or division that contains all the value chain functions it needs to pursue its business model successfully.

self-dealing managers using company funds for their own personal consumption, as done by Enron and Computer Associates in previous years.

self-managing teams teams where members coordinate their own activities and make their own hiring, training, work, and reward decisions.

share-building strategy a strategy that aims to build market share by developing a competitive advantage to attract customers by providing them with knowledge of the company's products.

shareholder value returns that shareholders earn from purchasing shares in a company.

share-increasing Strategy when a company focuses its resources to invest in product development and marketing to become a dominant industry competitor.

span of control the number of subordinates who report directly to a particular manager.

stakeholders individuals or groups with an interest, claim, or stake in the company, in what it does, and in how well it performs.

standardization the degree to which a company specifies how decisions are to be made so that employees' behavior become measurable and predictable.

stock options the right to purchase company stock at a predetermined price at some point in the future, usually within 10 years of the grant date.

strategic alliances long-term agreements between two or more companies to jointly develop new products or processes that benefit all companies which are a part of the agreement.

strategic groups the set of companies that pursue a similar business model and compete for the same group of customers.

strategic leadership creating competitive advantage through effective management of the strategy-making process.

strategic outsourcing the decision to allow one or more of a company's value-chain activities to be performed by independent, specialist companies that focus all their skills and knowledge on just one kind of activity to increase performance.

strategy a set of related actions that managers take to increase their company's performance.

strategy formulation selecting strategies based on analysis of an organization's external and internal environment.

strategy implementation putting strategies into action.

substandard working conditions arise when managers under-invest in working conditions, or pay employees below-market rates, in order to reduce their production costs.

supply-chain management the task of managing the flow of inputs and components from suppliers into the company's production processes to minimize inventory holding and maximize inventory turnover.

support activities activities of the value chain that provide inputs that allow the primary activities to take place.

sustained competitive advantage a company's strategies enable it to maintain above-average profitability for a number of years.

switching costs costs that consumers must bear to switch from the products offered by one established company to the products offered by a new entrant.

SWOT analysis the comparison of strengths, weaknesses, opportunities, and threats.

takeover constraint the risk of being acquired by another company.

tangible resources tangible resources Physical entities, such as land, buildings, equipment, inventory, and money.

team Strategic control systems the mechanism that allows managers to monitor and evaluate whether their business model is working as intended and how it could be improved.

technical standards a set of technical specifications that producers adhere to when making the product, or a component of it.

technological paradigm shifts in new technologies that revolutionize the structure of the industry, dramatically alter the nature of competition, and require companies to adopt new strategies in order to survive.

threats elements in the external environment that could endanger the integrity and profitability of the company's business.

total quality management increasing product reliability so that it consistently performs as it was designed to and rarely breaks down.

transfer pricing the problem of establishing the fair or "competitive" price of a resource or skill developed in one division that is to be transferred and sold to another division.

transferring competencies the process of taking a distinctive competency developed by a business unit in one industry and implanting it in a business unit operating in another industry.

transnational strategy a business model that simultaneously achieves low costs, differentiates the product offering across geographic markets, and fosters a flow of skills between different subsidiaries in the company's global network of operations.

two-boss employees employees who report both to a project boss and who report to a functional boss.

unrelated diversification a corporate-level strategy based on a multibusiness model that uses general organizational competencies to increase the performance of all the company's business units.

value chain the idea that a company is a chain of activities that transforms inputs into outputs that customers value.

values a statement of how employees should conduct themselves and their business to help achieve the company mission.

vertical integration when a company expands its operations either backward into an industry that produces inputs for the company's products (backward vertical integration) or forward into an industry that uses, distributes, or sells the company's products.

vertical disintegration when a company decides to exit industries either forward or backward in the industry value chain to its core industry to increase profitability.

virtual corporation when companies pursued extensive strategic outsourcing to the extent that they only perform the central value-creation functions that lead to competitive advantage.

virtual organization a collection of employees linked by laptops, smartphones, and global video teleconferencing who may rarely meet face-toface, but who join and leave project teams as their skills are needed.

vision the articulation of a company's desired achievements or future state.

Index

('f' indicates a figure; 't' indicates a table)